Margaret Schell Frazier • Connie Morgan

Clinical Medical Assisting
Foundations and Practice

Second Custom Edition for Condensed Curriculum International

Taken from:
Clinical Medical Assisting: Foundations and Practice, First Edition
by Margaret Schell Frazier and Connie Morgan

ISBN 10: 1-323-56797-6
ISBN 13: 978-1-323-56797-5

Dedication

To Dave, you continue to be my strength and love,

To my students, who taught me so much,

To my mentors and friends in AAMA.

-Margie Frazier

To my husband and children, you sacrificed family time and provided love and support for me to continue on this book.

To my students and fellow educators, you are my lifelong inspiration to high standards for learning and teaching.

To Margie, you are my loving, dedicated friend through all times and my encouragement for tenacity and endurance.

-Connie Morgan

CONTENTS

Chapter 24   Gastroenterology and Nutrition 499

PROCEDURES

PREFACE

According to U.S. Department of Labor statistics, medical assisting is one of the top ten fastest growing professions in the United States. This has been the trend for several years.

The increased employment opportunities for medical assistants in medical offices are, in part, a result of the nursing shortage. It is important to remember that nurses are trained to care for patients in the hospital, in bed. Many nurses now have specialized training in advanced care and are compensated according to their skills and time on the job. Medical assistants are trained in the care of ambulatory patients. Although working in the physician's office is the primary goal for employment, other options are available. Graduates find employment in clinics, pharmaceutical companies, insurance companies, medical laboratories, and in walk-in emergency and ambulatory care settings. Graduates should sit for the exams to become RMAs or CMAs, as the trend now is to hire credentialed assistants.

The Development of this Text

When we first set out to write this book, we were encouraged to develop a text we could use to teach clinical medical assisting in our classrooms. As educators with experience in medical assisting and nursing, we decided that a text using a body systems approach would be most useful to students. We felt it would fit with other courses such as medical terminology, anatomy and physiology, and pharmacology.

An outline was developed and modified many times along the way. Ideas for chapters were discussed and a body systems approach was determined to be the best avenue for the book. We felt it was necessary to include all the required clinical content and competencies delineated by the Accrediting Bureau of Health Education Schools (ABHES) and the Commission on Accreditation of Allied Health Education Programs (CAAHEP) for medical assisting programs. In this unique format, we include instruction of required clinical content and competencies in the body systems to which they apply.

How to Use This Text

The book can be used by both ABHES- and CAAHEP-accredited schools or those applying for accreditation to meet both content and competency requirements in the clinical area.

The material is divided into six general areas, with some unavoidable overlapping of concepts. Section I discusses the primary concepts and dynamics of medical assisting. The second section advances the student into the medical office, the physician office lab (POL), asepsis, and minor surgery. Pharmacology and medication administration are also addressed. The text moves on to the third section, diagnostic testing in the medical office. The fourth section covers medical specialties and testing,

and the fifth deals with medical specialties. The sixth, and final, section covers nontraditional medicine.

Section I

It was our intent to introduce entry-level students to the origins of medicine as we know it today, and the origins and progression of the medical assisting profession. Therefore, the first chapter is an introduction to the medical assisting field and describes the medical assistant's role in health care. It includes information about the Hippocratic Oath and the American Medical Association's *Principles of Medical Ethics* and the American Hospital Association's *Patient Bill of Rights.* Professional characteristics, work responsibilities, employment opportunities for medical assistants, professional associations, and credentials for medical assistants are discussed in this chapter.

An important factor in dealing with any individual or group of people is interpersonal communication. Chapter 2 was developed to aid the student in understanding the various concepts that come into play in communicating with patients in the health care setting.

Patient-centered care is the theme of Chapter 3. The holistic health concept is discussed along with pain, its causes, and its management. These early chapters are designed to introduce the beginning medical assistant to positive aspects of patient care in the medical office.

Chapter 4 addresses end-of-life considerations. Students should have some understanding of how to handle the difficult situations that often arise as patients face their mortality. This chapter provides students with background information on such matters as living wills and durable power of attorney for health care.

Section II

The clinical environment and safety are the topics covered in Chapter 5. The student will learn about measures that provide a safe, clean, and comfortable environment for their patients and themselves. OSHA and CDC guidelines, Universal Precautions, disaster guidelines, and office safety procedures are all discussed.

Chapter 6 addresses the clinical visit, including the medical assistant's role, triage, consent, medical records, documentation or charting, and obtaining patient history. Chapter 7 discusses the immune system and infection, medical asepsis and handwashing. Chapter 8 deals with surgical asepsis and preparation for assisting in a sterile procedure. Chapter 9, the pharmacology chapter, introduces the student to common medications prescribed in the medical office and how they are administered, both orally and parenterally. Chapter 10 presents hands-on training for the clinical medical assistant with a discussion of obtaining vital signs and positioning and draping the patient for examination. Assisting the physician is an important aspect of this chapter.

Section III

Section III begins with Chapter 11, which discusses surgical procedures performed in the medical office setting, the medical assistant's role in minor surgery, postoperative care, and patient teaching. Chapter 12 moves to the medical assistant's role in the medical laboratory. Content includes CLIA regulations, Quality Control and Quality Assurance, the Safe Medical Procedures Act, laboratory equipment, and precertification. Chapter 13 includes information about microscopes and microbiological testing. Bacteria nomenclature is discussed, along with preparation of smears, specimen collection for microbiological examination, and culture and sensitivity testing. Chapter 14 is the hematology-testing chapter. Blood and its components are described. Order of draw, venipuncture, capillary puncture, and specimen collection, handling, and transport are also covered. Basic hematology tests are demonstrated and blood chemistries and chemistry testing equipment described.

Section IV

Chapter 15 moves into the area of diagnostic tests and system-related conditions. This chapter deals with the collection of urine specimens, processing of the specimens (specifically urinalysis), the anatomy and physiology of the urinary tract, and the various conditions and diseases of the urinary system. Informative tables in the chapter list the diseases, signs and symptoms, causes, diagnoses, and treatments.

Chapter 16, the radiology chapter, discusses various imaging procedures, including the technology, safety issues, and patient instruction prior to, during, and after the procedures. Chapter 17 is the cardiology chapter: anatomy and physiology of the heart, common cardiovascular conditions, cardiac arrhythmias, diagnostic procedures, and the Holter monitor. As in other chapters, informative tables accompany this chapter. Various scans and diagnostic tests are discussed in Chapter 18, which covers pulmonology and pulmonary testing. This chapter discusses the anatomy and physiology of the pulmonary system, diagnostic testing, and nebulizer treatments.

Chapter 19, the EENT chapter, delves into the anatomy and physiology of the eye, ear, nose, and throat as well as visual acuity and hearing tests. Chapter 20 introduces the immune system, its anatomy and physiology, immunodeficiency diseases, and autoimmune disorders. Hypersensitivity and allergic reactions are also addressed. Chapter 21, on dermatology, discusses the anatomy and physiology of skin, skin disorders, and the medical assistant's role in the dermatology office. Chapter 22 discusses the endocrine system, the complex interactions among glands, and the many disorders that occur in this system.

Section V

This section begins with Chapter 23, which discusses emergency care for both the office and general emergency encounters. The 911 emergency system is described, along with accepted emergent situations for entry into the EMS system. The ABCDs of emergency care and cardiac and respiratory intervention are addressed as primary topics. Traumatic injuries and sudden illnesses, as well as appropriate interventions by the medical assistant, are also addressed.

Chapter 24 discusses the gastrointestinal system, its anatomy and physiology, and the importance of adequate and proper nutrition. Basic food components, the Food Guide Pyramid, caloric intake, and the effects of alcohol on the body are addressed, as are disorders associated with altered nutritional status and food allergies.

Chapter 25 covers the medical assistant's role in the orthopedic office and presents information on the musculoskeletal system, diagnostic procedures, and treatment options for musculoskeletal conditions. Chapter 26 discusses the female reproductive system, including the menstrual cycle, contraception, pregnancy, and the birth process. Chapter 27 is a discussion of the activities and procedures in the pediatric office: routine well-child visits, recommended immunizations, and recordkeeping. Tables listing information about communicable childhood diseases accompany this chapter.

Chapter 28 discusses the medical assistant's role in neurology and neurosurgery. The anatomy and physiology of the nervous system are described, as are disorders and diseases of the central nervous system. Assessment of the neurological system includes the Glasgow Coma Scale, lumbar punctures, and electroencephalography.

Chapter 29 discusses the medical assistant's role in the mental health field, including assessment, diagnosis, and treatment. Chapter 30 provides basic information on oncology: classification and physiology of cancers, diagnostic procedures and treatment options, hospice, and the cancer prevention lifestyle. Chapter 31 provides a general discussion of the geriatric office as well as the aging process, cultural views of aging, and health promotion among the elderly.

Section VI

Chapter 32 discusses complementary and alternative medical systems. Although not all such therapies are approved by medical societies, many people turn to them as alternative or complementary treatments when traditional methods are not working for them.

Pedagogical Features in this Textbook

The following special features appear throughout the text:

- **Learning Objectives:** Specific learning objectives appear at the beginning of each chapter, stating what will be achieved upon successful completion of the chapter.
- **MedMedia:** This link to the supplementary material available on the student CD describes the CD content as it relates to each chapter of the core text.
- **Medical Assisting Competencies:** Each chapter includes CAAHEP entry-level competencies for CMAs and ABHES entry-level competencies for RMAs.

- **Competency Skills Performance:** A list of competencies appears in chapters in which procedures are presented. For each competency, theory is discussed, required materials are listed, and the procedure is presented in the proper format with the task, conditions, and a space for the instructor to add the required standard (time limits, required accuracy, or necessary achievement).

- **Medical Terminology and Abbreviations:** Terms and their definitions appear at the beginning of each chapter as well as in the narrative and the comprehensive glossary. Phonetic pronunciations for difficult medical terminology are given in the comprehensive glossary.

- **The Medical Assistant's Role:** Each chapter begins with a description of the medical assistant's specific role as it pertains to the content presented in the chapter.

- **Case Studies with Critical Thinking Questions:** A thought-provoking case study is presented at the beginning of each chapter, with critical thinking questions interspersed throughout the chapter. Students must rely on the content in the text and their own critical thinking skills to answer the questions.

- **Keys to Success:** These are brief, helpful tips for professional success.

- **Concept Link:** This is a tool for providing references to concepts presented in earlier or later chapters.

- **Caduceus Chronicles:** Interesting historical facts are inserted where relevant to highlight the text.

- **Anatomy and Physiology:** A discussion of anatomy and physiology is included in each of the body systems chap-ters. This, along with the medical terminology, should be used to reinforce the material in the rest of the chapter.

- **Informational Charts and Tables:** These appear throughout the text and summarize pertinent information for the reader. They provide students with visuals and comparisons to reinforce the lesson. In the specialty chapters they provide a quick reference for the disorders described in the chapter. Most tables include signs and symptoms, causes, diagnosis, and treatment. Students should refer to these tables for information not included in the text.

- **Color Photos and Illustrations:** These support the textual material presented and reinforce key concepts.

- **Chapter Summary:** The chapter summary is an excellent review of the chapter content, and is often used for certification exams.

- **Chapter Review Questions:** End-of-chapter questions are provided in multiple-choice, true/false, short answer, and research format, and help reinforce learning. The review questions measure the students' understanding of the material presented in the chapter. These tools are available for use by the student or by the instructor as an outcomes assessment.

- **Externship Application Experience:** This feature places the student in an externship site with a simulated situation the student may encounter.

- **Resource Guide:** This listing provides additional information (organization contact information, websites, etc.) related to the chapter content.

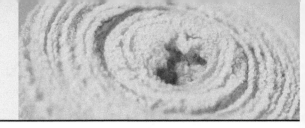

Margaret Schell Frazier, RN, CMA, BS, studied nursing at Parkview Methodist School of Nursing, completing an ADN at Purdue University, then a BS in Health Sciences at St. Francis University. She continued her formal education at Indiana State University, taking courses in technical education.

Margaret spent 13 years as an educator in the health careers field, specializing in medical assistant education. In addition to teaching mainly in medical assisting programs, she was assigned to curriculum development in pharmacology technology, physical therapy assistant, phlebotomy, massage therapy, EKG technician, and medical dictation. She also served twice on the statewide medical assisting curriculum review committee.

As an RN, she spent over 23 years at an intercity hospital working in maternal child health, including 8 years in labor and delivery. She then transferred to the emergency department where she worked for over 15 years. This experience also afforded an opportunity to work in the ambulatory care center on weekends while teaching medical assisting classes. She also worked in the office of an ENT practitioner and in addition to office duties served as a private surgical scrub.

Margaret has been a member of AAMA since 1988 and a CMA during that time. She has served the organization at all three levels, local, state, and national. Her work has been published twice in the national professional journal, and she has published other books. She has presented at several national meetings in continuing education seminars. She is recognized by schools around the country as an expert in curriculum development and implementation.

Retirement from nursing and the teaching arena was not a retirement from the medical field. Margaret is president and consultant of M and M Consulting and still works in both areas of a physician's office, administrative and clinical. She spends many hours at her computer writing books and in her flower shop, Margie's Rose, where she relaxes while arranging flowers.

As early as she can remember, Margie (as she is known to her friends, students, and colleagues) has been interested in the medical field. She would read anything she could about medicine and still does. Her childhood neighbor was a physician and he encouraged her, as did her father, to keep learning about medicine and to do her best in that field.

Margaret was married in 1957. She and her husband have four children, seven grandchildren, and one great-grandchild. They live on a small farm in rural northeast Indiana.

Connie Morgan, MEd, RN, CMA, graduated from Indiana Wesleyan University in 1978 with a BS in Nursing and received RN licensure the same year. She was certified as a medical assistant in 1993 and remains current in skill level and certification. She went on to earn a master's degree in Education in 1995. Connie became "hooked" on teaching when she started assisting nursing students during their clinical rotation. In the years since, she has taught nursing students at St. Joseph's Diploma School of Nursing in Fort Wayne, IN, as well as the public, the general and clinical staff at Munising Memorial Hospital in Munising, MI, and medical assistant and practical nursing students at Ivy Tech Community College in Kokomo, Logansport, and Wabash, IN.

Connie has worked in a variety of clinical areas, including nursing homes and surgical, oncology, orthopedic, urology, obstetric, pediatric, intensive care, and ambulatory care settings as a nurse, and as a medical assistant in insurance, pediatric, and podiatry settings. In addition, she has worked to promote the medical assistant profession by maintaining membership in the American Association of Medical Assistants since 1993, serving as a CRB/CAAHEP surveyor since 1996, and editing articles for the magazine *Certified Medical Assistant* for the past few years. She continues to teach in the medical assistant program at Ivy Tech Community College.

ACKNOWLEDGMENTS

Many individuals played important roles in the concept, development, and final production of this unique medical assisting clinical text. We would be remiss if we did not formally thank these wonderful people.

Our deepest gratitude goes to Julie Alexander, publisher, for your confidence in the project and for your many astute observations and insightful comments at the very first "meeting of the minds." Your continued support as the project unfolded and continued is most appreciated.

Barbara Krawiec, we thank you for your constant attempts at persuading us to take on this project. You never gave up and kept after your vision of what we could do with this book.

Mark Cohen, we met you in Upper Saddle River and you became our editor. We owe you a big thank you for all the many hours you spent working with us and for your positive attitude through the years.

Melissa Kerian, like Mark, your assistance was also invaluable to us.

Joan Gill, our present executive editor, thanks. You have shown patience and have given us direction as the book approached completion. We would have never made it to the end without you.

Alexis Ferraro, developmental editor, a big thanks for your constant pushing for material. Without that, we probably would have never made any deadlines. You had a very difficult job and brought everything together.

Michael Heron, your photography is exceptional as usual; thanks for the fine job.

Cindy Abel, thank you for providing your technical expertise and the direction necessary for the photos shot for the required illustrations.

Thank you to the following groups and individuals for their assistance with the photo shoot:

Arnett Clinic Orthopaedics
Tammy Dodt, CMA
Teresa Henry, CMA
Kim Smith, Surgical Spec. Adm.

The Care Group Lafayette
Tricia Crowe, CMA
Rhonda Johnston, CMA
Carrie Shipman, RN

Ivy Tech Community College
Cindy A. Abel, BS, CMA, PBT (ASCP), Associate Professor/Instructor
Vernon Jackson, Manager, Follet's Bookstore
Jolene Miller, Chair, Ivy Tech Community College
Missy Ticen
Amy Walters

Health Sciences Division
Marsha Duda, MSN
Deborah Dye, RN, BS

Amanda Guthrie, CST
Joy Ratcliff, CDA, EDDA
Nicky Smith

Purdue University Student Health (PUSH), Purdue University
Dr. James Westman
Dr. Sarah Sayger
Debra Steiner, AS, RT (R)
Tai Staller, AS, TR (R)

We extend a special thank you to Elizabeth Tinsley, who rewrote so much of our content, and to Stacia Reagan—the book would not have been finished without you. You stepped in when we needed help and were most gracious about helping us.

There are many more individuals at Prentice Hall that we need to thank; however it is impossible to remember all the names and titles. For anyone involved, a great big thank you.

We thank the experts who acted as contributing authors: James Thompson, Ph.D. MT (ASCP) and Christine E. Hollander, CMA, MA.

To others who have provided guidance and answers to so many questions, medical, technical, or otherwise, thank you. Dean Dauscher, MD and Carolyn Dauscher, RN, you both were most kind and were always available to answer any medical question asked. Others who provided answers to medical questions or to technical questions about office forms, policies, or procedures include Carolyn Steinbacher, ORT; John Csisco, MD; Kimberly Weaver, RN, ADN; Mischelle Musser, RN, ADN; Jodie Inskeep, RN, ADN; David Schlueter, MD; Eugenia Flucher, BSN, EdD; Bradley Boyd, MD; Mark Reecer, MD; and Jeffery Hudson, MD.

Ronald Buskirk, St. Joseph and Dupont Hospitals, you were readily available to answer technical questions about hospitals and compliance. Your help with providing forms was invaluable. Thank you.

Margaret Schell Frazier, RN, CMA, BS
Connie Morgan, MEd, RN, CMA

I can never express the depth of my gratitude to my husband and partner in life. Dave, your patience, your encouragement, and your love carried me through the many toils and turmoil of writing this book. Without you at my side, I would have given up many times. My family, children, and grandchildren have all been tolerant of the time I spent at the computer, at the libraries, and in general working on this project. Thank you all.

Finally, to Connie, my co-author, thank you. We started this roller-coaster ride in Indianapolis and managed to wear out a few vehicles with our many trips to the libraries midway between our homes. We shared so many joys and so many sorrows. I will never forget our trip home from Buffalo, NY on 9-11. The tears and the fears on that unforgettable day made us sisters. We've shared the loss of loved ones and the joys of new life and of graduations and other successes. Now we share the long awaited completion of this project.

Both joy and sadness are in my heart as this book is completed. It has been a big part of my life for the last few years. It is now time to move on and to look forward to other projects and work in my life.

Peace and blessings to all.

Margaret Schell Frazier, RN, CMA, BS —Margie

Reviewers

The authors and publisher wish to thank the following reviewers, all of whom provided valuable feedback and helped to shape the final text:

Cindy Abel, BS, CMA, Pbt (ASCP)
Medical Assisting Program
    Chair/Assistant Professor
Ivy Tech Community College
Lafayette, IN

Kaye Acton, CMA
Department Head, Medical Assisting
Alamance Community College
Burlington, NC

Deborah J. Bedford, CMA
Program Coordinator/Instructor
North Seattle Community College
Seattle, WA

Kay E. Biggs, BS, CMA
Advisor/Coordinator Medical Assisting
    Program
Columbus State Community College
Columbus, OH

Sue Boulden, BSN, CMA
Mount Hood Community College
Gresham, OR

Minda Brown, RMA
PIMA Medical Institute
Colorado Springs, CO

Susan Buboltz, RN, MS, CMA
Instructor and Co-director, Medical
    Assistant Program
Madison Area Technical College
Madison, WI

Ginger Burleson, RN, CMA
Director, Medical Assistant Program
Northeast State Technical Community
    College
Blountville, TN

Lisa L. Cook
MA Education Program Chair
Bryman College
Port Orchard, WA

Lorraine R. Fedorchak-Kraker, CMA-AC
Glen Oaks Community College
Kalamazzo, MI

Ann Kunze, BA, CMA
Instructor
Medical Careers Institute
Newport News, VA

Mary Marks, FNP-C, MSN, Pbt (ASCP)
Program Coordinator
Mitchell Community College
Mooresville, NC

Valerie Matson, BS, CLT
Adjunct Professor and Medical
    Technologist
Broome Community College
Binghamton, NY

Deborah H. McCloskey, M.Ed., MT
    (AMT), CLS (NCA), CLT (HHS)
Program Director, Medical Assistant
    Program
Western School of Health and Business

Natalie McBride
ICM School of Business and Medical
    Careers
Duquesne, PA

Charles Brown
Director of Career Services, MA
    Instructor
MedVance Institute
Stuart, FL

Janette Gallegos, RMA
Medical Assistant Instructor
Keiser College
Boca Raton, FL

Nikki A. Marhefka
Medical Assisting Program Director
Central Pennsylvania College
Summerdale, PA

DeLeesa Meashintubby
Medical Office Assistant/Health Records
    Technology Program Coordinator
Lane Community College
Eugene, OR

Karen Minchella, PhD, CMA
Consultant/Faculty
Baker College
Macomb Community College
Warren, MI

Kinasha Myrick, CMA, CAHI, BBA, MA
Medical Assisting/Billing and Coding
    Program Director
South Suburban College
South Holland, IL

Lisa Nagle, CMA BSed
Program Director, Medical Assisting
Augusta Technical College
Augusta, GA

Brigitte Niedzwiecki, RN, MSN
Medical Assistant Instructor/Program
    Director
Chippewa Valley Technical College
Eau Claire, WI

Theresa Errante-Parrino CMA, EMT-P
Indian River Community College
Fort Pierce, FL

Lauren Perlstein, RN, MSN
Associate Professor, Medical Assistant
    Coordinator
Norwalk Community College
Norwalk, CT

Stacia Marie Reagan, BA, CMA
Medical Assistant Program Director
Community Colleges of Spokane
Spokane, WA

Tiffany Rosta, CMA
Medical Assistant Instructor
ICM School of Business and Medical
    Careers
Pittsburgh, PA

Janet Sesser, RMA, CMA, BSed Admin.
Corporate Director of Education
High-Tech Institute, Inc.
Phoenix, AZ

Lisa Schostek, BA, RMA, CPC, CAHI
Adjunct Faculty, Science and Health
    Division
Lakeland Community College
Kirtland, OH

Lynn G. Slack, BS, CMA
Medical Program Director
ICM School of Business and Medical
    Careers
Pittsburgh, PA

Nancy S. Wright, RN BS CNOR
Instructor, School of Health Sciences
Virginia College
Birmingham, AL

THE LEARNING PACKAGE

The Student Package

- Textbook

- Interactive CD-ROM with exercises, learning games, skills review, medical office simulation for real-life application, skills videos, simulations, animations, resources, and audio glossary

- Student Workbook that contains Chapter Outlines; Chapter Reviews; Learning Activities; Medical Terminology Review; Critical Thinking Questions; Chapter Review Test, with multiple choice, true/false, and short answer questions; and Competency Check-off Skill Sheets

- Vango Notes: chapter highlights and in-depth summaries that are downloaded to an MP3

The Instructional Package

- Instructor's Resource Guide with Lesson Plans, Performance Objectives, Concepts for Lecture, PowerPoint Lecture Slides, Answers to all textbook and workbook questions; Syllabus; Teaching Tips; and Instructional Strategies

- CD-ROM with Test Gen, over 2,500 test questions, and Classroom Management software

- Hundreds of PowerPoint slides for in-class lectures

- Clinical Medical Assisting videos in VHS or DVD format

- Transition Guides to help make text implementation easy

Chapter Opener Features

Case Study

Thought-provoking case studies provide scenarios that help students understand how the material presented in the chapter relates to the medical assisting profession. Critical thinking questions are interspersed within the body of the chapter, and students must rely on the content in the text and their own critical thinking skills to answer the questions.

Objectives

Each chapter opens with a list of learning objectives, which can be used to identify the material and skills the student should know upon successful completion of the chapter.

MedMedia

This link to the accompanying CD ROM and Companion Website provides a description of the many interactive resources available to supplement the content in each chapter.

CHAPTER 5

The Clinical Environment and Safety in the Medical Office

Case Study

Objectives

Medical Assisting Competencies

This boxed feature identifies CAAHEP Entry-Level Competencies for the CMA and ABHES Entry-Level Competencies for the RMA discussed in each chapter.

MEDICAL ASSISTING COMPETENCIES

CAAHEP ENTRY-LEVEL COMPETENCIES FOR CMA	ABHES ENTRY-LEVEL COMPETENCIES FOR RMA
• Perform hand washing.	• Prepare and maintain examination and treatment area.
• Dispose of biohazardous materials.	• Apply principles of aseptic techniques and infection control.
• Obtain vital signs.	• Take vital signs.
• Prepare and maintain examination and treatment areas.	• Prepare patient for and assist with routine and specialty examinations.
• Prepare patient for and assist with routine and specialty examinations.	• Dispose of biohazardous materials.
• Recognize and respond to verbal communications.	• Practice Standard Precautions.
• Recognize and respond to nonverbal communications.	• Determine needs for documentation and reporting.
• Document appropriately.	• Document accurately.
• Explain general office procedures.	• Operate and maintain facilities and equipment safely.
• Instruct individuals according to their needs.	• Orient patient to office policies and procedures.

Medical Terminology and Abbreviations

The Medical Terminology and Abbreviations sections appear at the beginning of each chapter. The terms are listed in alphabetical order, a definition is provided, and the terminology appears in boldface on first introduction in the text. All terms are defined in the comprehensive glossary that appears at the back of the book, and phonetic pronunciations for difficult medical terminology are also provided.

Medical Terminology

cadaver—a dead body used for dissection, study, and tissue samples

empathy—understanding of and sensitivity to the feelings, thoughts, and experiences of others

epidemiology—branch of science that studies the incidence, spread, and control of disease in a population

indigestion—inability to digest, often with pain in the gastro-intestinal (GI) tract

practitioner—a person who practices in a profession, such as medicine

prognosis—a prediction of the outcome of an illness (literal meaning: knowledge before)

Abbreviations

AAMA—American Association of Medical Assistants

ABHES—Accrediting Bureau of Health Education Schools

AMT—American Medical Technologists

CMA—Certified Medical Assistant

HMO—health maintenance organization

NCCA—National Commission for Certifying Agents

PCP—primary care physician

RMA—Registered Medical Assistant

Additional Features

The Medical Assistant's Role in Neurology and Neurosurgery

There are numerous opportunities for the medical assistant in neurology and neurosurgery offices. Many of these opportunities are in the administrative arena; however, clinical positions are generally available as well.

As a medical assistant in a neurology office, you may be responsible for obtaining a preliminary history and information pertaining to the current office visit. You will assess and record vital signs, assist the neurologist with the patient examination, assist the patient as required, document the examination on the patient's chart, provide patient instruction, and make and confirm appointments for any additional diagnostic tests.

The Medical Assistant's Role

Each chapter begins with a description of the medical assistant's specific role as it pertains to the content presented in the chapter.

Competency Skills Performance/Procedures

A list of competencies appears at the beginning of those chapters in which procedures are presented. For each competency, theory is discussed, required materials are listed, and the procedure is presented in the proper format with the Conditions, Tasks, and Standards noted.

COMPETENCY SKILLS PERFORMANCE

1. Demonstrate correct use of the microscope.
2. Prepare a specimen smear for microbiologic examination.
3. Prepare a gram stain.
4. Instruct the patient in the collection of a fecal specimen for occult blood or culture testing.
5. Perform a wound or throat culture collection using sterile swabs.

PROCEDURE 13-2 Prepare a Specimen Smear for Microbiological Examination

Theory

A frosted-edge slide is easier to grasp during preparation and to label with patient information. Patient identification must be done with a labeling pen. Do not use felt-tip markers that might run during the staining procedure.

Specimens for smear preparation can be from a culture swab, a culture growing in a petri dish, or a liquid source. Spread the smear thinly to allow for better microscopic examination and faster air-drying time.

Heat fixation is performed to make sure the cells stick to the slide during the staining process. Heat also kills the microorganisms, thus lowering the possibility of disease transmission during slide preparation and handling. The slide should not become too hot to hold, as excess heat could damage the specimen and alter test results.

Materials

- glass slide (preferably with frosted edge)
- disposable gloves
- sterile distilled water
- inoculating loops or specimen swabs
- flame source
- biohazardous waste container
- sharps container

Competency

(**Conditions**) With the necessary materials, you will be able to (**Task**) prepare a slide (**Standards**) correctly for microscopic examination within 30 minutes.

1. Wash your hands.
2. Gather equipment and supplies.
3. Wash your hands again and put on disposable gloves.
4. Write the patient information on the frosted edge of the slide.
5. Prepare a thin film, or smear, on the slide.
   For a specimen from a swab: Roll and turn the swab across the slide (Figure 13-11 ◆).
   - Gather sterile distilled water with a sterile inoculating loop and place it on the slide.
   - Use the inoculating loop to gather the microbial specimen, without gathering any culture medium.
   - Mix the specimen into the distilled water on the slide.
   - Sterilize the loop over the flame.
   For a specimen from a Petri dish (Figure 13-12 ◆):
   - Dip the inside of the sterile inoculating loop in the culture until it appears covered with a film.
   - Touch the film to the center of the slide.
   - Allow the specimen on the slide to air-dry completely.
   - Hold and pass the slide through the flame several times. The slide is now ready to stain.
6. Clean the work area.
7. Dispose of the gloves and wash your hands.

Charting Example

Document in the designated log any quality control or safety measures you followed, such as looking at expiration dates or correctly storing the specimen.

Figure 13-11 ◆ Roll and turn the swab across the slide.

Figure 13-12 ◆ Using a loop with a Petri dish.

Figure 13-13 ◆ Using a loop with a liquid

Keys to Success
THE IMPORTANCE OF CLEANING INSTRUMENTS PROPERLY

What happens when a pathogenic outbreak is identified? In cooperation with the CDC, the local Public Health Department investigates each patient history for common factors. For example, did the patients eat at the same restaurant, go to the same medical office, use the same bathroom, or receive the same procedure at the same medical office? Microorganism cultures may be taken of food samples, disinfected or sterilized medical instruments, bathroom faucets, toilet handles, and so on.

Once the cause of the outbreak is determined, actions are taken to eliminate the possibility of recurrence. This might involve, but is not limited to, temporary or permanent closing of the facility, resterilization of items thought to be sterilized, and treatment of persons who might harbor the pathogen. If patients have been harmed during a procedure, malpractice lawsuits may be filed against the facility and all persons involved in the procedure or the cleaning of instruments, including the medical assistant.

Keys to Success

Helpful tips for career success are interspersed throughout the text to highlight the importance of professionalism.

Concept Link

This visual link is a tool for providing references to concepts presented in earlier or later chapters.

Axon branches secrete chemical messengers called **neurotransmitters** that transmit electrical impulses across the synaptic gap. Neurotransmitters function to cause or inhibit reactions of the connected neuron(s). (∞ For a discussion of the role of neurotransmitters in mental disorders, refer to Chapter 29.)

Caduceus Chronicles

Interesting historical facts relevant to chapter content are interspersed throughout the text to highlight the content presented.

Caduceus Chronicle
A BRIEF HISTORY OF BLOOD GROUPING

The ABO blood groups are the most important of several systems for classifying human blood. Type A blood contains A antigens, does not form A antibodies against its own blood type, and develops B antibodies when type B blood is introduced. Type B blood contains B antigens, does not form antibodies against its own blood type, and develops A antibodies if type A blood is introduced. Type AB blood contains antigens A and B, but neither A nor B antibodies. Type O blood does not contain either the A or B antigens or antibodies.

These blood groups were identified in 1901 by Karl Landsteiner (1868–1943), a U.S. immunologist. In 1902, the AB blood group was discovered by Alfred von Decastrello (1872–1960) and Adriano Sturli (1873–1964). Other "minor" blood group systems, such as Kell, Duffy, Lewis, and many others, have subsequently been discovered.

Color Photos and Illustrations

Color photos and illustrations appear throughout the book to support the textual material presented and reinforce key concepts.

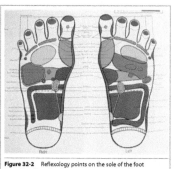

Figure 32-2 Reflexology points on the sole of the foot
Source: Photo Researchers, Inc.

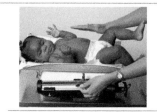

Figure 27-8 Weigh the infant on the balance baby scale.

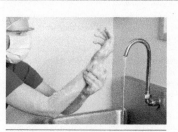

Figure 8-27 Scrub from the fingertips to the elbows with the sponge for 3 minutes.

Review

Chapter Summary

Each Chapter Summary is an excellent review of the chapter content.

Chapter Review Questions

End-of-chapter questions are provided in multiple-choice, true/false, short answer, and research format, and help reinforce learning. The review questions measure the student's understanding of the material presented in each chapter. These tools are available for use by the student or instructor as an outcome assessment.

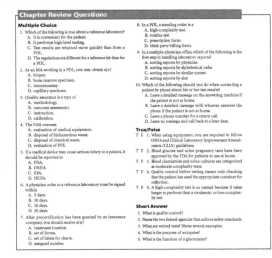

Externship Application Experience

This feature places the student in an externship site with a simulated situation the student many encounter. Critical thinking questions appear at the end of each brief scenario, and students must rely on the knowledge acquired in the chapter and their own critical thinking skills to answer each question.

Resource Guide

This listing provides additional information (organization contact information, websites, etc.) related to chapter content.

MedMedia

Reminds students to visit the Companion Website and explore the Student CD to supplement the chapter content.

MedMedia
www.prenhall.com/frazier

More on this chapter, including interactive resources, can be found on the Student CD-ROM accompanying this textbook and on the Companion Website at www.prenhall.com/frazier.

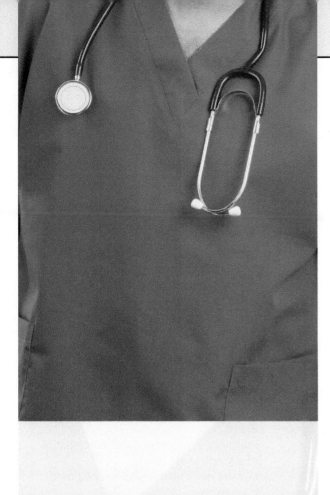

SECTION I

Introduction

My name is Johnna Connell, and I'm a Certified Medical Assistant. I worked as a medical assistant for 10 years before embarking on a teaching career.

One of the highlights of medical assisting is the diversity of the career. The training a medical assistant receives in both the clinical and administrative areas makes for a versatile employee. Some of my job duties included assessing patients; assisting the physician with exams; setting up and assisting with minor surgeries, x-rays, EKGs, PFS studies, and lab testing; preparing inventory of supplies; ordering supplies; purging files; and more.

Unlike other clinical employees, I could also flex and work in the front office. Even though my everyday duties involved the clinical areas, I also wanted to keep my administrative skills up to date. This administrative expertise became invaluable to my employers when the group decided to open a satellite office. I was given the job of setting up this office and working it singlehandedly several afternoons a week, including both administrative and clinical duties. It was a huge responsibility and challenge, but what a great feeling to know I could run an entire office alone!

One of my favorite parts of the job was getting to know the patients. I tried to treat each of them as I would want my own family members to be treated. Some of my patients did seem like dear friends after many years of assisting them. It was a joy to serve them. The desire to serve should be at the heart of every medical assistant.

Today, I have the challenge of serving medical assisting students—I teach medical assisting at the Winder campus of Lanier Technical College. I am so proud to promote such an exciting career.

CHAPTER 1

The Medical Assistant Profession and Health Care

Case Study

Janet has been working with Dr. Fletcher for many years as a medical assistant and really enjoys her chosen profession. Next week the office will be celebrating Janet's 30-year anniversary as a medical assistant, and everyone is excited about the celebration.

During Tuesday's staff meeting the office manager, Annette, announced that she will be updating files and implementing some employee certification changes that Dr. Fletcher learned about at a recent seminar. The biggest change will be that all medical assistants will have to be certified by taking and passing the AAMA certification exam within the next 12 months.

Janet is worried. She confides to a friend and coworker, Lucy, that she isn't really sure what Annette was talking about when she mentioned the AAMA certification exam. Lucy explains that she took the exam shortly after graduation last year and that is why her name pin bears the title "CMA."

Janet confesses that she has never taken a certification exam because she went to work right out of high school and got her first job in health care by being "grandfathered" in. When Janet started working 30 years ago, it was legal to train staff on the job, without certificates from accredited schools.

"You introduce yourself to patients as 'Dr. Fletcher's nurse,' so you must have gone to an RN program," Lucy says.

Janet looks offended. "No, I didn't. We're in the nursing profession, so I let my patients call me 'Nurse.' It's no big deal."

MedMedia

www.prenhall.com/frazier

Additional interactive resources and activities for this chapter can be found on the Companion Website. For audio glossary, legal and ethical scenarios, job scenarios, quizzes, and games related to the content of this chapter, please access the accompanying CD-ROM in this book.

 Assets Available:

Audio Glossary
Legal and Ethical Scenario: *The Medical Assistant Profession and Health Care*
On the Job Scenario: *The Medical Assistant Profession and Health Care*
HIPAA Quiz: *Medical Assisting: The Profession; Medical Science: History and Practice; Medical Law and Ethics*
Multiple Choice Quiz
Games: Crossword, Strikeout, and Spelling Bee

Objectives

After completing this chapter, you should be able to:

- Spell and define the medical terminology in this chapter.
- Define the medical assistant's role in the health-care profession.
- Discuss the history of medical assisting and the purpose of the Hippocratic Oath.
- Explain the American Medical Association's *Principles of Medical Ethics*.
- Describe the purpose of the American Hospital Association's *Patient Bill of Rights*.
- Identify the professional characteristics of a medical assistant.
- List the work responsibilities of a medical assistant.
- Discuss the various opportunities for employment for medical assistants.
- Identify the professional associations for medical assistants.
- Discuss the credentials of the American Association of Medical Assistants (AAMA) and American Medical Technologists (AMT).

✚ MEDICAL ASSISTING COMPETENCIES

CAAHEP ENTRY-LEVEL COMPETENCIES FOR CMA	ABHES ENTRY-LEVEL COMPETENCIES FOR RMA
▪ Identify and respond to issues of confidentiality. ▪ Perform within legal and ethical boundaries. ▪ Demonstrate knowledge of federal and state health-care legislation and regulations.	▪ Project a positive attitude. ▪ Maintain confidentiality at all times. ▪ Be a "team player." ▪ Be cognizant of ethical boundaries. ▪ Exhibit initiative. ▪ Adapt to change. ▪ Evidence a responsible attitude. ▪ Be courteous and diplomatic. ▪ Conduct work within scope of education, training, and ability.

Introduction

Medical assisting is a fairly new profession in the health-care delivery system, receiving professional recognition in the 1960s. Advances in medical science, a nursing shortage, and changes in the reimbursement system have made formal training and certification necessary for anyone wishing to work as a medical assistant in a medical office or clinic.

The Medical Assistant's Role in Health Care

Your role as a medical assistant (MA) is vital to the health-care field. You will be helping to fill the need for trained professionals. To do this you will need knowledge about the medical assisting profession and the evolution of medical science along with the practical skills to work in a fast-paced setting. Becoming an MA is stepping into a future filled with both challenges and an unlimited potential for growth.

The History of Medicine

Ancient treatments for illness and disease were practiced and passed down orally through the generations. Folk remedies evolved as certain plants were discovered to be harmful and others found to improve health. Early efforts to understand the origins of diseases and illnesses were largely based on belief in the supernatural.

Early Healing Practices

Early medicines were developed largely from plants and animals. Many plant remedies are still used today for heart conditions, **indigestion,** bleeding, and urinary tract infections. For example, garlic has recently been approved in Europe for treating cardiovascular conditions such as high cholesterol. Numerous other plant remedies are used around the world (Figure 1-1 ◆).

- Ginger treats conditions such as nausea, motion sickness, and lack of appetite.
- Licorice is used to soothe inflamed mucous membranes.

Medical Terminology

cadaver—a dead body used for dissection, study, and tissue samples

empathy—understanding of and sensitivity to the feelings, thoughts, and experiences of others

epidemiology—branch of science that studies the incidence, spread, and control of disease in a population

indigestion—inability to digest, often with pain in the gastrointestinal (GI) tract

practitioner—a person who practices in a profession, such as medicine

prognosis—a prediction of the outcome of an illness (literal meaning: knowledge before)

Abbreviations

AAMA—American Association of Medical Assistants

ABHES—Accrediting Bureau of Health Education Schools

AMT—American Medical Technologists

CMA—Certified Medical Assistant

HMO—health maintenance organization

NCCA—National Commission for Certifying Agents

PCP—primary care physician

RMA—Registered Medical Assistant

Figure 1-1 ◆ Numerous plant remedies are used around the world, such as (A) foxglove, (B) ginger, (C) licorice, (D) peppermint, (E) chamomile, and (F) green tea.

- The foxglove plant (*Digitalis lanata*) is the basis for digitalis preparations such as digoxin that are prescribed to slow and strengthen the heartbeat.
- Green tea is an antioxidant.
- Peppermint treats indigestion.
- Chamomile soothes the nerves.

Animals are another source of treatments and cures.

- Leeches are used to treat wounds that require the draining of blood, such as reconstructive surgery for grafted tissue.
- Snake venom is commonly used to produce antivenin, the treatment for poisonous snakebites.

The use of nonpoisonous snakes by early Greek physicians is the origin of the caduceus symbol (Figure 1-2 ◆). Snakes were thought to have regenerative powers, in part because they regularly sloughed, or shed, their skin.

Healing Based on the Supernatural

Diseases were often believed to be of supernatural origin, caused by evil spirits and angry gods. Treating these diseases was the responsibility of sorcerers and shamans and often consisted of torturing the patient to make the body unfit for demons to live in. *Trepanning,* or boring a hole into the patient's skull, was

Figure 1-2 ◆ Caduceus symbol

Caduceus Chronicle
THE WORKS OF HIPPOCRATES

■ The Hippocratic Oath was the first physician's code of ethics.
■ *On Airs, Waters, and Places* suggested that a physician could evaluate the health of a community's citizens based on data gathered on the weather, drinking water, and the town's placement with respect to the winds.
■ *Regimen* and *Regimen in Acute Diseases* presented the concept of preventive medicine and the effects of diet and living habits on health and recovery.

done to release evil spirits. Other, less painful treatments to ward off demons included dancing, the use of talismans, or magical charms, incantations, and magic (Figure 1-3 ◆).

Hippocrates and Early Contributors

Hippocrates (B.C.E. 460?–377?), known as the Father of Medicine, practiced and taught medicine on the island of Kos, Greece. He believed that disease was caused not by supernatural forces but by natural causes. He believed the four elements of earth, air, fire, and water were represented by the four humors (body fluids): blood, phlegm, black bile, and yellow bile. Good health depended on keeping the humors balanced within the body. This belief was the basis for many theories of disease until the late 1800s.

Hippocrates taught a philosophy of wellness based on diet, exercise, moderation, rest, and positive outlook. His descriptions of disease identified symptoms and included a **prognosis.** The time-honored medical rule "First, do no harm" is attributed to Hippocrates.

Other early contributors to the medical field were:

■ Galen (C.E. 129–199), who based his ideas about anatomy and physiology on his work with animal **cad-**

avers, a forerunner of later postmortem examinations. He also discovered that arteries carried blood instead of air and developed a technique for taking the pulse, a diagnostic tool used to this day.

■ Andreas Vesalius (1514–1564), who became known as the Father of Modern Anatomy through his dissections of the human body.

■ William Harvey (1578–1657), who discovered how the heart pumps blood through the circulatory system.

■ Thomas Sydenham (1624–1689), called the English Hippocrates, who founded the science of **epidemiology.** He is also considered an early **practitioner** of clinical medicine because of his detailed patient observations and records. He described and named scarlet fever and Sydenham's chorea (once known as St. Vitus' dance).

■ Antoni van Leeuwenhoek (1632–1723), who was the first to study bacteria and protozoa using a microscope.

Other important figures in the history of medicine will be discussed in later chapters.

Caduceus Chronicle
MEDICAL FIRSTS IN THE UNITED STATES

■ First medical college, May 3, 1765: College of Philadelphia Department of Medicine, now called the University of Pennsylvania School of Medicine
■ First African American to receive a medical degree, 1822: James Hall, Medical College of Maine
■ First woman physician, 1849: Elizabeth Blackwell, Geneva Medical College, New York
■ First blood bank established, 1940: Bernard Fantus, Cook County Hospital, Chicago (Fantus also coined the term "blood bank")

Ethics and Patient Rights

Ethics has been a part of medical practice since ancient times. In early Babylon, the Hammurabi Code set forth penalties for medical errors. The Hippocratic Oath followed. For close to 25 centuries, the oath has guided physicians on issues of confidentiality, training practices, nondiscrimination, honesty, integrity, healing, morality, euthanasia, and abortion. It established medicine as an art of healing, not harming. The oath serves as the basis for medical ethics today.

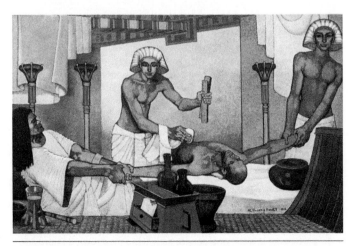

Figure 1-3 ◆ Diseases, often believed to be of supernatural origin, were treated by talismans.
Brian Warling/International Museum of Surgical Science

Caduceus Chronicle
HIPPOCRATIC OATH (CLASSICAL VERSION)

I swear by Apollo the physician, and Aesculapius, and Health, and All-heal, and all the gods and goddesses, that, according to my ability and judgment, I will keep this Oath and this stipulation—to reckon him who taught me this Art equally dear to me as my parents, to share my substance with him, and relieve his necessities if required; to look upon his offspring in the same footing as my own brothers, and to teach them this art, if they shall wish to learn it, without fee or stipulation; and that by precept, lecture, and every other mode of instruction, I will impart a knowledge of the Art to my own sons, and those of my teachers, and to disciples bound by a stipulation and oath according to the law of medicine, but to none others. I will follow that system of regimen which, according to my ability and judgment, I consider for the benefit of my patients, and abstain from whatever is deleterious and mischievous. I will give no deadly medicine to anyone if asked, nor suggest any such counsel; and in like manner I will not give to a woman a pessary to produce abortion. With purity and with holiness I will pass my life and practice my Art. I will not cut persons laboring under the stone, but will leave this to be done by men who are practitioners of this work. Into whatever houses I enter, I will go into them for the benefit of the sick, and will abstain from every voluntary act of mischief and corruption; and, further from the seduction of females or males, of freemen and slaves. Whatever, in connection with my professional practice or not, in connection with it, I see or hear, in the life of men, which ought not to be spoken of abroad, I will not divulge, as reckoning that all such should be kept secret. While I continue to keep this Oath unviolated, may it be granted to me to enjoy life and the practice of the art, respected by all men, in all times! But should I trespass and violate this Oath, may the reverse be my lot!

—Translated by Francis Adams

From Edelstein, Lugwig. *The Hippocratic Oath: Text, Translation and Interpretation.* © 1996 Harold Cherniss. Reprinted with permission of The Johns Hopkins University Press.

Caduceus Chronicle
HIPPOCRATIC OATH (MODERN VERSION USED IN MANY MEDICAL SCHOOLS TODAY)

I swear to fulfill, to the best of my ability and judgment, this covenant:

I will respect the hard-won scientific gains of those physicians in whose steps I walk, and gladly share such knowledge as is mine with those who are to follow.

I will apply, for the benefit of the sick, all measures which are required, avoiding those twin traps of overtreatment and therapeutic nihilism.

I will remember that there is art to medicine as well as science, and that warmth, sympathy, and understanding may outweigh the surgeon's knife or the chemist's drug.

I will not be ashamed to say "I know not," nor will I fail to call in my colleagues when the skills of another are needed for a patient's recovery.

I will respect the privacy of my patients, for their problems are not disclosed to me that the world may know. Most especially must I tread with care in matters of life and death. If it is given me to save a life, all thanks. But it may also be within my power to take a life; this awesome responsibility must be faced with great humbleness and awareness of my own frailty. Above all, I must not play at God.

I will remember that I do not treat a fever chart, a cancerous growth, but a sick human being, whose illness may affect the person's family and economic stability. My responsibility includes these related problems, if I am to care adequately for the sick.

I will prevent disease whenever I can, for prevention is preferable to cure.

I will remember that I remain a member of society, with special obligations to all my fellow human beings, those sound of mind and body as well as the infirm.

If I do not violate this oath, may I enjoy life and art, respected while I live and remembered with affection thereafter. May I always act so as to preserve the finest traditions of my calling and may I long experience the joy of healing those who seek my help.

—Written in 1964 by Louis Lasagna
Academic Dean of the School of Medicine at Tufts University

The American Medical Association (AMA), established in 1846, wrote a code of ethics for physicians in 1847. It has evolved to meet the changing needs of medical practice. The AMA *Principles of Medical Ethics* cover:

- Integrity
- Individual responsibility to society and community
- Respect for human dignity
- Lifelong study
- Professional autonomy, or self-rule

As a medical assistant you should understand the *Principles of Medical Ethics* as explained by the AMA's Council on Ethical and Judicial Affairs. For example, the *Principles* state: "The term 'ethical' is used in opinions of the Council on Ethical and Judicial Affairs to refer to matters involving (1) moral principles or practices and (2) matters of social policy involving issues of morality in the practice of medicine. The term 'unethical' is used to refer to professional conduct which fails to conform to these moral standards or policies."

The American Association of Medical Assistants (**AAMA**) also has a Code of Ethics that sets guidelines for medical assistants in the practice of the profession. All medical assistants should be familiar with its contents.

The ten Standards of Practice for all individuals certified by the AMT are related to professionalism, ethics, standards of competence, and patient safety and welfare. Standard VI states, "The AMT professional shall respect the law and will pledge to avoid dishonest, unethical, or illegal practices."

Keys to Success
AAMA CODE OF ETHICS

The Code of Ethics of AAMA shall set forth principles of ethical and moral conduct as they relate to the medical profession and the particular practice of medical assisting.

Members of AAMA dedicated to the conscientious pursuit of their profession, and thus desiring to merit the high regard of the entire medical profession and the respect of the general public which they serve, do pledge themselves to strive always to:

1. render service with full respect for the dignity of humanity;
2. respect confidential information obtained through employment unless legally authorized or required by responsible performance of duty to divulge such information;
3. uphold the honor and high principles of the profession and accept its disciplines;
4. seek to continually improve the knowledge and skills of medical assistants for the benefit of patients and professional colleagues;
5. participate in additional service activities aimed toward improving the health and well-being of the community.

Reprinted with permission of AAMA.

The American Hospital Association's Patient Bill of Rights (1973)

As patients have become more involved in their own care, the focus has shifted from physicians telling patients what to do to physicians involving patients in decisions about their care. Patients today want to know more about the treatments their physician recommends and any alternative treatments, including the benefits and risks of each. (∞ See Appendix A for the complete Patient Bill of Rights.) In 1992, hospitals were encouraged to adapt the revised bill to their facilities and communities.

Professionalism

As the average age of health-care workers and the general population rises, the need for trained health-care providers also rises. The training of nursing and allied health-care professionals has not kept pace with the growing demand for healthcare services. The recent recognition of medical assistants as multiskilled health professionals has expanded employment opportunities in the field (Figure 1-4 ◆).

Nurses traditionally carried out both clinical and administrative duties in the physician's office. As the shortage of nurses became chronic, medical assistants began to meet those needs. Depending on the medical office, MAs are expected to provide administrative and/or clinical assistance.

Medical assistants are trained to perform many administrative tasks, including, but not limited to, scheduling appointments and procedures, processing insurance claims, bookkeeping, and other clerical functions. Clinical training includes understanding and performing fundamental procedures, specimen collection, diagnostic testing, and patient care. Training in the general areas of medical assisting includes professional communications, legal concepts, patient instruction, and operational functions. This textbook focuses on clinical duties, including the written recording of a patient's history, placing the patient in an examining room, taking vital signs, and helping with diagnostic procedures.

Communication and Medical Terminology

Medical terminology is a basic language you will need to learn in order to speak with other health professionals, such as physicians and nurses. It comprises terms that are formed from roots, prefixes, suffixes, and combining forms. Learning medical terminology is the key to gaining medical knowledge and skills.

Another aspect of communication involves patients. When patients are ill or injured, they may be nervous or scared. It will be your duty to calm them as much as possible so that they do not overreact physically or emotionally to physical examination or treatment. Therapeutic touch and an assuring manner help to defuse a patient's fear or anxiety. (∞ Chapter 2, Interpersonal Communication, presents a more detailed discussion of this topic.)

Physical Requirements

Flexibility and strength are required for both clinical and administrative tasks. You must be strong enough to perform various duties and have the dexterity to operate a variety of equipment (Figure 1-5 ◆). For example, you may need to transfer patients to exam tables or to wheelchairs. You may have to reach for supplies from higher storage shelves. Your color vision must function normally to allow you to accurately describe the appearance of physical signs and symptoms. You must be able to hear the telephone, voices, and patient sounds, especially when patients are distressed, and to listen to a patient's heartbeat with a stethoscope.

Character

As a medical assistant you must possess certain personality traits, including **empathy** for the patient as a whole person. The following characteristics are essential for working effectively with other medical team members and caring for patients:

- Honesty and integrity
- Dependability

Figure 1-4 ◆ The recognition of medical assistants as multiskilled health professionals has expanded employment opportunities in the field.

Figure 1-5 ◆ The medical assistant must have the dexterity to operate a variety of equipment.

- Respect for individual and cultural differences
- Sense of humor
- Courtesy and patience, even in challenging situations
- Common sense
- Tact when dealing with problems and sensitive situations
- Discretion and confidentiality when caring for patients and handling medical records

Health-Care Team Members

To be an effective member of a health-care team, you should understand the role of every other team member in patient-centered general care. Understanding the interaction of various roles adds to the quality of patient care and the efficiency of the physician's office.

Physician

Physicians provide the diagnosis and direction for patient treatment. Their training is long and rigorous, requiring a bachelor's degree, completion of medical school, licensure examination, and residency. Some physicians choose to specialize in a specific body system or treatment. For example, a physician who specializes in gastroenterology treats the gastrointestinal system, and a physician who specializes in gerontology deals with aging patients.

A physician must follow ethical practices. A physician's license may be suspended—the physician is temporarily barred from practicing—until the case is reviewed, or the license may be revoked—taken back by the government—if the misconduct is serious.

Health maintenance organizations (**HMOs**), managed care, and preferred providers have created another title for physicians: primary care physician (**PCP**), also called the *gatekeeper*. The PCP replaces what used to be referred to as the general practitioner (GP) or family physician. The PCP takes on the primary responsibility for patient care, makes referrals for additional treatment as necessary, and acquires precertification for care and procedures.

Your training should allow you to work with most physicians at the entry level. With additional on-the-job training you may be able to help a physician in specific settings. Be aware of your responsibility to the physician(s) with whom you work. The physician is held as the *respondent superior* in court—if you make a patient error, both you and the physician are held responsible, or the physician employer is liable for his employee's actions.

Physician's Assistant

A physician's assistant (PA) provides patient care under the supervision of a physician. Training requirements and duties vary from state to state. Duties generally include taking the patient's medical history, performing physical examinations and diagnostic procedures, providing follow-up care, teaching patients, and, in some states, writing prescriptions.

Nurse

A licensed practical or vocational nurse (LPN, LVN) usually completes one year of training. A registered nurse (RN) can graduate from a two-year (associate), three-year (diploma), or

Keys to Success
YOUR TITLE

Medical assistants must *never* intentionally represent themselves as nurses. If a patient calls you "Nurse," carefully tell him or her your correct title. The best way to prevent misunderstandings is to wear a name pin with "CMA" or "RMA" following your name. *Never* refer to yourself as "the nurse."

four-year (baccalaureate) program. An RN receives more training in assessment and clinical skills, and as a result has greater responsibilities than an LPN or LVN. A nurse practitioner (NP) completes a master's degree, which includes additional clinical training. An NP may function independently, performing examinations and procedures, writing prescriptions, and providing education and counseling to patients.

—Critical Thinking Question 1-1—
Should Janet continue to allow her patients to call her "Nurse"? Why or why not? Can she be held civilly or criminally liable if she knowingly continues to do so?

Other Health-Care Team Members

Other members of the medical and dental health-care team are described below.

- Blood bank technologist—tests blood to ensure donor-recipient compatibility.
- Certified nursing assistant (CNA)—helps nursing staff by providing bedside patient care in nursing home and extended care facilities, such as bed baths, feeding, walking, and vital signs.
- Clinical dietitian—coordinates patient's diet and medications.
- Dental assistant—works chairside with the dentist by preparing patients for treatment, taking dental X-rays, and making dental impressions.
- Dental hygienist—cleans patient's teeth, discusses findings with the dentist, and teaches dental health to the

Keys to Success
LICENSING AND CERTIFICATION

Certification is written confirmation that an individual has met specified standards for the safe practice of a profession or service. Certified Medical Assistant (CMA) and Registered Medical Assistant (RMA) certificates are recognized nationally. Medical assistants and other health care professionals should complete an educational program and pass a national exam for voluntary certification.

Licensure is the granting of written permission to practice a profession. Physicians and nurses in all 50 states and the District of Columbia are required to have licenses. These licenses are recognized only in the state that grants them, although a license can be held in more than one state if the nurse or physician meets the requirements set by each state. State statutes (Practice Acts) define the scope of practice for these professionals.

patient; in some states, may perform more advanced procedures with training.

- Electrocardiograph technologist—takes EKGs to provide a patient record of cardiac electrical activity.
- Electroencephalograph technologist—takes EEGs to provide a patient record of brain activity.
- Emergency medical technician (EMT)—from basic to paramedic levels, provides emergency stabilizing care at the scene of injury or trauma, then transports the patient to the nearest medical center. Three levels of EMT are basic, advanced or intermediate, and paramedic (Figure 1-6 ◆).
- Medical laboratory technologist—tests clinical specimens such as blood, urine, and other body specimens; also manages the department.
- Medical records technician—files patients' charts, ensures that stored records are kept confidential, and follows procedures for release of chart information to patients, courts of law, and insurance companies.
- Medical secretary—does a variety of administrative duties as directed based on the needs of the office, the professional staff, and the office manager.
- Medical transcriptionist—transfers physician/surgeon data from audio recordings to hard copies for the patient chart.
- Nuclear medicine technologist—responsible for dispensing radioactive substances before X-rays are performed.
- Occupational or physical therapy assistant—helps therapists by working with patients on specific activities.
- Occupational therapist (OT)—works with individuals who have conditions that are physically, emotionally, or developmentally disabling; helps patients to function at work and with daily living.

- Office manager—directs the activities of the administrative and clinical staff, such as physicians, nurses, and lab and respiratory technicians.
- Pharmacist—highly trained in dispensing of medications; fills prescriptions and provides patient education; mixes prescription pharmaceutical preparations as directed by the physician.
- Pharmacy technician—helps the pharmacist with routine tasks such as counting pills and labeling and helps the patient with health-care items.
- Phlebotomist—specializes in taking blood specimens for laboratory analysis.
- Physical therapist (PT)—restores function, improves mobility, eases pain, and works to reestablish a patient in the workplace and community after an injury or illness (Figure 1-7 ◆).
- Radiology technologist—takes X-rays.
- Respiratory therapist (also called respiratory care practitioner)— evaluates, treats, cares for, and educates patients with respiratory diseases.
- Social worker—connects patients with special needs to agencies that may help them; needs may be financial or may the result of acute or long-term physical or mental illness.
- Ultrasound technologist—takes fetal and cardiac ultrasounds and others (Figure 1-8 ◆).

This list does not include every health-care team member. As the medical field changes, so do job descriptions and training.

Figure 1-6 ◆ Emergency medical technician (EMT)

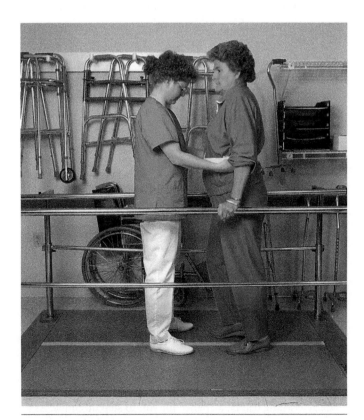

Figure 1-7 ◆ Physical therapist

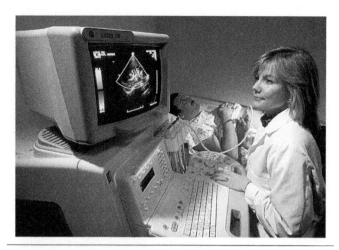

Figure 1-8 ◆ Ultrasound technologist
Browne Harris/The Stock Market

Scope of Practice for Medical Assistants

The American Association of Medical Assistants defines medical assisting as an allied health profession whose practitioners function as members of the health-care delivery team and perform administrative and clinical procedures. The medical assistant performs delegated clinical and administrative duties within the supervising physician's scope of practice consistent with the medical assistant's education, training, and experience. Such duties do not constitute the practice of medicine. Physician supervision shall be active and continuous but shall not be construed as necessarily requiring the physical presence of the supervising physician at the time and place that services are rendered.

It is not possible to devise a specific list of skills that covers all areas of performance for medical assistants. The AAMA defines and supports the medical assisting profession in its documents: *AAMA Role Delineation Study: Occupational Analysis of the Medical Assisting Profession,* the *Content Outline* for the Certified Medical Assistant Exam, the *Standards for an Accredited Educational Program for the Medical Assistant,* and *Advanced Practice of Medical Assisting.* To protect the public welfare and the right of the medical assistant to practice, and to provide a basis for legislation with the documents mentioned above, the AAMA has developed the *Scope of Practice for Medical Assistants.*

You will be considered a dependent professional because your performance is the result of assigned tasks within a job description and state law. Your duties will often overlap those of licensed health-care professionals.

It is your responsibility to know the laws concerning a medical assistant's scope of practice in the state in which you work. It is the responsibility of the employing agency to supply a job description that falls within legal regulations. It is the joint responsibility of the MA and the supervisor to monitor performance levels and provide training or supervision as necessary.

Job Opportunities

Medical assisting can be a chance for you to step up in life. As a medical assistant you will perform outpatient and inpatient services in many work settings, including medical offices, ambulatory clinics, hospitals, extended-care facilities, government agencies, rehabilitation facilities, and free-standing clinics. Jobs in a hospital or physician's office may include admissions, reception, billing, insurance, EKG, medical records, phlebotomy (with additional training), treatment/procedure, and emergency (registration or assistant). With further education and training you may also find work as a pharmacy technician, for example (depending on state regulations), or an assistant to other professionals such as dentists and physical therapists.

The job outlook for medical assistants is promising. Job opportunities are expected to expand rapidly because of the rising numbers of elderly in the United States and because of advances in technology. With the likely growth in clinics and group practices, outpatient settings will continue to have the most openings. The strength of your training in administrative and clinical tasks will allow you a greater variety of job choices that meet your goals and interests.

Getting a job as a medical assistant may require previous experience in the field. In addition to an externship, which is an on-the-job learning experience, you can gain experience in an office setting by volunteering at a clinic in your community. Other volunteer possibilities include health screening clinics or fairs, well-baby clinics, senior citizen centers, and hospitals. Check with the college placement service to see what your community offers.

You must have a proper resume when you look for a job. Most schools teach resume writing and also provide a chance to role-play a job interview. If you have access to the Internet, you may be able to get online help or advice on writing a resume.

Medical Assistant Educational Programs

In 1934, Dr. M. Mandl established the first school for training medical assistants. No longer just the physician's general helper, the medical assistant is now considered a multiskilled health-care professional. Training today combines formal and clinical education along with an externship.

You have two options for credentials. One is the Certified Medical Assistant (**CMA**) credential through the American Association of Medical Assistants (AAMA) (Figure 1-9 ◆). The second option is the Registered Medical Assistant (**RMA**) credential through the American Medical Technologists (**AMT**) (Figure 1-10 ◆). In 2001, AAMA and AMT reached an agreement on a model state law that recognizes the scope of medical assisting. They also established minimum qualifications for practicing as an MA.

AMT was founded in 1939. AAMA, founded in 1955, develops the necessary structures to protect the MA's rights to practice. Both groups certify and represent medical assistants. AMT also represents and administers allied health certification examinations for medical laboratory technicians, medical technologists, phlebotomists, laboratory technicians, medical administrative assistants, allied health instructors, laboratory consultants, and dental assistants. AMT is accredited by the National Commission for Certifying Agencies (**NCCA**).

Figure 1-9 ◆ Certified medical assistant (CMA) pin
Courtesy of the American Association of Medical Assistants

Along with the Committee for Accreditation of Allied Health Education Programs (CAAHEP), AAMA has established standards for accreditation (official approval) of medical assisting programs throughout the nation. The *Standards for an Accredited Educational Program for the Medical Assistant* may be viewed on the Internet at the CAAHEP site.

AMT is a member of the National Commission for Certifying Agents (NCCA), the accreditation arm of the National Organization for Competency Assurance (NOCA). NOCA sets standards for credentialing organizations in allied health fields.

The Accrediting Bureau of Health Education Schools (**ABHES**) is another accrediting agency. The U.S. Department of Education has granted recognition to ABHES as a specialized accreditor for training institutions with a health-care educational focus. The evaluation standards of an ABHES-accredited

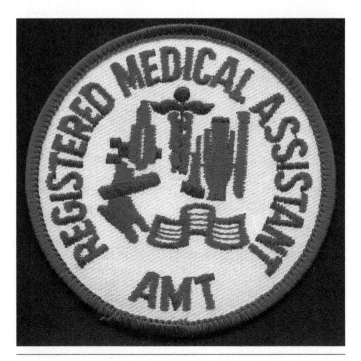

Figure 1-10 ◆ Insignia of the registered medical assistant
Courtesy of American Medical Technologists

program may be found on the Internet at www.abhes.org, in Chapter VI of the Accreditation Manual.

Certification Examination

To qualify for the CMA examination, you must meet the standards required by AAMA. The current standards require graduation from one of the following:

■ A CAAHEP-accredited program, including externship, by January 31, June 30, or October 31 before the June, October, or late January test dates each year.
■ An ABHES-accredited program completed by the deadline date.

To keep your CMA status, you must recertify by testing on a five-year cycle or by fulfilling continuing education requirements.

To qualify for the RMA examination, you must meet the standards set by AMT. The current standards require graduation from one of the following:

■ A medical assistant program accredited by ABHES or CAAHEP.
■ A medical assistant program accredited by a regional accrediting commission or a national accrediting organization approved by the U.S. Department of Education; the program must include 720 clock hours of medical assisting training and a clinical externship.
■ A formal medical services training program of the U.S. Armed Forces.

Another way to qualify is to be employed in the medical assistant profession for at least five years, with no more than two as an instructor in a postsecondary medical assisting program. Upon passing the test, you obtain RMA status.

AMT now has a Certification Continuation Program (CCP). AMT members are required to document activities supporting continuation of AMT certification every three years. Only newly certified members and reinstated members of AMT (after January 1, 2006) are required to attest to continuous employment while obtaining continuing education every three years. The goal is to promote, encourage, and reward practitioners who attempt to maintain the competencies required at initial certification throughout their careers.

Both AAMA and AMT offer networking possibilities at different levels within the organization and professional information through various publications. They also recognize the role of medical assistants during National Medical Assistant's Week, held yearly in October.

?—Critical Thinking Question 1-2—
Can Janet apply to take the AAMA exam at one of the three times offered this year? Why or why not? If not, explain what steps she might have to take to become eligible.

Chapter Summary

- The early medical treatment of illness and disease consisted of folk remedies and sorcery. Knowledge of effective treatments was based on trial-and-error experiments with a wide range of plant and animal products. Some traditional treatments derived from plants, such as digoxin, are now manufactured in synthetic form.
- Hippocrates is known as the Father of Medicine. In addition to teaching about health, he created the Hippocratic Oath, which sets ethical and professional guidelines for physicians. He also taught that disease had natural, rather than supernatural, causes.
- In 1847 the AMA wrote a code of ethics for physicians. The code stressed professional and community responsibilities and promoted respect for human dignity, lifelong professional learning, and independence. The *Patient Bill of Rights* was developed by the AHA in 1973 to ensure effective care and satisfaction.
- As the medical field grew, requiring more highly trained people, the nursing profession developed to handle patient care. Economic changes in health care and a shortage or nurses have shaped the need for the trained multiskilled health professionals known as medical assistants.
- A medical assistant needs solid communication, administrative, and clinical skills to project a professional image in the physician's office. Following ethical principles, including tolerance toward all persons, empathy, and maintaining patient confidentiality, is as important on the job as integrity, dependability, a sense of humor, and common sense. Good personal hygiene and certain physical capabilities are also necessary to perform the clinical aspects of patient care.
- Jobs for medical assistants maybe found in health-care settings such as ambulatory care, physicians' offices, nursing homes, and hospitals. To perform specialized treatments, you may need additional training specific to the physician's office. It is also very important to understand the roles of other health-care team members to work successfully on a team.
- It is the medical assistant's responsibility to maintain active membership in a professional organization. The AAMA and the AMT are two professional organizations for medical assistants, and their certification tests are nationally recognized. CMA recertification through continuing education is required to keep CMA credentials. RMA recertification encourages voluntary continuing education for previously registered AMT members and a Certification Continuation Program for members joining after January 1, 2006.

Chapter Review Questions

Multiple Choice

1. Which of the following is an early medicine that is still used in medical treatment?
   - A. cocoa
   - B. ephedra
   - C. foxglove
   - D. geranium

2. Trepanning was done to
   - A. relieve pressure on the brain.
   - B. release evil spirits.
   - C. drain fluid after a head injury.
   - D. allow good spirits to enter the head.

3. Who first used the term *prognosis?*
   - A. Hammurabi
   - B. Galen
   - C. William Harvey
   - D. Hippocrates

4. Which of the following is covered in the AMA's *Principles of Medical Ethics?*
   - A. lifelong study
   - B. humor
   - C. personal hygiene
   - D. personal gain

5. In a medical office, *respondent superior* means
   - A. You and everyone else in the office are held responsible for a mistake that you make.
   - B. Both you and the physician are held responsible for a mistake that you make.
   - C. Only you are held responsible for a mistake that you make.
   - D. Only the physician is held responsible for a mistake that you make.

Chapter Review Questions (continued)

6. On-the-job professionalism involves
   A. picking up and driving patients.
   B. scolding patients if they arrive late for an appoinment.
   C. avoiding contact with patients.
   D. courtesy and patience with patients.

7. To become an MA, you should
   A. pass a recognized national certification test.
   B. apply for a license within your state.
   C. meet with local regulatory officials.
   D. take an oath before starting your job.

8. Experience in the field when you are still a student is called a(n)
   A. internship.
   B. externship.
   C. apprenticeship.
   D. clerkship.

9. In 2001, the AAMA and AMT established
   A. a working agreement to merge both organizations.
   B. a joint certification test for MAs.
   C. joint guidelines for the teaching of medical assisting.
   D. minimum qualification requirements to practice as an MA.

10. To maintain your CMA, you must continue your education or retest in
    A. six years.
    B. four years.
    C. five years.
    D. ten years.

True/False

T F 1. Medical assisting is a fairly new profession in the health-care delivery system and did not receive professional recognition until the 1960s.

T F 2. In 1822, James Hall was the first African American to receive a medical degree.

T F 3. Physical flexibility and strength are not required if you plan to work only in the administrative section of the medical office.

T F 4. The PCP and gatekeeper function as two separate practitioners in general medicine.

T F 5. An RN has more training than an NP, but both can write prescriptions.

Short Answer

1. What is the term for the written confirmation that an individual has met specific standards for the safe practice of a profession or service?

2. What is the granting of written permission to practice a profession called?

3. Which member of the health-care team specializes in taking blood specimens for laboratory analysis?

Research

1. What is the contact number for your local AAMA? Does it hold monthly meetings?

2. What is the process for applying to become a member of your local AAMA chapter?

3. Where would you research the specific laws that pertain to medical assistants working in your state?

Resource Guide

Commission on Accreditation of Allied Health Education Programs (CAAHEP)
35 E Wacker Dr., Suite 1970
Chicago, IL 60601
1-312-553-9355
www.CAAHEP.org

American Association of Medical Assistants (AAMA)
20 N. Wacker Dr., Suite 1575
Chicago, IL 60606
1-800-228-2262
www.aama-ntl.org

Accrediting Bureau of Health Education Schools (ABHES)
7777 Leesburg Pike, Suite 314 N.
Falls Church, VA 22043
(703) 917-9503
www.abhes.org

American Medical Technologists
710 Higgins Road
Park Ridge, IL 60068
847.823.5169
www.amt1.com

MedMedia
www.prenhall.com/frazier

More on this chapter, including interactive resources, can be found on the Student CD-ROM accompanying this textbook and on the Companion Website at www.prenhall.com/frazier.

CHAPTER 2

Interpersonal Communication

Case Study

Oksana is working at the receptionist desk of Dr. Chen's ENT office during a slow lunch hour. Oksana is responsible for answering phones and checking in patients for their afternoon appointments. Most of the patients have been checked in and the phone isn't ringing very much, so Oksana decides to eat the sandwich she brought for lunch. As she sits at the desk eating, one of Dr. Chen's hearing-impaired patients walks up and makes eye contact. Oksana quickly places her sandwich on a stack of papers and, still chewing, says impatiently, "Yes?"

The patient tilts her head slightly and furrows her eyebrows, conveying the message "I don't understand." The patient attempts to communicate that she is here for her 1:00 appointment and that she has new health insurance. She speaks slowly and with some effort.

As Oksana tries to understand what the patient is saying, several phone lines begin to ring. She raises her hand and holds up her index finger as she turns away from the patient to answer the phone.

The patient continues to stand at the desk, waiting to provide a copy of her new insurance card to Oksana. Meanwhile, Oksana speaks with the callers, cradling the phone to her shoulder and crossing her arms over her chest. She avoids eye contact with the patient at the desk.

Moments later the office manager walks in to see the patient's look of frustration, Oksana on the phone with her arms crossed over her chest, and a half-eaten sandwich on a stack of office memos.

Objectives

After completing this chapter, you should be able to:

- Spell and define the medical terminology in this chapter.
- Define the medical assistant's role in communicating.
- Discuss verbal communication.
- Describe oral and written communication in the medical office.
- Explain symbolic language and how to communicate with patients who use it.
- Discuss nonverbal communication.
- Explain the concept of personal space.
- Describe the role of body language in communication.
- Discuss the importance of listening.
- Explain Maslow's hierarchy of needs.
- Describe some of the barriers to communication with patients.
- Explain how cultural and age factors can affect communication.
- List and explain common defense mechanisms.
- Discuss how to understand and help a grieving person.

 MedMedia

www.prenhall.com/frazier

Additional interactive resources and activities for this chapter can be found on the Companion Website. For videos, audio glossary, legal and ethical scenarios, job scenarios, quizzes, and games related to the content of this chapter, please access the accompanying CD-ROM in this book.

Assets Available:

Audio Glossary
Legal and Ethical Scenario: *Interpersonal Communication*
On the Job Scenario: *Interpersonal Communication*
Video Scenario: *When English Is Not the Language; Coping with Sales Calls; A Hospital Admission*
HIPAA Quiz: *Medical Assisting: The Profession; Medical Science: History and Practice; Medical Law and Ethics*
Games: Crossword, Strikeout, and Spelling Bee

MEDICAL ASSISTING COMPETENCIES

CAAHEP ENTRY-LEVEL COMPETENCIES FOR CMA	ABHES ENTRY-LEVEL COMPETENCIES FOR RMA
▪ Identify and respond to issues of confidentiality.	▪ Maintain confidentiality at all times.
▪ Perform within legal and ethical boundaries.	▪ Be cognizant of ethical boundaries.
▪ Demonstrate knowledge of federal and state health-care legislation and regulations.	▪ Exhibit initiative.
	▪ Adapt to change.
	▪ Evidence a responsible attitude.
▪ Respond to and initiate written communications.	▪ Be courteous and diplomatic.
▪ Recognize and respond to verbal communications.	▪ Conduct work within scope of education, training, and ability.
	▪ Be attentive, listen, and learn.
▪ Recognize and respond to nonverbal communications.	▪ Be impartial and show empathy when dealing with patients.
▪ Demonstrate telephone techniques.	▪ Adapt what is said to the recipient's level of comprehension.
	▪ Serve as a liaison between physician and others.
	▪ Use proper telephone technique.
	▪ Interview effectively.
	▪ Use appropriate medical terminology.
	▪ Receive, organize, and transmit information expediently.
	▪ Recognize and respond to verbal and nonverbal communication.
	▪ Use correct grammar, spelling, and formatting techniques in written works.
	▪ Principles of verbal and nonverbal communication.
	▪ Adaptation for individualized needs.
	▪ Applications of electronic technology.
	▪ Fundamental writing skills.
	▪ Professional components.
	▪ Allied health professions and credentialing.

Medical Terminology

anxiety—fear of the unknown; a feeling of fear or worry about the future

hearing impaired—unable to hear, or having a diminished sense of hearing

vocally impaired—unable to speak, or having a diminished ability to speak

Abbreviations

ASL—American Sign Language

HIPAA—Health Insurance Portability and Accountability Act

Introduction

Communicating involves two people who are each sending and receiving messages. These messages can be verbal and/or nonverbal. Communicating is a lifelong process. Some individuals believe that communication begins before birth with the *fetus* (unborn baby) hearing the voice and heartbeat of the mother, external voices of others, music, and sounds.

 ## The Medical Assistant's Role in Communication

As an MA student, and later as a CMA or RMA, how and why you send messages is important to the way you communicate with patients and staff in the medical office. You will use more professional language, including medical terminology, than when you converse with friends. With patients you will use a warm, professional approach combined with empathy for the patient's situation.

Written office communication must also be professional. Charting is an essential form of communication in the medical office. Medical charts are legal documents that must be accurate and legible. (∞ Chapter 6, Clinical Visit: Office Preparation and the Patient Encounter, discusses charting and medical records in greater detail.)

Verbal Communication

Verbal communication can be oral, written, or symbolic. Oral communication begins with the person who sends an auditory message to a recipient, or listener. Written communication consists of letters, memos, and e-mail. Writing allows you to edit the message for clarity and accuracy before sending. Symbolic communication uses a language that is not vocal, such as sign language. Regardless of the form of communication, patient confidentiality must be observed at all times.

Oral Communication

Talking with another person is the most common way to communicate. As an MA, you will be in contact with patients, patients' families, physicians, and other medical staff. Your voice tones and word choices are part of your professional image. Communicating by telephone requires more care because you cannot rely on nonverbal messages as well.

Office Procedures

Choose your words carefully. Be professional and avoid using slang. Keep your conversation focused and to the point.

When speaking with a patient, understand that he or she may be anxious, and messages may need to be repeated to be understood. Remain pleasant and repeat the message until the patient verbalizes understanding or appears to understand. Do not interrupt when the patient is speaking or try to finish the patient's sentences when he or she pauses.

The physician and staff deserve the same respectful communication as the patient. Make sure your descriptions and information are accurate and easy to understand. Ask questions if you are unclear about any instructions or information. Avoid gossip.

? — Critical Thinking Question 2-1—
How should Oksana have greeted the patient who walked up to her desk? What steps should she have taken before patients arrived to appear more professional and competent?

Telephone Procedures

It is important to answer the phone before the third ring. If circumstances dictate that the caller be placed on hold, ask the caller for permission first. Occasionally the call will be about an emergency situation, or there may be some other reason the caller should not be put on hold.

Greet the caller in a pleasant and professional manner. Your greeting should include:

- "Hello," "Good morning," "Good afternoon," or "Good evening"
- The name of the organization
- Your first name
- A service statement, such as "May I help you?"

Answering the phone properly establishes a good first impression. Smile when you greet the caller. A smile adds a friendly, welcoming note to your voice. Sitting up and feeling poised and alert also relay that message to the caller.

Being clear and courteous on the telephone avoids incorrect interpretation of your message by the caller and any misunderstandings that may result. Common telephone courtesy includes:

- Listening to the caller without interrupting
- Asking permission before putting a caller on hold, identifying the second caller and whether it is an emergency
- Obtaining enough information to determine if a call is an emergency situation
- Offering the caller an alternative time to call back if he or she cannot wait on hold
- Checking back with a caller on hold approximately every 15 to 20 seconds
- Keeping your mind on the call by avoiding distractions
- Never expressing hostility, a negative attitude, or vulgarities

? —Critical Thinking Question 2-2—
Do you think Oksana's posture affects her tone of voice and the way she delivers her message to the caller? Should she have asked the callers if they could be placed on hold so that she could return to the patient at the desk?

Non-English Speakers

People who are visiting or who have immigrated to the United States from a foreign country will also need health-care services. Since English is not their first language, you will need to find out how well these patients understand English. Some may understand English very well but may not be able to express their thoughts and responses verbally in English. Any instructions you provide must be repeated or demonstrated by the patient or support person before the patient leaves the office. You should also provide the non-English-speaking patient with an interpreter if necessary, since this is also a legal requirement.

In certain parts of the United States it is a good idea to learn a few phrases in the foreign languages commonly spoken in the area. Courtesy words, such as *hello, please,* and *thank you,* help make the patient feel welcome and respected. Speak slowly and use body language, such as facial expressions, to help convey your meaning. Be aware, however, that some kinds of body language mean different things in other cultures. If an interpreter is used, it is still very important that you talk directly to the patient.

Some medical dictionaries list foreign words and their translations in their appendices. Another option is to check with local hospitals, which often have resource staff people who speak languages other than English and can interpret in a medical situation. It is helpful to make a list of commonly used words in the other languages heard in your medical office. Some useful Spanish words and phrases are listed in Table 2-1.

TABLE 2-1 COMMON SPANISH WORDS AND PHRASES

English	Spanish
Yes	Sí
No	No
Don't be afraid.	No tenga miedo.
Here	Aquí
There	Allí
Every day	Todos los dias
Every hour	Cada hora
Show me.	Enséñeme.
Right	Derecha
Left	Izquierda
Say it once again, please.	Repita por favor.
At bedtime	A la hora de acostarse
At night	Por la noche
Early in the morning	Temprano por la mañana
Allergy	Alergía
Good	Bien
Bad	Mal
Have you any pain?	¿Tiene dolor?
Where does it hurt?	¿Donde le duele?
Show me where.	Enséñeme donde.
Is it worse now?	¿Está peor ahora?
Cough	Tosa
Take a deep breath.	Respire profundemente.

Written Communication

Written communication should be clear, well organized, and concise, or to the point. Choose your words carefully, citing only facts, not your opinion. Use correct grammar and spelling and avoid slang. Abbreviations, shortened medical terms, and symbols may be used with physicians and staff. With a patient it is best to use lay terms. Since mutual understanding is the goal of communication, the use of lay terms may save patients the embarrassment of having to ask for an explanation.

Documenting information on medical charts and records is vital to your job. Other written materials include memos, letters, messages, faxes, and e-mail. Make sure your handwriting or printing is neat and legible. Memos, letters, and messages are used in an office to pass information to physicians, staff, and patients. Keep these short and focused on the information requested or communicated. Faxing is an easy way to send messages and information to other medical facilities and business offices. Faxes *must* be kept confidential. Send only the exact patient information requested and make sure the reception site is secure. To ensure confidentiality, call ahead to let the receiver know that a fax is being sent. Note on the patient's chart what you sent by fax, to whom you sent it, and the date and time of transmission. A transaction log should be maintained and kept by the fax machine for a predetermined time (a minimum of 30 days is required by HIPAA), as established by office policy and required by law.

E-mail is a quick and efficient method of sending and receiving messages. As an MA, you will be able to use e-mail and the Internet to

- access patient records from other medical offices.
- obtain diagnostic test results.
- research information.

- transmit requested patient data.
- communicate with other medical facilities and business offices.

Often precertifications, reimbursement billing, and procedure scheduling can be done in minutes over the Internet. When sending confidential e-mail information, be sure you are using secure sites. An e-mail message should be edited before sending to prevent errors and avoid misunderstanding. Use office e-mail for business purposes only.

Many medical offices are now converting to "paperless" offices through the use of electronic medical records (EMR) programs. These EMR programs allow for easily accessible and up-to-date patient information to be transferred electronically between medical staff within the clinic or to medical staff at other locations.

While computers provide greater opportunities in the medical office environment, there is also a risk that patient privacy may be jeopardized. HIPAA includes rules for the use of EMR, which can be viewed at http://www.cms.hhs.gov/SecurityStandard/. The office must have policies and procedures in place outlining confidentially and security methods, and that backup methods are established.

Symbolic Language

Symbolic language refers to an alternative way of communicating. Sign language is the most common form of symbolic language. Braille is the written form of language for people who are blind. It uses symbolic tactile (touch) images.

Sign Language

Sign language is used by a person who has total hearing loss or is unable to speak. Those who are unable to hear or who have a diminished sense of hearing are **hearing impaired,** sometimes called deaf; those who are unable to speak are called

---

Keys to Success
E-MAIL ETIQUETTE

- Use a personal name if your system allows it. This will help to identify you on the e-mail faster than the Internet address alone.
- Fill in the subject line to identify your message. Send one message for each subject.
- Change the subject line if your reply changes the subject of a message.
- Use correct spelling and grammar.
- Do not write a message with all uppercase letters, which may be viewed by the receiver as expressing anger.
- Do not send messages expressing strong emotions. You are likely to regret it.
- Check the return address of an e-mail before sending. It can be very embarrassing to accidentally send an e-mail to the wrong person(s).
- Use a signature to identify who you are and add alternative means of contact. The average signature length is four to seven lines.
- Use "please" and "thank you" as you would in a spoken message. Do not expect immediate replies. Avoid personal or sensitive information because e-mail is not secure without encryption (special coding).
- Refrain from using any form of sarcasm, as the receiver cannot see your body language.

vocally impaired. The term *dumb* to denote inability to speak is less respectful. American Sign Language (**ASL**) is a complex language in its own right, with specific grammar rules, and signs for words, using hand movements. Hand signs can also represent the letters of the alphabet, but communicating by spelling out words is considered "baby talk" and does not ensure informed consent. (Figure 2-1 ◆). ASL is considered a formal communication method, where hand gestures, movements, and facial expressions enhance the meaning of signs.

When communicating with persons with hearing impairment, it is important to face them at all times, including when an interpreter is used. Many are able to read lips to some degree. Speak to the person in a normal tone of voice. Some patients can hear minimal sounds. It is also helpful to learn basic phrases in sign language, such as "please" or "thank you." Written communication can also be effective. Some patients are able to speak and be understood, while others make sounds

Caduceus Chronicle	
A SHORT HISTORY OF COMMUNICATION WITH THE DEAF	
1754	Abbé Charles Michel de l'Epée (1712–1789) established the first school for the hearing impaired in Paris.
1816	Dr. Thomas H. Gallaudet (1787–1851) traveled to Paris to study French Sign Language (FSL) in order to help a friend's deaf daughter. He studied Old French Sign Language (OFSL) under Laurent Clerc (1785–1869), who was deaf.
1817	The first U.S. school for the deaf was founded in Hartford, Connecticut, with Gallaudet as principal and teacher and Laurent Clerc as a teacher. American Sign Language (ASL) was developed as a combination of FSL and hand gestures already in use among the U.S. deaf population.
1864	Edward Miner Gallaudet (1837–1917) founded the first college for students with hearing impairment. It was later named Gallaudet University.
1880s	Teaching sign language was opposed by many who believed it isolated the deaf from the hearing community. By the early twentieth century, oralism—speaking and lip reading—became the accepted way to teach those with hearing impairment.
1950s	William C. Stokoe (1919–2000) began the modern linguistic study of sign language. His research led to acceptance of ASL as a fully formed language.
1960s	Total Communication gained popularity. It includes signing, speaking, and lip reading.

that represent certain words. Listen carefully. Remember also the legal requirement to provide an interpreter.

Braille

Braille is a system of writing for the blind. Raised dots in certain patterns on paper represent letters of the alphabet. A blind person touches these dots with the fingertips to read words and numbers (Figure 2-2 ◆). (∞ In Chapter 19, EENT, office procedures for blind patients are discussed.) Remember that it is not necessary to talk loudly to a person who is visually challenged; he or she is *not* hard of hearing.

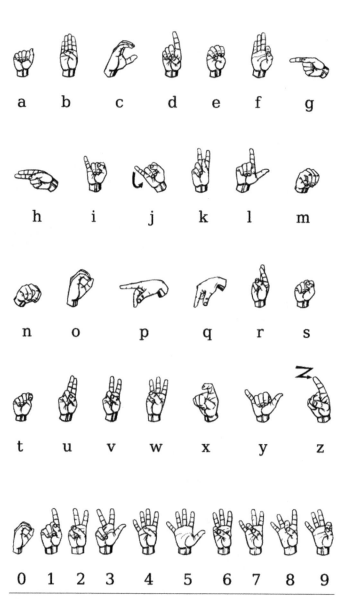

Figure 2-1 ◆ The American sign language alphabet

Figure 2-2 ◆ Braille is a system of writing for the blind.

Caduceus Chronicle
A SHORT HISTORY OF THE BRAILLE SYSTEM

1827	Louis Braille (1809–1852), a 12-year-old blind French student, created the Braille system.
1829	The Braille system was published in the United States.
1858	The American Printing House for the Blind was founded in Kentucky.
1866	The first raised-print book was published by the American Printing House.
1879	Congress voted to permanently fund the American Printing House.
1893	The stereotyping machine, which automated the Braille printing process, was invented.
1893	The first Braille book was published by the American Printing House.
1916	The Braille system was officially accepted in the United States.
1932	English Braille became the universal standard for English-speaking people.

Nonverbal Communication

Nonverbal communication is sending a message without words. A smile and a touch are examples of nonverbal communication. Body language shows emotion and feeling. Learning to use and being able to read nonverbal communication are vital to working in a medical office. A patient's facial expressions, gestures, posture, and positioning provide clues to his or her mental state and health.

Personal Space

Personal space is the area immediately surrounding a person (Figures 2-3 ◆ through 2-6 ◆). It is a comfort zone. In U.S. culture, standing too close to someone sends a message of intrusiveness, while standing too far away sends a message of disinterest, rudeness, or lack of commitment to the conversation. Personal space varies with different cultures. In Arab countries, people converse at a distance that would be considered intimate in the United

Figure 2-3 ◆ Intimate distance: shows affection, provides comfort and protection

Figure 2-4 ◆ Personal distance: most communication takes place at this distance

Figure 2-5 ◆ Social distance: less personal; used in social and business encounters

Figure 2-6 ◆ Public distance: least personal; observed in lectures, church, and impersonal social encounters

States, and backing away is considered an impolite gesture. As a medical assistant, it is important that you be knowledgeable about personal space issues and respect patients' boundaries.

To understand the U.S. concept of personal space, ask yourself the following questions:

1. How do I feel when I am in a crowded elevator?
2. How would I feel at the library if I saw another student who had books and papers spread out on a table and all the other tables were in use?
3. How do I feel when a person whom I do not know enters my personal space?
4. How do I feel when a health-care provider leans across me to reach for an item?

Often a person backs away when you enter his or her personal space. This is an immediate cue for you to stop or back away slightly. Some procedures will require that you be in a patient's personal space. Usually the patient is aware of this, but make sure you ease the discomfort as much as possible. Before you invade the patient's personal space or touch the patient, say, "I need to take your pulse, so I am going to hold your wrist for approximately one minute. Is that OK?" It is important for the patient to give implied or verbal consent prior to any type of touching.

Body Language

Eye contact, facial expressions, gestures, and posture are body language. They provide clues to a person's feelings and state of mind.

Eye Contact

Making eye contact shows you are listening to what the patient has to say or, as you are talking, if the patient understands what you are saying. The eyes express a range of emotions, including anger, love, and fear. Normal eye contact during conversation is not staring. Staring, a prolonged wide-eyed gaze, is a form of nonverbal communication. It can make a patient uncomfortable and can be interpreted as threatening.

Facial Expressions

Happiness, sadness, surprise, fear, anger, and disgust are basic facial expressions common to all cultures. Other, more subtle expressions are harder to read. For example, a raised eyebrow can mean that the patient is either questioning what you are saying or does not believe you.

Gestures

Gestures are movements that a person makes when he or she is talking. The hand may be used to indicate where the pain is located and if the pain is spreading to another area. Some people use gestures more than others, often to emphasize a point.

Posture

Posture involves body positioning and movement. A person who is listening carefully to what you are saying may lean toward you. Abruptly standing can indicate the conversation is over.

Keep in mind that your body language is a reflection of how you are relating to others. A gentle nod of your head can be read as understanding. Keep it positive and open. Avoid folding your arms over your chest, as this is a closed position. It separates you from the patient. *Never* point a finger at anyone or gesture improperly. Even if someone is annoying, remain professional.

Listening

A factor often overlooked in communicating is the importance of listening. Listening involves focusing on what the other person is saying and making sure you understand, so that you can respond appropriately.

Effective listening includes the following techniques.

- Make eye contact with the person, but do not stare.
- Pay attention to the person's behavior and body language.
- Allow the person to finish what he or she is saying without interrupting.
- Ask relevant questions to keep the person on the subject and for your understanding. For example, a patient states, "I started having this pain on Tuesday morning in my lower back and then it spread to my right hip." Since it is already Thursday, you might say, "So on Tuesday morning the pain was in your lower back. Did the pain spread to your right hip on Tuesday or Wednesday?"
- Paraphrase (restate) what the person says to make sure you have the correct information and interpretation. For example, the patient states, "I took two pills at 4:00 with my dinner and two more at 10:00 before I went to bed." You could repeat the information by saying, "You took your pills six hours apart—two at 4:00 P.M. and two at 10:00 P.M."
- Avoid interjecting your own stories or information. The goal of listening is to listen, not to share personal information with the patient.

Effective listening is vital in a medical office. It ensures that you accurately record patient information and fully understand the physician's instructions.

Developmental Stages of the Life Cycle

Human development is a lifelong process. The individual faces certain tasks during each stage, builds on previous growth when entering each new stage, and gradually progresses to a higher level of development. The physical and emotional stages of the life cycle are often presented in psychology courses; understanding these stages helps in communication with all patients, regardless of age.

The stages of development are a complex subject that is presented more in depth during psychology courses. Depending on what theorist you subscribe to, you may believe that individuals will pass through life stages one at a time in chronological order without ever returning to the previous stage, they may skip stages and successfully navigate others in a random order, or they may pass unilaterally through stages and remain in one or more at any given time. It is important to understand that there is no "appropriate" method of development with people, because they will develop at an individual pace according to their own needs and environment.

An individual's ability to communicate and to interpret messages is greatly affected by his or her developmental stage (Table 2-2). It is important to communicate with each person at his or her developmental level. As an example, an older female patient of 70-plus years might be beginning to prepare for the loss of her mate or for her own death. She may not hear or understand communication about medications, activity, or treatment because she is preoccupied with other concerns. A common mistake made by people who work with the elderly is to speak in baby-like, patronizing tones. The usual response is one of annoyance or feeling insulted, and the elderly person may simply stop listening.

In terms of personality and relationships, the United States psychoanalyst Erik Erikson (1902–1994) believed that the development of trust, or lack of trust, in the first year of life is the foundation for the development of an individual's coping skills (Table 2-3). In each of the developmental stages described by Erikson, the positive resolution of any crisis is based on positive coping characteristics: trust, independence, initiative, competence, and integrity. Negative coping characteristics that contribute to negative resolution include mistrust, insecurity, and dependency, among others. An awareness of Erikson's life stages will help you better understand what patients experience as they grow and age and provides a foundation for more effective therapeutic communication with patients.

Maslow's Hierarchy of Human Needs

Communication may be influenced by people's needs. Abraham Maslow (1908–1970) was a United States psychologist who studied human motivation and developed what is known as Maslow's hierarchy of human needs (Figure 2-7 ◆). According to Maslow's principles, individuals fulfill their needs, partially or totally, at a basic level before moving toward higher levels of emotional satisfaction. For example, people must satisfy the most basic needs for food, shelter, and clothing before they can

TABLE 2-2 APPROXIMATE PHYSICAL AND EMOTIONAL STAGES OF THE LIFE CYCLE, ACCORDING TO JEAN PIAGET

6 weeks	The baby begins to smile and develop facial expressions.
10 weeks	The baby begins to roll from prone to a supine position.
4 to 6 months	The baby raises its head and shoulders while lying in supine position.
6 to 8 months	The baby sits without support. Eye color may change.
8 to 12 months	The baby learns to crawl, stand, take steps, feed him- or herself, and develop autonomy.
1 year	The baby understands commands and simple conversation.
18 months	The toddler walks alone, feeds self, stacks objects, and is becoming more independent.
20 to 24 months	The toddler begins to learn bowel and bladder control and explores the environment.
3 to 4 years	The child talks in complete sentences.
4 to 5 years	The child dresses and undresses him- or herself.
5 to 6 years	The child's eye and body coordination improves. The child can skip and draw figures.
6 to 8 years	The child enters school, and physical skills improve.
8 to 13 years	The adolescent's rate of physical growth increases and adult sexual characteristics develop.
13 to 18 years	The teenager undergoes puberty and strives for independence.
18 to 20 years	The young adult becomes more independent, may continue his or her education, and/or may marry and have children.
20 to 30 years	The adult attempts to build a firm, safe foundation for the future. There may be a continuation of the educational process, marriage, and children.
30 to 40 years	The adult experiences more freedom, continuing to work and raise children.
40 to 50 years	The adult evaluates the first part of his or her life and continues working. The children may begin leaving the nest.
50 to 60 years	The adult experiences a sense of comfort, acceptance of life. Children continue leaving the home. The individual experiences freedom and success.
60 to 70 years	The adult looks forward to or begins retirement. Losing the mate and living alone become real possibilities. Less home committments mean greater sense of freedom to explore, travel, start a new hobby. Their rich fullfillment of life offers a great education they can pass on to younger generations.
70 plus years	The adult faces the facts of aging, may lose the mate and friends to illness and death, and begins to prepare for his or her own death. Less financial burdons bring the ability to fulfill wants and desires of traveling, gifts, vacations. More time can be spent enjoying family, friends and hobbies.

The last stage of life, old age, is often divided into three stages: early old age (55–65), old age (65–85), and very old age (85 and older). Adults in early old age become more aware of their own mortality, and significant lifestyle changes may occur. Some begin to acknowledge health problems, physical limitations, and a likely decline in earning power or working capacity in the years ahead.

Among the 65- to 85-year-old group, many have retired, are forced to live on lower incomes, and are experiencing progressively worse health problems. Living arrangements may change because of their financial situations or because they can no longer care for themselves. Some have lost partners, family members, and friends through death.

Most adults over age 85 have gone through all the experiences mentioned above. Many are in long-term-care facilities, many have severe memory problems, and many have no income. Others are in excellent health, are able to care for themselves, travel, and live life to the fullest.

The aging process affects different people in different ways. It is important not to stereotype the elderly—each person is unique in terms of genetic makeup, health status, financial status, and life experience.

TABLE 2-3 ERIK ERIKSON'S LIFE STAGES AND DEVELOPMENTAL TASKS

1. Infancy	Develop trust.
2. Early childhood	Develop independence and self-direction.
3. Play age	Develop initiative.
4. School age	Develop competence.
5. Adolescence	Develop self-identity.
6. Early adulthood	Develop intimacy and love.
7. Middle adulthood	Develop concern for others and continue productivity.
8. Old age	Develop integrity.

go on to fulfill their needs for family, employment, financial stability, or self-actualization.

Although the hierarchy is simplistic and cannot be applied to every situation, it does provide a perspective on communication problems in the clinical setting. Health is not listed in Maslow's hierarchy, but it is a basic physiological need. Illness affects a person's emotional state. When an individual experiences chronic illness, recovery can take precedence over job stability, friendships, and self-actualization. During times of illness, some people worry about their job, family, and income over their own physiological needs. An individual who puts others' needs above his or her own health may sacrifice present needs for worsening health in the future.

Barriers to Communication

It is sometimes difficult to communicate with a patient. Patients who are struggling with some of the problems of aging, who come from a different ethnic or cultural background, or who have very strong defense mechanisms may present particular challenges.

When people come to the doctor it is likely the result of injury of illness. People who have terminal, chronic, or acute illnesses may present a barrier in communication. They may be in significant pain, or consumed with worry and not able to freely express themselves as they normally would. Children pose another unique barrier to communication. Depending on their age, development, and maturity they simply may not be able to grasp the concept of the medical treatment and procedures. The MA must be very careful when attempting communications with anyone who looks as if they might have difficulty communicating. Looks can be deceiving and it would be a great disservice to your patient and your professional image to undermine the patient's ability to understand based on appearance.

Cultural and Age Factors

Cultural factors, religious or ethnic, affect a person's beliefs about health and disease. For example, stoicism is valued among the Vietnamese and can cause a patient to delay seeking health care. Koreans have a strong belief in diagnoses based on data from clinical testing. African Americans may combine religious, magical, and practical beliefs, depending on their cultural background. Hispanics may seek permission from the eldest family member. They may also say "Yes" out of respect and politeness even when they disagree with the treatment proposed by the physician.

Age can play an important role in health care. An older patient has had a number of life experiences that could cause him or her to delay or distrust treatment. Paying the medical bills may weigh heavily on an elderly person and can affect his or her attitude toward treatment. Also, an older patient often has more fears about entering a hospital.

When age and culture are factors in patient education, be patient. Listen carefully and be positive and supportive.

Belonging to a particular ethnic group or culture does not mean the patient will automatically follow the customs, traditions, or beliefs of that group. The best way to open communication is to include the patient as much as possible and respect their choices and boundaries.

Defense Mechanisms

Defense mechanisms are people's characteristic, usually unconscious, ways of protecting themselves in stressful situations. Just as everyone has physical defenses that combat disease, everyone also has mental and emotional defenses to deal with stress and **anxiety**. These mechanisms may be engaged consciously or unconsciously, usually in combination with others. Table 2-4 lists some common defense mechanisms you may encounter in patients. You should also examine your own defense mechanisms as they arise in your interactions with patients and coworkers.

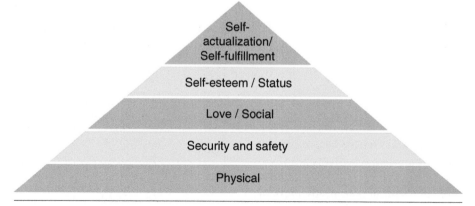

Figure 2-7 ◆ Maslow's hierarchy of needs
Source: Maslow, Abraham H., Frager, Robert D. (ed.), and Fadiman, James (ed.). Motivation and personality, 3rd ed. © 1987. Reprinted by permission of Pearson Education, Inc. Upper Saddle River, NJ.

The following are examples of different approaches to the same situation—a patient has just been diagnosed with insulin-dependent diabetes.

- You are teaching a 7-year-old boy how to give himself insulin injections. It is natural for the child to be worried. He may not listen well or remember instructions. One way to handle the situation is to find out more about the child's home situation, then instruct one or both parents in giving the insulin injection along with the child. The child will feel more secure when his parents are involved. It also satisfies the child's emotional needs, paving the way for easier learning. A parent or responsible caretaker should be present in the room during the teaching experience.
- A woman with a hearing impairment who is on Medicare and social security thinks she is going to die because she has no money for insulin and syringes. Explain that you will help her contact the appropriate agencies to help pay for the medications. Stress that she should contact you if she needs any other help. By relieving her concerns about money, you now have a patient ready to learn.
- A Chicano man learns he will have to take insulin for the rest of his life. He tells you, "I might as well die!" After talking with the man, you learn he is afraid he will no longer be able to work. Assure him that working should not be a problem. Tell him that learning how to take care of himself will help him continue taking care of his family.

Defense mechanisms protect a person's self-esteem but do not effectively deal with conflict. It is important to recognize the coping style of the patient, the patient's family, staff, and physicians. For example, one of the most common defense mechanisms is denial. A patient with a serious condition may refuse to believe what is happening. This refusal to accept reality is a factor in the patient's treatment and education.

An understanding of the psychological principles discussed in this chapter will improve your therapeutic communication skills and your interactions with patients.

The Grieving Process

Working in a medical office, you will have to deal with the emotional states of chronic and terminally ill patients. In 1965 Elisabeth Kübler-Ross, a physician, began working with terminally ill patients to help them as they faced death. Through this effort, she identified five emotional stages (Table 2-5). Although most patients move through all the stages before they reach acceptance, they may not move through them in sequential order.

Grieving is experienced by a dying patient as well as by anyone suffering a major loss, such as the loss of a loved one, a body part or function, one's health, employment, or income. It is essential to remember that family members also share in the grieving process and have to move through their own stages of grief.

Grieving is part of the healing process. Each person suffers loss in his or her own way, and the grieving process may be lengthy. Many turn to a spiritual source for comfort and stability; others may turn to family and friends. Health-care providers can help in the grieving process by offering support, but medical assistants must remain within the scope of their practice and refrain from counseling grieving patients or families.

TABLE 2-4 COMMON DEFENSE MECHANISMS

Compensation	Trying to overcome some inability or inferiority. It helps to maintain one's self-respect and raise self-esteem.
Conversion	Changing an emotional problem into a physical symptom or other method of release that eases tension and anxiety related to conflict.
Denial	Avoiding or escaping the unpleasant or distasteful realities of living by ignoring or refusing to admit their existence.
Displacement	Transferring into another situation an emotion that was felt in a past situation where its expression would have been socially unacceptable.
Identification	Unconsciously imitating the mannerisms, behavior, and feelings of another person.
Overcompensation	Repressing unconscious attitudes and wishes and replacing them with conscious attitudes and behavior that are the opposite of the unconscious ones. Often referred to as *reaction formation*.
Projection	Blaming someone else for one's own failures or for specific events.
Rationalization	Explaining, excusing, or defending ideas, actions, and feelings. It helps to "save face" in embarrassing and anxiety-producing situations.
Regression	Escaping frustration and conflict anxiety by returning to methods used at an earlier stage of life.
Repression	Unconsciously storing unpleasant, unacceptable thoughts, desires, and impulses in the mind. The repressed information does not enter conscious awareness and may not be remembered unless there is an emotional trigger. Repression is sometimes termed *selective forgetting*.
Substitution	Accepting something in place of a desired object or need when the original cannot be obtained. The substitution helps to achieve at least some fulfillment.
Suppression	Storing away or forgetting unpleasant, emotionally painful experiences. This is a conscious forcing of unpleasant, anxiety-producing experiences into the unconscious mind.

TABLE 2-5 KÜBLER-ROSS'S STAGES OF GRIEVING

Denial	Denial is usually the first stage of the grieving process, when the person refuses to believe the truth or face reality. The person may say, "No, this isn't happening to me," "This can't be," or "I don't believe it."
Anger	Anger surfaces as the person responds strongly with displeasure, irritation, and resentment.
Bargaining	Bargaining is the process of promising something in return for delaying death. It is an attempt to make a deal to change the situation or to postpone the inevitable.
Depression	Depression is a feeling of low spirits, deep sadness, or grief as the person begins to accept death.
Acceptance	Acceptance is the last stage, when the person is at peace with the truth or reality of the situation.

Certain types of statements should be avoided in loss situations, such as:

- "He is better off."
- "She's no longer in pain."
- "He's in a better place now."
- "It was God's will."

Often these statements are made in an attempt to comfort the survivor. It is hard to find the right words in such a difficult situation. Use tact and be sincere. "My thoughts are with you" or "You have my sympathy" are fairly safe statements to make. Since it is unlikely that you will know the grieving person's religious or spiritual beliefs, do not refer to your own beliefs.

Keys to Success
SCOPE OF PRACTICE

As an MA, you are not trained to advise or counsel at a professional level. However, you can listen, then accurately chart the comments of the grieving patient and family. You can also alert the physician as to the patient's status and statements of grief. Written documentation or the verbal sharing of information is helpful in the team approach to patient-centered care.

REVIEW

Chapter Summary

- Communicating consists of sending messages to and receiving messages from another person. It is a vital part of an MA's role in the medical office.
- Verbal communication can be oral, written, or symbolic. All communication should be professional. Grammar must be correct and slang should be avoided.
- Oral communication is talking with another person in the medical office or on the telephone. Conversations should be to the point and words must be chosen carefully. Being polite, respectful, and positive is key to building rapport.
- If English is the patient's second language, any instructions must be repeated or demonstrated by the patient or the patient's support person. Remember that providing an interpreter, if needed, is a legal requirement. Using body language and speaking slowly to the patient may also help to convey the message.
- Written communication should be clear, organized, and to the point. Written materials include medical charts, memos, letters, messages, faxes, and e-mail. All communication containing patient information must be kept confidential. Be aware of and follow requirements under HIPAA.

- Symbolic language includes sign language and Braille. Sign language is used by persons who have total hearing loss or are unable to speak. Braille is used by the blind.
- Nonverbal language consists of sending a message without using words. Personal space and body language are types of nonverbal language.
- Listening is extremely important in a medical office. What a patient relates to you provides clues for diagnosis. Listening also helps you connect with other people, whether they be medical staff or patients.
- According to Maslow's hierarchy of needs, individuals fulfill their needs at a basic level before moving toward higher levels of emotional satisfaction.
- A patient's age and cultural background can affect how the patient views health care. Careful listening and observing help with patient teaching.
- Defense mechanisms are the various ways people cope with life situations. Denial is a common defense mechanism shown by patients, especially those diagnosed with a serious illness.
- Elisabeth Kübler-Ross identified five emotional stages of grieving: denial, anger, bargaining, depression, and acceptance. Grieving applies to terminally ill patients as well as to patients who have experienced other kinds of losses.

Chapter Review Questions

Multiple Choice

1. Which of the following is verbal communication?
   A. facial expressions
   B. Braille
   C. posture
   D. emotion

2. If you put a caller on hold, how long should you wait before checking back with the caller?
   A. 15 to 20 seconds
   B. 40 to 50 seconds
   C. 1 to 2 minutes
   D. 3 to 4 minutes

3. Which of the following is the best way to maintain patient confidentiality when sending a fax?
   A. sending the fax after office hours
   B. sending the fax before office hours
   C. calling the receiver after the fax has been sent
   D. calling ahead to let the receiver know the fax is being sent

4. An e-mail should
   A. be worded strongly.
   B. be written in all uppercase letters.
   C. include a signature to identify who you are.
   D. include a minimum of three messages.

5. When communicating with a person who is hearing-challenged, it is important to
   A. learn to read lips.
   B. face the person at all times.
   C. become skillful in sign language.
   D. talk to the person loudly.

6. Which of the following should you do when a patient is talking to you?
   A. Avoid looking at the patient.
   B. Stare at the patient.
   C. Move in very close to the patient.
   D. Make eye contact with the patient.

7. A common defense mechanism for a patient who has just received a serious diagnosis is
   A. denial.
   B. identification.
   C. conversion.
   D. compensation.

8. Which of the following is one of Kübler-Ross's stages of grieving?
   A. rationalization
   B. substitution
   C. anger
   D. overcompensation

9. Which of the following is acceptable to say to a person who is grieving over the loss of his father?
   A. "Let's pray together."
   B. "You have my sympathy."
   C. "At least he isn't suffering anymore."
   D. "He's gone to the hereafter."

10. When you are listening to a patient, it is acceptable to
    A. interrupt the patient with questions.
    B. interject your own information.
    C. ask the patient relevant questions.
    D. answer a telephone call.

True/False

T F 1. A person who is leaning toward you is interested in what you are saying.

T F 2. A common mistake made by people who work with the elderly is to speak in babyish, patronizing tones.

T F 3. If a patient is slow in conveying a message, it is appropriate to guess what the patient is trying to say by finishing sentences for him or her.

T F 4. Defense mechanisms protect a person's self-esteem and effectively deal with conflict.

T F 5. Communicating by telephone requires less care because the caller cannot see you and you don't have to worry about your personal appearance or posture.

Short Answer

1. What term describes changing an emotional problem into a physical symptom or other method of release that eases tension and anxiety related to conflict?

2. What is nonverbal communication?

3. List six common defense mechanisms.

4. Which U.S. psychologist developed the hierarchy of human needs?

5. What are the five stages of grieving identified by Elisabeth Kübler-Ross?

Research

1. Does the Americans with Disabilities Act (ADA) require that Braille be printed on public buildings to indicate bathrooms, elevators, etc.?

2. In your local area, are sign-language classes available to the public?

3. In your local area, what are the resources for patients who speak English as a second language?

4. If a non-English-speaking patient comes to your office alone, what local agency can you contact for an interpreter?

Externship Application Experience

Elizabeth is assigned to assist at the reception desk. A male patient approaches the desk and complains that he has been waiting for 30 minutes and has to get to work. He is angry because other patients who arrived after he did have already been taken to the examination room. He demands to see the doctor immediately. How should Elizabeth respond?

Resource Guide

American Foundation for the Blind (AFB)
11 Penn Plaza, Suite 300
New York, NY 10001
1-800-232-5463
www.afb.org

American Association of the Deaf-Blind (AADB)
8630 Fenton Street, Suite 121
Silver Spring, MD 20910-4500
TTY Phone: (301) 495-4402
Voice Phone: (301) 495-4403
Fax: (301) 495-4404
E-mail: info@aadb.org

National Institute on Deafness and Other Communication Disorders
National Institutes of Health
31 Center Drive, MSC 2320
Bethesda, MD 20892-2320
www.nidcd.nih.gov

MedMedia

www.prenhall.com/frazier

More on this chapter, including interactive resources, can be found on the Student CD-ROM accompanying this textbook and on the Companion Website at www.prenhall.com/frazier.

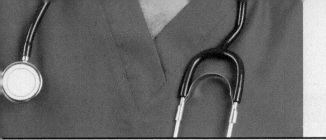

Objectives

After completing this chapter, you should be able to:

- Spell and define the medical terminology in this chapter.
- Define the medical assistant's role in patient-centered care.
- Define wellness.
- Discuss the holistic approach to health care.
- Explain the mind–body connection.
- Describe the types of pain, including physical, psychological, and phantom pain.
- Explain how pain is assessed.
- Describe different methods of pain management.
- Discuss the methods of assisting patients with special needs, including the physically challenged, visually impaired, hearing impaired, speech impaired, mentally impaired, elderly, and those who do not speak English.

Patient-Centered Care

Case Study

Marina successfully passed her RMA exam and was excited to start her career as a medical assistant. After applying to several positions, she obtained employment with Dr. Gerard, a doctor of naturopathic medicine. Marina enjoys her work and loves teaching her patients about different approaches to a healthy lifestyle and effective stress and pain management.

After a particularly long, stressful morning, Marina takes her assigned break outside in the building's patio area. One of Marina's patients passes by and stops to say hello. His expression changes from one of happy recognition to one of confusion as Marina quickly extinguishes the cigarette she has been smoking. Suddenly feeling like a teenager caught by her parents doing something wrong, Marina forces a nervous smile as she greets her patient.

MedMedia

www.prenhall.com/frazier

Additional interactive resources and activities for this chapter can be found on the Companion Website. For videos, audio glossary, legal and ethical scenarios, job scenarios, quizzes, and games related to the content of this chapter, please access the accompanying CD-ROM in this book.

 **Assets Available:**

Audio Glossary
Legal and Ethical Scenario: *Patient-Centered Care*
On the Job Scenario: *Patient-Centered Care*
Video Scenario: *Handwashing and Gloving: Prepping the Exam Room*
Multiple Choice Quiz
Games: Crossword, Strikeout, and Spelling Bee

Medical Terminology

acute—sharp, severe, sudden; having a sudden onset and usually of short duration

afferent nerves—sensory nerves that carry impulses to the central nervous system

analgesic—pain reducing

cerebral—pertaining to the cerebrum, the forepart of the brain

chronic—of long duration, often with slow progression

controlled substances—narcotics, stimulants, and certain sedatives

efferent nerves—motor nerves that carry impulses from the central nervous system to the peripheral nervous system

endorphins—proteins in the brain that have analgesic properties

referred pain—pain that is felt in a different area from the injured or diseased part of the body

risk factor—factor that makes a person particularly vulnerable to certain diseases or disorders

Abbreviations

BMI—body mass index

JCAHCO—Joint Commission on Accreditation of Health Care Organizations

PSA—prostate-specific antigen

✚ MEDICAL ASSISTING COMPETENCIES

CAAHEP ENTRY-LEVEL COMPETENCIES FOR CMA	ABHES ENTRY-LEVEL COMPETENCIES FOR RMA
■ Identify and respond to issues of confidentiality. ■ Perform within legal and ethical boundaries. ■ Demonstrate knowledge of federal and state health-care legislation and regulations. ■ Recognize and respond to verbal communication. ■ Recognize and respond to nonverbal communication.	■ Project a positive attitude. ■ Maintain confidentiality at all times. ■ Be a "team player." ■ Be cognizant of ethical boundaries. ■ Exhibit initiative. ■ Adapt to change. ■ Evidence a responsible attitude. ■ Be courteous and diplomatic. ■ Conduct work within scope of education, training, and ability. ■ Recognize and respond to verbal and nonverbal communication.

Introduction

Quality care involves focusing on the patient. Patient-centered care requires you to be professional, communicate properly, understand the legal concepts, teach patients, and maintain the medical office.

The Medical Assistant's Role in Patient-Centered Care

As an MA, one of your many roles will involve teaching patients how to manage their pain and how to maintain wellness. You may also be involved in:

- Charting patients' pain levels
- Obtaining patient medical data
- Assisting patients with special needs

Wellness

Wellness is the ongoing process of practicing a healthy lifestyle. It depends on a balance between a person's physical and psychological states. Wellness is a personal matter, as each person is unique and has different needs. **Risk factors** are determined to assess the level or degree of wellness (Table 3-1). Then the individual takes action to reduce or eliminate these factors.

?— Critical Thinking Question 3-1

In the case study, why do you think the patient looked confused when he noticed that Marina was smoking? Why do you think Marina felt guilty or uneasy about being seen by her patient while smoking? How would you feel if the person teaching you healthy habits and encouraging you did not follow his or her own advice?

TABLE 3-1 COMMON RISK FACTORS	
• Smoking or tobacco product use • Poor physical fitness • High alcohol intake • Poor diet and nutrition • Disregarding auto safety measures • High stress level • Occupational health and environmental hazards • Drug abuse	• Lack of immunizations • Poor dental care • High or very low blood pressure • Family history of cancer, heart attack, stroke, or diabetes • Unsafe sex • High or very low heart rate • Unhealthy body mass index (**BMI**) • Risk-taking behavior

The average life span in the United States is 76 years. Smoking, abusing drugs and/or alcohol, diet, exercise, using seat belts, weight management, performing breast or testicular self-exams, prostate-specific antigen (**PSA**) screening, blood pressure screening, cholesterol screening, Pap smears, and safe sex are personal choices that can affect life span. Ignoring healthy lifestyle practices puts people at risk for developing chronic illnesses and/or debilitating (weakening) conditions.

People's lifestyles are based on their personal attitudes, experiences, and role models. For example, a child whose role model eats healthy foods, exercises, and does not smoke is more likely to practice the same healthy habits later in life. On the other hand, if the role model uses drugs, smokes, and is involved in criminal activity, the child is more likely to take up risky behavior. Positive experiences reinforce a healthier lifestyle. A person who starts exercising three times a week soon discovers that she has more energy for daily tasks. The energy is a positive outcome of exercising, which, in turn, motivates the person to continue.

Some risk factors cannot be changed, such as a genetic predisposition (tendency) toward developing a disease. Others, such as smoking, *can* be changed if the person has the desire to change them. Some healthy habits and attitudes are listed in Table 3-2.

TABLE 3-2 WELLNESS GUIDELINES	
• Keep a positive attitude. • Cherish your values. • Exercise your mind, body, and spirit. • Control your stress. • Soothe your fears. • Think happy thoughts. • Stay active. • Challenge your mind. • Forgive and forget. • Avoid dangerous drugs. • Watch your sugar intake. • Walk briskly.	• Enjoy the outdoors. • Maintain a healthy weight. • Eat a well-balanced diet. • Rinse fresh fruits and vegetables before eating. • Practice cleanliness. • Take medications as directed. • Stop smoking. • Lower your blood pressure and cholesterol. • Learn to breathe deeply.

A Holistic Approach to Health Care

Health-care providers must understand the importance of the interaction between body and mind. A holistic approach to health care recognizes and addresses the complete care of the patient, including physical, social, psychological, spiritual, environmental, and economic elements. Holistic medicine facilitates healing and promotes wellness.

The patient should be involved in making decisions concerning the treatment or management of his or her general health. For example, stress is often a factor that contributes to illness or makes an illness worse. Part of holistic care consists of helping the patient learn how to control stress by using relaxation techniques, which contribute to overall healing.

The Mind–Body Connection

It has long been known that the human spirit and spirituality are driving forces in healing. Positive emotions such as joy, love, and happiness cause the brain to release endorphins. **Endorphins,** a group of proteins in the brain with **analgesic** properties, benefit physical functioning and boost immunity to disease. Negative feelings such as fear, anger, and grieving cause tightened muscles, faster heart and respiratory rates, and other heightened reactions.

Laughter, games, and relaxation activities have been used effectively in the treatment of chronic and terminal pain. Friendship, love, and spirituality give a sense of emotional security. The new area of pet therapy has been shown to be very beneficial for nursing home residents, hospital patients, and hospice patients.

Recognizing the connection between mental and emotional states and physical health is an important step in developing a healthier lifestyle. Finding ways to release or deal with negative emotions and replace them with positive, uplifting experiences is an excellent way to implement this step.

Pain

Pain is an unpleasant sensory and emotional experience. Each person responds differently to pain, depending on tolerance and pain threshold. Even when pain is seen as "imagined" by others, it can be very real to the person experiencing it. Factors that can affect how a person feels pain are cultural background and past experience. Anxiety, stress, and fear usually heighten the experience of pain.

In some cultures, people are taught not to show pain. Also, some patients may have a very high tolerance for pain, which means that some early warning signs may be ignored or undetected.

Pain is categorized as **acute** or **chronic.** Acute pain, such as surgical pain, usually lessens with treatment and time. Chronic pain, such as that of rheumatoid arthritis, lasts longer than a few weeks, often for a lifetime. It is the long-term effects of chronic pain on a patient's mental and physical state that are of the most concern. These effects include the following:

- Decreased activity or possibly inactivity
- Decreased sleep or poor quality of sleep
- Increased irritability and fatigue
- Chemical and/or medication dependency
- Mood swings
- Impaired ability to handle stress
- Lower self-esteem
- Anger
- Helplessness
- Sadness or depression

The treatment goal is to lessen the pain, keep it tolerable, and promote physical functioning.

Types of Pain

Physical Pain

Body pain is a signal of disease process or inflammation and serves as a protective mechanism. Pain causes a person to seek medical attention. For example, severe chest pain may be a heart attack, and severe abdominal pain could be internal bleeding. Without pain, there is no signal that something is wrong. Some patients have an impaired sense of pain. For example, a patient with diabetes may have reduced sensation in the feet. The patient may not be aware of a breakdown in tissues until it is so severe that the only treatment is amputation.

Pain intensity varies. Superficial pain is usually located on the body surface and does not penetrate deep into the tissue. Deep pain involves muscles, joints, and tendons. Visceral pain involves the internal organs and is usually the most severe.

Psychological Pain

Psychological pain can be either acute or chronic. Acute psychological pain may be described as terror, fear, despair, grief, rage, anger, helplessness, or hopelessness. If appropriate intervention does not take place to address and ease the pain, it often becomes chronic.

Chronic psychological pain may have a subtle onset. The person may not be aware of the symptoms he or she is experiencing. Diagnoses include anxiety disorders, posttraumatic stress disorder, major depression, and other psychological disorders.

Keys to Success
HOW THE BODY RESPONDS TO PAIN

The nervous system carries electrical impulses to and from the brain (Figure 3-1 ◆). The brain interprets these signals and directs the body's response through chemical, hormonal, and muscular reactions. **Afferent nerves,** found in muscles, joints, organs, and skin, transmit impulses to the spinal cord and brain via the central nervous system. The brain sends signals through the **efferent nerves** to produce the appropriate body response. Afferent nerves send fast and slow signals for pain to the brain. This explains the occurrence of sharp, then throbbing pain after traumatic blunt injury. **Referred pain** confuses the brain because it is felt in a different area from where the pain originates.

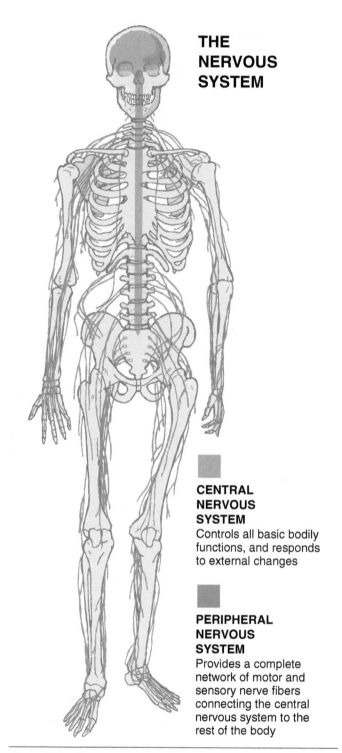

THE NERVOUS SYSTEM

CENTRAL NERVOUS SYSTEM
Controls all basic bodily functions, and responds to external changes

PERIPHERAL NERVOUS SYSTEM
Provides a complete network of motor and sensory nerve fibers connecting the central nervous system to the rest of the body

Figure 3-1 ◆ The nervous system

(∞ Chapter 29, Mental Health, discusses psychological pain in greater detail.)

Phantom Pain

Phantom pain occurs after the amputation of a body part (Figure 3-2 ◆). The severed nerve endings feel as if they are still receiving stimuli from the amputated part, causing painful sensations as if the body part were still attached. The pain is usually severe but eases and disappears over time.

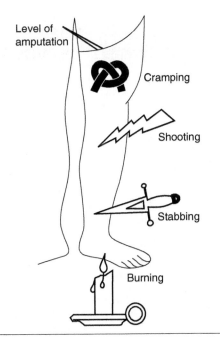

Figure 3-2 ◆ Phantom pain occurs after the amputation of a body part.

Pain Assessment

As an MA, part of your job may be to ask the patient to describe his or her pain (Table 3-3). It is best to use open-ended questions:

- When did the pain start?
- Where is the pain located?
- How frequently does the pain occur?
- Could you describe the pain for me?
- What actions or movements seem to lessen or increase the pain?

TABLE 3-3 COMMON WORDS USED TO DESCRIBE PAIN	
• Stabbing	• Intractable
• Sharp	• Unbearable
• Cutting	• Colicky
• Tearing	• Excruciating
• Burning, stinging	• Radiating
• Dull	• Penetrating
• Intermittent	• Aching
• Continuous	• Nagging, gnawing
• Throbbing	• Fleeting

Three methods are commonly used to rate pain:

- Numerical or symbolic scale: The patient is asked to "grade" his or her pain on a scale of 0 (no pain) to 10 (the most severe pain) (Figure 3-3 ◆).
- Face scale: The patient is shown a series of faces ranging from a happy smiling face to a very unhappy face and points to the face that best illustrates his or her pain (Figure 3-4 ◆). The face scale works well with children and adults who have trouble using the number scale.
- Full body picture (front and back): The patient marks the picture to indicate the areas where he or she feels pain, using different types of marks for different types of pain.

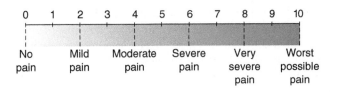

Figure 3-3 ◆ Numerical pain level chart with word modifiers

1. Explain to the child that each face is for a person who feels happy because he or she has no pain (hurt, or whatever word the child uses) or feels sad because he or she has some or a lot of pain.

2. Point to the appropriate face and state, "This face...":
   0—"is very happy because he (or she) doesn't hurt at all."
   1—"hurts just a little bit."
   2—"hurts a little more."
   3—"hurts even more."
   4—"hurts a whole lot."
   5—"hurts as much as you can imagine, although you don't have to be crying to feel this bad."

3. Ask the child to choose the face that best describes how he or she feels. Be specific about which pain (e.g., "shot" or incision) and what time (e.g., Now? Earlier before lunch?)

Figure 3-4 ◆ The Wong/Baker FACES Rating Scale
Source: From Hockenberry, M. J., Wilson, D., Winkelstein, M. L.: Wong's essentials of pediatric nursing, ed. 7, St. Louis, 2005, p. 1259. Used with permission. Copyright Mosby.

Keys to Success
GUIDELINES FOR PAIN ASSESSMENT AND MANAGEMENT

The Joint Commission on Accreditation of Health Care Organizations (**JCAHCO**) has set guidelines for pain assessment and management. The guidelines became effective January 1, 2001, for hospitals and other health-care facilities, including nursing homes, clinics, health maintenance organizations, and home health agencies. Agencies must comply with the regulations for pain assessment to remain fully accredited.

Pain assessment is now considered the fifth vital sign, to be charted along with temperature, pulse, respiration, and blood pressure. The patient evaluates the pain on a scale of 0 to 10. Happy and sad faces are used for children and those who cannot use the numerical scale. Pain relief is provided, and the patient is reassessed on a regular basis.

Pain Management

Pain management involves medication, comfort measures, alternative therapies, exercise, surgery, or a combination of methods. The choice of treatment depends on many factors including the severity or chronic nature of pain. Comfort measures include heat and cold therapy, elevation of the affected part, gentle massage, and other physical therapy. Surgery may involve severing the afferent nerve to stop the delivery of pain impulses to the brain. (∞ Chapter 25, Orthopedics and Physical Therapy, and Chapter 9, Pharmacology and Medication Administration, discuss pain management with physical therapy and medication.)

If these initial methods of pain control for patients with chronic pain are not effective, the physician may prescribe **controlled substances.** These medications are not prescribed over the phone or after office hours. The patient must be taught to strictly follow directions for dosage and use. The patient must keep scheduled appointments to obtain the next prescription. Additional medication is not supplied if the patient takes more than the prescribed dosage ahead of schedule. If the prescribing physician discovers the patient has obtained a controlled substance from another source, further pain management ceases. (∞ Refer to Chapter 9, Pharma-

Figure 3-5 ◆ Patient teaching is vital for pain management.

Keys to Success
HEALTHY MIND AND BODY—A PATIENT TEACHING GUIDE EXAMPLE

Take the time to keep healthy and prevent illness. If you already have a medical condition, make it a personal goal to stay as healthy as you can. Post the following reminders in a prominent place such as a refrigerator door or a bathroom mirror. Remember to focus on health even if you have a busy life.

■ **Eat a healthy diet.** A balanced diet provides basic nutrients to boost immunity, keep the mind alert, and meet general body needs.
■ **Exercise 30 minutes each day.** Regular exercise increases blood circulation, the movement of nutrients to the cells, muscle strength, and beneficial hormones. It also improves mental alertness and elevates the mood. Discuss an exercise plan with your physician before starting.
■ **Get sufficient sleep.** While you rest, your body and mind are repairing, restoring, and refreshing.
■ **Visit your physician for regular checkups and recommended screenings.** Come prepared with any questions you may have. If you are on medications, bring a list of drugs, dosages, and frequency of each. If you have a family pattern of medical conditions, tell the physician. Ask about periodic screening for those illnesses or diseases.

cology and Medication Administration, for additional information on controlled substances.)

A patient may choose to manage pain without medication because of potential side effects and drug dependence. Some examples of alternative therapy are relaxation exercises, herbal remedies, magnet therapy, biofeedback, acupuncture, acupressure, and chiropractic treatments. (∞ Refer to Chapter 32, Alternative Medicine, for a more detailed discussion of alternative therapies.)

Patient Teaching

Patient teaching is vital for pain management (Figure 3-5◆). The medical office should make information and guidelines available to patients, such as:

■ Discussion of the disease process that is causing the pain
■ General information on treatments available for the disease
■ Specific information relating to the individual patient
■ Medication dosage and treatment frequency, explained in terms the patient can understand
■ Changes in condition that should alert the patient to call the office immediately

Patients with Special Needs

Patients with special needs may:

■ Be physically challenged
■ Be visually challenged
■ Be hearing impaired
■ Be speech impaired
■ Not speak or understand English

- Come from different cultural backgrounds
- Be elderly
- Be emotionally challenged

Good observational skills on your part may alert you to a patient with a physical or emotional challenge. Some disabilities are very plain to see; others may be carefully hidden or guarded by the patient. The geriatric patient may have multiple challenges in addition to the normal process of aging.

Assisting Patients with Various Special Needs

As a medical assistant you will likely encounter patients with various special needs. Good communication skills, kindness, patience, and understanding are always helpful in these situations. Patients may be challenged physically or emotionally, may have visual, hearing, or speech impairments, or may come from different cultures and speak different languages. Geriatric patients often present with multiple special needs.

Physically Challenged Patients

Patients experiencing physical challenges usually require assistance with activities. It is best to ask the patient for direction before assisting. For example, a wheelchair is helpful when movement to another area of the office is required. Ask the patient if he or she would like a wheelchair. If the patient agrees, proceed. If the patient declines, take your time walking the patient to the area. (∞ Refer to Chapter 25, Orthopedics and Physical Therapy, for additional information on patients with physical challenges.)

Visually Impaired Patients

A patient with a minor vision loss may only need large-print forms. If the visual loss is more severe, you may need to read instructions and fill out the form for the patient. A patient with significant visual loss may use a white cane with a red tip or have a guide dog. A patient with severe visual impairment usually requires complete assistance or may be accompanied by a helper.

Be sure to announce your presence as you approach the patient. Explain each procedure before beginning. If the patient does not have a helper, offer your arm to guide him or her to the room. Never take the patient's arm without first asking permission. If the patient has a guide dog, ask the patient how he or she would like you to help. A guide dog often directs the patient. Never touch the guide dog without the owner's consent. Describe the surroundings to familiarize the patient and do not leave him or her alone for any length of time. (∞ Chapter 19, EENT, contains additional information on vision loss.)

Keep in mind that just because a patient's vision is impaired, his or her hearing is not necessarily impaired. When speaking to a patient who is blind or visually impaired, use normal tones. Do *not* shout.

Hearing-Impaired Patients

A patient may tell you he or she has hearing loss, or you may notice that the patient does not appear to be hearing what is said. A hearing aid device may be visible.

Speaking clearly and distinctly is usually all that is necessary. Face the patient when you speak. This is very helpful if the patient reads lips. Do not embarrass the patient by asking, "Can you hear me?" Instead, ask the patient to repeat the question or information. Again, it is important to avoid shouting. If necessary, written communication is helpful, especially printed instructions. (∞ Chapter 19, EENT, discusses hearing loss.)

Patients with Speech Impairments

Patients with limited speaking abilities are another challenge. A patient with a speech impairment can become very frustrated in the attempt to communicate. This is especially true if the patient has had a stroke. Do not rush the patient, fill in words, or try to finish the patient's sentences. Other forms of communication may be necessary, such as written communication, sign language, or hand gestures. (∞ Chapter 2, Interpersonal Communication, discusses speech impairment.)

Culturally Diverse Patients

It is not possible for a medical office to hire a multilingual staff to communicate with patients from all ethnic and cultural backgrounds. But you should try to identify and be familiar with your patients' backgrounds. Showing respect for different customs is essential. When working with a patient who speaks English as a second language, be patient and try to understand to the best of your ability. Ask for assistance when necessary. Again, remember that providing an interpreter when necessary is a legal requirement. (∞ Refer to Chapter 2, Interpersonal Communication, for additional information on cultural diversity and English as a second language.)

Emotionally Challenged Patients

A patient with emotional challenges may either acknowledge or deny those challenges. You may be able to detect an emotional problem by observing actions and behavior. While anxiety is common in patients experiencing pain or waiting for the results of diagnostic tests, anger is not generally a normal response. Being kind and understanding will help ease a patient's anxiety or anger. In particular, speak in quiet, even tones. (∞ Refer to Chapter 29, Mental Health, for a more thorough discussion of patients with emotional challenges.)

Geriatric Patients

In many geriatric patients, sight, hearing, and mobility may be compromised. Mental capacity may be diminished. Assisting with insurance forms, explaining how to take medications, providing information on outside agencies for assistance, and encouraging proper diet and social activities are some of the ways you can help a geriatric patient. (∞ Refer to Chapter 31, Geriatrics, for additional information on the elderly.)

Chapter Summary

- Wellness is the ongoing process of practicing a healthy lifestyle.
- Holistic medicine addresses the whole patient and his or her needs. It involves the patient in making informed decisions about the course of treatment.
- Pain may be acute (short-term) or chronic (long-term). Chronic pain is the most serious and debilitating.
- Types of pain include physical, psychological, and phantom. Physical pain, as a symptom of disease process, inflammation, or trauma, serves as a protective mechanism by causing the person to seek medical attention. Psychological pain, while very real, is rarely caused by a pathological process but by a mental or emotional condition. Phantom pain occurs after the amputation of a body part. For a period of time the patient continues to feel pain as if the body part were still attached.

- Pain can be measured in three ways. The numerical scale ranges between 0 (no pain) and 10 (severe pain). The face scale is a series of faces ranging from happy to unhappy. On a picture of the body, front and back, the patient points to the location of pain.
- Pain is managed with medication, comfort measures, alternative therapies, exercise, surgery, or a combination of methods.
- An important part of an MA's job is patient teaching. The patient should understand the cause of the pain as well as how to manage it safely.
- Special-needs patients include those who are physically challenged, visually impaired, hearing impaired, speech-impaired, and elderly. Other considerations are cultural diversity and language barriers.

Chapter Review Questions

Multiple Choice

1. Which of the following is most likely a risk factor?
   A. yoga
   B. brisk walking
   C. lower cholesterol
   D. high blood pressure

2. Positive emotions cause the brain to release proteins called
   A. endorphins.
   B. afferent neurons.
   C. efferent neurons.
   D. ganglia.

3. Phantom pain most likely occurs
   A. after strenuous exercise.
   B. before surgery.
   C. after an amputation.
   D. before resting.

4. Which of the following questions can you ask to assess a patient's pain?
   A. Are you sure you're in pain?
   B. Why didn't you come into the office sooner with this pain?
   C. How frequently does the pain occur?
   D. Do you really think the pain is serious?

5. Comfort measures for chronic pain include
   A. chiropractic treatments.
   B. heat and cold therapy.
   C. medications.
   D. surgery.

6. Controlled substances prescribed for chronic pain require the patient to
   A. schedule an appointment for the next prescription.
   B. call the office for a refill of the prescription.
   C. increase the dosage if the pain gets worse.
   D. seek alternative therapy.

7. When assisting a patient with a severe vision loss, it is acceptable to
   A. take the patient by the arm without asking because it is expected.
   B. announce your presence as you approach the patient.
   C. pet the guide dog when walking the patient to the examining room.
   D. tell the patient you are going to take him or her to the examining room in a wheelchair.

8. Which of the following questions is acceptable to ask a patient with a hearing impairment?
   A. Is your hearing aid turned on?
   B. Can you hear me?
   C. Do I have to talk louder?
   D. Could you repeat that information for me?

9. Which of the following is an acceptable practice with a patient who is speech-impaired?
   A. Hurry the patient.
   B. Fill in words for the patient.
   C. Be patient and understanding.
   D. Avoid looking at the patient.

Chapter Review Questions (continued)

10. A geriatric patient most needs you to
    A. speak loudly.
    B. assist him or her when necessary.
    C. assist during every phase of the office visit.
    D. speak softly.

True/False

T F 1. Pain is manifested only in physical complaints and does not affect mental ability.

T F 2. All types of stress have a negative impact on overall health.

T F 3. To assist stroke patients who are having difficulty speaking, it is appropriate to finish sentences for them.

T F 4. Your patient is on medications to control chronic pain. He had a particularly rough weekend and took an additional dose of medication. You may go ahead and refill the next prescription one day early to compensate for the change.

T F 5. All risk factors can be changed regardless of genetic predisposition.

T F 6. Challenging your mind frequently leads to additional stress and should be avoided in order to maintain a healthy lifestyle.

T F 7. The elderly are not considered a special-needs category for patient care.

T F 8. Wellness is the ongoing process of practicing a healthy lifestyle.

T F 9. It is important for a patient to know how to manage pain safely and effectively.

T F 10. People's lifestyles are based on their personal attitudes, experiences, and role models.

Short Answer

1. Which motor nerves carry impulses from the central nervous system to the peripheral nervous system?

2. Sometimes severed nerve endings feel as if they are still receiving stimuli from the amputated part, causing painful sensations. What is this phenomenon called?

3. What kind of pain is felt in a different area from the injured or diseased part of the body?

4. What is the difference between acute and chronic pain?

5. What is the term for proteins in the brain that have analgesic properties?

Research

1. In your local area, what phone number(s) can patients call for assistance to stop smoking?

2. Where can patients find out about low-cost exercise programs in your community? Are any offered at the local YMCA or college?

3. In your local area, is there a pain management clinic for inpatient and outpatient treatment, or are patients treated by their primary care providers?

Resource Guide

American Academy of Pediatrics
141 Northwest Point Blvd
Elk Grove Village, IL 60007
847-434-4000
www.aap.org

American Foundation for the Blind (AFB)
11 Penn Plaza, Suite 300
New York, NY 10001
1-800-232-5463
www.afb.org

American Holistic Health Association
P.O. Box 17400
Anaheim, CA 92817-7400
(714) 779-6152
www.ahha.org

National Council on Aging
300 D Street SW, Suite 801
Washington, DC 20024
202-479-1200
www.ncoa.org

National Institute on Deafness and Other Communication Disorders
National Institutes of Health
31 Center Drive, MSC 2320
Bethesda, MD 20892-2320
www.nidcd.nih.gov

 MedMedia

www.prenhall.com/frazier

More on this chapter, including interactive resources, can be found on the Student CD-ROM accompanying this textbook and on the Companion Website at www.prenhall.com/frazier.

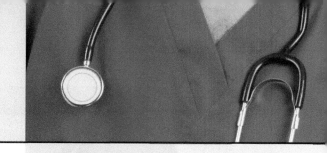

CHAPTER 4

Considerations of Extended Life

Case Study

One weekend, while home from college, Ori sat with his family watching a television special about organ transplants. Ori mentioned that when he renewed his driver's license he had chosen to become an organ donor. Ori's younger sister said that she, too, wanted to be a donor as soon as she turned 18, because she felt it was important to help others, even in death.

Their mother, Katrina, said vehemently that she would not allow either of her children to be organ donors.

"Well, you can't stop me. I'm an adult now!" Ori shouted.

"Yes, I can, and I certainly will!" replied his mother. She went on to explain that if they got into an accident they would not be saved. It was her belief that rescue workers did not perform CPR or other life-saving measures on people who were known organ donors because it would be easier and less expensive for the hospital to just let them die and take the organs later.

MedMedia
www.prenhall.com/frazier

Additional interactive resources and activities for this chapter can be found on the Companion Website. For audio glossary, legal and ethical scenarios, job scenarios, quizzes, and games related to the content of this chapter, please access the accompanying CD-ROM in this book.

 **Assets Available:**

Audio Glossary
Legal and Ethical Scenario: *Considerations of Extended Life*
On the Job Scenario: *Considerations of Extended Life*
Multiple Choice Quiz
Games: Crossword, Strikeout, and Spelling Bee

Objectives

After completing this chapter, you should be able to:

- Spell and define the medical terminology in this chapter.
- Define the medical assistant's role as it relates to extended life and terminal care.
- Discuss organ donation concepts, criteria, and resources for information.
- Discuss the selection of transplant recipients.
- Explain the uniform donor card and its importance.
- Summarize the Uniform Anatomical Gift Act.
- Explain how the 1987 amendments to the Social Security Act impact reimbursement for inpatient services.
- Discuss advance medical directives and the durable power of attorney in health care.
- Discuss living wills and life-prolonging declarations.
- Provide information regarding hospice.

✚ MEDICAL ASSISTING COMPETENCIES

CAAHEP ENTRY-LEVEL COMPETENCIES FOR CMA	ABHES ENTRY-LEVEL COMPETENCIES FOR RMA
■ Identify and respond to issues of confidentiality. ■ Perform within legal and ethical boundaries. ■ Demonstrate knowledge of federal and state health-care legislation and regulations. ■ Recognize and respond to verbal communications. ■ Recognize and respond to nonverbal communications ■ Instruct patients according to their needs. ■ Identify community resources. ■ Instruct patients with special needs.	■ Project a positive attitude. ■ Maintain confidentiality at all times. ■ Be a team player. ■ Be cognizant of ethical boundaries. ■ Exhibit initiative. ■ Adapt to change. ■ Evidence a responsible attitude. ■ Be courteous and diplomatic. ■ Conduct work within scope of education, training, and ability. ■ Be attentive, listen, and learn. ■ Be impartial and show empathy when dealing with patients. ■ Serve as a liaison between physician and others. ■ Use appropriate medical terminology. ■ Recognize and respond to verbal and nonverbal communication. ■ Adapt to individualized needs. ■ Instruct patients with special needs.

Medical Terminology

cadaver—dead body

hospice—facility or program that provides care for the terminally ill in a home setting or hospice center

ischemic—pertaining to a decreased blood supply to tissue due to impaired circulation to the organ or part

organ—a group of tissues making up a structure that has a particular function in the body

palliative—relieving pain or discomfort

tissue—a group of cells that act together for a particular body function

Abbreviations

DNR—do not resuscitate

Introduction

New treatment technologies and techniques have significantly advanced medical care, particularly in the field of organ and tissue transplantation. Legal and educational strides in the area of organ donation have raised public awareness and interest.

While transplantation improves the quality of life, life-prolonging measures have raised quality-of-life questions. A living will allows a healthy person or a person with a terminal disease or catastrophic injury to state his or her wishes about prolonging life. A durable power of attorney for healthcare tells the physician and the family that if the patient is no longer mentally competent, the appointed person with power of attorney can make decisions regarding medical care in the patient's best interest. Hospice is an alternative to hospitalization for the terminal patient who wishes to die in comfort and with dignity.

The Medical Assistant's Role in Extended Life Care

As an MA, you need to be aware of the rules regarding organ and tissue donations and transplants. Patients who need organ transplants or want to know about organ donation may ask you for information. You may also be asked about medical directives, durable power of attorney for health care, living wills, and life-prolonging declarations. You will direct the patient and family to the proper sources of information, such as physicians, nurses, brochures, and Internet sites. Documenting the patient's questions and understanding the information you give is another responsibility.

Organ and Tissue Donations

Modern technology and scientific advances have made it possible to endow very ill people with the gift of life through other people's organs and tissues. It is now possible for one donor to provide organs and tissue for as many as 50 recipients. Table 4-1 lists organs and tissues that may be donated and transplanted.

Organ transplantation has been performed for over a century. Table 4-2 lists the highlights of this life-saving procedure's history.

Organ and Tissue Harvesting

Removal of organs or tissues is based on three factors:

1. Source of the donation—**cadaver** or live donor
2. Waiting period—cold **ischemic** (the body is in refrigeration in a morgue) or warm ischemic (the body is not refrigerated)
3. Removal order

Certain **tissues,** inner parts of the bone and ear, skin, corneas, connective tissue, and veins can be harvested (removed) from a donor who has been pronounced dead. Tissue compatibility must be determined before transplanting to reduce the chances of rejection by the recipient's body. The tissues may be removed some time after circulation and respiration have ceased. Warm ischemic time, however, cannot exceed four hours; cold ischemic time 12 hours. The cornea, for example, remains suitable for removal for transplantation when harvested within approximately six hours after the donor's heart has stopped beating.

One method of processing donated tissue is cryopreservation, in which tissues are frozen at a super cold temperature. The processor makes arrangements to transport the tissue to the tissue procurement organization. In some facilities the local medical examiner or coroner can release tissue for transplant when residual tissue can be returned for examination. An alternative is having a pathologist do a complete pathological tissue study.

Organs such as the heart, lungs, kidneys, liver, pancreas, stomach, and intestines must be harvested after the patient has been pronounced brain dead. The donor must have sustained brain death under circumstances in which respiration and circulation can be supported artificially, by means of ventilators and medications. The heart is removed first, then the other organs, as quickly as possible.

Live donors may donate certain tissues, bone marrow, stem cells, cord blood, kidneys, or a portion of the liver.

Donation Issues and Concerns

There is generally very little religious objection to organ or tissue donation. Most religions view donation as morally and ethically acceptable as long as it benefits individuals and society and helps to ease the suffering of others. Jehovah's Witnesses, who do not believe in blood transfusions, do not object to organ and tissue transplants as long as all the blood has been removed before transplantation.

Obstacles to donation include distrust, fear of premature death, language differences, and family involvement. Some cultures may forbid organ donation because they believe the body should remain intact for burial.

? — Critical Thinking Question 4-1—
How should Ori try to educate his mother about the process of organ donation?

In the United States, the sale and purchase of tissue and organs is prohibited. The donor's physician or the physician who pronounces the donor dead should not be involved in any part of the harvest procedure. The United Network for Organ Sharing (UNOS) is the agency that oversees tissue and

TABLE 4-1 BODY PARTS THAT MAY BE DONATED	
Tissues	**Organs**
Skin	Heart
Heart valves	Lungs
Bone	Liver
Corneas	Kidney
Islet cells	Pancreas
Bone marrow	Stomach
Stem cells	Small and large intestines
Cord blood	
Saphenous (leg) veins	
Tendons and ligaments	

TABLE 4-2 A SHORT HISTORY OF ORGAN TRANSPLANTATION	
1905	First successful cornea transplant.
1933	First human-to-human kidney transplant (the kidney never functioned).
1954	First successful kidney transplant, identical twins.
1963	First successful lung transplant.
1967	First successful liver transplant.
1967	First heart transplant in South Africa.
1968	First successful heart transplant in the United States.
1968	Uniform Anatomical Gift Act passed.
1978	Uniform Brain Death Act passed, defining death as brain death.
1981	First successful heart/lung transplant.
1983	First anti-rejection drug approved for use.
1984	National Organ Transplant Act (NOTA) passed.
1986	Require Request Laws passed.
1989	First successful living-related liver transplant.
1990	First successful living-related lung transplant.
1991	First successful small intestine transplant.

Keys to Success
DONOR INFORMATION

Although there is no longer a specific age limit for donors, the recommended age is between birth and 75 years. The health and condition of the donor and of the organs and tissue at the time of death influence the suitability of the donation. Organs are harvested in such a way as to preserve the appearance of the body. Harvesting the heart may make the embalming procedure a little more difficult, but it can be done.

organ harvest, preparation and testing of the tissue or organ, and storage and distribution of the tissue or organ. The cost of the harvest procedure is not passed on to the donor's family but is usually covered by the facility harvesting the tissue or organ or the regional organ procurement organization.

? — Critical Thinking Question 4-2—

As you read in the case study, Ori's mother believes that hospitals save money if they let patients die and harvest organs later. Explain why the hospital cannot receive monetary compensation for organs. Also explain the difference between time frames in cold ischemic and warm ischemic donations.

When the organ or tissue comes from a live donor, it may go to a designated recipient. For example, if a mother is a match for a child who is experiencing kidney failure, she can donate her kidney to her child. The organ does not go into the general program.

In most states there is a statement on the front or the back of the driver's license that a person may sign declaring his or her wish to be a tissue or organ donor at the time of death (Figure 4-1 ◆). The person may designate what tissue or organs may be harvested. This statement is only a statement of intent, however, and may be overridden by the next of kin in most states. Usually the next of kin makes the final decision.

Most states consider a signed universal donor card a legal document permitting the procurement of organs and tissue (Figure 4-2 ◆). However, some states require a signature on a universal donor card in addition to a signature on the back of a driver's license. Also, many institutions request permission from family members before procuring any organs. The decision is granted to a family member or guardian in the following order of priority:

1. Spouse
2. Adult son or daughter
3. Either parent
4. Adult sibling
5. Grandparent
6. Guardian

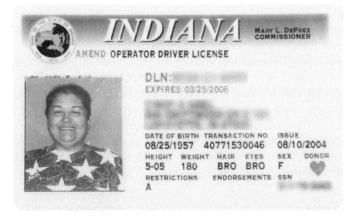

Figure 4-1 ◆ Individuals may declare their wish to be a tissue or organ donor on their driver's license.

Organ Donor Card

I, _____, hereby make the following anatomical gift, if medically acceptable, to take effect upon my death.

_____Any organs or parts   _____Entire body

Only the following specific organs or parts:

_____

Limitations or special wishes if any:

_____

(Signatures of donor and witnesses appear on reverse side.)

Front of card

Organ Donor Card (side two)

Signed by the donor and the following two witnesses in the presence of each other.

Donor Signature: _____

Date of Birth: _____ Date signed: _____

City and State: _____

Witness Signature: _____

Witness Signature: _____

This is a legal document under the Uniform Anatomical Gift Act or similar laws.

Back of card

Figure 4-2 ◆ Universal donor card

However, if the decedent, prior to the time of death, has indicated a refusal to make an organ donation, the institution or health-care provider must honor that decision.

Sometimes a family member lower on the priority list may object to the donation. Most institutions abide by the wishes of the family and do not harvest any tissue or organs if all members are not in agreement.

? — Critical Thinking Question 4-3—

Can Ori's mother disregard his signed intent to be an organ donor and refuse to allow the hospital to harvest organs upon his death?

Transplant Costs

Medical costs for transplants can include:

- Pretransplant evaluation and testing
- Hospital stay and surgical charges
- Follow-up care and testing
- Additional hospitalizations for complications or rejection
- Charges for anti-rejection drugs and other drug therapy
- Physicians' fees (including surgeons, radiologists, anesthesiologists, and pathologists)
- Procurement fees
- Rehabilitation, including physical, occupational, and vocational rehabilitation
- Insurance co-pays or deductibles

Out-of-pocket expenses include:

- Transportation to and from the transplant facility before, during, and after the transplant
- Food, lodging, and telephone charges for both the patient and the family
- Any child care
- Lost wages for patient and family members

Patients must research the full cost(s) for a transplant procedure. Medicaid and many insurance policies do not cover transplants.

Organ and Tissue Donation Rules and Regulations

Many states have laws regarding the declared intent to donate body tissues or organs upon death. In the past, laws varied among the states and some states had no laws at all in this area. To address this inconsistency, the National Conference of Commissioners on Uniform State Laws approved the Uniform Anatomical Gift Act in 1968.

Uniform Anatomical Gift Act

As transplant methods advanced, the supply of donor organs and tissues was not meeting the demand. In 1987 the Uniform Anatomical Gift Act was updated with statutes to educate the public to the need for donated organs and tissues. Greater public awareness has since increased donations.

The Uniform Anatomical Gift Act includes the following rules:

- The donor must be at least 18 years old.
- The intent to donate must be made in writing.
- The donor may designate specific organs or tissue for transplantation, the entire body for research or transplantation, or any acceptable organs or tissues.
- The donor's valid statement takes precedence over other individuals' wishes except when an autopsy is required by law.
- If the donor has not acted during his or her lifetime, the survivors, in a specified order of priority, may act on the donor's behalf.
- If aware of the donor's wishes, the attending physician may dispose of the body under the act.
- The physician accepting the donor's organs in good faith is protected from lawsuits.
- The death of the donor may not be determined by any physician involved in the transplantation.
- The donor may revoke the intent to donate, or the gift may be refused by the recipient or by the health-care provider (physician or facility).
- No financial arrangements can be made for donated organs.

Hospitals

A 1987 amendment to the Social Security Act requires written protocols, or sets of rules, from hospitals participating in Medicare or Medicaid that "assure that families of potential organ donors are made aware of the option of organ or tissue donation and their option to decline." Also, "No discussion or request is necessary if the medical record discloses a prior gift or a refusal to make a gift or if the gift would not be suitable according to accepted medical standards."

Hospitals generally ask certain routine questions during the admission procedure. They are now required to ask about organ donation in order to identify potential organ donors. With the consent of the attending physician, they are required to discuss organ donation with a person who answers in the negative.

When a patient agrees to donate, a request is made to see and document the organ donor card, driver's license, or other documentation of the intent to donate. Then it must be determined if there are any limitations (for example, a donor may wish to donate only his or her eyes or to donate for a single purpose, such as transplantation but not research). A copy is placed in the patient's medical record as evidence of a valid gift to be effective at death. This requirement is mandatory only during the admission process to hospitals.

Physicians are encouraged to ask their patients about donation. Hospitals are encouraged to ask patients who are scheduled for outpatient, emergency, or minor surgery, or any procedure that does not require being admitted to the hospital.

In 1998, the Organ Procurement and Transplant Network (OPTN) Final Rule was introduced by the Department of Health and Human Services. It requires that all hospitals performing transplants follow OPTN rules to receive Medicare or Medicaid reimbursement. Organ and tissue distribution was expanded from a local and regional system to a national system based on need. Also, three goals were established:

1. Minimum listing criteria establishing common guidelines for putting a patient on a waiting list.
2. Standard criteria for determining the medical status of a patient awaiting transplant, which allows a transplant center to release organs to patients with the most critical medical needs.
3. A reasonable collection policy permitting organs to be distributed over a larger geographic area, which has been made possible by newer methods of preserving organs for a longer period of time.

UNOS (United Network for Organ Sharing) established a national computer system for registering patients in need of transplants. Patient data entered into the system includes blood type, body size, medical urgency, length of time on the list, and tissue match. When a donor is identified, his or her data is entered to quickly find the closest matching candidate with the greatest need.

Tissue organizations process cardiovascular tissue, orthopedic tissue, and skin. The Food and Drug Administration (FDA) regulates tissue procurement, storage, and shipment.

Advance Medical Directives

Laws and guidelines for advance medical directives vary from state to state.

- *Advance medical directives* are signed legal documents in which an individual specifies his or her wishes concerning the provision of health care if he or she is ever in an incapacitated state.
- A *durable power of attorney for health care* tells the physician and the family that if the patient is no longer mentally competent, the appointed person with power of attorney can make decisions regarding medical care in the patient's best interests (Figure 4-3 ◆).

The patient should discuss these legal decisions with his or her family, the physician, and, if desired, with an attorney or clergy member. An attorney should be consulted to draft any documents and copies should be given to anyone who might be contacted in an emergency. The power of attorney can be revoked in writing.

Durable Power of Attorney for Health Care

General guidelines for the appointment of a Durable Power of Attorney for Health Care include the following (according to state law and requirements):

- The statement is voluntary, in writing, dated, and signed by the patient.
- If the patient is not capable of signing, another person may sign for the patient, in the patient's presence and at the patient's express direction.
- Two competent witnesses at least 18 years old, not related to the patient or responsible for the patient's health care, are usually required.
- The Power of Attorney must be notarized.
- Neither witness can sign on the patient's behalf.
- The person representing the patient must be at least 18 years old.
- The person representing the patient shall make decisions in the patient's best interest. The patient's family or physician cannot overrule the decisions without the court intervening.
- The appointment of this person becomes effective when the patient's physician certifies in writing that the patient is not able to consent.
- The appointment may be revoked by destroying the appointment document. Informing others in writing that the appointment is revoked will also revoke it. The final step in revoking the appointment is telling the physician. He or she must be aware of the revocation, or medical decisions will continue to be based on current knowledge of the durable power of attorney.

Living Wills

A living will is a document advising the physician of a person's wish to die naturally rather than be kept alive when death is inevitable (Figure 4-4 ◆). The living will may indicate treatments that should not be performed or treatments that should be terminated under clear circumstances. It can include a **DNR** order ("do not resuscitate"). Conditions of the declaration include certification in writing by the attending physician that:

- The patient has an incurable injury, disease, or illness.
- The patient's death will occur within a short time.
- Using life-prolonging procedures would serve only to artificially lengthen the dying process.

A provision in the will allows any medical procedure or medication necessary to provide comfort care and alleviate pain, even after other life-prolonging procedures have been withdrawn. Another possible provision addresses the wish to receive artificially supplied nutrition and hydration. If this provision is not included, the decision concerning nutrition and hydration will be made by the person with the power of attorney. States that do not honor living wills as legal documents recognize a person's right to decide to die naturally under the advance directive document.

Life-Prolonging Declarations

Some living wills include a "life-prolonging procedures" declaration, which states that the person wants health-care providers to perform all possible life-prolonging medical treatments (Figure 4-5 ◆). As with other medical directives, the decision to sign this declaration should be made while the person is in good health and not under stress. The document must be signed, dated, and witnessed by two people over the age of 18 in advance of any hospitalization or admission to an inpatient facility. Furthermore, the decision should be discussed with family members, an attorney, and the physician. The patient's family and physician should be made aware of the declaration when it is completed. A copy should be placed in the patient's chart.

Hospice

During the nineteenth and early twentieth centuries, the terminally ill were cared for at home. With the advances in modern medicine and technology, many terminally ill patients are now cared for in hospitals, where multiple attempts are often made to extend their lives. These interventions often deny the patient the chance to die with dignity. Some patients are shocked or defibrillated, only to be kept alive in a vegetative state.

Hospice, an alternative to these interventions, originated in Europe. Hospice is a facility or program that provides care for the terminally ill in a home setting or hospice center. In 1974, the first hospice in the United States was established in

Keys to Success
PROVIDING INFORMATION

As a medical assistant, you should acquire written information concerning tissue and organ donation, universal donor cards, living wills, advance medical directives, and durable power of attorney for health care. Create an information file for the office to provide resource material for other staff and patients as needed.

POWER OF ATTORNEY FOR HEALTH CARE

(1) **DESIGNATION OF AGENT:** I designate the following individual as my agent to make health care decisions for me: _____

_____
(Name of individual you choose as agent)

_____
(address) (city) (state) (zip code)

_____
(home phone) (work phone)

OPTIONAL: If I revoke my agent's authority or if my agent is not willing, able, or reasonably available to make a health-care decision for me, I designate as my first alternate agent:

_____
(Name of individual you choose as first alternate agent)

_____
(address) (city) (state) (zip code)

_____
(home phone) (work phone)

OPTIONAL: If I revoke the authority of my agent and first alternate agent or if neither is willing, able, or reasonably available to make a health care decision for me, I designate as my second alternate agent:

_____
(Name of individual you choose as second alternate agent)

_____
(address) (city) (state) (zip code)

_____
(home phone) (work phone)

(2) **AGENT'S AUTHORITY:** My agent is authorized to make all health care decisions for me, including decisions to provide, withhold, or withdraw artificial nutrition and hydration, and all other forms of health care to keep me alive, **except** as I state here:

(3) **WHEN AGENT'S AUTHORITY BECOMES EFFECTIVE:** My agent's authority becomes effective when my primary physician determines that I am unable to make my own health care decisions unless I mark the following box. If I mark this box [ ], my agent's authority to make health care decisions for me takes effect immediately.

(4) **AGENT'S OBLIGATION:** My agent shall make health care decisions for me in accordance with this power of attorney for health care, any instructions I give below, and my other wishes to the extent known to my agent. To the extent my wishes are unknown, my agent shall make health care decisions for me in accordance with what my agent determines to be in my best interest. In determining my best interest, my agent shall consider my personal values to the extent known to my agent.

(5) **AGENT'S POSTDEATH AUTHORITY:** My agent is authorized to make anatomical gifts, authorize an autopsy, and direct disposition of my remains, except as I state here or elsewhere in this form:

INSTRUCTIONS FOR HEALTH CARE
Strike any wording you do not want.

(6) **END-OF-LIFE DECISIONS:** I direct that my health care providers and others involved in my care provide, withhold, or withdraw treatment in accordance with the choice I have marked below: **(Initial only one box)**
[ ] (a) **Choice NOT To Prolong Life**
I do not want my life to be prolonged if (1) I have an incurable and irreversible condition that will result in my death within a relatively short time, (2) I become unconscious and, to a reasonable degree of medical certainty, I will not regain consciousness, or (3) the likely risks and burdens of treatment would outweigh the expected benefits, **OR**
[ ] (b) **Choice To Prolong Life**
I want my life to be prolonged as long as possible within the limits of generally accepted health care standards.

(7) **RELIEF FROM PAIN:** Except as I state in the following space, I direct that treatment for alleviation of pain or discomfort should be provided at all times even if it hastens my death:

DONATION OF ORGANS AT DEATH
(8) Upon my death: (mark applicable box)
[ ] (a) I give any needed organs, tissues, or parts,
OR
[ ] (b) I give the following organs, tissues, or parts only: _____
[ ] (c) My gift is for the following purposes:
(strike any of the following you do not want)
(1) Transplant
(2) Therapy
(3) Research
(4) Education

(9) **EFFECT OF COPY:** A copy of this form has the same effect as the original.

(10) **SIGNATURE:** Sign and date the form here:

_____   _____
(date)   (sign your name)

_____   _____
(address)   (print your name)

_____   _____
(city)   (state)

(11) **WITNESSES:** This advance health care directive will not be valid for making health care decisions unless it is either: (1) signed by two (2) qualified adult witnesses who are personally known to you and who are present when you sign or acknowledge your signature; or (2) acknowledged before a notary public.

Figure 4-3 ◆ Sample of power of attorney for health care

Source: Ramont, Roberta Pavy, Niedrighaus, Dee Maldonado, Towle, Mary Ann, Comprehensive nursing care, © 2006, pp. 845, 900. Reprinted by permission of Pearson Education, Upper Saddle River, NJ.

LIVING WILL DECLARATION

Declaration made this _____ day of _____, 20_____ . I, _____ _____
being at least eighteen (18) years of age and of sound mind, willfully and voluntarily make known my desires that my dying shall not be artificially prolonged under the circumstances set forth below, and I declare:

If at any time my attending physician certifies in writing that: (1) I have an incurable injury, disease, or illness; (2) my death will occur within a short time; and (3) the use of life prolonging procedures would serve only to artificially prolong the dying process, I direct that such procedures be withheld or withdrawn, and that I be permitted to die naturally with only the performance or provision of any medical procedure or medication necessary to provide me with comfort care or to alleviate pain, and, if I have so indicated below, the provision of artificially supplied nutrition and hydration. (Indicate your choice by initialling or making your mark before signing this declaration):

_____ I wish to receive artificially supplied nutrition and hydration, even if the effort to sustain life is futile or excessively burdensome to me.

_____ I do not wish to receive artificially supplied nutrition and hydration, if the effort to sustain life is futile or excessively burdensome to me.

_____ I intentionally make no decision concerning artificially supplied nutrition and hydration, leaving the decision to my health care representative appointed under IC 16-36-1-7 or my attorney in fact with health care powers under IC 30-5-5.

In the absense of my ability to give directions regarding the use of life prolonging procedures, it is my intention that this declaration be honored by my family and physician as the final expression of my legal right to refuse medical or surgical treatment and accept the consequences of the refusal.

I understand the full import of this declaration.

I am a resident of

The declarant has been personally known to me, and I believe her to be of sound mind, I did not sign the declarant's signature above for or at the direction of the declarant. I am not a parent, spouse, or child of the declarant. I am not entitled to any part of the declarant's estate or directly financially responsible for the declarant's medical care. I am competent and at least eighteen (18) years of age.

_____   _____
Witness Signature   City and State of Residence

_____   Date _____
Printed Name

_____   _____
Witness Signature   City and State of Residence

_____   Date _____
Printed Name

Figure 4-4 ◆ Sample living will declaration

New Haven, Connecticut. The objective is to improve the quality of the patient's last days by providing **palliative** care. No special interventions are used to prolong life. Pain medication is administered to keep the patient comfortable.

When the patient can no longer be cared for in the home setting, a long-term hospice center may be the next step. Family members care for the patient when they are able to do so. A team-oriented approach involves both family and professionals who offer emotional, social, and spiritual support to both the patient and the family along with bereavement counseling.

Life-Prolonging Procedures Declaration

Declaration made this _____ day of _____ (month, year). I, _____, being at least eighteen (18) years of age and of sound mind, willfully and voluntarily make known my desire that if, at any time I have an incurable injury, disease or illness determined to be a terminal condition, I request the use of life-prolonging procedures that would extend my life. This includes appropriate nutrition and hydration, the administration of medication and the performance of all other medical procedures necessary to extend my life, to provide comfort care or to alleviate pain.

In the absence of my ability to give directions regarding the use of life-prolonging procedures, it is my intention that this declaration be honored by my family and physician as the final expression of my legal right to request medical or surgical treatment and accept the consequences of the request.

I understand the full import of this declaration.

Signed _____
City, Country, and State of Residence _____

_____

The declarant has been personally known to me, and I believe (him/her) to be of sound mind. I am competent and at least eighteen (18) years of age.

Witness _____ Date _____
Witness _____ Date _____

Figure 4-5 ◆ Life-prolonging procedures declaration
Source: Lutheran Health Network, Fort Wayne, Indiana. www.lutheranhealthnetwork.com

REVIEW

Chapter Summary

- Organ and tissue donation has become increasingly common with new breakthroughs in transplantation.
- An MA should be familiar with advanced medical directives, durable power of attorney for health care, living wills, and life-prolonging declarations in order to answer patients' questions. An MA should also understand how organs and tissues are harvested.
- Some organs and tissues are harvested after a patient has died. Others are harvested after the patient has been pronounced brain dead but respiration and circulation have been supported artificially. Living donors can donate certain organs and tissues.
- Patients should research transplant costs. They include medical costs, such as hospital stay and surgery, and out-of-pocket expenses, such as child care and lost wages.
- The Uniform Anatomical Gift Act governs organ donation.

- Hospitals must have written protocols concerning informing families of the option to donate and the option to decline.
- Organs and tissues are distributed via a national computer system. Donors and recipients are matched as closely as possible to avoid rejection of the tissue or organ. Distribution is also based on critical need.
- A durable power of attorney tells a physician and family that if the patient is no longer mentally competent, a person appointed by the patient has the power of attorney to make decisions for him or her.
- A living will is a document declaring a person's wish to die naturally.
- A life-prolonging declaration indicates that the person wants all possible medical treatment used to prolong his or her life.
- Hospice offers an alternative way for the terminally ill to die with dignity. The patient may be cared for at home or in a hospice center.

Chapter Review Questions

Multiple Choice

1. Which of the following tissues can be transplanted?
   A. pancreas
   B. small intestine
   C. large intestine
   D. bone

2. Warm ischemic time cannot exceed
   A. 1 hour.
   B. 4 hours.
   C. 2 hours.
   D. 3 hours.

3. Cold ischemic time cannot exceed
   A. 4 hours.
   B. 8 hours.
   C. 10 hours.
   D. 12 hours.

4. Which of the following organs and tissues can be harvested after a donor has died and circulation and respiration have ceased?
   A. pancreas
   B. small intestine
   C. corneas
   D. kidney

5. Which of the following is true about a physician who pronounces the donor dead?
   A. The physician should not be involved in any part of the harvesting process.
   B. The physician should be involved in all parts of the harvesting process.
   C. The physician can oversee the harvesting by another physician.
   D. The physician cannot oversee harvesting but can oversee distribution.

6. A live donor understands that he or she
   A. cannot designate who receives the organ or tissue.
   B. can designate who receives the organ or tissue.
   C. is required to have a donor card.
   D. is responsible for all costs, including the patient's cost.

7. The updated version of the Uniform Anatomical Gift Act includes
   A. the ability to sue a physician who accepts the donor's organs in good faith.
   B. the provision that the donor may not revoke the donation.
   C. acceptable financial arrangements for donate organs.
   D. measures to raise awareness of the need for donated organs and tissue.

8. A durable power of attorney for health care allows
   A. a terminally ill patient to die naturally without life-prolonging medical procedures.
   B. a terminally ill patient to receive all possible life-prolonging medical treatments.
   C. an appointed person to make decisions for a patient who is no longer mentally capable.
   D. an appointed person to refuse any medication or treatment that eases the patient's pain.

9. A living will allows
   A. a terminally ill patient to receive all possible life-prolonging medical treatments.
   B. a terminally ill patient to die naturally without life-prolonging medical procedures.
   C. an appointed person to make decisions for a patient who is no longer mentally capable.
   D. an appointed person to refuse any medication or treatment that eases the patient's pain.

10. Hospice is
    A. an alternative to hospital care.
    B. life-prolonging care.
    C. an alternative to home and family care.
    D. a transplantation care center.

True/False

T F 1. Hospitals must have written protocols about informing families of the option to donate organs and the option to decline.

T F 2. Due to advances in modern medicine and technology, many terminally ill patients are now cared for in hospitals, where multiple attempts are often made to extend their lives.

T F 3. If the decedent, prior to the time of death, indicated a refusal to make an organ donation, the institution or health-care provider can choose not to honor that decision if the decedent had previously signed an organ donation card.

T F 4. The United Network for Organ Sharing (UNOS) is the agency that provides financing options for the family of the decedent making an organ donation.

T F 5. When a living will is signed advising the physician of a person's wish to die naturally rather than be kept alive when death is inevitable, the patient loses the right to receive any medication, including pain control.

Chapter Review Questions (continued)

Short Answer

1. What is a living will?

2. What is an alternative to hospitalization for the terminally ill patient who wishes to die in comfort and with dignity?

3. How many recipients can one donor provide organs and tissue for?

4. In which method of processing donated tissue are tissues frozen at a super cold temperature?

5. List the organs that must be harvested after the patient has been pronounced brain dead.

Research

1. Where do patients in your community go to have a living will drawn up? Must they use an attorney, or does someone offer this service free of charge?

2. Find the phone number and address of a local hospice your patients can utilize.

3. In your state, is the signed universal donor card a legal document permitting the procurement of organs and tissue? Does your state also require a signature on a universal donor card in addition to the signature on the back of the driver's license?

Externship Application Experience

A patient comes to the office to inquire about becoming a tissue and organ donor. She explains that her friend has been put on a waiting list for a heart and she wants information on how she and her family members can become donors upon their death. What would you do?

Resource Guide

Hospice Foundation of America
1621 Connecticut Ave., NW, Suite 300
Washington, DC 20009
1-800-854-3402
www.hospicefoundation.org

International Association for Organ Donation
PO Box 545
Dearborn, MI 48121-0545
313-745-2235
www.iaod.org

United Network for Organ Sharing (UNOS)
PO Box 2484
Richmond, VA 23218
804-782-4800
www.unos.org

MedMedia
www.prenhall.com/frazier

More on this chapter, including interactive resources, can be found on the Student CD-ROM accompanying this textbook and on the Companion Website at www.prenhall.com/frazier.

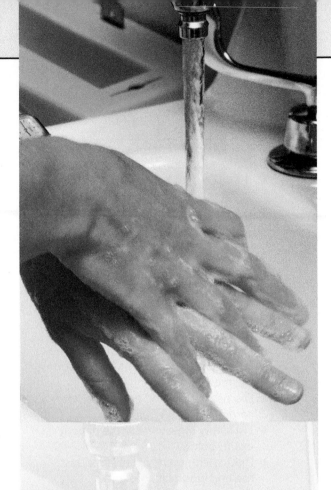

SECTION II

The Clinical Environment

My name is Walter R. Nicholas. At the present time I am a phlebotomist, but I am going to school to be a medical assistant. I would eventually like to become a registered nurse.

What I have learned so far is that a medical assistant takes vitals signs, performs height and weight assessments, assists the physician with minor office surgery, and sets up for procedures performed in the office. The MA may also administer medications and perform intramuscular, subcutaneous, and intradermal injections.

I really like my job; it makes me feel so good when I have a patient tell me that I do my job very well. It gets stressful at times, but I just think of the patients I am helping. I think that as a health care professional, if you smile no matter how bad the situation is, it will become better. A person's first impression is a lasting one.

CHAPTER 5

The Clinical Environment and Safety in the Medical Office

Case Study

Ian and Cora are busy completing the opening procedures for the wound care center where they work. At 5 minutes to opening time, Ian walks back through the reception area to check for wrinkles in the carpet and loose electrical cords from the lamps while Cora goes to the front door to unlock it.

As Cora walks back to the reception desk, a man stumbles through the front door, moaning, with blood running down his forehead. Just as he steps inside the door, he collapses.

Cora shouts to Ian, who is in the back. Hearing her cry for help, Ian quickly places the soda he is drinking in the mini-fridge the staff uses for injectable medications and rushes to offer assistance.

Objectives

After completing this chapter, you should be able to:

- Spell and define the medical terminology in this chapter.
- Define the medical assistant's role as it relates to safety in the medical office.
- Discuss proper body mechanics for the medical office employee.
- Describe procedures intended to provide a safe environment for everyone in the medical office.
- Discuss patient and employee safety according to OSHA guidelines.
- List safety measures for the patient exam room.
- Discuss emergency plans for disaster, fire, and workplace violence.
- Give an overview of OSHA's Bloodborne Pathogen Standards.
- List and describe the elements of OSHA's Bloodborne Pathogen Standards.
- Explain Standard Precautions.
- Discuss the disposal of biohazardous materials.

 **MedMedia**

www.prenhall.com/frazier

Additional interactive resources and activities for this chapter can be found on the Companion Website. For videos, audio glossary, legal and ethical scenarios, job scenarios, quizzes, and games related to the content of this chapter, please access the accompanying CD-ROM in this book.

 Assets Available:

Audio Glossary
Legal and Ethical Scenario: *Clinical Environment and Safety in the Medical Office*
On the Job Scenario: *Clinical Environment and Safety in the Medical Office*
Video Scenario: *Facing Office Emergencies*
Multiple Choice Quiz
Games: Crossword, Strikeout, and Spelling Bee

✚ MEDICAL ASSISTING COMPETENCIES

CAAHEP ENTRY-LEVEL COMPETENCIES FOR CMA	ABHES ENTRY-LEVEL COMPETENCIES FOR RMA
■ Perform within legal and ethical boundaries. ■ Demonstrate knowledge of federal and state health-care legislation and regulations.	■ Be cognizant of ethical boundaries. ■ Exhibit initiative. ■ Adapt to change. ■ Evidence a responsible attitude. ■ Be courteous and diplomatic. ■ Conduct work within scope of education, training, and ability.

Medical Terminology

decontamination—use of physical means or chemical agents to remove, inactivate, or destroy pathogens on a surface or object to the point where they are no longer capable of transmitting infectious disease, thereby rendering the surface or object safe for handling, use, or disposal.

pathogen—disease-causing microorganism

Abbreviations

ADA—Americans with Disabilities Act

AIDS—acquired immunodeficiency syndrome

HBV—Hepatitis B virus

HIV—human immunodeficiency virus

MSDS—material safety data sheet

OSHA—Occupational Safety and Health Administration

Introduction

Safety in the medical office is the responsibility of all employees. In 1970, the Occupational Safety and Health Administration (OSHA) was created by Congress to establish safety and health standards and regulations in the workplace. The Occupational Safety and Health Act (1970) which established OSHA, also set regulations for exposure to toxic chemicals, lead, asbestos, cotton dust, pesticides, and noise. In 1991, OSHA's Occupational Exposure to Bloodborne Pathogens Standards were developed. A **pathogen** is a disease-causing microorganism. The standards are designed to reduce employee risk of pathogen-caused diseases such Hepatitis B and AIDS.

The Medical Assistant's Role in Office Safety

As an MA, you will need to be aware of and trained in general and medical safety procedures. It is essential that you report any unsafe conditions to the proper person(s) immediately and follow all office safety rules. Following general and medical safety procedures will lower the potential for harm to employees and the public, and it will keep liability for injuries resulting from unsafe practices to a minimum.

Personal Safety Measures

For your safety, you should:

- Avoid loose and baggy clothing that could get caught in equipment.
- Keep jewelry to a minimum (it can get caught in equipment and may harbor bacteria).
- Wear shoes that are supportive and appropriate.
- Secure long hair back, as it can get caught in equipment.
- Store all personal items, such as your medication and jewelry, in a secure area away from patients.

Body Mechanics

Whether you are caring for patients or moving and lifting supplies and equipment, proper body mechanics are vital to your job. Know how to lift, carry, and move to protect yourself from injury. The following are some guidelines for proper body mechanics.

- Before lifting, check the object to be lifted. If it is too heavy, ask for help. When items in a box are likely to shift, grasp it properly or ask for help.
- Make sure the floor is clean and dry where you are going to lift.
- Face the object; move your feet apart to a distance equal to your shoulder width, and put one foot slightly forward.
- Bend at the knees, then firmly grasp the object with both hands (Figure 5-1 ◆).
- Tighten your stomach muscles and keep your back straight.
- Lift the object with your legs. This technique uses the stronger leg muscles to lift rather than the weaker back muscles.
- If you need to turn, use your whole body. Never twist your body.
- Carry the object close to your body and close to your center of gravity. Keep your back straight (Figure 5-2 ◆).
- Bend at the knees, using the legs to balance the weight and to put the load down.
- Push, rather than lift, larger objects.

Figure 5-2 ◆ Carry the object close to your body and keep your back straight.

General Office Safety

In the medical office, general safety measures include:

- Attending to possible hazards, such as spilled fluids and electrical cords on the floor, immediately.
- Storing food separately from medication in a designated refrigerator and/or cabinet.
- Following directions for the use of office equipment and machinery.
- Removing obstructions in hallways and reception area.
- Following traffic flow patterns.
- Exercising caution when passing through doorways.
- Replacing light bulbs or letting the appropriate person know when a light bulb needs to be replaced.
- Keeping reception areas clean and orderly.

If you are unable to correct a situation, bring it to the attention of the office manager or administrator.

Examination room safety includes:

- Keeping all medications locked in a cabinet.
- Disposing of expired medications by opening and flushing them or returning them to the manufacturer.

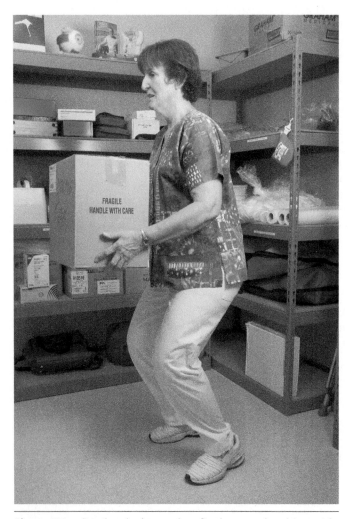

Figure 5-1 ◆ Bend at the knees, then firmly grasp the object with both hands.

- Keeping floors clean, dry, and free of obstructions.
- Securing equipment, such as sphygmomanometers and otoscopes, at the proper wall height.
- Storing other equipment in appropriate drawers and cabinets.
- Performing routine surface cleaning to prevent microbial growth.
- Disposing of all medical materials in appropriate containers.
- Offering assistance to patients getting on or off the examination table.

The office should always have supplies available to maintain dry floors to prevent slips and falls.

?— Critical Thinking Question 5-1—

Ian wants to save time and get to the reception area as quickly as possible. But what is the proper procedure for storing personal food items and medications in an office environment?

The Americans with Disabilities Act (**ADA**) of 1990 requires that every effort be taken to protect the civil rights of the disabled (Table 5-1). This includes making all areas of the office handicapped accessible. Should any barrier be brought to your attention, report it to the office manager or administrator.

The ADA is divided into five sections or titles. It is primarily intended to protect the civil rights of the disabled. It also applies to individuals who are associated with or assist persons with disabilities. Employment provisions apply to businesses of 15 or more employees. Public accommodations apply to businesses of all sizes.

Emergency Plans

As a new hire in a medical office, part of your training must include emergency plans. These should be permanently kept in a policy or procedure manual. Review this information on a regular basis.

Emergencies include fire, electrical accidents, explosions, and workplace-related violence. Disasters can be acts of nature or "acts of God." They include earthquakes, tornadoes, hurricanes, floods, snowstorms, and other weather-related events.

TABLE 5-1 AMERICANS WITH DISABILITIES ACT (ADA)	
Title I	Employers must provide reasonable accommodations to all employees with disabilities in all aspects of pre-employment and work performance.
Title II	Public services cannot deny services to persons with disabilities that are offered to persons without disabilities.
Title III	All new construction must meet ADA requirements. Present structures must remove barriers to access if easily achievable. Included in this section are parking lot ramp requirements.
Title IV	Telecommunications telephone service to the general public must also provide relay services, such as TTY.
Title V	This section prohibits coercing, threatening, or retaliating against the disabled or those aiding persons with disabilities.

It is essential that you:

- Remain calm during an emergency.
- Take care of patients first.
- Call the authorities, such as the fire department.
- Evacuate if necessary.

Know where evacuation plans are posted in each room and keep hallways and exit doors free from obstructions. Tell your office manager or administrator if an exit door is blocked or locked. It is a violation of fire codes to block exit routes. When an evacuation is announced, assist all patients from the office and/or building. Know your assigned meeting place.

?— Critical Thinking Question 5-2—

Once Ian is on the scene with Cora, who is assessing the patient's vital signs and status, what should he do next?

Fire and Electrical Safety

You should know the location of fire exits, alarms, and fire extinguishers. Follow all emergency plans. Keep all hallways and exit doors free from obstructions. *If you discover a fire, pull the alarm.*

If the alarm sounds:

- Call or direct someone to call 911 (only if it is safe to do so), or call from a safe place outside the building.
- Close all doors and windows (only if it is safe to do so).
- Check bathrooms and examination rooms to make sure all patients and staff are aware of the fire alarm.
- Evacuate with patients immediately.
- Meet at an assigned place.
- Never use the building elevator during a fire, as it can stop on the floor with the fire; use the stairs.

The only time a fire extinguisher should be used is when the fire is between you and the door. If you have to use the extinguisher, use the PASS method (Figure 5-3 ◆). It is important that you know how to use the appropriate kind of fire extinguisher before trying to use it. Local fire departments generally train employees regarding fire safety in the office. Practice fire drills and emergency carries.

Electrical safety requires exercising caution. Be careful with all equipment and make sure it is in good condition before using it. Tell your office manager or administrator if you see:

- frayed wires or cords
- overused extension cords
- lack of ground plugs or grounded outlets
- cracked or broken switch or receptacle plates
- sparking when a plug is inserted into or removed from an outlet
- broken lights

Disasters

Learn the guidelines for specific natural disasters in your area. The director of emergency preparedness or emergency management in your community is a source for these guidelines.

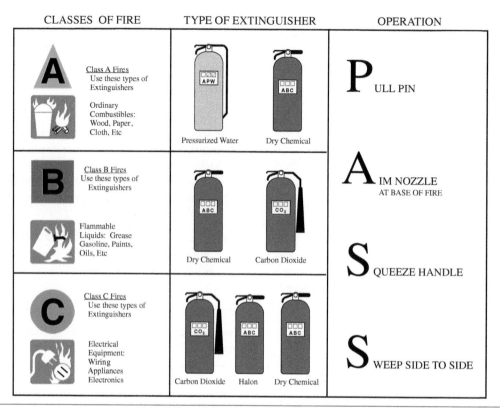

Figure 5-3 ◆ PASS method of firefighting: pull the pin, aim at the base of the fire, squeeze the trigger, and sweep from side to side.
Source: The University of Texas Health Science Center at Houston Environmental Health and Safety Department.

If a disaster happens, remain calm. The amount of time that you have to prepare before a disaster strikes can vary.

- The National Oceanic and Atmospheric Administration's (NOAA) National Weather Service issues watches and warnings for weather events such as tornadoes. A *watch* means conditions are favorable for the formation of a tornado. A *warning* means a tornado has been sighted in the area and immediate action must be taken. Patients and staff must move to a safe area, such as a basement or an inner room without glass windows. Everyone must get down on the floor and cover their heads. There is usually advance warning for hurricanes, and preparations can be made before the storm arrives.
- Earthquakes usually happen without warning. The best approach is to evacuate the building, away from possible falling debris. If you are unable to leave the building, get under a heavy piece of furniture and cover your head.

Be alert for secondary hazards after a disaster has occurred, such as ruptured gas or water lines, downed electrical or other wires, fires, broken pavement or earth, glass and debris, and fallen objects and trees. Common sense is the best guide before, during, and after natural disasters.

Workplace Violence

Violence in the workplace may be committed by an employee, former employee, patient, former patient, a patient's family member, or total stranger. If you are faced with a threatening person, speak in a calm and quiet voice. Alert another staff member who can call the police.

Workplace Security

Workplace security has become an issue in recent years. Medical offices have become a target for thieves and drug addicts. Some basic precautions should be followed.

- Doors and windows must be locked at the end of the day. Security keys or codes are usually assigned to select employees. If you are given keys and one is missing, tell the office manager or administrator. All locks must be changed when a key is lost.
- Keep prescription pads out of patients' sight. Account for all prescription pads at the end of the workday. If any pads are missing, an incident report should be filed and the appropriate law enforcement or drug enforcement agency notified.

Incident Reports

Incident reports are used to document unusual occurrences or accidents in the medical office (Figure 5-4 ◆). The persons involved, witnesses, a description of the event, and treatments given are among required information. Incident reports are a good tool for analyzing the event to prevent it from happening again.

INCIDENT REPORT

Name of injured party _____ Date _____

Address _____ Telephone _____

_____

The injured party was: ☐ Employee   ☐ Patient   ☐ Other _____

Date of accident/incident _____   Time of incident _____

Where did incident occur? _____

Names of witnesses (include titles):

_____   _____

_____   _____

What first aid/treatment was given at the time of the incident?

_____

_____

Who administered first aid? _____

Briefly describe the incident. _____

_____

_____

_____

_____

Names of employees present at time of incident/injury:

_____

_____

_____

Follow-up: What steps have been taken to prevent a similar accident? _____

_____

_____

_____   _____
Date   Employee's signature

_____   _____
Date   Supervisor's signature

Figure 5-4 ◆ An example of a typical incident report.

Examples of events that should be recorded on an incident report form include the following:

- Receiving a contaminated needle stick injury.
- Discovering that a wrong medication has been given.
- Finding a patient who has fainted in the reception area, examination room, or the parking lot.
- Discovering that prescription pads are missing.
- Seeing a patient or office staff member fall on a wet floor.
- Feeling an electric shock while plugging an EKG machine into an electrical outlet.

Keys to Success
DOCUMENTING INCIDENTS

The incident report is reviewed by the physician's office. It does not become part of the patient's chart, although the same information is recorded in the chart. Record only the facts. Do not record any opinions. If the chart information or the incident report is used as evidence in court, opinions could be viewed as an admission of fault by the physician's office or as an attempt to blur the facts.

—Critical Thinking Question 5-3—
After the situation in the reception area has been taken care of and the patient is no longer in need of medical assistance, how should the incident be recorded, and by whom?

OSHA Bloodborne Pathogen Standards

OSHA's Occupational Exposure to Bloodborne Pathogens Standards are important regulations for every medical office. These standards are designed primarily to reduce employee risk of infectious diseases such as hepatitis B virus (**HBV**) and human immunodeficiency virus (**HIV**) by limiting exposure (Table 5-2). (∞ Refer to Chapter 7, Medical Asepsis, for more information on HBV and HIV.) Although the goal is employee safety, any worker or employer with potential occupational exposure must follow these standards. Failure to comply could result in a citation and a fine up to $7,000 for each violation and a maximum penalty of $70,000 for repeat violations.

According to OSHA's standards, each medical office must have a written exposure control plan that addresses:

- methods of compliance
- infection control practices
- housekeeping and laundry **decontamination**
- Hepatitis B vaccinations
- engineering and work practice controls
- post-exposure evaluation and follow-up
- hazards communications
- documentation of training and record keeping

Patient Safety

Following OSHA standards greatly reduces the risk of pathogen transmission from health-care worker to patient. An employee who has been or is a known disease carrier and who performs high-risk procedures should know his or her HBV and HIV status. An employee with HIV or HBV should not perform patient care without first consulting a personal physician and a medical review committee. The affected employee must also tell patients of the potential risk, as appropriate. An employee with draining lesions should tell a supervisor, and patient contact will be restricted.

The Centers for Disease Control suggest TB screening of every health-care worker. Refer to state guidelines for your area's specific requirements. Initial screening by Mantoux skin test is usually an acceptable screening tool. The CDC also recommends that each health-care facility have an exposure plan developed

TABLE 5-2 POTENTIALLY INFECTIOUS (REGULATED) MATERIALS

Blood or body fluid visibly contaminated with blood
Vaginal secretions or semen
Body fluids, including cerebrospinal, peritoneal, synovial, pericardial, pleural, amniotic, and saliva in dental procedures
Pathology specimens, such as tissue culture, cells, any unfixed human tissue, or fluid known to be HIV infected

and in place. Again, refer to state and local guidelines for specific recommendations. Administrators responsible for plans should obtain medical and epidemiologic guidance from state and local health departments. Risk assessment should help to determine the types of administrative, environmental, and respiratory protection controls that are required and provide an ongoing evaluation tool of the quality of TB infection control. This assessment will also assist in the identification of any necessary improvements in infection control measures.

Exposure Control Plan

In the exposure control plan, each employee is classified according to the likelihood of exposure to blood and other potentially infectious materials. Employee categories are based on:

- Ongoing occupational exposure risk
- Accidental or potential exposure risk
- No exposure risk

For example, a medical assistant or other clinical person is at risk for ongoing occupational exposure. Custodial or laundry service staff are at risk of accidental or potential exposure to improperly discarded sharps in the trash or laundry.

The exposure control plan sets effective dates for other provisions of the standard. The plan must also establish procedures for evaluating exposure incidents. These written procedures must be readily available to employees and to OSHA. The plan must be evaluated annually.

Standard Precautions and Infection Control Practices

Standard Precautions, including both Universal Precautions and Body Substance Isolation, are infection control guidelines

Caduceus Chronicle
THE HISTORY OF BLOOD TRANSFUSIONS AND HIV DISCOVERY

1628	Circulation of blood discovered by William Harvey (1578–1657). First blood transfusion is attempted.
1665	First successful blood transfusion is performed in dogs.
1795	First successful blood transfusion in humans is performed.
1867	Antiseptics are used by Joseph Lister (1827–1912) to combat infections during transfusions.
1884	Saline becomes the substitute for blood transfusions because of adverse reactions to milk.
1932	A Leningrad hospital becomes the first blood bank.
1981	Signs and symptoms of, and medical conditions related to, HIV/AIDS are observed in homosexuals, including *Pneumocystis carinii*, Kaposi's sarcoma, and suppression of CD4 cells, also known as T cells.
1983	U.S. and French researchers describe HIV infection that causes **AIDS**.
1985	To eliminate the potential contamination of blood donations and reduce blood transmission of HIV/AIDS to noninfected individuals, blood centers in the United States begin testing every blood donation for HIV antibodies.
1996	Blood centers add another test called HIV antigen assay, making blood supply even safer.

Keys to Success
WRITTEN PROCEDURES

When procedures are written for the medical office or any health-care facility, standards of performance and safety are included:
- Materials and required steps
- Personal protective equipment (PPE) required
- Instructions for proper cleaning, sterilization, or disposal of used supplies and equipment
- Description of body fluid type and approximate exposure amount during the procedure

established by the Centers for Disease Control and Prevention (CDC). All human blood and body fluids are considered infectious. (Refer to Chapter 7, Medical Asepsis, for more complete information on Standard Precautions.)

Engineering and Work Practice Controls

Engineering controls reduce or eliminate the risk of occupational exposure. Examples include devices that isolate or remove health hazards, such as autoclaves, biohazard containers, and safety cabinets. In November 2000, President Clinton signed the Needlestick Safety and Prevention Act, which specifies employee involvement in evaluating needle devices in current use and in the selection of better, safer needle devices. Following OSHA work practice controls also reduces the risk of exposure.

Frequent hand washing is one of the most important ways to reduce risk. Other work practice controls include the following.

1. Keep the potential for spraying, spattering, and splashing moisture droplets from blood and body fluids to a minimum.
2. Know the appropriate color coding or labeling for biohazard containers and biohazard-containing appliances (Figure 5-5 ◆).
3. Bandage open wounds on the hands.
4. Wash the hands after each glove removal.
5. Wash any skin surface immediately after contact with blood or body fluids. Flush mucous membranes with water.
6. Dispose of contaminated needles and other sharps in the appropriate puncture-resistant container after use. (Refer to Chapter 14, Hematology and Chemistry, for more information on procedures for using, handling, and disposing of needles and sharps.)

Keys to Success
GOOD SAMARITAN ACT

If a worker assists another coworker who has become ill, is this occupational exposure? The answer is no. This is considered a "Good Samaritan" act, not part of the job.

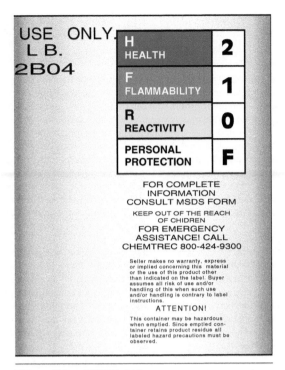

Figure 5-5 ◆ MSDS label

7. Never eat, drink, store food, smoke, or apply cosmetics in areas where blood or body fluids are present because of potential contamination.
8. Place potentially infectious blood or tissue into containers that prevent leakage during collection, handling, processing, storage, and transport. Containers should be closed, except during collections and processing, and specially labeled or color coded as containing biohazardous materials.
9. Decontaminate equipment contaminated with blood and body fluids before it is cleaned.
10. File an incident report if an employee is exposed to a potentially infectious material. The employer must begin the exposure procedures.

Personal Protective Equipment

Personal protective equipment (PPE) is required protective wear. PPE protects health-care employees from contact with potentially infectious blood and body fluids. Single or combined PPE

Caduceus Chronicles
NEEDLESTICK ACT, NOVEMBER 2000

On November 6, 2000, President Clinton signed the Needlestick Safety and Prevention Act, which revised OSHA's Bloodborne Pathogen Standard. Needlestick devices must be reevaluated annually. Frontline employees, such as nurses and laboratory technicians, are required to be part of the evaluation process. Employers are required to keep logs of all needlesticks and sharps injuries, including those in individuals remaining healthy and those succumbing to related illnesses. At all times, the privacy of the employee must be maintained. The CDC has estimated that since the act went into effect the use of safer devices has led to a 62 to 88 percent reduction in sharps injuries in hospital settings.

may be worn depending on the degree of anticipated exposure. PPE includes:

- gloves (for direct hand contact)
- face shields or masks (for sprays, splashes, or droplets)
- gowns or laboratory coats (for large amounts of infectious materials)
- masks (for airborne transmission)

OSHA requires that PPE be provided by the employer at no charge to the employee. The employer also covers the cost of replacing, maintaining, or cleaning PPE. More medical offices are using disposable items when they are more cost effective than cleaning and/or sterilizing. Examples include patient gowns and disposable suture removal sets. Gloves are *never* reused. Clothing or equipment such as masks must be strong enough that body substances do not penetrate and reach the employee's clothing, skin, or mucous membranes. Before leaving the medical office, the employee must place contaminated equipment or clothing in a designated container. (∞ Refer to Chapter 7, Medical Asepsis, for more information on PPE.)

Housekeeping and Laundry Decontamination

Housekeeping employees in a medical office are at risk for exposure to potentially infectious materials. They must receive OSHA-required training and offered immunization protection. All employees must follow OSHA standards regarding housekeeping and laundry decontamination procedures, which are defined by the facility. (∞ Refer to Chapter 7, Medical Asepsis, for complete information on cleanup and decontamination.)

Hepatitis B Vaccinations

OSHA requires that Hepatitis B vaccinations be offered to every health-care worker within 10 days of beginning employment. The employer must provide immunization at no charge to the employee, along with education regarding the benefits of the vaccination. The employee is given the opportunity to accept or decline immunization. If the employee declines, he or she must sign a form so indicating. The employee can later choose to accept immunization.

Hazard Communication Program

Orange or orange-red labels are required on items such as containers and refrigerators that contain regulated infectious waste (Figure 5-6 ◆). Items not labeled are to be stored and transported in red bags or containers. Decontaminated, regulated waste and tested HIV/HBV free blood does not need to be labeled. When all specimens and all laundry are handled according to Standard Precautions, red bags or hazard labels are not needed.

Radioactive waste occurs as a by-product of nuclear medicine or radiation therapy and must be clearly labeled. It is never incinerated or poured down the drain and must be disposed of by a licensed facility.

Medical offices are required to keep an inventory of toxic substances used on the premises. The Material Safety Data Sheet

Figure 5-6 ◆ Orange or orange-red labels are required on items such as containers and refrigerators that contain regulated infectious waste

(**MSDS**) (Figure 5-7 ◆) for each chemical includes such information as:

- product name and/or synonymous (identical) names
- the manufacturer's name, address, and phone number
- components of the chemical
- effects of exposure to the chemical
- first aid and emergency measures for exposure
- storage and disposal requirements
- procedures for cleaning leaks or spills
- use of PPE

Employees must read each MSDS. The employer must be able to provide evidence that all employees have read the MSDS. Usually, the signature or initials of each employee on the MSDS is sufficient. By signing or initialing, the employee accepts responsibility for the correct handling of the hazardous substance.

Training and Record Keeping

OSHA standards require that employers provide training to employees at occupational risk of exposure to infectious body substances. Training must occur during the first 90 days of employment, then every year thereafter. The training includes information and updates on the exposure control plan and methods of compliance.

Employers must keep training records for three years after the training session. Confidential records for each at-risk medical office employee are kept for 30 years post-employment (Table 5-3).

Exposure, Post-Exposure Evaluation, and Follow-up

Each medical office or other health-care facility must have a specified procedure to be followed for exposure incidents. If an

Keys to Success
THE CONTROVERSY OVER MERCURY THERMOMETERS

Exposure to even small amounts of mercury can be harmful. Swallowing mercury from a broken glass thermometer is an emergency, requiring a visit to the emergency room or a call to the poison control center. If a person with a healthy gastrointestinal (GI) tract swallows mercury, it is usually eliminated quickly, without causing symptoms. If the person has a history of gastrointestinal ulcers, fistulas, or inflammatory bowel disease, passage through the GI system is slower and exposure to the mercury is prolonged.

Mercury is a very heavy element that is not well absorbed through the skin or cuts. The most likely reaction to mercury contact is a skin rash. Mercury contact occurs mostly through inhalation of vapors with more than a one-time, short exposure. Mercury is an environmental hazard and must be disposed of properly.

If a mercury thermometer breaks, wear gloves when you clean up the spill. Mercury beads on a hard surface. It can be scooped up and lifted into a jar with stiff paper or cardboard. It can also be lifted with a small eye dropper. If mercury gets on a carpet, cut out the spot. Put the mercury or mercury-soaked carpeting in a jar and seal tightly. Never vacuum mercury, because the heat may cause it to evaporate. The objective when cleaning up is to prevent inhalation of the fumes.

Alcohol thermometers are an alternative; however, they may not be as accurate. Digital thermometers, although more costly, are becoming more common. Many facilities are removing mercury thermometers from use, and some communities have banned them.

employee is exposed to a hazardous substance, an exposure report form must be filled out.

Post-exposure medical evaluation and treatment are provided by the employer without charge to the employee. Employee information created by the medical evaluation must be kept confidential. The evaluation includes events of the exposure and blood testing of the source person and the employee. If consent is given, treatment and counseling are provided.

TABLE 5-3 OSHA RECORD REQUIREMENTS

Employee Records

Name
Social security number
Hepatitis B vaccination dates
Post-exposure examinations, testing, and follow-up (including medical evaluation and recommendations)
Copy of exposure report

Training Records

Content
Session dates
Names and qualifications of presenters
Names and titles of employee attendees

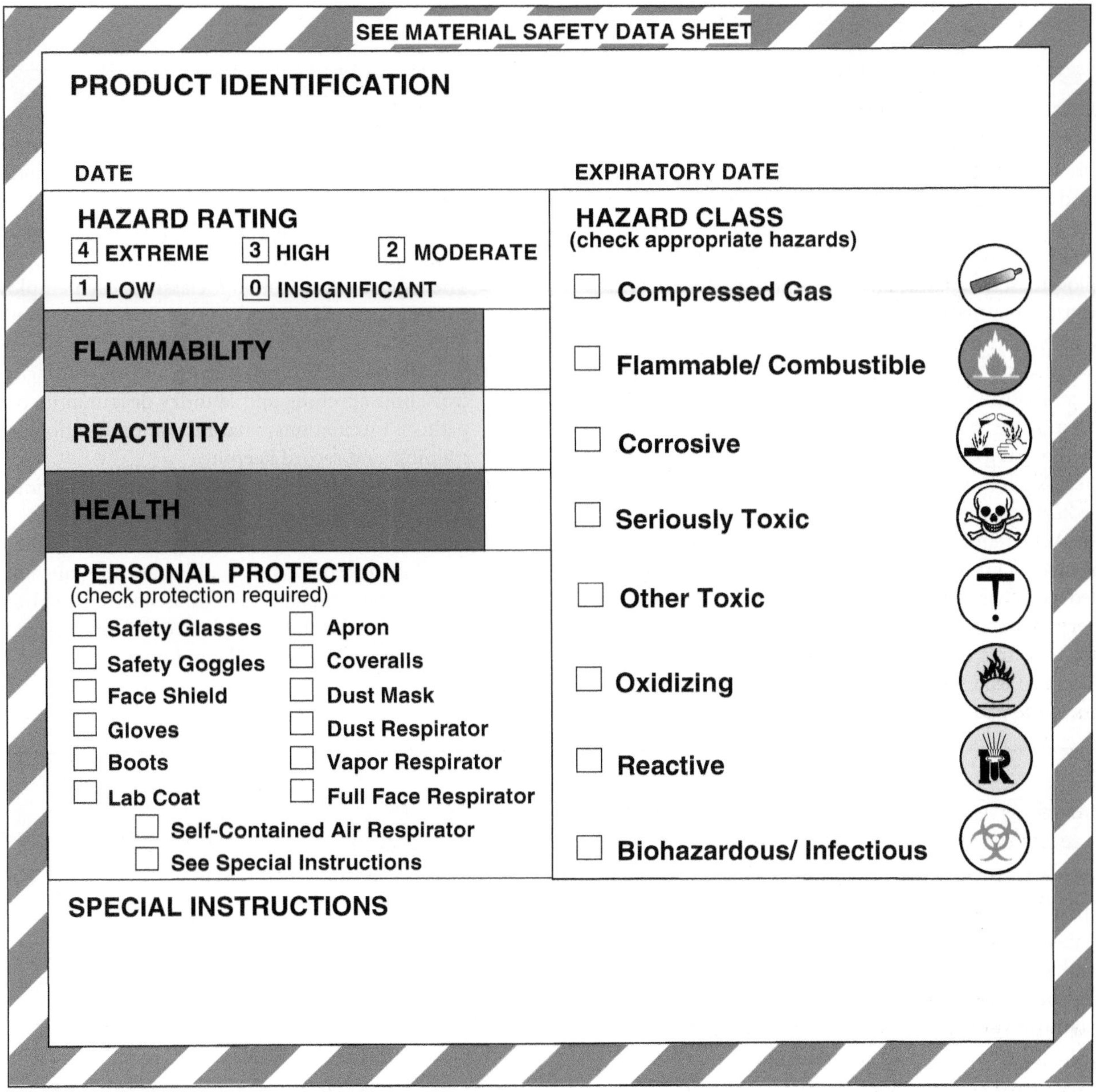

SEE MATERIAL SAFETY DATA SHEET

PRODUCT IDENTIFICATION

DATE   EXPIRATORY DATE

HAZARD RATING

4 EXTREME   3 HIGH   2 MODERATE
1 LOW   0 INSIGNIFICANT

FLAMMABILITY

REACTIVITY

HEALTH

PERSONAL PROTECTION
(check protection required)

☐ Safety Glasses   ☐ Apron
☐ Safety Goggles   ☐ Coveralls
☐ Face Shield   ☐ Dust Mask
☐ Gloves   ☐ Dust Respirator
☐ Boots   ☐ Vapor Respirator
☐ Lab Coat   ☐ Full Face Respirator
    ☐ Self-Contained Air Respirator
    ☐ See Special Instructions

HAZARD CLASS
(check appropriate hazards)

☐ **Compressed Gas**

☐ **Flammable/ Combustible**

☐ **Corrosive**

☐ **Seriously Toxic**

☐ **Other Toxic**

☐ **Oxidizing**

☐ **Reactive**

☐ **Biohazardous/ Infectious**

SPECIAL INSTRUCTIONS

Figure 5-7 ◆ An example of a Material Safety Data Sheet (MSDS)

REVIEW

Chapter Summary

- In 1970, the Occupational Safety and Health Administration was created to establish safety regulations and health standards for the workplace. In 1991, Occupational Exposure to Bloodborne Standards were developed to reduce employees' risk for infectious diseases. All employees must follow these standards. Employers must provide a written exposure control plan.
- As an MA, you must always be alert to the safety of your patients, yourself, and the office.
- General office safety includes basic safety measures, such as removing hallway obstructions and exercising caution when passing through doorways, and examination room safety, such as securing equipment and disposing of all medical materials in appropriate containers.
- The ADA requires that every effort be made to protect the civil rights of the disabled. This includes making the medical office handicapped accessible.
- Every medical office must have an emergency plan for disasters, fires, electrical problems, violence in the workplace, and security breaches. All employees must have access to the plan.

- It is most important to remain calm in an emergency. Follow all office procedures for evacuation and calling the police and fire department.
- Incident report forms must be filed for unusual occurrences and emergencies.
- The exposure control plan classifies each employee according to the likelihood of exposure to blood and other infectious materials. Included in the plan are Standard Precautions, PPE, engineering and work practice controls, housekeeping and laundry decontamination, Hepatitis B vaccinations, a hazard communication program, training, and record keeping.
- PPE protects wearers from contact with infectious blood and body fluids.
- A hazard communication program requires the proper handling and disposal of all hazardous substances, including contaminated, infectious, and radioactive wastes. Chemicals used in the medical office must have MSDSs on file and available to all employees.

Chapter Review Questions

Multiple Choice

1. The first thing you should do before lifting is to
   A. make sure the object is not too heavy for you to lift.
   B. ask someone else to do it.
   C. move it with your foot.
   D. remove your shoes, so you have better balance.

2. When you are lifting a box, you should
   A. keep your feet together.
   B. bend at the waist.
   C. lift with your legs.
   D. loosen your stomach muscles.

3. The ADA requires that
   A. access to a public building is required, but public services can be denied.
   B. the civil rights of a person with disabilities should be protected.
   C. access to a public building can be denied, but public services are required.
   D. the civil rights of a person with disabilities be considered different from those of persons without disabilities.

4. Workplace security involves
   A. learning how to use a fire extinguisher.
   B. listening to the weather band on the radio.
   C. reporting overused electrical outlets.
   D. keeping prescription pads out of patients' sight.

5. A written exposure control plan must include information on
   A. documenting of training.
   B. types of fire extinguishers.
   C. types of security alarms.
   D. documenting disasters.

6. Which of the following measures is most important for reducing exposure risk?
   A. decontaminating equipment
   B. washing hands frequently
   C. using an autoclave
   D. labeling biohazard containers

7. OSHA requires employers to provide PPE to an employee
   A. and for the employee to pay for cleaning of the item.
   B. on a one-time basis, after which the employee is responsible for replacing an item.
   C. and for the employer to pay for the cost of replacing any worn item.
   D. and allows the employee to reuse gloves.

8. Which of the following is true about Hepatitis B vaccinations?
   A. An employee may be charged for the vaccination.
   B. An employee must be vaccinated.
   C. An employee must be offered the vaccination after three months on the job.
   D. An employee may decline being vaccinated.

Chapter Review Questions (continued)

9. A hazard communication program covers
   A. only bloodborne pathogens.
   B. toxic substances used in the workplace.
   C. only chemicals.
   D. regulated waste in workplace.

10. OSHA requires that a new employee at occupational risk for exposure to infectious body substances be trained within the first
   A. 110 days of employment.
   B. 100 days of employment.
   C. 90 days of employment.
   D. 120 days of employment.

True/False

T F 1. As an MA, you will need to be aware of and trained in general and medical safety procedures.

T F 2. In 1950, the Occupational Safety and Health Administration (OSHA) was created by Congress to establish safety and health standards and regulations in the workplace.

T F 3. For your safety, you should avoid loose and baggy clothing that could get caught in equipment.

T F 4. The exposure control plan classifies each employee according to the likelihood of exposure to blood and other infectious materials.

T F 5. OSHA's Occupational Exposure to Bloodborne Pathogens Standards are designed to reduce employee risk of infectious diseases.

Short Answer

1. What did Joseph Lister use in 1867 to combat infections during transfusions?

3. According to OSHA, when must Hepatitis B vaccinations be offered to health-care workers?

3. What document will give you information about chemicals used in the medical office, such as the effects of exposure as well as storage and disposal requirements?

4. What should you wear to protect yourself from contact with potentially infectious blood and body fluids?

5. Which government agency issues watches and warnings for weather events such as tornadoes?

Research

1. Does your local area have a standard 911 system, or is there another number that must be dialed?

2. List the following emergency numbers for your community:
   Hospital _____
   Fire Department _____
   Poison Control _____
   Non-emergency Transport _____
   EMT _____

Externship Application Experience

As a student in the medical office, you bring your lunch for the day. You ask the receptionist where you should put it until lunchtime. She shows you a refrigerator in the clean utility room and tells you to put it there. When you open the door, you notice that medications are being stored in this refrigerator. What do you do?

Resource Guide

Centers for Disease Control and Prevention (CDC)
Emergency Preparedness and Response
1600 Clifton Road
Atlanta, GA 30333
1-800-CDC-INFO
www.bt.cdc.gov

Federal Emergency Management Agency (FEMA)
500 C Street, SW
Washington, DC 20472
202-566-1600
www.fema.gov

Joint Commission on Accreditation of Healthcare Organizations (JCAHO)
601 13th Street, NW
Suite 1150N
Washington, DC 20005
630-792-5000
www.jcaho.org

Occupational Safety & Health Administration (OSHA)
200 Constitution Avenue, NW
Washington, DC 20210
1-800-321-OSHA (6742)
TTY 1-877-889-5627
www.osha.gov

 **MedMedia**
www.prenhall.com/frazier

More on this chapter, including interactive resources, can be found on the Student CD-ROM accompanying this textbook and on the Companion Website at www.prenhall.com/frazier.

CHAPTER 6

The Clinical Visit: Office Preparation and the Patient Encounter

Case Study

Ali Keen, an RMA, is preparing the patient charts she will need for the day. She cannot locate the chart for her 1:00 patient. Ali looks on the physician's desk and in the vertical storage file, without luck. She then searches the computer schedule and sees that her patient came in as a walk-in appointment last week and was treated by Dr. Erin Strauser, her regular physician's partner.

Certain that Alexis, Dr. Strauser's MA, will have the chart, Ali goes to speak to her. After several minutes of shifting the clutter on Alexis's desk, she finds the chart. Ali notices that it's covered with coffee stains, which have soaked into several of the reports inside.

"Is this coffee? The chart can't be used like this," she says as she hands the chart back to Alexis.

Alexis takes the chart and hastily wipes off the cover and rips out several pages. She scribbles most of the information (incorrectly) onto new sheets and throws away the prescription refill notes. She says they are unnecessary since the medications have already been refilled and taken and the notes are more than 6 months old. Alexis then gives the chart back to Ali.

Objectives

After completing this chapter, you should be able to:

- Spell and define medical terminology within the chapter.
- Define the medical assistant's role in the clinical visit.
- Define triage and give examples of triage procedures in the medical office.
- Discuss the essentials of consent.
- Obtain consent for treatment.
- Discuss the importance of medical records in the medical office.
- Explain the documentation of a patient visit.
- List important elements contained in an initial patient history.

MedMedia

www.prenhall.com/frazier

Additional interactive resources and activities for this chapter can be found on the Companion Website. For videos, audio glossary, legal and ethical scenarios, job scenarios, quizzes, and games related to the content of this chapter, please access the accompanying CD-ROM in this book.

 Assets Available:

Audio Glossary

Legal and Ethical Scenario: *The Clinical Visit: Office Preparation and the Patient Encounter*

On the Job Scenario: *The Clinical Visit: Office Preparation and the Patient Encounter*

Video Scenario: *Taking Patient Histories* and *Explaining Office Policies*

Multiple Choice Quiz

Games: Crossword, Strikeout, and Spelling Bee

➕ MEDICAL ASSISTING COMPETENCIES

CAAHEP ENTRY-LEVEL COMPETENCIES FOR CMA	ABHES ENTRY-LEVEL COMPETENCIES FOR RMA
■ Obtain and record patient history. ■ Complete a patient history form. ■ Document a clinical visit and procedure. ■ Perform telephone and in-person screening. ■ Prepare and maintain examination and treatment areas. ■ Establish and maintain the medical record. ■ Document appropriately. ■ Explain general office procedures. ■ Perform maintenance of administrative and clinical equipment.	■ Interview and take a patient history. ■ Prepare and maintain examination and treatment area. ■ Perform telephone and in-person screening. ■ Determine needs for documentation and reporting. ■ Document accurately. ■ Follow established policy in initiating or terminating medical treatment. ■ Operate and maintain facilities and equipment safely. ■ Orient patient to office policies and procedures.

Introduction

The patient has the right to expect a safe, clean, and orderly environment in the medical office. A physician also requires the same clean and orderly environment to provide efficient and thorough care to the patient. Convenient placement of instruments, supplies, and equipment allows the physician to make best use of time and movement in the examination or treatment areas.

Carefully documented medical records are critical for patient care. Whether documenting an initial visit, patient history, or clinical visit, accuracy and attention to detail in these charts are a major responsibility in the medical office.

The Medical Assistant's Role in the Clinical Visit

As an MA, you usually do not have great input into the physical layout of a physician's office. However, you will be responsible for providing a clean, safe environment in the examination and treatment areas. Preparing and maintaining the examination and treatment areas depend on the type of specialty practice in which you will be employed.

Depending on the office duties that will be assigned to you, you may be involved in administrative responsibilities such as triage and preparing medical records, including consent forms and third-party information, or in clinical responsibilities—obtaining the patient's history, taking vital signs, and updating the patient's chart.

COMPETENCY SKILLS PERFORMANCE

1. Prepare and maintain a medical record.
2. Complete a patient history form.
3. Document a clinical visit and procedure.

Medical Terminology

charting—documentation of all the events of a patient's visit

diagnosis—conclusion made about the patient's condition by interpretation of data

implied consent—agreement implied by the patient for examination and treatment when presenting for a routine visit; also, in an emergency, consent that it is assumed the patient would give if the patient could do so

informed consent—consent given by a patient after all potential treatments and outcomes have been discussed for a specific medical condition, including risks and possible negative outcomes

ophthalmoscope—instrument used to examine the eyes

otoscope—instrument used to examine the ears

prognosis—an outcome prediction for the course of a disease and patient recovery

sign—that which can be seen, heard, measured, or felt by the examiner

sphygmomanometer—instrument used to measure blood pressure

stethoscope—instrument used to listen to sounds within the body

symptom—a perceptible change in the body related by the patient

thermometer—instrument used to measure body temperature

triage—prioritizing patient needs by assessing symptoms, situations, and external factors and arranging patients according to most immediate need

Abbreviations

POMR—problem-oriented medical record

SOAP—subjective, objective, assessment, plan

The Standard Medical Office

The majority of office complexes are designed to provide efficiency in the physical structure with each physician using at least two examination rooms. Nearly all examination rooms and treatment areas have a sink, a small cabinet for supplies, an examination table, a stool, a writing surface, auxiliary lighting, hazardous waste and sharps containers, a chair, and possibly a telephone (Figure 6-1 ◆). An area for dressing or a screen is often provided for patient privacy. The patient's coat or clothing may be hung on a hook or placed on a chair. Sheets or paper drapes provide the patient with privacy and warmth if necessary.

The area should be well lit and easily ventilated. The walls and door of the room should be soundproof for patient privacy and confidentiality. The door should be kept closed for patient privacy. There are racks for chart holders by the door on the wall outside the room. Temperature controls should be placed so that the rooms can be kept at a comfortable temperature for the patient.

Standard equipment may include the following:

- A wall-mounted or portable **sphygmomanometer,** which measures blood pressure
- An **otoscope,** which is used to examine the ears
- An **ophthalmoscope,** which is used to examine the eyes
- An examination table with stirrups and a pull-out foot rest
- A wall-mounted X-ray view box
- Portable lighting

Depending on the specialty, other equipment may be required. Equipment to monitor vital signs includes a **thermometer,** which is used to measure patient's temperature; a **stethoscope,** which is used to listen to sounds within the body; and a sphygmomanometer. A scale to weigh and to measure the patient's height is available in the clinical area of the medical office. A Snellen eye chart is usually mounted in a hall or other location that allows the patient's vision to be tested at a distance of 20 feet.

Equipment should be checked on a regular basis to make sure it is in working condition. It will be your responsibility to know how the equipment works and to be able to assist the physician in its use.

Storage for equipment and supplies includes the examination table, supply cabinet, and desk. The examination table

Keys to Success
EQUIPMENT MALFUNCTIONS

Do not forget or ignore broken equipment or assume someone else will take care of it. Follow office policy and take immediate steps to store the broken item in another location, label it as broken, and make repair arrangements. Also, keep a log on the item, noting labeling, removing, and repairing.

In a court of law, when involved in a legal case, it is usually a point to establish who knew about the equipment failure and when it occurred. Liability is more severe if it becomes known that staff knew of malfunctioning equipment and did not take safeguards to label and repair it.

has drawers in which to store equipment and supplies, such as patient gowns, drapes, sheets, vaginal specula, emesis basins, lubricant, and urine specimen containers. The supply cabinet is a storage unit for thermometers, alcohol prep pads, slides and specimen containers, tongue depressors, cotton-tipped applicators, a tuning fork, specula for the otoscope, disposable gloves, sterile gloves, laryngeal mirror, nasal speculum, reflex hammer, stethoscope, otoscope, ophthalmoscope, and tape measure. Tissues and writing materials are available on the small desk.

Preparing and Maintaining Examination and Treatment Areas

At the beginning of the day, you should check all examination rooms to see that they are clean, free of clutter, and in order. Make sure there are adequate supplies for the day and restock if necessary. Then check the patient roster for the day and why the patients are being seen. Any supplies for special examinations or procedures should be on hand in the supply area.

After the patient visit is completed and the patient has left the room, replace the examination table paper. When removing used table paper, turn all soiled surfaces inward and fold the paper into a small package for disposal (Figure 6-2 ◆). This way your hands come in contact with the clean side only. (The same principle applies to removing gloves.)

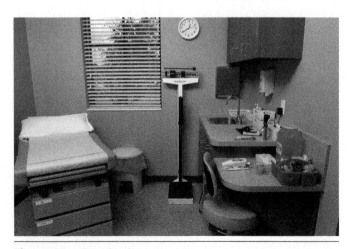

Figure 6-1 ◆ Examination room

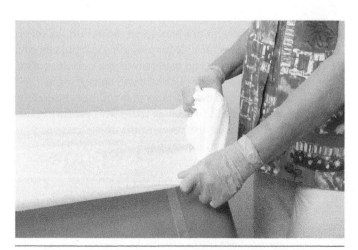

Figure 6-2 ◆ When removing used table paper, turn all soiled surfaces inward and fold the paper into a small package for disposal.

Any soiled areas are cleansed according to office protocol. Used or soiled equipment should be removed to the "dirty" area for cleansing and appropriate disinfection or sterilization. Waste receptacles should be emptied frequently. If necessary, use a disinfectant spray to combat germs and/or odor. Any spills should be cleaned immediately. Generally, professional cleaning services are contracted to maintain the floors, windows, and other structural components of the office.

At the end of the day, check all areas for cleanliness and make sure that adequate supplies are available for the next day. Dispose of hazardous materials according to office and OSHA guidelines. Clean and disinfect the restroom and restock it with paper supplies and urine specimen cups if necessary.

Triage

Triage is the process of prioritizing patient needs by assessing symptoms, situations, and external factors and arranging patients according to most immediate need. Triage can occur through direct patient contact to assess who is in the most immediate need of medical attention, or by phone to assess who has the most immediate need for a return phone call. Listening to the complaint and the information imparted by the patient is of utmost importance. Follow office policy or protocol concerning additional questions and the triage of critically ill or severely injured patients. It may be necessary to confer with an office nurse or physician for further instructions.

A patient with a possible contagious disease will need to be removed to an examination room that may be qualified as a designated isolation room. Patients who are nauseated and complain of possible vomiting should be removed to an appropriate room as soon as one is available. Take patients who have come for various other procedures to appropriate rooms. Keep the flow of patients moving to maximize the physician's time in the office.

Critically Ill or Severely Injured Patients

Office policy should be established concerning individuals calling in or presenting with chest pain and/or difficulty breathing. Most physician offices refer patients with any chest pain or those having difficulty breathing and not present in the office to Emergency Medical Services (EMS). Depending on the situation, the patient or the caller may or may not be able to call 911. In this situation, office staff should use another phone line to call EMS while keeping the caller on the phone for additional information, including location and continuing condition. Should the patient present at the office, take him or her into a treatment room WITHOUT DELAY and have the physician notified immediately while you begin assessing vital signs and symptoms. The physician will determine the course of treatment for these patients.

Other patients with sudden onset of severe pain should be considered emergency patients. Again, depending on office policy and the presence of the physician in the office, a patient contacting the office by phone may be instructed to call Emergency Medical Services (usually 911), proceed to an emergency facility, or come to the office as soon as possible. This patient will be taken into the treatment area upon arrival and assessed.

Keys to Success
PATIENT EMERGENCIES

If the physician is not present and a patient presents with life-threatening symptoms, **call 911** after explaining to the patient that it is unsafe for him or her to self-transport.

Symptoms, including onset and location of pain, should be assessed and documented. The patient will be asked about the onset and duration of the pain, what makes it better or worse, and if it has occurred before. As an MA, you should be aware of conditions that are considered serious or emergency conditions requiring immediate intervention. In addition to chest pain, other emergencies requiring immediate assessment or intervention include the following:

- Difficulty breathing
- Seizures
- Decreased level of consciousness
- Allergic reactions
- Diabetic reactions
- Drug overdose
- Head injuries
- Severe lacerations and bleeding
- Sudden onset of paralysis or loss of speech
- Severe dizziness

A patient must be placed in a treatment room and the physician notified immediately for

- Sudden onset of acute pain
- Sudden acute illness
- Severe vomiting
- Poisoning
- Foreign body in the eye
- Possible fractures
- Drug overdose

All of these conditions require intervention as soon as possible. In the meantime, you should assess the situation and have information available for the physician on his or her arrival in the examination/treatment room.

Common sense is a good guideline for triage. Office policy is the best principle to follow in these matters. All personnel must be familiar with these policies and follow them.

Consent

Many offices do not require consent for routine examinations and treatment. They rely on **implied consent,** meaning that the patient agrees to examination and treatment when presenting for a routine visit. The contract between a physician and a patient consists of the request for service, provision of the services, and compensation for the services. The patient also has the right to expect care that is customary, reasonable, and consistent with what a prudent provider should do within the scope of his or her practice and training.

Signed consent forms are required legal documents stating that the patient is giving his or her permission for certain

WINDY CITY CLINIC
Beth Williams, M.D.
123 Michigan Avenue
Chicago, IL 60610
(312) 123-1234

RECORDS RELEASE   Date _____

To _____
                                              Doctor

_____
                                              Address

I hereby authorize and request you to release

to _____
                                              Doctor

_____
                                              Address

all medical records in your possession concerning any
examination, diagnosis, and/or treatment rendered to me
during the period from _____ to _____

_____
Signature of patient or closest relative

_____
Relationship

_____   _____
Signature of witness   Address

Figure 6-3 ◆ Consent to release information form

procedures to be performed or for information or documents to be released. A completed form must contain the patient's signature (or that of the patient's representative), date of signing, and date the consent will expire. The signatures on all consent forms must be witnessed. Often it is the MA who witnesses the signing of the consent form. The witness also signs the document, with the date. In signing, the witness merely verifies that the signature is that of the patient.

A Consent to Release of Information form is signed by a patient before the care provider can apply for third-party reimbursement (Figure 6-3 ◆). Forms to release information should include the following:

- Name of the medical facility or practice that will be releasing the information
- Name of the individual who is to receive the information
- Patient's full name, specific information to be released
- Purpose of releasing the information

Informed Consent

Special procedures and surgical procedures require **informed consent** (Figure 6-4 ◆). The informed consent form includes a description of the procedure, the expected outcome, the risks involved, and possible negative outcomes. After the physician discusses the procedure with the patient, the patient agrees to treatment by signing the form, stating that he or she understands the procedure and the accompanying risks.

Keys to Success
CONSENT TO RELEASE INFORMATION

Only the information requested can be released to third parties after the patient signs the consent form. To release more than is requested and consented to by the patient is a breach of confidentiality.

Under the Doctrine of Informed Consent, all of the following must be explained to the patient in clear, easy-to-understand language before a procedure or surgery is performed:

- The patient's diagnosis, if it is known
- The purpose, advantages, and risks of the proposed treatment
- Alternatives available to the patient, along with their risks and benefits
- Potential treatment outcomes
- Potential outcomes if there is no treatment

Procedures in an office or outpatient facility that may require special consent forms include, but are not limited to:

- Administration of blood and blood products
- Invasive diagnostic procedures, including lumbar punctures, cystoscopies, biopsies, and endoscopies
- Chemotherapy
- Cardiac or pulmonary stress testing

Medical Records and Documentation

Accurate and thorough patient records, or charts, must be maintained. Charts are considered legal documents and must be legibly written in black or blue ink. Allergies are often noted in red ink or identified by a red label on the chart with the allergy-inducing substance written on the label. Confidentiality must be maintained concerning these records. All chart entries are written in ink and must be legible, dated, and signed. No erasures or changes are acceptable. When an error is made, a line is drawn through the error, notation of error is written above the error, and it is initialed and dated.

? — Critical Thinking Question 6-1—
What is the proper protocol for Alexis to follow after discovering the soiled chart? Who is responsible for the chart?

Although the paper medical record is the most common form, it usually requires a multimedia format to be considered comprehensive and complete. At present, the paper record can incorporate some electronic media, audiotapes, videotapes, X-rays, monitor strips, and photographs. Older records are stored on microfilm and microfiche.

As more privacy mechanisms become available on the Internet, sending medical records electronically will become more common. More and more health-care institutions and medical offices are switching to electronic medical records. With

MEMORIAL HEALTH

COMPLETE ORIGINAL IN INK FOR HOSPITAL CHART
PATIENT MUST BE AWAKE, ALERT AND ORIENTED WHEN SIGNING
DATE: _____ TIME: _____ ☐ AM ☐ PM

I AUTHORIZE THE PERFORMANCE UPON_____
OF THE FOLLOWING OPERATION (state nature and extent):_____
_____
_____

TO BE PERFORMED UNDER THE DIRECTION OF DR. _____

1. I HAVE BEEN ADVISED THAT THERE IS A FAVORABLE LIKELIHOOD OF SUCCESS, BUT I UNDERSTAND THAT A COMPLETELY SUCCESSFUL OUTCOME MAY NOT BE ACHIEVABLE, AND THERE ARE NO GUARANTEES REGARDING THE OUTCOME. I ALSO UNDERSTAND THAT CERTAIN ADVERSE EVENTS COULD OCCUR AS A RESULT OF THE PERFORMANCE OF THE PROCEDURE OR TREATMENT, INCLUDING PAIN, INFECTION, LACERATION OR PUNCTURE OF INTERNAL ORGANS, BLEEDING, NERVE DAMAGE OR EVEN IN RARE CASES, DEATH. I UNDERSTAND THAT HOSPITALIZATION OR OTHER INSTITUTIONAL CARE, HOME CARE OR CARE BY HEALTH PROFESSIONALS MAY BE NEEDED FOLLOWING THE PROCEDURE OR TREATMENT, RELATED TO FULL RECOVERY, RECUPERATION OR CONVALESCENCE. I UNDERSTAND THE ALTERNATIVES TO THIS PROCEDURE, INCLUDING MY RIGHT TO REFUSE TO CONSENT TO IT, AND I NEVERTHELESS HAVE DECIDED TO CONSENT TO PERFORMANCE OF THE PROCEDURE OR TREATMENT.

2. I CONSENT TO THE PERFORMANCE OF OPERATIONS AND PROCEDURES IN ADDITION TO OR DIFFERENT FROM THOSE NOW CONTEMPLATED, WHETHER OR NOT ARISING FROM PRESENTLY UNFORESEEN CONDITIONS WHICH THE ABOVE NAMED DOCTOR OR HIS/HER ASSOCIATES OR ASSISTANTS MAY CONSIDER NECESSARY OR ADVISABLE IN THE COURSE OF THE OPERATION.

3. I CONSENT TO THE DISPOSAL BY HOSPITAL AUTHORITIES OF ANY TISSUES OR PARTS WHICH MAY BE REMOVED.

4. THE NATURE AND PURPOSE OF THE OPERATION/PROCEDURE, POSSIBLE ALTERNATIVE METHODS OF TREATMENT, THE RISK AND BENEFITS INVOLVED, AND THE COURSE OF RECUPERATION HAVE BEEN FULLY EXPLAINED TO ME. NO GUARANTEE OR ASSURANCE HAS BEEN GIVEN BY ANYONE AS TO THE RESULTS THAT MAY BE OBTAINED.

5. I UNDERSTAND AND AGREE WITH THE ABOVE INFORMATION. I HAVE NO QUESTIONS WHICH HAVE NOT BEEN ANSWERED TO MY FULL SATISFACTION. I UNDERSTAND THAT I HAVE THE RIGHT TO ASK FOR FURTHER INFORMATION BEFORE SIGNING THIS CONSENT.

I have crossed out any paragraph above which does not apply or to which I do not give consent.

PATIENT SIGNATURE: _____ WITNESS SIGNATURE: _____
(OR PARENT OR GUARDIAN IF PATIENT IS UNDER 18 YEARS OF AGE) *(OF PATIENT, PARENT OR GUARDIAN SIGNATURE)*

RELATIONSHIP: _____ WITNESS SIGNATURE: _____
☐ **TELEPHONE CONSENT** *(2ND WITNESS NEEDED FOR TELEPHONE CONSENT)*

Figure 6-4 ◆ Sample of an informed consent form

consent and privacy procedures in place, physicians will be able to share and compare medical information concerning their patients. Patients will likely also have access to their own medical records through the Internet. There will be different levels of security for Internet medical records; non-patient-identifiable data will have the least restricted access.

HIPAA includes rules for the use of electronic medical records. Offices must have policies and procedures in place outlining security methods and confidentiality.

Third-Party Providers

When calling a third-party provider for precertification, it is essential to record the date and time of the contact, the name of the person to whom you spoke, and any numbers or information you are given. Be sure to sign and date the entry. Should you be advised that precertification is not necessary for the procedure, document that statement along with the name of the representative making the statement. Keep copies of any faxes or forwarded hard copies in the patient record.

Failure to obtain precertification or to document all information regarding it may result in denial of payment for the claim.

New Patient Medical Record Documentation

As an MA, it will be your responsibility to assemble the chart with the necessary forms and to add forms as needed to continue documentation. This may be accomplished by mailing the questionnaire to the patient before the scheduled appointment with instructions to complete and return it at the initial visit. Another method is to have the patient complete the history form while waiting in the reception area.

Some medical offices take photos of new patients. Polaroid or digital images are placed in the patient chart for reference. The physician and staff will have a picture of the patient available should the patient call in with questions or problems. Also, photo identification is now being required in some facilities to prevent insurance fraud.

PROCEDURE 6-1 Prepare and Maintain the Medical Record

Theory

Medical records contain information concerning the patient's medical history, including treatment records and previous outcomes, personal information, insurance information, and consent for treatment. Any signed releases of information or informed consent are also included, as well as a signed HIPAA form. Only information requested can be released to third parties after signed consent is obtained. To release more than requested and consented to is a breach of confidentiality. Offices have various forms and a variety of ways for compiling this information.

The patient registration form and health questionnaire may be completed by a new patient before or at the beginning of the first visit. This form includes current date, patient's name, address, and phone number, Social Security number, health-care insurance information, occupation, marital status, and next of kin or emergency contact person (Figure 6-5 ◆).

It may be necessary for you to assist the patient in completing these forms. For example, a patient who is illiterate or for whom English is a second language may have difficulty, as would an elderly patient with arthritic hands.

Medical records include the following.

Demographic information
- Patient name
- Address and telephone number
- Occupation
- Next-of-kin information

Administrative information
- Patient registration record (usually in patient's handwriting)
- Correspondence (from medical professionals, the patient, or other sources)
- Insurance coverage and copies of insurance cards
- Name of individual responsible for payment

PATIENT REGISTRATION FORM
(Please Print)

Date: _____

Patient's
Name: _____
    First   Middle   Last

DOB: _____ / _____ / _____
    Month   Day   Year

Address: _____
    Street   City   State   Zip

Phone: _____ / _____ - _____
    (Area code)

Patient's SS#: _____ - _____ - _____ Driver's License #: _____ Occupation: _____

Method of payment (circle):   cash   check   credit card   insurance co-payment

Primary Insurance Co.: _____ Policy/Group #: _____

Medicare #: _____ Medicaid #: _____

Person
Responsible
For Payment: _____
    First   Middle   Last   Relationship

Address: _____
    Street   City   State   Zip

Phone: _____ / _____ - _____
    (Area code)

Employer Name: _____
    First   Middle   Last

Dept: _____

Address: _____
    Street   City   State   Zip

Phone: _____ / _____ - _____
    (Area code)

Spouse or
Nearest Relative: _____
    First   Middle   Last   Relationship

Address: _____
    Street   City   State   Zip

Phone: _____ / _____ - _____
    (Area code)

How were you referred to this office? _____

_____

Statement of Financial Responsibility: I, _____,
do hereby agree to pay all medical charges incurred by the above listed patient. I further understand that these charges are my responsibility, regardless of insurance coverage.

Responsible Person's Signature: _____

Figure 6-5 ◆ Patient registration form

PROCEDURE 6-1 **Prepare and Maintain the Medical Record** *(continued)*

Consent documents
- Consent for treatment
- Consent to release information
- Signed HIPAA form

Clinical information
- Patient's medical or health history
- Progress notes
- Current complaint or condition
- Physical examination and assessment findings
- Allergies
- Medical treatment plan or services received
- Current medications and medications prescribed, dispensed, or administered
- Immunization record
- Consultation reports
- Home health-care reports
- Outcomes and response to care

Laboratory documents
- Chemistry reports
- Cytology reports
- Hematology reports
- Histology reports
- Microbiology reports
- Serology reports
- Urinalysis reports
- Miscellaneous laboratory reports

Diagnostic procedure reports
- Electrocardiogram and other cardiology testing reports
- Imaging and other radiology reports
- Respiratory therapy reports
- Miscellaneous diagnostic procedure reports

Hospital documents
- Admission notes
- Emergency room reports
- History and physical
- Operative reports
- Pathology reports
- Discharge summary report

Therapeutic service reports
- Nutritional therapy reports
- Occupational therapy reports
- Physical therapy reports
- Speech therapy reports
- Rehabilitation therapy reports

Materials
- File folder for chart
- Black or blue ink pen
- Allergy label or red pen for noting allergies
- Fasteners
- Chart dividers
- Double- or triple-hole punch
- Name and alphabetic, color-coded file labels
- Preprinted forms listed below (the practice or specialty of the medical office will determine if some or all of the forms will be used):
  - Administrative documents
  - Patient registration record (usually in patient's handwriting)
  - Correspondence (from medical professionals, the patient, or other sources)
  - Consent documents
  - Consent for treatment
  - Consent to release information
  - Clinical documents
  - Patient history (see the Patient History section following in this chapter)

Competency
(**Conditions**) Using the following listed materials (**Task**), you will prepare and maintain record readiness for the medical office (**Standards**) according to established office policy within the time and to the degree of accuracy designated by the instructor.

1. Greet and identify the new patient.
2. Instruct the patient to complete a registration form if he or she has not mailed one in.
3. Upon completion of the registration form, clarify any information the patient left blank or illegible.
4. Enter the registration data into the computer.
5. Organize forms and dividers according to office requirements and place in the record. Some charts require that forms be double- or triple-hole punched.
6. Label the record and each form with the patient's name and record identification number.
7. Place the registration form in the record location as directed by office policy.
8. If necessary, add an allergy label to the record folder and to appropriate chart forms.
9. For each patient return visit, check and place additional forms in the record as necessary.

Patient Education
Discuss with the patient the importance of filling out the forms completely and legibly. Answer any questions about the forms that the patient may ask.

Charting the Medical History and Clinical Visit

Charting is the documentation of all the events of a patient's visit. Along with the patient history, it is done by those involved with the treatment of the patient and is part of the medical record. Because it is a legal document, accuracy and correctness are critical. Unless a procedure is charted after completion, the documentation is considered incomplete by the legal system. Accurate charting requires skill and practice. Personal opinions are *never* to be charted.

Patient History

As part of the initial assessment, you will review the patient's health history by asking specific questions about general health and previous health conditions. The physician will review this history with the patient (Figure 6-6 ◆).
A patient history should include the following:

- Personal history/social and occupational history
- Past medical or health history, including allergies and medications
- Family medical history
- Chief complaint (CC)
- Present illness
- Assessment/review of body systems

Combined with diagnostic data and the physical examination, the physician draws on the history to make a **diagnosis,** which is a conclusion about the patient's condition. Finally, the physician anticipates the patient's response to treatment as well as the **prognosis,** which is a prediction of the outcome of a disease and patient recovery.

Personal History
Personal history may also be referred to as social and occupational history and includes the factors listed in Table 6-1.

Past Medical or Health History
Past medical or health history provides a background of previous or ongoing health concerns (Table 6-2).

Family Medical History
The family medical history provides the physician with an assessment of the patient's extended family health history. Questions are asked about the age, current health status, and disease occurrences of blood relatives, including parents, grandparents, siblings, and children, as well as of the spouse. If a family member is deceased, age and cause of death are noted. Some physicians have patients complete a health *genogram.* This chart, in the form of a family tree, illustrates any patterns of illnesses or health conditions in the patient's ancestors and siblings. Some diseases are genetic or hereditary, others show a familial tendency, and occasionally environmental factors affect some family members earlier or more intensely than others.

All this information provides the physician with an insight into the patient's present condition, clues to the cause of any health-related problems, and an indication of how the patient may comply with treatment options. Some physicians are selective about the questions they prefer to be asked, and some forms are tailored to specialty practices.

Chief Complaint
An important part of any history, whether during the initial encounter or on repeat visits, is the presenting chief complaint (CC). The patient describes the symptoms causing the most trouble or the reason for the visit. **Symptoms** are changes in body functions reported by the patient and indicating the presence of disease or injury. Symptoms like pain, pruritus, vertigo, and nausea are felt only by the patient and are considered subjective in nature. It is for you or another person to observe objective symptoms, such as rash, coughing, weight gain, edema, and cyanosis. Recording or charting the CC is essential to quality patient-centered care.

Figure 6-6 ◆ An example of a medical health history form used by the physician
Courtesy of Bibbero Systems, Inc., Petaluma, CA; Phone: 800-242-2376 Fax: 800-242-9330; Email: info@bibbero.com; Web: www.bibbero.com

TABLE 6-1 PERSONAL HISTORY INFORMATION

- Lifestyle
- Family situation
- Living environment
- Education
- Military service
- Occupation, both past and present
- Exercise habits
- Sleeping patterns

- Alcohol consumption
- Smoking or tobacco habits
- Caffeine consumption
- Dietary habits
- Health habits
- Foreign travel
- Living arrangements
- Seat belt use

TABLE 6-2 PAST HISTORY INFORMATION

- Allergies
- Past major illnesses
- Previous hospitalizations and surgical procedures
- Childhood diseases

- Any injuries or accidents
- Unusual infections
- Immunizations

- Previous medical tests
- Medications, both past and present

Present Illness

As the cause of the CC is explored, information about the present illness is expanded. Ask the patient for a detailed description of the present symptoms and illness. Open-ended questions such as "What brings you in today to see the physician?" are a good starting point. Record the patient's statement in his or her own words as closely as possible. Table 6-3 lists some of the signs and symptoms patients may describe.

TABLE 6-3 COMMON SIGNS AND SYMPTOMS RELATED BY AND OBSERVED IN PATIENTS

Circulatory System

Angina	chest pain occurring during exertion
Arrhythmia	irregular heartbeat
Bradycardia	slow heart rate, below 60 BPM
Cyanosis	bluish tint to skin
Dehydration	loss of body fluids
Edema	swelling, fluid in tissues
Palpitations	rapid, thumping heartbeat
Petechiae	small pinpoint hemorrhages on the skin
Tachycardia	rapid heartbeat, over 100 BPM
Varicosities	abnormally swollen and twisted veins, usually in legs

Gastrointestinal System

Anorexia	loss of appetite
Constipation	difficulty moving the bowels
Diarrhea	loose, watery stools
Dysphagia	difficulty swallowing, usually accompanied by pain
Eructation	belching
Flatus	intestinal gas
Jaundice	yellow color to skin and whites of eyes
Melena	blood in the stool
N & V	nausea and vomiting; unpleasant sensation of having to vomit and actually expelling the contents of the stomach orally

Integumentary System

Diaphoresis	sudden onset of intense perspiration
Flushing	sudden redness to skin
Pruritus	severe itching
Rash	an eruption on the skin, usually red in color

Nervous System

Ataxia	unsteadiness, a problem with coordination
Cephalgia	pain in the head, headache
Chill	feeling cold, usually with shivering
Convulsion/seizure	involuntary muscular contractions
Dementia	progressive impairment or decline of mental functioning
Dyslexia	a learning disorder involving ability to read or write
Fever or pyrexia	body temperature elevated above normal
Insomnia	difficulty sleeping
Neuralgia	severe and sharp pain along a nerve
Pain	unpleasant sensation
Palsy	inability to control muscle movement, shaking
Syncope	fainting
Vertigo	dizziness

Reproductive System

Amenorrhea	absence of menses
Dysmenorrhea	painful menses
Erectile dysfunction	inability to achieve or maintain an erection with stimulation
Menorrhagia	excessive bleeding during menses, heavy period

Respiratory System

Coughing	forceful, violent expiratory effort
Cyanosis	bluish tint to skin
Dyspnea	difficult or painful breathing
Epistaxis	nosebleed
Laryngitis	loss of voice, hoarseness with little volume
Orthopnea	difficulty breathing unless in a sitting position
Rhinorrhea	runny nose

Urinary System

Anuria	absence of urine output
Dysuria	painful urination
Enuresis	bedwetting
Incontinence	inability to hold urine
Nocturia	frequent urination during the night
Oliguria	scanty urine output
Polyuria	voiding large amounts of urine

Psychological or Emotional Symptoms

Aggression	a forceful action, physical, verbal, or symbolic
Anxiety	apprehension, uneasiness
Depression	hopeless, helpless, sad feeling; crying all the time
Hallucinations	imaginary perceptions of visual or auditory stimuli
Paranoia	feeling of being persecuted or pursued

Try to limit the chief complaint to one or two specific symptoms. Information about the symptoms should include:

- Onset
- Duration
- Location, indicating specific area of the body
- Frequency
- Intensity of the symptoms, from just bothersome to severe and interfering with sleep and normal activities
- Any changes over time

Patients may describe pain as aching, burning, cramping, crushing, dull, sharp, shooting, squeezing, or throbbing. They may also say it is constant, intermittent, radiating, transient, localized, deep, or superficial. Guide the patient with questions and write down the answers in his or her own words.

Assessment of Body Systems

The assessment of body systems is a physician review of all body systems with the patient to identify any symptoms not yet revealed. The physician asks questions regarding each body system and notes the answers on the chart. This preliminary step suggests specific areas of concern to the physician and provides a focus for the physical examination to follow.

Completing a Patient History Form

Collecting information on a patient's health history involves an oral interview. Information obtained from the health history and subsequent visits provides a complete historical record of the patient's health, including data to identify the patient, reason for the current visit, and family and patient history of disease conditions, illnesses, and hospitalizations. The physician uses past and family medical information to treat a patient for current and long-term medical conditions. The physician also uses the information to promote patient education and individual responsibility for prevention or progression of disease.

PROCEDURE 6-2 Complete a History Form

Theory

You escort the patient to a private area, usually the examination room, to interview him or her. Privacy encourages open communication and reduces anxiety and distractions for the patient. Your body language must show interest in the patient's concerns. Generally, patients respond more openly to a calm and caring approach. Address the patient in a formal manner unless the patient encourages a more informal manner. For the comfort of parent and child during a child's clinical visit, ask the parent or child what name the child prefers.

Materials

- Chart
- File folder for chart
- Patient history form
- Blue or black ink pen

Competency

(**Conditions**) With the necessary materials listed above, (**Task**) you will be able to complete the Patient History Form (**Standards**) following office policy and within the time and to the degree of accuracy designated by the instructor.

1. Greet the patient in a formal or age-appropriate manner.
2. Explain the health history form. Explain to the patient or parent that additional information beyond the original question is always important and can be added.
3. Observe patient's body language and respond appropriately or tactfully to encourage open sharing of medical information.
4. The order of interview for the Patient History Form follows the order of the form unless office policy dictates otherwise.
5. Instruct the patient to fill in the patient identification section. Review it to make sure the information is complete.
6. Use open-ended questions to obtain details of the patient's CC, or present illness, such as:
   - How long have the symptoms been occurring?
   - Where do the symptoms occur?
   - What activity brings on the symptoms or makes the symptoms worse?
   - Do the symptoms occur suddenly or gradually?
   - What activity helps the symptom(s) disappear or lessen?
   - When symptoms occur, how long do they last?
7. Proceed through questions about past medical history, family medical history, and social/occupational history as presented on the Patient History Form.

Patient Education

Discuss with the patient or parent the importance of complete and accurate information. Provide the patient with a pencil and paper to take notes on items that might need more information at a later or follow-up visit.

Keys to Success
OBTAINING DETAILS FOR A CC

Encourage the patient to describe the reason for the visit in his or her own words. Avoid using disease terminology. Using the patient's own words provides a more accurate picture for the physician.

Charting a Clinical Visit

Guidelines for charting include the following.

- Select the correct chart for the patient. Verify the patient's name and, if necessary, birth date.
- Write or print legibly, using black or blue ink. Red ink is acceptable for allergies.
- Check to make sure the patient's name is on each page.
- Date and initial every entry.
- Write brief but complete entries.
- Use only accepted medical abbreviations.
- Make sure all medical terms are spelled correctly.
- *Never* erase or white-out mistakes. Draw a line through any mistake, write the word "error" above the mistake, date, and initial. Follow the mistake with the correct information and sign the completed entry (Figure 6-7 ◆).

- Document phone conversations with the patient or significant other by any staff member with action taken or recommended.
- Document all missed appointments.

Charting or documenting the patient's medical record may be done in several formats.

Two primary methods are used to chart.

- The first method is chronological (Figure 6-8 ◆). It is a sheet of paper with the name at the top. Each entry is dated, vital signs are added, and reason for visit is documented. The physician adds narrative comments with each visit. New sheets of paper are added as needed.
- A second method, based on the patient's problems, is called the problem-oriented medical record (**POMR**). Information is charted by all employees providing care or treatment for the patient. All problems are recorded, and a numbered problem list is created. At each visit or encounter, information pertaining to a numbered problem is identified and recorded.

Charting for POMR is done by the subjective, objective, assessment plan (**SOAP**) method (Figure 6-9 ◆). When problems are identified, they are documented in a systematic manner.

Date	Time	Order	Doctor	Administered by
3/14/07	3 pm	Erythromycin ~~500 mg~~ ^{Error} 250 mg BT 9/9	Williams	J. Jones, RN

Figure 6-7 ◆ Example of a corrected chart notation

Patient's Name: Isabel Miranda
7/10/XX　*9:30 a.m.　37-year-old Spanish-speaking female presents with a CC of sore throat, difficulty swallowing and excessive coughing, onset 3 days ago and getting progressively worse. 15-year-old daughter accompanies to translate. Skin is very warm to touch and is flushed. Patient is alert and cooperative. Nonproductive cough is noted. Vital signs: T 102.7 F, P 114, R 28, BP 140/90. Wt, 150#, Ht, 65". LMP - 7-02-02. Allergies – Penicillin. Meds, aspirin for pain, BCP, Zantac. Husband is L&W; has two other children, L&W: parents are deceased. Recently immigrated to US from Mexico for husband's employment and to be with other children. Marjorie Nelson, CMA*

Figure 6-8 ◆ Sample completed chronological form

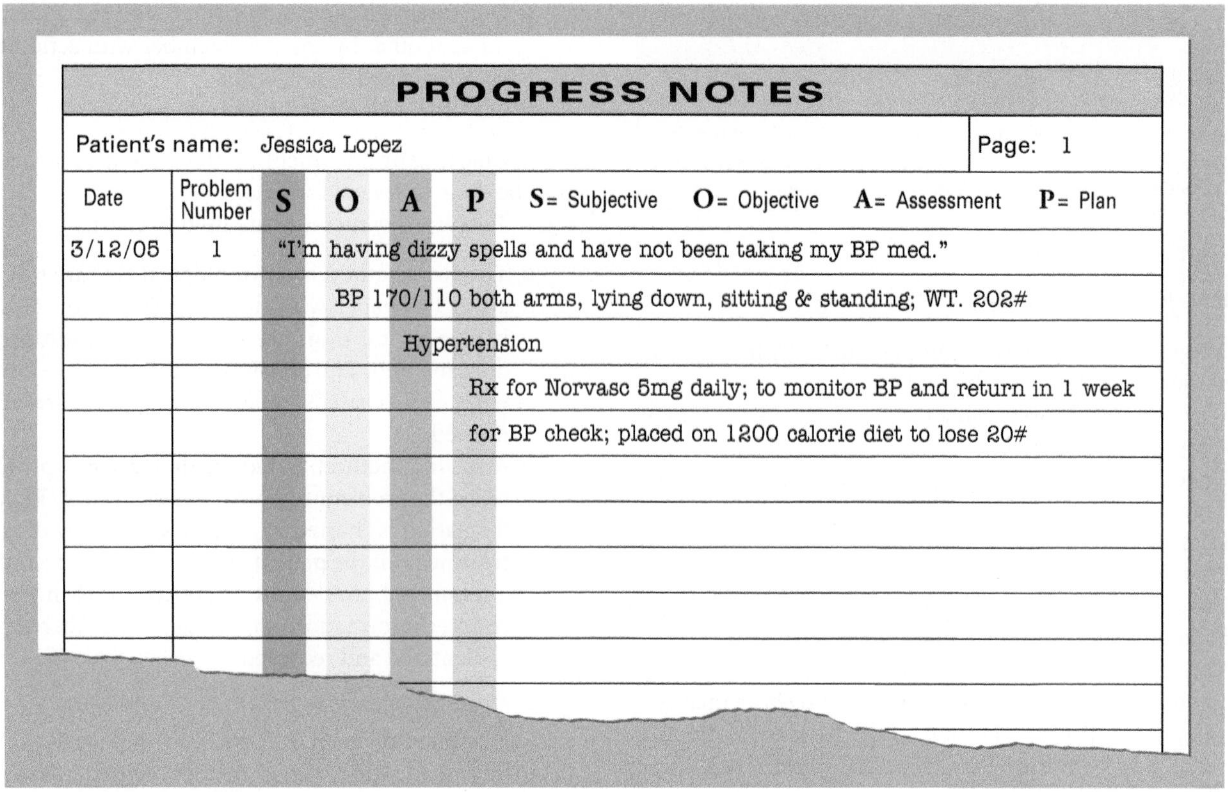

PROGRESS NOTES

Patient's name:	Jessica Lopez								Page: 1	

Date	Problem Number	**S**	**O**	**A**	**P**	S= Subjective	O= Objective	A= Assessment	P= Plan
3/12/05	1	"I'm having dizzy spells and have not been taking my BP med."							
			BP 170/110 both arms, lying down, sitting & standing; WT. 202#						
				Hypertension					
					Rx for Norvasc 5mg daily; to monitor BP and return in 1 week				
					for BP check; placed on 1200 calorie diet to lose 20#				

Figure 6-9 ◆ An example of a POMR SOAP form

S   Subjective; refers to the symptoms described by the patient and/or family. It is best to record the patient's actual words in quotation marks, or write "Patient states _____."

O   Objective; refers to findings elicited on the physical exam, the vital **signs,** and results of laboratory or other diagnostic testing.

A   Assessment; includes the physician's diagnosis or nurse's assessment.

P   Plan of action; includes any recommended treatments, additional testing, medications administered or prescribed, consultations recommended, surgery or physical therapy suggested.

In a medical office, you are responsible for charting the subjective and objective components. Other professionals, including physicians, nurses, laboratory technicians, and others, document some or all SOAP components, depending on the need for complete or partial documentation and established policies. Observations, test procedures, or results may be documented in partial SOAP format according to office procedures and within the scope of practice of each professional.

As an MA, you must remember that diagnosis is not within the scope of your training. When charting a history, you must be careful not to make diagnostic statements. Occasionally a patient may suggest a diagnosis. Document the patient's exact words and place quotations around them.

Charting Procedures

Procedures performed on the patient are mostly charted by you (Table 6-4 lists commonly used abbreviations and terminology). Extensive or operative procedures are usually dictated by the physician. Procedures should be charted immediately after performing them. For legal reasons, it is important to remember that a procedure was not done unless documented in the chart. Charting before a procedure is *illegal.*

The following information must be included in chart documentation: vital signs, including temperature, pulse, respirations, and blood pressure, as well as weight and height. New pain assessment guidelines for inpatient facilities are required, and some medical offices have adopted charting this aspect of patient assessment at each visit. Medication administration, specimen collection and laboratory tests, cardiac testing, and respiratory testing are also recorded.

Documenting a Clinical Visit

In the reception room, call the patient's name and ask him or her to accompany you to the examination room or a room that is quiet and comfortable with a door that can be closed for privacy. Introduce yourself and verify the patient's name. Offer the patient a chair and be seated yourself. Using professional communication skills, do the following.

TABLE 6-4   ABBREVIATIONS AND TERMINOLOGY COMMONLY USED TO CHART SYMPTOMS

ac	before meals	N/C	no complaints
AM	before noon	neg	negative
amt	amount	NKA/NKDA	no known drug allergies
ANS	autonomic nervous system	N&V	nausea and vomiting
ASAP	as soon as possible	NPO	nothing by mouth
ASL	American Sign Language	OB	obstetrics
BCP	birth control pills	opth	ophthalmology
BM	bowel movement	ortho	orthopedics
c̄	with	OPV	oral polio vaccine
CC	chief complaint	OT	occupational therapy
CMA	Certified Medical Assistant	OTC	over the counter
CNS	central nervous system	OV	office visit
c/o	complains of	pc	after meals
CXR	chest x-ray	peds	pediatrics
dc	discontinue	per	by or through
DOB	date of birth	PM	afternoon
DOI	date of injury	PNS	peripheral nervous system
DPT	diptheria, pertussis, tetanus injection	po	by mouth
dsg	dressing	post-op	postoperative
ea	each	pre-op	preoperative
EDC	expected date of confinement	prep	preparation
EENT	eyes, ears, nose, throat	PT	physical therapy
ENT	ears, nose, throat	pt	patient
FX,fx	fracture	qns	quantity not sufficient
GI	gastrointestinal	qs	quantity sufficient
GU	genitourinary	RMA	registered medical assistant
GYN	gynecology	ROM	range of motion
H₂O	water	Rx	prescription
HRT	hormone replacement therapy	s̄	without
h.s.	at bedtime	S&S	signs and symptoms
hx	history	SOB	shortness of breath
Lac	laceration	spec	specimen
LMP	last menstrual period	stat	immediately
meds	medications	TPR	temperature, pulse, respirations
MH	marital history	Tx	treatment
MMR	measles, rumps, rubella	VS	vital signs
MVA	motor vehicle accident	V&D	vomiting and diarrhea
NAD	no apparent distress	WNL	within normal limits
NB	newborn		

■ Ask the patient the name he or she prefers to be called.

■ Maintain good eye contact and display a sincere interest in and concern for the patient.

■ Use terminology that the patient can understand.

■ Listen carefully to the patient and observe his or her non-verbal body language.

■ Avoid making any judgmental comments.

■ Take your time and avoid hurrying the patient.

On the progress note of the patient's chart, note the date, time, and CC. List the CC as one or two major symptoms, being brief and concise. Note the patient's words in quotation marks.

What, *when*, and *where* are good words with which to elicit descriptions of symptoms. Note the answers on the chart, thank the patient for the input, then proceed to the next step, which is usually taking vital signs. Advise the patient that the physician will be with him or her shortly. Place the patient's chart in the proper place to inform the physician that the patient is ready to be seen.

— Critical Thinking Question 6-2 —
Do you think the situation in the case study should be reported to the office manager or physician? Why or why not?

PROCEDURE 6-3 Document a Clinical Visit and Procedure

Theory

It is your responsibility, along with other clinical staff, to document details of the clinical visit and the procedures performed. Accurate, concise, and complete documentation provides information for chart audits, medical insurance companies, courts of law, and the patient care team. If members of the health-care team are aware of all efforts being made on the patient's behalf, efforts can be coordinated, patient teaching can be reinforced, and errors can be reduced or eliminated. Documenting observations during patient visits can inform health-care team members whether the symptoms, illness, or patient's treatment response is progressing or regressing. As visit and procedure notes are compared, patient improvement will dictate the need for continuing or discontinuing the current treatment. Lack of patient progress or worsening symptoms will suggest the need for treatment changes.

Materials

- Patient chart
- Narrative or progress note forms to be added to the chart
- Blue or black ink pen

Competency

(**Conditions**) Using the listed materials, (**Task**) you will be able to document a clinical visit or procedure (**Standards**) in the time and with a score designated by the instructor.

1. Verify that the chart is the correct one for the patient.

2. If notes are insufficient for documentation, add the appropriate form.
3. With narrative charting or SOAP charting, avoid leaving blank areas.
4. Write the date and time in the left-hand column of the notes.
5. Continue writing in the charting format used by the medical office.
6. Document immediately after performance of procedures.
7. Use only standard, accepted abbreviations and describe clinical observations during performance of the procedure.
8. Document only facts. DO NOT make diagnoses or judgmental statements.
9. Sign your name and add your title at the end of the documentation.

Patient Education

Discuss with the patient the importance of complete and accurate information. Provide the patient with a pencil and paper to take notes on items that might need more information at a later or follow-up visit.

Charting Example

04/28/xx 1:30 P.M. Patient returned for blood pressure follow-up. BP lying 110/60, BP sitting up 100/60, BP standing 90/60. Physician notified of blood pressures taken on left arm at 10-minute intervals. Michael Richards, RMA

REVIEW

- As an MA you will have a primary role in the preparation and maintenance of examination and treatment areas of the medical office. In the performance of your duties you will also provide a clean, orderly, and safe clinical environment for the patient.

- Each examination room is usually soundproof or muted for confidential conversation and standardized with examination table, appropriate lighting, supply cabinets, a stool for the physician, a place for the patient to sit and to place clothes on, and a way to provide privacy for dressing/undressing. Necessary equipment includes a sphygmomanometer, stethoscope, thermometer, otoscope, ophthalmoscope, and a wall-mounted X-ray view box. You will ensure that all equipment is working and clean and that the examination room is adequately stocked. At the end of the clinical visit you will change the examination table paper and clean any soiled areas per office procedure.

- Established office triage procedures for making immediate or same-day appointments or referring patients to urgent care or emergency room for treatment may be part of your job. It is important that you listen carefully as the patient describes symptoms over the phone or at the reception desk. It may be necessary to confer with an office nurse or physician for additional instructions. In addition to urgent or emergency conditions, patients presenting with contagious diseases will need to be removed from the reception area immediately and placed in an examination room.

- For routine office visits, patients give implied consent for treatment. A Consent to Release Information form must be signed by the patient before the information can be sent to third parties. Only the requested information is sent. Special procedures, including invasive or surgical procedures, require the patient's signature on an Informed Consent Form.

- Many forms are part of the patient's medical record. It is often your responsibility to assemble the record and add more forms when needed to continue documentation. Before or during the initial visit, the patient completes patient registration, insurance information, and a health questionnaire.

- Charting, also known as medical documentation, provides a legal document. Guidelines, including the correction of errors and writing in dark ink, are to be followed at all times. Charting is done only after a procedure is completed and is signed by the person making the entry. Chart immediately after the procedure to document accurately. If documentation is not done, the courts will assume the procedure was not performed.

- Charting usually follows one of two formats. The first is chronological, with each entry dated and vital signs or other narrative notes following. A second format uses the SOAP method. *S* refers to subjective statements made by the patient about the reason for the clinical visit. *O* refers to objective data gathered by the clinical staff, such as vital signs, laboratory data, X-rays, or observations of the patient. *A* refers to the assessment by the physician or nurse relating to the subjective and objective data. *P* refers to the plan of care based on the assessment of the patient's clinical illness or symptoms.

- The Patient History covers the following areas: personal history/social and occupational history, past medical history, family medical history, CC, present illness, and assessment and review of body systems.

- Questions should be open-ended to encourage the patient to provide all the necessary information. Sample questions include: How long have you had the symptoms? When did the symptoms start? What makes the symptoms worse? What helps to lessen the symptoms? What were you doing when the symptoms started? Generally the patient's own words are used to describe symptoms. You do not make diagnostic statements because diagnosis is not in the scope of your practice.

- When communicating with the patient, use the name the patient prefers, maintain eye contact, use body language that shows interest and concern, and document the information in patient quotes as much as possible. After all information is obtained for the visit, inform the patient the physician will be in soon, and follow office procedure for informing the physician that the patient is ready to be seen.

- The physician reviews all initial information retrieved by others before conducting a review of body systems, identifying any other symptoms or findings not yet revealed. The physician then provides the patient with a diagnosis, prognosis, and treatment plan.

Chapter Review Questions

Multiple Choice

1. Doors to examination rooms are kept closed for
   A. equipment safety.
   B. room temperature regulation.
   C. patient privacy.
   D. storage.

2. Which of the following is a part of triage?
   A. immediately isolating a patient with a contagious disease in an examination room
   B. putting a patient who is calling in and experiencing chest pain on hold to talk with the physician
   C. asking a patient who is experiencing severe pain on arrival at the office to sit in the reception area until an examination room is available
   D. asking a patient who is in the office and experiencing chest pain to leave immediately for the emergency room because the physician is away from the office

3. A Consent to Release Information form allows a medical office to send
   A. requested information without the witness's signature.
   B. all information in the patient's medical record without signature.
   C. information without the patient's signature being witnessed.
   D. only requested information for which the patient signs.

4. It is acceptable to document allergies in
   A. black ink.
   B. blue ink.
   C. red ink.
   D. green ink.

5. Which of the following is included in a patient history?
   A. next-of-kin phone number
   B. insurance coverage
   C. individual responsible for payment
   D. military service

6. A CC is the patient's
   A. chief complaint.
   B. congestion/cough.
   C. cyanosis care.
   D. chill and cough.

7. Which of the following is an appropriate question to ask a patient about his or her symptoms?
   A. "When you cough, is it similar to COPD?"
   B. "Why didn't you phone this condition in sooner?"
   C. "Why didn't your other physician notice this symptom?"
   D. "When symptoms occur, how long do they last?"

8. When you make a mistake on a chart, you should
   A. erase it.
   B. draw a line through it.
   C. use white-out.
   D. block it out with a permanent marker.

9. Which of the following is a vital sign to be charted?
   A. pulse
   B. pain
   C. weight
   D. specimens

10. When conversing with a patient, you should
    A. avoid eye contact.
    B. avoid making any judgmental comments.
    C. automatically use a nickname for the patient.
    D. make sure you complete the process quickly.

True/False

T F   1. Whether documenting an initial visit, patient history, or clinical visit, accuracy and attention to detail are a major responsibility in the medical office.

T F   2. As an MA, you will be responsible for providing a clean, safe environment in the examination and treatment areas.

T F   3. To promote efficient use of the physician's time, the MA provides expert medical advice to patients when they call and request to speak to the doctor.

T F   4. Standard equipment in an exam room may include several types of lighting.

T F   5. Charting is the documentation only of the vitals taken during a patient's visit.

Short Answer

1. What elements does a physician use to make a diagnosis about the patient's condition?

2. What is triage?

3. What is the correct procedure for a patient with a possible contagious disease?

4. List at least eight emergencies requiring immediate assessment or intervention.

5. What is the difference between implied and informed consent?

Research

1. Call five clinics in your local area. Do they use electronic charting or paper charts?

2. Who invented the sphygmomanometer?

3. Research a medical malpractice case won by the plaintiff due to insufficient charting. How would you protect your physician employer from the same fate?

Externship Application Experience

1. Consider the following circumstances for triaging office appointments for the day, including room assignments. List each patient as a regular, a minor procedure, or isolation room. Already scheduled appointments:
   - Cast removal
   - Routine Pap
   - Well-baby check
   - Dressing change for a surgical wound
   - Recheck for respiratory TB diagnosed one week ago, on medication
   - Mole removal

   Call-ins for appointments that day:
   - HIV diagnosed patient c/o coughing and elevated temp
   - Child with suspected chicken pox, sibling diagnosed two weeks ago
   - Diagnosed hepatitis B with nausea and vomiting
   - Patient c/o possible elevated blood pressure
   - 5-year-old female with chest pain

2. Report the daily routine of checking supplies in the office where the externship experience is taking place.

Resource Guide

Center for Health Promotion and Education
Centers for Disease Control and Prevention
Building 1 South, Room SSB249
1600 Clifton Road NE
Atlanta, GA 30333
404-329-3492
www.cdc.gov

U.S. Department of Health and Human Services
200 Independence Avenue, SW
Washington, DC 20201
www.os.dhhs.gov

MedMedia

www.prenhall.com/frazier

More on this chapter, including interactive resources, can be found on the Student CD-ROM accompanying this textbook and on the Companion Website at www.prenhall.com/frazier.

Medical Asepsis

Case Study

Gloria is rushing around the office because everyone is running so far behind. It is late Friday afternoon and they have already accommodated several walk-in patients. Dr. Becan orders a throat swab from the last patient Gloria roomed to check for Strep-A. The patient presented with a fever and sore throat, and Strep-A has been a common diagnosis this winter.

In her hurry Gloria skips washing her hands when she reenters the exam room and simply dons gloves. She takes a sterile cotton applicator and begins to swab the patient's throat. The patient gags and coughs up mucus droplets on Gloria's hands.

Gloria realizes she has forgotten to bring the testing serums in the room with her, so with the swab in one hand she opens the door with her other hand and leaves the room. Still wearing the gloves, she grabs a coworker's pen and quickly jots down the patient information on the lab order form and hands it to the receptionist for coding and billing.

MedMedia

www.prenhall.com/frazier

Additional interactive resources and activities for this chapter can be found on the Companion Website. For videos, audio glossary, legal and ethical scenarios, job scenarios, quizzes, and games related to the content of this chapter, please access the accompanying CD-ROM in this book.

 Assets Available:

Audio Glossary
Legal and Ethical Scenario: *Medical Asepsis*
On the Job Scenario: *Medical Asepsis*
Video Scenario: *Sanitation, Disinfection, and Sterilization*
Multiple Choice Quiz
Games: Crossword, Strikeout, and Spelling Bee

Objectives

After completing this chapter, you should be able to:

- Spell and define the medical terminology in this chapter.
- Define the medical assistant's role in the promotion of infection control in the medical office.
- Explain the cycle of infection.
- Identify the body's natural defenses against infection.
- Describe the layers of the skin and their functions.
- Explain the function of the immune system.
- Explain how a person's general state of health may serve as a defense against infection.
- Identify other natural defenses against infection.
- Explain medical asepsis.
- Explain the roles of OSHA and the CDC in setting infection control guidelines.
- List and explain the importance of Universal and Standard Precautions.
- Identify the types of personal protective equipment and their uses.
- Describe hepatitis, its routes of transmission, and patient education measures.
- Describe the symptoms, diagnosis, treatment, and patient education considerations of HIV/AIDS.
- Discuss caring for the HIV/AIDS patient.
- Explain the theory of hand washing.
- Explain the theory of nonsterile gloving.
- Identify the symptoms of latex allergy and patient education measures.

MEDICAL ASSISTING COMPETENCIES

CAAHEP ENTRY-LEVEL COMPETENCIES FOR CMA	ABHES ENTRY-LEVEL COMPETENCIES FOR RMA
■ Identify and respond to issues of confidentiality. ■ Perform within legal and ethical boundaries. ■ Demonstrate knowledge of federal and state health-care legislation and regulations. ■ Perform hand washing. ■ Dispose of biohazardous materials. ■ Practice Standard Precautions.	■ Project a positive attitude. ■ Maintain confidentiality at all times. ■ Be a "team player." ■ Be cognizant of ethical boundaries. ■ Exhibit initiative. ■ Adapt to change. ■ Evidence a responsible attitude. ■ Be courteous and diplomatic. ■ Conduct work within scope of education, training, and ability. ■ Apply principles of aseptic technique and infection control. ■ Dispose of biohazardous materials. ■ Practice Standard Precautions. ■ Instruct patients with special needs. ■ Teach patients methods of health promotion and disease prevention.

Introduction

The medical environment can be hazardous to a patient's health. Patients who come to a medical office may appear healthy and be well, may appear healthy but carry disease-producing organisms, or may be experiencing the symptoms of infectious or noninfectious disease. If patients or staff members are not the source of infection, the clinical environment can be. Dust harbors very tiny insects and microorganisms that carry disease. Instruments that have not been cleaned properly may harbor infectious microorganisms. Door handles may be covered with microorganisms from ill patients. To promote health and to ensure a clean and safe environment for all patients and staff, medical offices must follow infection control practices and Universal Precautions. Understanding the basics of asepsis and infection control is essential to preventing or reducing the spread of disease.

The Medical Assistant's Role in Infection Control

As an MA it is your responsibility to learn and practice the measures formulated by the federal agencies OSHA and the CDC to prevent the transmission of disease in the medical setting. These measures are based on interrupting the cycle of infectious disease. They include frequent washing of the hands, correct gloving technique, using personal protective equipment, and other Universal and Standard Precautions. You will also instruct patients in the proper aseptic technique to follow at home.

—Critical Thinking Question 7-1—

How do you think Gloria's actions make her patient feel? How much time do you think Gloria really saved by not washing her hands and then not removing the gloves and washing her hands again?

Medical Terminology

aerobe—organism able to survive and grow only in the presence of oxygen

anaerobe—organism that survives and grows in the absence of oxygen

asepsis—practice of maintaining a pathogen-free or pathogen-controlled environment to prevent the spread of illness and disease

bactericidal—capable of killing or destroying bacteria

bloodborne pathogens—pathogens carried in the bloodstream

Body Substance Isolation (BSI)—procedures, equipment, and supplies used to prevent the transmission of communicable diseases by preventing direct contact with all body substances such as blood, body fluids, drainage from wounds, feces, urine, sputum, and saliva

carrier—person who has the capacity to transmit a disease and is usually unaware of infection

Centers for Disease Control (CDC)—agency of the Public Health Operating Division of the U.S. Department of Health and Human Services that studies and monitors diseases and disease prevention and works to protect public health and safety

cilia—hairlike processes projecting from the epithelial cells

contamination—making a sterile field unclean or having pathogens placed in it

dermis—middle layer of the skin

epidermis—outermost layer of the skin

epithelial—pertaining to the epithelium (cells covering the external and internal surfaces of the body)

follicle—small hollow or cavity with secretory functions (e.g., hair follicle, ovarian follicle, gastric follicle, etc.)

fomites—nonliving objects that may transmit infectious material

homeostasis—interaction between body systems that maintains optimum body function

immunity—ability to resist disease

incubation—period of time between exposure to infection and the appearance of symptoms

infection—invasion of the body by a pathogenic microorganism

Medical Terminology *(continued)*

integumentary—pertaining to the skin, hair, and nails

keratinocyte—any skin cell that produces keratin, the hard protein material found in the skin, hair, and nails

medical asepsis—the practice of reducing the number of pathogens and the transmission of disease; also known as clean technique

microorganism—organism that can be viewed under a microscope, but not by the naked eye

nonpathogen—harmless organism that does not cause disease

nosocomial infection—infection resulting from the hospitalization of a patient

personal protective equipment (PPE)—protective clothing and equipment such as gloves, gowns, and masks that are worn to prevent contamination by blood and other body fluids

phagocytosis—the engulfing and destruction of microorganisms or foreign matter by phagocytic cells

prodromal—period between earliest symptoms and appearance of physical sign, such as fever or rash.

Standard Precautions—precautions that replace Body Substance Isolation and Universal Precautions in institutional health care settings such as hospitals and nursing homes; the first level of care combines Universal and

Body Substance Isolation Precautions, and the second consists of Transmission-based Precautions

sterile—free from pathogens and all microorganisms

subcutaneous tissue—deepest layer of the skin

transmission-based precautions—care based on symptoms of disease and transmission method of the pathogen, such as contact, droplet, air, vector, or common vehicle

Universal Precautions—the CDC's original guidelines for preventing the transmission of AIDS and other blood-borne diseases

Abbreviation

ELISA—enzyme-linked immunosorbent assay

COMPETENCY SKILLS PERFORMANCE

1. Perform correct hand-washing procedure.
2. Demonstrate nonsterile gloving.

The Cycle of Infection

Microorganisms are organisms that cannot be seen by the naked eye but must be viewed under a microscope. All microorganisms require an optimum environment for growth. They grow well at normal body temperature (98.6 degrees F) and in the dark, moist environments of body cavities. Microorganisms also require nutrition, oxygen (**aerobes**) or the lack of oxygen (**anaerobes**), and usually a neutral pH (7.0).

Microorganisms can be pathogens or nonpathogens. Disease-producing organisms are pathogens (Figure 7-1 ◆). Harmless microorganisms are called **nonpathogens**. Bacteria, viruses, fungi, parasites, and protozoa are pathogens when disease conditions result from their presence. **Bloodborne pathogens** are disease-producing microorganisms carried in the bloodstream. Table 7-1 lists some bloodborne pathogens and diseases.

Nonpathogenic microorganisms can become disease-producing pathogens when they leave their natural environments. As an example, *Escherichia coli (E. coli)* may move

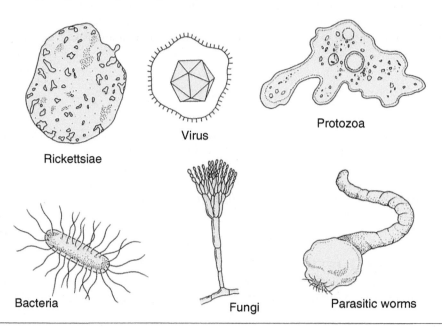

Figure 7-1 ◆ Pathogens

TABLE 7-1 BLOODBORNE PATHOGENS AND DISEASES	
Arboviral infections	Herpes simplex virus
Babesiosis	Human immunodeficiency virus (HIV)
Brucellosis	Human T-lymphotrophic virus Type I
Creutzfeld-Jakob disease	Leptospirosis
Hepatitis A virus (HAV)	Relapsing fever
Hepatitis B virus (HBV)	Syphilis
Hepatitis C virus (HCV)	Viral hemorrhagic fever

from its normal habitat in the colon to the urinary tract and cause a urinary tract infection. Nonpathogens can also become pathogenic when the body's immune system has been overwhelmed.

There are five elements, or links, in the cycle of infection in which pathogens are transmitted from one host to another (Figure 7-2 ◆):

- Reservoir host
- Means of exit
- Means of transmission
- Means of entrance
- Susceptible host

The cycle begins with a reservoir or **carrier** host. The host may exhibit symptoms of the disease or may be unaware that he or she may be spreading potentially pathogenic microorganisms. After a period of reproduction and **incubation,** the pathogen finds a portal of exit to leave the body. Blood and body fluids, including tears, saliva, sputum, feces, urine, and vaginal secretions, are common vehicles of transmission. During the entry, reproduction, and incubation phases of the cycle, the patient does not experience any clinical symptoms. Next, the pathogen is transmitted to a susceptible host. Microorganisms may be transmitted by air, contact, contaminated food, human carriers, animal carriers, insects, **fomites,** and soil. They enter the portals of the respiratory, genitourinary, and gastrointestinal tracts or the eyes, ears, and open areas of the skin. Pathogens may also cross the placental barrier to infect the fetus. Effective means of interrupting the cycle of infection include wearing barrier protection and following proper cleaning procedures.

?—Critical Thinking Question 7-2—
In the case study, who has been put at risk of possible exposure to Strep A by Gloria's actions?

Keys to Success
THE TRANSMISSION OF MICROORGANISMS

- Vector transmission: Parasitic insects carry disease via animals. An example is Lyme disease, which is carried by a tick commonly found on deer.
- Airborne transmission: Microorganisms are moved through the air on dust particles. Examples include rubeola and varicella viruses and *Mycobacterium tuberculosis.*
- Droplet transmission: The moist droplets from sneezing, coughing, and talking transfer pathogenic microorganisms. Respiratory infections such as the common cold and influenza are spread by droplet transmission.
- Indirect contact, also known as common vehicle transmission: Microorganisms are transferred to a susceptible host by physical contact or by touching a contaminated object such as a food tray, faucets, or equipment. HIV (human immunodeficiency virus) may be transferred from a contaminated needle to the puncture site.
- Direct contact: There is direct contact between an infected area and another skin surface or mucous membrane. Medical personnel are required to wash their hands between patients to avoid skin-to-skin transmission of microorganisms such as *Staphylococcus aureus.*

After the pathogenic organism reproduces in the new host, the body responds with pain, swelling, and redness at the infected sites. Other symptoms, such as higher temperature and pulse rate, indicate that the patient has entered the prodromal phase of the illness. Laboratory tests will indicate an elevated white blood cell count. In the acute phase the patient experiences the strongest symptoms of the illness. In the recovery phase, the patient's symptoms diminish.

If the body's natural defenses cannot overcome the infection, antibiotics and other medications may be ordered by the physician and administered by clinical staff.

Natural Defenses Against Infection

Interactions among body systems maintain **homeostasis.** Overall health and functioning depend on the body's natural ability to resist **infection.** The integumentary system, the immune system, general good health, and specific body mechanisms such as coughing and sneezing are among the body's natural defenses against infectious disease.

The Integumentary System

The **integumentary** system (skin) is the first line of defense against infection (Figure 7-3 ◆). Intact skin serves as a barrier against invasion by the microorganisms normally present on the skin's surface. When there is a break in the skin—such as an abrasion, laceration, or surgical wound—the risk of infection increases. The skin is the largest organ in the human body. In the average person, it measures approximately 20 square feet and weighs 5.6 pounds.

The skin consists of three layers (Table 7-2).

- The outermost, protective layer is called the **epidermis.** It is made up of five stratified layers of **epithelial** cells that have been pushed up from the lowest layer, called the stratum germinativum, where **keratinocytes** are

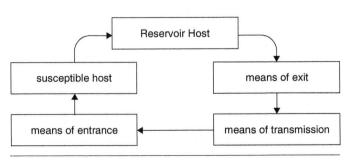

Figure 7-2 ◆ Five links in the cycle of infection

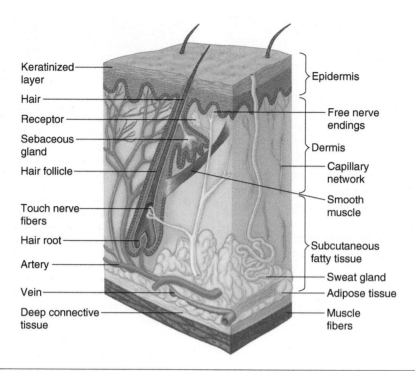

Keratinized layer
Hair
Receptor
Sebaceous gland
Hair follicle
Touch nerve fibers
Hair root
Artery
Vein
Deep connective tissue

Epidermis
Free nerve endings
Dermis
Capillary network
Smooth muscle
Subcutaneous fatty tissue
Sweat gland
Adipose tissue
Muscle fibers

Figure 7-3 ◆ Structure of the skin

TABLE 7-2 LAYERS OF THE SKIN
Epidermis (five sublayers)
■ stratum corneum
■ stratum lucidum
■ stratum granulosum
■ stratum malpighii
■ stratum germinativum
Dermis
Subcutaneous tissue

first formed. In the middle layer of the epidermis, the stratum granulosum, cells become cornified and are no longer living. These cells move upward to the outermost layer of the epidermis, the stratum corneum. This is the sloughing layer that sheds during showers or baths.

■ The middle layer is the **dermis.** It contains hair **follicles,** connective tissue, nerve endings, and sweat (sudoriferous) and oil (sebaceous) glands. Sebaceous glands secrete oil onto the skin that prevents dryness and cracking.

■ The deepest layer is the **subcutaneous tissue.** It contains fat, blood and lymph vessels, and other connective tissue. This layer helps to insulate and cushion internal organs from injury.

The Immune System

The immune system is another of the body's defenses against infection. It is a vessel system that serves as a filter for the plasma portion of the blood. **Immunity** is the ability to resist disease. There are two specific immunity defenses: cell-mediated immunity and humoral immunity.

■ T4 lymphocytes or helper cells play a dominant role in cell-mediated immunity.

■ Humoral immunity utilizes B cells, which are responsible for antibody production.

Cytokines are proteins produced by monocytes or lymphocytes that regulate other cell activities within the immune system. Immunizations assist the body in developing active and passive immunity. Active immunity develops antibodies or sensitized lymphocytes within the body that kill the infectious agent. Passive immunity utilizes previously developed antibodies for the same purpose. ∞ For further discussion of the immune system, see Chapter 20.

General Health

A person's general state of health is a third potential defense against infection and a major player in how the body fights all disease states. It is well documented that healthy individuals live longer, more productive lives. Individuals who are overweight and do not eat properly, do not exercise regularly, cannot relax, smoke cigarettes and abuse alcohol, or lead stressful lifestyles are placing extra physiological demands on their bodies. For example, if the body needs more oxygen because of improper lung functioning (as in chronic lung disease), the lungs will breathe faster and work harder to accomplish homeostasis and supply oxygen to the cells. Unhealthy lifestyles create new disease conditions or aggravate existing ones. Quick fixes such as diet fads are available, but only individual commitment over the long term provides a higher quality of health and life.

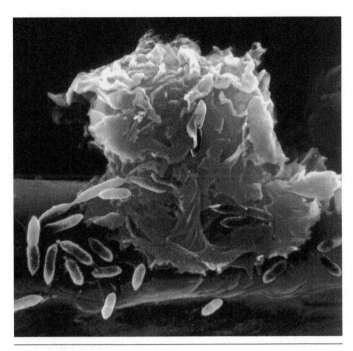

Figure 7-4 ◆ Phagocytosis
Source: Phototake

Other Natural Defenses

Other specific mechanisms in the body help to fight infection.

- The mucous membranes lining cavities and passages serve as barriers to microorganisms and produce secretions that inhibit microbial growth.
- **Cilia** are hairlike projections from epithelial cells that trap and prevent microorganisms from entering deeper into the body.
- Coughing, sneezing, and the movement of the respiratory tract cilia serve to expel pathogens. Tears, sweat, urine, and vaginal secretions are other excretory mechanisms.
- The acidic pH (lower than 7.0) of urine and vaginal secretions inhibits microbial growth. Under healthy conditions, urine is **sterile.** Urination expels microorganisms from the urinary tract and cleanses the external perineal area.
- The acidic pH of gastric juice serves as a **bactericidal** agent.
- The circulatory and lymphatic systems also play an important role in fighting infection. Leukocytes (white blood cells) surround and destroy pathogens in a process known as **phagocytosis** (Figure 7-4 ◆). Lymphocytes are activated to produce antibodies when antigens (foreign substances) are introduced into the body.

Asepsis and Infection Control

Asepsis is defined as the practice of maintaining a pathogen-free or pathogen-controlled environment to prevent the spread of illness and disease. There are two kinds of asepsis: **medical asepsis** and surgical asepsis. ∞ Surgical asepsis requires sterile technique and is discussed in Chapter 8. Every medical office develops infection control policies and procedures to prevent the transmission of disease-causing microorganisms.

Caduceus Chronicle
ANTISEPTIC METHODS IN CHILDBIRTH

Ignaz Semmelweis (1818–1865), a Hungarian obstetrician, was the first to use antiseptic methods in childbirth. He determined that puerperal fever (bacterial infection of the female genital tract after childbirth) was contagious after observing student doctors who performed autopsies and then examined women in labor without first washing their hands. He also noticed that women giving birth at home did not seem to contract puerperal fever. When he ordered students to wash their hands with chlorinated lime before examining patients, the maternal mortality rate dropped drastically. Throughout the remainder of his professional life, he encountered strong opposition from hospital officials who refused to enforce hand-washing policies. His published studies were rejected locally and abroad. After suffering a mental breakdown, he died from an infection contracted during the performance of surgery.

Infection control consists of aseptic procedures and Standard Precautions, described in greater detail later in this chapter.

The primary purposes of medical asepsis, also known as the clean technique, are to maintain a clean environment and prevent the transmission of disease by reducing the number of pathogens. The most important procedure in the maintenance of medical asepsis is hand washing. Other practices include keeping the office free of dirt, dust, and insects; proper disposal of biological waste materials according to OSHA's Bloodborne Pathogen Standards; ensuring adequate lighting and ventilation; and wearing minimal jewelry (Figure 7-5 ◆).

Occupational Safety and Health Administration (OSHA)

The Occupational Safety and Health Administration (OSHA) was established by Congress to ensure worker safety on the job

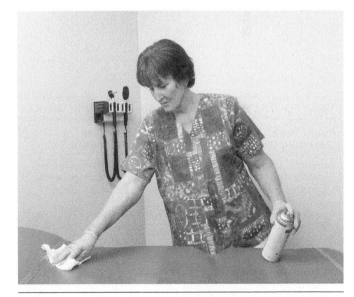

Figure 7-5 ◆ The primary purposes of medical asepsis are to maintain a clean environment and prevent the transmission of disease by reducing the number of pathogens.

Caduceus Chronicle
OSHA

The Occupational Safety and Health Administration (OSHA) was established by Congress in 1970. It is one of approximately 20 agencies of the Department of Labor. OSHA draws criticism from some businesses as an unfair regulatory agency enforcing excessive compliance, documentation, and penalties. On the other hand, many labor groups believe it does not do enough to protect the occupational health of U.S. workers. OSHA has its headquarters in Washington, DC, and 10 regional offices throughout the United States.

Caduceus Chronicle
CDC

Originally established in 1946, the Communicable Disease Center became known as the Centers for Disease Control (CDC) in 1970. Although the agency added "and Prevention" to its official title in 1992, Congress requested that its official initials remain CDC. The CDC's headquarters are in Atlanta, Georgia. Past accomplishments include the discovery of the causative pathogens of Legionnaire's disease and toxic shock syndrome.

by reducing hazards in any type of work setting. It has also established and maintained health programs for employees. In the medical office setting, OSHA enforces regulations for safety and infection control practices.

Centers for Disease Control and Prevention (CDC)

The **Centers for Disease Control and Prevention (CDC)** studies and monitors diseases and disease prevention and works to protect public health and safety. In addition to researching infectious disease, it provides immunization services and dispenses health information to the public and the medical community. The CDC is an agency of the Public Health Operating Division of the U.S. Department of Health and Human Services (Table 7-3).

Infection Control Precautions

OSHA requires that all health professionals follow "universal blood and body fluid precautions." **Universal Precautions** were established in 1985 by the CDC to reduce the risk of hepatitis and acquired immunodeficiency syndrome (AIDS). All blood, blood products, human tissue, and body fluids are considered potentially infectious materials. Examples include nasal and oral secretions, cerebrospinal fluid, amniotic fluid, and joint and other body cavity fluids. Sources of infectious

material include pathologic waste, microbiological waste, and body tissues, cells, or fluids previously identified as infected with HIV.

It is important for all health-care providers to consider *every* patient a potential source of AIDS, Hepatitis B, or other bloodborne pathogens. OSHA suggests the following guidelines.

- Every individual, even if healthy, should be considered a potential carrier host capable of transmitting infection.
- Wash the hands before and after gloves are used.
- Change gloves after each patient contact.
- Wear personal protective barriers according to anticipated exposure to blood and body fluids. Protective barriers include gloves, face or eye shields, gowns, and masks.
- After exposure to blood or body fluids, immediately remove protective barriers and thoroughly wash your hands.
- Follow proper technique when handling, cleaning, and disposing of sharps.
- Resuscitation devices must be available for mouth-to-mouth or mouth-to-tracheostomy artificial ventilations.
- Refrain from patient care if open or weeping skin lesions are present.
- Use 10% sodium hypochlorite solution immediately to clean any blood or body fluid **contamination** on hard surfaces. To make a 10% solution, mix one part sodium hypochlorite (common household bleach) with nine parts water. Make a fresh solution daily. Do not store the mixed solution, as it may deteriorate and lose its effectiveness.
- Report all sharps injuries immediately.

If Universal Precautions are not followed when caring for an asymptomatic patient, both worker and patient may become part of the transmission of disease. Because some microorganisms may be fatal to the health-care worker or other patients, strict adherence to universal precautions benefits the health of all medical professionals and patients.

In 1992, **Body Substance Isolation** (BSI) was developed. BSI regards all body substances as infectious materials. Under BSI precautions, all body substances of individuals seeking emergency and non-emergency medical treatment (including blood and body fluids, drainage from wounds, feces, urine, tears, sputum, and saliva) are isolated to prevent the transmission of pathogen-caused diseases. BSI went further than Universal Precautions to isolate substances not currently known to contain HIV.

TABLE 7-3 U.S. DEPARTMENT OF HEALTH AND HUMAN SERVICES	
Public Health Operating Division	**Human Services Operating Division**
National Institutes of Health	Health Care Financing Adminis
Food and Drug Administration	tration (Medicare and Medicaid)
Centers for Disease Control and Prevention	Administration for Children and Families
Agency for Toxic Substances and Disease Registry	Administration on Aging and Prevention
Indian Health Service	
Health Resources and Services Administration	
Substance Abuse and Mental Health Services Administration	
Agency for Healthcare Research Quality	

Neither Universal nor Body Substance Isolation Precautions addressed the transmission of airborne droplets or contact with pathogens that may be present on dry, unbroken skin. In 1996, the original Universal Precautions were expanded by the CDC to include **nosocomial infections** and became known as **Standard Precautions,** applicable to patients receiving care in institutional health-care settings such as hospitals and nursing homes. With broader applications, Standard Precautions are made up of two tiers:

1. Universal Precautions and Body Substance Isolation for all hospital patient care.
2. **Transmission-based precautions** for patients who are infected or suspected of being infected. Barrier protection, in addition to gloves, is based on anticipated exposure and the mode of infectious disease transmission.

Personal Protective Equipment (PPE)

Standard Precautions applying to **personal protective equipment** are based on actual and anticipated exposure to blood and body fluids (Figure 7-6 ◆). Correct procedures must be followed when using PPE or disease transmission will continue. For example, wearing gloves during patient contact is ineffective if the gloves are not discarded between patients and the hands are not washed. Protective clothing or equipment should be strong enough to prevent infectious material from reaching the wearer's clothing, skin, or mucous membranes.

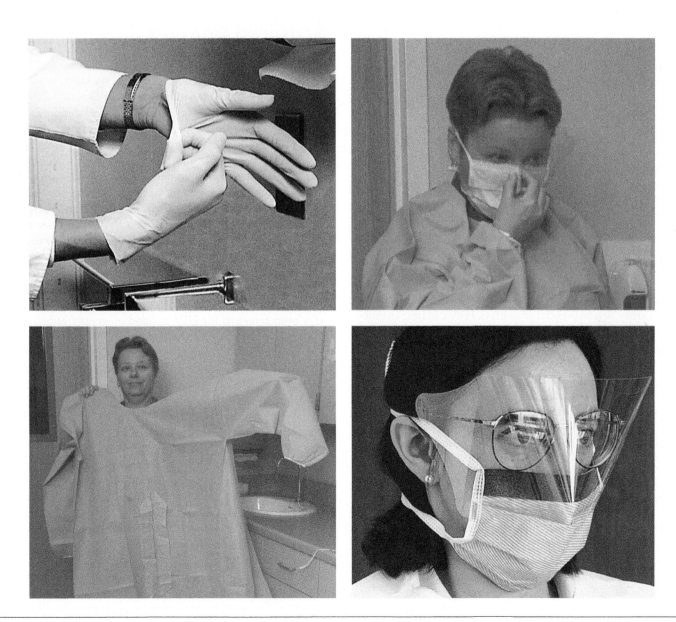

Figure 7-6 ◆ Personal protective equipment: gloves, gown, mask, and protective eyewear.

TABLE 7-4 PERSONAL PROTECTIVE EQUIPMENT	
PPE	**When to Use**
Gloves	■ Anticipated contact with blood or body fluids ■ Contact with open wounds, sores, or mucous membranes
Gowns	■ Anticipated contact with body fluid splashes or droplets ■ Contact with open wounds, sores, or mucous membranes
Masks, protective eyewear, or face shields	■ Anticipated contact with body fluid splashes or droplets ■ Anticipated droplet spread from patient's productive cough ■ Anticipated aerosol spread of body fluids or tissues during procedures
Disposable patient equipment	■ Easily transmitted infectious diseases (if disposable equipment is unavailable, disinfect and sterilize nondisposable equipment before use with another patient)

Contaminated PPE must be properly disposed of after use. Table 7-4 lists the uses for various PPE.

Hepatitis

Hepatitis, or inflammation of the liver, is usually caused by a viral infection. The severity of symptoms depends on the type of hepatitis and the health of the individual before infection. Five types of hepatitis have been identified: Hepatitis A (HAV), Hepatitis B (HBV), Hepatitis C (HCV), Hepatitis D (HDV), and Hepatitis E (HEV). New types continue to be identified. (∞ See Chapter 24, Gastroenterology and Nutrition, for more information.)

HAV and HEV are transmitted via oral and fecal routes. HBV, HCV, and HDV are transmitted through percutaneous contact, permucosal contact, blood, products for blood transfusion, and IV drug use. Renal-dialysis and multiple-transfusion patients may also be blood transmitters. HBV can be transmitted through sexual contact. HEV occurs in areas such as Asia, India, Africa, and Central America, but may also be seen in travelers to those areas. HAV, HBV, and HCV are the most common types in the United States.

Health-care workers are at risk for contracting hepatitis because of their daily occupational exposure to blood and body fluids. They can decrease that risk by practicing consistent hand washing and sharps precautions. Several forms of immunization for Hepatitis B are also available, including Heptavax B, developed in 1982.

Patient Education

After the first hepatitis immunization, the second dose is given one month later, and the third is given six months after the initial dose. When the immunization series has been completed, a blood sample should be tested for seroconversion. Occasionally the injections may need to be repeated.

Patients with multiple sexual partners or a history of intravenous drug use should be advised to receive the HBV vaccination. Some states, such as Indiana, require that children receive a series of three HBV vaccinations before kindergarten.

Keys to Success
HEPTAVAX B

Be sure to read directions about the route of administration prior to administering hepatitis B immunizations. In adults, the deltoid is the recommended site for the IM injection. In infants and young children, the anterolateral thigh is recommended. The gluteus muscle is no longer recommended because of the possibility of injecting into fatty tissue. If the medication does not reach the muscle, the individual could fail to seroconvert and reach the desired immunity.

Patients who have received blood transfusions cannot donate blood for six months. Patients who have been infected with HBV or HCV should never donate blood.

Acquired Immunodeficiency Syndrome (AIDS)

Acquired immunodeficiency syndrome, or AIDS, is a disease state caused by the human immunodeficiency virus (HIV). Approximately 1 million people in the United States are infected with HIV. Every year, 50,000 more people are infected, including 2,500 infants.

HIV can be transmitted only by contact with blood or body fluids from an infected person. The transmission is complete when the contaminated materials come in contact with the recipient's body membranes or skin breaks and then move into the bloodstream. Certain individuals or groups are at high risk of contracting HIV, including those with multiple sex partners and those who use contaminated needles. Other ways in which HIV is spread are blood transfusions, placental transfer to the fetus, and continued breastfeeding after nipples have been traumatized. Since 1985, blood transfusions in the United States have been screened for HIV antibodies, greatly reducing the risk to patients requiring blood transfusion.

There have been no documented cases of HIV infection from tears or saliva. However, during oral sex, the virus can be transferred into bleeding gums or open sores in the mouth.

The initial infection occurs when the virus attaches to the T4 lymphocytes (helper cells) at the CD4 receptor. HIV, a retrovirus, transfers its own DNA to that of the cell it has invaded. The lymphocyte function changes to that of the invasive HIV. Reproduction ensures the survival of the HIV-trained lymphocyte and the destruction of the T4 lymphocyte and impairs the immune system's capabilities. The immune system is progressively weakened until it fails completely. In the final stages of the disease, overwhelming and often repeated opportunistic infections eventually become fatal to the patient.

The early stages of HIV infection are characterized by nonspecific viral signs and symptoms such as fever, malaise, joint pain, rash, and swollen lymph glands. Many patients do not experience symptoms for years and may not be diagnosed for as long as seven to ten years after the initial infection. Even without symptoms, however, an infected individual is a carrier. Blood testing can be performed only after antibodies form, and antibodies take approximately three months to develop from the time of infection.

There are numerous ways to label or classify the progression of HIV infection to the final stage of AIDS. Most classifications of the stages of HIV infection involve the T4 count and the absence, presence, and degree of symptoms. There are four major stages in the diagnosis of HIV infection or AIDS.

Stage 1: The primary HIV infection stage may bring flu-like symptoms and last for a few weeks. Diagnosis is likely to be missed because antibodies have not yet developed.

Stage 2: The clinically asymptomatic stage may last up to ten years. The patient is likely to have swollen lymph glands, and the HIV antibody is detectable in the blood. HIV is actively replicating during this stage.

Stage 3: During the symptomatic HIV infection stage, the immune system becomes progressively impaired as it loses the struggle to replace T4 cells being destroyed by the HIV infection. Symptoms are usually mild in the beginning but worsen as the immune system deteriorates. Opportunistic infections and cancers begin during this stage.

Stage 4: During this final stage of progression from HIV infection to AIDS, the immune system is severely damaged, with a T4 count of less than 200 mm^3.

A diagnosis of HIV infection is based in part on a history of high-risk factors and behaviors. Then serologic testing by **ELISA** and Western blot is performed. ELISA is the first test for HIV antibodies, but results are not specific for HIV infection alone. The Western blot test, or immunofluorescent antibody (IFA), is the second and confirming test for HIV infection. Occasionally the Western blot is neither positive nor negative because of an error in interpretation or because testing is done too early. The test results of ELISA and Western blot can also be inaccurate if the tourniquet is applied for longer than one minute when the blood specimen is obtained. In this case the test should be repeated at intervals until results are confirmed as positive or HIV has been ruled out as a possible diagnosis. In rare cases HIV antibodies do not develop. The most recent criteria for positive diagnosis of AIDS is a CD4 or T cell count lower than 200 per cubic millimeter (mm^3) of blood. The count in a healthy individual is 1000/mm^3.

Other diagnostic findings include anemia, a decreased white blood cell count, and biopsies or imaging procedures that confirm involvement of opportunistic diseases in organs and systems. Home tests that use ELISA, Western blot, or IFA are identified by number only to ensure confidentiality.

The organisms of opportunistic infections are normally present in humans. But when the immune system is impaired or severely compromised, the body cannot inhibit the growth and reproduction of these organisms or of some types of cancer. During the initial and asymptomatic stages of HIV infection, the body has some immunity protection. During the symptomatic stages, the body is increasingly overwhelmed by the virus and by opportunistic infections. Table 7-5 lists

TABLE 7-5 COMMON OPPORTUNISTIC INFECTIONS	
Organism Name	**Organism Type/Infection Site**
*Candida albicans**	Fungus/mouth (thrush), vagina
Herpes simplex	Virus/vagina
Herpes varicella zoster (chickenpox, shingles)	Virus/skin
Cryptococcus	Fungus/liver, bone, brain
Histoplasmosis	Fungus/bone marrow, liver, lungs
Toxoplasmosis	Parasite/brain
Cryptosporidiosis	Parasite/gastrointestinal tract
Pneumocystis carinii (PCP)*	Protozoa/lungs
Salmonella	Bacteria/gastrointestinal tract
Cytomegalovirus*	Virus/eyes, gastrointestinal tract, lungs

The most common opportunistic infections in AIDS.

This list is not inclusive. Other infecting organisms may become opportunistic in a patient with immunologic compromise.

common opportunistic infections and the sites they affect. Ultimately the patient dies from repeated opportunistic infections or cancers, not from AIDS. The body fails because it cannot both fight the infections/cancers and support normal body functions.

Kaposi's sarcoma is not an opportunistic infection. It is a malignant neoplasm characterized by purplish or dark red blemishes on the skin. Biopsy confirms this clinical diagnosis. The disease spreads to other body tissues, but like opportunistic infections it is rarely the cause of death in the AIDS patient (Figure 7-7 ◆).

Current Treatment

There is no cure for HIV infection and AIDS, although drug therapy can slow the reproduction and invasiveness of HIV as well as damage to the immune system. The drug most commonly used is AZT (zidovudine), but others, including didanosine, zacitabine, lamivudine, and stavudine may also be given to inhibit the growth of HIV. AZT is also given to patients who are HIV-positive but have not progressed to the stage of full-blown AIDS. A new family of drugs called protease inhibitors, such as indinavir, has proven effective at maintaining a lower HIV count in the bloodstream. A triple-combination drug therapy is another approach that is increasingly being used. Physicians also give antibiotics to HIV-infected individuals before opportunistic infections set in. Researchers are seeking a vaccine for AIDS, but the most effective prevention is avoidance of behaviors that raise the risk of infection.

Caring for the Patient with HIV/AIDS

There are several guidelines for caring for a patient with HIV or AIDS.

■ Follow the CDC's Universal Precautions for handling blood and body fluids.

■ Wear eye protection, a mask, gloves, and a gown in anticipation of contact with blood and body fluids.

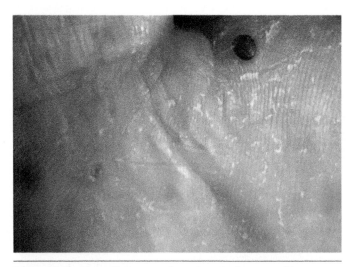

Figure 7-7 ◆ Kaposi's sarcoma found on the bottom of foot
Courtesy of the CDC/Dr. Steve Kraus, 1981.

- Avoid skin puncture by carefully disposing of needles in a sharps container immediately after use.
- Mark specimens with labels for "blood and body fluid precautions."
- Double-bag and label contaminated linens, equipment, and trash before processing.
- Educate the patient about the importance of frequent hand washing and avoiding oral or genital transmission of the infection.
- Instruct the significant other or the family on how to provide supportive care for symptoms the patient will experience, such as fever, anorexia, and fatigue. As the patient's

outside contacts learn of the disease, the patient is likely to experience isolation. During the terminal stage, the patient enters the grieving process, experiencing anger, guilt, denial, bargaining, and depression. Family and/or significant other(s) need to be aware that these psychological needs are normal and encouraged to continue providing emotional support.

- Assist the patient by providing information about social agencies that may provide assistance with food, housing, medical costs, or hospice care.

Patient Education

For patients at risk or those with HIV infection, the following behaviors should be discussed and encouraged.

- Avoid multiple sex partners, regardless of sexual orientation.
- Avoid unprotected sex. Use latex condoms correctly and consistently. (Keep in mind, however, that it is not entirely accurate to call condom use "safe sex" as it is not 100% effective against HIV transmission.)
- Do not share IV needles.
- Avoid irresponsible behavior that passes the infection to others.

Critical Thinking Question 7-3

How would you feel if you were a patient and Gloria enters the exam room and does not wash her hands before examining you?

PROCEDURE 7-1 Hand Washing

Theory

You must wash your hands frequently whether you are working in the office or in the clinical areas. *Washing your hands is one of the most important ways you can prevent the transmission of disease.* Washing your hands does not sterilize them, but it reduces the number of microorganisms present on the skin. Although gloves serve as barriers to the spread of infection, *do not* use gloves without taking the extra precaution of washing your hands.

You must wash your hands before and after physical contact with every patient. Keep your hands and fingers below the elbows to prevent contaminated or dirty water from running down onto your hands and fingers from your arms. Hands must be washed for a minimum of 2 minutes before beginning to work with patients and 30 seconds following each patient contact.

There are some simple but important points to keep in mind about hand washing:

- Hand washing with soap and water is best in situations of direct patient contact. Antiseptics that do not use water are used in certain circumstances; however, recent studies have questioned their effectiveness. Use warm water to wash the hands, as water that is too hot or cold can promote dry skin.
- Nails should be kept short. Microorganisms on the hands are found in greatest numbers around and under the nails.
- Jewelry should be kept to a minimum, as it creates more areas in which to trap microorganisms.
- Lotion should be applied nightly to the hands to keep the skin from drying and cracking. Broken integrity of the skin is an open invitation to pathogens.

PROCEDURE 7-1 **Hand Washing** *(continued)*

- Bar soap should be avoided unless it can be rinsed and placed on a drainable soap tray.
- Always wash your hands before and after using gloves. Gloves do not absolutely guarantee the prevention of disease transmission, as they may be torn or have holes too tiny to see.
- Faucets are contaminated. Use paper towels when turning them on or off.

In the clinical setting, *always* wash your hands:

- before starting and after ending the clinical day
- before and after assisting in the performance of procedures
- before and after physical contact with each patient
- before and after handling potentially contaminated equipment
- after cleaning in the medical office environment
- after sneezing, blowing your nose, covering your mouth to cough, or using the toilet
- before mealtimes or handling food

Materials
- Soap (bar or pump)
- Paper towels
- Waste container
- Nail brush or cuticle stick

Competency
(**Conditions**) With the necessary materials you will be able to (**Task**) wash your hands (**Standards**) following medically aseptic technique in the time designated by the instructor.

1. Remove and secure most jewelry. Wedding bands and professional watches are allowed. Push the watch higher than your wrist. Avoid touching the contaminated sink front with your uniform.
2. With a paper towel, turn on the water and adjust to a warm temperature (Figure 7-8 ◆). The water should run continuously until you have finished the procedure. Discard the paper towel.
3. With your hands and fingers lower than your elbows, wet your wrists and hands.
4. Apply soap and scrub lather over the hands and fingers, between the fingers, under and around the nails, and rinse (Figures 7-9 ◆ and 7-10 ◆). Apply soap and lather to the wrists and forearms (Figure 7-11 ◆). The purpose of this washing order is to wash the dirtiest areas first. A circular

Figure 7-8 ◆ Turn on water using a paper towel.

Figure 7-9 ◆ Scrub lather over the hands and fingers.

Figure 7-10 ◆ Rinse hands.

Figure 7-11 ◆ Apply soap and lather the wrists and forearms.

continued

PROCEDURE 7-1 **Hand Washing** *(continued)*

motion and friction rubbing will loosen dirt and micro-organisms. If you are using bar soap, rinse it before returning it to the soap dish.
5. Use the cuticle stick or nail brush to clean your nails (Figure 7-12 ◆). If you are wearing a wedding band, scrub around it with the nail brush.
6. Rinse off the lather, keeping your hands in a downward position. Avoid splashing and touching the sink or faucets.

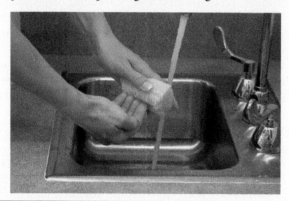

Figure 7-12 ◆ Use the nail brush to clean fingernails.

7. Dry your hands with a paper towel and discard it.
8. Turn off the faucet with another paper towel and discard it. Using a new paper towel prevents the contamination of clean hands.

Patient Education

Discuss with the patient and/or significant other(s) the importance of frequent hand washing. Assess for cultural, physical, emotional, or educational factors that may affect the patient's motivation or ability to learn and adjust your teaching methods accordingly.

Demonstrate hand washing technique and have the patient or significant other(s) perform a return demonstration. Document your teaching efforts.

Charting Example

01/22/xx 0900 Discussed with patient that hand washing would reduce germs that she could give to family members while she is recovering from pneumonia. Patient performed return demonstration and stated that she didn't want other family members to get sick. Alexis Smith, CMA

PROCEDURE 7-2 **Nonsterile Gloving**

Theory

Nonsterile gloving is a medically aseptic procedure used in the prevention of disease transmission. It serves as a barrier tool for personal protection.

You must wash your hands even when you use gloves. Gloves create a warm, moist environment around your hands—favorable conditions for microbial growth. Perspiration mixed with the powder in most gloves also contributes to these conditions. Washing your hands reduces the number of microorganisms on your skin before you put gloves on.

Nonsterile or clean gloves are worn for direct patient contact and for handling equipment that may be contaminated by patient or secretion contact. A sequential combination of clean and sterile gloves may also be used as appropriate. For example, clean gloves may be used to remove an old dressing, and sterile gloves may be used to clean the wound and to apply a sterile dressing.

Gloves should be readily available in patient exam rooms and other work areas. They should be used only once and then discarded. Rings, except for wedding bands, should be removed to prevent the accidental puncture of the glove(s).

Materials

■ Nonsterile exam gloves
■ Waste receptacle

Competency

(**Conditions**) With the necessary materials you will be able to (**Task**) put on, remove, and dispose of nonsterile gloves (**Standards**) following medically aseptic technique in the time designated by the instructor.
1. Wash and dry your hands.
2. Choose gloves of the right size. They should not be so loose that they fall off during a procedure. If they are too tight, they may tear and new gloves will have to be applied.
3. Take one glove from the box and pull it on over your hand to the wrist.
4. Take a second glove and pull it on to the wrist (Figure 7-13 ◆).
5. Adjust the gloves so that the wrists are covered.
6. To remove the first glove, grasp the outside of the glove at the wrist with the other gloved hand and pull down (Figure 7-14 ◆). This motion will keep the contaminated

PROCEDURE 7-2 **Nonsterile Gloving** (continued)

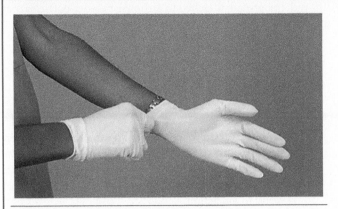

Figure 7-13 ◆ Pull the second glove on to the wrist.

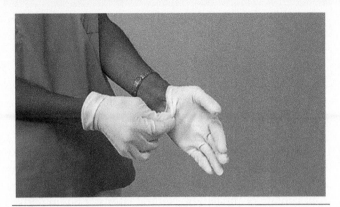

Figure 7-14 ◆ Grasp the outside of the glove at the wrist with the other gloved hand and pull down.

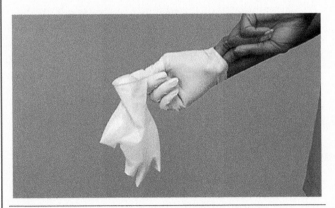

Figure 7-15 ◆ With your ungloved hand, reach inside the second glove.

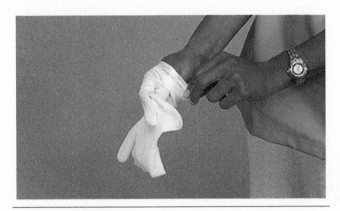

Figure 7-16 ◆ Grasp the inside of the glove and pull it down and off.

surface inside and is called "glove touch glove." Discard the glove immediately.

7. With your ungloved hand, reach inside the second glove (Figure 7-15 ◆). Grasp the inside of the glove and pull it down and off (Figure 7-16 ◆). This second glove removal also keeps the contaminated surface on the inside and is called "ungloved hand touch hand inside before removing." Discard the second glove immediately.

8. Wash and dry your hands.

Patient Education

Discuss with the patient and/or significant other(s) the importance of gloving and removing gloves correctly. Explain that the hands must be washed before and after glove use. Assess for cultural, physical, emotional, or educational factors that may affect the patient's motivation or ability to learn and adjust your teaching methods accordingly.

Demonstrate putting on, removing, and disposing of gloves and have the patient do the same. Document your teaching efforts.

Charting Example

01/22/xx 0915 Patient demonstrated how to glove, remove, and dispose of gloves properly. Patient washed hands after removing gloves without staff reminder. Michael Zheng, CMA

Keys to Success
JEWELRY ON THE JOB

Rings set with diamonds or gemstones are a natural breeding ground for microorganisms. During the gloving procedure, pronged settings may also catch and tear the gloves, rendering them ineffective as a protective barrier. It is best to leave most jewelry at home. In the medical office, a safety pin will secure jewelry to your uniform or scrubs.

Latex Allergy

In recent years, a growing number of health-care workers have been affected by latex allergies. The risk for allergy extends to all others who use natural latex gloves. Latex allergies result from contact or inhalation. Natural latex is a liquid derived from rubber trees. Some synthetic rubber products are referred to as latex, but it is exposure to proteins in *natural* latex that increases the risk for allergy and the severity of symptoms.

The most common reactions to latex are irritant contact dermatitis and allergic contact dermatitis. Irritant contact dermatitis results from exposure to the powder inside the gloves. Allergic contact dermatitis is a reaction to the chemicals added to the latex during the processing and manufacturing of the gloves.

Mild reactions can include rashes, hives, itching, and redness. Severe reactions may involve runny nose, sneezing, irritated eyes and throat, and asthma symptoms, progressing to life-threatening reactions. Reactions are not confined to the areas of contact with the skin. As powdered gloves are removed, the protein attached to airborne powder particles may be inhaled, thereby causing respiratory reactions.

Education for the Patient or Health Professional

- Use nonlatex gloves when working with noninfectious materials.
- If latex gloves are necessary, individuals with powder-related irritant contact dermatitis should use powder-free gloves. People with allergic contact dermatitis should wear hypoallergenic latex gloves to reduce the risk or severity of a reaction.
- Wash and dry your hands thoroughly after wearing latex gloves.
- Clean office areas and equipment that harbor latex-contaminated dust frequently to reduce allergens.
- Familiarize yourself with the common symptoms of latex allergy and consult a physician if symptoms arise. If latex allergy is diagnosed, wear medical alert identification and inform your friends, family members, and coworkers.
- Stay up-to-date about research in latex allergies.

REVIEW

Chapter Summary

- After it was scientifically established that infectious disease is caused by microorganisms, hand washing and the disinfection of instruments became the primary tools for breaking the cycle of infection. The cycle continues unless one or more of five elements are removed: the reservoir host, a means of exit, a means of transmission, a means of entrance, and a susceptible host.
- An intact integumentary system is the body's first line of defense against invasion by microorganisms, or infection. Other elements in the defense system include the immune system, a general state of good health, age, and natural mechanisms such as tears, coughing, and the acidic pH of urine. Cells in the immune system known as phagocytes engulf and digest microorganisms and foreign materials.
- Diseases such as hepatitis and AIDS place the health-care professional at great risk because of the potential for bloodborne transmission of pathogens during patient care.

- With the rise in bloodborne diseases, the Occupational Safety and Health Administration (OSHA) and the Centers for Disease Control (CDC) have developed Bloodborne Pathogen Standards and Universal and Standard Precautions, respectively. These guidelines are designed to prevent the transmission of pathogenic microorganisms, thereby breaking the cycle of infection, and to reduce the risk of infectious disease to the health-care professional.
- Universal and Standard Precautions are based on the assumption that all blood, blood products, human tissue, and body fluids are potentially infectious materials. They emphasize hand washing and the use of appropriate protective barriers. Gloves, gowns, and masks are examples of personal protective equipment (PPE). PPE is used for anticipated contact with blood and body fluids to prevent contact with pathogens.
- Hand washing and gloving procedures are effective only if they are performed correctly. Using gloves is not a

Chapter Summary (continued)

substitute for frequent hand washing, nor does it prevent the growth or transmission of microorganisms when the hands are not washed between patient contacts.

■ All professionals and patients who routinely use latex gloves should be aware of the symptoms of latex allergy and to seek treatment. Some allergy reactions are severe and can be fatal.

■ In addition to medical treatment, education of the patient and significant other(s) is important to health recovery and in the prevention of disease transmission. High-risk populations, health-care workers, and those in

certain other occupations should receive the hepatitis B vaccination series.

■ Following Universal and Standard Precautions is crucial. During the asymptomatic stage of infectious illness, transmission of pathogens may occur if the health-care professional chooses not to follow precautions. It is the responsibility of health-care professionals to stay current regarding bloodborne diseases and infection control practices. This commitment will ensure quality of care for patients and professional longevity in health-related occupations.

Chapter Review Questions

Multiple Choice

1. The cycle of infection includes all of the following except
   A. reservoir host.
   B. means of transmission.
   C. the use of personal protective equipment (PPE).
   D. susceptible host.

2. The body's first line of defense against infection is
   A. an intact integumentary system.
   B. the immune system.
   C. mucous membranes.
   D. the acidic pH of urine.

3. The most important medically aseptic procedure in preventing the transmission of disease is
   A. dusting with a moistened cloth.
   B. hand washing.
   C. disinfecting doorknobs.
   D. wearing nonsterile gloves.

4. The common source of HBV and HIV transmission is
   A. shared use of eye drop medication.
   B. air particles.
   C. moisture droplets.
   D. blood and body fluids.

5. Personal protective equipment (PPE) prevents the transmission of infectious materials and involves wearing gloves, gowns, masks, eyewear, and/or face shields based on
   A. actual and anticipated exposure to blood and body fluids during patient care.
   B. actual exposure to blood and body fluids by direct health-care personnel only.
   C. anticipated exposure to blood and body fluids for administrative and housekeeping personnel.
   D. anticipated exposure to airborne transmission of infectious materials.

6. In the HIV-infected patient, opportunistic infections
   A. cause the immune system to intermittently become compromised and then become stronger.
   B. strengthen the immune system due to repeated exposure to infection.
   C. weaken and severely compromise the immune system.
   D. are rarely cause for concern or adjustments in treatment.

7. *Resident flora* is defined as
   A. pathogenic viruses living and thriving on equipment surfaces.
   B. pathogenic bacteria living and thriving in tissue.
   C. nonpathogenic bacteria living in tissue.
   D. none of the above.

True/False

T F 1. Ignaz Semmelweis (1818–1865) discovered a connection between hand washing and reduced risk of infection, yet he died from an infection contracted during the performance of surgery.

T F 2. Door handles may be covered with microorganisms from ill patients.

T F 3. Understanding the basics of asepsis and infection control is essential to preventing or reducing the spread of disease.

T F 4. Microorganisms are organisms that can be seen by the naked eye.

T F 5. Microorganisms that require oxygen are anaerobes.

Short Answer

1. What is the difference between aerobes and anaerobes?

2. Name the five elements, or links, in the cycle of infection in which pathogens are transmitted from one host to another.

3. List six common vehicles in the transmission of microorganisms.

Chapter Review Questions (continued)

4. Name two microorganisms that are spread by airborne transmission.

5. What is another term for *common vehicle transmission?*

6. What is the first line of defense against infection?

7. Name the two primary purposes of medical asepsis.

8. What function do cilia perform?

9. How many cases of HIV infection from tears or saliva have been documented?

10. Name five nonspecific viral signs and symptoms of the early stages of HIV infection.

Research

1. Research the common symptoms of latex allergy. Compare the prices of latex and nonlatex gloves.

2. Where can patients in your community obtain free or low-cost HIV testing?

3. Are there HIV-specific clinics in your area that offer treatment and counseling?

Externship Application Experience

During your externship experience you observe hand-washing techniques in your assigned office. On one occasion you notice that an employee used the restroom and went back to work without washing her hands. What should you do?

Resource Guide

AIDS

National Center for HIV, STD, and TB Prevention
1600 Clifton Rd.
Atlanta, GA 30333
1-800-311-3435
http://www.cdc.gov/nchstp/od/nchstp.html
e-mail NCHSTP@cpsod1.em.cdc.gov
Information at this site applies to a general audience.

GOVERNMENT AGENCIES

Centers for Disease Control and Prevention (CDC)
1600 Clifton Rd.
Atlanta, GA 30333
1-800-311-3435
http://www.cdc.gov

Occupational Safety and Health Administration (OSHA)
Office of Public Affairs
200 Constitution Ave., Room N 3647
Washington, DC 20210
202-693-1999
http://www.osha.gov
For general safety and health-related inquiries, contact your OSHA area office or OSHA State Plan Office. To report emergencies, call 1-800-321-OSHA or 1-800-321-6742.

LATEX ALLERGY

American Academy of Family Physicians
http://www.aafp.org/afp

American Latex Allergy Association
http://www.latexallergyresources.org/

Latex Allergy Information Service (LAIS)
176 Roosevelt Ave
Torrington, CT 06790
860-482-6869

UNIVERSAL AND STANDARD PRECAUTIONS

Centers for Disease and Control and Prevention
http://www.cdc.gov/ncidod/hip/BLOOD/UNIVERSA.HTM
http://www.cdc.gov/ncidod/hip/isolat/std_prec_excerpt.htm

MedMedia
www.prenhall.com/frazier

More on this chapter, including interactive resources, can be found on the Student CD-ROM accompanying this textbook and on the Companion Website at www.prenhall.com/frazier.

Objectives

After completing this chapter, you should be able to:

- Spell and define the medical terminology in this chapter.
- Explain the principles of aseptic technique.
- Explain the differences between sanitization, disinfection, and sterilization.
- Describe the process of sanitization.
- Discuss the different types of disinfectants and how they are used in the medical office.
- Discuss the principles of autoclave sterilization.
- Describe how to wrap instruments and prepare sterile trays using sterile technique.
- Discuss the concept of the surgical field.

Surgical Asepsis

Case Study

Ian is preparing to help his physician employer during an in-office surgical procedure. Ian begins by thoroughly washing the Mayo stand, letting it air-dry, and placing the proper covering on it to create a sterile field. He then carefully opens the instruments and lets them drop to the stand. Shea, a coworker, enters the room and tells Ian he has a phone call. Ian drops the last instrument on the table and leaves the room.

When Ian returns, he notices that he is one instrument short for the necessary surgical setup, so he goes to the supply cabinet to get it. Not finding it there, he checks the autoclave machine that has just been run but not emptied. Ian takes the instrument and verifies that the indicator tape has changed color. Upon opening the package, Ian notices some drops of moisture in the hinge area, so he double-checks the package. Again he verifies that the indicator tape has changed color, so he knows the autoclave was run and proceeds to place the instrument on the sterile field.

MedMedia

www.prenhall.com/frazier

Additional interactive resources and activities for this chapter can be found on the Companion Website. For videos, audio glossary, legal and ethical scenarios, job scenarios, quizzes, and games related to the content of this chapter, please access the accompanying CD-ROM in this book.

 **Assets Available:**

Audio Glossary
Legal and Ethical Scenario: *Surgical Asepsis*
On the Job Scenario: *Surgical Asepsis*
Video Scenario: *Medical Waste Disposal; Surgical Fields and Sterile Packets; The Surgical Scrub*
Multiple Choice Quiz
Games: Crossword, Strikeout, and Spelling Bee

Medical Terminology

asepsis, surgical—practice that keeps objects and areas sterile or free from microorganisms using sterile technique

aseptic—without germs (literally, without sepsis)

autoclave—device used to sterilize instruments under steam and pressure

autoclave load—wrapped or unwrapped instruments, packs, and supplies placed in an autoclave to be sterilized

cold sterilization—sterilization with a chemical sterilant, performed when heat cannot be used

debris—organic or inorganic extraneous material that interferes with the proper functioning or cleaning of supplies or equipment

disinfection—method of decontamination that destroys or inhibits pathogenic microorganisms but does not kill spores and some viruses; used sometimes as an alternative to autoclave sterilization.

emesis—vomit

endoscope—fiber-optic instrument used to visualize the internal aspect of the GI tract

germicide—agent used to kill germs

Mayo stand—movable table used for placement of supplies and/or a sterile field during a procedure

noncritical—pertaining to objects that do not touch the patient or touch only intact skin

pH—measurement of hydrogen ion concentration in a substance or solution; a pH of 7.0 is considered neutral, below 7.0 is considered acidic, and above 7.0 is considered alkaline

sanitization—method of decontamination that reduces the numbers of microorganisms on an object or surface; removes organic material from equipment or instruments and must be performed before disinfection and sterilization

spore—capsule formed by some bacteria as a protective shell during their resting state; under favorable conditions the bacteria become active again

sterilant—chemical sterilizing agent

 MEDICAL ASSISTING COMPETENCIES

CAAHEP ENTRY-LEVEL COMPETENCIES FOR CMA	ABHES ENTRY-LEVEL COMPETENCIES FOR RMA
■ Perform hand washing. ■ Wrap items for sterilization. ■ Perform sterilization techniques. ■ Dispose of hazardous materials. ■ Perform maintenance of administrative and clinical equipment. ■ Prepare and maintain examination and treatment areas. ■ Prepare patient for and assist with procedures, treatments, and minor office surgeries.	■ Prepare patients for procedures. ■ Apply principles of aseptic techniques and infection control. ■ Prepare and maintain examination and treatment areas. ■ Prepare patient for and assist physician with routine and specialty examinations and treatments and minor office surgeries. ■ Use quality control. ■ Collect and process specimens. ■ Wrap items for autoclaving. ■ Perform sterilization techniques. ■ Dispose of biohazardous materials. ■ Practice Standard Precautions. ■ Operate and maintain facilities and equipment safely.

Introduction

Surgical asepsis is a very important practice for preventing the transmission of pathogenic microorganisms. Following the correct techniques for sanitization, disinfection, sterilization, and sterile technique, the medical assistant helps to ensure the patient's safety and normal healing and recovery after minor surgeries and treatments.

The Medical Assistant's Role in Surgical Asepsis

During ambulatory surgery and invasive treatments, part of the medical assistant's responsibility is to remember which areas are clean and which are required to be sterile. The physician performs a surgical scrub, then dons a surgical gown, mask, and gloves. The MA usually follows clean technique and is free to obtain more supplies, open sterile supplies but not touch the inside contents of packages, place sterile contents onto the sterile field by drop or sterile transfer forceps, and perform other necessary functions, including preparing specimens for the lab.

COMPETENCY SKILLS PERFORMANCE

1. Demonstrate the performance of sanitization.
2. Demonstrate disinfection procedures.
3. Demonstrate how to wrap surgical instruments and prepare sterile trays for autoclave sterilization.
4. Demonstrate the correct procedure for loading and operating an autoclave.
5. Demonstrate the correct procedure for opening a sterile surgical pack to create a sterile field.
6. Demonstrate the correct procedure for using transfer forceps.
7. Demonstrate a sterile scrub (surgical hand washing).
8. Demonstrate sterile gloving and removal.

Medical Terminology *(continued)*

sterile—free from all living microorganisms and bacterial spores

sterile field—microorganism-free environment used during procedures to prevent contamination by pathogens

sterilization—process of destroying all microbial forms of life, for which the autoclave is most commonly used

sterilization indicator—different forms of tape or inserts (strips or tubes, for exam-

ple) that provide verification of an autoclave's effectiveness

ultrasonic cleaning—use of ultrasound waves to loosen contaminants

Surgical Asepsis

The practice of **surgical asepsis** removes all microorganisms, including **spores**, from objects or designated areas. Removing all microorganisms eliminates all risk of contact with pathogens. Also known as **sterile** or **aseptic** technique, surgical asepsis is used at all times during invasive procedures and when skin integrity is or will be broken—such as during the suturing of a laceration, injections, minor surgical procedures, and the insertion of a catheter into a normally sterile environment. A sterile object remains sterile unless contaminated by violation of sterile procedure. Sterile procedure is breached when a contaminated object touches or crosses a **sterile field.**

The functions of the clinical team can be divided into clean and sterile. It is important that you and other clinical staff remember your roles as either sterile or clean and to function accordingly. (∞ To review medical asepsis, or clean technique, see Chapter 7). Table 8-1 compares the applications and effects of medical and surgical asepsis.

Caduceus Chronicle
THE ORIGINS OF ASEPTIC TECHNIQUE

Pasteurization, a heat process for killing bacteria in milk, is named for Louis Pasteur (1822–1895), who discovered that many diseases are caused by bacteria.

Joseph Lister (1827–1912), an English surgeon, discovered that carbolic acid killed germs. He advocated spraying surgical wound areas, as well as the surgeon's hands and instruments, with carbolic acid. Lister is known as the founder of antiseptic surgery.

TABLE 8-1 COMPARISON OF MEDICAL AND SURGICAL ASEPSIS

Medical Asepsis	Surgical Asepsis
Reduces or controls the numbers of microorganisms	Removes all microorganisms from an object or surface
Follows clean technique—using clean equipment and supplies	Follows sterile technique—using sterile equipment and supplies
Hands are washed or clean gloves worn before supplies and equipment are handled	Surgical scrub performed and sterile gloves donned before supplies and equipment are handled
Equipment and supplies placed on clean field	Equipment and supplies placed on sterile field
Used for noninvasive procedures such as taking vital signs	Used for invasive procedures such as suturing and endoscopic procedures

Sanitization, Disinfection, and Sterilization

Decontamination, the physical or chemical process that removes, inactivates, or destroys pathogenic microorganisms, including bloodborne pathogens, is accomplished by sanitization, disinfection, and/or sterilization.

- **Sanitization** inhibits bacterial growth or inactivates pathogens. It does not destroy microorganisms. It is used to remove organic materials from equipment or instruments.
- **Disinfection** destroys or inhibits pathogenic microorganisms but does not kill spores and some viruses. In addition to cleaning surfaces and equipment used for noninvasive procedures, it is also used to clean some invasive equipment that may be damaged by sterilization in an **autoclave.**
- **Sterilization** destroys all living forms of microorganisms, including spores. Using a sterile field for invasive procedures creates a microorganism-free environment that prevents contamination by pathogens.

Sanitization

After each patient examination or treatment, the treatment room must be sanitized and disinfected to prevent the transfer of microorganisms to other patients. Supplies and equipment with the potential for direct or indirect patient contact are sanitized by manual scrubbing with a neutral-**pH** detergent, using a brush if necessary, followed by hot water rinsing and air drying. Items not sanitized immediately after use are soaked according to the manufacturer's directions.

Instruments may also be sanitized by ultrasound. In **ultrasonic cleaning**, sound waves are used to loosen contaminants, and then the articles are rinsed. Because instruments are handled less, this method may be considered safer. However, because the instruments must not touch each other and different types of metal may not be placed in the same load, fewer instruments may be sanitized at one time and the process may take longer.

Keys to Success
CONTAMINATED OR NOT CONTAMINATED?

It is the responsibility of medical assistants and other clinical staff to consider an area or object contaminated if there is any doubt it is a sterile environment. In this situation, the correct action would be decontamination to create the required clean and/or sterile environment. To neglect action would be to risk patient and employee health.

PROCEDURE 8-1 Sanitization

Theory

After a minor surgery or treatment, rinse or soak the instruments immediately to prevent body tissue or fluids from drying on them. Take the used instruments from the treatment room to the cleaning area in a towel-covered basin. Add disinfectant to the basin after transporting the instruments to minimize spill hazards.

In compliance with OSHA's Bloodborne Pathogen Standards, you must wear gloves when handling contaminated instruments. Wear utility gloves over disposable gloves to protect your hands from chemicals and to add another barrier when cleaning sharp instruments.

Before using the cleaning agent or detergent, check the expiration date. An expired solution is not guaranteed to inactivate or reduce microorganisms. Read the product's MSDS safety precautions, such as the use of PPE, mixing, storage, and cleaning accidental spills. If the resulting mixture is too weak, microorganisms may not be reduced or removed effectively. If the mixture is too strong, skin contact or inhalation may be harmful.

Holding one instrument at a time, carefully use the scrubbing brush (nylon for the instrument surface and stainless steel for grooves, cracks, or serrated edges) to remove organic materials from all areas. Autoclaving does not sterilize any areas in which organic materials remain. Use a neutral-pH detergent to prevent staining the instruments. Thoroughly rinse off the detergent to prevent stains and deterioration, which could later interfere with the function of the instrument. Avoid dropping instruments, which could damage or impair their function. When the instruments are clean and dry, inspect them individually for defects and proper working function.

Materials for Manual Sanitization
- Contaminated instruments
- Basin for soaking instruments
- Examination gloves
- Utility gloves
- Neutral low-suds detergent
- Scrubbing brush
- Paper towel
- Cotton towel

Competency for Manual Sanitization

(**Conditions**) With the necessary supplies, (**Task**) you will be able to manually clean and sanitize instruments (**Standards**) correctly and safely, within the time frame designated by your instructor.

1. With examination and utility gloves on your hands, place the contaminated instruments in an empty basin, cover it with a cotton towel, and transport it to the cleaning area (Figure 8-1 ◆). Remove the towel and add disinfectant or water with detergent to the basin. After the patient is discharged, clean, disinfect, and supply the room for the next patient.
2. In the instrument cleaning area, drain off the disinfectant or detergent and remove the instruments. Carefully wipe away blood and/or any tissue **debris.** Hold the instruments by their finger openings when possible.
3. Place the instruments in a basin with the recommended amount of cleaning agent and water.
4. Cleaning one instrument at a time, use a soft brush on all serrated and smooth edges, grooves, and opened hinges (Figure 8-2 ◆).
5. Rinse all the instruments with hot water.
6. Dry each instrument with a paper towel and allow to air-dry completely on a cotton towel (Figure 8-3 ◆). Lubricate the hinges with a water-based lubricant.
7. Follow the manufacturer's directions for disposing of cleaning solution. *Do not reuse.*
8. Remove the gloves and wash your hands.
9. Inspect each instrument for defects and proper function. Package the instruments as needed to ready for sterilization

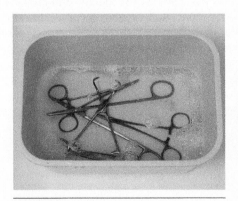

Figure 8-1 ◆ Place the contaminated instruments in an empty basin.

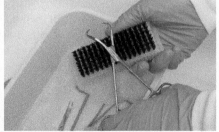

Figure 8-2 ◆ Use a soft brush on all serrated and smooth edges, grooves, and opened hinges.

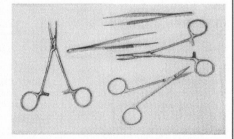

Figure 8-3 ◆ Allow instruments to air dry completely on a cotton towel.

PROCEDURE 8-1 Sanitization *(continued)*

Materials for Ultrasonic Sanitization
- Ultrasonic cleaner
- Ultrasonic cleaning solution
- Examination gloves
- Utility gloves
- Paper towel
- Cotton towel

Competency for Ultrasonic Sanitization

(**Conditions**) With the necessary supplies, (**Task**) you will be able to clean and sanitize instruments with ultrasonic equipment (**Standards**) correctly and safely.

1. With examination and utility gloves on your hands, prepare the cleaning solution for the ultrasonic cleaner as directed by the manufacturer. Observe all MSDS safety and accidental spill precautions.
2. Place instruments made of different metals in separate ultrasonic cleaning loads.
3. Place the instruments in the ultrasonic cleaner with their hinges open and sharp edges not touching other instruments. Make sure that all the instruments are covered with the ultrasonic cleaning solution (Figure 8-4 ◆). Turn on the ultrasonic cleaner.
4. When the recommended cleaning time has passed, remove the instruments and rinse each one with hot tap water.
5. Dry each instrument with a paper towel and allow to air-dry completely on a cotton towel. Lubricate the hinges with a water-based lubricant.

6. Follow the manufacturer's directions for changing the cleaning solution.
7. Remove the gloves and wash your hands.
8. Inspect each instrument for defects and proper function. Package the instruments as needed to ready for sterilization.

A

B

Figure 8-4 ◆ (A) Correctly position the instruments in the ultrasonic cleaner; (B) Make sure all instruments are covered in the cleaning solution.

Disinfection

Disinfection is the second level of microbial control and the second step of the sterilization procedure. Disinfection can destroy or inhibit pathogens but cannot kill spores and some viruses. It is accomplished by soaking in chemicals called **germicides,** by steam, or by boiling water. Chemical disinfectants are used to clean plastic and rubber items, floors, and furniture. Depending on the chemical and the manufacturer's instructions, immersion time can vary, up to several hours or more.

There are three levels of disinfection.

- Low-level disinfection kills most bacteria and viruses but does not kill microorganisms such as tuberculosis bacilli or bacterial spores. It is typically used for surfaces such as examination tables, countertops, and walls.
- Intermediate-level disinfection kills mycobacteria, most viruses and bacteria, and tuberculosis bacilli, but cannot kill bacterial spores. It is used for articles that come in contact with skin but not with mucous membranes, such as blood pressure cuffs and stethoscopes.

- High-level disinfection kills all microorganisms except bacterial spores. It is used for articles that come in contact with mucous membranes, such as those in the oral cavity, throat, and vagina. Flexible sigmoidoscopes and glass thermometers require high-level disinfection.

Noncritical items are those that do not touch the patient or touch only intact skin, such as crutches, blood pressure cuffs, and gooseneck lamps. These items are not usually involved in transmitting disease. Washing noncritical items with a detergent or low-level disinfectant is sufficient. If these items are contaminated with blood or body fluids, stronger disinfection measures, sterilization, or biohazardous disposal are mandatory.

After soaking in disinfectant, items are thoroughly rinsed. Some disinfectants can only be used on inanimate objects, but alcohol and Betadine are used to disinfect a patient's skin before a procedure is performed. Chemical disinfectants for soaking or wiping include 70% isopropyl alcohol, bleach, phenol, formaldehyde, hydrogen peroxide, and soap. Items that cannot be entirely soaked, such as **endoscopes,** must be

TABLE 8-2 COMMON DISINFECTANTS USED IN THE MEDICAL OFFICE

Disinfectant	Level of Disinfection	Common Names and Uses
Chlorine and compounds	Low	Sodium hypochlorite, also known as household bleach. Recommended by OSHA to clean blood spills. Used also as a surface disinfectant. Usually diluted to 1 part bleach to 10 parts water.
Phenolics	Low	Carbolic acid, phenylic acid, phenyl hydroxide, phenic acid, hydroxybenzene, hexachlorophene, Lysol. Used as a surface disinfectant.
Hydrogen peroxide	Low	Hydrogen peroxide. Used to clean objects or surfaces not intended for human contact.
Alcohol		
Isopropyl	Low to intermediate	Isopropyl alcohol. Used to disinfect rubber tops of vials, stethoscopes, percussion hammers.
Ethyl	High	Ethyl alcohol. Used to clean glass thermometers.
Glutaraldehyde	High	Cidex, Cidex Plus, Glutarex, Metricide, Procide, Omnicide, Wavicide. Can also be used as a chemical sterilant. As a disinfectant, is used to clean glass thermometers and flexible sigmoidoscopes.

wiped with disinfectant, and removable parts must be soaked in disinfectant or sterilized according to the manufacturer's directions.

Sodium Hypochlorite

Sodium hypochlorite is also known as household bleach. It is a low-level disinfectant used mostly to disinfect surfaces. It is effective against many microorganisms, including human immunodeficiency virus (HIV) and hepatitis B virus. It is also very inexpensive to use.

Phenolics

Phenolics are used to clean countertops, walls, floors, and furniture. Because of the corrosive nature of this group, it may be necessary to wear PPE to protect the eyes and skin.

Alcohol

Two types of alcohol are used in the medical office—isopropyl alcohol and ethyl alcohol. Isopropyl is used to clean the rubber tops of vials, such as those used for medication, and for stethoscopes and percussion hammers. Ethyl alcohol is used to clean mercury glass thermometers. Stronger concentrations of alcohol are not as effective as 70% because the absence of water decreases their effectiveness. Because alcohol can dissolve the cement used to hold lenses in instruments, it should not be used to clean endoscopes.

Glutaraldehyde

Glutaraldehyde is rapid acting and requires only 10 to 30 minutes for disinfection. It is not corrosive and can be used for rubber or metal materials and for disinfecting lenses. The presence of organic material does not inactivate glutaraldehyde as it often does with other disinfectants.

Hydrogen Peroxide

Although hydrogen peroxide is used to clean wounds, it can also be used as a disinfectant for objects or surfaces that are not used for human contact. As a disinfectant it should be used with caution as it may damage some metals and some rubber or plastic surfaces.

Table 8-2 summarizes the types of disinfectant and their uses in the medical office.

Sterilization

Sterilization is the third method of microbial control. All microorganisms, including spores, are killed by steam, dry heat, or chemical sterilization. The physical nature of the material determines the type of sterilization used. Because autoclave steam can damage certain materials, chemicals or dry heat may be used instead. In addition, some dense items require the use of dry heat. Items must first undergo sanitization and sometimes disinfection before they are sterilized.

Autoclave Sterilization

The autoclave consists of two separate compartments (Figure 8-7 ◆). An outer compartment surrounds the inner sterilizing chamber. Reducing the air in the inner chamber allows air pressure to build to 15 pounds of pressure per square inch. This pressure causes the distilled water in the chamber to reach a temperature of 250 degrees F, at which point it converts to steam. The steam penetrates the wrappers on the instruments and kills all microorganisms and bacterial spores. The high temperature of the steam must be maintained for over 15 minutes to assure the death of all living organism in the autoclave.

Certain guidelines for the use of autoclaves in the physician's office must be followed.

- *Location:* The autoclave must be on a level surface, close to the electrical outlet, with the front of the autoclave near the front of the support surface and providing a surface for the drain tube to drain.
- *Filling and loading:* The water must contain no minerals; therefore, distilled water is always used. The reservoir should be filled to the level indicated in the manual. Objects and packs must be properly loaded to ensure adequate steam penetration and air circulation.
- *Timing:* The processing must be timed once the desired pressure and temperature are reached. The sterilizing time is determined by the items to be sterilized (Table 8-3).

PROCEDURE 8-2 **Disinfection**

Theory

All instruments to be sterilized must first undergo sanitization, then disinfection. When performed correctly, sanitization removes all organic materials and prepares instruments for effective disinfection. All organic material must be completely removed for the disinfectant to reach all areas of the article or instrument. Instruments must be dried thoroughly before they are placed in the disinfectant, as any water may dilute the chemical disinfectant.

Before you proceed with the disinfection of contaminated articles, read the MSDS for the disinfectant. Look for general information regarding potential hazards, how to clean accidental spills, and which PPE to wear. Disposable gloves serve as a protective barrier against potentially infectious materials or contaminated instruments such as blood or body tissue. Additional utility gloves protect the skin from the irritating chemicals used for disinfection. Before you move the basin containing the contaminated instruments to another room, cover it with a cotton towel.

Materials

- Contaminated articles
- MSDS
- Disposable gloves
- Utility gloves
- Chemical disinfectant
- Soaking container
- Paper towels
- Cotton towel

Competency

(**Conditions**) With the necessary supplies, (**Task**) you will be able to perform the steps of disinfection (**Standards**) correctly and safely.

1. Review the MSDS, noting potential hazards, how to clean accidental spills, and whether PPE should be worn.
2. Apply disposable gloves to place the contaminated items into the basin. Then apply an additional layer of utility gloves.
3. Complete the sanitizing steps in Procedure 8-1. Remember to cover the basin of contaminated instruments with a cloth towel when you move them to the cleaning area.
4. Check the expiration date of the disinfectant and follow the manufacturer's directions for mixing and use (Figure 8-5 ◆).
5. With gloves on, completely immerse the contaminated articles in the container of disinfectant (Figure 8-6 ◆). Cover the container and soak the instruments for the length of time recommended by the manufacturer.
6. Remove and rinse each instrument thoroughly. Dry the instruments with paper towels.
7. Place the disinfected instruments on muslin or into sterilizing packets for the autoclave.

Figure 8-5 ◆ Follow the manufacturer's directions for mixing and use of the disinfectant.

Figure 8-6 ◆ Completely immerse the contaminated articles in the container of disinfectant.

Once the proper time has elapsed, the autoclave controls are turned to off and the pressure is allowed to return to normal. At that point the door of the autoclave is opened and air is allowed to circulate within the inner chamber until the items inside are dry. Then they can be safely removed and stored.

 — Critical Thinking Question 8-1—

In the case study, is the surgical instrument that Ian placed last, with noticeable moisture on it, considered sterile? Could the moisture possibly indicate that the autoclave is not working properly or that the cycle was not completed properly?

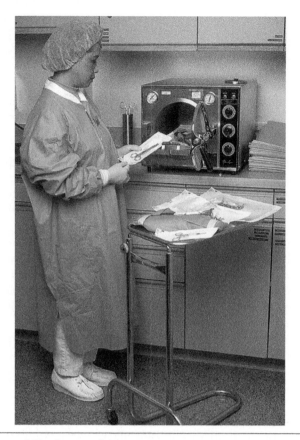

Figure 8-7 ◆ An autoclave

TABLE 8-3 MINIMUM TIME REQUIREMENTS FOR AUTOCLAVE STERILIZATION

Time	Articles
15 minutes	Unwrapped metal instruments on open tray, hinges open Open glassware or metal containers Needles and unassembled syringes Unwrapped rubber tubing
20 minutes	Wrapped or covered instruments Muslin fabric Wrapped rubber products such as tubing and catheters
30 minutes	Instrument packs wrapped in muslin or paper Syringes unassembled and wrapped in gauze or glass tubes Needles packaged individually in gauze or paper Sutures, needles, and materials wrapped in muslin or paper Dressings, loosely packed Liquids or semiliquids

Note: These times apply to the manual operation of an autoclave.

In automatic autoclaves, the sterilization countdown begins when 250 degrees F (121 degrees C) and 15 pounds of pressure per square inch have been reached.

Whether you use manual or automatic settings, follow the manufacturer's directions for operation, maintenance, cleaning, and recommended sterilization times. The autoclave should be cleaned with a manufacturer-recommended detergent and rinsed thoroughly so that it is free from lint or debris

before each load. Check all discharge lines, valves, and vents to eliminate the possibility of obstructions. Check the seals to make sure there are no cracks. Learn how to read the gauges for the outside jacket pressure, inner chamber pressure, timer, and temperature.

To ensure sterility quality, the Centers for Disease Control and Prevention (CDC) recommends keeping thorough records of all loads and quality control measures. Details of each load, such as operator, date, time, description, sterilization exposure time, and results of sterilization indicators are recorded. If there is an automatic printout for each sterilization cycle, that should be kept. Policies should also be established for regular monitoring by outside agencies—for instance, by sending samples from an **autoclave load** to a testing agency.

Other Methods of Sterilization

In addition to the autoclave, sterilization methods include the following.

■ The dry heat oven is used to sterilize items that are harmed by steam or cannot be penetrated by steam. For example, steam sterilization dulls needles and sharps, erodes ground glass, and does not penetrate substances such as petroleum jelly. Dry heat ovens operate like household ovens. Items are placed in protective foil before sterilization.

■ **Cold sterilization** involves immersion in a chemical agent for a specified period of time, usually 6 to 24 hours. Whenever an instrument is added, the timing must be restarted. Because cold sterilization can harm instruments

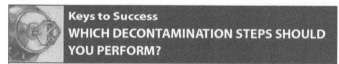

Keys to Success
WHICH DECONTAMINATION STEPS SHOULD YOU PERFORM?

Consider the following implements: bandage scissors, used **emesis** basin, sphygmomanometer, and suture removal scissors.

■ The bandage scissors are multipurpose and used in clean procedures. They are sanitized between patient uses.

■ The emesis basin can be reused by the same patient (after the emesis has been discarded and the container rinsed). Before it can be used by another patient, it must be sanitized, disinfected, and sterilized.

■ Sphygmomanometers are normally used with a number of patients without special cleaning. However, if a patient is very diaphoretic, the sphygmomanometer may need to be wiped with disinfectant, and in certain cases a disposable cuff may be used.

■ Suture scissors are used in sterile procedures to avoid introducing microorganisms to healed wounds.

To decide which steps are appropriate in the cleaning process, determine whether the procedure to be performed is dirty, clean, or sterile. For example, a dirty procedure involves instruments or equipment that are clean but not sterile or disinfected, such as a clean towel or a clean ace bandage. A clean procedure would require equipment or instruments that have been sanitized and disinfected. A sterile procedure requires equipment and instruments that have been sanitized, disinfected, and sterilized. Always follow product instructions.

and processing time must be periodically restarted, it is used only when other recommended methods of sterilization are not available.

■ Radiation is used only when heat or chemical sterilizing methods cannot be used. In this method, ionizing radiation is the sterilizing agent.

■ Heat-sensitive items or prepackaged instruments or equipment can be sterilized with ethylene oxide gas. These include plastic and rubber articles such as catheters and syringes. Because the process is complicated and expensive, it is not used in the medical office.

Wrapping Instruments and Preparing Sterile Trays

Procedures for wrapping instruments and preparing sterile trays vary from one medical office to another according to the clinical practice and physician preference. For example, packaging sterile hemostats and suture kits may be similar in all settings. However, some clinical settings may require sterile instrument packaging for Pap smears, and others may require sterile packaging for cataract surgery. In addition to the information in this chapter and in specialty chapters later in the text, you will incorporate specific applications in the clinical setting in which you work.

Table 8-4 lists examples of sterile tray packaging. Instruments may be wrapped individually or in packages. All instruments must be sanitized before sterilization. **Sterilization indicators** verify that a package or instrument has been placed in the autoclave, that steam heat has reached the inside of each package, and that sterilization has been achieved (Figure 8-8 ◆). Sterilizing tape is used on the outside of packages, with stripes that turn dark when a package has been sterilized.

A

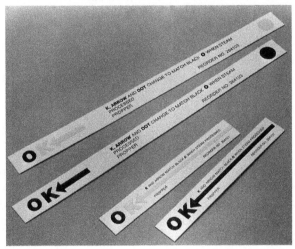

B

Figure 8-8 ◆ (A) Autoclave indicator tapes; (B) Sterility check strips
Reprinted by permission of Propper Manufacturing Co., Inc.

Preparing the Surgical Field

A surgical field is an area that is considered sterile. Sterile towels or sterile drapes on a table or tray provide a sterile field on which instruments and suture material can be placed. The wrapping of a sterile surgical pack may also provide a sterile or surgical field when it is opened.

You will use sterile supplies to prepare a sterile field by opening the surgical pack, adding to the surgical field, and sterile gloving. It is your responsibility and that of others involved in the sterile procedure to follow sterile field guidelines to prevent contamination and the potential transfer of microorganisms (Table 8-5, p. 106). If sterile technique is breached during an invasive procedure, the patient may be harmed and the medical office and clinical staff may be held liable.

? — Critical Thinking Question 8-2 —
Ian left the room to take a phone call after dropping one last instrument on the sterile field. When he reenters the room, is the setup still considered sterile?

TABLE 8-4 EXAMPLES OF STERILE TRAY PACKAGING FOR DIFFERENT PROCEDURES		
Incision and Drainage (I&D)	**Biopsy**	**Vasectomy**
Kelly hemostat	Hemostats	Scalpel handle and
Scalpel handle	Scalpel handle	blade (no. 15)
and blades (no. 11)	and blades	Curved mosquito
Tissue forceps	(nos. 10 and 15)	forceps
Thumb dressing forceps	Tissue forceps	Straight forceps
Curved iris scissors	Thumb dressing	Dressing forceps
Retractor	forceps	Suture scissors
4 × 4 gauze	Splinter forceps	Suture materials and
	Blunt probe	needles
	Suture materials	Retractor
	and needles	Towel clamps
	Needle holder	4 × 4 gauze
	Retractor	
	4 × 4 gauze	

PROCEDURE 8-3 Wrapping Surgical Instruments for Autoclave Sterilization

Theory

Some instruments that are used immediately or used in procedures that do not require sterilized instruments do not require wrapping. These instruments may be placed in an autoclaving tray. For other instruments, single or variety groups must be packaged for the appropriate procedure. Whenever possible, sterilize items in small packs that steam can penetrate more easily.

Materials used to package instruments for sterilization include porous plastic, paper, and fabric. Porous materials allow the moisture and heat to penetrate and sterilize the package contents. Muslin fabric is the most commonly used wrapping material. A sealer may have to be purchased for some types of plastic packaging.

Place instruments in the center of the wrapping material and alternate with any dressing materials required for the procedure. Position the instruments in such a way as to prevent metal-to-metal contact within the pack. Hinged instruments should be slightly open to allow for steam penetration and sterilization. Place the inside sterilization indicator tape within the package before folding and/or sealing the package.

Double-back folding is an important step in wrapping. Later, when you open the package to create a sterile field, it will provide edges to grab and help to prevent contamination. Place sterilization indicator tape across the last folded edge and write on the tape the type of tray and the expiration date. Each office has a specific policy concerning expiration dates—for example, sterilized packages may be used for up to one month after the autoclave date. Using an expired package would not guarantee sterility.

Materials

- Dry wrapping paper, muslin cloth, or sealable bags
- Sanitized and disinfected items to be sterilized
- Sterilization indicators for interior and exterior of packages
- Marker pen

Competency

(**Conditions**) With the necessary supplies, (**Task**) you will be able to package and wrap instruments and supplies to be placed in the autoclave (**Standards**) correctly, in the time designated by your instructor.

1. Place the sanitized items to be sterilized in the center of the dry wrapping paper, muslin, or sealable bag. Place an indicator tape inside the package (Figure 8-9 ◆). The sealable bag may need to be sealed if it is not manufacturer-prepared.
2. For cloth or paper packaging, fold up one corner to cover the items. Double-back a small fold to use as a pull corner for unwrapping (Figure 8-10 ◆). Do the same fold and double-back fold for the right side and left side. Fold the last side once toward the center and tuck the corner under before applying sterilization indicator tape (Figures 8-11 ◆ and 8-12 ◆).
3. Use the marker to label the tape with the date and contents.

Figure 8-9 ◆ Place the sanitized items in the center of the dry wrapping paper.

Figure 8-10 ◆ Double-back a small fold to use as a pull corner for unwrapping.

Figure 8-11 ◆ Do the same fold and double-back fold for the right side and left side.

Figure 8-12 ◆ Apply the sterilization indicator tape.

PROCEDURE 8-4 Loading and Operating an Autoclave

Theory

Sanitization and disinfection remove organic and inorganic debris from instruments before sterilization in the autoclave. Sterilization is the last defense against pathogenic bacteria.

The autoclave reservoir is filled with distilled water to produce steam for sterilization. Using distilled water prevents mineral corrosion inside the autoclave and mineral deposits that might block the air exhaust valves. Air pockets, created when the autoclave reservoir is emptied of water, can reduce the temperature during the sterilization process. To prevent air pockets, it is an important daily routine to fill the reservoir at the beginning of every day or every load, depending on the frequency of autoclave use.

The autoclave must be loaded correctly to ensure steam penetration and complete sterilization. Steam must reach all surfaces for the required time and at the required temperature to kill all microorganisms. Loading guidelines include the following.

- Position packs and instruments loosely in the inner chamber to allow steam to circulate, penetrate all porous materials, and make contact with all surfaces. Larger packs should be spaced 2 to 4 inches apart, and smaller packs 1 to 3 inches apart.
- Sterilization pouches should be placed on their sides, rather than flat, to allow better steam penetration and drying. Containers should also be placed on their sides, with their lids removed to allow air to escape. Trapped air in a side-lying container would prevent the steam from reaching all surfaces. Dressing packs should be arranged in a vertical position to allow the steam to penetrate each layer.
- Avoid leaning any item against plastic, as the heat will mold the plastic to the shape of the object.

Once the autoclave has been loaded, follow the operating instructions. As a safety measure, make sure the steam pressure has been automatically or manually released before you start the autoclave. Otherwise pressure in the inner chamber can "pop" the door open suddenly and forcefully and cause injury. Newer models are designed to keep the pressurized chamber door from opening this way. Be sure to read the instruction manual.

Sterilization time begins when the correct pressure and temperature have been reached. (See Table 8-3 for recommended sterilizing times.)

Remove the dry packs with heat-resistant gloves. Packs are considered contaminated if they are removed while wet or damp, if they are torn or have holes, or if the indicator tape color has not changed.

Materials

- Wrapped or unwrapped sanitized and disinfected instruments
- Distilled water
- Heat-resistant gloves
- Manual or automatic autoclave
- Manufacturer's instruction manual
- Sterile transfer forceps
- Storage containers or shelf areas

Competency

(**Conditions**) With the necessary supplies, (**Task**) you will be able to load and operate an autoclave correctly and safely (**Standards**) to ensure complete sterilization.

1. Wash your hands and assemble materials.
2. Check the level of distilled water in the autoclave reservoir and fill as necessary (Figure 8-13 ◆).
3. Load the autoclave, asking yourself the following questions:
   Are the autoclave trays 1 inch apart?
   Are small packs 1 to 3 inches apart?
   Are large packs 2 to 4 inches apart?
   Are any of the packs touching the inside of the autoclave chamber?
   Are glassware and jars on their sides?
   Are dressings and sterilization pouches in a vertical position, on their sides?
   Are any materials leaning against plastic items?
   For a mixed load of porous and nonporous materials, are materials such as dressings on the top shelf and instruments on the lower shelf?
4. Close and latch the door. Turn on the autoclave (Figure 8-14◆).
5. Sterilization time starts when the correct pressure and temperature have been reached.
6. After steam pressure has been manually or automatically released, open the autoclave door slightly to allow the load

Figure 8-13 ◆ Fill the reservoir as necessary.

Figure 8-14 ◆ Turn on the autoclave.

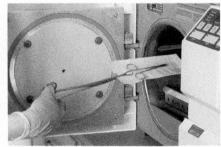

Figure 8-15 ◆ Remove instruments to a clean container using the sterile transfer forceps.

continued

PROCEDURE 8-4 **Loading and Operating an Autoclave** *(continued)*

to dry. Larger packs with dressings may take 45 to 60 minutes to dry.

7. Wearing heat-resistant gloves, remove the dry packages. Inspect for holes, tears, and indicator tape color change. Use the sterile transfer forceps to remove single instruments or items to a clean container (Figure 8-15 ◆). Place sterile items toward the back of the stock so that the oldest

dated materials are used first. Avoid storing in cool areas that may cause condensation, make the materials damp, and require additional wrapping and sterilizing.

8. Remove the gloves and wash your hands.

9. Record the date, autoclave load contents, and use of sterilization indicators and quality controls in the sterilization log book.

TABLE 8-5 GUIDELINES FOR A STERILE FIELD

- Never reach, lean, or pass over a sterile field. The air above a sterile field is considered sterile.
- Sterile areas should be set up away from areas with potential air currents such as doors, windows, and fans to avoid the transfer of microorganisms.
- Never cough, sneeze, or talk over a sterile field. Moisture droplets will contaminate the sterile air and sterile field.
- Wet areas on the sterile field lead to contamination. Depending on the extent of a spill, the area may be covered or a new sterile field may need to be created.
- Movement around the sterile field should be minimal and purposeful. Always face the sterile field and keep your arms above waist level. An extra sterile drape or towel can be kept close by for those times you may have to turn your back on the sterile field or leave the room.
- Place all items toward the center of the sterile field. Anything in the 1-inch perimeter is considered contaminated because of its proximity to clothing or other nonsterile work surfaces.

Keys to Success
THE IMPORTANCE OF CLEANING INSTRUMENTS PROPERLY

What happens when a pathogenic outbreak is identified? In cooperation with the CDC, the local Public Health Department investigates each patient history for common factors. For example, did the patients eat at the same restaurant, go to the same medical office, use the same bathroom, or receive the same procedure at the same medical office? Microorganism cultures may be taken of food samples, disinfected or sterilized medical instruments, bathroom faucets, toilet handles, and so on.

Once the cause of the outbreak is determined, actions are taken to eliminate the possibility of recurrence. This might involve, but is not limited to, temporary or permanent closing of the facility, resterilization of items thought to be sterilized, and treatment of persons who might harbor the pathogen. If patients have been harmed during a procedure, malpractice lawsuits may be filed against the facility and all persons involved in the procedure or the cleaning of instruments, including the medical assistant.

Sometimes sterile solutions for irrigation, infusion, or injection must be added to the sterile field, or vials must be ready for the withdrawal of medication. Certain techniques are followed for pouring solutions and withdrawing medication to prevent contamination of the sterile field.

- If a solution is to be added, the physician holds the sterile container just beyond the edge of the sterile field and the MA palms the label of the solution, pours some solution into a trash receptacle or sink, then pours the rest into the sterile container (Figures 8-16 ◆ and 8-17 ◆).

Palming the label before pouring avoids staining the label and making it difficult to read.

- If the physician needs to withdraw local anesthetic from a vial, the MA, with clean or gloved hands, uses an alcohol prep pad to clean the vial top, then holds the vial upside down just outside the sterile field with the label facing the physician so that the physician can verify it is the correct solution. The physician uses a sterile syringe and needle from the sterile field to withdraw medication.

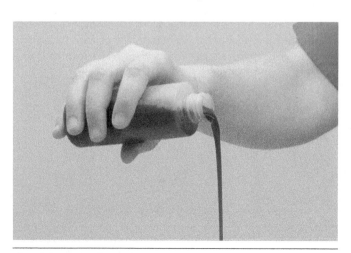

Figure 8-16 ◆ Palm the label.

Figure 8-17 ◆ Pour the remaining solution into the sterile container.

PROCEDURE 8-5 Opening a Sterile Surgical Pack to Create a Sterile Field

Theory

Creating a sterile field involves using "no-touch" sterile techniques. The first step is to adjust the height of the **Mayo stand** to provide a comfortable working level, prevent back strain, and help maintain a sterile field.

After noting the expiration date on the primary sterile surgical pack and determining that it is usable, open the pack. Lift the top flap away from your body to prevent contamination from reaching or crossing over the sterile field as the rest of the flaps are opened. Next, open the side flaps, then the last flap. In addition to the surgical pack contents, you should have already gathered other supplies, such as appropriate-size sterile gloves, suture materials, needles, instruments, dressings, and basins.

At all times during the opening and preparation of the sterile field, *do not* allow any part of your body or clothing to touch the sterile field. Touching the sterile field, even with clean clothing or skin, would result in contamination and the need to prepare a new sterile field. If additional supplies are needed, another person may open the outer pack while the sterile-gloved physician or medical assistant takes the sterile contents inside. Or the outer wrapping of the package may be opened and the items dropped on the sterile field. When all items are on the sterile field, they can be moved with transfer forceps or sterile gloves. A sterile cotton towel or drape is used to cover the completed sterile field.

Materials

- Mayo stand
- Sterile packet(s)
- Sterile transfer forceps
- Sterile gloves
- Sterile towels or drapes
- Waste container

Competency

(**Conditions**) With the necessary supplies, (**Task**) you will be able to use sterile technique to open a sterile surgical pack for a sterile field (**Standards**) correctly within the time frame designated by your instructor.

1. Wash your hands and assemble the equipment.
2. Adjust the height of the Mayo stand to a comfortable working position.
3. Position the sterile surgical pack on the Mayo stand so that the top flap will open away from you (Figure 8-18 ◆).
4. Remove the sterilization indicator tape from the pack, note whether the appropriate color change occurred to indicate sterility, and discard.
5. Pull the top flap away from you and down to hang over the edge of the Mayo stand. Pull each of the side flaps away from the packet and over the edge (Figure 8-19 ◆).
6. Without reaching over the sterile field, bring the last flap toward you and down to hang over the edge. Do not touch your body to any part of the sterile field while opening the pack or anytime during a sterile procedure.
7. The inside of the pack is now the sterile field.
   - To move items on the sterile field, use sterile transfer forceps

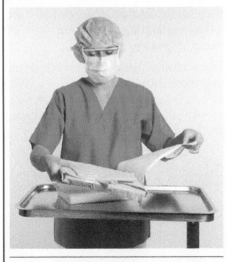

Figure 8-18 ◆ Position the sterile surgical pack on the Mayo stand.

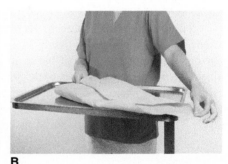

Figure 8-19 ◆ (A) Pull the top flap away from you and down to hang over the edge of the Mayo stand; (B) Pull each of the side flaps away from the packet and over the edge.

continued

PROCEDURE 8-5 Opening a Sterile Surgical Pack to Create a Sterile Field *(continued)*

- To add items to a sterile field, open other packages without touching the inner side of the package or contents, then dump the contents on the sterile field without crossing or touching it (Figure 8-20 ◆).
- To open the inner package of another sterile surgical pack during the procedure, a person with clean hands may open the outer package so that a person with sterile gloves may take the inner packet of instruments and supplies (Figure 8-21 ◆).

8. Cover the tray with sterile towels or drape until ready to use. Open a pack of sterile gloves and a pack of sterile drapes or towels, then put on the sterile gloves to unfold the drape or towel over the sterile field (Figure 8-22 ◆). Some sterile packets come with material for draping the sterile field.

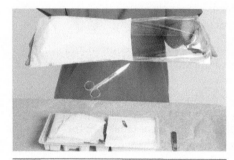

Figure 8-20 ◆ Place the contents of another package on sterile field without crossing or touching it.

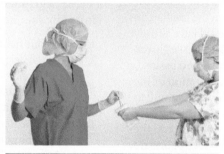

Figure 8-21 ◆ Another person wearing sterile gloves takes inner packet of instruments out.

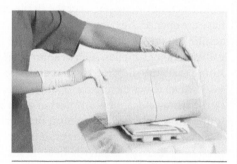

Figure 8-22 ◆ Place the drape or towel over the sterile field.

PROCEDURE 8-6 Using Transfer Forceps

Theory

The 1-inch perimeter around the outside of a sterile field is considered contaminated and is therefore kept empty of supplies or instruments. Sterile items must be placed toward the center of the sterile field. Only transfer forceps can be used to move items onto or within the sterile field. The forceps are kept in a container of chemical **sterilant.** The handles are clean and may be touched, but the jaws and tips are considered sterile.

Remove the transfer forceps vertically from the container, holding the handles firmly while keeping the tips together. Touching the sides of the container could contaminate the tips. Prepare an open package of 4 × 4s to dry the transfer forceps by contact and prevent dripping onto the sterile field. Transfer forceps must be cleaned and autoclaved weekly. The sterilant solution should also be changed weekly.

Materials

- Transfer forceps
- Sterile tray set up on a Mayo stand
- Forceps container 2/3 full of Cidex or other sterilant
- Sterile 4 × 4 gauze package
- Instrument or supply pack for use with sterile transfer forceps

Competency

(**Conditions**) With the necessary supplies, (**Task**) you will be able to move sterile instruments and supplies within a sterile field, onto a sterile field, or into a sterile gloved hand (**Standards**) without contaminating and within the time frame designated by your instructor.

1. Open the 4 × 4 gauze package using sterile technique and lay it on the countertop or Mayo stand.
2. Grasp the forceps handles, keeping the tips together. Remove the forceps vertically from the container without touching the sides (Figure 8-23 ◆).

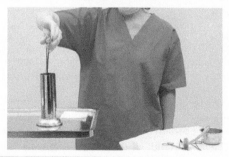

Figure 8-23 ◆ Remove forceps from the container without touching the sides.

PROCEDURE 8-6 Using Transfer Forceps *(continued)*

3. Touch the forceps tips to the 4 × 4s to dry them. Do not allow the forceps to touch the sterile field. Holding them vertically, pick up and move an item from the open pack to the sterile field. To move a sterile item on the sterile field, keep the forceps vertical, pick up the item, and lift it to the desired location without touching the sterile field (Figure 8-24 ◆).
4. Place the transfer forceps back into the standing container without touching the sides.

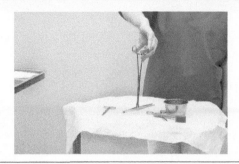

Figure 8-24 ◆ Keep the forceps vertical, pick up the item, and lift it to the desired location without touching the sterile field.

PROCEDURE 8-7 Performing a Sterile Scrub (Surgical Hand Washing)

Theory

Medical hand washing, recognized simply as hand washing, is required for most procedures in the clinical setting. Hand washing reduces the numbers of microorganisms and the possibility of cross-infection between staff and patients. For example, it is performed first thing in the morning before patient care, between patients, and after using the bathroom. Some procedures, because of their invasive nature or the lowered immunity of the patient, require surgical hand washing, or a sterile scrub.

Before beginning a sterile scrub, gather supplies. Open the sterile towel pack away from the splash area of the faucets to prevent moisture contamination of the sterile towel that you will use to dry your hands after the second rinse. You will need a clock or watch to time the first and second scrubs—5 minutes and 3 minutes respectively for each hand. Remove all jewelry. Microorganisms are likely to hide around jewelry sites, under the fingernails, and between the fingers. (It is best to leave jewelry at home; however, you may secure it to your uniform top.)

The general order of the procedure is:

■ Wetting
■ Scrubbing
■ Rinsing
■ Second scrubbing
■ Second rinsing
■ Drying

Start with your fingers and proceed to your hands, wrists, and lower arms. The second scrub and rinse are a precautionary measure to ensure the elimination of as many microorganisms as possible. To prevent chapping and cracking, use warm, not hot, water. Breaks in skin integrity could harbor microorganisms that may be transferred to patients. Keep the hands pointed upward and rinse them from fingertips to elbows to prevent contaminating the hands. Turn off the water only *after* you have dried your hands with the sterile towel. Use the towel to prevent contact between your hands and the faucet handles when you turn off the water. Touching the handles without a barrier would contaminate your hands and would require starting the sterile scrub from the beginning. Some sinks are equipped with knee handles or foot pedals that eliminate the possibility of hand contamination.

Materials

■ Germicidal liquid soap in dispenser
■ Large wall clock
■ Sink with hand, knee, or foot on/off controls
■ Sterile towel packet
■ Sterile scrub sponge
■ Orangewood stick or nail file

Competency

(**Conditions**) With the necessary supplies, (**Task**) you will be able to perform surgical hand washing using sterile technique (**Standards**) correctly within the time frame designated by your instructor.

1. Without touching the inside, open the sterile towel packet some distance from potential water spray.
2. Remove all jewelry from your hands and wrists. Use an orangewood stick or nail file to remove dirt from under your fingernails.
3. Turn on the water with hand, knee, or foot controls and adjust the temperature. Wet your arm from the fingertips to the elbows (Figure 8-25 ◆).

continued

PROCEDURE 8-7 Performing a Sterile Scrub (Surgical Hand Washing) *(continued)*

  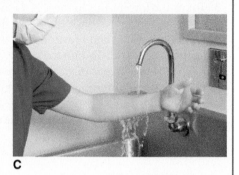

A **B** **C**

Figure 8-25 ◆ (A) Turn on the water with the hand, knee, or foot controls; (B) Adjust the temperature; (C) Wet your arms from the fingertips to the elbows.

4. Apply liquid soap to your hands and lower arms. For 5 minutes, use a circular motion to create lather, starting from the fingertips and working toward and including the elbows (Figure 8-26 ◆). Be sure to wash between the fingers and under the fingernails.
5. Rinse the lather from your arm, beginning at the fingertips and proceeding to the elbows. Keep your hands above your elbows.

6. Repeat the process, applying liquid soap to your hands and lower arms. Scrub from the fingertips to the elbows with the sponge for 3 minutes (Figure 8-27 ◆).
7. Rinse thoroughly and leave the water running. Use a sterile towel to dry your hands (Figure 8-28 ◆).
8. Use the towel to turn off a hand-controlled faucet or, if necessary, use your elbow. Otherwise release the foot pedal or move the knee control to turn off the water.

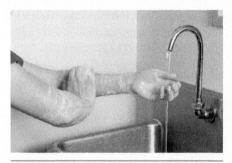 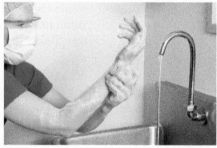 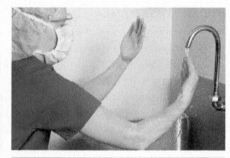

Figure 8-26 ◆ Use a circular motion to create lather, starting from the fingertips and working toward and including the elbows.

Figure 8-27 ◆ Scrub from the fingertips to the elbows with the sponge for 3 minutes.

Figure 8-28 ◆ Rinse thoroughly and leave water running.

Alcohol-Based Hand Rubs

The Centers for Disease Control and Prevention has presented new guidelines on the use of alcohol-based hand rubs, which suggest that these hand rubs can be used at the times usually required for hand washing.

The guidelines state that rings, watches, and bracelets should be removed before beginning the surgical hand scrub, and debris should be removed from underneath the fingernails using a nail cleaner under running water. Hands and forearms should be prewashed with a non-antimicrobial soap and then dried completely before using the alcohol-based surgical hand scrub product. When decontaminating hands with the alcohol-based surgical hand rub and following the manufacturer's instructions, apply the product to the palm of one hand and rub hands together, covering all surfaces of the hands and fingers (Figure 8-29 ◆). Apply the hand rub to the forearms as well and scrub persistently (Figure 8-30 ◆)

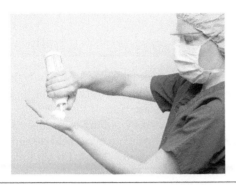

Figure 8-29 ◆ Apply the product to the palm of one hand and rub hands together, covering all surfaces of the hands and fingers.

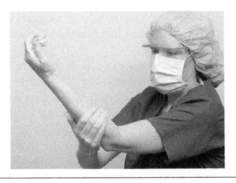

Figure 8-30 ◆ Apply the hand rub to the forearm.

Keys to Success
STERILE GOWNING

The outer surfaces of uniforms, scrub suits, and gowns harbor microorganisms that can contaminate a sterile surgical field. For some procedures it is necessary to cover this clothing with a sterile cover-up or gown. Sterile gowns may be made of washable cloth or disposable material. Disposable gowns have a protective moisture barrier on the inner surface and are more commonly used. Remember that nonsterile hands or surfaces must never touch the sterile gown's outer surface. The inner surface of the gown may be touched as it is considered contaminated.

A sterile gown may be donned mostly on one's own or with assistance.

1. After applying a surgical mask and hair cover, perform a surgical scrub. Pick up the gown by the inner neckline and hold it away from your body, high enough that the bottom does not touch the floor (Figure 8-31 ◆).
2. Insert your arms into the sleeves one at a time without touching the outer surface of the gown. Depending on how the sterile gloves are to be donned, you may or may not pull your hands completely through the sleeves (Figure 8-32 ◆). If you are donning the gown unassisted, your hands will advance only as far as the cuffs of the gown, and you will handle the gloves from within the cuffs. This takes a great deal of practice. If you are being assisted, you may pass your hands through the cuffs, making sure you touch nothing until you are assisted in the application of the sterile gloves.
3. The back of the gown is considered contaminated and you will need someone to tie the ties.
4. After gowning is completed, keep your hands above the waistline to prevent contamination.

You should receive specialized training in donning a sterile gown before you are required to do so in a surgical procedure.

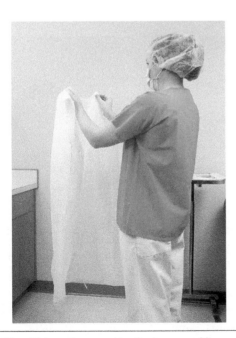

Figure 8-31 ◆ Pick up the gown by the inner neckline.

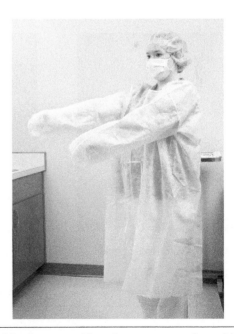

Figure 8-32 ◆ Insert arms into sleeves one at a time without touching the outer surface.

PROCEDURE 8-8 Sterile Gloving and Glove Removal

Theory

When you first learn to don and remove sterile gloves, you are likely to make errors that result in contamination. To help reduce errors, remember this phrase: skin to skin, sterile to sterile. For example, if you have the first sterile glove halfway on your hand, use the fingers of your other hand to pinch the inside or skin-side of the glove to pull it up further. Do *not* attempt to skin-touch the sterile glove fingers for proper fit at this time. Let them dangle and proceed with using the sterile portion of the glove to help get the other sterile glove on. Once both sterile gloves are on, you can adjust the fit by using the sterile surface of one to maneuver the sterile surface of the other.

Occasionally, one sterile-gloved hand could be contaminated while the other remains sterile. It takes a great deal of concentration to remember which hand can be used in the sterile procedure, and this situation should be avoided. You will also learn which size glove to use for yourself and for the physician and how to adjust an improperly fitting sterile glove.

Materials

- Sterile glove pack in correct size

Competency

(**Conditions**) With the necessary supplies, (**Task**) you will be able to apply gloves using sterile technique (**Standards**) correctly within the time frame designated by your instructor.

1. Open the pack of sterile gloves, touching only the outside of the pack. Touching only the outside of the inner packet, turn the cuff end toward you.
2. Open the inner packet by pulling each edge to the side. The gloves will be lying on the sterile field created by opening the inner pack (Figure 8-33 ◆). *Do not* touch the inside of the inner pack.
3. Perform a sterile scrub (see Procedure 8-7).
4. The following directions are for a right-handed person. Perform the opposite actions if you are left-handed. With the thumb and fingers of the left hand, grasp only the folded-back cuff area (skin to skin: your skin touches what is to be the inside of the glove). While dangling the glove with the left hand, carefully slide the right hand in (Figure 8-34 ◆). *Do not* touch the outside of the glove with your ungloved hand. Keep your hands above your waist and in front of you.
5. To don the second sterile glove, slide the fingers of your gloved hand under the cuff (sterile to sterile: the outside of the gloved hand is sterile against the sterile outside of the second glove). (Figure 8-35 ◆). With the second glove "hooked" by the fingers of your gloved hand, slide your second hand into the glove (Figure 8-36 ◆). Continue to keep your hands above your waist and in front of you.
6. Adjust the finger and thumb fit of the gloves (sterile to sterile).

Figure 8-33 ◆ Open the inner packet.

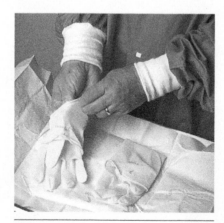

Figure 8-34 ◆ Carefully slide the right hand in.

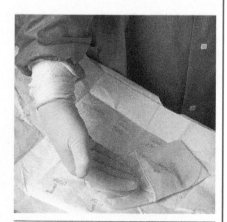

Figure 8-35 ◆ To don the second glove, slide the fingers of your gloved hand under the cuff.

PROCEDURE 8-8   Sterile Gloving and Glove Removal *(continued)*

7. To remove the gloves, use the fingers of one gloved hand to grasp the other glove at the wrist. Pull the glove over itself and hold it in the palm of the gloved hand. Slide the fingers of the ungloved hand under the cuff of the remaining glove, grasp the inside, and pull it down over the glove and off the hand (Figures 8-37 ◆ and 8-38 ◆).

8. Discard the gloves in a biohazard waste receptacle.

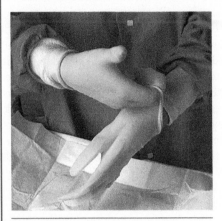

Figure 8-36 ◆ Slide your second hand into the glove.

Figure 8-37 ◆ Use the fingers of one gloved hand to grasp the other glove at the wrist.

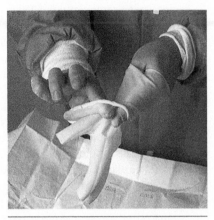

Figure 8-38 ◆ Pull the cuff of the remaining glove down over the glove and off the hand.

REVIEW

Chapter Summary

- Medical asepsis is used during clean procedures. Surgical asepsis, also known as sterile or aseptic technique, is used when assisting with minor surgery and treatment procedures. Surgical asepsis removes all microorganisms from an object or surface using sterile technique and sterile supplies. A sterile item that touches or is touched by a nonsterile or contaminated area or object is also contaminated. The medical assistant must be able to distinguish clean, sterile, and contaminated areas.

- Decontamination removes, inactivates, or destroys pathogens on a surface or object. Three methods of decontamination are sanitization, disinfection, and sterilization. Sanitization inhibits bacterial growth or inactivates pathogens. It is used to remove organic material from instruments and equipment. Disinfection destroys some microorganisms, inhibits others, but does not destroy spores and some viruses. Disinfection is used to clean surfaces and some noninvasive equipment. Sterilization is the only method that destroys all microorganisms, including spores and viruses. It is most commonly performed with the steam autoclave, although dry heat, chemical sterilization, and radiation are also used for specific materials. Individual and packaged instruments and supplies used in a sterile field must be sterilized.

- Supplies and equipment are sanitized by manual scrubbing, hot water rinsing, and air drying. Ultrasonic cleaning is another method of sanitization.

- Disinfection is accomplished by the use of germicides, steam, or boiling water. There are three levels of disinfection: low level, intermediate level, and high level. Commonly used chemical disinfectants are 70% isopropyl alcohol, sodium hypochlorite (bleach), phenol, formaldehyde, hydrogen peroxide, and soap.

Chapter Summary (continued)

- An autoclave consists of an inner sterilizing chamber and an outer compartment. Distilled water is heated to create steam, which, under pressure, sterilizes implements and supplies. Items for sterilization may be wrapped in procedure packs. Sterilization time varies according to the materials being processed and the size of the pack. It begins when a temperature of 250 degrees F (121 degrees C) inside the autoclave has been reached.
- Other methods of sterilization include the dry heat oven, cold sterilization, radiation, and ethylene oxide gas.
- Instruments are sanitized and sometimes disinfected before sterilization to remove all debris. They are wrapped individually and in procedure packs, with sterilization indicators inside each pack and dated autoclave tape on the outside. Each autoclave load must be correctly positioned. Some packs should be vertically placed, open containers should be placed on their sides, and packs should be 1 to 4 inches apart. Hinges of instruments are left open and dressings are layered to allow for more thorough steam penetration. At the end of the recommended sterilization time, any package whose indicators and tape have not changed color should not be used, as the sterility of the instruments and supplies cannot be guaranteed.

- The CDC requires that autoclave results be recorded. Culture samples may be sent to an outside agency to monitor quality control.
- To create a sterile field, follow sterile procedure to open sterile surgical packs, gloves, or individual dressings or instruments. The outer 1 inch of a sterile field is considered contaminated, so all instruments must be kept toward the center and within the sterile area. Open the surgical pack by pulling the first flap away from you, then opening the side flaps, then pulling the last flap toward you. This practice avoids crossing over the newly created sterile field and should be followed throughout the procedure to prevent contamination. The sterile glove package is opened by touching only the inner and outer wraps. It helps to remember "skin to skin" and "sterile to sterile" as you put on the gloves. Move items on the sterile field wearing sterile gloves or using transfer forceps. Single items may be added by spreading packages open and carefully dropping the items onto the sterile field.
- The manufacturer's directions must be followed when using chemical solutions or equipment for sanitization, disinfection, or sterilization. Diluting chemicals decreases their effectiveness and creates infection control hazards.

Chapter Review Questions

Multiple Choice

1. During ambulatory surgery and invasive treatments, part of the medical assistant's responsibility is to
   A. remember which areas are porous.
   B. remember which areas are safe for chlorine disinfectant.
   C. remember which are required to be sterile.
   D. remember which areas are nonporous.

2. The area that is considered contaminated on a sterile field is
   A. There is no contaminated area on a sterile field.
   B. 1/2 inch around the outer edge.
   C. only the outer edge not covered by the sterile drape.
   D. 1 inch around the outer edge.

3. The CDC requires that autoclave results be
   A. recorded.
   B. faxed in daily.
   C. mailed in monthly.
   D. none of the above.

4. To open a sterile packet you should
   A. don latex gloves, then open the package.
   B. don sterile gloves, then open the package.
   C. open the flaps away from your body and let them drop to the table.
   D. open the package with flaps toward you so you are less likely to drop the item.

5. Once you have donned a sterile gown and gloves you should keep your hands
   A. above the height of the surgical table.
   B. above your waistline.
   C. at shoulder level.
   D. at your sides, provided you do not touch anything.

6. If you must reach across a sterile field, you should
   A. never reach across for any reason.
   B. make certain your sterile gown does not touch the table.
   C. make certain you only reach across with sterile gloves on.
   D. not worry about it if you are already sterile.

7. When performing a surgical hand scrub, you should
   A. turn off the water using a disposable paper towel before you have dried your hands with a sterile towel.
   B. turn off the water before you have dried your hands with the sterile towel.
   C. turn off the water using a disposable paper towel after you have dried your hands with a sterile towel.
   D. turn off the water only after you have dried your hands with the sterile towel.

8. In ultrasonic cleaning, sound waves are used to
   A. loosen contaminants after the articles are rinsed.
   B. loosen contaminants before the articles are rinsed.
   C. disinfect the instruments.
   D. sanitize the instruments.

Chapter Review Questions (continued)

9. If a solution is to be added to the sterile field, the physician holds the sterile container
   A. over a biohazard container.
   B. over the sink.
   C. just beyond the sterile field.
   D. over the transfer container.

10. For the pouring procedure on a sterile field, the MA palms the label of the solution then
   A. pours some solution into a trash receptacle or sink, then pours the rest into the sterile container.
   B. pours the solution directly into the sterile container, holding it beyond the sterile field.
   C. pours the solution directly into a sterile transfer container, holding it over a sink, then transfers it to the sterile field.
   D. pours the solution into a sterile specimen cup to be placed on the sterile field.

True/False

T F 1. To place sterile contents correctly onto a sterile field, you must drop them or use sterile transfer forceps.

T F 2. To perform a sterile pour, you should place the rim of the solution bottle on the container the solution is being transferred to in order to prevent droplets from splashing onto the sterile field.

T F 3. Surgical asepsis is used at all times during invasive procedures and when skin integrity is or will be broken.

T F 4. Pasteurization, a heat process for killing bacteria in milk, is named for Joseph Lister, who discovered that many diseases are caused by bacteria.

T F 5. Louis Pasteur, an English surgeon, discovered that carbolic acid killed germs.

Short Answer

1. What two procedures must be performed on all instruments before they are sterilized?
2. In what type of procedure are sound waves used to loosen contaminants?
3. What are the two types of alcohol used in the medical office, and what are they used to clean?
4. What is cold sterilization?
5. What are sterilization indicators?
6. What is the second step of the sterilization procedure?
7. How does disinfection differ from sterilization?
8. Name three ways disinfection can be accomplished.
9. Why should you never reach, lean, or pass over a sterile field?
10. What instrument should you use to move items onto or within a sterile field?

Research

1. In your local area, do the clinics use autoclaves or do they send items out for sterilization?
2. How many hospitals in your community use gas sterilization for beds, wheelchairs, and other large equipment?

Externship Application Experience

You are assisting the clinical medical assistant in unloading the autoclave. She accidentally drops a sterile packet on the floor. She picks it up and puts it in the storage cabinet. What do you do?

Resource Guide

American Hospital Association
One North Franklin
Chicago, IL 60606
312-422-300
www.aha.org

Association of Surgical Technologists
7108-C South Alton Way, Suite 100
Englewood, CO 80112
1-800-637-7433
www.ast.org

**Liaison Council on Certification
for the Surgical Technologist**
7790 East Arapahoe Road, Suite 240
Englewood, CO 80012-1274
(303) 694-9264
(800) 707-0057
www.lcc-st.org

MedMedia
www.prenhall.com/frazier

More on this chapter, including interactive resources, can be found on the Student CD-ROM accompanying this textbook and on the Companion Website at www.prenhall.com/frazier.

CHAPTER 9

Pharmacology and Medication Administration

Case Study

Heidi has been a CMA for Dr. Wittig, a GI specialist, for six months. A patient, Claire, calls to say that she is now seven months pregnant and suffering from horrible heartburn. This is not a new medical condition for Claire. Heidi reads in her chart that Claire has suffered heartburn for several years and takes 150 mg of Zantac twice a day. Claire states that she has been taking her Zantac regularly and would like to know if she can increase the dose because the pregnancy is causing more heartburn. Heidi notes that Claire missed her regular six-month follow-up appointment with Dr. Wittig. In fact, she has not been seen in the office for ten months now but has been continuing to get medication refills.

MedMedia
www.prenhall.com/frazier

Additional interactive resources and activities for this chapter can be found on the Companion Website. For videos, audio glossary, legal and ethical scenarios, job scenarios, quizzes, games, and virtual tours related to the content of this chapter, please access the accompanying CD-ROM in this book.

 Assets Available:

Audio Glossary
Legal and Ethical Scenario: *Pharmacology and the Administration of Medications*
On the Job Scenario: *Pharmacology and the Administration of Medications*
Video Scenario: *Pharmacology, Injections; Capillary and Venipuncture; Syringe Prep*
A & P Quizzes: *The Skeletal System; The Muscular System; Body Structure and Function*
Multiple Choice Quiz
Games: Crossword, Strikeout, and Spelling Bee
3D Virtual Tour: Muscular System: Hand and Forearm, Hip and Thigh
Drag and Drop: Muscular System: Muscles of the Posterior; Muscles of the Anterior; Interior Muscle Structure

Objectives

After completing this chapter, you should be able to:

- Spell and define the medical terminology in the chapter.
- Discuss the medical assistant's role in administering and dispensing drugs.
- Explain the basic actions of drugs in the body.
- Differentiate the various types of effects of drugs in the body.
- List the basic functions of drugs.
- Explain the differences between prescription and over-the-counter drugs.
- List and describe the three names every drug is assigned.
- List the main drug reference resources.
- Explain how drugs are measured and conversions are calculated.
- Explain how drug dosages are calculated.
- List safety guidelines that must be followed when drugs are administered.
- Describe the various drug classifications and give examples of each.
- Explain the legal guidelines for prescribing and administering controlled substances.
- Describe the parts of a prescription.
- Explain how and why prescription pads should be safeguarded.
- Identify and describe the forms and routes of drug administration.
- Discuss the parenteral administration of medications.

✚ MEDICAL ASSISTING COMPETENCIES

CAAHEP ENTRY-LEVEL COMPETENCIES FOR CMA	ABHES ENTRY-LEVEL COMPETENCIES FOR RMA
■ Identify and respond to issues of confidentiality. ■ Perform within legal and ethical boundaries. ■ Demonstrate knowledge of federal and state health-care legislation and regulations. ■ Perform hand washing. ■ Dispose of biohazardous materials. ■ Practice Standard Precautions. ■ Use methods of quality control. ■ Apply pharmacology principles to prepare and administer oral and parenteral medications. ■ Maintain medication and immunization records.	■ Project a positive attitude. ■ Maintain confidentiality at all times. ■ Be a "team player." ■ Be cognizant of ethical boundaries. ■ Exhibit initiative. ■ Adapt to change. ■ Evidence a responsible attitude. ■ Be courteous and diplomatic. ■ Conduct work within scope of education, training, and ability. ■ Practice Standard Precautions. ■ Use quality control. ■ Dispose of biohazardous materials. ■ Prepare and administer oral and parenteral medications as directed by the physician. ■ Maintain medication and immunization records.

Introduction

Pharmacology is the study of **drugs** and their effects on the human body. It is a complex area of study that incorporates the chemical structure of a drug, its chemical action within the body, the desired or intended effects of treatment, and potential undesirable effects. Drug forms and methods of administration are part of pharmacology. Medical professionals who dispense and administer medications must have an understanding of pharmacological basics. They must also take into account the present functioning state of the healthy or diseased body and such factors as the individual's absorption, distribution, metabolism, and excretion capabilities.

The Medical Assistant's Role in Administering and Dispensing Drugs

Drug therapy is a major part of medical care today, and as a medical assistant you must be familiar with medications administered in or prescribed by the medical office. You must be familiar with the legal guidelines set by the Drug Enforcement Agency (**DEA**), a branch of the Department of Justice. Your responsibilities will include reading medication orders or prescriptions, administering medications, being aware of possible side effects, recognizing side effects, instructing patients, and consulting reference resources for additional information.

Upon the physician's order and following state law and office protocol, you may give the patient a supply of drugs for self-administration. You must obtain verification from another clinical staff person that the correct drug is being dispensed in the correct amount. All drugs must be clearly and completely labeled prior to dispensing. You will need to document the dispensing of any medication, including samples from pharmaceutical companies.

Medical Terminology

chemical name—official pharmaceutical name for a drug based on its chemical composition

contraindication—reason or condition for which a drug should not be administered, e.g., pregnancy

controlled substance—Drugs that have a potential for being addictive or abused.

drug—any substance capable of producing a change in function when administered to a living organism; commonly, a term for a substance used to treat or prevent disease; in the medical office, synonymous with the term *medication*

generic (nonproprietary) name—pharmaceutical name for a medication, often a shortened chemical name; used by all manufacturers that produce the medication; never capitalized

over-the-counter medications—nonprescription medications that can be purchased anywhere without a physician's prescription; examples include antacids, cold remedies, and aspirin

pharmacology—the study of drugs and their effects on the human body

side effect—effect other than the therapeutic effect

sympathomimetic—drugs that mimic the sympathetic nervous system

therapeutic effect—the desired or intended effect

toxic effect—potential harmful or life-threatening effect

trade (brand, proprietary) name—name registered by a manufacturer for use only by that manufacturer; has a registered trademark symbol; first letter is always capitalized

Abbreviations

CSA—Federal Controlled Substances Act

DEA—Drug Enforcement Administration

OTC—over-the-counter

PDR—Physician's Desk Reference

USP-NF—U.S. Pharmacopeia and National Formulary

COMPETENCY SKILLS PERFORMANCE

1. Demonstrate the preparation of a prescription for the physician's signature.
2. Demonstrate withdrawing medication from an ampule.
3. Demonstrate withdrawing medication from a vial.
4. Demonstrate the reconstitution of a powdered drug for injection administration.
5. Demonstrate the administration of medication during infusion therapy.
6. Demonstrate the preparation and administration of oral medication.
7. Demonstrate the administration of a subcutaneous injection.
8. Demonstrate the administration of an intramuscular injection to adults and children.
9. Demonstrate the administration of a Z-track injection.

—Critical Thinking Question 9-1—

Heidi notes that Claire has been receiving medication refills even though she has missed her follow-up appointments. How would you handle this situation?

Basic Pharmacology

Pharmacology studies the biological and chemical interactions between drugs and bodily organs and processes. The basic actions of drugs in the body are absorption, distribution, metabolism, and excretion (Figure 9-1 ◆).

Absorption refers to the time and process whereby a drug reaches the cells and produces the desired action. For example, oral tablets are absorbed slowly because digestion must take place before the medication can be absorbed into the bloodstream. Oral liquid medication passes through the digestive system more quickly, while intravenous medication is absorbed immediately into the bloodstream. The absorption time of medications absorbed through the mucous membranes (sub-

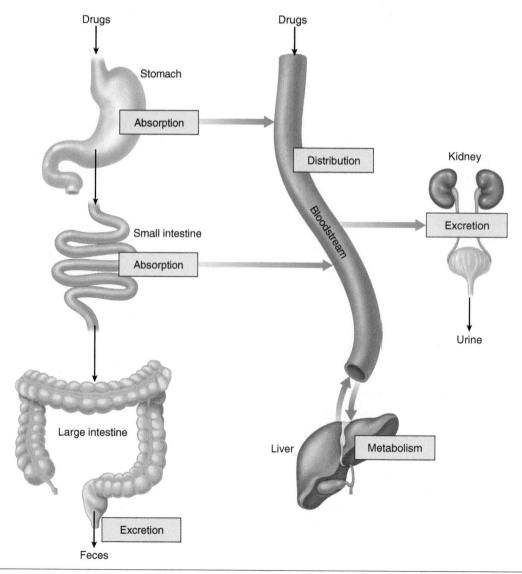

Figure 9-1 ◆ The four processes of drug movement

TABLE 9-1 FACTORS THAT AFFECT ABSORPTION	
Concentration (dose) of administered drug	Metabolic rate (lower in children and elderly patients)
Frequency of drug dosing	Genetics
Food-drug interactions	Excretion rate (rate of elimination)
Drug-drug interactions	Half-life ($t_{1/2}$) of administered drug
Absorption rate	Changing medical condition (liver or kidney disease)

Source: Holland, Norman; Adams, Michael Patrick, Core Concepts in Pharmacology, 2nd ed. © 2007. Reprinted by permission of Pearson Education, Inc. Upper Saddle River, NJ.

lingual or buccal tablets, vaginal or rectal suppositories) is between that of oral and intravenous medications because these medications do not undergo digestion but pass easily through the membranes and directly into the circulatory system. Table 9-1 lists and compares the factors that affect absorption.

Drug *distribution* refers to the circulation of the absorbed drug through the body. Impaired circulation in cardiovascular disease may impede the distribution of medication and decrease its therapeutic effects.

Drug *metabolism,* or processing, takes place in the liver before or after entering the bloodstream. This process facilitates the drugs' chemical and therapeutic action and inactivates unused portions. If liver function is impaired by acute or chronic conditions, more medication may be needed to achieve full therapeutic effects, or less medication may be prescribed to reduce unwanted side effects.

Excretion of the inactivated products of medication in the system is performed mostly by the kidneys, intestinal tract, lungs, and skin. When any of the excretory organs are impaired by acute or chronic disease conditions, the accumulated medication can reach toxic levels. In this case the physician may need to decrease the amount of medication.

General Effects of Drugs

The **therapeutic effect** is the desired effect or the reason the drug is being administered. Adverse reactions to medications may be classified as side effects, toxic effects, or idiosyncratic reactions. **Side effects** are the effects generated by the medication other than the intended or desired effects. Side effects can be therapeutic, nontherapeutic, or even dangerous. **Toxic effects** result from prescription overdose, accidental overdose, allergic reactions, interactions between two or more drugs taken at the same time, or the impaired functioning of the body organs that metabolize or excrete the drug. Idiosyncratic reactions are those that cannot be explained or predicted and may be genetically determined. Most drugs have **contraindications,** or reasons against prescribing and administering them to specific patients. A common contraindication is pregnancy.

? — Critical Thinking Question 9-2 —

Claire has not been seen in Dr. Wittig's office for the past ten months and is now seven months pregnant. Dr. Wittig may not be aware that Claire is pregnant and has continued taking Zantac, which may be contraindicated during pregnancy. Now that Heidi is aware of this situation, how should she proceed?

Basic Functions of Drugs

Treatment with drugs serves five basic functions.

- *Therapeutic drugs* treat and relieve symptoms in a disease process, as in pain relief, anesthesia, improved GI function, and stimulation of the pancreas to secrete insulin.
- *Diagnostic drugs* assist in the diagnosis of disease, as in the use of contrast materials in imaging studies and the assessment of endocrine hormones.
- *Curative drugs* intervene in the disease process and improve the patient's quality of life, as in the treatment of infections with antibiotic and antimicrobial agents.
- *Replacement drugs* restore a normal body substance, element, or chemical that is deficient in the body, as in insulin replacement and thyroid hormone replacement in hypothyroidism.
- *Preventive or prophylactic drugs* maintain a healthy state by preventing disease, as in childhood immunizations, tetanus prophylaxis, and flu vaccines.

Prescription versus Over-the-Counter Drugs

Medications may be classified as either prescription or over-the-counter. A prescription drug can be obtained only with a prescription written by a licensed physician or a physician's representative. An **over-the-counter (OTC) medication** may be purchased without a written prescription for the self-treatment of various symptoms. Many drugs that were once obtainable only by prescription have been approved by the FDA for OTC sale. Common OTCs are aspirin, Tylenol, Motrin, Aleve, Advil, Sudafed, Actifed, Benadryl, Mylanta, Maalox, Tums, and other medications for gastric upset and GERD (gastroesophageal reflux disease).

The quality and safety of nonprescription substances are controlled by the FDA just as prescription drugs are. These drugs are usually low-dosage and considered fairly safe, although they still have the potential for causing unwanted side effects, especially when directions are not followed. It is important that you ask all patients if they are taking any OTC drugs, as many people do not consider them medications to be reported to the

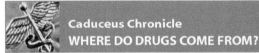
Caduceus Chronicle
WHERE DO DRUGS COME FROM?

Drugs are derived from plants, animals, and minerals or manufactured in a laboratory. Plant substances such as tree bark, roots, and blossoms were used by early cultures to treat a variety of symptoms. Native Americans used willow bark tea, which contains salicylates, to treat headaches and toothaches. In 1928 Alexander Fleming, an English bacteriologist, accidentally discovered that a mold growing on a culture of disease-causing bacteria was killing the bacteria. This discovery led to the development of penicillin. Insulin, a substance originally derived from the pancreas of pigs and cows, was discovered in the 1920s to be effective in the treatment of diabetes mellitus. Today, salicylates, penicillin, and insulin are manufactured synthetically. New drugs are often developed synthetically after they are discovered in a natural setting such as the rainforest in South America.

physician. Because interactions may occur between medications, you must instruct patients to report to the physician any use of OTCs to reduce the potential for a harmful reaction.

Patients must follow certain precautions when taking prescription drugs. These include reading and following all printed directions, following recommended dosages, not combining OTCs with prescribed medications unless approved by the physician, discarding outdated medications, and not using any medication a patient knows he or she is allergic to.

Drug Nomenclature

Drug nomenclature (the way drugs are named) comprises three general names: the *chemical name, generic name,* and *brand name.*

- A drug's **chemical name** is its official pharmaceutical name and is based on its chemical composition. The chemical name identifies the exact chemicals in the drug along with its molecular structure.
- The **generic or nonproprietary name**, also called the common name, is assigned to the drug by the manufacturer who first seeks approval of the drug by the FDA (Federal Drug Administration). The generic name is a pharmaceutical name, often a shortened chemical name, used by all manufacturers that produce the medication. It is never capitalized.
- The **trade, brand,** or **proprietary name** is registered by a manufacturer for use only by that manufacturer. It is used with a registered trademark symbol, and the first letter is always capitalized. The chemical and generic names of the drug are listed in the *Pharmacopoeia/National Formulary* (USP/NF) as the official name of the drug.

The manufacturer who originally proposes the drug to the FDA for approval and clinical trial owns exclusive rights to produce the drug for twenty years after the initial proposal. After that time, other manufacturers may produce the drug under other brand names, but it must have the same generic name and chemical structure. Generic forms of the drug are usually less costly than the brand-name or proprietary drug.

Drug Reference Sources

As an MA assisting the physican to fill out prescriptions, calling in prescriptions, and administering medications in the medical office, you should know how to use drug reference books and materials.

The *U.S. Pharmacopeia and National Formulary* (**USP-NF**) and the *Physician's Desk Reference* (**PDR**) are two standard drug reference books. As the recognized official source of drug standards, the USP-NF lists and describes all accepted therapeutic drugs and their chemical formulas. The PDR, published annually, contains information about approximately 2,500 drugs. It is one of the most widely used medical references and is available in most health-care settings. Categories of information include classification, generic names, recommended uses, and listings by manufacturer's name or trade name. Color photos assist in the identification of many drugs. A PDR supplement listing OTC medications is published every year.

Other sources of drug information are the package inserts that accompany medications and the computer-generated printouts dispensed by the pharmacy with every prescription.

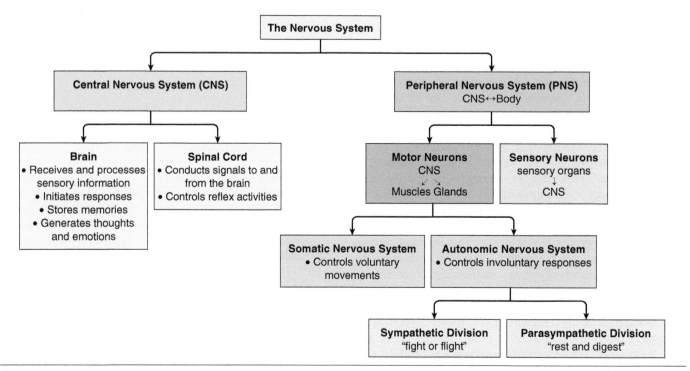

Figure 9-2 ◆ Functional divisions of the nervous system

Source: Holland, Norma; Adams, Michael Patrick, Core Concepts in Pharmacology, *2nd ed. © 2007. Reprinted with permission of Pearson Education, Inc. Upper Saddle River, NJ.*

TABLE 9-2 AUTONOMIC NERVOUS SYSTEM REACTIONS

Body System or Organ	Adrenergic Agonists, Sympathomimetics	Cholinergic Agonists, Parasympathomimetics
Vessels	Constrict	Dilate
Heart	Speeds up rate and increases contractility	Slows down rate and decreases contractility
Respiratory	Constricts bronchioles	Dilates bronchioles
GI tract	Slows peristalsis	Increases peristalsis
Urinary tract	Relaxes the bladder, contracts the sphincter	Contracts the bladder, relaxes the sphincter
Eyes	Dilates pupils (mydriasis)	Constricts pupils (myosis)

Drug Classifications

Drugs are classified according to function and the area of the body they affect. Some drugs affect specific organs or tissues, while others have a more general effect.

Many drug formulas are based on the functions of the autonomic nervous system (ANS). Understanding the normal functions of the sympathetic and parasympathetic divisions of the autonomic nervous system is essential to understanding the drugs that mimic these functions. Drugs that mimic the sympathetic nervous system are known as sympathomimetic.

The nervous system is divided into two general anatomical areas or systems, the central nervous system and the peripheral nervous system. (∞ The nervous system is more fully discussed in Chapter 28.) The central nervous system comprises the brain and spinal cord. The peripheral nervous system is composed of all nervous system structures outside the brain and spinal cord and includes twelve pairs of cranial nerves, thirty-one pairs of spinal nerves, peripheral smaller branching nerves, and the autonomic nervous system (Figure 9-2 ◆).

The brain is composed of different areas that exert control over conscious and unconscious actions of the body. The cerebrum or forebrain is responsible for cognitive functions, including thinking, reasoning, hearing, talking, seeing, and motor activities. The cerebellum is concerned primarily with balance, coordination, and equilibrium. The midbrain acts as a relay station as well as an area where the cerebrospinal fluid is managed. The brain is connected to the spinal cord through the medulla oblongata and the pons. The spinal cord and peripheral nerves transport impulses to and from the brain for interpretation and response.

The autonomic system is made up of two divisions, the sympathetic and parasympathetic nervous systems. The sympathetic nervous system initiates the body's response to

Keys to Success
REMEMBERING TARGET SYSTEMS OF THE ALPHA AND BETA-ADRENERGIC BLOCKERS

An easy way to remember target systems of the alpha and beta-adrenergic blockers is to think of it in this way. *Alpha* blockers exert activity on the *arteries, beta₁* blockers on the heart (the body has only *one* heart), and *beta₂* blockers on the lungs (the body has *two* lungs).

threat or danger. This is often referred to as the "fight or flight" response. Because the body cannot survive in the emergency state of response for extended periods of time, the parasympathetic nervous system applies the "brakes" to bring body functioning back to normal. The sympathetic nervous system's response is termed *cholinergic*, and that of the parasympathetic nervous system is *anticholinergic* (Table 9-2).

The neurotransmitters responsible for activities in the ANS are epinephrine, norepinephrine, and acetylcholine. Epinephrine and norepinephrine, adrenergic agonists, stimulate the sympathetic system in the event of a perceived threat to the organism and cause the typical fight-or-flight response. Norepinephrine, of the sympathetic nervous system, can be further divided into alpha and beta receptors. Acetylcholine is the main parasympathetic or cholinergic neurotransmitter that acts as a "housekeeping" agent to restore body systems to normal function. Sympathetic and parasympathetic agonists mimic the actions of the two systems, adrenergic and cholinergic, respectively. The sympathetic nervous system response can be inhibited by adrenergic blockers (alpha and beta-blockers) and the parasympathetic system can be inhibited by cholinergic blockers, or anticholinergics (alpha and beta-blockers) (Table 9-3).

Central nervous system drugs generally affect the whole system, although some target only one area. CNS drugs may

TABLE 9-3 TYPES OF AUTONOMIC RECEPTORS

Neurotransmitter	Receptor	Primary Locations	Responses
Acetylcholine (cholinergic)	muscarinic	parasympathetic target: organs other than the heart heart	stimulation of smooth muscle and gland secretions decrease in heart rate and force of contraction
	nicotinic	cell bodies of postganglionic neurons (sympathetic and parasympathetic pathways)	stimulation of smooth muscle and gland secretions
Norepinephrine (adrenergic)	alpha₁	all sympathetic target organs except the heart	constriction of blood vessels, dilation of pupils
	alpha₂	presynaptic adrenergic neuron terminals	inhibition of norepinephrine release
	beta₁	heart and kidneys	increase in heart rate and force of contraction; release of renin
	beta₂	all sympathetic target organs except the heart	inhibition of smooth muscle

Source: Holland, Norman and Adams, Michael Patrick, Core Concepts in Pharmacology, *2ⁿᵈ Edition © 2007. Reprinted with permission of Pearson Education, Inc. Upper Saddle River, NJ.*

help to reduce pain (analgesics), eliminate pain during surgical procedures (anesthetics), reduce elevated body temperature (antipyretic agents), prevent or stop seizures (anticonvulsants, antiepileptics), sedate or induce sleep (hyponotics/sedatives), reduce anxiety (antianxiety agents), help to relieve symptoms of Alzheimer disease, treat symptoms of depression (antidepressants), and treat psychotic disorders (antipsychotic drugs). Antianxiety, antipsychotic, and antidepressant medications are often referred to as psychotropic agents.

Analgesics are drugs that help to reduce pain without altering level of consciousness. They work by blocking the transmission of pain impulses to the brain or blocking the interpretation of pain impulses by the brain. Some analgesic drugs also have an antipyretic effect. Analgesics are normally classified as narcotic or non-narcotic. Narcotic analgesics are either derivatives of opium or synthetic opioids.

Anesthetic medications are available in two forms, general and local. General anesthetics achieve total loss of sensation in the body by inducing loss of consciousness. Local anesthetics provide a temporary loss of sensation from specific areas of the body. Anesthetics are used during surgical procedures to remove the sensation of pain and allow the procedure to progress in a therapeutic and humane manner.

Antiinflammatory drugs may be corticosteroids or NSAIDs (non-steroidal anti-inflammatory drugs). Corticosteroids are prescribed when the inflammatory process is severe and immediate reversal of the condition is indicated. These drugs often have serious side effects and are avoided whenever possible. NSAIDs help to relieve common inflammation, including arthritis and other chronic inflammatory conditions. Frequent blood studies are indicated to check for liver and kidney injury.

Cardiovascular drugs are used to treat conditions of the heart and blood vessels. (∞ The cardiovascular system is discussed in Chapter 17.) This family of drugs includes cardiac glycosides, antiarrhythmic agents, anticoagulants, platelet inhibitors, hemostatic agents/coagulants, thrombolytic agents, vasoconstrictors, vasodilators, and antihypertensive drugs. Cardiac glycosides are used in the treatment of congestive heart failure to slow and strengthen the heartbeat. Antiarrhythmic drugs help to restore the heart rhythm to normal. Anticoagulants and platelet inhibitors are used in the treatment of clot formations or any condition in which clot formation is likely. The function of hemostatic drugs is to treat uncontrolled bleeding and hemorrhage. Thrombolytics, often referred to as "clot busters," dissolve existing clots and restore blood flow. Vasoconstrictors are administered to treat shock by constricting blood vessels and maintaining a viable blood pressure. Vasodilators have the opposite effect—they dilate the vessels—and are used to treat arterial spasms, angina (chest pain), and certain vascular disorders. The antihypertensive group of drugs is used in the treatment of hypertension, or high blood pressure. Drugs used to treat hyperlipidemia or to lower cholesterol and triglyceride levels are often also classified as cardiovascular drugs.

Drugs that affect the gastrointestinal (GI) system can be classified according to the part of the system they target: the esophagus, the stomach, the small intestine, or the large intestine. Other GI drugs may be classified according to their specific action, such as laxatives, anti-flatulence drugs, or proton-pump inhibitors.

Antiinfective agents are used to treat infections caused by bacteria, viruses, parasites, fungi, or protozoa. A culture and sensitivity test is often performed to determine the optimum drug for the particular infective microorganism.

Respiratory system drugs include antihistamines, antitussives, bronchodilators, decongestants, and expectorants. Antihistamines help to relieve nasal congestion. Antitussive medications, both narcotic and non-narcotic, help to relieve coughing. Bronchodilators are used in the treatment of asthma and other obstructive airway conditions. Decongestants help to relieve congestion in the upper respiratory region and are helpful in treating the common cold, sinusitis, and rhinitis. Expectorants help to liquefy respiratory mucous membrane secretions and promote the expectoration of mucus.

Medications prescribed for common disorders of the endocrine system include drugs used to treat diabetes mellitus and thyroid disorders. Drug therapy prescribed for the reproductive system, whose functions are related to those of the endocrine system, has its own categories. Contraceptive drugs, hormone replacement drugs, and erectile dysfunction agents are the drugs most frequently prescribed for reproductive conditions. Contraceptives are available in oral, intradermal, and injectable form. Hormone therapy is often prescribed for women who have experienced natural or early surgical menopause.

Urinary system drugs include diuretics, which increase urine production and excretion; antibiotics and antiseptics to treat UTIs; analgesics; and drugs that relax bladder muscles. Conditions affecting the prostate gland in men, including urinary retention, frequency, and urgency, may be successfully treated with drug therapy.

Miscellaneous drugs include neoplastic agents, used to treat cancers and neoplastic disease; antihistamines, used to treat allergic reactions; and antiallergic drugs, used as a prophylactic measure to prevent allergic attacks.

Table 9-4 lists and briefly describes the various drug classifications.

Controlled Substances

Drugs with a potential for abuse have been identified in the Federal Controlled Substances Act (**CSA**), which is enforced by the DEA (Table 9-5). The CSA sets guidelines for the storage, record keeping, and safekeeping of these **controlled substances,**

Keys to Success
THE TOP 50

An excellent way to stay current in pharmacology is to find out which drugs are most commonly prescribed. *Pharmacy Times* publishes a list of the fifty most frequently prescribed drugs in its April issue each year. Peruse the list, check previous years' lists, and see if you can spot any trends. This will give you a snapshot of where drug therapy has been and where it is now.

TABLE 9-4 DRUG CLASSIFICATIONS

Classes and Examples	Main Functions
Analgesics, narcotic: morphine, Demerol, codeine, oxycontin, diladid, Duragesic, Darvon	Relieve severe pain, including postoperative pain, myocardial pain, pain from trauma and terminal illness.
Analgesics, non-narcotic or non-opioid: acetaminophen, aspirin, ibuprofen, naproxen	Relieve minor to moderate pain and chronic pain.
Antipyretic agents: acetaminophen, aspirin, ibuprofen, naproxen	Lower elevated body temperature.
General anesthetics: thiopental Na (Pentothal), midazolam (Versed), methohexital (Brevital)	Produce loss of sensation for surgical, dental, and other procedures. General anesthesia induces loss of consciousness.
Local anesthetics: lidocaine (Xylocaine), procaine (Novocaine), bupivacaine (Marcaine)	Produce regional or local anesthesia for specific area of body.
Anticonvulsants, antiepileptics: Dilantin, Zarontin, Tegretol, phenobarbital, Valium, Depakene, Mysoline, Klonopin, Neurontin, Keppra, Zarontin, Lyrica	Prevent seizures, treat and halt seizures in progress. Barbiturates used in all forms of epilepsy; Dilantin, Keppra, Neurontin for grand mal seizures; Zarontin for petit mal seizures. Neurontin also used to treat post-herpetic neuralgia and some nerve pain.
Hyponotics/sedatives: Amytal, Seconal, Noctec, Dalmane, Halcion, Ambien, Restoril, Lunesta	Promote rest and sleep.
Alzheimer treatment: Cognex, Aricept	Stimulate nerve transmitters as a means of improving memory and behavior.
Antianxiety: Valium, Xanax, Ativan, Tranxene	Relieve anxiety, some psychosomatic disorders, muscle tension, nausea and vomiting.
Antidepressants, tricyclic agents: Elavil, Triavil, Trifanil, Pamelor; **SSRI,** Prozac, Paxil, Zoloft; **MAO inhibitor,** Nardil	Treat depression; often referred to as mood elevators.
Antipsychotic drugs: Thorazine, Haldol, Eskalith, Risperdal, Mellari, Prolixin	Treat symptoms of psychosis and severe neurosis. Lithium levels must be routinely monitored. Eskalith is a lithium preparation used to treat bipolar disorders.
Anti-Parkinson's drugs: Symmetrel, Sinemet, Cogentin, Kemadrin, Artane	Treat symptoms of Parkinson's by increasing level of dopamine or dopaminergic activity. Anticholinergic drugs reduce activity of ACH. Goal is to stop or moderate tremors, muscle spasms, and muscle rigidity.
Antiinflammatory agents. *NSAIDS:* aspirin, acetaminophen (Tylenol), ibuprofen (Motrin, Advil), naproxen (naprosyn, Aleve), nabumetone (Relafen), celecoxib (Celebrex), valdecoxib (Bextra). *Steroids:* prednisone	Treat conditions caused by inflammation of the muscles and joints.
Antineoplastic agents: flurouracil (5-FU), cyclophosphamide (Cytoxan), methotrexate (Folex)	Chemotherapy prescribed to treat cancer and inhibit growth of neoplasms. Often used before surgery or radiation to shrink tumors or as adjunct therapy with surgery or radiation.
Antihistamines: diphenhydramine (Benadryl), chlorpheniramine (Chlor-Trimeton), clemastine (Tavist), fexofenadine (Allegra), loratadine (Claritin), cetirizine (Zyrtec). (See Histaminic II blockers)	Relieve symptoms of allergic response by blocking histamine reactions in tissue. Often used to treat runny nose and watery eyes connected with hay fever and other allergies.
Antiallergic: cromolyn (Intal)	Used prophylactically to prevent asthma attacks and associated bronchospasms, coughing, and wheezing.
Antipruritic: diphenhydramine (Benadryl), calamine lotion, corticosteroid ointments and creams, hydroxyzine HCl (Atarax), clemastine (Tavist)	Treat itching. Some used directly on skin, others systemic.
Antitussive drugs: codeine sulfate, dextromethorphan (Romilar, Robitussin DM, Benylin, Triaminic)	Treat or suppress cough.
Cardiac glycosides: digitoxin (Digitoline, Crystodigin), digoxin (Lanoxin)	Slow and strengthen the heartbeat. Used in treatment of congestive heart failure.
Antiarrhythmic agents: atenolol (Tenormin), propanolol (Inderal), verapamil (Isoptin, Calan), Topril	Treat arrhythmias and restore normal heartbeat.
Anticoagulants: dicumarol, warfarin sodium (Coumadin), heparin sodium	Prevent or delay blood clots from forming. Also prescribed to treat deep vein thrombosis and other thrombosis conditions.
Hemostatic/coagulants: menadiol sodium (Synkavite), phytonadione (AquaMEPHYTON, vitamin K)	Increase coagulating ability of blood, treat hemorrhage and excessive or uncontrolled bleeding.
Platelet inhibitors: aspirin, dipyridamole (Persantine), clopidogrel (Plavix)	Prevent platelet aggregation. Usually prescribed in combination with aspirin for better effect.
Thrombolytics: alteplase (Activase), streptokinase (Streptase), tenectoplase (tissue plasminogen activator, TPA)	Dissolve blood clots, especially in MIs and CVAs.
Vasoconstrictors: norepinephrine (Levophed), epinephrine (Adrenalin)	Treat shock; primary action is constriction of vessels.
Vasodilators: nitroglycerin (Nitro-stat), isoxsuprine (Isordil), hydralazine (Apresoline), sodium nitroprusside (Nipride)	Treat angina and hypertensive crisis.
Antihypertensive agents: rampapril (Altace), doxazosin (Cardura), benzothiazepine (Cardizem), clonidine (Catapres), methyldopa (Aldoril)	Treat hypertension. Altace inhibits angiotension-converting enzymes, Cardura dilates vessels.
Antihyperlipidemic or hypolipidemic drugs: simvastin (Zocor), pravastatin (Pravachol), atorvastatin (Lipitor), ezetimibe (Zetia)	Treat hyperlipidema by reducing blood cholesterol levels; statin drugs may reverse some plaque accumulation in blood vessels.
Antibiotics: penicillin (ampicillin, amoxicillin, Staphcillin, Unipen, Geocillin, Pipracil); cephalosporins (Duricef, Keflex, Cecloe, Suprax, Rocephin); aminoglycosides (Amikin, Garamycin, Nebcin); tetracyclines (Vibramycin Terramycin, Minocin); sulfonmide antimicrobials (Sulfonamide, Sulamyd, Gantanol, Gantrisin); macrolides (erythromycin, Zithromax, Biaxin, Dynabac); flruoquinolone antimicrobials (Cipro)	Treat bacterial infections.

continued

TABLE 9-4 *cont.*

Classes and Examples	Main Functions
Antifungal: fluconazole (Diflucan), Monistat 3, Mycelex vaginal tabs, Vagistat-1, griseofluvin (Grisactin), tolnaftate (Tinactin)	Treat candidiasis, coccidiodomycosis, tinea capitis, tinea pedis, and other miscellaneous fungal infections.
Antiparasitic: Vermox, Biltricide, Antiminth, Pin-Rid, Mintezol	Treat parasitic worm infections.
Antivirals: amantadine, rimantadine, ganciclovir, ribravirin, acyclovir, famciclovir, trifluridine, valacuclovir, vidarabine; **for HIV,** didanosine, delavirdine, nelfinavir, nevirapine, zalcitabine	Treat viral infections including influenza, CMV retinitis, RSV syncytial virus infections, herpes zoster, genital herpes, herpes simplex, keratitis, HIV (drugs used to treat HIV are fairly new; success uncertain).
Antiulcer treatment: Biaxin, Amozil	Peptic ulcer treatment; eliminates *H. pylori* from stomach
Proton pump inhibitors: Prilosec, Prevacid, Nexium, Aciphex	Treat peptic ulcers; reduce gastric acid secretion by blocking enzyme responsible for secreting hydrochloric acid.
Histaminic II blockers (antagonists): Tagamet, Axid, Zantac, Pepcid	Treat peptic ulcers; also reduce gastric acid secretion by blocking histaminic II receptors.
Antiemetics: Phenergan, Tigan, Reglan, Compazine, Zofran	Prevent vomiting, relieve nausea.
Cathartics and laxatives: CoLyte, mineral oil, citrate of magnesia, Dulcolax, castor oil, Surfak, Serutan	Stimulate evacuation of the bowel.
Antispasmodics: atropine, belladonna, Robinul, Pro-Banthine, Bentyl, Zelmac	Treat hypermotility in GI tract.
Asthma prophylactics: cromolyn sodium	Used before exposure to allergen to prevent allergic reaction.
Bronchodilators: Proventil, Theo-Dur	Relax smooth muscle in bronchi and slow or stop bronchial spasm.
Decongestants: Afrin, Sudafed	Used to constrict the nasal membrane to open air passageways. Constricts nasal mucousal vessels.
Expectorants: Robitussin, Organidin	Increases respiratory secretions, liquefies secretions for easier expectoration.
Thyroid medications: antithyroid (Tapazole, propylthiouracil) and thyroid replacement (Synthroid)	Inhibit production of thyroid hormone when too much is produced; replacement therapy when inadequate amounts are produced.
Hypoglycemic agents: Glucotrol, Glynase, Diabeta, Glucophage	Stimulate production of insulin by pancreas.
Insulin: NPH, Humulin	Replaces insulin not produced by pancreas.
Contraceptives: Ovral, Triphasic	Prevent pregnancy.
Hormone replacement therapy: Premarin, Estrace, Provera, Prempro	Treat symptoms of menopause.
Diuretics: Lasix, Bumex, HydroDIURIL	Used to treat fluid retention, CHF, hypertension.

TABLE 9-5 SCHEDULE OF CONTROLLED SUBSTANCES

Schedule I Substances (C-I): Substances with no accepted medical use in the United States and high potential for abuse. Illegal to obtain or prescribe for use in the United States.
- Narcotics, including heroin
- Stimulants, including amphetamine variations and Ecstasy
- Depressants
- Hallucinogens, including LSD, mescaline, peyote
- Cannabis, including marijuana

Schedule II Substances (C-II): Substances with accepted medical use and high potential for abuse. No refills without a new physician-written prescription.
- Narcotics, including Demerol, morphine, codeine, Dilaudid, Oxycodone
- Amphetamines, including Dexadrine, Ritalin
- Cocaine
- Short-acting barbiturates, including phenobarbital, Amobarbital, Seconal

Schedule III Substances (C-III): Substances with accepted medical use and lower abuse potential than Schedule I or Schedule II controlled substances. Prescriptions may be refilled five times within six months with physician authorization.
- Combination drugs containing lower amounts of narcotics or stimulants, including Tylenol with codeine

Schedule IV Substances (C-IV): Substances with accepted medical use and less potential for abuse than Schedule III substances. May be refilled five times within six months with physician authorization.
- Antianxiety drugs including Xanax, Valium, Librium
- Sedative hypnotics including Dalmane, Restoril, Halcion, Ambien, Versed

Schedule V Substances (C-V): Substances with accepted medical use and limited abuse potential. Prescription must be authorized by physician, and patient must be 18 years old and show identification.
- Cough medicines with codeine, antidiarrheal medication such as Lomotil

also called *schedule drugs.* Drugs with the potential for abuse include narcotics; drugs that are potentially addictive or habit-forming, such as depressants and stimulants; and drugs with hallucinogenic properties. The potential for abuse must be established before a drug is placed on the list.

All drugs must be accounted for at all times. Records concerning the purchase and management of controlled substances must be maintained for two years, kept in an area separate from the patient chart, and available for inspection by DEA personnel at any time. Any controlled substance administered to a patient must be recorded in a log with the date, time, patient name, dosage, and amount discarded, if appropriate. The controlled substance log is required in addition to documentation in the patient chart.

Schedule drugs must be stored in a safe or in a locked box inside another locked box that is securely fastened to the wall. The drugs must be counted by two staff members whenever keys are transferred. Two staff members must document any discrepancy in the drug count. Missing drugs must be reported immediately to the DEA and the local law enforcement agency. An investigation must also be initiated per established office policy. The disposal of an unused portion of a controlled substance must be witnessed by two staff members and documented on the controlled substance inventory form. All scheduled drugs must be returned to the pharmacy to be destroyed. Schedule II drugs must be counted by a licensed pharmacist, and that number verified by the office staff prior to being destroyed.

Medication Measurement and Conversion

Different systems are used to measure drugs before they are administered. Historically, narcotics, barbiturates, aspirin, acetaminophen, atropine, and thyroid hormone replacements have been prescribed in apothecary and metric dosages. The apothecary system of weights is rarely used today. The metric system is the most widely used measurement system. Other systems are medication-specific: mEq for electrolytes (e.g., potassium), units (e.g., insulin), inches (Nitrobid paste), and drops (liquid medication administered by dropper). Percentages are used to measure the mixtures used in intravenous solutions or ointments. Household measurements (teaspoon, tablespoon, etc.) cannot be standardized and are therefore not used often. When medication dosage is ordered in teaspoons, the pharmacy includes a standardized medication cup or spoon with the teaspoon level clearly marked.

The units of apothecary measurement include the minim (or drop), grain, and dram. The grain unit is based on the weight of one grain of wheat. The metric equivalent of one grain (gr ĭ) is 60 milligrams (60 mg). One dram (dr ĭ) equals 4–5 milliliters (4–5 ml), or one teaspoon (1 tsp). Apothecary dosages are written with the unit first, followed by a Roman numeral—for example, gr iv, meaning 4 grains.

As a medical assistant you should have a basic understanding of the apothecary system, because some physicians still write orders with these abbreviations. It is also important to remember that similarities between some abbreviations may cause inaccurate dosage administration. For example, the symbol for dram is ℨ, and the symbol for ounce is ℥. A medication error occurs if a patient receives an ounce (30 ml) when a dram (4–5 ml) was ordered. Another error is mistaking gr (grain) for gm (gram).

Metric measurements consist of units of length (meter), volume (liter), and weight or mass (gram). The first step in studying the metric system is to memorize the order of the metric prefixes: kilo-, hecto-, deka-, deci-, centi-, milli-, and micro-. Then pair the numerical value with the prefix: kilo- = 1000, hecto- = 100, and so forth. Converting from one metric unit to another is a matter of moving the decimal a specific number of places in one direction or the other. For example, 1 liter becomes X milliliters by moving three decimal places to the right: 1000.0 milliliters. To convert 1 liter to X kiloliters, move the decimal three places to the left: 0.001 kiloliters. Because of the extra three digit places between milli- and micro- units, an extra three decimal places would need to be added or subtracted, depending on the direction of the conversion.

The MA uses only some of the basic metric units for conversion: kilogram, meter, liter, gram, centimeter, millimeter, milliliter, milligram, and microgram. The other units are used more commonly in scientific research.

Table 9-6 lists the most common metric and apothecary/metric equivalents. Printed conversion charts are posted in most medication preparation workstations. Be sure to double-check any conversion you have calculated against the printed chart.

TABLE 9-6 COMMON METRIC AND APOTHECARY/METRIC EQUIVALENTS

	Metric
Weight	1 kilogram (kg) = 2.2 pounds (lb)
	1 kilogram (kg) = 1000 grams (gm)
	1 gram (gm) = 1000 milligrams (mg)
	1 milligram (mg) = 1000 micrograms (mcg)
Length	1 inch (in) = 2.5 centimeters (cm)
Volume	1 liter (L) = 1000 milliliters (ml) or 1000 cubic centimeters (cc)*

	Apothecary/Metric
Weight	1 ounce (oz) = 30 grams (gm)
	1 gram (gm) = 15 grains (gr)
	1 grain (gr) = 60 milligrams (mg)
	1/2 grain (gr) = 30 milligrams (mg)
Volume	1 gallon (4 quarts) = 4000 milliliters (ml)
	1 quart (2 pints or 32 fluidounces) = 1000 milliters (ml)
	1 pint (16 fluidounces) = 500 milliliters (ml)
	1 cup (8 fluidounces) = 250 milliliters (ml)
	1 fluidounce (8 fluidrams) = 30 milliters (ml)
	1 fluidram (60 minims) = 4 milliliters (ml)
	1 milliliter (ml) = 15 minims

*cc and ml are used interchangeably (e.g., 1 cc = 1 ml)

Dosage Calculation

Dosage calculations are based on adult dosages, pediatric dosages, or the patient's weight in pounds or kilograms. Although most drugs have standard adult dosages, other factors may need to be considered for the elderly, the extremely thin, the young, and patients with illness or disease conditions. The concentration of the drug is another factor that may enter into the calculation.

As an example, consider the following scenario. A patient weighs 110 pounds. The medication dosage to be given is 4 mg/kg. The medication comes in a vial of 200 mg/ml.

1. Convert pounds to kilograms if necessary. To convert pounds to kilograms, *divide* the patient's weight by 2.2. To convert kilograms to pounds, *multiply* the patient's weight by 2.2. When converting pounds to kilograms, you should always end with a smaller number. When converting kilograms to pounds, your final answer should always be larger than your starting number. To convert 110 pounds to kilograms: 110/2.2 = 50 kilograms. To convert 50 kilograms to pounds: 50 × 2.2 = 110 pounds.

2. Calculate the medication for the kg weight of the patient. The dosage to be given is 4 mg/kg.

$$\frac{X \text{ mg}}{50 \text{ kg}} = \frac{4 \text{ mg}}{1 \text{ kg}}$$

Cross-multiply and divide as above to find the unknown.

$$200 \text{ mg/kg} = X \text{ mg/kg}$$
$$200 \text{ mg} = X \text{ mg}$$
$$200 = X$$

The answer is 200 mg.

3. Calculate the amount of tablets or solution to be given to the patient.

$$\frac{100 \text{ mg}}{1 \text{ ml}} = \frac{200 \text{ mg}}{X \text{ ml}}$$

Cross-multiply and divide as above to find the unknown.

$$100 \text{ mg}/X \text{ ml} = 200 \text{ mg}/1 \text{ ml}$$
$$100 \text{ mg} = 200 \text{ mg}$$
$$100 X = 200$$
$$X = 1$$

The amount to be given to the patient for the correct amount of medication in this scenario is 1 ml.

Keep in mind that the physician will likely order the amount to be given based on his or her knowledge of the standard dose. If you are unfamiliar with the standard dose, look up the standard dose or the amount to be given per weight in kilograms and calculate as a double-check. Remember that most medication errors occur because of shortcuts or omission in following the rights of medication administration.

Metric and Household Systems of Measurement

As an MA, you may use one of two types of measurement in the medical office to calculate medication dosage: metric or household measurements. Although household measurements are approximate and used infrequently in the medical office, you should still be familiar with them. The metric system, considered the official measurement for scientific purposes, is used more frequently. Table 9-7 lists common household measurements. Metric measurements and their equivalent household measurements are listed in Table 9-8.

You will likely be required to calculate dosages using metric measurements. For example, the doctor orders 0.2 grams of

---

TABLE 9-7 COMMON HOUSEHOLD MEASUREMENTS

60 drops* = 1 teaspoon (tsp)
3 tsp = 1 tablespoon (tbsp)
2 tbsp = 1 ounce
8 ounces = 1 regular glass or cup
16 tbsp = 1 cup
2 cups = 1 pint (pt)
2 pints (pt) = 1 quart (qt)
4 quarts (qt) = 1 gallon (gal)

* The approximate measurement of drops depends on the thickness of the liquid and the opening in the dropper.

TABLE 9-8 METRIC AND HOUSEHOLD MEASUREMENTS: APPROXIMATE EQUIVALENTS

Metric	Household
1 gm	1/4 tsp
15 gm	1 tbsp
30 gm	1 ounce
1 kg	2.2 lbs
1 mL	15 drops
5 mL	1 tsp
15 mL	1 tbsp
30 mL	1 fl. oz.
500 mL	1 pt
1,000 mL	4 cups (1 qt)
2.5 cm	1 inch

Gatifloxacin for a patient. The medication is available in 400 mg tablets. Begin with an equation using proportions, or ratios.

1. 1,000 mg : 1 gm = X mg : 0.2 gm
   This equation is read as "1,000 milligrams is to 1 gram as X milligrams is to 0.2 grams." Always make certain you have an equal equation: mg : gm = mg : gm.

2. Solve for the unknown by multiplying the means by the mean and the extremes by the extremes. The means of a proportion are the inner two numbers, and the extremes are the outer two numbers. In the equation above, 1 gm and X mg are the means and 1,000 mg and 0.2 gm are the extremes.

$$1 \text{ gm} \times X = 1X$$
$$1,000 \times 0.2 = 200$$
$$1 X = 200$$
$$X = 200 \text{ mg}$$

3. Now calculate the number of tablets to be given.

Known unit on hand : known dosage form = dose ordered : unknown amount to be given
$$400 \text{ mg} : 1 \text{ tablet} = 200 \text{ mg} : X \text{ tablets}$$
$$400 : 1 = 200 : X$$

4. Multiply the means by the means and the extremes by the extremes.

$$400 \times X = 400X$$
$$1 \times 200 = 200$$
$$400X = 200$$
$$X = 0.5 \ (1/2 \text{ of a } 400 \text{ mg tablet})$$

Calculating Pediatric Dosages by Body Weight

According to the Institute of Medicine, 7,000 patients are killed and 375,000 are injured every year due to prescription error. Many medications, especially in the pediatric setting, are given in doses based on a patient's weight. In the past, Young's, Clark's, and Fried's methods of calculations were used to determine what percent of an adult dose was appropriate for a child. But because children do not develop and grow in steady, predictable patterns, these calculations are no longer used.

There are two ways to determine the exact dosage of medication for a child: according to body weight or according to body mass (BSA). The calculation based on body weight is the most widely used, and most people find it easier to calculate correctly. BSA calculations require the use of a formula and a nomogram.

As an example of body weight calculation, the doctor orders medication at 15 mg/kg/day for a young patient. The patient is to take the medication with a meal three times per day for 30 days, then be reevaluated. You weigh the patient before beginning your calculations. She weighs 55 pounds.

1. Convert pounds to kilograms.

$$55 \text{ lbs} \div 2.2 = 25 \text{ kg}$$

2. Calculate the dosage (15 mg/kg/day) for the client's weight, or 15 mg/25 kg/day.

$$15 \text{ mg} \times 25 = 375 \text{ mg/day}$$
$$375 \text{ mg/day} \div 3 \text{ doses/day} = 125 \text{ mg per dose}$$

Keys to Success
ZERO VS. 0

When dosage is communicated verbally, the word *zero* must be used rather than number 0 to avoid confusion with the letter O. For example, 0.05 mg is said as "zero point zero five milligrams." Likewise, a decimal point should always be preceded by a zero (for example, 0.3 mg, or "zero point three milligrams," not .3).

3. The patient should take 125 mg of medication with each meal for the next 30 days.
4. The total number of 125 mg tablets needed to fill the prescription would be 3 tablets per day × 30 days = 90 tablets.

Safety Guidelines for Administering Medications

Medications should be prepared in a well-lit environment with a minimum of distraction. Always wash your hands before beginning the procedure. Always practice the "six rights" and the three label checkpoints when preparing any medication. These factors are as follows:

1. Right patient:
   • Identify the patient by asking him or her to state name.
2. Right drug (medication):
   • Dispense or administer only medications you have prepared yourself.
   • Compare the medication with the physician's order three times:
      • when removing the medication from the storage area
      • before taking the medication from the container
      • before returning the medication to the storage area or disposing of the empty container
3. Right dose:
   • Confirm the adult or child dosage.
   • Verify the accuracy of your dosage calculation with another clinical staff member.
4. Right route:
   • Confirm the route on the physician's order.
   • Use the correct site for parenteral medication.
5. Right time: Confirm the specified time with the physician's order.
6. Right documentation:
   • Record the date, time, name, dosage, and administration route of the medication on the patient chart. All documentation must be signed by the individual dispensing or administering the medication.
   • If the medication is an injection, record the site.
   • For immunizations and allergy medications, also document the lot number and expiration date.
   • If the medication is not given, document the reasons and report to the physician.

The Prescription

The physician is responsible for prescribing medications, either in written form (physician's order or prescription) or verbally. A prescription is a legal document and should be typed or written in ink. Depending on state practice acts, you may complete a prescription blank according to the physician's order and have him/her sign it. All Schedule II, III, and IV drug prescriptions must be signed by the physician. Office protocol must be followed in every case. You may call a prescription in to a pharmacy, except for controlled substances.

A written prescription is usually a preprinted form with the physician's name, address, phone number, and DEA number (Figures 9-3 ◆ and 9-4 ◆). Some physicians write prescriptions on hospital or clinic forms printed with the hospital or clinic name and information. Prescription forms for controlled substances are printed on special paper that identifies any alterations to the prescription, especially attempted erasures.

In addition to the physician's data, the customary parts of a prescription are:

1. the patient's name and address, and the prescription date
2. superscription: the symbol Rx, which means "take"
3. inscription (main part of the prescription): drug name, form, and strength
4. subscription: directions to pharmacist for amount of drug to be dispensed
5. signature: patient instructions (Sig:) to be placed on label
6. refill information ("REPETATUR 0 1 2 3 PRN"): refill instructions for the physician to circle
7. physician's signature and "Dispense as written" or "Substitute Generic Medication"

Some preprinted prescriptions feature a box with the word "Label," which instructs the pharmacist to label the prescription container.

Table 9-9 lists the most common pharmacology abbreviations used in prescriptions and other medical forms. In May 2005, in order to reduce the number of medical errors related to the incorrect use of terminology, The Joint Commission on Accreditation of Healthcare Organizations (JCAHO) issued a "do not use" list of abbreviations, acronyms, and symbols. The ab-

---

IMA N. PAINE, M.D.
2105 Lancey Dr., Suite 1, Modesto, CA 95355
Phone (209) xxx-xxxx

Name _____ Date _____

Address_____

R̽

_____ M.D.

DEA#_____ Refills: 0   1   2   3   Other _____

Figure 9-3 ◆ Example of a prescription form used in a medical office

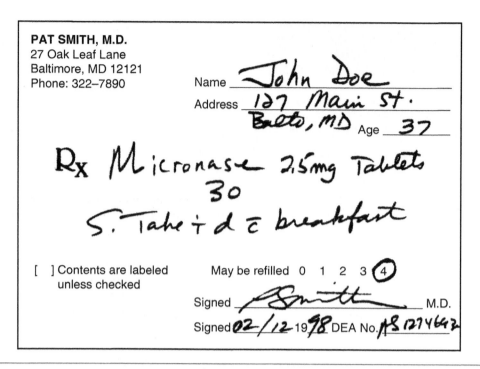

PAT SMITH, M.D.
27 Oak Leaf Lane
Baltimore, MD 12121
Phone: 322–7890

Name *John Doe*

Address *127 Main St.*
Balto, MD Age *37*

Rx *Micronase 2.5mg Tablets*
30
S. Take 1 d c̄ breakfast

[ ] Contents are labeled
unless checked

May be refilled   0   1   2   3 ④

Signed _____ M.D.

Signed *02/12*-19*98* DEA No. *AS 1274642*

Figure 9-4 ◆ Example of a completed prescription

TABLE 9-9 COMMONLY USED PHARMACOLOGY ABBREVIATIONS			
Abbreviation	**Medical Terminology**	**Abbreviation**	**Medical Terminology**
aa	equal parts, of each	kg	kilogram
ac	before meals	l	liter
ad lib	as desired	lb	pound
amp	ampule	mcg, µg	microgram
amt	amount	med	medicine
ante	before	mEq	milliequivalent
aq, aqua	water	mg	milligram
ad	right ear	npo	nil per os, nothing by mouth
au	left ear	noc	night
bid	twice a day	ns	normal saline
c, cum	with	oz	ounce
cap	capsule	pc	post cibum, after meals
cc	cubic centimeter	po	per os, by mouth
cm	centimeter	prn	whenever necessary
dc	discontinue	q	every
dil	dilute	qh	every hour
disp	dispense	qid	four times a day
dr	dram	qn	every night
elix.	elixir	qns	quantity not sufficient
et	and	qs	quantity sufficient
ext	extract	q2h	every 2 hours
fl	fluid	q4h	every 4 hours
fl oz	fluid ounce	rx	prescription
g	gram	s	sans, without
gr	grain	sol	solution
gtt	drops	ss	one-half
h or hr	hour	stat	immediately
hs	hours sleep, at bedtime	sc, sub-q	subcutaneous
H₂O	water	tab	tablet
inj	inject	tid	three times a day
im	intramuscular	to	telephone order
id	intradermal	ung	ointment
iv	intravenous	vo	verbal order

Keys to Success
PRESCRIPTION DRUGS TAKEN DURING PREGNANCY

The side effects of thalidomide taken during pregnancy called public attention in the 1960s to the teratogenic effects of certain medications. Babies whose mothers had taken thalidomide were born with partial or undeveloped limbs. Thalidomide was not approved for use in the United States but was available in Europe as a sedative. Pregnant women obtained the drug while traveling in Europe or from others who had traveled there. As a result of these birth defects, the FDA implemented a system for classifying drugs based on safety for consumption during pregnancy. The categories are A (lowest risk factor), B, C, D, and X (highest risk factor). Package inserts identify the level of risk.

breviations must be included on each accredited organization's "do not use" list. It is important to familiarize yourself with this list, which can be viewed at http://www.jointcommission.org/PatientSafety/DoNotUseList/.

Safeguarding Prescription Pads

The potential for theft and substance abuse exists in every medical office. You and other medical office staff are responsible for the safekeeping of prescription pads. The following guidelines help to prevent theft and drug abuse.

- Prescription blanks and preprinted prescriptions should be stored in a locked area. They must never be left lying around in the office.

PROCEDURE 9-1 Demonstrate the Preparation of a Prescription for the Physician's Signature

Theory

In compliance with the Controlled Substance Act of 1970, all physicians who prescribe any type of drug, either over-the-counter or controlled, must register with the DEA. Every physician must fill out a registration form, renewable every three years, with his or her state license number and signature. Physicians who write prescriptions in different states must be registered in each state. Physicians who practice in multiple locations in the same state must register each address. The certificate of approval from the DEA must be kept at each registered location and be available for inspection by officials.

Every prescription must bear the physician's name, address, and DEA number in permanent ink so that it can be traced back to the physician who authorized the medication. There is no approved medical use for Schedule I drugs, so prescriptions for these drugs are prohibited. Schedule II medications are controlled substances for which a written prescription is required. As refills for these drugs are not allowed, the patient must obtain a new prescription whenever additional medication is needed. In cases of emergency, the DEA allows for a one-time limited amount of Schedule II medications to be phoned in by the physician, with the signed, written prescription to be delivered to the pharmacy within 72 hours.

Once a prescription is filled, all identifying information, including an assigned prescription number, is entered into a computer. The paper version of the prescription is then filed and kept for a minimum of seven years. The pharmacy may file prescriptions according to schedule (II through V).

Materials

- physician's order for medication
- patient chart
- ink pen or computer if Rx is typed
- blank prescription

Competency

(**Conditions**) With the necessary materials, you will be able to (**Task**) write a prescription (**Standards**) correctly within 10 minutes.

1. Gather the equipment.
2. Obtain the prescription information (name, dose, amount, frequency, refills) from the physician.
3. Correctly write out the prescription according the information received from the physician.
4. Document the procedure. Include the date, time, medication, strength, dose, frequency, and refills allowed. Many offices will want a photocopy of the written Rx.

Patient Education

If office procedures indicate the need, instruct the patient when and how to obtain refills if any are needed. Some offices prefer that the patient call the pharmacy directly with the refill request, some have dedicated prescription refill lines, and others prefer to fax requests.

Charting Example

01/26/XX 8:00 am Patient received written prescription for Ambien 10mg #30 for treatment of idiopathic insomnia. Sig: Take 1 tablet by mouth 30 minutes prior to sleep on nights that are available to dedicate to a full 8 hours of sleep. No refills issued. Patient instructed to avoid taking medication on nights when 8 hours of sleep are not available and to watch for side effects, such as but not limited to hypersomnia. Photocopy of prescription filled in chart under medication flow sheet. Juanita Hernandez, CMA

- The physician should use one prescription pad at a time.
- Prescription blanks should be numbered and used in numerical order.

Forms and Routes of Medication Administration

Medications may be administered in several different forms. Solid forms include tablets (chewable, sublingual, enteric coated, and plain), capsules (sustained release and caplet form), lozenges, suppositories (vaginal, rectal, or urethral), and dermatological forms (creams and ointments, transdermal patches). Liquid forms include elixirs, solutions, suspensions, syrups, sprays, and tinctures. Injectables are available in powder form (to be mixed prior to administration) or in commercially prepared, ready-to-use liquid form.

Medications may also be administered via a number of routes: oral (swallowing), sublingual (under the tongue), transdermal, parenteral (intradermal, subcutaneous, intramuscular, and intravenous, buccal, inhalation, irrigation, instillation, rectal, topical. See Figures 9-5 ◆ and 9-6 ◆ and Table 9-10.

The form of medication prescribed for specific patients may be affected by certain factors. For example, if a patient is unable to take the oral form of digoxin, it may be administered intravenously. A physician may also prescribe the intravenous route to obtain rapid therapeutic action and later prescribe the oral form for daily use. Other factors in the choice of medication form and route include the present functioning of the healthy or diseased body as well as the patient's absorption, distribution, metabolism, and excretion capabilities. Age is another factor. In the elderly, medication is generally absorbed, distributed, metabolized, and excreted

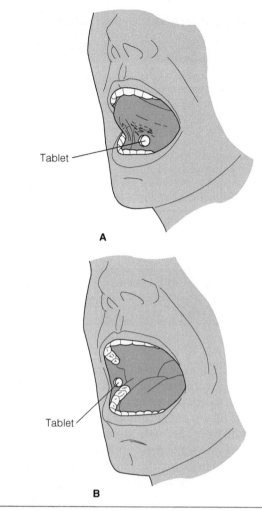

A

B

Figure 9-5 ◆ (A) Sublingual administration; (B) Buccal administration

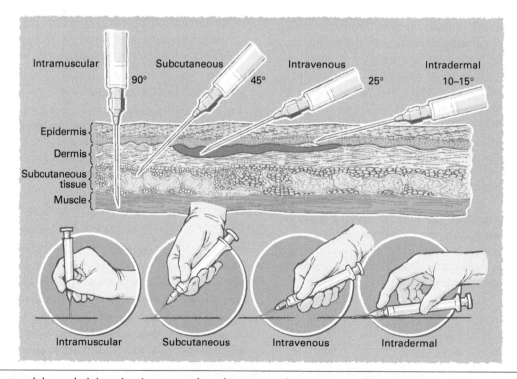

Figure 9-6 ◆ Parenteral drug administration: Intramuscular, subcutaneous, intravenous, and intradermal

TABLE 9-10 MEDICATION FORMS, ROUTES, AND PROCEDURES FOR ADMINISTERING

Medication Form	Route of Administration	Procedure
Capsule, pill, tablet, spansule, liquid, solution	Oral	Medication is given orally and swallowed.
Tablet	Buccal (oral cheek space)	The tablet is placed between the gums or teeth and the cheek and is absorbed as it dissolves.
Tablet, liquid, or solution	Sublingual	Medication is placed under the tongue for absorption through the oral mucous membrane.
Aerosol, mist, spray, or stream	Inhalation	Equipment (inhalation device, nebulizer, or ventilator) dispenses the medication in a mist or liquid form for inhalation.
Liquid medication in solution form	Irrigation	Solution is passed through a cavity or over a membrane, then allowed to drain.
	Instillation	Medication is released into a body cavity for absorption by tissue.
Sterile solution	Injection (intradermal, subcutaneous, or intramuscular)	Medication is injected into body tissue.
	Intravenous (infusion or injection)	Medication is injected or instilled into a vein.
Solution or suppository	Rectal	Medication is introduced into the rectum for absorption.
Cream, dermal patch (transdermal), lotion, spray, tincture, powder, and ointment	Topical	Medication is applied to the skin with gloved hands. Dermal patches are self-adhering.
Suppository, cream, ointment, foam, solution and liquid	Vaginal	Medication is introduced into the vagina by insertion, application, or irrigation.

more slowly. Dosages may also be smaller because of the potential for toxicity.

The oral route is the safest route of administration, because the medication can be retrieved, if necessary, in the immediate minutes after administration. Emesis can be induced and the drug expelled from the body. IV administration requires complete accuracy in administration because once the medication is injected into the bloodstream, its action is permanent and retrieval is not possible. The rapid action of sublingual and buccal medications is essential in emergency situations, but again, the action usually cannot be halted.

Medications administered by different routes are absorbed by the body at different rates, as follows.

1. *Oral:* Depending on the medication type (tablet, capsule, liquid, etc.) and whether the medication is to be taken on a full stomach, oral medications can take 10 to 30 minutes to be absorbed and distributed in the body. Most oral medications are absorbed through the wall of the small intestine, which accounts for the delay in absorption time. The oral route is the route most often prescribed because it is quick, easy, and can be done at home, which is convenient for patients who require multiple doses of the same medication.

2. *Injection:* Medications given by injection are absorbed quickly, due to the high blood flow in muscles. The medication is absorbed in the muscle fibers and transferred to the bloodstream, then throughout the body. The injectable route is often used for medications that may cause GI upset and possibly interfere with absorption, and for medications that are taken infrequently, such as monthly B$_{12}$ injections for pernicious anemia.

3. *Intravenous:* Medications given via IV have a rapid onset. The medication is administered directly into the bloodstream, causing an immediate effect. IV medications are generally given only in emergency situations and by a

trained physician. Medical assistants cannot administer IV medications.

Parenteral Administration

Parenteral routes of administration include all routes that do not involve the gastrointestinal tract. Common parenteral routes are intramuscular injections, intravenous injections or infusions, subcutaneous injections, inhalation, and topical or dermal application. Drugs administered through the GI tract usually have a slower onset of action than those administered by parenteral route. Also, some drugs are irritating to the stomach, and others may be destroyed or inactivated by gastric acids.

Drugs administered via dermal application are absorbed through the skin. The drugs placed in dermal patches have different release times, allowing for a more consistent blood level of the medication. Medications delivered by this route include cardiovascular drugs (Nitroderm), pain medications (Duragesic, Lidoderm patches), hormones (contraceptives and HRT), and antinausea medications (Transderm scop).

Table 9-11 describes various types of parenteral administration by injection. Injectable medications require the use of a syringe and needle. Although injections may be administered by intravenous route, the common routes used in the physician's office are intradermal, subcutaneous, and intramuscular. The different methods and sites of injection, as well as the different types and amounts of medication, require a variety of syringes and needles.

Syringes commonly used in the physician's office include the tuberculin, insulin, and 3 cc/ml syringe. The tuberculin syringe has very small calibration markings that allow injection of amounts as minute as 0.1 cc (Figure 9-7 ◆). Tuberculin syringes are used for Mantoux and allergy tests via the intradermal route. Insulin is administered with insulin syringes, usually U50 or U100 marked, via the subcutaneous route (Figure 9-8 ◆). The 3 cc/ml syringe (Figure 9-9 ◆) is used most often for intramuscular injections. If the amount of med-

TABLE 9-11 TYPES OF INJECTIONS

	Intradermal	Subcutaneous	Intramuscular
Purpose	Allergy tests and Mantoux testing	Slow absorption of medication	Quick absorption of medication
Sites	Distal to the antecubital space of the anterior aspect of the forearm	Outer aspect of the upper arm, abdomen, and anterior thigh	Dorsal aspect of the gluteus, deltoid, vastus lateralis of the thigh, and ventral aspect of the gluteus
Amount	0.1 to 0.3 ml	Less than 2 ml	2 to 5 ml. Dosages above 4 ml should be divided and administered at two different sites.
Needle Length and Size	1-1/2" to 5/8" length, 25 to 27 gauge	5/8" to 1" length, 22 to 27 gauge	1-1/2" to 2" length, 14 to 22 gauge

ication is greater than the size of the syringe, the dosage may be split and administered in different sites with two syringes.

Needle sizes vary according to the type and depth of tissue to be injected. Tuberculin and insulin syringe needles, which are used for intradermal and subcutaneous administration, respectively, are smaller than the needles used for intramuscular injections. Intradermal and subcutaneous injections are administered into the most exterior layers of the skin. Intramuscular injections penetrate into the deeper tissues below the skin.

Always follow safety procedures and universal precautions when handling sharps. Avoid recapping needles unless you use a slide cap procedure. In this method, you slide the exposed needle into the cap before lifting the syringe/needle combination to an upright position or to another surface before injection. Do not anchor the cap tightly to the syringe. A tight cap would be hard to remove and increase the risk of needle injury during removal. (Newer safety syringes have safety guards that prevent needle stick injury.) After use, dispose of syringe/needle combinations and other sharps, such as glass

ampules, into the nearest sharps container. (∞ See Chapter 5 for more information concerning the use and disposal of sharps.)

Ampules and Vials

Medication for parenteral administration comes in ready-to-use liquid form in vials and ampules and in powdered form for reconstitution. Ampules and vials are available in small and large sizes and in clear or darkened glass. Some medications are stored in plastic vials. Storage in a glass ampule prevents a chemical reaction with other materials, such as the rubber stopper of a vial or the plastic of a pre-filled syringe. An ampule also ensures sterility.

An ampule removed from storage or packaging may have fluid in the top portion above the neck or breaking line. Tapping lightly with a fingertip may be enough to release the fluid into the bottom portion. If bubbles develop, however, the final dosage amount may be affected. Another method is to hold the top of the ampule and twirl it so that the medication slides into the bottom.

Most ampules are painted with a break line at the upper portion of the neck, marking the expected break and weakest

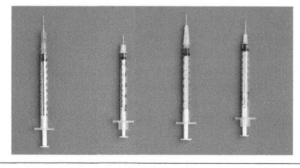

Figure 9-7 ◆ Tuberculin syringes

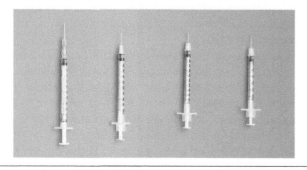

Figure 9-8 ◆ Insulin syringes

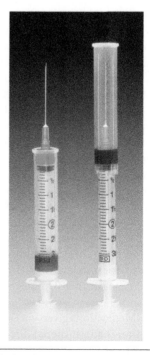

Figure 9-9 ◆ 3 cc/ml syringes

PROCEDURE 9-2 Demonstrate Withdrawing Medication from an Ampule

Theory

An ampule is a single-use, single-dose, sterile glass container of liquid medication. Many prepackaged surgical sets, such as disposable Thorascopy tray sets, contain Xylocaine or another medication in an ampule as part of the kit.

Materials

- sterile filter needle/syringe set
- ampule of medication
- sterile gauze 2×4s or 4×4s or safety ampule breaker
- alcohol wipes
- gloves
- sharps container
- patient chart

Competency

(**Conditions**) With the necessary materials, you will be able (**Task**) to withdraw medication from an ampule (**Standards**) correctly within 15 minutes.

1. Wash your hands and gather equipment.
2. Check to make sure the medication matches the physician's order. Calculate the dosage, if necessary. Look up information relating to the medication's function, usual doses, and side effects. Check for patient allergies.

3. Check the medication label a second time against the physician's order. Verify the medication, expiration date, and medication quality following the six rights.
4. Identify the patient and escort him or her to the treatment area. Verify allergy information in the chart and ask the patient if they have allergies.
5. Put on your gloves.
6. Dislodge any medication that may be trapped in the ampule neck by holding the ampule by the neck and quickly flicking your wrist in a downward motion.
7. Disinfect the ampule with an alcohol swab and check the label again for correct medication and dosage.
8. Completely wrap the neck of the ampule with the sterile cotton gauze and snap off the top by pulling it toward you (Figure 9-10 ◆). Discard the top in a sharps container.
9. With a filtered needle, withdraw the necessary medication amount. You can withdraw the medication with the ampule inverted or not (Figure 9-11 ◆).
10. Change needles and discard the filtered needle into a sharps container.
11. Identify the patient, if you have drawn up the medication in a separate room. If the medication will affect driving. Verify patient has a driver or ride home.
12. Administer the medication according to the physician's orders.

Figure 9-10 ◆ Snap off the top of the ampule.

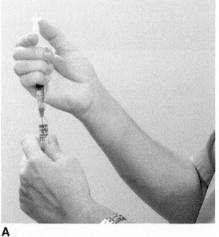

A

B

Figure 9-11 ◆ Withdraw the necessary medication amount. You can withdraw the medication with the ampule upright (A) or inverted (B).

continued

PROCEDURE 9-2 Demonstrate Withdrawing Medication from an Ampule *(continued)*

13. Discard the used needle into the sharps container.
14. Remove the gloves and wash your hands.
15. Document the procedure. Include date, time, site, medication, route, and amount administered. Follow office policy for recording the expiration date and lot number.

Patient Education

If office policy or potential side effects dictate that the patient wait in the reception area for a specified period of time, explain the reasons for the waiting period. Be prepared to ex-

plain side effects the patient should be alert for and report. Instruct the patient to report any sudden reactions to the medication, whether local or general.

Charting Example

04/18/XX 9:35 AM Phenergan 25mg injection administered to patient in the left ventrogluteal area for leg pain. Patient was instructed to wait in the exam room for 20 minutes for observation and was released. Dennis Benson, CMA

point of the glass. Breaking the top of the ampule usually requires only an alcohol pad to protect you. Safety ampule breakers are also available. For a larger ampule, wipe the neck with an alcohol wipe, then use 2 × 2 gauze to snap off the top. Discard the top into a sharps container. Using a filtered needle to withdraw medication will prevent glass fragments from entering the syringe. If it is necessary to invert the ampule to withdraw medication, note that the fluid will not drain because of the air pressure outside the ampule pushing up on the liquid at the smaller ampule neck. Do not inject air into the ampule while it is upside down, as this will force medication or diluent to drain. After the medication has been withdrawn, pull the plunger back to draw the medication into the syringe. Tap any bubbles to the top air pocket, then push the plunger up until the correct dosage is measured (Figure 9-12 ◆).

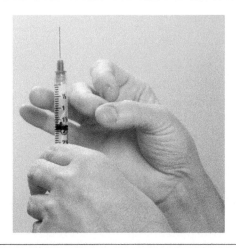

Figure 9-12 ◆ Tap syringe to remove any air bubbles.

PROCEDURE 9-3 Demonstrate Withdrawing Medication from a Vial

Theory

Medication comes in a variety of containers, and liquid medications are often supplied in vials made of glass or plastic, depending on the requirements of the medication.

Materials

- gloves
- alcohol wipes
- two appropriate-sized needles and a syringe
- vial of medication
- bandage strips
- sharps container
- patient chart

Competency

(**Conditions**) With the necessary materials, you will (**Task**) withdraw a medication for injection from a vial (**Standards**) correctly within 15 minutes.

1. Wash your hands and gather the equipment.
2. Select the correct-size needle to withdraw the medication. Viscous medications require a greater needle gauge.
3. Check the vial label against the physician's medication order (Figure 9-13 ◆).
4. Remove the plastic cap from the vial if necessary. If the vial has already been used, wipe the rubber stopper with an alcohol wipe (Figure 9-14 ◆).
5. Inject air into the vial in an amount equal to the medication being removed.
   - Place the vial on a firm surface and insert the needle through the rubber stopper.
   - Inject air into the vial.
   - Invert the vial with the needle tip under the surface of the medication to avoid getting air into the syringe (Figure 9-15 ◆).
   - Pull back the plunger to withdraw the necessary amount of medication (Figure 9-16 ◆).

PROCEDURE 9-3 Demonstrate Withdrawing Medication from a Vial *(continued)*

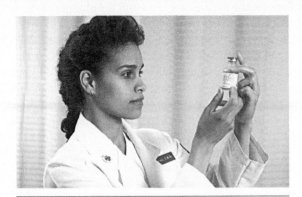

Figure 9-13 ◆ Check the vial against the physician's order.

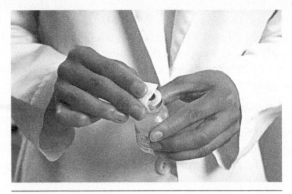

Figure 9-14 ◆ Wipe the rubber stopper with an alcohol wipe.

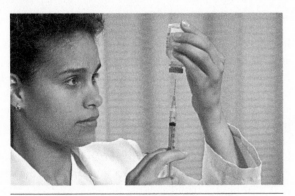

Figure 9-15 ◆ Invert the vial with the needle tip under the surface of the medication to avoid getting air into the syringe.

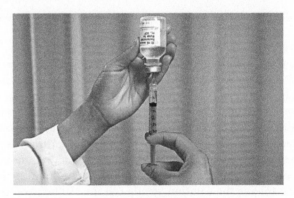

Figure 9-16 ◆ Pull back the plunger to withdraw the necessary amount of medication.

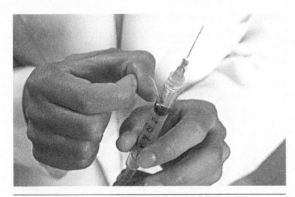

Figure 9-17 ◆ Tap firmly on the syringe to release air bubbles.

- If air bubbles are present, tap firmly on the syringe to release the bubbles and reinject them into the vial (Figure 9-17 ◆).
- Check the level of medication in the vial and withdraw more if needed.
- Withdraw the needle from the vial and replace the cap.

6. Remove the needle and discard it in a sharps container.
7. Replace the needle with a sharp, sterile needle of appropriate size.
8. Inject the medication at the appropriate site.
9. Document the procedure. Include the date, time, medication, site, route, and amount administered. Follow office policy for recording the medication expiration date and lot number.

Patient Education
See Procedure 9-1.

Charting Example
02/22/XX 4:45 PM Patient received monthly injection of B12, cyanocobalamin crystalline, for anemia. Maintenance dose of 100mcg (1 mL) administered subcutaneously in the right ventrogluteal area. Patient was observed in the waiting area for 20 minutes and told to report any unusual effects immediately. Elaine Rodgers, CMA

A vial may be made of glass or plastic, depending on the storage requirements of the medication or diluent, and may be single- or multiple-dose. All vials (even new ones) should be cleaned prior to use. When using a multiple-dose vial, always wipe the rubber stopper with an alcohol wipe before withdrawing the medication or diluent. Repeated use of a multiple-dose vial can damage the rubber stopper. If the stopper has been damaged or you can see rubber particles in the vial, follow office procedure for disposal of the vial and the unused portion of medication.

It is important to follow procedure for injecting air into a vial to prevent the creation of a vacuum. You will need two needles for this procedure, one to withdraw medication and the other to administer the medication to the patient. When you force the first needle through the rubber stopper to withdraw the medication, the tip is dulled and must be replaced for the injection.

First clean the rubber stopper of the vial and allow it to air-dry. Remove the needle cover and pull the plunger of the empty syringe back until the marked measurement side of the rubber stopper is at the correct dosage level. Puncture the rubber stopper of the vial and inject the air into the air space. (If air is injected into the fluid in the vial, bubbles will form. Bubbles may affect the accuracy of the dosage.) Keeping the syringe and needle in place, hold the vial with the index and second fingers of the other hand. Invert the vial with the needle and syringe in place. Keep the needle under the fluid level to withdraw the correct amount of medication. Aspirate a small amount of medication above the correct amount and withdraw the needle from

PROCEDURE 9-4 Demonstrate the Reconstitution of a Powdered Drug for Injection Administration

Theory

When an injectable medication is supplied as a powder, it must first be reconstituted into liquid form, usually with a sterile diluent such as water or saline. A sterile water vial is cleaned and the correct amount is injected into the vial containing the powdered medication and mixed. It is important to read the inserts that come with powdered medications. Many of these medications have a rapid expiration time, beginning as soon as the powder is mixed into liquid form. When mixing the solution, gently roll the vial between the palms of your hands. Do not shake or jolt the container, which would cause bubbles to form in the solution.

Materials

- gloves
- alcohol wipes
- two appropriate-size syringes with needles
- vial of medication
- sterile water
- sharps container
- fine-tip permanent marker
- patient chart

Competency

(**Conditions**) With the necessary materials, you will be able to (**Task**) reconstitute a powdered medication for injection (**Standards**) correctly within 15 minutes.

1. Wash your hands and gather the equipment.
2. Check to make sure the medication matches the physician's order. Calculate the dosage if necessary. Look up information relating to the function of the medication, usual dosage, and side effects. Follow the six rights.
3. Check the medication label again against the physician's order to make sure it is the right medication.

4. Remove the protective tops from the diluent (sterile water) and medication and wipe both with alcohol.
5. Insert one needle into the diluent, making certain to inject an amount of air equal to the amount of solution you are removing. Withdraw the necessary amount of diluent.
6. Inject the diluent into the powdered medication vial.
7. Discard the used needle in the sharps container.
8. Roll the vial containing the diluent and powder between your palms. It may take several minutes to mix the solution thoroughly. Avoid shaking the vial.
9. If the medication will not be used immediately, label the vial with the date and time prepared, your initials, and the expiration date/time.
10. With the second needle, draw up the correct amount of prepared medication to give to the patient.
11. Document the procedure. Include the date, time, medication, site, route, and amount administered. Follow office policy for recording the medication expiration date and lot number.

Patient Education

See Procedure 9-1.

Charting Example

04/28/XX 2:45 PM Patient came in for her monthly injection of Xolair (Omalizumab) 375 mg to be administered by subcutaneous injection as determined by serum total IgE level and patient weight. Xolair chart consulted for appropriate dose assignment. Medication prepared per manufacturer administration guidelines. The medication was administered with a 25-gauge needle, subcutaneous injection. Patient is familiar with common side effects and was given the package insert for reference and instructed to call if any unusual effects should occur. David Johnson, RMA

PROCEDURE 9-5 Demonstrate the Administration of Medication during Infusion Therapy

Theory

Depending on state regulations, a CMA or RMA may be allowed to administer medication to a patient during IV therapy under the supervision of a registered nurse and/or physician. There are several methods for administering medication to a patient receiving infusion therapy. Medications may be added to the primary infusate container, although this is rarely done as pharmacists perform this function in the pharmacy under strict asepsis, to ensure proper mixing and prevent the drug from infusing in the base of the container and being delivered as a bolus dose to the patient. The medication may also be administered directly into a vein that is not being used in the IV therapy. In the most common method, the medication is added through an injection port using the "S-A-S" method described below. Normal saline is injected into the cannula port to ensure the lock is clear ("S"). Then the medication is administered as prescribed by the physician into the cannula port ("A"), followed by more saline to ensure that the full amount of medication has cleared the lock ("S").

Materials

- three syringes with needles
- medication to be administered
- normal saline (0.9%) 4 mL
- alcohol wipes
- gloves
- sharps container
- patient chart
- artificial IV therapy arm, or vein block stimulator

Competency

(**Conditions**) With the necessary materials, you will be able to (**Task**) administer medication (**Standards**) through an intermittent infusion device correctly within 15 minutes.

1. Wash your hands and gather equipment.
2. Check to make sure the medication matches the physician's order. Calculate the dosage, if necessary. Look up information relating to the medication's function, usual doses, and side effects. Check for patient allergies by verifying in chart *and* asking the patient.
3. Check medication compatibility with the infusion product being used.
4. Put on gloves.
5. Disinfect the cannula port with the alcohol wipe.
6. Verify that the cannula and vein are freely open, with no blockages.
7. With the first of the three syringes, slowly inject 2 mL of the normal saline into the cannula port.
8. With the second syringe, administer the medication as prescribed by the physician into the cannula port.
9. With the final syringe, inject 2 mL of normal saline into the cannula port.
10. Remove the gloves and wash your hands.
11. Document the procedure. Include date, time, site, medication, route, and amount administered. Follow office policy for recording the expiration date and lot number.

Patient Education

Be prepared to explain side effects the patient should be alert for and report. Instruct the patient to report any sudden reactions to the medication, whether local or general.

Charting Example

04/18/XX 9:35 AM Injection of medication XXXXX given to patient via cannula port. Injections of 2 mL of normal saline used to ensure cleared lock before and after injection of medication. Infusion therapy continues in the cephalic vein above right dorsal venous arch. Patient reports that the vein is slightly "sore" but he reports he is in no significant pain. 2/10 on the pain scale. Page Wade, RMA

---

the vial. With the needle pointing up, pull the plunger back to create an air pocket at the top of the barrel. Tap all air bubbles to the air pocket. Push the plunger to move the stopper to the correct dosage level. Slide the needle into a cap cover if not administering the medication immediately.

Some medications must be mixed prior to administration because the solution does not remain chemically stable or evenly mixed for extended periods of time. Powdered medication is mixed with a diluent such as sterile saline or water. Diluents are stored in ampules or vials. It is important to follow procedures for removing the correct amount of diluent from a vial or ampule. Using the correct amount ensures correct dilution and the correct dosage as ordered by the physician. To calculate the

amount required for the dosage ordered by the physician, use the strength of the correctly mixed medication. For example, after a medication is reconstituted correctly according to directions, the strength is 50 mg/ml. The physician has ordered 75 mg. Therefore the correct amount of medication to administer is 1.5 ml.

Intravenous Therapy

Medications or therapeutic solutions may be injected directly into the bloodstream for immediate circulation and use by the body. State practice acts designate which health-care professionals can initiate intravenous (IV) fluid therapy and medication administration. Medical assistants must consult their state practice act before attempting any intravenous procedure. In

PROCEDURE 9-6 Demonstrate the Preparation and Administration of Oral Medication

Theory

The preferred route for administering medications is the oral route. Oral medications can be self-administered by the patient at home. The oral route is used when rapid absorption is not necessary and the medication is not destroyed by the gastrointestinal tract before absorption. Patients are more compliant when their medications can be swallowed and can be scheduled around other activities of the day—for example, before or after meals or at bedtime. Patients are also more compliant because of the relatively low cost of oral medications compared to that of other types of medication.

Medications packaged in single-use containers can be checked three times per standard routine and returned to storage if for some reason the medication is not used or the package has not been opened. Medications prepared as stock medications must be poured from the original container according to the prescribed dosage. Whether you are pouring tablets, pills, capsules, liquids, or suspensions, be careful to avoid contaminating the bottle against the container for the patient. Maintaining a small distance between the containers while pouring prevents contamination and enables the continued clean storage of the medication for later use by other patients. Some liquid suspensions separate during storage and must be shaken gently until thoroughly mixed to ensure an accurate dosage of all components. When pouring any liquid medication, hold the container with the palm covering the label. This action will prevent spills or drips from making the label illegible for future use.

Materials

- vial of medication
- gloves
- patient chart

Competency

(**Conditions**) With the necessary materials, you will be able to (**Task**) administer oral medication (**Standards**) correctly within 15 minutes.

1. Wash your hands and gather equipment.
2. Put on gloves.
3. Check to make sure the medication matches the physician's order. Calculate the dosage, if necessary. Look up information relating to the medication's function, usual doses, and side effects. Check for patient allergies by asking patient and verifying in the chart. Always follow the six rights of medication administration.

4. Check the medication label a second time against the physician's order.
5. Identify the patient and escort him or her to the treatment area.
6. Pour the correct amount of medication.
   - *For pills, capsules, and tablets:* Pour the correct amount from the container directly into a medicine cup.
   - *For liquids and suspensions:* If the ingredients are not evenly mixed, shake the bottle gently but thoroughly. Allow time for any bubbles to disappear. When pouring, hold the medication bottle with your palm over the label and hold the medicine cup at eye level.
7. Check a third time to match the medication against the physician's order.
8. If at any time you have doubts about the function of the medication, the dosage or route of administration, or the possibility of an allergic reaction, *immediately* consult the physician.
9. Give the medicine cup to the patient. Have drinking water available for pills, capsules, and tablets, as well as for liquids or suspensions, if necessary.
10. Observe as the patient takes the medication to ensure that it is swallowed completely, without difficulty.
11. Dispose of the used medication cup and preparation supplies. Wash your hands and return the multiple-use medication bottle to the storage shelf.
12. Document the procedure. Include date, time, site, medication, route, and amount administered. Follow office policy for recording the expiration date and lot number.

Patient Education

If office policy or potential side effects dictate that the patient wait in the reception area for a specified period of time, explain the reasons for the waiting period. Be prepared to explain side effects the patient should be alert for and report. Instruct the patient to report any sudden reactions to the medication, whether local or general. Make sure the patient has a ride home if necessary.

Charting Example

04/18/XX 9:35 AM Tylenol #3, two tablets given as ordered by mouth for lt. knee pain. Patient denies any allergy to the Tylenol or codeine components of the medication. Appointment made for follow-up X-ray of left knee upon arrival at the hospital X-ray department because of lingering pain and inability to use non-prescription pain medications. Julia Sanchez, CMA

some states the medical assistant may start IV fluid therapy with advanced training and physician supervision. Medical assistants should be aware of the dangers of administering medications by the intravenous route and recognize they do not have the training necessary to push IV medications (bolus). *The following information is provided only to acquaint you with the IV therapy process and should not be considered a competency.*

Generally, intravenous fluids are administered to replenish body fluid supply and electrolytes, most commonly solutions of 5% dextrose, normal saline, 45% normal saline, or 5% dextrose with normal saline. Dextrose contributes glucose to meet energy needs and saline contributes sodium, an electrolyte that maintains fluid balance and cellular functions. In addition, blood products, including packed cells or plasma; hyperalimentation (designed for patients too sick to meet their own nutritional needs); and medications may be administered by the IV route.

The intravenous administration of medications or solutions may be per unit dosage or may be continuous. Examples of unit dosage are bolus, IV push, or scheduled intermittent administration by heparin lock or piggyback medication into an IV port. An example of continuous dosage is an IV drip that may last several hours or around the clock. The flow rate of intravenous lines is regulated by a flow clamp or infusion pump.

Intravenous administration requires extra knowledge and precautions because of the direct access to the bloodstream. Adverse reactions, which can be fatal, may be caused by the specific medication, too many fluids administered too rapidly into the body, violation of any of the medication rights of administration, or certain pre-existing medical conditions. Nonfatal reactions include necrosis of tissue (sometimes a reaction to chemotherapy) or swelling or infiltration through the blood vessel into the tissue, obstructing IV flow. Any office in which IV fluid therapy is performed must have emergency equipment, emergency medical access, and established office policies for routine administration, dealing with adverse reactions, and the handling of emergencies. The patient and the infusion site must be assessed regularly during the infusion for signs of adverse reactions.

Starting an IV requires preparation. Before an intravenous site is chosen, tubing is selected and connected to the correct solution container, following sterile technique. The tubing is flushed to remove all air. Tape and dressing supplies for the site must also be prepared beforehand. A preparation tray with appropriate IV starter materials and the prepared IV is taken to the patient. An intravenous pole is used to hang the IV solution on.

The intravenous site and the appropriate size and type of catheter are selected. The IV is generally started in the arm, although different medical scenarios may require other sites. The intravenous catheter includes an outer cannula to thread into the vein and an inner needle to serve as a guide for insertion and then to be removed. A constricting tourniquet is placed above the site. The skin is cleansed and the catheter is introduced into the vein to obtain an open blood supply. The tourniquet is released and removed. The plastic cannula is advanced into the vein and the needle is removed. To reduce the patient's anxiety, it is important to mention that the needle has been removed and that only the plastic cannula remains. As soon as the needle is removed and blood supply has been established, the site is anchored with tape, the IV tubing is connected, and dressing of the site is completed. The IV is regulated with flow clamps or IV pump as prescribed by the physician. Gloves are worn during the procedure as part of standard precautions. All needles and biohazard materials are disposed according to office policy and OSHA standard precautions. Figure 9-18 ◆ illustrates the setting up and initiating of an IV.

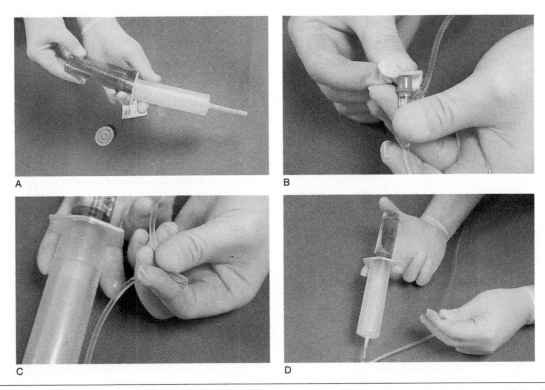

Figure 9-18 ◆ Delivery of an amp without the SAS method: (A) Prepare the drug; (B) Clean the administration port; (C) Pinch the line; (D) Administer the drug

PROCEDURE 9-7 Demonstrate the Administration of a Subcutaneous Injection

Theory

When a medication is administered by subcutaneous injection, it is absorbed slowly into the bloodstream. Sites for this injection are the outer upper arm, the scapular area of the back, the abdomen, and the anterior thigh. The scapular area is generally used by clinical staff because it is too hard for the patient to reach. A syringe that can hold 2 ml of solution and a needle that is 25 to 27 gauge and 5/8 inch long are used. Before the medication is injected, aspiration is performed to determine if the needle is within a blood vessel. If there is no blood in the syringe when aspiration is performed, the medication is administered. Medication injected when blood is aspirated would be detrimental to the patient because the medication would be administered directly into the bloodstream, with overly rapid, adverse effects.

Administering an IM injection is a common medical procedure, yet debate over the necessity to aspirate during the procedure is evident in the literature and reflected in practice. More recently, evidence-based guidelines do not advocate aspiration, and whilst these guidelines refer to vaccination, it is recommended that with the exception of the dorsogluteal site, the principles should be applied when administering any IM injection regardless of the context. The lack of policy in other practice areas should be addressed to support this."

Reference: Aspirating during the intramuscular injection procedure: a systematic literature review – Sisson – 2015 – Journal of Clinical Nursing – Wiley Online Library. (n.d.). Retrieved September 3, 2015, from http://onlinelibrary.wiley.com/doi/10.1111/jocn.12824/abstract
"Some nursing curricula do not include aspiration as part of the recommended technique for SC injection. One nursing guideline highlights the debate existing over aspiration prior to a SC injection, concluding that while the likelihood of piercing a vessel is slim, local guidelines should be followed in determining individual practices."
Reference: http://f1000research.com/articles/3-157/v1

Materials

- gloves
- alcohol wipes
- syringe with needle
- vial or ampule of medication
- Bandage strip(s)
- sharps container
- patient chart

Competency

(**Conditions**) With the necessary materials, you will be able to (**Task**) administer a subcutaneous injection (**Standards**) correctly within 15 minutes.

1. Wash your hands and gather the equipment.

2. Check to make sure the medication matches the physician's order. Calculate dosage if necessary. Look up information relating to the function of the medication, usual dosage, and side effects. Always follow the six rights to medication administration.
3. Check the medication label again against the physician's order to make sure it is the right medication.
4. Identify the patient and escort to treatment area. Verify the patient's allergies by asking the patient and checking the chart.
5. Select the subcutaneous site. Put on gloves.
6. Loosen the cap of the needle so that you can drop it on the counter just before you withdraw medication from the ampule or vial. Cleanse the skin site with an alcohol wipe and allow it to thoroughly air-dry.
7. Withdraw the correct amount of medication. If necessary, cover the needle by the slide cap method. Otherwise, if the patient is nearby, do *not* recap the needle.
8. Check a third time to match the medication against the physician's order.
9. If you have any doubts, consult the physician immediately before administering the medication. If you must leave the room, bring the medication with you.
10. Grasp the skin immediately surrounding the injection site with your nondominant hand.
11. Quickly insert the needle at a 45-degree angle. Hold the barrel of the syringe with your nondominant hand and pull (aspirate) the plunger with your dominant hand. If no blood appears in the syringe barrel, move your nondominant hand to the skin position and hold the syringe with your dominant hand. Push the plunger down with your index finger.
12. Withdraw the needle and blot the area gently with an alcohol wipe. Discard the syringe into the sharps container. Apply a bandage strip to protect the patient's clothing.
13. Remove the gloves and wash your hands.
14. Document the procedure. Include the date, time, medication, site, route, and amount administered. Follow office policy for recording the medication expiration date and lot number.

Patient Education

See Procedure 9-1.

Charting Example

03/28/XX 2:45 PM Regular insulin (20 units given) subcutaneous as ordered by the physician into rt. arm, directly above tricep muscle, for a blood sugar of 180. Patient has been diabetic for five years and states knowledge of low blood sugar symptoms. Pt instructed to report to laboratory for fasting glucose and glucose tolerance testing at 7 AM at the hospital outpatient area. Patient states awareness of nothing to eat or drink past midnight for the blood testing. Dwayne Lincoln, RMA

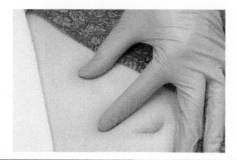

Figure 9-19 ◆ Stretch the skin with your nondominant hand.

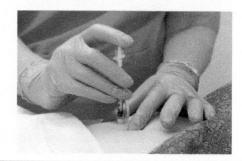

Figure 9-20 ◆ Push the plunger down with your index finger.

PROCEDURE 9-8 Demonstrate the Administration of an Intramuscular Injection to Adults and Children

Theory

Medication administered by intramuscular injection is quickly absorbed into the bloodstream. Sites are the deltoid, vastus lateralis of the thigh, dorsogluteal, and ventral gluteal muscles. Although all these sites may be used for adults, the vastus lateralis is used in children under 3 years old. The dorsogluteal site is not used until after the child has been walking for at least one year.

Syringe and needle size are different for adults and children.

■ For adults, injections of 2 to 5 ml can be given, although any dose 4 ml or above should be divided and administered as two injections. Needle size should be 22 gauge and 1 to 1-1/2 inches long, depending on the size of the patient. The needle gauge may have to be larger (smaller number) when more viscous medications are administered.

■ For young children, the medication amount should not exceed 1 ml because of the size of the vastus lateralis muscle. The needle size for an infant injection should be 25 gauge and one inch long, but may vary according to the size of the child and the viscosity of the medication.

As with a subcutaneous injection, aspiration is performed before an intramuscular injection is performed to determine if the needle has entered a blood vessel. If you are giving a medication injection to a child, there are additional forms that must be filled out prior to the administration of the medication. A consent form must be signed and a medication information form including common side effects, and pros and cons of the medication must be given to the parent for review.

Materials

■ gloves
■ alcohol wipes
■ syringe with needle
■ vial or ampule of medication
■ bandage strips
■ sharps container
■ patient chart

Competency

(**Conditions**) With the necessary materials, you will be able to (**Task**) administer an intramuscular injection to an adult or child (**Standards**) correctly within 15 minutes.

1. Wash your hands and gather the equipment.
2. Check to make sure the medication matches the physician's order. Calculate dosage if necessary. Look up information relating to the function of the medication, usual dosage, and side effects. Always follow the six rights to medication administration.
3. Check the medication label again against the physician's order to make sure it is the right medication.
4. Identify the patient and escort to treatment area. Ask parents to identify the child patient.
5. Select the intramuscular site. Put on the gloves.
6. Loosen the cap of the needle so that you can drop it on the counter just before you withdraw medication from the ampule or vial. Cleanse the skin site with an alcohol wipe and allow it to thoroughly air-dry.
7. Follow the procedure for withdrawing medication from a vial or ampule. Withdraw the correct amount. If necessary, cover the needle by the slide cap method. Otherwise, do *not* recap the needle.
8. Check a third time to match the medication against the physician's order.
9. If you have any doubts, consult the physician immediately before administering the medication.
10. Lightly stretch the skin immediately surrounding the injection site with your nondominant hand (Figure 9-19 ◆). For a small child, ask another clinical staff person to hold the child, then grasp the upper outer quadrant area of the vastus lateralis muscle (Figure 9-21 ◆).
11. Quickly but lightly thrust the needle at a 90-degree (perpendicular) angle. Hold the barrel of the syringe with your nondominant hand and with your dominant hand pull (aspirate) the plunger. If no blood appears in the syringe barrel, move your nondominant hand to the skin position and hold the syringe with your dominant hand. Push the plunger down with your index finger (Figure 9-20 ◆).

continued

PROCEDURE 9-8 Demonstrate the Administration of an Intramuscular Injection to Adults and Children *(continued)*

12. Withdraw the needle and apply pressure with an alcohol wipe. Massage the muscle unless contraindicated. Discard the syringe into the sharps container. Apply a bandage strip to protect the patient's clothing.
13. Remove the gloves and wash your hands.
14. Document the procedure. Include the date, time, medication, site, route, and amount administered. Follow office policy for recording the medication expiration date and lot number.

Patient Education
See Procedure 9-1.

Charting Example
10/13/XX 2:43 PM Demerol 50 mg given into rt. dorsogluteal site as ordered by physician for complaints of severe pain. Patient and significant other state awareness that patient is not to drive

Figure 9-21 ◆ For a small child, grasp the upper outer quadrant area of the vastus lateralis muscle.

for 24 hours. Patient and significant other have been instructed to seek continued emergency room evaluation for potential hospital admission for kidney stones. At time of discharge, additional written instructions given to significant other for kidney stone diagnosis and treatment. Janet Wahl, RMA

PROCEDURE 9-9 Demonstrate the Administration of a Z-Track Injection

Theory
The Z-track method, a type of intramuscular injection, is used when medication should not leak into subcutaneous tissues, when total intramuscular absorption of the medication is required, or when medication would discolor the tissue. The dorsogluteal site is preferred for the Z-track method, although the ventral gluteal and vastus lateralis sites may be also used. The medication is drawn into the syringe with 0.2 to 0.4 ml of air. When the injection is given, the additional air allows the medication to fully clear the needle and enter the muscle tissue. The needle should be 22 gauge and 1-1/2 to 2 inches long. The needle gauge may be larger (smaller number) if the medication is viscous. The skin is pulled laterally before the needle is inserted. When the needle is removed, a Z-track is left that allows the subcutaneous tissue to cover the muscular injection site.

Medications administered by this method include Vistaril, iron dextran, gamma globulin, antibiotics, narcotics, estrogen and testosterone, Procaine, and Imferon.

Materials
- gloves
- alcohol wipes
- tuberculin syringe with needle
- vial of medication
- bandage strips
- sharps container
- patient chart

Competency
(Conditions) With the necessary materials, you will be able to **(Task)** administer a Z-track injection **(Standards)** correctly within 15 minutes.

1. Wash your hands and gather the equipment.
2. Identify the patient and escort to the treatment area.
3. Select the appropriate intramuscular site. Put on the gloves.
4. Cleanse the skin with an alcohol wipe and allow to thoroughly air-dry.
5. Cleanse the top of the medication vial with an alcohol wipe and allow to air-dry. Withdraw the correct dosage from the vial and hold the syringe in your dominant hand.
6. With your nondominant hand, pull the skin laterally toward the side opposite the site (Figure 9-22 ◆).

PROCEDURE 9-9 Demonstrate the Administration of a Z-Track Injection *(continued)*

7. Quickly but lightly thrust the needle into the site at a 90-degree (perpendicular) angle. While still holding the skin away from the needle site, inject the medication and wait for 10 seconds (Figure 9-23 ◆).
8. After 10 seconds, quickly withdraw the needle and allow the skin to track back over the original injection site.
9. Blot the area gently with an alcohol wipe. Discard the syringe into the sharps container. Apply a bandage strip to protect the patient's clothing.
10. Do not massage the injection site.
11. Document the procedure. Include the date, time, medication, site, route, and amount administered. Follow office policy for recording the medication expiration date and lot number.

Patient Education
See Procedure 9-1.

Charting Example
03/27/XX 2:40 PM 2 mL of Vistaril given via Z-track injection per office procedure into the left dorsogluteal area. Patient and significant other state awareness that patient is not to drive for 24 hours. Patient and significant other have been instructed to seek continued emergency room evaluation if discussed potential side effects occur. Anthony Laden, CMA

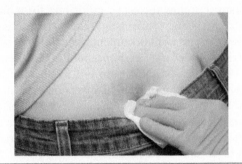

Figure 9-22 ◆ Pull the skin laterally toward the opposite side of the site.

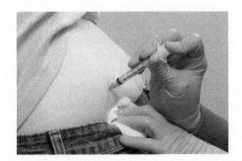

Figure 9-23 ◆ Inject the medication.

Keys to Success
LOW-INCOME PATIENTS AND THE COST OF MEDICATIONS

People with limited or fixed incomes often face the dilemma of deciding between paying for basic necessities such as food and heat and purchasing prescription drugs. Some lower-income patients choose to take intermittent or split dosages to make the medication last longer. Often the result is a decline in the patient's condition. Many people have turned to foreign sources, such as Canada or Mexico, for prescription medications at a reduced cost. However, drugs from outside the United States are not subject to FDA standards.

The medical community, including medical offices, hospitals, and clinics, provides some assistance through complimentary drug samples left by pharmaceutical sales representatives. The medical office may refer patients to free clinics, social service agencies, community trustees, or pharmaceutical programs. Recent Medicare reform includes a provision for prescription coverage to ease the financial burden of the elderly and chronically disabled.

REVIEW

Chapter Summary

- Pharmacology is a study of drugs and their effects on the human body. It focuses on the chemical structure of a drug, the chemical action within the body, the therapeutic effects of treatment, and potential side effects.
- A medical assistant's responsibilities in the physician's office include reading medication orders, ordering prescriptions, administering medications, using reference resources, recognizing side effects, and providing patient instruction.
- Drug absorption, distribution, metabolism, and excretion are factors that affect the biological and chemical reactions of medications within the body. Other factors, such as the patient's present state of health, medical conditions, and age, also require consideration before the physician prescribes medication.
- Drugs perform five basic functions: therapeutic, diagnostic, curative, replacement, and preventive.
- Drugs can be obtained with a physician's prescription or without prescription (over-the-counter). It is important to obtain information from the patient about nonprescription and prescription medications to prevent potential drug interactions.
- Drug classifications include (but are not limited to) the following categories.
  - Analgesics—relieve pain
  - Anesthetic medications—decrease or eliminate sensation or pain
  - Antianxiety medications—for emotional, behavior, or sleep deprivation or for treatment of seizures
  - Antiinflammatory drugs—decrease inflammation
  - Cardiovascular drugs—treat various heart and circulatory conditions
  - Gastrointestinal medications—treat conditions of the esophagus, stomach, small and large intestines
  - Antiinfectives—treat various system and organ infections
  - Respiratory medications—treat upper and lower, acute and chronic lung conditions
  - Endocrine drugs—replace or control hormones and hormonal reactions
  - Urinary system drugs—increase urine output, treat urinary infections and other kidney and bladder conditions

- Controlled substances, or schedule drugs, have a higher potential for abuse, and are classified into five categories by the Federal Controlled Substances Act. All schedule drugs are prescribed, administered, and monitored according to strict legal requirements.
- Every drug has three names: a chemical name, a generic name, and a trade name. The *Physician's Desk Reference* and the *U.S. Pharmacopeia and National Formulary* are important resources for information about drugs.
- The physician's prescription functions to communicate to the pharmacist the name and amount of the prescribed drug, directions for dispensing, instructions to the patient, the number of refills, and permission to use generic forms of the medication. Prescription pads must be kept in a secure, locked location.
- To eliminate the possibility of medication errors, it is important to follow the safety guidelines for administration ("six rights"): right patient, right drug, right dose, right route, right time, and right documentation.
- Metric, apothecary, and household measurement systems are used in the administration of medication. The metric system is used most often. Conversion equivalents can be used to convert one system to another when the medication order does not match the concentration of the medication available. The medical assistant must be able to use conversion tables and calculate dosages.
- Medications for oral routes of administration are available as liquids or solids. Other routes of administration include suppositories, dermatological, and parenteral routes.
- Needle gauge (size) and length are determined by the type and amount of medication to be administered. The type of medication administered results in immediate (intravenous), time-controlled (subcutaneous, intramuscular), or skin reaction (intradermal) absorption.
- The intravenous route is used primarily to replenish fluids, electrolytes, and blood products, but may also be used to administer medications. Intravenous medications may be administered only by designated licensed personnel.

Chapter Review Questions

Multiple Choice

1. The effect of a drug other than the intended therapeutic effect is known as a
   - A. toxic effect.
   - B. side effect.
   - C. therapeutic effect.
   - D. pharmacology effect.

2. The time and process whereby a drug reaches the cells and produces the desired action is known as
   - A. reception.
   - B. distribution.
   - C. elimination.
   - D. absorption.

Chapter Review Questions (continued)

3. The circulation of an absorbed drug throughout the body is called
   A. metabolism.
   B. distribution.
   C. absorption.
   D. reception.

4. Drugs that treat and relieve symptoms in a disease process are
   A. curative.
   B. diagnostic.
   C. therapeutic.
   D. preventive.

5. Drugs prescribed to improve a patient's quality of life by intervening in the disease process are
   A. curative.
   B. therapeutic.
   C. diagnostic.
   D. prophylactic.

6. Common OTC drugs include all of the following except
   A. Aleve.
   B. Pepcid AC.
   C. Claritin.
   D. Visteril.

7. Which common medication is not produced synthetically today?
   A. salicylates.
   B. penicillin.
   C. digoxin.
   D. bovine insulin.

8. Which of the following is not a neurotransmitter responsible for activities in the ANS?
   A. acetylcholine.
   B. epinephrine.
   C. norepinephrine.
   D. adrenergic agonists.

9. Which of the following drugs help restore heart rhythm to normal?
   A. antiarrhythmic.
   B. glycosides.
   C. anticoagulants.
   D. hemostatic agents.

10. Which drug is used to treat shock?
    A. vasodilator.
    B. antihypertensive.
    C. vasoconstrictor.
    D. cardiac glycosides.

True/False

T F 1. Antiinflammatory drugs may be corticosteroids or NSAIDs.

T F 2. Glycosides are administered to quicken the heart rate of patients with congestive heart failure.

T F 3. Thrombolytics dissolve existing blood clots but do not restore blood flow.

T F 4. Hemostatic drugs are used to control bleeding and hemorrhage.

T F 5. A laxative is considered a gastrointestinal drug.

T F 6. A vasodilator dilates vessels to control arterial spasms but has no effect on angina.

T F 7. Antiinfective agents are used to prevent infections caused by bacteria, viruses, and parasites.

T F 8. Drugs with potential for abuse are identified by the DEA, which is controlled by the CSA.

T F 9. Schedule I drugs include Ritalin, narcotics, barbiturates, and other drugs with a high potential for abuse.

T F 10. If a physician signs the Rx line "Substitute Generic Medication," the patient can still state he or she would like brand-name medications only.

Short Answer

1. Name four sources from which drugs can be derived.

2. What is the difference between analgesic and anesthetic drugs?

3. What is the function of thrombolytic drugs?

Research

1. Your patient cannot remember the name of the medication she is taking but knows the shape and color and says she would recognize it if she saw it or heard the name. She has no idea what the medication does for her. How can you verify what medication she is taking?

2. A patient states that every time he gets an antibiotic for an infection he "saves" some of the pills for future use. What can happen to the pathogen that causes the infection if the antibiotic is not taken at the prescribed strength for the correct duration of treatment?

Externship Application Experience

The physician has asked you to write a prescription for 25 mcg of Synthroid, "dispense 30." You write it for 25 mg of Synthroid. What are the possible implications if this error is not caught by the pharmacist? What is your response when the pharmacist calls the physician to report the error?

Resource Guide

Drug Enforcement Administration
Office of Diversion Control
2401 Jefferson Davis Highway
Alexandria, VA 22301
1-800-882-9539
www.dea.gov

Medline Plus
National Library of Medicine
National Institutes of Health
http://www.nlm.nih.gov/druginformation.html

Pharmacy Times
241 Forsgate Drive
Jamesburg, NJ 08831
www.pharmacytimes.com

RX List: The Internet Drug Index
www.rxlist.com/top200.htm

U.S. Pharmacopeia
12601 Twinbrook Parkway
Rockville, MD 20852
1- 800-822-8772
www.usp.org

 **MedMedia**
www.prenhall.com/frazier

More on this chapter, including interactive resources, can be found on the Student CD-ROM accompanying this textbook and on the Companion Website at www.prenhall.com/frazier.

Objectives

After completing this chapter, you should be able to:

- Define and spell the medical terminology for this chapter.
- Explain the principles of vital signs and state normal values for various age groups.
- Explain the significance of changes in body temperature.
- Define *pulse* and explain the factors that affect pulse rates.
- Discuss the importance of respirations in patient assessment.
- Discuss blood pressure and its role in patient assessment.
- Explain the significance of weight and height measurements in a patient's health status.
- Explain the medical assistant's role in patient preparation, including gowning, positioning, and draping.
- Describe the methods of assessment used during a medical examination.
- Explain the ways in which the medical assistant assists the physician during the medical examination.
- Discuss the medical assistant's role during recurrent clinical visits.

Vital Signs

Case Study

Chelsea has been working with Dr. Sevigney, a pulmonologist, for only a few weeks. Recently, while taking a patient's blood pressure, she was uncertain about what she was hearing. Chelsea first heard the blood pressure in the right arm at 130/110. Then she measured the blood pressure in the left arm and heard two distinct blood pressure starts and stops. She heard the first blood pressure sounds at 160/140 and then at 130/110 in the same arm.

MedMedia

www.prenhall.com/frazier

Additional interactive resources and activities for this chapter can be found on the Companion Website. For videos, audio glossary, legal and ethical scenarios, job scenarios, quizzes, games, and virtual tours related to the content of this chapter, please access the accompanying CD-ROM in this book.

 **Assets Available:**

Audio Glossary
Legal and Ethical Scenario: *Vital Signs*
On the Job Scenario: *Vital Signs*
Video Scenario: *Taking Vital Signs*
Multiple Choice Quiz
Games: Crossword, Strikeout and Spelling Bee
3D Virtual Tour: Lungs; Cardiovascular System: Heart; Ear: The Ear

Medical Terminology

accommodation—the adjustment of the lens of the eye to various distances

apical—at the apex of the heart

aural—pertaining to the ear

auscultation—listening to various areas of the body

axillary—under the arm

blood pressure—pressure the blood exerts on the vessel walls as a result of the pumping action of the heart

conduction—heat transfer by direct contact through fluids, solids, or other substances

convection—heat transfer by air

diaphoresis—profuse sweating

diastole—the relaxation phase of the heart muscle; lowest reading of the blood pressure

expiration—exhalation of carbon dioxide by physical or therapeutic means

hypertension—elevated blood pressure

hypotension—below-normal blood pressure

inspection—visual examination of both the external surface of the body and the interior portions of body cavities

inspiration—inhalation of atmosphere air or oxygen by physical or therapeutic means

malignant hypertension—rapidly developing, severe elevation of blood pressure, often fatal

mensuration—measurement

oral—by mouth

palpation—examination involving touch; examiner uses the hands and fingers to feel both the surface of the body (for abnormalities or irregularities) and various organs (for size, location, and tenderness) and feel generally for masses or lumps and assessing the texture and temperature of the tissue

percussion—examination consisting of tapping the fingertips lightly but sharply against the body to assess the size and location of underlying organs

pulse—the regular, palpable beat of the arteries caused by the contractions of the heart

radial—at the wrist over the radial artery

rhythm—time interval between pulses or breaths

✚ MEDICAL ASSISTING COMPETENCIES

CAAHEP ENTRY-LEVEL COMPETENCIES FOR CMA	ABHES ENTRY-LEVEL COMPETENCIES FOR RMA
■ Perform hand washing. ■ Dispose of biohazardous materials. ■ Obtain vital signs. ■ Prepare and maintain examination and treatment areas. ■ Prepare patient for and assist with routine and specialty examinations. ■ Recognize and respond to verbal communications. ■ Recognize and respond to nonverbal communications. ■ Document appropriately. ■ Explain general office procedures. ■ Instruct individuals according to their needs.	■ Prepare and maintain examination and treatment area. ■ Apply principles of aseptic techniques and infection control. ■ Take vital signs. ■ Prepare patient for and assist with routine and specialty examinations. ■ Dispose of biohazardous materials. ■ Practice Standard Precautions. ■ Determine needs for documentation and reporting. ■ Document accurately. ■ Operate and maintain facilities and equipment safely. ■ Orient patient to office policies and procedures.

Introduction

The medical assistant plays an integral role in assisting the physician and caring for the patient. The physician needs basic information about the patient to make an informed diagnosis. The patient history and vital signs provide the physician with an initial picture of the patient's general health status. This information establishes a baseline for future comparison of health status and an assessment of treatments. Medical assistants assist during the physical examination by providing the physician with assessment equipment and supplies, by positioning and draping the patient to facilitate a thorough examination, and by performing and documenting vital signs.

The Medical Assistant's Role in the Initial Clinical Visit

The medical assistant working in the clinical area of the medical office has many responsibilities in patient assessment. Before the physician begins the examination, a thorough patient history is essential. (∞ Refer to Chapter 6 for information on taking a patient history.) As you record the history and obtain vital signs, you will use your observational skills to assess the patient's general condition, including cooperation, skin condition, alertness, level of consciousness, and apparent presence of pain.

Vital signs include temperature, pulse, respirations, blood pressure, height, and weight. A visual and auditory examination may be required as part of the assessment. After vital signs and a patient history have been taken, you will prepare the patient for the physical examination by gowning, draping, and positioning. You may also assist the physician during the examination, and when it is completed you will assist the patient to dress, then prepare the room for the next patient.

Medical Terminology *(continued)*

sublingually—under the tongue

systole—the contraction phase of the heart; highest reading of the blood pressure

temperature—measurement of body heat produced and lost during metabolism,

respiration, elimination, and environmental fluctuation

turgor—normal appearance of the skin and its ability to return to normal after being pinched

vital signs—signs that measure the patient's general state of health, include temperature, pulse, respirations, and blood pressure

Abbreviations

BPM—beats per minute

CV—cardiovascular

TPR—temperature, pulse, respirations

COMPETENCY SKILLS PERFORMANCE

1. Obtain an oral temperature with an electronic digital thermometer.
2. Obtain an axillary temperature with an electronic digital thermometer.
3. Obtain a rectal temperature with an electronic digital thermometer.
4. Obtain an aural temperature with a tympanic thermometer.
5. Obtain a dermal temperature with a disposable thermometer.
6. Perform a radial pulse count.
7. Perform an apical pulse count.
8. Perform a respiration count.
9. Perform a blood pressure measurement.
10. Obtain weight and height measurements.
11. Demonstrate patient positions used in medical examinations.
12. Prepare the patient for medical examination and assist the physician.

Vital Signs

Vital signs measure the patient's general state of health and include temperature, pulse, respirations, and blood pressure (**TPR** and BP). TPR and BP, along with weight and height, are usually measured and recorded at each visit. The physician compares these findings to normal ranges to help determine a diagnosis, prognosis, and course of treatment for the patient. Vital signs are also taken during the course of treatment to evaluate the patient's reaction to any procedure or medication.

Temperature

Temperature is the measurement of body heat produced and lost during metabolism, respiration, elimination, and environmental fluctuation. Changes in a patient's body temperature may be an indication of a change in health status or illness.

The temperature is regulated by several organs and processes.

■ In the hypothalamus, various mechanisms regulate heat production and loss.

■ In the metabolic process, glucose from food is oxidized in body cells, producing heat. This heat is distributed throughout the body by the blood and blood vessels.

■ As blood vessels pass near the body's surface, heat is lost through the skin by **conduction**, **convection**, radiation, and evaporation of perspiration.

■ Heat is lost through respiration and the elimination of urine and feces.

Taking the Temperature

Body temperature is measured by either the Fahrenheit or Celsius scale (Table 10-1). It may be assessed in different ways, according to the patient's age and physical status.

■ One of the most common ways to take the temperature is to place a digital thermometer probe under the tongue until the reading is obtained. The patient must be alert, cooperative, and cognizant of the process.

■ For patients who are unconscious, uncooperative, or too young, a digital thermometer probe may be placed in the **axillary** space under the arm or in the rectum. The axillary temperature is considered less accurate because the thermometer has less direct contact with

TABLE 10-1 TEMPERATURE CONVERSION

■ To convert Celsius to Fahrenheit:
  Fahrenheit degrees = (Celsius degrees × 9/5) + 32
■ To convert Fahrenheit to Celsius:
  Celsius degrees = (Fahrenheit degrees − 32) × 5/9
Examples of Celsius and Fahrenheit readings in degrees:

Celsius (C)	Fahrenheit (F)
35.0	95.0
35.5	95.9
36.0	96.8
36.5	97.7
37.0	98.6 (normal oral)
37.5	99.5
38.0	100.4
38.5	101.3
39.0	102.2
39.5	103.1
40.0	104.0
40.5	104.9
41.0	105.8

the body's blood circulation (skin instead of mucous membranes).

- **Aural** thermometers read the temperature of the tympanic membrane. Dermal devices measure the temperature of the skin.
- Mercury thermometers are still used in some facilities; however, many states have passed laws that limit or prevent new production of mercury-containing equipment along with more stringent standards for disposal.
- A newcomer on the thermometer scene is the alcohol thermometer. It is calibrated like a mercury thermometer and works on the same principle.

Normal temperatures vary according to the method used to obtain them (Table 10-2). An **oral** temperature of 98.6 degrees F (Fahrenheit) or 37 degrees C (Celsius) is considered normal. A rectal temperature is considered normal at 99.6 degrees F or 37.6 degrees C. A normal axillary temperature is 97.6 degrees F or 36.4 degrees C. Historically, the oral temperature reading has been considered the baseline for normal at 98.6 degrees F. Rectal temperature readings are usually a degree warmer because of the internal environment of the rectum. Axillary temperatures are usually considered a degree lower than oral temperatures as the axilla is more exposed to air.

Rectal temperatures are considered the most accurate; however, particularly with small children, there is a risk of perforating the rectal wall with the thermometer. At present, rectal temperatures are rarely taken in medical offices or hospitals. Many pediatricians prefer to have patients' temperatures obtained by the axillary or aural method.

Many factors influence changes in body temperature. An elevated temperature may occur as a result of bacterial infection, increased food intake, physical activity, exposure to heat, metabolism-raising drugs, pregnancy, stress, or emotional reactions. Some women experience a slight increase in body temperature during ovulation. Age is a variable as well; an infant's or young child's body temperature may be one or two degrees higher than that of adults.

There are several kinds of abnormally elevated temperature, or fever:

- *Continuous:* body temperature remains fairly constant and above the patient's normal baseline
- *Remittent:* fluctuating body temperature remains above normal
- *Intermittent:* fluctuating body temperature returns to normal, then rises again
- *Relapsing:* fever returns after an interval of several days of normal temperature

TABLE 10-2 NORMAL TEMPERATURE RANGES (FAHRENHEIT)

Routes	Normal Ranges
Oral	97.6 – 99.6
Rectal	98.6 – 100.6
Axillary	96.6 – 98.6
Tympanic	similar to rectal range

Caduceus Chronicle
A SHORT HISTORY OF THE THERMOMETER

As early as the first century B.C.E., Hero of Alexandria and Philo of Byzantium made "thermoscopes" to measure the temperature of expanding air as it was heated. In 1592 Galileo made a primitive water thermometer and barometer. In 1612, Santorio Santorio adapted the air thermometer to incorporate a colored liquid that was forced down by the expansion of air. This was the first time a thermometer was used to measure body temperature during illness and recovery.

Daniel Gabriel Fahrenheit constructed a mercury thermometer in 1714, setting the melting point of ice at 32 degrees, blood heat at 96 degrees, and the boiling point of water at 212 degrees. Anders Celsius invented a centigrade scale in 1742, with the boiling point at 0 degrees and the freezing point at 100 degrees. In 1745 Carolus Linnaeus inverted the Celsius scale into the form we commonly use today, with the freezing point at 0 degrees.

Lowered body temperatures may result from viral infections, fasting, decreased muscular activity, exposure to cold, metabolism-lowering drugs, depression, hemorrhage, dehydration, and severe central nervous system insults. In the elderly, decreased metabolic and physical activity lowers the body temperature.

Time of day is another factor. The temperature is usually at its lowest early in the day, following rest, and during decreased activity and sleep. Muscular and metabolic activity throughout the day usually raises the body temperature, which reaches its peak in the evening.

Thermometers

Thermometers are used to measure body temperature.

- The traditional glass thermometer contains mercury, which expands and elevates in the column as it warms. There are glass thermometers for oral, rectal, and axillary routes. The thermometer used to take oral and axillary temperature has a slender, longer bulb, while the thermometer designed for rectal use has a short, round bulb. Both types are marked with both Fahrenheit and Celsius calibrations, and elevations are usually marked in red. Traditional mercury thermometers are no longer recommended for use in the medical setting, as the biohazards of mercury outweigh any of its benefits. Some professionals are also questioning the safety of glass thermometers now that alternative methods are readily available. Alcohol thermometers, like mercury thermometers, may be placed under the tongue, under the arm, or in the rectum.
- Battery-operated electronic thermometers allow a much more rapid reading. They come with two different probes, one for oral and axillary routes and the other for the rectal route, as well as disposable covers for the probes (Figure 10-1 ◆).
- Aural thermometers come with either a disposable or reusable ear speculum and give a reading within 3 seconds (Figure 10-2 ◆).

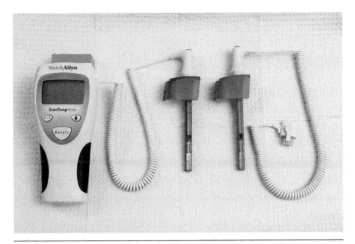

Figure 10-1 ◆ Electronic thermometers come with two different probes; one for oral and axillary routes, and the other for the rectal route.

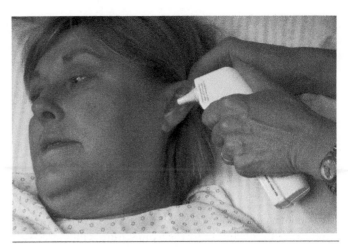

Figure 10-2 ◆ Aural thermometer

PROCEDURE 10-1 Obtain an Oral Temperature with an Electronic Digital Thermometer

Theory

Before taking the temperature, ask the patient if he or she has smoked or had any hot or cold liquids immediately before coming to the medical office. Taking a temperature under those conditions could yield inaccurate results. Install a cover on the electronic thermometer probe to allow multiple patient uses and prevent cross-contamination. Place the thermometer **sublingually** next to the frenulum linguae. Heat transferred by conduction from the blood supply under the tongue to the thermometer is measured as the patient's temperature.

Instruct the patient to keep the mouth closed while taking an oral temperature. Breathing through the mouth may transfer heat by convection and result in an altered temperature. The thermometer should remain in place until beeping indicates that the temperature has been measured.

You must remain in the room while an oral temperature is taken. You may need to help the patient hold the thermometer in the correct position in the mouth. If you are not doing that, you can count the radial pulse and respirations while waiting for the temperature to register.

Materials

■ electronic digital thermometer
■ thermometer probe covers
■ watch with second hand (for pulse and respiration count)
■ examination gloves

Competency

(**Conditions**) With the necessary supplies, (**Task**) you will be able to measure oral temperature (**Standards**) accurately and in the time designated by the instructor.

1. Identify the patient, escort to the examination room, and offer a place to sit on a chair or the examination table.
2. Wash your hands and apply gloves.
3. Ask the patient if he or she has had hot or cold drinks or food or smoked a cigarette within the last 10 minutes. If so, wait 10 minutes. If not, proceed with taking the oral temperature.
4. Remove the electronic thermometer from its charge base and place a cover on the probe (Figure 10-3 ◆).
5. Place the probe under the tongue near the frenulum linguae. Instruct the patient to close the mouth around the thermometer.
6. Explain to the patient that the thermometer will need to stay in place until the beep sounds. You may count pulse and respirations now (see Procedures 10-6 through 10-8) or after the temperature is taken.
7. When the beep sounds, remove the thermometer from the patient's mouth, note the temperature, and discard the probe cover in a waste receptacle (Figure 10-4 ◆).

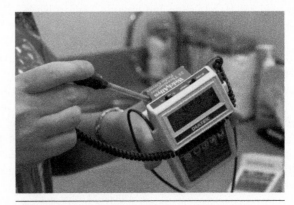

Figure 10-3 ◆ Place a cover on the probe

continued

PROCEDURE 10-1 Obtain an Oral Temperature with an Electronic Digital Thermometer *(continued)*

8. Remove the gloves and wash your hands. Return the thermometer to its charge base (Figure 10-5 ◆).

9. Record the temperature, pulse, and respirations in the appropriate place on the chart. Return the thermometer to its designated storage location.

Patient Education

Remind the patient that cold or hot substances that have been in the mouth shortly before the temperature is measured will affect the accuracy of the temperature. It is also important for the patient to hold the thermometer in the "pocket" on either side of the frenulum linguae.

Charting Example

10/11/XX 10:45 AM T 98.6°F, P 76, regular and strong, R 20. Patient states purpose of visit is for annual physical. Taylor Furber, RMA

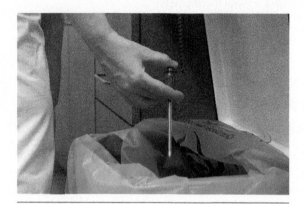

Figure 10-4 ◆ Discard the probe cover.

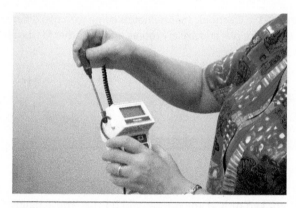

Figure 10-5 ◆ Return the thermometer to its charge base.

PROCEDURE 10-2 Obtain an Axillary Temperature with an Electronic Digital Thermometer

Theory

The axillary method of taking the temperature is recommended for mouth-breathing patients or for patients who have had oral surgery, trauma, or inflammation. It is also recommended for infants, toddlers, and preschoolers who are too young to hold the thermometer in their mouths. Parents can hold a sick child close and provide comfort while an axillary temperature is taken.

It may be necessary to remove clothing from the arm and shoulder area to allow correct placement of an axillary thermometer. Because diaphoresis may affect the measurement, the area should be gently patted dry. Rubbing the area to dry it stimulates local skin circulation, which may in turn raise the temperature. Once the thermometer is placed in the center of the axilla, in direct contact with the skin, the patient lowers the arm to the side and brings the forearm against the chest. This position reduces air currents to the thermometer.

Materials

- electronic digital thermometer
- thermometer probe cover
- watch with second hand (for pulse and respiration count)
- examination gloves

Competency

(**Conditions**) With the necessary supplies, (**Task**) you will be able to measure axillary temperature (**Standards**) accurately in the time designated by the instructor.

1. Identify the patient, escort to the examination room, and offer a place to sit on a chair or the examination table. Have the patient either unbutton or take off his or her shirt to allow access to the axilla.

2. Wash your hands and put on the gloves.

3. Observe the axillary area for dryness or **diaphoresis.** Pat the area dry with a washcloth or towel if it is diaphoretic.

PROCEDURE 10-2 Obtain an Axillary Temperature with an Electronic Digital Thermometer *(continued)*

4. Remove the electronic thermometer from its charge base and place a cover on the probe.
5. Ask the patient to raise an arm. Place the thermometer in direct contact with the skin of the axilla and have the patient lower the arm against the side of the chest (Figure 10-6 ◆). Explain that the thermometer will need to stay in place until the beep sounds. You may count pulse and respirations now or after the temperature is taken.
6. When the beep sounds, remove the thermometer and discard the probe cover in a waste receptacle.
7. Remove the gloves and wash your hands. Return the thermometer to its charge base.
8. Record the temperature (Figure 10-7 ◆), pulse, and respirations in the appropriate place on the chart. Write "A" after the temperature to indicate that the axillary route was used.
9. Return the thermometer to its designated storage location.

Patient Education

Inform the patient that the underarm must be dry and that the arm should be held against the side and chest for an accurate reading. Patients who take their own temperature at home should always reprt the route to the medical office staff because an axillary temperature is considered one degree higher than an oral temperature.

Charting Example

10/11/XX 11:00 AM T 101.4°F A, P 110. Unable to obtain respirations due to fussiness of 6-month-old. Mom states child has been fussy on and off for two days. Takes formula when Motrin brings fever down. Has had fever for one day. Philip Romo, CMA

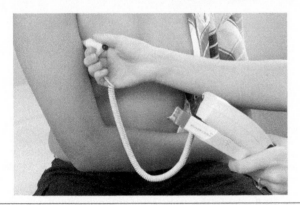

Figure 10-6 ◆ Place the thermometer in direct contact with the skin of the axilla.

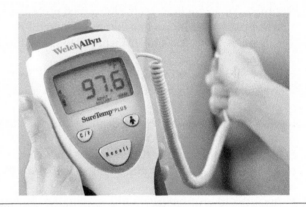

Figure 10-7 ◆ Record the temperature.

PROCEDURE 10-3 Obtain a Rectal Temperature with an Electronic Digital Thermometer

Theory

The rectal temperature is considered more accurate than both oral and axillary temperatures because the thermometer is in direct contact with mucous membranes rather than potentially exposed to the air. With the advent of the tympanic thermometer, this method is rarely used today, especially in the physician office. However, it can be used with unconscious patients, mouth-breathing patients, and small children. There may be a safety concern with patients who cannot lie still during the taking of a rectal temperature. The distal end of the thermometer probe stem must be held throughout the procedure. To avoid perforating the bowel, do *not* insert the thermometer if there is any possibility of an obstruction.

Safety note: Prepare equipment and place it in reaching proximity before positioning the patient. A young, old, or seriously ill patient may be at risk for falling from the examination table and should *not* be left in position before or during the procedure.

Materials

■ electronic digital rectal thermometer and probe covers
■ lubricant and tissue
■ examination gloves

continued

PROCEDURE 10-3 **Obtain a Rectal Temperature with an Electronic Digital Thermometer** (continued)

Competency

(**Conditions**) With the necessary supplies, (**Task**) you will be able to measure rectal temperature (**Standards**) accurately in the time designated by the instructor.

1. Identify the patient and escort to the examination room. Assist the patient in removing clothing from the waist down. Keeping the patient draped, assist him or her into a left side-lying position (Sim's position) on the examination table. Drape for exposure of the buttocks only.
2. Wash your hands and apply gloves.
3. Remove the electronic thermometer from its charge base and place a cover on the probe.
4. Place a small amount of lubricant on a tissue next to the patient. Dip the tip of the probe cover in the lubricant.
5. Inform the patient of procedure before you insert the rectal probe. For an adult, insert the lubricated probe cover approximately 1-1/2 inches into the anus (Figure 10-8 ◆). For an infant, insert it 1/4 to 1/2 inch, and for a child, 1/2 to 1 inch.
6. Hold the thermometer in place until it beeps. Remove the thermometer and discard the probe cover in a waste receptacle.
7. Remove the gloves and wash your hands. Return the thermometer to its charge base.
8. Record the temperature in the appropriate place on the chart. Write an "R" after the measurement to indicate the rectal route.
9. Return the thermometer to its designated storage location.

Patient Education

Rectal temperatures are taken only when the patient's medical condition dictates and with controls for safety concerns. Assure the patient that you will hold the rectal thermometer during the procedure.

Charting Example

11/13/XX 1330 J 102.6° R, P 100, R 40. Temperature taken rectally because patient had breathing difficulty and extreme diaphoresis. The head of examination table was raised about 30 degrees during the procedure. After temperature completed, patient was assisted to sitting position for remainder of office visit. McKenzie Adams, RMA

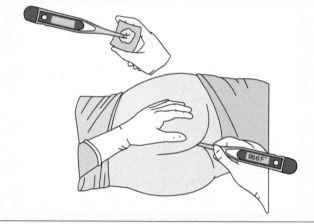

Figure 10-8 ◆ Insert the probe cover approximately 1-1/2 inches into the anus.

PROCEDURE 10-4 **Obtain an Aural Temperature with a Tympanic Thermometer**

Theory

Aural temperatures with an electronic tympanic thermometer are taken when a rapid temperature reading is needed and the patient's comfort is an issue. This method works well with pediatric patients. The parent or other family member can hug the child snugly and hold the child's head while the medical assistant takes the aural temperature.

The tympanic or aural thermometer measures the temperature of the warmth within the ear canal and the tympanic membrane with infrared light. The tympanic membrane reflects the central core temperature of the body and provides readings close to the temperature of the pulmonary artery. The tympanic thermometer is considered an accurate alternative to the mercury thermometer.

Because of the anatomical differences in the ear canal between the adult and the infant or child, the canal must be positioned differently to obtain the most accurate aural temperature. With an adult, gently pull the outer ear upward. With an infant or child, pull the outer ear downward. With your other hand insert the tympanic thermometer to obtain the reading. As the thermometer is inserted, the ear canal is closed to air currents that would affect the accuracy of the aural temperature.

Materials

- tympanic thermometer and probe covers
- examination gloves

PROCEDURE 10-4 Obtain an Aural Temperature with a Tympanic Thermometer *(continued)*

Competency

(**Conditions**) With procedure materials, (**Task**) you will be able to perform an aural temperatures (**Standards**) accurately, according to the patient's age, within the time designated by the instructor.

1. Identify the patient, escort to the examination room, and offer a place to sit on a chair or the examination table. If the patient is a child, encourage the parent to sit and hold the child.
2. Wash your hands and apply the gloves.
3. Explain the basic procedure to the patient or parent. Assess whether the patient has had an aural temperature before. Depending on the patient's age and previous experience or knowledge of the procedure, you may need to assure him or her that the procedure is painless or demonstrate on the parent before taking a child's temperature.
4. Remove the tympanic thermometer from its charge base and place a cover on the probe.
5. For an adult, pull the outer ear in an upward direction. For a child or infant, pull the outer ear in a downward direction.
6. With your hand insert the probe-covered earpiece of the thermometer into the ear canal and press the scan button to obtain the temperature reading (Figure 10-9 ◆).

7. When the thermometer beeps, withdraw it from the patient's ear and pop the probe cover into the waste receptacle. Read the temperature reading in the thermometer's display window (Figure 10-10 ◆).
8. Remove the gloves and wash your hands. Return the thermometer to its charge base.
9. Record the temperature on the patient's chart, followed by a "T" to indicate tympanic temperature.
10. Return the tympanic thermometer to its designated storage location.

Patient Education

Explain to the patient or parent the reason for pulling the outer ear upward for the adult patient or downward for the infant or child. Emphasize that a different probe cover should be used each time for the same person or for different persons within the same household to prevent the reintroduction of microorganisms.

Charting Example

10/23/XX 0935 AM Mother brings child to office. Child has runny nose, which mom states has been present for one week. Mother states that child has had on and off fever for three days and appetite has decreased. Aural temperature obtained, 97.8ℱ Wallace Banks, CMA

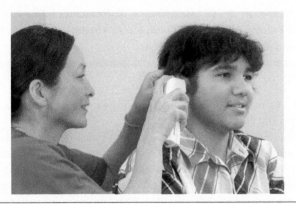

Figure 10-9 ◆ Insert the probe-covered earpiece of the thermometer into the ear canal.

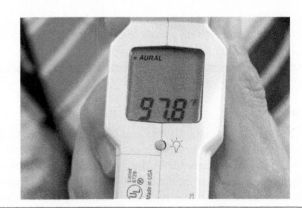

Figure 10-10 ◆ Read the temperature in the display window.

PROCEDURE 10-5 Obtain a Dermal Temperature with a Disposable Thermometer

Theory

Chemical thermometers can be either oral or dermal. Both types are single-use and consist of chemical reactant dots or tape that respond to heat by changing color. Chemical thermometers are generally used only in the home. Although they are not considered as accurate as other thermometers, they do provide a general assessment of the patient's temperature patterns.

Like electronic thermometers, disposable oral thermometers are placed under the tongue and left in place for about 60 seconds. Dermal thermometers are disposable strips that are held on the forehead for about 15 seconds. For both types, the last color change is the temperature reading.

Because these thermometers react chemically to heat and to the heat generated by light, they should be stored in a cool, dark place. Unwrap and handle them carefully to avoid touching the chemical dots.

Materials

- disposable dermal strips
- clean, dry washcloth
- examination gloves

Competency

(**Conditions**) With the necessary supplies, (**Task**) you will be able to measure dermal temperature (**Standards**) accurately in the time designated by the instructor.

1. Identify the patient, escort to the examination room, and offer a place to sit on a chair or the examination table.
2. Wash your hands and apply gloves.

3. Observe the forehead for dryness or diaphoresis. Pat the area dry with a washcloth if it is diaphoretic.
4. Carefully unwrap the dermal strip without touching the chemical dots and place it on the forehead.
5. Leave the strip on the forehead for the length of time recommended by the manufacturer, usually about 15 seconds.
6. After noting the temperature of the last color-changed dot, remove and dispose of the dermal thermometer in a waste receptacle.
7. Remove the gloves and wash your hands.
8. Record the temperature on the patient's chart, followed by the word "dermal."

Patient Education

Instruct the patient or parent to avoid touching the chemical dots because the temperature reading could be affected. Reinforce that the last dot affected indicates the temperature. The same procedure should be followed whenever the temperature is taken so that temperatures can effectively be compared. Patting the forehead dry allows the dermal temperature strip to stick for the required time.

Charting Example

11/11/XX 11:00 AM T 101.4 dermal, P 110. Unable to obtain respirations due to fussiness of 6-month-old. Temperature has been as high as 102 last midnight. Mother states infant has had three watery stools and has taken only 4 ounces of formula since midnight. Patricia Davis, RMA

Pulse

The **pulse** is the regular, palpable beat of the arteries caused by the contractions of the heart. It is an indication of the pressure exerted by the blood flow during the contraction (systole) phase of the heartbeat. Assessing the patient's pulse provides a rapid picture of the heart's pumping action, including rate, rhythm, and volume. It is also an indicator of the patient's response to treatments and medications as well as general cardiac status.

A normal heart beats 60 to 100 times a minute, or **BPM** (beats per minute). Table 10-3 lists normal pulse ranges. The **rhythm** is regular and is normally felt as strong. Deviations are called *arrhythmias* and are often indicative of underlying cardiac conditions (∞ refer to Chapter 17 for a discussion of cardiac arrhythmias).

In a medical office the most common site for obtaining a pulse is the **radial** artery in the wrist (radial pulse). Other sites where a pulse may be palpated include the brachial, temporal, facial, carotid, pedal, popliteal, and femoral sites (Figure 10-11 ◆). The carotid and femoral pulses are used to assess cardiac function

in a critically ill adult patient, and the brachial site is used in a critically ill infant or child.

An **apical** pulse is the pulse or heartbeat heard through a stethoscope at the apex of the heart. The apical pulse is counted for a full 60 seconds and is the most accurate assessment of the heartbeat. Apical pulses are usually taken on infants, individuals taking certain heart medications, and patients who are critically ill.

Occasionally an apical-radial pulse rate may be required. The preferred method involves one practitioner taking the apical pulse and another taking the radial pulse at the same

TABLE 10-3 AVERAGE PULSE RANGES BY AGE	
Newborns	130–160 BPM
Infants	110–130 BPM
Children 1–7 years	80–120 BPM
Children over 7 years	80–90 BPM
Adults	60–80 BPM
Elderly adults	50–70 BPM

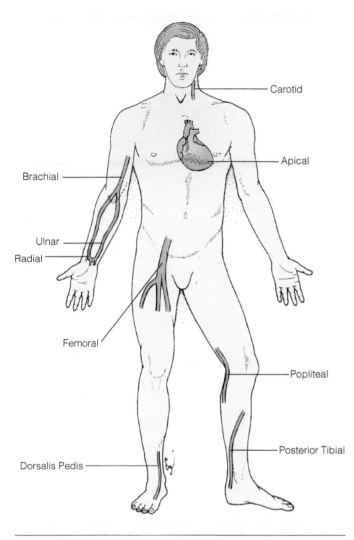

Figure 10-11 ◆ Points on the human body where pulse may be taken

TABLE 10-4 FACTORS THAT AFFECT HEART RATE AND RHYTHM	
Age	Infants and children normally have a more rapid heartbeat than adults. It is not unusual for a newborn to have a heart rate of 160 BPM. Likewise, it may be normal for an elderly individual to have a heart rate of 50–60 BPM.
Gender	Females tend to have a faster heartbeat than males, usually by about 10 BPM.
Exercise/ physical activity	Since increased activity requires more oxygen and nutrition to be delivered to the cells, the heart rate temporarily increases 20–30 BPM to accommodate for the greater need.
Size	Larger individuals usually have a slower heartbeat than smaller persons.
Physical condition	People who exercise vigorously and regularly tend to have heartbeats that are slower than normal. It is not unusual for an individual who runs on a regular basis to have a heartbeat in the range of 48–56 BPM.
Medications	Medications may either raise or lower the heart rate. Drugs that raise the heart rate include stimulants (caffeine), sympathetic agents (epinephrine, albuterol, terbutaline), and ACE inhibitors. Drugs that slow the heart rate include cardiac glycosides (digitalis), beta blockers (propanolol and atenolol), and parasympathetic drugs. ∞ Refer to Chapter 9 for drugs that affect the heart rate.
Presence of disease or illness	The raised metabolic rate of an individual experiencing illness or disease usually causes the heart to beat faster.
Anxiety, fear, anger	Any highly emotional state that causes an increase in sympathetic nervous system activity tends to raise the heart rate.
Depression	Depressed individuals tend to have a slower heart rate.
Increased intracranial pressure	This lowers the heart rate.
Thyroid disease	Hypothyroidism slows the heart rate. Hyperthyroidism causes a rapid heartbeat.
Shock	Shock speeds up the heart rate as the body attempts to compensate for dilated blood vessels.

Keys to Success
THE PATIENT ON DIGITALIS

When teaching a patient who is taking digitalis how to take an apical pulse, emphasize that the pulse should be counted for one full minute to ensure accuracy. The pulse should be measured prior to the administration or ingestion of the digitalis.

time. The person timing the minute usually lifts a finger to indicate when to begin counting, then lowers the finger when the minute has elapsed. Any difference in the pulse rates obtained is termed a *pulse deficit.*

Volume, or the pressure of the blood against the arterial walls, may range from normal, strong, or bounding to weak, feeble, or thready. The volume felt by the fingertips provides a general assessment of the strength or weakness of cardiac muscle effort during the contraction phase of the heartbeat. Factors affecting the strength of the heartbeat include the amount of blood in the **CV** system (which may be influenced by dehydration), the forcefulness of the heart contraction, and the condition of the arterial walls. Further assessment of volume may be made by the appropriate professional.

It is possible to assess both the rate and rhythm of the heartbeat with the pulse. The rate is the beats per minute. Rhythm is defined by the regularity or irregularity of the pulsation felt by fingertips or sounds heard with the stethoscope and is an indicator of cardiac condition. Many factors affect rate and rhythm (Table 10-4).

Respirations

Oxygen is necessary for life. The body breathes oxygen in and exhales carbon dioxide. Respiration, the act of breathing, includes inspiration and expiration (∞ see Figure 18-1, the respiratory system, on p. 366). **Inspiration** is the inhalation of atmospheric air or oxygen by physical or therapeutic means. **Expiration** is the exhalation of carbon dioxide by physical or therapeutic means. For most people the act of breathing is an "autonomic" body function that does not require thought. However, it is controlled by the medulla oblongata of the brain,

PROCEDURE 10-6 Perform a Radial Pulse Count

Theory

Taking a baseline pulse is important for monitoring changes in the patient's condition. The radial pulse is measured at a resting rate. Ask the patient about activity levels and smoking, which may increase the pulse rate above the baseline resting rate. Use only your fingertips when taking the pulse. If you use your thumb, you are likely to feel your own pulse as well as that of the patient. Do not apply too much pressure when palpating for the radial pulse, as you may close off the artery and the pulse will not be palpable.

Materials

- watch with second hand

Competency

(**Conditions**) With the necessary supplies, (**Task**) you will be able to perform a radial pulse count (**Standards**) accurately within the time frame designated by the instructor.

1. The patient has been identified, escorted to the examination room, and offered a place to sit on a chair or the examination table.
2. Wash your hands (unless you have already done so prior to taking the temperature).

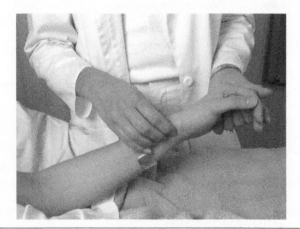

Figure 10-12 ◆ Obtaining a radial pulse count

3. Explain the procedure to the patient (unless you have already done so prior to taking the temperature). Do *not* mention that you will be counting respirations after taking the pulse.
4. Position the patient's arm at about heart level, with the palm facing down. Identify the radial artery with the three middle fingertips by feeling pulsation through the arterial wall (Figure 10-12 ◆).
5. Palpate for the pulsation of the radial artery on the inside of the wrist below the thumb. Note the strength and rhythm of the pulse. Do *not* palpate the pulse with your thumb.
6. Looking at your watch, start counting the pulse beats when the second hand is at 3, 6, 9, or 12. Count for one full minute.

   While still holding the wrist, observe the patient's respiratory efforts and count as instructed in Procedure 10-8.
7. Document the rate, strength, and rhythm of the pulse on the chart.
8. Wash your hands.

Patient Education

Teach the patient or significant other to feel for the radial artery with the fingertips rather than the thumb. The pulse should be counted for one full minute, and the strength, rhythm, and rate should be noted. Ask the patient or significant other to demonstrate how to take the radial pulse. Make sure the patient or significant other realizes that learning to perform a radial pulse may be challenging for some and easy for others. Be supportive and encouraging. Secondary arrangements may have to be made for monitoring the pulse. The patient or significant other should keep a record of daily pulse counts to show the physician at each visit.

Charting Example

11/15/XX 1425 Patient has been placed on digoxin for irregular heartbeat. She has seen video on taking pulse and has demonstrated correctly with fingertips how to take her own pulse. Patient verbalizes she will call the doctor's office if her pulse rate is less than 60 before she takes her medicine. Andrea Thomson, CMA

PROCEDURE 10-7 Perform an Apical Pulse Count

Theory

An apical pulse is usually taken when the patient is on heart medication for an irregular or weak pulse or an abnormal heart rate. The apical pulse is also taken on babies and critically ill patients.

The apical pulse is most audible at the apex of the heart and can be found at the fifth intercostal space below the midclavicular line. Count five rib spaces down from where the ribs join the sternum. In that intercostal space, imagine a line drawn down from the middle of the clavicle at the top of the left shoulder. The apex of the heart is anatomically just below the left nipple.

Before counting the apical pulse, wipe the earpieces and diaphragm of the stethoscope to prevent the transfer of microorganisms to the staff or the patient. If the chestpiece of the stethoscope (the part containing the diaphragm and bell) is cold, hold it in your hands for a short period. Placing a cold chestpiece on the patient may speed up the heartbeat from its normal resting state. If a second person is measuring the radial pulse at the same time, use one watch to count both. The person with the watch should indicate when the counting starts and stops to help ensure the accuracy of the pulse deficit.

Materials

- stethoscope
- alcohol prep
- watch with a second hand

Competency

(**Conditions**) With the necessary supplies, (**Task**) you will be able to perform an apical pulse count (**Standards**) accurately within the time frame designated by the instructor.

1. The patient has already been identified, and you have washed your hands to obtain vital signs.
2. Explain the procedure to the patient. Do *not* mention that you will be counting respirations after you have noted the apical pulse.
3. Wipe the stethoscope earpieces with the alcohol prep. With the earpieces pointed toward the nose, place the stethoscope earpieces in your ears Place the bell or diaphragm on the patient's chest in the area of the apex of the heart (Figure 10-13 ◆).

4. Begin counting heartbeats (each "lub-dub" counts as one heartbeat) when the second hand of the watch is at 3, 6, 9, or 12.
5. Count for one full minute. Note the quality and regularity of the heartbeat.
6. Chart the rate, rhythm, and any other pertinent information. If the radial pulse is also documented, write "RP" before the radial pulse rate and "AP" before the apical pulse rate.

Patient Education

Instruct patients that the apical pulse and the different sounds of the heart often give the physician important medical information. The patient and/or family should keep a record of the daily apical pulse to show the physician at each visit.

Charting Example

10/23/XX 2 PM 55-year-old male patient is visiting physician because of recent frequent episodes of chest pain and SOB that are relieved by periods of rest. T 98.6°F, RP 90, AP 110, R 24. Thomas Medley, RMA

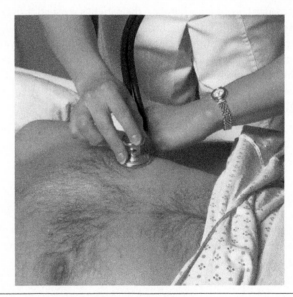

Figure 10-13 ◆ Place the bell or diaphragm on the patient's chest.

the diaphragm, and acid-base balance factors. Due to the process of acute or chronic illness, some individuals require assistance with breathing—by mask, nasal cannula, or ventilator.

A rapid assessment of a patient's respiratory function is accomplished by counting the number of breaths taken in one minute and noting the depth and regularity of the respiratory pattern. Rate, depth, and regularity of breathing affect the amount of oxygen inhaled and the amount of carbon dioxide exhaled. These two factors and additional factors listed below ultimately affect the patient's overall health status and ability to adjust to temporary healthy conditions or to chronic medical conditions. For example, breathing fast during a race is healthy and serves to bring more oxygen to the tissues. Breathing fast may also reflect an attempt by the body to lower abnormally high carbon dioxide levels caused by respiratory or other medical conditions. The examiner uses the assessment of rate, depth, and rhythm to request more definitive testing, make a diagnosis, and prescribe appropriate treatment.

Factors that affect the respiratory rate include:

- allergic reactions
- disease
- exercise
- excitement, anger
- stimulation of peripheral nervous system (PNS)
- fever, deviations from normal body temperature
- hemorrhage
- high altitude
- medications, drugs
- obstruction of airway
- pain
- shock
- decrease or increase of CO_2 in blood

PROCEDURE 10-8 **Perform a Respiration Count**

Theory

Assessment of the rate, rhythm, and depth of respirations is an essential part of taking vital signs. The respiratory rate is usually counted immediately after the radial or apical pulse is measured. Keep your hand on the patient's wrist after the radial pulse count (or the stethoscope on the chest after the apical pulse count), but glance toward the chest to observe and count respirations. The patient should be unaware that respirations are being counted. Otherwise he or she may consciously try to control the breathing, which will affect the resting respiratory count.

Materials

- watch with second hand

Competency

(**Conditions**) With the necessary supplies, (**Task**) you will perform a respiration count (**Standards**) accurately, in the time designated by the instructor, making sure the patient is unaware that you are doing so.

1. This procedure is a continuation of the radial or apical pulse count. The patient has been identified and you have washed your hands.
2. After counting the radial or apical pulse and mentally noting the rate, continue holding the patient's wrist or holding the stethoscope chestpiece in place.
3. Watch the patient's chest rise (inspiration) and fall (expiration) and count the respiratory cycles for 30 seconds. Observe the regularity and depth of the respirations (Figure 10-14 ◆). Make a mental note of the respiratory rate.
4. Multiply the 30-second count by two and record that figure as the respiratory rate. Record the pulse as well. Add

any appropriate comments about the regularity or depth of the respirations on the chart.

Patient Education

Instruct the patient's significant other to count respirations for one full minute following the radial or apical pulse, while the patient is unaware. If the patient is aware, the respiratory count could increase or decrease above the resting rate. It is also important to determine if the respirations are shallow or deep. The significant other should describe to the physician any abnormal sounds heard with the respirations.

Charting Example

09/21/XX 1530 Daughter states that patient has been getting weaker and breathing has been getting more difficult for the patient. T 99.6°F, P 100, R 28, B/P 140/90. Emeka Wright, CMA

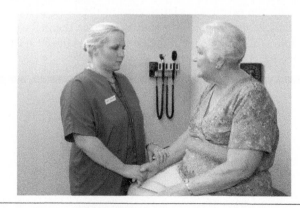

Figure 10-14 ◆ Performing a respiration count

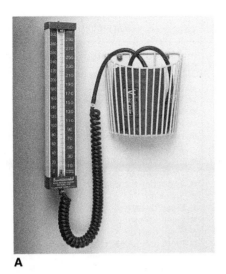 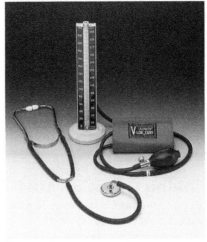

A **B**

Figure 10-15 ◆ (A) Wall mounted mercury sphygmomanometer; (B) Portable mercury sphygmomanometer
Reprinted with permission of W. A. Baum.

Blood Pressure

Blood pressure is the measurement of circulating blood pressure exerted on vessel walls by the pumping action of the heart. The pressure varies with the contraction and relaxation phases of the heartbeat. **Systole** refers to the contraction phase, and **diastole** refers to the relaxation phase.

Blood pressure readings provide the examiner with a quick overview of the patient's circulatory status. Excessive or abnormally low pressure on the vessel walls from high or low blood pressure, respectively, may lead to complications or related medical conditions. Deviations in blood pressure readings (high or low) provide information with which to formulate a possible diagnosis and treatment.

A sphygmomanometer is used to measure blood pressure in millimeters of mercury (mm Hg)—either in a calibrated column of mercury or with an aneroid dial (Figures 10-15 ◆ and 10-16 ◆). Mercury has been found to pose serious health risks, and thus mercury sphygmomanometers are being elim-

inated. Restrictions vary from state to state, so some offices may still have them in use. A stethoscope is used in conjunction with the sphygmomanometer to hear systolic and diastolic pressure, which are represented by the two numerical values in a blood pressure measurement.

- *Systolic pressure* is the period of highest pressure. It represents the force of the blood pushing against arterial walls when the ventricles of the heart are contracting.
- *Diastolic pressure* is the period of lowest pressure, when the ventricles relax.

A blood pressure reading is recorded as a fraction, with systolic over diastolic pressure. A normal blood pressure reading for an adult is 120/80—120 is systolic and 80 is diastolic (Table 10-5). The numerical difference is called the *pulse pressure*. Normal pulse pressure is 40 points. Pulse pressure lower than 30 points or greater than 50 points is considered abnormal and an indication of an underlying problem.

 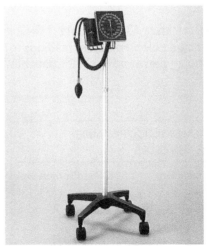

A **B**

Figure 10-16 ◆ (A) Portable aneroid sphygmomanometer; (B) Portable aneroid sphygmomanometer on wheels
Courtesy of Welch Allyyn, Inc.

TABLE 10-5 AVERAGE SYSTOLIC/DIASTOLIC VALUES FOR BLOOD PRESSURE BY AGE

Newborn	80/50 mm Hg
Infant	90/60 mm Hg
Child, 3 years	100/60 mm Hg
Child, 6 years	100/60 mm Hg
Child, 10 years	110/60 mm Hg
Child, 14 years	120/60 mm Hg
Adult	120/80 mm Hg
Elderly > 60 years of age	155/95 mm Hg

?– Critical Thinking Question 10-1–

Knowing that a normal pulse pressure is between 30 mm Hg and 50 mm Hg, what should Chelsea do next?

Blood pressure consistently elevated by 20 to 30 points over the baseline BP is termed **hypertension**. Several elevated readings are required for a diagnosis of hypertension. Blood pressure with significant elevation, usually with rapid onset, indicates **malignant hypertension**, and immediate intervention is required.

The American Heart Association issued the following guidelines concerning classifications of hypertension (Table 10-6): "The classifications in the table below are for people who aren't taking antihypertensive (blood pressure-lowering) drugs and aren't acutely ill. When a person's systolic and diastolic pressures fall into different categories, the higher category is used to classify the blood pressure status. Diagnosing high blood pressure is based on the average of two or more readings taken at each of two or more visits after an initial screening."

Readings 20 to 30 points *below* normal are indicative of **hypotension**. A sudden, significant drop in pressure is indicative of shock, and immediate intervention is required to prevent circulatory collapse. (∞ See Chapter 23 for information on emergency intervention.)

Table 10-7 lists the causes of abnormally elevated and lowered blood pressure.

?— Critical Thinking Question 10-2–

Chelsea heard two distinct blood pressure readings in the same arm. How should she record this in the patient's chart?

TABLE 10-6 CLASSIFICATION OF BLOOD PRESSURE FOR ADULTS AGE 18 YEARS AND OLDER

Category	Systolic (mm Hg)		Diastolic (mm Hg)
Normal*	less than 120	and	less than 80
Prehypertension	120–139	or	80–89
Hypertension:			
Stage 1	140–159	or	90–99
Stage 2	160 or higher	or	100 or higher

Unusually low readings should be evaluated for clinical significance.

Reproduced with permission www.americanheart.org. © 2006, American Heart Association, Inc.

TABLE 10-7 CAUSES OF VARIATIONS IN BLOOD PRESSURE

Increased or Elevated Blood Pressure	Decreased or Lowered Blood Pressure
■ Exercise	■ Weak heart
■ Stress, anxiety, excitement, fear	■ Massive heart attack
■ Pain	■ Hemorrhage
■ Increased arterial blood volume	■ Shock and vascular collapse
■ Loss of vessel elasticity as blood vessels age	■ Dehydration
■ Increased peripheral resistance, narrowing of blood vessels	■ Adrenal insufficiency
■ Endocrine disorders	■ Certain drug therapies
■ Smoking	■ Disorders of the nervous system
■ Renal disease	■ Hypothyroidism
■ Liver disease	■ Sleep
■ Heart disease	■ Infections, fevers
■ Right arm higher than left arm	■ Cancer
■ Certain drug therapies	■ Anemia
■ Increased intracranial pressure	■ Approaching death
■ Late pregnancy	■ Middle pregnancy
■ Obesity	■ Pain
■ Time of day	■ Starvation
	■ Sudden postural changes
	■ Time of day

Errors in Blood Pressure Readings

Factors that contribute to errors in blood pressure readings include the following:

■ Using a cuff of incorrect size
■ Air leaks in the valve
■ Failing to uncover the patient's arm (not rolling up the sleeve, etc.) before applying the cuff
■ Incorrectly positioning the patient's arm
■ Applying the cuff too loosely
■ Not centering the cuff over the brachial artery
■ Not securing the end of the cuff properly
■ Allowing the stethoscope tubing to touch something else
■ Improperly positioning the stethoscope earpieces in the ears
■ Placing the bell or diaphragm incorrectly over the brachial artery
■ Not inflating the cuff to 20 mm above the normal pressure
■ Closing the thumbscrew incompletely, allowing air to escape from the cuff
■ Deflating the cuff too rapidly
■ Retaking the blood pressure before waiting a minute or retaking the pressure in the same arm more than twice
■ Failing to calibrate the sphygmomanometer
■ Upset, anxious, or shaking patient

Weight and Height

The **mensuration,** or measuring of a patient's weight and height, establishes baseline information for future comparison and helps in the assessment of health status and response to illness and/or treatment. These measurements are used to diagnose obesity and aid in the management of conditions such as diabetes and congestive heart failure. Medication dosages are prescribed on the basis of weight. Children are weighed and measured on a routine basis to assess their growth.

PROCEDURE 10-9 **Measure Blood Pressure**

Theory

Blood pressure is measured as part of vital sign assessment during most patient visits to the medical office. The usual inflation is a minimum of 20 mm of mercury above the previous reading or to a level of 180 mm Hg as the starting point. The stethoscope tubing should not be touching anything during the procedure because the added noises may affect the accuracy of the measurement.

The width of the blood pressure cuff is important. To obtain an accurate reading, the cuff must fit the limb. Appropriate cuff widths are:

Newborns of average size:	2.5 cm (1 inch)
Children 1–4 years of age:	6 cm (2.3 inches)
Children 4–8 years of age:	9 cm (3.5 inches)
Adults:	13 cm (5.1 inches)
Obese adults:	20 cm (8 inches)

Routine blood pressure is measured in the sitting position. If it is measured while the patient is standing or lying down, note that on the chart.

Materials

- stethoscope
- 70% isopropyl alcohol wipes
- sphygmomanometer (aneroid or mercury)

Competency

(**Conditions**) With the necessary supplies, (**Task**) you will obtain an accurate blood pressure reading (**Standards**) accurately within the time frame designated by the instructor.

1. Wash your hands and assemble the equipment. Squeeze the bladder of the sphygmomanometer cuff to make sure it is completely deflated.
2. Identify the patient and escort to a central area or patient examination room. Have the patient sit either on a chair or on the examination table. Explain the procedure to the patient.
3. Cleanse the earpieces, diaphragm, and bell of the stethoscope with the alcohol wipes.
4. Expose the patient's upper arm and ask the patient to extend the arm with the palm facing upward. You may have to assist the patient in rolling up the sleeve.
5. Place the sphygmomanometer cuff around the patient's upper arm and secure it snugly, centering over the brachial artery (Figure 10-17 ◆).
6. Palpate the brachial pulse.
7. Hold the arm with the attached sphygmomanometer at heart level.
8. Place the sphygmomanometer gauge where you can monitor it easily or ask the patient to hold it (Figure 10-18 ◆).
9. Place the stethoscope earpieces in your ears. Place the diaphragm of the stethoscope over the location where you felt the brachial pulse. Hold the bell of the stethoscope in place with the thumb of your nondominant hand while supporting the elbow with your fingers (Figure 10-19 ◆).
10. With your dominant hand, close the thumbscrew on the hand bulb by turning it clockwise. Quickly and evenly pump the bulb to inflate the cuff.
11. Slowly turn the thumbscrew counterclockwise, releasing air at approximately 2–3 mm per second.

Figure 10-17 ◆ Place the sphygmomanometer cuff around the patient's upper arm.

Figure 10-18 ◆ Place the sphygmomanometer gauge where you can monitor it easily.

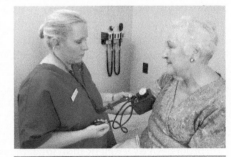

Figure 10-19 ◆ Hold the bell of the stethoscope in place with the thumb of your nondominant hand.

continued

PROCEDURE 10-9 Measure Blood Pressure *(continued)*

12. Listen and mentally note when you hear the first pulsation. Slowly continue to release air until the pulsation sounds cease, and make a mental note of that reading.
13. Quickly release the rest of the air, deflating the cuff. Remove the cuff.
14. If it is necessary to check the blood pressure reading because of an error in the procedure or an abnormally high or low reading, wait one minute before retaking the blood pressure on the same arm.
15. Clean the earpieces and diaphragm with 70% ethyl alcohol. Return the sphygmomanometer and stethoscope to their usual storage place.
16. Wash your hands.
17. After recording the date and time, document the first pulsation sounds as systolic and the last sounds as diastolic readings. Write the systolic over diastolic readings in fraction format. If the blood pressure was taken with the patient standing or lying down, specify the position in the chart. If the patient asks for the reading and office policy allows it, you may inform the patient of the reading.

Patient Education

Patients and significant others generally go to a medical supply or department store to buy a sphygmomanometer. Emphasize the importance of seeking help to find a properly fitting cuff. Kits are often available with a stethoscope but are also sold separately. The entire arm should be level with the heart during the procedure. Demonstrate ways to do this, such as placing the arm on a higher countertop or holding the arm elevated. Because of the potential for impairing circulation, instruct the patient never to inflate the cuff more than twice on the same arm. The patient or significant others should keep records of the blood pressures for the next medical office visit. This information will be used to adjust, add, or delete medications and evaluate the status of acute and chronic medical conditions.

Charting Example

06/29/XX 8:30 AM T 98.6 P 94 R 24 B/P 160/110. Patient states narrowly missed being in an auto accident before coming for office appointment. Carol Herns, RMA

06/29/XX 8:50 AM P 88 R 20 B/P 140/90. Carol Herns, RMA

Weight

An individual's weight is another valuable tool for assessing health status. Weight measurements are used to monitor the growth of an infant or child. The weight of any patient, child or adult, is an important factor in calculating drug dosages as well as the effectiveness of drug and nutritional therapies. Physicians use daily weight measurements as an assessment tool in the treatment of specific diagnoses. Patients with congestive heart failure or renal failure may require daily weighing. For example, rapid weight gain would indicate the need for additional diuretics or dialysis treatments.

While there are standard guidelines for normal weight based on height, variations are to be expected. An "ideal weight" must be individualized for body type, age, and health status. Being either underweight or overweight can have serious implications for the patient's well-being. An underweight individual may be experiencing nutritional problems or metabolic disorders. An overweight individual may also be experiencing nutritional or metabolic problems, but with the added complication of hypertension, heart disease, or diabetes.

The patient is usually weighed at every visit. On the initial visit the weight establishes a baseline for future comparison. It is good practice during the initial assessment to ask the patient what his or her usual weight is and whether the current weight is significantly different. You should be alert to any changes and call them to the physician's attention.

Some patients are very sensitive about their weight and do not want anyone to know what it is. Keep the scales in a private area. When you are weighing the patient, do not comment on

Keys to Success
POUNDS AND KILOS

Most scales measure weight in pounds and ounces. Canadian clients are used to measuring their weight in kilograms. To convert pounds to kilograms, divide the weight in pounds by 2.2. For example, 180 pounds is 81.8 kilos. To convert kilograms to pounds, multiply the weight in kilograms by 2.2. Patients from the United Kingdom may express their weight in stones. One stone is equal to 14 pounds, so a 126-pound woman weighs 9 stone.

the weight. Chart the results, return the balance weights to the zero position before the patient steps down from the scales, and escort the patient back to the examination room. If the patient is accompanied by another individual or support person, try to keep the weight a confidential matter between the physician and the patient.

Height

Like weight, height is a valuable tool in assessing the status of a patient's health. Height measurements are used to monitor the growth of an infant or child. Failure to grow is ascertained in a child or infant who shows little or no change in height. During the aging process, individuals may begin to lose height because of spinal compression or other disease processes.

Measurements of height or length are usually reported in feet and inches. However, some practitioners may prefer the metric system of measurement and report the measurement in meters and centimeters.

PROCEDURE 10-10 Obtain Weight and Height Measurements

Theory

The measurement of weight and height is considered part of the routine that includes the taking of temperature, pulse, respirations, and blood pressure. The following procedural steps are for patients who can stand and follow directions, and step on and off the scales with or without assistance. (∞ Measuring the length, weight, and head circumference of infants is covered in Chapter 26.)

The patient is weighed at each visit, initially to determine a baseline weight, and on following visits to observe for trends or sudden changes. You can measure a patient's weight quickly if the patient knows approximately what he or she weighs. The scales should be balanced to zero before the patient is weighed. On electronic models this calibration may be done with a button; on manual models a screw on the upper arm of the scale is loosened or tightened until the scale is balanced. To maintain patient confidentiality and privacy, the scales should be kept in a private area away from other patients. Return the weight to zero after you record the patient's results. Height is measured as the last step, and then the patient is returned to the examination room.

When measuring height and weight, note whether the patient is wearing shoes with thick soles or heels. Note on the chart any added height from shoes. If the patient has removed the shoes, note that on the chart. The same concept applies to clothing. Some offices prefer that the patient remove coats or bulky jackets and/or shoes before weighing. Other heavy or bulky clothes should be noted on the chart. If possible, ask patients to remove keys and other heavy objects from their pockets. Common sense should prevail in these situations.

Whether a patient's weight is measured in the office or at home, the same standards should be followed—for example, if shoes and/or socks are worn during weighing in the office, they should be worn for weighing at home. Other standards include wearing clothing or minimal clothing, weighing at the same time every day, and using the same scales. A change greater than three to five pounds in one day should be called in to the medical office.

The physician generally reads the weight figure when he or she looks over the entire set of vital sign measurements. If necessary, you can share weight results with the physician out of the patient's sight and hearing.

Materials

- upright balance scales with height bar
- paper towel

Competency

(**Conditions**) With the necessary supplies, (**Task**) you will be able to obtain weight and height measurements (**Standards**) accurately within the time frame designated by the instructor.

1. Identify the patient and escort him or her to the examination room.
2. Wash your hands.
3. Explain the procedure to the patient. Explain that most personal items may be left in the room, although a female patient may want to take her purse. Escort the patient to the scales.
4. Balance the scales to read zero.
5. Instruct the patient to step on the scales. You may need to place a paper towel on the scale for patients who wish to remove their shoes. Assist the patient onto the scales and provide support as needed.
6. Instruct the patient to stand still. Move the weights until the scale balances (Figure 10-20 ◆).
7. Note the weight and return the balance weights to zero.
8. Ask the patient to step off the scales, assisting as necessary.
9. Help the patient to step on the scales backwards so that his or her back is against the scale. Ask the patient to stand erect, eyes looking ahead.
10. Raise the height bar in a collapsed position above the patient's head (Figure 10-21 ◆). Extend the bar and slowly bring it down until it touches the top of the patient's head (Figure 10-22 ◆). Note the height.
11. Raise the entire height bar up over the patient's head, collapse it, and return it to its original position.

continued

PROCEDURE 10-10 Obtain Height and Weight Measurements *(continued)*

12. Ask the patient to step off the scales, assisting as necessary.
13. Record the height and weight on the patient's chart.

Patient Education

Instruct the patient or significant other to follow the same weighing procedure every day: weigh at the same time, use the same scales, wear shoes or not, wear regular or minimal clothing. The patient should also keep a daily record and call the physician about any weight changes greater than 3 to 5 pounds in one day.

Charting Example

08/23/XX 1120 Patient called to state that weight has been increasing by approximately a pound a day. Patient reports a 3-pound weight gain today. Physician informed. Lasix dosage has been increased from 10 to 20 mg/day by mouth and prescription has been called to Wellbetter Pharmacy as requested by patient. William Martinez, CMA

Figure 10-20 ◆ Move weight to balanced position

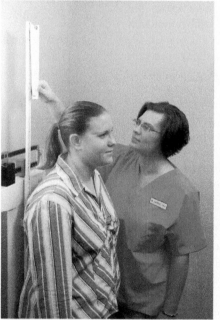

Figure 10-21 ◆ Raise the height bar in a collapsed position above the patient's head

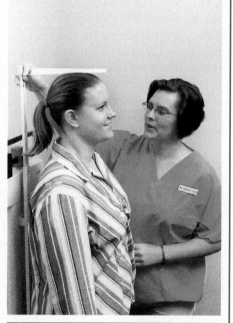

Figure 10-22 ◆ Bring the bar down until it touches the top of the patient's head

Visual Acuity

Visual acuity is an assessment of the acuteness or clarity of the patient's vision. This is an easy test to perform and is often included in a pre-employment physical. Visual acuity testing is part of the application for certain drivers' licenses. (∞ Refer to Chapter 19 for detailed information and skills proficiency on visual acuity screening.).

Hearing Assessment

Hearing assessment includes an evaluation with a tuning fork. An audiometer may be used for a more thorough and complete assessment of an individual's hearing range. (∞ Refer to Chapter 19 for additional information on hearing assessment.)

Preparing the Patient for a Physical Examination

The physician must be able to easily access the part of the body to be examined. The patient is asked to remove clothing as necessary and to don a patient gown, pants, or drape. Draping provides for modesty, comfort, and warmth. The patient is then properly positioned, usually on the examination table, for the physical examination.

Gowning

In preparation for examination by the physician, you will instruct the patient regarding the removal of clothing and donning the patient gown. During a complete physical examination, the physician visually inspects the entire body. The patient may need to remove all clothing and wear a gown, usually with closure in the back. Depending on the thoroughness of the examination, undergarments may be left on. However, if the examination or procedure includes exposure of the pelvic cavity, rectum, or chest/breast areas, undergarments will need to be removed and a gown with front closure worn.

Gowns are made of cloth or paper, with ties or snaps for closure. Half-paper gowns cover only the chest, and paper or cloth sheets allow for privacy and draping (Figure 10-23 ◆).

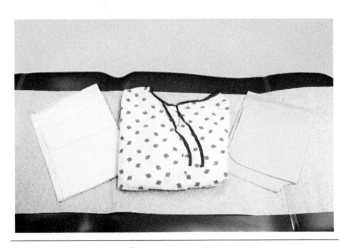

Figure 10-23 ◆ Types of gowns

Draping

Draping involves covering any area that may be exposed during the examination. A sheet over the legs is the usual drape for a patient in a sitting position. (Positions are described in the following section.) A sheet over the torso and legs is the usual drape for a patient in a lying position, both supine and prone. A sheet is placed over the lower torso and can be draped over the legs of a patient in lithotomy position. For a patient in the knee-chest position, a sheet is placed over the posterior torso and can be draped over the buttocks. Similarly, a sheet is draped over a patient in Sims' position, and the edge can be lifted to provide access to the buttocks and rectal region.

Positioning the Patient

Patient positioning for the examination is usually done by the medical assistant. A common position for the beginning of an examination is to have the patient sit upright on the exam table. As the examination progresses, you will assist the patient into various positions, depending on the area of the body being examined. Positions include the following:

- Anatomical—standing
- Sitting—sitting upright with the legs hanging over the side of the examination table (Figure 10-24 ◆)
- Fowler's—sitting erect on the table with the legs extended in front and the back rest at a 90-degree angle (Figure 10-25 ◆)
- Semi-Fowler's—sitting on the table with the legs extended and the back rest at 45 degrees (Figure 10-26 ◆)
- Supine—lying flat on the back
- Dorsal recumbent—lying flat on the back with the knees bent and the feet flat on the table (Figure 10-27 ◆)
- Prone—lying on the abdomen with the head to one side (Figure 10-28 ◆)
- Trendelenburg—lying flat on the back with the head lower than the feet (Figure 10-29 ◆)
- Knee-chest—kneeling on the table with the buttocks raised and the head and chest on the examination table (Figure 10-30 ◆).
- Jackknife—lying with the abdomen on the table, the knees on the table step, and the buttocks extended (Figure 10-31 ◆)
- Lithotomy—lying on the back in dorsal recumbent with the feet on the corners of the table or in the stirrups (Figure 10-32 ◆)
- Left lateral recumbent—lying horizontal on the left side
- Right lateral recumbent—lying horizontal on the right side
- Sims'—right or left lateral recumbent with the upper leg flexed (Figure 10-33 ◆)

Upon completion of the examination or procedure, the patient should be assisted to an upright sitting position and observed for any signs of light-headedness. Then the patient is assisted to a standing position and assisted to dress if necessary.

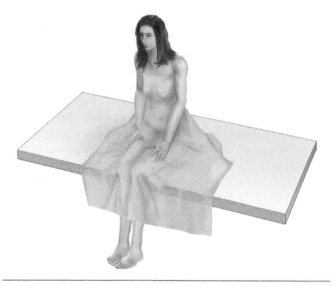

Figure 10-24 ◆ Sitting position

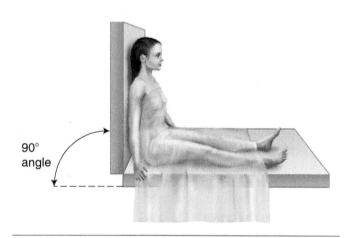

90°
angle

Figure 10-25 ◆ Fowler's position

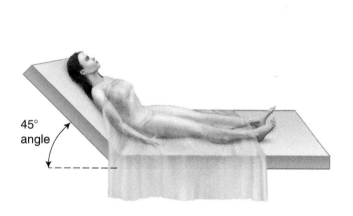

45°
angle

Figure 10-26 ◆ Semi-Fowler's position

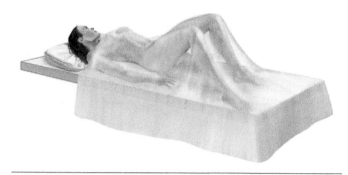

Figure 10-27 ◆ Dorsal recumbent position

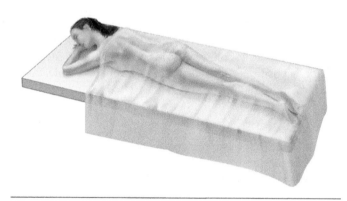

Figure 10-28 ◆ Prone position

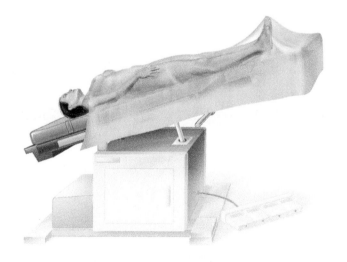

Figure 10-29 ◆ Trendelenburg position

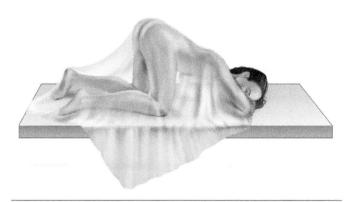

Figure 10-30 ◆ Knee-chest position

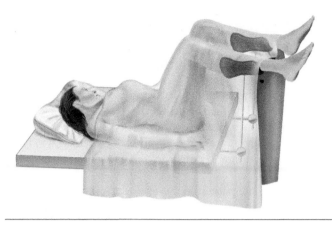

Figure 10-32 ◆ Lithotomy position

Figure 10-31 ◆ Jackknife position

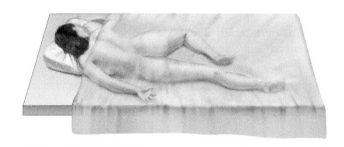

Figure 10-33 ◆ Sims' position

PROCEDURE 10-11 Demonstrate Patient Positions Used in a Medical Examination

Theory

When positioning the patient, some factors to be considered are the patient's range of motion, the patient's comfort, and the length of time the position will be maintained. You should not place the patient in any position other than sitting or lying until the examination or procedure is ready to begin. Children and the elderly should never be left alone. The patient should be covered with a drape that is lifted only when the body part is being examined.

Depending on the type of examination, the physician will have the patient shift from a sitting position to other positions. For a pelvic examination and Pap smear, the patient is moved from sitting to supine, then dorsal recumbent, and lastly to the lithotomy position. A patient experiencing shortness of breath should be placed in a Fowler's position to facilitate breathing. As you may not be present for the entire examination, it is important that you anticipate draping and positioning needs based on the patient's reason for visiting the medical office.

Materials

- patient gown, pants, and drapes
- examination table paper

Competency

(**Conditions**) With the necessary supplies, (**Task**) you will be able to assist the patient into the sitting, supine, Sims', prone, dorsal recumbent, and lithotomy positions (**Standards**) correctly within the time designated by the instructor.

continued

PROCEDURE 10-11 Demonstrate Patient Positions Used in a Medical Examination *(continued)*

1. Identify the patient and escort to examination room.
2. Wash your hands and gather drape materials.
3. Explain the procedure to the patient. Ask the patient to completely undress and to put on a patient gown. For a breast examination, instruct the patient to tie the gown in front.
4. Instruct the patient to sit on the examination table, assisting as necessary. Cover the patient with the drape.
5. Assist the patient into the supine position.
6. Assist the patient into the Sims' position.
7. Assist the patient into the prone position.
8. Assist the patient back into the supine position, then into the dorsal recumbent position.
9. Assist the patient into the lithotomy position.
10. Assist the patient in returning to the sitting position and stepping off the examination table.
11. After the examination has been completed and the physician has discussed the procedure with the patient, clean the examination room. Remove the used paper from the examination table and replace it with clean paper for the next patient.
12. Wash your hands and complete documentation in the patient's chart.

Patient Education

Explain to patient that he or she will be assisted/directed through change of positions for the examination. Provide reassurance that modesty will be provided. Inform patient that some discomfort may be experienced, but encourage patient to verbalize any additional needs that may need to be addressed throughout the examination.

Charting Example

12/05/XX 9:30 AM Assisted patient turning from supine to left-lateral position for rectal examination. Patient tolerated examination without discomfort. Danica Verdo, RMA

Assessment Methods Used in an Examination

Physicians use a variety of assessment methods during a physical examination: inspection, palpation, auscultation, percussion, and, in some instances, mensuration.

Inspection is the visual examination of both the external surface of the body and the interior portions of body cavities (Figure 10-34 ◆). The external surface is examined for asymmetry, the size of the individual, any unusual breaks in the skin, scars, color, and any unusual shapes or positions. Internal cavity surfaces that may be examined include the eyes, throat, nares, ears, vaginal walls, cervix, and rectum. These examinations require the use of certain instruments.

Palpation is an examination involving touch (Figure 10-35 ◆). The examiner uses the hands and fingers to feel both the surface of the body (for any abnormalities or irregularities) and various organs (for size, location, and tenderness). In addition to assessing the texture and temperature of the tissue, the examiner palpates for lumps or masses.

Figure 10-34 ◆ Inspection is an assessment method used by the physician.

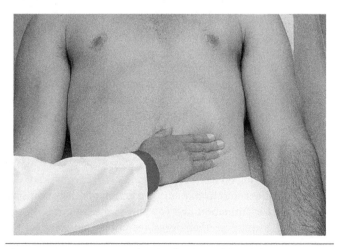

Figure 10-35 ◆ An example of palpation of the abdomen.

Figure 10-36 ◆ Auscultation consists of listening to various areas of the body.

Auscultation consists of listening to various areas of the body (Figure 10-36 ◆). It is possible to assess the status of the heart, lungs, and gastrointestinal tract by auscultation. The valves of the heart make a particular sound when they are healthy and a different sound in the presence of disease or irregularity. Breath sounds are assessed for depth and texture. Fluid in the chest cavity can be detected during auscultation. The presence, absence, strength, and quality of bowel sounds aid in detecting problems within the GI tract. The examiner usually uses a stethoscope for auscultation, although some breath sounds are audible without it.

In **percussion,** the examiner taps the fingertips lightly but sharply against the body to assess the size and location of underlying organs (Figure 10-37 ◆). The technique involves placing two fingers of one hand on the patient's skin and gently striking those fingers with the index and middle fingers of the other hand. Training allows for differentiation of the sounds of the percussion. For example, a deviation from normal may lead the examiner to suspect fluid or pus in a cavity

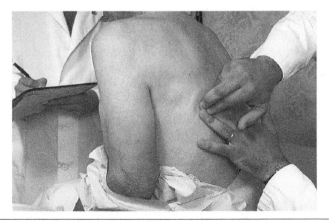

Figure 10-37 ◆ The physician uses percussion to assess the size and location of underlying organs.

or a change in the density of an organ. Another percussion method involves the use of a percussion hammer to test tendon reflexes.

Mensuration is the measurement of certain parts of the body or the length and height of the individual. Tissue calipers measure the size of certain tissues. A tape measure is used to measure the circumference of the head, neck, chest, abdomen, legs, ankles, arms, and wrists. A standing scale with a height measurement bar is used to measure height, except for infants, whose length is measured with a tape measure.

The medical assistant uses assessment tools to some extent. For example, taking blood pressure involves palpation of the brachial artery as well as auscultation with a stethoscope. The MA always uses the inspection method and documents and reports abnormal findings. If you are not sure if a finding is abnormal, ask the physician and/or nurse.

When the initial examination is complete, the physician may order diagnostic testing. It is your responsibility to schedule the tests and coordinate the time with the patient. You will give the patient instructions for the tests as well as directions to the testing facility (unless testing is to be done in the office). You will note on the chart when to schedule a return appointment and assist the patient in doing so. (∞ Refer to Chapter 12 for more information on scheduling diagnostic testing.)

Assisting the Physician During the Examination

Most complete physical examinations begin at the head and proceed downward. The skin is observed for color, warmth, moisture, and **turgor**. The physician notes the patient's level of consciousness, demeanor, and cooperativeness. Examination of the head includes the eyes, ears, nares, and oral cavity. The eyes are normally examined for pupil equality, reaction to light, and **accommodation**. Ocular muscle activity or coordination may also be assessed with an ophthalmoscope. The ears are examined with an otoscope, usually with a disposable speculum. A wider speculum may be added to the otoscope for examination of the nares. The otoscope may be used as a light source to examine the oral cavity. A tongue depressor is used to hold the tongue in place while the examiner visualizes the throat. It also aids in the inspection of the buccal surface of the cheeks and the teeth.

The examiner palpates the neck for any masses or abnormalities. Usually the patient is asked to grip the examiner's fingers and squeeze as an evaluation of muscle and nerve strength of the arms and hands. The carotid arteries in the neck are palpated for texture and lumps, then auscultated for any bruits or unusual sounds. A visual examination of the anterior chest wall will reveal any abnormalities, including asymmetrical rise and fall of the rib cage as well as any sternal retraction. The posterior chest is visually inspected, followed by auscultation of the chest cavity for any abnormal breath sounds or heart tones.

This portion of the examination is usually completed with the patient in a sitting position with the legs extending over the side of the exam table. The examiner may check knee reflexes, pedal pulses, and swelling of the ankles and feet as well as any other aspect of the legs and feet.

Examination of the abdomen requires that the patient lie down on the exam table. The examiner visually inspects the skin of the abdomen and observes for any unusual movement under the surface of the skin. This is usually followed by auscultation of the abdominal region—listening for bowel sounds with a stethoscope. The abdomen is usually palpated for masses, tenderness, and guarding. Palpation begins in the right upper quadrant and progresses clockwise through the right lower quadrant, left lower quadrant, left upper quadrant, and back to the starting point.

The pelvic region may be palpated for masses and tenderness just above the pubic bone. If the patient complains of midback or flank region pain, the examiner may palpate the area over the kidneys and just under the ribs posteriorly to ascertain tenderness and pain.

For a pelvic exam and Pap smear, the patient is assisted into stirrups and the lithotomy position. The patient may be placed in a knee-chest or Sim's position for a rectal examination. Other specialty examinations will be addressed in the appropriate chapters.

The patient may be asked to walk in the examination room so that the examiner can assess gait, posture, and any spinal abnormalities.

When the examination is complete, you assist the patient to dress, if necessary, and provide any other assistance the patient needs.

Recurrent Clinical Visits

On recurrent clinical visits, you will escort the patient to the appropriate examination room and obtain a brief history, including the reason for the visit, any changes noted since the last visit, and an update on medications. You will measure vital signs, including weight and height, and update the chart to reflect your observations and findings. Then you will prepare the patient for the physical examination in the usual manner.

PROCEDURE 10-12 Assist the Physician with the Physical Examination

Theory

Physical examinations require more of the physician's and medical assistant's time. Each medical office has an established protocol for blocking time for physical examinations. Depending on the patient's age, gender, and medical condition, you may leave or be required to stay during all or part of the physical examination.

The patient must disrobe completely or almost completely for this procedure. Some patients are very modest, and are resistive to completely undressing. Patients who are concerned about the cool temperature of the examination room may be allowed to wear underwear until it needs to be removed. Provide these patients with extra draping or cover. Protect the patient's dignity with draping and provide assurance by explaining the basic components of the procedure.

Throughout the procedure, observe the patient's body language for any signs of discomfort or anxiety. Before the procedure begins, ask if the patient needs to use the bathroom. Emptying the bladder helps the patient feel more comfortable during the physical examination. If a urine specimen is required, it can be obtained at this point.

Materials

- examination table with clean covering (sheet) and stirrups if pelvic examination is to be performed
- patient gown and appropriate drapes
- pillow with disposable cover
- scales with height rod
- Snellen chart and color vision charts
- disposable gloves
- lubricant and tissues
- emesis basin
- alcohol swabs
- laryngeal mirror
- nasal and ear speculums
- ophthalmoscope and otoscope
- pen light
- reflex hammer
- sphygmomanometer and stethoscope
- tape measure
- thermometer
- tongue depressors
- tuning fork
- urine specimen container
- gooseneck lamp

Competency

(**Conditions**) With the necessary supplies, (**Task**) you will be able to prepare the clinical room with the appropriate examination supplies, provide instruction and reassurance to the patient, and assist the physician as needed during the examination procedure (**Standards**) correctly within the time frame designated by the instructor.

1. Equip each examination room with the necessary supplies, equipment, and instruments. Ensure that instruments are in working order and the room temperature is comfortable.
2. Identify the patient and escort him or her to the examination room.
3. Wash your hands.

PROCEDURE 10-12 Assist the Physician with the Physical Examination *(continued)*

4. Obtain the patient's weight and height, usually in a semi-private but central location in the clinical area.
5. Obtain vital signs and pain assessment.
6. Instruct the patient to remove necessary clothing and to put on the gown or cover. Offer to assist the patient if necessary and explain where to place removed clothing.
7. Instruct the patient to sit on the examination table and provide a drape.
8. Obtain the patient history through interview and review of the completed forms (Figure 10-38 ◆).
9. Gather the instruments the physician will need.
10. Notify the physician that the patient is ready.

11. When the physician is ready, assist with positioning the patient and the physical examination. Be prepared to gather additional supplies and assist the physician with any instruments or supplies necessary for the examination.
12. Upon completion of the examination, assist the patient from the examination table.
13. Prepare specimens for examination and/or transport by labeling and completing appropriate forms.
14. Remove soiled instruments and equipment to the utility room for cleaning.
15. Clean the room and dispose of any waste. Wash your hands.
16. Prepare the room for the next patient.

Patient Education

Instruct the patient on the importance of accurate information. If the patient is unable to answer questions, reassure him or her that the information can be documented when the patient remembers. If the patient has specific questions for the physician and is worried about forgetting, provide a pen and paper for the patient to make notes while waiting.

Charting Example

04/27/XX 2:30 PM T 98.6°F, P 86, R 20. B/P 126/80. Pt states this is a routine physical. Medical history forms reviewed and completed with assistance from patient. Linda Anderson, RMA

Figure 10-38 ◆ Taking the patient's history

REVIEW

Chapter Summary

- Vital signs establish baseline values for present and future medical assessment and treatment. They vary according to age but are specific to the individual because of medical condition(s), medications and medication interactions, and other factors such as obesity or exercise level.
- Body temperature is generally lower in the morning before activity. Fever is an elevation of temperature and often indicates an infectious disease process that may or may not require antibiotic therapy.
- Deviations from average pulse or respiration rates may indicate a normal physiological reaction, such as during and immediately after exercise, or may indicate a disease process of the cardiovascular and/or respiratory systems.
- Blood pressure is the pressure the blood exerts on vessel walls during cardiac contraction and relaxation. The patient's baseline blood pressure and family and past medical history are useful in the diagnosis and treatment of medical conditions such as hypertension.

- Weight and height measurements are used as guidelines to diagnose obesity, but are also used to adjust medication dosages and dietary management for medical conditions such as diabetes mellitus.
- The medical assistant prepares the examination room and anticipates the physician's needs during the physical examination. The MA also prepares the patient by providing instruction and assistance in gowning, positioning, and draping. Draping protects the patient's modesty and provides warmth and comfort.
- The physician performs patient assessment using the tools of palpation, percussion, auscultation, and inspection during the medical examination.
- Recurrent patient visits include taking vital signs and preparing the patient and the examination room for the anticipated procedure.

Chapter Review Questions

Multiple Choice

1. The appropriate cuff width for a child 1 to 4 years old is
   A. 6 cm.
   B. 9 cm.
   C. 2.5 cm.
   D. 13 cm.

2. Heat is lost through the skin by
   A. respiration.
   B. contraction.
   C. conduction.
   D. elimination.

3. The body temperature is lowest
   A. in the evening.
   B. 10 minutes after consuming food or a beverage.
   C. in the afternoon.
   D. in the morning.

4. An oral temperature is not contraindicated when
   A. the patient is an infant.
   B. the patient is elderly.
   C. the patient is combative.
   D. the patient is unconscious.

5. The skin is not observed for which of the following?
   A. elasticity
   B. color
   C. warmth
   D. turgor

6. A blood pressure reading of 110/60 mm Hg is an average normal reading for a child who is
   A. 6 years old.
   B. 3 years old.
   C. 10 years old.
   D. 14 years old.

7. When taking a tympanic temperature on an adult, you should
   A. not move the ear at all.
   B. pull the ear downward.
   C. pull the ear upward and forward.
   D. pull the ear upward.

8. When taking a tympanic temperature on a child, you should
   A. pull the ear upward and forward.
   B. pull the ear upward.
   C. pull the ear downward.
   D. not move the ear at all.

9. The measurement of weight and height is considered part of the routine that also includes all of the following except
   A. chest circumference.
   B. temperature.
   C. pulse.
   D. respirations.

10. Breathing is regulated by the
    A. hypothalmus.
    B. medulla oblongata.
    C. pituitary gland.
    D. thyroid.

Chapter Review

True/False

T F 1. Temperature is the measurement of body heat produced and lost during metabolism, respiration, elimination, and environmental fluctuation.

T F 2. Most complete physical examinations begin at the head and proceed downward.

T F 3. The skin is observed for color, warmth, moisture, and turgor.

T F 4. The eyes are examined with an otoscope.

T F 5. Fluid in the chest cavity can be detected during palpation.

Short Answer

1. Name and describe the four different types of fever.

2. Define *pulse*.

3. For a pelvic exam and Pap smear, the patient is assisted into which position?

4. What blood pressure readings are indicative of hypotension?

5. List at least six factors that affect the respiratory rate.

Research

1. Research common vital signs and symptoms of patients with known cardiac conditions such as hypertension, CAGB, and so on. How do these conditions affect the vital sign readings?

2. Research common vital signs and symptoms of patients with known pulmonary conditions such as COPD, emphysema, and so on. How do these conditions affect the vital sign readings?

Externship Application Experience

A patient has come to the office for her annual pelvic exam and Pap smear. This is her first physical examination since her left radical mastectomy. She appears anxious. Describe psychological support that you might give her during both preparation and procedure.

Resource Guide

U.S. Department of Health and Human Services
200 Independence Avenue, SW
Washington, DC 20201
1-877-696-6775
www.os.dhhs.gov

 **MedMedia**

www.prenhall.com/frazier

More on this chapter, including interactive resources, can be found on the Student CD-ROM accompanying this textbook and on the Companion Website at www.prenhall.com/frazier.

CHAPTER 11

Minor Surgery

Case Study

Latesha is a new RMA in the office and Gwen, the CMA manager, is showing her the office protocol for nonroutine surgeries. First on the list of things to do is to check that a consent form has been signed and is available in the chart. When Latesha looks for it, she cannot find it and lets Gwen know. "Oh, I know it was signed. It just hasn't been filed yet. I'll bring it to you later," Gwen replies.

Next, Gwen takes Latesha to the room the surgery will be performed in. Latesha notices that the table paper is crinkled and a laryngoscope has been left on the counter. Latesha observes Gwen quickly change the table paper and place the laryngoscope back in its case and under the counter. Gwen does not use a disinfectant or sterilize any of the surfaces.

Objectives

After completing this chapter, you should be able to:

- Spell and define the medical terminology in this chapter.
- Define the medical assistant's role in medical office surgery.
- List and describe surgeries performed in the medical office.
- Explain the essentials of consent.
- Discuss preoperative care of the patient in the medical office.
- Discuss how to set up the room for surgery in the medical office.
- Identify the types and functions of instruments used during surgery in the medical office.
- Explain the principles of positioning and draping for minor surgical procedures.
- List the types of anesthesia used during surgery in the medical office.
- Discuss the ways in which the MA assists the physician during minor surgery.
- Describe the suture materials used in minor surgery.
- Discuss recovery and postoperative care of the patient following surgery in the medical office.
- Describe postoperative patient teaching and discharge.
- Describe the stages of wound healing.
- Discuss the types of dressings used in medical office surgical procedures.

MedMedia

www.prenhall.com/frazier

Additional interactive resources and activities for this chapter can be found on the Companion Website. For videos, audio glossary, legal and ethical scenarios, job scenarios, quizzes, games, and activities related to the content of this chapter, please access the accompanying CD-ROM in this book.

 Assets Available:

Audio Glossary
Legal and Ethical Scenario: *Minor Surgery*
On the Job Scenario: *Minor Surgery*
Multiple Choice Quiz
Games: Crossword, Strikeout and Spelling Bee
Drag and Drop: Integumentary System: Organization of the Body

MEDICAL ASSISTING COMPETENCIES

CAAHEP ENTRY-LEVEL COMPETENCIES FOR CMA	ABHES ENTRY-LEVEL COMPETENCIES FOR RMA
■ Identify and respond to issues of confidentiality.	■ Maintain confidentiality at all times.
■ Perform within legal and ethical boundaries.	■ Be cognizant of ethical boundaries.
■ Demonstrate knowledge of federal and state health-care legislation and regulations.	■ Exhibit initiative.
	■ Adapt to change.
	■ Evidence a responsible attitude.
■ Perform hand washing.	■ Be courteous and diplomatic.
■ Wrap items for autoclaving.	■ Conduct work within scope of education, training, and ability.
■ Perform sterilization techniques.	■ Be attentive, listen, and learn.
■ Dispose of biohazardous materials.	■ Be impartial and show empathy when dealing with patients.
■ Practice Standard Precautions.	■ Adapt what is said to the recipient's level of comprehension.
■ Prepare patient for and assist with procedures, treatments, and minor office surgeries.	■ Adaptation for individualized needs.
	■ Prepare patients for procedures.
	■ Apply principles of aseptic techniques and infection control.
	■ Wrap items for autoclaving.
	■ Perform sterilization techniques.
	■ Dispose of hazardous materials.
	■ Practice Standard Precautions.
	■ Prepare and maintain examination and treatment area.
	■ Assist physician with examination and treatments.
	■ Use quality control.
	■ Collect and process specimens.

Introduction

Changes within the insurance reimbursement system, along with advances in medical technology and surgical procedures, have resulted in many surgeries now being performed as outpatient procedures. Often referred to as ambulatory, minor, or office surgery, outpatient surgeries may range from a simple 10-minute procedure, such as the removal of a skin lesion, to the 23-hour outpatient stay for a surgical clinic procedure, such as disk repair and patient recovery time.

The Medical Assistant's Role in Office Surgery

As an MA, your role in office surgery can cover scheduling through the completion of the procedure and dismissal of the patient. Individual responsibilities may include obtaining precertification approval, making sure the consent form is signed, ordering supplies, and cleaning and/or sterilizing instruments.

Medical Terminology

abrasion—Scraping away of the surface such as skin or teeth, by friction. An abrasion can be the result of injury or by mechanical means, as in dermabrasion for scar removal

anesthesia—partial or complete loss of sensation

approximation—joining together of surgical wound edges

avulsion—Process of forcibly tearing off a part or structure of the body, such as a finger or a toe

biopsy—The obtaining of a representative tissue sample for microscopic examination, usually to establish a diagnosis

cannula—tube or sheath

closed wound—wound that involves trauma to the underlying tissue without a break in the skin or mucous membrane or exposure of the underlying tissue

colposcopy—The examination of vaginal and cervical tissue by means of a colposcope

contraction—Process of drawing up or thickening of a muscle fiber

cryosurgery—The use of extremely cold probes to destroy unwanted, cancerous, or infected tissues

cutting—using a knife or surgical scissors to separate or divide tissues

dissection—cutting into smaller parts for study and analysis of each part

distal—away from the center

drainage—The flow or withdrawal of fluids from a wound or cavity, such as pus from a cavity or wound

elective surgery—A treatment or surgical procedure not requiring immediate attention and therefore planned for the patient's or provider's convenience

electrocautery—Cauterization using a variety of electrical modalities to create thermal energy, including a directly heated metallic applicator, or bipolar or monopolar electrodes

emergency surgery—1. Any urgent condition perceived by the physician as requiring immediate medical or surgical evaluation or treatment

Medical Terminology *(continued)*

granulation—Fleshy projections formed on the surface of a gaping wound that is not healing by first intention or indirect union

hemostat—instrument used to stop blood flow

incision—A cut made with a knife, electrosurgical unit, or laser especially for surgical purposes

inflammatory—An immunological defense against injury, infection, or allergy, marked by increases in regional blood flow, immigration of white blood cells, and release of chemical toxins

intraoperative—pertaining to patient care during surgery

laceration—A wound or irregular tear of the flesh

local anesthesia—absence of feeling or pain in a localized area of tissue without the loss of consciousness

Mayo stand—stand that holds a flat metal tray for setting up a sterile field for instruments and supplies; usually has an open side that allows it to be moved over a gurney or table

open wound—break in the skin or mucous membrane that exposes underlying tissues

optional surgery—The patient is given the option of surgery or not. Surgery is not medically relevant, denial for surgery will have no adverse effects on the patient's health

postoperative (post-op)—pertaining to patient care following surgery

preoperative (pre-op)—pertaining to preparation before surgery

punctures—A hole or wound made by a sharp pointed instrument

Abbreviations

D & C—dilatation and curettage

I & D—incision and drainage

COMPETENCY SKILLS PERFORMANCE

1. Demonstrate skin preparation for a surgical procedure.
2. Demonstrate setting up a sterile tray and assisting the physician with a minor surgical procedure.
3. Demonstrate assisting with suturing.
4. Demonstrate suture or staple removal.
5. Demonstrate how to change a sterile dressing.

The term **preoperative** pertains to the period of preparation time before surgery. **Intraoperative** pertains to the period during surgery. **Postoperative** refers to the period involving patient care following surgery. Preoperative, intraoperative, and postoperative duties may include:

- setting up the room for surgery
- prepping the patient
- assisting the physician during the treatment or minor surgical procedure
- labeling and transporting any specimens
- applying dressings
- recovering the patient
- providing reassurance to the patient
- filing the insurance claim
- transcribing dictation

The physician explains the nature of the procedure and associated potential risks to the patient and also answers the patient's questions. Patient teaching by an MA, under the direction of the physician, can include wound care, signs of infection, postoperative activity level, and prescriptions.

During the actual surgical procedure, you may be involved in two different roles—scrub assistant or circulating assistant.

The scrub assistant is responsible for setting up the sterile field and assisting the physician in sterile procedures. Other responsibilities may include performing a 5-minute surgical scrub, sterile gowning, and gloving or assisting the physician with sterile gowning or gloving. During the surgical procedure, the scrub assistant hands instruments and other supplies to the physician and may also perform draping and cut sutures.

In some offices a circulating assistant is called a float assistant. The circulating assistant is considered "clean" rather than "sterile" and is responsible for obtaining supplies, equipment, and sterile packets for the "sterile" team. The circulating assistant completes any necessary requisitions, identifies specimens, and sends them to the laboratory. Positioning the patient and adjusting the surgical light are other duties. Occasionally an assistant may wear sterile gloves to assist with cutting sutures and applying dressings.

Occasionally the physician is the only one who scrubs, and one assistant may prepare the sterile field and assist the physician as needed. Cleaning the treatment room after the procedure, washing instruments, and discarding any disposables are also responsibilities of the scrub assistant.

Surgeries Performed in the Medical Office

Surgeries performed in a physician's office usually take 15 to 60 minutes. They include the following, also summarized in Table 11-1.

- **Biopsies** may be done with a needle, by shaving off a small area of the tissue, by punch, or by excision of the tissue.
- **Colposcopy** allows the physician to visually examine the vagina and cervix using light and magnification. During this procedure the physician may remove cells for biopsy.

TABLE 11-1 SIMPLE SURGICAL PROCEDURES THAT MAY BE PERFORMED IN A MEDICAL OFFICE OR SURGICAL CLINIC

Arthroscopies	Laser surgery
Biopsy specimen collection	Mastectomies
Cataract and other surgical eye procedures	Nail or part of nail removal
Colposcopy	Orthopedic repairs
Cryosurgery	Prostate biopsies
Disk repairs	Puncture wound
D & Cs (dilatation and curettage)	irrigation and cleansing
Electrocauterization	Small growth, lesion, or
Endoscopic procedures	cyst removal
ENT (ear, nose, and throat) procedures	Suture and staple removal
Foreign body removal	Tubal ligations
Incision and drainage	Vasectomies
Ingrown toenail excision	Wound cleansing and
Laceration repair	debridement
Laparoscopic procedures	

- **Cryosurgery**—freezing abnormal tissue and destroying abnormal cells—may be performed in combination with colposcopy.
- **Electrocautery** is the use of high-frequency alternating electric current to destroy, cut, or remove tissue and coagulate small blood vessels.
- **Incision** and **drainage** (**I & D**) involves draining pus from abscesses caused by infection. I & D relieves pain and pressure.
- Foreign bodies embedded in soft tissue may be surgically removed.
- Growths and tumors are often excised in the medical office.
- Suture and staple removal, while not a surgical procedure, requires sterile technique.
- Suturing lacerations and other wounds requires cleansing, **approximation** (joining together surgical wound edges), and sterile technique.
- Vasectomies are regularly performed as outpatient surgeries in a medical office.

More complex procedures, while still considered ambulatory, are more often performed in a surgi-center or an outpatient surgical clinic. Most of these facilities are situated close to a hospital or in the same complex as the physician's office. Some can accommodate a 23-hour outpatient procedure, meaning the patient stays less than 24 hours without an overnight stay. Although these facilities employ MAs, advanced training is necessary for these positions.

Another way to classify surgeries is elective, emergency, or optional. An elective surgical procedure is considered medically necessary but may be performed at the patient's convenience. Surgery that must be performed immediately is considered an emergency procedure. An optional surgery is not medically necessary but is one the patient wishes to have done.

Implied and Informed Consent

As you learned in Chapter 6, patient consent is required before all medical treatment. When a patient visits the physician's office, he or she "implies" consent for routine examination and procedures by body language or action. For example, a patient who sits on the examining table and raises her arm for blood pressure to be taken or lowers her arm for venipuncture is giving implied consent.

For a nonroutine procedure, however, informed consent is required. Special procedures and surgical procedures usually require a signed consent form. The physician must discuss with the patient details of the procedure, the expected outcome, the risks involved, and possible negative outcomes. In addition to the required signatures, the form should include the following elements:

- Consent to a specific procedure and any consequential procedures during the process by the listed physician or technician.
- Disclosure of potential risks.
- Consent to anesthesia.
- Consent to disposal of tissue removed.
- Consent to any photography or recording of the procedure.
- Consent to the presence of students or other qualified medical personnel for observation.
- Patient's diagnosis, if known.
- Nature and purpose of the proposed treatment or procedure.
- Risks and benefits of the proposed treatment or procedure.
- Alternative treatments.
- Risks and benefits of the alternative treatment or procedure.
- Risks and benefits of not receiving or undergoing a treatment or procedure.

Preoperative Care and Patient Preparation

In some cases, preoperative care may start a week before the scheduled procedure. Preoperative care includes the following:

- Obtaining the necessary laboratory tests.
- Instructing the patient in both preoperative preparation and postoperative care.
- Informing the patient about the time to arrive for the procedure.
- Instructing the patient to have someone available to drive him or her home after the procedure.

Keys to Success
SIGNING THE CONSENT FORM

Some physicians place a statement at the bottom of the consent form: "To assure that you have understood the information presented, please copy the following statement in your own handwriting: 'I understand the information presented and am willing to accept the fact that this procedure is not 100 percent guaranteed for success.'" This statement is usually specific to the procedure and may list possible unsuccessful results. It is meant to ensure that a patient reads and fully understands the consent he or she has given for surgery, including the risks.

As with other patient teaching, both oral and written instructions should be given. It is good practice to include a family member or significant other(s) in the teaching process, both in the preoperative preparation and in the postoperative release. The patient and/or significant other(s) should be advised concerning diet and any other preoperative requirements. Postoperative instructions may also be given at this time. The patient should be instructed to notify the office if he or she develops a fever or any other illness the day of the scheduled surgery.

—Critical Thinking Question 11-1—

Latesha cannot locate the signed informed consent paperwork that Gwen "knows" she had the patient sign and that she promised to bring to Latesha later. How should Latesha handle this situation?

Setting Up the Room

For each surgical procedure, nonsterile surgical supplies must be gathered and arranged in an area separate from the sterile field. Review the procedure book or card to see what supplies are necessary and in what order they will be used. Before setting up any supplies or equipment, confirm that the room is clean and that all surfaces are disinfected. Place clean table paper on the examination or surgical table. Check the sterilization dates on all sterile packets. Changes in JCAHO and AAMI standards reflect that sterility is event-related and not time-related. Packages that have not been compromised are now considered sterile indefinitely. The standard expiration date depends on the type of package; however, many offices will adhere to the following guidelines:

- 30 days for packages enclosed with non-woven paper
- 3 weeks for packages enclosed with muslin
- 9 to 12 months for packages enclosed in disposable pouches

Gather any necessary equipment or supplies.

Keys to Success
PROCEDURE CARDS AND BOOKS

To provide quality care and continuity, most facilities have procedure cards or books that list each procedure, the required supplies and equipment, and step-by-step instructions.

—Critical Thinking Question 11-2—

Latesha observed Gwen cleaning the room but not sanitizing it or confirming that the counters were disinfected. What should Latesha do?

Wash your hands before setting up the sterile field on a **Mayo stand**(s). Open the sterile packets and drop sterile instruments and supplies on the field without contaminating them. Cover or drape the sterile field with a sterile cloth and push the Mayo stand to the side out of the traffic pattern.

Instruments

Surgical instruments are classified by function, such as clamping, cutting, dilating, dissecting, grasping, probing, suturing, and visualization. Specialty areas, such as ear, nose, and throat (ENT), gynecology, neurology, obstetrics, orthopedics, proctology, and urology require special instruments. Some instruments are named for the surgeon who developed them. Most are made of steel and are rustproof, stainproof, heat-resistant, and durable. They are delicate and expensive and must be handled with care.

The tray for a minor surgical procedure usually includes a scalpel with or without a blade, scissors, **hemostat**, and needle holder (Figure 11-1 ◆). The physician indicates what type of blade and suture will be used. A syringe and needle are dropped on the sterile field for the physician to use for the local anesthesia. The physician may use a larger gauge needle to draw up the anesthetic and then change to a smaller-gauge needle for the injection.

Clamping and Grasping

Forceps are two-pronged instruments used to grasp tissue (Figure 11-2 ◆). Some are hinged at one end with a spring-type

Keys to Success
EASING A PATIENT'S ANXIETY AND FEARS

As an MA, you play an important role in helping to ease a patient's fears and anxieties. An informed patient is usually a less anxious patient. Some facilities mail or give printed materials to a patient when the procedure is scheduled. These materials provide instructions for any preoperative preparations, diet, or testing that is to be done, as well as instructions for the day of the surgery. Many are procedure-specific, explaining the procedure, the anesthesia, the recovery time and process, and anticipated activity restrictions.

If the procedure is done during an office visit as the result of findings during that office visit, you should be prepared to answer questions as you are prepping the patient. Should there be a question beyond your scope of training or knowledge, you should refer it to the physician before the start of the procedure. Remain calm and answer all questions honestly and confidently.

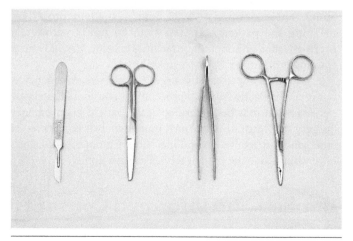

Figure 11-1 ◆ Tray for a minor surgical procedure

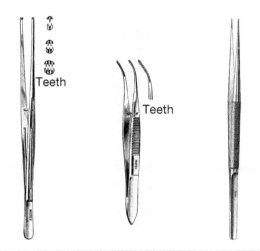

Figure 11-2 ◆ Types of forceps

hinge and can be opened and closed with the fingers and thumb. They may have either a smooth mouth or teeth to help with grasping.

Ring or sponge forceps have hinges farther down on the shanks, similar to scissors hinges. These forceps may be straight or curved and may have teeth or be smooth. A ratchet on the handle allows for securing or fastening the forceps. The operator end has a ring-like structure for a finger and a thumb. These forceps include Allis tissue forceps, small mosquito hemostats, longer Kelly hemostats, even longer hemostats, and hemostats with ring-like structures to grasp sponges. Hemostats are used specifically to clamp blood vessels.

Needle holders hold the needle for suturing. Like hinged hemostats, needle holders are hinged, usually close to the working end. There are grooves on the inner part of the holder shank to secure the needle. Placement of the needle is important. The needle holder should grasp the needle toward the eye, one-third of the length of the shaft. Care must be taken to face the needle in the correct direction for a right-handed or left-handed physician.

Towel clamps have sharp points to hold towels and drapes in place.

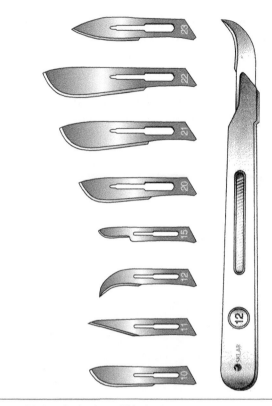

Figure 11-3 ◆ Scalpels and blades

Cutting

Cutting is using a knife or surgical scissors to separate or divide tissues. Scalpels are knives with different types and sizes of blades. They may consist of one piece and be disposable or have a reusable handle and a disposable blade (Figure 11-3 ◆). Surgical blades come in various sizes and shapes. Some are longer than others, some have straight blades, and others have curved blades. The physician indicates his or her choice by number. Scalpels and blades must be handled carefully and are disposed of as sharps.

Scissors are used for dissecting as well as for cutting (Figure 11-4 ◆). **Dissection** is the process of cutting into smaller

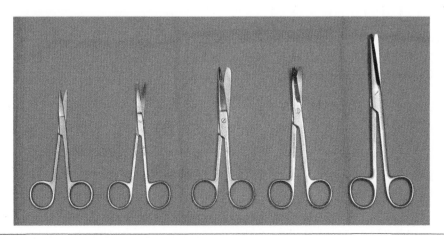

Figure 11-4 ◆ Types of scissors

parts for study and analysis. Scissors may have sharp (pointed) or blunt tips, and straight or curved blades.

Operating scissors have two sharp blades, two blunt blades, or one sharp blade and one blunt blade. They range in size from very small iris scissors to larger ones. Suture scissors have a hooked tip on one blade that is used to slip under a suture to clip it for removal. Angled scissors with a blunt tip on the longer end are bandage scissors, capable of sliding under a bandage or dressing and cutting it off without danger to the patient. In dissecting scissors both blades are blunt and may be either straight or curved.

Dilating, Probing, and Visualizing

Instruments used for dilating may also be used for probing and visualization (Figure 11-5 ◆). Probes are used to explore wounds and cavities. They have a curved blunt point for easier insertion. A trocar is a hollow **cannula** inserted into a body cavity to withdraw fluids. Punches are used to remove small samples of tissue for examination and detection of cancerous cells.

Various types of scopes, which are usually lighted, may be inserted into the body to visualize a cavity. A speculum may be opened after insertion into the body cavity to visualize the area or to remove samples of tissue for additional examination.

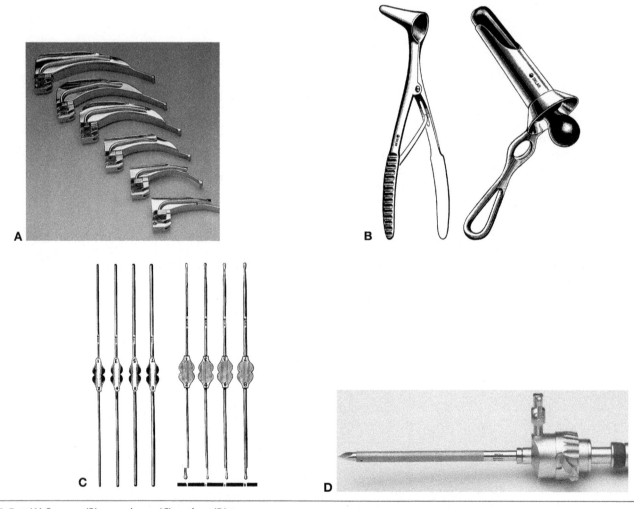

Figure 11-5 ◆ (A) Scopes; (B) speculums; (C) probes; (D) trocar

PROCEDURE 11-1 **Prepare the Skin for Surgical Procedure**

Theory

Proper skin preparation, including cleansing, disinfecting, and applying antiseptic, is critical to prevent contamination by microorganisms and lower the potential for infection during surgical procedures. The area prepped must be at least 2 inches beyond the surgical field or the area exposed by drapes. A plastic-backed drape is placed under the portion of the patient's body to be prepped in order to absorb or contain any liquids.

The basic skin prep consists of three steps:

1. Shaving, if necessary.
2. Scrubbing and rinsing with an antiseptic soap.
3. Applying antiseptic to the surgical area.

Sterile sponges held by sterile forceps or sterile gloved hands are used for each of these steps and for each area cleansed. Applying the sponges in concentric circles from the center outward removes microorganisms from the immediate surgical area. Most physicians prefer a 5-minute scrub of the area. Should the prep area be a hand or foot, the entire appendage must be cleansed, particularly between the fingers or toes, to remove microorganisms from crevices or folds.

Hair is considered a contaminant and may need to be removed from the surgical site by shaving. If shaving is required, a disposable razor is used to shave the hair from the cleansed area in the direction of growth.

The next step of the skin prep involves application of an antiseptic solution, such as Povidone iodine, chlorhexidine gluconate, or benzalkonium chloride. It is important to confirm that the patient is not allergic to iodine solutions before applying. The antiseptic solution is applied in the same manner as the cleansing process or may be applied with cotton-tipped applicators. The area is allowed to air-dry so that the disinfectant has time to reduce and kill microorganisms.

Either you or the physician places sterile drapes over the area until the procedure begins. Dispose of contaminated supplies and instruments used during skin preparation and tray setup. This keeps the procedure area organized and the clean, dirty, and sterile areas defined.

After the procedure, dispose of soiled dressings and material. Remove your gloves and place one hand inside an empty plastic bag. With this hand pick up and place all soiled materials in a bag. With the other hand pull the outside of the bag over the soiled dressings and material. Dispose of gloves and soiled materials in a biohazard bag or container.

Materials

- shave prep kit, including razor, sterile basin pack, antiseptic germicidal soap, sterile 4 × 4s, sterile applicators, sterile sponge forceps
- Mayo stand or side tray
- sterile water or saline
- waste receptacle
- hazardous waste container
- plastic bags for disposal of contaminated material
- sterile gloves
- sterile towels
- sterile drapes
- antiseptic

Competency

(**Conditions**) With the necessary materials, you will be able to (**Task**) prepare the patient's skin for a surgical procedure with a surgical scrub and shave (**Standards**) correctly, within the time designated by your instructor.

1. Wash your hands thoroughly. Gather equipment and supplies.
2. Identify the patient and guide him or her to the treatment area. Explain the entire procedure to the patient.
3. Instruct the patient to void if necessary.
4. Have the patient remove appropriate clothing and wear a patient gown until it is time for positioning and draping.
5. Wash your hands and apply non-sterile gloves. Position the patient and remove the gown as necessary.
6. Unwrap the outer wraps of all packs. Unwrap the basin pack.
7. Following correct technique for pouring liquids in a sterile field, pour germicidal soap into one basin, sterile water or saline into the second basin, and germicidal solution into the third basin. (Figure 11-6 ◆).
8. You may need to shave the area before it is surgically scrubbed. If so, apply soap solution to the area.
9. Remove the razor from the shave prep pack that has been placed outside the sterile field.
10. Pull the skin gently taut at the surgical site. Shave in the direction of hair growth (Figure 11-7 ◆).
11. Rinse the skin with sterile saline or water in an outward circular motion, then pat the area dry.
12. Wash your hands and put on sterile gloves.
13. Apply soapy solution to the patient's skin in a circular motion with a sterile sponge, starting at the center of the surgical site and moving outward (Figure 11-8 ◆). During

Figure 11-6 ◆ Pour germicidal soap into one basin, sterile water or saline into the second basin, and antiseptic into the third basin.

PROCEDURE 11-1 **Prepare the Skin for Surgical Procedure** (continued)

Figure 11-7 ◆ Shave in the direction of hair growth.

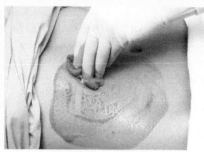

Figure 11-8 ◆ Apply soapy solution to the patient's skin in a circular motion with a sterile sponge.

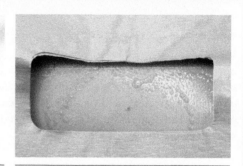

Figure 11-9 ◆ Drape 3 to 5 inches above and below the surgical site with sterile towels.

the application the circles should not overlap each other or repeat over the same area.

14. Rinse the area in the same circular manner with new sterile sponges.
15. Allow area to air dry.
16. Apply germicidal solution in concentric circles with a sterile sponge or cotton-tipped applicators.
17. After allowing the prep area to completely air-dry, drape 3 to 5 inches above and below the surgical site with sterile towels (Figure 11-9 ◆).
18. Drape the prepared surgical site with a sterile towel (Figure 11-10 ◆). If the patient must be left unattended

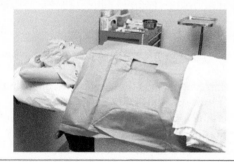

Figure 11-10 ◆ Drape the prepared surgical site with a sterile towel.

at any time after the surgical scrub, another Medical Assistant or scrub float will need to cover the prepped area with a sterile towel.

19. If the physician did not participate in the patient prep or setting up the surgical tray, alert him or her that the patient has been prepped.
20. Document the scrub procedure with patient education notes.

Patient Education

The patient should be instructed not to touch the prepped area. The patient should understand that the prepping procedure reduces the risk for infection by setting up a sterile surgical field.

Charting Example

03/17/xx   8:30 a.m. Right lower-quadrant prepped and draped for mole excision. Disinfected with Betadine. Patient instructed not to touch area. Patient nodded agreement. Richard McNeal, CMA

Keys to Success
SHAVING

Some practitioners feel that shaving may cause minute nicks or breaks in the skin, leaving open areas that are prone to infection. It is the policy of some physicians not to shave the area, or they may do it themselves, especially when areas of the scalp near the face are involved. Others may request that excess hair be carefully removed by trimming it close with scissors.

Positioning and Draping

Positioning and draping usually take place before local anesthesia is administered. Positioning provides support for the patient and proper exposure of the surgical area. You will assist the patient onto the examination or operating table and make him or her comfortable. Use small pillows to provide additional comfort. Place a drape, sheet, or blanket over any exposed areas to provide warmth and preserve the patient's dignity. If a general anesthesia is administered, the patient will be asleep before the final positioning and draping. Pay attention to any disabilities or special needs the patient may have.

Draping the patient and the area provides a sterile field for the procedure. The physician can work without contaminating instruments or equipment, which helps to prevent microorganisms from entering the wound.

Drapes are made of sterile muslin cloth or sterile paper, often with a vinyl or plastic backing. They come in various sizes and colors. The choice depends on the physician's preference. Drapes called *fenestrated drapes* have a slit or hole that exposes the surgical area.

Anesthesia

Anesthesia is the partial or complete absence of sensation. During many procedures, usually surgical procedures, anesthetic medications are administered to relieve the patient of feelings of pain. Sometimes an additional amnesiac drug or muscle relaxant may be needed. In most office procedures local anesthetics are used to achieve a painless state, with the patient alert during the procedure. Occasionally an anesthesiologist may administer a general anesthesia that induces loss of consciousness.

When drugs are administered to alter the patient's level of consciousness, the patient is placed on a cardiac monitor or a pulse oximeter. Emergency equipment and supplies, including oxygen, an Ambu bag, and a crash cart or emergency drug box, are all in close range of the anesthesiologist, who monitors the patient's vital signs throughout general anesthesia.

Local Anesthesia

Local anesthesia induces the absence of sensation in a specific area of tissue without the loss of consciousness. Table 11-2 lists some of the medications used in the three methods of administering local anesthesia. The physician determines which local anesthetic to use based on the patient's medical condition, history, and other medications the patient takes. The physician may also consider longer-lasting anesthesia to provide the patient with greater comfort during the procedure.

TABLE 11-2 TYPES OF LOCAL ANESTHESIA	
Method	**Pharmaceutical Example**
Topical or surface anesthesia (painted or sprayed on the skin or mucous membranes)	Lidocaine 4% Ethyl chloride spray, external only Cocaine with or without epinephrine
Nerve block	Procaine 1%–2% Lidocaine 1%–2%
Infiltration or injection	Procaine (Novocaine) 1%–2% Lidocaine (Xylocaine) 1%–2% Tetracaine (Pontocaine) 0.2, 0.3, & 1% Bupivacaine (Marcaine) 0.25–0.75% Lidocaine with epinephrine

Local anesthesia in topical form may be a cream, gel, liquid, or spray. It may be used on children or on small lacerations in adults and reduces or eliminates the pain caused by injected local anesthesia. It takes topical anesthesia 15 to 20 minutes to anesthetize an area. Liquid anesthesia is applied to a wound with a sterile cotton applicator in repeated applications until the area loses feeling. The patient should be advised that it may sting or burn briefly when it is first applied to an open wound. Epinephrine in the preparation causes constriction of the vessels and an obvious blanching (whitening) of the tissue where it is applied.

Injected local anesthesia may also contain epinephrine, a drug with vasoconstricting (reducing blood flow to the area) properties. In addition to increasing the duration of action of the anesthetic, it prevents extra blood from entering the surgical field and improves visualization for the physician. However, certain precautions must be taken when epinephrine is used with a local anesthesia. Because of its vasoconstricting properties, it must not be used in procedures on fingers, toes, nose, ears, penis, or any area where local blood supply would be compromised. Also, caution should be used with patients with heart or respiratory disease.

As an MA you may often assist the physician in drawing up the local anesthesia. The physician wears sterile gloves and takes a sterile syringe from a sterile field or from an opened, sterile package that you are holding with contaminated edges folded back. After checking that you have chosen the correct vial of local anesthesia, cleanse the rubber stopper of the vial with 70% isopropyl alcohol. Holding the vial firmly in one hand while supporting your wrist with your other hand, extend the rubber stopper end toward the physician. The physician must be able to read the label and confirm it is the correct medication. The physician inserts the needle into the rubber stopper, injects air from the syringe, and withdraws the desired amount of anesthesia medication. Occasionally the physician may change needles to a smaller gauge before injecting into the tissue.

Injected local anesthetics tend to burn for approximately 10 seconds after the injection. It is good practice to prepare the patient for the initial unpleasant sensation.

Nerve blocks may be administered for procedures that are more involved than simple laceration repair. Depending on the location of the nerve to be blocked, either the physician or the anesthesiologist may administer it.

Before any anesthetic is administered, the patient *must* be questioned about allergies and any previous reaction to local anesthetic. Questions about any cardiac problems or disease and any respiratory difficulties must also be asked. Patient reactions to local anesthetics may be as severe as anaphylactic shock. In an office where minor surgical procedures are preformed, one of your responsibilities will be to maintain the emergency drug box or cart and to see that it is within easy reach of rooms where surgical procedures are performed.

Caduceus Chronicle
A SHORT HISTORY OF ANESTHESIA

1774	Joseph Priestley (1733–1804), English Unitarian minister and scientist, isolates nitrous oxide and predicts in his research on gases that a medicinal application will be developed.	1842	Crawford Long (1815–1878), a physician, performs surgery to remove a neck tumor with ether as the anesthesia.
mid-1780s	James Watt (1736–1819) works with Thomas Beddoes (1760–1808) to develop applications and equipment for Joseph Priestley's "factitious airs" or gases.	1846	Oliver Wendell Holmes (1809–1894), U.S. physician and author, suggests the word "anaesthesia" for ether-induced unconsciousness.
1799	Sir Humphry Davy (1778–1829) experiments with nitrous oxide under Thomas Beddoes. He becomes the first person to breathe nitrous oxide.	1846	Robert Liston, an English surgeon, is the first to administer surgical anesthesia.
1824	Henry Hickman (1800–1830) describes his anesthetic experiments with carbon dioxide on animals.	1847	Ether is used for the first time in the U.S. war with Mexico.
		1868	Nitrous oxide is liquefied for storage in metal cylinders.
1829	Jules Cloquet (1790–1883), a French physician, performs breast amputation with patient under hypnosis.	1898	Heroin is introduced by the Bayer Company as a nonaddictive painkiller. It is removed from the market when it is found to be more addictive than morphine.
1830s	Samuel Colt (1814–1862) tours the United States entertaining audiences with demonstrations of nitrous oxide to raise money for his revolver prototype production.	1874	The first intravenous general anesthesia is used.
		1884	Dr. Carl Koller (1857–1944), Austrian ophthalmologist, uses cocaine as a local anesthetic.
1840s	Franz Mesmer (1734–1815), a German physician, uses hypnotism for pain relief during surgery. Known as "mesmerism," the technique was used before the introduction of anesthesia in the latter half of the decade.	1898	The first spinal anesthetic is administered by German surgeon August Bier (1861–1949).
		1900	Spinal analgesia is used for the first time in vaginal delivery.
		1934	Thiopental is used for the first time in humans.

Assisting During Minor Surgery

As an MA, you may assist the physician during minor surgical procedures by performing preoperative, intraoperative, and postoperative duties. You will also provide emotional support for the patient. On the day of the procedure you will ask the patient again about allergies to medications, especially to anesthesia. You will assess and record vital signs. If the patient expresses any concern or has any questions, the physician should be advised.

Passing instruments to the physician is a skill developed over time. If the scrub assistant is sterile, the instruments may be passed directly into the physician's extended hand. The scrub assistant grasps the working end of the instrument with care and firmly places the operator end in the physician's palm. It is not necessary to "slap" the instrument into the physician's hand but only to firmly place it there.

Should the physician be the only one with sterile gloves, you will open the sterile packaging of the instrument, folding

PROCEDURE 11-2 Set Up a Sterile Tray and Assist the Physician with Minor Surgical Procedures

Theory

Preoperative, intraoperative, and postoperative duties may include setting up the room for surgery, prepping the patient, assisting the physician during the procedure, labeling and transporting any specimens, applying dressings, and recovering the patient. As an MA you will likely assume the role of circulating assistant during minor surgery.

As a circulating assistant, you will add sterile supplies by folding back edges of packages and dropping items onto the sterile field. The sterile wrapper edges must hang over the edge of the Mayo stand to protect both the sterile field and the operator from contamination. Using sterile transfer forceps, place instruments in the correct position on the sterile field according to the physician's preference and clinical protocol.

Avoid reaching across the sterile field for any reason during the procedure. Crossing over a sterile field can contaminate it, in which case a new sterile tray setup will be required.

Upon completion of the procedure, you will cleanse and dress the operative area as directed. Wearing gloves, you will place any specimens or tissue in the appropriate container(s), label for the laboratory, and store in the appropriate area. Once the specimens have been collected, while you are still wearing gloves, you may cover the surgical tray, as it may be disturbing for some patients to view the used/blood-tinted surgical equipment. You should remove you gloves and wash your hands.

Next you should assist the patient with re-dressing as appropriate and provide education of what to expect in the days following the surgery. Once the patient has been removed from

PROCEDURE 11-2 Set Up a Sterile Tray and Assist the Physician with Minor Surgical Procedures *(continued)*

the surgical area, you may don the appropriate PPE and clean the surgical area by placing the disposable items in the biohazard containers and taking the non-disposable items to be sterilized in the appropriate area. Without leaving the patient, you will begin cleaning the area by gathering instruments and supplies used during the procedure. You will place any specimens or tissue in an appropriate container and label it for the laboratory.

Patient teaching concerning the procedure and postoperative care is usually your responsibility. Under the direction of the physician, you will give instructions regarding wound care, signs of infection, activity level, prescriptions, and so on. Simple procedures usually only require repeating postoperative instructions, reviewing printed instructions with the patient and/or family or significant other(s), and confirming follow-up appointments. More complex procedures may require a recheck of vital signs and having the patient upright for a short time to make sure he or she is clinically stable enough to leave.

Materials

- sterile surgical pack, including two pairs of sterile gloves, towel pack, 4 × 4 sponge pack, sterile drapes, needle pack and suture materials, sterile instrument pack, sterile syringe pack, two sterile surgical basins, and sterile specimen containers
- Mayo stand and/or a surgical instrument table
- transfer forceps and holder
- waste container lined with plastic bag
- sharps disposal container
- biohazard waste container
- local anesthetic
- alcohol preps

Competency

(**Conditions**) With the necessary materials, you will be able to (**Task**) assist the physician with minor surgery by preparing for the procedure, anticipating physician needs, and providing or reinforcing instruction to the patient or significant other(s) (**Standards**) correctly and within the time designated by the instructor.

1. Determine scrub and float assistant staffing needs for the procedure.
2. Wash your hands.
3. Sanitize and disinfect a Mayo instrument stand by using a 4 × 4 gauze square that has been soaked in 70% isopropyl alcohol. Starting from the middle of the tray, use a circular motion to cleanse the entire tray, including the rim. (Figure 11-11 ◆)
4. If your place of employment uses sterile disposable drapes, place the package on a counter and carefully peel back the

top layer to expose the fan folded drape. Grasping only the corner of the drape with your thumb and forefinger, raise it quickly to a height that allows it to carefully unfold, *without* touching the counter top, or any portion of your body. If your place of employment uses sterile towels, they will be folded in the same manner and placed inside towel canisters. Sterile towels will be removed the same way.

5. With the drape held firmly with the thumb and forefinger of one hand well above waist level, take your other hand and pinch the opposite corner of the drape between your thumb and forefinger. Both corners along the shortest side of the drape are now firmly held.
6. With the drape held above waist level, careful reach over the Mayo stand and pull the drape towards you as you lay it on the stand. It is critical that the bottom edge of the drape does not touch the stand as you are reaching across. The drape must also not swing and touch any portion of your body at any time.
7. At this point in the procedure the tray is now considered sterile. It must not be left unattended, reached over, or touched. If the sterile drape needs to be adjusted, you may reach under and use the draping portions to make minor adjustments.
8. Gather the appropriate supplies needed for the procedure. If you gather items that are wrapped twice you must apply them in a sterile manner:
   - Position the package in your non-dominant hand with the flap facing up. The package should look like an envelope, with the envelope opening on top and towards you fingertips. You may adjust the package as needed at this point, as this outer wrapping is not sterile and neither is your hand.
   - Pull open the top flap by gently grasping it with your other hand and pulling it up and underneath, tucking it into the fingers of the non-dominant hand.
   - Follow the same procedure, pulling the right flap to the right and the left flap to the left, without crossing over

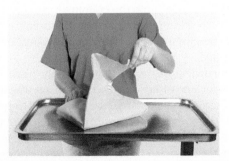

Figure 11-11 ◆ Open the sterile packs on the Mayo stand or surgery table.

continued

PROCEDURE 11-2 Set Up a Sterile Tray and Assist the Physician with Minor Surgical Procedures *(continued)*

your non-dominant hand. Rationale: This method allows the inner package to remain sterile while it is being exposed for removal. Gathering the loose ends into your fingers prevents them from being dragged across the sterile field or folding back onto the sterile package before it is placed on the tray.

- Carefully apply the package to the sterile field by holding it well above the tray and letting it carefully fall onto the tray.

Items that have been sterilized in plastic pouches must also be applied in a sterile manner:

- Carefully peel apart the package and allow the instrument to fall onto the sterile field.
- Do not allow the package to touch the sterile field and do not allow the instruments to slide or bounce as the land on the tray.

9. Once all items have been applied to the sterile field, you may wash your hands using a surgical scrub and apply sterile gloves. With sterile gloves on you may open the previously applied sterile package and verify its contents. You may also arrange the items on the tray according to physician preference. Note: If you drop your hands below your waist or touch any item outside of the sterile area you are once again contaminated. You must also pay very close attention to your clothes as scrubs that are worn too loosely will fall forward and contaminate the sterile tray. Once you have verified that all items are present and arranged according to physician preference you must cover the sterile tray. To cover the sterile tray follow the instructions for set up, but instead of crossing over the field and pulling the drape to you, you must hold the drape in front of you at a level so that the top towel and bottom towel are even and carefully lay it over the tray.

10. Identify the patient and guide him or her to the treatment area. Explain the entire procedure to the patient.

11. Instruct the patient to void if necessary.

12. Provide draping or a gown for the patient as required for the procedure. Sometimes patients disrobe and gown in another room before entering the treatment area.

13. Assist the patient onto the examination table.

14. Perform a skin prep as described in Procedure 8-1.

15. Assist the physician in scrubbing, gowning, and gloving as needed.

16. The physician may want you to open the packet of sterile gloves for him or her and place the packet where it can be easily accessed at the start of the procedure. (Depending on the duties of the scrub assistant during the procedure, you may be designated to scrub, and to gown, mask, and glove.)

17. When the physician is ready to proceed, he or she may remove the drapes from the tray setups without contaminating the trays or the sterile field. If you are directed to do this, grasp the towel or drape at the **distal** corners (away

from the center) (Figure 11-12 ◆). Lift the towel toward you without reaching over the tray and unprotected sterile field.

18. In anticipation of soiled dressings, place a bag or container to the side for the physician to discard them into.

19. Observe closely and anticipate the physician's needs.
    - If a specimen container is needed, hold it to receive a specimen.
    - *Note:* You may fulfill the role of scrub assistant or circulating assistant, depending on the procedure and the needs of the physician.

20. In most cases the physician will prefer to apply the first sterile dressing but occasionally may direct the scrub to do it. You will reinforce or anchor the dressing.

21. When the procedure has been completed, collect all soiled instruments in a basin and remove them from the patient's view. Dispose of soiled dressings in biohazard containers.

22. Remove your gloves and discard.

23. Wash your hands.

24. If specimen containers have been contaminated, use clean gloves to place and tighten lids on them.

25. Label and bag specimens before transporting or sending them to the lab.

26. Obtain and chart vital signs following office policy and document your recovery observations, including mental status, changes in drainage and size of drainage on dressings, and ability to ambulate and urinate. (Observation requirements may vary according to the medical office specialty.)

27. Review your observations with the physician.

28. When the physician determines discharge readiness, he or she discusses care instructions with the patient and significant other(s).

29. Give the patient a printed copy of the physician's discharge instructions, and review and reinforce them with the patient. Before the patient leaves the facility, help with any additional paperwork, such as follow-up appointments.

30. Assist or transport the patient to significant others or, in some cases, to the car.

31. Chart the results of patient instruction immediately.

Figure 11-12 ◆ Grasp the towel or drape at the distal corners.

PROCEDURE 11-2 Set Up a Sterile Tray and Assist the Physician with Minor Surgical Procedures *(continued)*

32. Don appropriate PPE to clean and sanitize the treatment room for the next patient.
33. Wash your hands.

Patient Education

It is important to inform the patient of each step of the procedure. A simple explanation about why a particular step or technique is performed decreases the patient's anxiety and ensures cooperation. Follow-up instruction is also vital. Ask the patient or significant other(s) to repeat discharge instructions to make sure of understanding and compliance.

Charting Example

04/29/xx 10:30 a.m. Discharge instructions reviewed with the patient and family. Patient displays some facial expression of pain. Wife able to verbalize correctly how to administer pain medication and antibiotic. Wife states correctly the signs of infection to report if they occur. Carlos Lopez, RMA

NOTE: The physician will also chart about the procedure and his or her observations immediately after the procedure.

---

it back over your hand. Be sure to open the package at the handle or operator end. Extend the operator end of the sterile instrument to the physician, who will grasp and remove it without touching the nonsterile outside of the package.

Sutures and Suture Removal

Sutures, or "stitches," hold the edges of tissue together as a wound heals. The wound may be accidental or intentional, such as a surgical incision. Sutures are also used in the ligation of vessels to stop bleeding.

Keys to Success
CHANGING ROLES

When you help the physician during minor surgery, you may be required to change roles. For example, a scrub assistant wearing sterile gloves must hold a bottle of lidocaine upside-down so that the physician can withdraw some for the local anesthetic. The hand holding the lidocaine is now nonsterile but clean. The nonsterile hand can still be used for clean technique and procedure, but cannot be used for sterile technique. This can be a confusing situation, as the scrub assistant must remember that one hand is sterile and the other is clean and that he or she cannot pass the nonsterile hand over sterile areas.

Remember that sterile gloves can be used for clean gloves when clean gloves are unavailable. However, clean gloves *cannot ever* be used as sterile gloves.

Keys to Success
LEAVING THE TREATMENT ROOM

Should you leave the treatment room once the sterile trays have been set up? The answer is no. For legal purposes, you are responsible and accountable for keeping the sterile field in sterile condition. You cannot guarantee that the sterile field remains sterile if you leave the room and the setup unattended.

Most suture material comes prepackaged with attached needles called *swaged needles*. Other sutures must be threaded into a needle. When opening prepackaged swaged sutures, grasp the needle with the needle holder and remove it first while grasping the suture close to the needle and guiding it through the thumb and finger. This will help straighten the suture as it is removed (Figure 11-13 ◆). Care must be taken not to contaminate the entire length of suture material.

Suture material is either absorbable or nonabsorbable. Absorbable suture material is dissolved by body fluids and does not need to be removed. It is usually absorbed five to twenty days after insertion. Absorbable suture is used on internal organs, including the intestines, bladder, and subcutaneous tissue, and to tie off blood vessels. It is occasionally used for skin sutures as well. Surgical gut (catgut) and synthetic materials, including polyglycolic acid and polyglactin 910, are types of absorbable suture material. Nonabsorbable sutures include sutures made of silk, nylon, steel, and other materials that cannot be absorbed. These sutures are often used in deep tissues to permanently hold tissue in place. They are also used for skin repair and must be removed. (See Procedure 11-4.)

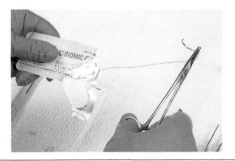

Figure 11-13 ◆ Remove the swaged needle from the package with the needle holder.

The size or gauge (diameter) of suture material is designated by numbers ranging from 0, the thickest, to 11-0 (00000000000), the smallest. On the delicate tissue of the face and neck, 5-0 or 6-0 is generally used. Areas where the skin or tissue is stronger and exposed to movement are usually sutured with 2-0 or 3-0. 10-0 and 11-0 may be used in neurological, possibly microscopic, surgery to suture very tiny vessels. In physician offices, other than ophthalmology or other specialty practices, only 1-0 to 6-0 size sutures are normally used.

Straight needles are used for suturing that passes directly through the tissue in a straight line. Curved needles allow for easier maneuvering in small spaces. The swaged needle, in which the suture and needle are one unit, is most commonly used as it causes the least amount of trauma to the tissue.

The physician assesses the wound and tissue before selecting the suture material and needle (Figure 11-14 ◆). A taper point needle, which tapers to a sharp point, is used on easily penetrated tissue and causes less trauma to the tissue. A cutting needle, which has at least two sharp edges, is used on tougher or stronger tissue that may be difficult to penetrate.

Other wound closure materials include wire staples and adhesive skin closure strips. Wire staples are considered the fastest way to close long incisions and wounds with approximated edges (Figure 11-15 ◆). Because the tissue is handled less, there is also less tissue trauma. The staples are inserted with a special staple gun and must be removed with a staple remover. Staplers containing a cartridge of staples may be disposable or reusable.

Nonallergic sterile strips of adhesive material may be used to hold the edges of a wound in place as healing takes place (Figure 11-16 ◆). The strips are often used in areas where there is little tension on the skin edges—for example, a laceration on the arm where no movement or stress is likely to occur. After the area is cleansed, the strips are applied crossways to bring the skin edges together. The advantages of adhesive skin closures are that local anesthetic is unnecessary, application and removal are easy, and less scarring usually results.

Suturing

The physician may require your help when suturing a simple repair of a laceration or tear. Suturing may also follow removal of

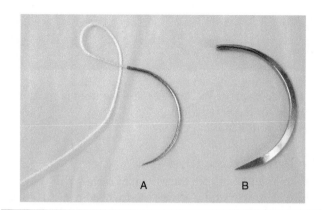

Figure 11-14 ◆ (A) Taper point needle; (B) Cutting point needle

a lesion or I & D of an infected wound. Assistance may include assembling supplies and equipment, setting up the sterile field, applying a dressing, gloving, passing instruments, and cutting sutures. Regardless of the complexity of the procedure, sterile technique must be maintained at all times.

When assisting the physician in a surgical procedure, you will be required to cut excess suture material after the suture is placed. You will wear sterile gloves and pick up sterile surgical scissors. The best way to hold and control the scissors is to place the thumb in one hole and the ring finger in the other. Placing the index finger on the hinge of the scissors allows excellent control of any downward movement of the scissors tips (Figure 11-17 ◆).

Recovery/Postoperative Care

Once the surgical procedure is complete, the patient may be moved to a recovery area. If a relatively simple procedure was done under local anesthesia, you will be responsible for cleansing the skin, applying pressure as directed, and then dressing the site with a sterile dressing. While doing this, you will observe the patient for any signs of reaction, dizziness, or light-headedness. The patient will need to be checked for orthostatic hypotension. The physical symptoms of orthostatic hypotension consist of dizziness, faintness or lightheadedness which appear when the patient stands up. The symptoms of orthostatic hypotension are caused by low blood pressure. Another condition that the Medical Assistant should be aware of is vasovagal

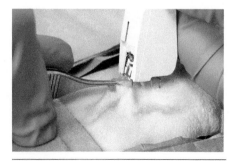

Figure 11-15 ◆ Physician stapling wound closed

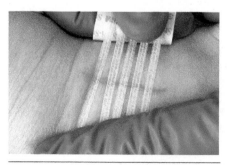

Figure 11-16 ◆ An example of the proper application of adhesive strips

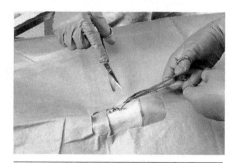

Figure 11-17 ◆ The proper way to hold scissors in a surgical procedure

PROCEDURE 11-3 **Assist the Physician with Suturing**

Theory

Any break in the skin may allow the entry of microorganisms into the tissue and subsequent infection. Most wounds and incisions require repair and closure to prevent infection, stop bleeding, promote healing, and reduce pain in the area. Sterile technique is required to achieve this goal.

In addition to passing instruments during the procedure, you may be required to sponge the area to clear any drainage and to keep the area visually clear. In anticipation of the physician's need for the scalpel, you will put the desired blade on the handle with a hemostat. Using the hemostat is a safety precaution to prevent cutting the fingers when manually adding the blade to the handle. As an additional safety precaution, pass the scalpel handle and blade to the physician carefully and with the blade edge down. If the edges of the wound need grasping, anticipate the physician's need for toothed forceps. Throughout the entire procedure, observe and reassure the patient.

When suturing is complete, each suture will extend 1/8 to 1/4 inch above the knot. This ensures that the knot is secure, visible, and easy to remove. As soon as the procedure is finished, soak the used instruments in disinfectant solution to remove residual tissue or body fluids. If debris is not removed, the contaminated, unclean portions are not sterilized during the sterilization process.

Materials

- sterile packs, including patient drapes, towels, and 4 × 4s, scalpels with blades or blades (size according to physician's preference)
- suture and needle pack (according to physician's preference)
- sterile suture pack, including scalpel handle, thumb forceps, needle holder, scissors, hemostats
- Mayo stand and side stand or table
- anesthetic (usually local)
- sterile transfer forceps and holder
- sterile basins
- sterile saline or water
- sterile gloves
- needle and syringe pack
- waste container with plastic bag liner
- biohazard waste container
- sharps container

Competency

(**Conditions**) With the necessary materials, you will be able to (**Task**) demonstrate sterile technique when assisting with suture repair of an incision (**Standards**) correctly and within the time frame designated by your instructor.

1. Wash your hands.
2. Identify the patient and guide him or her to the treatment area. Explain the entire procedure to the patient.
3. Position the patient on the exam table so that the area to be sutured is exposed.
4. Drape to cover the patient's clothing.
5. Follow the guidelines for prepping the skin and draping it for minor surgery.
6. Perform a 5-minute sterile scrub.
7. Put on sterile gloves.
8. Take a position standing opposite the physician.
9. Place two sterile sponges near the wound site. Have additional sponges ready as needed.
10. Pass instruments to the physician as requested, with a firm "snap" into the palm of the physician's hand.
11. Prepare a scalpel handle with blade according to the physician's preference. Pass the scalpel to the physician when necessary (Figure 11-18 ◆).
12. Sponge the area as necessary and as directed by the physician.
13. Pass other instruments, such as toothed forceps, as necessary (Figure 11-19 ◆).
14. Place the needle in the needle holder. Pass the needle holder, needle, and suture to the physician, keeping the suture material within the sterile field.
15. Keep a hold on the distal end of the suture until the physician sees it and takes it.
16. With suture scissors, cut sutures as directed by the physician 1/8 to 1/4 inch above the knot (Figure 11-20 ◆).
17. Sponge the closed wound during suturing and discard the soiled sponges (Figure 11-21 ◆).

Figure 11-18 ◆ Pass the scalpel to the physician when necessary.

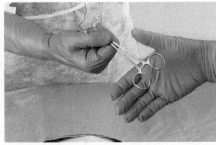

Figure 11-19 ◆ Pass other instruments as necessary.

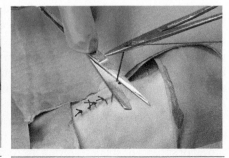

Figure 11-20 ◆ Cut sutures as directed by the physician, 1 /8 to 1/4 inch above the knot.

continued

PROCEDURE 11-3 **Assist the Physician with Suturing**(continued)

18. Place used instruments in a disinfectant-filled instrument basin immediately.
19. Add unused sterile instruments to the disinfectant at the same time, or use another disinfectant-filled instrument basin.
20. Remove the gloves and discard. Wash your hands.
21. Apply dressings as instructed by the physician.
22. Help the patient into a comfortable position. Monitor vital signs according to office procedures.
23. Provide the patient with both oral and written postoperative instructions, including the date and time of the follow-up appointment.
24. Make sure the patient is stable for discharge.

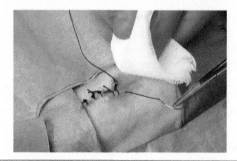

Figure 11-21 ◆ Sponge the wound during suturing.

25. Complete requisitions for specimens. Transport them to the laboratory or secure them for courier transport to the laboratory.
26. Clean, sanitize, and sterilize the instruments. Inspect them for residual tissue or body fluids and remove any you discover.
27. Clean and sanitize the room for the next patient.
28. Wash your hands.

Patient Education

Explain the basic elements of the procedure to the patient before the procedure begins. Explain that he or she should remain calm and still during the procedure. Follow-up instructions for the patient and/or significant others are also vital.

Charting Example

06/11/xx 11:00 a.m. Reviewed discharge instructions with patient. She verbalized the return appointment date and time and any signs of infection that should be reported. B/P 120/80, T 97.6°F, P 88, R 20. Ambulates steadily with husband escorting. Denies any nausea at time of discharge. Osi Kiwanuka, RMA

NOTE: The physician will also document the procedure and any observations immediately after the suturing procedure.

PROCEDURE 11-4 **Assist the Physician with Suture or Staple Removal**

Theory

Nonabsorbable suture materials are used on external surfaces and must be removed when they are no longer needed to support a healed and intact incision line. The healing rate of the sutured tissue depends on the blood supply to the area. Face and head tissue generally heals more quickly than tissue lower in the body. Depending on the location of the sutures, removal is directed by the physician, usually in three to five days on the face and head and five to ten days on the rest of the body. Nonabsorbable suture materials include cotton, silk, nylon, and stainless steel wire. Metal skin clips or "staples" may also be used.

Before discharge, the physician informs the patient, verbally and in written instructions, of the return date for removal of sutures or staples. During the return office visit, the physician assesses the condition of the incision area and may direct you to remove the sutures or staples. Immediately after

treatment, the physician and/or you must document observations of the approximated incision line, removal of suture materials, and instructions given to the patient.

To prevent the possibility of infection, antiseptic must be used before and after sutures or staples are removed. Use sterile saline or hydrogen peroxide to remove exudate and prevent the introduction of bacteria into the tiny open areas left by the sutures or staples. Another infection control measure is to cut one side of the suture as closely as possible to the skin, which reduces the amount of exposed suture material that is pulled through the skin.

Materials

- suture removal kit, including suture scissors, thumb forceps, and sterile 4 × 4 gauze, *or* staple removal kit, including staple remover and sterile 4 × 4 gauze

PROCEDURE 11-4 Assist the Physician with Suture or Staple Removal *(continued)*

- antiseptic swabs
- sterile 4 × 4 gauze
- gloves
- surgical tape
- biohazard waste container
- sharps container, if necessary

Competency

(**Conditions**) With the necessary materials, you will be able to (**Task**) demonstrate the procedure for removal of sutures or staples (**Standards**) correctly and within the time frame designated by the instructor.

1. Wash your hands.
2. Identify the patient and guide him or her to the treatment area. Explain the entire procedure to the patient.
3. Describe the sensation of pulling or tugging normally felt as the sutures or staples are removed.
4. Apply gloves.
5. Remove any dressing present. Moisten adhered dressing with sterile saline or hydrogen peroxide before removal, if necessary.
6. Grasp the edge of the dressing and lift it halfway to the point of the suture line. Then lift the other edge in the same manner. Once the dressing is free of the suture area, it can be disposed of in a biohazard container.
7. Cleanse the suture or staple area and surrounding skin.

8. Open the sterile suture or staple removal kit.
9. Wash your hands and put on sterile gloves.

For Sutures

1. With the thumb forceps, grasp the suture knot. Gently lift the knot upward.
2. With your other hand, slip the notched edge of the suture scissors under the suture as close to the skin as possible. Close the scissors to cut the suture (Figure 11-22a ◆).
3. Gently pull on the knot and pull the unexposed suture through the skin (Figure 11-22b ◆). Place it on the 4 × 4 gauze.
4. Continue until all the sutures are removed. Check the patient chart for total number of sutures applied to verify that all sutures have been removed. If the count is inconsistent you must report this to the physician for further instructions.
5. Cleanse the skin with an antiseptic swab.
6. Allow the skin to air-dry and apply adhesive skin closures or dressing as the physician directs.

For Staples

1. Slide the bottom jaw of the staple remover under the staple (Figure 11-23 ◆).
2. Squeeze the staple remover handles together. The staple will bend slightly into a "V" shape.

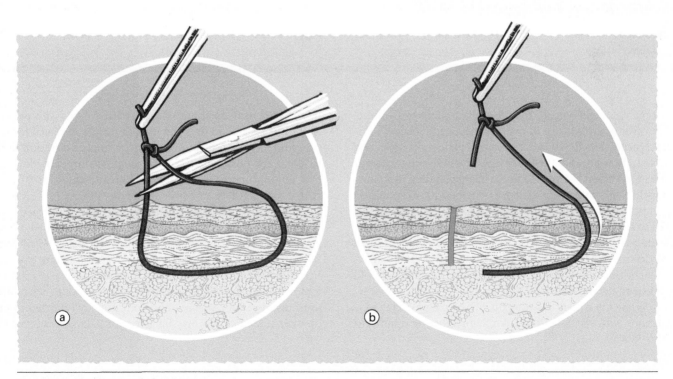

(a) (b)

Figure 11-22 ◆ Removal of sutures

continued

PROCEDURE 11-4 **Assist the Physician with Suture or Staple Removal** *(continued)*

3. Carefully lift the staple from the skin. Place it on the 4 × 4 gauze (Figure 11-24 ◆).
4. Continue the process until all the staples are removed.
5. Cleanse the skin with antiseptic swab.
6. Allow the skin to air-dry and apply adhesive skin closures or dressing as the physician directs.

Clean-up for Both Procedures

1. Dispose of contaminated materials in a biohazard or sharps container as appropriate.
2. Remove the gloves and discard.
3. Wash your hands.
4. Document the procedure.

Patient Education

The patient is usually allowed to shower after suture or staple removal, but check with the physician to confirm this before discussing it with the patient. To avoid irritation, the patient should pat the area dry rather than rub it. If the physician requires a dressing or adhesive skin closures, review and have the patient demonstrate correct application. The patient should be given both verbal and written wound care instructions and a list of signs to look for that may indicate a possible infection.

Charting Example

07/01/xx 9:30 a.m. Sutures intact and surgical incision approximated without signs of infection. Suture area cleansed with iodine and sutures × 15 removed from the abdominal incision per sterile technique. Iodine reapplied and allowed to air-dry before dressing applied. Incision and dressing care reviewed. Patient verbalized correct instructions for dressing changes. Abby McNair, CMA

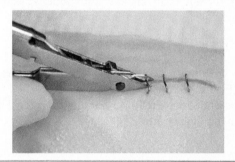

Figure 11-23 ◆ Slide the bottom jaw of the staple remover under the staple.

Figure 11-24 ◆ Place the staple on the 4 × 4 gauze.

syncope. Vasovagal syncope may also be referred to as fainting, neurocardiogenic syncope or neurally mediated syncope. Vasovagal syncope is believed to occur when a patient sits down and the blood flow pools in the lower legs, when the patient stands the trapped blood is returned to the heart, resulting in a fainting spell. Neither vasovagal syncope or orthostatic hypotension are life-threatening conditions but the patient must be monitored so that they do not fall, causing other injuries. You will assist the patient in sitting up on the side of the table until you have determined that he or she is stable enough to stand. If indicated by the procedure and by office policy, vital signs should be taken and recorded.

While the patient is sitting up, review the physician's instructions with the patient and family member or significant others and provide them with a written copy. The patient should be assisted in dressing if clothing was removed for the procedure. During the entire time, use your observation skills to assess any possible reaction to the procedure. Schedule the next appointment and dismiss the patient, who is usually escorted by a family member or significant other.

For more complex procedures and those performed with general anesthesia, vital signs are assessed and recorded. When general anesthesia has been administered, the level of consciousness and time of response to verbal stimuli are charted. Vital signs should be monitored and recorded every 15 minutes for the first hour, every 30 minutes for the next hour, then hourly until dismissal. Any nausea and vomiting are reported to the physician. Medication may be given for pain control and for prevention or control of nausea and vomiting. The patient is dismissed following facility guidelines when fully awake and able to ambulate. As with the less complicated ambulatory surgery, instructions are given and a follow-up appointment scheduled.

Patient Teaching and Dismissal

As with all patient teaching, feedback is important. Instructions are given both orally and in printed form. Depending on the nature of the procedure you will go over the postoperative instructions either with the attending family members or the patient individually. The patient or family member should be able to repeat the instructions back to you, or provide other demonstration of understanding. If you give the postoperative instructions to a family member you should ascertain that a release of information has been signed prior to the conversation to comply with HIPAA regulations. Typical postoperative instructions include keeping the dressing dry and reporting any blood or drainage that may appear on the dressing. Some instructions give a time frame in which to remove the dressing and describe how the incision should appear and how the area should be cleansed. Schedule the appointment for recheck and/or removal of sutures or staples. Give prescriptions and instructions for pain medication and any other medications indicated to the patient or the family member. Discuss any other anticipated outcomes.

Chart the patient's vital signs (if indicated), the patient's condition and apparent understanding of instructions, the method of discharge (ambulatory or wheelchair), and the person accompanying the patient.

Wound Healing

A wound is an insult or damage to an external skin surface or to the internal aspect of tissue. A wound is classified as accidental or intentional, and open or closed. An **open wound** is a break in the skin or mucous membrane that exposes underly-

ing tissues. Open wounds include abrasions, avulsions, incisions, lacerations, and punctures. (∞ Open wounds are discussed in greater detail in Chapter 23.)

A **closed wound** is a wound that involves trauma to the underlying tissue without a break in the skin or mucous membrane or exposure of the underlying tissue. Closed wounds include contusions, or bruises. Tissues under the skin are injured, blood vessels rupture, and blood seeps into the tissue, resulting in the bluish color of a bruise.

A wound must be cleansed and repaired to prevent infection, arrest any bleeding, promote healing, and reduce pain. The healing process begins with inflammation, which increases blood circulation to the wounded area to destroy the invading microorganisms. There are three phases in the process of normal healing: the inflammatory, granulation, and contraction phases (Table 11-3).

Dressings and Bandages

Dressings and bandages are used to cover wounds. Dressings also serve to:

- Act as a protective barrier against infection.
- Keep the surrounding skin clean and dry by absorbing drainage from wounds or surgical incisions.
- Reduce discomfort by restricting the movement of tissue surrounding the wound and by preventing irritation from clothing against the skin.

Bandages are also used to anchor dressings. Applying or changing a dressing allows for inspection of the wound. Observations of color, inflammation, edema, drainage, and healing stage should be noted and charted.

Keys to Success
MARKING DRAINAGE

Drainage on a dressing is marked by a line drawn around the edge of the drainage and the time the line is drawn. At intervals the drainage is checked and, if the area is expanding, another line is drawn and marked with the time by the patient or health-care person caring for the patient after dismissal. The physician will provide instructions as to when the office should be alerted.

TABLE 11-3 THE PHASES OF NORMAL HEALING	
Phase	**Process**
Inflammatory phase	■ Blood serum and cells form a network of fibrin in the wound. ■ A clot forms, filling in the wound and bringing the edges together with shreds of fibrin. ■ A scab begins to form.
Granulation phase (also called fibroblastic phase)	■ A network of granulation tissue absorbs fluid. ■ Epithelial cells begin to form from the edge of the wound. ■ A scar begins to form.
Contraction phase (also called maturation phase)	■ Small blood vessels are absorbed and fibroblasts contract. ■ The scar shrinks and becomes lighter in color.

PROCEDURE 11-5 Change a Sterile Dressing

Theory

Practicing sterile technique when applying or changing a dressing helps to reduce the chance of infectious organisms entering the body. The dressing must cover the wound but not be so large as to catch other materials. It is secured in place with tape or bandages. Gauze dressings come in various sizes, primarily 2×2, 3×3, and 4×4. The 4×4 is the most commonly used. Larger absorbent dressings are called ABD dressings.

As the wound drains, the gauze dressing absorbs the drainage. However, as the drainage dries, the gauze adheres to the wound. To prevent this, a nonadherent dressing is often used.

When the dressing is removed, you will assess the wound for color, inflammation, edema, drainage, and approximation. Document and report your observations to the physician to ensure proper treatment and continued healing.

After applying the appropriate dressing, secure it with either tape or a bandage. Tape can be used to make a complete seal around the dressing when you want to prevent drainage from leaking beyond the dressing onto other parts of the skin. Microbial growth can occur with a moist dressing or moist drainage beyond a dressing. When you remove or change a dressing, gently loosen the tape by applying slight fingertip pressure against the skin with one hand and using the other hand to pull up the tape perpendicular to the skin.

Materials

- prepackaged dressing pack, including sterile gauze or sponges, sterile thumb forceps, sterile dressings, adhesive tape (or tape most appropriate for skin condition and dressing function)
- Mayo stand and side tray
- antiseptic solution
- sterile transfer forceps
- sterile gloves
- scissors
- sterile basins
- thumb forceps
- disposable gloves
- waste container with plastic bag liner
- biohazard waste container

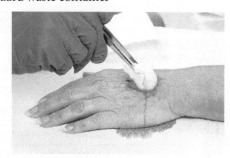

Figure 11-25 ◆ Clean the wound from the top downward or from the center outward.

Competency

(**Conditions**) With the necessary materials, you will be able to (**Task**) demonstrate a sterile dressing change (**Standards**) correctly within the time frame designated by the instructor.

1. Identify the patient and guide him or her to the treatment area. Explain the entire procedure to the patient.
2. Wash your hands.
3. Assemble the equipment on the Mayo stand or side table, using aseptic technique.
4. Apply non-sterile gloves, remove the dressing by pulling it in the direction of the wound.
5. Place the removed dressing into a biohazard bag, without touching the outside of the bag. Be careful not to pass it over your sterile tray.
6. Inspect the patient's wound and make a mental note to later document in the chart. A description of the wound size, shape, and any indication of infection, such as pus or inflammation should be noted.
7. Removed your soiled gloves.
8. Hold the antiseptic container with your palm covering the label. Pour some of the antiseptic into a sink or waste container. As the solution flows across the edge of the container, the edge will be disinfected. Pour the antiseptic into the sterile basin.
9. Wash your hands with a surgical scrub and apply sterile gloves.
10. Using sterile forceps and sterile cotton balls or sterile gauze pads, depending on the size of the wound, cleanse the wound. Disposable materials can be discarded in biohazard, and reusable items will be cleaned at the end of the procedure.
11. Cleanse the wound by moving from the inside to the outside, wiping from the top of the wound to the bottom, one time. The cotton ball must be changed with each stroke. (Figure 11-25 ◆)
12. Apply the sterile dressing to the wound and remove your gloves. Verify that your patient does not have an allergy to adhesives. If an allergy is present, secure the dressing with non-adhesive disposable bandage wrap such as Coban.
13. Secure the dressing with adhesive tape. Tape should not cover the entire dressing or be wrapped completely around the extremity.
14. Provide the patient with written and verbal instructions on wound care, signs of infection, and when they should follow up with the physician.
15. When the patient has exited the procedure area you may apply non-sterile gloves and clean the room in preparation for the next patient.
16. Remove your gloves and wash hands.
17. Chart the procedure, including the date, time, location, and condition of the wound. Chart and describe any drainage noted.

PROCEDURE 11-5 **Change a Sterile Dressing** *(continued)*

Patient Education

Instruct the patient and the patient's family or significant other(s) about the signs of infection: redness, increasing amount and odor of drainage, warmth, and hardness of the surgical site. Emphasize the importance of keeping the dressing dry to prevent the moist conditions in which microorganisms grow and reproduce. Ask the patient or significant other to verbalize the signs of infection. If dressings are to be changed as needed at home, it may be necessary to schedule a return visit to direct the patient or significant other through a supervised dressing change. Encourage the patient and/or family member or significant other to call the medical office if questions or problems arise.

Charting Example

05/01/xx 10:15 a.m. Abd drsg changed with sterile technique. Sutured wound was clean without signs of redness, swelling, or drainage. Patient asked when she could take showers. Reinforced physician's verbal instructions about waiting for showers until a few days after sutures were taken out. Return appointment scheduled for sutures to be taken out on 05/27/XX. Patient verbalized she would wait to take shower until after her next appointment. Joy Jones, CMA

REVIEW

Chapter Summary

- Minor surgeries range from a simple 10-minute procedure to 23-hour outpatient stay.
- As an MA, you could be responsible for any of the following.
  - scheduling outpatient testing and surgical procedures
  - assisting physician in the procedure
  - providing instructions
  - dismissing patients
  - obtaining insurance precertification and consent signature
  - ordering supplies for future surgeries
  - preparing instruments by cleaning, disinfecting, and sterilizing
  - setting up the room or treatment area
  - preparing the patient
  - properly handling specimens
  - processing insurance claims
- The scrub assistant sets up the sterile field and maintains sterile working conditions while assisting the physician during the procedure. The circulating assistant obtains supplies for the sterile team and performs all other procedures in which sterile procedure is not required.

- Many surgeries are performed in the medical office setting, including biopsy, colposcopy, cryosurgery, electrocautery, incision and drainage, removal of foreign bodies, suturing of lacerations, and suture or staple removal.
- Regardless of the type of minor surgery, implied or informed consent must be given by the patient. A patient must completely understand the procedure and risks before signing the consent form. A signed consent form is mandatory.
- Preoperative patient care involves instructing the patient about the procedure, time, diet, and someone to drive him or her home if necessary; obtaining laboratory tests; and easing the patient's concerns about the surgery. Setting up the room, positioning and draping the patient, taking vital signs, and assisting the physician with anesthesia are also part of preoperative care.
- Instruments are classified as clamping, cutting, dilating, dissecting, grasping, probing, suturing, and visualization. Forceps, scissors, scalpels, needle holders, and trocars are examples of surgical instruments.
- During the setup of sterile trays and during the procedure, it is important to know which areas are sterile, clean, and dirty.

Chapter Summary (continued)

By remembering whether an instrument, dressing, or step in a procedure is sterile, clean, or dirty, the medical assistant can move around and maintain a sterile field during the performance of all actions. It is critical that you *never* reach over the sterile field.

■ In the preparation of the surgical area, it is very important to follow cleaning from the surgical site outward and to use a separate sponge for each concentric circular area.

■ Anesthesia used in the medical office is generally local anesthesia, in topical form or as an injection. The MA assists by holding the vial while the physician draws the medication into a syringe for injection.

■ Intraoperative care varies according to the type of minor surgery and the physician's preference. Usually the MA is trained to perform all procedures related to minor surgery, including dressing changes, suturing, and suture removal.

■ In a wound, whether caused by trauma or surgery, the skin surface is broken. Wounds may be open, such as abrasions, avulsions, incisions, lacerations, and punctures, or closed, such as contusions. The phases of healing are the inflammatory, granulation, and contraction phases. You should be able to identify signs of wound infection, including redness, heat, and/or pain.

■ Applied correctly, dressings protect a wound site from further trauma and can protect it from infection.

■ During postoperative recovery, the MA is responsible for performing and monitoring patient vital signs and observing patient progress. Any abnormalities should be reported to the physician. When the patient is ready for discharge or dismissal, you will give verbal and written instructions as directed by the physician.

■ Documentation is another important aspect of minor surgery. Records of the procedure, outpatient testing, patient education, and patient progress are among the required documentation in the patient chart.

Chapter Review Questions

Multiple Choice

1. The circulating assistant's role is to
   A. assist with a five-minute surgical scrub.
   B. position the patient.
   C. hand instruments to the physician.
   D. assist the physician with sterile gloving.

2. Which of the following is most likely to involve a 23-hour outpatient procedure?
   A. cyst removal
   B. abscess incision and drainage
   C. D & C
   D. staple removal

3. Which of the following should you do after setting up the sterile field?
   A. Cover or drape the sterile field with a sterile cloth.
   B. Leave the room to get patient drapes.
   C. Leave the sterile field uncovered, ready for surgery.
   D. Push the Mayo stand next to the examination table.

4. Forceps are used for
   A. cutting.
   B. dissecting.
   C. grasping.
   D. probing.

5. A trocar is used for
   A. cutting.
   B. dissecting.
   C. grasping.
   D. probing.

6. When shaving a patient for surgery, you should
   A. shave the surgical site in the direction opposite that of hair growth.
   B. shave the surgical site in the direction of the hair growth.
   C. use antiseptic in concentric circles before shaving.
   D. avoid using germicidal soap because it causes irritation.

7. Which of the following is used as a local anesthesia?
   A. ether
   B. heroin
   C. ethyl chloride spray
   D. procaine

8. If a local anesthetic is used during surgery, you should
   A. hold the vial upside down with the label facing the physician.
   B. hold the vial upright with the label facing you.
   C. insert the needle into the rubber stopper and withdraw the desired amount.
   D. insert the needle into the rubber stopper, inject air from the syringe, and withdraw the desired amount.

9. A suture should be cut
   A. 1/16 inch above the knot.
   B. 1/4 inch above the knot.
   C. 1/2 inch above the knot.
   D. 1 inch above the knot.

Chapter Review Questions (continued)

10. Which of the following procedures should be done when changing a sterile dressing?
    A. Cleanse the wound from the center inward.
    B. Cleanse the wound from the bottom of the wound to the top.
    C. Cleanse the wound from side to side.
    D. Cleanse the wound from the top of the wound to the bottom.

True/False

T F 1. The term *preoperative* refers to the period during a surgery.

T F 2. The term *intraoperative* means "before surgery."

T F 3. The postoperative period follows a surgery.

T F 4. A scrub assistant is also known as a float or "clean" assistant.

T F 5. A scrub assistant may be responsible for setting up the sterile field and assisting the physician in sterile procedures.

T F 6. Optional surgery is medically necessary but can be done when it is most convenient for the patient.

T F 7. Elective surgery is not medically necessary and is only done when the patient requests it.

T F 8. Emergency surgery is performed when there is an immediate need.

T F 9. If a patient is having a nonroutine procedure, an informed consent is not needed.

T F 10. A circulating assistant can obtain supplies and sterile equipment for the "sterile team."

Short Answer

1. List the types of surgery.

2. Name a medically necessary surgery that can be done at the patient's convenience.

3. What must patients sign before all nonroutine procedures?

4. What is an I & D procedure? Why is it performed?

5. What is the difference between a closed wound and an open wound?

Research

1. In your local area, how many women have elective C-sections?

2. In your community, are there any outpatient surgery centers? Or are all surgeries, regardless of length and type, performed in a hospital?

Externship Application Experience

It is your second externship day in the office, and a mole removal is scheduled for a patient. You are to observe the procedure so that you can assist on the next scheduled minor surgery.

As an MA is opening the sterile packet, you notice she reaches across the sterile field on several occasions. How do you handle the situation?

Resource Guide

Allegiance Healthcare Corporation
1430 Waukegan Road
McGaw Park, IL 60085-6787
1-800-964-5227
www.cardinal.com

Miltex Instrument Company, Inc.
700 Hicksville Road
Bethpage, NY 11714
1-800-645-8000
www.miltex.com

SAMBA: Society for Ambulatory Anesthesia
520 N. Northwest Highway
Parkridge, IL 60068-2573
847-825-5586

MedMedia

www.prenhall.com/frazier

More on this chapter, including interactive resources, can be found on the Student CD-ROM accompanying this textbook and on the Companion Website at www.prenhall.com/frazier.

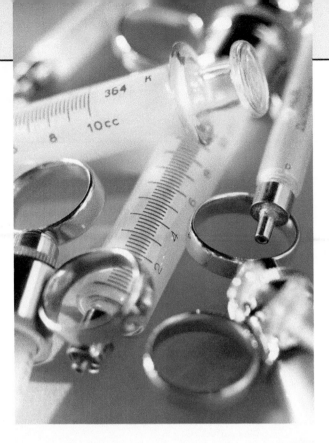

Diagnostic Testing in the Medical Office

My name is Glenda Gibson. I became a Medical Assistant in 1983. At the time, I was working at a semi-decent job, but it was one that had no future of growth or advancement. Then one day one I was watching television, I saw a commercial for the Missouri School for Doctor's Assistants. It sounded like just the right thing for me. I called and got an interview with the school director and signed up for classes.

My first job was at an internist's office. Here, the staff was responsible for performing EKGs on all new patients. We also set up and assisted in EKG stress testing. Since it was my first job, I had a lot to learn about drawing blood—drawing blood well was my biggest challenge. With all the practice I obtained, I turned out to be very good at drawing blood. The internist office's also had its own lab. It was part of my job to run protime, do CBCs, and get the lab ready for the morning lab person to come in and start testing. For a first-time job, this job really incorporated all aspects of my medical assistant training.

Now I am working for a large laboratory company. In the office where I am currently located, I am the only person working at the site. I use all skills from answering phone calls to coding diagnosis with my ICD-9 knowledge. I get a lot satisfaction from doing my job well. The customers who come to my site appreciate the work I do. These customers tell me that I have great phlebotomy and front office skills.

Medical assisting has been a great career for me. Now I am looking for future advancement by going back to school and getting certifications in Medical Office Administrator and Advance Medical Coding, as well as a B.S. in Social Work. My long-term goal is to run a medical office.

CHAPTER 12

Diagnostic Procedures

Case Study

Jason, a medical assistant, is busy working in a medical facility that utilizes an in-clinic laboratory. Some of the tests he has learned to perform are urine pregnancy tests, simple gross urinalysis, and glucose screening.

Objectives

After completing this chapter, you should be able to:

- Spell and define medical terminology in this chapter.
- Define the medical assistant's role in diagnostic procedures and the laboratory.
- Explain the role of Clinical Laboratory Improvement Amendments (CLIA) in setting standards for laboratory testing.
- Explain the differences between waived, PPMP, moderate-complexity, and high-complexity tests.
- Discuss quality control and quality assurance.
- Explain the roles of the FDA, EPA, and OSHA as they relate to laboratory testing.
- Explain the role of the Joint Commission on Accreditation of Healthcare Organizations in total quality management within the hospital setting.
- Discuss the Safe Medical Devices Act.
- Describe diagnostic testing in hospital laboratories.
- Identify equipment found in a physician office laboratory (POL).
- Explain how the physician's order is transmitted to the testing facility.
- Discuss the importance and process of obtaining precertification when required.
- Explain the procedure for scheduling diagnostic tests with outside agencies.
- Discuss the screening and following up of test results.

 MedMedia

www.prenhall.com/frazier

Additional interactive resources and activities for this chapter can be found on the Companion Website. For videos, audio glossary, legal and ethical scenarios, job scenarios, quizzes, games, and virtual tours related to the content of this chapter, please access the accompanying CD-ROM in this book.

Assets Available:

Audio Glossary
Legal and Ethical Scenario: *Diagnostic Procedures*
On the Job Scenario: *Diagnostic Procedures*
Video Scenario: *Specimen Collection* and *Urinalysis*
Multiple Choice Quiz
Games: Crossword, Strikeout, and Spelling Bee

⊕ MEDICAL ASSISTING COMPETENCIES

CAAHEP ENTRY-LEVEL COMPETENCIES FOR CMA	ABHES ENTRY-LEVEL COMPETENCIES FOR RMA
▪ Identify and respond to issues of confidentiality. ▪ Perform within legal and ethical boundaries. ▪ Demonstrate knowledge of federal and state health-care legislation and regulations. ▪ Perform hand washing. ▪ Dispose of biohazardous materials. ▪ Practice Standard Precautions. ▪ Use methods of quality control.	▪ Project a positive attitude ▪ Maintain confidentiality at all times ▪ Be a "team player." ▪ Be cognizant of ethical boundaries. ▪ Exhibit initiative. ▪ Adapt to change. ▪ Evidence a responsible attitude. ▪ Be courteous and diplomatic. ▪ Conduct work within scope of education, training, and ability. ▪ Interview and take a patient history. ▪ Prepare patients for procedures. ▪ Apply principles of aseptic techniques and infection control. ▪ Prepare and maintain examination and treatment area. ▪ Collect and process specimens. ▪ Perform selected CLIA waived tests that assist with diagnosis and treatment. ▪ Dispose of biohazardous materials. ▪ Practice standard precautions.

Introduction

Diagnostic testing is essential for a complete picture of the patient's health status. It also provides the physician with feedback concerning the effectiveness and proper dosage of prescribed medications.

A physician has two choices for laboratory testing—a reference laboratory or a physician office laboratory (**POL**). Both types of laboratories are governed by the same regulations and guidelines. A reference laboratory is independently owned and operated by an outside source and can perform high-level testing unavailable in the POL. Many reference labs have contracts with insurance providers and managed care providers.

One advantage of the POL is immediate testing, results, and treatment while the patient is still in the office. Other advantages are convenience and reduced time and travel for the patient.

The Medical Assistant's Role in Diagnostic Testing

As an MA working in a hospital or reference laboratory, you may schedule tests, maintain or file records of results, record or log calibrations, assist with quality control records, and obtain specimens. Depending on state regulations, and with immediate supervision, you may be able to perform a simple gross urinalysis and certain mechanized tests, procure capillary and venipuncture specimens, centrifuge urine and blood specimens, and plate specimens for culture. Also, depending on state and facility guidelines, you may be able to transmit test results to the physician's office.

Medical Terminology

centrifuge—instrument that spins substances at high speed to separate them into layers according to density

glucometer—instrument used to measure blood glucose levels

hematocrit—volume of RBCs in a given volume of blood, expressed as a percent of total blood volume

hemoglobin—iron-containing substance found in RBCs whose function is to carry oxygen from the lungs throughout the body

photometer—instrument used to measure the intensity of light rays; an electronic component of many instruments

Abbreviations

BUN—blood urea nitrogen

CBC—complete blood count, usually consisting of WBC count, RBC count, hemoglobin, hematocrit, RBC indices, and often platelet count and white cell differential

CLIA—Clinical Laboratory Improvement Amendments

CO_2—carbon dioxide

CPT—physician's current procedural terminology

C & S—culture and sensitivity

diff—differential white blood cell count

DOB—date of birth

ESR—erythrocyte sedimentation rate

Hct—hematocrit

HCFA—Health Care Financing Administration

Hgb—hemoglobin

ICD-9-CM—International Classification of Diseases, 9th Revision, Clinical Modification

POL—physician office laboratory

PPMP—provider-performed microscopy procedures

PT—prothrombin time

PTT—partial thromboplastin time

RBC—red blood cell count

SSN—social security number

WBC—white blood cell count

As an MA working in a POL, you may perform waived tests, provide patient education about obtaining specimens, and collect specimens within the scope of your training and physician supervision. Specimens you may obtain include urine, stool, cultures, and venous and capillary blood. You may set up certain microscopic tests; however, the physician must make the microscopic diagnosis. In some states you may read the microscopic results with further specialized training and with physician supervision and responsibility. Check state practice acts where you will be employed for what you are specifically and legally allowed to do in a POL.

When using equipment, you will be required to follow OSHA and Clinical Laboratory Improvement Amendments (**CLIA**) guidelines. In all procedures you must exercise caution to prevent accidents and exposure to biohazardous and chemical waste. Follow all OSHA, CLIA, and manufacturer's instructions when disposing of biohazardous and chemical waste.

COMPETENCY SKILLS PERFORMANCE

1. Check the accuracy of glucometer results using quality control methods.
2. Obtain a precertification by telephone.
3. Screen and follow up test results.

Clinical Laboratory Improvement Amendments (CLIA)

Accurate laboratory testing has been recognized as a critical element of correct diagnosis in medical office visits and in life-threatening situations. Decisions about diagnosis, care, medication, dosages, and procedures are based on the results of these tests.

In 1988, U.S. Congress passed the Clinical Laboratory Improvement Amendments (CLIA), establishing quality standards for all laboratory testing. Implementation of CLIA was the responsibility of the Health Care Financing Administration (**HCFA**). The goal of CLIA is "to ensure the accuracy, reliability and timeliness of patient test results regardless of where the test was performed." Certification by the Secretary of Health and Human Services is "required for all laboratories that examine materials derived from the human body fluids for diagnosis, prevention, or treatment purposes." Test categorization and CLIA studies are the responsibility of the CDC.

Quality standards are specified for proficiency testing (PT), quality control, quality assurance, patient test management, and personnel qualifications. The regulations are based on the complexity of the test method. The more complicated the test is, the more stringent the requirements. Tests fall into three categories:

- waived complexity
- moderate complexity, which includes the subcategory of provider-performed microscopy procedures (**PPMP**)
- high complexity

There are also specific cytology requirements.

Keys to Success
TYPES OF CLIA CERTIFICATES

Certificate of Waiver—issued to a laboratory that performs only waived tests
Certificate for PPMP (Provider-Performed Microscopy Procedures) issued to a laboratory in which a physician, midlevel practitioner, or dentist performs no tests other than microscopic tests; the laboratory may also perform waived tests
Certificate of Registration—issued to a laboratory that conducts moderate- and/or high-complexity laboratory testing until it is determined that the laboratory complies with CLIA regulations
Certificate of Compliance—issued to a laboratory after an inspection that confirms the laboratory complies with all applicable CLIA requirements
Certificate of Accreditation—issued to a laboratory on the basis of the laboratory's accreditation by an HCFA-approved accreditation organization.

Adapted from HCFA guidelines.

Enrollment in the CLIA program requires several steps. Laboratories must complete an application for registration, pay applicable fees, be surveyed, and, when necessary, become certified. Full-service providers (those performing moderate- and high-complexity tests) are surveyed routinely. Laboratories performing waived and PPMP testing may apply directly for the certificate and are not subject to routine inspections.

Waived Tests

Waived tests are the least complex tests to perform, so there is little danger of error or risk to the patient. Many of these tests have been approved by the FDA for patient use at home, such as blood glucose screening and urine pregnancy tests. Most waived tests are performed by physicians (MDs/DOs), registered nurses (RNs), licensed practical nurses (LPNs), and medical assistants (MAs). Very few medical technologists (MTs) and medical laboratory technicians (MLTs) regularly perform waived tests. Reading and following the manufacturer's instructions are required for any waived test.

Keys to Success
CLIA Waived Tests

1. Dipstick of tablet reagent urinalysis for:
   bilirubin
   glucose
   hemoglobin
   ketone
   leukocytes
   nitrite
   pH
   protein
   specific gravity
   urobilinogen
2. Fecal occult blood
3. Urine pregnancy tests: visual color comparison tests
4. Ovulation tests: visual color comparison tests for luteinizing hormone
5. Blood glucose using FDA approved glucose monitoring devices
6. Hemoglobin: copper sulfate, non-automated
7. Erythrocyte sedimentation rate, non-automated
8. Hemoglobin using single analyte instruments
9. Spun microhematocrit

Laboratories performing waived tests only, including POLs, apply for a Certificate of Waiver. The certificate exempts them from meeting various CLIA 1988 standards that apply to the other types of tests.

PPMP Tests

A waived laboratory with a PPMP certificate can perform tests using a microscope. Such tests are done during a patient visit on a specimen that is not easily transportable (Figure 12-1 ◆). Included in PPMP tests are pinworm examination, microscopic urinalysis, fecal leukocyte examination, and semen analysis (presence and/or motility of sperm, excluding the Huhner test, a postcoital test on cervical mucus).

Moderate-Complexity Tests

A moderate-complexity test is also simple to perform, but it may involve a more serious risk to the patient if results are inaccurate. Blood chemistries, red and white blood cell counts, **hemoglobin, hematocrit,** and urine cultures are categorized as moderate-complexity tests. Although many chemistries are performed with automated instruments, training beyond the MA level is required to perform these tests. Normal values as indicated in printed lab reports are variable according to the reference laboratory's values. (Where applicable, chemistries are discussed or listed in later chapters with the disease or condition to which they apply.)

Figure 12-1 ◆ The MA explains to the patient how to use a collection specimen kit.

High-Complexity Tests

A high-complexity test is complicated to perform and poses considerable risk to the patient if results are inaccurate. Bone marrow evaluations, immunoassays, flow cytometry, and electrophoresis are high complexity. These tests require sophisticated instrumentation and must be overseen by a pathologist or PhD-level scientist.

Quality Control and Quality Assurance

The objective of quality control is to ensure reliable and valid test results by applying the correct methods and detecting or eliminating errors. Quality control is essential for the physician to properly diagnose and treat a patient. Patient preparation and specimen collection, handling, transport, and testing are elements of quality control.

Quality control before testing includes confirming that the patient has followed the required preparation and selecting the appropriate container or system (Figure 12-2 ◆). The

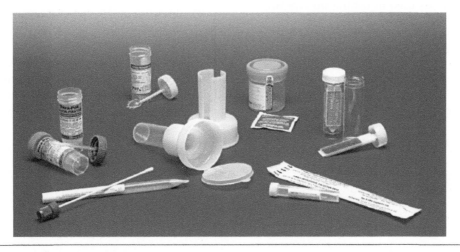

Figure 12-2 ◆ Specimen collection containers

PROCEDURE 12-1 Check the Accuracy of Glucometer Results Using Quality Control Methods

Theory

Quality control is performed to ensure standardized and accurate results of all manual and automated tests. A glucometer is used in the medical office and by patients at home to measure blood glucose, with immediate and accurate results. Whether performed at home by the patient or at the medical office, quality control requires keeping records of control testing, cleaning, equipment maintenance, and repairs. You will need to educate the patient on the importance of quality control at home because it directly affects the amount of insulin administered.

Materials

- quality control log book
- glucometer
- quality controls specific to brand of glucometer

Competency

(**Conditions**) With the necessary materials, you will be able to (**Task**) perform quality control testing of the glucometer (**Standards**) within the time and to the degree of accuracy designated by the instructor.

1. Wash your hands and assemble materials.
2. Perform control testing as recommended by the manufacturer and per office policy.
   - Check unsealed quality control vials and test strips for open and discard dates and expiration dates. Label the control vials and test strips if you are opening them for the first time.

- If you are changing code strips, calibrate and change the number per manufacturer's instructions.
3. Record the test results in a quality control log (Figure 12-3 ◆). If control results are abnormal, report them to the supervisor. Label the glucometer "Repair" and remove it from the clinical area to prevent other staff from using it. Return the glucometer to the clinical area only after the problem has been corrected.
4. Dispose of waste materials in the appropriate container.
5. Wash your hands and return the glucometer and quality test control equipment to the designated storage area.

Patient Education

Emphasize the importance of glucometer quality control in the treatment of diabetes. Instruct the patient in how to perform quality control tests, and have the patient do a return demonstration. Include instruction on keeping logs for quality control testing.

Charting Example

10/30/XX 11:45 A.M. Patient demonstrated quality control testing correctly and verbalized understanding of how to keep log records. Return appointment scheduled for one month to review logs of quality control testing and of blood glucose monitoring results. Patient verbalizes understanding of Regular Insulin sliding scale for elevated blood glucose and recording additional insulin on the glucose monitoring log. LaDanian Miller, CMA

---

container is labeled with the patient's name, any identification number, the date, and the technician's initials.

Quality control methods used in testing involve the following:

- Checking dated supplies and discarding outdated reagents.
- Calibrating and performing function checks on equipment.
- Maintaining equipment and documenting maintenance.

- Running and documenting control samples of each test for consistency.

Quality assurance is a type of outcome assessment. Monitoring laboratory testing begins at the start of the process, continues through the process, and ends with the results of the process. Each step in the process requires following instructions and methodology to ensure quality. Information, test results, and data are then assembled and reviewed. The data is compared to acceptable standards for testing. Services provided as

PROCEDURE 12-1 Check the Accuracy of Glucometer Results Using Quality Control Methods *(continued)*

Sample Form: Quality Control for Glucometer

Goal: Perform quality control testing and ensure accuracy of patient test results for blood glucose monitoring.

Glucometer serial number: _____

Code strip number: _____

Test strip lot number: _____

Check strip acceptable value range: _____

Low control solution lot number: _____

Low control solution expiration date: _____

Low control solution acceptable value range: _____

High control solution lot number: _____

High control solution expiration date: _____

High control solution acceptable value range: _____

Mark opened vials of low and high control solution with "open" and "discard" dates.

Year/Month/Day	Low Solution Test Results	High Solution Test Results	Check Strip Test Results	Action taken if control test results abnormal	Initials

Use back of sheet for additional information, if necessary. Date and initial each entry.

Figure 12-3 ◆ Sample form for quality control

well as results are compared. Written policies and documentation of the results are completed.

Regulations and Laboratory Safety

The Food and Drug Administration (FDA) and the Environmental Protection Agency (EPA) are the two federal agencies that enforce safety standards. The FDA evaluates equipment for clinical performance, medical relevance, and safety. The Safe Medical Devices Act of 1990 monitors and evaluates incidents involving equipment. The EPA enforces legal and proper disposal of hazardous chemical and biological materials. OSHA rules protect patients and health-care workers by mandating employee use of personal protective equipment (PPE) during blood and specimen collection. OSHA requires that MSDS sheets for all chemical substances be available in the medical office.

Joint Commission on the Accreditation of Healthcare Organizations

The Joint Commission on the Accreditation of Healthcare Organizations (JCAHO), a private, nongovernmental agency, has established guidelines regarding the quality of care in hospitals and health-care agencies, including laboratories. JCAHO provides accreditation for health-care agencies that establish a proven record of monitoring, evaluating, and implementing

---

Keys to Success
GENERAL GUIDELINES FOR LABORATORY SAFETY

1. *Always* wash your hands before and after all procedures.
2. Use PPE as required by OSHA and department policy. This includes gloves, gowns, and eye and face protective wear.
3. Avoid wearing loose clothing and wear long hair pulled back to prevent entangling it in the laboratory equipment.
4. Wear shoes that cover the entire foot and have slip-resistant soles to prevent injury from spills or falls.
5. *Always* walk or walk quickly, but never run.
6. *Never* recap needles. Put used needles immediately in a sharps container. Use caution when handling or transporting sharp instruments.
7. Cover biological specimens at all times when transporting and centrifuging.
8. Dispose of biological specimens, such as blood, urine, and tissue, in biohazardous waste containers.
9. Decontaminate specimen collection, preparation, and processing areas following procedures.
10. Use caution when handling chemicals to avoid eye splash.
11. Follow OSHA standards for cleaning accidental chemical or biological specimen spills.
12. Report all equipment or lighting malfunctions.
13. Keep traffic areas clear of debris and obstructions.
14. *Never* eat, drink, smoke, or place any item in the mouth while in the medical laboratory.
15. *Never* apply makeup, lipstick, or contact lenses in the medical laboratory.
16. *Never* store personal food or drinks in the laboratory specimen refrigerator.

---

policies and procedures for quality assurance in patient care. Departments such as laboratories are required to identify indicators of high-risk and high-volume procedures, establish minimal baselines for acceptable quality of care, and gather monitored data. When necessary, the health-care institution has to demonstrate a plan of correction, communication about the plan, and the effectiveness of correction. An accredited hospital laboratory or POL has demonstrated an effective quality assurance plan and established a high standard for patient care.

Safe Medical Devices Act

The Safe Medical Devices Act of 1990 was implemented to protect patients, visitors, and health-care facilities staff. The act requires anyone using a medical device to report to the manufacturer and/or the FDA any incidents that reasonably suggest that a medical device caused or contributed to a serious injury to or death of a patient. The act defines an injury or illness as "either permanent impairment of bodily function or permanent damage to a bodily structure or one that necessitates immediate medical or surgical intervention to preclude permanent impairment of a bodily function or permanent damage to a bodily structure." It also provides for enforcing the use of safe medical devices when drawing blood or handling blood or other body fluids, such as syringes or vacuum tube holders with retractable needles. Inspections and the training of employees in the use of these medical devices are mandatory. A log must be maintained to record any incidents regarding medical devices, and an exposure plan should be in place and reviewed on a periodic basis.

Hospital Laboratory Setting

The hospital laboratory setting provides for both inpatient and outpatient diagnostic testing. It is divided into functional areas for clinical analysis and surgical and anatomical pathology analysis (Table 12-1).

Blood chemistry tests include electrolyte levels (sodium, potassium, chloride, and carbon dioxide or CO_2); lipid studies, including cholesterol and triglycerides; creatinine; blood urea nitrogen (**BUN**); uric acid; liver and cardiac enzymes; serum protein; bilirubin; and blood glucose (Figure 12-4 ◆). Automated testing procedures are generally used, thereby ensuring better quality assurance and a more efficient, standardized level of testing.

Hematology and coagulation studies include the complete blood count (**CBC**) with its component parts as well as erythrocyte sedimentation rate (**ESR**); partial thromboplastin time (**PTT**); prothrombin time (**PT**); coagulation studies; and reticulocyte counts. A CBC with differential includes a red blood cell count (**RBC**), white blood cell count (**WBC**), hematocrit (**Hct**), hemoglobin (**Hgb**), platelet count, and differential white blood cell count (**diff**).

The microbiology department identifies the microorganisms in specimens such as blood, urine, stool, nose and throat

TABLE 12-1 HOSPITAL LABORATORY FUNCTIONAL AREAS

Clinical	Surgical and Anatomical
■ Hematology and coagulation studies ■ Microbiology ■ Virology ■ Toxicology ■ Immunology ■ Serology ■ Blood bank ■ Urinalysis	■ Surgical biopsy ■ Surgical histology ■ Cytology ■ Autopsy

tissues or mucus, other body fluids, and wound drainage. It then tests the microorganism sensitivity to various antibiotics to determine which medication is most effective for treatment. This procedure is referred to as culture and sensitivity (**C & S**). Bacteriology, virology, and mycology are part of the microbiology department.

Blood serum studies to determine antigen–antibody reaction are conducted in the immunology area of the laboratory. The serology area conducts tests for diseases associated with immune disorders, including AIDS, HIV, syphilis, rheumatoid arthritis, and mononucleosis. Tests on RBCs and serum, blood typing, compatibility, cross matching, and antibodies are performed in the blood bank area of the laboratory. Three forms of urinalysis tests are performed—physical, chemical, and microscopic—usually in a special area designated for urine studies.

Autopsies to determine the cause of death are performed in the surgical and anatomical pathology department of the laboratory. The surgical or histology area conducts tests on tissue specimens removed during surgical procedures. Histology tests help in the diagnosis of disease. In the cytology area of the laboratory, tests are conducted on cells from body fluids or tissues to determine the presence of abnormalities.

The Physician Office Laboratory

Physician office laboratories, or POLs, are small laboratories located in physicians' offices to provide a convenient place to perform simple tests on human specimens. According to CLIA regulations, these tests are classified as waived complexity because they require no interpretation and can be performed by medical assistants. Tests of higher complexity may be performed in the POL, but by a medical laboratory technician or medical technologist.

POL Equipment

Users must be trained in the operation of equipment in a POL. Training is a combination of formal education in the classroom, on-the-job training, and specific training by a sales representative for the equipment. Safety and CLIA guidelines are covered.

Equipment used in the laboratory includes centrifuges, microscopes, autoclaves, and electronic equipment, such as analyzers and measurement tools.

Centrifuge

The **centrifuge** is an instrument that separates specimens into their components using a rapid spinning action (Figure 12-5 ◆). Centrifugal force separates solids from liquids. For example, a centrifuge separates a blood specimen into red cells, white cells, and plasma, the lightest part of the blood. The heavier RBCs settle to the bottom of the tube, then a layer of WBCs, then the plasma on top. Urine specimens are also centrifuged to separate and obtain the portion required for microscopic study.

Figure 12-4 ◆ Chemcard™ cholesterol test
Courtesy of Chematics, Inc.

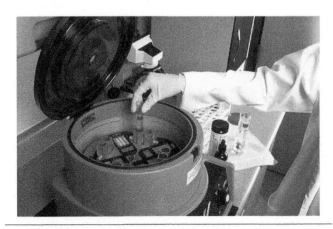

Figure 12-5 ◆ Example of a centrifuge used for blood and for urine

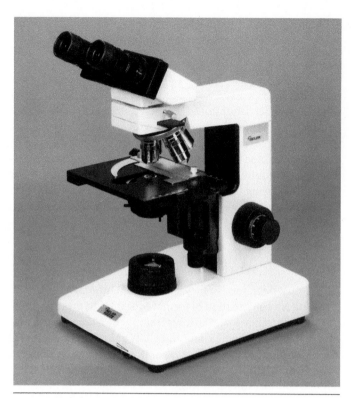

Figure 12-6 ◆ Clinical binocular microscope
Courtesy of Seiler Instrument.

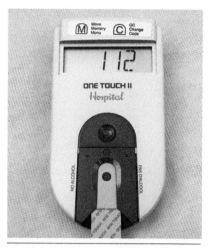

Figure 12-7 ◆ Example of a home glucometer

Microscope

A microscope is an optical instrument that magnifies minute objects (Figure 12-6 ◆). It is used in a POL to examine blood smears, perform microscopic blood cell counts, and identify microorganisms in body fluid samples. The optical microscope is the type most frequently used in the POL. Light is concentrated through a condenser to focus through the object being examined and project an image. A compound microscope contains two lenses that magnify the image created by the condensed light. Specimen slides and cover slips are used with the microscope.

Electronic Equipment

Electronic equipment in a POL may include various types of automated analyzers that permit the rapid and accurate analysis of a specimen. Calibration for quality control must be conducted on a daily basis. Preventive maintenance must also be scheduled on a routine basis. Calibration testing, preventive maintenance, and unscheduled maintenance must be documented.

A **glucometer** is a small, handheld electronic instrument used to measure glucose levels in blood samples (Figure 12-7 ◆). Several types are available; most provide a reading using a drop of blood. Usually the results are available on a screen in less than 60 seconds. A glucometer uses a **photometer**, a common electronic component in laboratory equipment, to reflect light and assist in the measurement of blood glucose levels.

Other types of electronic equipment are instruments that count red or white blood cells and complex chemical analyzers.

Ordering Diagnostic Tests

The physician initiates orders for diagnostic testing as needed. The medical assistant then calls third-party providers for precertification to initiate the process of obtaining financial reimbursement for the tests. You will also schedule in-house and outside-agency diagnostic testing. When test results are returned to the medical office, you will compare the normal values to the patient's values and forward abnormal values to the physician for follow-up.

The Physician's Order

Although physicians often give verbal orders for diagnostic testing, the orders must be in writing. If the physician or the office calls an order in to a reference laboratory, the order must be signed within 30 days.

Medical offices use preprinted forms or laboratory requisitions for common tests (Figure 12-8 ◆). The name of the test is circled, underlined, or checked. The patient's name, date of birth (**DOB**), and insurance information are entered on the form, which must be signed by the physician or the physician's representative (MA, RN, or LPN). In some states the encounter form or a prescription blank may be used to document the order in writing if a form is unavailable. The prescription blank must be printed with the physician's name, address, phone number, and other pertinent information. Office staff transcribing the order enter the patient's name, and DOB, and the diagnostic procedure ordered.

Many insurance companies, as well as Medicare and Medicaid, require a diagnosis and the *International Classification of Diseases, 9th Revision, Clinical Modification* (**ICD-9-CM**) code on the order. Following the practice guidelines of the specific state in which the practice is located, a designated staff member signs or stamps the physician's name, then signs his or her own name or initials. The completed order is given to the patient to take to the laboratory. It is accepted practice in most areas to fax a copy of the order to the diagnostic facility. The procedure is coded using the Physician's Current Procedural Terminology (**CPT**) and must agree with the diagnosis for the patient as listed by the ICD-9-CM code. For example, a CBC or EKG is not acceptable for a patient with a primary diagnosis of diabetes. A second diagnosis of

LABORATORY REQUISITION FORM

ORDER DATE: _____

COLLECTION DATE/TIME/BY: _____

FASTING
Y☐ N☐

Patient Name: _____ SS# _____ Sex: M☐ F☐ D.O.B _____
Address: _____ Parent/guarantor: _____
Ordering Physician: _____ Bill to: Patient ☐ or Insurance ☐
Insurance Company: _____ Policy Number: _____
Medicare number: _____ Medicaid Number: _____

Medicare Only Covers Medically Necessary Lab Tests

Narrative Diagnosis: _____
_____

Tests Performed At: _____

☐ ALBUMIN
☐ ALKALINE PHOSPHATASE
☐ ALT (SGPT)
☐ AMYLASE
☐ AST (SGOT)
☐ BETA HCG, QUAL (PREGNANCY)
____ SERUM ____ URINE
☐ BILIRUBIN
____ TOTAL ____ DIRECT ____ NEWBORN
☐ BUN
☐ CALCIUM
☐ CBC/AUTOMATED DIFF
☐ CBC/NO DIFF (HEMOGRAM)
☐ CHLORIDE
☐ CK-MB

☐ CPK
☐ CREATININE
☐ GLUCOSE
____ MEAL ____ GLUCOLA
☐ GLUCOSE
____ 1 HR PP ____ 2 HR PP
☐ GTT (ORAL)
____ 2 HR ____ 3 HR (PREGNANCY)
☐ HEMATOCRIT
☐ HEMOGLOBIN
☐ INFLUENZA A & B
☐ KOH PREP
☐ LDH
☐ LIPASE
☐ MAGNESIUM

☐ MONO SCREEN
☐ PLATELET COUNT
☐ POTASSIUM
☐ PROTEIN TOTAL
☐ PROTIME WITH INR
☐ RSV
☐ SED RATE, WESTERGREN
☐ SODIUM
☐ TROPONIN (FINGERSTICK)
☐ UA URINE DIP/REFLEXED MICROSCOPIC
☐ URIC ACID
☐ URINALYSIS, COMPLETE
☐ WET PREP

Tests Performed At: _____

☐ ALPHA FETO PROTEIN
(Complete separate form)
☐ ANTIBODY SCREEN
☐ ASO SLIDE 0 WITH REFLEXED TITER
☐ BETA HCG, QUANT
☐ CA-125
☐ CARCINOEMBRYONIC ANTIGEN (CEA)
☐ CHOLESTEROL
☐ HDL CHOLESTEROL ☐ LDL DIRECT
☐ CORTISOL, SERUM
____ AM ____ PM ____ RANDOM
☐ DIGOXIN
☐ DILANTIN
☐ DIRECT COOMBS

☐ DRUG ABUSE SCREEN, URINE
____ WITH ETOH
____ WITH CONFIRMATION
☐ ESTRADIOL
☐ FERRITIN
☐ FOLATE
☐ GLYCOSOLATED HEMOGLOBIN (A1C)
☐ HEPATITIS B SURFACE ANTIBODY
☐ HEPATITIS B SURFACE ANTIGEN (w/conf)
☐ HIV SCREEN WITH CONFIRMATION
☐ IRON
☐ IRON BINDING CAPACITY
☐ LITHIUM
☐ PHOSPHORUS

☐ PROSTATIC SPECIFIC ANTIGEN (PSA)
____ DIAGNOSTIC ____ SCREEN
____ FREE & TOTAL
☐ PTT (PARTIAL THROMBOPLASTIN TIME)
☐ RETICULOCYTE COUNT
☐ RH IMMUNE GLOBULIN
☐ RA WITH REFLEXED TITER
☐ RPR
____ WITH FTA CONFIRMATION
☐ T4 ☐ T3 UPTAKE ☐ T4, FREE
☐ THEOPHYLLINE

PANELS:
☐ COMPREHENSIVE PANEL: ALB, ALK PHOS, ALT, AST, T BIL, BUN, CA, CREAT, GLUC, CO2, NA, K, CL, TP
☐ BASIC METABOLIC: GLUC, BUN, CREAT, NA, K, CL, CO2, CALCIUM
☐ HEPATIC FUNCTION: T BILI, D BILI, ALBUMIN, ALK PHOS, AST, ALT, TOTAL PROTEIN
☐ ELECTROLYTES
☐ THYROID STIMULATING HORMONE (TSH)
☐ TRIGLYCERIDES
☐ TRIPLE SCREEN *(Complete separate form)*
☐ TROPONIN

☐ TYPE AND RH
☐ VITAMIN B12
☐ LIPID PANEL: CHOL, TRIG, HDL, CALCULATED LDL, CHOL: HDL
☐ HEPATITIS PANEL: HBSAG, HB CORE, HEP A, HEP C
☐ PRENATAL PROFILE 1 (OB PANEL): CBC/HISTO DIFF, RUBELLA, TYPE & RH, ANTIBODY SCREEN, RPR, HBSAG, GLUCOSE
☐ PRENATAL PROFILE 2: CBC/NO DIFF, RPR, ANTIBODY SCREEN, GLUCOSE
☐ RENAL FUNCTION PANEL: ALB, CA, CO2, CL, CREAT, GLUC, PHOS, NA, K, BUN

Physician's Signature: _____   Date: _____

White copy • Medical record   Yellow copy • Lab testing dept.   Pink copy • Coding (attach to fee ticket)

Figure 12-8 ◆ Sample diagnostic test request form

anemia would justify a CBC, and chest pain or complaints of palpitations would justify the EKG.

In-House Ordering

With a POL in the office, the physician may have certain routine tests performed on patients. An example is checking the urine sample of a pregnant patient for glucose and protein. This would be considered a standing order and would be conducted before the patient is seen by the physician. Other diagnostic tests may be performed after the patient sees the physician, while the patient waits for the results, or before the patient leaves the office. If the patient leaves before the physician knows the results, the patient is contacted for follow-up.

Keys to Success
PRECERTIFICATION AND REIMBURSEMENT

Reimbursement is often based on precertification. Payment for services can be denied if precertification is not obtained, in which case either the patient or the ordering physician is held responsible for paying the charges. *All* required precertifications *must* be obtained and documented on the patient's chart.

Standing orders are signed by the physician and placed in the patient's chart. Billing third-party providers requires a diagnosis appropriate for the test, test documentation, results, and any follow-up treatment or additional testing.

PROCEDURE 12-2 **Obtain a Precertification by Telephone**

Theory

When precertification is requested and granted, a number is usually assigned to it. This information may be necessary at a later time if an insurance claim reimbursement is denied. Record the number, date, time, and name of the contact person on the patient's chart. Make sure any required forms are completed. If a reasonable amount of time has passed without a response to a filed insurance claim, you may use the documented contact information to follow up. Either fax the form to the anticipated provider or give it to the patient to hand-carry to the provider, and place a copy in the patient chart.

Materials

- precertification log book
- telephone and telephone number
- tickler file containing contact information
- blue or black ink pen

Competency

(**Conditions**) With the necessary materials, you will be able to (**Task**) complete the precertification (**Standards**) within the time and to the degree of accuracy designated by the instructor.

1. Gather the patient chart and insurance contact information.
2. Telephone the insurance carrier and follow voice prompts if given.
3. When the telephone receptionist or voice prompt asks if the claim question is from a physician, medical office, or patient, state the physician's name or the medical office's name.
4. Ask the person at the insurance company for his or her full name. Document the name, time of telephone contact, and date in the precertification log book.
5. Give the necessary information: diagnosis, procedure(s) anticipated, treatment location, and whether it is an inpatient or outpatient procedure.
6. Document the precertification number in the log book as it is given and repeat the number to your contact person to verify. Thank the insurance contact person.

7. In the designated area of the patient chart, following office policy, document the name of the insurance contact person, the time, precertification number(s) given for the procedures anticipated, treatment location, and whether it is an inpatient or outpatient procedure.
8. Complete necessary an inpatient or outpatient procedure forms.
9. Make a copy and give it to the patient.
10. Place the original forms on the chart.

Patient Education

Inform the patient of the results of the precertification process. Instruct the patient to keep the precertification number with other information and to call the insurance company for further assistance if the precertification process does not bring the desired results or if payment is denied.

Charting Example

10/29/XX 10:45 a.m. Prudential Insurance called for Policy No. 393-29-3939. Contact was made with Mr. John Paymelater. Precertification No. 256789 was given for hospital admission, cancer of the colon, surgical resection of colon with colostomy. Pt also instructed to keep record of precertification number. Ashley Murdock, RMA

10/29/XX 2:30 p.m. Arrangements have been made for lab studies, EKG, and chest x-ray for 11/4. Arrangements have been made for hospital admission on 11/5. Precertification No. 256789 has been given to inpatient and outpatient areas. Pt called and instructed to report to the ambulatory clinic at 8 a.m. on 11/4 for outpatient registration and diagnostic testing. Pt also instructed not to drink or eat anything after midnight on mornings of diagnostic testing or surgery. Patient instructed to report to Caring Hospital by 6 a.m. on 11/5. Patient voiced understanding of instructions and repeated them correctly. Ashley Murdock, RMA

Precertification

Many third-party providers, or insurance carriers, require precertification for diagnostic testing. It is good policy to establish and maintain a file containing precertification requirements and guidelines for various third-party providers. Many providers contract with specific facilities to provide the services at a reduced rate for guaranteed reimbursement.

Precertification by Telephone

Before scheduling a diagnostic test, the medical office must contact the insurance carrier to confirm coverage and the facilities where the test may be performed.

Scheduling with Outside Agencies

Since not all diagnostic tests can be performed in the office, you will be responsible for coordinating test ordering and scheduling (Figure 12-9 ◆). Factors to consider when scheduling include the patient's condition, the timely or urgent need for diagnostic information, the patient's employment schedule, home and family responsibilities, and transportation availability. Discuss these factors with the patient before you contact the outside agency for scheduling.

Critical Thinking Question 12-1

Jason is scheduling a patient for a laboratory procedure to be done at another location. He has offered the patient several appointment times, but she has rejected each one, saying she has too many other things she needs to do. How should Jason handle this?

You should have the following information before scheduling procedures with outside agencies: the patient's name,

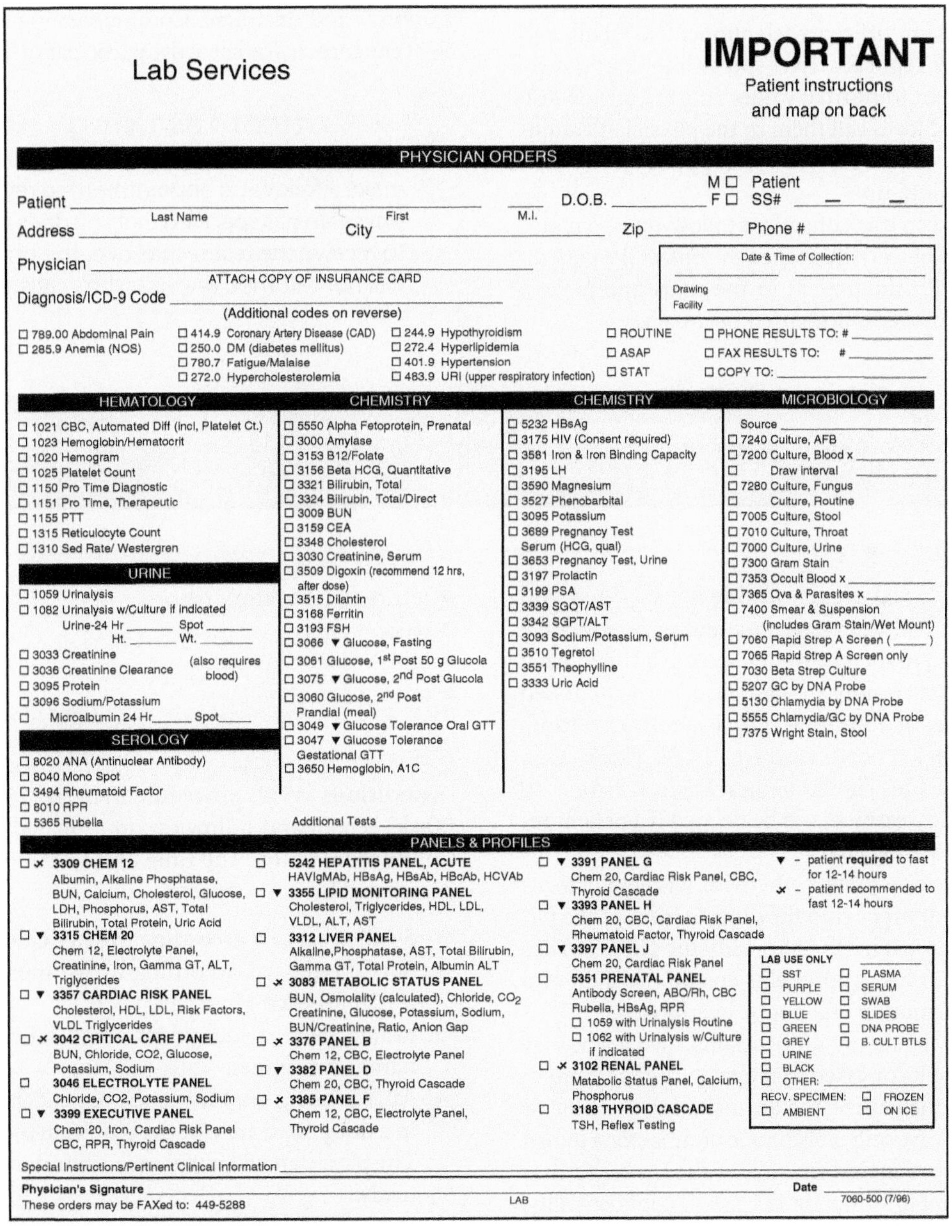

Lab Services

IMPORTANT
Patient instructions and map on back

PHYSICIAN ORDERS

Patient ______ (Last Name) ______ (First) ______ (M.I.) D.O.B. ______ M ☐ F ☐ Patient SS# ___ – ___ – ___
Address ______ City ______ Zip ______ Phone # ______
Physician ______
ATTACH COPY OF INSURANCE CARD
Diagnosis/ICD-9 Code ______
(Additional codes on reverse)

Date & Time of Collection: ______ ______
Drawing Facility ______

☐ 789.00 Abdominal Pain
☐ 285.9 Anemia (NOS)
☐ 414.9 Coronary Artery Disease (CAD)
☐ 250.0 DM (diabetes mellitus)
☐ 780.7 Fatigue/Malaise
☐ 272.0 Hypercholesterolemia
☐ 244.9 Hypothyroidism
☐ 272.4 Hyperlipidemia
☐ 401.9 Hypertension
☐ 483.9 URI (upper respiratory infection)
☐ ROUTINE
☐ ASAP
☐ STAT
☐ PHONE RESULTS TO: # ______
☐ FAX RESULTS TO: # ______
☐ COPY TO: ______

HEMATOLOGY
☐ 1021 CBC, Automated Diff (incl, Platelet Ct.)
☐ 1023 Hemoglobin/Hematocrit
☐ 1020 Hemogram
☐ 1025 Platelet Count
☐ 1150 Pro Time Diagnostic
☐ 1151 Pro Time, Therapeutic
☐ 1155 PTT
☐ 1315 Reticulocyte Count
☐ 1310 Sed Rate/ Westergren

URINE
☐ 1059 Urinalysis
☐ 1082 Urinalysis w/Culture if indicated
Urine-24 Hr ______ Spot ______
Ht. ______ Wt. ______
☐ 3033 Creatinine
☐ 3036 Creatinine Clearance (also requires blood)
☐ 3095 Protein
☐ 3096 Sodium/Potassium
☐ Microalbumin 24 Hr ______ Spot ______

SEROLOGY
☐ 8020 ANA (Antinuclear Antibody)
☐ 8040 Mono Spot
☐ 3494 Rheumatoid Factor
☐ 8010 RPR
☐ 5365 Rubella

CHEMISTRY
☐ 5550 Alpha Fetoprotein, Prenatal
☐ 3000 Amylase
☐ 3153 B12/Folate
☐ 3156 Beta HCG, Quantitative
☐ 3321 Bilirubin, Total
☐ 3324 Bilirubin, Total/Direct
☐ 3009 BUN
☐ 3159 CEA
☐ 3348 Cholesterol
☐ 3030 Creatinine, Serum
☐ 3509 Digoxin (recommend 12 hrs, after dose)
☐ 3515 Dilantin
☐ 3168 Ferritin
☐ 3193 FSH
☐ 3066 ▼ Glucose, Fasting
☐ 3061 Glucose, 1st Post 50 g Glucola
☐ 3075 ▼ Glucose, 2nd Post Glucola
☐ 3060 Glucose, 2nd Post Prandial (meal)
☐ 3049 ▼ Glucose Tolerance Oral GTT
☐ 3047 ▼ Glucose Tolerance Gestational GTT
☐ 3650 Hemoglobin, A1C

CHEMISTRY
☐ 5232 HBsAg
☐ 3175 HIV (Consent required)
☐ 3581 Iron & Iron Binding Capacity
☐ 3195 LH
☐ 3590 Magnesium
☐ 3527 Phenobarbital
☐ 3095 Potassium
☐ 3689 Pregnancy Test Serum (HCG, qual)
☐ 3653 Pregnancy Test, Urine
☐ 3197 Prolactin
☐ 3199 PSA
☐ 3339 SGOT/AST
☐ 3342 SGPT/ALT
☐ 3093 Sodium/Potassium, Serum
☐ 3510 Tegretol
☐ 3551 Theophylline
☐ 3333 Uric Acid

MICROBIOLOGY
Source ______
☐ 7240 Culture, AFB
☐ 7200 Culture, Blood x ______
☐ Draw interval ______
☐ 7280 Culture, Fungus
☐ Culture, Routine
☐ 7005 Culture, Stool
☐ 7010 Culture, Throat
☐ 7000 Culture, Urine
☐ 7300 Gram Stain
☐ 7353 Occult Blood x ______
☐ 7365 Ova & Parasites x ______
☐ 7400 Smear & Suspension (includes Gram Stain/Wet Mount)
☐ 7060 Rapid Strep A Screen (______)
☐ 7065 Rapid Strep A Screen only
☐ 7030 Beta Strep Culture
☐ 5207 GC by DNA Probe
☐ 5130 Chlamydia by DNA Probe
☐ 5555 Chlamydia/GC by DNA Probe
☐ 7375 Wright Stain, Stool

Additional Tests ______

PANELS & PROFILES
☐ ✗ **3309 CHEM 12** Albumin, Alkaline Phosphatase, BUN, Calcium, Cholesterol, Glucose, LDH, Phosphorus, AST, Total Bilirubin, Total Protein, Uric Acid
☐ ▼ **3315 CHEM 20** Chem 12, Electrolyte Panel, Creatinine, Iron, Gamma GT, ALT, Triglycerides
☐ ▼ **3357 CARDIAC RISK PANEL** Cholesterol, HDL, LDL, Risk Factors, VLDL Triglycerides
☐ ✗ **3042 CRITICAL CARE PANEL** BUN, Chloride, CO2, Glucose, Potassium, Sodium
☐ **3046 ELECTROLYTE PANEL** Chloride, CO2, Potassium, Sodium
☐ ▼ **3399 EXECUTIVE PANEL** Chem 20, Iron, Cardiac Risk Panel CBC, RPR, Thyroid Cascade
☐ **5242 HEPATITIS PANEL, ACUTE** HAVIgMAb, HBsAg, HBsAb, HBcAb, HCVAb
☐ ▼ **3355 LIPID MONITORING PANEL** Cholesterol, Triglycerides, HDL, LDL, VLDL, ALT, AST
☐ **3312 LIVER PANEL** Alkaline,Phosphatase, AST, Total Bilirubin, Gamma GT, Total Protein, Albumin ALT
☐ ✗ **3083 METABOLIC STATUS PANEL** BUN, Osmolality (calculated), Chloride, CO_2 Creatinine, Glucose, Potassium, Sodium, BUN/Creatinine, Ratio, Anion Gap
☐ ✗ **3376 PANEL B** Chem 12, CBC, Electrolyte Panel
☐ ▼ **3382 PANEL D** Chem 20, CBC, Thyroid Cascade
☐ ✗ **3385 PANEL F** Chem 12, CBC, Electrolyte Panel, Thyroid Cascade
☐ ▼ **3391 PANEL G** Chem 20, Cardiac Risk Panel, CBC, Thyroid Cascade
☐ ▼ **3393 PANEL H** Chem 20, CBC, Cardiac Risk Panel, Rheumatoid Factor, Thyroid Cascade
☐ ▼ **3397 PANEL J** Chem 20, Cardiac Risk Panel
☐ **5351 PRENATAL PANEL** Antibody Screen, ABO/Rh, CBC Rubella, HBsAg, RPR
☐ 1059 with Urinalysis Routine
☐ 1062 with Urinalysis w/Culture if indicated
☐ ✗ **3102 RENAL PANEL** Matabolic Status Panel, Calcium, Phosphorus
☐ **3188 THYROID CASCADE** TSH, Reflex Testing

▼ – patient **required** to fast for 12-14 hours
✗ – patient recommended to fast 12-14 hours

LAB USE ONLY ______
☐ SST ☐ PLASMA
☐ PURPLE ☐ SERUM
☐ YELLOW ☐ SWAB
☐ BLUE ☐ SLIDES
☐ GREEN ☐ DNA PROBE
☐ GREY ☐ B. CULT BTLS
☐ URINE
☐ BLACK
☐ OTHER: ______
RECV. SPECIMEN: ☐ FROZEN
☐ AMBIENT ☐ ON ICE

Special Instructions/Pertinent Clinical Information ______
Physician's Signature ______ **Date** ______
These orders may be FAXed to: 449-5288
LAB
7060-500 (7/96)

Figure 12-9 ◆ Requisition form for outside laboratory

address, phone number, DOB, social security number (**SSN**), insurance or financial responsibility, type of test to be ordered, precertification requirements, and individuals or agencies to whom the results are to be released. Once the test is scheduled, it must be confirmed with the patient both verbally and in writing.

Provide the patient with directions, verbally and in writing, to the testing facility. Instruct the patient on what to do before the test, again verbally and in writing, with understanding confirmed verbally. In the patient chart, document precertification, arrangements made, directions given to which facilities, instructions given for tests, and that instructions were verbal and written.

Screening and Following Up Test Results

Diagnostic reports on studies done in reference laboratories are returned to the physician office by telephone, fax, email, and U.S. mail. When these reports arrive, you will look at the results and compare them to normal values (norm) for the test. Flag any abnormal results to call them to the physician's attention. Record any intervention ordered by the physician and contact the patient for follow-up.

An easy way to keep track of patient follow-up is to maintain a tickler card file that alerts you when to contact the patient. Document contact with the patient in the chart and make a note on the card for further follow-up if necessary.

TABLE 12-2 INFORMATION ON A DIAGNOSTIC TEST REPORT
1. Diagnostic facility name, address, telephone number, fax number, and any identification number.
2. Ordering physician's name, address, telephone number, and other information
3. Patient name, address, telephone number, and other information
4. Patient's ID number
5. Date specimen was received by facility
6. Date of report of test results
7. Tests performed
8. Test results
9. Normal values or range for tests performed

Once all reports are reviewed and the physician has completed or delegated all necessary communication, the reports are filed with the patient chart (Table 12-2). Some offices file the reports in a special section identified as laboratory reports.

Diagnostic test results are an integral part of the physician's diagnosis and treatment. Communicating test results to the patient enhances his or her active participation in the treatment plan.

? —Critical Thinking Question 12-2—
Jason has called the patient several times this week to make a follow-up appointment to review test results. The physician has specified that she does not want the patient to receive the test results over the phone. But the patient has not returned any of Jason's calls. What can he do?

PROCEDURE 12-3 Demonstrate Screening and Follow-up of Test Results

Theory

When the procedure or laboratory testing is completed, you or other office staff will inform the patient approximately when the test results will be known. Designate a time to call the patient. Laboratory results are sent, faxed, or telephoned to the medical office. In a multiple-physician office setting, sort mailed laboratory reports according to physician, then alphabetically. Be alert for similar names. Medical errors can occur and therapeutic treatment can be delayed if a patient report is placed in the wrong chart.

Unless the physician prefers otherwise, it is helpful to attach the new laboratory report to the outside front of the patient chart. Do *not* place it in the chart until the physician has read and initialed it. This action helps ensure that new and critical medical information will not be overlooked.

Depending on the nature of the results, the patient may be called with the results or asked to return to discuss them in the office. If you call the patient and an answering machine or voicemail comes on, leave only a telephone number for a return call. Do *not* leave any patient information on the answering machine. Leaving medical information is a risk to confidentiality, as someone other than the patient may listen to the message.

Materials
- returned laboratory reports
- patient chart
- blue or black ink pen
- telephone

Competency

(**Conditions**) With procedure materials, you will be able to (**Task**) screen and follow up on returned laboratory results (**Standards**) within the time and to the degree of accuracy designated by the instructor.

1. Sort lab reports according to physician.
2. Sort the reports according to last name, first name, and initial for each physician.
3. Match patient identification numbers in cases where names are similar.
4. Attach the new reports to the patient chart and place them in a designated area for the physician to read and interpret. The physician will initial each laboratory test that he or she reads.

PROCEDURE 12-3 Demonstrate Screening and Follow-up of Test Results *(continued)*

5. Call patients with their laboratory results or set up appointments to discuss the results as designated by the physician. If an answering machine or voicemail is activated, do not include patient information in your message. Leave a phone number for the patient to return the call.
6. Place the laboratory reports in the chart according to office procedure.
7. On a tickler file, note the next scheduled date for routinely scheduled laboratory procedures.
8. Work with the patient to schedule the next appointment if the laboratory procedure is weekly or monthly.

Patient Education
Inform the patient approximately when the results will be known. Ask the patient what time of day would be best for you to call with the results.

Charting Example
07/19/XX 1:00 p.m. Results of Hgb and Hct performed on 07/18/XX within normal limits. Pt notified per physician's instructions. Jordan Leonard, CMA

REVIEW

Chapter Summary

- Diagnostic test information plays an important role in the diagnosis and confirmation of disease or wellness. Laboratory testing is done in either a POL or an independently owned and operated reference laboratory. The main advantage of POLs is quick testing and results. The primary advantage of reference laboratories is their capacity to perform higher-complexity tests.

- As an MA, you will perform waived testing. In some states, with supervision and training, you may be able to perform duties related to preparing specimens or doing mechanized testing.

- CLIA, a federal act, established quality standards for laboratory testing. The accuracy of laboratory testing affects diagnosis, treatment, medication, and dosages. Three categories of tests have been established: waived tests, moderate complexity-tests, and high-complexity tests. Quality standards are specified for proficiency testing (PT), quality control, quality assurance, patient test management, and personnel qualifications. Regulations affecting laboratory procedures are increasingly more stringent as tests become more complex to perform.

- Quality control ensures that test results are valid and reliable. It is the goal of quality control to detect and eliminate errors that may interfere with accurate test results.

- Quality assurance is a form of outcomes assessment that reviews documentation of test results, services provided, and other recorded data. This information is compared with acceptable standards of testing.

- A hospital usually has two laboratory divisions. One is the clinical division, which performs numerous diagnostic tests such as hematology and serology. The other is the surgical and anatomical laboratory, which performs autopsies, biopsies, surgical histology, and cytology. JCAHO has established guidelines regarding quality of care by hospitals and health-care agencies, including laboratory settings.

- FDA, EPA, and OSHA are federal agencies that regulate the safety of patients and health-care employees. The Safe Medical Devices Act of 1990 requires reporting to the manufacturer and/or the FDA any incidents that reasonably suggest that a medical device caused or contributed to a serious injury to or death of a patient. It also requires enforcing the use of safe medical devices when drawing or handling blood or other body fluids.

- Equipment used in the laboratory includes centrifuges, microscopes, autoclaves, measurement tools, and electronic equipment such as analyzers. Training in the use of laboratory equipment includes safety and CLIA guidelines.

- The physician writes an order for laboratory testing on a laboratory request or prescription form. Demographic and insurance data, along with ICD-9-CM and CPT, are included on the forms.

- Precertification is often required to ensure insurance provider payment. Some orders for laboratory testing within the physician's office are routine and are called standing orders.

Chapter Summary *(continued)*

Preprinted standing orders are placed in the patient chart for signing later by the physician. Precertification must be obtained or insurance claims filed for standing orders.

- As an MA, you may need to schedule procedures or laboratory testing outside the physician's office. When diagnostic reports are returned to the physician's office, you will review

and compare the results against norms and flag abnormal results for the physician. The physician will give you directions for following up test results with the patient or in some cases may personally call the patient. Diagnostic reports are placed in the chart and follow-up is documented.

Chapter Review Questions

Multiple Choice

1. Which of the following is true about a reference laboratory?
   A. It is convenient for the patient.
   B. It performs high-level testing.
   C. Test results are returned more quickly than from a POL.
   D. The regulations are different for a reference lab than for a POL.

2. As an MA working in a POL, you may obtain a(n)
   A. biopsy.
   B. bone marrow specimen.
   C. immunoassay.
   D. capillary specimen.

3. Quality assurance is a type of
   A. methodology.
   B. outcome assessment.
   C. instruction.
   D. calibration.

4. The FDA oversees
   A. evaluation of medical equipment.
   B. disposal of biohazardous waste.
   C. disposal of chemical waste.
   D. evaluation of PPE.

5. If a medical device may cause serious injury to a patient, it should be reported to
   A. FDA.
   B. OSHA.
   C. EPA.
   D. HCFA.

6. A physician order to a reference laboratory must be signed within
   A. 5 days.
   B. 30 days.
   C. 10 days.
   D. 20 days.

7. After precertification has been granted by an insurance company, you should receive a(n)
   A. treatment location.
   B. set of forms.
   C. set of labels for charts.
   D. assigned number.

8. In a POL, a standing order is a
   A. high-complexity test.
   B. routine test.
   C. prescription form.
   D. third-party billing form.

9. In a multiple-physician office, which of the following is the first step in handling laboratory reports?
   A. sorting reports by physician
   B. sorting reports by alphabetical order
   C. sorting reports by similar names
   D. sorting reports by size

10. Which of the following should you do when contacting a patient by phone about his or her test results?
    A. Leave a detailed message on the answering machine if the patient is not at home.
    B. Leave a detailed message with whoever answers the phone if the patient is not at home.
    C. Leave a phone number for a return call.
    D. Leave no message and call back at a later date.

True/False

T F   1. When using equipment, you are required to follow OSHA and Clinical Laboratory Improvement Amendments (CLIA) guidelines.

T F   2. Blood glucose and urine pregnancy tests have been approved by the FDA for patients to use at home.

T F   3. Blood chemistries and urine cultures are categorized as moderate-complexity tests.

T F   4. Quality control before testing means only checking that the patient has used the appropriate container for collection.

T F   5. A high-complexity test is so named because it takes longer to perform than a moderate- or low-complexity test.

Short Answer

1. What is quality control?
2. Name the two federal agencies that enforce safety standards.
3. What are waived tests? Name several examples.
4. What is the purpose of autopsies?
5. What is the function of a glucometer?

Chapter Review Questions *(continued)*

Research

1. Are medical assistants allowed to perform capillary and venipuncture mechanized tests in your local area?

2. Are MAs in your state allowed to centrifuge urine and blood specimens?

Externship Application Experience

As an extern, you are observing an MA in the office as she performs a glucose test using a glucometer. The quality control log specifies daily quality control checks on the glucometer. While cleaning and organizing the area after the test, however, you notice that no quality control checks have been logged in the past two days. What should you do?

Resource Guide

Environmental Protection Agency (EPA)
1200 Pennsylvania Ave., NW
Washington, DC 20460
www.epa.gov

Food and Drug Administration
5600 Fishers Lane
Rockville, MD 20857-0001
1-888-463-6332 (1-888-INFO-FDA)
www.FDA.gov

Health Care Financing Administration (HCFA)
www.hcfa.gov

MedMedia
www.prenhall.com/frazier

More on this chapter, including interactive resources, can be found on the Student CD-ROM accompanying this textbook and on the Companion Website at www.prenhall.com/frazier.

CHAPTER 13

Microscopes and Microbiology

Case Study

Irene has been working in a clinical laboratory for several months and is very comfortable obtaining specimens and using the microscopes. During one particularly busy day Irene identifies the organism *Escherichia coli* in the sample of a patient who has been complaining of urinary frequency, burning, and an inability to fully empty the bladder. The next sample she tests is from a toddler. The parents state that the little girl has had a runny nose for more than ten days and developed a rash with a crust over it directly under her nose. The doctor wants to check the toddler for impetigo, which is caused by *Staphyloccus aureus*, which Irene will be able to easily identify by shape.

Objectives

After completing this chapter, you should be able to:

■ Spell and define medical terminology in this chapter.
■ Define the medical assistant's role in microbiological testing and specimen collection.
■ Identify various types of microscopes and explain when each is used.
■ Identify the structures of a microscope and the function of each.
■ Explain how to use and maintain a microscope.
■ Discuss bacterial nomenclature and grouping.
■ Describe the normal flora present in the body.
■ Discuss how bacteria, parasites, and viruses cause disease.
■ Explain how to prepare a specimen smear.
■ Define gram staining and discuss when it is used.
■ Explain the three ways to prepare wet mount slides.
■ Discuss the role of stool specimens in the diagnosis of disease and how they are obtained.
■ Explain culture and sensitivity testing.
■ Describe how urine culture specimens are collected.

 MedMedia

www.prenhall.com/frazier

Additional interactive resources and activities for this chapter can be found on the Companion Website. For audio glossary, legal and ethical scenarios, job scenarios, quizzes, and games related to the content of this chapter, please access the accompanying CD-ROM in this book.

Assets Available:

Audio Glossary
Legal and Ethical Scenario: *Microscopes and Microbiology*
On the Job Scenario: *Microscopes and Microbiology*
Multiple Choice Quiz
Games: Crossword, Strikeout, and Spelling Bee

✚ MEDICAL ASSISTING COMPETENCIES

CAAHEP ENTRY-LEVEL COMPETENCIES FOR CMA	ABHES ENTRY-LEVEL COMPETENCIES FOR RMA
■ Identify and respond to issues of confidentiality.	■ Project a positive attitude.
■ Perform within legal and ethical boundaries.	■ Maintain confidentiality at all times.
■ Demonstrate knowledge of federal and state health-care legislation and regulations.	■ Be a "team player."
	■ Be cognizant of ethical boundaries.
■ Perform hand washing.	■ Exhibit initiative.
■ Dispose of biohazardous materials.	■ Adapt to change.
■ Practice Standard Precautions.	■ Evidence a responsible attitude.
■ Obtain throat specimen for microbiological testing.	■ Be courteous and diplomatic.
■ Instruct patients in the collection of fecal specimens.	■ Conduct work within scope of education, training, and ability.
	■ Practice Standard Precautions.
■ Use methods of quality control.	■ Use quality control.
■ Perform microbiology testing.	■ Collect and process specimens.
■ Screen and follow up test results.	■ Dispose of biohazardous materials.
	■ Obtain throat specimen for microbiological testing.
	■ Perform wound collection procedure for microbiological testing.
	■ Perform microbiology testing.
	■ Instruct patients in the collection of fecal specimen.

Introduction

The microscope is used to magnify and examine blood and urine specimens to detect the presence of pathogenic organisms. The diagnosis of an illness is not always clear based on the patient's complaints or symptoms and may require diagnostic testing using the microscope. Each step in preparing a slide for microscopic examination is time sensitive and critical to proper diagnosis.

The Medical Assistant's Role in Specimen Collection

The physician will require your assistance in preparing the patient, collecting the specimen, and processing and/or transporting the specimen. With classroom training and competency completion, you will help with microbiology testing by preparing the specimen for examination under the microscope. You will also be involved in patient education when the patient collects the specimen, as in the case of urine collection. Laboratory results are only as accurate as the specimen provided.

Medical Terminology

binocular—having two eyepieces (on a microscope)

eukaryotes—group of microorganisms, such as fungi and parasites, that have organized nuclear material and organelles to assist in reproduction

microbiology—the study of microorganisms

monocular—having one eyepiece (on a microscope)

morphology—the study of shape or form; in microbiology, a method of classifying bacteria according to shape

mycology—study of fungi, such as yeast and molds

normal flora—generally harmless microorganisms common in the human body

ocular—pertaining to the eye; also, the microscope's eyepiece

opportunistic pathogen—normally nonpathogenic microorganism that causes disease in a host whose immune resistance has been lowered by certain disorders or treatments

organelle—a very small organ-functioning unit within a living cell; mitochondria organelles are responsible for the metabolism of lipids and the synthesis (building) of proteins

parasitology—branch of biology that studies parasites

pathogenicity—ability of an organism to cause disease

prokaryotes—group of microorganisms, such as bacteria, that lack an organized nucleus and cytoplasmic organelles

serology—laboratory science in which blood serum is tested for the presence of antibodies

staph—*Staphylococcus*

strep—*Streptococcus*

ultramicroscopic—requiring magnification with an electron microscope to be seen

virology—specialized branch of microbiology that studies viruses and associated diseases

viruses—ultramicroscopic, nonliving organisms classified as microorganisms because they contain DNA or RNA and are capable of parasitic metabolism and reproduction

Abbreviations

KOH—potassium hydroxide
QNS—quantity not sufficient
QS—quantity sufficient
UTI—urinary tract infection

Keys to Success
OTHER TYPES OF MICROSCOPES

- The dissection microscope is used to look at larger specimens but cannot examine single cells because of its low magnification.
- In a confocal microscope, a laser light scans the specimen and the image appears on a computer screen for examination.
- Scanning electron and transmission electron microscopes use electron illumination for high magnification and 3D or 2D images, respectively. They are used in pathology examination and research.

Microscopes

In 1665, in his work *Micrographia,* Robert Hooke published intricate, highly accurate drawings of tiny creatures such as fleas that he had observed through an early microscope. Based on his work, Anton van Leeuwenhoek (1632–1723), a Dutch lens maker, proposed that illness and disease were caused by something too small to be seen with the naked eye. In an effort to see these mysterious entities, he invented the first light microscope. He examined water from a local pond and saw tiny, motile organisms living in it. His invention was a startling breakthrough for the scientific community and was the foundation for the field of **microbiology**, the study of microorganisms.

Types of Microscopes

Five kinds of microscopes are routinely used in laboratories (Table 13-1). The type of microscope you use is determined by the specimen and the particular examination the physician requests.

Structure and Parts of a Microscope

The magnification of an object by a microscope is accomplished by the interaction of visible light and the lens systems. The lenses of a microscope are convex (curved outward in the middle). The curvature refracts, or bends, the light waves as they pass through the lenses. Lens sizes and degree of curvature are directly related to the degree of magnification. When an object is illuminated by the light source, the light goes through the lens system and forms an optical replica from the refracted light. The real image is projected and magnified, forming a virtual image that is the reverse of the real image. The virtual image is the one the user sees.

The component parts of an optical microscope include the **oculars**, objectives (lenses), oil immersion objective, arm and focus controls, light source, stage, and substage (Figure 13-1 ◆).

Oculars

The microscope may be **monocular** (one eyepiece) or **binocular** (two eyepieces). The eyepieces on binoculars can be adjusted to compensate for differences in the visual acuity of the user's eyes and to comfortably fit the distance between the eyes. A

TABLE 13-1 TYPES OF MICROSCOPES

Type	Use	Magnification	Light	Stain
Compound or bright field	Most common type. Specimen is dark against an illuminated background.	Two magnification systems 100X to 1000X	Located below the specimen	Stained and unstained
Phase contrast	Thickness provides the contrast needed to see the live specimen. Thin areas are light; thick areas are dark. Background is dark.	100X to 1000X	Passes through or is deflected by the specimen	Unstained
Dark field	Light is deflected from the specimen, so the image is seen on a dark background.	100X to 1000X	Light source is projected from below. Condenser does not allow light to pass through the specimen. Light is directed at an angle.	Unstained
Fluorescence compound	Light rays are directed through a tube, a series of filters, a mirror, then through the ocular lens system, which illuminates the specimen on a black background.	100X to 1000X	Mercury lamp emits light rays.	Stained with special fluorescent stains. Colors range from bright yellow to orange to lime green.
Electron	Used to view ultramicroscopic organisms or individual cellular components. Image is formed on a screen, as in a television.	Up to 100,000 times normal size	Power source excites electrons through an electromagnetic field.	Stained and unstained

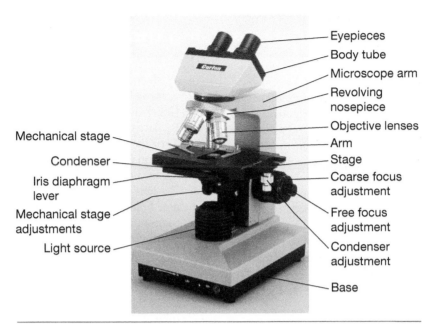

Eyepieces
Body tube
Microscope arm
Revolving nosepiece
Objective lenses
Arm
Stage
Coarse focus adjustment
Free focus adjustment
Condenser adjustment
Base

Mechanical stage
Condenser
Iris diaphragm lever
Mechanical stage adjustments
Light source

Figure 13-1 ◆ Binocular microscope with parts labeled

magnifying lens mounted at the top of the tube magnifies the image ten times and is called a 10X lens.

Objectives

The tube of the microscope contains a series of mirrors that reflect light and the image to be viewed. At the end of the tube is a revolving nosepiece that houses the objectives. Objectives include 10X (low power), 40X (high dry), and 100X (immersion oil) lenses. Total magnification of the microscope is the ocular magnification multiplied by the objective used. For example, if viewing an object with the 40X objective you have a total magnification of 400X, or ocular × objective (10 × 40 = 400). Other objectives may be added for special applications.

Oil Immersion Objective

Immersion oil must be used with the 100X lens to increase the resolution, or clarity. Higher resolution clarifies and sharpens the image. The oil fills the space between the slide and the objective, decreasing the number of deflected rays and wavelength changes that occur after the light passes through the specimen.

Arm and Focus Control

The arm is used to mount the focusing system and to suspend the ocular system over the stage area. Focus adjustment knobs are located on the arm near the base. Microscopes have fine and coarse adjustment knobs. One knob assembly often houses both. Coarse adjustment knobs are on the outside diameter, and fine focus knobs are contained in the inside diameter.

Light Source

The light source, the condenser, and the diaphragm are located under the mechanical stage. The condenser directs light rays from the light source through the diaphragm. The diaphragm

is adjustable, which allows the user to increase or decrease the amount of light from the source lamp. The microscope base contains a power cord, a tungsten lamp light source, and an on/off switch.

Stage

The mechanical stage is a flat surface on which specimens are placed. Stage clips hold the specimen slide in place. It can be moved forward or to the right or left so that the user can view the entire slide. An opening in the stage allows light to be directed through the condenser and diaphragm to illuminate the slide.

Substage

The condenser is located below the stage on the substage, where it directs concentrated light through the specimen. The iris, below the substage, opens and closes like a camera shutter, controlling the amount of light that illuminates the specimen.

Using the Microscope

The proper use of a microscope is crucial to examining specimens successfully. Remember that you are viewing the image in reverse and upside down. You turn the stage focus knob left to move the slide to your right. To move the image up or down, you turn the adjustment knob clockwise or counterclockwise. You can adjust the amount of light by opening the diaphragm, closing the diaphragm, adjusting the condenser, or, with some microscopes, using the built-in light adjustment system.

As an MA you will be responsible for cleaning, maintaining, and operating the microscope. When not in use, the microscope must be covered. Unplug the cord and wrap it loosely around the microscope. When you move it, hold it by the arm, supporting it at the base.

PROCEDURE 13-1 Demonstrate Using the Microscope

Theory

As you bring the slide closer to the objectives for examination, avoid direct contact with the slide or cover slip (Figure 13-2 ◆). Otherwise the specimen will be contaminated and a new one would have to be prepared. When you prepare the microscope and specimen for examination by the physician, remember that the objectives increase magnification, the iris controls the amount of light, and the fine and coarse controls adjust the clarity.

If magnification greater than 45x is needed, use the oil immersion lens.

Note the date and time on the maintenance log whenever a light bulb is replaced, repairs are needed, maintenance is called, and repairs are completed.

Materials

- microscope
- lens paper
- lens cleaner
- prepared slide (with or without cover slip)
- immersion oil
- disposable gloves
- tissues

Competency

(**Conditions**) With the necessary materials, you will be able to (**Task**) demonstrate how to use the microscope and focus all three objectives (**Standards**) correctly.

1. Wash your hands and put on disposable gloves.
2. Remove the cover from the microscope.
3. Check that the microscope is clean and in working order. Replace the light bulb if necessary.
4. Turn the light off until you are ready to focus the objectives on the specimen slide.
5. Clean the lenses and eyepieces (oculars) with lens paper. Use lens cleaner as necessary, but do *not* oversaturate the glue holding the lens in place.
6. Secure the slide on the stage with the slide clips.
7. Revolve the low-power objective into place until it is seated or you hear a click.
8. Adjust the oculars so that you see only one field rather than separate left and right views.
9. Using the coarse adjustment control knob, raise the body tube of the microscope, and swivel the 10X objective into place.
10. Turn the light on.
11. Lower the body tube with the coarse adjustment control knob to bring the slide into general focus.
12. With the iris controls, adjust the light to cover the slide. It is not important at this point to achieve clear focus.
13. Observing from the side, lower the body tube to bring the objective closer to the slide without touching it.
14. Look through the oculars, using the coarse adjustment to bring the specimen into focus. Adjust the iris if you need more light.

Figure 13-2 ◆ As you bring the slide closer to the objectives for examination, avoid direct contact with the slide or cover slip

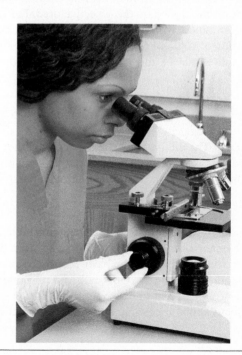

Figure 13-3 ◆ Adjust the fine focus

PROCEDURE 13-1 Demonstrate Using the Microscope *(continued)*

15. Observing from the side, switch to the high-power objective without touching the slide. The body tube may need to be adjusted during this process.
16. When the high-power objective (40X) is in place, adjust the fine focus controls to bring the specimen into clear focus (Figure 13-3 ◆).
17. If the slide specimen is dry and does not have a cover slip, apply a drop of oil and turn the oil immersion objective into place. Lower the objective until it is covered with oil.
18. After the specimen has been examined, lower the stage.
19. Remove the slide specimen and dispose of it in a biohazard waste receptacle.
20. Turn off the light.
21. Clean the lenses with lens cleaner and lens paper. Clean the stage.
22. Rotate the objectives to return the low-power objective directly above the stage.
23. Cover the microscope.
24. Clean the work area.
25. Dispose of the gloves and wash your hands.

Patient Education

Generally, the patient does not receive instruction on how to operate a microscope, although you might give a basic explanation of how some of the tests ordered by the physician are conducted with the microscope.

Charting Example

Operating the microscope is not documented in the patient chart. Maintenance, cleaning, and repairs are documented in the log.

Microscope Maintenance

The lens systems are the most important part of a microscope. Proper cleaning is essential to their proper operation. Artifacts such as eye makeup, eyelashes, and skin oil are often left on the oculars, and specimens and oil can leave residue on the stage or objectives, particularly the oil objective. Fibers may also be left behind when tissue paper or paper towels are used to clean the lenses.

After use, all lenses must be cleaned. Wipe the stage with lint-free cloth or paper to remove any oil or dirt. Then return the stage to its original position. Cover the microscope to keep it free of dust.

Microbiology

Microbiology is an area of biology focusing on organisms that are not visible to the naked eye but can be seen only with magnification. Many diseases and syndromes are the direct result of infection by a microorganism.

Microbiological testing in the medical office gives the clinician information with which to make a diagnosis. Some tests, such as direct gram stains and wet preps (wet mounts), may be processed before a patient leaves the office, while others, such as culture and sensitivity (C & S) tests, may require incubation of two or more days.

Scientific Nomenclature and Morphology

Microorganisms are classified into three major groups:

- **Prokaryotes** lack an organized nucleus and cytoplasmic **organelles**. Bacteria are the most important group of prokaryotic organisms (Figure 13-4 ◆).
- **Eukaryotes** are cells surrounded by a membrane. They have a nucleus and organelles that assist in reproduction. Fungi and parasites are eukaryotic organisms (Figure 13-5 ◆).
- **Viruses** are **ultramicroscopic**, nonliving organisms that are classified as microorganisms because they carry DNA or RNA and are capable of parasitic metabolism and reproduction (Figure 13-6 ◆).

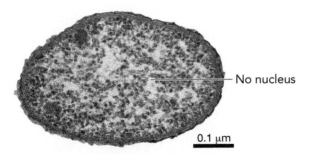

Figure 13-4 ◆ A prokaryotic cell

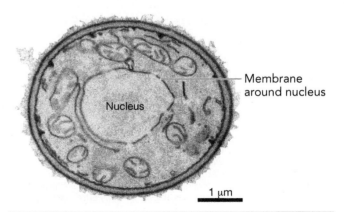

Figure 13-5 ◆ A eukaryotic cell

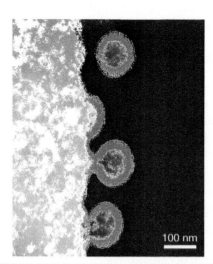

Figure 13-6 ◆ Viruses

All organisms are classified using scientific nomenclature. In the laboratory, a binomial system (two names) is used for prokaryotic and eukaryotic microorganisms. Each microorganism is named according to its genus and species. The first name represents the genus name and is capitalized. The second name is the species name and is always in lowercase letters. Both names are italicized. For example, in the name *Staphylococcus aureus*, the genus is *Staphylococcus* and the species is *aureus*.

Normal Flora

Normal flora are generally harmless but potentially pathogenic microorganisms that colonize in the human body (Table 13-2). Although normal flora inhabit every nonsterile major body system, these microorganisms can cause disease if they are transferred to another part of the body.

Pathogens

Pathogens are microorganisms capable of causing disease (Table 13-3). They possess a virulence factor that damages host cells directly or indirectly through the production of toxins.

TABLE 13-3 SOME COMMON PATHOGENS

Upper Respiratory Tract	Lower Respiratory Tract	Gastrointestinal Tract
Streptococcus pyogenes	*Streptococcus pneumoniae*	*Salmonella* species
Candida albicans	Enterobacteriaceae	*Shigella* species
Eikenella corrodens	*Haemophilus influenzae*	*Aeromonas* species
Actinomyces israelii	*Mycobacterium tuberculosis*	*Campylobacter* species
	Fungi	*Clostridium difficile*

Pathogenicity refers to the ability of an organism to cause disease. True pathogens cause disease whenever they are introduced into a living system. Microorganisms that cause disease only when the patient's immune system is compromised are called **opportunistic pathogens**.

Bacteria

Bacteria are classified in two ways:

1. By **morphology** or shape (Table 13-4)
2. By gram reaction (the result of staining the organism)

A gram stain is a simple diagnostic test that identifies types of bacteria by positive or negative classification (Table 13-5). Bacteria varieties stain or do not stain depending on the compounds in their cell walls. Gram-positive organisms retain the color reaction to the stain procedure and are seen as blue/purple under a microscope. Gram-negative organisms lose the primary stain and retain the red/pink secondary stain. Bacteria are the only organisms that stain well with this procedure. Its reliability is more limited with other organisms because of their complex cellular structure. Although yeast and fungi are not classified as bacteria, they stain positive.

Staphylococcus aureus is a gram-positive pathogen capable of causing a variety of infections: skin infections such as boils, carbuncles, and furuncles; subcutaneous infections such as cellulitis or abscesses; other infectious disease conditions such as osteomyelitis, foodborne illnesses, conjunctivitis, toxic

TABLE 13-2 NORMAL FLORA IN BODY SYSTEMS

Skin	Respiratory Tract	Gastrointestinal Tract
Staphylococcus aureus (**staph**)	*Micrococcus* species	*Escherichia coli*
Staphylococcus epidermidis	Peptostreptococci	*Enterococcus* species
Corynebacterium species	*Neisseria* species (other than *Neisseria gonorrhoeae*)	*Lactobacillus* species
Alpha (α) *Streptococcus* (**strep**)	*Corynebacterium* species	α *Streptococcus*
Bacillus species	α*Streptococcus*	*Pseudomonas aeruginosa*
Micrococcus species	*Candida albicans*	*Staphylococcus* species
Aerotolerant anaerobes, such as *Proprionibacterium acnes*	*Haemophilus parainfluenzae*	*Candida albicans*
	Many anaerobic organisms	*Bacteroides* species
		Clostridium species
		Klebsiella species
		Proteus species
		Enterobacter species
		Many other bacteria

TABLE 13-4 CLASSIFICATION OF BACTERIA ACCORDING TO MORPHOLOGY

Bacteria	Shape	Appearance	Examples
Coccus (plural: cocci)	Spherical	Often exist in pairs, groups, tetrads, or chains	*Staphylococcus* species *Streptococcus* species *Neisseria* species
Bacillus (plural: bacilli)	Rod-shaped	Parallel sides; different lengths and thickness depending on genus-specific characteristics	*Escherichia* species *Proteus* species *Campylobacter* species
Spirochetes	Spiral or corkscrew-shaped	Vary in length and thickness	*Treponema* species *Borrelia* species

TABLE 13-5 CLASSIFICATION OF MICROORGANISMS ACCORDING TO GRAM REACTION

Gram-positive	Gram-negative
Enterococcus faecalis	*Escherichia coli*
Streptococcus pyogenes or *Group A Streptococcus*	*Pseudomonas aeruginosa*
	Klebsiella species
Staphylococcus epidermidis	*Salmonella* species
Streptococcus agalactiae or *Group B Streptococcus*	*Shigella* species
	Campylobacter species
Streptococcus pneumoniae	*Bacteroides* species
Listeria monocytogenes	*Fusobacterium* species
Clostridium perfringens	

shock syndrome, urinary tract infections (**UTIs**), septicemia, and pneumonia (Figure 13-7 ♦). *Staphylococcus aureus* is found on the skin, in water and soil, and can live for long periods of time on inanimate objects. *Staphylococcus epidermidis* is associated with infections caused by prosthetic devices.

? — Critical Thinking Question 13-1
The sample of *Staphyloccus aureus* taken from the toddler's rash confirms the physician's diagnosis of impetigo. Irene knows what the pathogen will look like and that it will be gram-positive even before she begins the microscopic exam. How does she know this?

Enterococcus faecalis is a gram-positive organism that causes infections such as UTIs, wound infection, and septicemia. *Streptococcus pyogenes* or *Group A Streptococcus* is the causative agent of strep throat. Other diseases associated with *Group A strep* infections include scarlet fever, pyelonephritis, rheumatic fever, pneumonia, wound infections, cellulitis, osteomyelitis, flesh-eating disease, and impetigo.

Streptococcus agalactiae or *Group B Streptococcus* is mainly associated with neonatal infections, vaginal infections, UTIs, and wound infections. *Streptococcus pneumoniae* is the primary cause of community-acquired (but not hospital-acquired) pneumonia. *Listeria monocytogenes* causes septicemia in postnatal women. *Clostridium perfringens* is an anaerobic organism that causes gas gangrene. It is found in wound cultures, gunshot wounds, and other trauma-induced injuries.

Escherichia coli (*E. coli*) is the most common gram-negative pathogen. It is the primary cause of UTIs. Other diseases caused by *E. coli* include bacteremia, wound infections, pneumonia, foodborne illnesses, and abscesses. It is normally found in feces and can also inhabit the vaginal area. *Pseudomonas aeruginosa* causes many hospital-acquired or nosocomial infections such as pneumonia, UTIs, and wound infections, as well as folliculitis and external ear infections. It is often seen in cystic fibrosis patients.

? — Critical Thinking Question 13-2
Irene confirms that the patient is positive for an *E. coli* infection in her bladder. What are some possible causes for the bladder infection?

Other pathogenic gram-negative organisms include *Klebsiella* species, *Proteus* species, and *Enterobacter* species. These organisms are commonly associated with UTIs, wound infections, and pneumonia. *Salmonella* species, *Shigella* species, and *Campylobacter* species are causative agents in gastroenteritis and foodborne illnesses. *Bacteroides* and *Fusobacterium* species are anaerobic organisms often isolated from abscesses and trauma wounds.

Fungi

Yeast, molds, and other fungi are also capable of causing disease in humans (Figure 13-8 ♦). The study of these organisms is called **mycology**. Common mycological infections include oral thrush, vaginal yeast infections, and fungal infections of the hair, skin, and nails. Fungi are opportunistic pathogens that cause disease only when the normal balance of flora in the body is upset by traumatic injury, poor hygiene, or a compromised immune system. Treatment of fungal infection ranges from normal flora replacement to therapy with antifungal antibiotics.

Parasites

Parasitology is the study of parasites, organisms that infect living hosts and live at the expense of their hosts without contributing to their survival (Figure 13-9 ♦). Human parasites include protozoa, helminthes, and arthropods. Pathogenic

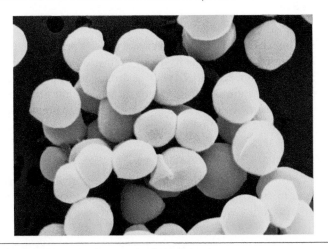

Figure 13-7 ♦ A microscopic view of staph
Source: Medical-on-Line/ Alamy

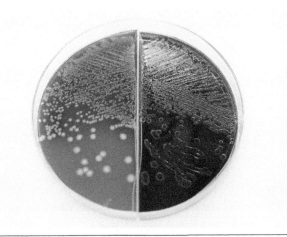

Figure 13-8 ♦ A microscopic view of a mold

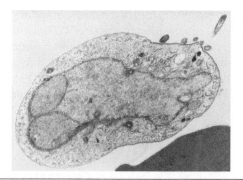

Figure 13-9 ◆ A microscopic view of a parasite
Source: London School of Hygiene & Tropical Medicine/Photo Researchers, Inc.

intestinal protozoa are transmitted through contaminated drinking water, animals, and poor hygiene. Transmission requires three elements:

1. A source of infection
2. A mode of transmission
3. A susceptible host

Parasites take vital nutrients from the host. Damage to the host is caused by the invasion or destruction of host cells, usually the intestinal mucosa, or by the inflammatory response. Diarrhea and abdominal discomfort are the most common symptoms of intestinal parasites. Treatment ranges from no treatment, if the infection is self-limiting, to antiparasitic drugs.

Viruses

Virology is a specialized branch of microbiology that studies viruses and resulting diseases (Figure 13-10 ◆). Although classified as microorganisms, viruses are actually nonliving organisms that cannot reproduce without invading host cells. Viruses cause hepatitis A, B, and C, and the human immunodeficiency virus (HIV) causes acquired immunodeficiency syndrome (AIDS).

Once a virus locates a target cell, it attaches itself to the cell, penetrates the cell membrane, and takes control of the nu-

Figure 13-10 ◆ The human immunodeficiency virus (HIV)
Source: Photo Researchers, Inc.

cleus. It uses the cell's resources to self-replicate, severely damaging and often killing the host cell in the process.

Diagnosis of a viral infection is generally done though indirect **serology** testing. Serum from the patient's venous blood specimen is tested for the presence of antibodies. The amount and type of antibody present can indicate disease progression to the physician. If necessary, direct specimens (tissue or secretions obtained by invasive or noninvasive techniques) may be tested for the presence of viral agents. Commercially available kits allow for testing for influenza virus in respiratory specimens, for example.

Preparing Specimens for Microscopic Examination

Microbiological specimens must be properly prepared on a slide before they can be examined under the microscope. You will be responsible for procuring the specimen, processing some slides, and preparing the microscope. The laboratory technician or physician develops slides and examines them under the microscope. Many slides require cover slips, which prevent contamination of the microscope by the specimen. Specimens that are stained or are examined with an oil immersion lens do not require cover slips.

Preparing a Specimen Smear

The gram stain, used to identify gram-negative and gram-positive microorganisms, is performed on a slide containing a thin smear of specimen.

Performing a Gram Stain

Hans C. J. Gram (1853–1928), a Danish physician, developed the gram stain procedure in the late 1800s. To this day, the gram stain is used to help identify bacteria, which are very small and almost colorless. The different appearances of colorized bacteria determine not only their gram-positive or gram-negative status but also their shape and grouping. With this information, the physician can make an initial diagnosis and determine the appropriate medication until the diagnosis is confirmed by a C & S test.

The gram stain procedure consists of four basic steps:

1. The cells are colorized with crystal violet, a primary stain.
2. A mordant (chemical fixative), Gram's iodine, is added.
3. The cells are decolorized with an alcohol/acetone mixture.
4. The last stain is safranin, a counterstain that provides contrasting color to cellular components not previously visible from the first stain.

Preparing Wet Mounts

A wet mount slide is another way to examine microorganisms under a microscope. There are three methods of preparing a wet mount slide:

■ normal saline (NS)
■ potassium hydroxide (**KOH**)
■ India ink

PROCEDURE 13-2 Prepare a Specimen Smear for Microbiological Examination

Theory

A frosted-edge slide is easier to grasp during preparation and to label with patient information. Patient identification must be done with a labeling pen. Do not use felt-tip markers that might run during the staining procedure.

Specimens for smear preparation can be from a culture swab, a culture growing in a petri dish, or a liquid source. Spread the smear thinly to allow for better microscopic examination and faster air-drying time.

Heat fixation is performed to make sure the cells stick to the slide during the staining process. Heat also kills the microorganisms, thus lowering the possibility of disease transmission during slide preparation and handling. The slide should not become too hot to hold, as excess heat could damage the specimen and alter test results.

Materials

- glass slide (preferably with frosted edge)
- disposable gloves
- sterile distilled water
- inoculating loops or specimen swabs
- flame source
- biohazardous waste container
- sharps container

Competency

(**Conditions**) With the necessary materials, you will be able to (**Task**) prepare a slide (**Standards**) correctly for microscopic examination within 30 minutes.

1. Wash your hands.
2. Gather equipment and supplies.
3. Wash your hands again and put on disposable gloves.
4. Write the patient information on the frosted edge of the slide.
5. Prepare a thin film, or smear, on the slide.
   For a specimen from a swab: Roll and turn the swab across the slide (Figure 13-11 ◆).
   For a specimen from a Petri dish (Figure 13-12 ◆):
   - Gather sterile distilled water with a sterile inoculating loop and place it on the slide.
   - Use the inoculating loop to gather the microbial specimen, without gathering any culture medium.
   - Mix the specimen into the distilled water on the slide.
   - Sterilize the loop over the flame.
   For a specimen from a liquid (Figure 13-13 ◆):
   - Dip the inside of the sterile inoculating loop in the culture until it appears covered with a film.
   - Touch the film to the center of the slide.
   - Allow the specimen on the slide to air-dry completely.
   - Hold and pass the slide through the flame several times. The slide is now ready to stain.
6. Clean the work area.
7. Dispose of the gloves and wash your hands.

Charting Example

Document in the designated log any quality control or safety measures you followed, such as looking at expiration dates or correctly storing the specimen.

Figure 13-11 ◆ Roll and turn the swab across the slide.

Figure 13-12 ◆ Using a loop with a Petri dish

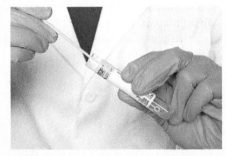

Figure 13-13 ◆ Using a loop with a liquid

PROCEDURE 13-3 Prepare a Gram Stain

Theory

Timing and rinsing techniques are critical to the correct identification of gram-positive or gram-negative bacteria. Stains are left on the slide for a period based on institution procedure and the manufacturer's directions and may be a minimum of 30 seconds or as long as 2 minutes.

It is important to rinse correctly but not excessively for the cells to retain the dye color. Excessive rinsing during the crystal violet phase can remove too much purple from gram-positive cells. After the Gram's iodine is added, the purple color remains to identify the gram-positive bacteria (Figure 13-14 ◆). During decolorization, the color must be removed according to the manufacturer's directions; otherwise it may also remove a degree of crystal violet from gram-positive cells. Organisms from which the primary stain is removed by decolorization exhibit a pink color from the safranin dye (Figure 13-15 ◆).

Materials

- disposable gloves
- slide with fixed smear
- crystal violet dye
- Gram's iodine
- alcohol/acetone mixture
- safranin dye
- wash bottle filled with distilled water
- rack and tray for slide staining
- forceps
- paper towel
- biohazardous waste container
- sharps container

Competency

(**Conditions**) With the necessary materials, you will be able to (**Task**) prepare a slide for microscopic examination of gram-negative and gram-positive bacteria (**Standards**) correctly, within 15 minutes.

1. Wash your hands.
2. Gather equipment, supplies, and the prepared slide (see Procedure 13-2).
3. Wash your hands again and put on disposable gloves.
4. Lay the slide on the slide rack and tray.
5. Pour crystal violet on the slide and allow it to stain for 1 minute.
6. Rinse the slide gently with water from the wash bottle.
7. Lay the slide on the slide rack and tray.
8. Pour Gram's iodine, also known as mordant, on the slide. Allow it to stain for 2 minutes.
9. Lift the slide diagonally with the forceps and rinse gently with water from the wash bottle.
10. Maintaining the vertical hold, gently pour the acetone/alcohol decolorizing mixture over the slide. Pour until the runoff is clear (approximately 1 minute).
11. Lay the slide on the slide rack and tray.
12. Pour safranin dye on the slide and allow it to stain for 30 seconds.
13. Lift the slide angled vertically with the forceps and rinse gently.
14. Let the slide air-dry vertically, or blot—do not wipe—the stained area with a paper towel.
15. Mount the slide on the microscope for examination.
16. Return supplies to storage.
17. Clean the work area.
18. Dispose of biohazardous waste and sharps in the appropriate containers.
19. Dispose of the gloves and wash your hands.

Charting Example

Document in designated logs any quality control or safety measures you followed, such as looking at expiration dates of dyes or other supplies; correct storage of specimen or prepared slide; or following OSHA precautions. The technician or physician performing the microscopic examination will document the results of the gram staining.

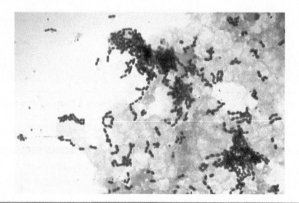

Figure 13-14 ◆ Gram-positive *Streptococcus pyogenes* bacteria in chains

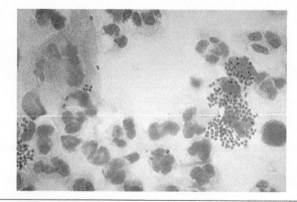

Figure 13-15 ◆ Gram-negative *N. gonorrhoeae*
Source: Biophoto Associates/Photo Researchers, Inc.

Saline

A saline mount involves placing a specimen smear on the slide, adding and mixing a drop of saline into the smear, placing a cover slip over it, and examining it immediately under the microscope. *Trichomonas vaginalis,* a sexually transmitted pathogen, is identified in this manner.

Potassium Hydroxide

Some microorganisms, such as fungi, are masked in a specimen because of the amount of protein they contain. Potassium hydroxide added to the specimen smear and left sitting at room temperature for 30 minutes dissolves the protein and makes fungal spores or hyphae visible under the microscope. Vaginal yeast infections are diagnosed with this method.

India Ink

India ink is used to visualize *Cryptococcus neoformans* in spinal fluid. After centrifugation, a drop of sediment and a drop of India ink are placed together on a slide.

Specimen Collection, Storage, and Transport

"Garbage in, garbage out." The quality of a test is only as good as the specimen submitted. Although this applies to all specimen collection, quality and procedural standards are especially important in microbial testing. There are several important considerations to keep in mind when you collect a specimen.

- A specimen should be collected before treatment has begun to ensure correct diagnosis.
- A specimen must measure "quantity sufficient" (**QS**) to ensure that all requested tests can be performed. If the quantity is not sufficient (**QNS**), more specimen will be needed.
- A specimen must be placed in a sterile collection device or sterile container.
- Specimens should be labeled at the time of collection with the patient's name (first and last), date of collection, time of collection, and body area or fluid source.
- Collection devices should be appropriate for the source to be cultured.
- When transport to the testing area is not immediate, transport media and packaging must be used. These ensure optimal recovery as well as the safety of transporting and testing personnel.

Collection of Stool Specimens

The physician may ask a patient to collect a stool specimen, or a series of three stool specimens, for a number of reasons, including microscopic examination for enteric pathogens, ova and parasite examination, and occult blood detection. Naturally passed stool is the preferred source for each specimen. Any stool for testing must be collected in a clean, dry container, free from

Keys to Success
INSTRUCTING THE PATIENT FOR SPECIMEN COLLECTION

Your role in specimen collection is extremely important. Whether you are assisting the physician in collection, collecting the specimen yourself, or instructing the patient in proper collection, you must follow strict guidelines to ensure accurate results. When the patient is collecting any specimen, verbal instructions must be clear and complete. Do *not* assume the patient will know proper collection technique. Provide written instructions to reinforce verbal information.

After explaining the procedure, ask the patient to describe what he or she has understood. Ask questions and encourage the patient to ask questions. The patient's level of understanding affects the quality of the specimen and the results of the test. Give additional verbal and written instructions if the specimen requires refrigeration and/or transport. Any specimen that is not collected, stored, and transported correctly must be discarded. Having to repeat the specimen collection delays diagnosis and treatment.

urine contamination, and transported to the testing area in a container with a tight-fitting lid. One specimen per 24 hours is the standard for stool cultures. Some physicians may request that three specimens be collected on the same day, if possible; others may request one specimen a day for three consecutive days.

Fecal Culture Testing for Ova, Parasites, and Other Infectious Organisms

Stool specimens for culture must be processed within one hour of collection or placed in appropriate transport media to recover enteric (intestinal) pathogens (such as Carey-Blair media) (Figure 13-16 ◆). Stool in transport media is viable for up to 24 hours. Follow the manufacturer's recommendations for transport times.

Stool specimen collection for ova and parasites is identical to collection for culture. A different type of transport media—a two-vial system—is used if the patient cannot return the specimen within one hour of collection. One vial contains PVA, a preservative used to permanently stain the specimen. The other vial contains formalin for preparing wet mounts of the specimen. All stools for ova and parasite examination are stained and examined on wet mounts to ensure the detection of all life stages of amoebae, helminthes, and pathogenic protozoa. Spec-

Keys to Success
PATIENT INSTRUCTIONS BEFORE SPECIMEN COLLECTION FOR CULTURE

- Obtain a clean, dry specimen.
- Alert the medical office if it will take more than one hour to transport the specimen to the laboratory, as this will require a different container to preserve the organisms.
- Obtain only one specimen in a 24-hour period.
- Do not take a stool specimen for 72 hours after a barium or radiology test.
- Do not use a urine-contaminated specimen.
- Do not use a specimen from a diaper.

Figure 13-16 ◆ Petri dish containing fecal bacterial cultures
Source: Jim Varney/Photo Researchers, Inc.

imens in this type of transport system are acceptable for testing for up to three days. Many physician offices and hospital laboratories do not perform ova and parasite examination on site because it requires extensive training. Specimens are usually referred to a reference laboratory. The patient is given verbal and written instructions for transferring the specimen to the vials.

Fecal Occult Blood Testing

Fecal occult blood testing, or stool guaiac, detects the presence of blood in the stool. The patient follows a modified diet for three days, then collects three different specimens. Because dietary guidelines may vary between test kits, it is important to follow the manufacturer's directions. Many foods, and even aspirin, can cause false positive results. A list of foods and medications to avoid is included in each kit.

Specimen collection for fecal occult blood testing can be done in the same manner as for an unpreserved stool culture. In the test preparation area, a clean, dry fecal specimen is taken from the container and placed on a testing card. An alternative method allows the patient to collect the specimen at home and place a smear directly on the testing card. The card is labeled with first and last name and the date and time of collection. The specimen is usable for testing for 14 days.

Fecal specimens may be collected for cultures or to examine for the presence of occult blood. While these tests are different in purpose, the specimen collection process is similar, and they are discussed together in the procedure.

Keys to Success
PEDIATRIC STOOL COLLECTION

Stool specimens taken from diapers are not acceptable for culture because of the absorbency of the material. If the diaper is lined with a non-absorbent material, however, a specimen may be taken and placed in a container or transport device.

Rectal swabs may be collected in the physician's office. Lay the child on his or her stomach, carefully insert the transport swab 1 to 1-1/2 inches into the rectum. Rotate the swab and withdraw. Place it in a transport sheath, label it with patient information, and send it to the testing area.

Keys to Success
PATIENT INSTRUCTIONS FOR SPECIMEN COLLECTION FOR FECAL OCCULT BLOOD TESTING

Follow the guidelines listed below for three days before the first specimen and until all three specimens have been obtained. These guidelines must be followed for accurate test results and comparisons.

■ Do not take medications containing aspirin, iron, steroids, or Vitamin C. Your physician has reviewed the medications that you are taking and will let you know which ones not to take until after all specimens have been collected. Inform your physician of any other medications or nutritional supplements he or she may not already be aware of.
■ Do not eat rare or red meat, liver or processed meats, cauliflower, broccoli, turnips, radishes, horseradish, or melons.
■ Do eat well-cooked pork, chicken, or fish; a variety of raw and cooked vegetables (except for cauliflower, broccoli, turnips, radishes, and horseradish); a variety of fruits, other than melons; and a variety of high-fiber foods.
■ Do *not* collect any specimens for testing in the presence of hemorrhoidal bleeding. For female patients, do not take any specimens during and for three days following a menstrual period.
■ Store the three test slides at room temperature until you use them.

Culture and Sensitivity Testing

The term *culture* refers to a process in which a direct specimen of tissue or secretion is cultivated in prepared media. When the specimen has grown, it is examined for pathogenic bacteria. Specific protocols are set up for each specimen type to maximize the recovery of these organisms. Special media are used to inhibit the growth of normal flora, allow for visual differentiation of bacteria groups, allow the pathogen to be easily recognized, and aid in the recovery of fastidious organisms (microorganisms that require special conditions and nutrients for culture, such as anaerobic bacteria, which grow only in the absence of oxygen). You will obtain the specimen and the laboratory technician will process the culture by inoculation, incubation, inspection, and identification.

Keys to Success
CULTURE PROCESS FOR IDENTIFICATION OF MICROORGANISMS

Step 1: Inoculation
The specimen is aseptically transferred to plate and/or tube media.
Step 2: Incubation
The plate and/or tube media are placed in an appropriate environment to optimize the recovery of organisms—usually 35° to 37° Celsius, with increased CO_2 and humidity. Some exceptions, such as stool cultures, are not kept in elevated CO_2. Total incubation times range from 48 hours to four days. Each culture should be examined every 24 hours.
Step 3: Inspection
After the initial incubation of 24 hours, each plate is visually examined and any suspected pathogen is subcultured for purity and prepared for Step 4.
Step 4: Identification
Any suspected pathogen must be identified. A variety of manual and automated methods can be used to identify organisms to genus and species levels. Gram staining is an important part of this procedure. Enzymatic testing, carbohydrate assimilation testing, and antigen detection tests are other ways to identify organisms.

PROCEDURE 13-4 Instruct a Patient in Collecting a Fecal Specimen for Occult Blood or Culture Testing

Theory

Fecal occult blood testing is important to the early diagnosis and treatment of colon cancer. The patient must follow dietary modifications and medication adjustments for three days. Specimens should not be collected during the active bleeding of menstruation or hemorrhoids. Always check the expiration date of the test kit, as chemical changes may affect the accuracy of results.

Fecal culture testing for ova, parasites, or other infectious organisms plays a role in the diagnosis of intestinal infestation or infection. The patient often experiences symptoms of abdominal pain, diarrhea, and vomiting caused by new, transient organisms that upset the balance of normal flora in the intestinal tract. For accurate test results and appropriate diagnosis and treatment, it is important that the fecal specimen is obtained without urine and that storage and transport are in line with institutional policy and the manufacturer's directions (Figure 13-17 ◆). Because certain microorganisms' growth and death are affected by temperature, oxygen, and nutrition, be sure to follow standard procedure and the manufacturer's guidelines for specimen storage and processing to accurately reflect the microbial population at the time the specimen is obtained. Fecal testing for occult blood does not require live cells; therefore, the patient may complete the fecal occult blood sample cards at home and bring them to the office.

Materials

Fecal Occult Blood

- patient chart
- testing kit
- clean and dry large-mouth container with spatula
- patient label and laboratory requisition form, if needed
- disposable gloves
- black ink pen

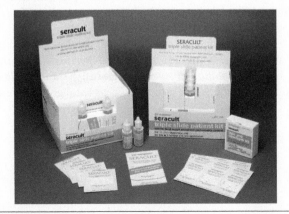

Figure 13-17 ◆ Test for occult blood
Courtesy of Propper Manufacturing Company.

Fecal Culture Testing

- patient chart
- specimen container for transport
- spatula
- patient label and laboratory requisition form, if needed
- disposable gloves
- black ink pen

Competency

(Conditions) With the necessary materials, you will be able to **(Task)** provide verbal and written instruction to the patient **(Standards)** correctly within 30 minutes.

1. Wash your hands.
2. Gather supplies.
3. Check the kit to make sure it has not expired.
4. Greet and identify the patient. Escort him or her to the examination room.
5. Ask the patient what he or she understands about the reason(s) for the test. Clarify the information as needed to help the patient understand.
6. Inform the physician if further discussion would benefit the patient.
7. Provide verbal instructions for fecal occult blood or culture testing. Reinforce them by giving the patient a written copy of the instructions and the appropriate test kit supplies, lab requisitions, and patient identification labels.
8. For *fecal occult blood specimen collection*, instruct the patient as follows.
   - Using the spatula provided for each slide, place a thin smear over the first square (labeled A).
   - Take a small specimen from a different area and smear it over the second square (labeled B).
   - Close the flap covering the slide.
   - Allow the slide to air-dry.
   - Repeat these steps for the remaining two slides, according to the physician's order.
   - Return the three slides to the medical office as soon as possible.

   For *fecal culture specimen collection*, instruct the patient as follows.
   - After collecting the specimen in a clean, dry container, tighten the container lid.
   - Transport the specimen immediately or transfer it to a preservative container.
9. Document on the chart the instructions you gave and the patient's understanding.
10. Wash your hands.

continued

PROCEDURE 13-4 Instruct a Patient in Collecting a Fecal Specimen for Occult Blood or Culture Testing (continued)

Patient Education

Fecal Occult Blood Specimen: Inform the patient that testing for fecal occult blood is performed to diagnose the cause of rectal and/or intestinal bleeding. Rectal bleeding is symptomatic of many disease conditions, including hemorrhoids, gastrointestinal tract ulcers, diverticulosis/itis, polyps, and colorectal cancer. Following the instructions for testing correctly will help to eliminate false results. If results indicate bleeding, there will be further diagnostic procedures, diagnosis, and treatment.

Culture for Ova, Parasites, or Other Infectious Organisms: Inform the patient that stool culture testing is performed to diagnose ova, parasites, or other organisms that cause intestinal infestation or infection. Abdominal pain, diarrhea, and vomiting are symptoms. Although the intestinal tract contains normal, resident microorganisms, it is newly hosted, transient microorganisms or parasites that cause symptoms.

Following the instructions for testing correctly will help to eliminate false results and assist in the accurate diagnosis and treatment of the pathogen.

Charting Example

Document in designated logs any quality control or safety measures you follow, such as looking at expiration dates of dyes or other supplies used; correct storage of specimen or prepared slide; or OSHA precautions taken. The technician or physician performing the microscopic examination will document the results of the gram staining.

11/22/xx 9:30 a.m. Pt given verbal and written instruction for collection of fecal occult testing specimens. Pt able to state correctly in own words the importance of following instructions. Lea Harden, CMA

Once identification is made, sensitivity testing may follow. Sensitivity testing determines which antimicrobial medication would be effective against the pathogen. Some organisms follow very predictable patterns and do not require routine testing. Others must be tested to ensure proper treatment. The organism is tested for sensitivity to selected drugs by either disc diffusion or broth dilution methods. Effectiveness is measured by the drug's ability to stop or inhibit the organism's growth in a controlled situation.

With the Kirby-Bauer disc diffusion (KBDD) method of sensitivity testing, the organism is designated as susceptible, intermediate, or resistant to particular concentrations of antibiotic. Microscan plates are manufactured to perform culture and sensitivity (C & S) or just sensitivity tests.

Broth dilution, or minimum inhibitory concentration (MIC) testing, is more specific. The results indicate the lowest dilution of the drug that stops the growth of the organism. Results are reported with a numerical MIC value and the interpretation of that value (susceptible, intermediate, or resistant).

Performing a Wound or Throat Culture

Bacterial wound cultures are requested by the physician to determine the causative agent of an infection. Some typical sites cultured are abscesses, animal bites, diabetic ulcers, and superficial skin wounds. Deep wounds require both aerobic and anaerobic cultures, but superficial wounds and skin infections require only aerobic cultures.

Throat cultures aid in the diagnosis of *Group A strep,* the main pathogen implicated in pharyngeal infections. Identification of the *Streptococcus* organism is important because of other disease conditions that can result, such as rheumatic fever, endocarditis, or acute glomerulonephritis. Rapid antigen testing (Rapid Strep testing) for the bacteria *Group A Strep* (*Streptococcus pyogenes*) is a commonly performed test in physician office laboratories. Built-in test controls confirm that proper procedure is followed.

Other pathogenic organisms that can be cultured from throat specimens include *Bordetella pertussis* (whooping cough), *Haemophilus influenzae* (epiglottitis), *Candida albicans* (oral thrush), and *Neisseria gonorrhoeae* (oral gonorrhoeae).

PROCEDURE 13-5 Perform a Wound or Throat Culture Using Sterile Swabs

Theory

For a wound culture, collect the exudate (pus or fluid accumulation) by removing the coating of the lesion and inserting a syringe with needle to aspirate the fluid. After a specimen is obtained, detach and dispose of the needle, cover the syringe end, and label the specimen with the patient's first and last name and the date and time of collection. Transport the syringe to the testing area immediately for processing.

If aspiration is not possible, a swab can be inserted into the lesion to collect the exudate or drainage. Label the swab and transport it to the testing area as soon as possible.

If no exudate is present, roll the swab over the surface of the uncovered lesion and place it in transport media.

Specimens on aerobic swabs are acceptable for culture for approximately 12 to 16 hours after collection. Specimens in syringes should be processed within one hour to optimize the recovery of anaerobic organisms. Use anaerobic transport media and swabs if inoculation of the specimen must be delayed for longer than an hour. A double-swab system is best for wound specimen collection if both a direct gram stain and a culture are both anticipated. Always check institutional procedure and the manufacturer's directions before proceeding with specimen collection.

Throat specimens can be obtained by using two swabs instead of one if the physician orders both Rapid Strep and C&S testing. Use a noncotton swab, such as Dacron®, to collect the throat specimen. Instruct the patient to open the mouth widely by saying "Ahh." Hold the tongue down with a clean tongue depressor to clear a path to the posterior pharynx. Being careful not to touch the inside of the mouth, the teeth, or the tongue, wipe the opened swabs against the throat and tonsil area in a circular or figure "8" pattern to collect a representative sample of microorganisms. Gather specimens only from the infected area, not the area surrounding it. Remove the swab carefully, without touching other parts of the oral cavity. Following procedure, place the swabs in a collection container, usually a tube with culture media, and transport them to the processing area.

Materials

Wound

- patient chart
- single- or double-swab collection device (one swab for culture inoculation and one for gram stain)
- setup for anaerobic culture (for nonsuperficial wound, if physician ordered)
- specimen label
- disposable gloves

Throat

- patient chart
- tongue depressor
- sterile swab and transport device
- specimen label
- disposable gloves

Competency

(**Conditions**) With the necessary materials, you will be able to (**Task**) perform swab culture collection and prepare it (**Standards**) correctly for transport and processing within 15 minutes.

1. Wash your hands.
2. Gather equipment and supplies.
3. Identify and greet the patient, then escort him or her to the examination room. Explain the process of specimen collection.
4. Wash your hands again and put on disposable gloves.
5. Wound specimen collection:
   - Mentally note the type and amount of drainage; any redness, warmth, or swelling in the surrounding area; any other abnormalities.
   - Swab the inside of the wound(Figure 13-18 ◆). Do not swab the surrounding skin area.
   - Place the swab in the transport container and medium, if used (Figure 13-19 ◆).

   Throat culture specimen collection:

   - Ask the patient to open the mouth wide and extend the tongue forward.
   - Examine the throat and make observe for redness, swelling of throat tissue, amount and type of drainage, or the presence of white patches or pustules.
   - Place the tongue depressor firmly on the tongue and press down.
   - Swab the posterior pharynx between the tonsillar pillars. Place the swab in the transport container and medium, if used (Figure 13-20 ◆).
6. Label the container with the patient's name (first and last), date and time of collection, and source of specimen.
7. Dispose of any waste materials in the appropriate container(s).
8. Remove and dispose of gloves. Wash your hands.
9. Transport the specimen to the testing area.
10. Perform the required charting or laboratory documentation relating to specimen collection.

continued

PROCEDURE 13-5 Perform a Wound or Throat Culture Using Sterile Swabs *(continued)*

Patient Education

Ask the patient to verbalize his or her understanding of why the test was performed. Usually the physician prescribes an antibiotic based on clinical symptoms and the usual microorganisms present in a wound or throat infection. If so, reinforce medication instructions. Inform the patient that C & S results usually take three days, but this can vary depending on the type of pathogen present. The test results will determine if the patient will remain on the same antibiotic or receive another prescription for a more effective medication.

Charting Example

9/30/xx 9:30 a.m. Throat culture specimen obtained per office procedure. Specimen placed in culturette tube and transported to laboratory immediately. Pt medication instructions reviewed. Pt repeated back medication instructions correctly. Pt informed that he would be called with results, and adjustments in treatment would be made, if necessary, in 3-4 days. Kirk Peters, RMA

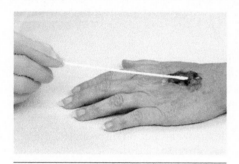

Figure 13-18 ◆ Swab the inside of the wound.

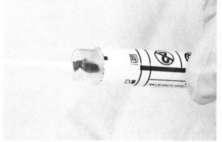

Figure 13-19 ◆ Place the swab in the specimen container.

Figure 13-20 ◆ Swab the posterior pharynx between the tonsillar pillars.

Urine Cultures

Specimens for urine culture are obtained from clean-catch or voided-midstream urine and catheterized urine (Figure 13-21 ◆). Random urine specimens commonly used for routine urinalysis tests are not used for cultures as they may be contaminated.

A clean-catch or voided-midstream specimen is obtained when the patient voids into a sterile container. The container is labeled with the patient's full name, the date and time of collection, and the type of specimen collected. Transport it to the testing area or store appropriately until testing is completed.

Before collecting a urine specimen for culture, the patient must clean the urogenital area with cleansing towelettes or sterile gauze, soap, and water. A female patient must cleanse the labia majora, labia minora, and vaginal area from front to back, then repeat the procedure two more times to remove normal flora. A male patient cleanses the urethral opening and foreskin, if present, using the three cleansing wipes provided.

After cleansing, the patient holds the vaginal folds (female) or foreskin (male) away from the urethral opening, then begins urinating in the commode. After a few seconds the patient stops the urine flow, positions the sterile container, and begins urinating again, catching approximately 20 to 50 ml of urine. The patient may then finish voiding in the commode.

Figure 13-21 ◆ Container for clean-catch urine specimen
Image courtesy of Cardinal Health, Inc. or one of its subsidiaries.

The container must be closed securely with a lid. The patient must not touch the inside of the lid.

For a patient unable to provide a specimen, a nurse or physician performs a catheterization. The catheter is inserted through the urinary meatus and passed through the urethra into the bladder. Catheterization requires sterile technique to avoid introducing bacteria into the urinary tract.

Catheters can be temporary or indwelling. Straight (temporary) catheterization, or "in and out catheter," involves threading the catheter into the bladder, collecting the urine in a sterile container, and removing the catheter. Indwelling catheters are anchored in the bladder, and urine is continuously collected in an attached bag. A specimen collected from an indwelling catheter must be taken from the port of the tubing. First, the catheter tubing must be drained of all urine. Then it is bent just below the withdrawal port, the port is cleaned with an alcohol swab, and a specimen is aspirated with a syringe and needle.

Small infants and toddlers in diapers pose a greater challenge. Special sterile collection devices can be used in place of straight catheterization. After the urogenital area is cleaned, a urine bag or "wee" bag is placed over the child's external genitals and secured with an adhesive. After the child urinates, the device is removed and placed in a sterile container for transport to the testing laboratory.

Storage and Transport of Urine Specimens

Unrefrigerated urine should be received in the testing area within one hour of collection. When this is not possible, urinalysis specimens may be refrigerated for up to four hours and urine culture specimens for up to 24 hours without compromising results. If specimens must be transported to an outside facility and constant refrigeration is impossible, special transport devices containing preservatives and buffers keep the pH stable and bacteria recoverable without refrigeration.

REVIEW

Chapter Summary

- The invention of the microscope greatly advanced the study and discovery of the causes of disease. The microscope helps to identify the tiny, pathogenic microorganisms that cause many diseases. Although there are five basic types of microscopes, the compound microscope is the one most commonly used.
- As an MA, you will prepare specimens for microscopic examination, assist in instructing and preparing the patient for specimen collection, and maintain logs related to laboratory testing in the medical office or laboratory setting.
- In the field of microbiology, it is important to differentiate between normal, resident flora and pathogenic, or disease-causing, microorganisms. Bacteria, fungi, parasites, and viruses are microorganisms.
- Bacteria are classified in two ways—by morphology and by gram stain reaction. Based on morphology, they are grouped into cocci, bacilli, and spirochetes. Based on gram stain reaction, they are either gram-positive or gram-negative. Bacteria generally have a genus name (beginning with a capital letter) and a species name (in lowercase). *Staphylococcus aureus* is an example.
- Specimen collection before treatment with antibiotics helps in the identification of causative pathogens. The accuracy of any test and of the resulting diagnosis depends on the quality and quantity of the specimen collected.

- When clinical symptoms are present, wet mounting and gram staining are two methods of examining specimens for pathogens before the patient leaves the medical office. Wet mount slide preparation usually involves placing a saline drop on a specimen smear and covering it with a cover slip before examining it under the microscope. Gram staining identifies whether pathogens are gram-positive or gram-negative.
- Many pathogens are common to specific infections, such as gram-positive *Staphylococcus aureus* (skin infections and abscesses), and gram-negative *E. coli* (urinary tract infections). An antibiotic is usually prescribed by the physician during the office visit to treat the suspected gram-negative or gram-positive organism. Later, if culture and sensitivity testing indicates there is a more effective medication, the physician changes the treatment.
- If specimen collection requires patient preparation and instruction, the MA provides verbal and written instructions. Reinforce to the patient that following the instructions exactly will ensure accurate, timely results and appropriate medical treatment.
- Throat, wound, urine, and stool specimens are used in C & S testing as appropriate to the clinical symptoms.

Chapter Review Questions

Multiple Choice

1. Which of the following objectives requires oil immersion?
   A. 10X
   B. 100X
   C. 20X
   D. 40X

2. When cleaning a lens, you should
   A. use lens paper.
   B. use a disposable paper towel.
   C. completely soak the lens with lens cleaner.
   D. completely soak the lens with distilled water.

3. A eukaryote has
   A. organelles but no organized nucleus.
   B. no organized nucleus or organelles.
   C. organelles and a cell nucleus surrounded by a membrane.
   D. a cell nucleus surrounded by a membrane but no organelles.

4. Which of the following is bacteria?
   A. yeast
   B. *Listeria monocytogenes*
   C. protozoa
   D. Hepatitis A

5. The leading cause of UTIs is
   A. *Staphylococcus aureus.*
   B. *Clostridium perfringens.*
   C. *Pseudomonas aeruginosa.*
   D. *E. coli.*

6. The gram-stained color of gram-positive pathogens is
   A. purple.
   B. blue.
   C. red.
   D. yellow.

7. When applying heat fixation to a specimen smear, you should
   A. keep the slide over the flame until it is hot.
   B. blow on the slide to cool it after heating.
   C. pass the slide through the flame.
   D. refrigerate it immediately.

8. Sensitivity testing is used to
   A. identify the causative pathogen.
   B. verify the gram staining procedure.
   C. decolorize the pathogen for identification.
   D. determine the most effective medication for treatment.

9. How long after a radiology procedure with barium salt can a stool specimen be collected?
   A. 8 hours
   B. 72 hours
   C. 24 hours
   D. 48 hours

10. Without compromising the results, a urinalysis specimen may be refrigerated for up to
    A. 6 hours.
    B. 8 hours.
    C. 4 hours.
    D. 24 hours.

True/False

T F 1. The lenses of a microscope are concave.

T F 2. Objectives on the microscope include 10X, 20X, 40X, and 100X power lenses.

T F 3. Using immersion oil with the 100X lens makes items clearer.

T F 4. The light source, the condenser, and the diaphragm are located under the mechanical stage.

T F 5. Normal flora inhabit every nonsterile major body system.

Short Answer

1. What is a dissection microscope used for?

2. What are the three classifications of bacteria according to morphology?

3. What is pathogenicity?

4. Why are viruses classified as microorganisms?

5. Why are fungi considered opportunistic pathogens?

Research

1. Are there wound-care centers in your community designed specifically for the treatment of patient wounds and/or identification of infectious pathogens?

2. Research a type of Group A Strep known as "flesh-eating disease." How is it contracted? How is it treated? What is the mortality rate?

Externship Application Experience

A wound drainage specimen obtained by syringe was not processed within the recommended hour after collection. You are aware of this because the specimen was marked as 12/16/XX 6 A.M., and it is now 10 A.M. Why is it important to process a syringe specimen within the hour time frame, and what do you do?

Resource Guide

American Association of Blood Banks (AABB)
8101 Glenbrook Road
Bethesda, MD 20814-2749
301-907-6977
www.aabb.org

American Medical Technologists (AMT)
710 Higgins Road
Park Ridge, IL 60068
847-823-5169
www.amt1.com

American Society for Clinical Laboratory Science
6701 Democracy Blvd, Suite 300
Bethesda, MD 20817
301-657-2768
www.ascls.org

American Society for Clinical Pathology (ASCP)
2100 West Harrison St.
Chicago, IL 60612
312-738-1336
www.ascp.org

National Accrediting Agency for Clinical Laboratory Sciences (NAACLS)
8410 W. Bryn Mawr Ave., Suite 670
Chicago, IL 60631
773-714-8880
www.naacls.org

National Credentialing Agency for Laboratory Personnel (NCA)
PO Box 15945-289
Lenexa, KS 66285-5935
913-438-5110
www.nca-Info.org

MedMedia

www.prenhall.com/frazier

More on this chapter, including interactive resources, can be found on the Student CD-ROM accompanying this textbook and on the Companion Website at www.prenhall.com/frazier.

CHAPTER 14

Hematology and Chemistry

Case Study

Kathleen is working in a medical laboratory as part of her externship and does a lot of routine blood draws. She is running behind, and many patients are getting angry because of the long wait time. While setting up to perform a CBC, CMP, and prothrombin time, Kathleen gathers the vacutainers, alcohol wipes, cotton balls, and tourniquets. She cannot find a disposable gown to wear and decides to perform the draw without it.

Kathleen begins to perform the tests, but one of the tubes, the light blue one, has a faulty vacuum and isn't filling properly. She didn't bring extra blue tubes to the station, so she quickly grabs the extra "brick-top" tube to collect the sample. After she completes the draw, Kathleen notices that some blood has spilled on her uniform shirt.

Objectives

After completing this chapter, you should be able to:

- Spell and define the medical terminology in this chapter.
- Define the medical assistant's role in blood specimen collection in the POL.
- Describe the components of blood.
- Explain how blood cells are formed.
- Define immunohematology.
- Identify the equipment used in blood collection.
- Explain the importance of following the correct order of draw.
- Describe the differences between venipuncture and capillary puncture.
- List important considerations in the transport of blood specimens.
- Identify and describe basic hematology tests.
- Explain the use of chemistry analyzers in common blood chemistry tests.
- Discuss the basics of blood typing.

MedMedia

www.prenhall.com/frazier

Additional interactive resources and activities for this chapter can be found on the Companion Website. For videos, audio glossary, legal and ethical scenarios, job scenarios, quizzes, games, and activities related to the content of this chapter, please access the accompanying CD-ROM in this book.

 **Assets Available:**

Audio Glossary
Legal and Ethical Scenario: *Hematology and Chemistry*
On the Job Scenario: *Hematology and Chemistry*
Video Scenario: *Blood Test Basics*
Multiple Choice Quiz
Games: Crossword, Strikeout and Spelling Bee
Drag and Drop: Circulatory System: Blood Types; Circulatory System: Blood Cells; Circulatory System: Circulatory System

Medical Terminology

agglutination—process in which platelets clump or aggregate together to form a plug or clot

anticoagulant—substance that inhibits blood clot formation

coagulation—blood clot formation

diluent—diluting agent

dyscrasia—abnormal blood or bone marrow condition, such as leukemia

erythrocytes—red blood cells; contain hemoglobin, which carries oxygen from the lungs to the body's cells

hematology—study of blood

hemostasis—process by which the body spontaneously stops bleeding and maintains the blood in a fluid state within the vascular compartment

immunohematology—study of antigens, antibodies, and their interactions

leukocytes—white blood cells; different types of cells that protect against bacterial infection and other foreign invaders

phagocytic—having the ability to ingest particulate material, such as bacteria

phlebotomist—individual trained to draw blood

phlebotomy—process of blood collection, sometimes defined as "an incision into a vein"

plasma—liquid portion of anticoagulated blood

serum—liquid portion that remains when the blood has been allowed to clot

spectrophotometric—measurement or estimate of the amount of color in a solution

thrombocytes—platelets; smallest cells found in blood

venipuncture—method of obtaining venous blood for analysis of hematology and chemistry studies

---

➕ MEDICAL ASSISTING COMPETENCIES

CAAHEP ENTRY-LEVEL COMPETENCIES FOR CMA	ABHES ENTRY-LEVEL COMPETENCIES FOR RMA
■ Identify and respond to issues of confidentiality.	■ Project a positive attitude.
■ Perform within legal and ethical boundaries.	■ Maintain confidentiality at all times.
■ Demonstrate knowledge of federal and state health-care legislation and regulations.	■ Be a "team player."
	■ Be cognizant of ethical boundaries.
	■ Exhibit initiative.
■ Perform hand washing.	■ Adapt to change.
■ Dispose of biohazardous materials.	■ Evidence a responsible attitude.
■ Practice Standard Precautions.	■ Be courteous and diplomatic.
■ Use methods of quality control.	■ Conduct work within scope of education, training, and ability.
■ Screen and follow-up test results.	■ Interview and take patient history.
	■ Prepare patients for procedures.
	■ Apply principles of aseptic techniques and infection control.
	■ Prepare and maintain examination and treatment areas.
	■ Use quality control.
	■ Collect and process specimens.
	■ Perform selected tests that assist with diagnosis and treatment.
	■ Screen and follow up patient test results.
	■ Dispose of hazardous materials.
	■ Practice Standard Precautions.
	■ Perform venipuncture.
	■ Perform hematology.

Introduction

Hematology is the study of blood. **Phlebotomy** is the process of blood collection, the surgical opening of a vein to withdraw blood. Properly collected, labeled, and transported blood samples are the basis for accurate laboratory results. It is the role of the **phlebotomist** to make sure that appropriate blood samples are collected and properly processed.

The Medical Assistant's Role in Hematology and Chemistry

As an MA, you must be familiar with the basic anatomy and physiology of the blood and veins to perform phlebotomy. Your training in phlebotomy will cover various methods of **venipuncture** and capillary blood collection. Responsibilities include properly identifying the patient, reviewing the physician's order, completing the laboratory requisition, and knowing which tubes to use and how much blood to collect.

You must wear the PPE required by OSHA for blood collection, particularly gloves. Snugly fitting latex gloves are most commonly used. Gloves made of other materials, such as polyethylene or nitrile, are available for health-care professionals and patients who are allergic to latex. If there is a possibility that blood will be spilled or will contaminate your clothing, a water-repellent

Abbreviations

FBS—fasting blood sugar

HGB—hemoglobin

MCH—mean corpuscular hemoglobin; a measure of the average hemoglobin content of RBCs

MCHC—mean corpuscular hemoglobin concentration; a measure of the concentration of hemoglobin in the average RBC

MCV—mean corpuscular volume; a measure of the average volume (size) of RBCs in cubic microns

NCCLS—National Committee for Clinical Laboratory Standards

PMN—polymorphonuclear WBCs

COMPETENCY SKILLS PERFORMANCE

1. Perform a butterfly draw using a hand vein.
2. Perform a venipuncture.
3. Perform a capillary puncture.
4. Fill a Unopette for a WBC and platelet count.
5. Prepare a blood smear for a differentiated cell count.
6. Prepare a smear stained with Wright's stain.
7. Perform a microhematocrit test.
8. Perform an ESR using the Wintrobe method.
9. Perform a blood glucose measurement using the Accu-Chek™ Glucometer.
10. Perform a blood cholesterol measurement using the ProAct testing kit.
11. Perform a test for infectious mononucleosis.

---

coat may be required. In some situations, such as working with isolation patients, you will need to wear special protective gowns and masks.

The Anatomy and Physiology of Blood

There are five to six liters of blood in the body of an average adult. Blood consists of **plasma** and cellular components. Solids (formed cells) comprise approximately 45 to 50 percent of blood, and plasma comprises approximately 50 to 55 percent. Approximately 90 percent of plasma is water. Formed elements include **erythrocytes, leucocytes,** and **thrombocytes.** Erythrocytes account for most of the 45 to 50 percent of blood volume; leucocytes and thrombocytes, also referred to as the buffy coat, account for less than 1 percent.

Plasma

Plasma is the liquid portion of blood and comprises approximately 55 to 65 percent of the blood volume. Plasma consists of a high percentage of water. Other components are sugars, salts, gases, hormones, antibodies, minerals, vitamins, **coagulation** factors, and waste products. Plasma appears light yellow in color when it is separated from the cells by centrifugation.

Plasma is the liquid portion of blood in its unclotted or anticoagulated state; **serum** is the liquid portion that remains when the blood has been allowed to clot. Some laboratory tests require serum and others require plasma, so it is important to understand the difference.

Blood Cells

The cellular components of blood include the red blood cells, white blood cells, and platelets.

Red Blood Cells

Red blood cells (also called RBCs or erythrocytes) contain the pigment hemoglobin (**Hgb**), which provides the blood's reddish color (Figure 14-1 ◆). Oxygen from the lungs is bound to hemoglobin and transported through the blood to the tissues, where it is released to the cells. Carbon dioxide (CO_2) is a waste product that is picked up by the blood and carried back to the lungs. RBCs are produced in the bone marrow and live approximately 120 days.

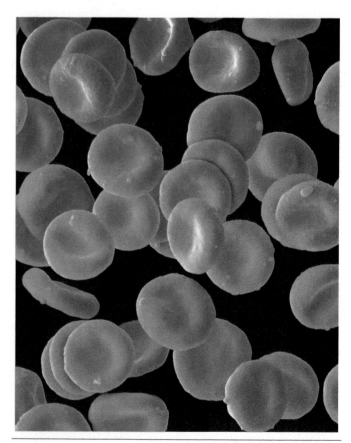

Figure 14-1 ◆ Red blood cells (RBCs) as seen under a microscope
Source: Power and Syred/Photo Researchers, Inc.

Hemoglobin blood test results are directly proportional to the oxygen-carrying capacity of the red blood cells. Because RBCs may have varying amounts of hemoglobin, the number of RBCs does not accurately indicate the blood's hemoglobin content. Hematocrit indirectly measures red blood cell mass by comparing packed red blood cell volume to the volume of whole blood in the test specimen.

White Blood Cells

Five types of white blood cells (WBCs or leukocytes) are found in normal blood. The type can be identified by performing a WBC differential. In this procedure, a stained blood smear is examined under a microscope, 100 WBCs are counted, and each WBC is identified. The differential is often performed by an automated analyzer that flags abnormal results for a technologist's review. WBCs and platelets appear as a white layer (buffy coat) between the plasma and RBCs when whole blood is centrifuged.

The five types of WBCs are neutrophils, lymphocytes, monocytes, eosinophils, and basophils.

- Neutrophils (polymorphonuclear white blood cells, also known as **PMNs** or segs and bands) are the most common WBCs and function to defend the body against infectious diseases, especially bacterial diseases (Figure 14-2 ◆).
- Lymphocytes are the second most common WBCs in adults, and often the most common in children (Figure 14-3 ◆). The primary role of lymphocytes is to aid in the immune defense of the body and to respond to viruses.
- Monocytes are the largest cells in normal blood, two or three times the diameter of erythrocytes (Figure 14-4 ◆). Monocytes are **phagocytic** cells and play a role in cell-mediated immunity.
- Eosinophils are similar in size to neutrophils (Figure 14-5 ◆). They function mainly in allergic or inflammatory responses, but also increase in some types of parasitic infections.

- Basophils are the least numerous WBCs, with a normal range of 0 to 2 percent (Figure 14-6 ◆). They contain histamine and appear to react in allergic states.

Platelets

Platelets (thrombocytes) are the smallest cells found in blood, ranging in size between 2 and 4 microns in diameter (Figure 14-7 ◆). Platelets function in **hemostasis,** during which the body spontaneously stops bleeding and maintains the blood in a fluid state within the vascular compartment. Platelets are an important factor in coagulation, which is the formation of blood clots that occurs when a blood vessel is damaged. A patient with a very low platelet count usually bleeds for an extended period, so extra care must be taken when performing venipunctures. **Agglutination** is the term for the process in which platelets clump or aggregate together to form a plug or clot.

Blood Cell Formation

The hematopoietic system is responsible for the production and maturation of all blood cells. This process takes place in the red bone marrow and other body tissues and organs. All blood cells start as stem cells that grow into blast cells (immature cells). The blast cells then differentiate by function to become mature erythrocytes, platelets, or leukocytes. The five basic kinds of leukocytes, or WBCs, are neutrophils, eosinophils, and basophils, which are all granular, and lymphocytes and monocytes, which are agranular. Agranulocytic monocytes, or mobile, immature, phagocytic leukocytes, circulate in the blood, migrate into the tissues, and become nonmobile, mature, phagocytic macrophages. Some cells are also designed to become precursor lymph cells that later develop into B- and T-lymphocytes, which help the body's immunological defenses. A **dyscrasia,** or blood disorder, can develop from aberrations in the blood cell differentiation and development process. Figure 14-8 ◆ illustrates some simplified examples of how a

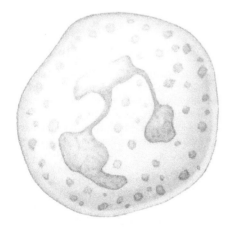

Figure 14-2 ◆ Neutrophil
Source: Dorling Kindersley

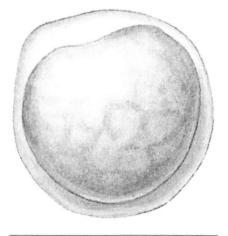

Figure 14-3 ◆ Lymphocyte
Source: Dorling Kindersley

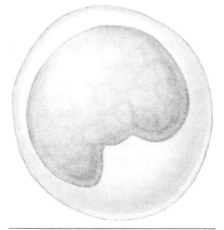

Figure 14-4 ◆ Monocyte
Source: Dorling Kindersley

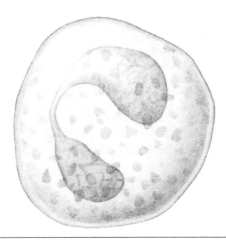

Figure 14-5 ◆ Eosinophil
Source: Dorling Kindersley

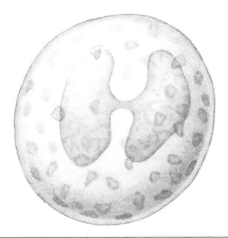

Figure 14-6 ◆ Basophil
Source: Dorling Kindersley

stem cell can differentiate into one of several different types of mature cell.

Altered functioning of the body's hematopoietic system affects CBC laboratory results. For example, an elevated RBC count indicates a different disease diagnosis than an elevated reticulocyte (an earlier stage of RBC development) count.

Immunohematology

Immunohematology is the study of antigens, antibodies, and their interactions. Antigens recognize foreign substances or organisms and stimulate an antibody reaction and the production of lymphocytes, granulocytes, and monocytes. Most clinical laboratories work with RBC antigen/antibody systems only. Immunology testing procedures with WBCs and platelets are often quite complicated and are most commonly performed by specially trained technologists in the blood bank area of the laboratory.

Knowledge of antigen-antibody reactions is important in the treatment of allergies, organ donation and transplantation, blood typing (A, B, AB, and O), and Rh factor (positive or neg-

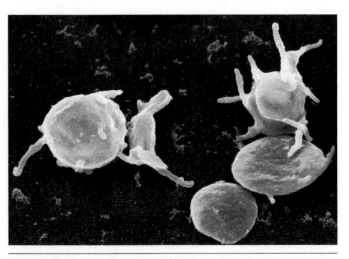

Figure 14-7 ◆ Platelet (thrombocyte)
Source: SPL/Photo Researchers, Inc.

ative). For example, A (blood type) positive (Rh factor) blood has antigen markings for A blood type and positive Rh factor to stimulate antibody formation against a transfusion of B negative blood. An A positive blood transfusion to a patient with A positive blood prevents antibody formation, prevents antibody reaction, and prevents blood transfusion reaction, in that order. Administration of the wrong blood type or Rh factor may cause the donor's blood cells to clump together, plug vital blood vessels, and cause the recipient's death.

Blood group antigens consist of protein molecules with specific groups of sugar molecules attached in precise locations. Blood group antibodies are plasma proteins, usually produced by the body as a defense mechanism in response to exposure to a foreign antigen. Antibodies in the ABO blood group system occur naturally but are usually not detectable until a child is at least 3 months old. Antibodies in other blood group systems usually occur only after exposure to the corresponding RBC antigens, through either transfusion or pregnancy. For additional information on blood typing and grouping, see pages 266–267.

Caduceus Chronicle
A BRIEF HISTORY OF BLOOD GROUPING

The ABO blood groups are the most important of several systems for classifying human blood. Type A blood contains A antigens, does not form A antibodies against its own blood type, and develops B antibodies when type B blood is introduced. Type B blood contains B antigens, does not form antibodies against its own blood type, and develops A antibodies if type A blood is introduced. Type AB blood contains antigens A and B, but neither A nor B antibodies. Type O blood does not contain either the A or B antigens or antibodies.

These blood groups were identified in 1901 by Karl Landsteiner (1868–1943), a U.S. immunologist. In 1902, the AB blood group was discovered by Alfred von Decastrello (1872–1960) and Adriano Sturli (1873–1964). Other "minor" blood group systems, such as Kell, Duffy, Lewis, and many others, have subsequently been discovered.

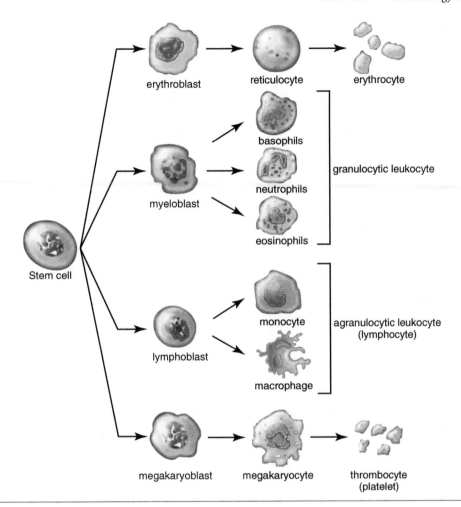

Figure 14-8 ◆ Diagram of differentiation of stem cells

Blood Collection Equipment and Procedures

Equipment used for blood collection includes tourniquets and various blood collection tubes and devices. Procedures include order of draw, puncture methods, and specimen transport.

Tourniquets

Tourniquets are used to make the veins more prominent and easier to find for venipuncture. They are usually latex bands measuring 1 to 1 1/2 inches wide and about 15 inches long. Latex-free tourniquets are available for patients with latex allergy. Velcro-type tourniquets, also commonly used, have the advantage of being quick and easy to apply and allow for easy adjustment of the venous pressure.

A blood pressure cuff may be used in place of a tourniquet. The patient's blood pressure should be taken first. During the phlebotomy procedure, maintain the cuff pressure below the level of the patient's diastolic pressure.

Blood Collection Tubes

Evacuated or vacuum tubes are used for laboratory blood collection. Vacutainer tubes are the type most commonly used, but the color coding for each tube type is consistent across all brands (Figure 14-9 ◆).

The color of the tube stopper indicates which additive, if any, is present in the tube. Additives include the following:

- **Anticoagulants**—contained in most blood collection tubes; each type of anticoagulant works to prevent clotting in a specific way.
- Clot activators—substances that produce clot formation within a specific time frame when mixed properly with the blood specimen; examples are citrate-phosphate-dextrose (CPD), acid-citrate-dextrose (ACD), oxalates; citrates, ethylene-diamine tetra-acetic acid (EDTA), heparin.
- Preservatives—substances that maintain blood cell components in the "drawn" and stable state by decreasing cellular metabolic activity.

Table 14-1 describes the most common tube types according to stopper color. Plasma collected in tubes with different

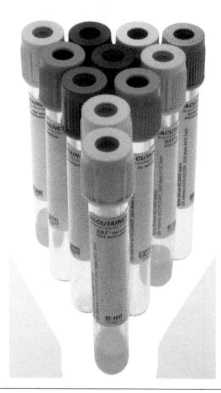

Figure 14-9 ◆ Vacutainer evacutated specimen tubes with Hemogard™ Closure blood collection tube
Courtesy and © Beckton, Dickinson and Company.

types of anticoagulant is not interchangeable. For instance, plasma collected in a blue sodium citrate tube may *not* be used for chemistry studies, as the sodium value would be grossly elevated. Other types may be required by reference laboratories for specific tests. Sterile tubes containing a nutrient broth or enrichment media are required for blood cultures in cases of suspected septicemia.

Order of Draw

Order of draw is important and is determined by the lab tests to be performed and the type of tubes to be used for collecting and processing the blood specimen. Blood being drawn for cultures must be drawn first to prevent contaminating the specimen. It is especially important that no tube containing other anticoagulants or clot activators be drawn before the blue tube, as coagulation testing is very sensitive to even small amounts of anticoagulant or clot activator. Any additive carryover has the potential to cause inaccurate results. It is recommended that when only a blue-top tube is drawn, a red-top tube be drawn first and set aside to prevent thromboplastin release from the cells during the venipuncture, which would contaminate the blue-top tube and skew the results of the coagulation testing. The Clinical and Laboratory Standards Institute (**CLIS**), formally the National Committee for Clinical Laboratory Standards (**NCCLS),** has instituted a recommended order of draw to minimize the effects of additive carryover (Table 14-2).

? —Critical Thinking Question 14-1—

Kathleen is assuming that because the "brick-top" tube does not contain additives, it will be fine to obtain the prothrombin time sample in. Why is this incorrect?

Venipuncture

There are three basic means of collecting venous blood samples:

- evacuated tube system
- syringe and needle
- winged infusion set (butterfly) method

These methods allow for a choice of needle gauge and length. *Needle gauge* refers to the diameter of the needle. The larger the gauge number, the smaller the needle diameter. A needle gauge of 21 to 23 is most commonly used for routine blood collection. Needle length is usually 1 to 1 1/2 inches. Deeper veins may require longer needles.

Evacuated Tube

The evacuated tube system consists of a plastic holder, attachable needles of various gauges, and vacuum tubes (Figure 14-10 ◆). The needle screws into the holder and has two pointed ends. The longer, beveled end is used for venipuncture. The short end is covered with a retractable sheath that is pushed into the tube stopper and allows blood to flow into the vacuum tube when venipuncture is performed. This is the fastest and most efficient system for venous blood collection.

Needle and Syringe

The needle and syringe are used if the veins are fragile or if there is concern that the vein may collapse with the pressure of the evacuated tube system (Figure 14-11 ◆). A needle of the appropriate gauge is attached to a syringe of the desired size. The basic phlebotomy steps are followed and the blood is transferred from the syringe to the appropriate tubes.

Winged Infusion (Butterfly)

The winged infusion or butterfly set consists of a very small needle attached to a length of tubing (Figure 14-12 ◆). This device is used on very small or fragile veins. A syringe is attached to the tubing.

Patient Reactions to Venipuncture

The patient may have significant reactions to the phlebotomy procedure such as dizziness, light headedness, fainting, upset stomach, and even vomiting. The medical assistant must be aware that the potential for these problems exists and must take adequate steps for patient safety. Some patients who come in for a blood draw will have been fasting for several hours per physician instructions. These patients will have a greater likelihood of adverse reactions such as fainting due to low blood sugar.

The best way to protect the patient from an adverse effect is to be prepared for the possibility that something will happen. Most phlebotomy stations come with a phlebotomy chair that includes a padded cross bar that is lowered across the patients lap. In the event that the patient faints, the padded bar will prevent them from slipping out of the chair or striking the head.

No matter how many times the patient reports they have had their blood drawn they should be instructed to take several slow deep breaths and move from the phlebotomy station only when they feel comfortable enough to do so. Rushing a patient before they are ready increases the likelihood that they will become dizzy and fall.

TABLE 14-1 ADDITIVES FOR BLOOD SPECIMEN VACUTAINER TUBES

Color of Stopper	Additive	Description and Use	Special Requirements
Red, large glass	No additive or clot activator	15 ml red-top tube used when serum is required for: ■ chemistry testing ■ blood bank testing ■ immunology ■ many reference lab tests	No mixing required.
Blue	Sodium citrate	Used primarily for coagulation tests (PT, PTT, D-dimer, fibrinogen). Sodium citrate prevents coagulation by binding calcium. Correct blood volume is required for accurate coagulation test results. *Never* use a blue tube as the first tube in an evacuated tube draw as there may be some fluid contamination from surrounding tissues. Draw 2 to 3 ml of blood in a tube containing no additives before drawing the blue tube.	Gently mix 8 to 10 times.
Red, small plastic	Clot activator	Small 7 ml red-top tube. The serum may be used for chemistry and immunology testing.	Gently mix 8 to 10 times.
Red, black mottled (also called serum separator tubes or SST brand) tubes	Clot activator and serum gel separator	Separator consisting of an inert gel works as a barrier by settling between the clot and the serum during centrifugation. This tube is especially useful for "send out" tests, as the serum does not need to be transferred to another tube. Serum may be used for most chemistry and immunology testing but is not recommended for blood bank antibody testing.	Gently mix 8 to 10 times.
Green	Heparin	Heparin is a natural anticoagulant that inhibits thrombin and thus prevents fibrin formation from fibrinogen. Plasma and whole blood are collected in these tubes and are often used for routine chemistry testing, as heparin does not interfere with common blood chemistry elements.	Gently mix 8 to 10 times.
Lavender	EDTA	Used for most hematology testing (CBC, reticulocyte count, sedimentation rates) and for some specialized testing. The anticoagulant EDTA binds the calcium needed for clot formation.	Mix gently 8 to 10 times.
Gray	Sodium fluoride and potassium oxalate	Sodium fluoride is a preservative that inhibits glycolytic action, and potassium oxalate is an anticoagulant that binds calcium. These tubes are usually used to collect specimens for glucose and lactic analysis.	Mix gently 8 to 10 times.

TABLE 14-2 ORDER OF DRAW

1. Blood cultures (yellow) SPS sterile; sometimes a non-additive discard tube
2. Light blue (sodium citrate tube)
3. Red (plain) or Tiger-Top mottled red (gel separator tube)
4. Green and light green (heparin tubes)
5. Lavender (EDTA)
6. Pink or white (EDTA)
7. Gray (sodium fluoride/oxalate)
8. Dark blue (FDP)
9. Royal Blue last

2003 CLIS/NCCLS recommendation.

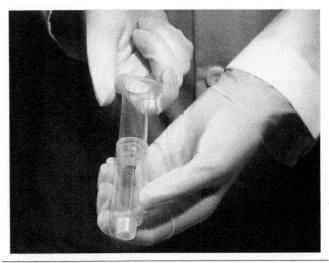

Figure 14-10 ◆ Vacutainer™ brand safety lock needle holder
Courtesy and © Beckton, Dickinson and Company.

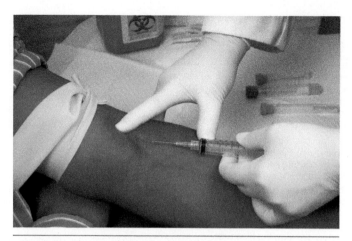

Figure 14-11 ◆ A needle and syringe

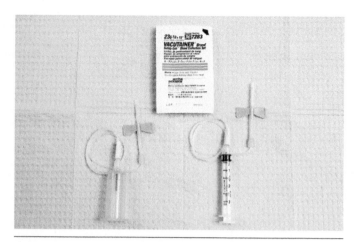

Figure 14-12 ◆ Winged infusion or butterfly set

PROCEDURE 14-1 Perform a Butterfly Draw Using a Hand Vein

Theory

For patients with weak or compromised veins, or veins that are not easily seen or felt, venous blood specimens can be drawn more easily with a butterfly needle (winged infusion) system. This system can be used with a vacutainer or syringe. Veins that are weak or compromised are at risk for collapse under the strong pressure caused by an evacuated tube system, so syringes are generally used. The sites most commonly chosen for the butterfly method are the back of the hand or the antecubital space in the arm. If you are obtaining a blood sample from the back of the hand, always use a syringe to collect the blood sample with the winged infusion system to prevent vein collapse. Also, have a variety of bandages available. Some patients may be allergic to the adhesives in bandage strips or paper tape, or they may have fragile skin that will tear easily with adhesives. For these patients make sure you have Coban, an adhesive-free self-adhering wrap, or a similar material available.

Materials

- gloves
- sterile butterfly package
- cotton balls
- tourniquet
- vacutainer or syringe
- bandage, Coban, or paper tape
- alcohol

- sharps container
- permanent pen for marking lab sample
- patient chart

Competency

(**Conditions**) With the necessary materials, you will be able to (**Task**) obtain a venous blood specimen from the back of the hand using a butterfly system (**Standards**) correctly within 15 minutes.

1. Wash your hands and gather the equipment.
2. Identify the patient and escort him or her to the treatment area.
3. Select the appropriate hand site. Put on gloves.
4. Cleanse the skin with alcohol.
5. Open the sterile butterfly package and stretch the tubing slightly to prevent it from recoiling when you begin the blood draw.
6. Apply the tourniquet to the patient's wrist area, proximal to the wrist bone, at least 3 inches above the injection site.
7. Have the patient make a fist or hold a stress ball or roll of gauze to slightly elevate the hand.
8. Enter the vein with the needle. The bevel should face upward, at a 30-degree angle to the skin. Advance the needle into the vein (Figure 14-13 ◆). Some people prefer to pinch the wings upward to hold the needle, while others prefer to hold just one wing from the side. If you enter

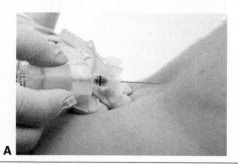

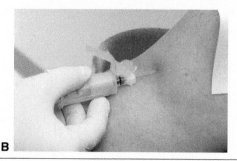

Figure 14-13 ◆ (A) Enter the vein with the needle at a 30-degree angle; (B) Advance the needle into the vein.

continued

PROCEDURE 14-1 Perform a Butterfly Draw Using a Hand Vein *(continued)*

the vein correctly, you will see blood "flash" into the hub of the needle, occasionally into the tubing. Hand veins have a tendency to roll, so you may want to do a single-finger or double-finger anchor.

- Single-finger anchor: With your thumb, pull the skin taut toward the patient's knuckles to hold the vein in place. Do not put excessive pressure on the vein, as it will collapse and be difficult to enter.
- Double-finger anchor: Place your thumb below the puncture site and pull the skin toward the knuckles. Place the index finger of the same hand above the puncture site with slight pressure. You will insert the needle between your two fingers, so take great care to avoid an accidental needle stick.

9. When blood appears in the tubing, release the tourniquet.
10. With the needle secured in the vein, pull back on the plunger to obtain the necessary amount of blood for testing. If you are taking blood from the anetcubital space with a vacutainer, advance the tube onto the collection-hub with your other hand, using the wings for support.
11. When you have obtained the correct amount of blood, break the suction of the vacutainer by removing the tube. (If you are using a syringe, there is no suction.)

12. Place a cotton ball or gauze pad over the puncture site without pressure and remove the needle.
13. Discard the needle and butterfly collection tubing into a sharps container.
14. Bandage as necessary.
15. Remove gloves and wash hands.
16. Label the blood specimen and fill out the laboratory paperwork.

Patient Education

Inform the patient about puncture site care and when to expect to receive test results, if required by your medical office.

Charting Example

12/16/XX 10:48 AM Venous blood sample obtained from back of patient hand, left, through butterfly collection. Blood specimen sent to laboratory for CBC, CMP, and LFTs. Patient was told to keep bandage over puncture site for approximately 10 minutes and report any unusual bleeding, swelling, or bruising. Blake Singer, RMA

Venipuncture Sites

The antecubital fossa, a triangular area below the elbow, is the most commonly used venipuncture site (Figure 14-14 ◆). The veins here are usually larger, better supported by surrounding tissue, and less painful to puncture than any other site. The median cubital vein is the vein of choice because it is large and well anchored. The cephalic vein may be more difficult to find and has a tendency to move. Extreme care must be taken if the basilic vein is used because of its proximity to the brachial artery.

Dorsal wrist and hand veins are also acceptable sites for venipuncture. Alternate sites, such as ankle or lower extremity veins, may be used when the usual sites are difficult to access. The physician's permission may be required in these cases.

Keys to Success
VENIPUNCTURE SITES TO AVOID

Do *not* draw blood:
■ Above an IV, as IV fluid dilution or contamination may yield inaccurate results that may lead to misdiagnosis.
■ From the side on which a mastectomy was performed, because of the potential harm to the patient from lymphostasis.
■ Near hematomas, as specimens may yield erroneous results.
■ Near burned areas, which are very susceptible to infection.
■ From an area reserved for dialysis access.
■ Near an area with edema, as the specimen may be diluted with tissue fluids that could affect the test results.

Using the Evacuation System

Before proceeding with the actual venipuncture, be sure to follow the appropriate preparation steps: verifying the physician's orders, preparing the laboratory requisition, checking availability of supplies, identifying the patient, verifying patient preparation, and comfortably and securely seating the patient.

Verifying the Orders

Verify that the physician's orders for laboratory tests are legible and contain all the necessary information (Figure 14-15 ◆). Your health-care organization may be subject to legal action if laboratory tests are performed based on incomplete orders. Transcribing the physician's order for tests may involve entering the orders into a computerized laboratory information system or writing the information on a laboratory form. Always order tests accurately to avoid having the patient return because of laboratory personnel errors. If possible, have someone else check your test orders for accuracy before collecting the blood sample.

When assigned to complete a lab requisition for a patient to take to a laboratory, you must complete all required information: the patient's name, date of birth, insurance, and contact information; the ordering physician's name and contact information; and the tests ordered and the diagnosis or reason for the test, usually in ICD-9CM codes. Additionally, a notation should be entered if fasting is required, along with the length of the fasting period prior to the test. Any other pertinent information should also be included.

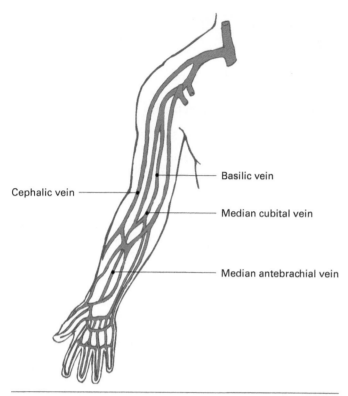

Figure 14-14 ◆ The antecubital fossa is the most commonly used venipuncture site.

Figure 14-15 ◆ Physician's order for lab test

Obtaining Supplies

Make sure all routine phlebotomy supplies are readily available. Avoid searching for supplies while the patient is sitting in the phlebotomy chair. Your lack of preparation can make the patient anxious and does not reflect well on the institution or you.

Some tests require special tubes that may need to be obtained from a different storage area within the laboratory or from the reference laboratory. Also, check to see if special handling is required for the ordered tests. For instance, ammonias should be transported on ice; cold agglutinins should be allowed to clot in a 37°C heat block.

Blood draws are usually performed using evacuated, or vacuum, tube systems. The needle for puncture and procurement of the blood specimen is attached securely to a holder, and the different evacuated tubes are placed in and removed from the holder in correct order of draw. This method is preferred because it eliminates the possibility of cell hemolysis, prevents clot adherence to the wall of the collection container, and reduces the chances of needle injury and exposure to blood that occur during other types of blood draw. A butterfly needle is used if the blood specimen is more difficult to collect, as in the case of some pediatric, geriatric, and cancer patients. The butterfly needle can be secured to the holder for evacuated tubes or to a syringe for later placement in an evacuated tube.

Identifying the Patient

In a doctor's office or hospital outpatient setting, ask the patient to tell you his or her name. Avoid asking questions such as "Are you Susie Smith?" There may be other patients nearby and enough sound interference to make it difficult for the patient to hear you clearly. The patient may say yes out of confusion. Check the birthdate. It is common to have two patients with the same name but different birthdates.

Verifying Patient Preparation

Make sure the patient has followed instructions for the tests ordered. Some laboratory tests require special preparation beforehand. Lipid profiles and fasting blood sugars (**FBS**) must always be collected after the patient has fasted. Drug levels may need to be checked at certain times after the patient has taken a medication. Other tests, such as CBCs, require no special preparation.

Proper Patient Care

Make every attempt to help the patient feel comfortable and more at ease. Follow these steps to ensure a successful venipuncture:

- Seat the patient in a phlebotomy chair. *Never* attempt to collect blood from a patient who is standing or sitting on a high stool.
- The phlebotomy chair should have a solid armrest that can be locked into position in front of the patient. Supported by the armrest, the patient's arm should not be significantly bent at the elbow (Figure 14-16 ◆).
- It is usually easier to collect blood from a child who is lying down. The child feels more comfortable, and it is

easier to prevent the child's arm from moving in that position. Some adult patients may also need to lie down, usually because they have previously experienced faintness or some other difficulty with blood collection.

■ Try to make unthreatening, professional statements such as "I need to collect a blood sample," rather than "I need to stick you to get some blood." Avoid telling the patient, especially a child, that the venipuncture will not hurt. Instead, use minimizing phrases such as "This will sting for a moment."

Capillary Puncture Collection

Capillary or dermal puncture collection is used with infants or small children and, in certain cases, with adults

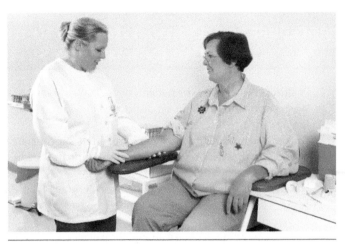

Figure 14-16 ◆ Phlebotomy chair

PROCEDURE 14-2 Demonstrate a Venipuncture Using the Evacuation System

Theory

Make sure the proper tubes are available for the ordered tests. For backup, it is a good idea to keep an extra tube of each type in your lab coat pocket or in a venipuncture supply tray in case a tube is found not to have a vacuum.

In routine inpatient situations, do *not* collect blood samples from patients without hospital identification bracelets. Ask the nursing staff to attach an identification bracelet to the patient before you collect blood. In a true emergency, such as with an ER trauma patient, there may not be time for a hospital bracelet. In this case, ask the patient to tell you his or her name or have the patient identified by the nurse.

Test result accuracy and patient comfort are your main concerns when applying the tourniquet. Prolonged application can result in the formation of a hematoma as blood infiltrates the tissue and can alter some test results. Leave the tourniquet on as briefly as possible, preferably no longer than one minute per application. The tourniquet may need to be applied twice, once before the procedure to select the vein, then just before the vein is punctured.

Verify that the patient does not have latex allergies. If the patient indicates a possible latex allergy, use a latex-free tourniquet and gloves.

Asking the patient to make a fist will help to make the veins more prominent and prevent them from rolling.

Cleanse the site with an antiseptic, usually 70 percent isopropyl alcohol. *When you collect blood for blood alcohol levels, you must use an aqueous, not alcohol-based, antiseptic to ensure valid results.*

After performing the venipuncture, fill the tubes in the correct order of draw to ensure the proper blood-to-anticoagulant ratio. Apply pressure and monitor bleeding from the puncture site after you withdraw the needle. A patient who is on anticoagulant therapy, such as Coumadin or heparin, may bleed from the venipuncture site for longer than normal. You can ask an able patient to apply pressure to the site. Make sure that bleeding has completely stopped before bandaging the site. Firmly apply an adhesive bandage over the pressure gauze to ensure continued clotting.

Materials

■ phlebotomy tray *or* individual items (antiseptic pads, appropriate vacutainers, holder, and needle)
■ tourniquet
■ handwritten or preprinted specimen labels
■ disposable gloves
■ sharps container

Competency

(**Conditions**) With the necessary materials, you will be able to (**Task**) demonstrate a venipuncture using an evacuation system (**Standards**) correctly within 15 minutes.

1. Review the physician's order. Verify that the order is legible, includes a diagnosis and other necessary information, and is signed by the physician or his or her assigned person. If any test order is not legible, or if there is any confusion about which test has been ordered, contact thephysician or the office nurse for confirmation. Document on the physician's order the correct tests and the name of the person who confirmed the order.
2. Wash your hands.
3. Prepare the laboratory requisition from the physician's order.
4. Make sure all routine and special supplies are available for venipuncture and transporting the specimen.
5. Identify the patient and escort him or her to the treatment area.
6. Verify that the patient has been properly prepared.

continued

PROCEDURE 14-2 Demonstrate a Venipuncture Using the Evacuation System (continued)

7. Position and reassure the patient.
8. Wash your hands and put on disposable gloves.
9. Prepare the needle.
   For evacuated tubes and holder: Thread the appropriate needle into the holder until it is secured, using the needle sheath as a wrench (Figure 14-17 ◆).
   For a syringe: Insert the needle into the syringe (Figure 14-18 ◆). Move the plunger within the barrel to check movement.
10. Apply the tourniquet. Wrap it around the patient's upper arm 3 to 4 inches above the antecubital fossa (Figure 14-19 ◆). Cross the ends of the tourniquet and pull them snugly against the patient's arm (Figure 14-20 ◆). With your thumb and forefinger, hold the tourniquet in place while pulling a loop of one end behind the joined area (Figure 14-21 ◆).
11. Select the venipuncture site.
12. Ask the patient to make a fist.
13. Palpate the antecubital area with your index finger to determine the exact vein location and needle entry site.
14. Clean the antecubital area (or other selected site) with an antiseptic wipe, cotton ball soaked in antiseptic, or alcohol wipe. Use a circular motion from the venipuncture site outward.
15. Allow the site to air-dry, or dry it with a clean gauze pad.
16. Insert the blood collection tube into the holder and onto the needle up to the recessed guideline on the needle holder. Avoid pushing the tube beyond the guideline to prevent loss of vacuum.
17. Remove the plastic protective cover from the needle.
18. To perform the venipuncture:
    - Make sure the patient's arm (or other venipuncture site) is in a downward position to prevent reflux or backflow.
    - Grasp the patient's arm firmly but gently.
    - Draw the patient's skin taut with your thumb to anchor the vein.
    - Line the needle bevel-up with the vein.
    - With a single, direct puncture, enter the vein at a 15- to 30-degree angle.
19. Hold the needle holder firmly and steadily, and then push the tube forward in the holder until the stopper is punctured with the rear of the needle.

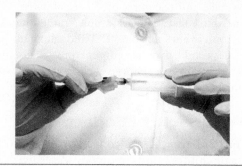

Figure 14-17 ◆ Thread the appropriate needle into the holder.

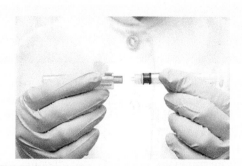

Figure 14-18 ◆ Insert the needle into the syringe.

20. As soon as blood is flowing freely, release the tourniquet by pulling on the free end above the loop.
21. Ask the patient to release his or her fist.
22. Fill the tubes in the correct order of draw. Invert any tubes containing anticoagulant.
23. Remove the last tube from the holder.
24. Withdraw the needle from the patient's arm.
25. Immediately place a clean gauze pad over the site. Apply pressure or instruct the patient to apply pressure.
26. Remove the needle from the hub and discard the needle in an approved container. Or, if using a syringe, after filling the tubes in the correct order of draw, discard the syringe in an approved container.
27. Label each tube with the patient's first and last name, identification number, date and time of collection, and your

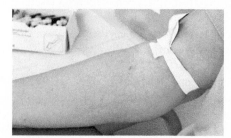

Figure 14-19 ◆ Apply the tourniquet around the patient's upper arm 3 to 4 inches above the antecubital fossa.

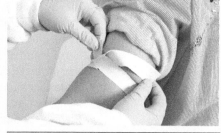

Figure 14-20 ◆ Cross the ends of the tourniquet and pull them snugly against the patient's arm.

Figure 14-21 ◆ Form the tourniquet loop.

PROCEDURE 14-2 Demonstrate a Venipuncture Using the Evacuation System *(continued)*

initials or identifying code. *Or,* if preprinted computer labels are available, initial each label and attach the labels to the appropriate tubes.

28. Check the venipuncture site to make sure bleeding has stopped, and bandage it. Instruct the patient to leave the bandage on for at least 15 minutes.
29. Remove and dispose of your gloves. Wash your hands.
30. Evaluate the patient for signs of faintness or color loss. If the patient appears stable, thank the patient for cooperating and escort him or her back to the waiting room.

Patient Education

Instruct the patient beforehand in the general procedure. Do *not* promise the patient that the procedure will not hurt. It is more tactful to say that it might feel like a "brief sting." Let the patient know when the actual puncture is about to happen. As necessary, provide information about how long the results will take and how they will be transmitted to the patient.

Charting Example

Sometimes charting may not be required for phlebotomy procedures because laboratory processing documentation is sufficient. If charting is required, it might look like this:

08/25/XX 7:30 a.m. Pt anxious about phlebotomy procedure. General explanations given before each step. Pt voiced concern over the amount of pain she would experience and that her veins were hard to get blood from. Venous specimen obtained for a CBC, Na, K, and Cl with appropriate tubes. Pt held pressure gauze onsite, site was bandaged, and pt was instructed to leave the bandage in place for 15 minutes. Pt escorted to the exit. Decon Ramirez, CMA

(Figure 14-22 ◆). It is performed with special lancets, usually disposable self-contained lancets with a trigger that releases the actual puncturing device. A capillary tube (stoppered with clay sealant after the specimen has been collected), microcontainer with scoop, or micropipette with dilution system may also be used to collect the specimen.

Performing a Capillary Puncture

A dermal (capillary) collection is performed when only a small amount of blood is required for testing, or when venipuncture is not appropriate, such as with infants, small children, or adults whose veins are difficult to find. Dermal collections are also recommended for burned or scarred patients, patients being monitored with a glucose monitoring device, patients

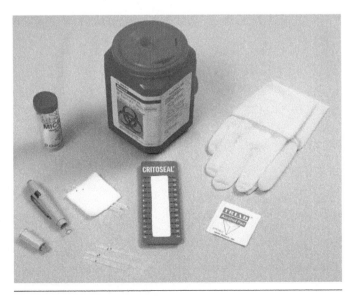

Figure 14-22 ◆ Capillary puncture equipment

Keys to Success
SPECIAL-NEEDS BLOOD TESTING

Special considerations or adaptations of procedure should be made for the following patients.

■ Diabetics: Before you take a blood specimen, ask the patient when he or she took diabetic medication last, and the name and dosage of the medication. Note this information on the laboratory requisition. Take blood specimens only from patients who have fasted. This is based on the fact that the test deals with glucose content of the blood. CBC, blood type, and other tests that normally do not require fasting may be drawn on a diabetic who has eaten. Ascertain whether you will need to help the patient obtain food after the test.

■ Children: Probably the most important step is to reassure the child and parents or guardian and be truthful about the minor discomforts of the procedure. Allow parental involvement in reassuring and immobilizing the child. If the parents are more of a hindrance than a help, escort them to an adjacent room, if possible, and explain tactfully that the procedure will be less stressful for the child if they are not present. They will likely feel less anxious if they are close by.

■ Elderly patients: Always consider how the individual has been affected by age. The patient may need assistance with transfer and ambulation. Proceed cautiously with venipuncture, as the veins may be more fragile or scarred. Smaller needles, such as the butterfly, are used more often with elderly patients, and the tourniquet may not be necessary. Elderly patients should be encouraged to carry a current list of medications and dosages with them.

■ "Bleeders": A patient who is a hemophiliac or on anticoagulant therapy or chemotherapy will often tell you. However, it is a good habit to scan each patient's diagnosis information before the procedure. Note on the laboratory requisition any medications, last time/dosage taken, or diagnoses that indicate bleeding tendencies. Plan extra time for pressure on and observation of the venipuncture site.

■ Difficult or other emotionally needy patients: Start by asking the patient to state why he or she is refusing to have blood drawn. While listening to the response, remain nonjudgmental. If the patient knows the reason and it can be resolved, you will likely gain the patient's cooperation. If the patient remains difficult and uncooperative, request assistance from the supervisor or a physician. Remember, performing venipuncture on an unwilling patient would be considered battery.

with thrombotic tendencies, or patients whose veins must be saved for chemotherapy or dialysis. Skin puncture blood is a mixture of blood from arterioles, venules, capillaries, and some cellular fluids. Some chemical blood elements may differ significantly between venous and capillary blood, so it is impor-

tant to document on the report whether a capillary collection was performed.

If you or another employee is accidentally exposed to a needle stick or puncture, follow the directions for institutional post-exposure follow-up testing. Employers are required to pro-

PROCEDURE 14-3 Perform a Capillary Puncture with Microcollection Tubes

Theory

Select an age-appropriate dermal puncture site where there is no danger of contact with bone. For an infant less than 1 year old, use the medial and lateral areas of the heel (Figure 14-23 ◆). For safety and convenience, an infant should be on his or her back in a bassinet. Hold the foot firmly to avoid any sudden movement.

The preferred site for finger sticks is the middle or ring finger, halfway between the center of the ball of the finger and its side (Figure 14-24 ◆). Avoid the thumb and index finger, as the thumb has a pulse and the index finger may be more sensitive or callused. The patient must be sitting or lying down for finger sticks.

If possible, warm the puncture site. Warming increases the capillary blood flow and makes blood collection much more efficient.

After cleansing the puncture site, allow the antiseptic to dry or wipe it with clean, dry gauze. Failure to dry properly may contaminate the specimen with antiseptic, hemolyze or destroy the blood cells, or cause stinging at the puncture site.

Choose a capillary puncturing device in an age-appropriate size. There are different sizes for infant heel sticks and for finger sticks.

The order of draw for capillary puncture is different than for venipuncture: lavender, other additive tubes, and red. Fill the tubes to the appropriate fill line using the collection scoop. Do not squeeze the heel or finger to obtain the sample, as squeezing releases tissue that may dilute the blood and lead to inaccurate results. Lightly touching the underside of the blood drop will prompt the blood to flow through the scoop and into the collection tube. Gently tap the tubes containing anticoagulant after each drop of blood to ensure adequate mixing. Invert each tube eight to ten times after filling.

Materials

- phlebotomy tray *or* individual items (antiseptic pads and capillary puncture and collection devices)
- handwritten or preprinted specimen labels
- disposable gloves
- sharps container

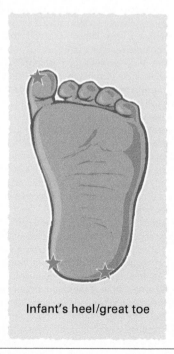

Infant's heel/great toe

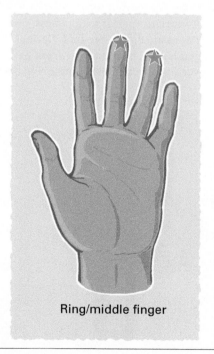

Ring/middle finger

Figure 14-23 ◆ Capillary puncture site: infant's heel/great toe

Figure 14-24 ◆ Capillary puncture site for adult: middle or ring finger

PROCEDURE 14-3 **Perform a Capillary Puncture with Microcollection Tubes** *(continued)*

Competency

(**Conditions**) With the necessary materials, you will be able to (**Task**) demonstrate a capillary puncture (**Standards**) correctly within 15 minutes.

1. Review the physician's order (see Procedure 14-1) and prepare the laboratory requisition.
2. Gather the supplies for capillary puncture and specimen transport.
3. Wash your hands.
4. Ask the patient to state his or her name. Ask the parents or guardian of babies or young children for identification information. Escort the patient or the parent/guardian with the child to the treatment area.
5. Verify that the patient has followed test preparation instructions such as changing the diet or taking special medications and is not allergic to latex.
6. Position and reassure the patient.
7. Select an age-appropriate dermal puncture site where there is no danger of contact with bone.
8. If possible, warm the site with a warming device or a warm, moist cloth (no warmer than 40°C/105°F) for three minutes.
9. Wash your hands and put on disposable gloves.
10. Clean the site with an antiseptic wipe, usually 70 percent isopropyl alcohol. Allow the area to thoroughly air-dry, or dry it with clean gauze.
11. Choose a puncturing device of the appropriate size. Remove the safety indicator and discard it in the appropriate biohazardous waste container.
12. Place the puncturing device firmly on the prepared skin surface, so that the lancet cuts across the grooves of the finger or heel print. Press the safety trigger to release the puncturing lancet (Figure 14-25 ◆).
13. For a finger stick, massage gently from the hand to near the puncture site, keeping the hand below elbow level to obtain the required blood sample.

14. Wipe away the first drop of blood with clean gauze. The first drop contains tissue fluids and may contaminate the blood sample (Figure 14-26 ◆).
15. Follow the correct order of draw for capillary puncture specimens to fill the tubes to the fill line: lavender, the other additive tubes, then red.
16. Collect the specimen by holding the scoop of the microcollection tube directly beneath the puncture site. Apply gentle pressure at the puncture site ends, opening the puncture slightly to maximize blood flow. (For a finger stick, apply gentle, intermittent pressure on the entire finger to allow the capillaries to refill with blood and to help ensure continuous blood flow.) (Figure 14-27 ◆)
17. Lightly touch the collection scoop to the underside of the drop of blood so that the blood flows through the scoop and into the collection tube.
18. Gently tap each tube containing anticoagulant after the addition of each drop of blood to ensure that the blood falls to the anticoagulant/blood mixture.
19. After filling the tube, invert it back and forth eight to ten times.
20. When the blood collection is complete, wipe the site dry and apply pressure with clean gauze until the bleeding stops.
21. Apply a cloth tape bandage to the puncture site.
22. Dispose of all used sharps and biohazardous waste in the appropriate containers.
23. Label each tube with the patient's first and last name, identification number, date and time of collection, and your initials or identifying code. Or, if preprinted computer labels are available, initial each label and attach the labels to the appropriate tubes.
24. Remove the disposable gloves and discard appropriately. Wash your hands.
25. Instruct the patient, or the patient's parent or guardian, to remove the bandage after at least 15 minutes. Thank the patient or parent/guardian for cooperating or assisting.
26. Escort the patient to the waiting room for further instructions.

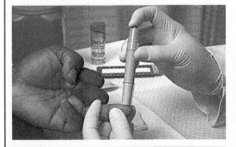

Figure 14-25 ◆ Place the puncturing device firmly on the prepared skin surface.

Figure 14-26 ◆ Wipe away the first drop of blood with clean gauze.

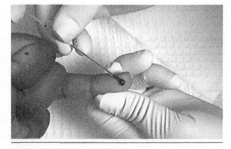

Figure 14-27 ◆ Collect the specimen using the microcollection tube.

continued

PROCEDURE 14-3 Performing a Capillary Puncture with Microcollection Tubes (continued)

Patient Education

Instruct the patient beforehand in the general procedure. Do *not* promise the patient that the procedure will not hurt. It is more tactful to say that it might feel like a "brief sting." Let the patient know when the actual puncture is about to happen. As necessary, provide information about how long the results will take and how they will be transmitted to the patient.

Charting Example

Sometimes charting is not required for phlebotomy procedures because laboratory processing documentation is sufficient. If charting is required, it might look like this:

08/25/XX 9:30 A.M. Hgb, Hct capillary specimen obtained from the ring finger of the patient's hand. Pressure applied, site checked and absent of bleeding, and bandage applied. Joan Houston, RMA

Keys to Success
MAINTAINING PATIENT CONFIDENTIALITY

Regardless of the kind of test involved, a breach of confidentiality concerning lab test results is considered *negligence*. Testing could include standard CBCs and urinalysis, but it could also include tests relating to illegal drug use or HIV. Treat all testing with the same high standard of confidentiality. All patient or employee results, chart information, and verbal and nonverbal communication must be kept between the patient and employee and or the physician.

Keys to Success
DIAGNOSIS FROM BLOOD TESTING

Diagnostic tests such as CBC, electrolytes, and many others measure present values in the patient's venous or arterial blood. These are compared to normal blood values, which are often stated on the same laboratory report. In addition to the patient complaint associated with the office visit and the physician's examination of the patient, laboratory results confirm or rule out the presence of particular diseases. If lab results do not yield diagnostic answers, the physician may order further tests.

Also, the disease process can be monitored for progress or relapse, and treatment can be monitored for effectiveness with blood tests. For example, an antibiotic is given to treat a particular infection. A WBC can determine if the disease is present or if it is reacting correctly to the antibiotic. Drug levels can be monitored to determine if they are at therapeutic level. Other tests, such as BUN and creatinine, can determine if the treatment is affecting kidney function. (See Appendix C for Normal Blood Values/Disease Conditions evaluated for abnormal values.)

vide this service. The CDC bases its recommendations for better safeguards on statistics from new disease or clinical information.

Transporting Specimens

Place blood specimens in an approved leakproof container, such as a sealed biohazard bag, before transporting them to the laboratory. Be attentive to any time constraints or special handling. For instance, sedimentation rates should be performed within two hours of collection. Place the specimens in the designated location in the laboratory and make sure that laboratory staff are aware they have been delivered.

Performing Basic Laboratory Testing

As an MA working in a hospital laboratory, you will usually be responsible only for blood collections. As an MA in a physician's office laboratory, you will often be required to perform some basic laboratory testing. Each laboratory has a written procedure for every test performed in that laboratory. It is essential that the tests be performed *exactly* as written.

Every laboratory has its own set of reference values, sometimes referred to as "normal values," based on the patient population in its area. In addition to reference values, each laboratory also has critical values, formerly referred to as panic values, for many tests. Critical values are abnormal values that indicate a possible threat to the patient's health status. They must be immediately communicated to the physician or healthcare professional responsible for the patient's care.

If you perform laboratory tests, it will be your responsibility to make sure that any applicable quality control has been performed and that all reagents are "in date," meaning their expiration dates have not passed. Quality control is necessary to assure results as accurate as possible for all tests performed. All facets of laboratory activity must be monitored from specimen collection to processing, testing, and reporting the results. Quality control assessment includes checks of supplies, reagents, personnel, machinery, and test performance. The results of all quality control procedures must be recorded and maintained.

Basics of Hematology Testing

Basic hematology testing includes WBC counts, RBC counts, hemoglobin, hematocrit (Hct), RBC indices, and platelet counts. WBC differentials are often considered basic tests as well.

Hemoglobin and hematocrit measurements are helpful to the physician in diagnosing many conditions. An abnormally high hemoglobin value may be indicative of dehydration, and an abnormally low value may indicate anemia. Other possible implications include but are not limited to high concentration or value: polycythemia, congestive heart failure, chronic obstructive lung disease, high altitudes, or severe burns. Likewise, other possible implications include but are not limited to low concentration or value: kidney disease, excessive IV fluids, cancers, and Hodgkin's disease. Normal values for adult males are 13.5 –18 g/dL, and for adult females 12–16 g/dL.

Hematocrit values, expressed as a percentage, indicate the concentration of packed red blood cells in 100 ml of blood. Normal values for the adult male are 40–54% and for the adult female 36–46%. Decreased percentages are indicative of but not limited to acute blood loss, anemia, leukemia, Hodgkin's disease, multiple myeloma, malnutrition, bone marrow failure, chronic renal disease, vitamin B and C deficiencies, cirrhosis of the liver, pregnancy, peptic ulcer, rheumatoid arthritis, and SLE. Increased percentages are indicative of but not limited to dehydration, polycythemia vera, eclampsia, trauma, pulmonary emphysema, hypovolemia, severe diarrhea, diabetic acidosis, surgery, trauma, and transient ischemic cerebral accident (TIA).

Most POLs have an automated cell counter (Figure 14-28 ◆). This device accurately counts and sizes cells by detecting and measuring changes in electrical resistance when a cell, in a conductive liquid, passes through a small aperture. Hemoglobin concentration is determined by **spectrophotometric** methods. Hematocrit, **MCHC,** and **MCV** are calculated based on the measured RBC count, **MCH,** and hemoglobin. When using an automated counter, it is important to follow institutional as well as manufacturer's guidelines for maintenance, calibration, and quality control.

Manual Tests

The following procedures may be performed manually in a POL:

- a WBC and platelet count with a Unopette vial and hematocytometer
- a blood smear for a differentiated cell count

Figure 14-28 ◆ Sysmex™ automated cell counter.
Courtesy of Sysmex America.

- a microhematocrit
- an erythrocyte sedimentation rate (ESR) using the Wintrobe method

Performing a WBC and Platelet Count with a Unopette Vial and Hematocytometer

When an automated counter or analyzer is not available, you may have to rely on manual methods to do cell counts and hematocrits. Manual cell counts are performed with a hemacytometer, a heavy glass slide with a depressed central area of precise volume specifications. Unopettes are vials that contain **diluent** solutions and are used to prepare blood dilutions for manual WBC and/or platelet counts. This test is no longer done on a regular basis in physician office labs. However, the basics are presented here for the practitioner who does not have access to an automated counter or analyzer.

White Blood Cell Differential

WBC differentials (diff) are a very useful diagnostic tool. Many disease states are diagnosed by the presence of certain WBC populations. For instance, increased polys and bands

---

PROCEDURE 14-4 **Perform a WBC and Platelet Count with a Unopette Vial and Hemacytometer**

Theory

Most hemacytometers use the Neubauer ruling, which consists of a square measuring 3×3 mm (9 mm^2) and subdivided into nine secondary squares, each 1×1 mm. This counting area is 0.1 mm deep (Figure 14-29 ◆).

When counting the WBCs and platelets, use the average count in the calculation formula. To ensure standardization and accurate results, check the laboratory's standard policy regarding the similarity of the side count numbers. Laboratory policy usually dictates that the side count numbers vary by less than 10 to 15 percent.

The 10/9 in each of the following formulas is a correction factor for the depth of the hemacytometer. For a healthy individual, the normal values of white blood cells range between 4,000 and 10,500 per cubic millimeter (mm^3), and platelets range between 150,000 and 450,000/mm^3.

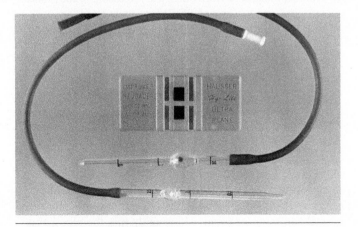

Figure 14-29 ◆ Hemacytometer
U.S. Department of Agriculture.

continued

PROCEDURE 14-4 **Perform a WBC and Platelet Count with a Unopette Vial and Hemacytometer** *(continued)*

The white blood cell calculation formula is: average count $\times$ 10/9 $\times$ 100 = WBC/mm^3. For example:

$$\text{Side 1} = 90$$
$$\text{Side 2} = 88$$
$$\text{Average} = 89$$
$$89 \times 10/9 \times 100 = 9888.9/\text{mm}^3 \text{ or } 9.8 \times 10^3/\text{mm}^3$$

The platelet calculation formula is: average count $\times$ 9 $\times$ 10/9 $\times$ 100 = PLT/mm^3. For example:

$$\text{Side 1} = 490$$
$$\text{Side 2} = 510$$
$$\text{Average} = 500$$
$$500 \times 9 \times 10/9 \ 100 = 500,000/\text{mm}^3$$

Materials

- Unopette vial and pipette unit
- hemacytometer with Neubauer ruling
- petri dish
- sterile gauze squares
- disposable gloves
- sharps container
- biohazardous waste container

Competency

(**Conditions**) With the necessary materials, you will be able to (**Task**) complete a manual counting of WBCs and platelets using a hemacytometer with Neubauer ruling and Unopette vial (**Standards**) accurately within 30 minutes.

1. Wash your hands.
2. Gather equipment and supplies.
3. Place the Unopette vial on a flat surface. Push the pipette shield through the diaphragm into the neck of the vial.
4. Remove the pipette assembly from the vial, then remove the pipette shield.
5. Holding the pipette horizontally, touch the tip to the blood sample—venous, mixed EDTA anticoagulated, or capillary. The capillary action filling the pipette will stop when the blood reaches the capillary bore end in the pipette neck.
6. Clean any blood from the outside of the pipette, being careful not to remove any blood from the pipette bore.
7. Squeeze and maintain a slight pressure on the Unopette vial to force out air but not the liquid.
8. With your index finger, cover the opening of the pipette overflow chamber. Insert the pipette into the punctured neck opening of the Unopette vial.
9. Remove your index finger from the pipette opening. The resulting negative pressure draws blood into the diluent.
10. Rinse the capillary pipette bore by gently squeezing the vial two or three times. Thoroughly mix the blood and diluent by swirling the vial.
11. Leave the vial standing for 10 minutes to hemolyze the red blood cells.

12. Invert the vial to thoroughly remix and suspend the cells in the fluid.
13. Convert to a dropper assembly by withdrawing the pipette from the reservoir and reseating it in the reverse position.
14. Gently squeeze the sides of the vial and discard the first three or four drops. Fill the chamber of the Neubauer hemacytometer with the diluted blood.
15. Place the hemacytometer on moistened paper in a petri dish. Cover the petri dish and leave it standing for 10 minutes so the cells settle.
16. Count and calculate for WBCs and platelets:
    - For WBCs, examine under 40X microscope power with lower light. Count all the white blood cells in the nine large squares of the counting chamber. Count the opposite side in the same manner. Add both sides and divide by two to obtain the average.
    Calculation formula: average count $\times$ 10/9 $\times$ 100 = WBC/mm^3
    - For platelets, examine under 40X microscope power with lower light. Count all the platelets in center secondary square of the Neubauer ruling of the counting chamber. Count the opposite side in the same manner. Add both sides and divide by two for the average.
    Calculation formula: average count $\times$ 9 $\times$ 10/9 $\times$ 100 = PLT/mm^3
17. Dispose of all used sharps and biohazardous waste in the appropriate containers.
18. Remove the disposable gloves and discard appropriately. Wash your hands.

Patient Education

Instruct the patient beforehand in the general procedure. Do *not* promise the patient that the procedure will not hurt. It is more tactful to say that it might feel like a "brief sting." Let the patient know when the actual puncture is about to happen. As necessary, provide information about how long the results will take and how they will be transmitted to the patient.

Charting Example

Sometimes charting may not be required for phlebotomy procedures because laboratory processing documentation is sufficient. If charting is required, it might look like this:

08/25/XX 7:30 a.m. Pt anxious about phlebotomy procedure. General explanations given before each step. Pt voiced concern over the amount of pain she would experience and that her veins were hard to get blood from. Venous specimen obtained for a CBC, Na, K, and Cl with appropriate tubes. Pt held pressure gauze onsite, site was bandaged, and pt was instructed to leave the bandage in place for 15 minutes. Pt escorted to the exit. Barbara Nelson, CMA

are found in cases of bacterial infections, appendicitis, and other disorders; infectious mononucleosis is characterized by increased numbers of atypical lymphocytes; allergy patients have higher levels of eosinophils; and, of course, immature and abnormal white blood cells are found in patients with leukemia.

In a manual diff, a drop of capillary or well-mixed EDTA anticoagulated blood is placed at the end of a glass microscope slide. A second slide is used to "push" the blood evenly to cover approximately three-quarters of the slide. The end of the blood smear must have a "feathered edge," where the blood is one cell thick (Figure 14-30 ◆). After the blood has dried, the slide is stained with Wright's stain and allowed to dry. The slide is then examined under a microscope with either the 50X or 100X oil objective. The technologist first counts 100 white blood cells as a group and then counts the 100 WBCs by type.

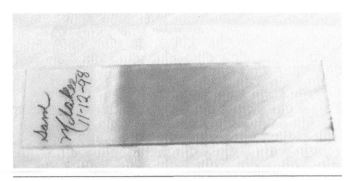

Figure 14-30 ◆ Blood smear on a slide, with feathered edge

Preparing a Blood Smear

Blood smears are made from venous or arterial blood for the purpose of examination under the microscope. Fresh drops of blood or anticoagulated specimens are used.

PROCEDURE 14-5 **Prepare a Blood Smear for a Differentiated Cell Count**

Theory

It is important to be precise at each step of this procedure. Accurate technique ensures that the blood smear is only one cell thick, which is ideal for microscopic analysis. High-quality smears have a feathered edge without lines, holes, or ridges. Low-quality smears result from failing to spread the smear before the blood dries, using a blood drop that is too large, or smearing the specimen with a cracked or chipped slide. Resist the temptation to blow on the specimen to dry it, as this could spread biological materials into the air or affect the quality of the smear. Because fingerprints could obscure a damp smear, the slide should be labeled after the specimen has air-dried. The dry, labeled slide is placed in a protective folder and transported to the laboratory. The medical technologist evaluates the slide for quality and performs staining procedures with Wright's stain.

Materials

- materials for venipuncture or capillary puncture
- microscope
- two glass slides
- gauze squares
- disposable gloves
- sharps container
- biohazardous waste container

Competency

(**Conditions**) With the necessary materials, you will be able to (**Task**) prepare a blood smear slide for microscopic examination (**Standards**) correctly within 10 minutes.

1. Wash your hands.
2. Gather equipment and supplies.
3. Ensure that the microscope is clean and working properly.
4. Greet and the identify patient and escort him or her to the laboratory draw area.
5. Wash your hands and put on disposable gloves.
6. Obtain a drop of blood by any one of the following methods. Place the blood drop 1/2 to 1 inch from the label end of the slide (Figure 14-31 ◆).

   For a capillary puncture:
   - Puncture the skin per the capillary puncture method.
   - Wipe the first drop of blood away with a sterile gauze square.
   - Lightly touch the second drop of blood to a slide.

Figure 14-31 ◆ Place the blood drop 1/2 to 1 inch from the label end of the slide.

continued

PROCEDURE 14-5 Prepare a Blood Smear for a Differentiated Cell Count *(continued)*

For a fresh venous specimen:

- After you withdraw the needle from the venipuncture site, immediately touch the drop of blood lightly to a slide.

For a venous specimen from a vacutainer:

- Place a capillary tube in the vacutainer. It will automatically draw the correct amount of blood.
- With sterile gauze, wipe away any blood from the outside of the tube, being careful not to remove the blood from the tip.
- Lightly touch the drop of blood from the capillary tube to a slide.

7. Place the second slide lengthwise, in front of, and in contact with the drop of blood (Figure 14-32 ◆). Allow the blood to spread along the edge of the slide by capillary action.

8. At a 30 degree angle and applying only light pressure, pull the second slide toward the opposite edge of the first slide (Figure 14-33 ◆). After approximately 1 inch and as the specimen is feathering, lift the second slide in a sliding arch away from the first slide.

9. Allow the slide to air-dry.

10. Label the slide and place it next to the microscope for examination.

11. Follow institutional procedure for the cell count, which is performed by a designated individual.

12. Dispose of all used sharps and biohazardous waste in the appropriate containers.

13. Remove the disposable gloves and discard appropriately. Wash your hands.

14. Document the procedure in the chart or log per institutional procedure.

Patient Education

Instruct the patient beforehand in the general procedure. Do *not* promise the patient that the procedure will not hurt. It is more tactful to say that it might feel like a "brief sting." Let the patient know when the actual puncture is about to happen. As necessary, provide information about how long the results will take and how they will be transmitted to the patient.

Charting Example

Sometimes charting may not be required for phlebotomy procedures because laboratory processing documentation is sufficient. If charting is required, it might look like this:

08/25/XX 7:30 a.m. Pt anxious about phlebotomy procedure. General explanations given before each step. Pt voiced concern over the amount of pain she would experience and that her veins were hard to get blood from. Venous specimen obtained for a CBC, Na, K, and Cl with appropriate tubes. Pt held pressure gauze onsite, site was bandaged, and pt was instructed to leave the bandage in place for 15 minutes. Pt escorted to the exit. Shawna Phillips, RMA

Figure 14-32 ◆ Place the second slide lengthwise, in front of, and in contact with the drop of blood.

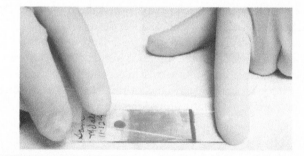

Figure 14-33 ◆ Pull the second slide toward the opposite edge of the first slide.

PROCEDURE 14-6 Prepare a Smear Stained with Wright's Stain

Theory

Performing a blood smear allows the technician to view the cellular components of a blood specimen. Different stains dye different cell components different colors. Most stains contain methylene blue, a blue stain, or eosin, a red-orange stain. When the cells are stained, their structures can be easily visualized and differentiated. Wright's stain is the most commonly used differential blood stain.

Label the thick end of the smear with a pencil, not a pen. Labeling the thick end will ensure that the name does not wash off in the staining process.

Materials

- clean glass slides (more than needed, in case of a break)
- transfer device, either a pipette or a capillary tube
- blood specimen
- Wright's stain
- disposable gloves

Competency

(**Conditions**) With the necessary materials, you will be able to (**Task**) prepare a blood smear stained with Wright's stain (**Standards**) correctly within 15 minutes.

1. Have all the necessary materials in your laboratory workstation.
2. Wash your hands and put on the gloves.
3. Mix the blood sample. If it has separated, gently swirl it in the tube.
4. With a pipette, take a small sample of the blood and drop it on the slide, approximately 1/4 inch from the end of the slide.

5. Hold the end of the slide with one hand. With your other hand, place the other slide directly in front of the blood specimen at a 30-degree angle.
6. Pull the spreader slide back into the drop of blood, just until contact is made. This will cause the blood to spread out along the edge of the slide in a thin line. You should be pulling the blood back toward the closer end of the slide.
7. To avoid air bubbles, push the spreader slide back toward the opposite end of the slide in a quick, smooth motion, being careful to maintain the 30-degree angle.
8. Allow the slide to dry.
9. When the slide is dry, label the thick end of the smear with a pencil.
10. Place the slide on a staining rack with the blood side up (Figure 14-34 ◆). Flood the smear with Wright's stain (Figure 14-35 ◆).
11. Follow the instructions for the waiting time, generally 1 to 3 minutes.
12. Add a buffer in an amount equivalent to the Wright's stain. Mix the stain and buffer and blow gently on the mixture for several minutes until a green, metallic sheen appears.
13. Rinse the slide completely with distilled water (Figure 14-36 ◆).
14. Allow the excess water to drain off the slide and stand it on end to allow it to dry.

Patient Education

Let the patient know that although the staining will be done immediately, the results will not be available until they have been reviewed by the physician. Give the patient a time frame in which to expect the test results.

Figure 14-34 ◆ Place the slide on a staining rack with the blood side up.

Figure 14-35 ◆ Flood the smear with Wright's stain.

continued

PROCEDURE 14-6 Prepare a Smear Stained with Wright's Stain *(continued)*

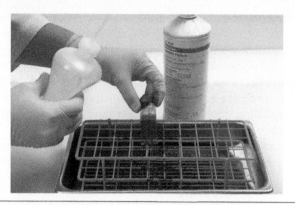

Figure 14-36 ◆ Rinse the slide with distilled water

Charting Example

09/05/XX 12:05 PM Wright's stain prepared for examination using 2-step method. Ellen Woods, CMA

Manual Hematocrit

A blood hematocrit is defined as the volume of erythrocytes (RBCs) in a given volume of blood and is usually measured as a percentage of the total blood volume. A hematocrit is a quick, easy test and is commonly used to screen for anemia. In a manual hematocrit, a blood-filled capillary tube is rapidly centrifuged, which packs the erythrocytes at the bottom.

The patient's age affects normal values for hematocrit. Adults have higher values than children. Normal values vary among institutions, but the generally accepted range for hematocrits in normal adult females is 36–46% and in normal adult males 40–54%.

MCV, MCHC, and MCH are used to differentiate specific types of anemia by examining the size of red blood cells and by measuring hemoglobin and hematocrit. Red blood cells can be macrocytic (large), normocytic (normal), and microcytic (small). RBCs with normal amounts of hemoglobin and normal color are normochromic. In anemic states, RBCs may be hypochromic (having less than normal color). MCV indicates the size of the red blood cells, MCHC measures the average RBC hemoglobin concentration, and MCH measures the average hemoglobin weight in each red blood cell. The MCHC is considered most accurate because both hemoglobin and hematocrit are used in the calculation of the

PROCEDURE 14-7 Perform a Microhematocrit by Capillary Tube

Theory

The centrifuged capillary tube is placed on a reading device and the volume of packed red blood cells is compared to the total amount of blood (RBC, WBC, platelets, and plasma) in the tube. There are several microhematocrit methods; the following is one example.

When placing capillary tubes in the centrifuge, counterbalance each tube with another in the opposite position. Place the tubes with the sealant side away from the center. These measures ensure that the specimen is properly spun. Close the lid of the centrifuge so that any accidental breakage of tubes is contained.

After the two- to five-minute spin, turn the centrifuge off. After it has stopped spinning, open the lid. Read the results from the line created between the plasma and the blood cells.

Materials

- heparinized capillary tubes
- microhematocrit centrifuge
- microhematocrit reader
- tube sealer or sealing clay
- gauze squares
- disposable gloves
- sharps container
- biohazardous waste container

Competency

(**Conditions**) With the necessary materials, you will be able to (**Task**) perform a microhematocrit (**Standards**) correctly within 15 minutes.

PROCEDURE 14-7 Perform a Microhematocrit by Capillary Tube *(continued)*

1. Wash your hands.
2. Gather equipment and supplies.
3. Greet and identify the patient and escort him or her to the laboratory draw area. Explain the procedure.
4. Wash your hands and put on disposable gloves.
5. Perform a capillary puncture or venipuncture.
6. Fill a capillary tube with capillary or well-mixed anticoagulated blood approximately three-quarters full.
7. Wipe excess blood off the outside of the tube.
8. Repeat steps 6 and 7. You will use the second tube as a counterbalance weight in the centrifuge or as a second test to confirm the accuracy of the results (Figure 14-37 ◆).
9. Holding each capillary tube by its sides, place the blood-filled end in the sealing clay to form a plug. Pull the tube straight up and out of the sealing clay.
10. Place the capillary tubes in the microhematocrit head grooves opposite each other. Make sure the sealed ends of the tubes face away from the center of the centrifuge and are touching the outside rim of the centrifuge head.
11. Attach and secure the lid of the centrifuge.
12. Centrifuge the capillary tubes at 12,000 RPM for the optimum time stated on the instrument, usually 2 to 5 minutes.
13. Remove the capillary tubes after the centrifuge has stopped spinning.
14. Place one centrifuged capillary tube into the groove on the clear plastic piece of the microhematocrit reader with the

plug end toward the reader bottom center. The reference line near the top of the groove should be under the separation line in the capillary tube where the clay plug and the RBCs meet.
15. Rotate the bottom of the reader plate so that the metal stop on the outer rim makes contact with the left edge of the grooved piece.
16. Holding the bottom plate steady, rotate the top plate to align the outer edge of the spiral line with the outer edge of the plasma meniscus.
17. Rotate the entire bottom portion of the reader clockwise until the spiral line intersects the line separating the buffy coat and plasma layer.
18. Read the results on the ruled scale where the red line intersects it.
19. Dispose of all used sharps and biohazardous waste in the appropriate containers.
20. Remove the disposable gloves and discard appropriately. Wash your hands.
21. Document the percentage results on the laboratory requisition or other designated area of the chart.

Patient Education

Instruct the patient beforehand in the general procedure. Do *not* promise the patient that the procedure will not hurt. It is more tactful to say that it might feel like a "brief sting." Let the patient know when the actual puncture is about to happen. As necessary, provide information about how long the results will take and how they will be transmitted to the patient.

Charting Example

Sometimes charting may not be required for phlebotomy procedures because laboratory processing documentation is sufficient. If charting is required, it might look like this:

08/25/XX 7:30 a.m. Pt anxious about phlebotomy procedure. General explanations given before each step. Pt voiced concern over the amount of pain she would experience and that her veins were hard to get blood from. Venous specimen obtained for a CBC, Na, K, and Cl with appropriate tubes. Pt held pressure gauze onsite, site was bandaged, and pt was instructed to leave the bandage in place for 15 minutes. Pt escorted to the exit. Kelly Abrams, CMA

Figure 14-37 ◆ Loading a centrifuge
Photos of StatSpin products provided by StatSpin, Inc. a wholly owned subsidiary of IRIS, Chadsworth, CA.

diagnostic value. Types of anemia include pernicious anemia, with macrocytic RBCs; aplastic anemia, with normocytic, normochromic RBCs; and iron deficiency anemia, with microcytic RBCs.

Erythrocyte Sedimentation Rate

The ESR or sed rate is useful in monitoring the progression of disease processes. The blood test results are standardized by using calibrated Wintrobe tubes and mixing the anticoagulated blood specimen before the procedure. When well-mixed blood is placed in a vertical tube, erythrocytes settle out or "sediment." The sedimentation process in the healthy person is slow, but the sedimentation rate increases at an accelerated rate in disease processes, depending on the severity of the disease. A greater tendency of the RBCs to sediment is commonly found in inflammatory disorders such as subacute bacterial endocarditis, rheumatic fever, rheumatoid arthritis, and pelvic inflammatory disease, as well as in other disease conditions such as respiratory infections, pulmonary embolism, and cancer. There are several methods for performing sed rates, including some automated methods. Manual methods include the Westergren method, the Zeta sedimentation rate, and the Wintrobe method.

Blood Chemistry Testing

There are hundreds of blood chemistry tests that aid in clinical diagnosis. The most commonly performed are tests for blood glucose levels, glycosylated hemoglobin, electrolytes (sodium, potassium, chloride, and CO_2), creatinine, BUN, total protein, albumin, and bilirubin levels. Some tests are very useful as a relatively rapid diagnostic tool, such as those for CPK and troponin I, which are elevated in cases of heart attack. Liver function tests and lipid profiles are also considered important in the diagnosis or monitoring of diseases. These tests and the importance of their values are discussed in appropriate chapters. It is important to remember that reference laboratories have different values for the testing they do. Suggested values will be referenced in chapters in which the disease or condition applicable to them are discussed.

Laboratories often combine commonly ordered groups of tests into a chemistry panel. For instance, glucose, electrolytes, BUN, and creatinine may be combined into a test panel called a basic metabolic panel. Test panels may also be organized based on organ function. For example, a liver function panel could consist of total bilirubin, serum glutamic oxaloacetic transaminase (SGOT), and serum glutamic pyruvic transaminase (SGPT).

Automated Chemistry Analyzers

A wide variety of automated chemistry analyzers are available. Many are programmed to perform specific organ panels or chemistry profiles, or individual chemistry tests on each sample. These analyzers are designed for use in hospital or reference laboratory settings and require sophisticated calibration and quality control protocols. They are maintained and operated by trained technologists.

Other analyzers are designed to perform a single test and can be operated by a patient or MA at the patient's bedside (point-of-care testing). A glucometer is the most common point-of-care analyzer, and you will be expected to know how to operate it. Portable cholesterol monitors are also commonly used and are operated in much the same way glucometers are.

Measuring Blood Glucose

Many types of glucometers are available for patient use. The timing of each step in the procedure contributes to the accuracy of the test results. Some monitors require waiting for the blood to soak into the test strip before placing it in the glucometer for reading. With other glucometers there is a waiting period as the blood moistens and reacts with the strip, and then excess blood is removed before the strip is placed in the glucometer. Because of these timing and procedural differences, always follow the manufacturer's directions for the particular model you are working with.

General instructions for an Accu-Chek™ glucose monitor are given in the Procedure 14-9. Follow the quality control and calibration guidelines of your health-care institution before using any glucometer. Perform calibration each time a new lot number of test strips is put into use. Refer to the user's manual for calibration and quality control instructions as well as for care and maintenance recommendations.

Measuring Blood Cholesterol

Cell membranes hold a fatty substance known as cholesterol. Cholesterol is a substance necessary for the formation of bile acids and hormones. Diet, caloric intake, physical activity, and family heritage all play a factor in the amount of cholesterol formed in the body. It is important for patients to understand that there are different types of cholesterol: the type that comes from the foods we eat and the type that is produced in the body. LDL cholesterol is considered "bad" cholesterol, and lower blood levels indicate a lower risk of heart disease. When too much LDL cholesterol builds up, it sticks to the walls of the arteries, decreasing the blood flow to the heart and brain. HDL

Keys to Success
HOME DISPOSAL OF SHARPS

Instruct a patient using puncture devices and syringes at home that these devices must be disposed of carefully, in a strong, puncture-resistant container. A hard plastic detergent container is an example of a safe container.

PROCEDURE 14-8 *Perform an ESR Using the Wintrobe Method*

Theory

A well-mixed anticoagulated blood sample is drawn into a Wintrobe tube and left upright for an hour. The full length of red cells from the top of the column in that hour is the erythrocyte sedimentation rate, or sed rate. Reference ranges vary among institutions, but the generally accepted reference range is 0 to 20 mm/hr for women and 0 to 9 mm/hr for men.

Materials

- Wintrobe tube (calibrated in millimeters)
- Wintrobe pipette rack
- pipette bulb
- EDTA-anticoagulated patient blood sample
- gauze squares
- disposable gloves
- sharps container
- biohazardous waste container

Competency

(**Conditions**) With the necessary materials, you will be able to (**Task**) demonstrate performing an ESR using the Wintrobe method (**Standards**) correctly in one hour.

1. Wash your hands.
2. Gather equipment and supplies.
3. Greet and identify the patient and escort him or her to the laboratory draw area. Explain the procedure.
4. Wash your hands and put on disposable gloves.
5. Perform a capillary puncture or venipuncture.
6. Mix thoroughly an EDTA-anticoagulated tube of patient blood.
7. Attach a disposable pipette bulb to the top of the Wintrobe tube (Figure 14-38 ◆).
8. Place the tip of the Wintrobe tube in the blood specimen. With the pipette bulb, draw a blood sample to the 0 mark.
9. Place the filled Wintrobe tube in an exactly vertical position in the rack. Set a timer for 60 minutes.
10. At the end of 60 minutes, record the number of mm the red blood cells have fallen. This result is the sed rate in mm/hr.
11. Dispose of all used sharps and biohazardous waste in the appropriate containers.
12. Remove the disposable gloves and discard appropriately. Wash your hands.
13. Document the sed rate in mm/hr on the laboratory requisition or other designated area of the chart.

Patient Education

Instruct the patient beforehand in the general procedure. Do *not* promise the patient that the procedure will not hurt. It is more tactful to say that it might feel like a "brief sting." Let the patient know when the actual puncture is about to happen. As necessary, provide information about how long the results will take and how they will be transmitted to the patient.

Charting Example

Sometimes charting may not be required for phlebotomy procedures because laboratory processing documentation is sufficient. If charting is required, it might look like this:

08/25/XX 7:30 a.m. Pt anxious about phlebotomy procedure. General explanations given before each step. Pt voiced concern over the amount of pain she would experience and that her veins were hard to get blood from. Venous specimen obtained for a CBC, Na, K, and Cl with appropriate tubes. Pt held pressure gauze onsite, site was bandaged, and pt was instructed to leave the bandage in place for 15 minutes. Pt escorted to the exit. Robert Larin, RMA

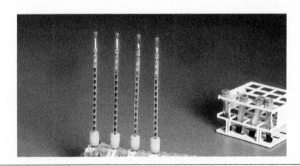

Figure 14-38 ◆ Wintrobe tube

PROCEDURE 14-9 Measure Blood Glucose Using Accu-Chek™ Glucometer

Theory

The light of the glucometer passes through the test strip to read the blood glucose level. Do not let the strip touch the patient's skin when you obtain the specimen, because oils from the skin may affect the test results. Also, to maintain accuracy, make sure the blood drop completely covers the specimen square on the strip.

Some patients may complain of pain after the capillary puncture. To ease discomfort, instruct the patient to hold a 2 × 2 gauze firmly against the site for a few minutes. Normal values vary among institutions, but the generally accepted normal range for adults is 70–110 mg/dl, and 30–70 mg/dl for newborns.

New glucometers appear on the market frequently. Newer models can process testing faster, use less blood supply, and store results in memory. Glucometers also store memory of the patient test strips used. Whichever model is used at home or in the POL, the glucometer must be calibrated and tested for accuracy with control solutions and calibration test strips. In your patient instruction, reinforce the importance of following the manufacturer's directions to ensure accuracy. Following instructions becomes even more important if the patient changes glucometer models.

Materials

- Accu-Chek™ glucometer
- Accu-Chek™ test strips
- glucose control solutions
- puncture device
- sterile 2 × 2 gauze
- disposable gloves
- sharps container
- biohazardous waste container

Competency

(**Conditions**) With the necessary materials, you will be able to (**Task**) measure blood glucose with a glucometer and record patient results (**Standards**) correctly within 15 minutes.

1. Wash your hands.
2. Gather equipment and supplies.
3. Verify that calibration and quality control have been performed and are acceptable.
4. Greet and identify the patient and escort him or her to the laboratory draw area. Explain the procedure.
5. Wash your hands and put on disposable gloves.
6. Check the expiration date on the test strip bottle. Obtain a different bottle if the expiration date has passed.
7. Turn on the glucometer by pressing the ON button (Figure 14-39 ◆).
8. Follow the manufacturer's directions for entering the 3-digit test-strip code in the display if the glucometer code does not match the code on the test strip bottle (Figure 14-40 ◆).
9. Enter the patient identification number. (Home glucometers may not require this information.)
10. Wait for the indicator that the monitor is ready for a test strip. Within the short time frame specified by the glucometer model, insert one test strip as directed into the monitor (Figure 14-41 ◆).
11. Remove the monitor from the charging station.
12. Obtain a capillary blood specimen from the patient following standard procedure for capillary blood collections. Venous or arterial specimens may also be used.
13. Touch the edge of the test strip to the drop of blood. The blood will be pulled into the strip. Fill the target area of the strip completely (Figure 14-42 ◆).
14. The glucose result will appear in the time frame specified by the manufacturer, usually within 30 seconds (Figure 14-43 ◆).
15. Remove the test strip and discard in a biohazard container. Dispose of the lancet or blade in the sharps container.
16. Return the monitor to the charging/storage unit.

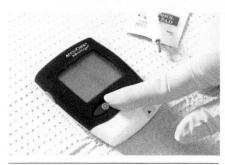

Figure 14-39 ◆ Turn on the glucometer.

Figure 14-40 ◆ Enter the 3-digit test code.

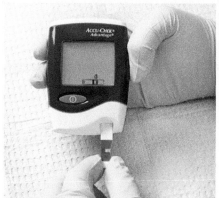

Figure 14-41 ◆ Insert one test strip into the monitor as directed.

PROCEDURE 14-9 Measure Blood Glucose Using Accu-Chek™ Glucometer *(continued)*

Figure 14-42 ◆ Touch the edge of the test strip to the drop of blood.

17. Remove the disposable gloves and discard appropriately. Wash your hands.
18. Document the date, time, finger used, patient's tolerance of the procedure, and results in the designated area of the chart.

Patient Education

Instruct the patient beforehand in the general procedure. Do *not* promise the procedure will not hurt. It is more tactful to say that it might feel like a "short sting."

Teach the patient to keep a record of home testing with the glucometer or to monitor the stored results in the memory of the glucometer. The patient should document the date, time, results, and symptoms if the results are above or below normal limits. The physician will refer to these records at the next office visit to make any necessary insulin or dietary adjustments.

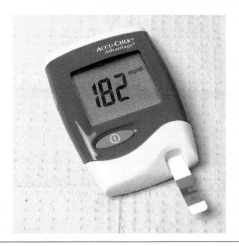

Figure 14-43 ◆ Glucose results

Charting Example

Sometimes charting may not be required for phlebotomy procedures because laboratory processing documentation is sufficient. If charting is required, it might look like this:

08/25/XX7:30 a.m. Pt anxious about phlebotomy procedure. General explanations given before each step. Pt voiced concern over the amount of pain she would experience and that her veins were hard to get blood from. Venous specimen obtained for a CBC, Na, K, and Cl with appropriate tubes. Pt held pressure gauze onsite, site was bandaged, and pt was instructed to leave the bandage in place for 15 minutes. Pt escorted to the exit. Gregory Fuller, RMA

PROCEDURE 14-10 Determine Cholesterol Level with the ProAct Testing Device

Theory

High cholesterol levels have been linked to stroke and heart disease. As part of their overall health maintenance, patients should understand the importance of regular cholesterol testing. They should know their cholesterol numbers, including HDL and LDL, and how to improve them.

In 2001, in response to continuing high rates of heart disease, the National Heart, Lung and Blood Institute of the National Institutes of Health issued new guidelines for cholesterol levels. According to the new guidelines, total cholesterol is less important than HDL and LDL cholesterol numbers.

Materials

- ProAct testing device
- capillary tube containing lithium heparin
- lancet device
- 2 × 2 gauze pads, sterile
- alcohol pads
- disposable gloves
- patient's chart

Competency

(**Conditions**) With the necessary materials, you will be able to (**Task**) measure cholesterol level using a ProAct testing device (**Standards**) correctly within 15 minutes.

continued

PROCEDURE 14-10 Determine Cholesterol Level with the ProAct Testing Device *(continued)*

1. Wash your hands and put on the gloves.
2. Verify the physician's order and the patient's identity. Explain the procedure to the patient.
3. Load the lancet device according to the directions.
4. Choose a puncture site free of broken skin or bruising.
5. Wipe the patient's finger with an alcohol wipe and allow to dry.
6. Puncture the finger and wipe away the first drop of blood that forms with the sterile gauze.
7. Hold the capillary tube horizontal to the patient's finger, making sure no air bubbles enter the tube. If air bubbles enter, you must throw away the tube and start over again.
8. When the tube has filled, remove it and have the patient put pressure on the puncture site with a sterile gauze square.
9. Remove a testing strip from the container and peel away the protective foil. Place the strip on a hard work surface.
10. Attach the filled capillary tube to the pipette.
11. Without touching the tip of the capillary tube to the testing strip, place one drop in the center of the application zone (Figure 14-44 ◆).
12. Allow the blood droplet to soak into the testing mesh for 15 to 20 seconds.

13. Place the strip in the ProAct device port (Figure 14-45 ◆). The device will start to count down approximately 160 seconds.
14. While the machine is running, clean the test area. Throw the pipette and capillary tube into a sharps container.
15. When the LED screen indicates, remove the test strip and observe it for uneven color development. (If the color is uneven, you will need to perform the entire test again.)
16. Discard the test strip into a biohazardous container.
17. Record the test results as displayed in the patient's chart.

Patient Education
Give the patient the cholesterol results after the physician has reviewed them, along with verbal and written dietary recommendations to help improve the patient's overall cholesterol numbers.

Charting Example
09/05/XX 12:05 PM Cholesterol level obtained using ProAct device. Patient reported no additional bleeding from puncture site and a pain level of 1/10. Cholesterol level reported to physician for analysis and lab report letter sent to patient with dietary recommendations. Jackie Chin, CMA

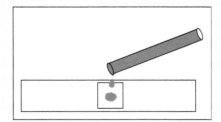

Figure 14-44 ◆ Place one drop in the center of the application zone.

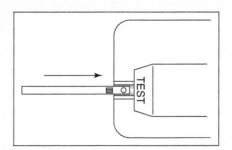

Figure 14-45 ◆ Place the strip in the ProAct device port.

cholesterol is "good" cholesterol, and higher levels are beneficial to health. HDL cholesterol binds to LDL cholesterol, moves it away from the heart and brain, and deposits it in the liver, where it can be processed and passed from the body. Too low a level of HDL cholesterol indicates a greater risk of heart attack.

Blood Typing and Grouping
When a blood group antigen and its corresponding antibody unite, agglutination (clumping) is the result. This reaction is the basis for the blood typing procedure. Commercially available antiserum (antibody) is mixed with whole blood. Agglutination is considered a positive reaction; it indicates that the antigen corresponding to the antiserum is present on

the tested red blood cells. The absence of agglutination is considered a negative reaction, indicating that the antigen corresponding to the testing antiserum is absent on the RBCs.

Transfusions are compatible when the recipient's blood does not have antibodies that interact with the donor's blood antigens. Type A blood has A antigens and anti-B antibodies. If type A blood were given to a patient with type B blood, the antibodies present would cause a transfusion reaction. Similarly, Type B blood contains B antigens and anti-A antibodies. If type B blood were given to a patient with type A blood, the anti-A antibodies would cause a transfusion reaction. Type AB blood has both A and B antigens but lacks antibodies and is known as the "universal recipient." A transfusion patient with type AB blood can receive any blood type. Type O blood has neither the A nor B antigen, but it does have anti-A and anti-B antibodies. Type O blood is known as "universal donor" because it can be transfused to any receiving patient regardless of blood type—it lacks antigens to interact with antibodies in type A, B, or AB blood.

Most immunohematology testing is performed in laboratories by specially trained technologists. Some office laboratories, however, offer slide blood typing. Table 14-3 includes blood group interpretation of slide reactions.

Immunology Testing

Test kits are used in immunology testing, including tests for infectious mononucleosis, rheumatoid arthritis, and anti-streptolysin O (ASO). One of the most commonly requested immunology tests is that for infectious mono.

Keys to Success
BLOOD TYPING USING THE SLIDE METHOD

1. Use whole blood.
2. On a glass slide at room temperature, place one drop (approximately 50 µL) of the appropriate reagents. When using anti-A, anti-B, and anti-D (for Rh positive and Rh negative testing) concurrently, anti-A may be placed on one-third of the slide, anti-B on one-third, and anti-D on one-third.
3. With a pipette, add one drop (approximately 50 µL) of whole blood to each drop of reagent on the slide.
4. With separate wooden applicator sticks, mix the blood and reagents well.
5. Tilt the slide back and forth and observe for agglutination. Tests with the anti-A and anti-B reagent that show no agglutination within 2 minutes are considered negative. (Do not interpret peripheral drying or fibrin strands as agglutination.) Negative reactions with anti-D reagent should undergo further testing for a weak D (Du). The presence of agglutination is considered a positive reaction.

TABLE 14-3 BLOOD GROUP INTERPRETATION OF SLIDE REACTIONS

Anti-A	Anti-B	Blood Group
Negative	Negative	O
Positive	Negative	A
Negative	Positive	B
Positive	Positive	AB

PROCEDURE 14-11 Perform a Mononucleosis Test

Theory

Once called the "kissing disease," mononucleosis is an acute infectious disease caused by the Epstein-Barr virus (EBV). EBV is a common virus worldwide. It is a member of the herpes virus family, although it has nothing to do with cold sores or genital herpes. A person can contract EBV and never have been infected with any other herpes virus. EBV most frequently infects people between 10 and 25 years of age. Symptoms such as swollen tonsils, sore throat, fever, and swollen lymph nodes that may last only a few days are often indistinguishable from those of other mild illnesses. For this reason, EBV infection is not always recognized. Infectious mononucleosis is almost never fatal but can lead to serious complications such as heart problems or swollen spleen and liver.

Materials

- Mono-Test kit
- nonsterile disposable gloves
- blood serum or plasma
- disposable capillary tube

Competency

(**Conditions**) With the necessary materials, you will be able to (**Task**) test for infectious mononucleosis (**Standards**) correctly within 15 minutes.

1. Bring all liquid reagents to room temperature. Check the expiration date of all reagents in the kit.
2. Wash and dry your hands and put on disposable gloves.
3. After obtaining a blood sample from the patient and processing it to separate the serum, fill the capillary tube to the marked line with the serum.
4. Using the glass slide and rubber bulb in the kit, place a small drop of the specimen serum in the first of the three circles on the slide.
5. Place a single drop of the negative control in the second circle on the slide.
6. Place a single drop of the positive control in the third circle.
7. Holding the bottle of Mono-Test reagent upright between your palms, gently roll it back and forth, making certain that the reagent RBCs that have settled in the tube are mixed thoroughly.
8. Hold the dropper 1 inch above the slide and place one drop of reagent into each of the three circles. Make certain the dropper does not come into contact with the slide and become contaminated.
9. Using the enclosed stirrers, one for each circle, quickly and thoroughly mix each area and spread it out to the full 1-inch diameter of the circle.
10. Observe the slide as you rock it back and forth gently for exactly 2 minutes.

continued

PROCEDURE 14-11 **Perform a Mononucleosis Test** (continued)

11. Agglutination is a positive test result; no agglutination is negative. Verify the test results by comparing them to the positive and negative controls on the slide.
12. Clean the work area, disposing of the test in a biohazardous container. Wash your hands.
13. Record the test results.

Patient Education

If the test results are positive, the patient should know what to expect over the standard course of infectious mononucleosis. Advise the patient to get plenty of rest, use throat lozenges to soothe sore throat, and take acetaminophen (such as Tylenol) or ibuprofen (such as Advil) to reduce fever and relieve sore throat and headaches, as prescribed by the physician. The feeling of weakness and fatigue may take weeks to subside and for some people can last several months. The patient should avoid heavy lifting and excessive physical activity until energy levels return to normal.

Charting Example

04-8-XX 4:28 p.m. Patient presented with acute fatigue, swollen lymph nodes, and aching muscles. Mono-Spot test was ordered and results were positive for EBV. Patient was given written and verbal instructions for care and released. Beth Loman, CMA

REVIEW

Chapter Summary

- A medical assistant plays a vital role in the laboratory. Key preparation steps before blood collection include checking the doctor's orders for clarity and completeness, preparing the laboratory requisition, checking supplies, identifying the patient, verifying patient preparation, and seating the patient.
- Blood consists of plasma and cellular elements: RBCs, WBCs, and platelets. The RBCs contain hemoglobin, which transports oxygen through the body. The RBCs are also the site of the blood group antigens. WBCs play an important role in the body's immune defenses and in the defense against infectious disease. Platelets function primarily in blood clotting. A variety of blood chemistry, immunology, and coagulation tests may be performed with plasma or serum.
- There are several types of blood collection tubes. The type of anticoagulant contained in each tube is indicated by the color of the stopper and written on the label. The order of collection using these tubes is important, as there may be some carryover from one tube to the next that could result in erroneous lab results. Different types and sizes of puncture devices are used in blood collection, depending on the size and accessibility of the patient's veins and the amount of blood required.
- The most common venipuncture site is the antecubital fossa. Other sites are hand veins and sometimes foot veins. In some cases blood may be collected from finger sticks, or heel sticks in infants.

- Key steps in actual blood collection are to make the patient as comfortable as possible, wash your hands, use appropriate personal protection equipment, and prepare the appropriate collection device. Apply the tourniquet, select the actual site, clean the venipuncture site with antiseptic and avoid retouching the site before sticking, fill tubes in the correct order of draw, mix tubes containing anticoagulant, release the tourniquet before removing the needle, and apply firm pressure to the site until the bleeding stops. Dispose of all sharps immediately and appropriately. Similar steps are followed for capillary punctures. Label all tubes with the patient's name, date and time of collection, and your initials. Some laboratories require the patient's medical record number on each tube as well.
- A hemacytometer is used for a manual WBC and platelet count. A microhematocrit is performed by spinning capillary tubes in a centrifuge and placing them on a reading device. The ESR can be measured using the Wintrobe method. A glucometer is a hand-held chemistry analyzer used by the patient at home and by health-care professionals. Automated cell counters and chemistry analyzers reduce the chances of human error and are preferred over manual methods of testing.
- Every laboratory or medical office has specific written procedures in place for each test it performs. It is important to follow each laboratory's procedure exactly as written for specimen quality, test standardization, accurate results, and the health and safety of patient and personnel.

Chapter Review Questions

Multiple Choice

1. The most common WBCs are
   - A. PMNs.
   - B. lymphocytes.
   - C. eosinophils.
   - D. basophils.

2. The main function of platelets in blood is to
   - A. ingest bacteria.
   - B. transport oxygen.
   - C. form blood clots.
   - D. respond to allergies.

3. Which of the following tubes must be drawn first because of potential anticoagulant carryover?
   - A. green top
   - B. blue top
   - C. red top
   - D. lavender top

4. It is safe to leave a tourniquet on a patient for
   - A. 3 minutes.
   - B. 5 minutes.
   - C. 6 minutes.
   - D. 1 minute.

5. Which of the following methods for collecting blood is the best to use with infants?
   - A. capillary puncture
   - B. winged infusion
   - C. needle and syringe
   - D. evacuated tube

6. The preferred site for a finger stick is the
   - A. thumb.
   - B. index finger.
   - C. little or pinkie finger.
   - D. middle finger.

7. Normal values for hematocrit in adults range from
   - A. 10 to 20 percent.
   - B. 32 to 48 percent.
   - C. 60 to 65 percent.
   - D. 21 to 26 percent.

8. The ESR is used most commonly for
   - A. diagnosing allergies.
   - B. detecting anemia.
   - C. monitoring disease progression.
   - D. diagnosing bacterial infections.

9. Which of the following blood groups tests positive for both anti-A and anti-B reagents?
   - A. AB
   - B. A
   - C. B
   - D. O

10. When collecting blood from an elderly person, you should
    - A. use smaller needles because the veins may be more fragile.
    - B. securely tighten the tourniquet because the arm is smaller.
    - C. do the procedure as quickly as possible.
    - D. avoid requesting a list of medications.

True/False

T F 1. RBCs may have varying amounts of hemoglobin.

T F 2. Hematocrit is the protein-iron bond substance in red blood cells that carries oxygen from the lungs to the cells and transports carbon dioxide from the cells to the lungs.

T F 3. Vacutainer collections are recommended for burned or scarred patients.

T F 4. Dermal collections are recommended for children and the elderly.

T F 5. You can obtain a blood sample from the side on which a mastectomy was performed.

T F 6. You cannot obtain a blood sample from or near burned areas, which are very susceptible to infection.

T F 7. Plasma appears light yellow when it is separated from the cells by centrifugation.

T F 8. Unopettes are vials that contain diluent solutions and are used to prepare blood dilutions for manual WBC and/or platelet counts.

T F 9. An abnormally high hemoglobin value may be indicative of dehydration, and an abnormally low value may be indicative of anemia.

T F 10. A glucometer is the most common point-of-care analyzer.

Short Answer

1. How is Type O blood different from other blood types in terms of antigens and antibodies?

2. Name the cellular elements in blood.

3. What do hematocrit values indicate?

4. Why should the thumb and forefinger be avoided for finger sticks?

5. What is the ESR or sed rate used for?

Research

1. What are the five vacutainer tubes most commonly used in phlebotomy?

2. What is the normal range of RBCs in men and women? What factors influence that number?

Externship Application Experience

As an extern, this is the first day you will perform phlebotomy in the laboratory section of this clinical site. You observe that the MA is not following the order of draw that you have been taught. What should you do?

Resource Guide

American Academy of Family Physicians
Office Lab Proficiency Testing
1-800-274-7911
http://www.aafp.org/pt.xml

American Diabetes Association
ATTN: National Call Center
1701 North Beauregard Street
Alexandria, VA 22311
1-800-DIABETES
http://www.diabetes.org/

American Medical Technologists
710 Higgins Road
Park Ridge, IL 60068
1-800-275-1268
http://www.amt1.com

Clinical Laboratory Improvement Amendments
http://www.cms.hhs.gov/clia/

National Accrediting Agency for Clinical Laboratory Sciences
8410 W Bryn Mawr Ave, Suite 670
Chicago, IL 60631
http://www.naacls.org

MedMedia
www.prenhall.com/frazier

More on this chapter, including interactive resources, can be found on the Student CD-ROM accompanying this textbook and on the Companion Website at www.prenhall.com/frazier.

SECTION IV

Medical Specialties and Testing

My name is April Minger and I chose to become a Medical Assistant because I enjoy being with people and because I wanted to make a difference in the lives of others. Being a mother of two children really helped me in my pursuit to become a medical assistant. I always tell my children you can be and do anything you set your heart to. I figured the best way to teach them was to show them.

I currently work for a medical group and have the opportunity to work for seven physicians and two physician's assistants. I have a lot of responsibility working for a medical group; working with so many different physicians means being flexible, able to multitask and think on your feet. I perform EKGs, treadmill stress tests, and placement of Holter monitors on a regular basis. I schedule patients for surgical procedures such as heart catheters and pacemakers. I also aid physicians with pre- and postoperative procedures. I prepare numerous laboratory specimens for the physicians. I perform many urinalyses and give countless injections such as Hepatitis A, and B, tetanus, TB skin test, vitamin B-12, and many more.

Being a medical assistant is both rewarding and challenging. The gratification I feel from knowing that I have in some small way touched the life of someone else, just by doing what I love to do, is remarkable. As a medical assistant, I'm not only an employee and coworker but also a confidante, liaison, a warm smile, and a voice of compassion.

CHAPTER 15

Urology and Nephrology

Case Study

Gina has been given instructions that each of the pregnant women at her externship site are to leave a clean-catch urine sample prior to being seen by the doctor. It is Gina's responsibility to ask each patient to leave a sample after checking in and to give them collection instructions. One patient mentions that she has experienced greater urinary frequency in the last two weeks than during the rest of her pregnancy and that it has become painful to empty her bladder. She also admits that she is nervous about telling anyone because she thinks she may have caused it and that there will be no safe treatment for her due to the pregnancy.

Objectives

After completing this chapter, you should be able to:

- Spell and define medical terminology in this chapter.
- Explain the medical assistant's role in urology and nephrology.
- Identify the important structures of the urinary system.
- Explain how urine is formed in the kidneys.
- List and describe common renal diseases.
- List and describe common urinary tract infections.
- Explain the process of dialysis.
- Explain neurogenic bladder and incontinence.
- List and describe common obstructive disorders of the urinary system.
- Discuss the procedures used in the diagnosis of urinary diseases and disorders.
- Explain the methods of urine specimen collection.
- List the characteristics of a normal physical urinalysis.
- Explain the principles of the chemical test strips used in urinalysis.
- Discuss the findings of the microscopic examination of urine.
- Identify the important structures of the male reproductive system.
- List and describe the diseases and disorders of the male reproductive system.

 **MedMedia**

www.prenhall.com/frazier

Additional interactive resources and activities for this chapter can be found on the Companion Website. For audio glossary, legal and ethical scenarios, job scenarios, quizzes, games, vitural tours, and activities related to the content of this chapter, please access the accompanying CD-ROM in this book.

 Assets Available:

Audio Glossary
Legal and Ethical Scenario: *Urology and Nephrology*
On the Job Scenario: *Urology and Nephrology*
A & P Quiz: *The Urinary System*
Multiple Choice Quiz
Games: Crossword, Strikeout and Spelling Bee
3D Virtual Tour: Reproductive System: Male Reproductive System; Urinary System: The Urinary System
Drag & Drop: Urinary System: Kidney Structure

MEDICAL ASSISTING COMPETENCIES

CAAHEP ENTRY-LEVEL COMPETENCIES FOR CMA	ABHES ENTRY-LEVEL COMPETENCIES FOR RMA
▪ Identify and respond to issues of confidentiality.	▪ Project a positive attitude.
▪ Perform within legal and ethical boundaries.	▪ Maintain confidentiality at all times.
	▪ Be a "team player."
▪ Demonstrate knowledge of federal and state health-care legislation and regulations.	▪ Be cognizant of ethical boundaries.
	▪ Exhibit initiative.
▪ Perform hand washing.	▪ Adapt to change.
▪ Dispose of biohazardous materials.	▪ Evidence a responsible attitude.
▪ Practice Standard Precautions.	▪ Be courteous and diplomatic.
▪ Instruct patients in the collection of a clean-catch midstream urine specimen.	▪ Conduct work within scope of education, training, and ability.
	▪ Practice Standard Precautions.
▪ Use methods of quality control.	▪ Use quality control.
▪ Perform urinalysis.	▪ Collect and process specimens.
▪ Screen and follow-up test results.	▪ Dispose of biohazardous materials.
	▪ Collect and process specimens.
	▪ Instruct patients in the collection of a clean-catch midstream urine specimen.

Introduction

A combined urology and nephrology practice treats patients with any disease or disorder of the urinary system and kidneys. **Urology** is the study of the urinary system and diseases that affect it; the **urologist** specializes in treating urinary system diseases and conditions as well as conditions involving the male reproductive system. **Nephrology** is the study of diseases of the kidney; a **nephrologist** is a physician specializing in diseases and disorders of the kidney.

Urinary system diseases and disorders include changes in the structure and function of the kidneys; problems arising in the ureters, bladder, and urethra; chemical or traumatic insult to any parts of the system; and the effects of other disease processes on the urinary tract. Disorders of the male reproductive system include fertility problems, erectile dysfunction, prostate conditions, and sexually transmitted diseases. Infectious processes can affect both systems.

Urinalysis (UA), the physical and chemical examination of urine, provides physicians with information not only about a patient's **renal** function but also about his or her physiology. Although urine is a fluid that is easy to collect and examine, tests must be performed carefully and under controlled conditions to ensure accurate results.

The Medical Assistant's Role in Urology and Nephrology

As an MA in the urology/nephrology office, you will encounter patients of all ages. Some may present with seemingly minor or trivial problems, while others may have life-threatening conditions. You will obtain a medical history, especially relating to the current complaint; vital signs; and specimens, as indicated. You will assist the physician. After proper training, you will perform chemical strip testing and some microscopic examination of specimens. Advanced training is required for catheterization.

Medical Terminology

aliquot—representative sample of a well-mixed specimen

anuria—absence of urine

bilirubin—substance formed by breakdown of hemoglobin

crescentic—crescent-shaped; term used to describe abnormalities found on biopsy of the kidney in rapidly progressive glomerulonephritis

cryptorchism (also cryptorchidism)—a condition in which one or both of the testes fail to descend into the scrotal sac during fetal development

cystitis—inflammation of the urinary bladder

dialysis—cleansing of waste products from the blood with a dialysis machine, or dialyzer

distal tubule—farthest tubule from the glomerulus

electrolytes—ionized substances in blood, cells, and tissues

fistula—abnormal tube-like structure connecting one body structure to another or to the surface of the body

flank—region in the lateral aspect of the midback, between the ribs and the upper border of the ilium

glomerulonephritis—inflammation and possible infection of the glomerulus

glomerulus—tuft or cluster of capillaries inside the capsule of the nephron

hematuria—blood in the urine

hydronephrosis—enlargement of the kidney caused by retention of urine due to an obstruction

incontinence—involuntary leakage of urine or feces

jaundice—yellow color in the skin and mucous membranes

kidney—one of two-bean shaped organs located retroperitoneally that filter blood, remove waste products, and manufacture urine

lithotripsy—breaking up a renal calculus with ultrasound waves aimed at the calculus from outside the body

nephrologist—physician specializing in the treatment of kidney diseases and conditions

nephrology—study of the kidney and the diseases that affect it

nephrons—microscopic tubular structures of the kidney

nocturia—increased urine output at night

Medical Terminology *(continued)*

oliguria—diminished urine output, less than 400 ml per day

periorbital edema—abnormal, excessive fluid surrounding the eye that usually occurs in the morning upon waking

plasmapheresis—daily replacement of blood plasma in the body with other fluids or donated plasma for two or more weeks

polyuria—excessive urine production and frequent, urgent, and excessive urinary output

prodromal—pertaining to the initial stage of a disease, before symptoms appear

prostatitis—inflammation and/or infection of the prostate gland

proteinuria—presence of abnormally large amounts of protein in the urine

proximal tubule—tubule closest to glomerulus

pyelonephritis—inflammation and/or of the pelvis of the kidney

pyuria—pus in the urine

renal—pertaining to the kidney

renal calculus (plural: calculi)—kidney stone

sequela (plural: sequelae)—outcome

testis (plural testes, also called testicle)—oval structure in the scrotal sac that produces sperm

trigone—triangular area in floor of urinary bladder where ureters enter and urethra exits

turbidity—cloudiness, lack of clarity

ureter—tube leading from the kidney to the urinary bladder

urethra—tube leading from urinary bladder to outside the body

urinalysis—visual and chemical examination of the urine

urinary bladder—receptacle for urine that has been manufactured by the kidneys

urinary meatus—external sphincter of the urethra

urobilinogen—derivative substance formed by conversion of direct bilirubin by bacteria in the intestinal tract

urologist—physician who specializes in treating urinary system diseases and conditions, as well as conditions involving the male reproductive system

urology—study of the urinary system in males and females and the diseases that affect it

Abbreviations

BPH—benign prostatic hypertrophy

DRE—digital rectal examination

ESRD—end stage renal disease

UA—urinalysis

UTI—urinary tract infection

COMPETENCY SKILLS PERFORMANCE

1. Demonstrate patient instruction for collecting a clean-catch midstream specimen.
2. Demonstrate patient instruction for collecting a 24-hour urine specimen.
3. Perform catheterization of a female patient.
4. Perform catheterization of a male patient.
5. Perform urinalysis using chemical test strips.
6. Demonstrate patient instruction for testicular self-examination.

The Anatomy and Physiology of the Urinary System

The urinary system is composed of four primary structures: the **kidneys, ureters, urinary bladder, urethra** (Figure 15-1 ◆). The human kidney is fist-sized and bean-shaped. Kidneys are well supplied with blood from the renal arteries. Blood circulating through the kidneys is filtered to remove toxins, water, sugar, urea, and certain salts. Each kidney is divided into:

- an outer layer, the cortex, where the bulk of the urine-forming tissue is located
- an inner medulla, where the urine is collected for drainage to the urinary bladder

Urine is produced from blood plasma by a system of **nephrons,** microscopic processing tubules in each kidney. Each kidney contains approximately one million nephrons. Once formed, the urine is collected by a system of internal pipes, the collecting ducts, and drained by another pipe, the ureter. The ureters deliver the urine to the urinary bladder for storage. The urine enters the bladder at the **trigone,** where both ureters enter and the urethra exits the bladder. When the smooth muscle of the bladder contracts, usually under the voluntary control of the central nervous system, the urine is delivered to the external environment through the urethra and the **urinary meatus.**

Kidney Function

In addition to the excretion of waste molecules, the kidneys have three other important physiological functions:

1. Maintaining the body's water balance by adjusting the amount of water in the urine.
2. Maintaining the acid-base balance of the body by adjusting the amount of acid.
3. Producing two internal regulatory substances, erythropoietin and renin.

The kidneys are secondary endocrine organs. Erythropoietin is a hormone that stimulates the red bone marrow to generate more red blood cells. Individuals with serious kidney disease often develop secondary anemia because the damaged kidneys do not produce adequate amounts of erythropoietin. Renin is an enzyme that activates angiotensin, a hormone involved in a complex regulatory process that maintains adequate blood volume and blood pressure.

Nephrons

The nephron (Figure 15-2 ◆) is a microscopic tubular structure connected at one end to the arterial blood supply of the

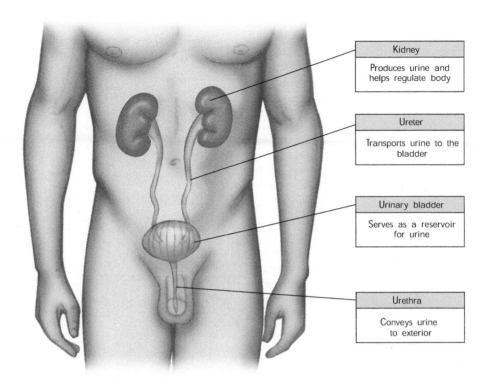

Figure 15-1 ◆ The urinary system

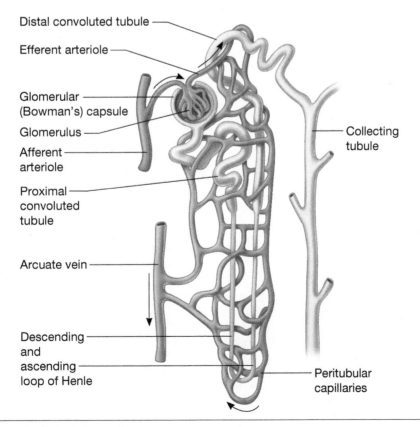

Figure 15-2 ◆ The nephron and enlarged glomerulus

kidney, and at the other end to the urine drainage system. Each nephron consists of five structural parts:

- **glomerulus,** tuft or cluster of capillaries inside the capsule of the nephron, also called Bowman's capsule
- **proximal tubule,** the tubule closest to the glomerulus
- loop of the nephron, also called the loop of Henle
- **distal tubule,** the tubule farthest from the glomerulus
- collecting ducts

Each region of the nephron plays a major role in the kidney formation of urine. The three major activities of the nephron in the formation of urine are filtration, reabsorption, and secretion. Filtration of substances from the blood, including water, takes place in the glomerulus. The proximal tubule begins the reabsorption process by reabsorbing water, sodium ions, and chloride ions. Glucose, other simple sugars, amino acids, potassium, vitamins, calcium magnesium bicarbonate, phosphates, urea, and lipid soluble materials are also absorbed. Secretion of hydrogen ions, ammonium ions, and creatinine occurs in the proximal tubule. The loop of the nephron continues the reabsorption of water and sodium and chloride ions. A small amount of water is reabsorbed in the distal tubule, along with some sodium, chloride, and bicarbonate ions. Secretion of hydrogen ions, ammonium ions, creatinine, some drugs and toxins occurs in the distal tubule. The collecting ducts continue reabsorption of water, sodium ions, bicarbonate ions, and urea under the stimulation of ADH (anti-diuretic hormone). Potassium and hydrogen ions are secreted in the collecting ducts.

Specific types of hematology testing (blood studies and chemistries) can reflect kidney function by measuring the reabsorption of certain components. Conversely, urine testing can reflect kidney function by measuring amounts of certain components that are excreted rather than reabsorbed.

Urine Formation

Urine formation is a complex process that can be broken down into five contributing functions (Figure 15-3 ◆):

1. Renal blood supply
2. Glomerular filtration
3. Tubular reabsorption
4. Tubular secretion
5. Water conservation

In reality, all these functions operate at the same time and influence one another. The kidneys are capable of self-regulation at the level of the cells of the nephron, but they also receive regulatory commands from the central nervous and endocrine systems.

Keys to Success
USING FUNCTIONING NAMES

The structures sometimes called the loop of Henle and Bowman's capsule were named after the physicians who identified them. Modern science has dropped this naming convention and these structures are now referred to as the loop of the nephron and the glomerular capsule. The trend in medicine today is to refer to anatomical structures, equipment, or accessories by their functioning names.

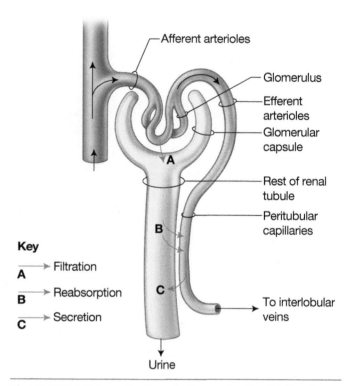

Figure 15-3 ◆ Schematic view of urine production: (a) filtration; (b) reabsorption; (c) secretion

The wastes carried by urine are individual molecules dissolved in water. The major types of waste found in urine are molecules absorbed from meals that were of no use to the body or were in excess of the body's nutritional needs or generated as metabolic byproducts of the many biochemical pathways of the body.

Some of these molecules are charged ions, termed salts or **electrolytes.** Examples are hydrogen, sodium, potassium, calcium, chloride, bicarbonate, sulphate, and phosphate ions. Other excreted molecules are organic, carbon-based compounds, such as sugars, amino acids, vitamins, hormones, organic acids, and alkaloids. One special group of important compounds is nitrogenous wastes, metabolic byproducts of protein and nucleic acid breakdown. The four main nitrogenous waste compounds are:

- Urea
- Uric acid
- Creatinine
- Ammonium salts

Measured over the course of a day and with adequate water intake, a normal person produces approximately 1-1/2 to 2 liters of urine. Heavy physical exertion, exposure to a hot environment, or fever can lead to unusual water loss by profuse sweating. Also, illness with vomiting and/or diarrhea can cause water loss. These conditions might reduce urinary output by 90 percent, generating as little as 150 mLs of urine in a day, and still maintain a satisfactory water balance. The kidneys do their job and are not overly stressed. If water loss exceeds a person's ability to replenish lost water, the kidneys attempt to conserve water by lowering the urine volume even more. Kidney damage may occur alongside the negative consequences of dehydration.

Urinary System Infections

The urinary system is a common site for infectious processes (Table 15-1). Many infections of the urethra and bladder migrate upward to the pelvis of the kidney, causing **pyelonephritis**. In the female patient, **cystitis** may be caused by the introduction of bac-

teria following sexual relations or by incorrect cleansing after a bowel movement (the correct way is front from the meatus back toward the rectum). Females are more prone to urinary tract infections (**UTIs**) than males due to the close proximity of the urinary meatus to the rectum. In both male and female patients, UTIs may be the result of sexually transmitted diseases. UTIs could also be the result of being prone to them, poor hygiene, or sexual activity not associated with STDs.

TABLE 15-1   INFECTIONS OF THE URINARY SYSTEM

Infection	Symptoms	Diagnosis	Treatment
Urethritis ■ Infection of urethra ■ Usually transmitted by sexual contact ■ In males, gonococcus is frequent source of infection ■ Often accompanied by cystitis in females	■ Frequent and painful urination ■ Pus in urine ■ Penile discharge in males	■ Patient presenting symptoms ■ Urinalysis	■ Antibiotics to treat infection
Cystitis ■ Inflammation of urinary bladder caused by bacteria ■ More commonly found in women because of shorter urethra and proximity of meatal opening to vagina and rectum, which tends to increase risk of contamination ■ Common source is *E. coli,* which is spread through fecal matter in the process of wiping after a bowel movement ■ Sexual intercourse is another source of infection	■ **Polyuria** ■ **Pyuria** ■ Hematuria ■ Malodorous urine ■ Burning during urination ■ Pressure in lower abdomen ■ Lower back pain	■ Patient presenting symptoms ■ Urinalysis ■ Blood test	■ Antibiotics for infection ■ Eight glasses of water per day to lower urine concentration ■ Voiding after sexual intercourse to eliminate microorganisms from lower urinary tract ■ Wiping from front to back after urination to prevent spread of fecal matter to urethra
Acute pyelonephritis/nephritis ■ Infection of renal medulla and upper urinary tract ■ Develops from untreated bladder infections, usually in women, which progress upward to involve renal pelvis but rarely invade nephrons ■ Recurrences are common	■ Frequent urination ■ **Flank** and lumbar back pain ■ Pyuria ■ Cloudy urine ■ High fever ■ Chills ■ Burning during urination	■ Patient presenting symptoms ■ Patient history ■ Urinalysis ■ Microscopic examination	■ Antibiotics for infection
Chronic pyelonephritis ■ Long-standing infection of renal medulla and upper urinary tract ■ Untreated, may involve nephrons and urine-collecting duct system and progress to uremia and renal failure ■ Scarring of kidneys may occur, reducing overall kidney function	■ Frequent urination ■ Flank and lumbar back pain ■ Cloudy urine ■ Blood in urine ■ High fever ■ Chills ■ Burning during urination ■ Hypertension	■ Patient presenting symptoms ■ Patient history ■ Urinalysis ■ Microscopic examination ■ Blood test ■ Intravenous pyelogram (IVP) ■ CT scan of abdomen	■ Long-term antibiotic treatment to prevent kidney damage
Uremia ■ Toxic condition resulting from kidney failure or insufficiency ■ Kidneys do not remove nitrogenous substances from blood	■ Nausea ■ Vomiting ■ Diminished vision ■ Coma, convulsions, stupor ■ Elevated blood pressure ■ Urine odor in breath ■ Dry skin ■ Oliguria	■ Patient presenting symptoms ■ Reduced amounts of urea in urine	■ Dialysis

? **─Critical Thinking Question 15-1─**
When Gina's patient mentions her urinary frequency and painful urination, what can Gina do to relieve some of her nervousness?

Renal Diseases

Many factors, including infection, trauma, obstructions, and autoimmune disorders, cause diseases of the renal system (Table 15-2). Most renal diseases occur commonly, but some are fairly rare.

Chronic renal failure is the end-stage outcome of all the chronic disorders described in Table 15-2. Patients develop uremia, loss of concentration, **nocturia, oliguria,** or **anuria,** and the prognosis is poor. Acute renal failure has the same symptoms but results from a different set of causes, such as sudden shocks to the kidney that weaken or destroy functional tissue, sudden loss of blood supply, exposure to toxic agents, trauma, surgical shock or injury, burns, transfusion reactions, and other

TABLE 15-2 RENAL DISEASES

Disease	Symptoms	Diagnosis	Treatment
Acute glomerulonephritis ■ May occur one to two weeks after an infection, commonly after a streptococcal sore throat ■ Usually no permanent tissue damage	■ Oliguria ■ **Hematuria** ■ **Periorbital edema**	■ Patient presenting symptoms ■ Urinalysis ■ Microscopic examination	■ Restriction of salt and water to reduce fluid retention and swelling ■ Dietary changes to restrict protein but maintain high calories ■ Hypertension medication if cause is not an infection ■ Antibiotics if cause is infection ■ Bed rest in certain cases
Crescentic (rapidly progressive) glomerulonephritis ■ Also called Goodpasture's syndrome ■ Acute onset progresses to oliguria and renal failure, which have a poor prognosis unless diagnosed early	■ Urine: blood, decreased output, dark color ■ Cough with bloody sputum ■ Weakness	■ Patient presenting symptoms ■ Urinalysis ■ Microscopic examination	■ Corticosteroids and anti-inflammatory drugs to reduce immune response ■ **Plasmapheresis** to slow the disorder ■ Dialysis if kidney is not functioning properly ■ Kidney transplant
Chronic glomerulonephritis ■ Membranous glomerulonephritis: generally occurs in patients over 40; slow progression; remission sometimes occurs but about one-third of patients eventually progress to nephrotic syndrome or chronic renal failure	■ Swelling ■ Weight gain ■ Protein in urine ■ Hypertension ■ Usually associated with other diseases: infections (hepatitis B, syphilis), connective tissue diseases (systemic lupus erythematosus, sarcoidosis), cancers, drug side effects (gold, mercurial compounds, penicillin)	■ Patient presenting symptoms ■ Patient history ■ Urinalysis ■ Microscopic examination	■ Early diagnosis critical to preventing more serious complications ■ Medication for hypertension ■ Dietary changes to reduce amount of protein, salt, and phosphate
■ Membrano-proliferative glomerulonephritis: each variety (Types I, II, and III) has a different characteristic change in microscopic anatomy of glomerulus; Type I is most common form; disease occurs mainly in people under 30 years old; prognosis extremely poor for young adults and children; patients often die within five years of diagnosis, although among children spontaneous remission may occur	In children and adolescents: ■ Protein in urine ■ Abnormal immune response ■ Antibodies in the kidney ■ Edema ■ Hypertension	■ Patient presenting symptoms ■ Patient history ■ Urinalysis ■ Microscopic examination	■ Steroids and cytotoxic agents for symptoms. ■ Dietary changes to restrict sodium, fluids, and protein intake ■ Antihypertensive medications to control hypertension ■ Diuretics to reduce edema ■ Dialysis or kidney transplant when necessary
Acute renal failure ■ Sudden onset ■ Caused by decreased blood flow to kidneys post surgical shock, traumatic shock, severe dehydration, poisoning, and kidney disease ■ May be result of incompatible blood transfusion	■ Sudden drop in urine output ■ Headache ■ GI distress ■ Odor of ammonia on breath ■ Altered LOC	■ Hyperkalemia ■ Elevated serum creatinine levels ■ Elevated BUN	■ Identification of cause and attempt to correct ■ Restoration of blood volume ■ Dialysis ■ Monitor intake and output

TABLE 15-2 RENAL DISEASES (*continued*)

Disease	Symptoms	Diagnosis	Treatment
Chronic renal failure ■ Irreversible loss of nephrons ■ Progressive ■ Gradual onset of uremia ■ Systemic effects in most or all body systems	■ Progressive weakness ■ Edema ■ Muscle weakness ■ Dyspnea	■ Elevated creatinine ■ Elevated BUN ■ Hyperkalemia ■ Decreased hemoglobin and hematocrit levels ■ 24-hour urine studies ■ Radiographic studies	■ Identification of cause and attempt to correct ■ Diet modification to control protein and sodium intake ■ Diuretic medications ■ Antihypertensive drug therapy ■ Dialysis ■ Monitor intake and output ■ Supportive care ■ Kidney transplant
Nephrotic syndrome ■ Generally develops when worsening glomerulonephritis is accompanied by circulatory problems, such as hypertension ■ Often progresses to chronic renal failure	■ Edema ■ Elevated serum lipids ■ Proteinuria ■ Poor appetite	■ Patient presenting symptoms ■ Patient history ■ Urinalysis ■ Microscopic examination	■ Prednisone to decrease protein content ■ Dietary changes to restrict sodium, fluids, and protein intake ■ Diuretics to reduce edema
Polycystic kidney disease ■ Slowly progressive disease that affects both kidneys and occurs when multiple cysts form on dilated nephrons and collecting ducts, resulting in enlarged kidneys ■ Most cases are inherited, but may be acquired following long-term chronic kidney disease and/or dialysis ■ No cure	■ Lumbar pain ■ Hematuria ■ Hypertension	■ Patient presenting symptoms ■ Physical examination	■ Supportive care for patient and family ■ Dialysis ■ Kidney transplant ■ Hypertension and infection management
Diabetic neuropathy ■ Often a **sequela** to diabetes mellitus ■ Cellular membranes of glomeruli harden or sclerose; deterioration in filtration system is the result of hypertension and elevated blood glucose levels ■ Infectious process often involved	■ Decrease in urine output ■ Nausea ■ Vomiting ■ Vision problems ■ Decreased mental alertness ■ Convulsions ■ Coma	■ Patient presenting symptoms ■ Physical examination ■ Urinalysis	■ Blood pressure and blood glucose controlled to forestall long-term effects ■ Supportive care ■ Dialysis ■ Kidney transplant is only long-term option

episodes of significant intravascular hemolysis. Prognosis depends on both the cause and the effectiveness of the treatment.

Blood studies and chemistries ordered in kidney diseases include the CBC (including hemoglobin and hematocrit), electrolytes, creatinine levels, and blood urea nitrogen (BUN). The patient's total clinical picture must be considered when deviations from normal in any of these tests occur. Repeat studies are used to monitor levels and the progress of the disease. (Please refer to a reference lab in your community for suggested normal levels.)

The list of important renal diseases is much longer than that in Table 15-2, but little information is derived from the routine urinalysis to assist in their diagnosis. These diseases include inborn errors of renal metabolism, defects in specific tubular reabsorptive or secretive functions, congenital malformations, progressive wasting diseases, and many more.

Dialysis

When a patient is diagnosed with end stage renal disease (**ESRD**), the first option of treatment is one of two forms of **dialysis.**

■ Hemodialysis is the cleansing of urea and other chemical substances from the blood with a dialysis machine, or dialyzer (Figure 15-4 ◆). Joining an artery and a vein, usu-

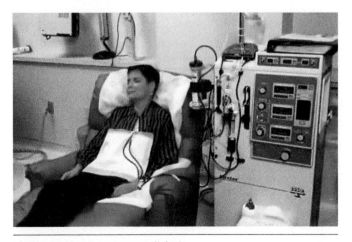

Figure 15-4 ◆ A patient on dialysis.
Source: Michal Heron Photography.

ally in the arm or leg, surgically creates an access, or **fistula.** Two needles are inserted into the fistula, one to remove blood from the body and the other to return it. The blood that is removed passes on one side of a membranous filter while the dialysis solution is on the other side. Although the blood and the solution do not mix, urea and other waste products pass across the membrane into the dialysis solution. A pump keeps the blood flowing through the machine and then back into the body. Patients usually require hemodialysis three times a week, and the procedure takes from three to five or eight to twelve hours. Although there are special centers equipped for hemodialysis, some patients opt for home dialysis. Family members or the patients themselves are trained to maintain the equipment as well as perform the procedure at home.

■ In peritoneal dialysis, the peritoneal membrane acts as the filter. Dialyzing fluid is infused into the peritoneum through a catheter. Wastes accumulate in the fluid, which is drained and replaced by clean fluid. The procedure can be performed in three different ways for the patient's comfort and mobility.

- Continuous ambulatory peritoneal dialysis is done three to five times a day and at night. The solution is drained into a bag the patient wears around the waist.
- Continuous cycling peritoneal dialysis (CCPD) is done by a machine while the patient sleeps.
- Intermittent peritoneal dialysis is usually done three to five times a week in a clinic and requires several hours to complete.

Both forms of dialysis are treatments, not cures, intended to be replaced when a suitable donor is found and the diseased kidney can be replaced by transplant.

Keys to Success
STRESSING DIETARY TREATMENT

Patients with kidney disease should be made aware of the importance of diet in their treatment. Protein- and sodium-restricted diets are usually indicated when kidney function is compromised. Referral to a dietician may be indicated.

Neurogenic Bladder and Urinary Incontinence

Neurogenic bladder is usually the result of an insult to the nerves supplying the bladder. The patient may have difficulty starting a stream of urine or emptying the bladder or, conversely, be unable to control the release of urine (**incontinence**). Incontinence may also be caused by nerve damage, especially in the lower spinal cord. The perineal sphincter muscles may be weak. Pregnancy and childbirth may be contributing factors in the female patient.

When the bladder becomes full, the patient usually experiences pain. Treatment may involve exercises to strengthen the perineal sphincter muscle to help with pain and incontinence. Other treatments are self-catheterization and pressing on the lower abdomen over the bladder to force stored urine out of the bladder. If the leaking of urine cannot be controlled, the patient may have to wear an absorbent pad to protect clothing.

Obstructive Conditions

Obstructive disorders that prevent urine from flowing down the urinary tract to be eliminated from the body may involve one or both kidneys (Table 15-3). **Hydronephrosis** is a condition in

TABLE 15-3 OBSTRUCTIVE CONDITIONS

Condition	Symptoms	Diagnosis	Treatment
Renal calculi ■ Stones may be single or multiple, large or small, and of a variety of compositions, such as uric acid, calcium salts, and cholesterol; may be round and smooth, sharp with rough edges, or, as "staghorn" stones, may take on form of renal pelvis ■ Obstruction must be relieved in approximately eight weeks to avoid permanent damage	■ Pain beginning in flank and moving downward to groin, vulva, or testicle as stone moves ■ Renal colic (severe pain in lower back over kidney) ■ Persistent urge to urinate ■ Blood in urine ■ Nausea or vomiting ■ Chills ■ Fever ■ Family or personal history	■ Patient presenting symptoms ■ Urinalysis ■ Radiographs (flat plate KUB, IVP, or CT scan)	■ Eight glasses of water per day to dilute the urine ■ Analgesics for pain ■ Dietary changes ■ **Lithotripsy,** less invasive treatment to remove the stones (Figure15-5 ◆) ■ Surgery
Bladder calculi (bladder stones) ■ Diagnosed almost solely in men ■ Stones formed in bladder when urine is concentrated and materials crystallize. ■ Obstruction must be removed to avoid permanent damage to bladder or kidneys	■ Frequent and difficult urination ■ Pain in abdomen and/or penis ■ Blood in urine ■ Abnormal color to urine	■ Urinalysis ■ Urine culture ■ Bladder x-ray ■ Cystoscopy	■ Eight glasses of water per day to dilute the urine ■ Lithotripsy to remove stones ■ Cystoscopy to remove stones and examine bladder

TABLE 15-3 OBSTRUCTIVE CONDITIONS (*continued*)

Condition	Symptoms	Diagnosis	Treatment
Cysts ■ Noncancerous lesions of the kidney ■ Commonly found in patients over 50 ■ Large cysts can impair renal function	■ Blood in urine ■ Flank pain	■ Patient presenting symptoms ■ MRI, CT scan, or ultrasound examination	■ Surgery or needle aspiration to remove pressure or pain and prevent kidney damage
Kidney or ureter cancer ■ Several types ■ Tumors sometimes erode walls of blood vessels, producing small to moderate hemorrhages of blood into the urine ■ Cancer hastens destruction of surrounding kidney tissue and alters ability of involved kidney(s) to form urine	■ Blood in urine ■ Flank pain ■ Abdominal mass ■ Weight loss ■ Intermittent fever ■ Fatigue	■ Patient presenting symptoms ■ Patient history ■ Ultrasound examination ■ CT scan or MRI	■ Removal of mass at early stage of development to prevent spreading ■ Removal of kidney and possibly lymph nodes to prevent spreading ■ Radiation therapy to prevent spreading ■ Chemotherapy or immunotherapy at more advanced stages
Bladder cancer ■ Men more likely than women to develop ■ Occurs rarely in people under 40 ■ Early detection critical for favorable prognosis	■ Blood in urine ■ Difficulty voiding ■ Pelvic pain	■ Patient presenting symptoms ■ Patient history ■ Cystoscopy ■ IVP ■ CT scan or MRI	■ Tumor removal at early stage to prevent spread ■ Cancer drug infusion into bladder to reduce likelihood of recurrence ■ Bladder removal to prevent spread ■ Removal of prostate for men and of ovaries, uterus, and part of the vagina for women, to prevent spread ■ Chemotherapy at later stages

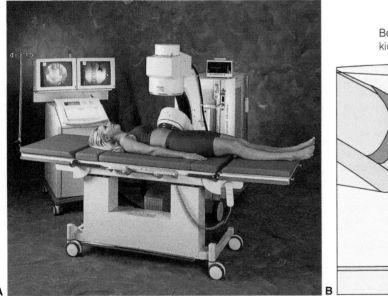

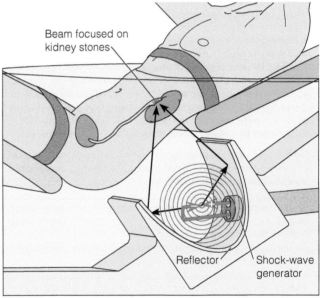

Beam focused on kidney stones

Reflector **Shock-wave generator**

A **B**

Figure 15-5 ◆ Extracorporeal shock-wave lithotripsy: (A) A shock-wave generator that does not require water immersion; (B) Water immersion lithotripsy procedure

which the kidney becomes dilated and enlarged with urine during an obstructive condition. Once the obstruction is relieved, the kidney usually returns to its normal status.

A frequent obstruction that affects one kidney is the **renal calculus** (kidney stone). Carcinoma (cancer) of the renal pelvis may also be extensive enough to cause an obstruction. An enlarged prostate is a common obstruction in older males. Cancer of the bladder is less common and occurs more frequently in males than in females.

Diagnostic Procedures

Laboratory tests for diagnosing renal diseases are invasive or noninvasive. Urinalysis testing is the most common noninvasive test. A clean-catch midstream urine test is used to diagnose the causal microorganism of urinary tract infections. Some invasive tests may be ordered to assist the physician in making or confirming a diagnosis. The invasive tests described in the following boxes are usually performed in a specialized area with radiography.

Keys to Success
PATIENT INSTRUCTIONS FOR INTRAVENOUS PYELOGRAM (IVP)

In an intravenous pyelogram (IVP), the kidneys are examined by x-ray for renal stones. IVPs are also used to diagnose disease conditions that cause hematuria, frequent urination, and side, abdominal, and lower back pain, as well as enlarged prostate; kidney, ureter, or bladder tumors; and trauma from an accident.

A contrast medium is used to enhance details of the kidneys, ureters, and bladder. Because of potential allergies to the contrast medium, tell your physician and/or clinical staff of any medication allergies that you have. Also inform your physician and clinical staff if you are diabetic or pregnant. Special accommodations will be made if you are diabetic, and if you are or may be pregnant, the physician will likely postpone the IVP or discuss other procedures to help diagnose and treat your symptoms.

1. On the day before the procedure, the physician will prescribe a laxative medication for you. Your prescriptions for the procedure and the times for taking them are as follows: _____

2. On the day before the procedure, your dietary instructions are as follows:_____. Do not eat or drink or take medication after midnight.

3. On the day of the procedure and before the procedure, you may take the following medications with only sips of water:_____

   You will receive instructions for resuming the other medications after the procedure.

4. On the day of the procedure, please leave valuables at home.

5. Go through the admissions area, and you will be escorted to the radiology department. After you change into a gown, the radiologic technician will take a "before" x-ray.

6. The contrast media will be given through an IV and a series of x-rays will be taken at intervals.

7. Because individuals are different, the process of taking radiographic films after the contrast medium has been administered may take one-half to three or four hours. Please be patient. The time will go faster if you bring some reading materials.

Keys to Success
PATIENT INSTRUCTIONS FOR CYSTOSCOPY

Your physician has ordered a cystoscopy to look inside your bladder. This procedure is done to assess the size and condition of the prostate gland in males or to look for obstructions, stones, tumors, and other abnormalities. Other conditions that warrant a cystoscopic examination include hematuria, frequent UTIs, incontinence or overactive bladder, painful urination, or the need of a catheter for urination. Stones or tumors are sometimes removed or a biopsy sample is obtained during this procedure. The physician uses a gel to numb the urethra, and it is rare that any other type of anesthesia is needed.

1. On the day before the procedure, do not eat or drink or take medication after midnight. Exceptions, if any, are as follows:
   _____

2. On the day of the procedure, please go to the admissions area and you will be escorted to the ambulatory outpatient department. You will be asked to change into a gown.

3. A nurse or technician will apply a numbing gel (local anesthetic) to the urethral opening.

4. The physician will give you instructions and information during the procedure. You may feel some discomfort and the urge to urinate during the procedure, particularly as the bladder is filled with sterile water or saline and stretched for better visualization.

5. The examination usually lasts only 15 to 20 minutes, but additional procedures, such as removal of stones or biopsy, will make it longer.

Keys to Success
PATIENT INSTRUCTIONS FOR VOIDING CYSTOGRAM

Your physician has ordered a voiding cystogram to look inside your bladder for obstructions, stones, tumors, or other abnormalities. If you are a female patient, this procedure is not done during your menstrual period.

1. On the day before the procedure, do not eat or drink or take medication after midnight. Exceptions, if any, are as follows:
   _____

2. On the day of the procedure, please go to the admissions area and you will be escorted to the radiology department. You will be asked to change into a gown.

3. A radiography film will be taken of your bladder before the procedure.

4. You will be asked to lie on the x-ray table for placement of a urinary catheter into the bladder.

5. A liquid contrast medium will be inserted via the catheter, and the catheter will then be removed.

6. When your bladder feels full, x-rays will be taken at intervals and you will be asked to turn from side to side. After x-rays are completed, you will be allowed to empty your bladder and a final x-ray will be taken.

Urinalysis

A routine urinalysis tests certain aspects of the first three functions of the kidney—waste excretion, acid-base balance, and water balance—but not the fourth function, endocrine regulatory activity. Measurements of various endocrine activities of the kidneys require specialized urine testing that is usually performed in a reference lab.

Urinalysis Specimen Collection

Different types of urine specimens are required for different testing goals.

1. A random voided specimen is adequate for routine screening.
2. A first morning specimen is best for routine screening, pregnancy tests, cytology (to detect abnormal cells), or orthostatic protein determination.
3. A fasting sample is required for diabetic monitoring. This is not the first but the second morning specimen, which eliminates much of the urine accumulated in the bladder overnight.
4. A midstream clean-catch is also appropriate for routine screening and best for a bacterial culture.
5. Timed or 24-hour specimens are required for quantitative analyses.
6. A catheterized specimen is sometimes requested for bacterial culture.
7. A suprapubic needle aspiration is rarely required for a bacterial culture (especially if anaerobes or other problem organisms must be identified) or for cytological examination for abnormal cells, such as cancer cells. Needle aspiration may be necessary for some pediatric specimens when a true sterile collection is required.
8. Pediatric specimens are difficult to obtain, particularly in clean-catch form. Plastic bags with adhesive may be used but require care.
9. Urine for drug testing must be collected in a very specific manner, according to the clinic's policy. Some clinics will place color altering tablets in the toliet water to verify urine has been expelled, check for warmth (to verify the urine was not brought in pre-packaged), and check for concentration (to verify the patient is not attempting to "flush" their system). Always check with your clinics drug-testing policies before attempting a patient's urine drug screening test.

Urine Containers

It is important to handle containers and specimens properly and to follow each collection procedure carefully for accurate results. Three major rules apply to containers.

- They vary according to the type of specimen required.
- They must be clean, dry, and of sufficient volume to hold the routine urinalysis sample.
- They must be sterile when a microbial culture and sensitivity is ordered.

If the specimen is to be transported, it should be placed in a proper biohazard bag to ensure it does not leak. Single specimens of 50 to 100 mLs are typically adequate for testing. Twenty-four-hour specimens usually require at least a one-gallon or three-liter bottle, usually made of rigid plastic or glass (Figure 15-6 ◆).

General Specimen Handling

Correct and complete labeling is essential. At the minimum, you must include the patient's name and the date and time of day of collection. In a hospital, a patient's hospital number may also be mandatory. Any unlabeled or incompletely labeled container should be considered unsatisfactory, such as a container

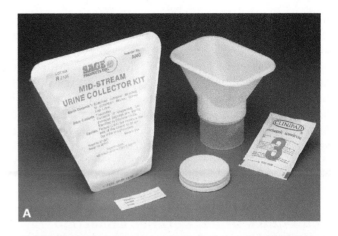

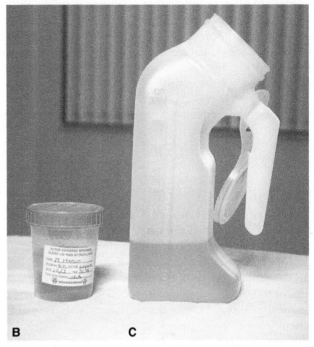

Figure 15-6 ◆ Urine specimen containers: (A) midstream clean-catch container; (B) urine collection cup; (C) 24-hour urine container

with a requisition slip around or under it. The requisition slip may be moved or stained with urine and difficult to read. The label must be affixed to guarantee the identification of the specimen source.

The most accurate results come from testing fresh urine. If the test must be delayed, the specimen should be refrigerated. Some values begin to change immediately if testing is delayed. All values are likely to be altered, some markedly, after 24 hours. The urine specimen should be allowed to come to room temperature and should be well mixed before testing.

The specimen should be delivered promptly, then either refrigerated or frozen immediately, have an appropriate preservative added immediately, or tested within one to two hours. There are many types of urine preservatives. Most are antimicrobial compounds, such as benzoic acid, boric acid, chloroform, formaldehyde, and preservative tablets with a mix of compounds. These compounds may also preserve cells, or alcohol can be mixed with the urine in equal portions for the same purpose.

Preservation kits are also available for transporting specimens to other facilities. Since preserved specimens are usually transferred to reference laboratories for special testing, follow the written procedures provided by the reference laboratory to prepare the specimen. Urine standing unpreserved at room temperature begins to change immediately, and test results will be less accurate. If the urine is to be preserved by refrigeration or chemical means, it should be done quickly.

Clean-Catch Urine Specimen Collection

Although the bladder and urethra are normally sterile, a urine specimen can be contaminated with microorganisms from the lower portion of the urethra and the meatus. After proper training, you will teach the patient how to obtain a clean-catch specimen. Thorough instruction will ensure that the collected specimen is not contaminated.

Keys to Success
UNDERSTANDING CHANGES IN UNPRESERVED URINE SPECIMENS

1. Exposure to light decreases **bilirubin** and **urobilinogen.**
2. Exposure to the atmosphere decreases CO_2. This raises the pH; permits nitrogen gas to evolve from dissolved nitrites, lowering nitrite levels; and permits volatiles to escape, such as acetone and other ketones. Evaporative water loss is only rarely significant.
3. Microbial growth:
   - breaks down urea to ammonia, raising the pH
   - changes the odor and perhaps the color
   - oxidizes urobilinogen to urobilin
   - decreases glucose and ketone bodies, lowering the pH
   - reduces nitrates by converting them into nitrites
   - increases the **turbidity**
   - alters the proportions of organisms
4. Changes in pH can:
   - precipitate crystals or dissolve crystals already present
   - break down or alter chemical constituents, and perhaps urine color
   - disintegrate cells and casts that were present (casts are discussed later in this chapter)

PROCEDURE 15-1 Demonstrate Patient Instruction for a Clean-Catch Urine Specimen

Theory

Proper instruction keeps the patient from returning to the medical office to repeat the test. The specimen is tested immediately or refrigerated, or preservative is added. Remind the patient not to touch the inside of the container or lid to prevent contamination of the specimen. Voiding some urine into the toilet before voiding into the specimen cup will wash microorganisms away from the meatus and will also prevent contamination of the specimen.

Materials

- sterile specimen container
- label
- antiseptic wipes
- chart
- requisition slip, if necessary

Competency

(**Conditions**) With the necessary materials, (**Task**) you will be able to instruct the patient on obtaining a clean-catch specimen (**Standards**) correctly within the time frame designated by the instructor.

1. Wash your hands. Gather equipment and supplies.
2. Identify the patient and guide him or her to the treatment area.

3. Instruct the patient to:
   - Label the container, not the lid, with their first and last name
   - Wash the hands.
   - Open the sterile urine container and place the lid on a flat area with the inside facing up.
   - Open the antiseptic wipes and place them on top of their packaging.
   - If male: Retract the foreskin, if present. Cleanse the glans penis with the antiseptic wipes with a circular motion from the meatal opening and proceeding outward. Repeat, using all the antiseptic wipes.
   - If female: Spread the labia apart with one hand. Wipe from front to back. Use one wipe to cleanse one side, then discard the wipe. Cleanse the other side with a new wipe and discard it. Finally, with a new wipe, cleanse down the middle across the meatus, and discard the wipe.
4. After cleansing, the patient should:
   - Discard all the used wipes in an appropriate waste container.
   - Void some urine into the toilet and stop (an uncircumcised male should also bring the foreskin forward)
   - Restart voiding to half-fill the sterile container.
   - Finish voiding into the toilet.
   - Wash the hands.
   - Put the lid on the container without touching the inside of the lid.
   - Place it in the designated receiving site.

PROCEDURE 15-1 Demonstrate Patient Instruction for a Clean-Catch Urine Specimen *(continued)*

5. Wash your hands.
6. Chart your observations of the urine specimen as well as the date, time collected, and tests ordered.
7. If the specimen is to be tested at another laboratory, complete a laboratory requisition slip. Take the specimen to the lab or refrigerator or add preservative.

Patient Education

Ask the patient to repeat his or her instructions to verify understanding. Inform the patient that the physician will review the results and call if additional or new treatment is needed.

Instruct the patient to call the medical office if symptoms worsen or if he or she would like to know more about the test results.

Charting Example

03/11/XX 8:30 a.m. Pt instructed on how to obtain clean-catch midstream. Pt expressed understanding of procedure and left the labeled specimen in the bathroom. Cloudy specimen was taken to the lab at 0840 and placed in the refrigerator. Megan Steed, CMA

24–Hour Specimen Collection

A 24-hour specimen is performed to measure specific urine components. Calcium, potassium, creatinine, urea nitrogen, protein, and lead levels are affected by hydration, activity and exercise, and metabolic rate and can vary throughout the day. Because of these fluctuations, a 24-hour specimen gives a more accurate picture of the composition of the urine. It may also be ordered to determine the content of existing kidney stones or ways to prevent further kidney stone formation.

PROCEDURE 15-2 Demonstrate Patient Instruction for Collection of 24-Hour Specimen

Theory

A large container of 3000 mLs, often with preservative, is used to collect a 24-hour urine specimen. The urine must be refrigerated or kept in a portable cooler to prevent deterioration and other changes. The patient should be advised to moderate fluid and alcohol intake to avoid producing more urine than the collection container can hold. The physician will evaluate the medications the patient is taking to decide if any can be discontinued for a short period. Some medications can alter the test results.

The test is started *after* the patient's first morning void and continued for the next 24 hours. If any portion of the 24-hour urine is not placed in the collection container, the results of the test are invalid and the test must be started again. The 24-hour specimen is returned to the medical office or laboratory the same morning the test is completed.

Materials

- 24-hour specimen container
- smaller collection container
- patient instruction sheet
- chart
- requisition slip

Competency

(**Conditions**) With the necessary materials, (**Task**) you will be able to instruct the patient to obtain a quality 24–hour specimen for accurate testing, diagnosis, and treatment (**Standards**) correctly within the time frame designated by the instructor.

1. Wash your hands. Gather equipment and supplies.
2. Identify the patient and guide him or her to the treatment area.
3. Instruct the patient to:
   - Label the container, not the lid, with first and last name.
   - Wash the hands.
   - Void into the toilet upon arising.
   - Record the time (from this time and for the next 24 hours, all urine will go into the 24-hour collection container).

continued

PROCEDURE 15-2 Demonstrate Patient Instruction for Collection of 24–Hour Specimen (continued)

- Void all urine into the smaller collection container to pour into the larger container.
- Each time wash, rinse, and air-dry the smaller container.
- After each specimen is placed in the larger specimen container, screw the lid tightly and put it in the refrigerator or portable cooler.
- At the end of the 24-hour period, bring the large container to the medical office or laboratory. (The first voided specimen of the second morning is the last specimen to be added to the container, ending the collecting period.)

4. Ask the patient if any problems occurred during the specimen collection. If too much urine was collected or if some was spilled during collection, tell the patient a new collection must be started.
5. Fill out a lab requisition slip for the specimen when it is brought to the office or taken directly to an outside laboratory.
6. Chart your observations of the urine specimen, the date, time collected, tests ordered, and any other pertinent information.

Patient Education

Ask the patient to repeat his or her instructions to verify understanding. For the test to be accurate, *all* urine after the initial morning void must go into the collection container. Inform the patient that the physician will review the results and call if additional or new treatment is needed. The patient should call the medical office if symptoms worsen or if he or she would like to know more about the test results.

Charting Example

03/13/XX 11:30 a.m. Pt said he understood the process of collecting all urine within the 24-hour period. Written instructions also sent with patient. Ivory Smith, RMA

03/15/XX 9:00 a.m. Pt started 24-hour urine collection after 8:00 a.m. voiding on 3/14. Pt stated that urine has been kept in portable cooler during that time and that all urine has been collected. Lab requisition prepared for calcium, potassium, creatinine, urea nitrogen, and protein. Specimen sent via courier to the lab for testing. Ivory Smith, RMA

Keys to Success
24-HOUR URINE COLLECTION FROM A CHILD

If a child patient wets the bed, the 24-hour collection must begin again with a new collection container. The 24-hour specimen must consist of *all* the urine voided by the child in a 24-hour period.

Specimen Collection by Catheterization

For certain procedures and tests, a thin tube (catheter) is inserted into the urinary bladder to withdraw urine. The three most common reasons a catheterization is performed are the relief of urinary retention, the need for a sterile urine sample, and the need to instill a medication directly into an empty bladder. Catheterization may also be done to empty the bladder prior to a surgical procedure and to measure the amount of residual urine in the bladder of individuals with bladder-emptying problems. The collected urine can be tested for a variety of microorganisms and used in a number of tests.

Physical Urinalysis

A number of physical components are determined in a routine urinalysis: appearance (color and clarity), odor, pH, specific gravity, and many others, summarized in Table 15-4 (page 290).

PROCEDURE 15-3 Perform Catheterization of a Female Patient

Theory

Catheterization ensures a sterile sample but is not always the ideal method of obtaining a sample. Because a foreign object is introduced into the body, there is the possibility of also introducing pathogens. It is imperative, especially when catheterizing female patients, that the surrounding area be appropriately and thoroughly cleaned.

Materials

- lighting source, preferably a gooseneck lamp
- sterile specimen container
- sterile drapes
- sterile catheterization kit or straight catheter
- sterile K-Y gel or other lubricant
- sterilized Mayo stand
- sterile gloves, two pairs
- nonsterile latex gloves
- biohazardous waste receptacle
- several 2 × 2 sterile gauze squares (minimum of 6)
- Betadine or other iodine solution
- maxipad or pantyliner
- patient chart
- lab order forms

PROCEDURE 15-3 **Perform Catheterization of a Female Patient** (continued)

Competency

(**Conditions**) With the necessary materials, (**Task**) you will be able to catheterize a female patient (**Standards**) correctly within the time frame designated by the instructor.

1. Gather all needed supplies to bring into the room. Generally, the patient will already be disrobed and covered with a drape. Bringing all supplies into the room on one trip avoids opening the door more than once while your patient is in a potentially embarrassing position.
2. Explain the procedure to the patient and obtain verbal permission to begin touching her.
3. If the patient is not unclothed, explain the correct dorsal recumbent position and draping.
4. Position the gooseneck lamp so that it is directed at the genital area, but do not turn it on, as it may heat up quickly and make the patient uncomfortable.
5. Wash your hands and put on nonsterile gloves. Open the catheterization kit.
6. Ask the patient to keep her knees apart and take slow deep breaths while lifting her hips off the table surface.
7. When her hips have cleared the surface, slide a sterile drape beneath her by encircling the corners with your hands. Avoid touching the patient or the table with your hands.
8. Open a second sterile drape and place it over the patient's genital area, making sure that the vulvar area is exposed.
9. Place the insertion portion of the kit on the sterile drape you placed under the patient's hips, between her knees.
10. Remove the gloves and wash your hands.
11. Following sterile technique, put on sterile gloves.
12. Soak the 2 × 2 gauze pads in Betadine or other iodine solution.
13. Open the sterile lubricant and place it on the sterile field on the Mayo stand. Open the remaining items, including the sterile container, and place them on the tray.
14. Cleanse the patient with the Betadine-soaked gauze squares. Separate the labia with the thumb and index finger of your nondominant hand (Figure 15-7 ◆). With your other hand, take a gauze square and wipe one side of the labia from top to bottom in **one pass.** Throw the square away (Figure 15-8 ◆). Take another square, repeat on the other side, and discard. Do not let the hand that is separating the labia touch and thereby contaminate your other hand.
15. With a third gauze square, cleanse the urinary meatus with a circular motion, working from the inside to the outside. Discard the square.
16. With your dominant hand, pick up the catheter, your thumb and index finger approximately 3 inches from the end to be inserted.
17. Dip the insertion end of the catheter into the sterile lubricant. Make sure the opposite end of the catheter is in the collection portion of the kit's tray.

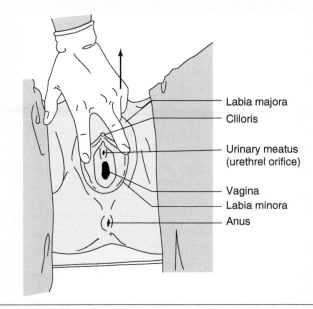

Figure 15-7 ◆ Separate the labia with the thumb and index finger of your nondominant hand.

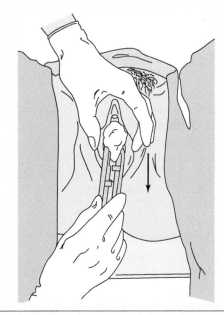

Figure 15-8 ◆ When cleansing the urinary meatus, move the swab downward.

18. Thread the catheter into the urinary meatus approximately 2 to 3 inches, until urine begins to flow into the collection tray.
19. If you meet resistance when threading the catheter, do not force it in. Resistance can be an indication of a problem. Remove the catheter and notify the physician.
20. After a small amount of the urine has flowed into the collection tray, move the end of the catheter into the sterile collection container.

continued

PROCEDURE 15-3 **Perform Catheterization of a Female Patient** *(continued)*

21. Measure the urine that has flowed from the bladder. Emptying more than 500 ml at one time may cause the bladder to spasm. If more than 500 ml has been released, clamp the catheter, wait 10 to 15 minutes, and release the remainder of the urine.
22. When the bladder is completely empty, gently remove the catheter.
23. Secure the collection container's lid in place and prepare the paperwork for laboratory testing.
24. Remove all supplies and dispose of them in a biohazardous container.
25. Assist the patient in sitting up and dressing if necessary.
26. Inform the patient that the Betadine used to cleanse the labia may stain her undergarments, and offer her a maxipad or pantyliner to protect her clothing.
27. Document the procedure in the patient's chart.

Patient Education

The patient should feel no discomfort or pain after the catheter is removed. Instruct her to report any discomfort, pain with urination, stinging, irritation, or fever. Also advise her to avoid using perfumed toiletries such as soaps, tissues, and tampons. Female patients should also avoid wearing overly tight pants and nylon underwear, which traps moisture and heat in the genital area.

Charting Example

05/23/XX 9:25 a.m. Sterile urine sample obtained through catheterization. Patient tolerated procedure well and does not report any pain, tingling, or burning. Urinary sample sent to laboratory for culture and sensitivity testing. Mary Brady, CMA

PROCEDURE 15-4 **Perform Catheterization of a Male Patient**

Theory

As with a female patient, it is imperative that the male patient's genital area be appropriately and thoroughly cleaned before catheterization to prevent the introduction of pathogens.

Materials

- lighting source, preferably a gooseneck lamp
- waterproof underpad
- sterile specimen container
- sterile catheterization kit or straight catheter
- sterile drapes
- sterile K-Y gel or other lubricant
- sterilized Mayo stand
- sterile gloves, 2 pairs
- nonsterile latex gloves
- biohazardous waste receptacle
- several 2 × 2 sterile gauze squares (minimum of 6)
- Betadine or other iodine solution
- fenestrated drape
- patient chart
- lab order forms

Competency

(**Conditions**) With the necessary materials, (**Task**) you will be able to catheterize a male patient (**Standards**) correctly within the time frame designated by the instructor.

1. Wash your hands. Collect all the needed supplies and bring into patient's room.
2. Explain the procedure to the patient and explain that it will be necessary to remove all articles of clothing from the waist down.
3. Assist the patient, if needed, into the supine position.
4. Wash your hands and put on nonsterile gloves.
5. Following sterile technique, open the catheterization kit and place the items on the sterile field on the Mayo stand.
6. Wrap the corners of the sterile underpad over your hands and place it over the patient's thighs, sliding it under the penis (Figure 15-9 ◆).
7. Remove the gloves, wash your hands, and put on sterile gloves.
8. Being careful not to touch the patient or the table, place a fenestrated drape over the genital area so that the penis is exposed (Figure 15-10 ◆).
9. Soak the 2 × 2 gauze pads in Betadine and place them on the patient's thighs for easy access.
10. With your nondominant hand, grasp the penis below the glans and hold it upright. If the patient is uncircumcised, retract the foreskin to expose the meatus.

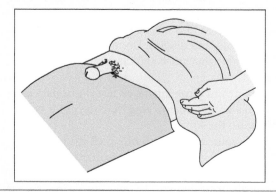

Figure 15-9 ◆ Place the sterile underpad over the patient's thighs, sliding it under the penis.

PROCEDURE 15-4 **Perform Catheterization of a Male Patient** (*continued*)

11. With your dominant hand, cleanse the meatus with a gauze square in a circular motion, working from the inside to the outside (Figure 15-11 ◆). Discard the gauze.
12. Repeat step 11 a total of three times, using a fresh gauze square each time you cleanse.
13. Dip the insertion tip of the catheter into lubricant to cover the 7 or 8 inches that will be inserted into the penis. Place the opposite end of the catheter in the collection tray.
14. Hold the penis firmly at a straight, upward angle to straighten the urethra for easier insertion.
15. Ask the patient to constrict the penis muscles in the same manner as when trying to urinate. While he is doing this, gently thread the catheter into the penis until urine begins to flow, generally 6 to 8 inches(Figure 15-12 ◆).
16. *Never* force the catheter. If you meet resistance, discontinue the procedure and notify the physician.
17. After a small amount of the urine has flowed into the collection tray, move the end of the catheter into the sterile collection container.

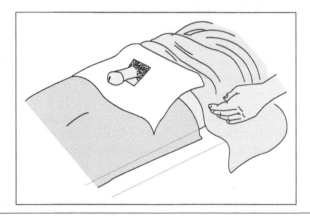

Figure 15-10 ◆ Place a fenestrated drape over the genital area so that the penis is exposed.

Figure 15-11 ◆ Clean around the meatus in a circular motion

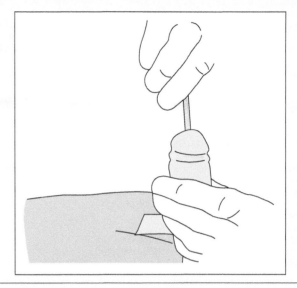

Figure 15-12 ◆ Gently thread the catheter into the penis until urine begins to flow, generally 6 to 8 inches.

18. Measure the urine that has flowed from the bladder. Emptying more than 500 ml at one time may cause the bladder to spasm. If more than 500 ml has been released, clamp the catheter, wait 10 to 15 minutes, and release the remainder of the urine.
19. When the bladder is completely empty, gently remove the catheter.
20. Secure the collection container's lid in place and prepare the paperwork for laboratory testing.
21. Remove all supplies and dispose of them in a biohazardous container.
22. Assist the patient in sitting up and dressing if necessary.
23. Inform the patient that the Betadine used to cleanse the glans may transfer to his undergarments and stain them.
24. Document the procedure in the patient's chart.

Patient Education

The patient should feel no discomfort or pain after the catheter is removed. Instruct him to report any discomfort, pain with urination, stinging, irritation, or fever. Remind the patient of the importance of voiding when the urge is present, as waiting stresses and irritates the bladder. The patient should also drink plenty of fluids to flush the urinary system and avoid caffeine, which may also irritate the bladder.

Charting Example

04/04/XX 9:25 a.m. Sterile urine sample obtained through catheterization. Patient tolerated procedure well and does not report any pain, tingling, or burning. Urinary sample sent to laboratory for culture and sensitivity testing. Joseph Baker, RMA

TABLE 15-4 CHARACTERISTICS OF A NORMAL URINALYSIS

Appearance	Normal pigments color the urine yellow. Clear urine is normal, although turbid (cloudy) urine is not necessarily a sign of pathology. The lighter the color of the urine, the greater the patient's degree of hydration. The darker the urine, the lower the patient's degree of hydration. Color can range from pale yellow to amber.
Odor	Normal fresh specimens have a faint, characteristic odor.
pH	5.0–8.0 normal < 7.0 acid urine > 7 alkaline urine
Specific gravity	1.016–1.030
Protein	0
Glucose	None present
Ketones	None present
Bilirubin	0
Urobilinogen	2
Blood	None detected
Leukocytes	None detected
Nitrite	None

Appearance

The color of the urine should be determined by looking down into the sample against a white background and with a good light source. Yellow is the normal color of urine (Figure 15-13 ◆). Urochrome, the pigment that colors urine, is derived from urobilin, a brown pigment. Intensity of color is usually related to the degree of concentration or dilution of the urine.

The following colors may indicate a possible disorder.

- Red or red-brown is the most common set of abnormal shades. A pink cast can be caused by several foods, such as beets or rhubarb, certain dyes, and drugs. Although hematuria, which is the introduction of RBCs, can be caused by menstrual flow, more serious conditions are likely.
- Yellow-brown or green-brown usually develops because of the presence of bile pigments, especially bilirubin (Figure 15-14 ◆). Severe **jaundice** may be accompanied by dark green urine. Other greens and blue-greens may be caused by pigmented microbes, such as *Pseudomonas*, or pigments in foods or drugs.

Figure 15-13 ◆ Pale yellow urine alongside a glass of concentrated urine with a dark yellow color
Source: Dorling Kindersley.

Figure 15-14 ◆ The deep yellow color of this urine is due to an excess of bilirbuin, a bile pigment in the body.
Source: SPL/Photo Researchers, Inc.

- Orange-red or orange-brown urine typically has large quantities of urobilin.
- Dark brown or black urine is usually the result of hemoglobin darkening upon standing, or more rarely a genetic disease, alkaptonuria.

Turbid or cloudy urine generally contains some sort of suspended particulate or cellular material). The urine may be treated with acid, heat, or a lipid solvent to help identify the specific source of turbidity.

- Leukocytes can form a white cloud that is not eliminated by the addition of acid. High numbers of neutrophils are indicative of pyuria. Bacteria or yeasts in high numbers create an opalescent turbidity. Hematuria may produce a turbid or smoky appearance.
- Prostatic fluid or mucus may produce a whitish turbidity. Small renal calculi or bladder stones, nicknamed "gravel," produce turbidity, as can fecal contamination. Larger material, or "clumps," can be created by pus, fecal contamination, calculi, or menstrual discharge. Contamination with powders and some antiseptics can produce turbidity. Emulsified paraffin from some vaginal creams can produce a milky appearance.
- Very rarely there may be leakage of lymph into the urine. Lipoproteins may also enter the urine in nephrosis and in some crush injuries.

Odor

Normal fresh specimens have a faint, characteristic odor. Upon standing, bacterial metabolism may impart an odor of rotting or ammonia to the urine. Certain foods, such as asparagus, give the urine a characteristic odor. Disease-causing states that produce characteristic odors include diabetes mellitus, in which ketones give the urine a sweet or fruity odor, and a variety of hereditary amino acid disorders. Urine odors associated with these disorders include "sweaty feet," "maple syrup," "cabbage hops," "mousy," "rotting fish," and "rancid."

Amino acid disorders, being hereditary, are quite rare, and detection is critical when the individuals are very young, so that appropriate treatment can be administered as soon as possible.

Specific Gravity

Specific gravity is the measurement of a specific volume of urine to an equal volume of water. Solutes in the urine contribute to the measurement. The concentrating and filtrating status of the kidneys, as well as the body's hydration status, are assessed by measuring urine specific gravity.

The normal range of specific gravity of urine for adults with normal diets and normal fluid intake is moderately concentrated, from 1.016 to 1.022, compared with the specific gravity of blood plasma, which remains very close to 1.010 at all times. In conditions such as diabetes insipidus, in which the urine is more dilute, the specific gravity is lower. In conditions such as diabetes mellitus, in which the urine is more concentrated, the specific gravity is higher.

The specific gravity of urine can be measured with a refractometer, a urinometer (also called a hydrometer), or a chemical test strip. Urinometers are now used infrequently, as other devices, such as dipsticks, are easier and more accurate. Some PLOs prefer to use the refractometer.

Urinalysis with Chemical Test Strips

The presence of abnormal body processes that affect the metabolism of carbohydrates, acid-base balance, and liver and kidney functions can be determined by testing the urine with chemical reagent test strips, or dipsticks (Figure 15-15 ◆). The same test is also used to detect infections or assess for drugs.

Each reagent pad on a test strip is saturated with chemicals that react with urine components to produce a predictable color change. The color can be observed with the naked eye and compared to color change charts and graphics provided by the manufacturer. Results are reported on standardized forms or

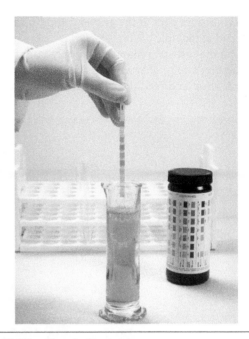

Figure 15-15 ◆ Chemical test strips

entered into computer databases. Test strips may also be read by specially designed instruments that recognize and measure the same color changes that the human eye detects. This method is referred to as *reflectance spectrophotometry.* Each manufacturer may place the reagent pads in their own specific order; verify order and results with manufacturer's instructions.

The test strip is immersed for one second in the urine. The back of the strip is wiped against a blotter, such as a paper towel, then turned at a right angle to drain excess urine (Figure 15-16 ◆).

Strip reactions occur rapidly and should be read quickly after the appropriate incubation time, which ranges from 30 seconds (bilirubin and glucose) to 2 minutes (leukocytes). The test strip pad is designed so that you begin reading with the

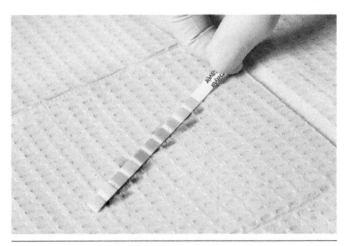

Figure 15-16 ◆ The back of the strip is wiped, then turned at a right angle to drain excess urine.

Keys to Success
CHECKLIST FOR URINE SPECIMEN EVALUATION

1. Is the specimen properly labeled?
2. Is it the proper type of specimen for the requested test?
3. Is the specimen properly preserved, if necessary?
4. Has the specimen been received in a timely fashion?
5. Are there any signs of contamination?
6. If the specimen is for multiple tests, has the bacteriologic examination been done first?
7. How many **aliquots** must be taken?

glucose and bilirubin pads at the grip end and finish with the leukocytes pad at the tip.

To read the test strip manually, simply hold it close to the manufacturer's color chart on the side of the container or on a separate sheet and read the color change under a bright

Keys to Success
TESTING STRONGLY PIGMENTED URINE

A strong abnormal color to the urine, regardless of the shade, may interfere with the accurate reading of some or all of the test strip pad reagent reactions, whether the reading is done visually or by instrument. Multistix® 10 SG Reagent Strips read visually or on the Clinitek® 50 instrument are waived under CLIA guidelines.

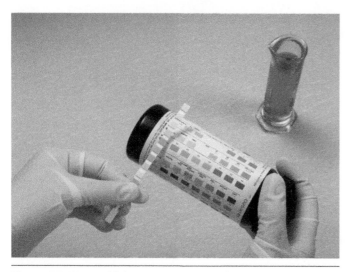

Figure 15-17 ◆ Hold the test strip next to the color chart and take the reading.

white light source (Figure 15-17 ◆). If an automated reader is available, simply insert the strip onto the reader tray after blotting and allow the instrument to read the results.

Urinalysis test strips should always be kept tightly sealed in their containers, at room temperature, until use. Discolored pads indicate damage and should be discarded. CLIA 1988 regulations require the use of a positive and a negative or normal control at least once in each 24-hour period when testing is performed and whenever a new container of dipsticks is opened. Patient and quality control results must be recorded and maintained for reference. Factors that affect test strip testing are summarized in Table 15-5.

The chemical tests typically performed in a routine urinalysis are pH, specific gravity, protein, glucose, ketones, bilirubin, urobilinogen, blood, leukocytes, and nitrite.

TABLE 15-5 FACTORS THAT AFFECT TEST STRIP TESTING

Test	Renal disease	Systemic disease	False positives	False negatives
Specific gravity	Urine-concentrating disorder	Fluid status changes	Proteinuria	Alkaline urine
pH	Renal tubular acidosis UTIs may produce alkaline pH	Acid-base disorders	None	None
Protein	Glomerular disease Infection Tubular disorders	Infection Exercise-caused transient proteinuria Bence-Jones protein in myeloma and related disorders	Alkaline pH Detergents	Dilute urine Bence-Jones protein
Microalbumin	Early renal disease	(See protein)	Timing errors	Timing errors
Glucose	Rarely increased in tubular disorders	Diabetes mellitus	Detergents Hypochlorite Peroxide	Vitamin C Aspirin
Ketones	None	Ketotic states	L-Dopa	Old specimens
Blood	Any site of bleeding in urinary tract (glomerulo-nephritis, tumor, stones, infection)	Coagulopathy Hemoglobinuria in hemolysis Myoglobinuria with muscle damage	Colored meds	Vitamin C Exposure to air
Ascorbic acid	None	Treatment with vitamin C	Other reducing substances	None
Bilirubin	None	Liver and biliary disease	Colored meds	Light exposure
Urobilinogen	None	Hemolysis Cirrhosis	Colored meds	Light exposure Nitrite Formalin
Nitrite	Infection with most gram-negative organisms	None	Colored meds	Vitamin C
Leukocyte esterase	Infection of genitourinary system Interstitial nephritis	None	Oxidizing detergents	Glucose Protein High specific gravity

pH

Normal urine pH ranges from moderately acidic (pH 5) to moderately alkaline (pH 8). Most individuals produce a slightly acidic urine (pH 5.0–6.0). Compounds in the diet have a great influence on urine pH, as do a variety of drugs. The pH reaction should be read at 60 seconds. No pH reading from a test strip indicates an abnormal situation by itself. There are no conditions that produce a false positive (pH result too high or alkaline) on the pH pad. However, improperly stored urine may have a genuine change of pH to the alkaline because of bacterial conversion of urea to ammonia. A false negative pH (pH result too low or acid) can occur in the presence of runoff of the acid buffer in the adjacent protein pad. This can be prevented by proper blotting.

Specific Gravity

No specific gravity reading with a dipstick indicates an abnormal situation by itself because other factors, such as exercise or high fluid intake before the test, can affect the results.

Protein

The normal level of urinary protein is insignificant. The urine dipstick is adjusted so that this normal background protein does not trigger a reaction on the pad. A positive reaction indicates clinically a significant increase in urine proteins. Normal individuals may experience **proteinuria** after strenuous exercise or other circumstances that create a transient dehydration through sweating, such as fevers or prolonged exposure to a hot environment.

Glucose

The normal urinary glucose level should be zero because normally all the glucose filtered at the glomerulus is rapidly reabsorbed in the proximal tubule. Occasionally, after a very rich meal, a normal individual may have a transient blood glucose level high enough to be read; otherwise, glucose enters the urine only if the patient is consistently hyperglycemic.

Ketones

Acetacetic acid, B-hydroxybuteric acid, and acetone are normal intermediary metabolites of fat metabolism, termed ketones or "ketone bodies." Ketones are normally recycled by the liver into other usable organic nutrient compounds. Small quantities are normal in the blood and may spill over into the urine. They become markedly increased and of clinical significance in uncontrolled diabetes mellitus, particularly in diabetic ketoacidosis; in starvation or the temporary starvation that accompanies disorders whose symptoms include severe vomiting and/or diarrhea; and in acute febrile illnesses.

Caduceus Chronicle
EARLY GLUCOSE TESTING

Before more sophisticated glucose tests became available, some physicians determined the presence of elevated blood glucose by dipping their finger in the urine sample and tasting it on the tongue to detect sweetness.

Bilirubin and Urobilinogen

Bilirubin levels rise in the blood and other body fluids, including urine, under three main conditions:

- Any major hemolytic episode in which blood escapes into a tissue space and must be broken down
- Liver disease
- Obstructions

Blood

The test strip pad for blood responds not only to intact RBCs but also to free hemoglobin and free myoglobin suspended in the specimen. Blood in the urine may indicate conditions such as hemorrhagic tissue injury, infection, coagulation disorder, kidney disorders, certain drug responses, and cancer.

Leukocytes

With their ability to use ameboid movements, leukocytes can enter the urinary tract anywhere along its length. A few leukocytes in anyone's urine specimen are considered normal. Increased leukocytes, however, are an excellent indicator of an inflammatory process occurring somewhere within the urinary tract. A positive result on the test strip leukocytes pad should be confirmed and compared to urine microscopy results.

Nitrite

The presence of nitrite in the urine is strong indirect evidence of bacteria in the urine. Nitrite is the metabolic product of the enzyme nitrate reductase. Although not all bacterial species capable of causing a urinary tract infection (UTI) produce nitrate reductase, most of the common ones do.

? — **Critical Thinking Question 15-2**
Given the patient's complaint, what tests do you think Gina should prepare to perform?

Sediment Examination

Before proceeding with a microscopic urinalysis, the specimen should be spun in a centrifuge. Centrifuging separates the sediment, which is the insoluble material, from the soluble material. Sediment settles to the bottom of the test tube after centrifuging.

The centrifuged urine sediment is examined with a standard bright field microscope with a low-power (10X) and high-power (40X) objective. Stains that color cellular structures, such as the Sternheimer-Malbin stain, are often used to assist in identification.

The formed elements that can be viewed under the microscope consist of the following:

crystals	bacteria
yeast and fungi	protozoa
parasites	epithelial cells
renal tubular epithelial cells	RBCs
WBCs	sperm cells
casts	artifacts

PROCEDURE 15-5 Perform a Urinalysis with a Chemical Test Strip and Prepare the Specimen for Microscopic Examination

Theory

Check the expiration date of the chemical test strips to ensure accurate test results. Keep the test strips dry and avoid touching the reactive reagent materials on the strips. Tighten the lid of the bottle immediately after removing a strip.

The test strip must be immersed completely to cover all the reagent squares. To prevent dilution of the chemicals and inaccurate results, pull out the strip in less than one second and remove excess urine. Hold the strip carefully above but close to the color chart. Any urine from the strip that touches the bottle could affect the colors of the chart. Finally, read the test strip areas at the correct times to ensure accuracy. The time for reading results ranges from 30 seconds to 2 minutes.

Although used less commonly, Acetest® (for ketones) and Clinitest® (for glucose) tablets may be used in urine testing of the diabetic.

Materials

- chemical reagent urine test strips
- blotting paper
- urine container
- centrifuge and test tubes
- microscope
- slide and cover slip
- pipette
- disposable gloves
- biohazardous waste receptacle
- urinalysis report form

Competency

(**Conditions**) With the necessary materials, (**Task**) you will be able to perform a urinalysis with chemical test strips (**Standards**) correctly.

1. Wash your hands. Gather equipment and supplies. Check the expiration date on the reagent strip container.
2. Identify the patient and guide him or her to the treatment area.
3. Provide the patient with a labeled urine container. Instruct the patient on how to obtain the specimen and where to leave it.
4. Wash your hands. Put on disposable gloves.
5. After the patient leaves the specimen in the designated area, move it to the testing area.
6. Observe and describe the urine's color, quantity, and odor. Inform the physician that the sample is ready for viewing.
7. Remove one reagent strip and recap the bottle tightly and immediately. Do not touch the test area of the strip. If necessary, place the strip temporarily on a dry paper towel while you open the urine specimen container.

8. Dip the test strip briefly in the urine, making sure to cover all testing areas (Figure 15-18 ◆). Pull the strip gently back against the inner edge of the container mouth, then place the length of the strip at a right angle to the blotting paper to remove excess urine.
9. Hold the reagent test areas of the strip next to, but not touching, the matching areas on the test strip bottle. Note the reaction reading at the time mentioned on the bottle for each square of reagent.
10. Dispose of the urine test strip in the biohazardous waste container.
11. Prepare urine for microscopic examination by the physician.
    - Put approximately 10 cc in a tube on one side of the centrifuge, and on the opposite side an equal amount of liquid in another tube (Figure 15-19 ◆).
    - Run the centrifuge for 5 minutes.
    - Pour out most of the liquid (supernatant) from the tube, but keep the sediment (Figure 15-20 ◆).
    - Mix the remaining liquid with the sediment and pipette a couple of drops of moistened sediment onto a slide (Figure 15-21 ◆).
    - Cover with a cover slip. Position and focus the slide under the lighted microscope.
12. Remove the gloves and discard in proper container. Wash your hands.

Figure 15-18 ◆ Dip the test strip into urine, covering all testing areas.

Figure 15-19 ◆ Load the centrifuge.

PROCEDURE 15-5 Perform a Urinalysis with a Chemical Test Strip and Prepare the Specien for Microscopic Examination *(continued)*

Figure 15-20 ◆ Pour out most of the liquid (supernatant) from the tube, but keep the sediment.

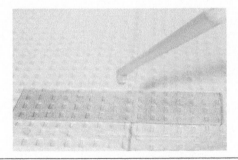

Figure 15-21 ◆ Place the urine sample on the slide.

13. Chart the results on the reporting urine lab slip immediately, including the date, time, and urine test strip brand name. Record the color, odor, volume, and cloudiness or sediment.
14. On the patient's chart, chart the date and time of specimen collection and procedure performance.
15. Return to the microscope examination area for cleaning and disposal.

Patient Education

Inform the patient that urine test strip testing will identify components in the urine and that the physician will review the results and call if additional or new treatment is needed.

Charting Example

04/8/XX 1:30 p.m. Routine urinalysis specimen provided by pt. Immediate testing showed traces of protein and glucose. Information placed in chart and physician notified. Jennifer Wilson, CMA

Table 15-6 lists significant microscopic findings that may be found in urine by the medical technologist or physician. The physician may examine the centrifuged specimen under the microscope, record his or her observations, diagnose the problem, and prescribe treatment and medication while the patient is still in the office. The information in the table is useful for a basic understanding of the correlation between the report and the diagnosis and treatment.

Crystals

Crystals form in the urine as salts (Figure 15-22 ◆) and can be found in the urine of a healthy patient. The number of crystals in a urine specimen is affected by cooling and by aging. After a specimen has been collected and begins to cool, especially if it is refrigerated, additional crystals may form that were not present in the fresh specimen. On the other hand, as a urine specimen ages and the pH changes, crystals that were initially present in the fresh specimen may degrade or even disappear. The addition or degradation of crystals affects the accuracy of the test results. Assessing crystal formation helps in the diagnosis and treatment of disorders.

A given patient specimen may contain several different kinds of crystals in various proportions. Normal crystals tend to form in neutral to alkaline urines. All the abnormal crystals of significance generally tend to form in acid urines. They include certain amino acids, such as cystine, leucine, and tyrosine, which

TABLE 15-6 SIGNIFICANT MICROSCOPIC FINDINGS IN URINE

Finding	Normal	Urinary Tract Disease	Systemic Disease
RBCs	3/high power field; higher in menstruating women	Glomerular injury Nephrolithiasis Inflammation (especially hemorrhagic cystitis) Neoplasms	Rarely with sickle cell anemia, disseminated intravascular coagulation
WBCs	3–5/high power	Infections of bladder or kidney Interstitial nephritis (eosinophils)	Infection of prostate, cervix, or vagina
Hyaline casts	After exercise, dehydration stress	Any cause of proteinuria, especially glomerular disease	Dehydration, fever, other causes of proteinuria, such as diabetes
Granular casts	Similar to hyaline casts	Heavy proteinuria Pigmented granular casts with acute tubular necrosis	Rarely with non-glomerular causes of proteinuria
Cellular casts	Not found	RBC casts in glomerulonephritis WBC casts in pyelonephritis	Not commonly found
Epithelial cells	Squamous, transitional epithelial cells	Renal tubular cells with tubular injury (tubular necrosis, transplant rejection)	None
Crystals	Uric acid, calcium oxalate, triple phosphate	Cystine in some tubular disorders Uric acid, calcium oxalate rarely with nephrolithiasis	Congenital aminoacidurias, drug crystals
Organisms	Present from contamination or prolonged storage before examination	Cystitis Pyelonephritis	Prostatitis may also give positive culture

(A) Crystals in Acid Urine

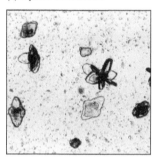  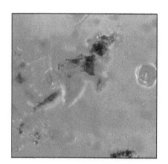 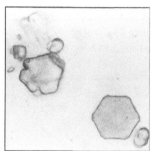

(B) Crystals in Alkaline Urine

 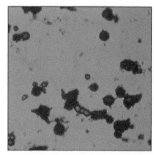 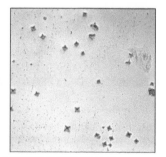

Figure 15-22 ◆ (A) Crystals in acid urine; (B) Crystals in alkaline urine
Courtesy of Bayer Diagnostic

are observed in some renal tubular disorders. Bilirubin and cholesterol are two other abnormal crystals.

A variety of drugs, such as sulfonamides, penicillins, and cephalosporins, form abnormal crystals when the urine is concentrated and the pH is favorable for crystallization. Drug crystals take a variety of forms and are difficult to identify without the patient's medication records for confirmation.

The Male Reproductive System

The male reproductive system uses part of the urinary tract in its function. The urological medical office is where male reproductive system disorders are often treated. These include prostate disorders, fertility problems and disorders, testicular disorders, and sexually transmitted diseases.

Anatomy and Physiology

The male reproductive system is composed of two major external structures and several internal structures (Figure 15-23 ◆). The penis and the scrotum are the external structures.

Penis

Tubular in shape and hollow, the penis provides a route for sperm to leave the male reproductive system and be directed into the female reproductive system. Arteries in the penis engorge with blood during sexual stimulation, promoting an erection. The firmness of the penis allows penetration into the vagina. Ejaculation releases sperm into the vagina; the sperm meet with and fertilize the ovum. The reproductive function of the penis is secondary to the excretion of urine from the urinary bladder through the urethra.

Scrotum

The scrotum contains two walnut-sized ovoid structures, the **testes** or **testicles.** Each testicle is made up of fibrous tissue and many lobes containing small tubes, the seminiferous tubules. Sperm cells, or spermatozoa, develop in these tubes. Testosterone is also produced in the testes. Secondary sex characteristics are

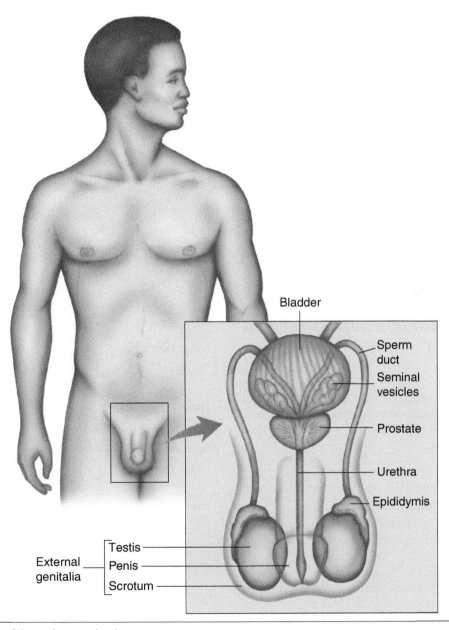

Figure 15-23 ◆ Diagram of the male reproductive system

stimulated by testosterone. Located posterior to each testicle is the epididymis. The tubules from the testicle join to form efferent tubules that open into the epididymis. Sperm is stored here to mature before moving on in the system. Spermatozoa are sensitive to heat and are destroyed by normal body temperature;

therefore, the testes are suspended down from the body in a cooler environment.

All males between the ages of 15 and 40 should be taught and encouraged to perform routine self-examination of the testicles.

PROCEDURE 15-6 Demonstrate Patient Instruction for Testicular Self-Examination

Theory

Examination of a man's testicles should be part of a general physical exam. The American Cancer Society (ACS) recommends a testicular exam as part of a routine cancer-related checkup. The ACS advises men to be aware of testicular cancer and to see a doctor right away if a mass is found. Identifying masses promptly is an important factor in getting early treatment, and it is recommended that all men do monthly testicular self-exams after puberty.

The patient should be aware that each normal testis has an epididymis, which appears as a small "bump" on the upper or middle outer side of the testis. Normal testicles also contain blood vessels, supporting tissues, and tubes that contuct sperm. Other noncancerous conditions, such as hydroceles and varicoceles, can sometimes cause enlargement or lumpiness around a testicle. Some men may confuse these with cancer. If the patient has any doubts, he should speak with the doctor. Whether the abnormality is a possible tumor or another condition, early treatment is often less complicated and severe.

Materials

■ Pamphlet for with instructions for performing an at-home testicular exam.

Competency

(**Conditions**) With the necessary materials, (**Task**) you will be able to instruct the patient on performing a testicular self-examination (**Standards**) correctly within the time frame designated by the instructor.

1. Wash your hands. Gather equipment and supplies.
2. Identify the patient and guide him to the treatment area.
3. Instruct the patient to:
   - Take a warm bath or shower to relax the scrotum. In the clinical setting, the patient should take several deep breaths.
   - Observe the contour of the scrotum. If one testicle is slightly larger or lies somewhat lower than the other, this is considered normal (Figure 15-24 ◆).

- Elevate the right leg to the level of a toilet, chair, or bed to expose the right testicle.
- With the left hand, lightly support the right testicle. With the right hand, palpate the right testicle for hardness, lumps, or anything unusual (Figure 15-25 ◆).
- Reverse the process by elevating the left leg to examine the left testicle. Support the left testicle with the right hand and, with the left hand, palpate the left testicle.
4. If the patient finds any abnormalities or has any questions, he should contact the physician.

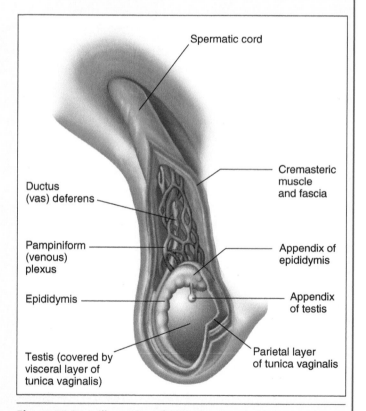

Figure 15-24 ◆ Illustration of normal scrotum

Labels:
- Spermatic cord
- Cremasteric muscle and fascia
- Ductus (vas) deferens
- Appendix of epididymis
- Pampiniform (venous) plexus
- Appendix of testis
- Epididymis
- Testis (covered by visceral layer of tunica vaginalis)
- Parietal layer of tunica vaginalis

PROCEDURE 15-6 Demonstrate Patient Instruction for Testicular Self-Examination (continued)

Patient Education

Ask the patient to repeat the instructions to verify that he understands them. Provide him with written instructions, if available.

Charting Example

02-28-XX 9:25 a.m. Patient given written and verbal testicular self-exam instructions. Patient demonstrated correct technique and understanding of the importance of monthly self-examinations. Erin Janson, RMA

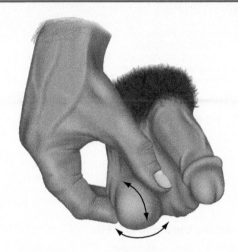

Figure 15-25 ◆ Palpate the testicle for hardness, lumps, or anything unusual.

Internal Structures

Internal structures ascend into the anterior pelvis as the epididymis transforms into the vas deferens. The vas deferens passes over the bladder and descends posterior in another tubular structure, the seminal vesicle. The seminal vesicles produce an alkaline fluid that becomes the semen that transports the sperm. The seminal vesicle descends and makes an anterior turn to pass through the posterior portion of the prostate gland to join at an approximate midpoint, the prostatic urethra that has descended from the urinary bladder. The urethra continues anterior and then descends down the penis to exit at the urinary meatus. The bulbourethral gland lies under the prostate gland and connects to the urethra as the urethra descends from the prostate gland. These glands, also called Cowper's glands, produce a mucus-type fluid that becomes part of semen, the product ejaculated during intercourse.

Diseases and Disorders of the Male Reproductive System

Diseases and disorders of the male reproductive system include not only reproductive and fertility conditions but often urinary conditions as well.

Diseases and Disorders of the Prostate

The prostate gland is located just below the male urinary bladder and encircles the urethra. Any condition affecting the prostate gland may cause enlargement, followed by pain and urinary retention. Conditions that affect the prostate gland include **prostatitis,** benign prostatic hypertrophy (**BPH**), and cancer (carcinoma) (Table 15-7). Evaluation of prostate con-

ditions usually includes a digital rectal examination (**DRE**) by the physician. The prostate gland is palpated by inserting a finger into the rectum and evaluating for size, tenderness, and any nodules or lumps present. The prostate-specific antigen (PSA) test is a screening tool for prostate cancer. The blood for a PSA must be drawn before any digital rectal examination. A DRE can cause the prostate gland to release PSA into the bloodstream, resulting in an inaccurate value.

Male Reproductive Disorders

Sexually active couples who do not conceive after one year of unprotected sexual intercourse are considered to have a fertility problem. The urologist may be involved in diagnosing and treating male fertility disorders (Table 15-8). Evaluation of the male reproductive system involves a thorough medical history, physical examination, and evaluation of semen for sperm count and motility. Causes of problems in the male include structural anomalies, low sperm count and motility, trauma to the per-

Keys to Success
VALUES FOR PROSTATE-SPECIFIC ANTIGENS (PSAs)

The PSA test is recommended annually for males over age 50. It is important for men to establish a baseline at some point between the ages of 40 and 50. Any sudden elevation in the value requires further evaluation. A continuous climb in values is a good indication of the presence of carcinoma. Fluctuations up and down indicate BPH or prostatitis. Patients should be cautioned that the PSA test is a screening tool and that the DRE is a major part of the diagnosis.

TABLE 15-7 DISEASES AND DISORDERS OF THE PROSTATE

Disease or Disorder	Symptoms	Diagnosis	Treatment
Prostatitis ■ Inflammation of the prostate gland ■ Can be acute bacterial, chronic bacterial, or chronic noninfectious in nature. Causative agents in both bacterial forms commonly are *E. coli* and Proteus ■ Bacterial condition usually affects younger males and is often recurrent	Acute: ■ Fever ■ Chills ■ Rectal, low back, or perineal pain Chronic bacterial: ■ Recurrent UTIs ■ Dysuria ■ Genital and ejaculatory pain Chronic nonbacterial: ■ Chronic pelvic pain ■ Ejaculatory pain	■ Patient presenting symptoms ■ Urinalysis ■ Digital rectal examination (DRE)	■ Antibacterial medications ■ Anti-inflammatory drugs, alpha blockers and allopurinol for inflammatory condition ■ 20-minute hot sitz baths two or three times a day to help relieve pain of inflammatory conditions ■ Application of ice two to three times a day for 20 minutes to help relieve pain of inflammatory conditions when sitz baths fail ■ Increased fluid intake (especially water) to dilute urine ■ Avoidance of caffeine-containing beverages to avoid dehydration
Benign prostatic hypertrophy (BPH) ■ Progressive enlargement of prostate gland that eventually causes obstruction of urethra and interferes with urination ■ Common in older men with increasing age ■ Cause is unknown	Hematuria Urination: ■ Frequent ■ Difficulty starting ■ Decreased force ■ Dribbling after voiding ■ Feeling bladder is not empty after voiding	■ Patient presenting symptoms ■ Physical examination ■ DRE ■ Urinalysis ■ Urine culture ■ Bladder x-ray ■ Cystoscopy	■ Drug therapy to relax neck of bladder and possibly shrink prostate ■ Laser treatment less invasive treatment to remove offending tissue ■ Cystoscopy for transurethral resection less invasive treatment with cystoscope, which is passed up the urethra; portions of prostate gland are shaved off and flushed from bladder ■ Surgery to remove enlarged gland through incision in lower abdomen, just above pelvis
Cancer (Carcinoma) ■ Second most common cause of male cancer deaths ■ Has a tendency to metastasize ■ Prostate feels hard and lumpy on palpation during a DRE	■ Similar to BPH ■ Elevated PSA	■ Patient presenting symptoms ■ DRE ■ Biopsy	■ Radiation ■ Chemotherapy ■ Hormonal drug therapy ■ Surgery (side effects of radical surgical excision include urinary incontinence, erectile dysfunction, and/or impotence) ■ Treatment factors include patient's age and physical condition, treatment side effects, and extent of cancer

Keys to Success
PATIENT EDUCATION

African American males are at greater risk for prostate and bladder cancers. The importance of routine PSA screenings and DREs should be stressed in public awareness campaigns and in patient education in the medical office.

ineum and testicles, exposure to radiation, previous infectious diseases of the system, hormonal imbalances, and stress. Treatment depends on the cause, and not all male fertility problems can be corrected.

Testicular disorders include but are not limited to **crypt-orchism,** torsion of the testicles, and cancer of the testicles.

Sexually Transmitted Diseases

Sexually transmitted diseases (STDs) or infections take many forms (Table 15-9). Common STDs in men include chlamydia, gonorrhea, syphilis, genital herpes, genital warts (*Condylamata acuminata*) and trichomoniasis. Many of these conditions present no symptoms at the onset. STDs are transmitted not only through sexual contact but by blood and body fluids. Untreated STDs are spread unknowingly, can cause sterility, and may even become life-threatening.

Keys to Success
THE SIDE EFFECTS OF VIAGRA

Viagra® is a vasodilator with specific activity directed to the penile arteries and has some dangerous side effects. Men with a history of cardiovascular disease, cerebral vascular accident, hypo- or hypertension, angina, or glaucoma should not take Viagra. Vascular dilation could be life-threatening in men with these disorders.

TABLE 15-8 MALE REPRODUCTIVE DISORDERS

Disease or Disorder	Symptoms	Diagnosis	Treatment
Erectile dysfunction ■ Inability to achieve erection with stimulation and maintain it for ejaculation ■ Experienced by most men at some time in their lives ■ Caused by failure of arteries that supply blood to penis to dilate and engorge penis; by nerve damage to spinal cord or other nerves supplying penis; by medical conditions such as diabetes, hypertension, heart disease; by drugs for these conditions; by alcohol consumption, smoking, stress	■ Failure to achieve erection	■ Patient presenting symptoms	■ Vasodilator such as Sildenafil citrate (Viagra®) ■ Penile implants and suction pumps for artificial erection ■ Counseling for couples
Cryptorchism ■ One or both testes fail to descend into scrotal sac during fetal development ■ Must be treated in first year of child's life to prevent infertility and possible predisposition to tumors later in life	■ Undescended testes	■ Examination of scrotal sac after birth and at well-baby check-ups	■ Hormone injections to help testes descend ■ Orchidopexy, RA surgical procedure to move testes to scrotal sac
Torsion of the testicles ■ Spermatic cord is twisted, resulting in diminished venous flow ■ Often result of traumatic insult to scrotum and testicles or result of congenital problem	■ Severe pain ■ Swelling ■ Redness ■ Tenderness	■ Patient presenting symptoms ■ Physical examination	■ Surgery if problem does not resolve on its own
Testicular cancer ■ Leading cancer in males 25 to 40 ■ Risk factors: family history, age under 40, Caucasian, undescended testes at birth, history of testicular infections ■ Painless lump in testicle is often first indication ■ Favorable outcome if discovered early and treated aggressively	■ Presence of lump	■ Physical examination ■ Biopsy	■ Surgery to remove lump ■ Radiation ■ Chemotherapy

TABLE 15-9 SEXUALLY TRANSMITTED DISEASES IN MALES

Disease	Symptoms	Diagnosis	Treatment
Chlamydia ■ Caused by *Chlamydia trachomatis* ■ Often no symptoms until irreversible damage has occurred	■ Frequent and painful urination ■ Pus in urine ■ Penile discharge	■ Patient presenting symptoms	■ Antibiotics (other than penicillin) for bacterial infections ■ Abstinence or protected (safe) sex for prevention
Gonorrhea ■ Caused by *Neiserria gonorrhoeae* ■ Transmitted by sexual contact ■ May become systemic	■ Pus or purulent discharge from urethra	■ Patient presenting symptoms ■ Physical examination	■ Antibiotics: penicillin, tetracycline, and ceftriaxone ■ Abstinence or protected (safe) sex for prevention
Syphilis ■ Caused by *Treponema pallidum;* can become systemic if undiagnosed and untreated ■ Transmitted by sexual contact; contagious in first and second stages ■ May go dormant for a number of years but remains in bloodstream ■ At end stage, cannot be reversed	■ First stage: ulcer or chancre on genital area ■ If untreated, second stage: rash appears on any part of body ■ If still untreated, damage to cardiovascular system, cerebral areas, and nervous system	■ Patient presenting symptoms ■ Physical examination	■ Antibiotics: Penicillin G and others ■ Abstinence or protected (safe) sex for prevention
Genital herpes ■ Ulcerative infection of genital skin ■ Caused by *Herpes simplex* virus type 2 ■ Contagious not only when lesions are present, but also in **prodromal** period ■ No cure at present	■ Blister-like eruptions ■ Systemic flu-like symptoms: fever, headache, general aching ■ Dysuria	■ Patient presenting symptoms ■ Physical examination	■ Antiviral drugs, acyclovir and valacyclovir, shorten duration and severity and reduce frequency of outbreaks ■ Abstinence or protected (safe) sex for prevention ■ Stress reduction to reduce frequency
Genital warts (*Condylamata acuminata*) ■ Caused by human papillomavirus ■ Transmitted by sexual contact ■ Recurrence is common	■ Raised growths on perineal region, in or near rectum	■ Patient presenting symptoms ■ Physical examination	■ Chemical or surgical removal to remove growths ■ Abstinence or protected (safe) sex for prevention
Trichomoniasis ■ Protozoal infection of genitourinary tract ■ Caused by *Trichomonas vaginalis*	■ Itching ■ Painful urination ■ Possibly urethritis	■ Patient presenting symptoms ■ Physical examination ■ Wet prep test of male urethral discharge	■ Antiprotozoal medications such as Flagyl® to treat both or all partners ■ Abstinence or protected (safe) sex for prevention

Chapter Summary

- Urinalysis is an important diagnostic tool that provides information about a patient's physiology and renal function. Proper standards and procedures must be followed to ensure accurate results.

- You have a vital role in the urology and nephrology medical office. Key instructions for the patient include obtaining a clean-catch urine specimen, preparing for a urological procedure, and what to expect during the procedure. You may be trained to test or microscopically examine urine. With more extensive training you may be asked to catheterize a patient.

- The urinary system consists of two kidneys, two ureters, a urinary bladder, and a urethra. Urine is formed in the kidneys, passes through the ureters to the bladder, then passes through the urethra to exit the body at the meatus. Urine is a combination of waste molecules and water. Some of the excreted molecules are electrolytes, sugars, amino acids, vitamins, hormones, organic acids, alkaloids, and nitrogenous wastes.

- In addition to the excretion of waste products, the kidneys have three other important physiological functions: 1) maintaining the water balance of the body; 2) maintaining the acid-base balance; and 3) producing the hormones erythropoietin, to stimulate the bone marrow to generate more red blood cells, and renin, to assist angiotensin to maintain adequate blood volume and blood pressure.

- Urinalysis provides information about waste excretion, acid-base balance, and water balance. Diagnostic information gained from the waste products in urine can give clues to different disease processes, such as glomerulonephritis, renal failure, nephrotic syndrome, pyelonephritis, and kidney stones.

- A routine urinalysis requires a clean container, a clean-catch requires a sterile container, and a 24-hour requires a large container that must be kept cold as the specimen is collected. A routine urinalysis and clean specimen require a freshly voided specimen.

- All urine, if not tested immediately, must be protected from deterioration, which affects the accuracy of results. Deterioration or other changes in urine occur if the specimen is not refrigerated or frozen or if preservative is not added. Specimens of 50 to 100 mL are adequate for testing; 12 mL or cc is the typical standardized amount for specific testing. The total volume of urine is important in qualitative and quantitative measurements and in the analysis of results.

- A routine, or normal, urinalysis consists of physical observation, chemical testing, and microscopic analysis. Chemical testing involves the use of reagent test strips or tablets. A rapid urine culture test, a chemical reagent test strip, is performed to immediately determine if a urinary tract infection is present. If results are positive, a culture and sensitivity test or Gram stain is performed to identify the causative organism.

- Chemical reagents used for testing must be kept in tightly sealed containers and at room temperature. The expiration date must always be checked. CLIA 1988 regulations require that controls be run to ensure accuracy and that records be kept and monitored.

- The specific gravity of urine can be measured with chemical test strips or a urinometer.

- Microscopic analysis involves spinning a specimen in the centrifuge and preparing a slide for the physician, who will examine the specimen for RBCs, white blood cells, casts, crystals, epithelial cells, mucus, bacteria, parasites, yeast, and sperm cells.

- The function of the male reproductive system is to produce, store, and transfer sperm cells to the female. Diseases and disorders of the male reproductive tract include prostate disorders, fertility problems and disorders, testicular disorders, and STDs. Conditions that affect the prostate gland include prostatitis, benign prostatic hypertrophy, and prostate cancer. The DRE is a common diagnostic procedure performed by the physician to differentiate the particular prostate condition.

- Male fertility disorders include erectile dysfunction and testicular disorders—cryptorchism, torsion of the testes, and testicular cancer. Monthly self-examination of the testes is recommended for all males aged 15 to 40.

- Sexually transmitted diseases are transmitted not only through sexual contact but by blood and body fluids. Common STDs include chlamydia, gonorrhea, syphilis, genital herpes, genital warts (*Condylomata acuminata*), and trichomoniasis. Untreated STDs can cause sterility and even become life-threatening.

Chapter Review Questions

Multiple Choice

1. Which of the following structures contains the nephrons?
   A. ureters
   B. kidneys
   C. urinary bladder
   D. urethra

2. Cystitis is a(n)
   A. disorder of the kidneys.
   B. infection of the nephritis.
   C. inflammation of the bladder.
   D. obstruction of the ureter.

3. Which of the following disorders is diagnosed almost solely in men?
   A. bladder calculi
   B. kidney cysts
   C. ureter cancer
   D. renal colic

4. An unpreserved urine specimen is likely to show a(n)
   A. decrease in turbidity.
   B. increase in cells and casts.
   C. increase in nitrates.
   D. decrease in glucose and ketone bodies.

5. Normal urine has a(n)
   A. faint, characteristic odor.
   B. opalescent turbidity.
   C. yellow-brown color.
   D. pH greater than 7.

6. In a urinalysis, pH reactions should be read at
   A. 20 seconds.
   B. 35 seconds.
   C. 60 seconds.
   D. 40 seconds.

7. When you examine a urine specimen under a microscope, motile bacteria may appear as
   A. RBCs.
   B. rods.
   C. gel.
   D. sand.

8. Abnormal crystals form in
   A. alkaline urine.
   B. nephrons.
   C. urinary tract mucus.
   D. acid urine.

9. Cryptorchism is normally diagnosed in
   A. men over the age of 50.
   B. men over the age of 60.
   C. infants.
   D. teenagers.

10. Which of the following is the cause of genital herpes?
    A. a bacterium
    B. a virus
    C. a protozoan
    D. a parasite

True/False

T F 1. Nephrology is the study of diseases of the bladder.

T F 2. Angiotensin is an enzyme that activates renin, a hormone involved in a complex regulatory process that maintains adequate blood volume and blood pressure.

T F 3. Each kidney contains approximately 1 million nephrons.

T F 4. For a 24-hour urine sample, the patient should collect each void, starting with the very first one in the morning.

T F 5. To calibrate a refractometer, you may use distilled or tap water.

T F 6. The human kidney is walnut-sized and bean-shaped.

T F 7. Urine enters the bladder at the trigone.

T F 8. The loop of Henle and Bowman's capsule were named after the physicians who identified them.

T F 9. A normal person produces approximately 1-1/2 to 2 liters of urine per day.

T F 10. Neurogenic bladder is usually the result of an insult to the nerves supplying the bladder.

Short Answer

1. Name the four primary structures of the urinary system.

2. What are the main symptoms of neurogenic bladder?

3. What are the uses of an IVP?

4. Which three kidney functions can a routine urinalysis be used to test?

5. What does light-colored urine indicate? What about darker-colored urine?

Research

1. In what states are MAs allowed to perform catheterization on patients?

2. What are the best exercises women can perform after childbirth to recondition the pelvic floor muscles?

Externship Application Experience

1. You have been assisting another office MA during a test strip procedure on a patient's urine specimen. She has given the report to the physician. You notice the date on the test strip container and realize the expiration date was six months ago. How do you handle this situation?

2. As a female MA, you are bringing an elderly male to the examination room. You note on the chart this is a return visit to discuss drug therapy prescribed for erectile dysfunction. During the usual assessment, you inquire about the reason for the visit. The patient appears embarrassed and reluctant to answer your questions. How do you proceed?

Resource Guide

American Association of Clinical Urologists
1111 North Plaza Drive, Suite 550
Schamburg, IL 60173
www.aacuweb.org

American Foundation for Urologic Disease
1128 North Charles Street
Baltimore, MD 21201
1-800-242-2383
www.afud.org

American Society of Nephrology
2025 M Street NW, Suite 800
Washington, DC 20036
1-202-367-1190
www.asn-online.org

American Society of Transplantation
17000 Commerce Parkway, Suite C
Mt. Laurel, NJ 08054
1-856-439-0500
www.a-s-t.org

American Urological Association, Inc.
1120 North Charles Street
Baltimore, MD 21201-5559
1-410-727-1100
www.auanet.org

National Kidney Foundation (NKF)
30 East 33rd Street
New York, NY 10016
1-800-622-9010
www.kidney.org

MedMedia
www.prenhall.com/frazier

More on this chapter, including interactive resources, can be found on the Student CD-ROM accompanying this textbook and on the Companion Website at www.prenhall.com/frazier.

CHAPTER 16

Medical Imaging

Case Study

Olivia is excited to begin work in a radiology facility, which is her first MA job since graduation. During her externship, Olivia worked in a pulmonology office where she was taught how to instruct patients in preparing for simple X-rays. At her new job, Olivia has a chance to practice with different types of medical imaging. Her orientation included learning more than fifteen different types of tests and the safety precautions for each.

Objectives

After completing this chapter, you should be able to:

- Spell and define medical terminology in this chapter.
- Define the medical assistant's role in medical imaging.
- Describe X-rays and how they function in radiology.
- Describe the information obtained from radiography and contrast studies, fluoroscopy, computed tomography, magnetic resonance imaging, sonography, and nuclear medicine.
- Describe the equipment used in medical imaging.
- Identify safety guidelines that protect both patient and technician during radiographic procedures.
- Define limited-scope radiography.
- Explain how radiographs are scheduled.
- Discuss how to prepare the X-ray room for a radiographic procedure.
- Define the terms commonly used in radiology procedures.
- Discuss patient preparation and instructions for contrast upper GI, lower GI, IVP, cholecystogram, and mammography procedures.
- Describe patient positioning for various chest X-ray projections.

MedMedia

www.prenhall.com/frazier

Additional interactive resources and activities for this chapter can be found on the Companion Website. For audio glossary, legal and ethical scenarios, job scenarios, quizzes, games, and activities related to the content of this chapter, please access the accompanying CD-ROM in this book.

Assets Available:

Audio Glossary
Legal and Ethical Scenario: *Medical Imaging*
On the Job Scenario: *Medical Imaging*
Multiple Choice Quiz
Games: Crossword, Strikeout and Spelling Bee
Drag and Drop: Skeletal System: The Skeleton; Skeletal System: The Skull; Skeletal System: Long Bone

MEDICAL ASSISTING COMPETENCIES

CAAHEP ENTRY-LEVEL COMPETENCIES FOR CMA	ABHES ENTRY-LEVEL COMPETENCIES FOR RMA
■ Identify and respond to issues of confidentiality. ■ Perform within legal and ethical boundaries. ■ Demonstrate knowledge of federal and state health-care legislation and regulations. ■ Practice Standard Precautions. ■ Prepare patient for and assist with routine and specialty examinations. ■ Instruct individuals according to their needs.	■ Project a positive attitude. ■ Maintain confidentiality at all times. ■ Be a "team player." ■ Be cognizant of ethical boundaries. ■ Exhibit initiative. ■ Adapt to change. ■ Evidence a responsible attitude. ■ Be courteous and diplomatic. ■ Conduct work within scope of education, training, and ability. ■ Prepare patients for procedures. ■ Prepare and maintain examination and treatment area. ■ Practice Standard Precautions. ■ Document accurately. ■ Use appropriate guidelines when releasing records or information.

Introduction

Medical imaging is a specialty that today encompasses radiology, sonography, fluoroscopy, computed tomography (**CT**), magnetic resonance imaging (**MRI**), and nuclear medicine. **Radiology** traditionally has involved the use of **radiographs,** or developed X-ray film, to produce images of bones and internal body structures. Computers have made it possible to scan a body part in dissecting planes or "slices," then assemble them to produce a three-dimensional, 360-degree image—a process called computed tomography. An MRI also produces a three-dimensional view, using magnetic fields rather than radiation. Medical imaging is an invaluable diagnostic tool for the physician.

The Medical Assistant's Role in Medical Imaging

As an MA, your role will involve patient education, preparation, and positioning, and following safety precautions. You may be required to schedule X-ray studies. Advanced training is required to become a radiology technician (rad tech) or radiographer. A radiographer maintains and uses radiology and imaging equipment in a safe manner to produce images of the body on X-ray film or screens, including fluoroscopic and CT screens. Advanced training is also required for the performance of MRIs, CT scans, mammograms, and ultrasound examinations. Nuclear medicine technologists are specialists who aid the physician in nuclear medicine procedures, and **radiation** therapy technologists assist in the delivery of radiation therapy.

Medical Terminology

angiography—radiograph of the vessels usually with contrast medium

arthrography—radiographic examination of a joint

cholecystography—radiograph of the gallbladder, using oral contrast; often referred to as gallbladder series

echocardiogram—type of sonogram used to study the internal structures of the heart

fluoroscopy—radiographic study in which structures are visualized in motion

mammogram—radiograph of breast tissue

myelography—radiographs of the spinal cord using a contrast medium

radiation—radiant energy

radiology—medical specialty that uses radiant energy forms, ultrasound, and magnetic waves to study, diagnose, and treat disease and injury

radiologist—physician who specializes in radiology

radiograph—developed X-ray film

radiography—study or practice of radiology using X-rays

radiolucent—easily penetrated by X-rays

radiopaque—capable of obstructing the passage of X-rays

sonography—use of ultrasound waves to view internal body structures

ultrasound—use of high frequency sound waves being projected and bounced back to the transmitter resulting in an image being projected

X-rays—form of electromagnetic radiation that travels in waves at the speed of light and can penetrate matter and produce a visible image on film

Abbreviations

ALARA—as low as reasonably achievable

AP—anteroposterior view; central ray is directed from front to back

CAT—computerized axial tomography

CT—computed tomography

IVP—intravenous pyelogram

LL—left lateral view; left side of the body faces the film

MRI—magnetic resonance imaging

PA—posteroanterior view; central ray is directed from back to front

PET—positron emission tomography

RL—right lateral view; right side of the body faces the film

COMPETENCY SKILLS PERFORMANCE

1. Perform the general procedure for an X-ray examination.
2. File and loan radiographic records.

Radiology

Radiology uses radiant energy—**X-rays**—to view body parts and functions. This specialty is an important aid in the study, diagnosis, and treatment of disease. There are several methods, or modalities, for visualizing the human body through diagnostic imaging. They include **radiography,** contrast studies, **fluoroscopy,** computed tomography, MRI studies, **sonography,** and nuclear medicine. Although they do not involve radiant energy, MRI (magnetic fields) and sonography (**ultrasound** waves) are usually considered part of the radiology department. Every specialty requires the core knowledge and skills common to all **radiologists.**

X-rays

X-rays are a form of electromagnetic radiation, similar to light rays but invisible to the human eye. They travel in waves at the speed of light, are capable of penetrating most matter, and can be directed through the body to record an image on radiographic film. The four different tissue densities—air, fat, water, and bone—develop on the film in different shades of black and white. Air, the least dense, is easily penetrated by X-rays (**radio-**

?—Critical Thinking Question 16-1—

Olivia's previous experience with X-rays has made her comfortable with patient preparation, gowning, and draping instructions. The X-ray technician has been ordered to take chest X-rays of a female patient who is believed to have pneumonia. The patient is elderly and has come to the appointment alone. She needs help removing her clothing and getting the drape set up and is not steady enough on her feet to stand alone in the X-ray room. What instructions or assistance should Olivia give her?

Caduceus Chronicle
A BRIEF HISTORY OF X-RAYS

William Crookes (1832–1919), an English scientist, explored the conduction of electricity in gases. His invention, the Crookes tube, allowed the passage of electricity through a tube from which air had been partially removed. This technique was the foundation for cathode rays and the work of another scientist, Wilhelm Conrad Roentgen (1845–1923). Roentgen, a German physicist, announced the discovery of radiant energy in 1895. He covered a Crookes tube with black paper, turned on the electric current, and created a dark image on a photographic plate near the tube. In 1901, Wilhelm Roentgen received the first Nobel Prize in physics for discovering the mysterious, invisible rays he called "X-rays."

lucent) and shows on the film as very dark. Bone, a very dense, calcium-containing substance, is much harder to penetrate. It is **radiopaque** and appears white on X-ray film. Physicians, especially radiologists, are trained to identify the structures of the body by studying the dark areas, lighter areas, and shadows.

Radiographs and Contrast Studies

Diagnostic radiography allows the radiologist to view internal body structures and aids physicians in disease diagnosis and treatment. Common procedures include the following:

- Venous studies
- Trauma procedures
- Head, neck and spinal studies
- Bone and joint studies
- Chest, abdomen, pelvic studies
- KUB (kidneys, ureters, bladder) radiography/urinary system studies, including retrograde pyelography
- Surgical procedures
- Myelography

Flat-plate, or plain film, X-rays are taken of the chest, abdomen, skull, skeleton (including long bones and spine), and the kidneys, ureters, and bladder (KUB) (Table 16-1).

TABLE 16-1 FLAT-PLATE RADIOGRAPHY FINDINGS

Anatomical Structure	Normal Findings	Examples of Abnormal Findings
Chest	Normal bony structure and lung tissue	Pneumonia, TB, atelectasis, pneumothorax, tumor, abscess, sarcoidosis, sarcoma, incidental findings of scoliosis and kyphosis
Heart	Normal shape and size of heart and blood vessels	Cardiomegaly, aneurysms, and aortic anomalies
Abdomen	Normal size and shape of abdominal structures, including gallbladder, liver, stomach, pancreas, spleen, and small and large intestines; normal gas patterns	Abdominal masses, intestinal obstructions, abdominal tissue trauma, ascites, blood in the peritoneal space
Kidney, ureters, bladder (KUB)	Normal size and structure of the kidneys, ureters, and bladder	Abnormal size and structure of kidneys, ureters, and bladder, renal calculi, masses, obstructions, urinary system abscesses
Skull	Normal structures	Intracranial pressure caused by fluid and swelling, cranial vault fractures, bone defects, congenital anomalies
Skeleton	Normal structures	Fractures, osteomyelitis, arthritic conditions, bone growth

PROCEDURE 16-1 Perform General Procedure for X-ray Examination

Theory

X-rays are used to view the body's bony and soft structures on flat film. The patient's reproductive organs must be protected from radiation with a lead apron. You should also avoid unnecessary exposure by wearing the proper protective garments and a dosimeter badge and remaining behind a lead wall whenever possible.

Materials

- physician's order
- patient chart
- dosimeter badge
- X-ray film
- X-ray film holder
- X-ray machine
- processing machine
- lead aprons for MA and patient
- paper drapes, as needed

Competency

(**Conditions**) With the necessary materials, (**Task**) you will be able to X-ray a patient (**Standards**) correctly within the time frame designated by the instructor.

1. Verify the patient's identity and the physician's order.
2. Check the X-ray equipment.
3. Explain the procedure to the patient.
4. Instruct the patient to remove the appropriate clothing for the X-ray. Provide paper drapes for modesty. For chest and neck X-rays, the patient should remove all jewelry and large hair bands, which may obstruct the view of the structures.
5. Position the patient according to the X-ray view(s) required (Figure 16-1 ◆).
6. Set the controls with the X-ray tube and cassette at the proper distance (Figure 16-2 ◆).
7. If necessary, ask the patient to take a deep breath and hold it.
8. Stand behind the lead wall or shield to take the X-ray.
9. Instruct the patient to adjust to a comfortable position while you develop the X-rays and have them reviewed. The patient should not dress or leave the X-ray suite until the physician has indicated that the X-rays are satisfactory.
10. With the physician's approval, assist the patient in dressing, if necessary.
11. Label the X-ray and X-ray sleeve according to office procedure.
12. Document the procedure in the patient's chart.

Patient Education

To ensure that the patient goes to the correct place and follows the correct pre-exam procedures, instructions should be given both verbally and in written form. Following instructions correctly saves time and money by preventing the need to reschedule or perform the tests more than once. The patient should be aware of when the results will be available. You may see abnormalities on the film as soon as it is developed, but be careful not to give the patient any advice without the physician's direct permission.

Charting Example

02/14/XX 4:25 p.m. Views obtained through X-ray as ordered.
Candace Jones, RMA

continued

PROCEDURE 16-1 Perform General Procedure for X-ray Examination *(continued)*

Figure 16-1 ◆ Position the patient properly.

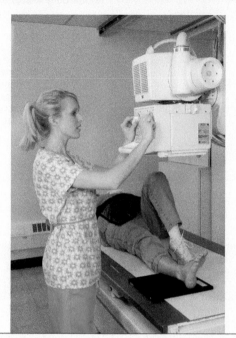

Figure 16-2 ◆ Align the X-ray tube to the cassette at the correct distance.

A contrast medium is a radiopaque substance. It provides a more accurate visualization of the internal body organ(s) and tissues adjacent to the point of interest (Table 16-2). The contrast medium may be a gas, such as air, oxygen, or carbon dioxide; the heavy metal barium sulfate; or organic iodine, either oil based or water-soluble. Contrast media may be administered orally, parentally, or via enema. Each one is specific for the examination of a particular organ or tissue (Figure 16-3 ◆).

Specialized radiographic examinations include mammography, angiography, arthrography, and cholecystography.

Mammography

A **mammogram** is an X-ray of the breast tissue taken to detect possible abnormalities, such as tumors, cysts, or malignant tissue (Figure 16-4 ◆). Two views are taken of each breast. When lesions without clinical symptoms are detected, early treatment leads to a higher survival rate. Regular mammograms are usually part of a woman's routine gynecological examination. However, men who may require mammograms to detect breast cancer or trauma injury are often overlooked.

A mammographer is a technologist who specializes in the imaging of the breast. He or she must be knowledgeable

TABLE 16-2 COMMON CONTRAST STUDIES

Contrast Study	Systems Examined	Reason for Examination
Upper GI, small bowel series, barium swallow	Upper GI tract including esophagus, stomach, small intestines	To diagnose ulcers, tumors, obstructions, hiatal hernia, or esophageal varices; to study size and shape of organs and structures
Lower GI, air contrast colon study or barium enema	Large intestines	To examine for disease or disorders of the large intestine and to diagnose conditions such as polyps, diverticuli, obstructions, tumors, and lesions
Cholecystogram or gallbladder series	Gallbladder	To diagnose disease or disorders such as blockage, tumors, calculi, and inflammation
Intravenous pyelogram (IVP)	Urinary tract including kidneys, ureters, urinary bladder, and urethra	To diagnose disease or disorders such as obstruction, narrowing, tumors, and calculi; to study size of organs and structures

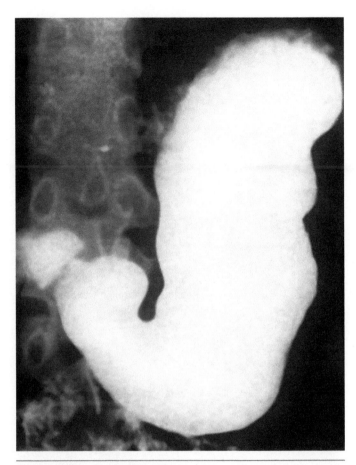

Figure 16-3 ◆ Upper GI series
Source: BSIP/agefotostock

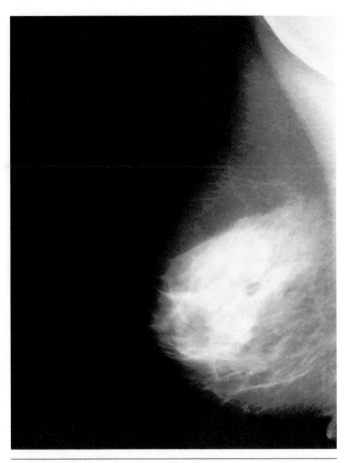

Figure 16-4 ◆ Normal mammogram
Source: Kings College School of Medicine/Photo Researchers, Inc.

Keys to Success
PREVENTING ALLERGIC AND MEDICAL REACTIONS

Before administering any contrast medium, question the patient about allergies and any medications being taken. Iodine can cause reactions from mild to severe to life-threatening. Mild reactions include the following:

nausea and vomiting	coughing	headache
dizziness	pallor	flushing
anxiety	itching	altered taste
shaking	chills	sweating
rash	nasal stuffiness	

More serious reactions include the following:

cardiovascular: pulse changes, hypotension, hypertension
respiratory: dyspnea, wheezing, bronchospasm, laryngospasm

Life-threatening reactions include the following:

unresponsiveness	convulsions	serious arrhythmias
anaphylactic shock	cardiopulmonary arrest	

Medications with the potential to interact with iodine and cause serious reactions include beta-blockers, calcium channel blockers, and metformin (Glucophage®). A patient with diabetes who takes metformin (Glucophage®) to control non-insulin-dependent diabetes mellitus (NIDDM) is at risk for developing lactic acidosis if iodine contrast is administered within 48 hours of the last metformin dose. The next metformin dose must be withheld for 48 hours following the administration of iodine. Many physicians prefer to avoid the risk and order ultrasound examinations or CT scans, neither of which requires a contrast medium.

in breast anatomy, mammography equipment and procedure, the correct positioning of the breast, and quality assurance related to patient care. An advanced certification examination given by the American Registry of Radiologic Technologists (ARRT) is required for employment as a mammographer.

Angiography

Angiography, an invasive examination of the blood vessels, helps in the evaluation of the patency of vessels and in the identification of abnormal vascularization, a possible result of tumors (Figure 16-5 ◆). In cerebral angiography, the carotid and vertebral arteries are outlined by injected dye. Information about the circle of Willis and small cerebral arterial branches may also be obtained. In pulmonary angiography, injected dye helps to visualize pulmonary vessels. Renal angiography is used to view and evaluate renal circulation and to find causes for hypertension such as thrombi, vascular stenosis, and lesions. Angiography is also employed in cardiac catheterization.

Arthrography

In **arthrography**, the radiographic examination of a joint, air and dye are injected into the joint space so that it can be viewed before an arthroscopic procedure.

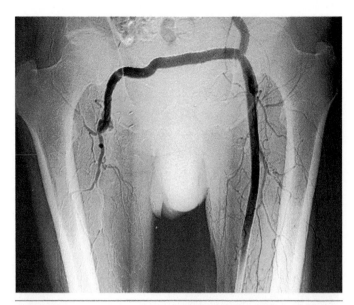

Figure 16-5 ◆ Digital angiogram of the lower limbs, front view, showing atheromatous stenoses of the femoral arteries
Source: Zephyr/Photo Researchers, Inc.

Cholecystography

Cholecystography, sometimes referred to as a gallbladder series, is an examination of the gallbladder using oral (swallowed) contrast to provide a visual picture of the gallbladder. It is used in the diagnosis of gallstones or obstruction of the cystic duct. For further diagnosis, IV cholangiography may be performed.

Fluoroscopy

A fluoroscopy procedure studies internal organ(s) as they function—for instance, the heart, stomach, intestines, and fallopian tubes (Figure 16-6 ◆). An X-ray instrument, a fluoroscope, projects visual images on a fluorescent screen rather than on a film. The radiographic tilt table is used for this procedure. The technician can view internal structures on a monitor as well as take pictures for diagnosis or documentation.

   Myelography uses both fluoroscopic and radiographic means to examine the spinal subarachnoid space. Air and a contrast medium are injected into the space at the lumbar region so that any abnormalities in that space, such as herniated intervertebral disks, can be viewed. MRIs have replaced most myelography procedures. However, MRIs cannot be performed on patients with metal implants or pacemakers, and for these patients myelograms are the preferred diagnostic procedure.

Computed Tomography

Until the 1970s, only two-dimensional X-rays were available for viewing the internal human body. A new technique, the computer tomography scan (CT scan, formerly called computerized axial tomography or **CAT** scan), is a nonharmful procedure that provides tomographic information far superior to that obtained by serial sectioning. Tomography allows for a specific level or

Figure 16-6 ◆ A fluoroscopic unit with upper GI study on screen
Source: Jim Pickerell/The Stock Connection.

plane of the body to be imaged by removing images of the tissue above and below the selected plane. Two issues influence its scientific usefulness: the clarity of image resolution and the tissue density of the image illuminated by the X-ray beam.

   This technique rotates a specific plane of an internal object as it is illuminated by a narrow X-ray beam. By sequentially merging many two-dimensional radiographs of an internal structure, a three-dimensional image can be recorded for further study (Table 16-3).

Magnetic Resonance Imaging

Magnetic resonance imaging (MRI) is used primarily in a medical setting to produce high-quality images of the inside of the human body (Figure 16-7 ◆). A CT scan specializes in larger images, whereas MRI images are smaller. MRI uses wavelengths of energy to produce the images based on spatial variations in the phase and frequency of the radio frequency energy absorbed and emitted by the imaged object. Abscesses, aneurysms, thrombi, congenital heart disease, cysts, edema, hemorrhage, infarctions, multiple sclerosis, muscular disease, skeletal abnormalities, thrombosis, and vascular plaque formation are all clinical problems that can be detected with MRI.

TABLE 16-3 CT FINDINGS

Anatomical Structure	Examples of Abnormal Findings
Head	Abscess, atrophy, cysts, edema, hematomas, hydrocephalus, infarction, tumors
Abdomen	
Adrenal	Tumors
Biliary	Obstructions due to calculi
Kidney	Abscesses, calculi, congenital anomalies, cysts, perirenal hematomas, tumors
Liver	Abscesses, cirrhosis with ascites, cysts, hematomas, tumors
Pancreatic	Acute and chronic pancreatitis, pancreatic lesions including abscesses, pseudocysts, and tumors
Chest and thorax	Aortic aneurysm, abscesses, cysts, tumors, pleural effusion, enlarged lymph nodes in the mediastinum
Spine	Herniated intervertebral disks, congenital spinal anomalies, tumors, paraspinal cysts, vascular malformations

Keys to Success
PREVENTING PATIENT MOVEMENT DURING A CT SCAN OR MRI

Both CT scans and MRIs involve surrounding the patient with a circular camera. Some patients experience claustrophobia during the procedure, and a sedative may have to be administered before the procedure is performed. Even children may require sedation, as any motion causes a distortion of the image and the reading may not be accurate.

- any type of metal implant or metal surgical clip, which can get hot.
- a pacemaker and/or aneurysm clips.
- body tattoos made with dye containing metal.

Sonography

In sonography, very high-frequency sound waves are bounced off internal body structures (Figure 16-8 ◆). An echo is passed back to the monitor and recorded, forming a composite picture. Ultrasounds also display movement of the structure at the time of examination (Table 16-4).

Ultrasound is performed on pregnant women to assess fetal growth and size, the number of fetuses, placental location, and possible birth defects (Figure 16-9 ◆). Ultrasound is considered safe for both mother and child. Newer ultrasound equipment shows a three-dimensional view of the fetus (3-D ultrasound).

An **echocardiogram** is a type of sonogram that can detect abnormalities in the internal structures of the heart. It is used to assess general anatomy, valve function, myocardial function, blood flow, and heart chamber size. A transducer is passed over the chest, and an ultrasonic echo is displayed on a monitor called an oscilloscope. An ultrasonic gel is applied to the skin under the transducer to ensure a clearer projection.

Ultrasounds are considered a low risk to the patient. Patients who cannot undergo contrast studies because of allergies or other risks often have ultrasound examinations instead. Although an ultrasound is effective at ruling out a defect, it is less effective at identifying one. A video film of the ultrasound

MRIs cannot be performed on patients with pacemakers, metal hardware, metal staples in the chest, or metal foreign bodies in the eye. The magnetic field may damage a pacemaker or disrupt its settings and pacing. Metal implants may be dislocated and would contribute to artifact, rendering the MRI inaccurate.

CAT scans and MRIs are used for similar tissue studies. Often the physician's choice depends on the contrast medium required for the procedure. Patients occasionally exhibit an allergic response to contrast medium, so the physician decides which procedure is least harmful and has the most diagnostic benefits for those patients. The magnetic field in an MRI is negatively affected by a patient with

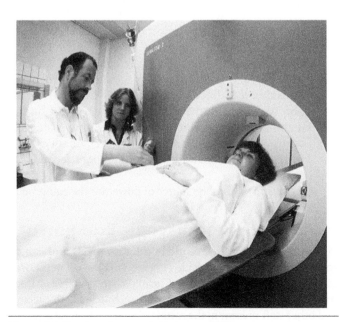

Figure 16-7 ◆ A patient undergoing an MRI

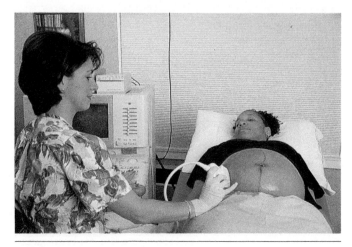

Figure 16-8 ◆ Ultrasound scanning

TABLE 16-4 SONOGRAPHIC FINDINGS

Anatomical Structure	Abnormal Findings
Abdominal aorta	Aortic aneurysm, aortic stenosis
Arteries and veins	Arterial occlusion (partial or complete), arterial trauma, chronic venous insufficiency, deep vein thrombosis (DVT)
Brain	Intracranial hemorrhage, hydrocephalus, lesions (tumors or abscesses)
Gallbladder	Acute cholecystitis, biliary obstruction, cholelithiasis
Heart	Cardiomegaly, aortic stenosis and insufficiency, congenital heart disease, mitral valve stenosis, pericardial effusion
Kidney	Acute glomerulonephritis, acute pyelonephritis hydronephrosis, renal cysts and tumors, perirenal abscesses, renal calculi
Liver	Hepatomegaly, abscesses, hepatic cysts, hepatic metastasis, hepatocellular disease
Pancreas	Acute pancreatitis, pancreatic tumors, pseudocysts
Pelvic, uterus, and/or pregnant uterus	Uterine fibroids, uterine tumors, fetal death, abruptio placenta, placenta previa, breech fetal presentation, fetal hydrocephalus
Spleen	Splenomegaly, abscesses, splenic cysts, tumor
Thyroid	Lesions (benign or malignant), goiters, cysts

procedure is made for more thorough examination by the radiologist and cardiologist.

Nuclear Medicine

In nuclear medicine, the patient either swallows or is injected with a radioactive material called a tracer that is absorbed by the target tissue or organ. A special scanner then detects the tracer

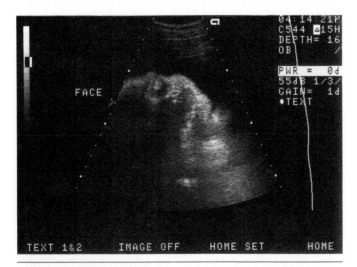

Figure 16-9 ◆ Ultrasound of the fetal face

and provides information about the function, chemical activity, or metabolism of the tissue or organ.

Positron emission tomography (**PET**) is a nuclear medicine technique that produces three-dimensional, multicolored scans with radioisotopes and a computer. PET scanning is used to identify amyloid plaques and tangles that are believed to cause Alzheimer's disease. Before the PET scan was available, Alzheimer's could be truly identified only through autopsy. Identifying the disease with a PET scan is critical to tracking the progression of dementia and planning its treatment.

Nuclear medicine treatments for cancer include brachytherapy and teletherapy. Both techniques use radiation to damage cancer cells during frequent cellular division. Because normal cells undergo a lower division rate, radiation kills the cancer cells and causes less harm to surrounding healthy tissues. In brachytherapy, also called internal radiation therapy, small radioactive materials are implanted within or near the malignant tumor. In teletherapy, or external beam radiotherapy, radiation is directed at the malignancy from outside the body.

Equipment

The equipment used in radiology is complicated and expensive. It is used primarily by physicians with many years of education and training and the support of trained technicians.

The X-ray machine consists of four major components.

- Tube: The cylindrical radiographic glass tube contains a vacuum that produces radiation.
- Table: The X-ray table comes in many shapes and sizes to meet the needs of an office, clinic, or diagnostic center (Figure 16-10 ◆). Some tables tilt to aid the patient in a fluoroscopy procedure, and some have a floating tabletop that is helpful in positioning the patient. All tables contain a Bucky tray, which holds the film cassette and can be moved from one end of the table to the other. A lead strip around the top of the table helps absorb the scatter radiation between the patient and the film.
- Control panel: Unless the X-ray equipment is a mobile unit that takes portable images, the control panel is inside a lead-lined area with a lead-treated observation window. Control panels vary, depending on the manufacturer, but all operate on the same basic concepts: quantity (milliamperes, or mA), quality (kilovoltage, or KVP), and time (milliampere seconds, or mAS).
- Generator: This is the source of power for the equipment.

Portable or Fluoroscopic Equipment

Portable equipment is mounted on large wheels and can be rolled to the patient's bedside (Figure 16-11 ◆). The fluoroscopic camera is mounted on a C arm. When portable or fluoroscopic films are being exposed, the technicians, physicians, and other staff present in the room wear lead aprons and gloves for protection against radiation exposure.

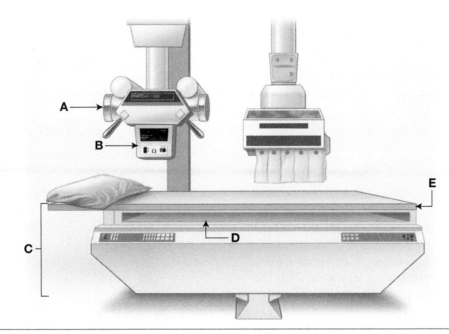

Figure 16-10 ◆ Diagram of the X-ray table: (A) X-ray tube; (B) collimeter; (C) radiographic table; (D) Bucky tray for cassette and film; (E) movable table

Safety Precautions and Patient Protection

Because the effects of radiation are cumulative, it presents a potential hazard to anyone who is frequently exposed to it (Table 16-5). Excessive exposure can cause biological changes, including cell and tissue destruction, with effects that may include temporary or permanent damage to the skin, eyes, thyroid gland, and blood-forming and reproductive organs. X-rays may also be harmful to developing embryos or fetuses, damage germ cells, and cause genetic mutations.

All radiation exposure must be kept as low as reasonably achievable (**ALARA**). The physician must weigh the risks of radiation exposure to the patient against the benefits that will be derived. The procedure should be explained to the patient and adequate preparation should be performed to eliminate any repeat exposure.

TABLE 16-5 SAMPLE SOURCES OF RADIATION			
Natural			
Internal (occur naturally in the human body)	**External**	**Artificial**
Potassium Carbon	Cosmic rays—radiation emitted from the sun Terrestrial—radiation produced in the earth, such as from uranium Radionuclides—interact with cosmic rays	Medical and dental X-rays Nuclear power Mining Radiopharmaceutical isotopes

The patient must always be protected. Before any exposure to X-rays, females of childbearing age must be asked if they could be pregnant. Follow the ten-day rule: A woman in her childbearing years can be safely X-rayed during the first ten days following the onset of her menses.

Three primary principles govern radiation exposure for the radiography technician and the patient:

- Time: The length of exposure should be kept as short as possible.
- Distance: The distance between the technician and the radiation source should be the maximum distance at all times.
- Shielding: Lead aprons, lead gloves, and thyroid shielding should be worn to protect the reproductive organs at all times by the employee and the patient. A radiation exposure badge (dosimeter badge) must also be worn at all times by all employees who are required to spend time in radiation areas (Figure 16-12 ◆).

Figure 16-11 ◆ A fluoroscope and portable equipment
Source: Novastock/The Stock Connection.

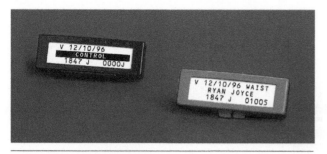

Figure 16-12 ◆ A radiation exposure badge (dosimeter badge)

An ambulatory patient may require assistance onto the table. Always offer a hand to the patient as he or she sits on the table. Help the patient lift the feet and legs up on the table, moving them together as a unit rather than separately. Offer the same consideration when the procedure is over and the patient is getting off the table.

Respect the patient's modesty and provide privacy. Blankets or sheets should cover legs and exposed body parts when it is not necessary to view them. Provide a pillow if possible for comfort as well as blankets for warmth if they are needed.

Radiation Shields

A variety of shields containing 1/16 inch of lead equivalent is available for both patient and technician (Figure 16-13 ◆):

- Full aprons (cover the breasts and abdominal–pelvic areas)
- Half aprons (cover the abdominal–pelvic area)
- Gonadal shields
- Thyroid shields
- Eye shields

Full aprons should be worn by both males and females when the extremities are X-rayed, half aprons when the chest is X-rayed, and gonadal shields when the abdomen is X-rayed. Thyroid shielding is worn primarily for skull X-rays and eye shields for lower jaw or larynx X-rays. Lead gloves should be worn to protect the hands when they may be exposed to radiation (Figure 16-14 ◆).

Personnel or family members who assist with patients should be provided with lead aprons, gloves, and thyroid shields. If someone must remain in the room when a radiograph is performed, the person should be positioned to the back of the tube.

The room where the X-rays are taken is also protected. Walls painted with lead equivalent (usually 1/16 inch) thick

Keys to Success
RADIATION EXPOSURE TIME

A good way to keep a patient safe from radiation is to remember the acronym ALARA—as low as reasonably achievable. Maintain the shortest exposure time, the lowest radiation strength, and the greatest distance possible from the source of radiation to achieve the required X-ray results.

A

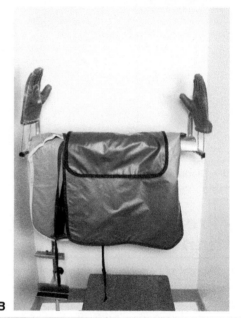

B

Figure 16-13 ◆ (A) A variety of shields: half apron, gonadal shield, and apron; (B) Storage rack for aprons and gloves

capture any bouncing radiation in the room and absorb radioactive ions that may scatter from the primary beam. A lead strip at the base of the wall and a strip around the X-ray tabletop absorb scattered radiation as well. Using grids in the film cassette and reducing the field size protect the patient further.

All lead protective barriers, including the lead strips on the X-ray table, should be checked periodically for cracks and signs of wear. Inform the physician or office manager of any wear.

Figure 16-14 ◆ Lead gloves

Keys to Success
MEDICAL PRACTICE ACTS

You must be aware of medical practice acts in your community and state regarding limited-scope radiography. In some states MAs are allowed to perform this activity, but other states prohibit it. Some state statutes prohibit the presence of students other than radiology students in a room where radiographs are exposed.

Current licensure information can be obtained from the American Registry of Radiologic Technologists (AART). In order to comply with states' current regulations regarding the dispensing of ionizing radiation, schools that provide training for limited-scope radiology must be officially recognized by each individual state. The state certification exam is customized in each state. After successful completion of training and examination, the limited-scope radiographer may seek employment. Continuing education is mandatory to maintain certification.

—Critical Thinking Question 16-2—
The patient tells Olivia that she is not steady on her feet and would like Olivia's assistance during the X-ray procedure. What precautions should Olivia take to avoid unnecessary exposure to radiation?

Limited-Scope Radiography

Some physicians have equipment in the office with which to perform simple X-ray procedures. After the appropriate training and if it is allowed in your state, you may be asked to expose and develop film in addition to preparing the patient. Limited-scope radiography allows you to perform limited numbers and types of X-ray procedures, typically upper and lower extremities, chest, and some skull procedures. As a limited-scope radiographer you are subject to state regulations.

Scheduling Radiographs

Some radiology testing can be performed in the medical office. Otherwise, it is scheduled with a radiology facility in a clinic, freestanding facility, or hospital radiology department.

- On-site: If the procedure is not performed immediately in the office, the physician writes an order for one. An appointment is scheduled, and an appointment card and verbal and written instructions are given to the patient.
- Off-site: After the physician writes the order, the patient is asked to confirm whether his or her insurance covers the suggested facility. If so, the order is relayed to the facility, usually by phone. An appointment date and time are confirmed with the patient. The facility then relays preparation instructions, which are given in verbal and written form to the patient along with an appointment card containing the name, address, and phone number of the facility. Transportation requirements may need to be discussed, and written directions are provided as necessary to the patient or patient's family member or caregiver.

Assisting with an X-ray

Simple X-rays may be performed in a physician's office depending on the office location and the availability of radiographic equipment. X-rays of limbs and appendages are often taken in an office where the physician treats fractures and simple trauma. Chest X-rays may be taken when the physician needs a rapid diagnosis of a respiratory complaint or condition. Podiatrists often take X-rays of the feet as a diagnostic tool. A flat plate or plain film radiograph of the abdomen or a KUB may be taken if a radiology facility is not readily accessed. Many physicians' offices are located in clinic complexes where the patient may have an X-ray taken, then return to the medical office for treatment.

Patient Preparation and Instructions

Any female of childbearing age must be asked if she could be pregnant. Usually, signs are posted in radiology departments instructing female patients to inform the technician or staff if they are or think they may be pregnant.

Jewelry and any metal objects must be removed from the area to be filmed and stored in a secure place. Any clothing or undergarments with metal closures must also be removed.

Preparation of the X-ray Room

Preparation for the X-ray room is minimal. A film cassette is stored upright, on its end, in a cabinet. It should *never* be stored flat or on its side. All film is stored flat in a dark cabinet. X-ray accessories, such as calipers, foam spacers, and risers, are kept in a place that is convenient for the technician but away from patients' reach.

Nothing should be kept in the X-ray room except the equipment to be used. The X-ray table should be cleaned with a mild disinfectant after each patient. Be careful not to damage the lead strip that surrounds the table as this could interfere with the capture of scattered radiation. Clean the chin rest as well as anything else that a patient may have touched after each use.

Terminology and Landmarks for Positioning

To obtain the best radiographic image possible, it is important to understand the relevant terminology (Tables 16-6 through 16-10) and the use of anatomical landmarks to position the patient properly. Anatomical landmarks are reference points or body structures used to perform procedures correctly.

TABLE 16-6 BODY HABITUS (SHAPE)	
Sthenic body habitus	Average body shape and size
Hyposthenic body habitus	Tall and slender body shape
Asthenic body habitus	Extremely tall and slender body shape
Hypersthenic body habitus	Short and stout body shape

TABLE 16-7 RADIOGRAPHIC POSITIONING TERMS

Projection	Path of the central rays from the source though the object
Tangential	Describing the path of the central ray along a body part as the part is seen in profile
Axial	Describing the path of the central ray along the long axis of the body part
Axillary	Describing the path of the central ray toward the axilla (underarm)
Cephalic	Describing the central ray toward the head
Caudal	Describing the central ray toward the feet
View	How the image is seen from the image receptor; the opposite of projection
Anteroposterior view (**AP**)	Central ray is directed from front to back
Posteroanterior view (**PA**)	Central ray is directed from back to front
Right lateral view (**RL**)	Right side of the body faces the film
Left lateral view (**LL**)	Left side of the body faces the film

TABLE 16-8 BODY PLANES (FIGURE 16-15 ◆)

Midsagittal plane	Division of the body into equal right and left halves
Sagittal plane	Vertical division of the body or body part into equal or unequal right and left sections
Coronal plane	Division of the body into front and back portions
Horizontal or transverse plane	Horizontal division of the body into upper and lower portions

TABLE 16-9 BODY POSITIONS

Position	Placement of the body or body part
Erect	Sitting or standing
Recumbent	In a reclining position or lying down
Decubitus	Lying down position
Left decubitus	Lying on the left side, recumbent
Right decubitus	Lying in the right side, recumbent
Supine or dorsal recumbent	Lying face up
Prone or ventral recumbent	Lying face down
Left lateral recumbent	Lying on the left side
Right lateral recumbent	Lying on the right side
Lateral	Body or body part placed at a 90-degree angle
Oblique	Body or body part placed at less than a 90-degree angle

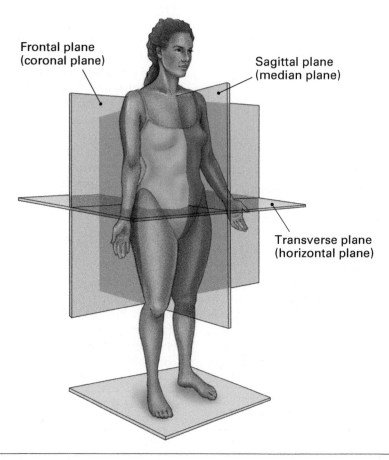

Frontal plane
(coronal plane)

Sagittal plane
(median plane)

Transverse plane
(horizontal plane)

Figure 16-15 ◆ Planes of the body

TABLE 16-10 BODY MOVEMENTS

Flexion	Decreasing the angle between two bones; bending at the joint
Extension	Increasing the angle between two bones; straightening at the joint
Abduction	Moving a body part toward the midline of the body
Adduction	Moving a body part away from midline of the body
Eversion	Turning a body part toward the outside
Inversion	Turning a body part toward the inside
Supination	Turning the palm of the hand upward
Pronation	Turning the palm of the hand downward

Preparing a Patient for a Mammogram

Baseline mammograms are recommended for women around 35 years of age, and yearly mammograms for women over 40 (see box below). Medicare and most insurance companies cover the procedure.

Preparing the Patient for Abdominal Contrast Studies

Patients may require radiographs made with a contrast medium, such as upper GI and intravenous pyelogram (**IVP**) (see the following boxes). Preparation for radiographic examinations of organs in the trunk area includes evacuation of GI contents. Failure to comply with these instructions and complete the prep may result in X-rays that do not supply adequate information for diagnosis. The entire procedure, including prep, may have to be repeated, resulting in additional stress on the patient as well as additional expense.

Keys to Success
PATIENT PREPARATION AND INSTRUCTIONS: MAMMOGRAPHY

Purpose: Radiographic examination of both breasts to detect any disease or disorders such as lesions, tumors, or cysts.

Patient preparation:

■ The patient should make an appointment for one week after the menses, when the breasts are less tender.
■ Mammography does not require GI tract preparation.

Day of procedure:

■ The patient will undress from the waist up and wear a gown.
■ The patient should wear no lotions, powders, perfume, or deodorant under the arms.

Procedure steps:

■ Both breasts are X-rayed.
■ The patient is placed in several positions with the breast placed between two plastic plates.
■ Two views are routinely taken of each breast.

Scheduled time: 30 to 40 minutes

Keys to Success
PATIENT PREPARATION AND INSTRUCTIONS: UPPER GI (BARIUM SWALLOW)

Purpose: Radiographic examination of the esophagus, stomach, and small intestines for diagnosis of ulcers, tumors, obstructions, hiatal hernia, or esophageal varices.

Patient preparation:
Day before procedure:

■ Light evening meal.
■ NPO 12 hours prior to X-rays.

Post-procedure:

■ Increase fluid intake.
■ Laxative if prescribed.

Procedure steps:

■ The patient drinks a barium mixture (chalky mixture) while standing in front of the fluoroscope.
■ The radiologist observes and X-rays the passage of the fluid through the digestive tract as the patient turns in various positions.

Scheduled time: 1 hour to 1-1/2 hours

Keys to Success
PATIENT PREPARATION AND INSTRUCTIONS: LOWER GI SERIES (BARIUM ENEMA)

Purpose: A radiographic examination of the large intestines for disease or disorders such as polyps, obstructions, tumors, and lesions.

Patient preparation:
Day before procedure:

■ Clear liquids only, such as coffee, tea, clear gelatin, broth, and carbonated beverages.
■ No milk or milk products.
■ In late afternoon or early evening, drink 3.2-oz bottle of magnesium citrate.
■ In early evening, prescribed laxative and NPO except water 12 hours before procedure.

Day of procedure:

■ NPO.
■ Cleansing enema if needed.

Procedure steps:

■ The colon is filled with a barium sulfate mixture.
■ The patient is moved into various positions to allow barium to fill the entire colon. Air may be used to push the barium further into the colon.
■ X-rays are taken.

Post-procedure:

■ Increase fluid intake.
■ Laxative if needed after 24 hours.

Scheduled time: 2 hours

Keys to Success
PATIENT PREPARATION AND INSTRUCTIONS: INTRAVENOUS PYELOGRAM (IVP)

Purpose: Radiographic examination of the urinary tract to diagnose disease or disorders such as blockage, narrowing, tumors, and calculi

Precautions: A contrast medium of iodine is used to view the urinary tract. Warn the patient of a warm flushed sensation when the medium is injected into the bladder and a possible metallic taste for several hours after the procedure. This procedure should not be performed on a patient who is allergic to iodine or shellfish. The physician may order an ultrasound study of the kidneys if the patient cannot tolerate the iodine.

Patient preparation:

Day before procedure:
- Light evening meal.
- Prescribed laxative in the early evening.
- NPO except water for 12 hours before exam.

Day of procedure:
- Enema in the a.m. if necessary.

Procedure steps:
- The patient is asked to dress in a patient gown and to urinate, to ensure his or her comfort while lying still during the procedure.
- An initial X-ray may be taken with the patient in a supine position.
- An IV is started and contrast medium injected.
- X-rays are taken.
- The patient is asked to urinate again, and a final X-ray is taken.

Post-procedure:
- Increase fluid intake.

Scheduled time: 45 minutes to 1 hour

Keys to Success
PATIENT PREPARATION AND INSTRUCTIONS: CHOLECYSTOGRAM (GALLBLADDER)

Purpose: Radiographic examination of the gallbladder to diagnose disease or disorders such as blockage, tumors, calculi, and inflammation.

Precautions: Iodine is taken the night before the examination. If the patient is allergic to iodine or shellfish, another type of examination, such as ultrasound, should be performed. Warn the patient of a metallic taste after the medication is taken.

Patient preparation:

Day before procedure:
- Light, fat-free meals.
- Take iodine tablets with water after dinner.
- Laxative if prescribed.
- NPO except for water after iodine tablets are taken.

Day of procedure:
- NPO before procedure.

Procedure steps:
- X-rays are taken of the gallbladder.
- A fatty meal is given to stimulate the gallbladder.
- X-rays are taken again.

Post-procedure:
- Increase fluid intake.

Scheduled time: approximately 30 minutes

Filing and Loaning Radiographic Records

Maintaining X-rays is the same as maintaining any other medical record. The original transcription report of the X-ray is kept in the facility and a copy sent to the primary physician.

Mammograms are generally kept for ten years, minor injury X-rays for five years, and asbestos X-rays permanently.

The procedure for loaning X-rays may differ with each facility. The general procedure must include the verbal and written consent of the patient. The patient or another facility can usually check out any X-ray for up to thirty days. The hospital, diagnostic center, or clinic may also copy an X-ray for another facility and charge the cost to the owner of the record.

PROCEDURE 16-2 File and Loan Radiographic Records

Theory

When X-ray films are taken by the patient to another facility or physician, notation must be made on the patient record along with the name of the receiving physician. All films leaving the department are recorded in a log or file along with the time, date, patient's name, and physicians' names.

Most radiology facilities require a written request from the requesting facility before releasing any X-ray films. The patient must sign a consent form as well. The films are placed in a large envelope or jacket labeled with the patient's name, DOB, physician's name, and the date when the films were taken.

Materials
- X-ray films
- consent form
- larger envelope or film jacket
- labels

Competency

(**Conditions**) With the necessary materials, you will be able to (**Task**) file and loan X-rays (**Standards**) correctly.

1. Place the films in a large film envelope labeled with the patient's name, DOB, date of procedure, and physician's name (Figure 16-16 ◆). The films will be taken to a radiologist to be read.
2. If the films are to be taken by the patient to another facility or physician, note the destination and receiving physician's name on the patient record.
3. Record the transfer of all films in a log or file, along with the time, date, patient's name, destination, and receiving physician.
4. Obtain the patient's signed consent for any films the patient takes from the ownership facility to another physician or diagnostic center.

continued

PROCEDURE 16-2 File and Loan Radiographic Records *(continued)*

Patient Education

Instruct the patient that the receiving or reviewing site returns most loaned X-rays. In other cases the patient has to hand-carry the X-rays back to the loaning facility.

Charting Example

8/24/XX 1:30 p.m. Bilateral mammography X-rays released to patient after signing consent for release for consultation with Dr. Brown. Simon Allen, CMA

Figure 16-16 ◆ A correctly labeled X-ray envelope, front and back

REVIEW

Chapter Summary

- Medical imagining encompasses radiology, sonography, and magnetic resonance imaging. Radiographs or X-rays produce images of bones and internal body structures. CT scans produce images of a specific body part by dissecting planes and reassembling them to produce a 360-degree image. MRIs produce 360-degree images with the use of magnetic fields rather than radiation.
- Radiologists are physicians who specialize in radiology. Radiology procedures include several specialty areas such as diagnostic radiology, fluoroscopy, mammography, computer tomography, radiation therapy, and nuclear medicine.
- X-rays can penetrate matter. They pass through the body to a specialized radiographic film, where images of light/dark contrast are recorded.
- Flat plate films are taken of the chest, abdomen, skull, skeleton (including long bones and spine), and the kidneys, ureters, and bladder. Contrast studies focus on the functioning of the GI tract, urinary tract, gallbladder and biliary system, circulatory system, cerebrospinal canal, and circulation of cerebral fluid in the brain.
- X-ray equipment includes the X-ray table, X-ray tube, and control console. The X-ray table can usually be tilted or moved from side to side. All equipment, unless portable, is housed in a lead-lined room for safety.

- Excessive exposure to radiation can cause harmful biological changes, including cell and tissue destruction. Harmful effects may include temporary or permanent damage to skin, eyes, thyroid, blood-forming and reproductive organs, and germ cells.
- The patient must be protected at all times. All females of childbearing age must be asked if they may be pregnant. According to the "ten-Day Rule," radiographs should be taken in the ten days following the onset of menses.
- Shields are used to protect both patient and worker against radiation. Full aprons, half aprons, gonadal shields, and eye and thyroid shields protect specific parts of the body; lead gloves should always be worn when there is a possibility of radiation exposure to the hands. A radiation detection badge must be worn at all times.
- Limited-scope radiology such as simple X-rays may be performed in the physician's office. Typical X-rays include the upper and lower extremities, chest, and some skull films. Depending on state statutes defining practice acts, medical assistants may be able to expose and develop film after preparing the patient for the procedure. Current licensure from AART is also recommended.
- Diagnostic modalities include venous studies; trauma procedures; head, neck, and spinal studies; bone and joint studies;

Chapter Summary (continued)

chest, abdomen, and pelvic studies; KUB (kidneys, ureters, and bladder) and urinary system studies; surgical procedures; and myelography. Contrast media include air, oxygen, carbon dioxide, barium sulfate, and organic iodine.

■ Before administering any contrast media, medication history and information about allergies must be obtained. Iodine can cause serious allergic reactions. Certain medications such as beta-blockers, calcium channel blockers, and metformin (Glucophage®) may cause potentially lethal reactions.

■ Fluoroscopy employs a screen rather than a photographic plate to obtain images. Internal organs are observed in motion. The patient's position may be changed while the physician views the movement of the organs on the screen.

■ Computer tomography (CT) is a noninvasive and nondestructive means of studying internal structures of the human body. With sequential merging of two-dimensional "slices." a 360-degree image of the body part can be viewed.

■ Magnetic resonance imaging (MRI) is similar to CT scanning in its sequential merging of "slices" into a 360-degree image. MRIs use a magnetic field to obtain the image, so the patient is not exposed to radiation. Contrast media may be used to define specific areas.

■ Sonography facilitates the viewing of internal body structures by projecting very high-frequency sound waves into the body and recording the echo passed back to the monitor. Ultrasound studies are used to determine fetal age and position and in echocardiograms to study the internal structures of the heart.

■ PET scans use radioisotopes and a computer to produce three-dimensional multicolored scans.

■ The MA may be called on to assist with patient preparation and instruction for radiography in the medical office. Documentation of film transfer may also be the MA's responsibility.

■ Scheduling X-rays with outside agencies should be done with the patient present. Insurance coverage is verified, any necessary preauthorization is obtained and charted, and verbal and written instructions are given to the patient.

■ Positioning is important in radiography. You must be familiar with the terminology of positioning and body movement.

Chapter Review Questions

Multiple Choice

1. Bone, a dense calcium-containing substance, appears on an X-ray film as a shade of
   A. light gray.
   B. white.
   C. dark gray.
   D. black.

2. Flat-plate X-rays that do not require a contrast are taken of the
   A. skull.
   B. urinary tract.
   C. gallbladder.
   D. GI tract.

3. ALARA is the acronym for
   A. as low as reasonably accurate.
   B. as long as reliably accurate.
   C. as long as reliably applied.
   D. as low as reasonably achievable.

4. Which of the following is a more serious reaction to a contrast medium?
   A. itching
   B. pallor
   C. pulse changes
   D. headache

5. Which of the following medical imaging is done while the structure is functioning?
   A. CT scan
   B. fluoroscopy
   C. MRI
   D. X-ray

6. How long should a female patient wait after her menstrual period to have a mammogram?
   A. three days
   B. four days
   C. five days
   D. one week

7. The day before a lower GI series, a patient may consume
   A. clear liquids only.
   B. milk and yogurt.
   C. a light evening meal.
   D. a full evening meal.

8. Which of the following is the standard maximum time a patient or facility can check out an X-ray?
   A. 60 days
   B. 30 days
   C. 90 days
   D. 120 days

True/False

T F 1. X-rays are a form of electromagnetic radiation and can be seen with the naked eye.

T F 2. Flat-plate or plain film can be used to view KUB.

T F 3. Arthrography is an invasive examination of the blood vessels.

T F 4. CT scans specialize in smaller images, whereas MRI images are larger.

T F 5. Both CT scans and MRIs involve surrounding the patient with a circular camera.

Chapter Review Questions (continued)

Short Answer

1. Who received the first Nobel Prize in physics for discovering X-rays?

2. What is an echocardiogram?

3. Which nuclear medicine technique is used to identify Alzheimer's disease?

4. What type of radiation shield should be worn by a patient when the extremities are X-rayed? What about when the abdomen is X-rayed? The skull?

5. Generally, how long are mammograms kept as part of a patient's medical record?

Research

1. In recent years, lung cancer was a focus of media attention with the deaths of Peter Jennings and Dana Reeve. What is the survival rate of patients diagnosed with lung cancer?

2. In your state, are medical assistants allowed to perform limited radiographs? What must you do to qualify?

Externship Application Experience

As a student, you are asked to assist with a limited radiographic procedure. What are your duties and responsibilities to ensure patient safety and comfort as well as your own safety?

Resource Guide

American Board of Radiology (ABR)
5255 E. Williams Circle, Suite 3200
Tucson, AZ 85711
520-790-2900
http://theabr.org

American Registry of Radiologic Technologists (ARRT)
1255 Northland Drive
St. Paul, MN 55120-1155
651-687-0048
www.arrt.org

American Society of Radiologic Technologists
15000 Central Ave. SE
Albuquerque, NM 87123-3917
505-298-4500
www.asrt.org

MedMedia

www.prenhall.com/frazier

More on this chapter, including interactive resources, can be found on the Student CD-ROM accompanying this textbook and on the Companion Website at www.prenhall.com/frazier.

CHAPTER 17

Cardiology and Cardiac Testing

Case Study

Rachel is checking on a patient, Ray, who has come to the office for his regular appointment to follow up on his cardiac surgery. Ray mentions that he almost canceled this appointment because he thinks he may have the flu. He complains of a sudden onset of fatigue, weakness, and a fever that comes and goes. He also mentions that he has been really tired the last couple of days and has had no appetite. He even canceled a dental appointment to get a tooth abscess taken care of, which has been bothering him for a while.

MedMedia
www.prenhall.com/frazier

Additional interactive resources and activities for this chapter can be found on the Companion Website. For videos, audio glossary, legal and ethical scenarios, job scenarios, quizzes, games, virtual tours and activities related to the content of this chapter, please access the accompanying CD-ROM in this book.

 Assets Available:

Audio Glossary
Legal and Ethical Scenario: *Cardiology and Cardiac Testing*
On the Job Scenario: *Cardiology and Cardiac Testing*
Video Scenario: *The Electrocardiogram*
A&P Quiz: The Circulatory System
Multiple Choice Quiz
Games: Crossword, Strikeout and Spelling Bee
3D Virtual Tour: Cardiovascular System: Head & Neck; Cardiovascular System: Chest & Abdomen; Cardiovascular System: Arm & Shoulder; Cardiovascular System: Leg; Virtual Tour of the Heart: Heart
Drag and Drop: Circulatory System: Circulatory System; Circulatory System: Brain Blood Vessels; Circulatory System: Digestive Blood Vessels; Cardiovascular System: Anterior & Posterior of the Heart; Cardiovascular System: Interior of the Heart

Objectives

After completing this chapter, you should be able to:

- Spell and define medical terminology in this chapter.
- Discuss the role of the medical assistant in a cardiology practice.
- Describe the anatomy and physiology of the heart.
- Explain the electrical conduction system of the heart.
- Discuss coronary artery disease.
- Describe the symptoms of and treatment for angina.
- Explain the symptoms, causes, and treatments for myocardial infarction.
- Describe sudden cardiac arrest.
- Explain the symptoms, causes, diagnosis and treatment of hypertension.
- Discuss congestive heart failure.
- Discuss pulmonary edema.
- Explain the symptoms, causes, diagnosis, and treatment of cardiomyopathy.
- Discuss cardiac arrhythmias and their various classifications.
- Compare the infective heart disorders: endocarditis, myocarditis, pericarditis, and rheumatic fever and rheumatic heart disease.
- Compare the various valvular disorders.
- Compare the vascular disorders, including embolisms, arteriosclerosis, aneurysms, phlebitis, thrombophlebitis, deep-vein thrombosis, Raynaud's disease, and Buerger's disease.
- Explain the electrocardiogram and its importance in cardiology.
- Explain the Holter monitor and discuss its importance in cardiology.
- Discuss stress testing and its function in cardiology.
- Explain the echocardiogram and its importance in cardiology.
- Explain the thallium scan.
- Describe a MUGA scan.
- Identify important arrhythmias.
- Discuss the importance of consent for procedures.

✚ MEDICAL ASSISTING COMPETENCIES

CAAHEP ENTRY-LEVEL COMPETENCIES FOR CMA	ABHES ENTRY-LEVEL COMPETENCIES FOR RMA
■ Perform electrocardiography. ■ Perform telephone and in-person screening. ■ Obtain vital signs. ■ Obtain and record patient history. ■ Prepare and maintain examination and treatment areas. ■ Prepare patient for and assist with routine and specialty examinations. ■ Prepare patient for and assist with procedures, treatments, and minor office surgeries. ■ Screen and follow up test results.	■ Interview and record patient history. ■ Prepare patients for procedures. ■ Apply principles of aseptic techniques and infection control. ■ Take vital signs. ■ Recognize emergencies. ■ Perform first aid and CPR. ■ Prepare and maintain examination and treatment area. ■ Prepare patient for and assist physician with routine and specialty examinations and treatments and minor office surgeries. ■ Use quality control. ■ Collect and process specimens. ■ Screen and follow up patient test results. ■ Prepare and administer oral and parenteral medications as directed by physician. ■ Maintain medication and immunization records. ■ Dispose of biohazardous materials. ■ Practice Standard Precautions. ■ Perform electrocardiograms. ■ Perform respiratory testing. ■ Perform telephone and in-person screening.

Introduction

The medical assistant in a cardiology office encounters many types of heart disease. A significant complaint is chest pain. Patients who complain of irregular heartbeats, shortness of breath (SOB), tissue swelling (edema), and exhaustion or fatigue are also treated on a regular basis. Complaints of nausea, excessive sweating, and denial of possible heart attack are serious symptoms that demand immediate intervention.

A variety of diagnostic tests are used in a cardiology office to identify possible cardiac disorders. An ECG measures the electrical activity of the myocardium (heart muscle). A Holter monitor 24-hour test is ordered if an electrocardiogram does not show significant findings and the patient is having persistent symptoms. An echocardiogram provides a visual concept of the heart structures coordinated with the conduction system and the contractility of the myocardium. Other diagnostic tests include stress tests, thallium scans, and MUGA scans.

Patients who have experienced a myocardial infarct, with subsequent cardiac arrest and resuscitation with CPR and/or automatic defibrillation are sometimes given follow-up care in the medical office, as are some patients who have had coronary artery bypass surgery. Patients with congestive heart failure, pulmonary edema, hypertension, arrhythmias, cardiomyopathy, cardiomegaly, vascular disorders, valve disorders, and inflammatory or infectious conditions are also treated in the cardiology office. Cardiologists perform cardiac catheterizations, angioplasty, and stent insertions in the hospital setting.

Medical Terminology

amplitude—abundance, amount, extent, fullness, or size

aneurysm—weakening and dilation of an artery

angina—left-sided chest pain brought on by exertion

angioplasty—procedure in which a balloon on the distal aspect of a cardiac catheter is inflated to compress plaque against coronary artery walls, increasing the lumen of the artery

anterior—toward the front

apex—pointed end of the ventricles

arrhythmia—absence of rhythm

arteriosclerosis—arterial hardening caused by the buildup of atherosclerotic plaque

artifact—appearance of electrical activity or waveforms from sources outside the heart

asystole—absence of cardiac activity; cardiac standstill, without systole

atherosclerosis—buildup of plaque in the arteries over a period of years

atrium (plural: atria)—right or left upper chamber of the heart

augmented lead—unipolar lead, one positive electrode; has very low voltage and must therefore be augmented by the electrocardiograph to equal the voltage of the other leads

automaticity—ability of the heart to initiate and maintain rhythmic activity without the nervous system

bradycardia—heart rate below 60 beats per minute (BPM)

cardiac catheterization—diagnostic procedure in which a catheter is threaded through a major artery back to the heart through the aorta; catheter may be threaded into the left ventricle or into the coronary arteries

cardiomegaly—enlarged heart

cardiomyopathy—diseases of the myocardium

conduction system—wiring and paths that initiate and maintain rhythmic contraction of the myocardium

conductivity—ability of a cardiac cell to transfer impulses to the next cell, allowing all areas of the heart (myocardium) to depolarize at one time

contractility—ability of the heart muscle to shorten or reduce in size

Medical Terminology *(continued)*

coronary artery bypass—surgery in which the ischemia or obstruction in the coronary arteries is bypassed with a graft of a vessel

coronary artery disease—condition in which the coronary arteries are narrowed by constriction caused by plaque buildup

depolarization—condition in which the cardiac cell environment becomes positive

diastole—period of ventricular relaxation

dysrhythmia—abnormal, irregular, or disturbed heart rhythm

ejection fraction—measurement of the fraction of the total amount (volume) of blood filling the ventricle that is ejected during the ventricular contraction

embolism—condition in which an embolus that is moving through the vascular system becomes lodged in a vessel

embolus (plural: emboli)—mass of material or tissue in a vessel; may be a blood clot, air, fat, bone fragments, bacterial clumps, amniotic fluid, or other materials

endocarditis—inflammation of the endocardium

excitability—response of cardiac cell to electrical stimulus

fibrillation—irregular contractions of the heart; ECG shows waveforms without definite pattern or shape. Atrial fibrillation: Atria are quivering and do not have a forceful beat to push blood into ventricles. Ventricular fibrillation: lethal arrhythmia; ventricles are quivering and do not contract with force to push blood into aorta.

Rhythm is chaotic, with no recognizable P waves, QRS complexes, or T waves; without immediate intervention and conversion of rhythm, asystole will follow.

focus (plural: foci)—specific site; the origin of an electrical cardiac impulse

hemoptysis—coughing up blood from the respiratory tract

interatrial septum—wall between the right and left atria

internodal pathway—the three tracts that carry the electrical impulse as it leaves the SA node, transmit the impulse to the AV node, and distribute it throughout the atria; the three divisions are the anterior, middle, and posterior divisions

interventriclular septum—wall between the right and left ventricles

isoelectric line—flat, horizontal line on an ECG strip representing the beginning and ending point of all waves of the ECG cycle

mitral valve prolapse—valvular disorder in which cusps of mitral valve prolapse into right atrium, failing to close and resulting in back pressure into left atrium

multifocal—originating from more than one area or focus

myocardial infarction—death of myocardial tissue due to obstructed blood supply to the tissue

myocarditis—inflammation of the myocardium

palpitations—irregular and often erratic heartbeats felt by the patient

pericarditis—inflammation of the pericardium

precordial lead—ECG lead that views the heart in a horizontal plain

premature ventricular contraction (PVC)—a beat that comes early in the cardiac cycle, is not preceded by a P wave, and has a widened and distorted QRS complex; sometimes referred to as premature ventricular complex or premature ventricular beat (PVB)

repolarization—return of the cardiac cell to the resting state

sinoatrial (SA) node—pacemaker of the heart

stenosis—narrowing or constriction of a passage

stent—device implanted in a vessel to maintain its patency (openness)

systole—contraction of the myocardium

tachycardia—heart rate above 100 beats per minute (BPM)

thromboembolism—obstruction of a blood vessel by a thrombus

thrombosis—condition of having a blood clot in a blood vessel

thrombus (plural: thrombi)—blood clot in the vessel that can form an obstruction in the vessel

unifocal—originating from same area or focus

ventricle—right or left lower chamber of heart

Abbreviations

ABG—arterial blood gases

A-fib—atrial fibrillation

AV—atrioventricular node

BBB—bundle branch block

CAB—coronary artery bypass

CABG—coronary artery bypass graft

CAD—coronary artery disease

CHF—congestive heart failure

DVT—deep-vein thrombosis

ECG/EKG—electrocardiogram

EF—ejection fraction

MI—myocardial infarction

MVP—mitral valve prolapse

NSR—normal sinus rhythm

PR—P-R interval in the complex

PVC—premature ventricular contraction

QRS—QRS interval or waveform in the complex

SA—sinoatrial

ST—S-T interval or waveform in the complex

V-fib—ventricular fibrillation

V-tach—ventricular tachycardia

The Medical Assistant's Role in Cardiology

Diagnostic procedures in cardiology include blood testing and various electronic assessments of the cardiovascular system, such as electrocardiograms (ECG or EKG), echocardiograms, the Holter monitor, stress testing, thallium scans, and MUGA scans. A newer procedure involves a three-dimensional view of the coronary arteries by MRI. Many offices now assess cardiac functioning by evaluating the oxygenation of the blood with a pulse oximeter (∞ discussed in Chapter 18 on respiratory testing). Medical assistants are trained to perform ECGs and in some offices may be responsible for Holter monitor application. With specialized training, they may assist in advanced procedures.

As a medical assistant, you will routinely perform ECGs, especially in a cardiology office. It is therefore important that you understand not only the anatomy and physiology of the heart, including the electrical conduction system, but the interpretation of rhythm strips as well.

You will be responsible for having the patient gowned and properly draped for a cardiac examination. The room temperature should be at a comfortable level and privacy should be afforded to the patient and the physician or any technicians. An electrocardiograph may need to be moved into the room and calibrated. The physician may select his or her personal stethoscope to assess heart tones or may expect one to be available. Supplies for the ECG, including leads, sensors, and paper, should be readily available in the room or in the ECG cart. If office protocol includes an O₂ saturation, this is obtained with the pulse oximeter and recorded for the physician to note. All necessary supplies should be available in the room so that you do not have to leave during the procedure.

COMPETENCY SKILLS PERFORMANCE

1. Perform an electrocardiogram.
2. Demonstrate the application of a Holter monitor.

Anatomy and Physiology of the Heart

The heart is a muscle that pumps the blood throughout the body (Figure 17-1 ◆). Deoxygenated blood enters the right **atrium,** the upper right chamber of the heart, through two large veins, the *inferior* and *superior vena cava.* The blood passes through the tricuspid valve into the right **ventricle,** the lower right chamber of the heart, then through the pulmonary valve into the pulmonary arteries. The pulmonary arteries transport the oxygen-poor blood to the lungs, where a gas exchange takes place by way of the pulmonary alveolar-capillary network. In the alveoli, oxygen is transferred to the blood and carbon dioxide is removed, to be exhaled through the lungs. The oxygen-rich blood then returns through the pulmonary veins to the left atrium, or left upper chamber of the heart. From there the blood is pumped through the bicuspid or mitral valve into the left ventricle, or left lower chamber of the heart. The blood then passes through the aortic valve into the aorta to be transported to the coronary arteries of the heart, the carotid arteries of the head, and other major arteries of the circulatory system. Blood then returns to the right atrium via the superior and inferior vena cava.

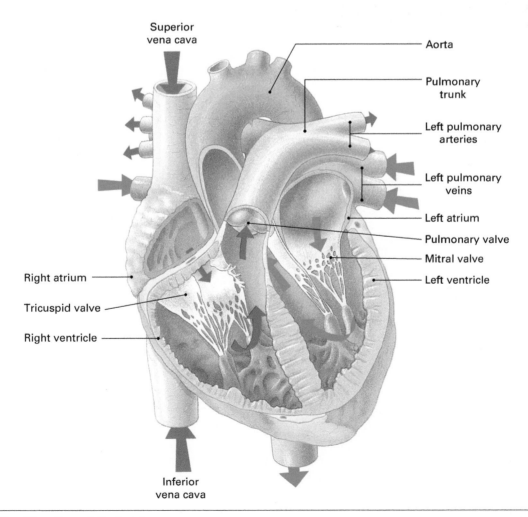

Figure 17-1 ◆ Blood flow through the heart

Caduceus Chronicle
ARTERIES AND VEINS

Historically, arteries have commonly been described as carrying oxygenated blood, and veins as carrying deoxygenated blood. Although this is largely true, the pulmonary arteries and veins do not follow this definition. The pulmonary arteries carry deoxygenated blood to the lungs, where it is oxygenated and reenters the heart through the pulmonary veins.

From outside to inside, the heart consists of three layers (Figure 17-2 ◆):

- Pericardium
- Myocardium
- Endocardium

The myocardium of this two-sided pump contains contractile filaments in each cardiac muscle cell. When the contractile filaments are stimulated by the conduction system, the healthy heart muscle contracts and relaxes 60 to 100 times a minute. Blood flow from the heart is generated by the physical contraction of the myocardial tissue.

Keys to Success
HEART VALVES

Here's a memory aid to help you remember which side of the heart the tricuspid and bicuspid (mitral) valves are on. The right lung has three lobes. The valve between the right atrium and right ventricle has three cusps and is called the tricuspid valve. The left lung has two lobes. The valve between the left atrium and left ventricle has two cusps and is known as the bicuspid (mitral) valve.

Heart Conduction

An electrical **conduction system** within the myocardium regulates the pumping action of the heart. The pacemaker cells, specialized cellular units of the cardiac conduction system, control the rate and rhythm of the heart and are also responsible for the generation and conduction of the electrical impulses that cause the myocardium to contract. Cardiac muscle cells have the unique characteristics of **excitability, conductivity, contractility,** and **automaticity.** In addition, neurological stimulation of cardiac muscle cells, and the resulting mechanical cardiac function, are affected by abnormally high or low electrolyte levels.

Electrolyte imbalance influences both mechanical and electrical cardiac functions. Potassium, sodium, calcium, and magnesium affect the cardiac cycle. When the cardiac cell is at rest, the concentration of potassium is greater inside the cell than outside the cell wall, while the concentration of sodium is greater outside the cell wall. Using the sodium–potassium exchange pump process, sodium and potassium ions are moved in and out through the cell wall. Venous blood samples measure extracellular amounts of electrolytes.

Cardiac **depolarization** and **repolarization** occur when a conduction impulse develops and spreads through the myocardium. Depolarization occurs as sodium ions rush into the myocardial cell and calcium slowly enters the cell; potassium exits the cell, resulting in the contraction of the cell. This process is followed by potassium returning to the cell and sodium exiting the cell. Repolarization, which is slower than depolarization, returns the cell to a recovered state. The next step in the progression of cardiac muscle cell activity is a refractory or total relaxation of the myocardial cell. After this period of rest, the myocardial cell is ready for the cycle to continue.

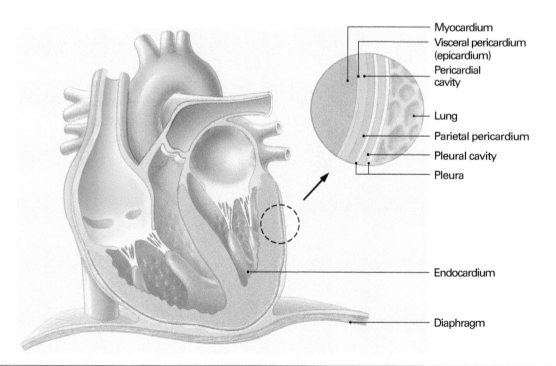

Myocardium
Visceral pericardium (epicardium)
Pericardial cavity
Lung
Parietal pericardium
Pleural cavity
Pleura
Endocardium
Diaphragm

Figure 17-2 ◆ Layers of the heart

The conduction system originates in the **sinoatrial (SA) node,** also known as the pacemaker (Figure 17-3 ◆). The SA node initiates the impulse. When it fails to do so, lower pacemaker cells can initiate the conduction as a "survival" effort. The impulse travels the **internodal pathway** through the right atrium to the atrioventricular **(AV)** node and through Bachmann's bundle in the **interatrial septum** to the left atrium. The impulse then travels through the bundle of His (AV bundle) to the right and left branches of the bundle of His, the **interventricular septum,** and then on to the Purkinje fibers in the ventricular myocardium. As the impulse travels through the conduction system, depolarization and repolarization take place, resulting in the contraction, or **systole,** and relaxation, or **diastole,** of the myocardium. The atrial stimulation causes the initial contraction of myocardial cells of the atria, allowing blood from the atria to be pumped into the ventricles. The sequential stimulation of the ventricular myocardium then causes the ventricles to contract, sending the blood into the pulmonary and general circulation of the body.

Diseases and Disorders of the Heart

Coronary Artery Disease

Coronary artery disease (CAD) is the result of plaque buildup, or **atherosclerosis,** in the arteries over a period of years. The plaque causes the arteries to harden, a condition called **arteriosclerosis,** and to become weak in some areas and thick in others. The arteries become narrow or are partially obstructed, and blood flow to the surrounding tissue is reduced. Consequently, oxygen and nutrition to the tissue are also reduced (ischemia), causing cramping of the myocardium and discomfort in the form of pain. If the condition is severe enough, complete obstruction and an infarction of the myocardial tissue result. Depending on the size of the infarction, the damage may affect a small area or may be catastrophic enough to cause sudden death.

Symptoms of CAD include angina-type pain, shortness of breath, weakness or dizziness, rapid heartbeat, **palpitations,** nausea, and perspiration.

Coronary artery disease may result in two forms of "heart attack":

- Myocardial ischemia: This type of "heart attack" is the result of reduced blood flow to the myocardium, which causes angina-type pain. It may be reversed if circulation is restored to the tissue within the six-hour time frame before tissue death, or infarction, results.
- Sudden cardiac death: The second type of "heart attack" occurs when the conduction system suffers an insult. In addition to **arrhythmias** caused by coronary artery obstruction, lethal arrhythmias may be caused by electrocution, trauma, and drug overdose. Sudden cardiac death may also be the result of respiratory arrest, drowning, or massive hemorrhage. (See *Myocardial Infarction, Arrhythmias,* and *Sudden Cardiac Death* below for additional information.)

Risk factors for coronary artery disease are classified as nonmodifiable and modifiable. The risk factors over which the individual has no control include a family history of heart disease at an early age, male gender, postmenopausal female, age over 45 years. Risk factors that can be reduced by the individual include smoking, high blood cholesterol levels, hypertension, blood glucose levels, lack of exercise, excess weight, and stress.

Angina

The patient experiencing **angina** will complain of pressure-like pain, usually in the chest region, possibly radiating down the left arm, to the left jaw, and to the right chest and arm. This discomfort is generally experienced on exertion and ceases

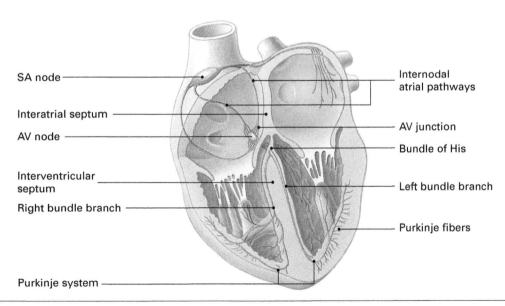

SA node

Interatrial septum

AV node

Interventricular septum

Right bundle branch

Purkinje system

Internodal atrial pathways

AV junction

Bundle of His

Left bundle branch

Purkinje fibers

Figure 17-3 ◆ Cardiac conduction system

after a few minutes of rest. Until it is confirmed that the pain is angina, the patient is considered to be in an emergent state with possible impending MI. Immediate assessment and intervention are essential. When such a patient presents in the office, the physician is notified and assessment is begun immediately (∞ refer to the section on triage in Chapter 23). If the patient calls from home, he or she is usually instructed to call 911 or to be transported to an emergency facility with cardiac resuscitation capabilities. Once the pain has been established as anginal, intervention may be in the form of a vasodilator such as nitroglycerin (Nitro-stat) or a calcium-channel blocker such as verapamil (Calan, Isoptin), diltiazem (Cardizem), or nifedipine (Procardia). Modifications in lifestyle, including diet, activity, and stress relief, are helpful in the course of treatment.

Myocardial Infarction

Myocardial infarction (**MI**) results when an obstruction to the myocardial tissue is followed by ischemia over a period of approximately six hours. The ischemia may be caused by plaque buildup in the arteries, spasm of the arteries, or a **thrombus** that has broken loose from an arterial wall or has formed and moved from the left atrium or ventricle. Intervention with **angioplasty, stent** insertion, or coronary artery bypass surgery may prevent permanent damage.

Post-Myocardial Infarction

Post-MI patients are seen in the office for follow-up care or possible referral to a cardiovascular surgeon. As with all cardiac patients, ECGs, vital signs, oxygen saturation levels, and body weight are important components of the office visit. Diagnostic procedures may be ordered and any previous diagnostic results may be discussed. Patient signs are assessed and symptoms or complaints are recorded. The physician reviews the chart and listens to (auscultates) the heart and breath sounds. The feet and legs are examined for edema and detection of pedal pulses. The color, temperature, and moistness of the skin are noted. (Examples: Skin warm, pink, and dry, or skin pale and dusky, cool and slightly moist.) Pulse oximeter readings are recorded. The patient is scheduled for follow-up appointments and rehabilitation is discussed and scheduled. It is important to realize there may be a psychological factor involved for the post-CAB patient, whose heart has been stopped and restarted during the procedure.

Sudden Cardiac Arrest

Sudden cardiac arrest occurs when the conduction system of the myocardium sustains a massive insult. This can be the result of ischemia in the area of essential cardiac conduction path, a lethal arrhythmia that causes cardiac standstill, electrocution, major trauma to the chest and heart, massive hemorrhage, or drug overdose. Respiratory arrest and drowning may also lead to sudden cardiac death. Immediate intervention with CPR and automated external defibrillator (AED) may successfully resuscitate the victim. (∞ Refer to Chapter 23 for additional information on CPR and AED.)

Hypertension/Hypertensive Heart Disease

Hypertension is often referred to as "high blood pressure." It is also called "the silent killer" because so many people who have hypertension are unaware of it. The blood pressure range accepted as normal by the American Heart Association is less than 120 systolic and less than 80 diastolic. A reading of 120–139 systolic and 80–89 diastolic is considered prehypertension. For a diagnosis of hypertension to be made, blood pressure readings over a period of time must be persistently elevated. Many patients experience what has been called "white coat syndrome"—a high initial blood pressure in the medical office due to the patient's anxiety. For this reason, many physicians prefer to have a second blood pressure reading taken close to the end of the visit, before any procedures or before the patient is dismissed.

An elevated blood pressure makes the heart work harder to pump blood through constricted vessels. The constriction may be caused by arteriosclerosis, atherosclerosis, or renal disease. Stress is considered a factor in hypertension, as is being overweight (Table 17-1).

Essential hypertension results when a prolonged state of elevated blood pressure develops without apparent cause. With an insidious onset, it is possible for the disease process to be in an advanced state by the time it is diagnosed, as many individuals are asymptomatic. The condition may go undetected until a blood pressure reading is elevated. Symptoms include light-headedness, headaches, dizziness, syncope, tinnitus, nosebleeds, palpitations, and malaise. Malignant hypertension may follow essential hypertension, with extreme stress often being the precipitating factor.

There is no cure for essential hypertension. Treatment is lifelong and involves decreasing the heart's workload and dilating the vascular system. The first line of defense and treatment is the modification of risk factors. Dietary changes to reduce salt and fat intake are helpful in controlling hypertension. Cessation of smoking, increased activity and exercise, weight reduction, and stress reduction are also helpful. If these lifestyle modifications do not help, drug therapy is prescribed. Drugs for hypertension include diuretics, vasodilating drugs, ACE inhibitors, and beta-blocking drugs.

Congestive Heart Failure

The patient with congestive heart failure (**CHF**) complains of shortness of breath, weight gain, swelling (edema), and possibly exhaustion. He or she will exhibit fluid retention, possibly with swollen feet and hands and facial puffiness, and may report

TABLE 17-1 RISK FACTORS IN HYPERTENSION	
Nonmodifiable Risk Factors	**Modifiable Risk Factors**
Family history of hypertensive disease Being of African American descent Older age Diabetes Kidney disease	Chronic stress Obesity Diet high in salt and fat Oral contraceptives Sedentary lifestyle Smoking

difficulty putting on shoes and rings. These symptoms usually have an insidious onset; the dyspnea gradually increases to a severe state. Other signs include distended neck veins, respiratory distress, and pitting edema of the legs, ankles, and feet. Radiographs of the chest are taken to assess the size of the heart and are compared with previous films to measure the progression of enlargement.

Treatment of CHF includes drug therapy to reduce the workload of the heart. Additional drugs such as cardiac glycosides and digitalis preparations (Lanoxin) slow and strengthen the heartbeat, making it more efficient. Diuretics reduce blood volume and decrease the fluid in the tissues. Vasodilators reduce vascular pressure. Fluid and sodium intake is restricted. Daily weight and apical pulse assessments are also part of the treatment.

Pulmonary Edema

Pulmonary edema follows CHF as the lungs fill with interstitial fluid and pressure builds in the lung tissue, increasing the workload of the heart. Left-sided heart failure, mitral valve disorders, hypertension, renal failure, and cardiac arrhythmias may also cause pulmonary edema. The patient experiences shortness of breath, dyspnea, and coughing. Bloody, frothy sputum may be present. The symptoms often worsen at night after the patient has gone to bed and is in a reclining position.

Treatment is aimed at decreasing the fluid levels in the lung tissue, with subsequent reduction of cardiac workload. Drug therapy includes diuretics, Lanoxin, vasodilators, and bronchodilating drugs. Most patients require aggressive treatment in a hospital environment.

Cardiomyopathy

Cardiomyopathy, a noninflammatory disease of the myocardium, often has no identifiable cause. The muscle thickens, possibly as a result of hypertension and increased workload, and its ability to pump blood is affected.

In *dilated cardiomyopathy,* as the workload of the myocardium increases, the heart muscle fibers are stretched, the chambers are dilated, and the walls become weaker and thinner. The heart compensates and the chambers enlarge and stretch more, a condition called **cardiomegaly.** The thinning walls of the heart can no longer keep up with the circulatory demands of the body. Symptoms may be insidious or may appear fairly rapidly. They are similar to those of CHF, including fatigue, weakness, shortness of breath, edema of the legs and feet, and

respiratory congestion. Diuretics are prescribed to decrease fluid volume and thus reduce the workload of the heart. Digitalis helps to strengthen and slow the heartbeat. Vasodilators help to reduce the workload by reducing the resistance of constricted vessels. If arrhythmias occur, they are controlled with antiarrhythmic drugs, including beta-blockers and calcium-channel blockers. When drug therapy is no longer effective, a heart transplant is the only solution.

Another form of cardiomyopathy is termed *hypertrophic cardiomyopathy.* The fibers of the myocardium exhibit abnormal growth and arrangement and the wall of the heart thickens, mostly in the left ventricle. As the wall thickens, it loses the ability to contract and relax completely. Blood flow diminishes, causing a breathless feeling. The patient experiences fainting, or syncope, as the brain receives inadequate blood supply. Chaotic heartbeats may occur, occasionally resulting in sudden cardiac death. Hypertrophic cardiomyopathy is often diagnosed in young asymptomatic males when exertion from exercise causes the symptoms and an awareness of the condition.

Echocardiograms and auscultation of heart sounds aid in the diagnosis of this condition. The treatment objective is to prevent lethal arrhythmias. Antiarrhythmic drugs and diuretics are usually prescribed, and exercise is limited in some cases.

Arrhythmias

Arrhythmias may be classified in different ways: by disturbance of impulse formation or origin, by disturbance of conduction, by consistency of the point of origin, and by prognosis.

The heart is autorhythmic—it initiates the impulse. This impulse normally originates in the SA node and travels through the atrium to the AV node, down the septal wall by way of the bundles of His to the Purkinje fibers. Various conditions may cause the impulse not to originate in the SA node or cause interruptions in the pathway of the impulse through the heart. Areas of ischemic or infarcted tissue block the pathway of the impulse.

Arrhythmias Resulting from Impulse Formation or Origin

The SA node normally generates rhythmic impulses at the rate of 60 to 100 per minute. When the impulse originates in the atrium at a normal rate and travels the normal pathway through the conduction system, it is called a normal sinus rhythm (**NSR**). Common cardiac arrhythmias resulting from impulse formation are categorized by the point of origin (Table 17-2).

Arrhythmias Resulting from Conduction Disturbances

Conduction disturbances refer to abnormal delays or blocks in the conduction of the cardiac impulse from the SA node through the AV node, the bundle of His, and the Purkinje fibers. Common cardiac arrhythmias resulting from conduction disturbances are listed in Table 17-3. Blocking of the impulse results in first-degree, second-degree, Mobitz second-degree, and third-degree heart blocks. Drugs and chemicals can also cause irregular impulses. Impulses may

TABLE 17-2 TYPES AND EXAMPLES OF ARRHYTHMIAS RESULTING FROM IMPULSE FORMATION

Sinoatrial Arrhythmias	Atrial Arrhythmias	AV Nodal (Junctional) Arrhythmias	Ventricular Arrhythmias
Sinus **tachycardia** Sinus **bradycardia** Sinus arrhythmia Wandering pacemaker Sinoatrial arrest	Premature atrial contraction Paroxysmal atrial tachycardia Atrial flutter Atrial **fibrillation** Atrial standstill	Premature junctional contractions Paroxysmal junctional tachycardia Nonparoxysmal junctional tachycardia	Premature ventricular contractions Ventricular tachycardia Ventricular fibrillation

TABLE 17-3 CLASSIFICATION OF ARRHYTHMIAS RESULTING FROM CONDUCTION DISTURBANCES

General Location	Sinus or atrial	Atrioventricular Node	Ventricular
Type and Name of Arrhythmia	Sinoatrial block	First-degree AV block Second-degree AV block Mobitz, Type I Mobitz, Type II Third-degree (complete) AV block	Bundle-branch blocks, right or left Bilateral bundle-branch blocks Ventricular standstill

originate in other areas of the myocardium and are often identified relative to this point of origin.

Arrythmias Classified According to Consistency of Point of Origin

Another origin categorization relates to the consistency of the point of origin. **Unifocal** impulses have the same point of origin, while **multifocal** rhythms have various points of origin. Multifocal rhythms are potentially life-threatening and are identified on an ECG. Additionally, the SA node may not fire every time, causing a delayed complex or interval.

Atrial rhythms have their origin in the atria. Sinus rhythms originate in the SA node, nodal rhythms in the area of the AV node, and ventricular rhythms in the ventricles.

Arrhythmias Classified According to Prognosis

Another method of general classification is by the degree of seriousness of the arrhythmia or the prognosis of the condition (Table 17-4). This group includes minor arrhythmias that usually do not lead to more serious arrhythmias and do not affect the circulation. Major arrhythmias may lead to the onset of lethal arrhythmias and often have serious effects on the circulation. Death-producing arrhythmias require immediate and aggressive intervention.

As a medical assistant, you are expected to recognize potentially lethal rhythms when performing an ECG or if the patient is on a cardiac monitor. If these rhythms appear, immediate assistance is required and must be requested. The physician must be notified immediately so that aggressive intervention may be instituted.

Treatment

Once arrhythmia is diagnosed, antiarrhythmic drugs are prescribed. The patient is assessed frequently during the first few months until the heart rhythms return to near-normal status or the patient is asymptomatic. The drugs do not cure the

Caduceus Chronicle
EINTHOVEN'S TRIANGLE

Willem Einthoven (1860–1927) introduced the concept that, when properly applied, leads I, II, and III have a relationship in which they form a triangle over the body. Limb leads are placed on the right and left arms and the left leg, forming a triangle, called Einthoven's triangle (Figure 17-4 ◆). Einthoven's Law states the following equation: lead I + lead III = lead II. The height and depth of the recordings in lead I added to those of lead III are equal to the height and depth of lead II. When the P wave is positive in lead II, it should be negative in leads I and III. Also, the height of the QRS wave in lead I plus the height of the QRS in lead III is equal to the height of the QRS wave in lead II.

underlying cause of the arrhythmias but are used to control them. Patients with potentially life-threatening arrhythmias may require implants of cardiac pacemakers or internal automatic

TABLE 17-4 CLASSIFICATION OF ARRHYTHMIAS ACCORDING TO PROGNOSIS

Type of Arrhythmia	Examples
Minor Arrhythmias	Sinus bradycardia Sinus tachycardia Wandering pacemaker Premature atrial contractions Premature junctional contractions
Major Arrhythmias	Sinus bradycardia consistently <50 BPM Sinus tachycardia consistently >100 BPM Sinoatrial arrest Sinoatrial block Atrial tachycardia Atrial flutter Atrial fibrillation Paroxysmal junctional tachycardia Premature ventricular contractions >6 BPM or in pairs Ventricular tachycardia First-, second-, and third-degree heart block Bundle-branch block
Lethal Arrhythmias	Ventricular fibrillation Ventricular standstill

The inability of the valve leaflets to close completely results in a murmur that may be detected during auscultation of heart sounds. Depending on the extent of the condition, the individual displays sudden onset of a febrile illness with symptoms that include chills, intermittent fever, weakness, anorexia, and fatigue. In addition, thrombi may form on the valves or chordae tendineae and eventually break loose, becoming emboli. These emboli not only have the potential for occluding a vessel but may also carry the infection to other parts of the body.

Sources of the invading bacterium may be a respiratory infection, tooth abscess, urinary tract infection, or skin infection. Individuals with a history of rheumatic fever, valvular difficulties, cardiac surgery, and extensive orthopedic surgeries are at risk for this type of infection. Therefore, prior to any dental procedure, prophylactic antibiotics are administered. Treatment involves aggressive therapy with antibiotics.

?—Critical Thinking Question 17-1–

Knowing that Ray has a history of cardiac surgery and is planning to have dental surgery, what should Rachel's response to his presenting symptoms be?

Myocarditis

Myocarditis is an inflammation of the cardiac muscle caused by a virus, bacteria, or parasite. Vague symptoms, including mild fever, dyspnea, shortness of breath, palpitations, fatigue, and tachycardia are exhibited. Blood studies indicate an elevated WBC, increased ESR, and elevated cardiac enzymes. A chest x-ray shows left-sided cardiac enlargement, and the ECG is abnormal. Treatment includes antibiotics for infection and medication to control arrhythmias.

Pericarditis

Pericarditis is an inflammation of the pericardium, the outer surface or sac covering of the heart. The pericardial space between the pericardium and the myocardium normally contains a small amount of lubricating pericardial fluid that allows the myocardium to move within the sac during heartbeats. Pericarditis results from infection, inflammation, or other conditions in the body. Signs and symptoms include fever, chills, chest pain, dyspnea, and malaise. A friction rub may be heard during auscultation. Elevated WBC and ESR and echocardiogram abnormalities help confirm the diagnosis. Treatment includes pain relief and addressing the underlying cause.

Rheumatic Fever and Rheumatic Heart Disease

Rheumatic fever and the resulting rheumatic heart disease follow a sore throat caused by Group A beta-hemolytic *Streptococcus*. The endocardium and valves become inflamed. The bacteria settle on the valves and grow into vegetations that scar the endocardial tissue. This scarring leads to valvular insufficiency and/or stenosis.

A history of recent upper respiratory infection, sore throat, and fever followed by inflamed, painful joints leads to suspicion of strep infection. Patients have an elevated temperature and complain of joint pain and swelling, especially in the

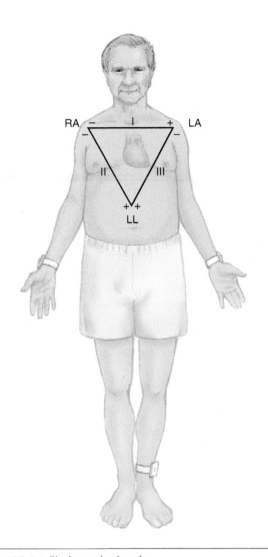

Figure 17-4 ◆ Einthoven's triangle

defibrillators. Some cardiology offices assist pacemaker clinics in the monitoring and control of these devices.

Infective Heart Disorders

Infective and inflammatory disorders of the heart include endocarditis, myocarditis, pericarditis, and rheumatic heart disease resulting from rheumatic fever. The causative agents of these disorders may be bacterial, viral, fungal, or parasitic. These cardiomyopathies often lead to cardiomegaly and heart failure and require aggressive treatment, including IV antibiotics and cardiac and oxygen saturation monitoring.

Endocarditis

Endocarditis, an inflammation of the lining of the heart chambers and valve surfaces, is usually the result of a bacterial infection. Pyogenic bacteria such as *Staphylococci* and *Streptococci* are often the source; viruses and trauma are other possible sources. The majority of these infections occur in the left side of the heart. Valvular involvement results in surface defects on the valves, followed by scarring and stiffness. **Stenosis** is the narrowing or constriction of a passage.

fingers, knees, and ankle joints. They may also experience weight loss, loss of appetite, malaise, weakness, and a rash on the trunk. Often a cardiac murmur is heard. Diagnosis is confirmed by taking a culture.

Prevention is the best strategy. To prevent rheumatic fever, a Rapid Strep test should be performed on children with sore throats. If the causative agent is Group A beta-hemolytic *Streptococcus,* an intense regimen of antibiotic therapy is instituted. Bed rest is helpful, along with analgesics for the pain and antipyretics for the fever.

Valvular Disorders

The heart has four valves: the tricuspid, pulmonary, mitral or bicuspid, and aortic (Figure 17-5 ◆). Any of the valves may be affected by disease or disorder. When a valve fails to close completely, it is termed *insufficient.* Blood flows back into the previous chamber, creating a back pressure on that chamber. When the valve fails to open completely because of a constriction, the condition is called stenosis. As the blood slows in the narrowed or "hardened" valve, a back-pressure is also created in the previous chamber. Heart murmur may be detected in the presence of these valvular conditions. Diagnosis may be made with the aid of ECG, echocardiogram, radiograms of the chest, and cardiac catheterization.

The mitral valve is the valve most often affected. The bacteria responsible for rheumatic heart disease migrate to the mitral valve and vegetations develop, scarring the valve cusps and preventing the valve from either completely closing or completely opening. Patients experience symptoms similar to those of many heart disorders, including dyspnea, shortness of breath, and occasionally cyanosis. Patients with mitral stenosis may experience **hemoptysis.**

Treatment of valvular conditions includes reduction of the workload of the heart with bed rest and fluid restriction or administration of diuretics. Oxygen therapy is helpful in some cases. Antibiotics are often prescribed to slow or halt any infectious process. In mitral stenosis, a surgical procedure, commissurotomy, may be performed to free up the cusps and allow the blood to flow through more easily. Valve replacement may be required in severe cases.

Table 17-5 describes common valvular disorders.

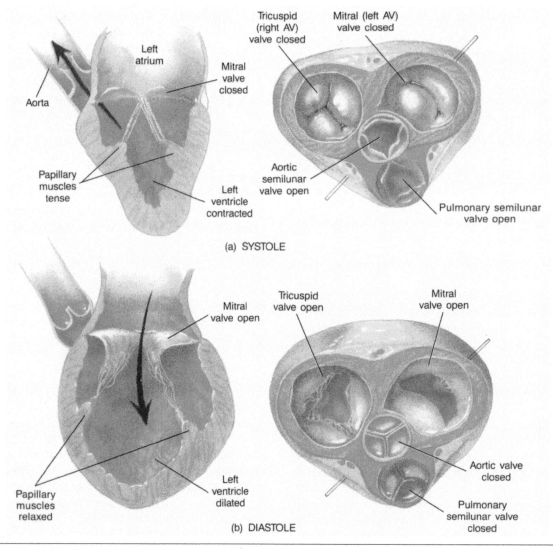

(a) SYSTOLE

(b) DIASTOLE

Figure 17-5 ◆ Valves of the heart

TABLE 17-5 VALVULAR DISORDERS

Valvular Disease	Physiology	Diagnosis	Treatment
Mitral insufficiency	Mitral valve does not close completely, allowing blood to flowback into left atrium. Extra workload results in increased volume of blood and elevated pressure in left atrium, leading to hypertrophy of the left atrium and right ventricle, with possible right ventricular failure.	*Symptoms:* dyspnea, fatigue, orthopnea, palpitations *Signs:* rales, peripheral edema, distended neck veins, hepatomegaly *Diagnostic tests:* cardiac catheterization, radiographs, ECG, echocardiogram	Valvotomy and repair or valve replacement. As with other cardiac conditions, symptoms are treated with diuretics to reduce blood volume and drug therapy to strengthen heartbeat.
Mitral stenosis	Mitral valve does not open completely, causing the blood to flow slowly into the left ventricle. The results are the same as for mitral insufficiency.	*Symptoms, signs, and diagnostic tests:* see Mitral insufficiency.	See Mitral insufficiency.
Mitral valve prolapse (MVP)	Chordae tendineae, either too long or too short, prevent mitral valve from closing completely, allowing blood to flow back into left atrium. As left ventricle contracts, blood regurgitates into left atrium.	*Symptoms:* Usually asymptomatic; otherwise chest pain, dizziness, syncope, dyspnea, fatigue *Signs:* Murmur heard on ascultation leads to further investigation.	Asymptomatic patient: no treatment required. Symptomatic patient: beta blockers, avoidance of caffeine and large, heavy meals *Diagnostic tests:* echocardiogram
Aortic insufficiency	Blood flows back into left ventricle, causing ventricle to enlarge and eventually leading to left ventricular failure. Condition may be result of rheumatic fever, endocarditis, hypertension, or syphilis. As ventricular failure occurs, CHF and pulmonary failure begin.	*Symptoms:* angina, syncope, fatigue, dyspnea, palpitations *Diagnostic tests:* ECG, echocardiogram, cardiac catheterization, radiogram	Progress of condition is monitored to note when surgical intervention with valve replacement is necessary
Aortic stenosis	Blood flow into aorta is compromised, causing increased pressure in left ventricle and subsequent enlargement that eventually leads to left ventricular failure. May be result of infectious process or may be congenital.	*Symptoms, signs, and diagnostic tests:* see Aortic insufficiency	See Aortic insufficiency.
Tricuspid insufficiency	Tricuspid valve unable to close completely, forcing blood back into right atrium. Condition may be result of rheumatic heart disease and right-sided heart failure.	*Symptoms:* Initial symptoms include dyspnea and fatigue, followed by peripheral edema, distended neck veins, hepatomegaly, and ascites; systolic murmur is present. *Diagnostic tests:* cardiac catheterization, radiogram, ECG, echocardiogram	Valvular replacement may be only treatment option. Treatment of symptoms is helpful for patient.
Tricuspid stenosis	Tricuspid valve fails to open completely, so blood remains in right atrium. Condition often associated with mitral valve disease.	*Symptoms:* Initial symptoms include dyspnea and fatigue, followed by peripheral edema and distended neck veins; diastolic murmur is present. *Diagnostic tests:* cardiac catheterization, radiogram, ECG, echocardiogram	See Tricuspid insufficiency.
Pulmonic insufficiency	Blood flows back into right ventricle, creating increased pressure. This is followed by right ventricular hypertrophy and right-sided heart failure. Condition a result of pulmonary hypertension.	*Symptoms:* chest pain, fatigue, syncope, dyspnea *Signs:* distended neck veins, peripheral edema, hepatomegaly; diastolic murmur may be present. *Diagnostic tests:* cardiac catheterization, radiogram, ECG, echocardiogram	When symptoms are controlled, no intervention may be necessary. Surgical intervention includes valve reconstruction or replacement.
Pulmonic stenosis	Blood flow into pulmonary artery is obstructed, creating increased pressure in right atrium. Pulmonic stenosis is followed by right ventricular hypertrophy and right-sided heart failure.	*Symptoms:* chest pain, fatigue, syncope, and dyspnea *Signs:* distended neck veins, peripheral edema and hepatomegaly; systolic murmur may be present *Diagnostic tests:* echocardiogram, cardiac catheterization (including digital angiography)	See Pulmonic insufficiency.

Vascular Disorders
Phlebitis

Phlebitis, an inflammatory condition of the veins, usually occurs in the deep veins of the lower limbs. Tenderness in the affected area often alerts the individual to the condition. Increasing pain with redness and swelling follow, signaling advancement of the condition. A history of insult to the tissue along with possible stasis of the blood is another indication of phlebitis. Analgesic medications are given and the individual is instructed not to rub or massage the area, as massage could stimulate clot formation or release emboli that have already formed into the bloodstream. Treatment involves analgesics for pain and avoiding stimulation, such as massage, to the affected area.

Thrombophlebitis

Thrombophlebitis, an inflammatory condition, occurs in a vein where a thrombus has formed on the wall. Blood flow in the vein is compromised and edema occurs. Insult to the vessel, particularly to the walls, venous stasis, and hypercoagulating blood are all causes of thrombophlebitis. The individual experiences systemic chills and fever, as well as pain, edema, warmth, and redness in the area. Tenderness is exhibited with palpation of the affected area. These symptoms, along with swelling of the affected limb, lead to diagnosis, which is confirmed by venograms and ultrasound. Treatment involves immobilization of the affected limb and the administration of anticoagulant drugs and antibiotics.

Embolisms, Deep-Vein Thrombosis, and Thromboembolism

An **embolus** is a mass of material that forms an obstruction, or **embolism,** in a blood or lymphatic vessel (Figure 17-6 ◆). The material or mass may be solid, such as a blood clot (**thrombus**); liquid, such as amniotic fluid; gaseous, such as an air bubble; or it may be composed of fat, bone tissue, bacteria, tumor cells, or any material that may be in the bloodstream. Emboli (more than one embolus) occlude the vessel, resulting in infarction of the tissue supplied by that vessel. Many emboli are thrombi that travel from the deep vessels of the legs to the lungs, where they become pulmonary embolisms.

Deep-vein **thrombosis (DVT)** is frequently the result of stasis of the blood in the deep vessels of the legs due to inactivity. Other causes include an insult to the endothelial tissue and blood that has a tendency to clot quickly. Individuals at risk for developing emboli or thrombi are those who have experienced recent trauma or surgical procedures (especially those involving knee, hip, and prostate), CHF, severe infections, or malignancies, or who are inactive, obese, or pregnant, taking oral contraceptives, or over the age of 50. A **thromboembolism** occurs when the thrombus occludes the vessel. For those who travel great distances or for long periods of time, moving the legs frequently is a good preventive measure.

Patients with DVT usually complain of pain and tenderness in the affected leg, which may be swollen and warm to the touch. Many patients, however, are asymptomatic.

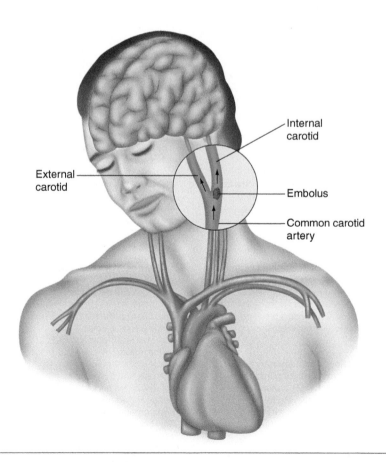

External carotid

Internal carotid

Embolus

Common carotid artery

Figure 17-6 ◆ Embolus

Diagnostic studies include contrast venography, Doppler ultrasound, real-time ultrasound, and clotting and coagulation blood studies. Treatment includes drug therapy to prevent enlargement of the thrombus, placement of inferior vena caval barriers, thrombolytic drug therapy, and immobilization of the affected part. Prevention is the best strategy with DVT.

Progression to pulmonary embolism is extremely serious. Aggressive intervention should be instituted as soon as possible.

Arteriosclerosis and Atherosclerosis

Arteriosclerosis is a condition, usually part of the aging process, in which the arterial walls lose elasticity. As the vessels harden, their ability to expand is compromised. Another condition affecting the internal lumen of the arteries is atherosclerosis. Deposits of plaque of saturated lipids, cholesterol, and other debris from the bloodstream adhere to the internal vessel walls, causing the walls to thicken and narrow (Figure 17-7 ◆). The cerebral and coronary vessels are most likely to be affected. Risk factors for both conditions include lipid accumulation, possibly due to lack of exercise, a diet high in saturated lipids, diabetes mellitus, obesity, hypertension, a sedentary lifestyle, smoking, and trauma to the vessels.

Many individuals are asymptomatic. The first sign of arteriosclerosis or atherosclerosis may be angina or transient ischemic attacks, precursors to acute myocardial infarction or cerebral vascular accident. Less dramatic symptoms include elevated blood pressure, dizziness, and shortness of breath. Doppler studies aid in verifying the diagnosis of atherosclerosis.

A change in dietary habits, especially a lower intake of saturated fats, lipids, and high-cholesterol foods, is one way to manage progression of the condition; another is giving up smoking. Hyperlipidemic drugs are often prescribed, and hypertension and diabetes mellitus must be controlled.

Aneurysms

An **aneurysm** is the weakening and dilation of an artery. Plaque buildup from atherosclerosis contributes to the formation of an aneurysm. While aneurysms may occur in any artery, the usual sites are the aorta and cerebral arteries. Aneurysms develop over a period of time. It is common for an aortic aneurysm to be found on physical examination when a pulsating mass is observed and palpated. In some instances, a previously undetected aneurysm is discovered when it ruptures, causing severe pain and loss of blood. Cerebral aneurysms are usually undetected until a rupture causes a cerebral bleed and the resulting cerebral vascular accident. Many of these bleeds, whether in the aorta or in the cerebral arteries, are fatal. Treatment consists of surgical intervention to repair the defect before the aneurysm ruptures.

Raynaud's Disease

Raynaud's disease results when small vessels in the fingers, hands, toes, and feet spasm, causing pain, numbness, and tingling. These areas frequently become very pale, sometimes to the point of blanching, because of the compromised blood flow. The condition is aggravated by cold and stress, and as it progresses, the affected areas turn blue. As spasms subside, the areas turn purple, then red. Women are more likely than men to suffer from Raynaud's disease.

Application of mild warmth provides relief as the vessel spasms subside. Prevention is important and includes not smoking. The hands and feet should be protected from sudden exposure to very cold temperatures with warm gloves, socks, and heavy shoes.

Buerger's Disease (Thromboangiitis Obliterans)

Buerger's disease, or thromboangiitis obliterans, is an inflammation of the peripheral vessels of both arteries and veins, with possible clot formation in the extremities. Smoking is a primary causative factor, and males who smoke are at greatest risk. Exercise tends to initiate severe pain in the legs and feet. Rest usually relieves the pain.

Arteriograms and ultrasound studies showing the site of the clot or obstruction confirm the presence of the disease. Aggressive intervention is important to preserve the integrity of the tissue supplied by the vessels. The obstruction should be resolved before permanent damage develops. Failure to intervene can lead to tissue necrosis, followed by amputation of the affected limb.

Keys to Success
TEDS® ANTIEMBOLISM STOCKINGS

Teds are often prescribed for patients who have had pelvic trauma, hip replacement, or knee replacement surgeries or other surgeries or illness that require immobilization in bed for long periods. These stockings may also be used on cardiac patients. Teds exert uniform pressure on the venous system of the legs, promoting circulation to the heart. They help to prevent venous stasis and dependent edema in the lower extremities.

Teds come in various lengths and calf sizes. Patient teaching in their use is often necessary. The patient should be in a recumbent position so the vessels in the legs are not distended. The Teds are pulled over the toes and gently worked over the heels up to the knee or groin area, depending on their length. Any wrinkles must be smoothed out to prevent uneven pressure on the legs. The stockings should be removed daily to assess skin condition and to provide any necessary skin care. Sometimes the stockings are removed for an hour or so while the patient is resting and not ambulatory or sitting with the legs down.

Figure 17-7 ◆ Arteriosclerosis and atherosclerosis

Diagnostic Tests

Assessment of all cardiology patients includes vital signs (T, P, R, BP, and weight). Many physicians prefer an apical pulse and notations regarding strength and rhythm of the heartbeat. Notations are made of any irregularities, gasping or rapid breathing, pedal edema, and the color, temperature, and moisture content of the skin. It is customary to check for the presence and strength of pedal pulses.

Radiographs, usually chest x-rays, are done to assess the size, location, and position of the heart in the chest (pleural) cavity and the presence of fluid in the lungs. Blood tests including a CBC, cardiac enzymes, electrolytes, and, on occasion, **ABGs** are done. The pulse oximeter provides a rapid and noninvasive evaluation of the oxygen saturation of arterial blood. Coagulation studies often are performed.

Some cardiology offices are located close to facilities where cardiac catheterizations, including angiocaths, are performed to evaluate the status of the coronary arteries. These facilities perform angioplasties and/or stent insertions. **Coronary artery bypass (CAB)** procedures, also known as coronary artery bypass graft **(CABG)**, are referred to a cardiovascular surgeon. Treatment for post-MI or impending MI patients may include cardiac catheterization with angioplasty and/or stent insertion. When this type of intervention cannot be achieved, coronary artery bypass surgery may be performed.

Electrocardiogram

An electrocardiogram (**ECG** or **EKG**) is a recording of the electrical activity of the heart. This record is a tool the clinician uses, along with symptoms and signs, to assess the condition of the heart. The ECG often indicates ischemic areas of the myocardium, information useful in the diagnosis of cardiac pathology.

An electrocardiograph is used to perform the ECG (Figure 17-8 ♦). This machine amplifies low-voltage electric

Keys to Success
UNDERSTANDING CARDIAC PROCEDURES

During a **cardiac catheterization,** a catheter is threaded through an artery in the arm or groin to the aorta and the coronary vessels. Dye is injected into the vessels, and the radiologist and cardiologist assess the circulation through the coronary arteries. Dye can also be injected into the chambers of the heart to view valve and myocardial function.

If narrowing of the arteries is detected, angioplasty may be attempted. A balloon near the distal end of the catheter is expanded, compressing the plaque against the arterial walls and thereby expanding the lumen of the vessels and allowing for increased blood flow. Stents are often inserted into the arteries after angioplasty to maintain the wider lumen. The location and extent of the occlusion or partial occlusion determine if angioplasty and/or stent insertion should be attempted. Aspirin and other anticoagulant medications are prescribed following stent insertion.

When angioplasty and/or stent insertion cannot be performed, coronary artery bypass (CAB) is done. During this surgical procedure, arteries (mammary) or veins from the legs are grafted to bypass the narrowed or occluded artery. This revascularization procedure reestablishes circulation to the compromised areas of the myocardium.

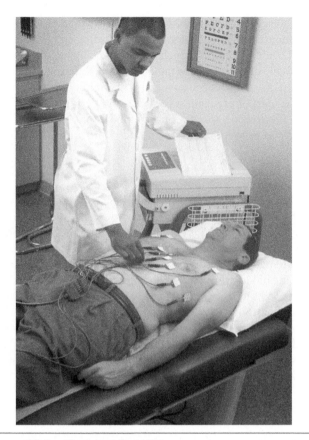

Figure 17-8 ♦ Electrocardiograph

impulses detected on the skin and provides a printed record of that electrical activity. A cardiac monitor displays the heart's electrical impulses on a screen called an *oscilloscope*. Electrodes—adhesive pads containing a conductive gel—are placed on the patient's skin. They are attached to color-coded wires called *leads* that connect to the electrocardiograph. Three leads—a positive, a negative, and a ground lead—are required to transmit the electrical activity to the electrocardiograph.

A 12-lead ECG provides images of the various planes of the heart (Table 17-6). Lead II is usually used for the rhythm strip on a monitor because of its ability to show P waves. (P waves are discussed below.) Leads I, II, and III are often referred to as limb leads (Figure 17-9 ♦). Additional limb leads are the **augmented leads,** aVL, aVR, and aVF (Figure 17-10 ♦). The **precordial leads** V1, V2, V3, V4, V5, and V6, placed on the chest in a semicircular pattern around the heart, provide a horizontal plane view of the heart (Figure 17-11 ♦). Lead II provides an image from the upper area of the heart where cardiac conduction starts. Chest leads V5 and V6 provide images from the lower area as conduction approaches the **apex** of the heart.

Wires are identified or coded by color and lead number. The right arm lead is usually white and marked RA; the left arm lead, black and marked LA: the right leg lead, green and marked RL: and the left leg, red and marked LL. The limb leads are placed over fleshy areas of the arms and legs. Placement of the chest leads (brown wires) begins with the identification of the third intercostal space and the sternum.

- V1 is placed over the fourth intercostal space and to the right of the sternum (right sternal margin).
- V2 is placed over the fourth intercostal space and to the left of the sternum (left sternal margin).
- V3 is placed midway over the fourth and fifth intercostal spaces and halfway between the base of the sternum and the nipple (midway between leads 2 and lead 4).
- V4 is placed over the fifth intercostal space and in line with the nipple (junction of midclavicular line).
- V5 is placed in the same line midway between the nipple and midpoint of the axilla, **anterior** to the midaxillary line.
- V6 is placed over the intercostal space at the axilla midpoint (left midaxillary line).

Interpreting Waveforms on the ECG Tracing

ECGs are printed on special standardized graph paper (Figure 17-12 ◆). The paper travels through the electrocardiograph at a speed of 25 millimeters per second. The horizontal line measures time, and the vertical line measures **amplitude** or voltage. The ECG paper is divided, both vertically and horizontally, into squares 5 millimeters in width and height,

TABLE 17-6: ECG LEADS
Limb Leads
Lead I: Records electrical activity from right arm to left arm
Lead II: Records electrical activity from right arm to left leg
Lead III: Records electrical activity from left arm to left leg
Augmented Leads
aVR: Records electrical activity away from midpoint between left arm and left leg to left arm (across heart to right shoulder)
aVL: Records electrical activity from midpoint between right arm and left leg to left arm (across heart to left shoulder)
aVF: Records electrical activity from midpoint between right arm and left arm to left leg (across heart toward feet)
Chest or Precordial Leads
V1: Records electrical activity between center of heart and the chest wall where V1 electrode is placed
V2: Records electrical activity between center of heart and chest wall where V2 electrode is placed
V3: Records electrical activity between center of heart and chest wall where V3 electrode is placed
V4: Records electrical activity between center of heart and chest wall where V4 electrode is placed
V5: Records electrical activity between center of heart and chest wall where V5 electrode is placed
V6: Records electrical activity between center of the heart and chest wall where V6 electrode is placed.

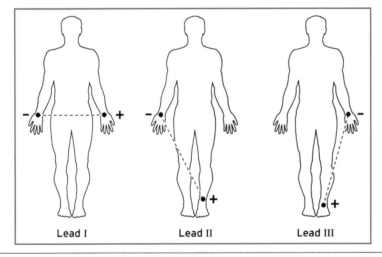

Figure 17-9 ◆ The bipolar leads

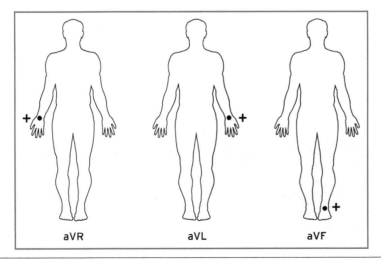

Figure 17-10 ◆ The augmented leads

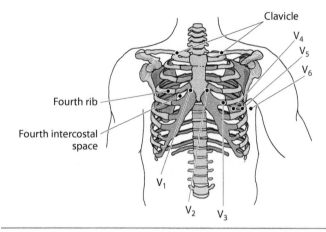

Figure 17-11 ◆ The precordial leads

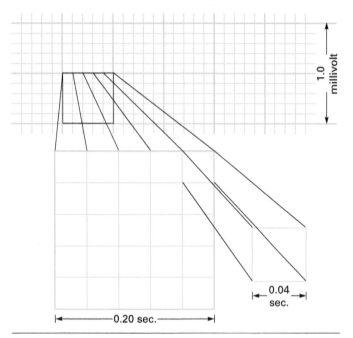

Figure 17-12 ◆ ECG paper and markings

each representing a time interval of 0.20 second. It is further divided into smaller squares 1 millimeter wide, each representing a time interval of 0.04 second. Proper interpretation of cardiac rhythms depends on understanding the time represented on the ECG paper.

The second aspect of the ECG is the waveform. The electrical impulse originates in the SA node and produces a waveform

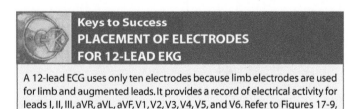

Keys to Success
PLACEMENT OF ELECTRODES FOR 12-LEAD EKG

A 12-lead ECG uses only ten electrodes because limb electrodes are used for limb and augmented leads. It provides a record of electrical activity for leads I, II, III, aVR, aVL, aVF, V1, V2, V3, V4, V5, and V6. Refer to Figures 17-9, 17-10, and 17-11 to identify the placement of the ten electrodes.

on the graph paper. The resting state of the myocardial cells is depicted by a baseline or **isoelectric line,** which is a straight line on the ECG strip. The beginning and ending point of all waves is represented by this line. There are five major waves during a cardiac cycle: the P wave, the Q, R, and S waves, and the T wave (Figure 17-13 ◆).

- The cardiac cycle begins with the firing of the SA node and is characterized by a P wave on the ECG. Representing the depolarization of both the right and left atria, the P wave is approximately 0.10 second in length and appears as a smooth, upward deflection.
- The time interval during which the impulse travels from the SA node through the atria to the ventricles is the **PR** interval. The time from the beginning of the P wave to the beginning of the next complex (QRS) should measure three to five small squares or 0.12 to 0.20 second (Figure 17-14 ◆). If the SA node does not initiate the impulse, lower pacemaker cells can initiate the conduction as a "survival" effort. These impulses are termed *ectopic.*
- The next portion of the waveform is the **QRS** complex—the Q, R, and S waves representing the conduction of the impulse from the bundle of His through the ventricles. The Q wave deflects down from the baseline, and the R wave follows with an upward deflection and reflects the patient's heart rate. The downward deflection following is the S wave. The QRS complex is measured from the beginning of the Q wave to where the S wave meets the baseline. The QRS complex normally measures less than 0.12 second or less than three small squares (Figure 17-15 ◆). There may be variations in the waves of the QRS complex

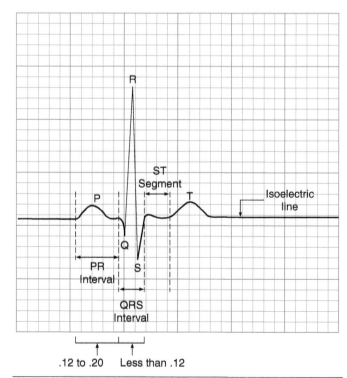

Figure 17-13 ◆ ECG waveforms

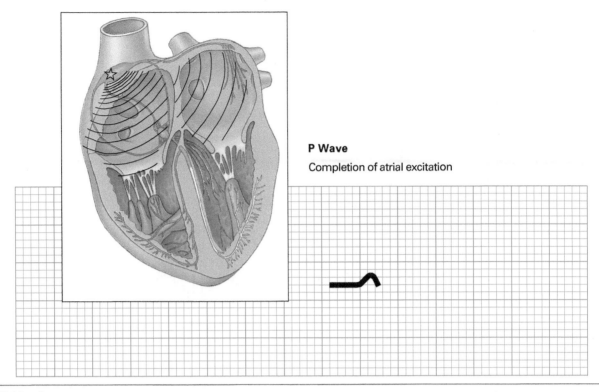

P Wave

Completion of atrial excitation

Figure 17-14 ◆ P wave

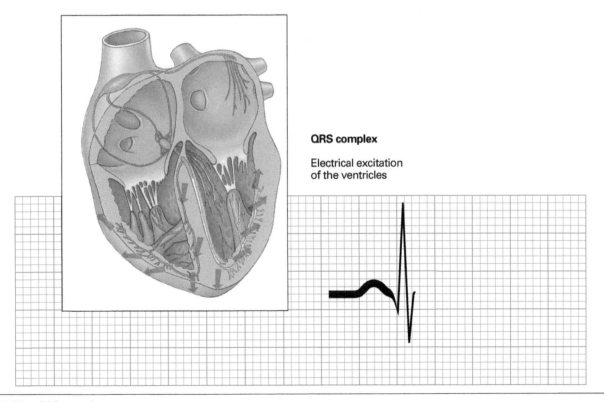

QRS complex

Electrical excitation
of the ventricles

Figure 17-15 ◆ QRS complex

among individuals, and all three waves are not always present.
■ During the **ST** segment, the ventricles are depolarized and repolarization begins. Usually the ST segment is isometric.

■ The final portion of the waveform is the T wave, which indicates the repolarization or recovery phase of the ventricles. The normal shape of the T wave is slightly asymmetrical, slightly rounded, with a positive deflection (Figure 17-16 ◆). The T wave is the "resting phase"

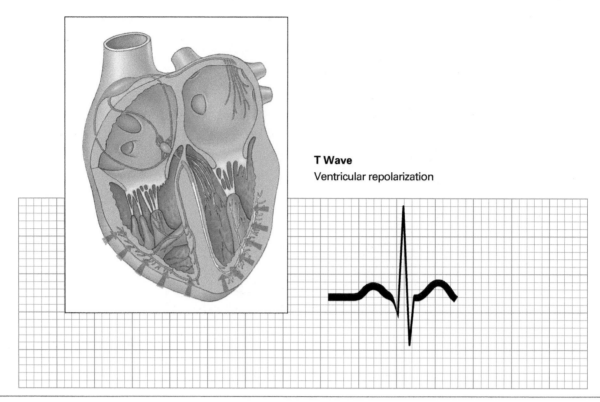

T Wave
Ventricular repolarization

Figure 17-16 ◆ T wave

of the cardiac cycle, during which the heart is most vulnerable to impulses that may lead to arrhythmias.

Artifacts

An **artifact** is any electrical activity on an ECG that is noncardiac in origin and represents unwanted marks on the ECG paper. There are two types of artifacts.

- Intentional artifacts include standardization marks and pacemaker spikes (Figure 17-17 ◆).
- Unintentional interferences (Figure 17-18 ◆) may be caused by loose, corroded, or dirty electrodes, broken cables or wires, improper grounding, or the patient's muscular tremors, movement, talking, or nervous disorder. In addition, 60-cycle interference is caused by alternating current of electrical equipment such as IV pumps, ventilators,

or electric beds. Changing outlets or moving to a different location may alleviate this type of interference.

Keys to Success
AGE, CULTURAL, AND DISABILITY CONSIDERATIONS

The elderly are sometimes fearful of electrocardiographs. Assess the patient's facial, behavioral, and verbal expressions as you explain the procedure. Body language or conversation may indicate a fear of electrocution or even death. Ask the patient to restate what is involved, and clarify any misconceptions.

A patient with bilateral above-knee amputation (AKA) needs a preoperative ECG. Where are the leg electrodes placed? How would they be placed for a right AKA? In both cases, the leg electrodes are placed on the upper thigh areas. When they cannot be placed in the correct position, they must be directed away from the heart.

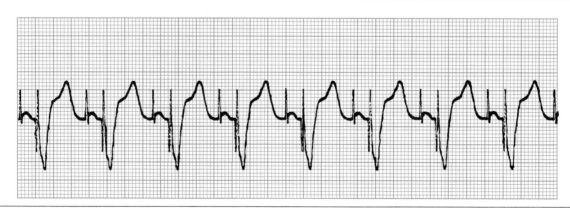

Figure 17-17 ◆ Intentional artifacts include standardization marks and pacemaker spikes

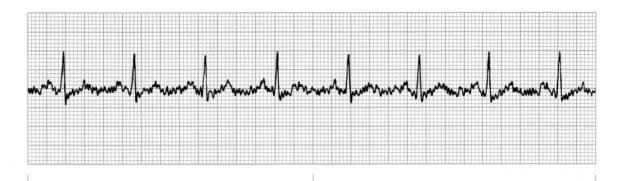

Figure 17-18 ◆ Artifact

PROCEDURE 17-1 **Perform an Electrocardiogram**

Theory

An electrocardiogram is used in conjunction with other diagnostic testing and physical assessment to establish baseline and medical information about the patient. To reduce patient nervousness or movement that could affect the quality of the electrocardiogram, it is important to provide a relaxing, calm, and warm environment. You can alleviate any patient anxiety by explaining the basic procedure. Some patients are unaware that an ECG records electrical activity already present in the heart and may fear that the electrocardiogram may cause shock and pain. Watch the patient's facial expressions to assess understanding or fear, and encourage the patient to ask questions or describe previous experiences with the same kind of procedure.

Your responsibilities during the procedure include the following:

■ Prevent unnecessary electrical-interference artifacts on the ECG by pointing the power cord away from the patient. Avoid taking the cord under the bed to the electrical outlet.

■ Cleanse any oils from the skin and dry it thoroughly for better contact with the electrodes. Remove the adhesive backing and place each electrode on the skin with the tab pointing toward the cable of the ECG machine. This will minimize the "pull" on the electrodes and the potential for artifacts.

■ Use anatomical landmarks (intercostal spaces, midclavicular line, midaxillary line, etc.) to place the electrodes in the correct position (Figure 17-19 ◆).

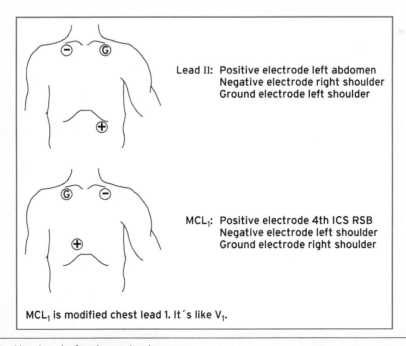

Lead II: Positive electrode left abdomen
Negative electrode right shoulder
Ground electrode left shoulder

MCL₁: Positive electrode 4th ICS RSB
Negative electrode left shoulder
Ground electrode right shoulder

MCL₁ is modified chest lead 1. It´s like V₁.

Figure 17-19 ◆ Anatomical landmarks for electrode placement

continued

PROCEDURE 17-1 **Perform an Electrocardiogram** *(continued)*

- Attach the lead wires only after the electrodes are in place. Reduce the potential for artifacts by laying the wires along body contours.
- Before beginning the procedure, you will need to calibrate the ECG machine. This process, also called standardization, verifies that the machine deflects 10 mm in response to 1mv of electricity in sensitivity 1. With older machines this may have to be done manually, but newer models calibrate automatically before the electrocardiogram is printed. The paper moves 25 mm per second, and the recording stylus moves the same distance.
- Older machines do not automatically identify which lead is being recorded. In this case, you will be expected to identify each lead strip with a specified marking (Table 17-7).
- The ECG should not leave the testing area without patient identification. With newer electrocardiograph models the patient's name, age, height, weight, sex, and current medications can be entered into the machine before the procedure begins. With older models you may need to write the patient data on the ECG after it has been printed out.
- If the quality of the electrocardiogram is poor, you will need to run a second one. You should look for and correct the reasons for the poor ECG quality. Explain the problem to the patient to ensure cooperation and ease the patient's anxiety.

Materials

- electrocardiograph with wires, electrodes, and ECG paper
- patient gown and drape as necessary for privacy and warmth
- alcohol pads
- supplies for shaving, if needed

Competency

(**Conditions**) With the necessary materials, (**Task**) you will be able to perform a 12-lead ECG (**Standards**) correctly within the time frame designated by the instructor.

1. Wash your hands. Assemble the equipment and supplies.
2. Identify the patient and escort him or her to the patient examination room.
3. Explain the procedure to relieve the patient's apprehension.
4. Ask the patient to disrobe from the waist up. Assist the patient into a gown, with the opening in front. Assure the patient that his or her privacy will be respected.
5. Help the patient recline on the examination table or bed where the procedure will be performed.
6. Cover the patient with the drape, leaving the arms and legs exposed. You may need to raise pant legs to expose the calves of the lower legs.
7. Cleanse the skin with alcohol pads where the electrodes will be applied. If chest hair will interfere with contact between the electrodes and the skin, remove the hair with soap and/or shaving cream and a disposable razor.

8. Apply the electrodes in the correct positions, making sure the wires do not touch the cart or examination table and that they follow the normal contours of the body (Figure 17-20 ◆). The power cord should not cross under the examination table or bed.
9. Explain to the patient that the electrocardiograph is a sensitive machine and that he or she must remain as still as possible during the procedure.
10. Calibrate the electrocardiograph and run the ECG (Figure 17-21 ◆). Mark the leads if necessary.
11. When the ECG is complete, remove the electrodes and cleanse any residual conduction gel from the patient's skin.
12. Assist the patient in dressing. Discard the gown, if it is disposable; otherwise, place it in a laundry hamper.
13. Cleanse the equipment. Sanitize the leads by wiping them with antiseptic solution, then store them in the appropriate compartment of the electrocardiograph cart. Replace any necessary supplies. Wash your hands.
14. Label the electrocardiograph paper with the patient's name, DOB, and the date and time. Document the patient's tolerance of the procedure.
15. Per physician preference, instruct the patient to wait to discuss the test with the physician or make a follow-up appointment.

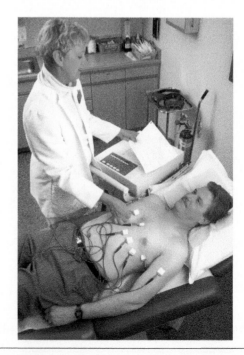

Figure 17-20 ◆ Apply the electrodes in the correct position.

PROCEDURE 17-1 **Perform an Electrocardiogram** (continued)

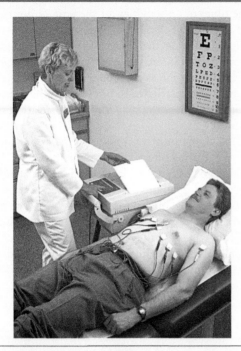

Figure 17-21 ◆ Calibrate the ECG

Patient Education

If it is not an emergency electrocardiogram, the patient should bathe or shower beforehand. Clean skin will ensure good contact with the electrodes for a quality ECG.

The patient should be informed that the procedure—taking a "picture" of the electrical activity of the heart—is painless. Instruct the patient to remain still during the procedure and to ask for an extra cover if he or she feels cold.

If it is necessary to run a second ECG, instruct the patient on how to help and explain that the second run is not an indication of medical problems.

Charting Example

11/25/XX 2:30 PM 12-lead ECG performed with patient cooperation. States recent episodes of chest pain occurring after stressful events at work. Daniel Trees, CMA

11/25/XX 3:30 PM Physician ordered additional study of Holter monitor. Holter monitor attached and patient instructions given orally and in written handout. Patient verbalized understanding of instructions and phone number if there are questions. Daniel Trees, CMA

TABLE 17-7 SENSOR (LEAD) PLACEMENT AND MARKING CODES

Limb Leads	Placement	Abbreviation	Marking Code
Lead I	Right arm to left arm	RA-LA	•
Lead II	Right arm to left leg	RA-LL	• •
Lead III	Left arm to left leg	LA-LL	• • •
Augmented Leads			
aVR	RA-midpoint (LA-LL)	(LA-LL) RA	-
aVL	LA-midpoint (RA-LL)	(RA-LL) LA	- -
aVF	LL-midpoint (RA-LA)	(RA-LA) LL	- - -
Chest Leads	**Placement**		**Marking Code**
V1	4th intercostal space, right sternal border		- •
V2	4th intercostal space, left sternal border		- • •
V3	Midway between V2 and V4		- • •
V4	5th intercostal space, mid-clavicular left		- • • • •
V5	Left anterior axillary fold horizontal to V4		- • • • • •
V6	Left mid-axillary horizontal to V4 and V5		- • • • • • •

Note: The right leg is never used for the tracings, but is an electrical ground.

Source: Fremgen, Bonnie F. Essentials of Medical Assisting, 1st Edition © 1998. Reprinted by permission of Pearson Education, Inc., Upper Saddle River, NJ.

Holter Monitor

Many ECGs are recorded using three seconds of electronic cardiac monitoring. It is possible for **dysrhythmias** not to occur during this brief period. The physician may therefore order a portable form of monitoring, called the Holter monitor, that allows noninvasive recording of the patient's cardiac condition over a 24-hour period. This testing is useful in identifying events and unexplained symptoms in patients with arrhythmias and in monitoring the effectiveness of current medications or pacemaker function. The clinician can observe cardiac rhythms over a period of time while the patient engages in the normal activities of daily living. A 48-hour Holter monitor test may be ordered when the physician wants a longer time frame for evaluation.

Keys to Success
INTERPRETING DYSRHYTHMIAS

When interpreting dysrhythmias, the most important component is the patient's clinical appearance. A dysrhythmia without clinical symptoms may or may not need treatment, depending upon the diagnosis.

The patient may continue with daily activities except for bathing, showering, or swimming to keep monitor and electrodes dry. A diary is given to the patient with instructions to record the times of all activities for the next 24 hours, including bowel and bladder elimination, emotional changes or stressful situations, smoking, drinking caffeinated beverages, taking medications, sexual intercourse, rest or sleeping periods, and clinical symptoms, such as chest pain and shortness of breath. The patient is also instructed to briefly push the event button of the monitor to mark the strip for later correlation of activities and times.

A return appointment is made for 24 hours later, when the monitor is turned off and the leads are removed. The strip is removed from the monitor, labeled, and correlated with patient information, date, and time. It is attached to the diary and forwarded to the cardiologist for interpretation. The patient is instructed as to a return visit and a discussion of the test results. The lead wires and the recorder are cleaned according to the manufacturer's guidelines and the Holter monitor is returned to the proper storage place. The recorder cartridge is removed and attached to the diary.

PROCEDURE 17-2 Applying a Holter Monitor

Theory

The Holter monitor is battery-powered and has a strap for the patient to place over the shoulder. The medical assistant's role in Holter monitoring includes the application and removal of the monitor leads, identification of the monitor strip, and patient instruction. Applying the monitor leads is very similar to applying EKG leads. The skin must be clean, dry, and shaved for optimum contact with the electrodes. A new battery and a blank magnetic tape should be installed in the recorder before each patient use (Figure 17-22 ◆).

It is very important to test the Holter monitor before the patient leaves the office to ensure that waveforms are clear and artifacts are minimal or absent. The monitor should be kept in its case. Electrodes should not be touched to avoid causing interference and degrading the quality of the information obtained.

Materials

- medical order for the Holter monitor
- Holter monitor
- ECG electrodes
- ECG
- recording cassette
- fresh batteries (or recharged batteries)
- patient gown and drape as necessary for privacy and warmth
- supplies for shaving if needed
- alcohol pads
- 4 × 4 gauze pad
- liquid abrasive
- adhesive tape
- patient diary
- patient chart
- gloves

A   B

Figure 17-22 ◆ (A) Install a new battery into the Holter monitor; (B) Install a blank tape.

PROCEDURE 17-2 Applying a Holter Monitor *(continued)*

Competency

(**Conditions**) With the necessary materials, (**Task**) you will be able to apply a Holter monitor (**Standards**) correctly within the time frame designated by the instructor.

1. Run a test of the equipment to make sure it is functioning properly and that the batteries are fresh.
2. With the patient sitting on the exam table, explain the procedure while showing the patient the equipment (Figure 17-23 ◆)
3. Instruct the patient to remove all clothing from the waist up. If the exam room is cool, offer the patient a blanket.
4. Because the electrodes of the Holter monitor must be in constant contact with the skin, you may have to shave the electrode sites. If so, explain the reason for shaving before you begin.
5. Wash your hands and put on gloves.
6. Cleanse the skin with alcohol wipes to remove all lotions, cologne or perfume, and body oil.
7. Moisten a 4 × 4 gauze with liquid abrasive and abrade the skin at the electrode sites until it is slightly red to ensure the electrodes adhere (Figure 17-24 ◆).
8. Take the electrodes from their packaging and remove the adhesive covering from each one.
9. Check for moist gel on each electrode and apply the adhesive side to the skin site, using circular pressure from the center outward (Figure 17-25 ◆).
10. Attach the lead wires to the electrodes and tape a loop of the electrode wires to the skin (Figures 17-26 ◆ and 17-27 ◆).
11. Cover each electrode site with nonallergenic tape, which will remain in place over the next 24 hours.
12. Verify the correct electrode placement by connecting the electrodes to the ECG machine and obtaining a test strip.
13. Help the patient to dress, if necessary, being careful not to disturb any of leads.
14. Test the Holter monitor by placing a cassette into it and making certain it runs smoothly. Plug the electrode cable into the recorder, and note the starting time in the patient diary and patient chart.
15. Make an appointment for 24 hours later to review the monitor and remove the electrodes.
16. Document the procedure in the patient's chart.

Patient Education

Explain to the patient the importance of keeping an activities diary in a simple spiral-bound notebook. Any activities such as eating, sleeping, and exercising must be noted, as well as changes in energy level or breathing and feelings of chest discomfort. The exact time of each occurrence should be reported so the physician can review it simultaneously with the cardiac readout from the Holter monitor.

Charting Example

11/25/XX 3:30 PM Physician ordered additional study of Holter monitor. Holter monitor attached and patient given instructions orally and in written handout. Patient verbalized understanding of instructions and phone number if there are questions. Darren Brimsek, RMA

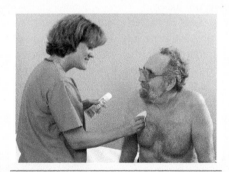

Figure 17-23 ◆ Explain the unit to the patient.

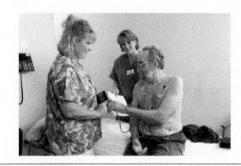

Figure 17-24 ◆ Abrade the electrode site.

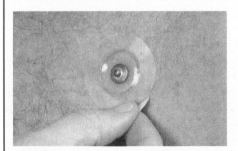

Figure 17-25 ◆ Apply electrode to the skin.

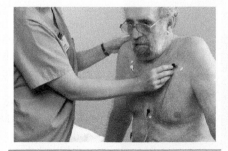

Figure 17-26 ◆ Attach the lead wires to the electrodes.

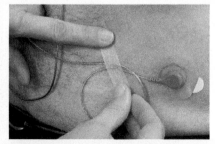

Figure 17-27 ◆ Tape a loop of the electrode wires to the skin.

Stress Testing

After an electrocardiogram, the physician may need additional diagnostic information about the patient's cardiac status. The treadmill stress test, also known as stress or exercise testing, provides valuable information about how the patient's heart reacts to moderate, controlled exercise on a treadmill or stationary bicycle (Figure 17-28 ◆). Stress testing is used to evaluate patients with a cardiac history and those who have had cardiovascular surgery or a heart attack.

A 12-lead ECG is done prior to the treadmill exercise. Blood pressure readings are taken both prior to and during the test. Respiratory efforts are monitored. The leads on the patient are connected to a monitor during the test to monitor and record the heart's electrical activity in response to the exercise. The speed and incline of the treadmill are gradually increased. The test is terminated either when the patient can no longer tolerate the activity or when the goal of the test has been achieved. Should the patient complain of chest pain, the test is terminated immediately.

If the patient is unable to engage in routine stress testing because of a physical disability, dipyridamole or adenisene may be administered to simulate physical stress without the exercise.

The physician is present during the test. The medical assistant's role is to assist the technician in patient preparation. You will instruct the patient beforehand to wear comfortable walking shoes and loose-fitting clothes. Female patients should wear a blouse that opens in the front. During the test, it will be your responsibility to check all equipment and make sure the crash cart and emergency medications are in the procedure room. You will assist the physician by monitoring the patient and taking vital signs. You may also operate the treadmill as directed by the physician. If the patient reaches a target heart rate or exhibits abnormal symptoms (chest pain, severe weakness or tiredness) or abnormal arrhythmias (displayed on the ECG machine), the test is stopped. The patient is observed and the physician provides appropriate medical intervention. It is important to document accurately and thoroughly during the procedure. After the procedure, the patient is monitored per office protocol. Then the electrodes are removed.

Cardiac patients can be very apprehensive about performing the stress test because of a previous heart attack or the potential medical risks. The medical office gives patients printed preparation instructions as well as verbal instructions because anxious patients may not remember verbal directions. Patients who know what to expect during the procedure and what to report feel less anxiety and a greater sense of control.

When giving verbal and printed instructions, focus on these major points:

1. Instruct the patient to wear comfortable clothing and shoes for the procedure.
2. Inform the patient about normal symptoms: sweating, slight shortness of breath, some increase in pulse rate, and some fatigue.
3. Emphasize that the patient should report abnormal symptoms and may stop the procedure if he or she experiences chest pain or severe weakness or tiredness.
4. Inform the patient of safety precautions followed during the procedure. The physician is present to monitor the patient's condition and provide any necessary emergency treatment, and emergency equipment is close at hand in the testing area.

Review any further physician instructions with the patient and make follow-up appointments as directed.

Echocardiogram

An echocardiogram is an examination of the cardiac structure using ultrasound (acoustic imaging). It allows the clinician to measure and define the size, shape, thickness, position, and movements of various cardiac structures, including the valves, myocardial walls, septum, and chambers. The arteries and veins, aorta, pulmonary veins and arteries, and superior vena cava are also viewed in an echocardiogram (Figure 17-29 ◆).

Echocardiograms are noninvasive tests. A transducer with conductive gel is placed on the chest wall over the ribs near the sternum, directed toward the heart. Sound waves are sent into the chest cavity by the transducer and bounced off the heart walls and valves. Images of the moving heart and its structures are transmitted to an oscilloscope and recorded on paper and videotape. The Doppler measures the direction and velocity of the blood through the heart. This measurement—the fraction of blood ejected from the left ventricle with each heartbeat—is referred to as the **ejection fraction (EF)**. Normal EF is 55%.

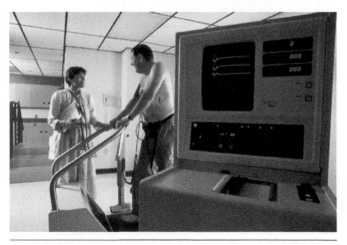

Figure 17-28 ◆ Treadmill stress test
Source: David Scott Smith.

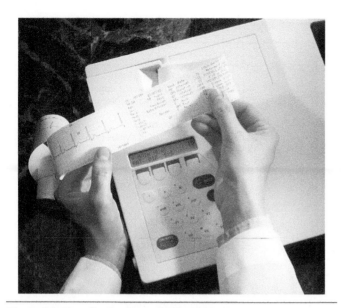

Figure 17-29 ◆ Single-channel echocardiograph

Abnormal EF results from abnormal contractions of the heart muscle and the changing velocity of blood through the heart. Cardiac muscle enlargement and valve malfunctioning are among the structural or functional abnormalities that may be diagnosed.

As a medical assistant you will not perform echocardiograms unless you are specifically trained as an echocardiographic technician. The MA's role is to provide information to the patient and the patient's family and provide assistance to the technician.

The patient is asked to lie still, but may be asked to make minor adjustments to help the technician obtain additional information or a clearer picture. The technician applies a clear gel to the transducer, which is then applied to the chest, over the heart. The patient should be forewarned that the first touch of gel to the chest will be cold but that the sensation is temporary.

Patient Preparation and Instructions

You will prepare the patient room and provide patient care and support during the procedure. Explain to the patient that the procedure examines the structure and function of the heart and will help the physician prescribe the most appropriate medical treatment, if any is required. Inform the patient that no preparation is necessary for the procedure. Mention that it is a painless procedure, although there might be some minor discomfort from lying still for approximately an hour. Document vital signs, observations, and the patient's tolerance of the procedure. Emphasize the need for a follow-up appointment as directed by the physician to discuss the test results. The physician may request that preprinted or internally developed written materials be given to the patient to reinforce verbal instructions.

Thallium Scan

In a thallium scan, an IV infusion of the radioisotope thallium-201 is used to assess myocardial perfusion. First, the patient is stressed on a treadmill. At the peak of stress, the thallium is in-

fused and is taken up by the myocardium. The patient is then placed under a gamma camera and pictures are taken of the heart. Healthy tissue absorbs the thallium, but ischemic areas or areas of coronary artery disease do not absorb the isotope immediately and are thus identified. Infarcted areas never absorb the isotope, so the location and extent of myocardial ischemia or infarction can be identified as well. A thallium scan may also be used to determine the possible prognosis of a myocardial condition.

MUGA Scan

MUGA (multiple gated acquisition, also multinucleated gated angiography) scans assess the function of the left ventricle and identify abnormalities of the myocardial walls. Following injection of an isotope, a series of images are taken that show left ventricular function and allow the calculation of the ejection fraction.

A summary of cardiac diagnostic tests is given in Table 17-8.

Blood Studies

Blood studies aid the physician in the diagnostic process. Table 17-9 lists blood diagnostic tests often ordered by physicians to assess various stages of cardiac conditions.

Identifying Arrhythmias/Dysrhythmias

Anyone performing an ECG must recognize which arrhythmias, also known as dysrhythmias, are usual or unusual and which are life-threatening. Although atrial arrhythmias may cause symptoms of light-headedness or weakness, they usually are not life-threatening. Arrhythmias originating in the ventricles may be more serious, however, and some are considered life-threatening. The health-care professional performing an ECG must recognize waveforms and rates and be able to rapidly interpret irregularities in order to alert the physician when necessary.

- Rhythms originating in the SA node with normal conduction through the heart are called sinus rhythms. They may be within normal time limits (normal sinus rhythm, NSR), fast, or slow.
- Rhythms originating in the AV node are called junctional or nodal rhythms and usually proceed through the conduction system from that point. If the conduction system is blocked for some reason, rhythms take a detour around the damaged tissue that is causing the block and are blocking-type rhythms.

 Keys to Success
CONSENT

Some cardiac procedures, such as stress tests or thallium scans, may cause serious arrhythmias as the need for oxygen and nutrition to the myocardium increases. An informed consent should therefore be signed, witnessed, and placed in the chart.

TABLE 17-8 CARDIAC DIAGNOSTIC TESTS

Diagnostic Test	Indications	Clinical Notes
ECG/EKG	Records electrical activity of the heart	■ Noninvasive study ■ May indicate need for Holter monitor testing
Holter monitor	Arrythmias of undetermined cause and abnormal ECG/EKG	■ Detects abnormal cardiac rhythm over a 24-hour period ■ Noninvasive study ■ Patient records activities in a diary
Echocardiogram	Visual diagnostic study to examine various structures, size, and cardiac output of the heart	■ Noninvasive study ■ Uses ultrasound with transducer Doppler
Stress test(s)	Assess cardiac response to stressors, including exercise	■ Usually noninvasive test using treadmill ■ May include thallium scan ■ Medications can be given to a patient physically unable to tolerate activity on the treadmill
Angiogram	Patency and structure of blood vessels	■ Invasive imaging study ■ May indicate and include angioplasty and stent
Cardiac catheterization	Patency and structure of blood vessels; also heart structure and size, cardiac and pulmonary vascular pressures	■ Invasive imaging study ■ May indicate and include angiogram, angioplasty, and stent insertion
Chest X-ray	Determines heart size and condition of lungs	■ Noninvasive radiation exposure ■ Two views

TABLE 17-9 BLOOD STUDIES

CBC (complete blood count)	Detects anemias, blood cell changes, or infections	■ Specimens must be obtained in an EDTA tube ■ Platelet count ■ Includes measurement of RBCs, WBCs, Hgb, Hct, MCV, MCH, MCHC
Cholesterol	Screen tool used for family or medical history of heart disease	■ Serum required for test ■ NPO for 12 hours pretest ■ HDL:LDL ratio provides confirmation of cholesterol screening ■ Elevated levels are precursor to diagnosis of atherosclerosis
Triglycerides	Screening tool used for arterial diseases	■ As triglycerides increase, LDL also increases
Coagulation studies	Screening tool for thromboembolic conditions and medication adjustment	■ Include PTT or PT ■ Used to adjust medication regime
Cardiac enzymes	Chest pain, myocardial status	■ CPK (CK), LDH, AST (SGOT) ■ Elevations occur after cardiac trauma, including MI ■ For additional studies, isoenzymes are ordered

■ Rhythms originating in the ventricles present a danger and may cause the heart to stop beating in some cases. **PVCs, or premature ventricular contractions,** originate in the ventricle and not the pacemaker cells of the heart. They prevent the atria from filling with blood, and when they cause the ventricles to contract, no blood is pumped out of the ventricle. This phenomenon may be what a patient refers to as a "skipped beat." The danger arises when there are more than six PVCs in one minute, when they occur in pairs or every other beat, or when they arise from different foci in the ventricle. Unifocal PVCs originate from the same **focus** (site) in the ventricle, whereas multifocal PVCs arise from different foci. This can be a life-threatening arrhythmia that demands immediate intervention.

The various cardiac rhythms are described in Table 17-10. The medical assistant performing ECGs must know when to alert the physician to an abnormal ECG or a life-threatening situa-tion. The MA must therefore be familiar with waveforms and rates and be able to rapidly interpret irregularities.

Using ECG calipers, you will measure P-to-P or R-to-R intervals to determine if atrial (P waves) and ventricular (QRS complexes) rhythms are regular. You will calculate measurements of the PR interval (normal range 0.12 to 2.0 seconds) and QRS complex (normal range less than 12 seconds). Atrial and ventricular rates are both calculated because the rates may be different with some cardiac arrhythmias. If P waves or QRS complexes are not visible, you will not be able to calculate atrial and ventricular rates, respectively, by multiplying each number in a six-second strip × 10. If you cannot identify QRS complexes, the patient is in a life-threatening clinical situation or an electrode and wire have become disconnected. *Always* check the patient for clinical signs and symptoms of cardiac and respiratory arrest, and look for signs of disconnection between the ECG, the electrodes, or the wires before initiating CPR.

(text continues on p. 358)

TABLE 17-10 CARDIAC RHYTHMS

Normal sinus rhythm (NSR)	P wave originates in SA node, measures 0.12 to 2.0 seconds. QRS complex has normal waveform and is complete in less than 0.12 seconds. T wave has a positive deflection. Beats per minute (BPM) are 60–100 (Figure 17-30 ◆).
Sinus bradycardia	Normal waveform and complex, only less than 60 BPM (Figure 17-31 ◆).
Sinus tachycardia	Normal waveform and complex, only greater than 100 BPM (Figure 17-32 ◆).
Atrial fibrillation (**A-fib**)	Irregularly spaced QRS complexes with noticeable absence of P waves, replaced by F waves (Figure 17-33 ◆)
Atrial flutter	Electrical impulses are generated at a rapid rate in a single irritable source in the atria. Normal P waves are not present with F waves; flutter or sawtooth patterns instead (Figure 17-34 ◆).
Supraventricular tachycardia (SVT)	Encompasses all tachycardias originating above the ventricle with BPM over 100: sinus tachycardia, atrial tachycardia, paroxysmal atrial tachycardia, paroxysmal supraventricular tachycardia, paroxysmal junctional tachycardia, and junctional tachycardia.
Paroxysmal atrial tachycardia (PAT)	Atrial tachycardia with sudden onset.
Premature atrial contractions (PACs)	Occur when a single electrical impulse originates outside the SA node (Figure 17-35 ◆).
Premature junctional rhythm (PJC)	Electrical impulse originates from a single site in the AV junction and earlier than the next expected complex (Figure 17-36 ◆).
Bundle branch block (**BBB**)	Normal P wave. QRS complex is notched.
First-degree AV block	PR interval is greater than 0.20 second (Figure 17-37 ◆).
Second-degree heart block I, Mobitz Type I	P:P waves are normal interval, but R:R intervals are irregular. There is a progressive lengthening of the PR interval until a QRS complex is not conducted or present (Figure 17-38 ◆).
Second-degree heart block II, Mobitz Type II	More P waves than QRS complexes, but the PR wave has a constant interval, resulting in a slowed ventricular rate (Figure 17-39 ◆).
Third-degree heart block	No consistent relationship between P waves and QRS complexes (Figure 17-40 ◆).
Premature ventricular contractions (PVCs)	Individual complexes, not a rhythm, originate from an ectopic or irritable focus in the ventricle. No blood is pumped from the heart during a PVC, and the individual feels as if the heart is "skipping a beat."
Unifocal PVCs	PVC arises from the same focus each time, and the complexes are uniform in shape or appearance (Figure 17-41 ◆).
Multifocal PVCs	PVCs arise from different foci in the ventricle and have different shapes or configurations (Figure 17-42 ◆).
Ventricular tachycardia (**V-tach**)	Three or more PVCs in a sequence with a rate of more than 100 BPM (Figure 17-43 ◆).
Ventricular fibrillation (**V-fib**)	Often described as a fatal arrhythmia; contains no coordinated atrial or ventricular contractions and no palpable pulse (Figure 17-44 ◆).
Asystole	Straight line, cardiac standstill. No atrial or ventricular activity is present (Figure 17-45 ◆).

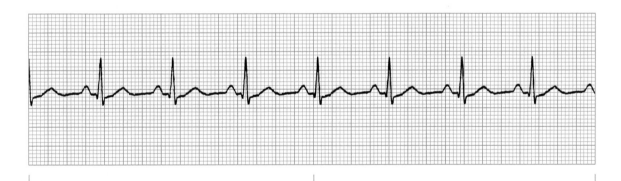

Figure 17-30 ◆ Normal sinus rhythm

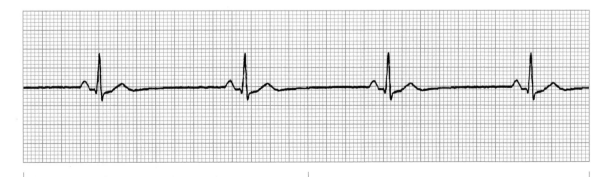

Figure 17-31 ◆ Sinus bradycardia rhythm

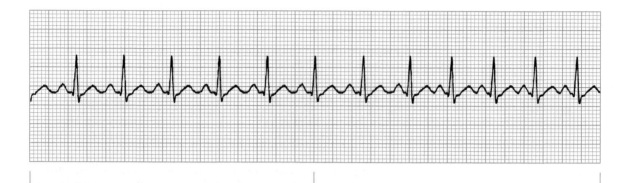

Figure 17-32 ◆ Sinus tachycardia rhythm

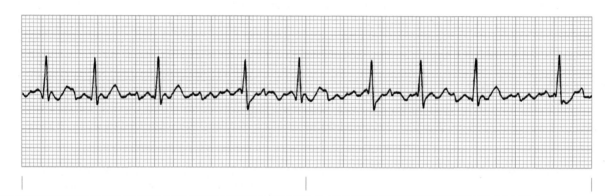

Figure 17-33 ◆ Atrial fibrillation (a-fib)

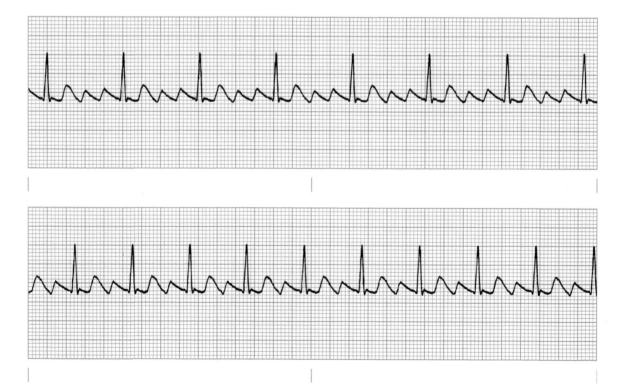

Figure 17-34 ◆ Atrial flutter

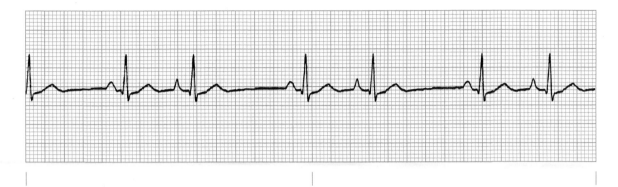

Figure 17-35 ◆ Premature atrial contractions (PAC)

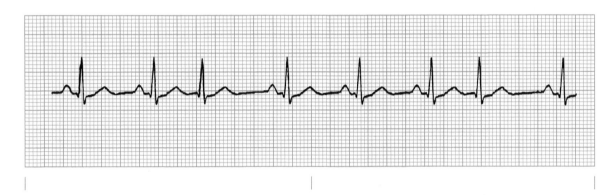

Figure 17-36 ◆ Premature junctional contractions (PJC)

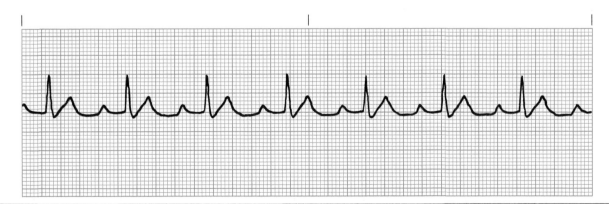

Figure 17-37 ◆ First-degree AV block

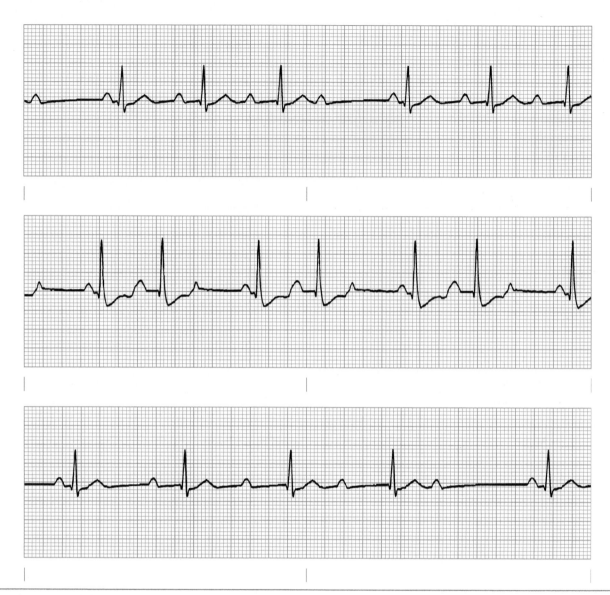

Figure 17-38 ◆ Second-degree heart block I, Mobitz Type I

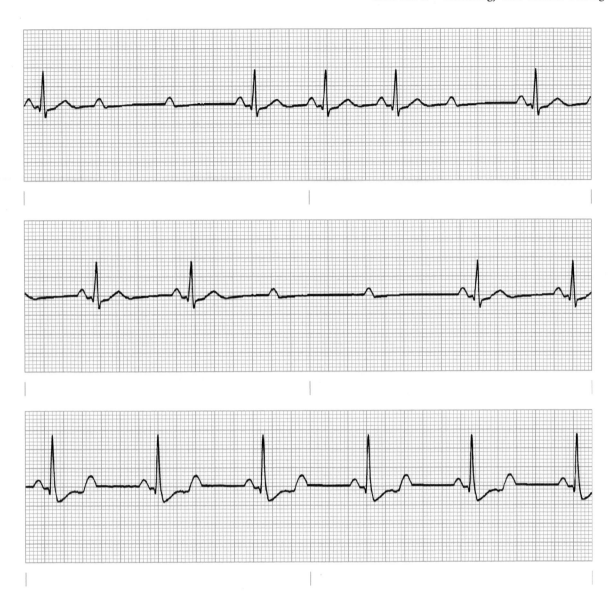

Figure 17-39 ◆ Second-degree heart block II, Mobitz Type II

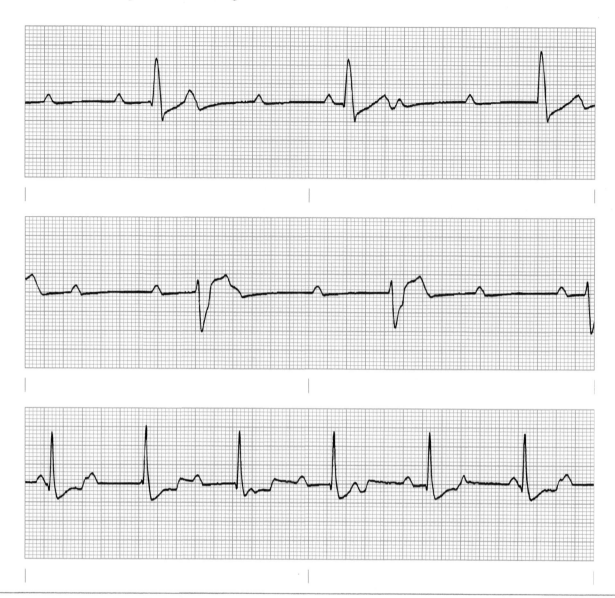

Figure 17-40 ◆ Third-degree heart block

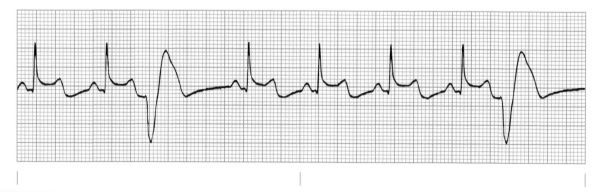

Figure 17-41 ◆ Unifocal PVCs (premature ventricular contractions)

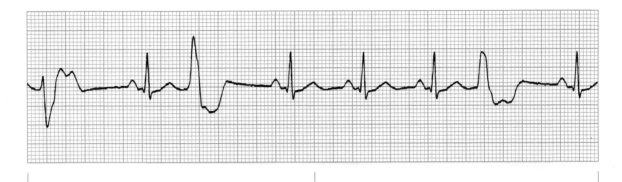

Figure 17-42 ◆ Multifocal PVCs (premature ventricular contractions)

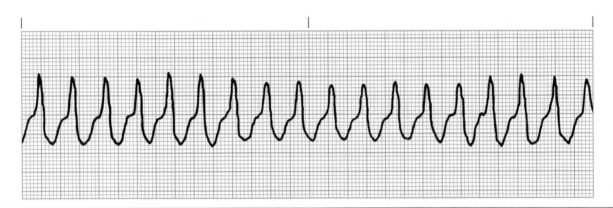

Figure 17-43 ◆ Ventricular tachycardia (V-tach)

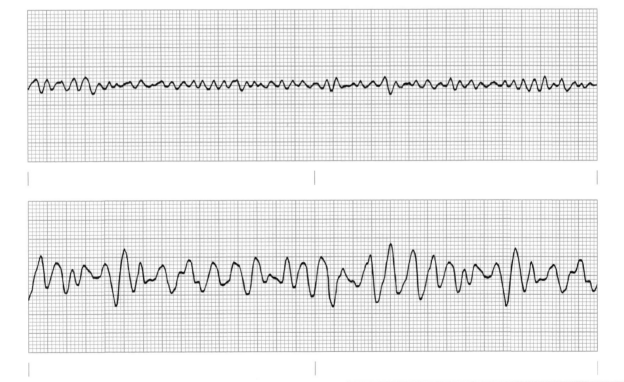

Figure 17-44 ◆ Ventricular fibrillation (V-fib)

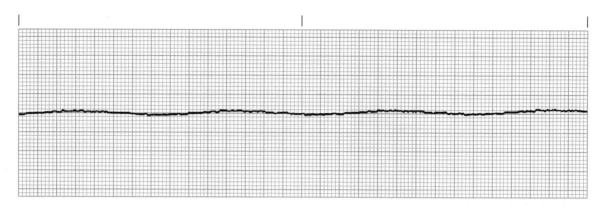

Figure 17-45 ◆ Asystole

The following are additional considerations when analyzing ECG conduction patterns.

1. Are some QRS complexes wider, premature to the regular rhythm, or different in appearance? Is there a pattern to the irregular, premature QRS complexes?
2. With the ECG calipers, measure the PR interval. Multiply the number of small squares by 0.4 seconds. Is the measurement within or outside the normal range of 0.12 to 0.20?
3. Present your ECG calculations to the physician for further analysis and interpretation. If the clinical condition of the patient changes and deteriorates rapidly, take the ECG to the physician and report signs and symptoms immediately.

As an example, the abnormal P waves, or flutter waves, of atrial flutter occur at a much faster rate. The high rate of P wave conduction is blocked along the conduction pathway to the ventricles. Therefore, the reduced number of conducted impulses to the ventricles, or number of QRS complexes, is less than the atrial rate or P wave count. The P-to-P and R-to-R intervals are both regular. The QRS complex may be normal, wider, or have a "rabbit ear" appearance due to past or current cardiac events.

All ECGs are given to the physician for interpretation. The measurements of the PR interval and QRS complex and the shape of all waveforms or segments may be within normal limits or may be affected by medications or past and current history of cardiac disease or heart attack. Some ECG equipment automatically provides an interpretation, but the physician analyzes, interprets, and verifies the programmed findings. ECGs are kept together in the same area of the patient chart so the physician can compare present and past electrocardiograms.

REVIEW

- Medical assistants in a cardiology office perform selected procedures and assist with others. Assessment of the cardiac patient includes taking vital signs, measuring height and weight, and assisting with ECG, rhythm assessment, and evaluation of various pulse points.

- Understanding heart anatomy and conduction is crucial to performing or assisting with cardiac testing. Deoxygenated blood enters the right atrium, passes through the tricuspid valve to the right ventricle, and continues to the lungs, where it is oxygenated. The blood then passes to the left atrium, through the left ventricle, and to all parts of the body. After the blood circulates oxygen and other nutrients to the cells, it returns to the right atrium, deoxygenated.

- The heart is a mechanical pump that is stimulated to contract by the sinoatrial node. If the SA node does not initiate the impulse, lower pacemaker cells in the heart can do so as a "survival" effort. The conduction of a healthy heart originates at the SA node of the right atrium and spreads through each atrium to the atrioventricular node, the bundle of His, and the Purkinje fibers in each ventricle. Many factors can affect the function of the mechanical and electrical systems of the heart. Electrolyte imbalance, previous or current cardiac history, and other existing medical conditions can cause or predispose a patient to cardiac events.

- Cardiac patients often complain of chest pain, irregular heartbeats, dyspnea, edema, and fatigue. Complaints of nausea, sudden onset of extensive sweating, and denial of heart attack are symptoms of an impending MI and demand immediate intervention.

- Coronary artery disease is the result of plaque buildup, or atherosclerosis that causes the coronary arteries to harden (arteriosclerosis). Blood flow is impeded to the point of complete obstruction. Pain results as oxygen and nutrition to the myocardium are denied; when deprivation is severe, the tissue dies, causing a myocardial infarct and possible death. There are two forms of "heart attack." One occurs when the reduced blood flow to the myocardium causes anginal pain and myocardial ischemia. The second type occurs when the conduction system suffers an insult. Arrhythmias may be caused by coronary artery obstruction. Lethal arrhythmias may be caused by electrocution, trauma, and drug overdose.

- Angina is a pressure-like pain, usually in the chest region, the left arm, possibly the left jaw, occasionally the right chest and arm. It is generally experienced on exertion and ceases a few minutes after rest. Until angina is confirmed, the patient must be treated as if experiencing an impending heart attack. The physician must be notified immediately. Vasodilating drugs and calcium channel blocking drugs are used to treat angina.

- Myocardial infarction demands immediate intervention to restore blood flow to the myocardium. Angioplasty, stent insertion, and coronary artery bypass surgery are invasive techniques used to reverse the blockage. Post-myocardial patients are often treated in the cardiology office.

- Sudden cardiac arrest occurs when the conduction system of the heart fails, often following a sudden and severe occlusion of the coronary arteries. It may also be the result of respiratory arrest, drowning, or massive hemorrhage. Immediate intervention consists of CPR and AED.

- Hypertension, or high blood pressure, occurs when blood pressure readings are consistently over 140/90. Elevated blood pressure increases the workload of the heart as it pumps blood through constricted vessels. Arteriosclerosis, atherosclerosis, and renal disease often are precursors to hypertension and hypertensive heart disease. Stress and being overweight are contributing factors. Essential hypertension is chronic hypertension with no identifiable cause. There is no cure, and drug therapy with diuretics, vasodilating drugs, ACE inhibitors, and beta-blocking agents must be continued for life. Nondrug therapy includes stress reduction, weight reduction, dietary changes, and exercise.

- A patient with congestive heart failure (CHF) complains of shortness of breath (SOB), weight gain, edema, and possibly exhaustion. Symptoms have an insidious onset and dyspnea becomes severe. Pitting edema, distended neck veins, and respiratory distress are other signs. Radiographs of the chest are helpful in the diagnosis. Treatment includes diuretics, cardiac glycosides, vasodilators, restriction of fluid and sodium intake, and daily weighing.

- Pulmonary edema follows CHF as fluid fills the lungs, increasing the workload of the heart. Dyspnea and coughing of frothy, bloody sputum occur, especially at night. Treatment is aimed at decreasing fluid in the lungs with diuretics, Lanoxin, vasodilators, and bronchodilating drugs.

- Cardiomyopathy is a noninflammatory disease of the myocardium often with no identifiable cause. The muscle in the heart wall thickens, with resulting inefficiency of the heartbeat. The only treatment may be a transplant.

- Arrhythmias, or irregular heartbeats, are classified in different ways: by disturbances of impulse formation, by disturbances in conduction, or according to prognosis. When the impulse does not originate in the SA node, it is a disturbance in origin. When the impulse does not follow the normal pathway through the conduction system (SA node, AV node, bundle of His, and Purkinje fibers), it is a disturbance in conduction.

- Infective and inflammatory diseases of the myocardium include rheumatic heart disease, endocarditis, myocarditis, and pericarditis. These diseases may lead to cardiomyopathies and cardiomegalies. Rheumatic heart disease is a sequela to rheumatic fever, which is a sequela to a Group A beta-hemolytic *Streptococcus* infection of the throat. Aggressive drug therapy with antibiotics is the usual course of action.

(continued)

Chapter Summary (continued)

■ Valvular diseases occur on any of the four heart valves. Inflammation and infectious processes in the endocardium may result in scarring of the valves. If the valve fails to open completely, as in stenosis, not all the blood is emptied into the next chamber, and pressure increases in the previous chamber. If the valve fails to close completely, blood is forced back into the previous chamber, also increasing the pressure in that chamber. Symptoms include dyspnea, shortness of breath, and sometimes cyanosis. ECGs, echocardiograms, radiographs of the chest, and cardiac catheterization are used to diagnose valvular conditions. Treatment includes bed rest, fluid restriction, diuretics, and oxygen therapy. Infectious processes are treated with antibiotics. Surgery to free up the stenosis or replace the damaged valve may be performed.

■ Phlebitis, an inflammatory condition of veins, usually occurs in the deep veins of the lower limbs. Tenderness in the affected area is often the first symptom, followed by increasing pain, redness, and swelling. Analgesics are given and the individual is instructed not to rub or massage the area.

■ Thrombophlebitis, an inflammatory condition, occurs in a vein where a thrombus has formed on the wall. Blood flow in the vein is compromised and edema occurs. The individual experiences pain, edema, warmth, redness in the area, systemic chills, and fever. Insult to the vessel, particularly to the walls, venous stasis, and hypercoagulating blood are all causes. Venograms and ultrasound confirm diagnosis. Treatment involves immobilization of the affected limb and administration of anticoagulant drugs and antibiotics.

■ An embolus is a mass of material that forms an obstruction, or embolism, in a blood or lymphatic vessel. Emboli that occlude the vessel cause infarction of the tissue supplied by that vessel. Deep-vein thrombosis is often the result of stasis of the blood in the deep vessels of the legs brought on by inactivity. Other causes include blood that has a tendency to clot quickly, insult to the vessels, and surgery such as hip and knee replacement and prostate surgery.

■ Conditions of the peripheral vessels of the hands and feet include Raynaud's disease and Buerger's disease. Raynaud's occurs when the small vessels in the extremities spasm as a result of exposure to cold or stress. Cigarette smoking aggravates the condition. Buerger's disease affects mainly males and results from inflammation of the vessels of the legs and feet. Obstruction of the vessels may lead to clot formation and severe pain in the extremities. Smoking is a primary causative factor.

■ The 12-lead ECG takes a short snapshot of the electrical activity of the heart from different angles of the conduction system. A Holter monitor allows for a 24-hour study of the conduction system.

■ The echocardiogram is a noninvasive ultrasound that examines the movements and anatomical structures of the heart while the patient rests. Stress testing is performed while the patient is exercising, usually on a treadmill or stationary bicycle. Thallium and MUGA scans are invasive tests that identify damaged, unhealthy areas of the heart.

■ Procedures performed on cardiac patients include cardiac catheterization to evaluate the status of the coronary arteries. Stent insertion may follow angioplasty to help keep the coronary artery lumen patent. Coronary artery bypass graft surgery is performed when other attempts to maintain patent coronary arteries will not achieve the goal.

■ MAs play an important role in cardiac testing. They perform procedures such as blood testing or assist with ECGs, echocardiograms, Holter monitor recording, stress testing, thallium scans, and MUGA scans. The MA must be able to identify and alert the physician to abnormal electrocardiograms.

Chapter Review Questions

Multiple Choice

1. The mitral valve is located between the
   A. left atrium and right atrium.
   B. left atrium and respiratory circulation.
   C. left ventricle and right ventricle.
   D. left atrium and left ventricle.

2. Cardiac muscle cells have all the following properties except
   A. reproductivity.
   B. excitability.
   C. automaticity.
   D. contractility.

3. The pacemaker of the heart is the
   A. atrioventricular node.
   B. sinoatrial node.
   C. ventricular node.
   D. bundle node.

4. Angina-type pain, shortness of breath, weakness or dizziness, rapid heartbeat, palpitations, nausea, and perspiration are symptoms of
   A. hypertension.
   B. sinus bradycardia.
   C. coronary artery disease.
   D. phlebitis.

Chapter Review Questions (continued)

5. Myocardial infarction occurs because of
   A. opening blood flow from coronary bypass surgery.
   B. obstruction of blood flow, ischemia, and resulting death to tissues.
   C. a change in heart rate or respiratory rate.
   D. a change to reduce cardiac risk factors.

6. Treatment for congestive heart failure includes
   A. diuretics, digitalis preparations, and vasodilators.
   B. diuretics, digitalis preparations, and sodium-enriched diet.
   C. diuretics, vasodilators, and laxatives.
   D. none of the above.

7. Arrhythmias usually result from
   A. normal activities of daily living.
   B. maintaining a healthy lifestyle.
   C. reducing cardiac risk factors.
   D. disease conditions that impair the normal electrical conduction of the heart.

8. In sinus bradycardia, the heart rate is abnormally slow and the electrical impulse originates in the
   A. sinojunctional node.
   B. sinus of the left atrium.
   C. sinoatrial node.
   D. sinus of the right atrium.

9. The causative agent of endocarditis, myocarditis, and pericarditis is
   A. caffeine-containing substances.
   B. viral, fungal, bacterial, or parasitic.
   C. working and living in smoke-filled environments.
   D. working without personal protective equipment (PPE).

10. Rheumatic heart disease is caused by
    A. bacterial infection.
    B. fungal infection.
    C. viral infection.
    D. parasitic infestation.

True/False

T F 1. Nausea, excessive sweating, and denial of a possible heart attack should be taken seriously.

T F 2. An ECG measures the electrical activity of the myocardium.

T F 3. Arteries (except the pulmonary arteries) carry oxygenated blood and veins carry deoxygenated blood.

T F 4. A healthy heart contracts and relaxes no more than 60 times per minute.

T F 5. The AV node is known as the "pacemaker" of the heart.

Short Answer

1. What is the difference between arteriosclerosis and atherosclerosis?

2. What are the two kinds of risk factors for coronary artery disease?

3. Describe pulmonary edema.

4. Name two dietary changes that are helpful in controlling hypertension.

5. What is the function of a Holter monitor?

Research

1. Are MAs in your state allowed to assist in a thallium scan? If so, what is their role in the procedure?

2. Are MAs in your state allowed to assist in a treadmill stress test? If so, what is their role?

Externship Application Experience

What would you do if a flat line appeared on the screen while you were performing an ECG? A flat line means that the electrocardiograph is not receiving any record of cardiac electrical activity. Does this mean that your patient has had cardiac arrest? What should you do? What should you not do?

Resource Guide

American College of Cardiology
9111 Old Georgetown Road
Bethesda, MD 20814
1-800-253-4636
www.acc.org

American Heart Association
7272 Greenville Ave.
Dallas, TX 75231
1-800-AHA-USA1
www.amhrt.org

American Red Cross
www.redcross.org

Med**Media**

www.prenhall.com/frazier

More on this chapter, including interactive resources, can be found on the Student CD-ROM accompanying this textbook and on the Companion Website at www.prenhall.com/frazier.

Objectives

After completing this chapter, you should be able to:

- Spell and define medical terminology in this chapter.
- Define the medical assistant's role in a pulmonology practice.
- Identify lower airway structures and their functions.
- Discuss lung and chest mechanics and the gas mechanics of respiration.
- Describe the symptoms, causes, and treatments for obstructive respiratory conditions, infectious and inflammatory pulmonary conditions, pulmonary malignancies, and mechanical insults.
- Describe breathing patterns and other signs and symptoms of pulmonary disorders.
- List pulmonary function tests that may be performed in a medical office.
- Discuss the role of inhalers and nebulizers in pulmonary treatment.
- Explain oxygen therapy and how it is administered.

Pulmonology and Pulmonary Testing

Case Study

Keera is assigned to work in a pulmonology office as part of her externship. Since she started working, she has learned to take patients' vital signs and chief complaints and perform spirometry and peak flow testing. Today her preceptor is teaching her how to obtain a sputum sample from a patient and give inhaler instructions for several new types that have come on the market.

MedMedia
www.prenhall.com/frazier

Additional interactive resources and activities for this chapter can be found on the Companion Website. For audio glossary, legal and ethical scenarios, job scenarios, quizzes, games, virtual tours, and activities related to the content of this chapter, please access the accompanying CD-ROM in this book.

 **Assets Available:**

Audio Glossary
Legal and Ethical Scenario: *Pulmonology and Pulmonary Testing*
On the Job Scenario: *Pulmonology and Pulmonary Testing*
A & P Quiz: The Respiratory System; TB Testing & Analysis
Multiple Choice Quiz
Games: Crossword, Strikeout and Spelling Bee
3D Virtual Tours: The Respiratory System: Respiratory System
Drag & Drop: Respiratory System: Interior of the Lung; Respiratory System: The Lungs;
    Respiratory System: Diaphragm

Medical Terminology

alveolus (plural: alveoli)—microscopic air sacs that are the primary unit of gas exchange in the lungs

asthma—lung disease characterized by wheezing and shortness of breath; often caused by an allergic response; also known as reversible airway obstruction

bronchiole—airway less than 1 mm in diameter

bronchitis—lung disease characterized by large volumes of pulmonary secretions and air trapping; can be chronic or acute in nature

bronchodilator—medication that dilates the walls of the bronchi

bronchus (plural: bronchi)—one of two primary airways that branch into the lungs

diaphragm—primary muscle of breathing; separates chest and abdominal cavities

dyspnea—difficult breathing

emphysema—disease of chronic airways obstruction (COLD) in which air is trapped; usually caused by either smoking or heredity

eupnea—normal breathing

hemopneumothorax—accumulation of blood and air in the pleural cavity, resulting in the partial or complete collapse of the lung

hemoptysis—coughing up sputum containing blood

hemothorax—accumulation of blood and fluids in the pleural cavity that limit the expansion of the lung

hepatotoxicity—harmful effect of drugs on the liver

immunocompetence—body's ability to fight infection; capacity for normal immune response

intradermal—between the layers of the skin

noninvasive—pertaining to a procedure or technique that does not require entry into the body by incision or inserting an instrument

orthopnea—ability to breathe only in a standing or upright sitting position

ototoxicity—harmful effect of drugs on the nerves or organs in the ear

pneumothorax—the collection of air or gas in the pleural cavity that causes the lung to partially or completely collapse

pulmonary function testing—testing performed to evaluate airflow and lung volume

septum—a thin wall dividing the two sides of the interior nose

tachypnea—rapid breathing

➕ MEDICAL ASSISTING COMPETENCIES

CAAHEP ENTRY-LEVEL COMPETENCIES FOR CMA	ABHES ENTRY-LEVEL COMPETENCIES FOR RMA
▪ Identify and respond to issues of confidentiality.	▪ Project a positive attitude.
▪ Perform within legal and ethical boundaries.	▪ Maintain confidentiality at all times.
▪ Demonstrate knowledge of federal and state health-care legislation and regulations.	▪ Be a "team player."
	▪ Be cognizant of ethical boundaries.
▪ Perform hand washing.	▪ Exhibit initiative.
▪ Dispose of biohazardous materials.	▪ Adapt to change.
▪ Practice Standard Precautions.	▪ Evidence a responsible attitude.
▪ Use methods of quality control.	▪ Be courteous and diplomatic.
▪ Perform respiratory testing.	▪ Conduct work within scope of education, training, and ability.
▪ Perform telephone and in-person screening.	▪ Interview and take a patient history.
▪ Obtain vital signs.	▪ Prepare patients for and assist physician with routine and specialty examinations and treatments and minor office surgery.
▪ Obtain and record patient history.	▪ Apply principles of aseptic techniques and infection control.
▪ Prepare and maintain examination and treatment areas.	▪ Prepare and maintain examination and treatment area.
▪ Prepare patient for and assist with routine and specialty examinations.	▪ Collect and process specimens.
▪ Prepare patient and assist with minor procedures, treatments, and minor surgery.	▪ Dispose of biohazardous materials.
▪ Apply pharmacology principles to prepare and administer oral and parenteral medications.	▪ Practice Standard Precautions.
▪ Maintain medication and immunization records.	▪ Prepare and administer oral and parenteral medications as directed by the physician.
	▪ Maintain medication and immunization records.
	▪ Perform respiratory testing.

Introduction

Pulmonary testing is performed to decide which part of the pulmonary system is involved in a disorder. Testing includes determining

- The patient's ability move to air in and out of the upper airway.
- The compliance of the patient's lungs.
- The effectiveness of bronchodilators and other medications.
- Therapy treatments.

A licensed respiratory care practitioner usually evaluates and analyzes pulmonary disorders.

The Medical Assistant's Role in Pulmonology

Respiratory disorders are divided according to the part of the system affected: the upper or lower area. An ear, nose, and throat (**ENT**) specialist usually treats upper respiratory disorders. Pulmonologists treat lower pulmonary, or lower respiratory, disorders. As a medical assistant

Abbreviations

ABG—arterial blood gases

AFB—acid-fast bacillus

BCG—bacillus Calmette-Guérin

COPD—chronic obstructive pulmonary disease

EENT—ears, eyes, nose, throat

ENT—ear, nose, and throat

MDI—metered dose inhaler

O₂ sat—oxygen saturation

PaCO₂—partial pressure of carbon dioxide

PaO₂—partial pressure of oxygen

PEF—peak expiratory flow

PFT—pulmonary function testing

PPD—purified protein derivative

TB—tuberculosis

COMPETENCY SKILLS PERFORMANCE

1. Demonstrate performance of spirometry.

2. Demonstrate performance of peak flow testing.

3. Demonstrate performance of the Mantoux test by intradermal injection.

4. Demonstrate patient instruction in the use of an inhaler.

5. Demonstrate patient instruction in the use of a nebulizer.

---

in the pulmonology office, you will help patients by giving emotional support, carrying out or assisting the physician with treatments, and giving educational support to the patient as directed by the physician and respiratory technicians.

State practice acts must be followed regarding the procedures you can do.

The Anatomy and Physiology of the Pulmonary System

The respiratory tree consists of the lungs, air passages serving the lungs, and anatomical structures of the thoracic and abdominal cavities that surround the lungs (Figure 18-1 ◆). Each structure is dependent on the others to function.

The Upper Airway

The upper airway consists mainly of the nose, but also includes the adjacent zone structures of the pharynx, where the nasal, oral, and laryngeal cavities meet. The two sides of the interior nose are separated by the nasal **septum.** (∞ Refer to Chapter 19, EENT, for a more detailed discussion of the anatomical structures of the upper airway.)

The Lower Airways

The lungs are located inside the thoracic cavity (chest) in a sealed system with only one opening—the upper airway. Twelve pairs of ribs surrounding the entire cavity protect the lungs. The ribs also aid in the respiratory process as the muscles surrounding them bring air into and out of the lungs during contraction and relaxation. The **diaphragm** forms the bottom of the pleural cavity and also aids in respiration. As it rises, it helps push the air out of the lungs; as it retracts, it makes the pleural cavity larger, allowing air to enter the lungs.

The area containing the heart, lungs, and trachea is called the pleural cavity. The right lung, with three lobes, is slightly larger than the left lung, which has two. The heart is nestled in a sulcus, or fold, of the left lung. Each lung has a double-folded membranous covering, called a pleura. The inside layer is the visceral pleura, and the outer aspect is the parietal pleura. A serous, watery substance acts as a lubricant between the two layers.

The trachea is the beginning of the lower airway. The trachea divides into two branches, the right and left bronchi. The **bronchi** lead to the right and left lungs, dividing into smaller and smaller tube-like structures, eventually becoming **bronchioles.** At the end of the bronchioles are clusters of air sacs called **alveoli.** The alveolar walls are only one cell thick, facilitating the exchange of gas with surrounding capillaries. Capillary blood absorbs inhaled oxygen from the alveoli while exchanging carbon dioxide (CO_2), which is then exhaled from the lungs.

Pulmonary Physiology

Pulmonary physiology can be separated into lung tissue elasticity, chest mechanics, and gas exchange.

The physical mechanics of respiration are divided into inhalation and exhalation. Lungs are elastic—they return to their normal shape after being stretched. When the diaphragm falls, or relaxes, the lungs expand, creating a negative or lower pressure in the airways and cellular lung tissue. Oxygen-rich atmospheric air, of higher pressure, enters and expands the lungs. This is inhalation. This is followed by a contraction of the diaphragm and thoracic muscles, which raise and squeeze lung tissue, creating higher lung pressure and lower atmospheric pressure. CO_2-laden is exhaled (Figures 18-2 ◆).

Patients with obstructive lung disease, such as **emphysema, bronchitis,** and **asthma,** have less elastic (more compliant) lungs. They can inhale fairly easily; however, their lungs do not return to their normal shape, and they trap the air.

On the other hand, some patients have more difficulty expanding their lungs. This means their lungs are more elastic (less compliant) and hold less air. Restrictive lung diseases include pulmonary edema, pneumoconiosis (also called *black lung*), and asbestosis. Black lung disease is often associated with coal miners.

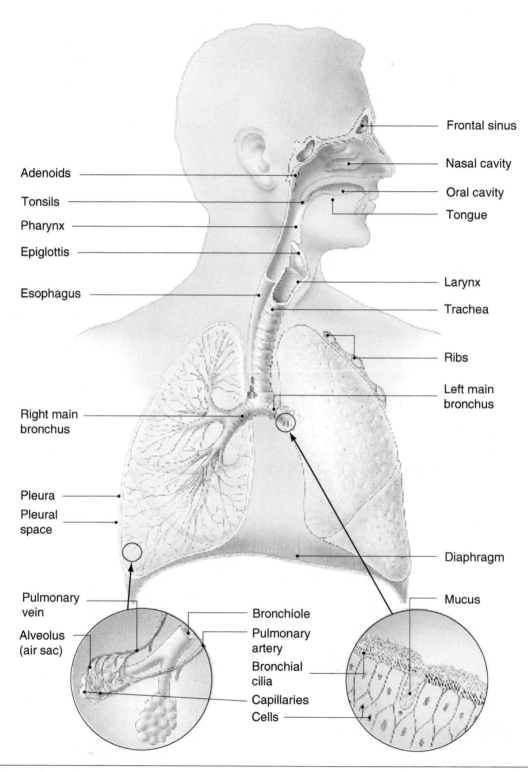

Figure 18-1 ◆ The respiratory system

Both conditions, the inability to expand the lungs or the inability to expel air, cause the patient to suffer apnea—the inability to breathe. Long-term episodes of apnea lead to hypoxemia, which may cause dizzy spells.

The Mechanics of Gas Exchange

Gases move from point to point because of the physical law of diffusion. Diffusion occurs when molecules move across a membrane from an area of high concentration to an area of low concentration. The process requires no energy expenditure. Oxygen and carbon dioxide are exchanged in the lungs through the process of diffusion.

Blood from the right side of the heart that circulates to the lungs is oxygen-poor and carbon-dioxide-rich. As this blood enters the lung during inhalation, the available oxygen from inhalation diffuses into the blood and raises the oxygen level to

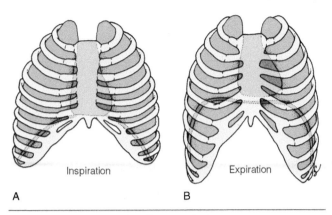

Figure 18-2 ◆ (A) Inhalation; (B) Exhalation

Keys to Success
COAL MINER'S HEALTH SAFETY ACT

"Black lung" is the common term for pneumoconiosis or anthracosis. This chronic disease is caused by breathing coal dust over an extended period and is aggravated by cigarette smoking. The Coal Miner's Health and Safety Act of 1969 was enacted to ensure the safety of coal miners, whose livelihood exposes them daily to the risk of black lung. Under the Act, coal miners must be compensated for the permanent lung damage they suffer on the job. The claim filing process requires a skilled medical claims filer in the medical office.

100 mmHg. The extra carbon dioxide from the blood diffuses into the lung and is exhaled. As the blood leaves the lungs, it is ready for transport to the rest of the body, replenished with oxygen and holding normal amounts of carbon dioxide. This oxygen-rich blood returns to the left side of the heart to be pumped to the heart muscle, to the head, and to all of the organs and tissues of the body.

Diseases and Disorders of the Pulmonary System

Upper respiratory disease conditions, such as acute rhinitis (common cold), rhinitis (hay fever), sinusitis, pharyngitis, and laryngitis, involve the nose and throat. The common cold is the most common upper respiratory infection and is usually caused by a viral group known as rhinovirus. (∞ See Chapter 19, EENT, for further discussion of upper respiratory diseases.)

Diseases that affect the lower respiratory system can be broadly classified into obstructive diseases, infection and inflammatory diseases, malignancies, and mechanical insults.

Lower Respiratory Obstructive Diseases

Chronic obstructive pulmonary disease (**COPD**) is the collective name for lung diseases characterized by long-term, steadily worsening airway blockage. COPD is most often caused by smoking, but long-term exposure to chemicals, fumes, or organic dust is another causative factor. Air pollution worsens symptoms. Chronic bronchitis and emphysema are the most common diagnoses linked to COPD; some patients suffer from both. Treatment includes oxygen therapy, medications, preventing infection, and quitting smoking.

Other obstructive diseases of the lower respiratory system include asthma, acute bronchitis, and pneumonoconiosis (Table 18-1). All these conditions involve airway obstruction at the bronchi, bronchioles, or alveoli.

TABLE 18-1 LOWER RESPIRATORY OBSTRUCTIVE DISEASES

Disease	Symptoms	Diagnosis	Treatment

Asthma
■ Lung disease also called bronchial asthma
■ Leading cause of childhood illness and school absences
■ Asymptomatic unless triggered by individual specific allergen or non-allergen factors
■ Attacks vary in severity
	■ SOB
	■ Wheezing
	■ Productive or nonproductive cough
	■ Leaning forward over chair, table, or counter to use accessory muscles for exhaling
	■ Skin pale and moist
	■ Cyanosis of nail bed in severe attacks
		■ Patient presenting symptoms
		■ PFT
			■ Avoid triggers
			■ Inhaler for preventive use and at onset of attack
			■ Nebulizer (used mainly in hospital setting)
			■ Asthma triggers
			  1. Allergens including mold, animal dander, dust, cockroach excrement, various foods, pollen, and household mites
			  2. stress and/or anxiety
			  3. infection
			  4. inhalation of allergens
			  5. exercise and/or overexertion
			  6. exposure to cigarette smoke
			  7. aerosol sprays or perfume

Legionellosis/Legionnaire's disease ■ Form of pneumonia caused by infection with the bacteria *Legionella pneumophila*	■ Initial generalized flu-like symptoms include malaise, cough, headache.	■ Radiographs of the chest ■ Sputum cultures positive for *Legionellosis pneumophila*	■ Antibiotic therapy ■ Antipyretics ■ Fluid replacement if indicated

continued

TABLE 18-1 LOWER RESPIRATORY OBSTRUCTIVE DISEASES *(continued)*

Disease	Symptoms	Diagnosis	Treatment
Legionellosis (*cont.*) ■ Acute respiratory tract infection ■ Identified after epidemic occurred at the 1976 American Legion convention in Philadelphia; over 200 people contracted the disease and 34 died as a result of the infection. ■ Bacteria live and grow in warm aquatic environments such as cooling towers, areosolized droplets from air conditioners, spas, and showers.	■ Pneumonia-like symptoms, including fever, chills, dyspnea, chest pain, anorexia, vomiting, diarrhea	■ Elevated WBC, elevated liver emzyme levels	■ Oxygen therapy
Emphysema ■ Chronic lung disease ■ Caused by trapped air in overextended, inflated alveoli	■ Mucus ■ Able or unable to cough ■ Thin, barrel-chested body type ■ Leaning forward (see "Asthma" above)	■ Patient presenting symptoms ■ Physical examination ■ Testing: PFT, chest X-rays, blood tests	■ Mucolytic agents to liquefy and loosen mucus in pulmonary airways, along with **bronchodilator**, steroid, and antibiotic medications ■ Quitting smoking, for medical reasons and for safety when using oxygen ■ "Pursed-lip" breathing to push trapped air out of the alveoli ■ Frequent, small meals and snacks to maintain health. ■ Mental health counseling and support group access when physical condition worsens and patient becomes more disabled and dependent
Acute bronchitis ■ Lung disease resulting from severe cold, flu, or no clear cause ■ Short in duration, usually lasting about 10 days ■ May progress farther down bronchial tree to bronchioles and air sacs, resulting in bronchopneumonia	■ Mucus ■ Cough ■ Possible chest pain and fever	■ Patient presenting symptoms ■ Physical examination ■ PFT	■ Rest to ease fatigue and strengthen immune system ■ Staying inside during cold weather to help prevent coughing ■ High fluid intake to thin mucous secretions and promote productive cough to clear airways ■ Avoiding cough suppressants except to allow rest. ■ Expectorants to help loosen mucus and promote productive cough ■ Antibiotics if sputum changes from gray to yellow or yellow-green, indicating possible bacterial infection ■ Quitting smoking
Chronic bronchitis ■ Lung disease resulting from repeat attacks of acute bronchitis, prolonged chemical inhalation, or cigarette smoking (main cause) ■ Occurs yearly and lasts a few months or more	■ Increase in mucus ■ Swelling and narrowing of airways ■ Chronic cough ■ Decreased ability to cough mucus from narrow airways ■ Possible increase in dyspnea ■ Greater risk for hypoxia ■ Bacterial infections possible	■ Patient presenting symptoms ■ Physical examination ■ PFT	■ See "Acute Bronchitis" ■ Yearly flu vaccination ■ Pneumonia vaccination ■ Supplemental oxygen as necessary. ■ Bronchodilators or steroids orally or via inhaler or nebulizer ■ Long-term medical management and psychological counseling

TABLE 18-1 LOWER RESPIRATORY OBSTRUCTIVE DISEASES *(continued)*

Bronchiectasis

■ Lung diseases that occur when bronchial tube walls enlarge and obstruct airway, and distended pockets below develop into sites of infection ■ May be a result of immunologic deficiency, cystic fibrosis, pneumonia-related, or obstruction ■ May progress to pneumonia	■ Productive cough with yellow or green sputum ■ Possible hemoptysis ■ Halitosis	■ Physical examination ■ Patient presenting symptoms ■ Sputum culture ■ PFT ■ Chest x-ray ■ CT scan ■ Bronchoscopy ■ Other testing (sweat test or Mantoux test)	■ Bronchodilators ■ Antibiotics ■ Postural drainage (support person helps place patient in upside-down position, so fluids drain to trachea) ■ Pulmonary percussion (support person massages patient by striking body part with light rapid blows) ■ Surgery to remove affected portion of lung

Pneumonoconiosis

■ Group of chronic obstructive lung diseases caused by inhaling dust: anthracosis or "black lung" (coal dust), silicosis (silicon), asbestosis (asbestos fibers)
■ Takes 2 to 20 years to develop; average is after 10 years of continuous exposure
■ Often considered occupational disease
■ No cure
	■ Dyspnea
	■ Dry cough
	■ Bronchitis, asthma, and emphysema may be sequelae
		■ Radiographs
		■ PFT
		■ ABGs
			■ Avoiding exposure to causative agents with mask or respirator
			■ Support treatment
			■ Causative agents
			  1. cigarette smoking
			  2. air pollution
			  3. chronic bronchitis/repeated respiratory tract infections
			  4. long-term exposure to chemical irritants
			  5. inhalation of corrosive gases
			  6. family tendency

Keys to Success
THE EFFECTS OF SMOKING

■ Physical and psychological addiction to nicotine.
■ Decreased growth of lung tissue.
■ Increased respiratory and cardiac symptoms and diseases.
■ Higher risk of premature and low-weight births.
■ Higher risk of different types of cancer.
■ Shorter life expectancy.

Infectious and Inflammatory Conditions

Infectious and inflammatory conditions include pneumonia, influenza, histoplasmosis, pulmonary tuberculosis, Legionnaire's disease, and pleuritis (Table 18-2). In these conditions, infection and inflammation are usually caused by pathogenic microorganisms, usually bacteria or viruses.

Malignancies

Respiratory system malignancies include cancer of the lung(s) and larynx. Often these malignancies show symptoms of an obstructed airway because tumor growth in any respiratory area reduces the amount of oxygen flow. A patient at risk for cancer, such as one who smokes or has a family history, needs constant support and encouragement to practice a healthier lifestyle. (∞ For further discussion of cancers related to the respiratory system, see Chapter 30, Oncology).

Mechanical Insults

Mechanical insults include pulmonary emboli, atelectasis, and the symptoms of **hemoptysis** (Table 18-3). Major traumatic

TABLE 18-2 INFECTIOUS AND INFLAMMATORY CONDITIONS OF THE PULMONARY SYSTEM

Disease	Symptoms	Diagnosis	Treatment
Pneumonia			
■ Lung disease with lower respiratory inflammation of bronchioles and alveoli resulting from infection ■ Can be fatal ■ Bilateral pneumonia affects both lungs; lobar pneumonia affects particular lobe or lobes ■ Tuberculous pneumonia caused by *Mycobacterium tuberculosis* ■ Secondary pneumonia is complication of another medical problem	■ Chills ■ Fever ■ Chest pain or aching ■ Cough ■ Weakness ■ SOB	■ Patient presenting symptoms ■ Physical examination ■ Chest X-ray ■ Sputum culture	■ Antibiotics ■ Rest to ease fatigue and strengthen immune system ■ Higher fluid and calorie intake to strengthen immune system ■ Oxygen as needed ■ Analgesics as needed ■ Pneumonia vaccination for prevention

continued

TABLE 18-2 INFECTIOUS AND INFLAMMATORY CONDITIONS OF THE PULMONARY SYSTEM *(continued)*

Disease	Symptoms	Diagnosis	Treatment
Influenza ■ Upper respiratory viral infection that affects lungs ■ Many varieties of virus ■ Virus spread by moisture droplets from sneezing, coughing, or by contact with contaminated articles, such as facial tissue ■ May put patient at risk for secondary pneumonia	■ Cough ■ Sore throat ■ Sneezing ■ Runny nose ■ Fever ■ Chills ■ Muscle aches ■ Headache ■ Gastrointestinal symptoms (vomiting and diarrhea)	■ Patient presenting symptoms ■ Physical examination	■ Rest ■ Higher fluid intake ■ Analgesics for pain ■ Antipyretics to reduce fever ■ Yearly influenza vaccination to prevent most likely flu strain(s) for that year
Histoplasmosis ■ Fungal infection of lungs ■ May progress to pneumonia ■ When symptoms appear, fungus has already spread through lung tissue	■ Weakness ■ SOB ■ Fever	■ Patient presenting symptoms ■ Chest X-ray ■ Skin test ■ Blood test ■ Sputum or other tissues	■ Antifungal medication if needed ■ Other supportive measures and medications as needed
Pulmonary tuberculosis (TB) ■ Infection of lung tissue, usually by *Mycobacterium tuberculosis* ■ Spread by moisture droplets from sneezing, coughing, or contact with contaminated facial tissue; can also be inhaled through dust carrying inactive bacteria, which become active when moistened ■ Although incidence of TB has been greatly reduced in the United States, case numbers are rising again	■ Loss of appetite, energy, and weight ■ As infection progresses, other symptoms include dyspnea, fever, productive cough, night sweats	■ Patient presenting symptoms ■ Physical examination ■ Chest x-ray ■ Sputum test ■ Blood test ■ Mantoux test	■ Preventive antibiotics when patient has been exposed to TB but does not have the active disease. (Note: Hearing and liver function must be monitored because of **ototoxicity** and **hepatotoxicity** of many anti-tuberculosis drugs) ■ Antibiotics (after a prescribed period of time, patient on antibiotic therapy is no longer contagious) ■ In countries where TB is prevalent, bacillus Calmette-Guérin (**BCG**) vaccine is administered
Extrapulmonary tuberculosis ■ Disease that affects tissues and organs outside of the lungs. ■ Causative organism travels to other oxygen- and blood-rich areas of the body via lymphatic or circulatory systems ■ Accounts for about 15% of patients affected by TB ■ Other nonpulmonary organs or tissues that can be infected include bones and joints, lymph nodes, pleural space surrounding lungs, meninges surrounding brain and spinal cord, peritoneum covering abdominal organs, reproductive organs, and urinary tract	■ Symptoms relate to organ being affected	■ Patient presenting symptoms ■ Physical examination	■ TB medications ■ Other supportive measures
Pleuritis (also called pleurisy or pleuritis) ■ Lung disease with inflammation of visceral pleura membranes caused by infection, trauma, or tumor ■ Usually a secondary result of pneumonia or another infection	■ Sharp chest pains on inhaling and/or coughing	■ Patient presenting symptoms ■ Patient history ■ Physical examination ■ Auscultation of rubbing sounds ■ Chest X-ray	■ Pain medication as needed ■ Antibiotics ■ Heat compresses ■ Encircling chest bandages to decrease chest movement and pain

TABLE 18-3 MECHANICAL INSULTS TO THE PULMONARY SYSTEM

Mechanical Insult	Symptoms	Diagnosis	Treatment
Pulmonary embolus ■ Obstruction of pulmonary artery circulation usually caused by thrombus formed in deep veins of legs but also by foreign matter such as a piece of fat, air bubble, amniotic fluid, tumor cells, piece of bone marrow) ■ Requires immediate emergency treatment (death may be sudden without treatment)	■ Usually sudden, severe chest pain ■ Cough, possibly producing bloody sputum ■ SOB ■ Tachypnea ■ Syncope ■ Skin possibly cool and clammy, pale, or cyanotic ■ Blood pressure drop ■ Rapid, weak pulse ■ Anxiety ■ Oxygen SAT drop	■ Patient presenting symptoms ■ Patient history ■ Radiograph of chest ■ Perfusion scan ■ Pulmonary angiogram ■ Doppler ultrasound studies of deep leg veins for deep vein thrombosis (DVT)	■ Supplemental oxygen ■ Thrombolytic and anticoagulant drugs to ease fatigue and strengthen immune system ■ Anti-embolism (TED™) stockings after surgery or during inactivity ■ Ambulation as soon as possible after surgery ■ Blood coagulation studies ■ Activity to avoid lengthy periods of sitting ■ Quitting smoking, especially females using hormonal birth control
Atelectasis ■ Partial lung collapse that affects alveoli ■ Caused by obstruction in airway, such as mucus plug, tumor, or foreign body ■ Possible complication following surgery ■ Requires rapid and/or emergency treatment	■ Dyspnea ■ SOB ■ Rapid heartbeat ■ Diaphoresis ■ Cyanosis ■ Substernal retraction	■ Auscultation ■ Radiographs ■ Bronchoscopy ■ CT examination	■ Suction, coughing, or bronchoscopy to remove obstruction ■ Antibiotics for infection ■ Surgery to remove any tumor ■ Preoperative deep breathing (incentive spirometry) and deep cough training for the immediate postoperative period
Hemotypsis ■ Consequence of disease process or trauma to respiratory tract ■ Causes include respiratory infection, trauma, drug abuse, especially cocaine, vascular disorders, bronchitis, inhaled foreign bodies, blood clotting disorders ■ Copious amounts of blood may be life threatening	■ Blood in sputum (bright red, dark red, or pink-tinged) ■ Spitting up blood ■ Coughing up blood ■ Pain possible	■ Patient presenting symptoms ■ Patient history ■ Physical examination ■ Imaging studies ■ Bronchoscopy	■ Intervention to halt blood flow ■ Removal of foreign bodies ■ Cauterization or ligation of blood vessels
Sleep apnea ■ Intermittent cessation of breathing ■ Usually caused by relaxation of tongue muscles, allowing tongue to fall back into oral pharynx and block airway ■ Apneic periods may last 60 to 90 seconds and occur 30 to 500 times during 7-hour sleep cycle ■ Condition may lead to heart attacks and strokes ■ Sleepiness may cause motor vehicle accidents and other accidents involving machinery	■ Excessive daytime sleepiness ■ Restless sleep ■ Snoring with apneic spells ■ Memory loss ■ Nighttime chest pain ■ Hypertension ■ Choking sensation during sleep ■ Depression ■ Morning headaches	■ Polysomnography (sleep studies)	■ Continuous positive airway pressure (CPAP) to keep airway open ■ Surgery (uvulopalato-pharyngoplasty [UPPP] or radio frequency ablation, both of which have limited success) ■ BiPAP

insults to the chest may cause pneumothorax, hemothorax, or hemopneumothorax. **Pneumothorax** is a condition of air in the pleural cavity that causes the lung to partially or completely collapse. **Hemothorax** is an accumulation of blood and fluids in the pleural cavity that limit the expansion of the lung. **Hemopneumothorax** is an accumulation of both blood and air in the pleural cavity, resulting in the partial or complete collapse of the lung. Depending on the severity of the condition, the patient will require observation and immediate or emergency treatment. (∞ Other emergency respiratory conditions are discussed in Chapter 23, Emergency Care.)

Pulmonary Assessment and Diagnosis

Patients with pulmonary conditions exhibit one or more of a variety of symptoms.

- Sounds: wheezing (continuous musical sound), rales (crackles), rhonchus (wheeze, snore, or chest squeak heard on auscultation), or stridor (high-pitched, harsh sound)
- Cyanosis: a symptom of hypoxemia; often accompanies breathing difficulty or shortness of breath over a long period
- Cough: productive (with sputum) or nonproductive (dry)
- Sputum: may be blood-tinged (hemoptysis) or yellow/green (indicates infection)
- Chronic respiratory conditions: clubbing (abnormal curvature of the nail bed), barrel chest appearance, using accessory muscles (muscles that aid in a secondary way) to make up for weakened respiratory muscles and help with breathing

Respiratory breathing patterns are classified as follows:

- **Eupnea:** normal breathing
- **Dyspnea:** difficult breathing
- **Orthopnea:** breathing in a standing, or upright sitting position
- **Tachypnea:** rapid breathing

Keys to Success
MUCUS OR MUCOUS?

It is important that you use the terms *mucus* and *mucous* correctly.
- *Mucus* is a noun. It refers a thick fluid secreted by the mucous membranes of the respiratory, gastrointestinal, reproductive, and urinary tracts. Mucus serves as a lubricant and contains substances that slow microbial growth.
- *Mucous* is the adjective form of *mucus* and is used to describe a noun—for example, mucous membrane.

Caduceus Chronicle
THE HISTORY OF CARDIOPULMONARY RESUSCITATION (CPR)

Since 3000 BCE, people have attempted to "reawaken" the deceased in a variety of ways.

3000 BCE: Rectal fumigation (blowing smoke into the rectum) was first practiced by the Peruvian Incas to resuscitate the dead. In the early 1700s, (Native Americans and the colonists followed this practice as well.

1700 BCE: The inversion method was used by the Egyptians on drowning victims. The victim was hung upside down and pressure was applied to the chest.

800–900 BCE: According to the Bible (2 Kings 4:34), Elijah, the prophet, performed mouth-to-mouth resuscitation on a child.

500–1500 CE: Victims were whipped to bring them back to life. In another method, the victim's body was warmed with hot water or ashes to prevent the coldness that represented death. In a third method, a fireplace bellows was used to blow into the victim's mouth. The success of this technique served as the basis for modern-day bag-valve-mask resuscitators. In 1829, it was discovered during an animal experiment that overfilling the lungs with the bellows could cause death, and the method was abandoned.

1543: Andreas Vesalius (1514–1564), after introducing a tube into the trachea of an animal, performed "intratracheal intermittent positive pressure ventilation."

Late 1700s: A resuscitation society called the Dutch Society for Recovery of Drowned Persons recommended treatment that included:

- use of the bellows for ventilation
- stimulating and warming the victim
- bloodletting
- tilting the body or lowering the head and tickling or applying pressure to the abdomen to induce vomiting and remove water from the victim's lungs

1800s: The "Russian method" reduced the body's metabolism with ice. The "trotting horse method," used at beaches, involved draping the victim over a horse. The bouncing of the running horse alternated compressing and relaxing the victim's chest. The "roll method" involved rolling the victim from stomach to side 16 times per minute. Backpressure was added when the victim was prone. Marshall Hall (1790–1857) suggested that laying the victim flat on the back allowed the tongue to block the airway, body warmth without ventilation was harmful, and transporting the victim wasted valuable time that could have been spent on treatment. A new method of artificial respiration was named for him.

1891: Closed chest massage was first performed on humans.

1947: The first successful defibrillation was performed at Case Western Reserve University, the birthplace of clinical defibrillation, a result of the pioneering work of the great U.S. physiologist Carl J. Wiggers, MD, and the U.S. surgeon Claude S. Beck.

1950s: The mouth-to-mouth method was rediscovered and used shortly after WWII. In 1954, James Elam documented the use of the mouth-to-mask method on patients recovering from general anesthesia. The "push-pull" method of placing the victim supine with the arms folded under the face, pushing on the ribs, then pulling or lifting up the folded arms was developed.

1960s: Mouth-to-mouth resuscitation was added to lifeguard training. Closed cardiac massage was introduced and used with mouth-to-mouth resuscitation. "Resusci Annie," a realistic, life-size CPR training mannequin, was developed by Asmund Laerdal. The Red Cross and the American Heart Association offered training in CPR to the general public during the period of the Vietnam War.

The acronym ABCD refers to the series of steps followed in modern CPR:

A—Airway
B—Breathing
C—Circulation
D—Defibrillation

Pulmonary Function and Other Common Diagnostic Testing

Pulmonary function testing (PFT), an assessment of the performance level of respiratory system structures, is done to confirm that a patient has lung disease or to evaluate and manage diagnosed pulmonary disorders. PFT is not used to identify a specific respiratory disease but to measure the effects of disease. There are several types of PFTs, including spirometry, lung volume, and diffusion capacity.

- Spirometry, a noninvasive test, measures the exhalation capacity of the lungs and is very helpful in tracking the progression of acute or chronic respiratory conditions such as asthma, COLD, and respiratory infections or the effects of asthma medication. Spirometry is also used as a postoperative treatment.
- Lung volume measures the inhalation capacity of the lungs, such as in emphysema.
- Diffusion capacity measures the amount of test-administered carbon monoxide absorbed in one cycle of inhalation and exhalation. The difference between the amount of carbon monoxide inhaled and the amount exhaled is an estimate of how long it takes inhaled gas to travel from the lungs to the capillary system. Adult Respiratory Distress Syndrome (ARDS) is an example of a traumatic respiratory condition that severely affects gas diffusion capabilities.

Other common diagnostic studies include chest X-ray, arterial blood gases, pulse oximetry, methacholine challenge, sputum collection for cytology and for culture and sensitivity, sweat test, and bronchoscopy.

- Chest X-rays are a **noninvasive** tool for diagnosing or screening for respiratory infections (including pneumonia, tuberculosis, and lung abscess), lung tumors, or conditions of sudden respiratory distress, such as pneumothorax (Figure 18-3 ◆). They are contraindicated for pregnant women.
- Arterial blood gases (**ABGs**) are used to analyze the acid/base balance of blood in chronic respiratory and acute respiratory, metabolic, and traumatic conditions. Examples of these conditions include COLD, ARDS, emphysema, pulmonary embolism, pneumonia, bronchitis, anxiety, fever, and diabetic ketoacidosis. ABGs also measures oxygen saturation and the carbon dioxide level of the arterial blood. Arterial blood gases are drawn from an artery, often a painful procedure. Pressure must be maintained on the puncture site for at least 3 to 5 minutes to seal the arterial wound and prevent bleeding. After an arterial blood sample is obtained, the sealed tubes containing the arterial blood are placed in a container of ice and must be transported to a laboratory and processed immediately. The laboratory values direct the treatment procedures, which are directed largely toward returning the values of pH, pCO_2, pO_2, and HCO_3 to normal for the patient.
- Pulse oximetry is an early, noninvasive screening test of blood gas status or oxygen saturation (O_2 sat) of tissues

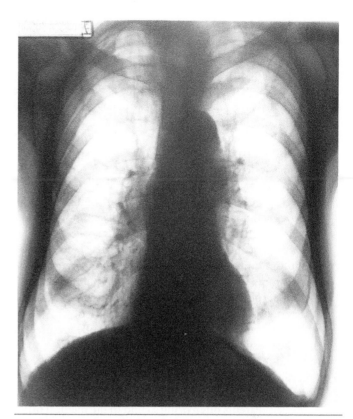

Figure 18-3 ◆ Chest X-ray of a patient with emphysema
Source: Scott Camazine, Photo Researchers, Inc.

(Figure 18-4 ◆). It is used to analyze symptoms of cardiac, circulatory, or respiratory distress such as chest pain, dyspnea, nasal flaring, decreased consciousness, wheezing, skin color changes (paleness or cyanosis); clinical signs of shock; and symptoms following exposure to intense heat, smoke, or flame. Pulse oximetry has replaced ABGs to some extent.

- The methacholine challenge test is used in the diagnosis and treatment of asthma. The patient inhales periodic and increasing amounts of the medication methacholine and

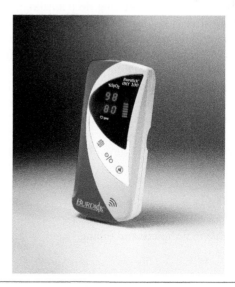

Figure 18-4 ◆ Burdick pulse oximeter.
Courtesy of Burdick Cardiac Science.

undergoes PFTs to assess the reaction of the bronchial airways and the effect on the respiratory system. Patients with certain medical conditions—including a known history of aneurysm, heart attack, stroke, chronic uncontrolled hypertension, myasthenia gravis, or who are presently pregnant or nursing—are advised not to take the methacholine challenge.

■ Sputum cultures obtained by a respiratory therapist are used to diagnose respiratory infections, such as pneumonia. A deep pulmonary sputum sample is obtained by deep thoracic coughing, stimulation, or suctioning. A specimen of saliva, rather than sputum, obtained by any individual not trained in sputum collection procedures may yield inaccurate test results. Sputum collection is beyond the scope of training of medical assistants.

■ Sputum samples for cytology are used to diagnose lung carcinoma (malignant tumor). A deep pulmonary sputum sample is obtained by deep thoracic coughing, stimulation, suctioning, or during a bronchoscopy.

■ Sputum samples for acid-fast bacilli (**AFB**) are used in culture testing for pulmonary tuberculosis.

■ Blood tests for theophylline level reveal inadequate, excessive, or toxic medication levels within the bloodstream.

■ A sweat test is performed to confirm diagnosis of cystic fibrosis. Parents often bring a child to the medical office stating that the child tastes like salt when kissed. A colorless, odorless chemical is applied to the child's skin and a sweat collection device is attached for 30 minutes to one hour. The sweat specimen is analyzed for sodium and chloride. The initial diagnosis is based on several symptoms, including foul-smelling, frothy stool; heavy pulmonary secretions; and other GI symptoms. The sweat test is not a primary diagnostic test.

■ Bronchoscopy is a tool for visualizing the bronchial tree, clearing mucous obstructions, and obtaining a biopsy. It is an invasive procedure that requires operative consent. It may be performed under a general or local anesthetic. Patients are required to take nothing by mouth (NPO) for at least 8 hours before the test. They are also restricted from drinking or eating until the gag reflex has returned (usually about 8 hours postprocedure).

■ Other diagnostic tests include the peak flow test and Mantoux test, which are discussed in greater detail later in this chapter.

?—Critical Thinking Question 18-1–

Keera has been given the directions for obtaining a sputum sample and has observed the technique being performed. Now that it is her turn, what precautions should she take?

Keys to Success
SPUTUM SPECIMEN

Saliva is a clear fluid secreted from the salivary glands into the mouth to begin digestion. Sputum is material that is coughed up from the lungs and expectorated through the mouth. When obtaining a sputum specimen, ask the patient to take a deep breath and cough up secretions from deep within the lungs. This lessens the chance of getting a "spit" or saliva specimen.

PROCEDURE 18-1 Demonstrate Performance of Spirometry

Theory

With spirometry PFT, baseline information can be obtained about a patient's normal breathing, deep inhaling, or exhaling. The patient should be instructed not to eat a large meal or smoke for 4 to 6 hours before the PFT. The physician will also order bronchodilator drugs to be used during testing.

A nose clip helps focus the patient's efforts on sealing his or her lips around the mouthpiece and prevents air leaks from the nostrils. Make sure the patient puts forth the greatest possible effort for the best results.

During the PFT you will stay with the patient to instruct and provide emotional coaching. Your presence can decrease the patient's anxiety.

Materials

■ spirometer
■ disposable mouthpiece and tubing
■ nose clip
■ chart
■ forms and lab slips for documentation and testing

Competency

(**Conditions**) With the necessary materials, (**Task**) you will be able to assist the patient in the performance of spirometry testing (**Standards**) correctly within 30 minutes.

1. Wash your hands. Gather equipment and supplies.
2. Identify the patient and guide him or her to the treatment area.
3. Record the patient's history and main complaint. Explain the entire procedure.
4. If the patient is chewing gum, ask him or her to dispose of it (to prevent choking during the test). If a female patient is wearing lipstick, ask her to remove it to create a tight seal.
5. Ask the patient to place the mouthpiece in his or her mouth and to close the lips tightly around the mouthpiece to make a good seal (Figure 18-5 ◆).
6. Place the nose clips on the patient's nose, sealing the nostrils closed (Figure 18-6 ◆).
7. Ask the patient to inhale as deeply as he or she possibly can and hold the breath for a short time. Then tell the patient to blow the air out into the mouthpiece as hard and as fast

PROCEDURE 18-1 **Demonstrate Performance of Spirometry** *(continued)*

as possible—until he or she cannot blow out any more air (Figure 18-7 ◆).

8. Repeat this procedure two more times, giving the patient a few minutes in between.

9. The electronic equipment will usually "select" the best of the three breathing tests.

10. Document patient compliance with and tolerance of the testing procedure.

11. Follow cleaning procedures to prepare the equipment and the area for the next patient.

12. Wash your hands.

Patient Education

Explain to the patient that the purpose of the procedure is to monitor the progress of a disease or how well treatment is working and that medical treatment is based on the findings of regularly scheduled PFTs. Encourage the patient to tell the physician if the treatment is not working.

Charting Example

08/12/XX 9:00 a.m. Pt stated that last meal was at 6:00 a.m.— one egg, one toast slice, and one cup coffee. Pt stated physician wanted no bronchodilator medication until after the test. Pt followed test instructions with slight shortness of breath, but recovered within 2 minutes to repeat. Results given to physician for evaluation. Margaret Jones, CMA

Figure 18-5 ◆ The patient should close the lips tightly around the mouthpiece.

Figure 18-6 ◆ Place the nose clips on the patient's nose.

Figure 18-7 ◆ Direct the patient to blow the air out into the mouthpiece as hard and as fast as possible.

Keys to Success
COMPLIANCE VS. COMPLIANCE

When referring to the lungs, *compliance* means the elasticity of the lungs for breathing. When referring to the patient, *compliance* means ability to follow instructions.

ABGs and Pulse Oximetry

It is critical to determine a patient's oxygen status. In an acute care setting, an invasive procedure known as arterial blood gas (ABG) analysis has been widely used. An ABG measures oxygen status (**PaO_2** values), acid-base status (pH values), the body's ability to expel cellular waste products (**$PaCO_2$** values), and possible causes of respiratory disease (Table 18-4). The information from this study reveals how well the lungs are functioning to meet the body's oxygen needs. Only specially trained professionals can perform ABGs. Check the practice acts of your state.

TABLE 18-4 NORMAL VALUES FOR ABGs

ABG	Normal Range
Arterial pH	7.35–7.45 ■ <7.35 indicates acidosis ■ >7.45 indicates alkalosis
Arterial $PaCO_2$	35–45 mm Hg ■ When CO_2 is abnormal, the condition has a respiratory cause and the HCO_3 is normal.
Arterial HCO_3	22–26 mEq/L ■ When HCO_3 is abnormal, the condition has a metabolic cause and the pCO_2 is normal. ■ This value reflects the metabolic function of the kidneys.
Arterial PaO_2	80–100 mm Hg ■ If pO_2 is < 50 mm Hg, oxygen therapy is required
Arterial O_2 sat	95% or greater

A newer, noninvasive method called pulse oximetry has gained popularity in both medical offices and acute care settings. Although it measures oxygen saturation (SAT) indirectly rather than by blood sample analysis, pulse oximetry is a fairly simple procedure for testing a patient's oxygen status. In the clinical setting, you may hear the abbreviated terms "pulse ox" or "O₂ sat" used to refer to this procedure.

Pulse oximeters light up the tissues with infrared light. Oxygen-rich tissues emit a different wavelength of light than oxygen-poor tissues, and oxygen saturation is measured with these wavelengths. The lower limit of acceptable oxygen saturation is 85 percent. A patient with saturations below this level requires oxygen from a supplemental source.

Attachment points for pulse oximetry include the fingertip (most common site), earlobe, and tip of the toe. Wherever it is attached, the oximeter must fit securely. On a fingertip, nail polish, poor fit or contact with the sensor, very low blood pressure, severe anemia, or a poorly calibrated pulse oximeter can have a negative affect on a pulse oximetry reading.

Peak Flow Testing

Peak flow testing measures a patient's maximum ability to exhale (pulmonary airflow). It is one of a variety of pulmonary function tests that measures air capacity of the lungs (spirometry). Peak flow, or air flow, rates are also used to monitor the effectiveness of medication or determine the need for different medical treatment. Peak flow rates change according to the patient's medical condition, body frame, and age, as well as the time of the day the test is taken.

Airflow rate is measured with a peak flow meter after the patient has inhaled as deeply as possible and then exhaled as rapidly and fully as possible (Figure 18-8 ◆). The test is repeated at least three times for accuracy.

A peak flow meter measures liters per second or liters per minute. Because there are many types of peak flow meters, it is important to use the same kind for each patient to maintain uniform and accurate tests results. These meters can be mechanical or computerized.

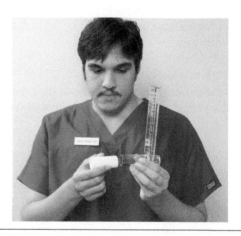

Figure 18-8 ◆ Peak flow meter

PROCEDURE 18-2 Demonstrate Performance of Peak Flow Testing

Theory

A peak flow meter can detect an asthma attack before symptoms occur. This information allows the patient to prevent symptoms or reduce their effect. Peak flow testing gives the patient greater control over monitoring and managing the condition.

Taking peak flow readings under different conditions, such as before and after exercise, after exposure to pets, or after exposure to tobacco smoke or allergens, makes the symptoms easier to identify. If an asthma attack occurs, the patient and/or medical staff can make decisions based on the readings about whether the patient can manage the situation at home or will require emergency medical treatment at the hospital.

Materials

- peak flow meter
- patient log or diary of peak flow readings
- patient chart

Competency

(**Conditions**) With the necessary materials, (**Task**) you will be able to assist the patient in the performance of peak flow testing (**Standards**) correctly within 30 minutes.

1. Wash your hands completely. Gather equipment and supplies.
2. Identify the patient and guide him or her to the treatment area.
3. Instruct the patient to take as deep a breath as possible, place the mouthpiece just in front of the teeth, then use his or her lips to make a complete seal. Ask the patient to exhale as hard and as fast as possible (Figure 18-9 ◆).
4. Have the patient repeat step 3 three times.

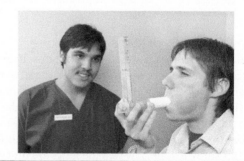

Figure 18-9 ◆ Ask the patient to exhale as hard and as fast as possible.

PROCEDURE 18-2 Demonstrate Performance of Peak Flow Testing *(continued)*

5. If test results also need to be taken after medication, allow the patient to rest. Administer the medication, then repeat the test.
6. Clean the equipment and dispose of contaminated materials appropriately.
7. Wash your hands.
8. Record the results. Compare the results with previous readings.

Patient Education

The physician determines the pattern for peak flow testing. He or she may require that the patient be tested after awakening, before going to bed, before and after taking medications (such as inhalers), or in the presence of asthma attack triggers.

Stress to the patient the importance of following the testing schedule and the proper procedure. Give the patient a form to keep track of peak expiratory flow (**PEF**) readings, which measure highest rate of airflow that can be forced during expiration. Instruct the patient to bring the form to medical office visits and to keep and carry a medication list for medical visits or emergencies.

Charting Example

01/27/XX 12:30 p.m. ↑ shortness of breath & asthma attacks. Pt states ↑ in asthma attacks are probably due to additional emotional stress at work. A copy of the pt's PEF readings attached for physician review. John Banks, RMA

**Keys to Success
PATIENT REASSURANCE**

A patient who is dependent on supplemental oxygen and must undergo PFT can be very frightened. The thought of having the oxygen flow interrupted and not being able to breathe is very difficult to handle. To calm the patient:

- Explain the entire procedure.
- Explain that you will be there throughout the entire testing procedure and an oxygen supply will be available.
- Stay with the patient until the procedure is complete.
- Help the patient to restore the supplemental oxygen flow.

**Keys to Success
INTRADERMAL TESTING**

Intradermal injection is used in allergy testing as well as in the Mantoux test. For allergy testing, a permanent marker is used to label each site after the allergy substance is injected.

Mantoux Test

The Mantoux test is used to screen patients for contact with or presence of the active disease state of **TB.** Each positive result is followed by another Mantoux test and/or chest x-ray to

PROCEDURE 18-3 Demonstrate Performance of the Mantoux Test by Intradermal Injection

Theory

Find a site on the patient's lower forearm without hair or blemishes. Because the medication's composition may be affected by exposure to light, prepare the medication syringe immediately prior to administration. The administration of a PPD via intradermal injection is a uniquely different method of injection and has rules for administration that vary greatly from all other types of injections. Unlike other types of injections, the administration of PPD also specifies that the medical assistant should not aspirate, doing so will cause skin and tissue damage. The final unique difference with PPD application is that a bandage must not be applied over the administration site. The bandage can create pressure, expelling the solution from the wheal, invalidating the test results. If the patient has slight bleeding, a small cotton ball can be

placed directly above the site but should not be allowed to wick any of the medication from the wheal. Preparing the medication immediately before administering it also helps to maintain the needle's sterility and allows you to proceed without recapping the needle.

After administration of the Mantoux, a return visit is scheduled so that test results may be measured and documented. Only induration, not redness, is measured. Usually, an induration less than 2 millimeters (mm) across is considered a negative result. An induration greater than 2 mm must be reported to the local health department.

Materials

- patient chart
- disposable gloves

PROCEDURE 18-3 Demonstrate Performance of the Mantoux Test by Intradermal Injection *(continued)*

- sterile water and cotton balls
- sharps container
- tuberculin syringe with needle
- vial of medication
- bandage strips

Competency

(Conditions) With the necessary materials, **(Task)** you will be able to perform the Mantoux test **(Standards)** correctly within 15 minutes.

1. Wash your hands and gather the equipment.
2. Identify the patient and guide him or her to the treatment area.
3. Wash your hands again and put on disposable gloves.
4. Ask the patient to reach out with one hand and turn the palm upward. Find a site without hair or blemishes on the forearm.
5. Cleanse the top of the PPD vial with an alcohol wipe and allow it to air-dry (Figure 18-10 ◆). Withdraw 0.1 cc from the vial and hold it in your dominant hand (Figure 18-11 ◆).
6. Place your nondominant hand under the patient's forearm and gently pull the skin tight. Ask the patient to keep the arm still. Insert the needle bevel just into and under the skin at a 10- to 15-degree angle (Figure 18-12 ◆).
7. Inject the medication slowly to create a raised blister, or wheal (Figures 18-13 ◆ and 18-14 ◆).

8. Release the skin, then withdraw the needle and blot the area gently with an alcohol wipe.
9. Discard the syringe in the sharps container.
10. Make an appointment for the patient to return and have the injection site checked after 48 to 72 hours.
11. Document the procedure, including a description of the Mantoux test site.
12. When the patient returns, measure only the induration, *not* the redness. For positive results, measure in millimeters (mm) and follow local public health guidelines for reporting.

Patient Education

Discuss the procedure with the patient beforehand, including what to expect afterwards and on the return visit. Tell the patient not to irritate the test site by scratching or wearing scratchy clothing. Explain that some redness is to be expected and that a return check will be necessary to measure the induration, if any, and to observe the test site.

Charting Example

03/27/XX 2:40 p.m. Mantoux test was given following office procedure into pt's R forearm area. The pt was instructed to make a return appointment 48 to 72 hours after the test for observation and test results. Michelle Carter, RMA

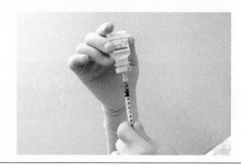

Figure 18-11 ◆ Withdraw medication from the medication vial.

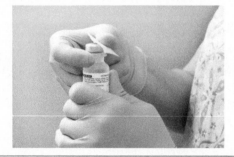

Figure 18-10 ◆ Clean the top of the medication vial.

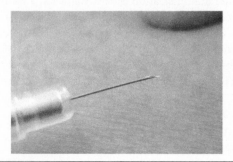

Figure 18-12 ◆ Needle bevel

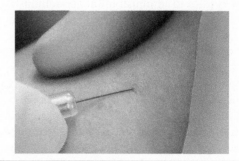

Figure 18-13 ◆ Insert the needle bevel just into and under the skin of the patient's forearm.

PROCEDURE 18-3 Demonstrate Performance of the Mantoux Test by Intradermal Injection (continued)

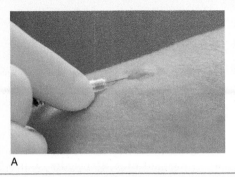
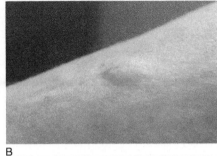

A   B

Figure 18-14 ◆ (A) Inject the medicine slowly to create a raised blister, or wheal; (B) Wheal on patient's arm

Keys to Success
VACCINATIONS

Pneumonia immunization can prevent pneumonia-related deaths and is generally recommended once for elderly patients over 65 and nursing home patients. It is also suggested for patients with chronic illness(es), a compromised immune system, or organ transplant(s).

Influenza vaccinations are recommended yearly for elderly patients, patients with chronic illnesses, and health-care workers. Flu shots should not be given to individuals who are sensitive or allergic to eggs because the vaccination is made from viruses grown in eggs. Any allergic reaction usually occurs immediately after the injection. It is also common to experience mild flu symptoms, such as malaise, fever, and muscle pain, after immunization.

The BCG (bacillus Calmette-Guérin) vaccine is used for TB prevention in countries outside of the United States. The effectiveness varies from zero to 80 percent. Once the vaccination is given, the patient shows a positive reaction to tuberculin skin testing and needs chest x-rays to diagnose or rule out TB. The Centers for Disease Control (CDC) has guidelines for the use of the BCG vaccination for specific groups in the United States.

negate or confirm the earlier results. Positive results indicate only that the patient carries the TB bacteria. It does not indicate an active TB disease process. (*Note:* The first Mantoux test may not yield a reaction in a patient with lowered immunity and a more severe infection. Later, as the patient regains **immunocompetence,** repeated Mantoux testing with PPD will cause the expected induration at the injection site.)

The Mantoux test is administered by **intradermal** injection of purified protein derivative (**PPD**). Institutions such as nursing and retirement homes require repeat testing before admitting a patient. A positive reaction occurs more slowly in an elderly person and may not show unless a repeat test is given.

Inhalers and Nebulizers

Inhalers and nebulizers are devices used to treat obstructive airway conditions. Patient and caregiver teaching are essential to successful treatment with either device.

Inhalers are pocket-sized, portable devices for the self-administration of medication directly into the respiratory system. In addition to portability, inhalers have several advantages. They are available in many different medications. They deliver a consistent, metered dose of medication to the airways. Proper technique is very important, however, and the oral route must be easily accomplished by the patient. Another drawback is the high out-of-pocket cost per dose.

?—**Critical Thinking Question 18-2**—
Keera has just instructed the patient in the correct way to use a metered dose inhaler (**MDI**). What other instructions or methods should she mention to the patient?

The nebulizer delivers fine particles of medication to the patient via compressed air or oxygen through tubing and a mask (Figure 18-15 ◆). This delivery method is effective even if the patient has a severe problem with breathing. Nebulizers are used mainly in hospitals, but can also be used in outpatient

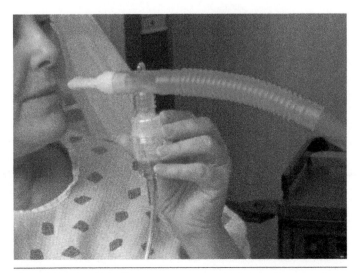

Figure 18-15 ◆ Nebulizer

or ambulatory care settings. With its reusable mouthpiece and mask, the nebulizer is a good alternative for those who have difficulty using inhalers. The mask is the easiest delivery route for pediatric patients. The major disadvantage of nebulizers has been that they are difficult to carry; however, a battery-operated nebulizer without a mask has recently been developed.

PROCEDURE 18-4 Demonstrate Patient Instruction in the Use of an Inhaler

Theory

When you instruct a patient in the use of an inhaler, keep these points in mind:

■ Take note of any physical problems that may prevent correct handling. For example, a patient with arthritic hands may not be able to use an inhaler.

■ The inhaler canister should be thoroughly shaken to mix the medication particles evenly.

■ Holding the canister in the upright position (not at an angle) ensures that the metered dose is delivered correctly.

■ It can be helpful to encourage the patient to exhale before inhaling the medication. This ensures deeper inhalation for the inhaled medication. Follow local policy and the procedures of your employer, clinic, or hospital.

■ The patient must inhale slowly and as deeply as possible and hold the breath to ensure that the medication penetrates deeply into the bronchial tree and lungs.

Materials

■ patient's prescription inhaler
■ patient's chart

Competency

(**Conditions**) With the necessary materials, (**Task**) you will be able to instruct and/or help the patient use an inhaler for the first time (**Standard**) correctly within one hour.

1. Wash your hands and gather the equipment.
2. Identify and guide the patient to the treatment area.

Figure 18-16 ◆ Patient with inhaler held upright.

3. Give the patient the following instructions.
   • Shake the canister thoroughly.
   • Hold the canister upright within 2 inches of the mouth. Place the mouthpiece in your mouth, sealing the opening with your lips (Figure 18-16 ◆).
   • Activate the inhaler (usually by pressing the canister down) to spray (Figure 18-17 ◆). Breathe slowly but deeply after the medication is delivered.
   • Hold your breath for as long as possible, up to 10 seconds.
   • Begin breathing normally again.
   • Follow the physician's instructions for immediate repeat use.
4. Document the patient's ability to follow instructions. Inform the physician if the patient has any problems with self-administration. Give the patient backup written instructions.

Patient Education

Inform the patient about the side effects of the medication at normal prescription levels and the consequences of overuse. Tell the patient to call the physician if the medication appears not to help or if symptoms worsen.

Charting Sample

11/23/XX 2:30 p.m. Pt demonstrated correct use of the inhaler with instruction. Written instructions were given with the office's phone number. Pt states that medication has helped make breathing easier. Parker Clay, CMA

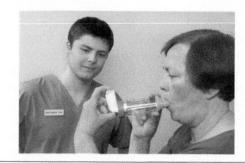

Figure 18-17 ◆ Activate the inhaler.

PROCEDURE 18-5 Demonstrate Patient Assistance in the Use of a Nebulizer

Theory

Nebulizer treatments may be given after baseline PFT. Testing is then repeated to measure the patient's response to medications in the nebulizer. Medications (usually pre-mixed) are placed in the nebulizer, which is then attached to a compressor source, and an aerosol mist is produced for the patient to inhale through a mask.

Materials

- compressor
- nebulizer with mask and tubing
- medications
- patient's chart

Competency

(Conditions) With the necessary materials, **(Task)** you will be able to assist the patient in the use of a nebulizer **(Standards)** correctly within 30 minutes.

1. Wash your hands. Gather equipment and supplies.
2. Identify the patient and guide him or her to the treatment area.
3. Obtain vital signs.
4. Wash your hands again.
5. Prepare the nebulizer cup with medication(s) as ordered and/or prescribed (Figure 18-18 ◆).
6. Turn on the compressor (Figure 18-19 ◆).
7. Instruct, or help, the patient to hold the mask while the medication is being delivered.

8. Continue treatment until no medication remains in the nebulizer. Monitor the patient's pulse every 5 minutes throughout the treatment (Figure 18-20 ◆). If the pulse rises to 120 beats per minute or the patient's condition worsens, *stop the treatment and tell the physician.*
9. Dispose of used materials in the appropriate containers.
10. Wash your hands.
11. Document the patient's vital signs at the beginning, middle, and end of the treatment. Also describe patient signs and symptoms at beginning and end of treatment.

Patient Education

Instruct the patient or significant other in how to do this procedure at home, and how often. After you demonstrate the procedure, have the patient or significant other return the demonstration and show you how to monitor the pulse during the procedure. If the pulse rises above 120 beats per minute, the treatment should be stopped. The physician will have to change the medication or adjust the dosage or frequency.

Charting Example

12/27/XX 2:45 p.m. Instructions given to pt's wife to perform the nebulizer treatment. She demonstrated the procedure correctly. She described the correct frequency and symptoms to observe and demonstrated the correct procedure for counting a radial pulse. Susan Tucker, RMA

Figure 18-18 ◆ Prepare the nebulizer cup with medication(s) as ordered and/or prescribed.

Figure 18-19 ◆ Turn on the compressor.

Figure 18-20 ◆ Monitor the patient's pulse.

Oxygen Therapy

Oxygen therapy is administered for three primary reasons:

- To decrease the work of breathing
- To decrease the work of the heart
- To reverse or prevent low blood oxygen levels

In an outpatient setting, the oxygen is usually delivered by way of a nasal cannula (also called *nasal prongs*) (Figure 18-21 ◆). The patient is attached by tubing to a portable oxygen concentrator or oxygen tank. The oxygen can also be delivered by mask.

Oxygen is a prescription drug that is administered only after a physician has written an order describing the method and concentration of oxygen delivery—for example: "Oxygen via nasal cannula at 2 liters per minute." Instruct the patient *not* to change the flow rate without the physician's permission or direction. Doing so may worsen the patient's medical condition. Also teach the patient how to pad the skin where the oxygen tubing may rub against it and cause irritation.

Instruct the patient in the safe use of oxygen. Although oxygen does not burn or explode, it can "fuel" a small spark or flame. Tell the patient when oxygen is being used to avoid substances considered flammable, such as oil-based lubricants, smoking materials, open gas, or heat sources. If a patient tries to smoke in the medical office with oxygen running, reinforce no-smoking office policies. If a patient is smoking, stop the oxygen flow and ask the patient to put out the cigarette. Restart the oxygen only after the cigarette is put out. If the patient needs to moisten dry lips or nostrils caused by oxygen therapy, *only* a water-soluble lubricant may be used.

Traveling requires additional preparation. Tell the patient to always carry his or her oxygen prescription. Before flying, the patient should check with the airline about proper procedures to follow. The physician should be alerted as well. He or she will provide the patient with specific instructions about oxygen flow rate during the high-altitude phases of the trip.

Common Oxygen Therapy Equipment

The following are different types of oxygen therapy equipment:

Oxygen Tanks: Oxygen tanks come in a variety of sizes according to use and need for portability.

E Tank: Small tank that holds approximately 500 liters of oxygen for patient home use in the event of power failure.

H Tank: Kept in the medical office and holds approximately 6900 liters of oxygen. Used for in-office emergencies and testing patient's need for oxygen therapy.

C Tank: This is a standard size, small portable tank that the patient may use for short trips away from the home. This tank holds approximately 240 liters of oxygen.

Liquid oxygen: Liquid oxygen is also commonly referred to as cryogenic liquid, its scientific name. When oxygen is liquefied it will have a boiling point of $-297.3°F$ ($-183.0°C$). Although great care must be taken in the storage system of liquid oxygen it is much less bulky than in gas form and therefore costs much less to store. A typical storage system consists of a cryogenic storage tank constructed much like a metal thermos container with inner and outer shells, one or more vaporizers, a pressure control system, and all piping necessary for the fill, vaporization, and supply functions.

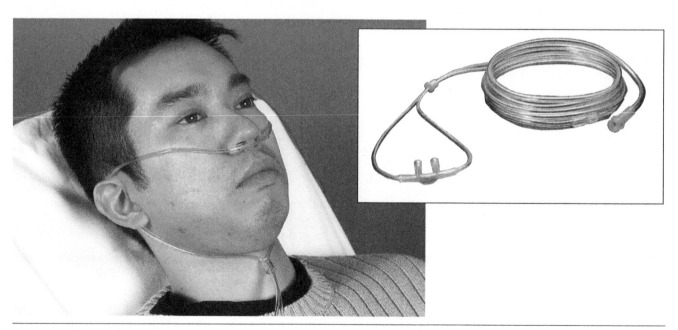

Figure 18-21 ◆ Nasal cannula

Conserving device: During normal inhalation and exhalation a shift in pressure in the diaphragm occurs. This shift in pressure sends a signal that travels through the nasal cannula to a pressure sensor in the conserving device. An electronic circuit then opens an electrical valve to deliver a precisely metered dose of oxygen that has been prescribed by a physician. After the initial dose of oxygen is delivered, the system will automatically re-set in anticipation for the next inhalation from the patient. Oxygen does not continue to flow when the patient is exhaling so there is much less oxygen wasted.

Concentrator: If oxygen is ordered for home use, the Medical Assistant will order a concentrator that runs off electricity and makes its own oxygen without the need for refilling.

Tubing: Oxygen can be delivered to the patient via a nasal cannula, which is disposable, lightweight and easily slips into the nasal openings, or a full face mask. The face mask is used much less often because it is cumbersome, uncomfortable and can give the patient a sense of being smothered, causing anxiety.

Typical flow rate: A patient's oxygen is ordered as a flow rate per liters in minute increments. For example a patient that requires 2 liters of oxygen continuous will have a prescription that may read: Oxygen: 2 lpm via nasal cannula/continuous. Oxygen can be ordered as a supplement when the patient is being physically active, at rest, at night, or continuous. Individual diagnoses will determine the amount of oxygen ordered and for what extent of time. Patients may also have multiple orders for oxygen therapy, such as 2 liters per minute while at rest, increase to 4 liters per minute with exertion.

REVIEW

Chapter Summary

- Pulmonary testing measures the patient's lung elasticity and ability to breathe and has an impact on medications and treatment.
- Upper respiratory diseases are usually treated by an ENT. Lower respiratory disorders are treated by a pulmonologist. As a medical assistant you will assist with examinations, perform treatments, and provide emotional and educational support to the patient.
- The respiratory tree comprises the lungs, air passages serving the lungs, and anatomical structures of the thoracic and abdominal cavities that surround the lungs.
- In the respiration process, oxygen is inhaled and carbon dioxide is exhaled. Blood from the right heart is oxygen poor and carbon dioxide rich. As this blood enters the lungs, oxygen diffuses into the blood and raises the oxygen level to 100 mm Hg.
- Pulse oximetry is a noninvasive form of testing that measures the oxygen content of the blood. Peak flow testing examines pulmonary airflow by measuring rapid, full, forced exhaling. It is used to evaluate pulmonary conditions or the medical management of those conditions.
- Respiratory breathing patterns include eupnea, dyspnea, orthopnea, and tachypnea.

- Obstructive diseases of the lower respiratory system include asthma, acute bronchitis, chronic bronchitis, emphysema, and bronchiectasis. In these conditions, the bronchial tree or portions of the alveoli are obstructed, decreasing oxygen to the body tissues.
- Inhalers are portable devices for the self-administration of medication directly into the respiratory system. Nebulizers are used to treat respiratory conditions when oral medications or inhalers do not produce the required results. Oxygen therapy helps patients who use their accessory muscles to breathe by decreasing the workload of a weakened heart and preventing or reversing low blood oxygen levels.
- Infectious and inflammatory pulmonary conditions include pneumonia, influenza, histoplasmosis, pulmonary tuberculosis, and pleuritis. In these conditions, infection and the resulting inflammation are usually caused by bacteria or viruses.
- Mechanical insults include pulmonary emboli, atelectasis, and the signs and/or symptoms of hemoptysis (spitting or coughing up blood).

Chapter Review Questions

Multiple Choice

1. The lower airways begin at the
   A. nose.
   B. true vocal cords.
   C. upper palate.
   D. sinuses.

2. Pulse oximetry is gaining use over arterial blood gas tests because it is
   A. noninvasive.
   B. invasive.
   C. more accurate.
   D. more mechanical.

3. The lowest acceptable oxygen sat limit for a patient is
   A. 55 percent.
   B. 65 percent.
   C. 75 percent.
   D. 85 percent.

4. Peak flow testing is used to measure a patient's
   A. maximum ability to inhale.
   B. minimum ability to exhale.
   C. maximum ability to exhale.
   D. minimum ability to inhale.

5. Nebulizer treatment must be stopped immediately and the physician alerted if the patient's pulse is
   A. higher than 120 beats per minute.
   B. 90 beats per minute.
   C. 100 beats per minute.
   D. lower than 110 beats per minute.

6. When oxygen therapy is ordered for a patient for home use, he or she would use
   A. E tank
   B. C tank
   C. liquid oxygen
   D. all of the above

7. Which of the following is acceptable for use during oxygen therapy?
   A. water-based lubricants
   B. hairspray
   C. cigarette
   D. oil-based lubricants

8. Which of the following steps is used to reduce the patient's bleeding after an intradermal test?
   A. pulling the patient's forearm skin more tightly before removing the needle.
   B. injecting the site on the patient's forearm without gently pulling it tight.
   C. selecting a site on the patient's forearm with hair.
   D. releasing the patient's forearm skin gently before removing the needle.

9. An induration is a
   A. rash.
   B. scratch.
   C. swelling.
   D. cut.

10. Which of the following is a mechanical insult?
    A. pneumonia
    B. pulmonary embolism
    C. TB
    D. asthma

True/False

T F 1. The upper airway includes the pharynx and the nasal, oral, and laryngeal cavities.

T F 2. The lungs are in a sealed system with only one opening.

T F 3. The right lung has more lobes than the left lung.

T F 4. The diaphragm is located in the chest cavity, above the pleural cavity.

T F 5. The trachea branches into several different branches like a tree.

Short Answer

1. Describe the condition of the lungs in obstructive lung disease.

2. Describe the condition of the lungs in pulmonary edema.

3. What is a sweat test used to confirm?

4. What is the function of the Mantoux test?

5. What does lung volume measure?

Research

1. Find a "float diagram" for MDI inhaler use. It will show your patients a quick and easy method for seeing how much medication is left in the inhaler.

2. Do some research to find patient instructions on how to correctly use an MDI inhaler, a spacer device, and a disc inhaler.

Externship Application Experience

A patient using supplemental nasal oxygen starts to light a cigarette in the medical office. As a medical assistant, what should you do?

Resource Guide

American Lung Association
61 Broadway, 6th Floor
New York, NY 10019
1-800-586-4872
www.lungusa.org

Committee on Accreditation of Respiratory Care (COARC)
1248 Harwood Rd.
Bedford, TX 76021-4244
817-283-2835
www.coarc.com

National Board for Respiratory Care (NBRC)
8310 Nieman Rd.
Lenexa, KS 66214-1579
913-599-4200
www.NBRC.org

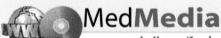

MedMedia
www.prenhall.com/frazier

More on this chapter, including interactive resources, can be found on the Student CD-ROM accompanying this textbook and on the Companion Website at www.prenhall.com/frazier.

CHAPTER 19

EENT

Case Study

Stacy has a busy day ahead of her at the EENT office where she is finishing her externship. First on the list of patients is a 4-year-old girl who got sand in her right eye after falling off the swing at the school playground. Next is a college student who must take a Snellen eye test for her sports physical. The receptionist has just alerted Stacy that a mother is bringing in her 3-year-old son, who stuck a small toy in his nose and then pushed it up too far for his mother to retrieve with her finger.

Objectives

After completing this chapter, you should be able to:

- Spell and define medical terminology in this chapter.
- Define the medical assistant's role in the EENT office.
- List and describe the roles of EENT health-care providers.
- Describe the anatomy and physiology of the eye.
- List and discuss diseases and disorders of the eye.
- Discuss diagnostic procedures and assessments related to the eyes.
- Describe the anatomy and physiology of the ear.
- List and discuss diseases and disorders of the ear.
- Discuss diagnostic procedures and assessments related to the ears.
- Describe the anatomy and physiology of the nose and nasal passages.
- List and discuss diseases of the nasal passages and sinuses.
- Describe the anatomy and physiology of the throat.
- List and discuss diseases of the throat.

 MedMedia
www.prenhall.com/frazier

Additional interactive resources and activities for this chapter can be found on the Companion Website. For audio glossary, legal and ethical scenarios, job scenarios, quizzes, games, virtual tours and activities related to the content of this chapter, please access the accompanying CD-ROM in this book.

Assets Available:

Audio Glossary
Legal and Ethical Scenario: *EENT*
On the Job Scenario: *EENT*
Multiple Choice Quiz
Games: Crossword, Strikeout and Spelling Bee
3D Virtual Tours: Ear: The Ear; Eye: The Eye
Drag & Drop: Ear; Eye

➕ MEDICAL ASSISTING COMPETENCIES

CAAHEP ENTRY-LEVEL COMPETENCIES FOR CMA	ABHES ENTRY-LEVEL COMPETENCIES FOR RMA
■ Identify and respond to issues of confidentiality.	■ Project a positive attitude.
■ Perform within legal and ethical boundaries.	■ Maintain confidentiality at all times.
■ Demonstrate knowledge of federal and state health-care legislation and regulations.	■ Be a "team player."
	■ Be cognizant of ethical boundaries.
■ Perform hand washing.	■ Exhibit initiative.
■ Dispose of biohazardous materials.	■ Adapt to change.
■ Practice Standard Precautions.	■ Evidence a responsible attitude.
■ Use methods of quality control.	■ Be courteous and diplomatic.
■ Obtain throat specimen for micro-biological testing.	■ Conduct work within scope of education, training, and ability.
■ Use methods of quality control.	■ Interview and take a patient history.
■ Perform telephone and in-person screening.	■ Prepare patients for and assist physician with routine and specialty examinations and treatments and minor office surgery.
■ Obtain vital signs.	■ Apply principles of aseptic techniques and infection control.
■ Obtain and record patient history.	
■ Prepare and maintain examination and treatment areas.	■ Prepare and maintain examination and treatment area.
■ Prepare patient for and assist with routine and specialty examinations.	■ Collect and process specimens.
■ Prepare patient and assist with minor procedures, treatments, and minor surgery.	■ Dispose of biohazardous materials.
	■ Practice Standard Precautions.
■ Apply pharmacology principles to prepare and administer oral and parenteral medications.	■ Prepare and administer oral and parenteral medications as directed by the physician.
■ Maintain medication and immunization records.	■ Maintain medication and immunization records.
	■ Obtain throat specimen for microbiological testing.

Introduction

Physicians who specialize in eye, ear, nose, and throat conditions include the following:

- **Ophthalmologist**—eye diseases and conditions
- **Otorhinolaryngologist**—ear, nose, and throat diseases and conditions
- **Otolaryngologist**—ear and throat diseases and disorders
- **Laryngologist**—throat diseases and disorders
- **Rhinologist**—nose diseases and disorders
- **Otologist**—ear diseases and disorders

Optometrists and **opticians** are not physicians, although an optometrist (Doctor of Optometric Medicine) may refer a patient to an ophthalmologist for evaluation if a condition or disease is noted. Optometrists are trained to examine eyes, test visual **acuity,** and prescribe adaptive lenses and contact lenses. Opticians are trained to grind lenses, insert lenses into frames, and fit eyeglasses.

Medical Terminology

acuity—keenness or sharpness

audiologist—professional trained to assess hearing levels

audiometry—measuring and testing hearing acuity

cerumen—earwax; waxy substance secreted in external ear canal

decibel—unit for measuring the intensity of sound

degenerative—impaired in function or condition over time

intraocular—within the eye

laryngologist—physician specializing in disorders and diseases of the throat

nasal septum—cartilage wall that divides the nasal cavity

ophthalmologist—physician who specializes in the treatment of eye diseases and disorders

optician—trained professional who grinds lens, inserts the lens into frames, and fits the patient's glasses

optometrist—licensed professional (Doctor of Optometric Medicine) who examines eyes, tests for visual acuity, and prescribes and adapts lens for patients

otic—pertaining to the ear

otologist—physician who specializes in the treatment of ear diseases

otolaryngologist—physician who specializes in the treatment of ear and throat diseases

otorhinolaryngologist—physician who specializes in ear, nose, and throat diseases

purulent—containing pus

rhinologist—physician who specializes in the treatment of nasal passage and sinus diseases

tinnitus—ringing in the ears

vertigo—dizziness

Abbreviations

dB—decibels

EENT—eye, ear, nose, and throat

FB—foreign body

OD—right eye

OS—left eye

The Medical Assistant's Role in an EENT Practice

You can use your skills and knowledge in an **EENT** practice by:

- Obtaining and recording vital signs and patient history.
- Testing visual acuity.
- Performing **audiometry.**
- Performing eye and ear irrigations and instillations.

You may be offered additional specialty training that will enable you to do advanced audiometric exams and fit glasses.

COMPETENCY SKILLS PERFORMANCE

1. Demonstrate the measurement of distance visual acuity with a Snellen chart.
2. Perform an Ishihara color vision test.
3. Demonstrate an eye irrigation.
4. Demonstrate the instillation of eye medication.
5. Demonstrate the performance of simple audiometry.
6. Demonstrate an ear irrigation.
7. Demonstrate the instillation of an ear medication.

The Anatomy and Physiology of the Eye

The eye is the organ of sight. It is protected by the eyebrows, lids that open and close, eyelashes, and the frontal orbital sockets of the skull (Figure 19-1 ◆). The conjunctiva, the mucous membrane covering the eyeball and lining the eyelid, moistens the eye.

The eyeball is made of three concentric (having a common center) layers of tissue: the sclera, the choroid, and the retina.

- The sclera is a tough white fibrous tissue that covers the outside of the eyeball. The extrinsic muscles that move the eye are attached to the sclera. A clear or transparent area of the sclera, the cornea, is located in the frontal portion of the eye and is covered with delicate epithelium.
- The middle layer of the wall of the eyeball is the choroid or vascular tunic. This layer contains numerous blood vessels, lymphatics, and the intrinsic eye muscles. The iris, the ciliary body, and the choroid are all contained in the middle layer. Functions of the choroid include regulating the amount of light entering the eye, supplying a route for blood vessels that provide nourishment and oxygen to the eye, secretion, and absorption.
- The retina, the innermost layer of the eye, contains sensory receptors called rods and cones. The cones are responsible mainly for color vision and daytime vision, and the rods are responsible for black and white vision and vision in dim light. The area of sharpest or most distinct vision is a concentration of cones in a small depression in the center of the posterior portion of the retina called the fovea centralis. Images are transmitted from the retina to the brain by the optic nerve.

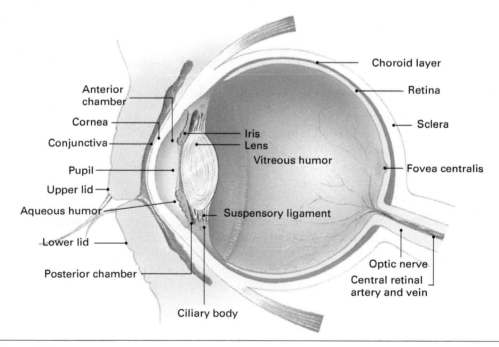

Figure 19-1 ◆ Anatomy of the eye

The globe of the eye is filled with humors, watery fluids that help maintain the eye's internal pressure. Aqueous humor fills the space before the lens, and vitreous humor fills the space behind the lens. The lens lies at the rear of the anterior chamber of the eyeball.

The iris, the colored part of the eye, regulates the amount of light that enters the eye. The black spot in the middle of the iris is the pupil. Bright light reduces pupil size as the circular muscle of the iris contracts. The pupil dilates in the dark or in dim light as those muscles relax.

Vision is the result of light refraction (bending from a straight path). Light enters the sclera at the transparent cornea (the first part of the eye that refracts light). It then passes through the pupil. It is kept from scattering in the choroid. The rod and cone cells of the retina receive the light refraction image. The optic nerve at the back of the eye transmits the image through the thalamus (a division of the brain) and ends in the vision region of the cerebral cortex. At first the image is upside down. The cerebral cortex inverts it, and the image becomes what people see (Figure 19-2 ◆).

Intrinsic muscles within the eye are the iris (colored membrane) and the ciliary muscle. The iris controls the size of the pupil and the amount of light that reaches the retina. The ciliary muscle changes the shape of the lens and how light is refracted to the retina.

Six extrinsic (outside) muscles control the movement of each eye:

- Superior rectus muscle: moves the eye to look upwards
- Inferior rectus muscle: moves the eye to look down
- Lateral rectus muscle: moves the eye laterally (corner to corner)
- Medial rectus muscle: moves the eye medially (to the middle)
- Superior oblique muscle: rolls the eye as it looks down and to the side
- Inferior oblique muscle: rolls the eye as it looks up and to the side

Disorders and Diseases of the Eye

Common problems affecting vision and the eyes can be broadly classified as refractive, infectious, or **degenerative,** with additional disorders resulting from injury or foreign bodies in the eye.

- Refractive disorders: As light passes through the eye to the retina, a break in the direct path may occur, with the result that the image is not focused directly on the retina. This change in the path of the image is a refractive error. There are four variations from normal—myopia, hyperopia, astigmatism, and presbyopia.
- Infectious disorders: These include conjunctivitis, keratitis, blepharitis, and styes (Figures 19-3 ◆ through 19-7 ◆).
- Degenerative disorders: Include cataracts, diabetic retinopathy, macular degeneration, strabismus, nystagmus, and glaucoma. As a patient ages, visual acuity typically becomes impaired. The condition may result in blindness.
- Other disorders: Retinal detachment may be the result of a degenerative process or a traumatic insult. Regardless of the cause, medical care is necessary to prevent permanent vision loss. Foreign bodies (**FB**) are a common cause of eye injuries.

Table 19-1 summarizes common eye diseases and disorders in these categories.

Diagnostic Procedures

The eyes are examined with a variety of instruments, including the following:

- Ophthalmoscope: used to examine the retina and other internal structures of the eye (Figure 19-8 ◆)

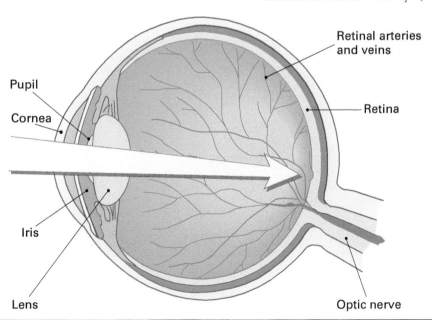

Pupil

Cornea

Iris

Lens

Retinal arteries and veins

Retina

Optic nerve

Figure 19-2 ◆ Light entering the eye

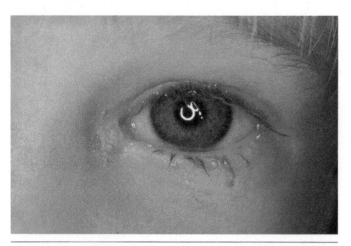

Figure 19-3 ◆ Eye with conjunctivitis
Source: Dorling Kindersley Media Library.

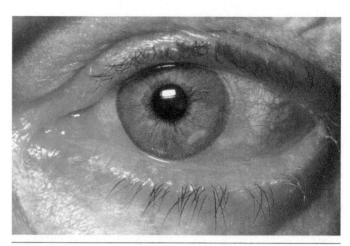

Figure 19-4 ◆ Eye with keratitis
Source: Dr. P. Marazzi/Photo Researchers, Inc.

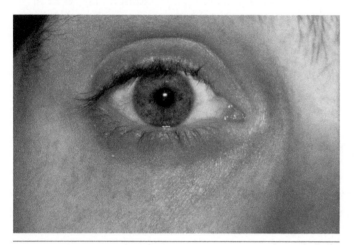

Figure 19-5 ◆ Eye with blepharitis
Source: Jane Shemilt, Cosine Graphics/Photo Researchers, Inc.

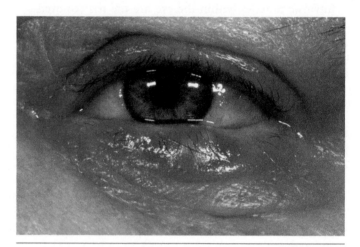

Figure 19-6 ◆ Eye with stye
Source: Dr. Chris Hale/Photo Researchers, Inc.

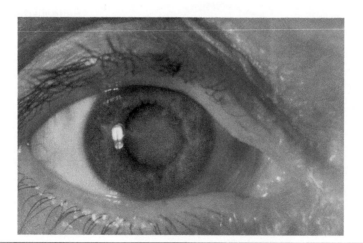

Figure 19-7 ◆ Eye with cataract
Source: Biophoto Associates/Photo Researchers, Inc.

TABLE 19-1 DISEASES AND DISORDERS OF EYE

Disorder or Disease	Symptoms	Diagnosis	Treatment
Astigmatism ■ Eyeball is shorter than normal and image focuses behind retina	■ Inability to focus on objects (blurry vision)	■ Ophthalmologic exam ■ Astigmatoscopy ■ Jaeger chart ■ Snellen chart	■ Corrective lens
Blepharitis ■ Inflammation and infection of hair follicles and glands at margins of eyelids. ■ Caused by virus, bacterial infection (*Staphylococcus*), allergic response, exposure to irritants	■ Red, tender, sore eyelids with sticky drainage ■ Watering of eyes ■ Possible eyelid inversion ■ Possible loss of eyelashes	■ Patient presenting symptoms	■ Moist heat to provide relief ■ Ophthalmic drops or ointment ■ Patient care
Cataract ■ Condition of lens of eye that develops slowly. ■ As cataract becomes opaque, vision diminishes ■ Onset usually occurs with aging	■ Impaired vision ■ Eventual blindness	■ Patient presenting symptoms	■ Surgical removal ■ Lens implant
Chalazion ■ Small, localized, hard cystic mass on the eyelid ■ Caused by blockage of a meibomian gland on eyelid	■ Usually painless but if infected may be swollen, inflamed, and painful	■ Observation of mass on the eyelid and patient history	■ Watchful waiting if no symptoms present ■ Surgical removal may be indicated
Conjunctivitis ■ Inflammation and infection of conjunctiva ■ Infection may be viral or bacterial ■ Inflammation caused by allergens or irritations from chemicals and UV light	■ Conjunctiva red and swollen ■ Infection may cause **purulent** drainage	■ Patient presenting symptoms	■ Gentle cleansing of discharge from eyelid and eyelashes (eye may be sealed shut) ■ Moist heat to provide relief ■ Antibiotics for bacterial infection
Diabetic retinopathy ■ Caused by diabetes ■ Causes microaneurysms (microscopic abnormal expansion of blood vessels) and hemorrhages (blood loss) in vessels of retina ■ Retinal veins become dilated and new blood vessels develop near optic disk	■ Painless ■ Blurred vision	■ Patient presenting symptoms ■ Ophthalmic examination	■ Laser surgery
Foreign bodies in eye ■ Include dust, insects, metal particles, wood splinters, or any small, airborne objects ■ Cause eye to tear in an effort to wash out offending substance	■ Pain ■ Decreased visual acuity ■ Photophobia ■ Feeling that something is under eyelid or stuck in cornea	■ Examination under eyelids	■ Irrigation with normal saline solution ■ Fluorescein to stain eye and help detect any corneal damage ■ Grinding (used when foreign body is metal and leaves a rust ring; eye and eye spud are anesthetized and rust ring is ground away)
Glaucoma ■ Increased fluid pressure within eye ■ Two forms: acute (closed angle) and chronic (open angle) ■ Causes damage to optic nerve and eventual blindness, if untreated	■ Visual loss	■ Patient presenting symptoms ■ Ophthalmic examination	■ Medication to release fluid ■ Laser surgery ■ Early detection, diagnosis, and treatment vital to save vision

(continued)

TABLE 19-1 DISEASES AND DISORDERS OF EYE (*Continued*)

Disorder or Disease	Symptoms	Diagnosis	Treatment
Glaucoma (*cont.*)			
■ If aqueous humor does not drain due to obstruction, pressure is created in eye ■ Visual loss results from death of nerve cells			
Hyperopia (farsightedness)			
■ Eyeball is shorter than normal and image focuses behind retina	■ Inability to focus on close objects	■ Ophthalmologic exam ■ Astigmatoscopy ■ Jaeger chart ■ Snellen chart	■ Biconvex (convex on both sides) lens in front of eye to focus image on retina
Keratitis			
■ Inflammation and ulceration of surface of cornea ■ Caused by infection (bacterial, fungal, or viral), corneal trauma, or exposure to light from welding	■ Pain ■ Photosensitivity ■ Tearing ■ Impaired vision	■ Patient presenting symptoms	■ Eye drops ■ Ointments ■ Systemic antibiotics if necessary ■ Eye patch to protect eye from further damage
Macular degeneration			
■ Gradual destruction of sharp central vision ■ Progressive disease related to aging ■ No cure	■ Painless ■ Blind spot in middle of visual field ■ Distorted vision; straight lines appear crooked	■ Ophthalmic examination ■ Patient presenting symptoms ■ Two types: dry and wet	■ Laser photocoagulation (allows limited improvement)
Myopia (nearsightedness)			
■ Eyeball is longer or deeper than normal and image focuses in front of retina	■ Inability to focus on objects in distance	■ Ophthalmologic exam ■ Astigmatoscopy ■ Jaeger chart ■ Snellen chart	■ Biconcave (concave on both sides) lens in front of eye to focus image on retina
Nystagmus			
■ Involuntary, repetitive, rhythmic movements of the eyes ■ May be caused by lesions in the brain or inner ear	■ Horizontal, vertical, or circular movement of one or both eyes ■ Possible blurred or impaired vision	■ Ophthalmologic exam	■ Treatment of underlying cause
Presbyopia			
■ Focusing of light rays is delayed due to aging of structures in eye	■ Eyes take longer to focus	■ Ophthalmologic exam ■ Astigmatoscopy ■ Jaeger chart ■ Snellen chart	■ Corrective lens
Retinal detachment			
■ Occurs when retina separates from choroids ■ May be result of traumatic insult to head or eye, or may be spontaneous	■ Floaters ■ Light flashes ■ Dark shadow appearing and progressing upward or to one side of visual field ■ Sudden, painless onset	■ Ophthalmologic examination to confirm separation ■ May follow cataract surgery	■ Photocoagulation (use of laser to treat detachment and retinal bleeding) ■ Cryotherapy
Strabismus			
■ Failure of the eyes to focus on the same position at the same time. ■ Exotropia: when one or both eyes turn outward. Esotropia: when one or both eyes turn inward.	■ One or both eyes turning inward or outward ■ Possible double vision	■ Patient presenting symptoms	■ Corrective glasses ■ Eye exercises ■ Surgery
Stye (hordeolum)			
■ Inflammation of one or more sebaceous (oil-secreting) glands of eyelid ■ Caused by bacterial infection	■ Redness ■ Pain ■ Purulence	■ Patient presenting symptoms	■ Moist heat to provide relief ■ Antibiotics

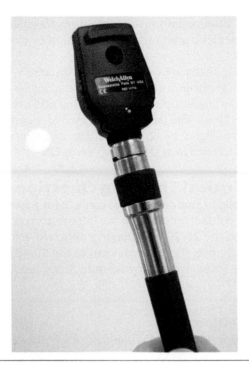

Figure 19-8 ◆ Ophthalmoscope

Keys to Success
USING A TONOMETER

Eye care professionals use different types of tonometers.

■ The mechanical tonometer is the most accurate type. After the eye is anesthetized with eye drops, the eye care professional touches the cornea with the tonometer. The amount of pressure needed to make an indentation on the cornea is measured and recorded. Caution must be taken because the eye is numb and therefore at risk for corneal injury until the anesthetic wears off.

■ The noncontact tonometer blows a puff of air across the eye as the individual looks into the tonometer. The cornea is flattened slightly to obtain a reading. The "air-puff" or "puff-of-air" test involves no contact with the cornea, is painless, and does not require a local anesthetic in the eye.

An increase in intraocular pressure often indicates the onset of glaucoma. Any tonometer reading above 21 mm is considered elevated, but not necessarily a diagnosis of glaucoma.

■ Slit lamp: used to examine and perform specialized procedures within the front structures of the eye (Figure 19-9 ◆)
■ Eye spud: used to remove a foreign particle or rust ring from the cornea
■ Tonometer: used to measure **intraocular** pressure (Figure 19-10 ◆)

Visual Acuity

A patient's visual acuity is measured in his or her ability to read letters on a special chart at a specific distance. Testing is performed to assess degree of eye injury or disease process. It

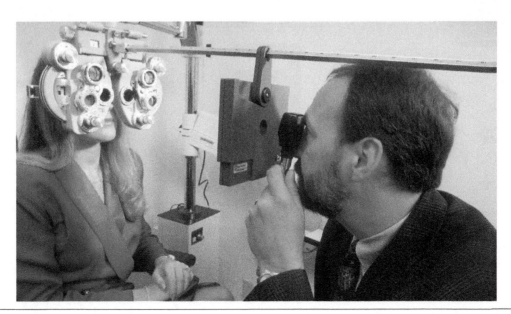

Figure 19-9 ◆ Slit lamp

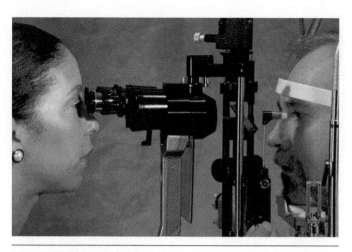

Figure 19-10 ◆ Tonometer
Source: Photo Researchers, Inc.

establishes baseline information, monitors the effectiveness of a treatment, or monitors the progression of chronic eye conditions.

Snellen charts are used to measure distance visual acuity. They are available in different forms—for English-speaking patients, non-English-speaking patients, and pediatric patients (Figure 19-11 ◆). The Jaeger chart is used to measure near-vision acuity (Figure 19-12 ◆). In patient documentation, the right eye is referred to as **OD,** the left eye as **OS.**

─ Critical Thinking Question 19-1 ─

The college student who has come in for a Snellen test wears contact lenses. With her left eye, the patient can read to the 20/20 line, making only two errors. With her right eye, she can only read to the 20/40 line and makes three errors. How should Stacy record these results?

Color Blindness

Color blindness (also called color deficiency) is an abnormal condition characterized by an inability to identify one or more primary colors. It is an inherited trait found mostly in males and results from a deficiency of or defects in the cones of the retina. There are two types of color blindness: achro-

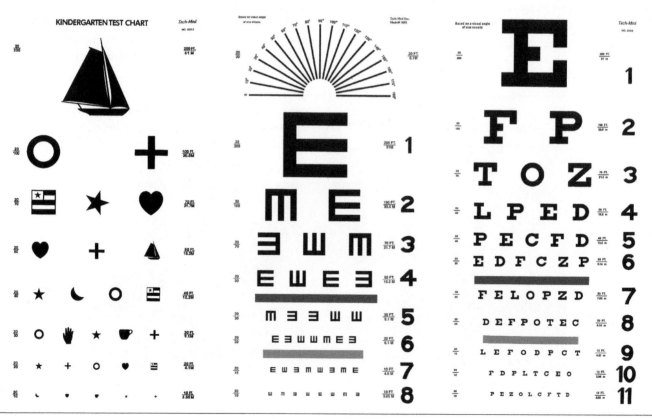

Figure 19-11 ◆ Various types of Snellen charts

PROCEDURE 19-1 Measure Distance Visual Acuity with a Snellen Chart

Theory

A line is marked on the floor 20 feet from the wall where a Snellen chart hangs. The patient stands, toes at the line, and is instructed to cover one eye with an occluder (spatula or card if an occluder is not available) to test the vision of the uncovered eye. The covered eye must be kept open to prevent squinting. If the patient tilts the head, tears, or squints during the test, he or she likely has vision problems. Note this on the patient's chart. Also note whether the patient performed the test with or without glasses or contact lenses.

Record the lowest readable level for each eye. Measurements are recorded as a fraction with the number 20 first or on top. The first number indicates the chart was 20 feet away from the patient. The second or bottom number indicates normal, uncorrected vision. For example, a score of 20/30 indicates that the patient is able to read at 20 feet what a person with normal vision could read at 30 feet.

Materials

- Snellen chart
- occluder, spatula, or card
- patient chart

Competency

(Conditions) With the necessary materials, **(Task)** you will be able to assist the patient in testing the visual acuity of both eyes **(Standards)** correctly within 30 minutes.

1. Wash your hands. Gather equipment and supplies.
2. Identify the patient and guide him or her to the treatment area.
3. Record the patient's history and main complaint. Explain the entire procedure to the patient.
4. Position the patient, standing or sitting, at the 20-foot line. Give the patient the occluder. Observe patient during the procedure for head tilting, squinting, and tearing.
5. Ask the patient to cover the left eye, keeping it open, and to read aloud from the top line to the smallest line of readable letters.
6. Record the right-eye vision with the number of errors. For one or two errors, record the vision fraction and minus one or two. For more than two errors, record the vision fraction as noted one line above on the Snellen chart. For example, if the patient reads the 20/40 line with the right eye and two errors, the result is recorded as OD 20/40-2. If the patient reads the 20/40 line with the right eye and three errors, the result is OD 20/50, or one line above the 20/40 line.
7. Next, ask the patient to repeat the procedure, covering the right eye and reading with the left.
8. Record the left-eye vision with the number of errors.
9. Wash your hands and report the results to the physician.

Patient Education

Explain to the patient that the procedure is done with both eyes open, even though one will be covered. Tell the patient that reading the Snellen chart should not be painful, but to report any symptoms during the procedure. If the patient does not speak English and is being tested with the Snellen E chart, have the patient practice pointing his or her fingers in the direction of each E before testing begins.

Charting Example

01/23/XX 9:30 a.m. Pt tested with corrective glasses. OS reading was 20/30 −2. OD reading was 20/40. Observed the pt squinting during the testing of OD. Patient referred by physician to local optometrist. Grant Reilly, RMA

Figure 19-12 ◆ A patient using a near-vision acuity card

matic vision and Daltonism. Achromatic color blindness is very rare. The affected individual cannot see any color at all, only shades of black, white, and gray. People with Daltonism, a more common disorder, cannot distinguish between red and green.

In addition to the two types of color blindness, there are three types of color deficiency: deuteranopia, protanopia, and tritanopia. Individuals with deuteranopia have difficulty distinguishing among neutral shades, bluish reds, and different shades of green. Protanopia, or "red blindness," is characterized by difficulty seeing reds or, occasionally, the difference between yellows and greens. Tritanopia, or "blue blindness," is the rarest condition, in which the individual is unable to see any shade of blue.

As an MA you may be asked to do color blindness testing with Ishihara color plates. The Ishihara book contains fourteen images of colored dots arranged in the shape of a numeral set against a background of dots in a contrasting color. Patients with color blindness have difficulty distinguishing the numerals from the background.

Eye Treatments

Dust, dirt, chemicals, or other substances may get onto the surface of the eye and can be difficult for patients to safely remove on their own. Eye irrigations are an easy and comfortable way to remove these substances in the medical office. The procedure involves flowing a fluid across the eye and flushing the irritating substance from the surface.

PROCEDURE 19-2 Perform the Ishihara Color Vision Test

Theory

The ability to see colors is a function of the cones of the retina. People who can no longer see color or who have never seen color most likely have defective cones or no cones at all. If the color blindness is not congenital, it may indicate damage to or disease of the retina, optic nerve, or even the thyroid.

The Ishihara test should be administered in a well-lit room out of direct sunlight.

Materials

- Ishihara color plates book
- pen
- patient chart

Competency

(**Conditions**) With the necessary materials, (**Task**) you will be able determine color vision acuity using Ishihara color plates (**Standards**) correctly within the time frame designated by the instructor.

1. Explain the procedure to the patient.
2. Follow the physician's directions for administering the total book or in sections.
3. Ask the patient to identify the number in each plate with both eyes.
4. Have the patient cover the left eye and read the book again, then the right eye.
5. Write down the page number of any plates the patient misses. (The correct answer is on the back of each page.)
6. Follow the directions on the last page of the book to determine the level of color blindness, if any.
7. Document the procedure in the patient's chart.

Patient Education

A patient who reads ten Ishihara plates correctly is considered to have normal color vision (Figure 19-13 ◆). A patient who reads seven plates or fewer correctly has color vision abnormalities and is referred to an optometrist or ophthalmologist for further review and treatment.

Charting Example

11/25/XX 3:30 PM Ishihara color plates examined by patient. No visual abnormalities noted. Shannon Reese, RMA

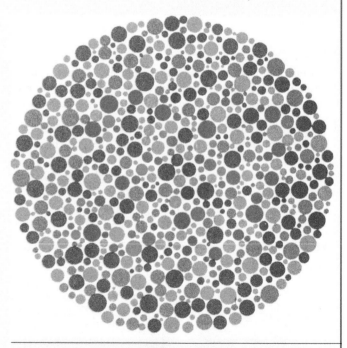

Figure 19-13 ◆ Color vision plate
Source: Alexander Kaludov/Fotolia

In the treatment of eye disorders, as well in preparation for eye examinations, a variety of topical drugs may be administered. Make sure that any medication you instill in a patient's eye is labeled "For Ophthalmologic Use."

- Local anesthetics are often dropped onto the surface of the eye before a procedure. They also are used to relieve pain from a foreign body or abrasion of the cornea. Tetracaine 0.5 percent ophthalmologic is a local anesthetic.
- Fluorescein ophthalmologic drops or strips are used to stain the eyes.

- Mydriatic eye drops dilate the pupils.
- Miotic medications cause the pupils to constrict.
- Other medications are prescribed to treat conditions such as glaucoma, infections, and corneal abrasions.

? — Critical Thinking Question 19-2-

The young girl with sand in her eye is frightened about having her eye flushed. She squeezes her eye shut and will not hold still. What are Stacy's options?

PROCEDURE 19-3 Perform Eye Irrigation

Theory

Eye irrigation may be performed on one or both eyes with a sterile solution. As with any medication or solution used for treatment, check the label when removing the medication from the storage shelf, immediately before using, and against the physician's order. Wear protective gear—gown, face shield, and disposable gloves—to protect against possible splashing.

The solution is irrigated from the center of the face or the inner corner of the eye to the outside. This prevents cross-contamination and the movement of the foreign substance or infectious material to the other eye. The patient helps by lying or sitting and turning the head toward the eye to be irrigated. It is also important that you irrigate toward the inside of the lower eyelid, or conjunctival sac. To avoid force and trauma to the eye, do *not* irrigate directly at the corneal surface.

For safety reasons, have the patient lie or sit still during the procedure. Be sure to ask the patient about medication allergies, and check the chart as well.

Materials
- irrigating solution
- sterile basin
- irrigating syringe
- protective gear (gown, face shield, disposable gloves)
- towels
- kidney-shaped basin
- tissues
- patient chart

Competency

(**Conditions**) With the necessary materials, (**Task**) you will be able to irrigate the patient's eye (**Standards**) safely and correctly within 30 minutes.

1. Wash your hands. Gather equipment and supplies.
2. Identify the patient and guide him or her to the treatment area.
3. Record the patient's history and main complaint.

4. Review the physician's order for the patient's name, the volume and name of the irrigating solution, and which eye to irrigate.
5. Ask the patient about medication allergies. Explain the entire procedure.
6. Check the label of the irrigating solution against the physician's order before pouring it into the sterile basin for irrigation.
7. Wash your hands.
8. Put on the gown, face shield, and gloves before proceeding with irrigation.
9. Ask the patient to lie or sit down with the head tilted toward the eye to be irrigated. Place a towel and the kidney-shaped basin next to the patient's face to catch irrigating fluid.
10. With your dominant hand, fill the irrigating syringe with the prescribed irrigating solution.
11. With your nondominant hand, press with a tissue against the patient's cheekbone beneath the eye to expose more of the eye surface.
12. While holding the syringe approximately 1/2 inch from the eye, gently direct the fluid toward the inside surface of the lower conjunctiva and from the inner to outer corner of the eye (Figure 19-14 ◆).
13. Continue irrigating until the prescribed volume is used. Depending on the cause and symptoms, the physician may order further irrigation.
14. When irrigation is complete, dry the area around the affected eye with tissues.
15. Remove your protective clothing and place it in the proper laundry and waste containers.
16. Wash your hands.
17. Document the patient's tolerance of the procedure, the amount and kind of irrigating solution, and the eye irrigated.

Patient Education

Describe the procedure completely to ensure the patient's cooperation. For safety reasons, the patient will need to

continued

PROCEDURE 19-3 Perform Eye Irrigation *(continued)*

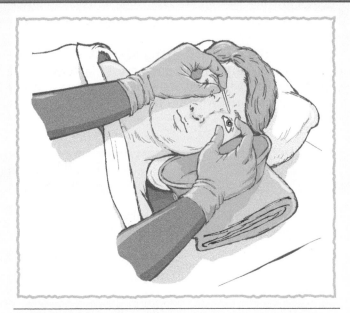

Figure 19-14 ◆ Irrigation of the eye

remain very still. Tell the patient that eye irrigation will ease the discomfort and help the eye heal faster. Schedule a follow-up visit.

Charting Example

07/15/XX 2:45 p.m. Fussy 8-year-old pt presents with sand in both eyes from a sibling scuffle in the family's sandbox. Per physician's order, each eye was irrigated per procedure with 180 cc normal saline with holding assistance from mother. Both right and left conjunctival sacs and cornea are clear after irrigation. Child stated that both eyes now feel better. Ann Maynard, CMA

PROCEDURE 19-4 Perform Instillation of Eye Medication

Theory

Eye medication, whether eye drops or ointment, is often used for successive patients. Ophthalmologists often use the same bottle of medication to instill drops in multiple patients' eyes, especially when dilating pupils or for anesthesia. To maintain the sterility of the container tip and prevent microbial contamination, keep it covered with the cap when you are not using it and during storage. Check the label on the medication or solution package when you take it from the storage shelf, immediately before using it, and against the physician's order.

A patient who requires eye medication often has not only a medication prescribed for one eye, but another medication for both eyes. Provide the patient with written as well as verbal instructions concerning the correct medication and dosage for each eye as prescribed by the physician. Ask the patient about medication allergies and check the chart. Only ophthalmic preparations may be used in the eye, as other preparations have a different concentration that may harm or damage eye tissue.

Materials

- prescription medication (drops or ointment)
- disposable gloves
- tissues
- patient chart

Competency

(**Conditions**) With the necessary materials, (**Task**) you will be able to instill eye medication (**Standards**) safely within 30 minutes.

1. Wash your hands. Gather equipment and supplies.
2. Take the medication from the storage shelf. Check the label against the physician's order.
3. Identify the patient and guide him or her to the treatment area. Check the patient's identification against the physician's order and medication name.
4. Note the medication dosage to be administered.
5. Ask the patient about allergies. Explain the entire procedure.
6. Wash your hands and put on disposable gloves.
7. Ask the patient to lie down or sit with the head tilted back with both eyes open. (It may be necessary to ask the sitting patient to look at the ceiling.) If the patient is wearing an eye patch, remove it.
8. Give the patient a tissue to hold in each hand until after the procedure.
9. With your nondominant hand and a tissue, press on the lower cheekbone and gently pull the lower eyelid down to expose the cornea and conjunctival sac.

PROCEDURE 19-4 Perform Instillation of Eye Medication *(continued)*

10. To administer eye drops, fill the eyedropper with your dominant hand. Hold the dropper approximately 1/2 inch away from the patient's eye, and administer the prescribed dose into the conjunctival sac (Figure 19-15 ◆). To administer the ointment, rest your dominant hand on the patient's forehead, hold the tube, and lightly squeeze ointment into the conjunctival sac from the inner to outer corner of the patient's eye.
11. Release the patient's lower eyelid and tell the patient to close the eye.
12. Repeat the procedure in the other eye, if ordered by the physician.

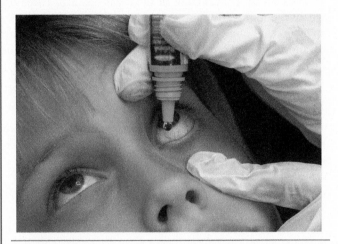

Figure 19-15 ◆ Administer the prescribed dose into the conjunctival sac

13. Instruct the patient to use a separate tissue for each eye to wipe away excess medication.
14. Apply an eye patch, if ordered by the physician.
15. Provide a waste container for the patient to discard the used tissue into.
16. Dispose of the gloves and tissue.
17. Wash your hands.
18. Document the patient's tolerance of the procedure, the amount and kind of medication administered, and the eye(s) treated.

Patient Education

Give the patient or the patient's significant other verbal and written instructions for administering eye medications at home. If the patient has not done it before, talk him or her through the instillation procedure. If the patient has done it but had a problem, observe how he or she does it. Tactfully discuss how the patient's technique might be improved, if necessary. Give the patient written instructions about each medication, including frequency and amount. Warn the patient to use only ophthalmic preparations in the eye.

Charting Example

02/25/XX 9:00 a.m. One eye gtt of Timoptic solution administered OS as prescribed. Instructions given to pt about the administration of eye drops and the pt demonstrated correctly how to administer one gtt OD as prescribed by physician. Patrick Cooper, RMA

Keys to Success
PATCHING THE EYE

The physician may order that a patient's eye be patched to keep the eyelid from passing back and forth over the cornea as the eyeball moves. The eye patch must apply a gentle pressure on the closed lid to prevent it from opening and closing in the normal process of blinking.

When one eye has a foreign body or abrasion, both eyes are usually patched to limit eye movement and further trauma to the cornea or eyelid, since the eyes move together (Figure 19-16 ◆).

Also, if only one eye is patched, warn the patient that depth perception will be impaired. The patient should use caution when going up and down stairs and when trying to see distant objects. The patient should be advised not to drive.

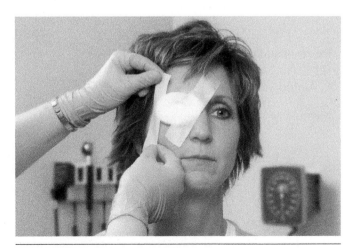

Figure 19-16 ◆ Patching the patient's eye

The Anatomy and Physiology of the Ear

The ear is the organ for hearing. It is divided into three areas—the external ear, middle ear, and internal ear (Figure 19-17 ◆).

- The external ear comprises the auricle, or pinna, which is the visible portion that projects from the side of the head, and the external auditory canal. The auditory canal is the pathway to the middle ear. It is lined with glands that secrete **cerumen,** or earwax, which protects the canal from infection.
- The tympanic membrane (eardrum) separates the outer or external ear from the middle ear. There are three small bones, called ossicles, in the middle ear: the malleus, incus, and stapes. The oval window connects the middle ear and the inner ear.
- The inner ear, or labyrinth, is made up of three compartments: the cochlea, vestibule, and semicircular canals. Perilymph and endolymph are fluids that transmit vibrations through the canals in the inner ear. The cochlea, a snail-shaped structure, houses the organ of Corti with its sound receptors. The vestibule and semicircular canals assist with equilibrium by transmitting information about the position of the body to the brain via the vestibular nerve.

The process of hearing occurs when sound waves move through the ear. The sound waves:

- enter the auditory canal from the auricle,
- then vibrate the tympanic membrane (eardrum),
- move the three tiny ossicles in the middle ear (malleus, incus, and stapes),
- pass through the oval window,
- continue into the inner ear or labyrinth, which contains the cochlea,
- enter the cochlea, where the fluids perilymph and endolymph allow the sound waves to continue to the auditory receptors in the organ of Corti,
- move to the tiny hairs in the receptors to be relayed on the auditory nerve fibers,
- are sent to the auditory center in the cerebral area of the cortex. These impulses are interpreted as sound by the brain.

An additional function of the ear is balance. Three organs in the inner ear maintain equilibrium: the semicircular canals, saccule, and utricle. Endolymph and tiny, sensitive hair cells move with the movement of the head to help maintain the body's balance.

Diseases and Disorders of the Ear

In conduction disorders, hearing loss may result when sounds are blocked from reaching the auditory nerve by one of a number of factors.

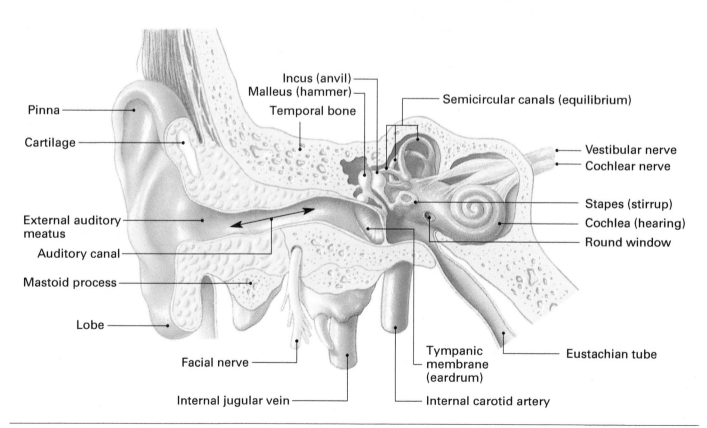

Figure 19-17 ◆ Anatomy of the ear

- Cerumen may block the passage of sound waves to the middle ear.
- Inflammatory and infectious disorders may cause edema and block the passage of sound waves to the inner ear.
- Otosclerosis prevents the ossicles from vibrating and sending the sound waves on.

Infectious disorders of the ear include otitis externa, otitis media, and labrynthitis (otitis interna). Injury to the ear may take the form of nerve trauma or a foreign body in the ear.

Table 19-2 summarizes common disorders and diseases of the ear.

Diagnostic Procedures

Instruments used in otic examinations include:

- Otoscope: a handheld device that beams light into the ear canal (Figure 19-18 ◆)
- Vienna speculum: a device used to examine the external auditory canal and eardrum (Figure 19-19 ◆)
- Zeiss microscope: magnifies the tympanic membrane

Hearing tests include audiometry and tuning fork testing.

Simple Audiometry

Simple audiometry testing helps determine a patient's hearing level in each ear and can also be used to confirm the presence

---

TABLE 19-2 DISEASES AND DISORDERS OF THE EAR

Disorder	Symptoms	Diagnosis	Treatment
Impacted cerumen ■ Conducted disorder ■ Earwax becomes hardened ■ May result from using cotton swabs to clean the ear	■ Impaired hearing ■ Tinnitus (ringing in the ears) ■ Plugged or stuffed feeling in outer ear	■ Patient presenting symptoms ■ **Otic** examination	■ Irrigation to soften or loosen plug ■ Cryotherapy
Labyrynthitis ■ Inflammation and infection of labyrinth or semicircular canals of the inner ear ■ Cause may be bacterial or viral infection	■ Impaired hearing ■ Vertigo ■ Nausea ■ Vomiting ■ Tinnitus	■ Patient presenting symptoms	■ Antibiotics for bacterial infection ■ Corticosteroids for viral infection
Ménière's disease ■ Conduction disorder characterized by sudden onset of symptoms ■ Abnormality caused by change in volume of endolymph fluid, edema, or rupture of membranous labyrinth ■ No cure	■ Pressure or pain in ear ■ Impaired hearing ■ Vertigo (dizziness) ■ Tinnitus	■ Hearing tests ■ Balance tests ■ Physical examination	■ Drug therapy to control symptoms ■ Surgery—either cutting of vestibular nerve or labyrinthectomy (portion of inner ear is removed, resulting in total hearing loss)
Nerve trauma ■ Injury caused by extended exposure to high noise levels (loud music, loud radio, jackhammers, sirens, machinery, gunshots, jet engines)	■ Impaired hearing	■ Hearing tests	Prevention (damage is not reversible)
Otitis externa ■ Inflammation of outer ear, also called swimmer's ear (often occurs after swimming); other ear also inflamed and reddened	■ Impaired hearing ■ Pain ■ Fever	■ Visual inspection of outer ear	■ Antibiotic drops for infection ■ Steroid drops ■ Keeping ear dry
Otitis media ■ Inflammation or bacterial infection of middle ear, usually with fluid that cannot drain ■ Eardrum bulges and may be reddened ■ Often comes before or just after upper respiratory or a cold ■ Two forms: serous and purulent	■ Pain ■ Fever ■ Discharge ■ Impaired hearing ■ Young children cry, pull at their ears, or sit with head held to one side	■ Audiology testing ■ Balance tests ■ Physical examination	■ Antibiotics to treat the infection

(continued)

TABLE 19-2 DISEASES AND DISORDERS OF THE EAR *(Continued)*

Disorder	Symptoms	Diagnosis	Treatment
Otosclerosis ■ Conductive disorder caused by fusion of three main bones of middle ear ■ Movement of stapes is restricted, so sound waves cannot be sent to inner ear	■ Progressive hearing impairment	■ Hearing tests ■ Physical examination	■ Surgery to replace stapes with a metal or plastic prosthesis
Ruptured tympanic membrane ■ Conductive disorder caused by injury or infectious process of otitis media. ■ Scarring and impaired hearing may remain after membrane heals	■ Impaired hearing	■ Otic examination	■ Antibiotics for otitis media
Foreign bodies ■ Injury caused by object placed in ear or by insect flying or crawling into ear ■ Children often place peas, beans, or other small foods into ear that absorb moisture in ear and swell, further obstructing canal	■ Impaired hearing	■ Physical examination	■ Earwax spoon to remove object ■ Gentle suction ■ Gentle irrigation ■ For insect: in a dark room, shining a light into ear (insect often moves toward light and out of ear)

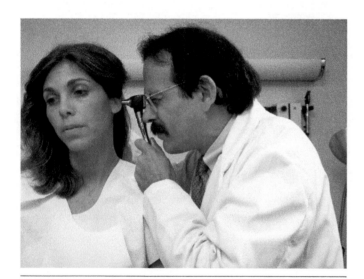

Figure 19-18 ◆ Examination of the ear using an otoscope
Source: Michal Heron Photography.

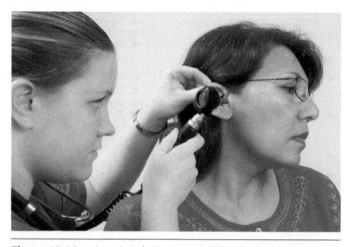

Figure 19-19 ◆ A patient being examined with vienna speculum

Keys to Success
ASSISTING THE HEARING OR VISUALLY IMPAIRED

The visually impaired patient may require assistance when completing office forms. To provide privacy and prevent embarrassment, politely and discreetly escort the patient to a private area and offer your assistance. Do not assume the visually impaired patient has hearing problems and speak loudly.

The hearing-impaired patient may require written instructions to complete medical forms. Face the patient directly and speak in normal tones.

of underlying disease. The audiometer measures the patient's response to acoustic stimuli of specific frequencies. Employers often order an audiometry exam to establish baseline information for new hires and monitor the hearing status of long-term employees. You will need additional training from an **audiologist** or physician to perform this procedure.

Ear Treatments

Irrigating the ear clears the external auditory canal of cerumen or other foreign material. The physician may order an ear irrigation to make the tympanic membrane easier to see.

Drugs instilled in the ear include antibiotics, topical anesthetics, and solutions or oils that soften cerumen. These drugs must be labeled for use in the ear.

PROCEDURE 19-5 Perform Simple Audiometry

Theory

Audiometry provides information about sound frequencies the patient is able and unable to hear. The test is performed in a quiet room or soundproof booth because outside noises affect the accuracy of the results. You should begin testing tones on the ear with better hearing, if known. Earphones are marked for the right or left ear. It is important that earphones are placed correctly for tones to be delivered to the correct ear and results to be accurate.

    Make sure the tones do not follow a rhythm, as the patient may guess correctly when the next increasing tones are done. If the patient finds the test too long or the results are inconsistent, inform the physician and reschedule the test. Before performing the rescheduled test, try to correct or improve on the failed first test.

Materials

- audiometer
- earphones
- audiometric test report form
- patient chart

Competency

(**Conditions**) With the necessary materials, (**Task**) you will be able to perform bilateral audiology testing (**Standards**) correctly within 30 minutes.

1. Wash your hands. Gather equipment and supplies.
2. Prepare the testing area to ensure quiet during the procedure.
3. Identify the patient and guide him or her to the testing area.
4. Inform the patient that only one ear at a time will be tested. Instruct the patient to raise one finger or nod when he or she first hears the sound, no matter how soft.
5. Place earphones on the patient.
6. Administer low-frequency sounds to one ear to determine the patient's baseline hearing measurements and ability to follow test instructions (Figure 19-20 ◆).

7. Plot the results from each tone on the graph immediately.
8. Continue raising the tone frequency by 10 **dB** (**decibels**) and recording the results until the patient can no longer hear in the first ear.
9. Lower the tone by 5 dB until the patient signals, to confirm the lowest frequency the patient can hear in that ear.
10. Repeat the procedure with the other ear.
11. Give the audiometric test results to the physician.
12. Prepare the audiometric equipment and room for next the patient.

Patient Education

It is important that the patient understand the testing instructions to obtain the most accurate results. Always ask the patient to repeat the instructions back to you before testing.

Charting Example

09/26/XX 1:30 p.m.   Pt demonstrated understanding of audiometry test instructions before the procedure. Results given to physician for discussion with pt. Lauren Willis, RMA

Figure 19-20 ◆ Hearing test
Source: adam james/Alamy

PROCEDURE 19-6 Perform Ear Irrigation

Theory

Check the condition of the external auditory canal with an otoscope before and after the procedure to observe any changes. Additional otoscopic examination may be required during the procedure if the patient complains of pain.

The patient's head is tilted toward the affected ear to allow fluid to enter the canal. If it is expected that the earwax will be difficult to remove, the physician may order that a couple of drops of hydrogen peroxide or oil be placed on the surface of the ear canal. As the hydrogen peroxide or oil slides toward the tympanic membrane, the earwax is softened.

For a child 3 years old or an adult, the auricle is pulled back and up to position the ear canal. For a child under 3, whose external auditory canal is narrower, the auricle is pulled back and down.

When you are ready to begin, instruct the patient or other office staff to hold the basin under the ear and next to the neck. Place a towel under the basin to protect the patient's clothing. Place the solution-filled syringe at the opening of the external auditory canal and direct the tip toward the side or top.

Severe pain, and possibly the rupture of the tympanic membrane, will result if you irrigate with the tip aimed straight at the canal because of the force of the irrigating fluid moving directly through the canal.

When you have completed the procedure, examine the auditory canal with the otoscope. Help the patient lie down on the side of the irrigated ear to allow complete drainage. Some physicians also perform a final otoscopic examination to check the ear canal and tympanic membrane.

Note: Store the solution at room temperature to maintain the correct temperature for irrigation.

Materials

- irrigating solution
- sterile basin
- irrigating syringe
- towels
- cotton ball(s)
- patient chart

Competency

(**Conditions**) With the necessary materials, (**Tasks**) you will be able to irrigate the patient's ear (**Standards**) safely and correctly within 30 minutes.

1. Wash your hands. Gather equipment and supplies.
2. Identify the patient and guide him or her to the treatment area. Explain the entire procedure.
3. Check the label of the irrigating solution when you take it from the shelf and against the physician's order.
4. Position the patient in a sitting position and instruct him or her to lean the head toward the side to be irrigated.
5. Check the condition of the external auditory canal with the otoscope.
6. Drape a towel across the patient's shoulder, under the ear.
7. Fill the irrigating syringe with prescribed solution.
8. Place the basin under the ear and against the skin (Figure 19-21 ◆). Instruct the patient or other office personnel to hold the basin in place.
9. For a child under 3 years, gently pull the auricle down and back (Figure 19-22 ◆). For a child over 3 years or an adult, gently pull the auricle ear up and back (Figure 19-23 ◆).
10. Gently place the tip of the irrigating syringe into the external auditory canal and point to the side or top. Do *not* point directly toward the tympanic membrane.
11. Instill the irrigating solution with gentle pressure on the plunger of the syringe (Figure 19-24 ◆).
12. Place the irrigation basin aside.
13. Use the otoscope to determine if more irrigation is needed.
14. Repeat the procedure until the desired results are obtained. If the patient experiences discomfort or other difficulties, report to the physician.

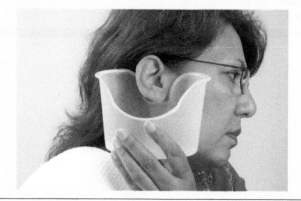

Figure 19-21 ◆ Position the basin for ear irrigation.

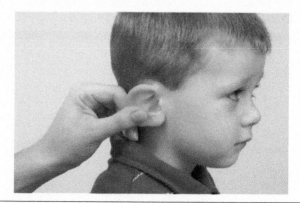

Figure 19-22 ◆ Proper holding position of the ear lobe for children

PROCEDURE 19-6 **Perform Ear Irrigation** *(continued)*

15. After irrigation, instruct and/or assist the patient to lie down with the head tilted toward the irrigated ear.
16. Place a towel under the head to catch the drainage.
17. Help the patient to a sitting, then standing position. Assess the patient for light-headedness or dizziness. Escort the patient to the waiting room.
18. Clean the treatment area and remove reusable equipment to the utility cleaning area.
19. Wash your hands.
20. Document the patient's tolerance and the results of the procedure.

Patient Education

Explain the procedure before and during the irrigation, including the normal feeling of fullness and flushing discomfort. Instruct the patient to report any new or increased pain.

Charting Example

10/09/XX 9:30 a.m. Otoscope showed moderate amount of cerumen present in the rt external auditory canal. Ear irrigation was done. Pt stated no additional discomfort. Post-otoscopic examination shows clear auditory canal with pearly gray membrane visible. Pt states she can hear better with the rt ear. Liam Marks, RMA

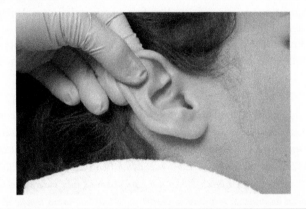

Figure 19-23 ◆ Proper holding position of the outer ear for adults

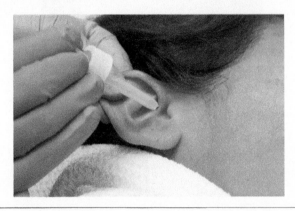

Figure 19-24 ◆ Instill the irrigating solution into the patient's ear

PROCEDURE 19-7 **Perform Instillation of Ear Medication**

Theory

Ear medication is generally prescribed for the patient in multiple doses, and it is important to keep the dropper or bottle tip sterile. This is done by storing it in the bottle when it is not in use and avoiding contact with any surface other than the medication in the bottle.

Ear medication should be at room temperature as the internal ear is sensitive to temperature extremes. If the medication is cold, the patient may experience nausea and/or vertigo.

Check the label when removing the medication from the storage shelf, immediately before using, and against the physician's order. Check the written instructions to verify the correct medication and dosage for each ear as prescribed by the physician. Ask the patient about medication allergies and check the chart as well. After administering the medication, instruct the patient to lie still for approximately 10 minutes to allow the medication to coat the external auditory canal and eardrum.

Materials

■ medication
■ disposable gloves
■ cotton balls
■ patient chart

Competency

(**Conditions**) With the necessary materials, (**Task**) you will be able to instill medication into the patient's ear (**Standards**) safely and correctly within 30 minutes.

1. Wash your hands. Gather equipment and supplies.
2. Check the label when removing the medication from the shelf and against the physician's order. Do *not* administer the medication unless it is at room temperature.
3. Identify the patient and guide him or her to the treatment area. Check the patient name against the physician's order and against the medication.

continued

PROCEDURE 19-7 **Perform Instillation of Ear Medication** *(continued)*

4. Explain the entire procedure to the patient. Ask about any allergies.
5. Instruct the patient to lie on the side opposite the ear to be treated.
6. Position the auricle as in Procedure 19-6.
7. Hold the ear dropper or bottle tip about 1/2 inch above the external auditory canal and gently squeeze the bulb to administer the prescribed number of drops (Figure 19-25 ◆).
8. Instruct the patient to lie still for 10 minutes.

9. Loosely place a small cotton ball, if the physician orders it, at the opening to the canal.
10. Repeat the procedure for the other ear, if ordered.
11. Recap the medication bottle and dispose of waste materials.
12. Remove and dispose of the gloves. Wash your hands.
13. Escort the patient back to the waiting room.
14. Document the patient's tolerance of the procedure, the medication, the dosage administered, and which ear received treatment.

Patient Education

Provide verbal and written instructions for administering ear medications at home, including frequency and dosage. If the patient is new to instillation, talk him or her through the procedure. If the patient is physically unable or too young to perform the procedure, give the instructions to a significant other.

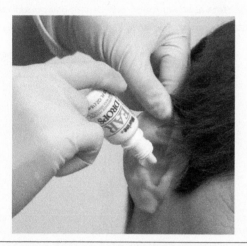

Figure 19-25 ◆ Instilling medication drops in the patient's ear

Charting Example

03/08/XX 9:00 a.m. Auraglan five gtts instilled into each ear per procedure and physician's order. Cotton ball loosely placed at opening to each ear canal. Pt demonstrated ability to instill medication correctly in right ear after demonstration and instilling by undersigned. Pt did not complain of any side effects. Pt said he understood how to instill eardrops at room temperature for seven days, twice daily. Jill Franklin, CMA

Keys to Success
TYMPANOMETRY

Tympanometry is a process that measures the flexibility of the patient's tympanic membrane when sound waves and pressure are applied. A tympanometer (Figure 19-26 ◆) has an earpiece that is positioned against the ear canal. If fluid is present behind the tympanic membrane (as in otitis media), the machine will record the absence of tympanic membrane movement.

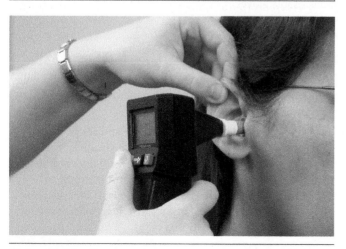

Figure 19-26 ◆ Tympanometer

The Anatomy and Physiology of the Nose

The nose and throat comprise the upper airway. The two sides of the interior nose are separated by the **nasal septum** (dividing wall). The interior of the nose has three zones (Figure 19-27 ◆):

- The vestibular zone is the outermost opening of the nose. The holes in the nose are known as *nares;* the anterior nares are the nostrils. The cilia (nasal hair) filter inhaled air by trapping particles.
- The olfactory zone is the most interior portion of the nose where the sense of smell is located. The chonchae (nasal bones) are located here, covered with membranous tissue. The entering air is warmed and humidified before it reaches the respiratory zone.
- The respiratory zone is located above the soft palate. This is where the airflow begins its downward journey toward the oral cavity.

Surrounding the nose in the skull are the sinuses. The functions of the sinuses are believed to include lightening the weight of the skull and enhancing phonation (the production of vocal sounds).

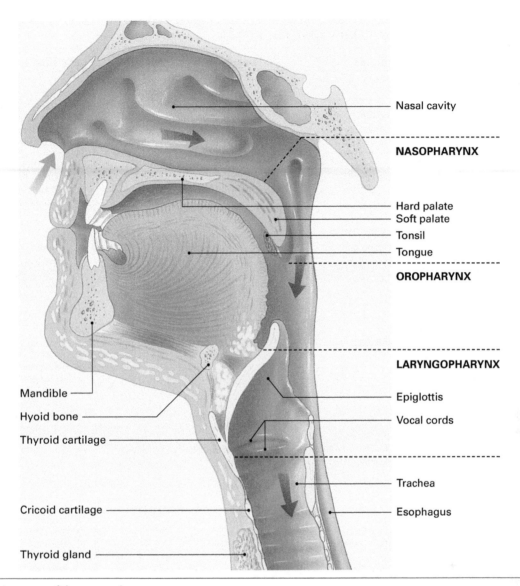

Figure 19-27 ◆ Anatomy of the upper airway.

Diseases and Disorders of the Nose and Nasal Passages

Disorders of the nose or nasal passages include the inflammatory conditions of rhinitis and paranasal sinusitis, structural conditions of the septum, nasal polyps, epistaxis, traumatic insult, the common cold, and foreign bodies (Table 19-3). An allergic response may be the cause of both rhinitis and sinusitis. Hay fever is typically an allergic response. Therefore, patients who experience chronic or recurrent episode of both upper respiratory conditions may be referred to an allergy specialist.

Diagnosis and Treatment

There are several instruments that facilitate the examination of the nasal passages.

■ The otoscope is used to examine not only the ear, but also the nasal cavities. A speculum with a larger opening is usually placed on the scope. The light source enables the examiner to see the mucous membranes lining the nasal cavities.
■ The Vienna speculum is used to open the nares and see the nasal membranes. An outside light source is required as well.
■ A pharyngeal mirror helps the examiner see into the posterior part of the nasal cavity, or nasopharynx, with an external light source (Figure 19-28 ◆).

Decongestants and steroid-containing nasal sprays are among the drugs used in the care of nose-related conditions.

? —Critical Thinking Question 19-3-
What items should Stacy lay out for the physician so that he can remove the toy from the child's nose?

TABLE 19-3 DISEASES AND DISORDERS OF THE NOSE AND NASAL PASSAGES

Disease or Disorder	Symptoms	Diagnosis	Treatment
Common cold/Upper respiratory tract infection ■ Inflammatory process affecting upper respiratory tract ■ Caused by viruses	■ Nasal congestion ■ Runny nose ■ Coughing, sneezing ■ Watery eyes ■ Hoarseness ■ Sore throat	■ Patient presenting symptoms and patient history ■ Cultures of nasal discharge and sputum may be necessary to rule out other conditions or to confirm diagnosis of viral cause	■ Condition is usually self-limiting to less than ten days' duration ■ Decongestants and steam vaporizer for nasal congestion, cough syrup for cough, antipyretic agents for fever; mild analgesics ■ Rest and fluids
Epistaxis (nosebleed) ■ Nasal hemorrhage that may occur spontaneously or as result of traumatic injury ■ Often caused by upper respiratory infections or may be recurrent and secondary to other diseases	■ Bleeding from one or both nostrils	■ Patient presenting symptoms ■ Physical examination	■ Blowing nose, then compressing soft tissues just below nasal bones for 5 to 10 minutes (usually stops bleeding, except in case of traumatic injury)
Foreign bodies ■ Objects inserted, usually accidentally, in nares, where they absorb moisture from nasal mucosa (children often insert small objects such as dried peas or grapes into nose)	■ Difficulty breathing	■ Patient presenting symptoms	■ Removal by physician (child may have to be mildly sedated) ■ Squeezing nose if object is something like cereal or small grape; child can then blow object out after it has been crushed
Nasal polyps ■ Masses develop from nasal mucosa and hang down in nasal cavity	■ Difficulty breathing ■ Sinusitis	■ Patient presenting symptoms	■ Surgery to improve airway
Rhinitis ■ Inflammation and/or infection of nasal mucosa ■ Usually caused by virus; part of common cold ■ Causes nasal congestion and rhinorrhea (sneezing and/or itching of nose) ■ Inflammation results in increased mucus secretion and runny nose	■ Runny nose ■ Fever ■ Congestion ■ "Stuffy" head	■ Patient presenting symptoms	■ Liquids ■ Vaporizer to humidify room ■ Over-the-counter (OTC) medications to relieve symptoms—antipyretics for fever and analgesics for discomfort ■ Rest ■ Decongestant sprays (continued use is not recommended)
Septal defects ■ Septum is deviated ■ May be congenital or result of physical injury	■ Sinusitis and nosebleed when there is nasal obstruction	■ Patient presenting symptoms	■ Surgery to improve airway
Sinusitis ■ Inflammation and/or infection of paranasal sinuses ■ Often the forerunner of a cold ■ May be caused by bacteria or virus ■ Acute sinusitis may become chronic	■ Pain and tenderness in cheeks and forehead above eyes	■ Patient presenting symptoms ■ Sinus X-ray	■ Antibiotics and decongestants for bacterial sinusitis ■ OTC medications—antipyretics for fever and analgesics for discomfort ■ Decongestant sprays (continued use is not recommended)

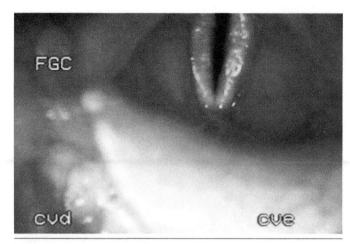

Figure 19-29 ◆ Vocal cords
Source: Point-of-view/Alamy

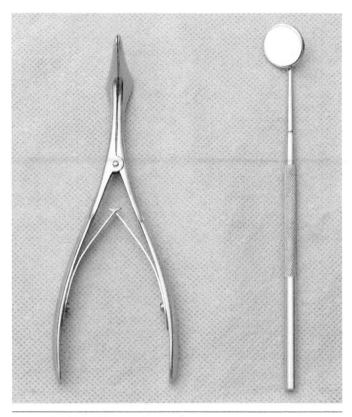

Figure 19-28 ◆ Nasal speculum and pharyngeal mirror

The Anatomy and Physiology of the Throat

The pharynx is where the nasal, oral, and laryngeal cavities meet. The pharynx has three regions:

- The nasopharynx is just above the soft palate. It includes the pharyngeal tonsils (adenoids) and the eustachian tubes. Each eustachian tube connects the nasopharynx to the middle ear and maintains equal pressure between these two areas.
- The oropharynx is the region you see when you look into a patient's mouth. The palatine tonsils flank either side of this region and the tongue. This region, also called the oral cavity, contains the teeth, the tongue and its taste buds, the inner portion of the cheeks (buccal membranes), and the salivary glands.
- The laryngopharynx is just above the vocal cords. The lingual tonsils (at the base of the tongue), and the epiglottis are located here. The epiglottis is the cartilage (elastic tissue) that covers the trachea (windpipe) during swallowing. The epiglottis prevents food or liquids from entering into the airway.

The vocal cords are housed in the larynx and mark the beginning of the lower airway (Figure 19-29 ◆). They vibrate during exhalation, which creates the sound of the voice.

Diseases of the Mouth and Throat

Common infectious conditions of the throat include pharyngitis, laryngitis, and strep throat. Tonsillitis and adenoiditis are the inflammation and usually infection of the tonsils and adenoids. Thrush is a fungal infection usually affecting infants. Oral cancer may occur in a number of locations in the mouth, lips, and tongue (Table 19-4).

Diagnosis and Treatment

Structures in the oral cavity and pharynx are viewed with the following instruments:

- External light source and tongue depressor
- Laryngeal mirror and external light source—mirror is usually warmed under warm running water to prevent fogging by the patient's breath
- Laryngoscope—requires sedation of the patient and application of a topical anesthetic

Drug therapy includes lozenges, gargles, throat sprays, and antibiotics.

TABLE 19-4 INFECTIOUS CONDITIONS OF THE MOUTH AND THROAT

Disease	Symptoms	Diagnosis	Treatment
Laryngitis ■ Inflammation and/or infection of larynx ■ Inflammation of vocal cords makes it difficult to speak ■ May be bacterial or viral in origin ■ May be caused by irritation of respiratory passage or excessive use of the voice	■ Difficulty speaking ■ Sore throat ■ Fever ■ Chills	■ Patient presenting symptoms ■ Visual examination with laryngeal mirror	■ Voice rest ■ Drinking liquids ■ Humidified air ■ Antibiotics for bacterial infections ■ Removing the cause
Oral cancer ■ Cancer on the lips, buccal mucosa, anterior tongue, hard palate, floor of the mouth, or lower gingivia ■ May be in the form of squamous cell carcinoma or adenocarcinoma	■ White patchy lesions in the mouth that do not heal ■ Ulcers on lips and tongue are or become painful ■ Possible difficulty eating, chewing, or swallowing ■ Reduced appetite ■ Possible weight loss	■ If not painful, lesions often discovered on a dental visit ■ Patient history and exam	■ Depends on extent and location of lesion ■ Radiation and surgery (surgery may have to be extensive to remove diseased tissue)
Pharyngitis (sore throat) ■ Inflammation and/or infection of pharynx ■ Caused by bacteria or virus, sometimes smoke or foreign objects ■ May precede a cold or sinusitis or be secondary to a virus	■ Dry or burning sensation in throat ■ Fever ■ Chills ■ Difficulty swallowing and speaking ■ Enlarged cervical lymph nodes ■ Red or swollen membranes	■ Patient presenting symptoms ■ Visual examination	■ Antipyretics and analgesics for bacterial infections ■ Saltwater gargles and throat lozenges to ease discomfort ■ Tonsil removal for chronic pharyngitis that may be result of tonsillitis ■ Rhinitis and sinusitis treatment when these conditions are present
Thrush ■ Fungal infection in mouth caused by *Candidiasis albicans* ■ Occurs most often in infants and young children, but the elderly and immunodeficient individuals also susceptible	■ Usually noticed in infants as slightly raised yellow patchy areas in mouth on inner aspects of cheeks, tongue, and upper palate, and on mucous membrane of inner lip ■ Burning sensation	■ Patient history, oral examination, and laboratory examination of tissue samples	■ Antifungal medications ■ Antifungal mouthwash
Tonsillitis and adenoiditis ■ Inflammation and infection of tonsils and adenoids ■ Patient may refer to this condition as sore throat ■ Most common in children ages 5 to 10; may lead to rheumatic heart disease ■ Non-streptococcal tonsillitis resolves in a few days	■ Pain ■ Difficulty swallowing ■ Fever ■ Chills ■ Earache ■ Muscle aches ■ General malaise ■ Cervical lymph nodes swollen and tender to touch	■ Patient presenting symptoms ■ Visual examination	■ Strep screen or a culture to identify infection ■ Antibiotics ■ Tonsillectomy for patients, especially children, who have more than four sore throats in a year (removal of adenoids in children is common during this procedure)

REVIEW

Chapter Summary

- Eye specialists include:
  - *ophthalmologists*—diagnose and treat eye diseases and conditions
  - *optometrists*—examine eyes, test visual acuity, and prescribe adaptive lenses
  - *opticians*—grind lenses, insert lens into frames, and fit patient glasses
- Ear, nose, and throat specialists include:
  - *otorhinolaryngologists*—ear, nose, and throat diseases and conditions
  - *otolaryngologists*—ear and throat diseases and conditions
  - *laryngologists*—throat diseases and disorders
  - *rhinologists*—nose diseases and disorders
- As an MA, you may take vital signs, record patient histories, and perform visual acuity testing, simple audiometry, and irrigation and instillation of the eyes and ears.
- Refractive errors of the eye cause myopia, hyperopia, astigmatism, and presbyopia.
- Infectious disorders of the eye include conjunctivitis, keratitis, blepharitis, and styes. Conjunctivitis is an inflammation and infection of the conjunctiva, the mucous membrane covering the eyeball and lining the eyelid. Keratitis is an inflammation and ulceration of the surface of the cornea. Blepharitis is an inflammation and infection of the hair follicles and glands of the eyelid margins. A stye is an inflammatory and infectious process of an eyelid sebaceous gland.
- Degenerative disorders of the eye include cataracts, diabetic retinopathy, macular degeneration, and glaucoma. Visual

acuity typically becomes impaired with aging. Retinal detachment may be the result of a degenerative process or of a traumatic insult.
- Foreign bodies in the eye cause tearing, pain, and occasionally impaired visual acuity or photophobia.
- Visual acuity testing and eye irrigations and instillations are the assessments and diagnostic procedures commonly performed by an MA. Instruments used in eye care include the ophthalmoscope, slit lamp, eye spud, and tonometer.
- Ear disorders include impacted earwax; inflammatory and infectious disorders such as Ménière's disease, otitis externa, otitis media, and otitis interna (labyrinthitis); otosclerosis, a fusion of three main ear bones (ossicles); ruptured tympanic membrane; nerve trauma; and foreign bodies. Diagnostic procedures and hearing assessments performed by an MA include simple audiometry and ear irrigations and instillations. Instruments used in ear care include the otoscope, Vienna speculum, and Zeiss microscope.
- Nose or nasal passage disorders include the inflammatory conditions of rhinitis and sinusitis, structural conditions of the septum, nasal polyps, epistaxis (nosebleed), traumatic insult, and foreign bodies. Instruments used in nose care include the otoscope, Vienna speculum, and pharyngeal mirror.
- Common throat disorders include pharyngitis, laryngitis, strep throat, tonsillitis, adenoiditis, and thrush. Oral cancer may affect a number of locations. Instruments used in throat care include the tongue depressor, laryngeal mirror, and laryngoscope.

Chapter Review Questions

Multiple Choice

1. A patient being tested for visual acuity must keep both eyes open, because
   - A. it prevents squinting.
   - B. it is easier to see through the spatula.
   - C. the patient is standing 20 feet away from the chart.
   - D. it helps the patient keep his or her balance.

2. Which of the following specialists is trained to grind lenses?
   - A. ophthalmologist
   - B. optometrist
   - C. optician
   - D. otolaryngologist

3. Myopia is a/an
   - A. infection.
   - B. refractive disorder.
   - C. foreign body.
   - D. inflammation.

4. When you irrigate a patient's eye, the patient should
   - A. lie flat on his or her back.
   - B. sit and look straight at you.
   - C. turn the head away from the eye being irrigated.
   - D. turn the head in the direction of the eye being irrigated.

5. Ear medication must be administered at
   - A. room temperature.
   - B. 35°F.
   - C. 40°F.
   - D. 45°F.

6. A child with otitis media often
   - A. smiles and laughs.
   - B. falls asleep easily.
   - C. pulls at the ear.
   - D. keeps the head totally straight.

Chapter Review Questions (continued)

7. The sense of smell is located in the
   A. vestibular zone.
   B. respiratory zone.
   C. nasopharyngeal zone.
   D. olfactory zone.

8. Which of the following is a function of the sinuses?
   A. sinusitis
   B. phonation
   C. balance
   D. filtration

9. Which of the following is a function of the Eustachian tube?
   A. phonation
   B. filtration
   C. balance
   D. sinusitis

10. A tonsillectomy is usually recommended if a patient has more than how many sore throats in a year?
    A. four
    B. one
    C. two
    D. three

True/False

T F 1. The mucous membrane covering the eyeball and lining the eyelid is conjunctivitis.

T F 2. The iris is responsible for regulating the amount of light that enters the eye.

T F 3. The superior rectus muscle moves the eye to look down.

T F 4. The ophthalmoscope is used to examine the ear.

T F 5. A tonometer is used to test the pressure within the eye.

Short Answer

1. What does the top number or first number recorded on a Snellen measurement indicate?

2. What does the second or bottom number on a Snellen measurement indicate?

3. Which medications cause the pupils to constrict?

4. What is the purpose of simple audiometry testing?

5. Name the three zones of the interior of the nose.

Research

1. Is there a low-cost clinic for patients in your community who need hearing aids?

2. Optometrists' services offered in "superstores" such as Walmart are gaining in popularity. What are some of the pros and cons of these practices?

Externship Application Experience

The medical assistant has prepared to irrigate the eyes of a 5-year-old patient who has sand in her eyes from playing in a sandbox. The MA has explained the procedure to the patient and her mother. When the MA begins the procedure, the patient begins screaming and squirming. What should the medical assistant do?

Resource Guide

American Academy of Ophthalmology
655 Beach Street
San Francisco, CA 94109-7424
(415) 561-8500
http://www.aao.org

American Optometric Association
243 Lindbergh Boulevard
St. Louis, MO 63141
(314) 991-4100
http://www.aoanet.org

American Diabetes Association
1701 N. Beauregard Street
Alexandria, VA 22311
(703) 549-1500
1-800-342-2383
http://www.diabetes.org

Juvenile Diabetes Foundation International
432 Park Avenue South
New York, NY 10016
(212) 889-7575
http://www.jdfcare.com

National Diabetes Information Clearinghouse
National Institute of Diabetes and Digestive and Kidney Diseases
1 Information Way
Bethesda, MD 20892-3560
(301) 654-3327
http://www.niddk.nih.gov

Resource Guide (continued)

National Eye Institute
2020 Vision Place
Bethesda, MD 20892-3655
(301) 496-5248
http://www.nei.nih.gov

Prevent Blindness America
500 East Remington Road
Schaumburg, IL 60173
1-800-331-2020
(847) 843-2020
http://www.preventblindness.org

MedMedia
www.prenhall.com/frazier

More on this chapter, including interactive resources, can be found on the Student CD-ROM accompanying this textbook and on the Companion Website at www.prenhall.com/frazier.

CHAPTER 20

Immunology and Allergies

Case Study

Eric is assisting an AIDS patient who has come in for an assessment of a rash on his left and right flanks that wraps around to his back. The rash itself is not itchy, but the area is very painful and nothing seems to be helping. After Eric checks in the patient, he will assist the doctor in performing a prick skin test on another patient to determine if she can have a new puppy for her eighth birthday. The child's mother is concerned because she has other allergies, and she wants to make certain they won't bring a puppy home only to have to return it a few days later.

Objectives

After completing this chapter, you should be able to:

- Spell and define the medical terminology in this chapter.
- Define the medical assistant's role in the immunology office.
- Discuss the anatomy and physiology of the immune system.
- List and describe immunodeficiency diseases.
- List and describe common autoimmune disorders.
- Explain hypersensitivity and allergic reactions.

MedMedia
www.prenhall.com/frazier

Additional interactive resources and activities for this chapter can be found on the Companion Website. For audio glossary, legal and ethical scenarios, job scenarios, quizzes, and games related to the content of this chapter, please access the accompanying CD-ROM in this book.

 **Assets Available:**

Audio Glossary
Legal and Ethical Scenario: *Immunology and Allergies*
On the Job Scenario: *Immunology and Allergies*
A & P Quiz: The Immune System
Multiple Choice Quiz
Games: Crossword, Strikeout and Spelling Bee

⊕ MEDICAL ASSISTING COMPETENCIES

CAAHEP ENTRY-LEVEL COMPETENCIES FOR CMA	ABHES ENTRY-LEVEL COMPETENCIES FOR RMA
■ Identify and respond to issues of confidentiality. ■ Perform within legal and ethical boundaries. ■ Demonstrate knowledge of federal and state health-care legislation and regulations. ■ Perform hand washing. ■ Dispose of biohazardous materials. ■ Practice Standard Precautions. ■ Perform immunology testing. ■ Obtain vital signs. ■ Obtain and record patient history. ■ Prepare and maintain examination and treatment areas. ■ Apply pharmacology principles to prepare and administer oral and parenteral medications. ■ Maintain medication and immunization records. ■ Instruct individuals according to their needs. ■ Provide instruction for health maintenance and disease prevention. ■ Identify community resources.	■ Project a positive attitude. ■ Maintain confidentiality at all times. ■ Be a "team player." ■ Be cognizant of ethical boundaries. ■ Exhibit initiative. ■ Adapt to change. ■ Evidence a responsible attitude. ■ Be courteous and diplomatic. ■ Conduct work within scope of education, training, and ability. ■ Be impartial and show empathy when dealing with patients. ■ Adapt what is said to the recipient's level of comprehension. ■ Serve as a liaison between the physician and others. ■ Interview effectively. ■ Use appropriate terminology. ■ Recognize and respond to verbal and nonverbal communication. ■ Adaptation to individualized needs. ■ Apply principles of aseptic techniques and infection control. ■ Take vital signs. ■ Recognize emergencies. ■ Prepare and maintain examination and treatment areas. ■ Collect and process specimens. ■ Prepare and administer oral and parenteral medications as directed by the physician. ■ Maintain medication and immunization records.

Introduction

An immunologist is a physician who specializes in the immune system and its functions. An allergist is a physician who specializes in diagnosing and treating allergies. Immunology and allergy are often combined within one practice, where allergy testing, allergy desensitization, and laboratory testing are performed.

 ## The Medical Assistant's Role in Immunology and Allergy

As an MA in an immunology and allergy medical office, you will:

■ Obtain the patient's medical history.
■ Take vital signs.
■ Instruct the patient about removing clothing, provide a gown and drape, and help the patient, if necessary.

Medical Terminology

allergen—substance that is not necessarily harmful, such as dust or eggs, but that produces a hypersensitive reaction in some individuals

ankylosis—condition of joint immobility

antibody—substance produced by the body in response to a specific antigen

antigen—foreign substance that stimulates the production of antibodies against it when it is introduced into the body

antipyretic—fever reducing

autoimmunity—body's negative reaction to its own cells

carditis—inflammation of the heart

dysfunction—abnormal or impaired function

dysphagia—difficulty swallowing

dysphasia—difficulty speaking

ecchymosis—bruise; area of bleeding under the skin

electromyography—procedure in which a needle is inserted into muscle tissue to record electrical activity

hematopoietic—pertaining to normal blood cell development in the bone marrow

hemolytic—pertaining to the breakdown of RBCs

immunodeficiency—inability of the immune system to function normally to protect the body from infection

interphalangeal—between the joints of the fingers or toes

intrinsic factor—substance secreted by the gastric mucosa that is necessary for the absorption of vitamin B_{12} and the development of RBCs

megakaryocytes—large bone marrow cells that play an important role in the production of platelets in the bone marrow

neuritis—inflammation of a nerve or nerves

petechiae—small hemorrhages under the skin

reactive—able to respond to a stimulus

subcutaneous—under the epidermal and dermal layers of the skin

Abbreviations

AIDS—acquired immunodeficiency syndrome
CSF—cerebral spinal fluid
EMG—electromyography

LE—lupus erythematosus
N & V—nausea and vomiting
RA—rheumatoid arthritis

SCID—severe combined immuno-deficiency disease

- Assist the immunologist or allergist, as necessary, with the examination and procedures.
- Watch for signs of allergic reaction when allergy desensitization injections are given.
- Instruct the patient about medication orders, written pre- or postprocedure instructions, and any other written instructions.
- Stress the importance of keeping follow-up appointments.

The Anatomy and Physiology of the Immune System

The immune system provides physical and chemical barriers to bacterial and viral infection and foreign bodies. Barriers include intact skin, secretions, the mucous membranes of organs, the actions of coughing and sneezing, and the acidity of body fluids such as urine and gastric juices.

Allergens are substances that are capable of producing a hypersensitive allergic reaction but may not be harmful to the organism. **Antigens** are foreign substances, usually proteins, that can evoke an allergic response. When an antigen enters the body, the immune system reacts to deactivate, neutralize, or kill it.

There are four components to the body's immune response.

- The *cell-mediated response* is responsible for the production of T-cell lymphocytes. It is part of the response to some infections, malignancies, and delayed hypersensitivity reactions. It is also responsible for tissue transplant rejection.
- The *humoral immune response* is responsible for the production of B-cell lymphocytes with antigen exposure and the resulting **antibody** development. This process renders the patient immune or hypersensitive to the specific antigen.
- Body tissues respond to injury with inflammation, also known as a *nonspecific immune response*. The inflammatory response involves chemical, vascular, and leukocyte activities. Signs of inflammation include redness, swelling, pain, and warmth.
- The *specific immune response* activates when the inflammatory response is not adequate to manage the infectious or inflammatory process. This response is controlled by the T and B cells of the cell-mediated and humoral immunity processes, respectively.

The lymphatic vessel system filters infectious microorganisms from the lymph system and uses substances within the plasma portion of the blood to activate the inflammatory response. When blood, tissue, or organs are transplanted, a transfusion reaction or tissue rejection may result in response to the presence of foreign, or non-self, cells, tissue, or fluid. Suppression of the inflammatory response to prevent tissue rejection is accomplished with medication for the remainder of the recipient's life. Blood transfusion reactions are temporary, are often prevented by administering medications during the procedure, or are treated at the onset of symptoms.

The immune system (Figure 20-1 ◆) is made up of:

- A primary set of organs, the thymus gland and bone marrow, that are responsible for the development of lymphocytes.
- A secondary set of organs—the lymph glands and vessels, tonsils, liver, and spleen—that filter substances and stimulate the production of lymphocytes.
- **reactive** leukocytes.

There are five kinds of leukocytes.

- Polymorphonuclear leukocytes (PMNs), also known as polys or neutrophils, react to infection threatening the health of body cells and protect cells from damage.
- Monocytes, which mature into macrophages, are the first line of defense in phagocytosis, a process in which specific cells ingest foreign agents and substances. Other phagocytes include Kupffer's cells of the liver and lymph node reticular cells (Figure 20-2 ◆).
- Eosinophils are attracted to cells and parasites coated with C3B substance, such as helminths. The eosinophils then secrete chemicals to erode the walls of the invading organism.
- Basophils are important in hypersensitivity reactions in the allergic response.
- Lymphocytes (B cells and T cells) are responsible for the antigen–antibody response and sensitization, or memory, of cells to previous antigen exposure.

All lymphocytes form in the bone marrow. B lymphocytes (also called B cells) mature in the bone marrow, whereas T lymphocytes (T cells) migrate and mature in the thymus gland. Macrophages absorb the foreign substance or infection after T cells and B cells destroy it. This process is called cell-mediated immunity when only T cells are involved, and humoral or antibody-mediated immunity when T and B cells are involved.

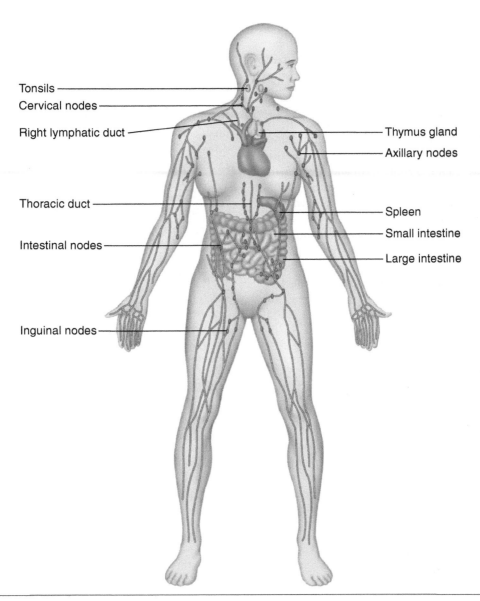

Tonsils
Cervical nodes
Right lymphatic duct
Thymus gland
Axillary nodes
Thoracic duct
Spleen
Small intestine
Intestinal nodes
Large intestine
Inguinal nodes

Figure 20-1 ◆ The lymphatic system

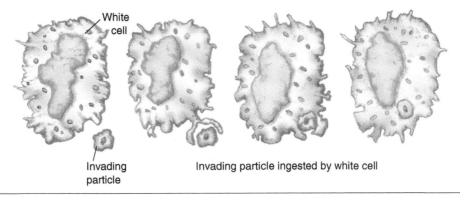

White cell

Invading particle

Invading particle ingested by white cell

Figure 20-2 ◆ Phagocytosis

Immunity is the ability to resist a particular disease or condition. *Natural immunity* is inherited. *Acquired immunity* results from being exposed to the disease or being immunized. Natural immunity and immunity acquired by exposure stimulate the development of antibodies to create active immunity.

Active immunity is long-term and often lifelong. For example, a patient who has had chickenpox is immune for life and will never need a chickenpox vaccination. Immunizations (administered vaccines) also lead to active immunity. *Passive immunity*, on the other hand, is short-term and involves the administration of already formed antibodies. Further vaccination is required to acquire immunity. For example, newborns, because of the placental transfer of the mother's antibodies, have passive immunity to some diseases for a short time after birth. Breast-fed babies keep this immunity even longer because of the transfer of antibodies in breast milk. However, the child requires vaccinations when the antibody protection wears off. (∞ See Chapter 27 for more information on childhood immunizations.)

Diseases and Disorders of the Immune System

Diseases and disorders of the immune system fall into three general categories: immunodeficiency diseases, autoimmune disorders, and hypersensitivity and allergy reactions. Immunodeficiency diseases occur when the immune system is unable to fight the disease and protect the body. In autoimmune conditions, the body fails to recognize its own cells as self and develops self-antigens, which leads to the destruction of the perceived foreign cells. Hypersensitivity and allergy reactions result from the entry of a foreign body or substance into the system with resulting inflammation and organ **dysfunction.**

Immunodeficiency Diseases

Immunodeficiency diseases result when the immune system is unable or becomes unable to fight and protect the body from disease (Table 20-1). Some immunodeficiency diseases are caused by hereditary, or genetic, patterns. More commonly, however, the immune system is weakened by chemotherapy or radiation, immunosuppressive drugs for organ/tissue transplants, or disease. Treatments such as chemotherapy, radiation, or immunosuppressive drugs decrease the ability of white blood cells to fight infection or foreign substances. The patient may suffer severe or recurrent opportunistic infections, and it is often these complications that prove life-threatening or fatal (Table 20-2).

?—Critical Thinking Question 20-1

What precautions should Eric take when setting up the patient with AIDS for examination by the physician?

HIV/AIDS Transmission Prevention Strategies

HIV/AIDS is transmitted by person-to-person contact. The following are suggestions for avoiding direct contact with the transmission source while still living as normal a life as possible.

- Avoid sex with multiple partners. Maintain a monogamous relationship.
- Use condoms and spermicides to prevent the transmission of body fluids during sex.

TABLE 20-1 IMMUNODEFICIENCY DISEASES

Disease	Symptoms	Diagnosis	Treatment
Acquired Immunodeficiency Syndrome (AIDS) ■ Caused by human **immunodeficiency** virus (HIV) ■ Virus is easily killed outside body with diluted bleach or other solutions ■ Virus destroys lymphocytes, particularly T cells and macrophages, leaving immune system defenseless against all infections ■ Inability to fight infections, even with antibiotic treatment, results in death	■ Influenza ■ Kaposi's sarcoma ■ Pneumocystis carinii pneumonia (PCP) ■ Candida albicans ■ Tuberculosis ■ Herpes zoster (shingles)	■ Patient presenting symptoms ■ Serologic studies ■ ELISA test detects HIV antibodies ■ Western blot test confirms AIDS diagnosis ■ T cell count, in addition to clinical symptoms, defines early, late, or advanced stages of HIV infection	■ Antibiotics for infections ■ Antiviral medications for viruses ■ AIDS drugs—various drugs in most effective combination for patient ■ Rebuilding lymphocytes to increase patient's immunity; T cells especially important ■ Support and counsel
Severe Combined Immunodeficiency Disease (SCID) ■ Inherited condition that puts infant in danger of severe infection ■ No T cell mediated or B cell antibody-mediated immunity ■ Most infants die within the first year	■ Failure to thrive (grow and gain weight) ■ Various infections such as pulmonary, ear, and systemic infections	■ Difficult to diagnose before six months to one year of age ■ Serologic tests	■ Bone marrow transplant to increase healthy T and B cells ■ Sterile environment to prevent exposure to any infection

TABLE 20-2 OPPORTUNISTIC CONDITIONS COMMON TO AIDS

Malignancies	Gastrointestinal Symptoms
■ Kaposi's sarcoma ■ Lymphomas	■ Nausea and vomiting (**N & V**) ■ Diarrhea ■ Lack of appetite
Infections	**Neurological Symptoms**
■ Pneumocystis carinii pneumonia ■ Candida albicans ■ Herpes zoster (shingles) ■ Tuberculosis ■ Toxoplasmosis ■ Herpes simplex	■ Confusion and memory loss ■ Headache and visual changes

- Do not use intravenous (IV) drugs or share used needles of any kind with another person.
- Make sure that people providing tattoo and body piercing services use new needles.
- Control your behavior. Avoid using drugs or overindulging in alcohol, both of which lower your guard in social situations and place you at risk for unprotected sex.

Autoimmune Diseases

Autoimmune diseases result from antigens that develop from aggressive activity by the body's immune system against itself (Figures 20-3 ◆ and 20-4 ◆). This type of disorder can affect any body area, including collagen (protein found in connective joints), **hematopoietic** tissue, cardiovascular system tissue, and nervous system tissue (Table 20-3). For example, in hemolytic anemia, the body fails to recognize its own blood cells and destroys RBCs and lymphocytes that have been produced in its own hematopoietic system. Autoimmune disorders may result from unknown causes, but may also be awakened by genetic weaknesses or in combination with other disease complications.

Autoimmune disorders may also affect other systems of the body:

- Gastrointestinal system: ulcerative colitis (a colon disease), atrophic gastritis (a stomach disease)

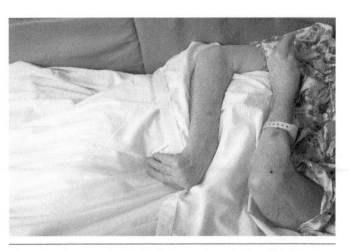

Figure 20-3 ◆ A patient with rheumatoid arthritis in the hands

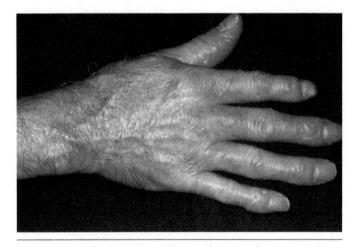

Figure 20-4 ◆ Systemic scleroderma of the hand
Source: Dr. P. Marazzi/Photo Researchers, Inc.

TABLE 20-3 AUTOIMMUNE DISEASES

Disease	Symptoms	Diagnosis	Treatment
Autoimmune hemolytic anemia ■ RBCs are not recognized and are destroyed by B cells ■ Decreased numbers of RBCs, platelets, hemoglobin, and hematocrit ■ Destroys lymphocytes, particularly T cells and macrophages, leaving immune system defenseless against all infections	■ Weakness ■ Fever ■ Chills ■ Dyspnea ■ Bruising ■ Skin color pale and jaundiced	■ Patient presenting symptoms ■ Serologic studies ■ Coombs' test for presence of antibodies	■ Immunosuppressive drugs to suppress antigen–antibody response ■ Antiviral medications for viruses ■ Transfusions of washed RBCs, platelets, and plasma in some cases ■ Splenectomy to halve RBC destruction; can increase patient's immunity; T cells especially important

(continued)

TABLE 20-3 AUTOIMMUNE DISEASES *(Continued)*

Disease	Symptoms	Diagnosis	Treatment
Idiopathic thrombocytopenic purpura ■ Bleeding into skin and other organs ■ Results when platelets are destroyed by body's own immune response ■ Hematopoietic conditions may result after some viral infections ■ Decreased platelet count and longer bleeding time ■ **Megakaryocytes** in bone marrow	■ **Petechiae** ■ **Ecchymosis** ■ Epistaxis ■ Hematuria ■ Gastrointestinal bleeding	■ Serologic tests	■ Blood transfusions to increase platelet count ■ Vitamin K to stop prolonged bleeding ■ Steroids to stop capillary bleeding ■ Plasma exchange and splenectomy to increase circulating platelets
Multiple sclerosis (MS) ■ Chronic and progressive neurological disorder affecting myelin sheath (covering that insulates and protects some nervous system cells) ■ May be autoimmune disorder but may also result from genetic tendency or viral infections	■ Double vision ■ Muscle weakness ■ Lack of coordination, progressing to paralysis ■ Numbness ■ Prickling ■ Tingling ■ **Dysphasia** ■ Incontinence ■ Mood swings from depression to euphoria	■ Patient presenting symptoms ■ Medical history ■ MRI ■ Cerebrospinal fluid (**CSF**) analysis	■ Physical therapy to increase muscle strength ■ Muscle relaxants for muscle spasms ■ Antidepressants for depression ■ Steroids to suppress autoimmune process ■ Psychological support for patient and significant others
Myasthenia gravis ■ Neuromuscular disease that results in chronically sporadic and progressive periods of weakened muscles ■ Muscle weakness usually occurs after strenuous activity or during afternoon/ evening ■ Progresses to complete muscular and respiratory paralysis	■ Fatigue ■ Muscle weakness ■ Double vision ■ Ptosis (drooping eyelids) ■ Difficulty swallowing ■ Backward flow of fluids through nose ■ Other symptoms of cranial nerve dysfunction (∞ see Chapter 28)	■ Patient presenting symptoms ■ **Electromyography (EMG)** ■ Neostigmine injection	■ Anticholinesterase drugs to reduce muscle weakness ■ Corticosteroid and immunosuppressive drugs to suppress autoimmune process ■ Thymectomy for a select number of patients ■ Psychological support for patient and significant others
Pernicious anemia ■ May be inherited or autoimmune blood cell production disorder ■ Results from deficiency of **intrinsic factor** ■ Macrocytic (abnormally large) RBCs develop when B_{12} is deficient ■ Patient's life will be normal	■ Weakness ■ Fatigue ■ Pallor ■ Light-headedness ■ Tachycardia and/or palpitations ■ Nausea and/or vomiting ■ **Neuritis** ■ Numbing and tingling of extremities	■ Patient presenting symptoms ■ Medical history ■ Laboratory studies ■ CBC ■ B_{12} serum levels ■ Schilling test to assess gastrointestinal absorption of B_{12} ■ Gastric analysis ■ Bone marrow test	■ **Subcutaneous** injections of cyanacobalamin on a weekly, biweekly, or monthly basis
Rheumatoid arthritis (RA) and juvenile rheumatoid arthritis ■ Chronic disease causing inflammation and destruction of synovial membranes of multiple joints; cartilage and bone erode and joints become deformed ■ May be hereditary; generally thought to be autoimmune disorder ■ **Ankylosis** can cause joint immobility ■ Edema may be present in **interphalangeal** joint areas in severely affected patients	In adults: ■ Joint pain ■ Mild or low-grade fever ■ Fatigue ■ Malaise ■ Weight loss In children: ■ Joint pain ■ Weight loss ■ High fever in the evening ■ Red rash over trunk and limbs	■ Patient presenting symptoms ■ Serologic test	■ Balanced activity and rest to control pain and inflammation ■ Salicylates (e.g., aspirin) to control pain and inflammation ■ Ibuprofen or other enteric coated anti-inflammatory drugs for patients with gastric irritation or gastric ulcers to reduce pain and inflammation (medication dosages for children based on weight)

TABLE 20-3 AUTOIMMUNE DISEASES *(Continued)*

Disease	Symptoms	Diagnosis	Treatment
Rheumatoid arthritis (RA) and juvenile rheumatoid arthritis (*cont.*) ▪ Rheumatoid arthritis in children is also called Still's disease	▪ Swollen neck and axillary area lymph glands ▪ Acute pericarditis ▪ Growth may be affected		▪ Physical therapy, paraffin wax therapy, and braces to improve mobility ▪ Surgery—complete joint replacement for severe cases
Rheumatic fever and rheumatic heart disease ▪ Rheumatic fever is caused by development of hypersensitive antibodies to group A hemolytic streptococci; reaction causes lesions to grow at cardiac tissue (myocarditis) and joints (arthritis) ▪ Characterized by elevated WBCs, cardiac enzymes, ESR	▪ Strep throat (about 4 weeks before fever) ▪ Malaise ▪ Fever ▪ Joint pain	▪ Patient presenting symptoms ▪ Medical history ▪ Laboratory tests such as ESR	▪ Antibiotics for strep throat to prevent it from progressing to rheumatic heart disease ▪ Analgesics, cardiac medications, and rest to prevent heart damage ▪ Surgery to replace damaged heart valves
Scleroderma (systemic sclerosis) ▪ Chronic disorder involving skin and connective tissue ▪ Ranges in severity from mild (only skin or part of skin involved) to severe (skin and internal organs involved) ▪ Collagen production leads to hardening and thickening of tissue, with decrease in function ▪ Usually slowly progressive disease, but sometimes can progress rapidly toward death	▪ Pain ▪ Stiffness ▪ Joint swelling ▪ Leathery, shiny, tightly stretched skin ▪ Raynaud's phenomenon (small artery and arteriole disease) ▪ Difficulty eating ▪ Gastric symptoms: efflux heartburn, **dysphagia**, diarrhea, constipation	▪ Patient presenting symptoms ▪ Skin biopsy ▪ Urinalysis	▪ Analgesics for pain ▪ Anti-inflammatories for inflammation ▪ Immunosuppressive drugs to control or slow autoimmune process ▪ Vasodilator and/or antihypertensive drugs to treat Raynaud's phenomenon
Systemic lupus erythematosus (SLE) ▪ Chronic systemic disorder affecting any part of connective tissue throughout the body ▪ Prognosis is grave; high mortality rate within 5 years of onset	▪ Butterfly rash on face ▪ Fever ▪ Malaise ▪ Weakness ▪ Weight loss ▪ Photosensitivity ▪ Joint symptoms ▪ Raynaud's phenomenon ▪ Pleuritis (inflammation of pleural membranes) ▪ **Carditis** ▪ Spotty alopecia (hair loss) ▪ Ulcerations in nose, pharynx, oral cavity	▪ Patient presenting symptoms ▪ Patient history ▪ Serologic tests, including CBC, ESR, anti-DNA, LE, and bone marrow	▪ Aspirin to relieve inflammation ▪ Corticosteroids to relieve inflammation ▪ Clothing protection (hats, long sleeves, and long pants) for patients with photosensitivity

▪ Endocrine system: Hashimoto's thyroiditis (a thyroid gland disease), thyrotoxicosis (a thyroid gland disease)
▪ Renal system: Goodpasture's syndrome (a kidney disease)
▪ Circulatory system: vasculitis (a blood vessel disease)

A Coombs' test assesses the development of antibodies to **hemolytic** diseases. Antinuclear antibody testing can be performed to assist in the diagnosis of LE or RA. Treatment focuses on steroids and immunosuppressive drugs to reduce the self-antigen/antibody response. Support treatment prevents possible further harm to the organ system(s) affected. Analgesics are prescribed for pain as necessary. Psychological support and therapy may be needed for these progressive and physically debilitating diseases.

Keys to Success
ACETAMINOPHEN VS. ASPIRIN

Aspirin has **antipyretic,** analgesic, and anti-inflammatory properties. Acetaminophen has only antipyretic and analgesic properties. It is not used to treat inflammatory disease conditions except to enhance the pain-relieving properties of another medication.

Hypersensitivity and Allergic Reactions

An allergy is an immune system response to a foreign body that results in inflammation and organ dysfunction. Hypersensitivity,

Keys to Success
AGING AND IMMUNITY

The thymus gland, which aids in the maturing of T cells during childhood, gradually decreases in size and function from puberty on. T cells in the shrinking thymus gland also decrease the immune system's fighting ability. B cell antibody function decreases as the body ages, too. It is thought that the decline in function of the immune system leads to a higher risk of disease development in the elderly. But there are other factors, such as general health, medications, nutrition, psychological stresses, and lack of social activity, that may raise their vulnerability to disease.

an abnormal condition, is an exaggerated response of the immune system. Allergies develop after repeated exposure to an antigen (Table 20-4). Allergic reactions include the following.

- Hay fever is a respiratory reaction to allergens such as pollen. It is usually seasonal.
- Asthma is a more serious respiratory reaction. It can be life-threatening if the person experiences status asthmaticus (severe and prolonged asthma attack).
- Urticaria, also known as hives, is characterized by a spreading area of reddened and elevated lesions (Figure 20-5 ◆). Causes include insect bites, stress, drugs, and food.
- Food allergies can be severe and life-threatening. For example, people who are allergic to peanuts cannot eat them or touch anything that has been touched by peanuts.
- Anaphylactic reactions are increasingly severe antigen–antibody reactions to repeated exposure to an allergen. They can be mild or life threatening. If symptoms progress toward swelling of airway passages and increasingly severe shortness of breath, emergency treatment is necessary. Anaphylactic reactions can occur after unexpected exposure to allergens or planned exposure to weakened allergens used in allergy desensitization injections (explained later in the chapter).

Diagnostic Procedures and Treatments

There are four methods of diagnostic allergy testing:

- Intradermal: injecting a small amount of potential antigen under the skin (Figure 20-6 ◆).
- Skin patch: putting a patch soaked with potential antigen on the skin.

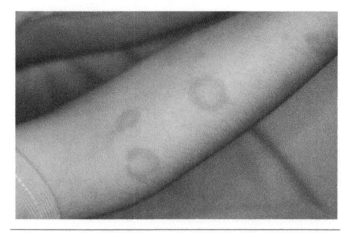

Figure 20-5 ◆ Urticaria is characterized by a spreading area of reddened and elevated lesions

Caduceus Chronicle
A BRIEF HISTORY OF IMMUNOLOGY

1798—Edward Jenner (1749–1823) discovered, through observation and experiments, that milkmaids exposed to cowpox were immune to smallpox. Based on this discovery, he developed the smallpox vaccination. The medical community was initially suspicious of the new theory of vaccination, but by 1840 smallpox vaccination was offered free of charge to all infants in Britain and became mandatory in 1853.

1862—Louis Pasteur developed the pasteurization process for killing bacteria and molds in milk.

1879—Louis Pasteur developed an attenuated chicken cholera vaccine. An attenuated vaccine uses live, but weakened bacteria. The attenuated vaccine causes mild symptoms of the disease, as the body develops antibodies to fight the actual disease if encountered at a later time.

1884—Ilya Metchnikoff (1845–1916), a zoologist studying single-cell organisms, proposed that certain cells defend the body against microorganisms through phagocytosis (cellular immunity theory).

1891—Robert Koch (1843–1910) discovered that necrotic tissue developed around tuberculosis bacteria in the lungs. When the bacteria was transferred to another animal, it caused the same reaction. Originally called the Koch phenomenon, that reaction is now known as "delayed type hypersensitivity."

1900—Humoral immunity was accepted by the medical community as the explanation for the body's immune system.

Early 20th century—Physicians noticed certain skin reactions—itching, rash, and other skin lesions—in response to contact with substances or compounds such as cosmetics and poison ivy. It was also noted that further contact with the same substances caused faster and stronger reactions.

1906—The word *allergy* was coined by Clemens Peter Pirquet (1874–1929). He was also known for the Pirquet test for TB.

1943—Sir Peter Brian Medawar (1915–1987) and Thomas Gibson performed research on graft rejection that contributed to the treatment of burned and wounded soldiers.

1950s—The cellular immunity theory was revived with the study of **autoimmunity** and immunodeficiency.

TABLE 20-4 COMMON ALLERGENS

Environment:

dust	animal dander
plant pollen	insect stings
mold	medications
latex	chemicals
cockroaches	strong aerosol odors
hair	cigarette smoke

Food:

peanuts and peanut products	nuts
shellfish	eggs
fish	milk

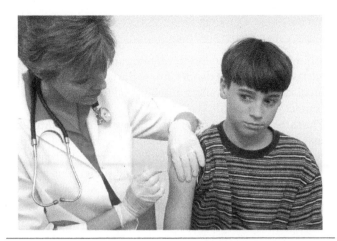

Figure 20-6 ◆ Diagnostic allergy testing: intradermal injection

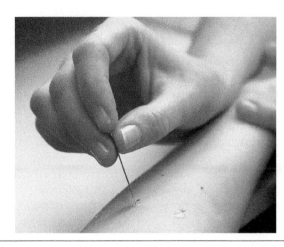

Figure 20-7 ◆ Diagnostic allergy testing: performing a scratch test on a patient

- Scratch testing: putting the potential antigen into a scratch made on the skin (Figure 20-7 ◆).
- CBC for RBCs, platelets, and WBCs, including B and T lymphocytes.

? **— Critical Thinking Question 20-2—**
Before Eric assists the doctor in performing a prick skin test, he must explain the four methods of diagnostic allergy testing. Because the child being tested is a minor, what else does Eric need to do?

Treatment of allergic reactions involves first trying to identify the cause. If possible, the allergen is removed from the patient's environment. Antihistamines are prescribed to treat symptoms and halt their progression. Allergy injections may be recommended to desensitize the patient to certain allergens. If the patient cannot be removed from environmental exposure to the allergen, a special serum may be prescribed. Each prescription is specially formulated to introduce very weak concentrations of the allergen and stimulate the patient's body to produce immunity to the allergen.

REVIEW

Chapter Summary

- Obtaining the medical history and routine vital signs and assisting patients and the physician are key functions of the MA in an immunology and allergy practice.
- Procedures performed in an immunology and allergy office are allergy testing, allergy desensitization, electromyography, and laboratory testing.
- The immune system provides a physical and chemical barrier to bacterial and viral infection and foreign bodies. It has a primary set of organs, a secondary set of organs, and reactive leukocytes.

- All lymphocytes form in the bone marrow, but B cells mature in the bone marrow and T cells migrate and mature in the thymus gland. T cells defend the body with a cell-mediated response. B cells defend the body with an antibody-mediated response.
- When the immune system malfunctions, a patient can become immunodeficient, autoimmune, and/or hypersensitive to allergens. A patient who receives a transplant may experience a transfusion reaction or tissue rejection.
- Immunodeficiency diseases result when the immune system no longer functions to protect the body against disease.

(continued)

Chapter Summary (continued)

Some immunodeficiency diseases are caused by hereditary, or genetic, patterns, but generally the immune system is weakened by chemotherapy or radiation, immunosuppressive drugs for organ/tissue transplants, or disease. Examples of immunodeficiency diseases are AIDS and SCID.

■ Autoimmune diseases result from developed self-antigens that stimulate aggressive activity by the immune system against itself. This disorder can affect any body area. Examples of autoimmune diseases are RA and MS.

■ Allergy responses are hypersensitive reactions of the immune system to allergen and antigens. Reactions include hay fever, asthma, urticaria, and life-threatening anaphylaxis. Common allergens include pet dander, house dust, mold, plant pollen, medications, foods, and household solutions that come in contact with the skin.

■ The three methods of diagnostic allergy testing are intradermal, skin patch, and scratch testing. Treatment of allergic reactions involves identifying the cause, removing the patient from the environment, if possible, and prescribing antihistamines. Allergy injections may be recommended to desensitize the patient to certain allergens.

Chapter Review Questions

Multiple Choice

1. Which of the following organs is responsible for producing lymphocytes?
   A. spleen
   B. liver
   C. thymus gland
   D. heart

2. Which of the following organs filters and removes foreign substances?
   A. spleen
   B. thymus gland
   C. bone marrow
   D. heart

3. Active immunity is
   A. an outcome of breastfeeding a child longer than is recommended.
   B. short-term, with the need for further vaccination.
   C. long-term and results from being exposed to and having the disease.
   D. an outcome of placental transfer of the mother's antibodies to the child.

4. AIDS can be transmitted by
   A. kissing.
   B. shared needles.
   C. hand contact.
   D. drinking alcohol.

5. SCID is a disease that affects
   A. elderly.
   B. teens.
   C. adults.
   D. children.

6. Autoimmune hemolytic anemia is treated by
   A. hysterectomy.
   B. appendectomy.
   C. splenectomy.
   D. lumpectomy.

7. Vitamin K is prescribed for idiopathic thrombocytopenic purpura to
   A. stop prolonged bleeding.
   B. increase platelet count.
   C. increase megakaryocytes.
   D. stop viruses.

8. Which of the following is a symptom of juvenile RA?
   A. vomiting
   B. strep throat
   C. pallor
   D. acute pericarditis

9. A serious anaphylactic reaction requires
   A. an MRI.
   B. a blood test.
   C. emergency care.
   D. a skin biopsy.

10. Which of the following is used to test for allergies?
    A. Schilling test
    B. intradermal test
    C. Coombs' test
    D. ESR

True/False

T F 1. Immunology and allergy treatment are combined into one practice.

T F 2. Coughing, sneezing, and the acidity of body fluids such as urine and gastric juices are all types of barriers to bacterial and viral infection and foreign bodies.

Chapter Review Questions (continued)

T F 3. Allergens are foreign substances, usually proteins.

T F 4. Antigens are substances capable of producing a hypersensitive allergic reaction.

T F 5. All lymphocytes are initially formed in the bone marrow.

Short Answer

1. What is another term for *inflammation?*

2. List the organs that make up the immune system.

3. What are the five kinds of leukocytes?

4. What is the difference between active and passive immunity?

5. Name the four methods of diagnostic allergy testing.

Research

1. How many AIDS cases were reported in your state last year?

2. Are there any AIDS/HIV support groups or activity centers in your community?

Externship Application Experience

An adult patient presents with redness, swelling, fluid-filled vesicles, and itching on the hands and lower arms. The patient states he has no history of allergies. What questions should you ask this patient?

Resource Guide

American Lupus Society
260 Maple Court, Suite 123
Ventura, CA 93003
1-800-331-1802

Arthritis Foundation
3400 Peachtree Rd. NE
P.O. Box 7669
Atlanta, GA 30357-0669
1-800-283-7800
www.arthritis.org

Lupus Foundation of America
2000 L Street NW, Suite 710
Washington, DC 20063
800-558-0121
www.lupus.org

National AIDS Hotline
P.O. Box 13827
RTP, NC 27709
1-800-342-AIDS, 24 hours a day
www.ashastd.org/nah
www.hivmail@cdc.gov

National Multiple Sclerosis Society
733 Third Ave.
New York, NY 10077
1-800-344-4867 (FIGHT-MS)
www.nmss.org

**Primary Immunodeficiency Association,
United Kingdom**
+44(0)20-7976-7640
www.pia.org.uk

MedMedia
www.prenhall.com/frazier

More on this chapter, including interactive resources, can be found on the Student CD-ROM accompanying this textbook and on the Companion Website at www.prenhall.com/frazier.

CHAPTER 21

Dermatology

Case Study

Manny is busy rooming patients at the dermatology office where he works and notices that he has two walk-in patients today. The first is a teenage girl who has come with her mother to check on what she describes as a "suspicious mole" she found while sunbathing. In the next room, a mother has brought in her four children after being notified of a lice outbreak at school.

Objectives

After completing this chapter, you should be able to:

- Spell and define medical terminology in this chapter.
- Define the medical assistant's role in the dermatology office.
- List and describe common types of dermatitis.
- List and describe common types of congenital skin disorders.
- List and describe common types of infectious skin disorders.
- List and describe common types of fungal skin diseases.
- List and describe common types of parasitic skin diseases.
- List and describe common types of pigmentation disorders.
- List and describe common types of benign skin disorders.
- List and describe the three types of skin cancer.

MedMedia
www.prenhall.com/frazier

Additional interactive resources and activities for this chapter can be found on the Companion Website. For audio glossary, legal and ethical scenarios, job scenarios, quizzes, games, and activities related to the content of this chapter, please access the accompanying CD-ROM in this book.

Assets Available:

Audio Glossary
Legal and Ethical Scenario: *Dermatology*
On the Job Scenario: *Dermatology*
A & P Quiz: The Integumentary System
Multiple Choice Quiz
Games: Crossword, Strikeout and Spelling Bee
Drag and Drop: Integumentary System: Anterior view of the Body; Integumentary System: Posterior view of the Body; Integumentary System: Hair Follicle; Integumentary System: Layers of the Skin; Integumentary System: Features of the Integumentary System

MEDICAL ASSISTING COMPETENCIES

CAAHEP ENTRY-LEVEL COMPETENCIES FOR CMA	ABHES ENTRY-LEVEL COMPETENCIES FOR RMA
▪ Identify and respond to issues of confidentiality. ▪ Perform within legal and ethical boundaries. ▪ Demonstrate knowledge of federal and state health-care legislation and regulations. ▪ Perform hand washing. ▪ Dispose of biohazardous materials. ▪ Practice Standard Precautions. ▪ Screen and follow-up test results.	▪ Project a positive attitude. ▪ Maintain confidentiality at all times. ▪ Be a "team player." ▪ Be cognizant of ethical boundaries. ▪ Exhibit initiative. ▪ Adapt to change. ▪ Evidence a responsible attitude. ▪ Be courteous and diplomatic. ▪ Conduct work within scope of education, training, and ability. ▪ Practice Standard Precautions. ▪ Use quality control. ▪ Dispose of biohazardous materials.

Introduction

A **dermatologist** is a physician who specializes in treating skin diseases and conditions. Procedures performed in the **dermatology** office include biopsies, **cryosurgery,** and the surgical removal of lesions. Suture removal and dressing application may be the responsibilities of the MA.

 ## The Medical Assistant's Role in Dermatology

As an MA in a dermatology office, you will:

▪ Obtain the patient's medical history.
▪ Take vital signs.
▪ Instruct the patient about removing clothing, provide a gown and drape, and help the patient as necessary.
▪ Assist the dermatologist, as necessary, with the examination and procedures.
▪ Instruct the patient about medication orders, written pre- or post-procedure instructions, and any other written instructions.
▪ Stress the importance of keeping follow-up appointments.

Medical Terminology

appendage—anything attached to a larger or major body part

cauterization—destruction of tissue with a caustic, electric current, hot iron, or by freezing

collagen—fibrous connective tissue

cryosurgery—freezing lesions with nitrous oxide

dermatitis—skin inflammation

dermatologist—physician who specializes in the treatment of skin diseases and conditions

dermatology—study and treatment of integumentary system diseases and conditions

dermatophytoses—superficial fungal infections of the skin and its appendages

integumentary system—the skin and its supporting structures (nails, hair, and sebaceous and sweat glands)

keratin—tough protein substance found in hair, nails, and horny tissue

lesion—tissue abnormality that may be hard or soft, small or large, flat or raised, crusted or filled with fluid or pus, and, when associated with skin, on or within the skin tissue

melanin—pigment (color) in the skin and hair

melanocytes—cells that produce melanin

neuralgia—sharp, stabbing, or burning pain that occurs along the course of a nerve

sebaceous glands—small glands in the dermis that secrete sebum, usually through ducts that empty into the hair follicles

Abbreviations

AK—actinic keratosis
BCC—basal cell carcinoma
SCC—squamous cell carcinoma
UV—ultraviolet

The Anatomy and Physiology of the Skin

The **integumentary system** is the largest organ of the body. The other structures of the integumentary system are the nails, hair, and sweat and **sebaceous glands**. The skin serves several bodily functions, including the following:

- Barrier to prevent microorganisms and other foreign bodies from entering.
- Temperature regulator.
- Protection against dehydration.
- Environmental sensor, including pain, temperature, and touch.
- Synthesizing vitamin D from sunlight.
- Excreting toxins in perspiration.

Skin is composed of three layers (Figure 21-1 ◆):

- Epidermis.
- Dermis.
- Subcutaneous tissue.

Skin cells originate in the basal layer of the epidermis (just above the dermis) and progress upward. As they move toward the surface, the cells die and are eventually sloughed off, or shed. The life cycle of epidermal cells lasts approximately four weeks. They are made up largely of **keratin**, a protein found also in hair and nails. **Melanin**, also produced in the epidermis, is the pigment that colors the skin, hair, and iris of the eye. It also serves to protect the skin from harmful ultraviolet (**UV**) rays.

The dermis contains blood and lymph vessels, nerve cell endings, and skin support organs—nails, hair follicles, and sweat and sebaceous glands. The elasticity of the skin depends on the connective cells and **collagen** within the dermis. The nerve cell endings in the dermis sense touch, pain, and temperature.

The innermost layer, the subcutaneous tissue, is made up of connective tissue and fat cells. This layer acts as insulation for the body. It provides protection against extreme heat and cold and against heat loss. The layers of fat cells cushion and protect underlying structures

The **appendages** of the skin are the following:

- Hair, which covers most of the body surface.
- Nails, which protect the finger and toe tips.
- Sweat glands, which regulate body temperature.
- Sebaceous glands, which prevent the skin and hair from drying.

Hair is a nonliving keratin tissue. Each hair is formed within a sheath-like follicle and extends upward to the skin surface (Figure 21-2 ◆). Nails, also nonliving keratin, grow from the nail root (Figure 21-3 ◆). The condition of the nails can reflect a person's overall health. Sweat glands are located in the dermis and subcutaneous tissue (Figure 21-4 ◆). They have excretory tubes extending to the surface of the skin, where they open as sweat pores. Sweat evaporating from the pores cools the body. The sebaceous glands open into the hair follicles and secrete an oily substance, sebum, that lubricates the skin and hair (Figure 21-5 ◆).

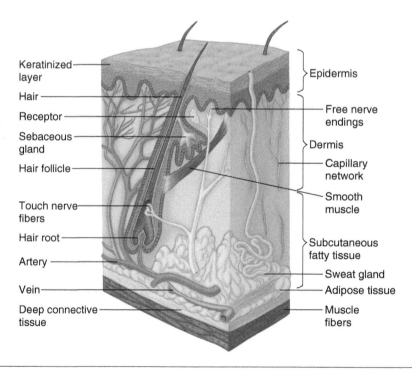

Figure 21-1 ◆ Structure of the skin

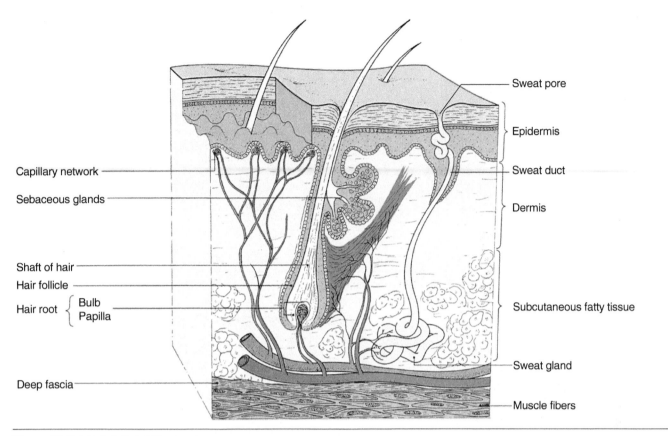

Figure 21-2 ◆ Hair follicle/skin structures

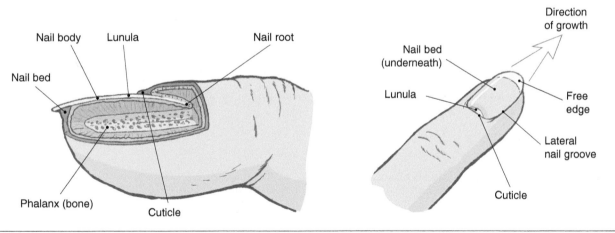

Figure 21-3 ◆ Nail bed and structure

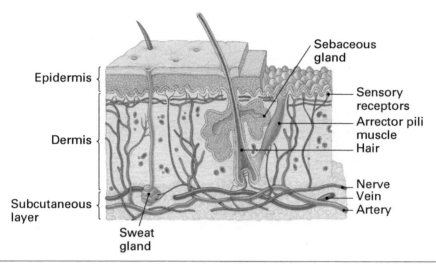

Figure 21-4 ◆ The sweat glands are located in the dermis and subcutaneous tissue

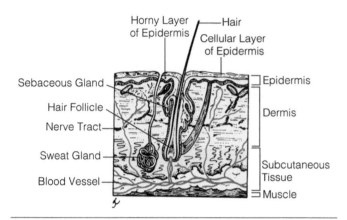

Figure 21-5 ◆ The sebaceous glands open in the hair follicles and secrete sebum.

Diseases and Disorders of the Skin

As the largest organ of the body, the integumentary system has a large exposed surface and is the site of many diseases and disorders. A break in this defense system of the body may result in generalized illness as well as localized irritations or **lesions**. Insults or injuries to the skin may disrupt any of several bodily functions involved with the skin.

Dermatitis

Dermatitis is an inflammatory condition that occurs on or in the layers of the skin. It may be chronic or acute. There are several types of dermatitis: seborrheic dermatitis, allergic contact dermatitis, contact dermatitis, eczema, and urticaria (hives) (Table 21-1; Figures 21-6 ◆ through 21-9 ◆).

TABLE 21-1 DERMATITIS

Type of Dermatitis	Symptoms	Diagnosis	Treatment
Allergic Contact Dermatitis			
■ Skin condition resulting from contact with an allergen	■ Skin redness ■ Swelling	■ Patient presenting symptoms	■ Removing the source when possible; irritation continues to spread as long as skin is in contact with source
■ Common allergens are plants (poison oak, poison ivy, sumac), latex, preservatives, laundry products, detergents, dyes, drugs, furs, fragrances, and cosmetics; sometimes radiation from sun or tanning beds	■ Oozing small vesicles that may burn, itch, and sting	■ Patient history	■ Cleansing skin to remove irritant from skin surface ■ Steroid cream to ease irritation and help healing ■ Oral steroids at decreasing dosages for more involved cases to reverse reaction and for healing
Contact Dermatitis			
■ Skin irritation caused by contact with a chemical substance on skin's surface ■ Common chemicals are latex, fragrances, dyes, detergents, laundry products, acids, and cleaning products	■ Skin redness ■ Swelling ■ Small, oozing vesicles that may burn, itch, and sting	■ Patient presenting symptoms ■ Patient history	■ See "Allergic Contact Dermatitis"

TABLE 21-1 DERMATITIS (*continued*)

Type of Dermatitis	Symptoms	Diagnosis	Treatment
Eczema (Atopic Dermatitis) ■ Inflammation of the skin ■ Generally found in people with family history of eczema or other allergic conditions ■ May be triggered by stress and sudden, severe weather changes; in infants, may be triggered by milk and orange juice ■ No known cure, but heals in time	■ Rash on face, neck, elbows, knees, and upper trunk ■ Severe itching ■ In children: rash with small blisters and oozing ■ In adults: rash with small, dry, leathery blisters	■ Patient presenting symptoms ■ Patient history	■ Steroid cream to control symptoms ■ Antihistamines to relieve itching ■ Antibiotics when necessary for bacterial infection due to scratching ■ Pimecrolimus cream (steroid-free anti-inflammatory) in place of steroids
Seborrheic Dermatitis ■ Chronic, inflammatory, and noncancerous ■ Caused by increased secretion by sebaceous glands ■ Called cradle cap in infants and toddlers	■ Skin redness ■ Itching ■ Yellow-tinged and greasy-looking scales	■ Patient presenting symptoms	■ Hydrocortisone or low-strength cortisone cream for topical application ■ Other, stronger medications prescribed when creams are ineffective
Urticaria (Hives) ■ Acute allergic response to allergen contact ■ Life-threatening when respiratory system is involved because of sudden and acute edema of airway tissue. ■ Contact with allergen may be through dermal contact, ingestion, injection (for example, bee stings), or inhalation	■ Eruptions on body, skin surfaces, or mucous membranes ■ Local swelling ■ Skin redness	■ Patient presenting symptoms ■ patient history	■ Antihistamines to relieve itching and allergy ■ Epinephrine to reduce swelling and edema ■ Immediate treatment necessary when respiratory system is involved

Figure 21-6 ◆ Acute facial seborrheic dermatitis
Source: Hercules Robinson/Alamy

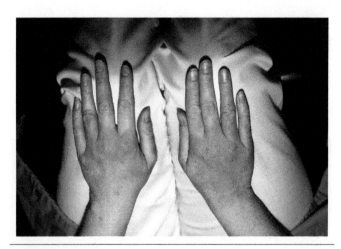

Figure 21-7 ◆ Contact dermatitis on the hands
Source: Custom Medical Stock Photo/Alamy

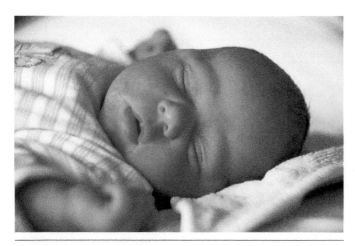

Figure 21-8 ◆ An infant afflicted by atopic eczema
Source: age footstock/SuperStock

Congenital Skin Disorders

A congenital disorder is one that is present at birth. Psoriasis is considered a congenital skin disorder (Figure 21-10 ◆). It is chronic, noninfectious, and inflammatory, with an unknown cause and no known cure. It is characterized by plaques (patches) of various sizes that are thick, flaky, red, and dry, with silvery scales. Patches are usually found on the patient's scalp, knees, elbows, and trunk. Other symptoms are itching, soreness, and pustules. Treatment consists of exposure to UV light to slow cell growth, steroid creams to reduce inflammation, and antihistamines to control mild cases. For more severe cases, chemotherapy may be necessary.

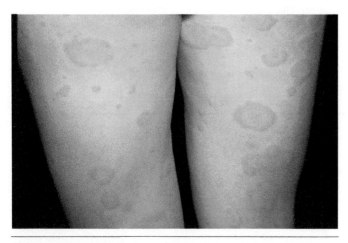

Figure 21-9 ◆ Urticaria
Source: Phanie/SuperStock

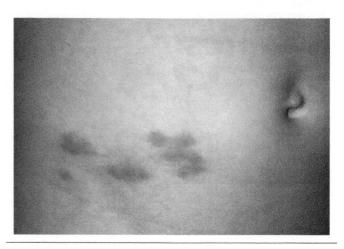

Figure 21-11 ◆ Shingles on the torso
Source: Dr. P. Marazzi/Photo Researchers, Inc.

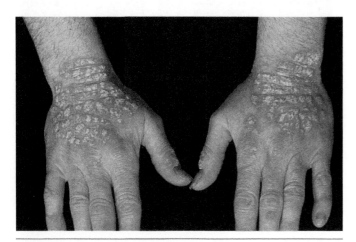

Figure 21-10 ◆ Psoriasis lesions

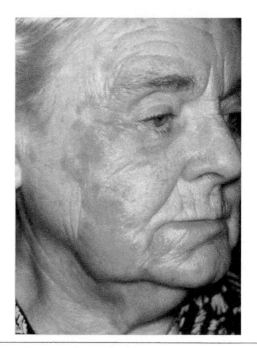

Figure 21-12 ◆ Shingles on the face
Source: Dr. P. Marazzi/Photo Researchers, Inc.

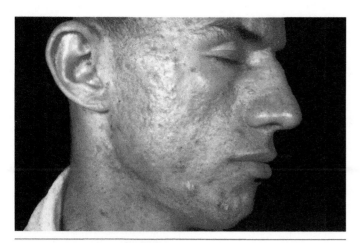

Figure 21-13 ◆ A patient with acne
Source: Custom Medical Stock Photo

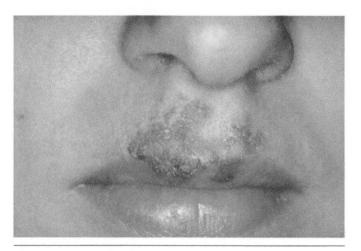

Figure 21-14 ◆ Impetigo
Source: Biophoto Associates/Photo Researchers, Inc.

Infectious Skin Disorders

Infectious skin disorders include herpes zoster (shingles), herpes simplex, acne, furuncles/carbuncles, and impetigo (Figures 21-11 ◆ through 21-14 ◆). See also Table 21-2.

Fungal Skin Conditions

Dermatophytoses—superficial skin conditions caused by fungi—affect the epidermal layer of the skin (Table 21-3). General symptoms include blisters, itching, scales, and swelling. These conditions thrive on moist, close skin surfaces. Tinea, or ringworm, occurs on the scalp, body, feet, groin, and nails, and each type is named for the body area of habitation (Figures 21-15 ◆ through 21-17 ◆).

Parasitic Skin Conditions

Two common parasites of the skin are itch mites, which cause scabies, and lice. The location of lice infestation on the body determines the name of the resulting skin condition. In school-age children, *Pediculus humanus capitis* (head lice) are spread easily through the sharing of hats, combs, brushes, and common coat rooms (Figure 21-18 ◆). *Pediculus humanus corporis* (body lice) and itch mites are frequently spread by poor hygiene and close body contact or the sharing of clothing or bedding (Figures 21-19 ◆ and 21-20 ◆). *Pediculus humanus pubis* (pubic lice) are spread through sexual contact. Table 21-4 describes various common parasitic conditions.

—Critical Thinking Question 21-1—

The mother is very concerned that her children may have lice and is under the impression that they will be labeled "dirty" or that she will be seen as an unfit mother. In addition, she has assumed that all lice are the same and attach to all types of hair. What should Manny tell her about the different kinds of head lice and how they're transmitted?

Caduceus Chronicle
LEPROSY

Leprosy, also called Hansen's disease, is caused by *Mycobacterium leprae*. It is not certain when the first case of leprosy occurred. Some Egyptian mummies from the second century BCE show evidence of the disease. Ancient records indicate that leprosy was spread from Egyptian soldiers to Roman soldiers and continued to spread during the Middle Ages, to Jerusalem and beyond. Victims of the disease were labeled "lepers" and isolated in colonies. They were shunned because the disease was incurable and extremely disfiguring.

Leprosy is spread by respiratory droplets. Mainly, the skin and nerves are attacked by the disease process. White, flat, or raised rashes or a combination of both appear on the skin. The affected skin loses sensation and cannot feel touch, heat, or pain. Numbness of the extremities and muscle weakness are other characteristics. Treatment consists of combined antibiotic therapy for approximately two years.

Today there are few cases of leprosy in the United States, and they are usually identified in persons who have traveled in foreign countries. Most of the cases diagnosed around the world occur in Central and South America, Africa, Asia, and other areas in the Pacific region.

TABLE 21-2 INFECTIOUS SKIN DISORDERS

Disease	Symptoms	Diagnosis	Treatment
Acne Vulgaris (commonly called Acne) ■ Condition of plugged pores, pimples, and cysts involving sebaceous glands and hair follicles ■ Appears on face, neck, arms, and upper back ■ Onset usually begins with puberty and increased levels of testosterone (sex hormone) ■ Pore becomes plugged with dead cells and sebum that does not reach skin surface, allowing bacterial growth; pore becomes inflamed and wall breaks, spilling sebum, dead cells, and bacteria into skin	■ Pimples ■ Pustules ■ Tender, reddened areas ■ Skin redness ■ White pustules	■ Patient presenting symptoms	■ Avoiding picking or squeezing pimples to avoid spread of bacteria, damage to skin, and scarring ■ Vitamin A acid cream or lotion for topical treatment to reduce bacteria and unblock pores ■ Antibiotic for topical treatment to reduce bacteria and help healing ■ Oral antibiotics for more involved cases when topical treatments fail ■ Female hormones to counteract testosterone
Furuncles and Carbuncles ■ Furuncle: localized infection or abscess involving entire hair follicle and surrounding subcutaneous tissue ■ Carbuncle: very large furuncle or multiple furuncles in surrounding tissue often connected by several drainage canals ■ Usually caused by bacterial infection; *S. aureus* is common causative microbe	■ Reddened tissue ■ Swelling around hair follicle/follicles ■ Pain ■ Discharge or drainage through the skin or internally ■ Carbuncles are larger	■ Patient presenting symptoms ■ Culture to identify causative agent	■ Hot compresses ■ Surgical incision and drainage ■ Antibiotics
Herpes Simplex ■ Systemic disorder resulting from previous infection with herpes simplex virus; virus moves to nerve root, where it is dormant until triggered by stress	■ Severe pain on lips and in mouth ■ Possible fever ■ Possible headache ■ Malaise ■ Blisters within hours to 1 day, lasting 4–5 days, eventually turning to scabs	■ Patient presenting symptoms	■ Cool compresses to ease pain ■ Antiviral drugs ■ Corticosteroids ■ Pain medication ■ Antiviral cream for application to lips
Herpes Zoster (Shingles) ■ Systemic disorder resulting from previous infection with herpes varicella (chickenpox) virus; virus moves to nerve root, where it is dormant until triggered by stress ■ Immunocompromised people at high risk for developing shingles; many suffer from post-herpetic **neuralgia** for weeks or months after blisters have disappeared ■ Repeat cases are rare ■ Not contagious to anyone who has had chickenpox ■ Newborns and adults who have never had chickenpox or have decreased immunity are at risk when exposed to fluid from blisters	■ Severe pain ■ Fever ■ Headache ■ Malaise ■ Rash ■ Blisters within 2 to 3 days, lasting 2 to 3 weeks, followed by pus or dark blood in blister pockets, eventually turning to scabs ■ Trunk of body most often affected, but cranial and spinal nerve dermatomes (bands of skin supplied by one nerve) may also be affected	■ Patient presenting symptoms	■ Cool compresses to ease pain ■ Antiviral drugs ■ Corticosteroid drugs ■ Pain medications
Impetigo ■ Contagious skin infection caused by *Streptococcus* or *Staphylococcus aureus* ■ Found around nose, mouth, cheeks, and extremities ■ Fluid from pustules can spread infection to nearby skin areas	■ Lesions that are yellow or red, weeping, crusted, pustular, and swelling	■ Patient presenting symptoms	■ Antibiotics for topical treatment to reduce bacteria and help healing

TABLE 21-3 FUNGAL SKIN CONDITIONS

Disease	Symptoms	Diagnosis	Treatment
Tinea Capitis (Scalp Ringworm) ■ Affects scalp	■ Lesions: round, scaly, itchy	■ Patient presenting symptoms	■ Antifungal cream to reduce fungus and help healing ■ Oral antifungal drugs when antifungal creams are not recommended
Tinea Corporis (Body Ringworm) ■ Affects hairless body skin ■ May be transmitted by infected animals, including cats.	■ Red scaly patches (center of patch clears, leaving a ring) ■ Vesicles ■ Itching	■ Patient presenting symptoms	See "Tinea Capitis"
Tinea Cruris (Jock Itch) ■ Affects groin area	■ Patches on groin area and inner part of upper thigh ■ Redness ■ Vesicles ■ Itching	■ Patient presenting symptoms	■ Antifungal cream to reduce fungus and help healing. ■ Oral antifungal drugs when antifungal creams are not recommended
Tinea Pedis (Athlete's Foot) ■ Affects the feet ■ Commonly found in athletes	■ Cracks and blisters between toes and on soles ■ Burning ■ Itching	■ Patient presenting symptoms	■ Antifungal cream to reduce fungus, itching, and burning and help healing
Tinea Unguium (Yellow Nail) ■ Affects fingernails and toenails	■ Nails: thickened, hardened, brittle, yellow-tinged (usually toenails)	■ Patient presenting symptoms	■ Antifungal cream for application to nail and nail bed

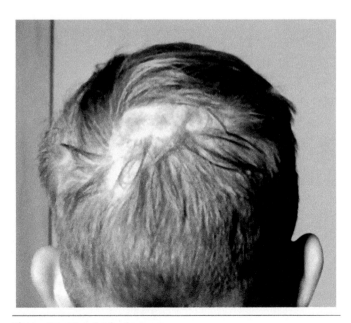

Figure 21-15 ◆ Scalp ringworm
Source: Courtesy of the CDC, 1959.

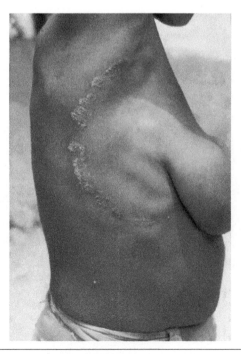

Figure 21-16 ◆ Body ringworm
Source: Courtesy of the CDC/Lucille K. Georg, 1964.

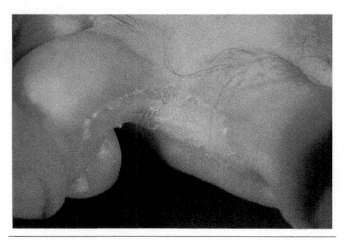

Figure 21-17 ◆ Athlete's foot
Source: Courtesy of the CDC/Dr. Lucille K. Georg, 1964.

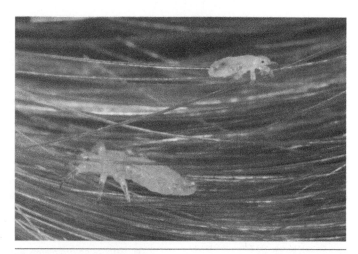

Figure 21-18 ◆ Head lice
Source: Darlyne A. Murawski/National Geographic Image Collection.

Pigmentation Disorders

Pigmentation refers to the natural coloring of the skin and hair. Pigmentation disorders include albinism, vitiligo, and chloasma (Table 21-5; Figures 21-21 ◆ through 21-23 ◆).

Benign Neoplasms

Benign neoplasms are lesions or localized growths that do not invade surrounding tissue. They do not metastasize, or spread, to distant sites in the body, although they may affect tissue func-

tion and cause physical symptoms. Malignant neoplasms are invasive and metastasize to distant sites. Benign skin disorders include actinic keratosis (**AK**), seborrheic keratosis, moles, warts, keloids, sebaceous cysts, and skin tags (Table 21-6; Figures 21-24 ◆ through 21-30 ◆).

Cancerous Skin Disorders

Many skin conditions seen in the dermatology office are benign and, while troublesome, are not life-threatening. Basal cell

Figure 21-19 ◆ Body lice
Source: Darlyne A. Murawski/National Geographic Image Collection.

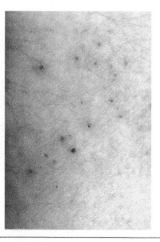

Figure 21-20 ◆ Itch mites
Source: Biophoto Associates/Photo Researchers, Inc.

TABLE 21-4 PARASITIC SKIN CONDITIONS

Parasite	Symptoms	Diagnosis	Treatment
Pediculus humanus capitis/ Pediculosis capitus (head lice) ■ Highly contagious ■ Affects the head ■ Commonly found among school-age children	■ Rash ■ Itching ■ Presence of lice and nits on hair shafts on head	■ Patient presenting symptoms	■ Special shampoo, cream, and sulfur preparation to thoroughly wash hair and body ■ Washing all contaminated clothing and bedding in hot water with bleach, then drying in dryer ■ Patient education to prevent re-exposure ■ Special hair combing to remove lice and nits
Pediculus humanis corporis/ Pediculosis corporis (body lice) ■ Highly contagious ■ Affects the body	■ Rash ■ Itching ■ Presence of lice and nits on body and clothing	■ Patient presenting symptoms	■ Special shampoo, cream, and sulfur preparation to thoroughly wash hair and body ■ Washing all contaminated clothing and bedding in hot water with bleach, then drying in dryer ■ Patient education to prevent re-exposure
Pediculus humanus pubis/ Pediculosis pubis (pubic lice or crabs) ■ Highly contagious ■ Transmitted sexually	■ Presence of lice and nits on pubic, groin, and armpit hair ■ Intense itching, especially at night ■ Brown-red dust in underwear ■ Blue-gray flat rash on trunk, thighs, or armpit	■ Patient presenting symptoms	■ See "Pediculus humanus corporis"
Scabies ■ Highly contagious ■ Caused by itch mites ■ Affects entire body	■ Rash ■ Intense itching ■ Feeling of something crawling on the body ■ Presence of scabies on the body and on clothing	■ Patient presenting symptoms	■ See "Pediculus humanus corporis"

TABLE 21-5 PIGMENTATION DISORDERS

Disorder	Symptoms	Diagnosis	Treatment
Albinism ■ Genetic disorder resulting in partial or total lack of skin color ■ No known cure	■ Very pale skin ■ Light or white hair ■ Eye color varies, but extreme is light or red irises ■ Visual difficulties: nystagmus (irregular or rapid eye movement), strabismus (eye muscle imbalance), astigmatism (distorted viewed image), photophobia (sensitivity to bright light)	■ Patient presenting symptoms	■ Sunscreen used outdoors ■ Treatment for specific vision difficulties
Chloasma (also called Melasma) ■ Skin disorder characterized by tan to brown patches ■ More common in women than men ■ Chloasma gravidarum is called mask of pregnancy but can also affect women using hormonal contraceptives ■ Also occurs in patients with underlying liver disease ■ No cure	■ Tan and brown patches found on forehead, temples, cheeks, and upper lip	■ Patient presenting symptoms	■ Sunscreen used outdoors ■ Makeup to cover patches
Vitiligo ■ Characterized by large white patches of skin ■ Cause unknown ■ No known cure	■ Large white patches of skin, commonly on hands and face	■ Patient presenting symptoms	■ Sunscreen used outdoors ■ Makeup to cover patches

Figure 21-21 ◆ Albinism

Source: Dr. P. Marazzi/Photo Researchers, Inc.

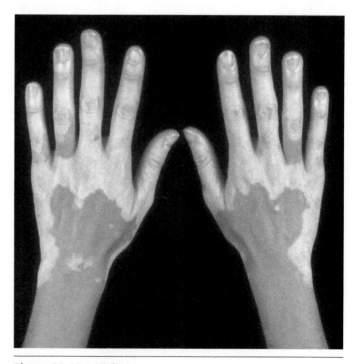

Figure 21-22 ◆ Vitiligo

Source: Custom Medical Stock Photo

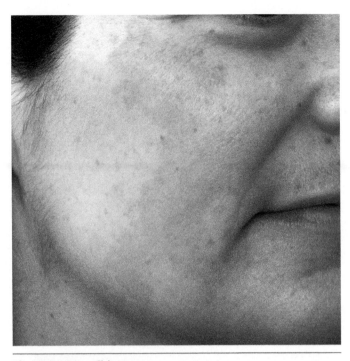

Figure 21-23 ◆ Chloasma

carcinoma (**BCC**), squamous cell carcinoma (**SCC**), and malignant melanoma are cancerous conditions affecting the skin (Figures 21-31 ◆ through 21-33 ◆). Skin cancers are the most common type of cancer as well as the most curable when diagnosed early (Table 21–7).

Skin cancers are initially diagnosed according to their appearance. Malignant melanoma is often identified by the "ABCD rule":

A = Asymmetry (the shape of one half is different from the shape of the other half)

B = Border (the edges of the lesion appear irregular and ill-defined, ragged, and uneven)

C = Color (commonly a mix of tan, black, and brown, but can also include blue, red, and white)

D = Diameter (lesions can be larger than 6 millimeters in diameter, or bigger than a pencil eraser)

Exposure to the sun is considered the main risk factor for skin cancer. Certain common-sense guidelines may be followed to reduce harmful exposure.

TABLE 21-6 BENIGN SKIN DISORDERS

Disorder	Symptoms	Diagnosis	Treatment
Actinic Keratosis (AK, also called solar keratosis) ■ Benign skin disorder, but can also be precancerous (squamous cell cancer) ■ Usually caused by exposure over time to solar or artificial UV rays ■ Biopsy of tissue is recommended after removal	■ Scaly, bumpy, crusty areas on face, ears, neck ■ Affected area may be flesh-colored, light or dark tan, pink, red, or combination ■ Itch ■ Tenderness	■ Patient presenting symptoms	■ Immediate examination by physician ■ Topical medication ■ Cryosurgery, curettage (scraping), electrosurgery, minor surgery, or laser surgery for removal ■ Routine examinations to track changes
Keloids (hypertrophic scars) ■ Benign overgrowths of collagenous scar tissue, often raised and hard ■ Secondary to surgical process or traumatic injury and form over incision scar ■ Surgery can cause further scarring ■ Some disappear by themselves	■ Flesh- or light-colored growths	■ Patient presenting symptoms	■ Cryotherapy for small keloids ■ Surgery followed by x-ray treatment or steroid injection at site as necessary
Moles (nevi) ■ Usually benign ■ Cause unknown ■ Should be monitored for changes in color or size; itching, pain, or bleeding may be sign of cancer ■ Almost everyone has moles, often developed in childhood	■ May be flesh-colored, brown, black, or blue	■ Patient presenting symptoms	■ Routine examinations to track any changes in people who have had extensive exposure to UV rays ■ Surgery only for cosmetic purposes
Sebaceous Cysts ■ Growths arising from epidermal tissue ■ Result of blocked sebaceous gland duct	■ Soft, smooth lump	■ Patient presenting symptoms	■ Incision and drainage (I & D) to drain cyst ■ Antibiotics as needed

(*continued*)

TABLE 21-6 BENIGN SKIN DISORDERS (*continued*)

Disorder	Symptoms	Diagnosis	Treatment
Seborrheic Keratosis ■ Benign skin disorder on outer ■ Cause unknown ■ Looks like waxy growth stuck onto skin surface ■ Lesions appear as individual ages and grow larger over time	■ Single or in clusters ■ Very light to very dark brown ■ Minute to over 2 inches in diameter	■ Patient presenting symptoms ■ Any lesion removed is sent to pathology lab to identify any malignant condition	■ Cryosurgery, curettage, or electrosurgery when growth becomes unsightly or irritated by clothing
Skin Tags (Acrochordons) ■ Small, skin-colored, benign outgrowths of skin tissue ■ Become more common after midlife	■ Small overgrowths of skin attached by narrow stalk	■ Patient presenting symptoms	■ Cryotherapy, electrical burning, or minor surgery for removal
Warts (Verrucae) ■ Small, contagious growths on skin ■ Often caused by a virus ■ Most occur on hands and feet	■ Small ■ Hard ■ May be flesh-colored, white, or pink ■ Painful if on bottom of foot	■ Patient presenting symptoms	■ Over-the-counter (OTC) medication to remove warts ■ Cryosurgery, electrical burning, minor surgery, or laser surgery for removal

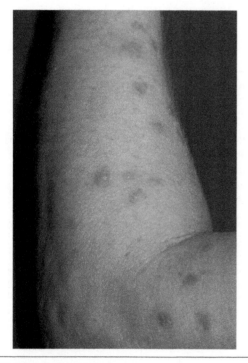

Figure 21-24 ◆ Actinic keratoses
Source: Doug Diamond/Alamy

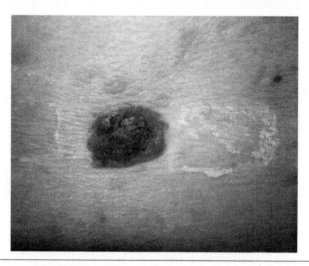

Figure 21-25 ◆ Seborrheic keratoses
Source: Courtesy of the CDC/Dr. Steve Kraus, 1981.

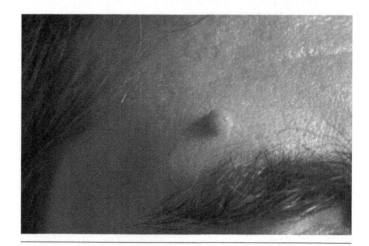

Figure 21-26 ◆ Raised mole
Source: © Custom Medical Stock Photo

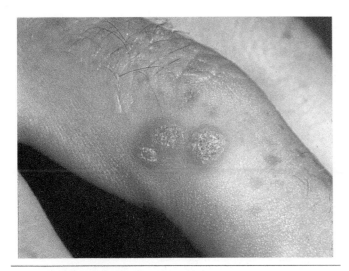

Figure 21-27 ◆ Warts

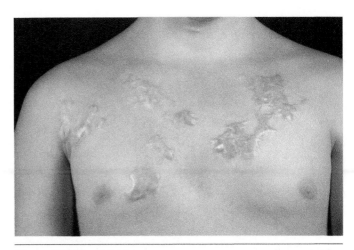

Figure 21-28 ◆ Keloids
Source: Biophoto Associates/Photo Researchers, Inc.

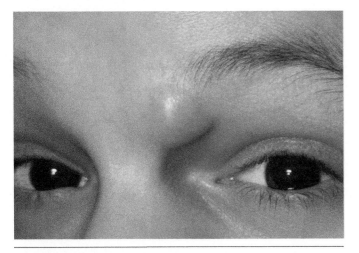

Figure 21-29 ◆ Sebaceous cyst
Source: Dr. P. Marazzi/Photo Researchers, Inc.

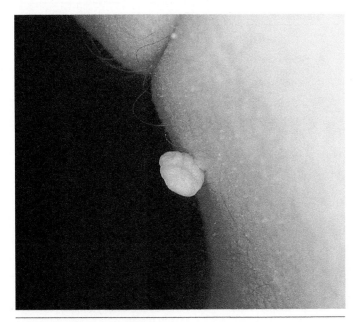

Figure 21-30 ◆ Skin tag
Source: Leonard Lessin/Peter Arnold, Inc.

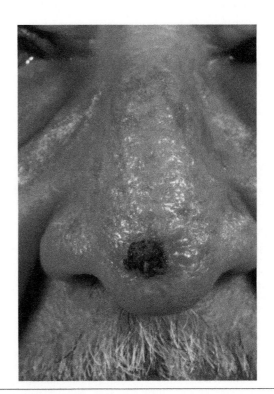

Figure 21-31 ◆ Basal cell carcinoma
©Caliendo/Custom Medical Stock Photo

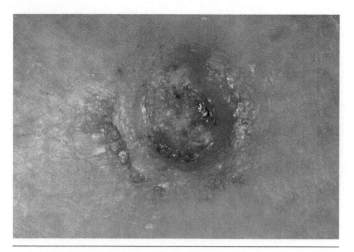

Figure 21-32 ◆ Squamous cell carcinoma
Source: Dr. P. Marazzi/Photo Researchers, Inc.

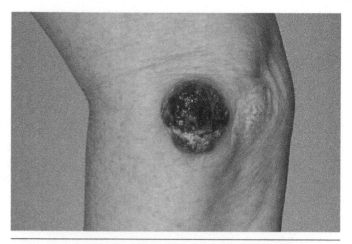

Figure 21-33 ◆ Malignant melanoma
Source: BioPhoto Associates/Science Source/Photo Researchers, Inc.

1. Avoid sun exposure when UV rays are strongest, from 10 am to 3 pm.
2. Apply sunscreen with UV protection greater than SP15, following product instructions.
3. Wear protective clothing outdoors, including a hat and clothing with sleeves and pant legs.
4. Plan outside activities for the periods of weaker UV rays.

?— Critical Thinking Question 21-2-

The teenage girl with the mole admits to sunbathing regularly in the summer at the lake and describes her mole only as "suspicious." What questions should Manny ask her regarding this condition? What advice should he give?

Miscellaneous Integumentary Conditions

In addition to the common disease conditions described above, the following may also be encountered in the medical office setting.

- Cellulitis is a condition of inflammation and infection of the skin and subcutaneous tissue. *Staphylococcus* is usually the cause. IV antibiotics are generally prescribed, along with pain medication, elevation of the extremity, and/or heat treatment to address the impaired circulation of the swollen tissue.
- Folliculitis is the inflammation and infection of a hair follicle, usually caused by *Staphyloccus*. This condition is

TABLE 21-7 CANCEROUS SKIN DISORDERS

Disorder	Symptoms	Diagnosis	Treatment
Basal Cell Carcinoma (BCC) ■ Slow-growing malignancy in basal cell layer of epidermis ■ Most common skin cancer ■ Lesions do not heal but are not likely to spread ■ Treatment based on depth and location of the lesions	■ Pearly nodule with a rolled edge when found on face, ears, or neck ■ Flat, flesh-colored, or brown scar-like lesion when found on chest or back ■ Itching ■ Bleeding	■ Patient presenting symptoms ■ Skin biopsy	■ X-ray radiation ■ Scraping and **cauterization**, surgical excision, cryosurgery, or Mohs' surgery (controlled shaved excisions) for removal ■ Sunscreen used outdoors
Squamous Cell Carcinoma ■ Malignant tumor in squamous cells of middle portion of epidermis ■ Can metastasize to other organs, such as lymph nodes ■ May start as a precancerous tumor	■ Firm red nodules that crust and bleed ■ May appear on face, ears, neck, hands, arms ■ Pain (later)	■ Patient presenting symptoms ■ Skin biopsy	■ X-ray radiation ■ Surgical excision for removal ■ Mohs' surgery for removal if cancer returns ■ Sunscreen used outdoors
Malignant Melanoma ■ Deadliest form of skin cancer ■ Metastasizes rapidly ■ Commonly occurs on normal skin, but some arise from a mole ■ Begins in **melanocytes**	■ Lesions of various colors and with irregular edges ■ Mole with color change, size change, itch, or soreness	■ Patient presenting symptoms ■ Skin biopsy	■ Surgical excision for removal; surrounding normal skin or lymph nodes also usually removed to stop spread

Keys to Success
FLUOROURACIL TREATMENT

Older Americans are at greater risk for BCC and AK as a result of long-term exposure to the sun's UV rays in the days before the link between such exposure and skin cancer was scientifically established. BCC and AK are often treated with a noninvasive topical cream or solution containing fluorouracil, which interferes with the cells' ability to reproduce. Since precancerous and cancerous cells reproduce much faster than normal cells, treatment with the drug causes them to die. However, fluorouracil may also affect the growth of normal body cells, and any serious side effects must be reported to the physician.

characterized by small pustules at the hair follicle and is usually treated by daily cleansing with antiseptic cleanser. Oral antibiotics may be required as well.

- Alopecia is a condition of partial or complete hair loss. Causative factors include heredity, aging, iron deficiency, thyroid disease, skin infection of the scalp, chemotherapy, and radiation. Some hair loss is temporary if the causative factor is addressed or removed.

- Hirsutism is a condition of excessive hair growth. Polycystic ovaries or tumors of the adrenal glands and ovaries may be the cause. Treatment varies but may include medications to suppress production of the hormone causing the condition or removal of tissue or organs causing the hormonal imbalance.

- Lyme disease is transmitted by ticks found on deer and other outdoor animals. It affects multiple systems of the body and is first recognized by a red ringed area with a white or faded center around the bite. If the disease is not diagnosed shortly after the tick bite, a range of mild flu-like symptoms and joint and muscle pains can progress to severe neurologic involvement. Complete recovery can occur over time with antibiotic treatment.

- Rosacea often occurs in middle-aged and elderly individuals, and the cause is unknown. Signs of rosacea include varying degrees of pustules (elevated and pus-filled skin lesions), papules (small, red, elevated skin lesions), and rhinopyema (hyperplasia, or overgrowth of nasal soft tissue). Rosacea is treated with medications, including antibiotics.

Cosmetic Treatment for Skin Conditions

In addition to traditional medical treatment for skin diseases and disorders, many patients are interested in removing residual effects, such as scarring or color changes, and in improving the skin's cosmetic appearance. Treatments include dermabrasion, chemical peel, and laser resurfacing. Dermabrasion involves a controlled scraping of the skin that gives it a smoother surface. The procedure removes or softens scars from acne, surgery, or accidents; smooths facial wrinkles; and removes some precancerous karatoses. A chemical peel removes the damaged outer layers of the skin, including blemishes, wrinkles, uneven skin coloration, and some precancerous skin growths. Laser resurfacing, also called laser peel, uses a carbon dioxide laser to remove wrinkles, scars, and uneven skin coloration.

REVIEW

Chapter Summary

- A dermatologist is a physician who specializes in treating skin diseases and conditions. Procedures performed in the dermatology office include biopsies, cryosurgery, and surgical removal of lesions.

- The integumentary system is the largest organ of the body. Its functions include barrier protection, temperature regulation, and toxin excretion. Other structures of the integumentary system are the nails, hair, and sweat and sebaceous glands.

- Skin is composed of three layers: the epidermis, dermis, and subcutaneous tissue. The epidermis is the outermost layer. Melanin (the pigment in the skin, hair, and iris) and keratin (a protein that makes up epidermal cells) are produced in the epidermis. Melanin protects the skin from harmful ultraviolet (UV) rays. The dermis, the middle layer, contains blood and lymph vessels, nerve cell endings, sweat and sebaceous glands, and hair follicles. The innermost layer, or subcutaneous tissue, is composed of connective tissue and fat cells and acts as insulation for the body.

- There are several types of dermatitis, including seborrheic dermatitis, allergic contact dermatitis, contact dermatitis, eczema, and hives (urticaria).

Chapter Summary (continued)

- Psoriasis is considered a congenital skin disorder. It is characterized by thick and flaky red patches covered with white, silvery scales. This condition is noninfectious, and its cause is unknown.
- Infectious skin disorders include shingles (herpes zoster), acne, and impetigo.
- Fungal skin conditions or dermatophytoses affect the epidermal layer of the skin. General symptoms include blisters, itching, scales, and swelling. Ringworm and athlete's foot are common fungal conditions.
- Common parasites of the skin include itch mites and lice.
- Pigmentation refers to the natural coloring of the skin and hair. Pigmentation disorders include albinism, vitiligo, and chloasma.
- Seborrheic keratosis, actinic keratosis, moles, warts, keloids, sebaceous cysts, and skin tags are all benign (noncancerous) skin disorders.
- Basal cell carcinoma (BCC), squamous cell carcinoma (SCC), and malignant melanoma are cancerous skin conditions.

Chapter Review Questions

Multiple Choice

1. Which of the following is a function of the integumentary system?
   A. blood sensor
   B. environmental sensor
   C. kidney regulator
   D. growth regulator

2. The dermis is the layer that
   A. is made up of connective tissue and fat cells.
   B. sloughs skin cells.
   C. is considered an appendage of the skin.
   D. contains nerve cell endings.

3. The epidermis is the layer that
   A. sloughs skin cells.
   B. is made up of connective tissue and fat cells.
   C. contains nerve cell endings.
   D. is considered an appendage of the skin.

4. The subcutaneous tissue is the layer that
   A. contains nerve cell endings.
   B. sloughs skin cells.
   C. is made up of connective tissue and fat cells.
   D. is considered an appendage of the skin.

5. Psoriasis is
   A. curable.
   B. not curable.
   C. not congenital.
   D. contagious.

6. Which of the following is a pigmentation disorder?
   A. albinism
   B. actinic keratosis
   C. scabies
   D. impetigo

7. A skin tag is a
   A. fungal infection.
   B. red surface bump.
   C. flat lesion.
   D. benign tumor.

8. Which of the following is a leading cause of skin cancer?
   A. unprotected sun exposure
   B. contact with chemicals
   C. contact with allergens
   D. untreated fungal skin infections

9. Actinic keratosis can develop into
   A. melanoma.
   B. moles.
   C. birthmarks.
   D. squamous cell cancer.

10. Melanoma is a(n)
    A. infection.
    B. precancerous condition.
    C. highly cancerous disease.
    D. fungal condition.

True/False

T F 1. Biopsies, cryosurgery, and lesion removal can all be performed in a dermatology office.

T F 2. Suture removal and dressing application may be the responsibility of the medical assistant.

T F 3. Structures of the integumentary system include nails, hair, and sweat glands but not nerves or sebaceous glands.

T F 4. The skin synthesizes vitamin D from sunlight.

T F 5. Skin cells originate in the basal layer of the dermis, above the epidermis.

Short Answer

1. How long is the life cycle of epidermal cells?

2. What are the functions of subcutaneous tissue?

3. What is melanin?

4. List four symptoms of psoriasis.

5. Which parasite causes scabies?

Chapter Review Questions (continued)

Research

1. Research leprosy and find out if there are still any leper colonies in the United States.

2. Find the most recent report on head lice outbreaks in schools in your community. How many children were affected?

Externship Application Experience

You are assisting a male dermatologist as he examines a 65-year-old female patient. He has discovered what he thinks are several malignant melanoma lesions on her face, neck, arms, and legs. A visual examination of her entire body is required, and she is asked to disrobe. He steps out of the room. The patient holds her clothing tightly and refuses to disrobe. What should you do?

Resource Guide

American Academy of Dermatology
930 N Meacham Road
P.O. Box 4014
Schamburg, IL 60168-4014
1-888-462-DERMx22
www.aad.org

American Cancer Society
1-800-ACS-2345
www.cancer.org

Melanoma Research Foundation
P.O. Box 747
San Leandro, CA 94577
1-800-MRF-1290
MRFI@melanoma.org

National Pediculosis Association
P.O. Box 610189
Newton, MA 02161
781-449-NITS (6487)
www.headlice.org

National Psoriasis Foundation
6600 SW 92nd Ave, Ste 300
Portland, OR 97223
503-244-7404
www.psoriasis.org/

National Skin Cancer Prevention Education Program
1-888-842-6355
www.cdc.gov/cancer/nscpep

Skin Cancer Foundation
245 5th Ave, Suite #1403
New York, NY 10016
1-800-SKIN-490
www.skincancer.org

MedMedia
www.prenhall.com/frazier

More on this chapter, including interactive resources, can be found on the Student CD-ROM accompanying this textbook and on the Companion Website at www.prenhall.com/frazier.

CHAPTER 22

Endocrinology

Case Study

Dr. Cabe has asked her CMA, Charles, to provide instructions to her patient, Mr. Wiat, who was recently diagnosed with adult Type 2 diabetes. The patient is more than 50 pounds overweight, does not participate in any type of exercise, and continues to eat a high-carbohydrate, high-fat diet. Reviewing Mr. Wiat's three-day diet journal, Charles notes that he consumes more than 2 liters of soda per day and regularly consumes fast food. When Charles mentions the danger of continuing this lifestyle, Mr. Wiat responds that he has lived this long with these lifestyle habits and isn't about to change. "It's not like it's going to kill me," he says.

Objectives

After completing this chapter, you should be able to:

- Define and spell medical terminology in this chapter.
- Define the medical assistant's role in the endocrinology office.
- Label the structures of the endocrine system.
- Discuss the physiology of the endocrine system.
- Identify and discuss pituitary gland disorders.
- Identify and discuss thyroid disorders.
- Identify and discuss parathyroid disorders.
- Identify and discuss glucose metabolism disorders.
- Identify and discuss adrenal gland disorders.

 **MedMedia**

www.prenhall.com/frazier

Additional interactive resources and activities for this chapter can be found on the Companion Website. For audio glossary, legal and ethical scenarios, job scenarios, quizzes, games, virtual tours, and activities related to the content of this chapter, please access the accompanying CD-ROM in this book.

 Assets Available:

Audio Glossary
Legal and Ethical Scenario: *Endocrinology*
On the Job Scenario: *Endocrinology*
A & P Quiz: The Endocrine System
Multiple Choice Quiz
Games: Crossword, Strikeout and Spelling Bee
3D Virtual Tour: Endocrine System: The Endocrine System; The Lymphatic System: The Lymphatic System
Drag & Drop: The Lymphatic System

⊕ MEDICAL ASSISTING COMPETENCIES

CAAHEP ENTRY-LEVEL COMPETENCIES FOR CMA	ABHES ENTRY-LEVEL COMPETENCIES FOR RMA
▪ Obtain and record patient history.	▪ Apply principles of aseptic techniques and infection control.
▪ Perform hand washing.	
▪ Prepare and maintain examination and treatment areas.	▪ Prepare and maintain examination and treatment areas.
▪ Prepare patient for and assist with routine and specialty examinations.	▪ Prepare patients for procedures.
	▪ Assist physician with examinations and treatments.
▪ Maintain medication and immunization records.	▪ Maintain medication records.
▪ Screen and follow up test results.	▪ Interview effectively.
▪ Recognize and respond to verbal communication.	▪ Recognize and respond to verbal and nonverbal communication.
▪ Recognize and respond to nonverbal communication.	▪ Maintain confidentially at all times.
▪ Identify and respond to issues of confidentiality.	▪ Use appropriate medical terminology.
	▪ Document accurately.
▪ Document appropriately.	▪ Adapt what is said to the recipient's level of comprehension.
▪ Instruct individuals according to their needs.	▪ Instruct patients with special needs.
▪ Provide instruction for health maintenance and disease prevention.	▪ Teach patients methods of health promotion and disease prevention.
▪ Identify community resources.	▪ Locate resources and information for patients and employers.

Introduction

The endocrine system consists of ductless glands that affect the functions of targeted organs in the body by secreting hormones. Disorders of the endocrine system usually involve the overactivity or underactivity of these glands. An endocrinologist diagnoses and treats disorders of the endocrine system such as diabetes and thyroid dysfunction.

The Medical Assistant's Role in the Endocrinology Office

In an endocrinology office the MA may perform a variety of assessment and other tasks, including the following:

- Obtaining and recording vital signs, history information, and reason for current visit, as requested by the physician.
- Obtaining blood and urine specimens for laboratory analysis.
- Performing blood glucose tests with a glucometer (∞ discussed in Chapter 12).
- Discussing with the patient written instructions concerning diet, diabetic foot care, the use and care of glucose self-monitoring equipment, or preparation for diagnostic testing.

Medical Terminology

endocrine glands—glands that secrete and release hormones directly into the bloodstream; also known as ductless glands

exocrine glands—glands that secrete substances through ducts, such as sweat glands

gluconeogenesis—conversion of noncarbohydrate sources stored in the liver into glucose

hormones—chemical messengers secreted by the endocrine glands

hypothalamus—very small structure in the midbrain, below the thalamus, that controls many body functions and endocrine processes

Abbreviations

ACTH—adrenocorticotropic hormone

ADH—antidiuretic hormone

FBS—fasting blood sugar

FSH—follicle-stimulating hormone

GHB A1c—glycohemoglobin/glycosylated hemoglobin

GH—growth hormone

IDDM (type I)—insulin-dependent diabetes mellitus

LH—luteiniziing hormone

MSH—melanocyte-stimulating hormone

NIDDM (type II)—non-insulin-dependent diabetes mellitus

PTH—parathyroid hormone

T₃—triiodothyronine

T₄—thyroxine

TSH—thyroid-stimulating hormone

Anatomy and Physiology of the Endocrine System

There are two control systems in the body: the nervous system and the endocrine system.

■ The nervous system, including the autonomic system, exerts control over body functions in a way similar to an electrical system. Impulses travel through the nerves at an extremely rapid speed and elicit an immediate response.

■ The endocrine system is slightly slower in its elicited response, which is chemically mediated by **hormones.** The endocrine system is composed of **endocrine glands** that secrete and release hormones directly into the bloodstream (Figure 22-1 ◆). These glands include the pituitary gland, thyroid gland, parathyroid gland, pancreas, adrenal glands, gonads (testicles and ovaries), pineal gland, and thymus gland. (∞ Refer to Chapter 15, Urinalysis, and Chapter 26, Obstetrics and Gynecology, for a discussion of the sex hormones.)

Endocrine disorders are the result of too much or too little of a particular hormone being stimulated or released. Therefore, most endocrine disorders are referred to as either the hyper- or hypoactivity of the gland.

Hormones are chemical substances that influence and control body functions such as growth and development, sexual maturity, and metabolism. Hormones send messages to other glands and target organs (Figure 22-2 ◆). Regulation of this system is accomplished by a positive–negative feedback process. Negative feedback originates when blood hormone levels are elevated and a message is sent slowing or stopping of the gland's activity, thereby ceasing or reducing the production of the hormone. In this manner, blood levels of various hormones control the secretion of other hormones and their resulting blood levels.

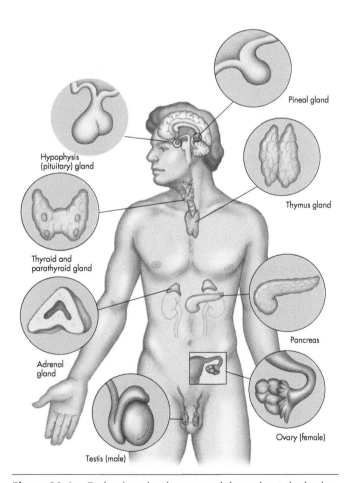

Hypophysis (pituitary) gland

Pineal gland

Thyroid and parathyroid gland

Thymus gland

Adrenal gland

Pancreas

Testis (male)

Ovary (female)

Figure 22-1 ◆ Endocrine glands scattered throughout the body

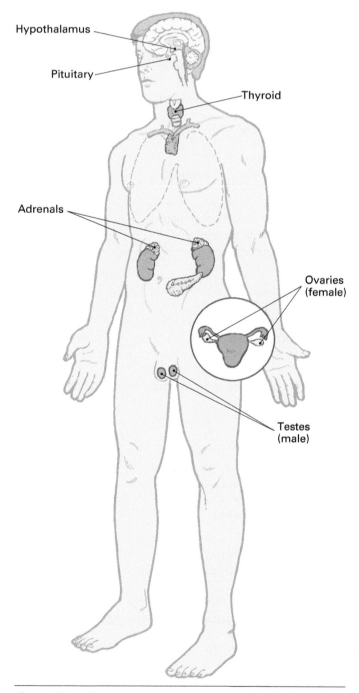

Hypothalamus

Pituitary

Thyroid

Adrenals

Ovaries (female)

Testes (male)

Figure 22-2 ◆ Hormones send messages to other glands and target organs

The Endocrine Glands

The *pituitary gland* is a minute structure located in the midbrain, in the middle of the skull. It consists of two lobes, the anterior lobe and the posterior lobe. This gland is controlled by the **hypothalamus** and its releasing factors. Hypothalamic releasing factor causes the anterior pituitary to release growth hormone (**GH**), prolactin, follicle-stimulating hormone (**FSH**), thyroid-stimulating hormone (**TSH**), luteinizing hormone (**LH**), adrenocorticotropic hormone (**ACTH**), and melanocyte-stimulating hormone (**MSH**). The function of the posterior lobe is to secrete vasopressin (also called antidiuretic hormone, or **ADH**) and oxytocin.

The *thyroid gland*, also composed of two lobes, is located in the neck on either side of the trachea. It secretes thyroxine (T_3), triiodothyronine (T_4), and calcitonin. T_3 and T_4 are under the control of TSH, stimulate cell metabolism, and are essential for energy and cell building and repair. When blood calcium levels are high, calcitonin stimulates some of the calcium to exit the blood and go into the bones, returning blood calcium levels to normal.

The *parathyroid glands*, usually four in number, are attached to the surface of the thyroid gland. Parathyroid hormone (**PTH**) affects calcium levels in the blood. It functions in concert with calcitonin to maintain appropriate calcium levels in the body.

The *pancreas* is both an endocrine and **exocrine gland.** As an endocrine gland, it produces insulin and glucagon in the islets of Langerhans. Insulin is produced in the beta cells of the islets and glucagon in the alpha cells. These two hormones are responsible for maintaining glucose levels in the blood. Exocrine functions of the pancreas are related to the digestive process, and the ducts empty into the GI tract.

The *adrenal glands* are two small glands on the upper surface of each kidney. Each gland has two portions.

- The *adrenal medulla,* or inner portion, works in concert with the sympathetic nervous system during activation of the sympathetic response, producing epinephrine (adrenaline) and norepinephrine (noradrenaline)
- The *adrenal cortex,* or outer portion, produces hormones called corticosteroids (steroids), including mineralcorticoids, glucocorticoids, androgens, estrogens, and progestins.

The *thymus gland* functions early in life, helping to develop the immune system. It is located in the mediastinum and is composed of lymphoid-type tissue. The thymus usually shrinks or atrophies during adolescence.

The *pineal gland* is located in the central portion of the brain. This gland is believed to secrete melatonin. It has a tendency to calcify during the aging process.

Table 22-1 summarizes the endocrine glands, the hormones they secrete, and the functions the various hormones perform.

TABLE 22-1 THE ENDOCRINE GLANDS

Gland	Location	Hormone(s) Secreted
Pituitary, anterior lobe	Cranial cavity, brain	■ Growth hormone: stimulates growth, protein synthesis, and lipid mobilization and catabolism ■ Thyroid-stimulating hormone: stimulates secretion of thyroid hormones ■ Adrenocorticotropic hormone: glucocorticocoid secretion ■ Follicle-stimulating hormone: stimulates estrogen secretion and follicle development (female) and sperm maturation (male) ■ Luteinizing hormone: stimulates ovulation, corpus luteum development, secretion of progesterone
Pituitary, posterior lobe	Cranial cavity, brain	■ Antidiuretic hormone: absorbs H_2O, elevates blood pressure and volume ■ Oxytocin: stimulates uterine contractions and milk ejection (female), and contractions of the prostate (male)
Thyroid	Neck	■ Thyroxine (T_3): increases metabolic rate ■ Triiodothyronine (T_4): increases metabolic rate ■ Calcitonin: increases calcium storage in bones
Parathyroid	Neck, attached to thyroid	■ Parathormone (PTH): increases calcium removal from the bones
Adrenal cortex	Retroperitoneal (above kidneys)	■ Mineralocorticoids (aldosterone): stimulate reabsorption of sodium in kidney tubules, accelerate loss of potassium ions from urine ■ Glucocorticoids (cortisol, corticosterone, cortisone): influence metabolism of food, exhibit anti-inflammatory effect ■ Gonadocorticoids (androgens, estrogens, progestins): possible support of sexual function
Adrenal medulla	Retroperitoneal (above kidneys)	■ Catecholamines, epinephrine, norepinephrine: enhance and prolong effects of sympathetic nervous system

(continued)

TABLE 22-1 THE ENDOCRINE GLANDS *(continued)*

Gland	Location	Hormone(s) Secreted
Pancreas islets	Abdomen	■ Insulin: promotes movement of glucose across cell membranes ■ Glucagon: promotes movement of glucose from storage into the blood
Thymus	Mediastnum	■ Thymosin: involved with immune response, essential for maturation of T cells
Pineal gland	Cranial cavity, brain	■ Melatonin: may affect circadian rhythms
Ovaries	Pelvic cavity	■ Estrogens: develop and maintain female sex characteristics and female reproductive cycle ■ Progesterone: maintains lining of uterus during pregnancy
Testes	Scrotum	■ Testosterone: develops and maintains male sex characteristics and sperm production

Endocrine Disorders

Most endocrine disorders are the result of either hyposecretion (diminished activity) or hypersecretion (increased activity) of the gland. For example, hypersecretion of the pituitary gland during the years of growth results in gigantism and, during post-growth years, in acromegaly (Figure 22-3 ◆). Hypopituitarism in children results in a condition called dwarfism (Figure 22-4 ◆). Table 22-2 lists a few of the disorders caused by hyper- and hyposecretion.

Pituitary Gland Disorders

The pituitary gland is often referred to as the master gland. The hypothalamus controls the activity of the gland by releasing factors to the anterior pituitary gland. Releasing factors, peptides produced by the hypothalamus, are secreted directly into the anterior pituitary gland to stimulate the secretion of specific tropic hormones. Tropic hormones control or stimulate the activities of other glands. Growth hormone (GH) secreted by the pituitary gland reaches all body tissues. Hypersecretion causes excessive growth, and hyposecretion retards growth. The overstimulation of bone and other tissue by GH results in abnormal growth during the growth period and gigantism. If overstimulation occurs after the growth period has ended, the result is acromegaly—overgrowth of the bones of the hands, feet, and face. In both conditions, the usual cause is a pituitary tumor. Although the overproduction of growth hormone can be controlled, excessive growth cannot be reversed.

Hypopituitarism is a reduction in the excretion of any of the pituitary hormones. This complex condition may involve

Figure 22-3 ◆ Gigantism
Source: Bettina Cirrone/Photo Researchers, Inc.

Figure 22-4 ◆ Dwarfism
Source: Spencer Grant/Photoedit, Inc.

TABLE 22-2 EXAMPLES OF ENDOCRINE DISORDERS CAUSED BY HYPERSECRETION AND HYPOSECRETION

Gland	Hypersecretion	Hyposecretion
Pituitary gland	Growth hormone: gigantism in childhood, acromegaly in adulthood	Growth hormone: dwarfism in childhood, hypopituitarism in adulthood
Thyroid gland	Thyroid hormones: Graves' disease	Thyroid hormones: simple goiter or hyperplasia of thyroid gland
Parathyroid gland	Parathyroid hormone: hypercalcemia	Parathyroid hormone: hypocalcemia
Pancreas	Insulin: hypoglycemia, or insulin shock	Insulin: hyperglycemia, or diabetic coma
Adrenal glands	Glucocorticoids: Cushing's syndrome	Adrenocortical hormones: Addison's disease

retarded growth, retarded or delayed sexual maturation, or metabolic dysfunction. Growth retardation in children results in dwarfism, and growth hormone is administered to encourage growth.

Diminished release of vasopressin, or antidiuretic hormone, by the posterior lobe of the pituitary gland causes excessive amounts of very dilute urine to be secreted by the kidneys. This condition is known as diabetes insipidus. Individuals with this condition may secrete as much as 3 to 6 liters of dilute urine in a 24-hour period. Injections of vasopressin or the use of nasal spray containing vasopressin help to replace the diminished supply and slow the excessive output of urine.

Thyroid Gland Disorders

Iodine must be supplied in the diet to assure the proper functioning of the thyroid gland. Hyperplasia or enlargement of the thyroid gland, also known as simple goiter, results from inadequate iodine intake and the inability of the gland to secrete thyroid hormones. The hyperplasia must be halted before it compromises the airway. Treatment options include iodine supplements, drug therapy to provide required amounts of T_3 and T_4, and surgical intervention to remove the overgrowth of tissue.

Hypothyroidism, the result of underproduction and undersecretion of thyroid hormones, is a common condition that is treated with hormone replacement therapy that must continue for life. Signs of hypothyroidism include a slowed metabolic rate, low levels of T_3 and T_4, pale, cool skin, slow heart rate, lethargy, decreased appetite, weight gain, intolerance to cold, and possible goiter.

Several conditions are related to hypothyroidism.

- Hashimoto's disease, also known as chronic thyroiditis, is a form of hypothyroidism and occurs as an autoimmune reaction.
- Myxedema is a severe or acute hypothyroid state in adults that may lead to hypoglycemia, hypotension, hypothermia, reduced levels of consciousness, and, when untreated, to death.
- Cretinism is a congenital condition of hypothyroidism resulting from iodine deficiency during fetal development or during early life development. This condition is characterized by mental retardation and impaired growth patterns.

Hyperthyroidism, an oversecretion of thyroid hormones, is also known as Graves' disease. This condition is often accompanied by an outward protrusion of the eyes, called exophthalmos. Other symptoms include a feeling of unusual nervousness, excessive perspiration, insomnia, palpitations and rapid heart rate, and intolerance to heat. Individuals may also experience weight loss, excessive thirst, muscle weakness, and fatigue. Treatment involves drug therapy with antithyroid drugs (propylthiouracil and methimazole) to slow the production of thyroid hormones, and cardiac drugs, including beta-blockers, to treat the cardiac arrhythmias. When drug therapy does not bring about a sufficient response, radioactive iodine or surgical removal of a portion of the thyroid gland may be necessary.

Parathyroid Disorders

Parathyroid disorders include hypoparathyroidism and hyperparathyroidism. Hypoparathyroidism causes low serum calcium levels, or hypocalcemia. Two consequences of hypocalcemia are increased nerve excitability (spontaneous muscle contractions or twitching), also known as tetany, and weak cardiac muscle contractions. Treatment involves lifelong calcium replacement therapy along with vitamin D supplements.

Excessive production and secretion of parathyroid hormone causes an elevation in blood calcium levels, or hypercalcemia, as calcium migrates from bone tissue into the blood serum. Symptoms of this condition include joint pain, kidney stones, CNS and gastrointestinal disturbances, and brittle bones. Treatment varies depending on the cause and includes partial resection of the parathyroid glands, hydration of the patient, and drug therapy to inhibit reabsorption of calcium from bone tissue.

Disorders of the Pancreas

The pancreas is both an endocrine gland and an exocrine gland. As an exocrine gland it secretes enzymes necessary for the digestive process that are released into the GI tract through the pancreatic duct. Endocrine activity occurs in the alpha and beta cells of the islets of Langerhans. In response to low blood glucose levels, the alpha cells secrete glucagon. Glucagon increases blood glucose levels by stimulating the liver to convert stored noncarbohydrate substances into glucose, a process called **gluconeogenesis.**

Insulin is produced in and secreted by the beta islet cells. Insulin is necessary for the transport of glucose across cell membranes into cells for cellular metabolism. When insulin is not available to assist in this transport, blood levels of glucose increase. The condition that results from the continued decrease of available insulin and the increase in blood glucose levels is diabetes mellitus. Normal blood glucose levels generally range between 60 and 120 mg/dl, although a 10 percent variable is considered within normal range.

Diabetes mellitus is classified into two different forms, insulin-dependent diabetes mellitus (**IDDM, type I**) and non-insulin-dependent diabetes mellitus (**NIDDM, type II**).

- IDDM often has an abrupt onset, usually appears before the age of 30, and is sometimes called juvenile-onset diabetes. In this condition, the pancreas does not secrete insulin. Treatment consists of insulin administration by injection or parenteral insulin pump.
- NIDDM often has a gradual onset, usually appearing in adults over the age of 40, and is often referred to as adult-onset diabetes. The pancreas still secretes some insulin, and it is possible to stimulate it to secrete more.

?—Critical Thinking Question 22-1

Mr. Wait is apparently unaware of how adult-onset diabetes occurs and what the treatment options are. How should Charles educate him?

Two serious glucose metabolism disorders, hypoglycemia and hyperglycemia, are complications of diabetes mellitus. Too much insulin, whether by injection or beta cell production stimulation, results in a dramatic drop in blood glucose levels, or hypoglycemia, also referred to as insulin shock. Other causes are inadequate food intake, excessive exercise, or other underlying illnesses. Hypoglycemia is a life-threatening condition that requires immediate intervention. The individual experiences a feeling of weakness, shakiness, light-headedness, and sweating. Without immediate intervention—ingestion or infusion of glucose—an altered level of consciousness follows and the individual may become agitated and uncooperative. ∞ This condition constitutes a true medical emergency, as described in Chapter 23, Emergency Care.

The opposite of hypoglycemia or insulin shock is hyperglycemia, or diabetic coma. The glucose level of the blood rises well above 120 mg/dl, the upper end of the normal range. As this condition evolves, the blood pH level drops, creating a condition of metabolic acidosis. As the body tries to rid itself of the excess glucose in the blood, more urine is produced and the respiratory system excretes acetones (ketones). Skipping or delaying an insulin injection, illness, and ingestion of too much food, especially food high in sugar content, can cause this complication. Symptoms include a fruity odor to the breath, intense thirst, lethargy, dry skin, occasionally abdominal pain, and possible coma. Intervention consists of hydration and the administration of insulin.

?—Critical Thinking Question 22-2

Mr. Wiat seems to be in denial about his condition and how his lifestyle may cause additional health problems and even death. How should Charles proceed in educating him?

Caduceus Chronicle
DIABETES

The medical condition of diabetes was described as early as 150 C.E. by Aretus the Cappadocian. The symptoms he listed included an incessant flow of urine, unquenchable thirst and drinking, parched mouth and dry body, nausea, vomiting, and restlessness. Life was difficult and painful, and death was quick.

Insulin was discovered in 1920 by Frederick Banting, a Canadian surgeon. With his partner, Charles Best, at the University of Toronto, he made an extract from dog pancreas. Two other colleagues, J. J. R. Macleod and J. B. Collip, joined the team to produce a purified form of insulin. Testing of the drug began in 1922, and Banting and Macleod received the Nobel Prize for medicine in 1923. Their discovery was one of the most important in the history of medicine and revolutionized the treatment of diabetes.

Gestational diabetes mellitus is a form of diabetes that has its onset during pregnancy. The inability to produce adequate amounts of insulin or to utilize it effectively is usually first noticed during the second or third trimester. Many physicians routinely order glucose tolerance tests or two-hour postprandial glucose during the last half of the pregnancy as a screening for gestational diabetes. Management of this disease is similar to the usual management of diabetes mellitus. It involves the monitoring of blood glucose levels and the administration of oral hypoglycemic agents and, on occasion, insulin.

The signs, symptoms, and treatment of hypoglycemia and hyperglycemia are summarized in Table 22-3.

Drug therapy for diabetes mellitus includes insulin replacement. Research is currently being conducted on new methods of insulin administration in addition to the current methods—injection or, in an emergency, IV. Oral hypoglycemic agents work in various ways to stimulate the pancreas to secrete more insulin by blocking gluconeogenesis, increasing insulin sensitivity, reducing insulin resistance and allowing better utilization of available insulin, and slowing absorption of dietary glucose in the gut.

In addition to daily "finger sticks" for glucose monitoring, the physician may order laboratory blood tests on a regular basis. A fasting blood sugar (**FBS**) drawn first thing in the morning is an accurate determination of blood glucose levels. A second blood test, also a fasting test, is the glycohemoglobin or glycosylated hemoglobin (**GHB A1c**) test. This test indicates an average of blood glucose levels over the previous 120 days as an indication of how well blood glucose has been controlled in that time frame.

The medical assistant may play one or more roles in dealing with the diabetic patient, including the following:

- Teaching the patient about insulin administration (depending on state practice acts and physician direction).
- Instructing the patient in how to use a glucometer and record the information in a "diabetic diary," if the glucometer is not equipped with an internal memory.
- Discussing the importance of foot care.

TABLE 22-3 HYPOGLYCEMIA VS. HYPERGLYCEMIA

	Hypoglycemia, Insulin Reaction	Hyperglycemia, Diabetic Coma
Signs and Symptoms	Rapid, abrupt onset Patient complains of hunger Cool, moist skin and profuse perspiration (diaphoresis) Pale, clammy skin Blood glucose level below 70 mg/dl Rapid onset of decreased level of consciousness	Slow, insidious onset Patient complains of intense thirst and dry mouth Dry, warm skin Flushed skin Blood glucose level elevated above normal Increased urine output Rapid and deep respirations Abdominal pain and vomiting Slow onset of decreased level of consciousness Acetone-smelling breath
Treatment	Give patient a simple sugar source such as hard candy, soda pop, or orange juice. If patient is unable to swallow or is comatose, give dextrose or glucagon by intravenous route.	Give patient insulin by subcutaneous injection, plus fluids and sodium (such as salt) by mouth. If patient is unable to swallow or is comatose, give insulin, fluids, and sodium by intravenous route.

■ Encouraging the patient to follow dietary plans, glucose monitoring, and medication instructions and to keep follow-up appointments as scheduled. (∞ Refer to Chapter 12 for glucose monitoring information and Chapter 24 for dietary information.)

■ Encouraging patients to discuss possible side effects of drugs with their physician or pharmacist and to immediately report to the physician any side effects that do occur.

Keys to Success
HELPING PATIENTS WITH THE COST OF DIABETIC SUPPLIES

The treatment of disease conditions usually involves medication or a specific therapy for a certain amount of time. But the diabetic patient needs medical supplies for a lifetime: a glucometer, glucometer strips, insulin syringes, insulin, lancets, lancet holders, syringe waste disposal, and healthier food. Patients may not understand the importance of preventive health maintenance and may risk hospitalization and other complications when their budgets are limited. The medical assistant can help patients by researching pharmaceutical companies that provide free or low-cost insulin and medical supplies. The MA should also know how to help patients contact the local trustee office or welfare office and provide assistance with filing insurance claims for Medicaid, Medicare, and other third-party payers.

Adrenal Gland Disorders

There are two major adrenal gland disorders.

■ Cushing's syndrome is caused by hypersecretion of glucocorticoids. The individual takes on an appearance typical of obesity, with the characteristic round or moon face. There is a wasting away of muscle tissue as well as the development of a thick trunk and a "buffalo hump" at the back of the neck. These individuals are at high risk for infection and have a poor stress response. They experience fatigue, weakness, hypertension, glucose intolerance, and delayed healing. Drug therapy, radiation, and surgery are intervention options for this disorder.

■ Addison's disease is caused by the hyposecretion of adrenocortical secretions. Possible causes are autoimmune response and infectious processes. The individual experiences weight loss, fatigue, frequent infection, anorexia, nausea and vomiting, syncope, and poor stress response. Replacement of the deficient hormones and dietary and electrolyte balance are the usual forms of treatment.

Chapter Summary

- The MA in an endocrinology office may perform typical assessment tasks, such as obtaining and recording vital signs and history information, as well as obtaining blood and urine specimens and performing blood glucose tests. The MA may also discuss dietary instructions, diabetic foot care, and glucose self-monitoring equipment with the patient.

- The nervous and endocrine systems are the two control systems in the body. The endocrine system is composed of glands that secrete and release hormones directly into the bloodstream. They include the pituitary gland, thyroid gland, parathyroid gland, pancreas, adrenal glands, gonads, thymus gland, and pineal gland. Hormones are chemical messengers that influence and control body functions.

- Endocrine disorders are the result of too much hormone being stimulated or released (hyperactivity) or too little (hypoactivity).

- The pituitary gland is controlled by the hypothalamus and its releasing factors. The anterior pituitary lobe releases growth-stimulating hormone, prolactin, follicle-stimulating hormone, thyroid-stimulating hormone, luteinizing hormone, adrenocorticotropic hormone, and melanocyte-stimulating hormone. The posterior lobe's function is to secrete vasopressin and oxytocin. Hyperfunctioning of the pituitary gland results in gigantism or acromegaly. Hypopituitarism in children causes dwarfism. Decreased secretion of the posterior lobe results in diabetes insipidus.

- The two lobes of the thyroid gland are located in the neck on either side of the trachea. The thyroid gland secretes thyroxine (T_3), triiodothyronine (T_4), and thyrocalcitonin (TCT). T_3 and T_4 stimulate cell metabolism and are essential for energy, cell building, and repair and are under the control of TSH. TCT or calcitonin serves to maintain normal blood calcium levels. Iodine deficiency causes simple goiter, or enlargement of the thyroid gland. Hypothyroid conditions include Hashimoto's disease, myxedema, and, in children, cretinism. Graves' disease is a hyperthyroid condition. Hypothyroidism is treated with lifetime hormone replacement therapy. Treatment options for hyperthyroidism include iodine supplements, drug therapy to replace required amounts of T_3 and T_4, or surgical intervention to remove the overgrowth of tissue.

- Parathyroid hormone (PTH) affects calcium levels in the bone. With calcitonin it maintains appropriate calcium levels in the body. Hypoparathyroidism causes low serum calcium levels, or hypocalcemia. Hyperparathyroidism causes elevated blood calcium levels, or hypercalcemia.

- The pancreas produces insulin and glucagon in the islets of Langerhans and is responsible for maintaining glucose levels in the blood. Glucose metabolism disorders include diabetes mellitus and hypoglycemia. There are two forms of diabetes mellitus: insulin-dependent diabetes mellitus (IDDM, type I) and non-insulin-dependent diabetes mellitus (NIDDM, type II). Drug therapy for diabetes mellitus includes insulin replacement. Hypoglycemia, or insulin shock, is a life-threatening condition resulting from too much insulin and requiring immediate intervention. In hyperglycemia, or diabetic coma, blood glucose levels rise well above normal. Intervention includes hydration and insulin administration.

- The adrenal glands are two small glands on the kidneys. They produce epinephrine (adrenaline), norepinephrine (noradrenaline), and corticosteroids (steroids). Cushing's syndrome is caused by hypersecretion of glucocorticoids. Drug therapy, radiation, or surgery are treatment options for this disorder. Addison's disease is caused by hyposecretion of adrenocortical secretions and is treated with replacement of the deficient hormones and dietary and electrolyte balance.

- The thymus gland helps to develop the immune system. It is located in the mediastinum and usually shrinks or atrophies during adolescence. The pineal gland, located in the brain, is believed to secrete melatonin.

Chapter Review Questions

Multiple Choice

1. The conversion of noncarbohydrates stored in the liver into glucose is known as
   A. gluconeogenesis.
   B. absorption.
   C. endocrine release.
   D. hypothalamus conversion.

2. Which of the following is not part of the endocrine gland system?
   A. ovaries
   B. testicles
   C. mammary glands
   D. thymus

3. The pituitary gland is controlled by the
   A. pineal gland.
   B. parathyroid.
   C. adrenal gland.
   D. hypothalamus.

4. Which of the following is *not* released by the anterior pituitary?
   A. LH
   B. ADH
   C. MSH
   D. TSH

Chapter Review Questions (continued)

5. How many parathyroid glands are there?
   A. 5
   B. 3
   C. 2
   D. 4

6. The two small glands on the upper surface of each kidney are
   A. adrenal medulla glands.
   B. adrenal glands.
   C. adrenal cortex glands.
   D. thymus glands.

7. The gland in the central portion of the brain that is believed to secrete melatonin is the
   A. pineal gland.
   B. thymus gland.
   C. adrenal gland.
   D. parathyroid gland.

8. Which hormone is *not* secreted by the anterior lobe of the pituitary gland?
   A. follicle-stimulating hormone
   B. luteinizing hormone
   C. antidiuretic hormone
   D. thyroid-stimulating hormone

9. Which of these is *not* secreted by the adrenal cortex?
   A. mineralocorticoids
   B. parathormone (PTH)
   C. glucocorticoids
   D. gonadocorticoids

10. Which of these hormones is *not* secreted by the thyroid?
    A. thymosin
    B. thyroxine
    C. triiodothyronine
    D. calcitonin

True/False

T F   1. Most endocrine disorders are the result of hyposecretion.

T F   2. Hypopituitarism in children results in a condition called *dwarfism.*

T F   3. The hypothalamus is often referred to as the "master gland."

T F   4. Hypopituitarism is a reduction in the excretion of a single pituitary hormone.

T F   5. An excessive urinary output may be caused by a diminished release of vasopressin.

T F   6. Hashimoto's disease is a form of hypothyroidism and can occur as an autoimmune reaction.

T F   7. Elevation of blood calcium levels is a reaction to excessive secretion from the thyroid gland.

T F   8. The pancreas is both an endocrine and an exocrine gland.

T F   9. Hyperglycemia is a life-threatening disorder in which skin appears cool and moist.

T F 10. Hypoglycemia is known as *insulin shock* and can cause a diabetic coma.

Short Answer

1. What is the range of normal blood glucose levels?

2. Which form of DM has its onset during pregnancy?

3. What is the difference between hypoglycemia and hyperglycemia?

Research

1. Does the hospital or other facility in your community run patient education programs for diabetic patients?

2. If you were to help your local clinic create a patient education brochure about endocrine disorders, which diseases, symptoms, and organs would you include? What would you leave out and why? What additional information would your brochure include?

Externship Application Experience

A patient is waiting in the reception area to be seen by the physician for nausea and vomiting. You notice that the patient is pale and very diaphoretic. Her spouse approaches you and says that the patient has had insulin but nothing to eat. The patient is conscious at present. What do you do?

Resource Guide

American Diabetes Association
1701 North Beauregard St.
Alexandria, VA 22311
1-800-DIABETES, 1-800-342-2383
www.diabetes.org

American Thyroid Association
6066 Leesburg Pike, Suite 650
Falls Church, VA 22041
703-998-8890; patients 1-800-THYROID
www.thyroid.org

Endocrine Society
8401 Connecticut Ave., Suite 900
Chevy Chase, MD 20815-5817
301-941-0200
www.endo-society.org

National Diabetes Information Clearinghouse (NDIC)
PO Box NDIC
Bethesda, MD 20892
301-468-2162
http://www.niddk.nih.gov

National Institute of Diabetes and Digestive and Kidney Diseases
NIH – Building 31, Room 9A04
31 Center Drive, MSC 2560
Bethesda, MD 20892-2560
www.niddk.nih.gov

MedMedia

www.prenhall.com/frazier

More on this chapter, including interactive resources, can be found on the Student CD-ROM accompanying this textbook and on the Companion Website at www.prenhall.com/frazier.

SECTION V

Medical Specialties

My name is Terri O'Connell, and I'm proud to say that I became a Certified Medical Assistant in June 2005. The path that led me to my goal began shortly after my youngest child entered first grade. I have a BA in Communications and had worked for over fifteen years in the advertising profession as a businessperson before taking time off to raise a family. The idea of recreating myself in a career that I could feel a great sense of accomplishment and contribution at the end of the day brought me back to our local community college. I became really interested in the Allied Health profession after taking a Medical Terminology course.

A Medical Assistant performs a combination of both clinical and administrative skills. While in the final months of our training, the clinical experiences we had in various offices and facilities led me to take a first job at a busy pediatric practice in my town. I knew I would have two patients in a pediatric office, the child and the parent. Sometimes either one of them could be difficult to work with. I had to learn how to keep the flow in the office moving, as the provider needed to be kept busy at all times. This entails finding the chief complaint of the patient quickly and making decisions as to what data the provider might need in order to make the final assessment and diagnosis.

In addition to lab and tests that we performed in the office, such as capillary draws, spirometry, audiometry and other tests, I was trained to screen for amblyopia. We used an EEG machine to do the test. I had babies as young as 6 months up to 6 years old to test. Amblyopia, or lazy eye, can cause blindness in children under the age of 8 if it's not detected and treated. A child who tested positive was referred by the provider to be seen by an ophthalmologist. At the end of the day, it feels good to make a contribution to help make someone else's life better. This work has a lot of value to me.

CHAPTER 23

Emergency Care

Case Study

Ariko, a medical assistant, receives a phone call from a young mother, Brenna, who is frantic and crying. Brenna explains that her 2-year-old was playing in the living room while she was doing dishes in the kitchen, one room away. Brenna reports hearing a loud thud against what she believes was the hardwood floor. When she rushed in, she found her daughter curled in a fetal position between a chair and an ottoman.

Brenna says her daughter did not say anything or explain what had happened. The child appears normal, with no bump or bruising and no bleeding that Brenna can see.

Objectives

After completing this chapter, you should be able to:

- Spell and define the medical terminology in this chapter.
- Define the medical assistant's role in emergency care.
- Describe the role of the EMS.
- List the equipment and supplies maintained for emergencies in a medical office.
- Explain the principles of early intervention with CPR and AED.
- Discuss how chest pain emergencies are handled in the medical office.
- Describe the types of respiratory distress and appropriate interventions.
- Identify the different types of shock.
- Compare the different types of bleeding.
- Compare open and closed wounds and their treatment.
- Describe burns, frostbite, and other thermal insults and their appropriate treatment.
- Discuss the appropriate interventions for musculoskeletal injuries.
- Explain allergic reactions and appropriate interventions.
- Describe neurological emergencies and interventions.
- Discuss interventions for acute abdominal pain, diabetic crises, poisoning, and foreign bodies in the eyes, ears, and nose.
- Describe appropriate interventions for psychosocial emergencies.

MedMedia
www.prenhall.com/frazier

Additional interactive resources and activities for this chapter can be found on the Companion Website. For videos, audio glossary, legal and ethical scenarios, job scenarios, quizzes, and games related to the content of this chapter, please access the accompanying CD-ROM in this book.

Assets Available:

Audio Glossary
Legal and Ethical Scenario: *Emergency Care*
On the Job Scenario: *Emergency Care*
Video Scenario: *Facing Emergencies*
Multiple Choice Quiz
Games: Crossword, Strikeout and Spelling Bee

MEDICAL ASSISTING COMPETENCIES

CAAHEP ENTRY-LEVEL COMPETENCIES FOR CMA	ABHES ENTRY-LEVEL COMPETENCIES FOR RMA
■ Identify and respond to issues of confidentiality.	■ Project a positive attitude.
■ Perform within legal and ethical boundaries.	■ Maintain confidentiality at all times.
■ Demonstrate knowledge of federal and state health-care legislation and regulations.	■ Be a "team player."
	■ Be cognizant of ethical boundaries.
	■ Exhibit initiative.
■ Perform hand washing.	■ Adapt to change.
■ Practice Standard Precautions.	■ Evidence a responsible attitude.
■ Perform telephone and in-person screening.	■ Be courteous and diplomatic.
	■ Conduct work within scope of education, training, and ability.
■ Prepare patient for and assist with routine and specialty examinations.	■ Practice Standard Precautions.
	■ Recognize emergencies.

Introduction

A positive outcome for a medical office emergency depends on prompt and effective assessment and intervention by the medical team members. Medical emergencies in the office can range from a nosebleed or simple laceration to shortness of breath, chest pain, and full cardiac arrest. They can occur on site or over the phone. It is the responsibility of each team member to know his or her role in any medical emergency. At all times, Universal Precautions and office protocol for emergency situations must be followed.

The Medical Assistant's Role in Emergencies

Medical assistants and other staff members must stay up to date on the emergency plans of the office, facility, and community. These plans should be reviewed on a regularly scheduled basis. For major or catastrophic events, the disaster plan of the American Red Cross (**ARC**) should be considered. Local law enforcement and emergency management agencies direct rescue, treatment, and transportation efforts after catastrophic events. The standard policy is to treat the least seriously injured, also called the walking wounded, as soon as possible so they can assist in any rescue attempts.

After the appropriate training, you will be expected to render emergency care as directed. Your role will include:

- Applying CPR, AED, and the Heimlich maneuver.
- Bandaging and manipulating pressure points.
- Immobilizing head, neck, and limbs.

More advanced responsibilities will be determined by the physician and the clinical specialty.

Medical Terminology

abrasion—open wound in which the outer layer of skin is scraped away, leaving underlying tissue exposed

Ambu bag—bag-valve-mask unit used to provide ventilation to a non-breathing patient or to assist ventilations for a patient whose breathing (respiratory effort) is inadequate to support life

anaphylaxis—severe allergic reaction

avulsion—open wound in which skin or tissue is torn loose or pulled completely from underlying tissue

cyanosis—bluish tint in skin or mucous membrane, usually appearing in fingernail beds, oral mucous membranes, and circumoral tissue (tissue surrounding the mouth) and indicating excessive deoxygenated hemoglobin or reduced hemoglobin in the blood

epistaxis—nosebleed

hyperglycemia—condition in which blood glucose is elevated above normal

hypertension—continued elevation of blood pressure above normal

hyperthermia—condition in which body temperature is much higher than normal for a prolonged period of time

hypoglycemia—condition in which blood glucose is below normal

hypothermia—condition in which body temperature is below normal for a prolonged period of time

incision—open wound with smooth edges made with a knife or other sharp object

laceration—open wound in which the skin and underlying tissue are torn and skin integrity is broken

patent—open

sepsis—febrile state characterized by pathogens in the bloodstream

status epilepticus—continuous seizure activity

venous—pertaining to blood vessels that carry blood toward the heart

Abbreviations

ABCD—airway, breathing, circulation, defibrillation
AED—automatic external defibrillator
AHA—American Heart Association
ARC—American Red Cross

CPR—cardiopulmonary resuscitation
CVA—cerebrovascular accident/stroke
ED—emergency department
ETA—estimated time of arrival

LOC—level of consciousness
NS—normal saline
SOB—shortness of breath
TIA—transient ischemic attack

COMPETENCY SKILLS PERFORMANCE

Training in cardiopulmonary resuscitation (CPR), clearing an obstructed airway, and using an automated external defibrillator (AED) must be supervised by an instructor certified by the American Red Cross (ARC) or the American Heart Association (AHA). Because it is an educational requirement for medical assistants, certification training must be at the same level as that required for all health care employees. The general information presented in this chapter for CPR, obstructed airway, AED use, and first aid skills is superseded by AHA or ARC skill training and certification. For this chapter, you will be responsible for learning the following emergency procedures:

1. Adult rescue breathing and one-rescuer CPR.
2. Use of an automated external defibrillator (AED).
3. Response to an adult with an obstructed airway.
4. Administration of oxygen.
5. Application of a pressure bandage.
6. Application of triangular, figure 8, and tubular bandages.
7. Application of splints.

Emergency Resources

Those seeking medical care in an emergency have several options.

- During normal office hours, minor emergencies may be handled in a medical office. Some physician group practices may have an emergency clinic where emergency service is provided both during and after office hours.
- Freestanding clinics or urgent care centers provide emergency care during and after hours until late in the evening and often on weekends. However, many of these facilities do not offer critical care intervention.
- Hospitals usually have 24-hour emergency departments (**ED**s) that are open seven days a week. These "24-7 EDs" can usually handle most emergencies and transport patients to critical care trauma centers.
- Critical care centers, such as cardiac, burn, and surgical centers, have specialty trained physicians, surgeons, anesthesiologists, and other critical care staff on duty at all times.

You should be aware of the emergency care options available in your community.

EMS

The Emergency Medical System (EMS) was established to provide prehospital care and safe and prompt transportation to an emergency facility. Guidelines have been established for consistency in care and for ongoing evaluation of the system services. The role of the EMS is to:

- Provide on-the-scene intervention and treatment.
- Prepare the victim with injuries, trauma, or illness for transport.
- Transport the victim to the emergency facility.

Emergency transportation is accomplished by ambulance, helicopter, or fixed-wing aircraft (Figure 23-1 ◆). Once the patient is safely delivered to the receiving facility, the patient's care is passed to medical personnel at that facility.

Good Samaritan Laws

A health-care professional who volunteers in an emergency situation is generally protected by various state laws that hold the medical professional *not* legally liable when rendering first aid. These laws are often referred to as Good Samaritan laws. A health-care professional has a commitment to render care to a victim(s) according to the scope of his or her license, certification, or training. He or she must remain with the victim until relieved by another health-care professional with an equal or higher level of training. It is important that every health-care professional be aware of the laws in his or her own state and remember that the standard of care must be met within his or her license, certification, or training.

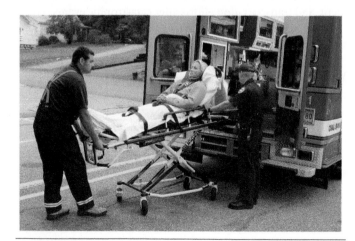

Figure 23-1 ◆ Ambulance transport

Caduceus Chronicle
A BRIEF HISTORY OF 911 AND EMS

In 1968 a universal system access number (911) was established through the efforts of Congressman J. Edward Roush. Initially available in Congressman Roush's hometown of Huntington, Indiana, 911 was so successful that he pushed to make it the emergency access number throughout the country. Almost the entire United States uses 911; some areas use "enhanced" 911, in which the phone number and address of the caller are displayed to the dispatcher. As a toll-free number, 911 may be called from any pay or cellular telephone at no charge. Using 911 under false pretenses is a crime that may be prosecuted in most states.

In 1973 the National Emergency Medical Services Systems Act was passed by Congress to oversee EMS across the country. Although the federal government continues to provide guidance and support, the states now have significant control of EMS systems. Standards for education and coordination of services have been established for providers.

Medical Office Preparedness

Most offices keep supplies specifically for emergencies. The office specialty often determines the choice of supplies.

Emergency Equipment and Supplies

Most offices have a crash cart fitted with equipment and supplies appropriate for the office specialty (Figure 23-2 ◆). For example, an allergy office has medications and injections to treat allergic responses.

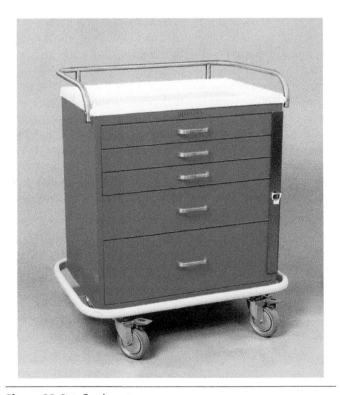

Figure 23-2 ◆ Crash cart

Crash Cart and Emergency Medical Box

The crash cart is usually kept in an emergency area with easy access from other areas of the office. It is mounted on wheels for easy transport of the equipment and various supplies to any part of the office. Respiratory aids on the cart should include the following:

- Oxygen tank with flow meter and wrench for opening the tank (Figure 23-3 ◆)
- Airways of all sizes, both nasal and oral
- Tubing
- Nasal cannula
- Oxygen masks, both adult and pediatric
- Ambu bags
- Resuscitation masks in a variety of sizes
- Bulb syringe for suctioning

The following IV supplies are also kept on the crash cart:

- IV fluids, including D5W, **NS,** D10W, and Ringer's lactate in 500-ml bags
- At least three butterflies of each size (#19, #21, #23, #25)
- At least three angiocaths of each size (#16, #18, #20, #22)
- Hemostats
- Tourniquets
- Iodine
- Alcohol preps
- IV tubing
- A collapsible IV pole

Keys to Success
LEGAL ISSUES CONCERNING CRASH CARTS

Offices with crash carts, AEDs, and emergency drug boxes face certain liability concerns. During office hours, office personnel trained in the use of emergency equipment and the administration of medications must be present. A physician must also be present during office hours to supervise the emergency and administer emergency medication (or supervise administration by qualified staff). Many offices choose to rely on EMS to provide advanced emergency care. The type of office, its location (proximity to a major medical center), and the availability of trained staff are decisive factors in determining what supplies and equipment to keep on hand.

Figure 23-3 ◆ Oxygen tank with flow meter and wrench

TABLE 23-1 DRUGS COMMONLY STOCKED IN AN EMERGENCY MEDICAL BOX

◼ Activated charcoal	◼ Nitroglycerin
◼ Atropine	◼ Normal saline
◼ Diphenhydramine	◼ Phenobarbital and diazepam
◼ Epinephrine	◼ Sodium bicarbonate
◼ Furosemide	◼ Solu-Cortef™
◼ Instant glucose	◼ Spirits of ammonia
◼ Insulin	◼ Syrup of Ipecac
◼ Lidocaine	◼ Verapamil
◼ Local anesthetics	

The emergency medical or drug box is kept on or close to the crash cart. Table 23-1 lists some of the drugs that may be stocked in an emergency medical box. Each office determines which drugs are appropriate for its practice, as established by emergency algorithms (Figure 23-4 ◆).

Other supplies usually stocked on a crash cart include alcohol prep pads, blood pressure cuffs (in standard, pediatric, and large sizes), a sphygmomanometer, a stethoscope, scissors, sterile 4 × 4s, sterile Kling™ gauze, pressure bandages in various sizes, sterile and examination gloves, prepackaged needles and syringes in assorted sizes, hypoallergenic tape, nasogastric tubes, a catheter tip syringe, water-soluble lubricant, a pen light, batteries, hot/cold packs, and a pen and note paper.

Emergency Intervention

Emergency intervention is called for in any situation that may be life-threatening (Table 23-2). The responder provides appropriate intervention and stays with the injured or ill person until more advanced care can be provided. Triage of emergency patients is a critical care issue.

Emergency Assessment

In any emergency, even if you are familiar with your office surroundings, the first step is to survey the scene. *Never* put yourself in harm's way. You could become injured or incapacitated. If the scene is safe, the next step is to conduct a primary survey of the injured or ill person, evaluating the airway, breathing, and circulation. If EMS services are required, call or designate an individual to call 911.

Do not move the victim of a fall or injury involving a sudden stop or acceleration, such as in a car. If the victim is conscious, tell him or her not to move, then introduce yourself and ask permission to render care. Ask the victim his or her name and use it. If you are given permission to proceed or if the victim is unconscious, immobilize the neck and possibly the spine. The victim must be log-rolled (moving the head, spine, and legs as a single unit to prevent additional spinal injury), or the spine must be immobilized and splinted. Ask the victim what happened and for medical information, including:

- The presence and location of pain.
- Any history of medical problems, such as diabetes or seizures.
- Last time the patient ate or drank.
- What medications were taken and when.
- Allergies.

Determine the cause of the injury, perform a rapid, focused trauma assessment and baseline vital signs, and plan for the victim's transport, if necessary.

? — Critical Thinking Question 23-1-
What questions should Ariko ask Brenna regarding the accident and the child's behavior?

Primary and secondary surveys follow. Check or recheck vital signs, including pulse, respirations, and blood pressure. Assess the skin for color, moisture, and temperature. Check for cuts, bruises, and any other signs of injury while assessing the victim from head to toe. Examine the pupils of the eyes for reactivity and equality of size, then the ears, nose, and mouth for fluid drainage. Palpate the sides of the victim's neck for pain, tenderness, or injury, then the shoulders, collarbones, rib cage, and chest. Feel the patient's abdomen in all quadrants for any signs of tenderness or rigidity. Check the arms, hips, legs, and feet.

In the event of sudden illness, acute pain, bleeding, or reduced level of consciousness in the medical office, move or assist the patient to an examination room where an assessment can be made. As with a trauma victim, the severely ill person should be assessed following established office guidelines. Evaluate the person's mental status. If the patient is responsive, obtain a rapid medical history. If the victim is unresponsive, quickly do a physical assessment and take vital signs. If the physician is unavailable

TABLE 23-2 EMERGENCY INTERVENTION

Life-Threatening Condition	Not Life-Threatening: Immediate Intervention	Not-Life Threatening: Intervention as Soon as Possible
◼ extreme **SOB** (airway or breathing problems) ◼ cardiac arrest ◼ severe, uncontrolled bleeding ◼ head injuries ◼ poisoning ◼ open chest or abdominal wounds ◼ shock ◼ severe burns, including face, hands, feet, and genitals ◼ potential neck injuries	◼ decreased levels of consciousness ◼ chest pain ◼ seizures ◼ major or multiple fractures ◼ neck injuries ◼ severe eye injuries ◼ burns not on face, hands, feet, or genitals	◼ severe vomiting and diarrhea, especially in the very young and the elderly ◼ minor injuries ◼ sprains ◼ strains ◼ simple fractures

PATIENT ASSESSMENT

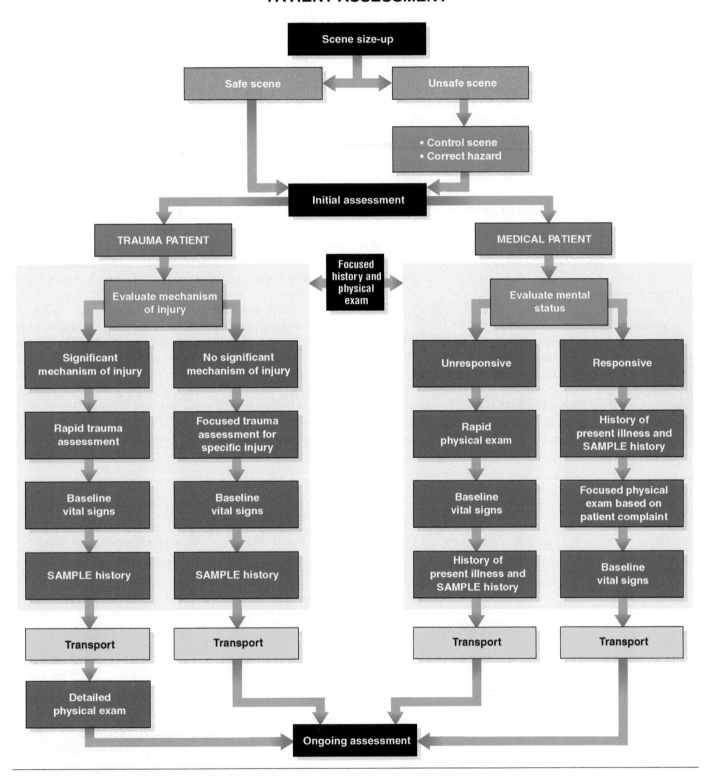

Figure 23-4 ◆ Example of emergency algorithm

Source: Limmer, Daniel; O'Keefe, Michael F.; Dickinson, Edward V.; Grant, Harvey; Murray, Bob; Bergeron, David J., Emergency Care, 10th Edition, ©2005. Reprinted by permission of Pearson Education, Inc. Upper Saddle River, NJ.

to provide direction and orders, call EMS, then prepare the victim for transport to an emergency facility.

As a rescuer, remain calm and in control of the situation. Office personnel not involved in the emergency response should return to work. One person should be designated to keep family members informed of the situation. Both the patient and the family need emotional support. If necessary, maintain crowd control. Another person should be designated to document or take notes about all the events. Record vital signs, times, symptoms and signs elicited, and any action or intervention, then complete an incident report.

OSHA Guidelines

OSHA guidelines apply to emergency as well as routine medical office procedures.

- Wear examination gloves when handling body fluids and infectious materials and when hands come in contact with mucous membranes, non-intact skin, or contaminated instruments or equipment.
- Dispose of any biohazardous materials in an appropriate waste receptacle.
- Wash your hands immediately after removing gloves and before caring for another patient.
- Wear additional PPE, such as a face shield or mask, whenever there is a risk of exposure.
- If you perform **CPR,** use a face mask barrier device.
- If your hands, arms, or any uncovered skin come into contact with blood or body fluids, wash with soap and water immediately. Flush mucous membranes, such as those in the mouth, eyes, and nose, immediately with water.
- To prevent accidental or careless exposure, *do not* eat, drink, or touch your face during emergencies without first washing your hands.
- Follow sharps precautions when using syringes and needles, and handle accidents involving glass carefully and without direct contact to avoid injury.
- Follow the correct sanitization, disinfection, and sterilization procedures when cleaning surfaces and instruments.

CPR, AED, and Obstructed Airway

Respiratory and cardiac arrest may be caused by an occluded airway, electrocution, shock, drowning, heart attack, trauma, **anaphylaxis,** drugs, poisoning, or traumatic head or chest injury. Intervention must be immediate if resuscitation is to be successful. For individuals experiencing acute chest pain, loss of consciousness, or respiratory arrest, follow CPR protocol.

Guidelines are similar for respiratory arrest, cardiac arrest, and obstructed airway but vary somewhat according to age group. Table 23-3 lists the major differences in the performance of CPR-related skills as defined by the **AHA.** Early access to EMS is important. Access for the adult victim is initiated by calling 911 as soon as it has been determined that the victim is unconscious and not breathing. With children and infants, EMS access is made after one minute of CPR. The sequence normally followed is airway, breathing, circulation, and defibrillation (**ABCD**).

TABLE 23-3 ADULT, CHILD, AND INFANT CPR SKILLS			
CPR Skill	**Adult: 8+ years**	**Child: 1 year–puberty (approximately 12–14 years)**	**Infant: under 1 year**
EMS access by calling 911 and giving emergency information	If victim found to be unresponsive, immediately activate EMS. If asphyxiation suspected, first perform 2 minutes of CPR (or 5 cycles), then activate EMS.	If sudden collapse is witnessed, immediately activate EMS. Otherwise perform 2 minutes of CPR (5 cycles), then activate EMS.	If sudden collapse is witnessed, immediately activate EMS. Otherwise perform 2 minutes of CPR (5 cycles), then activate EMS.
Assessment of unresponsiveness	Shake the shoulders.	Shake the shoulders.	Snap or poke the feet. Do *not* shake the shoulders.
Rescue breathing rate of 1 second long, normal breath until chest rises	10–12 breaths per minute or one breath every 5–6 seconds	12–20 breaths per minute or one breath every 3–5 seconds	12–20 breaths per minute or one breath every 3–5 seconds
Obstructed airway foreign object sweep	Slide a finger into one side of the mouth and sweep it toward the other side.	No blind sweep	No blind sweep
Pulse check location	Carotid	Carotid	Brachial
Compression technique	One hand linked over second hand, with heel of second hand on sternum	Heel of one hand on sternum	Single rescuer: two fingertips on sternum Two rescuers: two thumbs touching on sternum and hand encircling chest and back technique
Compression location	Center of chest 2–3 finger widths above sternum notch	Center of chest between nipples	Center of chest, just below nipple line
Compression depth	1-1/2—2''	1/2 to 1/3 depth of chest	1/2 to 1/3 depth of chest
Compression rate	100 per minute	100 per minute	100 per minute
Compression ratio to rescue breathing	Single rescuer: 30:2 Two rescuers: 30:2	Single rescuer: 30:2 Two rescuers: 15:2	Single rescuer: 30:2 Two rescuers: 15:2

Airway

First, roll the victim onto his or her back, using the log-roll technique. Next, assess the unconscious victim for responsiveness. With an adult or child, shake the shoulders and ask, "Are you choking?" With an infant, poke or snap the feet. Do not shake the shoulders, as shaking may cause Shaken Baby Syndrome.

If the victim does not respond, check the airway. With an adult, child, or infant, place the palm of one hand on the forehead and two or three fingers under the lower jawbone to gently tilt the head backward (Figure 23-5 ◆). If cervical or other spinal injuries are suspected, a jaw-thrust maneuver must be used to open the airway (Figure 23-6 ◆). When the airway is opened, the victim may begin spontaneous breathing because the tongue is lifted from covering the trachea. While keeping close to the victim's mouth, listen for air movement, look for chest movement, and feel for air movement on your cheek. If you do not feel air on your cheek, remove any clothing from the victim's neck. It is possible the victim has a tracheotomy, a surgically created opening for breathing, which may be the reason you do not feel air movement.

Breathing

If you have looked, listened, and felt for breathing and found none, pinch the patient's nose shut, seal your lips tightly around the patient's mouth, and deliver two breaths, each lasting 1 to 1-1/2 seconds. You will know the artificial ventilation

Keys to Success
SHAKEN BABY SYNDROME

Shaken Baby Syndrome is the term given to the act of shaking an infant or child without supporting the head and neck. It can result in intracerebral bleeding from the repeated striking of the brain against the inside of the skull. This trauma causes vessels to rupture and bleed within and around the brain tissue. Bleeding and the resulting swelling exert pressure on the brain tissue. Diminished blood flow, nutrition, and oxygen comprise a major insult to the child's brain that lead to severe brain damage and/or death.

is effective if the victim's chest rises with each delivered breath. For a victim with a tracheotomy, it may be necessary to close the mouth and nose and administer breaths to the tracheotomy.

Keys to Success
USING A MASK

In the medical setting, a mask is used to deliver breaths and serves as a barrier device to prevent transmission of infectious disease. The mask is often attached to an **Ambu bag** for delivery of artificial ventilations and oxygen (Figure 23-7 ◆). (The use of an Ambu bag requires CPR training.) The Ambu bag is more effective when one person holds the mask to the victim's face and the second person squeezes the bag.

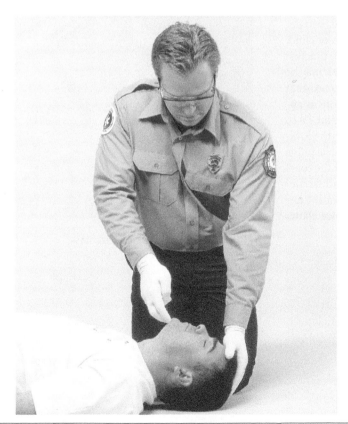
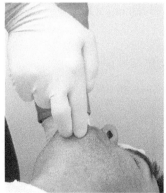

Figure 23-5 ◆ Head-tilt, chin-lift maneuver

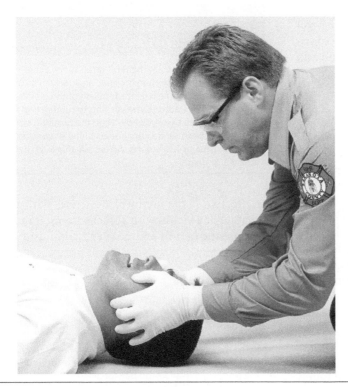
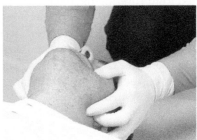

Figure 23-6 ◆ Jaw-thrust maneuver

Circulation

According to the most recent AHA Basic Life Support guidelines, the rescuer should check for signs of circulation, defined as pulse, color and warmth of skin, and victim movement. After you deliver breaths to the victim, check the pulse. In an adult or child, feel the carotid pulse in the neck. In an infant, feel the brachial pulse. Count the pulse for at least 10 seconds, because it may be erratic and weak. If the pulse is very weak, erratic, or nonexistent and there are no signs of circulation, begin compressions as appropriate to the victim's age (Figures 23-8 ◆, 23-9 ◆, and 23-10 ◆). If a second rescuer is available, instruct him or her to monitor compression quality by checking the carotid or brachial pulse. If your compressions are effective, a pulse will be felt. If the compressions do not generate a palpable pulse, the second rescuer should take over the compressions in two-man CPR or the entire sequence in one-man CPR. The one-man sequence allows the original rescuer to rest or get help.

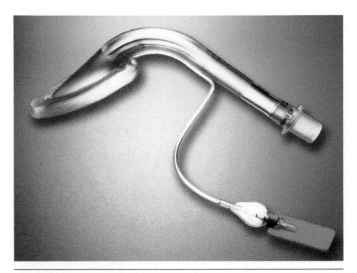

Figure 23-7 ◆ Ambu laryngeal mask.
Ambu Inc., Glen Burnie, MD

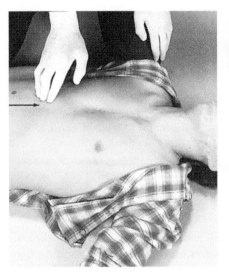
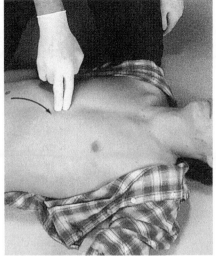
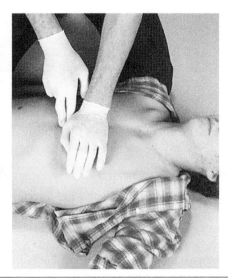

Figure 23-8 ◆ Compressions for an adult

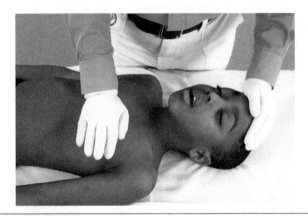

Figure 23-9 ◆ Compressions for a child

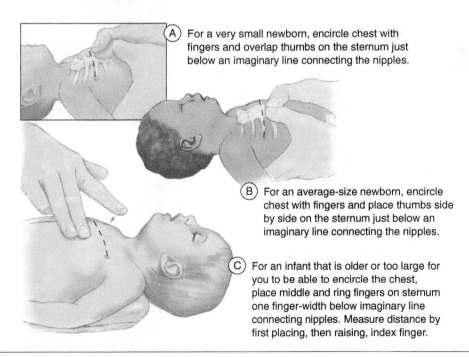

(A) For a very small newborn, encircle chest with fingers and overlap thumbs on the sternum just below an imaginary line connecting the nipples.

(B) For an average-size newborn, encircle chest with fingers and place thumbs side by side on the sternum just below an imaginary line connecting the nipples.

(C) For an infant that is older or too large for you to be able to encircle the chest, place middle and ring fingers on sternum one finger-width below imaginary line connecting nipples. Measure distance by first placing, then raising, index finger.

Figure 23-10 ◆ Compressions for an infant

PROCEDURE 23-1 Perform Adult Rescue Breathing and One-Rescuer CPR

Theory

Chest compressions and rescue breathing are performed on adults with an absence of respiratory and cardiac function. For the third time since 1992, the American Heart Association has changed the guidelines for CPR and rescue breathing. In 1992, rescuers were told to perform 15 chest compression for every 2 breaths given until a second rescuer arrived, at which point the compressions switched to 5 compressions to every 1 breath. In 2000, the AHA revised these guidelines to 15 compressions for every 2 breaths given, regardless of how many rescuers are present. In 2006, the AHA changed the guidelines again in an effort to simplify the CPR process. These new guidelines require rescuers to give 2 breaths for every 30 chest compressions. Laypersons are advised *not* to attempt to check the patient's pulse or attempt rescue breathing. Instead, laypersons should concentrate on applying correct chest compressions.

Using a mouth guard with a one-way valve prevents vomit or other body fluids from contaminating the rescuer's mouth.

Materials

- approved mannequin
- gloves
- ventilator mask
- mouth guard

Competency

(**Conditions**) With the necessary materials, (**Task**) you will be able to administer rescue breathing for an adult and one-rescuer CPR for an adult (**Standards**) correctly, within the time frame designated by the instructor.

1. Assess the victim and determine if help is needed. Shout "Are you OK?" while gently shaking the victim's shoulders.
2. If there is no response, assess the ABCs. Airway: Perform a head-tilt chin lift, or, if a neck injury is suspected, a jaw thrust (Figure 23-11 ◆). Look and feel for breath and chest

movements (Figure 23-12 ◆). Attempt to get another person to call 911. If you are alone, begin the rescue sequence for 1 minute and then attempt to call yourself. If gloves are available, put them on. If you have a ventilator mask, place it on the victim.

3. If breathing is absent, put on a mouth guard and administer two rescue breaths (Figure 23-13 ◆). If your breaths do not cause the chest to rise, tilt the head again and make a second attempt.
4. If the breath still does not enter the chest, proceed to the Heimlich maneuver for unconscious victims.
5. If the breaths cause the chest to rise, assess the patient's circulation by feeling for a pulse at the carotid artery (Figure 23-14 ◆). If you feel a pulse, begin rescue breathing. Administer 1 breath every 5 seconds, or 10–12 every minute. After 1 minute, reassess the victim for breathing and pulse.
6. If you do not feel a pulse, begin chest compressions. Kneel at the victim's side. Find the sternum and place the heel of one hand 2–3 fingers' width above that space (Figure 23-15 ◆).
7. Place your other hand on top of the first hand, making sure to lift your fingers off the chest, using only the heels of your hands to administer compressions.

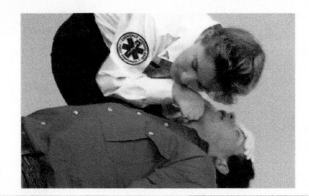

Figure 23-12 ◆ Look and feel for breath and chest movements.

Figure 23-11 ◆ Establish an open airway.

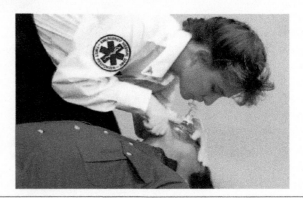

Figure 23-13 ◆ Administer two rescue breaths.

PROCEDURE 23-1 Perform Adult Rescue Breathing and One-Rescuer CPR *(continued)*

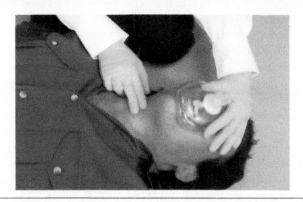

Figure 23-14 ◆ Assess the patient's circulation by feeling for a pulse at the carotid artery.

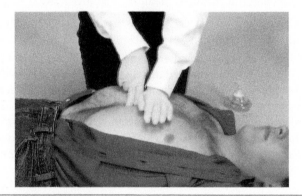

Figure 23-15 ◆ Locate the site for chest compressions.

8. Keeping your shoulders directly over your hands, compress the chest 1-1/2 to 2 inches, then allow the sternum to relax (Figure 23-16 ◆). Do not lift your hands off the chest.

9. Continue to compress the chest a total of 30 times, then administer 2 breaths.
10. Repeat this sequence for 4 total cycles. Reassess the victim.
11. If necessary, continue CPR until pulse and breathing return or you are relieved by more advanced medical personnel.

Patient Education

Advise the patient to follow up with his or her personal physician after release from the EMS.

Charting Example

08/05/XX 7:30 PM Patient found collapsed in bathroom and unresponsive. 911 call placed and CPR started. EMS arrived in approximately 10 minutes and took over care. Patient was transferred to Deaconess Medical Center. Vivian Nagle, RMA

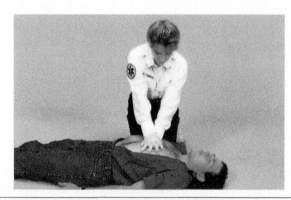

Figure 23-16 ◆ Compress the chest 1-1/2 inches, then allow the sternum to relax.

Defibrillation

Automated external defibrillation (**AED**) is highly effective when provided immediately after or within minutes of an adult cardiac arrest. Most cardiac arrests in adults are related to fatal electrical arrhythmias of the heart and are correctable with defibrillators. The defibrillator gives verbal directions to the rescuer or rescue team that are easy and safe to follow. AED is not applied to infants.

PROCEDURE 23-2 Use an Automated External Defibrillator (AED)

Theory

The use of AEDs as lifesaving devices is becoming more and more common. AEDs are now found in doctors' offices, malls, airplanes, and private residences (Figure 23-17 ◆). An AED works by sending an electrical current through the myocardium of the heart, briefly causing the heart to stop and allowing the heart's natural pacemaker to take over. The goal is for the heart to resume function. All AEDs function in the same manner.

The AED is brought by a second- or third-party rescuer after the initial chest compressions and rescue breathing have begun.

Materials
■ AED machine
■ patient chart

Competency

(**Conditions**) With the necessary materials, (**Task**) you will use an AED (**Standards**) correctly within the time frame designated by the instructor.

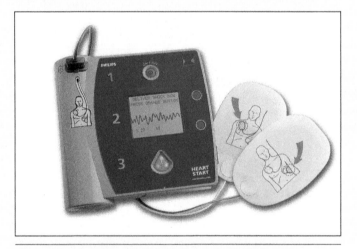

Figure 23-17 ◆ Philips Medical Systems SMART Biphasic Automated External Defibrillator, Model Heart Start FR2+.
Reprinted by permission of Philips Medical Systems.

1. Place the AED next to the victim's left ear. This position allows the rescuers clear access to the chest and airway for continued rescue measures.
2. Turn the AED on and follow the voice prompts.
3. You will be prompted to attach the electrode pads to the patient's chest, on the sternum and at the apex of the heart, following the diagram for correct placement.
4. Next, you will be directed to allow the machine to analyze the heart rhythm to determine if it is a shockable rhythm. CPR should cease while the machine is analyzing.
5. The machine will begin a charging sequence prior to shocking and warn rescuers to stand back. The voice prompt will then tell you to press the "shock" button to administer the electrical current to the patient.
6. If the machine indicates "No shock is advised," assess the patient for breathing and circulation. Continue CPR as needed until advanced medical personnel arrive.

Patient Education

If a friend or family member of the patient is present at the time of rescue, you will need to help that person remain calm and out of the way so that advanced rescue personnel can treat the victim. It is also helpful if you can explain to friends or family members what is happening and to what hospital the victim will be transported. Be careful not to make comforting statements that may not be accurate, such as "He'll be all right" or "She's going to be just fine."

Charting Example

11/25/XX 3:30 PM Patient found in stairwell, unresponsive, with absence of pulse and respirations. 911 protocol initiated with 2 rescuer CPR. Third rescuer initiated AED response and patient was analyzed for shockable rhythm. CPR and AED shocks administered a total of 8 cycles prior to advanced medical support arriving. Patient released to EMS care and transferred to Sacred Heart Medical Center. Martin Cowan, CMA

Guidelines have recently been established for the use of AED on children 1 to 8 years old. AED may be used after one minute of CPR. It is recommended that child defibrillator pads and cables, rather than adult, be used; however, adult pads can be used if the pads do not overlap on the chest.

Heimlich Maneuver

An obstructed airway prevents the movement of air into or out of the respiratory tract. Certain disease conditions, such as anaphylactic shock or epiglotitis, can cause an anatomical blockage, but most obstructions are caused by foreign objects. With small children, the cause is usually food or small toys. With adults, an obstructed airway may be the result of:

■ Not chewing large pieces of food properly.
■ Talking too excitedly or laughing too much while eating.
■ Drinking alcohol before and during eating.
■ Choking on body or extraneous fluids, such as vomit or blood.

You should know how to respond to the following choking scenarios:

1. Partial airway obstruction with good air exchange: The victim is conscious, is capable of speaking, and is making a strong effort to cough.

Keys to Success
EFFECTIVE ABCD

Breaths that are not successfully delivered do not help the victim. If you do not see the chest rise and fall with the first delivery of artificial ventilation, reposition the head and neck and attempt ventilation again. If it is still unsuccessful, change the ABCD sequence to obstructed airway. Call for help, reposition the head, and apply 6 to 10 abdominal thrusts to the patient's abdomen. If the obstruction is not cleared, perform a finger sweep of the adult mouth to dislodge any foreign object that may be occluding the airway. It does not help to proceed from artificial ventilation to a pulse check and compressions if the airway is not partially or totally open and oxygen cannot be delivered to the lungs and bloodstream. *Do not* proceed with the ABCD sequence unless you have restored an open airway to deliver artificial ventilations.

If you find a pulse, provide breaths only. Monitor the victim's pulse every few minutes. If you can still feel the pulse, continue to provide only breaths. If the pulse ceases, continue breaths and begin compressions.

2. Partial airway obstruction with poor air exchange: The victim is conscious but is weakening in clinical condition and ability to cough.
3. Total obstructed airway: The victim is unconscious, and there are no signs of breathing or the victim is unable to vocalize.

The conscious choking adult may use the universal choking sign—crossing the hands at the throat—to signal for help (Figure 23-18 ◆).

A partial airway obstruction may allow some air into the respiratory tract and is characterized by a high-pitched noise from the victim. The victim may be able to cough and expel the foreign object. *Do not* pat the victim on the back—it may lodge the object in the airway. If a phone call comes in to the medical office and the caller states, "My child is not breathing" and you hear the child crying in the background, the airway is not obstructed. Anytime the victim can speak or cry, air is moving in and out of the airway.

As a rescuer, ask the victim, "Can you speak?" If the victim responds by shaking the head, the airway is obstructed and immediate intervention is required. Perform the Heimlich maneuver for the adult or child (or abdominal thrusts for the supine victim) and back blows and chest thrusts for the infant

Figure 23-18 ◆ The universal choking sign

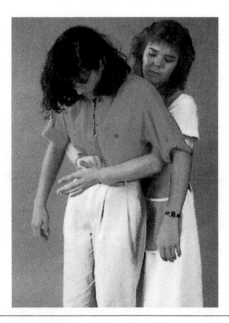

Figure 23-19 ◆ Heimlich maneuver

(Figure 23-19 ◆). You should also use the Heimlich maneuver if the victim's coughing weakens or if the victim cannot speak.

To perform the Heimlich maneuver, stand behind the victim and put your arms around his or her chest halfway between the xiphoid process of the sternum and the umbilicus. Make a fist with one hand, with the thumb turned into the fist. Wrap your other hand around the fisted hand and pull the fisted hand in and up toward the diaphragm. This force against the diaphragm is usually sufficient to loosen the foreign object and propel it out of the mouth. If the victim becomes unconscious, ease him or her to the floor to prevent any additional injuries, and proceed with the technique described below for unconscious obstructed airway. The Heimlich (or abdominal thrusts in the supine victim) is adjusted for infants, very obese people, and visibly pregnant women to chest thrusts that are identical to the chest compressions of CPR.

If the victim is unconscious, you will need to add artificial ventilations to the obstructed airway procedure. If the obstruction is loosened during the procedure, it may be possible to get oxygen around the object and into the bloodstream. Reposition the airway each time ventilations are attempted.

Keys to Success
SAVING CHILDREN AND INFANTS

Blind sweeps of the mouth are *never* attempted on children and infants. A child's or infant's airway is narrow, and it is possible to push the foreign object farther into the respiratory tract. You can look in the mouth of a child or infant for an object that can be removed.

Use chest thrusts followed by back blows for obstructed airways in infants and in children in an upright position (Figure 23-20 ◆). Attempt ventilations, reattempt ventilations, then return to chest thrusts and back blows. For children in a supine position, use a similar sequence, but use abdominal thrusts only.

Abdominal thrusts are done by placing the child on a flat surface. Place the middle and index fingers of both hands below the rib cage and above the navel. Make a quick upward thrust. *Do not* squeeze. Repeat until the object is expelled.

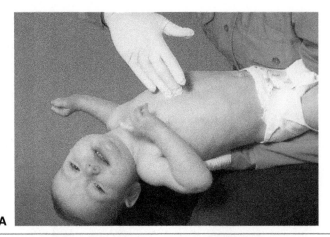
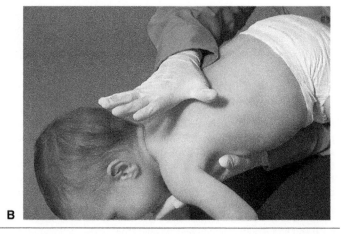

A   B

Figure 23-20 ◆ (A) Use chest thrusts followed by (B) back blows.

PROCEDURE 23-3 **Respond to an Adult with an Obstructed Airway**

Theory

A bolus of food is the most common object adults choke on. When the food is lodged in the upper airway, the person may put his or her hands around the throat, the universal sign of choking, to let bystanders know he or she cannot breathe properly. If the person can wheeze, make a high-pitched sound, cough, or speak, do not take any action. Instead call 911 and encourage the person to continue to cough forcefully to try to dislodge the object. If the person is unable to speak or cough, he or she is in immediate danger and action must be taken.

It is important that the rescuer call 911 even if the victim's airway is not completely blocked or the Heimlich maneuver was successful. Once the object has been expelled, the throat is likely to continue to swell as a result of the irritant, so the victim should be assessed in an emergency room.

Materials

- approved mannequin
- gloves
- ventilation mask with one-way valve for unconscious victim

Competency

(**Conditions**) With the necessary materials, (**Task**) you will administer the Heimlich maneuver to an adult (**Standards**) correctly within the time frame designated by the instructor.

1. Once it has been established that the victim is choking, with no air exchange, direct someone to call 911 and shout, "Are you choking?" or "Can you speak?" If the answer is no—as indicated by a head shake—tell the victim you are going to begin emergency treatment.
2. Stand behind the victim with your feet slightly apart, placing one foot between the victim's feet and one to the outside. This stance will give you greater stability, and if the

victim should pass out, you can safely guide him or her to the ground by sliding him or her down your thigh.
3. Place the index finger of one hand at the person's navel or belt buckle. If the victim is a pregnant woman, place your finger above the enlarged uterus.
4. Make a fist with your other hand and place it, thumb side to victim, above your other hand. If the person is very pregnant, the uterus is pushing the stomach and other internal organs under the rib cage and you may have to do chest compressions.
5. Place your marking hand over your curled fist and begin to give quick inward and upward thrusts (Figure 23-21 ◆).
6. There is no set number of thrusts to give to an adult who remains conscious. Continue to give thrusts until the object is removed *or* the victim becomes unconscious.
7. If the victim becomes unconscious, gently lower him or her to the ground.

Figure 23-21 ◆ Deliver a firm thrust into the patient's abdomen in an upward direction toward you.

PROCEDURE 23-3 **Respond to an Adult with an Obstructed Airway** *(continued)*

8. If gloves are available, put them on, open the victim's mouth, and perform a finger sweep to try to remove the foreign object (Figure 23-22 ◆).

9. If the object cannot be removed, perform a head-tilt chin lift (in case of possible neck injury, use a jaw thrust) and administer two rescue breaths.

10. If the air does not cause the chest to rise, tilt the head again and attempt two more breaths.

11. If your attempts are unsuccessful, straddle the victim's thighs and place the heel of one hand 2 to 3 finger widths above the navel and place your other hand on top, interlocking the fingers.

12. Give five quick inward and upward abdominal thrusts (Figure 23-23 ◆). If there is a second rescuer available the primary rescuer should stay at the head for rescue breaths while the second rescuer performs the abdominal thrusts.

13. Move to the head of the victim and perform another finger sweep. If the object has not been expelled into the mouth, tilt the head again and attempt two more rescue breaths.

14. Continue the cycle of five thrusts, finger sweep, and two breaths until the object is expelled or advanced medical personnel arrive to relieve you.

15. The victim may lose the pulse, but you cannot proceed to CPR chest compressions until the foreign airway obstruction is cleared.

Patient Education

If the object has been successfully removed and the patient did not lose consciousness, the patient may feel he or she no longer needs medical treatment. As a rescuer you must insist that the victim seek medical attention anyway. The lodged object may have caused swelling in the lining of the esophagus, constricting the throat and impairing the breathing.

Charting Example

10/25/XX 11:30 AM Jason Jones, CMA, exhibited signs of choking at lunch. Jason grabbed his throat and was unable to cough or make noise. Tina Muller, RMA, alerted the physician and placed a call to 911. Abdominal thrusts were given until the piece of apple was expelled. EMS arrived and checked Jason for signs of throat irritation and swelling. Janice Walker, CMA

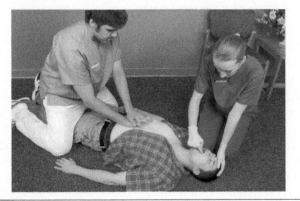

Figure 23-22 ◆ Open the victim's mouth and perform a finger sweep.

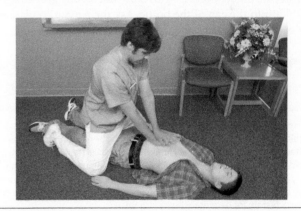

Figure 23-23 ◆ Straddle the victim's thighs and place the heel of one hand 2 to 3 finger widths above the navel and place your other hand on top, interlocking the fingers.

For an unresponsive, nonbreathing adult with an obstructed airway, the sequence is:

- Performing abdominal thrusts (chest thrusts if extremely obese or clearly pregnant).
- Sweeping the mouth.
- Attempting ventilations.
- Reattempting ventilations.
- Returning to abdominal thrusts.

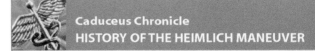

Caduceus Chronicle
HISTORY OF THE HEIMLICH MANEUVER

In 1974, Henry Heimlich (born 1920), a Cincinnati physician and thoracic surgeon, developed the concept of applying a squeezing pressure under the rib cage to dislodge a foreign object stuck in the tracheal airway. The method was later named for him—Heimlich maneuver. It is often referred to as an abdominal thrust to clear an obstructed airway.

Chest Pain

Heart attacks are the leading cause of death for both men and women. The patient experiencing chest pain may display various symptoms. The primary complaint will be pain in the middle or left side of the chest, described as sharp, stabbing, crushing, squeezing, or aching. The pain may radiate to the left arm, to the back, or up the neck. Sometimes the pain is brought on by exertion, but other times onset is sudden and unexplained. Other symptoms are nausea, weakness, SOB, apprehension, and the feeling of impending doom. The skin may be clammy, moist, pale, or cyanotic. Denial is common, as the individual tries to explain the pain as heartburn or indigestion.

The first intervention is to have the individual stop what he or she is doing and sit down, with the feet elevated if possible. Request help and/or call EMS, and inform the physician. If oxygen is available, administer it according to office protocol by nasal cannula at six to eight liters per minute until the physician or emergency personnel arrive.

If the victim has previously been diagnosed with angina and has nitroglycerin tablets, insert one tablet under the tongue.

Administering Nitroglycerin

Nitroglycerin is a vasodilator. Wear gloves when handling a patient's nitroglycerin tabs to prevent your own blood vessels from suddenly dilating (Figure 23-24 ◆). Be sure to check the expiration date on the bottle. If gloves are not readily available, put a tablet into the cap of the bottle. Ask the patient to place the tablet under his or her tongue or to raise the tongue so you can

Keys to Success
SYMPTOMS OF HEART ATTACK IN WOMEN

A heart attack in a woman is usually more difficult to diagnose because typical chest pain is not described. A burning sensation in the chest is often dismissed as heartburn. Flu-like symptoms of nausea, clamminess, cold sweats, and vomiting are common. Unexplained fatigue, weakness, or dizziness may also occur. A woman is therefore more likely to ignore the symptoms. It is important to monitor symptoms and check the patient's history for hereditary heart disease.

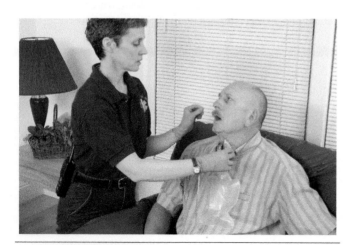

Figure 23-24 ◆ Administering nitroglycerin tablets

Figure 23-25 ◆ Self-administration of nitroglycerin tablets

drop the tablet there (Figure 23-25 ◆). Ask the patient if the tablet is "fizzling" under the tongue. A fizzle indicates the tablet is dissolving. Tablets may be administered every 5 minutes up to three doses. If the pain is not relieved, inform the physician and/or EMS on the scene.

If a patient calls complaining of chest pain:

- Keep the caller on the line while asking for help from another office staff member.
- Write down the caller's name and location (if someone is calling for the victim, ask the caller for the victim's name and location).
- Advise the caller that you are calling EMS.
- Instruct the caller to stay on the line with you.

The other staff member contacts EMS to relay the information and to enter the victim's name into the EMS system. Remain calm and assure the caller that help is on the way. The EMS dispatcher will keep you advised of the location of the EMS unit dispatched and an estimated time of arrival (**ETA**). End the phone conversation with EMS *only* when directed to do so or when EMS personnel have arrived on the scene. In all emergency situations, record times and interventions and add this documentation to the patient's chart.

Another cardiac emergency is congestive heart failure (CHF). The patient complains of SOB, swelling in the feet and hands, palpitations, and rapid heartbeat. He or she may appear anxious, cyanotic, diaphoretic, and slightly confused. Inform the physician immediately. Take the patient to an examination room and seat him or her on the examination table. If oxygen is available and the physician orders it, administer oxygen according to orders. Usually EMS is called to transport the patient to an emergency facility. Monitor and record vital signs, any medication administered, and treatment performed.

Respiratory Distress

Respiratory distress may be a reaction to a long-term debilitating disease, such as chronic pulmonary obstructive disease (COPD), or to an emergency situation, such as anaphylactic response to medication. It can also be the result of other disease processes, including obstructive conditions, such as asthma, chronic bronchitis, and emphysema, pneumonia, and acute pulmonary edema. Conscious control is usually not a factor in respiratory distress. Being unable to get enough oxygen causes extreme anxiety, and medical staff should be prepared to give the patient emotional support.

Signs and symptoms vary, depending on the cause. One of the most serious is an occluded airway that causes the patient to grasp at the neck and attempt to cough. Unconsciousness soon follows, then cardiac arrest. Other conditions of respiratory distress may cause symptoms such as:

- Acute anxiety with gasping breaths
- Bradypnea, abnormally slow breathing (fewer than eight breaths a minute)
- **Cyanosis**
- Failure of the chest to rise and fall
- Nasal flaring
- Pursing of the lips
- Noisy breathing (snoring, gurgling, wheezing, rattling, sternal retraction, stridor)
- Tachypnea, abnormally rapid breathing (more than 24 breaths per minute)

If respiratory distress is the result of a known diagnosis, the patient will need medical follow-up with an emergency facility and/or physician, depending on the severity or change in the condition. If respiratory distress is caused by an obstructed airway, the appropriate sequence for obstructed airway should be initiated.

Shortness of Breath (SOB)

Any individual experiencing SOB needs immediate intervention. A **patent** airway is necessary to support life. If the person can speak, air is moving in and out. Ask the patient about the onset for difficult breathing and what activity caused it. This information helps to identify the problem.

The patient experiencing SOB may be gasping for air, pale or cyanotic, and may exhibit nasal flaring and extreme anxiety (Figure 23-26 ◆). Usually the patient sits in an upright position and may be quite weak. If the airway is partially obstructed, the patient may cough in an attempt to clear the passages. It the patient is not in a sitting position, help him or her to a sitting position with support to the back. Call out for assistance.

Hyperventilation

Hyperventilation is quick, shallow breathing or rapid, deep breathing that results in decreasing carbon dioxide in the blood, dilation of blood vessels, and lowered blood pressure. The patient feels faint or light-headed and may experience:

- Chest tightness
- Cardiac palpitations
- Rapid pulse
- Deep sighing breaths
- Anxiety
- Tetany

Inform the physician and encourage the patient to breathe slowly. Have the patient breathe into an oxygen mask (not connected to any oxygen), block one nostril, or breathe into a brown paper bag. One of these methods is usually effective. This condition can generally be resolved quickly and without further intervention.

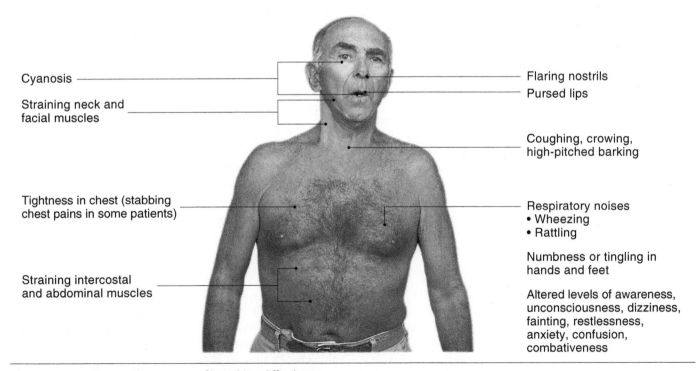

Cyanosis

Straining neck and facial muscles

Tightness in chest (stabbing chest pains in some patients)

Straining intercostal and abdominal muscles

Flaring nostrils
Pursed lips

Coughing, crowing, high-pitched barking

Respiratory noises
• Wheezing
• Rattling

Numbness or tingling in hands and feet

Altered levels of awareness, unconsciousness, dizziness, fainting, restlessness, anxiety, confusion, combativeness

Figure 23-26 ◆ Signs and symptoms of breathing difficulty

PROCEDURE 23-4 Administer Oxygen

Theory

Patients with chronic lung conditions often require oxygen therapy to breathe more easily. The delivery of oxygen helps improve the status of most patients' breathing. However, patients with severe lung conditions such as emphysema, COPD, and lung cancer should be transferred to a hospital immediately.

Materials

- portable oxygen tank
- pressure regulator
- oxygen flow meter
- sterile, prepackaged, disposable nasal cannula with tubing
- gloves
- oximeter
- patient chart

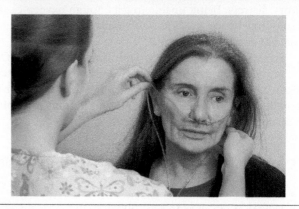

Figure 23-27 ◆ Adjust the tubing around the back of the patient's ears.

Competency

(**Conditions**) With the necessary materials, (**Task**) you will be able to administer oxygen therapy to an adult (**Standards**) correctly within the time frame designated by the instructor.

1. Gather all needed equipment.
2. Wash your hands.
3. Identify the patient and confirm the physician's order for oxygen therapy.
4. Check the pressure reading on the oxygen tank to make sure it has enough oxygen in it.
5. Start the flow of oxygen by opening the cylinder.
6. Attach the cannula tubing to the flow meter. Adjust the oxygen flow to the physician's order.
7. Hold the cannula tips over the inside of your wrist, without touching the skin, to determine if the oxygen is flowing.
8. Don gloves, if necessary. You may prefer to wear gloves with patients who demonstrate a chronic cough, nasal drip, or other situation of potential exposure.
9. Place the tips of the nasal cannula into the patient's nostrils. Wrap the tubing behind the patient's ears (Figure 23-27 ◆).
10. Instruct the patient to breathe normally through the mouth and nose. Some patients instinctively hold their breath or avoid breathing through the nose when an object is placed in the nostrils.

11. Check the patient's oxygen level with an oximeter. Place the probe over the index finger and record the reading. If necessary, have the patient take a short walk to verify that the oxygen flow rate is sufficient for activity.
12. Document the procedure in the patient's chart.

Patient Education

Instruct the patient on the safety protocol for oxygen use, such as refraining from smoking, not laying the oxygen container on its side, and other manufacturer instructions. If the oxygen will be required on a continuous basis, you will need to set the patient up with a portable oxygen unit for home use. Once a patient account has been established with a home healthcare company, per the physician's instructions, the respiratory therapy representative will explain different models and mobile units available to the patient for home use, as well as the necessary safety precautions.

Charting Example

10/25/XX 11:30 AM Patient evaluated for oxygen use. Patient tested on 2 lpm [liters per minute] continuous flow while at rest. 4 lpm needed for activity to maintain 90% blood oxygen saturation. Order for O₂ two lpm rest / four lpm with exertion faxed to Apria Home Health Care. Connie Hughes, CMA

Chronic Obstructive Pulmonary Disease (COPD)

Asthma, chronic bronchitis, and emphysema are considered chronic obstructive pulmonary diseases. Air is trapped in the lungs and the patient is unable to expel all the carbon dioxide from the alveoli. Although each condition has specific signs and symptoms, they share many of the same problems. A person with COPD has SOB and a rapid heart rate and experiences weakness. Asthma may also be characterized by audible wheezes, diaphoresis, and tightness in the chest. Inform the physician in all cases and, if ordered, administer oxygen. Depending on the situation, the physician may order medications to be administered, oxygen to be delivered, or transport to an emergency facility by EMS.

Pulmonary Edema

Fluid accumulation in the lung tissue and alveoli result in a condition known as pulmonary edema. The patient presents with difficulty breathing, wheezing sounds, cyanosis, rapid heartbeat, distended neck veins, extreme anxiety, and orthopnea. Inform the physician. Place the patient in a sitting position with feet and legs up on a bed or cart. Administer supplemental oxygen if ordered and available. Call EMS for transport to an emergency facility.

Shock and Anaphylactic Shock

Shock, the collapse of the cardiovascular system, is caused by insufficient cardiac output. Blood supply and nourishment (oxygen and nutrients, including glucose) to the tissue and perfusion to the organs are inadequate. Untreated shock can progress very rapidly to death. Shock may be the result of many insults to the body, including anaphylaxis, cardiac failure, hemorrhage, extreme emotional upset, respiratory distress, neurological collapse, severe metabolic insult, and **sepsis.** The types and causes of shock are summarized in Table 23-4. Some of the symptoms that may occur after the initial crisis are listed in Table 23-5.

Regardless of the cause, immediate, aggressive intervention is required to stop the progression of the condition and the possible death of the patient. Have the patient lie down, keep him or her warm, maintain a patent airway, control all bleeding, monitor vital signs, and provide emotional support. Inform the physician and call EMS for further assessment and transport. Oxygen may be administered, if ordered and available, by trained personnel.

Anaphylactic Shock

Anaphylactic shock is a severe allergic reaction to a foreign substance, characterized by antigen formation and physiological reaction. See Table 23-6 for symptoms. Examples of foreign

---

TABLE 23-4 CLASSIFICATIONS OF SHOCK

Type of Shock	Cause
anaphylactic shock	severe allergic reaction
cardiogenic shock	heart failure
hemorrhagic shock	blood loss
metabolic shock	loss of body fluids and electrolytes
neurogenic shock	nervous system failure
psychogenic shock	dilated blood vessels
respiratory shock	respiratory failure
septic shock	infection in bloodstream

TABLE 23-5 SYMPTOMS OF SHOCK FOLLOWING A CRISIS SITUATION

■ Weakness	■ Cool skin
■ Rapid heartbeat	■ Clammy skin
■ Thirst	■ Cyanosis
■ Nausea	■ Confusion
■ Dizziness	■ Disorientation
■ Restlessness	■ Unresponsiveness
■ Pallor	■ Shallow breathing

TABLE 23-6 SYMPTOMS OF ANAPHYLACTIC SHOCK

■ sudden onset of anxiety	■ cardiac arrhythmias
■ sneezing	■ respiratory arrest
■ difficulty breathing	■ cardiac arrest
■ hives	■ cyanosis
■ itching and rash	■ weakness
■ nasal congestion	■ weak rapid pulse
■ swelling of the lips and tongue	■ hypotension
■ flushed or dry skin	■ altered levels of consciousness

---

substances include medications, bug bites, and latex gloves. Inform the physician immediately. Call EMS. The physician may order epinephrine and/or an antihistamine. An IV may also be started.

Prevention is the most important factor in anaphylactic shock. Always ask the patient about allergies to any medication before administering it and record this information on the front of the chart in red. After administering medication, ask the patient to wait 20 minutes before leaving the office and observe for any potential reactions. In offices where antibiotics and allergy injections are given on a regular basis, you must be alert to possible reactions and be prepared with an emergency drug box for rapid intervention.

Bleeding

Bleeding can be either external or internal. External bleeding occurs when the skin is broken. Internal bleeding occurs with tissue damage, while the skin remains intact. Bleeding can originate from any of the three types of blood vessels—arteries, veins, and capillaries.

Arterial bleeding is usually copious, rapid, and bright red. The blood often spurts, echoing the heartbeat. Arterial bleeding must be brought under control as soon as possible. Pressure applied directly over the exit wound may halt the flow of blood. If this is not successful, external pressure on the pressure points (see below) may be. Elevating the injured part higher than the heart may also slow the blood flow.

Venous blood flows more slowly, is darker in color, and can usually be controlled by direct pressure. Blood from capillaries oozes rather than flows and can also be halted with direct pressure. Bleeding from the scalp or face is often copious because of the many circulatory vessels in the area. Caution must be exercised if a fracture in the area is suspected.

Direct pressure is applied by placing a sterile dressing over the wound and holding it in place (Figure 23-28 ◆). A pressure bandage may be wrapped around the injured part to maintain pressure on the site. If blood seeps through, reinforce the bandage by applying more dressings and bandages over it. Do *not* remove the original dressing.

Pressure Points

Pressure points may be used to help control external bleeding (Figure 23-29 ◆). Pressure is applied to the artery where it lies close to the skin and can be compressed against an underlying bone. These arteries include the temporal, carotid, facial, brachial, radial-ulnar, subclavian, femoral, and dorsalis pedis

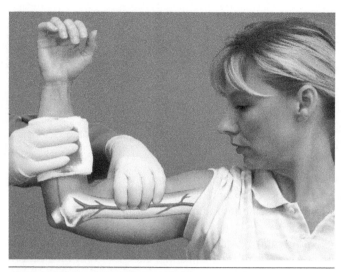

Figure 23-28 ◆ Apply direct pressure to the patient's wound.

(Table 23-7). It is possible to control external bleeding in regions distal to the pressure point.

Application of Direct Pressure

When direct pressure alone is not effective, direct pressure and bandaging must be applied while the EMS system is activated.

Internal Bleeding

Internal bleeding may be obvious or insidious. Bruising or discoloration of the skin may be an indication of bleeding in the underlying tissues. Be alert for signs and symptoms of internal bleeding and initiate intervention before the condition becomes grave. Observe the injured person for bruising, tenderness, and swelling at the site of injury. He or she may complain of pain in the area of injury. The systemic signs that are precursors to shock include a rapid pulse, cold, clammy and pale skin, nausea and vomiting, extreme thirst, anxiety, a drop in blood pressure, and possibly a decreased level of consciousness. Inform the physician of the signs and symptoms of internal bleeding. Call EMS for transport.

Until advanced intervention is available, try to prevent or slow the onset of shock. Keep the victim quiet, warm, and lying down with the feet slightly elevated.

Epistaxis

Epistaxis is the medical term for nosebleed. As an external form of bleeding, epistaxis can occur spontaneously or following a blow to the nose. Spontaneous forms may be the result of upper respiratory infection, low humidity in the environment, **hypertension,** strenuous activity, or exposure to high altitudes. While most nosebleeds are only a nuisance, those caused by hypertension are a signal of a more serious underlying problem.

Intervention begins with the patient sitting in a chair and the head tilted forward. Ask the patient to apply direct pressure by pinching and holding the sides of the nose together. It may take up to 15 minutes for the blood to clot and bleeding to be controlled. Apply an ice or cold pack after bleeding is controlled. An additional measure is to apply pressure to the upper lip just below the nose. Instruct the patient not to blow the nose for

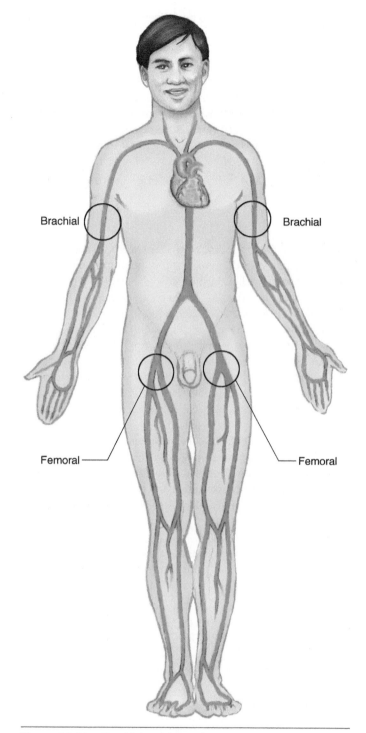

Figure 23-29 ◆ Brachial and femoral pressure points

several hours after the bleeding is controlled to prevent the nosebleed from recurring. If the bleeding cannot be controlled, alert the physician and EMS.

Open Wounds

With an open wound, the integrity of the skin and its defenses are compromised. Open wounds include abrasions, avulsions, amputations, lacerations, incisions, and punctures. The area

TABLE 23-7 MAJOR ARTERIES AND PRESSURE POINT SITES

Arteries	Location	Area in Which Bleeding Is Controlled
Temporal arteries	Temples in front of ears	Temporal region of scalp
Carotid arteries	Front of neck on either side of trachea ,face, ears, scalp	Face, ears, scalp area above pressure point
Facial arteries	Under mandible	Nose and mouth
Brachial arteries	Just above the hand, arm, elbow	Inner aspect of elbow below pressure point
Radial-ulnar arteries	Just above or at wrists	Hands and fingers below pressure point
Subclavian arteries	Just above clavicles	Hand, arm, shoulder, and portion of anterior chest wall
Femoral arteries	Anterior aspect midthigh	Leg below pressure point
Dorsalis pedis arteries	Anterior aspect of the foot	Toes and foot below pressure point

PROCEDURE 23-5 Demonstrate the Application of a Pressure Bandage

Theory

In the medical office setting, wear gloves and any other PPE necessary and available to prevent contact with blood and body fluids. Direct pressure is applied with a dressing. If clean or sterile dressings are not available, handkerchiefs, washcloths, sanitary napkins, socks, or other cloth material may be used. Do *not* remove the original pressure dressing but add dressings as needed to help form clots and slow the bleeding. Removing the original dressing would remove any clot formation and start fresh bleeding. If possible, elevate the bleeding area. If bleeding continues with pressure dressing, apply pressure at the pressure point above the injury.

It is important to be cautious when working with bleeding injuries because of the possibility of fractures or internal injuries. Apply only mild pressure if, for example, you see or suspect a fracture.

Materials

- dressing supplies or makeshift materials
- gloves and/or other PPE available

Competency

(**Conditions**) With the necessary materials, (**Task**) you will be able to demonstrate the application of a pressure dressing (**Standards**) correctly.

1. Escort the patient immediately to an examination room.
2. Wash your hands.
3. Put on disposable gloves.
4. Under physician's supervision, apply direct pressure with a dressing placed on the open wound. If possible, elevate the affected part.
5. After assessment, the physician will decide EMS should be activated.
6. Apply additional dressings as needed. Do *not* remove the original dressing.
7. Apply pressure to pressure points as necessary and with the physician's supervision.
8. If bleeding is controlled, anchor the dressing to maintain pressure.
9. Prepare the patient for transport to an emergency care facility.
10. Dispose of waste in a biohazardous container.
11. Remove your gloves and discard.
12. Wash your hands.
13. Document the procedure.

Patient Education

The patient will be anxious. Explain the basic procedure in a calm, quiet, authoritative manner. The physician will answer patient questions based on the patient's ability to deal with information. Engage the patient in general conversation as a focused distraction. This may help maintain the patient's consciousness, as the patient may be prone to fainting.

Charting Example

08/31/xx 8:00 a.m. Pt came to office with 6" laceration to right forearm. Injury occurred from fight with 7-year-old brother when older brother fell into glass patio door. Bleeding profusely. Physician called to examination room. B/P 96/60 P 100, regular but weak. R 26. Pt appears very nervous. Pt transported to Emergency to further control bleeding and take to surgery. Pt is alert and talking to parents. Stephen Porter, CMA

Keys to Success
STOPPING A NOSEBLEED

Some practitioners prefer to have the patient blow the nose before applying pressure to the outside of the nose. This step removes any clots that may be in the nasal passages.

must be cleansed, and most wounds require some type of dressing to promote healing and prevent infection. Tetanus prophylaxis should be administered if appropriate. The size, length, depth, location and condition of the wound should be noted and recorded on the chart.

Tetanus, also referred to as *lockjaw,* is an infection caused by an anaerobic bacillus, *Clostridium tetani.* This bacillus may be introduced into the body through an open wound or a burn. It affects the central nervous system and causes muscle spasms. If not promptly diagnosed and treated, tetanus can be fatal. Tetanus can be prevented with prophylactic immunizations. In the event of an insult to the skin or tissue, it is recommended that the previously immunized person be given a booster injection of tetanus toxoid. If the patient has never been immunized or immunization cannot be confirmed, an injection of tetanus immune globulin is administered, followed by a series of tetanus toxoid injections.

Anyone with soft tissue trauma, especially a puncture wound, should be asked about his or her tetanus immunization status.

Abrasions

An **abrasion** occurs when the outer layer of skin is scraped away, leaving the underlying tissue exposed (Figure 23-30 ◆). Common terms for abrasions include friction burns, rug burns, road rashes, and scrapes. Bleeding is usually in the form of oozing and the injury is quite painful because nerve endings are exposed and/or damaged. As with all open wounds, the area is cleansed and any debris removed. Depending on the physician's choice, antibacterial ointment may be applied to the area and covered with a sterile dressing. Large areas of abraded tissue may require burn treatment.

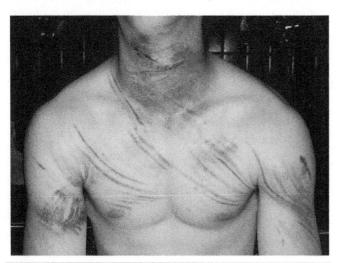

Figure 23-30 ◆ Abrasion
Courtesy of Charles Stewart, M.D. and Associates

Avulsions and Amputations

An **avulsion** is the tearing away of skin or tissue (Figure 23-31 ◆). Avulsions usually occur on limbs and appendages, including fingers, toes, hands, arms, feet, legs, nose, and penis. The body part may become entangled in machinery or be injured in a motor vehicle accident or a confrontation with an animal. Cleanse minor avulsion wounds with soap and water and return any skin flap to its normal position. Apply direct pressure, then apply a dressing when bleeding is controlled.

If the body part has been amputated and recovered, cleanse the dismembered part with sterile saline. Wrap it with moist, sterile gauze, seal it in a plastic bag, and place the plastic bag in a container on ice. Prompt medical attention and preservation of the body part enhance the chances for successful reattachment. Cover the wound or stump with a sterile dressing until advanced treatment is available.

Lacerations and Incisions

A **laceration** is an open wound in which the skin and underlying tissue are torn (Figure 23-32 ◆). It usually has jagged edges that may interfere with the healing process. When vessels are torn, bleeding results and must be controlled by direct pressure, pressure on pressure points, or eventual suturing or application of Steri-strips™. Cleanse the laceration with soap and water or an

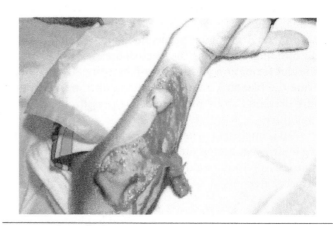

Figure 23-31 ◆ Avulsion
Courtesy of Edward T. Dickinson.

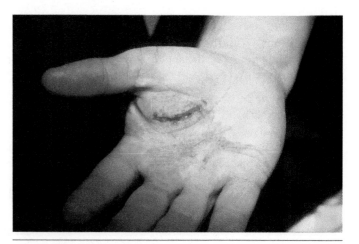

Figure 23-32 ◆ Laceration

antiseptic solution, removing all debris and foreign matter. If bleeding is severe, a physician should direct the cleansing process.

On minor lacerations, after cleansing, the edges are approximated and then held together with a small dressing, such as a Band-aid™, Steri-strip™ or sterile butterfly. Lacerations over a joint may require joint immobilization for a few days as healing progresses.

An **incision** is a cut with smooth edges made with a knife or other sharp object. It is treated in the same manner as any laceration. If the wound is deep or extensive, the physician usually performs a surgical intervention consisting of debridement, hemostasis, and trimming away of the jagged wound edges. If there is damage to underlying tissue, such as a tendon or ligament, further surgical intervention is required.

Puncture Wounds

A puncture wound results from a pointed foreign body penetrating the skin and tissue (Figure 23-33 ◆). Often the wound edges close, trapping pathogens and debris in the tissue. Depending on the nature of the pointed object, cleansing may consist of simply soaking the area or may require invasive irrigation. After cleansing, a dressing is applied. Bleeding from a puncture wound is usually minimal.

Impaled Objects

A patient who has been impaled by an object such as a large piece of glass or sharp metal requires special treatment. The general rule is to leave the object in place until it can be safely removed by trained personnel. Stabilizing the object is critical to preventing further damage (Figure 23-34 ◆). Control bleeding and stabilize the impaled object with a bulky dressing held in place with tape or other bandages. Splint the area to prevent movement. For a small penetrating object, a small paper cup may be used. Make a hole in the bottom of the cup, place it over the object with the lip of the cup against the skin, and secure it with bandages (Figure 23-35 ◆).

Soft-Tissue Injuries

Soft-tissue trauma involves both the skin and underlying tissue. Abrasions, incisions, lacerations, and puncture wounds are easily identified as open-wound skin injuries. Avulsions, amputations,

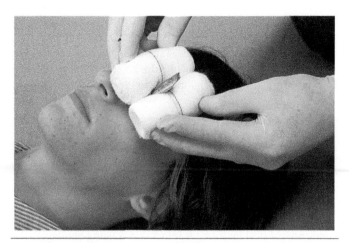

Figure 23-34 ◆ Stabilizing an impaled object

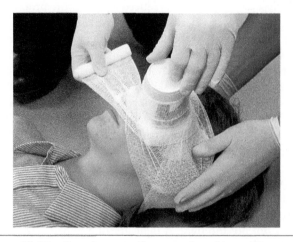

Figure 23-35 ◆ Securing a small penetrating object with a paper cup

and thermal insults are considered soft-tissue injuries because tissue as well as skin is involved.

Contusions are closed wounds in which the skin is not broken. Damage to the underlying tissue may involve blood vessels, nerves, muscles, and subcutaneous tissue. The tearing of minute to larger blood vessels results in bleeding into the tissue and discoloration of the area. Swelling may exert pressure on nerve endings, creating pain.

Crush injuries result when force is applied to the tissue. Depending on the area involved, the crush may be similar to pinching of tissue or it may be so severe as to involve organs and bones.

Elevating the body part above the heart and applying cold are often the only intervention needed. With a more severe injury, the body part should be immobilized. Monitoring vital signs and observing skin color, temperature, and moisture are essential to deciding whether more extensive intervention is needed.

Traumatic Injury Emergencies

Traumatic insults to the body may result in minor to very severe injuries. These injuries may be classified as soft-tissue

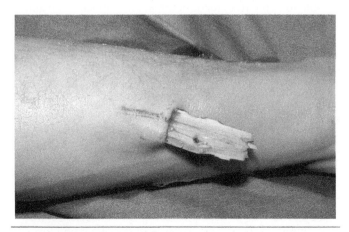

Figure 23-33 ◆ Puncture wound
Courtesy of Charles Stewart, M.D. and Associates.

injuries and musculoskeletal injuries. Soft-tissue injuries involve the skin and underlying tissue, including subcutaneous tissue, nerves, blood vessels, fat, muscles, fibrous tissues, membranes, and glands. Musculoskeletal injuries involve bones, joints, cartilage, ligaments, tendons, and muscles.

Pressure Bandages

Bandages anchor dressings in place, prevent contamination of a recent wound or surgical site, support and immobilize injured extremities, and may be used to apply pressure to slow and/or stop bleeding.

PROCEDURE 23-6 Demonstrate the Application of Triangular, Figure 8, and Tubular Bandages

Theory

Bandage application varies according to whether an open wound, surgical incision, or intact skin is being bandaged. For an open wound or surgical wound, a sterile dressing must be applied before the bandage. For application to intact skin, medical asepsis must be practiced for the entire procedure.

If necessary, clean and dry the area to be bandaged. If the skin integrity were to be broken under a dirty bandage, the new wound would be easily contaminated. As bandages are applied, avoid skin-to-skin contact. Microbial growth can occur when skin touches other skin and moisture develops. Protect bony prominences from rubbing, irritation, and potential skin breakdown by padding before wrapping with bandages. Position any extremities in a slightly flexed position before bandaging for additional comfort and protection from injury.

To help venous blood flow return to the heart, always apply bandages distally to, proximally, or far to near. Leave as much of the fingers and toes exposed as possible to monitor circulation (Figure 23-36 ◆). Ask the patient if the bandage is snug but not too tight. A tight dressing impairs circulation and predisposes the patient to complications. Check beneath the distal end of the bandage for signs of impaired circulation. Loosen the bandage and inform the physician if signs of impaired circulation occur.

Bandages come packaged in rolls and are often easy to drop. If you drop a bandage on a clean surface, you may use it again. A bandage dropped on a dirty surface should not be used.

In the medical office, three basic types of bandages are used:

- Elastic—often known by name brand, such as Ace™; washable for repeat use; secures bandages for comfort and support; if applied too tightly, can impair circulation
- Roller—made of sterilized gauze; molds to extremities or body parts
- Kling™—made of sterilized gauze; stretches to mold easily; layers cling together to stay in place

Different turns are used to apply bandages smoothly and to fit the body parts. They include figure 8, spiral and spiral reverse turn, circular turn, and recurrent turn. A tubular gauze bandage is applied to extremities with an applicator. A triangular bandage supports and immobilizes the arm. Regardless of type of bandage material, remember to choose the appropriate width for proper fit and patient comfort.

Materials

- elastic bandage
- roller bandage
- Kling™ bandage
- tubular gauze and applicator
- triangular bandage
- tape
- scissors

Competency

(**Conditions**) With the necessary materials, (**Task**) you will be able to apply triangular, figure 8, and tubular bandaging (**Standards**) correctly.

1. Escort the patient immediately to an examination room. You may need to assist the patient, depending on the severity, location, and type of injury.
2. Explain the procedure to the patient.
3. Wash your hands.
4. Gather necessary supplies.
5. Apply the bandage as follows.

Triangular bandage

- Keep the injured arm as immobile as possible.
- Carefully slide the triangular bandage under the area to be held. The two shorter sides of the triangle should be pointing toward the elbow, and the remaining longer edge should be parallel to the opposite body side.

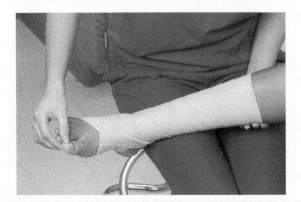

Figure 23-36 ◆ Bandage the patient's foot with toes exposed for monitoring circulation.

PROCEDURE 23-6 Demonstrate the Application of Triangular, Figure 8, and Tubular Bandages *(continued)*

- Bring the lowest side of the triangle up and over the arm.
- Tie the ends of the bandage behind and slightly to the side of the neck. Tuck the peak of the bandage in toward the elbow point of the bandage.
- The triangular bandage may also be wrapped around the head as a turban to anchor dressings onto the head.

Figure 8 bandage

- Place the thumb of one hand on one end of the bandage to hold it in place.
- Anchor the bandage with your other hand, then complete one circle around the extremity or body part (Figure 23-37 ◆).
- Continue to alternate wrapping above and below the body joint or dressing and circling behind the joint or dressing area until the injured area is covered adequately (Figure 23-38 ◆).

Tubular bandage

- Choose an applicator that is larger than the extremity to be bandaged.
- Cut an approximate amount of tubular gauze bandage and slide the gathered bandage onto the applicator (Figure 23-39 ◆).
- Slide the applicator over the extremity (Figure 23-40 ◆).
- Hold the bandage against the proximal end of the extremity and pull the applicator approximately 1 inch past the distal end (Figure 23-41 ◆).
- Twist the bandage gauze one complete turn.
- Next, slide the applicator toward the proximal end of the injury (Figure 23-42 ◆).
- Hold the proximal end of the tubular bandage gauze in place, and pull the applicator toward the distal end.
- After pulling past the distal end, complete one twist.

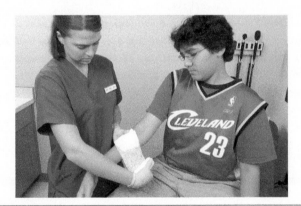

Figure 23-37 ◆ Complete one circle around the extremity or body part.

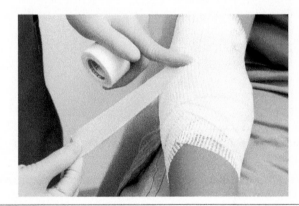

Figure 23-38 ◆ Wrap above and below the body joint or dressing.

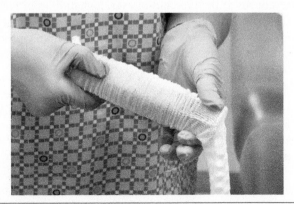

Figure 23-39 ◆ Gather the gauze bandage onto a tubular gauze applicator.

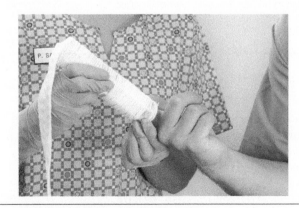

Figure 23-40 ◆ Slide the applicator on the body part.

continued

PROCEDURE 23-6 Demonstrate the Application of Triangular, Figure 8, and Tubular Bandages *(continued)*

Figure 23-41 ◆ Position the applicator one inch past the distal end.

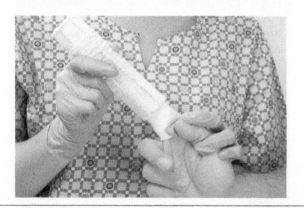

Figure 23-42 ◆ Slide the applicator toward the proximal end of the injury.

- Slide back and forth and twist the distal end of the dressing until the injured area is adequately covered.
- Cut excess dressing, but remember to anchor the bandage at the proximal end.

6. Instruct the patient to watch for signs of circulation impairment (Table 23-8).
7. Wash your hands.
8. Document the procedure and patient teaching.

Patient Education

Instruct the patient to watch for increasing pain, numbness, skin tightness, pale skin color, swelling, cold fingers and toes, and blue nail beds. Explain that some swelling, pain, numbness, and color changes may be expected for a short period, but to check with the physician for more specific information.

Charting Example

07/22/xx 9:30 a.m. Figure 8 bandage applied to arm as instructed by physician. Pt stated that arm feels supported and less painful. Pt stated awareness of return appointment and that he will call if pain and swelling become worse. Monica Mason, RMA

TABLE 23-8 SIGNS OF IMPAIRED CIRCULATION	
■ Pain, numbness ■ Tight skin ■ Pale skin color	■ Swelling ■ Cold fingers, toes ■ Cyanotic fingernails and/ or toenails

Thermal Injuries: Integumentary and Systemic

Thermal insults are integumentary or systemic injuries caused by extremes of heat or cold. Integumentary system injuries include burns and frostbite. Systemic injuries include heat exhaustion, **hyperthermia,** and **hypothermia.**

Integumentary Insults: Burns

Burns may be the result of thermal, chemical, electrical, light, or radiation insults to the skin and underlying tissue. Physical contact with heat sources, such as flames or fire, radiation, steam, hot liquids, or hot objects, can cause a thermal burn. Acids, bases, and caustics can cause chemical burns. Electrical current, including

lightning, enters the body, causing burns at the point of entry, the traveled pathway, and the point of exit. Intense light can cause radiation burns to the skin and/or eyes. Radiation from nuclear sources is also capable of causing burns. Without endangering yourself, your first priority is to remove the victim from the source.

Burns are classified by depth, area involved, and source of burn (Table 23-9). Classifications by depth are:

- Superficial or first-degree burns, involving the epidermis (Figure 23-43 ◆)
- Partial-thickness or second-degree burns, involving the epidermis and dermis (Figure 23-44 ◆)
- Full-thickness or third-degree burns, extending through all the layers of the skin to the underlying tissue, including muscle, fat, blood vessels, nerves, and bone (Figure 23-45 ◆)

Age also plays an important part in the outcome of burns. Adults over the age of 55, children under the age of 5, and infants are all at greater risk for unfavorable outcomes and complications.

TABLE 23-9 BURNS ACCORDING TO DEGREE OF INJURY, SYMPTOMS, AND TREATMENT

Burn Type	Symptoms	Treatment
First degree: superficial burns; heal without scarring	Reddened skin; no blisters; painful	Submerge in cool water 2 to 5 minutes. If patient is young or elderly, or if hands, face, feet, or genitals are involved, see physician.
Second degree: partial-thickness burns; heal with very little scarring	Reddened skin; fluid-filled blisters within 48 hours; very painful; white spots possible	Stop the burning. Do not break blisters. If patient is young or elderly, or if hands, face, feet, or genitals are involved, see physician.
Third degree: full-thickness burns; scarring is likely	Gray, black, or charred skin; underlying tissue involved; extremely painful or no pain if nerve endings are damaged	Call EMS. Treat for shock. Physician evaluation is necessary for treatment. Skin grafting may be necessary.

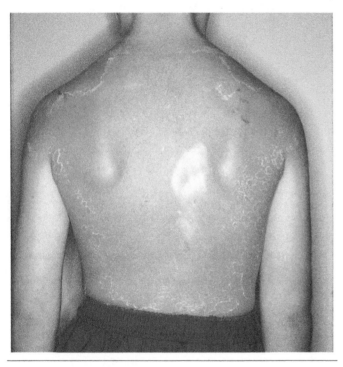

Figure 23-43 ◆ First-degree burn
Courtesy of Charles Stewart, M.D. and Associates.

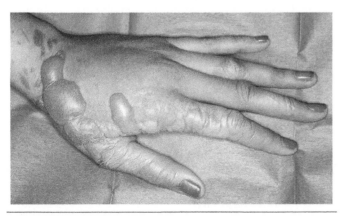

Figure 23-44 ◆ Second-degree burn
Courtesy of Charles Stewart, M.D. and Associates.

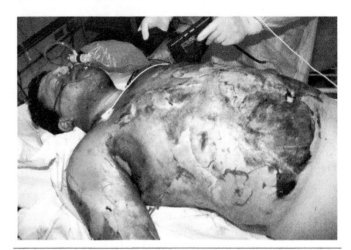

Figure 23-45 ◆ Third-degree burn
Courtesy of Edward T. Dickinson

The Rule of Nines is a common way to calculate the extent of the burn area. Specialty burn treatment centers make a more detailed calculation. On the Rule of Nines chart, anterior and posterior outlines of the body are shaded to indicate the burned surface areas (Figure 23-46 ◆). Note if the face, hands, feet, or genitals are involved. While these areas do not comprise a large percentage of the body's surface, they require special attention to promote healing and future functioning.

Burns from flames and intense heat may involve areas other than the skin. The respiratory system is often affected. As you assess a burn victim, note any singeing of the eyebrows, nasal hair, or facial hair, as well as any charring or soot. These signs indicate respiratory involvement and possible airway compromise.

Halt the burning process by immersing the injured part in cool water, if possible. If not, soak sterile gauze with cool normal saline and place it over the burned area. When the area has cooled, cover it with dry sterile towels or gauze until the burn can be assessed and treatment prescribed by the physician. Full-thickness burns are left untouched, covered with sterile dressings, and the victim is transported to an emergency facility, usually by EMS. Keep the patient warm to prevent shock.

If a liquid chemical is the cause of a burn, remove it from the skin by flushing with copious amounts of water. A dry or powdery chemical should be carefully wiped from the victim while avoiding exposure to yourself or bystanders. After all the powder has been brushed away, flush the area with a copious but gentle stream of water.

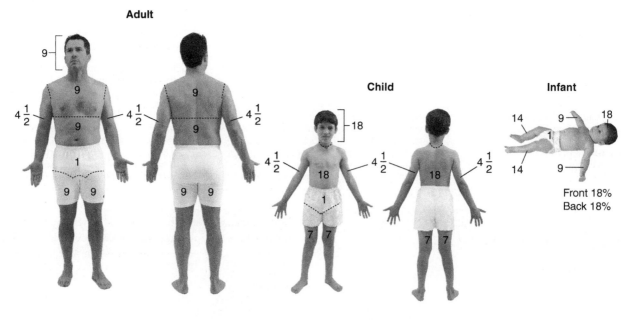

Adult

9

9

4½ 4½ 4½

9

1

9 9

Child

18

4½ 4½

18

1

7 7

Infant

14 9 18

1

14 9

Front 18%
Back 18%

Note: Each arm totals 9% (front of arm 4½%, back of arm 4½%)

Figure 23-46 ◆ Rule of nines

When an electrical burn is involved, the entry and exit points of the electrical current are evident, but the internal damage is difficult to assess. Therefore, first aid consists of covering the wounds with sterile material and transporting the victim to an emergency facility. If the victim is still touching the electrical source, *do not* attempt to remove him or her until the power has been disconnected. You could be electrocuted. If the electrical impact has thrown the victim, assess respiratory status. If cardiac arrest occurs, start CPR. Other considerations include musculoskeletal involvement.

Exposure to lightning also causes burns. If the victim is hit directly by lightning, the electrical charge usually travels through the body in a forceful or violent manner. Treat the entry and exit wounds the same way you would electrical burns. If respiratory arrest has occurred, start rescue breathing. Often cardiac arrest rapidly follows the cessation of breathing. CPR with AED must follow if the victim is to survive. Most lightning strike survivors are transported to an emergency facility. Cardiac and respiratory functions are monitored and the victim is observed for shock and blood pressure fluctuations. Other possible effects include ruptured tympanic membranes, caused by the shock of the impact, and damage to the eyes, such as eventual cataract development from the intense brightness of the lightning.

Radiation burn treatment is similar to thermal burn treatment after the victim is removed from the source. Radiation burns can include overexposure to the ultraviolet rays of the sun and tanning booths, x-rays, and radiation therapy for cancer.

Frostbite

Extreme cold can cause local injuries as severe as frozen soft tissue, or frostbite (Figure 23-47 ◆). Cold air, moisture, water, and wind may all be contributing factors. Body areas most com-

Caduceus Chronicle
THE ORIGINS OF SKIN GRAFT TREATMENTS

Many burn treatments used today are the results of research and treatments implemented during the Korean and Vietnam Wars. For example, skin harvested from cadavers is used to cover open areas left by partial- and full-thickness burns. This treatment enables the blood supply to regenerate. In approximately one week, the body can reject this foreign tissue without medical intervention. The main concern with treating a wound with a cadaver graft is preventing infection until a suitable skin graft is available or the patient has the strength to undergo surgery.

Many skin banks are maintained by the American Red Cross. Burn treatment centers that perform skin grafts and other treatments are located around the country. Shriners Burn Hospitals provide medical care without charge to children with burns.

monly affected by exposure to cold are the hands and fingers, ears, nose, face, feet, and toes. Ice crystals form in the soft tissue as circulation is compromised by the cold. The first sign of frostbite is a developing redness to the skin in a light-skinned individual and a lightening of the skin of a darker-skinned person. This is followed by blanching of the skin. The skin and underlying tissue become numb, all sensation ceases, and the area turns white. Tissue death and loss of the affected body part are possible outcomes (Table 23-10).

Move the victim from the cold to a warmer environment so the tissue can be gently warmed. A person with early frostbite may start the warming process by gently blowing on the area. If the fingers are involved, placing the hands under the armpits or immersing the affected part in tepid water often starts the warming process.

If the tissue has been frozen and is hard to the touch, call EMS or the physician. *Never* rub, squeeze, or massage frozen

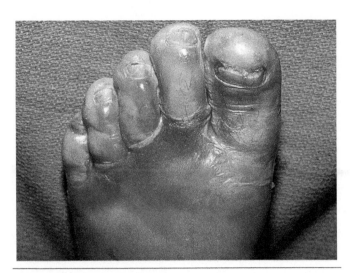

Figure 23-47 ◆ Frostbite
Courtesy of Charles Stewart, M.D. and Associates.

tissue. Wrap it in sterile gauze, if available, and clean towels in preparation for transport to an emergency facility or until the physician can intervene.

Heat Exhaustion

Heat exhaustion occurs as the result of sodium and water depletion from the body. Strenuous activity often precedes heat exhaustion, as the individual becomes overheated and perspires profusely. The skin is moist, pale, and cool, and body temperature is normal. The individual may complain of headache, muscle cramps, weakness, dizziness, and nausea. He or she should be moved to a cooler environment and encouraged to lie down. Apply cool compresses and give sips of water if the individual is conscious. Heat exhaustion can usually be prevented by taking salt pills and drinking lots of water before, during, and after strenuous activities in a warm environment.

Hyperthermia

Prolonged exposure to extremely hot temperatures often results in hyperthermia. The loss of water and salt through perspiration leads to a state of mild shock. If the body's cooling mechanisms fail, heat exhaustion can progress into heat stroke.

An individual experiencing heat stroke usually fails to perspire and has a body temperature of 105°F or higher. The skin is dry, red, and hot to the touch. Headache, shortness of breath, nausea or vomiting, dizziness, weakness, and dry mouth are common symptoms. At the onset the pulse is rapid, but it gradually slows and becomes weak, and the blood pressure begins to drop. Mental confusion may appear, possibly accompanied by irritability and hysterical behavior. In some cases the victim collapses. If he or she remains exposed to heat, brain cells begin to die and permanent brain damage or even death may eventually result.

The victim must be removed from the environment immediately. Loosen the clothing and cool the body down as quickly as possible by pouring cool water over the victim or sponging with a cool, wet cloth. If heat stroke is suspected, EMS should be contacted after the initial emergency treatment to transport the victim to an emergency facility where vital signs and cardiac status can be monitored. The victim should not be left alone and should be assessed by a physician as promptly as possible.

Hypothermia

The victim of hypothermia is also at great risk. Prolonged exposure to cold or cold water can cause the core temperature to drop below 95°F. The victim shivers and experiences a numbness and tingling over the body. The skin becomes very cool to the touch and is pale with a blue or ashy tinge. Respirations are slow and shallow, and the victim becomes disoriented and eventually unconscious as body functions and organs slow down to the point of complete shutdown.

Treatment involves removing any cold, wet clothing and wrapping the victim in warm blankets. Heat packs may be used, but not directly on the skin. Once the victim is conscious, offer sips of warm liquid. When possible, the victim should be transported to a treatment facility for assessment by a physician.

Table 23-11 summarizes the symptoms, causes, and treatment of thermal insults.

Musculoskeletal Injuries

Musculoskeletal injuries involve bones, muscles, tendons, and ligaments and include fractures, dislocations, sprains, and strains. Definitive diagnosis is made by X-ray, but these injuries must be considered fractured bones until determined to be otherwise. Therefore, the affected part must be immobilized.

TABLE 23-10 FROSTBITE INJURIES		
Injury	**Symptoms**	**Prognosis**
Frostnip: involves tips of ears, nose, cheeks, fingers, toes, or chin	Numbness Tingling	Completely reversible
Superficial frostbite: water freezes in upper layers of the skin	Edema Blisters	Reversible
Frostbite: tissue beneath skin is frozen solid	Light skin: redness Dark skin: lightening Small blisters Blanching Numbness No sensation Finally, area all white	Permanent damage may occur

TABLE 23-11 THERMAL INSULTS

Insult	Causes	Symptoms	Treatment
Heat stroke	Continued exposure to extremely hot temperatures Failure of the body to cope with excessive heat	Body temperature >105°F Dry, hot, red skin Dry mouth Nausea Vomiting Dizziness Weakness SOB Rapid pulse Decreasing BP Anxiety, confusion Possible seizures	Cool the body rapidly. Pour cool water over the body to bring the core temperature down below 100°F. Transport to an emergency facility.
Heat exhaustion	Continued exposure to extremely hot temperatures Depletion of salt or water in the body	Normal or below normal body temperature Profuse sweating Skin: moist, cool, pale Headache Dizziness Fatigue Nausea Muscle cramps Pulse: weak, rapid Dilated pupils	Move to a cool place. Apply cool compresses. Elevate the feet. If conscious, give small amounts of liquid.
Hypothermia	Continued exposure to wind, cold, or cold water.	Numbness or cold feeling Fatigue Core body temperature < 95°F Skin: blue, puffy Pulse: weak, slow Confusion Decreased level of consciousness	Remove wet clothing. Warm the patient by wrapping in warm blankets. Transport to an emergency facility.

Fractures

In a closed or simple fracture, the bone is broken but does not penetrate the skin (Figure 23-48 ◆). In an open or compound fracture, the bone pierces the skin, or the skin is torn open by the bone or by an external force (Figure 23-49 ◆). Fractures may also be single or multiple breaks in the bone (Figure 23-50 ◆). Bone breaks can be complete, twisted, or splintered. The affected part is immobilized and examined for impaired circulation to the distal aspect. The location of the fracture and the possible presence of heavy bleeding or bruising are also determined. Knowing the cause of the injury is very helpful in this assessment.

A fracture may occur in any bone. Special precautions must be taken for suspected fractures of the spinal column or skull. For any injury caused by sudden acceleration and deceleration, the cervical spine must be immobilized. Other injuries to the spinal column require extreme caution when moving the victim. The best response is to call 911. Allow EMT professionals to immobilize the cervical spine with a cervical collar and

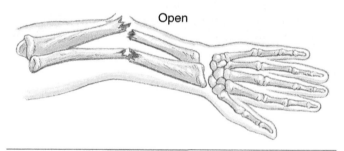
Open

Figure 23-49 ◆ An open fracture

log-roll the victim onto a spine board for transport to a facility where X-rays can be taken to determine the extent of the injury. Suspected fractures of the thigh (femur) and pelvis also require immobilization and transport and are best handled by the EMS.

In open or compound fractures, the soft-tissue injury must be tended. Cover the open wound with a sterile, saline-moistened dressing, then place a sterile occlusive dressing over that. Generally, the tissue must be surgically cleaned and debrided.

∞ Descriptions of specific fractures and their treatment are given in Chapter 25.

Splint Application

Fractures of long bones require immobilization by splinting to prevent joint movement above and below the fracture. In addition to preventing additional damage to the bone and surrounding soft tissue, the splint helps to relieve pain and allows safe movement of the injured part. Another comfort measure is the application of cold, usually after splinting, to prevent swelling.

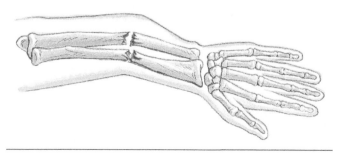

Figure 23-48 ◆ A closed fracture

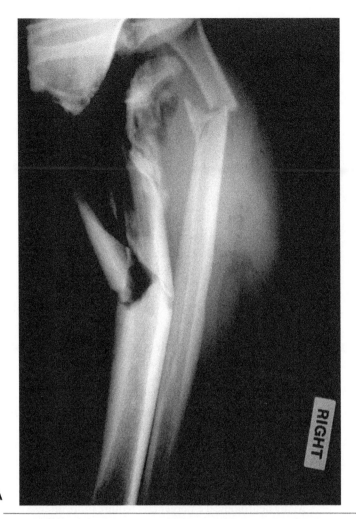
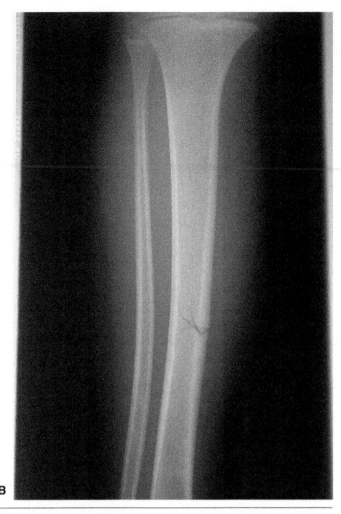

Figure 23-50 ◆ Fractures may be single or multiple breaks in the bone. (A) Severe fracture; (B) Subtle fracture; difficult to detect without an X-ray
Courtesy of Charles Stewart, M.D. and Associates.

PROCEDURE 23-7 Demonstrate the Application of a Splint

Theory

Manufactured splints may be available in the medical office. However, it may sometimes be necessary to improvise a splint using materials at hand, such as narrow boards, before a physician examines the victim. Rolled-up newspapers, magazines, a pillow, a folded blanket, or a rigid object may also be used. Pad the splint with a towel or other soft material before placing it under or beside the injured limb. The secured splint should be snug, but not so tight as to impair circulation or neurological status. If possible, leave a "window" or open area in the splint to allow observation of the extremity. Elevating the limb, especially a lower limb, is helpful in preventing pain and swelling.

Materials

- makeshift or sterile dressing supplies
- stiff or solid materials to immobilize the extremity
- bandages or strips of material to secure splint materials

Competency

(**Conditions**) With the necessary materials, (**Task**) you will be able to apply a splint (**Standards**) correctly with minimal movement to the extremity and without impairment to circulation or neurological status.

1. Identify yourself to the patient.
2. Obtain vital signs.
3. Ask the patient, if conscious, to speak his or her name.
4. Ask about medical allergies and medications and whether the patient has a medical history.
5. Assess the area of suspected fracture for bruising, bleeding, and open areas or protruding bones.
6. Moving the limb as little as possible and with gentle traction on the distal side, place the splint with padding under the limb or alongside the limb. You may have to ask other clinical staff for help to ensure the least amount of discomfort for the least amount of time.

continued

PROCEDURE 23-7 **Demonstrate the Application of a Splint** *(continued)*

7. Place sterile dressings or clean makeshift dressings gently over open areas.
8. Secure the splint by wrapping bandages or strips of material around the splint and the limb. The ties must be above and below the joints on both sides of the suspected fracture.
9. Add additional ties as necessary along the length of the splint.
10. If possible, leave an exposed area, such as toes or fingers, so that circulation can be monitored.
11. The splint should be snug enough to immobilize the limb, but not tight.

Patient Education

If the patient is conscious or significant others are present, instruct them to watch for increased pain, numbness, discoloration, and swelling. Emphasize the importance of immobilization and the need for physician and X-ray follow-up for additional diagnosis and care.

If the patient is unconscious, give the family or friends basic information and make EMS transport arrangements immediately.

Charting Example

12/23/xx 8:30 a.m. Pt came to office with splint applied to lower leg and foot. Pt states that brakes failed on bike, he swerved to miss a dog, and was thrown from bike when it ran into a tree. A passerby called his wife, who splinted the lower leg. Pt complains of severe pain and has pliable cold pack applied to area of leg pain. Pt is able to move toes and toes are pink and warm. William Hughley, CMA

Sprains, Strains, and Dislocations

A sprain occurs when muscles, tendons, or ligaments are torn. It may be the result of trauma or cumulative overuse of the joint.

A strain, often called a pulled muscle, occurs when a muscle or tendon is overextended by stretching. The patient complains of pain and may be unable to use the joint. In the lower extremities, weight-bearing is painful and sometimes impossible.

In a dislocation, the bone is actually pulled away from the joint, stretching or tearing the ligaments and tendons. A deformity is generally noted. Dislocations must be reduced and the bone reinserted into the joint.

The injured body parts should be immobilized to prevent additional damage and reduce pain. Applications of cold also help with the pain and slow edema. The physician assesses the injury and usually orders radiographs to eliminate the possibility of fracture and diagnose sprain, strain, or dislocation.

Allergic Reactions

Allergic reactions can range from possibly catastrophic anaphylaxis to the troublesome itching of hives. Respiratory reactions may be triggered by such common factors as perfume, hair spray, insect repellents, and other airborne irritants. Symptoms may range from hives, welts, wheezing, and anxiety, to airway constriction, respiratory arrest, vascular collapse, and cardiac arrest.

Each exposure to the same allergen may cause more intense symptoms. Many individuals with known allergic conditions wear identification, such as a bracelet, charm, or necklace, to alert health-care providers or emergency responders to the allergy.

Treatment consists of removing the allergen or removing the victim from the environment causing the reaction. In the medical office setting, if a physician is available, antihistamines or steroids may be ordered and administered to neutralize, slow, or stop the histamine-induced reaction. Cold-water compresses may be helpful in relieving the itching.

Neurological Emergencies

Neurological emergencies include head trauma, seizures, **status epilepticus,** sudden onset of paralysis or hemiparesis, spinal cord involvement, and altered level of consciousness. An insult to the brain or spinal cord can be either internal or external. External insults with open wounds require additional attention.

Many neurological emergencies require more intense intervention, monitoring, and treatment than is possible in a physician's office. Usually the best course of action is to place the victim in a supine or semi-Fowler's position (at a 45-degree angle), inform the physician, complete a rapid assessment, and stay with the patient. Have another person call 911 to transport the patient to an emergency facility. Take and record vital signs, note the level of consciousness (**LOC**), and implement shock prevention measures. Evaluate pupil reaction, if possible (Figure 23-51 ◆). Keep the patient quiet and remain calm.

The basic neurological assessment includes level of consciousness, pupil reaction, motor and sensory skills, and ability to cooperate. Emergency medical personnel may use the Glasgow Coma Scale to establish a baseline assessment of a head injury patient. The lower the score, the greater the chance of a negative outcome. Throughout the course of treatment, comparing scores may provide an indication of trauma progression or condition improvement.

A more complete and thorough examination is conducted by the physician and includes six components:

1. Cerebral function (mental status)
2. Cranial nerve function
3. Cerebellar function
4. Motor function
5. Sensory function
6. Deep tendon reflexes (DTRs)

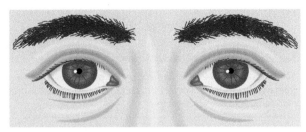

Constricted pupils

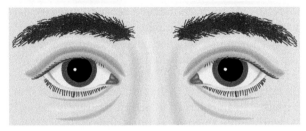

Dilated pupils

Unequal pupils

Figure 23-51 ◆ Evaluate pupil reaction

Keys to Success
GLASGOW COMA SCALE

Eye opening	Spontaneous	4	___
	To voice	3	___
	To pain	2	___
	None	1	___
Verbal response	Oriented	5	___
	Confused	4	___
	Inappropriate words	3	___
	Incomprehensible sounds	2	___
	None	1	___
Motor response	Obeys commands	6	___
	Localizes pain	5	___
	Withdrawal (pain)	4	___
	Flexion (pain)	3	___
	Extension (pain)	2	___
	None	1	___
	Glasgow Coma Score total		___

Total Glasgow Coma Scale Points (conversion = approximately one-third total value):

14–15 = 5   5–7 = 2
11–13 = 4   3–4 = 1
8–10 = 3

Neurological Assessment   ___

It is important to note and compare the functions on the right and left sides of the body. If the findings are not symmetrical, that is usually an indication of an abnormal condition.

Decreased Level of Consciousness

Decreased levels of consciousness range from dizziness and light-headedness to complete loss of consciousness. As the patient's level of consciousness drops, he or she may fall to the ground or floor, possibly sustaining an injury. If a patient complains of light-headedness or feeling faint, assist him or her to a sitting position, with the head between the knees. Or help lower the patient to a lying position and slightly elevate the feet and legs about 12 inches. Observe the airway to ensure that it remains open. Check and record vital signs and inform the physician. Light-headedness often passes quickly once sufficient blood flow has been reestablished to the brain.

If the patient is completely unresponsive, immediately have someone notify the physician, remain with the patient, contact EMS for transport, assess vital signs, administer oxygen if available, and follow office procedure.

?—**Critical Thinking Question 23-2**-
After Ariko has collected all the information on the accident as reported by Brenna, how should she advise Brenna?

Seizures

Seizures are involuntary muscular contractions or a series of muscular contractions that result from abnormal cerebral stimulation. Since the primary concern with a person experiencing a seizure is to prevent injury, you should do the following.

■ If the person is in an upright position when the seizure begins, ease him or her to the floor. Move furniture and other objects out of the way to minimize the risk of injury to the patient (Figure 23-52 ◆)

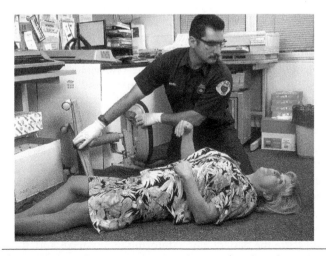

Figure 23-52 ◆ Emergency personnel protecting the seizure patient from injury

- Do *not* attempt to force open the mouth to hold the tongue from blocking the airway. Forcing the mouth open will break teeth and cause mouth injuries.
- Stay with the person and provide privacy.
- Loosen any constricting clothing.
- Ensure the airway is patent when the seizure stops.
- If the victim is not breathing, open the airway with the head tilt or jaw thrust maneuver. These maneuvers lift the tongue away from the airway (the tongue is never swallowed but only relaxes against the airway), and spontaneous breathing usually returns.
- If mucus and saliva are present in the person's mouth, turn the head to the side to drain the fluids and prevent aspiration.
- Note the length of the seizure, the part of the body involved, and any other pertinent information.
- Ask a family member to assist the person home after the seizure because the person may experience a postictal period during which he or she is responsive but disoriented. Do *not* allow the individual to drive or be alone.

Status epilepticus, a condition of continuous seizure activity, is considered a life-threatening emergency. Respiratory activity may be compromised and the seizures must be brought under control. Activate EMS and inform the physician immediately. The victim will need oxygen, and anti-seizure medication must be administered intravenously. If the physician is not available, the patient must be transported to an emergency facility for treatment and observation.

Cerebrovascular Accidents and Transient Ischemic Attacks

Cerebrovascular accidents (**CVA** or stroke) occur when circulation to the cerebral tissue in the brain is compromised, resulting in an interruption of neurological functioning. A plaque-narrowed artery may be occluded by a cerebral thrombosis or an embolism. Hemorrhage may also occur in an artery, causing bleeding into the tissue, pressure on other vessels, and the interruption of blood circulation in the area.

The onset of an occlusion is usually very sudden. Signs and symptoms are unilateral paralysis, impaired or slurred speech, confusion, dizziness, facial droop, arm drift, loss of balance and coordination, visual difficulties, and/or loss of consciousness (Figure 23-53 ◆). The patient with cerebral hemorrhage may experience a slower onset over a few minutes, and a headache may be one of the symptoms.

A transient ischemic attack (**TIA**) is temporary in nature but similar to a CVA. Usually the symptoms are less severe, do not involve a loss of consciousness, and resolve within 24 hours.

Since it is not possible to determine the seriousness of the attack, emergency treatment for both CVA and TIA victims is the same. In the medical office, take the patient to an examination room and assist him or her onto an examination table. The patient is usually more comfortable in a semi-sitting position. Do not leave the patient alone. Inform the physician and, if it is available and ordered, administer oxygen. Call EMS for transport to an emergency facility. Monitor and record vital signs.

Keys to Success
ASPIRIN AND STROKES

At the first sign of an impending stroke, the patient should chew one 5-grain aspirin tablet. Patients should consult a physician before adding aspirin to their treatment regimen.

Head Injuries

The severity of trauma to the head depends on what caused the injury, the force of the offending object, and the location of the trauma. Injuries may be open or closed and involve a fracture of the skull and soft-tissue damage (Figure 23-54 ◆). Most severe head and facial injuries, including open skull fractures, require advanced medical treatment, and the patient should be transported to an emergency facility. If severe bleeding is present, gently apply an absorbent dressing.

A neurological assessment is helpful to EMS and the physician. If the victim is conscious, attempt to keep him or her quiet and ask what happened.

Other Medical Emergencies

Other medical emergencies you may encounter include sudden onset of abdominal pain, diabetic crises, and poisoning.

Acute Abdominal Pain

Acute abdominal pain with a sudden onset often signals a serious underlying condition and must be assessed by the physician to determine the cause. Assessment is done in quadrants. Palpation begins in the upper right quadrant and moves clockwise around the abdomen, terminating in the lower right quadrant. While not definitive in a diagnosis, pain located in certain quadrant(s) signals possible acute conditions:

- Upper right quadrant—gallbladder disorders
- Lower right quadrant—appendicitis
- Back or flank region (retroperitoneal)—kidney disorders
- Pelvis—urinary infection, pelvic infection, or problem in lower GI tract; patient may guard the abdomen and sit with the knees drawn up

In the medical office, make the patient as comfortable as possible, preferably sitting with the knees drawn up on an examination table. Keep the patient warm, and take and record vital signs. Do not allow the patient to eat or drink or take pain medication unless you have the physician's permission. If the patient becomes unconscious and vomits, there is a risk of aspiration and further complications. If an undiagnosed condition is found, the patient may have to have surgery. Keep the patient NPO if there is the potential need for general anesthesia and until the physician gives orders to provide food and fluids.

For acute abdominal, flank, or pelvic pain, the patient must be examined by a physician. Laboratory and radiographic studies along with the examination and history assist the physician in a diagnosis and subsequent orders for treatment.

Figure 23-53 ◆ Stroke symptoms: (A) Facial droop; (B) Speech difficulties; (C) Arm drift
Source: Photo A) Michal Heron.

Diabetic Coma or Insulin Shock

A patient with diabetes may exhibit signs of either **hypoglycemia** or **hyperglycemia.** Both conditions may cause the rapid onset of altered levels of consciousness. The greatest risk for a patient is hypoglycemia.

Hypoglycemia, in which blood sugar falls below 70 mg per deciliter, may be the result of a skipped meal, vomiting after taking diabetic medications, excessive exercise, or an unknown reason. A patient may appear to be intoxicated (slurred speech, balance disturbances, and uncharacteristic behavior), have cold clammy skin, and be anxious or combative. Intervention must be immediate and consists of some form of glucose administration. If the patient is conscious, ask about the last intake of food and diabetic medication. If the patient is able to swallow, glucose paste may be placed inside the mouth behind the lip and along the cheek, or the patient may drink orange juice with added sugar. If the patient is unconscious, IV glucose is administered. The person experiencing hypoglycemia is in grave danger when the blood glucose drops below 40. The brain requires glucose to survive, and brain cells begin dying unless glucose is administered promptly. If possible, blood glucose levels should be checked with a blood glucose monitor. Contact EMS if a physician is not available to administer IV glucose.

If there is doubt about whether the patient is hypoglycemic or hyperglycemic, glucose may be administered. It will raise the glucose 25 to 50 points, but this rise can be reversed with an insulin injection as soon as an elevated glucose is diagnosed.

The hyperglycemic individual may experience acidosis. As this condition progresses the patient's breath develops a sweet, fruity odor, indicating the presence of ketones. The patient may progress to an unconscious state, reversible with insulin. The physician orders the amount and route of the insulin.

CONCUSSION
- Mild injury, usually with no detectable brain damage
- May have brief loss of consciousness
- Headache, grogginess, and short-term memory loss common

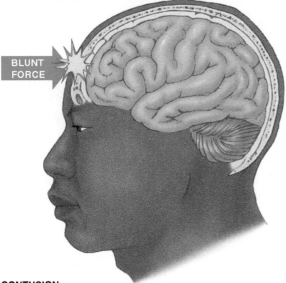

BLUNT FORCE

CONTUSION
- Unconsciousness or decreased level of responsiveness
- Bruising of brain tissue

Figure 23-54 ◆ Closed head injuries

Whether the patient is hypoglycemic or hyperglycemic, keep him or her as warm and comfortable as possible on an examination table until the physician arrives.

∞ Table 22-3 (p. 453) compares hypoglycemic and hyperglycemic reactions.

Poisoning and Overdose

Poisoning and overdoses may be accidental or intentional. The poison and its means of entry must be identified before appropriate treatment can begin. Poisons can be introduced into the body in four ways.

- Ingestion (swallowing): Ingested poisons include drugs, cleaning materials, food toxins, poisonous plants, and petroleum products. Depending on the substance, the patient drinks water or milk, or vomiting is induced. Vomiting is never induced when petroleum products or caustic substances have been ingested or when the patient is unconscious. Activated charcoal is often administered after emesis has been successfully induced to absorb any poison left in the GI tract.
- Injection: Injected poisons include drugs and any other poisonous substance delivered by insect sting, bite, sharp or piercing object, or needle. A patient who has been injected with a poison usually requires an antidote to counteract it.
- Absorption: Some poisons, such as insecticides, may be absorbed through the skin. The process of absorption can be slowed if the area is cleansed immediately with copious amounts of water.
- Inhalation: Inhaled poisons such as carbon monoxide enter the body through the respiratory tract. The patient

Keys to Success
TREATING INSECT STINGS

Insect stings may be insignificant or life-threatening. Some are quite painful, while others cause no pain and the victim is unaware of the sting until itching, redness, or a reaction develop. Help the victim by following these steps.

1. Remove the stinger by scraping across the affected area with a credit card or other rigid object. This is usually the only treatment necessary to remove the stinger.
2. Apply a paste of baking soda and water to the area.
3. If the victim is allergic to certain types of insect stings (bees, wasps, hornets), administer antihistamine or epinephrine, as ordered by the physician.

must be given respiratory support—usually supplemental oxygen—and an antidote, if applicable.

Poison Control Centers

Poison Control Centers have been established in most areas of the United States. The American Association of Poison Control Centers and Rocky Mountain Poison Control Centers offer telephone contact information for local centers. Telephone books usually list toll-free numbers as well.

Poison Control Centers offer emergency advice concerning accidental poisoning and overdose. In most cases there is no charge for this service. Registered nurses, pharmacists, and often physicians are available 24 hours a day, seven days a week, to provide emergency treatment instructions. The caller's name and phone number are recorded for follow-up contact within 24 hours after the initial patient contact and instructions. After follow-up, the caller's identity is discarded and the remaining information is used for statistics and for events reportable to the CDC. The caller provides the following information: sex, age, and weight of the poisoning victim; the substance ingested, including amount and any information on container; the time of occurrence; any other pertinent information; and any intervention made. Instructions are then given for the appropriate intervention.

Foreign Bodies in the Eye, Ear, and Nose

Foreign bodies present a unique challenge in the medical office. They include dirt, rust particles, metal, insects, and other small objects.

Keys to Success
ANIMAL BITES

Any animal, including humans, can inflict bites. First aid in the medical office involves cleansing the wound with soap and water and covering it with a sterile dressing until the physician assesses it and decides on the next step. Depending on the extent and location of the bite, sutures may be necessary. When children are bitten on the face, arms, and hands, they are often referred to a plastic surgeon for repair with minimal scarring.

Obtain information regarding the animal that inflicted the injury. Contact your local law enforcement agency for the name of the appropriate agency to call. A law enforcement officer may notify the agency for you. In many communities, animal bites are reported to an animal control department. You should familiarize yourself with local guidelines.

Keys to Success
TEACHING CHILDREN ABOUT POISONS

Mr. Yuk and Officer Ugg are two television characters who teach children how to identify potential poisons and containers containing poisonous materials.

Mr. Yuk was developed by the Children's Hospital of Pittsburgh to promote awareness of poisons among children by telling them never to touch anything with the picture of Mr. Yuk on it. Mr. Yuk has a green face and is sticking out his tongue. Stickers with Poison Control Center telephone number and a picture of Mr. Yuk are available to place on telephones.

Officer Ugg is used by Rocky Mountain Poison Control Centers as a symbol to warn children about poisonous substances. Officer Ugg wears a blue uniform and has a green face with white hands across the mouth.

A foreign body in the eye requires immediate attention to prevent further damage. Sterile eyewash may be used in some cases. Have the victim turn the head toward the affected side. Apply sterile wash across the eye from the inner cannula outward, gently letting it flow across the eye. If sterile eyewash is not available, you may use sterile IV fluid and tubing to wash the eye. As a last resort, have the victim place his or her head under water running in a slow stream, also from the inner cannula out. If both eyes are affected, irrigate one eye, then the other.

Impaled objects must be secured. Both eyes are closed and patched to prevent further damage, as the eyes are sympathetic and move together. The good eye is patched first to limit movement of the injured eye. Rust in the eye causes a rust ring residue that must be removed by a physician. Patients are often referred to an ophthalmologist for additional treatment. Surgery may be required to remove the impaled object.

An insect in the ear is easily removed by placing the patient in a dark room and shining a flashlight into the ear. If the insect is alive, it will migrate to the light source and come out of the ear on its own accord. If the insect is dead, gentle irrigation of the outer ear canal with a solution of 50 percent hydrogen peroxide and 50 percent warm water will wash it out.

Children sometimes push small objects up their noses. If the object is a dry item, such as a bean or dried pea, it will absorb moisture from the nasal mucosa and swell, blocking air passage through that nostril. Encourage the patient to blow the nose. If the object does not come out, a physician will have to remove the object, usually with instruments.

Psychosocial Emergencies

Psychosocial emergencies presenting on the phone or in person require prompt attention. They include child abuse, domestic violence, elder abuse, rape or sexual abuse, drug abuse, threatened suicide, depression, alcoholic intoxication, rage, and psychotic behavior.

Child and elder abuse are often detected during a routine office visit, or the victim may be seeking treatment for injuries resulting from abuse. By law these incidents are considered mandatory reportable incidents. Record all the information the victim or a family member provides. Reassure the victim that he or she does not deserve to be abused and is not responsible for the abuser's action. Treat any injuries and provide emotional support as required.

Domestic Violence

A victim of domestic violence may be reluctant to reveal any information, and according to state law that wish must be respected. If the victim chooses to share information about the abuse, listen in a calm, nonjudgmental manner, and inform the physician, who will determine the course of action. In most states, reporting is mandatory only in cases of child or elder abuse. Familiarize yourself with state and local statutes pertaining to abuse.

Sexual Abuse and Rape

Most states have statutes regarding rape and sexual abuse victims, and medical office protocol is designed accordingly. A calm and understanding approach helps the victim feel comfortable and secure. Assure her that she did not ask for this treatment and did not deserve to be sexually abused or raped. If the victim requests that no law enforcement agency be contacted, her wishes should be honored unless state law dictates otherwise.

Depression

Severely depressed persons look sad, may be tearful, and avoid eye contact. They require understanding and someone to listen to their problems. In an emergency situation, the physician must be notified as soon as possible, and the patient should not be left alone. ∞ Depression is a complex disorder that is further discussed in Chapter 29, Mental Health.

Suicide

The patient or individual who voices the intent to commit suicide on the phone or in the office should be taken seriously. Note if the person refers to the future or to details of the planned suicide. If the suicide threat is made over the phone, ask the following specific questions:

- "What is your name?"
- "How old are you?" or "When were you born?"
- "Where are you right now?"
- "Do you have an address?"
- "What is the telephone number from where you are calling?"
- "Are you alone?"
- "Have you ever felt this way before?"
- "Do you have access to any weapons, pills, or other means of suicide?"

These questions demonstrate your concern while providing you with the necessary information to get help. If the person is in the office, ask why he or she feels this way and if he or she has attempted suicide before.

When dealing with any potential suicide victim, help him or her identify reasons to go on living. Ask who will take care of the children, pets, home, and so on. Ask how you can help. Make the physician aware of the situation as soon as possible. Individuals at risk for suicide are often referred to a mental health facility for further intervention and treatment. Document any information you obtain and any action taken.

Rage

If the patient or other individual is agitated or hostile, the primary intervention is to defuse the situation. It is important to remain calm and speak in a quiet voice, which may help convince the person to accept assistance. Address the person by name. Do *not* interrupt, and do not respond in anger. Listen and try to understand the person's feelings. Sometimes an angry person just wants to air his or her frustration. Take notes so the person feels you are taking him or her seriously and repeat back the information.

If the individual has been diagnosed with psychotic behavior, recognize that you may need help. Attempt to redirect the rage to an inanimate object or to something outside the office environment. If you cannot defuse the situation, follow office protocol for contacting local law enforcement for assistance. An agitated psychotic individual is a danger to him- or herself and to everyone else in the building. Keep in mind that the leading cause of death in the workplace is homicide.

Alcohol Intoxication

The intoxicated patient may be unruly and uncooperative or very subdued. The odor of alcohol is usually noticeable. The patient should not be left alone; help should be requested and the physician notified for orders. It is best not to confront the alcohol-intoxicated patient until the physician is present to direct treatment and assist in handling the situation.

Psychotic Behavior

∞ Psychotic behavior is discussed in Chapter 29, Mental Health. It is best to be cordial to a patient exhibiting psychotic behavior and to request help from other staff. Ask the patient to sit down so you can talk quietly together. During a psychotic episode a patient may experience hallucinations (auditory or visual) and will require immediate intervention by a physician. Have someone advise the physician that his or her presence is required immediately.

REVIEW

Chapter Summary

- Each team member must know what procedures to follow in a medical emergency. As an MA, you will need advanced training in CPR, AED, and treating specialty office emergencies, such as allergic reactions.
- Patients may experience fainting, seizures, anaphylactic shock, and other conditions when visiting the medical office for other health reasons. Contacting the physician and EMS, if necessary, is part of office protocol. Good Samaritan laws were established to encourage health-care professionals to volunteer in emergencies without fear of financial liability. It is important that you and other health-care professionals render emergency care according to scope of license, certification, or training until relieved by another health professional.
- EMS may be called for on-the-scene care, stabilization of the victim, and transport to the appropriate emergency room for further assessment and treatment.
- Equipment is kept for medical emergencies in the medical office. The amount and type of equipment vary according to the types of patients seen and proximity to advanced emergency care. Examples of emergency equipment are the crash cart, oxygen supplies, emergency drugs, and intravenous supplies.
- In an emergency, you must first determine if the scene is safe to enter. If it is not safe, wait for emergency assistance. If it is safe, a primary survey determines the care for life-threatening conditions, followed by a secondary survey to assess and set priorities for additional care.
- For individuals experiencing acute chest pain, loss of consciousness, or respiratory arrest, CPR protocol is followed. First, establish whether the individual is unconscious. If the patient is conscious, there is no need to proceed with CPR. If the patient is unconscious, you will need to open the airway. If it is obstructed, determine whether the obstruction is total, partial with good air exchange, or partial with poor air exchange. If the breathing is obstructed, reposition the airway and attempt to ventilate. If you cannot ventilate the victim, proceed with the obstructed airway sequence until the obstruction is removed. When the airway is functioning, the third step is to check the pulse—carotid in the adult and child and brachial in the infant. If there is no pulse, begin compressions. Use AED on adults, but not on children or infants. If CPR is not needed, keep the victim comfortable, warm, and in the recovery position until EMS help arrives.
- Other cardiac and respiratory emergencies include chest pain, respiratory distress, SOB, hyperventilation, congestive heart failure, chronic obstructive pulmonary disease, and pulmonary edema. Chest pain may require emergency treatment with oxygen and/or nitroglycerin. If a patient with chest pain calls the medical office, keep the caller on the line and arrange for EMS to transport the patient to an emergency facility for evaluation and treatment.

Chapter Summary (continued)

■ Shock is the collapse of the cardiovascular system and may occur in any of several forms, including anaphylactic, cardiogenic, hemorrhagic, metabolic, neurogenic, psychogenic, respiratory, and septic. Shock may be life-threatening and require emergency treatment.

■ Vascular and soft tissue emergencies include bleeding, open wounds, and closed wounds. Pressure bandages on the bleeding site and direct pressure on pressure points are part of the treatment. You should be aware of and monitor the signs and symptoms of internal bleeding, bruising, tenderness, swelling, and pain at the site of the injury. Treatment varies according to type and extent of injury but includes elevation and ice, cleansing and bandages, and pain medication.

■ Thermal injuries to the skin and body systems caused by cold or heat may be considered medical emergencies. Burns and frostbite are integumentary insults. Treatment varies according to the depth of the injury. Systemic insults are often life-threatening and include hyperthermia and hypothermia.

■ Musculoskeletal injuries include fractures, dislocations, sprains, and strains. Fractures may be closed or open, simple or compound, and may lead to circulatory and neurological complications. The injured body part should be immobilized and observed for pain, numbness, swelling, bruising, bleeding, and circulation. If there is a skin break, dressings should be applied to prevent infection.

■ Allergic reactions can be life-threatening if they progress to anaphylactic shock, but can be treated in the office with follow-up evaluation, additional treatment, and patient education. Neurological emergencies, such as seizures and head trauma, require advanced evaluation and treatment in an acute-care hospital setting. Medical emergencies include sudden acute pain, diabetic coma or insulin shock, and poisoning. The physician assesses the patient, provides initial treatment, and refers the patient to an acute-care facility. Foreign bodies in the eyes, ears, and nose may be removed in the medical office or an emergency care facility, depending on the extent of the injury. If an object is impaled in the eye, it is necessary to cover the good eye first before the affected eye.

■ When handling psychosocial emergencies—rape, domestic violence, drug abuse, depression, psychotic behavior, suicide attempts, and other situations—it is important to know the laws that apply to treatment in the medical office. Encourage the patient to talk, ask questions, and take notes.

Chapter Review Questions

Multiple Choice

1. Which of the following is a life-threatening medical emergency requiring immediate intervention?
   A. open chest wound
   B. seizure
   C. severe vomiting
   D. major fracture

2. The victim of a sudden stop in a vehicle should
   A. receive pain medication before the primary survey.
   B. be moved immediately before splinting.
   C. be treated even if he or she refuses.
   D. have his or her neck and possibly spine immobilized.

3. The Heimlich maneuver on a child is performed by
   A. using abdominal thrusts.
   B. using chest thrusts.
   C. strongly shaking the child.
   D. strongly squeezing the child.

4. Which of the following should you do when administering nitroglycerin?
   A. Ask the patient to swallow the tablet immediately.
   B. Put the patient's tablet directly on his or her tongue.
   C. Wear disposable gloves before handling the patient's tablet.
   D. Call EMS and wait before administering the nitroglycerin.

5. If a patient has a partial airway obstruction, you should
   A. help the patient lie down.
   B. assist the patient to a sitting position.
   C. start CPR.
   D. perform the Heimlich maneuver.

6. Septic shock is caused by
   A. infection in the bloodstream.
   B. heart failure.
   C. loss of body fluids and electrolytes.
   D. an allergic reaction to a substance.

7. Blood from capillaries
   A. flows rapidly, echoing the heartbeat.
   B. flows rapidly and copiously.
   C. flows slowly and is darker in color.
   D. oozes slowly.

8. Which of the following steps should you perform when applying a pressure bandage?
   A. Add dressings every 10 minutes.
   B. Add dressings every 5 minutes.
   C. Keep the original dressing in place.
   D. Remove the original dressing and add a new dressing.

Chapter Review Questions (continued)

9. Which of the following procedures should be used in the treatment of a full-thickness burn?
    A. Immerse the burn in cool water.
    B. Leave it untouched and cover with a sterile dressing.
    C. Soak sterile gauze and apply it to the burn.
    D. Apply burn ointment immediately.

10. When a patient in the medical office experiences a seizure, you should
    A. never force open the mouth.
    B. force open the mouth.
    C. keep the patient in an upright position by holding him or her in place.
    D. keep the patient's head straight, even if saliva has formed in his or her mouth.

True/False

T F   1. A laceration is an open wound in which the outer layer of skin is scraped away.

T F   2. Hypoglycemia is a condition in which blood glucose is below normal.

T F   3. EMS technicians provide on-the-scene intervention and treatment but do not transfer patients.

T F   4. Since its introduction in 1968, the 911 emergency access number has been so successful that it is used in every single U.S. state.

T F   5. Decreased levels of consciousness are not a life-threatening condition.

T F   6. The first step in any emergency is to check if the victim is alert.

T F   7. You should not move a victim or help a victim move after a fall or sudden stop, such as a car accident, unless the victim is conscious.

T F   8. Cardiac arrest and heart attack have exactly the same symptoms from onset to death.

T F   9. AED can be used on children 1 year old or younger as long as the rescuer uses pediatric-size pads.

T F 10. If a child is choking on an object but can still move air past the object, a sharp, quick blow to the back between the shoulder blades may help move the item out of the airway.

Short Answer

1. When is the Heimlich maneuver used?

2. Blind finger sweeps can be performed on patients of what age?

3. What is the leading cause of death in both men and women?

Research

1. In your community, is Healthcare Providers CPR and First Aid required for medical assistant certification?

2. Is there a Good Samaritan Law in your community?

Externship Application Experience

While waiting for a scheduled appointment for a pre-employment physical, a 36-year-old female comes to the receptionist's window and states that she does not feel well. You observe that her face is pale and ashen. You check her pulse and note that it is fast and thready. She drops to the floor. What do you do next?

Resource Guide

American Heart Association (AHA)
American Heart Association National Center
7272 Greenville Ave.
Dallas, TX 75231
1-800-AHA-USA1
!-888-4STROKE
www.americanheart.org

American Red Cross
www.redcross.org

National Highway Traffic Safety Administration
1-888-327-4236
www.nhtsa.dot.org

U.S. Department of Transportation (USDOT)
400 7th St. SW
Washington, DC 20590
www.dot.gov

MedMedia
www.prenhall.com/frazier

More on this chapter, including interactive resources, can be found on the Student CD-ROM accompanying this textbook and on the Companion Website at www.prenhall.com/frazier.

Objectives

After completing this chapter, you should be able to:

- Spell and define the medical terminology in this chapter.
- Define the role of the medical assistant in the GI medical office.
- Describe the basic anatomy and physiology of the gastrointestinal system and accessory organs.
- Identify disease and disorders of the gastrointestinal system and accessory organs.
- List and describe the basic food components: proteins, carbohydrates, fiber, lipids, vitamins, minerals, and water.
- Explain how the Food Guide Pyramid/MyPyramid is used for healthy meal planning.
- Describe how individual health is affected by nutritional status.
- Discuss the factors that may affect caloric intake.
- Explain the effects of alcohol on nutritional status.
- Describe the relationship between aging and nutrition.
- List and describe the types of disorders associated with altered nutritional status.
- List some common food allergies and how they are diagnosed.
- Name the anatomical divisions and clinical quadrants of the body.
- List the diagnostic procedures performed for GI disorders.
- List and describe special and therapeutic diets commonly prescribed for GI patients.

Gastroenterology and Nutrition

Case Study

Reggie, an MA, is rooming a teenage patient, Serena, when her mother asks to speak to him regarding her care. Reggie takes the appropriate measures and makes sure he has the patient's permission to discuss her care with a family member. During the conversation, Serena's mother mentions that her daughter has decided with some of her friends at school to become a vegetarian. The mother is concerned that she is not going to get enough protein and will become anemic.

MedMedia
www.prenhall.com/frazier

Additional interactive resources and activities for this chapter can be found on the Companion Website. For audio glossary, legal and ethical scenarios, job scenarios, quizzes, games, virtual tours and activities related to the content of this chapter, please access the accompanying CD-ROM in this book.

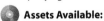 **Assets Available:**

Audio Glossary
Legal and Ethical Scenario: *Gastroenterology and Nutrition*
On the Job Scenario: *Gastroenterology and Nutrition*
A & P Quiz: The Digestive System
Multiple Choice Quiz
Games: Crossword, Strikeout and Spelling Bee
3D Virtual Tour: Digestive System: The Digestive System
Drag and Drop: Digestive System: Digestive System; The Intestinal Wall

Medical Terminology

absorption—passage of digested food products through the wall of the intestine into the bloodstream

alimentary canal—tube-like structure of the gastrointestinal system that originates in the mouth and terminates at the anus

alimentation—entire process of providing nourishment to the body that includes mastication, swallowing, digestion, and absorption

amino acids—chief components of protein, synthesized in the body and obtained from the diet

anastomosis—surgical joining of two tubular structures

anorexia—diminished desire to eat or diminished appetite.

anus—terminal aspect of the gastrointestinal tract through which dietary waste is expelled

bolus—mass of masticated food that is swallowed

calorie(also called small calorie)—energy released from the metabolism of proteins, fats, and carbohydrates; amount of heat required to raise 1 gram of water 1 degree Celsius

carbohydrates—simple and compound sugars that are the primary source of energy for metabolism

cholesterol—steroid alcohol formed in the liver and also found in plant and animal fats; may be responsible for fatty deposits of plaque in blood vessels

chyme—mixture of partially digested food and enzymes that enters the small intestines

colonoscopy—visual examination of the colon using a colonoscope

colostomy—surgically created opening connecting the colon to the abdominal surface for fecal evacuation

complete protein—protein containing all the essential amino acids

digestion—physical and chemical conversion of food into substances that can be used by the body

dyspepsia—painful digestion

dysphagia—difficulty swallowing

electrolytes—substances present in the bloodstream, cells, and tissues that are involved in homeostatic changes in acid-base balance, movement of tissue fluid, and activities of the cells and cellular walls

elimination—expulsion of waste products from the body

⊕ MEDICAL ASSISTING COMPETENCIES

CAAHEP ENTRY-LEVEL COMPETENCIES FOR CMA	ABHES ENTRY-LEVEL COMPETENCIES FOR RMA
■ Identify and respond to issues of confidentiality.	■ Project a positive attitude
■ Perform within legal and ethical boundaries.	■ Maintain confidentiality at all times
■ Demonstrate knowledge of federal and state health care legislation and regulations.	■ Be a "team player."
■ Perform hand washing.	■ Be cognizant of ethical boundaries.
■ Dispose of biohazardous materials.	■ Exhibit initiative.
■ Practice standard precautions.	■ Adapt to change.
■ Use methods of quality control.	■ Evidence a responsible attitude.
■ Obtain vital signs.	■ Be courteous and diplomatic.
■ Obtain and record patient history.	■ Conduct work within scope of education, training, and ability.
■ Prepare and maintain examination room and treatment areas.	■ Provide patient education for post-procedural care.
■ Prepare patient for and assist with routine and specialty examinations.	■ Prepare patients for procedures.
■ Prepare patient for and assist with procedures, treatments, and minor office surgeries.	■ Apply principles of aseptic techniques and infection control.
■ Screen and follow up test results.	■ Prepare and maintain examination and treatment area.
	■ Collect and process specimens.
	■ Perform selected CLIA waived tests that assist with diagnosis and treatment.
	■ Dispose of biohazardous materials.
	■ Practice standard precautions.
	■ Inform patients of dietary needs and treatment options.

Introduction

The gastrointestinal system is responsible primarily for the nourishment of the body. Salivation, mastication, and the process of **digestion** break food down into nutritional substances. Further processes of **metabolism** and **absorption** convert the products of digestion into fuel and nutrients for cellular functions.

Good nutritional habits help the body maintain a strong immune system and maintain healthy energy levels and mental alertness. During times of impaired health, a healthy nutritional status can speed recovery. For example, when nutritional supplements are given to hospitalized or nonhospitalized patients during the recovery process from surgery, wounds heal faster.

 # The Medical Assistant's Role in the Gastroenterology Office

Obtaining and recording the patient's medical history and vital signs are routine and essential functions of the medical assistant in the **gastroenterology** or **proctology** medical office. As an MA, you will need to be familiar with the anatomy of the GI tract as well as the regions of the abdomen. You will record specific symptoms as reported by the patient. Assisting the physician as

Medical Terminology *(continued)*

emesis—regurgitation of partially digested food from the stomach; vomit

emulsification—transformation of ingested particles of fat into small globules with bile

fat—food component that is a source of energy and aids in growth and development by providing fatty acids

feces—waste product of digestion that is expelled through the rectum and anus

fiber—nondigestible substances found in food, such as cellulose and pectin, that provide bulk and roughage for the evacuation of fecal waste

flatulence—excessive gas or air generated in the stomach or intestinal tract

gastric—pertaining to the stomach

gastroenterology—the study of diseases affecting the gastrointestinal tract

gastroscopy—visual examination of the stomach using a gastroscope

hematemesis—vomiting of blood, an indication of bleeding in upper GI tract

hepatomegaly—enlargement of the liver

ileostomy—surgical opening of the ileum onto the surface of the abdomen for the elimination of fecal material

incomplete protein—protein lacking one or more of the essential amino acids

intrinsic factor—A glycoprotein secreted by the parietal cells of the gastric mucosa

jaundice—yellowing of skin and mucous membranes resulting from deposit of bile

pigment; usually a symptom of a biliary disease process

kilocalorie—1000 small calories; amount of heat required to raise 1 kilogram of water 1 degree Celsius

large intestine—extending from the ileum to the anus and is approximately 5 ft. in length; includes the cecum and colon.

lipids—fat-related substances not soluble in water (triglycerides, fats, oils, phospholipids, sterols)

malnutrition—condition of excess or deficient nutrient and caloric intake

melena—black, tarry stools

metabolism—process of changing nutrients from food into substances for anabolic or catabolic activity

mineral—element essential to every cell, naturally occurring in nature, and used by the body in the processes of blood clotting, muscle contraction, and nervous system impulse conduction

obesity—excess body weight 20 to 30 percent above average for gender, age, and height, with abnormal amounts of body fat

overweight—general term for early stage of excess body weight above standard for gender, age, and height

peristalsis—rhythmic, involuntary, wavelike motion in the hollow tubes of the body that assists the passage of contents

polyps—fingerlike growths on the mucous membranes throughout the body

portal hypertension—condition of increased blood flow pressure through the blood vessels of the liver (portal circulation), often caused by cirrhosis of the liver or compression of the hepatic blood vessels

proctology—medical practice specializing in disorders of the rectum and anus

protein—food component composed of amino acids; provides a source of energy and assists in building and renewing body tissues

saturated fats—fats derived from animal sources that are solid at room temperature

small intestine—starting from the duodenum to the large intestine; includes the jejunum and ileum.

total parenteral nutrition—nutrition ingested by means other than oral intake

triglycerides—chief form of fat found in foods

unsaturated fats—fats derived from plant sources that are liquid at room temperature

upper gastrointestinal tract—oral cavity (mouth), pharynx, esophagus, duodenum, and stomach

vitamins—components required for metabolism, growth, and development

Abbreviations

BMI—Body Mass Index

DGA—Dietary Guidelines for Americans

DHHS—Department of Health and Human Services

ERCP—endoscopic retrograde cholangiopancreatography

FNB—Food Nutrition Board

GI—gastrointestinal

HDL—high-density lipoproteins

LDL—low-density lipoproteins

LGI—lower gastrointestinal

LLQ—left lower quadrant

LUQ—left upper quadrant

N & V—nausea and vomiting

RDA—recommended dietary allowance

RLQ—right lower quadrant

RUQ—right upper quadrant

S & S—signs and symptoms

TPN—total parenteral nutrition

UGI—upper gastrointestinal

USDA—U.S. Department of Agriculture

necessary during examinations and procedures is a routine function, along with instructing the patient in the removal of necessary clothing and providing a gown and drape. You will also arrange appointments for diagnostic tests and procedures and provide patient instruction concerning dietary guidelines and the collection of specimens. You should be aware of community resources for gastroenterology patients such as cancer screening, food pantries, and **colostomy** support.

The Anatomy and Physiology of the Gastrointestinal System

The gastrointestinal **(GI)** system, or digestive tract, is composed of the **alimentary canal** and accessory organs (Figure 24-1 ◆). The alimentary canal, a tubelike structure, begins with the **upper gastrointestinal tract (UGI),** or upper digestive tract,

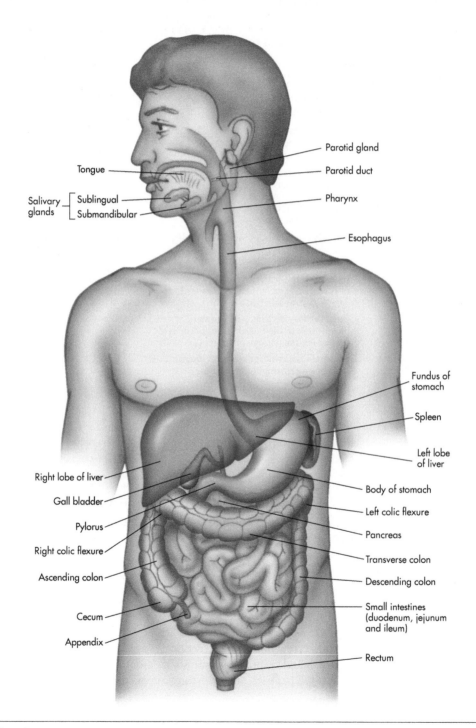

Figure 24-1 ◆ The digestive system

which includes the mouth, pharynx, esophagus, stomach, and duodenum. The next portion, called the **lower gastrointestinal tract (LGI)** or lower digestive tract, includes the small intestine, large intestine, cecum, appendix, sigmoid portion, rectum, and **anus.** The small intestine consists of the duodenum, jejunum, and ileum. The large intestine is made up of the cecum, ascending colon, transverse colon, descending colon, and sigmoid regions of the colon, terminating in the rectum. The accessory organs of the GI system are the pancreas, liver, gallbladder, and connecting ducts. The structures of the GI system and their functions are summarized in Table 24-1.

The alimentary canal is composed of four layers: the mucosa, submucosa (containing the main blood vessels of the GI tract), mucularis, and serosa (Figure 24-2 ◆). The outer surface of the stomach and intestines is covered and protected by a serosal-type surface called the parietal peritoneum. The peritoneal surface next to the GI organs is referred to as the visceral peritoneum. Blood is supplied to the GI system by the upper and lower mesenteric arteries and is drained away by the portal system.

The liver performs several functions. One primary function is assisting in the metabolism of proteins, fats, and carbohydrates. The liver removes nutrients from the blood, and during a process called glycogenesis, it stores glucose as glycogen and converts glycogen as needed into glucose. In another process called glyconeogenesis, the liver stores fat and protein for conversion into glucose. The liver also helps in the formation of clotting factors and blood plasma proteins as well as in the detoxification of drugs and some toxic substances.

The biliary tract comprises the organs and ducts involved in the secretion, storage, and transport of bile and digestive enzymes to the duodenum (Figure 24-3 ◆). The liver secretes bile, which functions in the emulsification of fats (lipids). The bile leaves the liver via the common hepatic duct to be stored in the gallbladder. When stimulated by the presence of fat in the duodenum, the gallbladder contracts and releases bile into the cystic duct. The cystic duct and the hepatic duct join to form the common bile duct, which empties into the duodenum. Pancreatic enzymes are also released through the common bile duct into the duodenum at an opening called the ampulla of Vater. The components of the biliary tract and their functions are listed in Table 24-2.

The Functions of the Gastrointestinal System

The major functions of the GI system are digestion and **alimentation,** which provide nourishment for the body, and the **elimination** of the waste products of digestion. This process is divided into the following steps:

- Ingestion: Food is taken through the mouth.
- Mastication (chewing): The initial, mechanical breaking up of food starts in the mouth with the teeth, mandible, maxilla, cheeks, tongue, and salivary glands. The resulting food mass is called a **bolus.**

TABLE 24-1　THE ALIMENTARY CANAL

Structure	Related Structures	Function
Oral cavity (mouth)		Initial entry into digestive tract; receives food and liquid for transformation and transport to rest of gastrointestinal tract.
	Teeth	Chew food (mastication). Mix saliva with food.
	Tongue	Assists in swallowing food.
	Salivary glands	Secrete saliva to add water and begin digestion of carbohydrates.
Esophagus		Moves bolus (masticated food) into stomach.
	Epiglottis	Closes to prevent food from entering bronchi.
	Cardiac sphincter—at distal aspect of esophagus	Prevents passage of gastric acid and other gastric contents back into esophagus.
Stomach	Muscular walls contain folds (rugae) for expansion; gastric mucosa contains glands that secrete hydrochloric acid, pepsinogen, and intrinsic factor	Mixes and dilutes swallowed mass as continuation of the digestive process. Acidic gastric secretions help in digestion of protein. Intrinsic factor makes absorption of Vitamin B_{12} possible.
	Pyloric sphincter at distal aspect of stomach	Prevents regurgitation of contents of duodenum into stomach.
Small intestine	Composed of duodenum (which contains ampulla of Vater at proximal junction), jejunum, ileum	Absorbs nutrients. Emulsifies fat with the help of bile and digests carbohydrates, fat (lipids), and protein with the help of pancreatic enzymes.
Large intestine (also known as colon)	Composed of cecum, ascending colon, transverse colon, descending colon, sigmoid colon	Absorbs water and electrolytes.
Rectum	Terminates at anus at body surface	Stores waste for defecation.

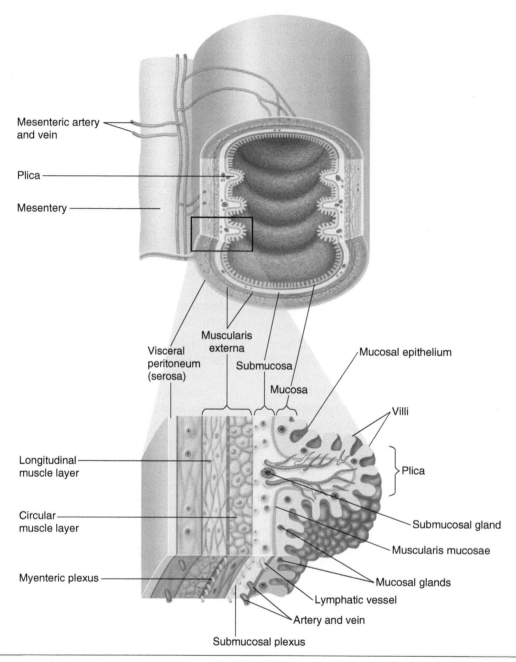

Mesenteric artery and vein

Plica

Mesentery

Muscularis externa

Visceral peritoneum (serosa)

Submucosa

Mucosa

Mucosal epithelium

Villi

Plica

Longitudinal muscle layer

Circular muscle layer

Submucosal gland

Muscularis mucosae

Mucosal glands

Myenteric plexus

Lymphatic vessel

Artery and vein

Submucosal plexus

Figure 24-2 ◆ Mucosal surface of the small intestine

- Deglutition (swallowing): This process involves the tongue, pharynx, and esophagus. **Peristalsis** begins in the esophagus.
- Digestion: The food is chemically broken down into substances that can be absorbed into the bloodstream. This process begins in the mouth when the salivary glands release amylase, which begins the digestion of starches, and progresses to the stomach, where hydrochloric acid and **gastric** enzymes (pepsin, gastrin, **intrinsic factor**) enter the digestive process. The end product of this process is called **chyme.** In the duodenum, bile for the **emulsification** of **fats** is joined by pancreatic enzymes (lipase and

protease) and intestinal enzymes (enterokinase, cholecystokinin, and secretin) to break down **carbohydrates, lipids,** and **proteins.**
- Absorption: In the small intestine, nutrients from the chemically digested food are absorbed into the bloodstream for transport to body cells. Water, fluids, and **electrolytes** are absorbed mainly in the large intestine.
- Excretion: Food that has not been digested, miscellaneous secretions, and the excretory products of metabolism are eliminated from the body through the rectum and anus. This final waste product of digestion is termed **feces.**

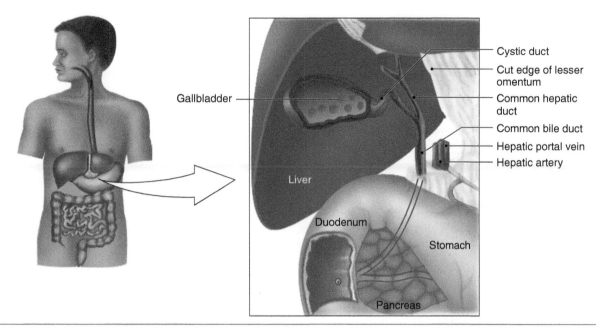

Figure 24-3 ◆ The gallbladder

TABLE 24-2 THE BILIARY TRACT	
Accessory Organ	**Function**
Liver	■ Manufactures bile for emulsification of fat (lipids) ■ Stores glucose as glycogen and converts glycogen as needed into glucose (glycogenesis) ■ Stores fat and protein for conversion into glucose (glyconeogenesis) ■ Detoxifies drugs and some toxic substances ■ Helps in the formation of clotting factors and blood plasma proteins
Common hepatic duct	Joins with the common cystic duct to form the common bile duct; carries bile from the liver to the common hepatic duct
Gallbladder	Stores bile from the liver
Common bile duct	Exits from the gallbladder and joins the pancreatic duct to deliver bile and pancreatic enzymes to the duodenum
Pancreas	■ Manufactures amylase for carbohydrate digestion, lipase for fat (lipids) digestion, trypsinogen, chymotripsinogen to digest proteins ■ Produces insulin, which transports glucose from the bloodstream into body cells for metabolism
Ampulla of Vater	Hepatopancreatic duct opening into the duodenum; releases bile and pancreatic enzymes from common bile duct into duodenum

Diseases and Disorders of the GI Tract

Diseases of the GI system include inflammatory conditions, obstructive conditions, infectious disorders, disorders due to increased or decreased peristalsis, circulatory and hemorrhagic disorders, congenital disorders, functional disorders, neoplasms, parasitic invasion, and food poisoning (Tables 24-3 and 24-4).

Nutrition

Food is required for the growth and repair of body tissues, provides nutrients that regulate body processes, and serves as the fuel for heat production. The basic components of food are carbohydrates, proteins, fats, **minerals, vitamins, fiber,** and water (Table 24-5).

■ Carbohydrates are the body's primary source of energy and are found primarily in breads and cereals, pasta products, rice, fruit, and potatoes.

■ Proteins assist in the building and renewing of body tissues. **Amino acids** are the building blocks of protein. There are eight *essential* amino acids, which cannot be manufactured by the body and must be supplied in the diet. The other 11 amino acids are *nonessential,* which means they can be manufactured internally by the body. A **complete protein** is one that supplies all the essential amino acids; meat, fish, eggs, and other animal products are a common source. Nuts, legumes, whole grains, and other vegetable sources provide **incomplete proteins.** Strict vegetarians, or vegans, must combine certain foods—such as beans and rice—to ensure an adequate intake of complete proteins.

(text continues on p. 509)

TABLE 24-3 DISORDERS AND CONDITIONS OF THE GASTROINTESTINAL TRACT

Condition or Disorder	Signs/Symptoms	Area Affected	Diagnosis	Treatment
Abnormal Function				
Constipation	Inability to move bowels, distension of abdomen, abdominal cramping	Small intestine, colon, rectum	Palpation of abdomen, auscultation of abdomen, imaging studies*	Laxatives, colonic irrigations, dietary changes
Diarrhea	Loose, watery stools, abdominal cramping	Colon, rectum	Reports of loose, watery stools	Antidiarrheal medications and dietary changes
Paralytic obstruction, also called paralytic ileus	Vomiting, abdominal distension, no bowel movements, severe abdominal pain	Esophagus, stomach, small intestine, colon, rectum	Palpation of abdomen, auscultation of abdomen, imaging studies	Drug therapy, surgical intervention
Vomiting	Expulsion of gastric contents through the mouth	Esophagus, stomach, small intestine	Visual exam, palpation, auscultation, imaging studies	Drug therapy, surgical intervention
Anatomical and Congenital Abnormalities				
Diverticulosis	Abdominal pain, abdominal distension, flatulence, difficulty and pain in defecation; small outpouching of intestinal lining that makes little pockets	Colon	Palpation, auscultation, imaging studies	Dietary changes, increase in roughage and fluids, avoiding seeds, nuts, and foods with skins
Gastroesophageal reflux disease (GERD)	Regurgitation of stomach and duodenal contents up into the esophagus. Usually occurs at night or when patient lies down	Esophagus, stomach, duodenum	Palpation, auscultation, imaging studies	Drug therapy, avoiding lying down for at least one hour after eating, elevating head of bed
Hiatal hernia	Portion of stomach slips up above the diaphragm into thoracic cavity	Esophagus, stomach, diaphragm	Imaging studies	Drug therapy, avoiding lying down for at least one hour after eating, elevating head of bed
Organic obstructions	Mechanical obstructions anywhere in GI tract. May be caused by tumors, strictures, foreign bodies, fecal impactions, adhesions, strangulated hernias	Esophagus, stomach, small intestine, colon, rectum	Visual exam, palpation, auscultation, imaging	Usually surgical intervention to relieve obstruction; fecal impaction may be removed digitally through rectum
Abdominal hernia	Lump appears in abdominal wall that can be painful or painless	Organ or part of an organ (usually the bowel) breaks through weak portion of muscles and membranes of a wall	Visual exam, palpation, auscultation, imaging studies	Surgical intervention usually the only way to resolve a hernia
Infections				
Gastroenteritis	Abdominal pain and cramping with or without vomiting and/or diarrhea	Stomach, small intestines, colon; commonly caused by rotavirus and Norwalk virus	Visual examination of individual, palpation and auscultation of abdomen	Drug therapy, hydration, diet modifications until condition improves
Enteritis	N & V, diarrhea, abdominal cramping, fever, malaise	Caused by invasion of protozoa or bacteria	Patient history, blood and stool cultures	Fluid and electrolyte replacement by mouth or IV therapy; nutritional support; antimicrobial, antinausea, and antiemetic medication; bed rest
Acute appendicitis	Sudden onset of acute pain in lower right quadrant of abdomen	Infection in appendix, causing inflammation, usually caused by bacteria	Palpation of abdomen, positive reaction to pressure on McBurney's point	Surgical excision of appendix to prevent rupture and peritonitis, accompanied by antibiotic therapy
Food Poisoning				
Salmonellosis	Abdominal pain, diarrhea, vomiting, abdominal cramping, fever	Stomach and intestines	Presence of salmonella in stool specimen	Usually resolves within a week; IV therapy may be required

TABLE 24-3 DISORDERS AND CONDITIONS OF THE GASTROINTESTINAL TRACT (*Continued*)

Condition or Disorder	Signs/Symptoms	Area Affected	Diagnosis	Treatment
Clostridium botulinum	Initial vomiting or diarrhea, later neurological complications, blurred vision, slurred speech, difficulty swallowing, paralysis, and respiratory failure	GI tract and nervous system	Presence of toxin in blood or stool	Antitoxin and support of systems when necessary
Escherichia coli	Abdominal cramping, vomiting, watery diarrhea possibly containing blood and mucus	GI tract	Presence of *E. coli* in stool specimens	Usually resolves without antibiotic intervention; supportive therapy may be required
Staphylococcus aureus	Severe nausea and vomiting, abdominal cramping, hypotension, reduced body temperature	Upper GI tract	Presence of *S. aureus* in suspected food	Usually resolves but supportive therapy may be required
Inflammation				
Esophagitis	Inflammation of mucosa lining the esophagus, causing pain	Irritation of mucosa caused by chemical or bacterial sources or reflux of gastric contents	Visual exam of esophagus, often with a gastroscope	Drug therapy and dietary modification
Gastritis	Pain, vomiting, eructation (belching). Acute: shallow lesions or erosions of gastric lining. Chronic: atrophy of gastric mucosa, mild and chronic inflammation.	Irritation of mucosa lining the stomach, caused by chemical or bacterial sources.	Symptoms aid in diagnosis. Visual exam, palpation, auscultation, imaging studies, often including gastroscopic exam	Drug therapy and dietary modification. Acute gastritis usually self-limiting
Peritonitis	Sudden, severe, general abdominal pain localizing at causal site; cool, clammy skin; possibly N & V and rigidity of abdomen	Inflammation of peritoneum caused by infection or foreign substance entering peritoneal cavity	Auscultation of bowel sounds, abdominal and chest x-rays, blood studies	NPO and nasogastric tube to keep GI tract empty; fluids and electrolytes by IV therapy; aggressive antibiotic therapy; surgery if perforation of GI tract occurs
Gastric/duodenal ulcer	Abdominal pain, possible bloody emesis or occult blood in the stool, abdominal distension and tenderness	Erosion of gastric or duodenal mucosa with or without bleeding, *H. pylori*	Visual exam, palpation, auscultation, imaging studies, including endoscopic examination (gastroscopy)	Drug therapy, diet modification, stress reduction, surgical intervention if other treatments unsuccessful
Stomatitis	Inflammation of tissue in the mouth	May be caused by bacteria, virus, or fungus	Visualization of oral cavity, microbiological smear or culture	Warm water mouth rinses, topical anesthetic for pain, bland or liquid diet; antiseptic mouthwashes further irritate condition and should not be used
Proctitis	Feeling of rectal fullness, constant urge to defecate, abdominal cramps, constipation, involuntary straining; pain; blood and mucus in stool	Inflammation of mucosa lining the rectum	Patient history, sigmoidoscopy, biopsy, microbiological smear or culture	Tranquilizers for emotional stress; elimination of laxatives; soothing enemas or suppositories to counteract effects of radiation
Diverticulitis	Abdominal pain, abdominal distension, flatulence, difficulty and pain in defecation	Colon inflammation in small outpouching of intestinal lining, occasionally infection of area	Palpation, auscultation, imaging studies	Dietary changes, increase in roughage and fluids, avoiding seeds, nuts, foods with skins; hydration and antibiotics if infection is present
Regional enteritis (Crohn's disease)	Abdominal pain, abdominal distension, flatulence, watery stools often containing blood, anorexia, weight loss, anemia, fatigue	Usually small intestine and ascending colon of large intestine, with inflammation of mucosa	Patient history, symptoms	There is no cure; antibiotics, corticosteroids, and surgical removal of the affected part
Chronic ulcerative colitis	Abdominal pain, abdominal distension, flatulence, watery stools often containing blood	Usually large intestine with inflammation of mucosa	Symptoms, patient history, colonoscopy	Antibiotics, corticosteroids, pain medication, possible surgical removal of affected area

(continued)

TABLE 24-3 DISORDERS AND CONDITIONS OF THE GASTROINTESTINAL TRACT *(continued)*

Condition or Disorder	Signs/Symptoms	Area Affected	Diagnosis	Treatment
Malignancies				
Carcinoma of the lip and tongue	Lesion on tongue or lip that does not heal; may be painful or painless	Tongue, lip, or mucosa inside mouth	Visual examination and biopsy	Surgical removal, possible radiation
Cancer of the esophagus	Lesion on esophagus that causes difficulty swallowing, spitting up of blood; may be asymptomatic	Esophagus may become obstructed, causing inability to swallow	Visual examination with endoscope, biopsy	Surgical removal, possible radiation and chemotherapy
Stomach cancer	Lesion in stomach that may cause pain or be painless, vomiting with mucus and blood	Usually on lesser curve of stomach; may cause obstruction in addition to pain	Tenderness in upper abdomen, possible pain, auscultation and palpation of upper abdomen, endoscopic exam with biopsy, ultrasound of stomach	Surgical removal, possible chemotherapy and radiation
Colon cancer	Weight loss, presence of blood in stool or melena, changes in character of stool, fatigue	Colon	Discovery of polyps during colonoscopy, occult blood in stool, imaging studies, confirmation by biopsy	Surgical removal of involved area, possible chemotherapy and radiation, possible colostomy
Rectal cancer	Weight loss, presence of blood in stool or melena, changes in character of stool, fatigue	Rectum	Proctoscopic exam, sigmoidoscopy, imaging studies, biopsy	Surgical removal, possible chemotherapy and radiation, possible colostomy
Vascular-Related Conditions				
Esophageal varices	Abdominal pain and distension; in emergency conditions, presence of bloody emesis	Blood vessels of esophagus, often resulting from **portal hypertension**	Endoscopic examination	Ice water lavage and epigastric tamponade with NN tube anchored by esophageal balloon
Hemorrhoids	Rectal and lower back pain, bloody stools	May be internal or external (protruding)	May be result of obesity, pregnancy, straining at stools, hard dry stools	Stool softeners, drug therapy, surgical excision

Imaging studies can include MRI, ultrasound, CT, PET, or X-ray, depending on the needs of the physician. The physician will order the study based on patient symptoms, suspected diagnosis, and location. Other factors may include patient allergies, claustrophobia, and availability. MRI is used to view alterations of living tissues, such as tumors or structural abnormalities in locations such as the lungs or brain. MRI gives multiple views or "cuts" as it passes over the body. The images produced by an MRI can be thought of as slices in a loaf of bread, with the entire body being the loaf of bread and each slice being a single MRI image. Ultrasound is commonly used during pregnancy to obtain an image of the fetus and its internal structures. Ultrasound is also used to view the structure, size, and location of internal organs, muscles, and tendons. Positron emission tomography (PET) scans are used to create a 3D image of the body, including the organs and other structures. PET scans allow physicians to see anatomic blood flow, or lack thereof, to different organs. X-rays are most commonly used to view the bony structures of the body but can also be useful in identifying abnormal conditions in soft tissues. Some organs such as the gallbladder create stones that can be identified by X-ray because the gallbladder is normally radiolucent and the gallstones appear radiopaque.

TABLE 24-4 DISEASES AND CONDITIONS OF THE DIGESTIVE ACCESSORY ORGANS

Condition or Disorder	Signs/Symptoms	Area Affected	Diagnosis	Treatment
Abnormal Function				
Cholelithiasis (gallstones)	Pain in right upper quadrant radiating to right shoulder blade, nausea and vomiting, bile-colored emesis and stool, **jaundice**	Stones may be present in gallbladder and/or in common bile duct	S & S, physical exam, tenderness in right upper quadrant, imaging studies including cholecystogram and ultrasound of gallbladder	Pain medication, surgical intervention (laparoscopy or endoscopy) to remove stones

TABLE 24-4 DISEASES AND CONDITIONS OF THE DIGESTIVE ACCESSORY ORGANS (*continued*)

Condition or Disorder	Signs/Symptoms	Area Affected	Diagnosis	Treatment
Infections				
Hepatitis A (infectious)	Jaundice, anorexia, fatigue, weakness, fever, joint pain, enlarged liver, lymph node involvement	Liver and blood	Virus or antibodies in the blood identified; liver function tests, possible liver biopsy	Immune globulin vaccination upon exposure; bed rest, low-carbohydrate diet; individual symptoms treated
Hepatitis B (serum)	Jaundice, anorexia, nausea and vomiting, general malaise, pruritic rash, enlarged liver, dark-colored urine, swollen joints	Liver and blood, body fluids	Virus or antibodies in the blood identified; liver function tests, possible liver biopsy	Prevention by vaccination is primary goal; bed rest, supportive treatment of symptoms
Hepatitis C (non A, non B)	Acute onset consisting of fever, chills, nausea and vomiting, malaise	Liver and blood	Virus or antibodies in the blood identified; liver function tests, possible liver biopsy	There is no cure; rest, well-balanced diet; interferon alpha to treat symptoms; additional symptom treatment
Inflammation				
Acute pancreatitis	Severe pain and tenderness in epigastric region and over pancreas, nausea and vomiting	Pancreas, ampulla of Vater, common bile duct, duodenum	S & S, physical exam, upper abdominal tenderness, imaging studies, ultrasound of pancreas	Pain medication, antibiotics, hydration, supportive therapy
Cholecystitis	Inflammation of gallbladder caused by gallbladder disease or gallstones	Gallbladder	S & S, physical exam, ultrasound or CT scan, stool test for fat	Surgery
Cirrhosis	Anorexia, weight loss, nausea and vomiting, indigestion, abdominal distention, dependent edema (edema of any body part lower than the heart regardless of vertical or horizontal body position) and ascites, jaundiced skin, greater tendency to bleed (including nosebleeds and bruising); untreated advanced cirrhosis leads to hepatic failure and death	Liver, usually caused by alcoholism; may also be caused by some forms of hepatitis, malnutrition parasites, toxic chemicals	Hard, palpable, enlarged liver, elevated liver enzymes and bilirubin levels; liver scan and biopsy for confirmation	Prevention of further damage by treating cause; rest, vitamins, minerals, diuretics, transplant in some cases
Liver cancer	Weight loss, anemia, **hepatomegaly**, pain, jaundice	Liver, usually metastatic from another site	Physical exam, liver scan, biopsy	Surgical removal of as much affected portion as possible, chemotherapy, radiation therapy
Pancreatic cancer	Weight loss, anemia, enlargement of pancreas, pain, nausea and vomiting	Pancreas may be primary site	Physical exam, ultrasonic examination and other imaging studies, biopsy	Surgical removal of as much affected portion as possible, chemotherapy, radiation therapy

Caduceus Chronicle
TREATING ULCERS

Historically, ulcer treatment consisted of dietary restrictions, a bland diet, and antacids. Histaminic II blockers that reduce gastric secretion were an advanced drug therapy. It has since been established that *H. pylori* is the microbe that causes peptic ulcers. Current treatments include antibiotics, histaminic II blockers, antacids, proton pump inhibitors that block the production of gastric acid, and coating agents, including Carafate, that protect the mucosa.

■ Fats are also a source of energy, and fatty acids aid in growth and development. Saturated, unsaturated, and polyunsaturated fatty acids are components of **triglycerides.** The amount of hydrogen holding the fatty acids together determines the degree of saturation. **Saturated fats** such as butter, with the greatest hydrogen hold, are solid and are usually derived from animal sources. **Unsaturated fats,** with the lowest hydrogen hold, are softer or liquid and usually come from plant sources. Polyunsaturated fats from such sources as fish and corn, soybean, and safflower oils contain two or more unfilled

TABLE 24-5 FOOD CATEGORIES AND FOOD SOURCES

Category	Functions	Sources
Carbohydrates (CHO) ■ Simple sugars ■ Complex carbohydrates (starch) ■ Dietary fiber	■ Supply fuel for energy, metabolism, and all cellular activities ■ Metabolize at a rate of 4 kcal/g ■ Converted by the body for use as glucose ■ Fiber/roughage provides bulk for elimination of intestinal wastes	■ Simple sugars: table sugar, corn and maple syrup, honey, candy, molasses, milk, fruits, sweets (cakes, cookies, pastries) ■ Complex carbohydrates: legumes, potatoes, seeds, vegetables, grain and grain products, cereal, whole-grain breads, pasta, corn, barley, rice ■ Fiber: bran, fruits, vegetables, dried fruits, beans, oatmeal, seeds, whole-grain breads and cereals
Fats (lipids)	■ Concentrated form of fuel; secondary energy source ■ Metabolize at the rate of 9 kcal/g ■ Necessary for essential fatty acids and absorption of fat-soluble vitamins ■ As adipose tissue, provides protection, insulates body, regulates temperature, and supports body organs	■ Saturated fats: animal sources (dairy products, eggs, fish, meat), coconut and palm oils ■ Unsaturated fats: polyunsaturated fats (fish, walnuts, corn, soybeans, sunflower seeds, safflower oil) and monounsaturated fats (fowl, almonds, pecans, cashews, peanuts, olive oil, avocados)
Protein	■ Builds and repairs tissues ■ Aids in body's defense against disease ■ Provides energy and regulates body secretions and fluids ■ Metabolizes at the rate of 4 kcal/g	■ Complete proteins: beef, chicken, poultry, fish, eggs, dairy products ■ Incomplete proteins: rice, whole grains, legumes, soybeans, nuts, soy flour
Vitamins: ■ Water soluble: B1, B2, B6, B12, niacin, folic acid, biotin, C ■ Fat soluble: A, D, E, K	■ Regulate the formation of body tissues ■ Aid in food metabolism ■ Prevent diseases resulting from nutritional deficiency	See Table 24-6
Minerals: ■ Calcium ■ Chlorine ■ Magnesium ■ Phosphorus ■ Potassium ■ Sodium Trace elements: ■ Iron ■ Copper ■ Chromium ■ Iodine ■ Fluorine ■ Manganese ■ Zinc ■ Selenium ■ Cobalt	■ Required in small amounts for electrolytes, water, and acid-base balance ■ Essential component of enzymes ■ Involved in regulation of heart rhythm, blood clotting, neuromuscular activities, and the building and maintenance of bones, muscles, and teeth	See Table 24-6
Water	■ Transport vehicle for nutrients, hormones, antibodies, and metabolic waste ■ Helps regulate body temperature ■ Solvent for most biochemical reactions ■ Lubricant for joints and mucous membranes	■ Healthy diet, eight glasses of water daily

hydrogen bonds. Monounsaturated fats in avocados, peanuts, and olive oil contain one unfilled hydrogen bond. Maintaining a diet lower in saturated fats and higher in unsaturated fats is one way to lower the risk of heart disease.

Lipoproteins are simple proteins that combine with lipid components, including **cholesterol,** phospholipids, and triglycerides. High-density lipoprotein (**HDL**) and low-density lipoprotein (**LDL**) are transport media that carry fats in the bloodstream. LDLs transport fats manufactured in the liver to body cells, while HDLs transport fats from body cells to the liver for disposal. A diagnostic test called a lipid profile provides information concerning LDL and HDL ratios as an assessment for possible heart and vascular disease.

■ Water, an element in almost every body process, is essential to life. The body can sustain life longer without food than without water. The body is composed of approximately 70% water. Water regulates body temperature, lubricates the joints, carries nutrition to and waste materials from body cells, and aids in other body processes. A healthy body maintains a normal balance of intake and excretion of water through the function of the circulatory, renal, and endocrine systems. Water is excreted from the body by urination, perspiration, respiration, and through the GI tract. When excessive water is lost through vomiting, diarrhea, bleeding, or burns, electrolyte imbalances may occur to a life-threatening degree. When body systems do not function properly and retain fluids, edema and possibly pulmonary congestion result. Other than plain water, sources of water include liquids such as juice, milk, coffee, tea, fruits, vegetables, broths, and soups. Drinking six to eight glasses of water daily is recommended to maintain water balance.

■ Vitamins are organic compounds required in small amounts for metabolism, growth, and development (Table 24-6). They are classified as fat-soluble (A, D, E, and K) and water-soluble (B complex and C). Antioxidants such as lycopene, lutein, beta carotene (a form of Vitamin A), and vitamins A, C, and E are substances believed to prevent cellular damage that may lead to cancer, atherosclerosis, and other conditions.

■ Minerals play an important role in specific regulatory processes and in tissue development and repair. They are essential to every cell, occur naturally in nature, and are used by the body in the processes of blood clotting, muscle contraction, and nervous system impulse conduction. The term *trace element* is applied to any mineral required in very small amounts.

■ Dietary fiber—carbohydrates that the body does not digest—promotes intestinal health and helps to prevent intestinal disease. Fiber is found in food plants, including fruits, vegetables, grains, and legumes. Good sources of dietary fiber include whole-grain products (wheat, barley, oats, brown rice, bran), apples, pears, berries, avocados, carrots, celery, nuts, seeds, and legumes (dried peas, beans, and lentils).

Keys to Success
SIMPLE VS. COMPLEX CARBOHYDRATES

Simple carbohydrates are sugars found in natural sources such as fruit and honey as well as in candy and other sweets. Complex carbohydrates are the starches in foods such as bread, potatoes, and whole grains. Ultimately, all carbohydrates are digested into simple sugars that are used by the body for cellular energy and as fuel for body activities. Digesting complex carbohydrates into glucose takes longer than digesting simple carbohydrates. Eating simple carbohydrates can give you a quick "energy boost" but can also lead to a rapid drop in blood glucose levels when the energy has been "spent." Ingestion of simple carbohydrates without complex carbohydrates can result in fluctuating blood glucose and energy levels. For diabetic patients, it is sometimes necessary to ingest simple carbohydrates to raise blood glucose levels quickly, but a combination of simple and complex carbohydrates not only allows levels to rise to normal quickly but also supplies a developing and longer-term source of glucose.

Energy released from the metabolism of proteins, fats, and carbohydrates is measured in units called **kilocalories** (kcal). One kilocalorie is equal to 1,000 small calories (calories as counted in food intake). The amount of energy released through metabolism is 4 kcal per gram of carbohydrate, 4 kcal per gram of protein, and 9 kcal per gram of fat.

TABLE 24-6 VITAMINS AND MINERALS

Vitamins/Nutrient	Source	Functional Deficiency	Toxicity	Recommended Dietary Allowances (RDA)[a]
Vitamin A (carotene): necessary for formation and maintenance of skin, mucous membranes, teeth and hair, and normal vision	Egg yolk, fish-liver oils, liver, green leafy or yellow vegetables, yellow and orange fruits, dairy products	Night blindness, fatigue, scaly skin	Headache, skin peeling, bone thickening, liver and spleen enlargement	5000 IU/day
Vitamin B$_1$ (thiamine): carbohydrate metabolism, nerve cell function, heart muscle function	Dried yeast, whole grains, meat (liver and pork), nuts, enriched cereals, potatoes, legumes	Beriberi, fatigue, mental confusion		1.5 mg/day
Vitamin B$_2$ (riboflavin): releases energy during protein metabolism	Milk, cheese, eggs, liver, enriched cereals, almonds	Anemia, dermatosis, skin cracks		1.2 mg/day
Vitamin B$_6$ (group): nitrogen and protein metabolism, assists in building body tissue	Dried yeast, liver, whole grain cereals, fish, legumes, bananas, avocados	Anemia, seborrheic dermatitis, nervous system disorders, convulsions, skin cracks	Nerve damage	2 mg/day
Vitamin B$_{12}$ (cyanocobalamin): nervous system function, fat and protein metabolism	Milk products, seafood, meat, liver, cheese	Pernicious anemia, fatigue, nervousness		6 mcg/day
Niacin (nicotinic acid): carbohydrate, fat, and protein metabolism	Dried yeast, fish, liver, meat, legumes, enriched cereals, eggs, peanuts, and poultry	Pellagra, dermatosis, glossitis, CNS dysfunction, fatigue		20 mg/day
Vitamin C (ascorbic acid): needed to build bones, muscles, blood vessels, and connective tissue; aids in iron absorption	Citrus fruits, tomatoes, broccoli, potatoes, cabbage, green peppers, berries, and strawberries	Scurvy, loose teeth, hemorrhoids, gingivitis, fatigue	Nausea and diarrhea	60 mg/day

(continued)

TABLE 24-6 VITAMINS AND MINERALS (*Continued*)

Vitamins/Nutrient	Source	Functional Deficiency	Toxicity	Recommended Dietary Allowances (RDA)[a]
Vitamin D: necessary for calcium and phosphorous absorption, bone and tooth development and maintenance; helps maintain nervous system and heart muscle action	Fortified milk, butter, margarine, eggs, fish-liver oils, liver, sunlight	Rickets, tetany, loss of bone calcium	Diarrhea, weight loss, renal failure	400 IU/day
Vitamin E: protects blood cell membranes, body tissues and fatty acids from destruction	Vegetable oil, wheat germ, margarine, egg yolks, leafy vegetables, legumes, cereals	Anemia, nerve damage, RBC hemolysis, muscle damage		30 IU/day
Vitamin K: normal blood coagulation, prothrombin formation	Leafy vegetables, liver, pork, vegetable oils, fruit, dairy	Hemorrhage in newborn and in person taking blood thinner		No RDA for Vitamin A
Biotin: metabolism of protein, carbohydrates, and fats	Yeast, liver, kidney, egg yolks, nuts, legumes, cauliflower	Dermatitis, glossitis		0.5 mg/day
Folic acid: RBC production	Dried legumes, green leafy vegetables, organ meats	Anemia, GI disorders, mouth cracks		0.4 mg/day
Pantothenic acid: aids in energy release from carbohydrates and fats	Whole grains, meats, vegetables, fruits, legumes	Muscle cramps, fatigue, vomiting		10 mg/day
Calcium: bone and tooth formation, muscle contractility, blood coagulation, myocardial conduction, neurom- uscular function	Milk and milk products, meat, fish, eggs, beans, cereals, fruits, vegetables, tofu, fortified orange juice	Hypocalcemia, tetany, neuromuscular excitability, osteoporosis	Hypercalcemia, kidney stones, renal failure	800 mg/day
Chromium: part of glucose tolerance factor (CTF)	Brewer's yeast and widely distributed in other foods	Impaired glucose tolerance in malnourished children and diabetics		No RDA
Cobalt: part of vitamin B$_{12}$ molecule	Green leafy vegetables	Anemia in children		20 mg/day
Copper: enzyme component	Oysters, organ meats, nuts, dried legumes, whole grain cereals	Anemia in malnourished children		0.3 mg/kg per day
Fluorine: bone and tooth formation	Coffee, tea, fluoridated water	Dental caries	Mottling and pitting of permanent teeth	No RDA
Iodine: thyroxine (T$_4$) and triiodothyronine (T$_3$) formation, necessary for energy formation	Seafood, iodized salt, dairy products	Goiter, cretinism	Myxedema	150 mcg/day
Iron: hemoglobin, enzymes	Soybean flour, kidney, beef, liver, beans, peaches	Anemia		30 mg/day
Magnesium: bone and tooth formation, nerve conduction, muscle contractility, enzyme activity	Green leafy vegetables, cereals, nuts, wheat bran, grains, seafood, chocolate	Neuromuscular irritability, weakness	Hypotension, respiratory failure, cardiac disturbances	280 mg/day
Phosphorus: bone and tooth formation, acid–base formation	Milk, cheese, meat, fish, poultry, cereals, nuts, legumes	Irritability, weakness, blood cell disorders		300 mg/day
Potassium: muscle activity, nerve transmission, intracellular acid–base balance, water retention	Milk, bananas, kiwi, raisins, vegetables	Hypokalemia, paralysis, cardiac arrhythmia (irregular heartbeat)	Hyperkalemia, paralysis, cardiacarrhythmia	2000 mg/day
Sodium: maintain acid–base balance, muscle contractility, nerve transmission	Meat (beef, pork), cheese sardines, olives, potato chips, table salt	Hyponatremia, muscle cramping	Hypernatremia, coma, confusion, high blood pressure	500 mg/day
Zinc: growth, wound healing component of insulin and enzyme	Vegetables	Growth retardation		30 mg/day

[a]IU, international units; mg, milligrams; mcg, micrograms.

Source: Beaman, Nina; Fleming–McPhillips, Lorraine. Pearson's Comprehensive Medical Assisting, *1st Edition, © 2007. Reprinted by permission of Pearson Education, Inc.*

Keys to Success
CONSEQUENCES OF DEHYDRATION

One consequence of dehydration is decreased blood volume. The felt pulse is weaker and described as "thready," and the person is susceptible to hypotension and therefore fainting or falls. The individual may also experience hypotension when sitting or standing abruptly. To compensate, the heart beats faster to circulate blood around the body. Dehydration may also affect kidney function, as the filtering of waste products and production of urine are decreased. Dehydration can be gradual and limited or sudden and severe. Severe dehydration can lead to hypovolemic shock and possibly death.

The Food Guide Pyramid/MyPyramid Food Guidance System

"We are what we eat" is a statement often made by nutritionists and health care providers. How do we decide what makes a nutritious diet? Guidelines have been established by various agencies and organizations, including the American Dietetic Association, the U.S. Department of Agriculture (**USDA**), and the American Home Economics Association.

The Food Guide Pyramid was an educational tool developed by the USDA to help healthy Americans maintain good eating habits. The pyramid recommended eating a specified number of servings of different food groups to meet daily nutritional needs. Since the creation of the first food pyramid, other versions have been developed for specific groups such as Asians, Latinos, vegetarians, the elderly, and children aged 2 through 6. Persons with medical needs require the assistance of professional dieticians and physicians to maintain healthful eating habits within the constraints of their particular situations.

In April 2005, the USDA replaced the Food Guide Pyramid with MyPyramid Plan, establishing a new nutritional attitude: "One size does not fit all." MyPyramid is suitable for all individuals of normal health over the age of 2. It can be found online at www.MyPyramid.gov and can be tailored to each individual based on eating habits, exercise levels, and nutritional requirements (Figure 24-4 ◆).

The USDA bases its recommendations on scientific information and consensus from a variety of sources and experts. Since 1985, Dietary Guidelines for Americans (**DGA**) have been developed and published jointly by the USDA and the Department of Health and Human Services (**DHHS**). The DGA serves

Anatomy of MyPyramid

One size doesn't fit all

USDA's new MyPyramid symbolizes a personalized approach to healthy eating and physical activity. The symbol has been designed to be simple. It has been developed to remind consumers to make healthy food choices and to be active every day. The different parts of the symbol are described below.

Activity
Activity is represented by the steps and the person climbing them, as a reminder of the importance of daily physical activity.

Moderation
Moderation is represented by the narrowing of each food group from bottom to top. The wider base stands for foods with little or no solid fats or added sugars. These should be selected more often. The narrower top area stands for foods containing more added sugars and solid fats. The more active you are, the more of these foods can fit into your diet.

Personalization
Personalization is shown by the person on the steps, the slogan, and the URL. Find the kinds and amounts of food to eat each day at MyPyramid.gov.

Proportionality
Proportionality is shown by the different widths of the food group bands. The widths suggest how much food a person should choose from each group. The widths are just a general guide, not exact proportions. Check the Web site for how much is right for you.

Variety
Variety is symbolized by the 6 color bands representing the 5 food groups of the Pyramid and oils. This illustrates that foods from all groups are needed each day for good health.

Gradual Improvement
Gradual improvement is encouraged by the slogan. It suggests that individuals can benefit from taking small steps to improve their diet and lifestyle each day.

MyPyramid.gov
STEPS TO A HEALTHIER YOU

USDA
U.S. Department of Agriculture
Center for Nutrition Policy
and Promotion
April 2005 CNPP-16

USDA is an equal opportunity provider and employer.

| GRAINS | VEGETABLES | FRUITS | OILS | MILK | MEAT & BEANS |

Figure 24-4 ◆ MyPyramid
Source: www.MyPyramid.gov.

as the basis for federal policy regarding federal nutritional programs, including school lunches.

In general, the DGA recommends a variety of foods for energy, essential nutrients, and a healthy physical and emotional state. Another recommendation is to limit intake of alcohol, sugar, salt or sodium, fat, saturated fat, and cholesterol. Eating a variety of whole-grain products, fruits, and vegetables provides complex carbohydrates, vitamins, minerals, and fiber and helps to decrease fat intake. Maintaining a healthy body weight by balancing caloric intake with an exercise program is also recommended.

The Food and Nutrition Board (**FNB**), which helps develop the DGA, also provides criteria for setting Recommended Daily Allowances (**RDA**). RDAs represent the amount of nutrients required to meet the daily nutritional needs of most healthy people. These recommendations cover caloric, vitamin, mineral, and water intake.

There are many variables in nutritional guidelines, such as cultural and religious background, age, social status, physical status, and availability of dietary components. Table 24-7 lists some typical religious and other restrictions.

How to Read a Food Label

Reading a food label is an important tool in maintaining a healthy lifestyle (Figure 24-5 ◆). In 1994 the federal government made reading food labels easier with the Nutrition Labeling and Education Act. Under this law, any special health claims on a product label must be stated using specific terms, and the nutritional content must meet USDA standard definitions for those terms. For example, if the label contains the term "reduced fat" or "low fat," that food must contain a minimum of 25% less fat per serving than the regular offered product. Any food that has

Nutrition Facts

Serving Size 6 Crackers (28g)
Servings Per Container About 10

Amount Per Serving

Calories 130   Calories from Fat 40

                                   % Daily Value*

	% Daily Value*
Total Fat 5g	7%
Saturated Fat 0.5g	4%
Trans Fat 0g	
Polyunsaturated Fat 2.5g	
Monounsaturated Fat 1g	
Cholesterol 0mg	0%
Sodium 50mg	2%
Total Carbohydrate 19g	6%
Dietary Fiber 3g	13%
Sugars 0g	
Protein 3g	

Vitamin A 0%	●	Vitamin C 0%
Calcium 0%	●	Iron 8%

*Percent Daily Values are based on a 2,000 calorie diet. Your daily values may be higher or lower depending on your calorie needs:

		Calories:	2,000	2,500
Total Fat	Less than		65g	80g
Sat Fat	Less than		20g	25g
Cholesterol	Less than		300mg	300mg
Sodium	Less than		2,400mg	2,400mg
Total Carbohydrate			300g	375g
Dietary Fiber			25g	30g

INGREDIENTS: WHOLE WHEAT, SOYBEAN OIL, MONOGLYCERIDES, SALT.

72% LESS SODIUM THAN ▓▓▓▓▓ ▓▓▓▓▓. LOW SODIUM HAS 50mg SODIUM VS. 180mg SODIUM IN ORIGINAL.

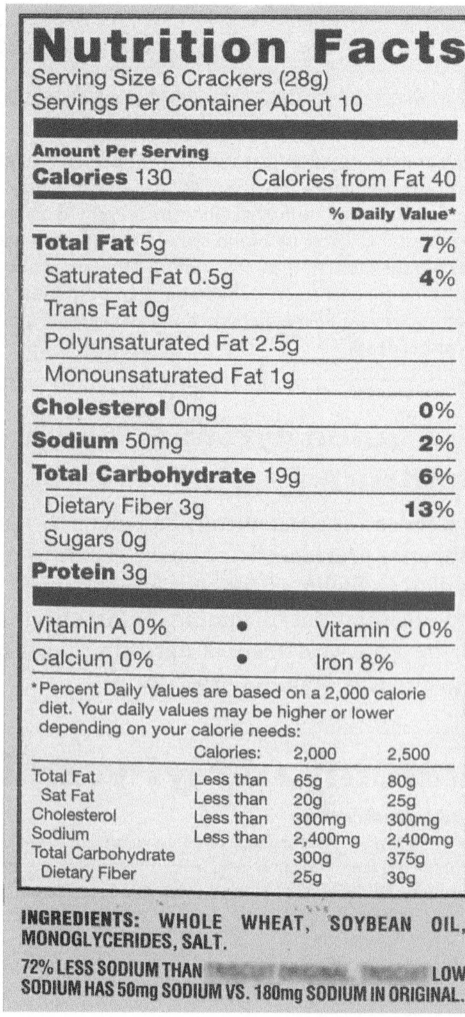

Figure 24-5 ◆ Food label listing nutritional information

the words "low fat" on the label must contain no more than 3 grams of fat per serving. A "fat-free" food must contain no more than 0.5 gram of fat per serving. Foods labeled "lite" or "light" must have a minimum of 1/3 fewer calories than the regular product or at least 50% less fat. Food manufacturers are allowed to use words that are not federally regulated, such as "right," "smart choice," or "natural," at their own discretion.

It is important to note that the percentages on a nutrition label are based on a 2,000-calorie-per-day diet, so if you eat more or less than 2,000 calories per day, you will need to adjust the nutritional values accordingly.

Another important component of the food label is the ingredients list. All manufacturers must list ingredients in descending order of predominance and weight. For example, if the first ingredient is sugar, then sugar makes up the majority of the product. Food manufacturers are allowed to list similar ingredients as separate compounds, a fact consumers should be aware of. In ketchup, for example, sugar, high-fructose corn syrup, and sucrose may be listed as separate ingredients, but they are all forms of sugar.

TABLE 24-7 RELIGIOUS AND PERSONAL DIETARY RESTRICTIONS

Buddhist	See Vegetarian.
Greek Orthodox	Avoid meat on fast days.
Hindu	See Vegetarian.
Mormon	Avoid alcohol and caffeine-containing products, including coffee and tea.
Muslim	Abstain from pork, pork products, and alcohol.
Orthodox Jewish	■ Abstain from pork, shellfish, and nonkosher meats. ■ Abstain from leavened bread during Passover. ■ Observe fasting days. ■ Do not serve milk and meat products together.
Roman Catholic	■ Avoid meat before Communion, Ash Wednesday, and Good Friday. ■ Observe religious fasting days.
Seventh-Day Adventist	■ Primarily vegetarian. ■ Do not eat meat from cloven-hoofed animals, such as cows, pigs, sheep. ■ Do not eat shellfish and other scavenger sea animals. ■ Discourage intake of caffeine-containing products.
Vegetarian	■ Diet consists mainly of vegetables, fruit, and grains. ■ Some may eat dairy product

Keys to Success
READING FOOD PRODUCT LABELS

Consumers can obtain important nutritional information by reading labels on food products. Since the early 1990s, under USDA regulations, all food products must carry a label listing nutritional information, including:

- the serving size for each product, in both household and metric measurements
- the number of servings per container
- total **calories** per serving and calories from fat
- grams of total fat, saturated fat, cholesterol, total carbohydrates, protein, and sodium by serving size
- a breakdown of total carbohydrates into dietary fiber and sugars
- a list of ingredients in the order of importance
- daily percentage of RDA for vitamins A, B complex, C, iron, and calcium
- any special health claim
- artificial color(s)

— Critical Thinking Question 24-1-

What questions should Reggie ask Serena about her newfound interest in vegetarianism so that he can more accurately assess her nutritional needs?

Nutrition and Health

Nutritional status has single, seesaw, or cascading effects on an individual's health. Single problems are caused by single deficiencies. Seesaw effects occur when the body overcompensates for a deficiency in nutrients, resulting in breakdown of tissue or other problems. Cascading occurs when a deficiency in one nutrient causes deficiencies in other nutrients because of impaired ability to transport, create, or absorb the other nutrients.

Busy lifestyles can contribute to poor eating habits and a deterioration in health. Individuals with existing health problems often have poor eating habits. Dental health is another contributing factor to nutritional status. Proper chewing is the essential first step in the breakdown and digestion of foods for maximum absorption of nutrients. Persons with poor dental health, missing teeth, or dentures cannot chew fiber and other foods thoroughly, which contributes to decreased motility of the GI system and may result in constipation or diarrhea. Persons with painful or malodorous mouth conditions also may not eat well.

Healthy habits include good oral hygiene; eating nutritious foods, including fiber to assist in peristalsis and evacuation; and exercising regularly. These basic practices help prevent disease as well as a declining nutritional status resulting from disease or illness. They also help prevent the additive effects of poor nutritional status on a disease condition.

The physician will evaluate if a patient is able to manage his or her own nutritional needs or if a regimen of diet, exercise, medications, or other treatments is required. If a patient cannot take nutrients orally, the physician will prescribe **total parenteral nutrition (TPN)** by tube feedings directly into the stomach or by IV therapy.

— Critical Thinking Question 24-2-

Once Reggie has established what type of vegetarian Serena would like to become, how should he proceed to help her reach her nutritional as well as lifestyle goals?

Factors That May Affect Caloric Intake

Caloric intake is affected by many potentially harmful cultural, economic, and lifestyle factors.

- Economic: People with low incomes tend to buy more high-carbohydrate foods in an effort to get more food on a limited budget.
- Culture: In some cultures social gatherings are often centered around large meals, and it is an insult to decline the offer of food.
- Lifestyle: As people's lives become busier, they tend to eat more fast food and exercise less.

Education and individual motivation are the best tools for counteracting these harmful influences. Most people need to eat higher-quality food in smaller quantities. The money "saved" from buying foods high in simple carbohydrates is actually money wasted, as **obesity** and other medical conditions lead to poor health. The influence of culture on dietary habits is a bigger challenge, but higher caloric intake can be balanced with more exercise, and modest daily intake can allow for family feasts. Lifestyle changes are also a challenge, and short-term and long-term individual goals must be established to achieve lasting benefits.

Obesity

Excess ingested food is metabolized, converted, and stored as fat. Obesity, a symptom of caloric intake greater than the body requires, is both a cause and a result of medical conditions. It is often directly linked to diabetes, cardiovascular disease, hypertension, and many other disease conditions. Obesity may also be a residual

Keys to Success
FAD DIETS, AT BEST, ARE TEMPORARY MEASURES

Americans spend over $30 million a year on weight loss programs and products. Fad diets promising rapid weight loss and beautiful figures contribute to this big business. Some examples are the Atkins Diet, the Cabbage Soup Diet, the Grapefruit Diet, and the Zone Diet. Fad diets have a common theme: restricting a particular food or food group and promoting high intake of another food or food group. For example, the Atkins Diet promotes restriction of carbohydrates in favor of proteins and fats. The Cabbage Soup Diet promotes a steady regimen of cabbage-based soups and restriction of other food groups. The Grapefruit Diet promotes an excess of grapefruits. The Zone Diet promotes a slightly higher intake of carbohydrates and dividing the remaining calories equally between protein and fat. The advantage to following a fad diet is usually rapid weight loss. The disadvantages are rebound weight gain, compromised self-image because of weight loss failure, and the absence of healthy, permanent lifestyle changes. Studies continue to prove that maintaining a balance between caloric intake and exercise is the only way to effectively manage weight.

effect of disease conditions that may cause a decrease in activity, such as myocardial infarction and congestive heart failure.

In addition to weight measurement, body fat and body mass index (BMI) figures may be used to determine the extent of obesity. Body mass index is calculated by dividing a person's weight in pounds by total body surface area, or height in inches squared, then multiplying the result by 703. (Several online sites have BMI calculators.) The normal range is between 18.5 and 24.9. A person with a BMI below 18.5 is considered underweight, over 24.9 **overweight,** and 30 or above obese.

Body fat is measured by hydrostatic weighing or with body fat scales or skinfold calipers. Hydrostatic weighing, in which the individual is floated in a hydrostatic weighing tank, is based on Archimedes' principle of water displacement. Body fat scales use bioelectrical impedance, passing a low-level current through the body. The measurement of impedance, height, weight, and other factors is used to determine body fat. Skinfold calipers measure folds of skin and their underlying layers of fat at specific locations on the body. Physicians, nutritionists, and physical fitness professionals use the body fat measurement to prescribe customized regimens of diet and exercise. Patients with medical conditions should consult with their physician, who can monitor the effects of the program and change the treatment plan if necessary.

Maintaining a balance between caloric intake and caloric expenditure is the most reliable way to control weight (Figure 24-6 ◆). Table 24-8 lists examples of caloric expenditure during different types of activity or exercise.

The Effects of Alcohol on Nutrition

Alcohol is a non-nutrient that yields 7 kcal/gram. It is absorbed by the stomach and small intestine and broken down by the liver before it is excreted from the body. Although small amounts have some therapeutic benefits, in general, alcohol

TABLE 24-8 CALORIC EXPENDITURE DURING SELECTED ACTIVITIES OR EXERCISE	
Activity	**Caloric Expenditure per Hour**
Sitting	80 calories
Weight lifting	215 calories
Walking (4 mph)	325 calories
Aerobics (high impact)	505 calories
Tennis	505 calories
Bicycling (15 mph)	720 calories
Running (10 minutes/mile)	720 calories
Swimming (crawl stroke)	790 calories

interferes with metabolism and contributes to the development of liver and other medical conditions.

■ When too much alcohol is delivered to the liver, it accumulates as fat and may eventually cause cirrhosis.

■ The metabolism of alcohol prevents enzyme use for other necessary nutritional reactions.

■ Long-term use leads to other medical disorders, including **malnutrition,** obesity, ulcers, cancer, hypertension, and diabetes mellitus.

■ Pregnant women are advised against taking *any* alcohol because of its devastating effects on the fetus, a condition known as fetal alcohol syndrome.

Recent studies suggest that one drink per day for women and two drinks per day for men may be beneficial for overall health status. A drink unit is 1.5 ounces of liquor, 5 ounces of wine, or 12 ounces of beer. Research is inconclusive as to whether beer or wine offers more health benefits. At this time, however, this finding is not generally accepted in medical practice.

The Effects of Aging on Nutritional Status

The physiological functioning of the gastrointestinal system becomes less efficient as an individual ages. Teeth, so important in the initial breakdown of food, often are absent or have been replaced by less effective false teeth. The sense of taste and sense of smell become dull, and the declining function of the nervous system results in slower peristalsis of the esophagus, stomach, and small and large intestines. The metabolism slows and, in general, activity levels decrease. Elderly persons also tend to lose the capacity or desire to shop and/or cook. Medications may affect digestion and food absorption. These conditions heighten the challenge of maintaining a balanced diet as a person ages.

Social interaction aids in the digestion process in people of all ages. Among the elderly, social interaction often decreases, leading to isolation from family and friends. One common reason for growing isolation is the loss of spouse. Elderly individuals also often become depressed as they fail to cope with the effects of aging.

The nutritional status of the elderly is the result of lifestyle habits and choices made during their younger years. The individual who establishes wellness habits early in life avoids inactivity, malnutrition, obesity, and the development or advancement of

Figure 24-6 ◆ Maintaining a balance between caloric intake and caloric expenditure is the most reliable way to control weight.
Source: Jim Cummins/Getty Images, Inc.

medical and dental conditions later. As an individual ages, nutritional status can affect or cause medical conditions. For example, obesity contributes to the development or advancement of hypertension, diabetes, arthritis, and other conditions. The loss of teeth affects the chewing, swallowing, and digestion of food. A person who cannot chew, lacks roughage in the diet, and is not active has slower GI motility and becomes constipated more easily.

Under the direction of dieticians and physicians, you should encourage elderly patients to eat nutritious foods and maintain or increase physical activity. Regular activity increases appetite, mobility, physical endurance, and immune response.

Diseases and Disorders Involving Nutrition

Disease conditions result from and are the cause of altered nutritional states.

- Heart disease, hypertension, and atherosclerosis often result from dietary intake of foods high in lipids (fats) and cholesterol (hyperlipedimia, hypercholesteremia).
- Prolonged nausea and vomiting, with the resulting loss of fluids, often lead to electrolyte imbalances.
- Parasitic infestation and infections caused by contaminated food and/or water, malabsorption syndrome, irritable bowel syndrome, gastric bypass surgery, cancer of the colon and other organs in the digestive tract, starvation (self-induced or otherwise), and starvation-related conditions including **anorexia,** bulimia, and binge eating are other factors in compromised nutritional status.
- Gastrointestinal obstructions, which can occur at any point along the GI tract, cause an interruption in the absorption of nutrients.
- Constipation and diarrhea are symptoms of altered gastrointestinal mobility.
- Inborn errors of metabolism negatively affect the normal absorption of nutrients by altering the metabolic process involved in digestion.
- Eating disorders include anorexia nervosa and bulimia.

Food Allergies and Food Intolerances

Food allergies and food intolerances occur in both children and adults (Table 24-9). Food intolerances are unpleasant reactions to certain foods, but they do not cause severe or life-threatening medical emergencies. Food allergies result from a hypersensitivity of the immune system to certain foods. Persons with food allergies often have a genetic predisposition and a history of other allergies. Children often outgrow allergies, but adults have their allergies for life. The frequency of particular allergies may be enhanced by geographic location; an example is the high rate of rice allergies in Japan.

Food allergies are similar to other allergies, such as drug allergies, in the way they develop. When a person with a genetic predisposition eats an allergy-causing food, the body's immune system produces immunoglobulin E (IgE), a protein antibody that circulates in the bloodstream. IgE attaches to mast cells that may be present in all body tissues but mostly in the nose,

TABLE 24-9 COMMON FOOD ALLERGIES AND INTOLERANCES	
Food Allergies: Adults	**Food Allergies: Children**
■ Shellfish: crab, crayfish, lobster, shrimp ■ Legumes: peanuts ■ Tree nuts: walnuts, Brazil nuts ■ Fish ■ Eggs ■ Cantaloupe and other fruit	■ Eggs ■ Milk ■ Legumes: peanuts, soy products ■ Fish ■ Shrimp ■ Fruit juices
Food Intolerances: Adults and Children	
■ Lactose-containing products ■ Sulfites ■ Monosodium glutamate (MSG) ■ Yellow dye #5 ■ Red dye	

throat, lungs, gastrointestinal tract, and skin. After a person has been exposed to the food and initiated IgE production and mast cell attachment, histamine is released. The area of histamine release directly relates to the symptoms. If it is released in the nasopharyngeal region, itching, difficulty swallowing, and difficulty breathing may develop. If histamine is released in the gastrointestinal system, symptoms may be diarrhea and/or pain, and when released in the skin, hives.

It is important to differentiate between a food allergy and food intolerance to prevent serious illness and fatality. After clinical assessment and intervention, food allergy percentages in the adult population decrease to 1 percent and in the pediatric population to 3 percent. To confirm a diagnosis of food allergy, the physician first rules out other possibilities.

- The reaction may be caused by the toxins in contaminated food.
- Some foods have a naturally high histamine content, such as mackerel, tuna, some wines, and cheeses.
- Lactase deficiency and food additives (MSG, sulfites) may cause food intolerances that are mistaken for food allergies.
- The symptoms of other medical conditions, such as ulcers and gastrointestinal cancers, can mimic those of food allergy.
- Psychological triggers may mimic food allergy symptoms.

When considering a diagnosis of food allergy, the physician performs a detailed health history. Often the patient is asked to keep a detailed food diary. Elimination diets are often used to determine if the absence of a food is related to the absence of symptoms. Skin and patch testing may be performed, but is not preferred if the person has experienced a severe anaphylactic reaction. Blood tests such as RAST and ELISA are performed to measure the presence of IgE.

The first step in treating a food allergy is avoiding the offending food. The patient must learn to read all food labels. Even then, however, anaphylactic reactions are possible, and the patient must be prepared to react quickly. The patient should wear an allergy bracelet, carry an emergency kit with adrenaline (epinephrine), and get help immediately. Emergency medication may also include antihistamines and bronchodilators, among others. It is important to communicate to the patient that cross reactivity may result, in which the patient may become allergic to similar foods. The patient should also be made aware of the possibility of exercise-induced food allergy, when a certain food eaten before exercise causes symptoms that range from light-headedness and itching to anaphylaxis and death.

Diagnosis and Treatment of GI Disorders

The location of patient signs and symptoms can be significant in guiding the physician to a diagnosis of conditions and disorders (Table 24-10). There are two methods for describing the location of the abdominopelvic regions: by the nine anatomical divisions or by the four clinical quadrants (Figures 24-7 ◆ and 24-8 ◆). You and other clinical staff assist the physician by listening to the patient's description and accurately documenting symptom location.

Warning signs of GI problems include:

- Nausea: motion sickness, pregnancy, emotional distress, gallbladder disease, intestinal obstruction, food poisoning, enteroviruses

- Vomiting, especially **emesis** containing blood (**hematemesis**): food poisoning, intestinal obstruction, esophageal varices, ulcers, early pregnancy
- Coffee-ground emesis: bleeding in GI tract from ulcers, esophageal varices
- Diarrhea: enteroviruses, food poisoning, gallbladder disease
- Constipation: intestinal obstruction, lack of fiber and fluids in diet, constipating foods
- Bright red blood in stools: hemorrhoids, rectal polyps, cancer of rectum or lower GI tract
- Black stools (**melena**): bleeding in GI tract, usually in stomach, upper GI tract, or upper portion of large intestine
- Abdominal pain: intestinal obstruction, food poisoning, enteroviruses, flatus, constipation, appendicitis, many other conditions
- Abdominal distension: intestinal obstruction, constipation, food poisoning, many other conditions
- Dyspepsia: Difficulty in digestion.
- Anorexia: Loss of appetite, not to be confused with Anorexia Nervosa, the mental condition in which an individual refuses to eat due to poor self-image.

TABLE 24-10 ABDOMINAL REGIONS AND DISORDERS

Structures	Possible Disorders
Right Upper Quadrant (RUQ)	
Liver	Cancer of the liver, cirrhosis, Hepatitis: A (infectious), B (serum), C (non A, non B), D (delta virus), E, G
Gallbladder	Cholecystitis, cholelithiasis, obstruction of bile ducts
Duodenum	Duodenal cancer, duodenal ulcer
Head of pancreas	Pancreatitis, cancer of pancreas
Right kidney and adrenal glands	Pyelitis, pyelonephritis, renal calculi, adrenal disorders
Hepatic flexure of the colon	Obstruction, cancer of colon
Portion of ascending and transverse colon	Obstruction, cancer of colon
Right Lower Quadrant (RLQ)	
Cecum	Obstruction, cancer of colon
Appendix	Appendicitis
Right ovary and fallopian tube	Cancer of ovary, ovarian cyst, ectopic pregnancy, endometriosis, PID
Right ureter	Renal calculi, UTI
Left Upper Quadrant (LUQ)	
Stomach	Gastric ulcer, gastric cancer, hiatal hernia
Spleen	Traumatic injury to spleen, enlarged spleen due to disease
Left lobe of liver	Cancer of liver, cirrhosis, Hepatitis: A (Infectious), B (serum), C (non A, non B), D (delta virus), E, G
Body of pancreas	Pancreatitis, cancer of pancreas
Left kidney and adrenal gland	Pyelitis, pyelonephritis, renal calculi, adrenal disorders
Splenic flexure of colon	Splenic flexure syndrome
Portion of transverse and descending colon	Obstruction, cancer of colon, diverticulosis, diverticulitis
Left Lower Quadrant (LLQ)	
Portion of descending colon	Obstruction, cancer of colon, diverticulosis, diverticulitis
Sigmoid colon	Obstruction, cancer of colon, diverticulosis, diverticulitis
Left ovary and fallopian tube	Cancer of ovary, ovarian cyst, ectopic pregnancy, endometriosis, PID
Left ureter	Renal calculi, UTI
Middle of Abdomen, Midline	
Aorta	Dissecting aorta
Abdominal wall	Umbilical hernia
Uterus (when enlarged)	Pregnancy, fibroid tumors, cancerous tumors
Bladder (when distended)	Urinary retention

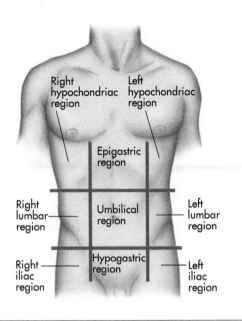

Figure 24-7 ◆ Anatomical divisions of the abdomen

- Flatulence: Excessive gas in the stomach and intestines.
- Dysphagia: Difficulty in swallowing

Diagnostic Procedures

Various diagnostic procedures may be ordered for GI disorders, some of which are performed in the office setting. Procedures include but are not limited to:

- palpation, auscultation, and visualization of the abdomen
- upper GI series
- lower GI series (barium enema, air contrast study)
- gallbladder series (cholecystography)
- endoscopic examination (**gastroscopy, ERCP, colonoscopy**)
- stool specimen studies for ova/parasites (∞ refer to Chapter 13)
- occult fecal blood specimen tests (∞ refer to Chapter 14)
- blood tests (CBC, bilirubin studies)
- ultrasound studies of abdomen and abdominal organs
- MRI of abdomen

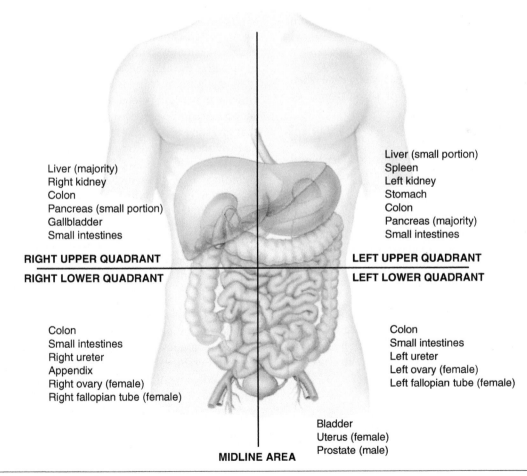

Figure 24-8 ◆ Clinical divisions of the abdomen

Obstructive conditions of the colon may require surgical intervention, including colostomy, either temporary or permanent, or resection (surgical removal) of the affected length of the colon. In resection, the ends of the remaining sections of the colon are sutured together in a procedure known **anastomosis.** Temporary colostomies are reversed, also by anastomosis, after the patient has healed and recovered from the causative factor.

Obstructive conditions involving the small intestine, including the ileum, are often treated with an **ileostomy.** During this procedure, the involved structure may be removed and an opening created through the wall of the abdomen for the expulsion of waste products. This procedure may also be reversed, or it may be permanent.

Colonoscopy

A colonoscopy is performed to assess healthy or disease states of the colon (Figure 24-9 ◆). The American Cancer Society recommends that all individuals over the age of 50 have a colonoscopy to screen for cancer. The procedure is also done to check for hemorrhoids, polyps, fistulas, and abscesses within the colon.

To properly view the entire length of the large intestine, the physician performs the colonoscopy in a hospital setting, where sedation is available for the patient's comfort. There are several types of flexible colon fiberscopes that allow that physician to view the colon, rectum, anus, sigmoid colon, and descending, transverse, and ascending colon sections as an in-office procedure.

The procedure serves to:

- obtain baseline information during a healthy state when the patient has a family history of colon cancer or **polyps**
- evaluate symptoms such as abdominal pain, persistent diarrhea, or unexplained blood in the stool
- evaluate the type and extent of an inflammatory bowel condition such as Crohn's disease or ulcerative colitis

The physician explains to the patient why a colonoscopy is necessary and what the risks are. Risks include possible bowel perforation, which requires surgical repair, bleeding from tissue biopsy or polypectomy (removal of polyps) performed during the procedure, reactions to sedative or anesthetic medications, possible infections, and GI symptoms relating to preparation for the procedure.

Many patients are apprehensive about having a rectal exam. To ease their apprehension, you should carefully explain the procedure, what it will feel like, sedation methods (if used), recovery time, and how to prepare the colon, if necessary.

Sigmoidoscopy

To correctly evaluate suspected lower gastrointestinal disorders, tumors, positive fecal occult blood tests, bleeding, polyps,

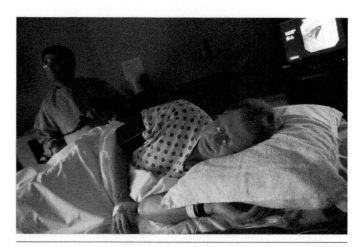

Figure 24-9 ◆ A gastroenterologist and enterological surgeon with staff performing a colonoscopy
Source: Renee Jones Schneider/Minneapolis Star Tribune/ZUMA Press/ Newscom

or suspected cancer, the physician must examine the lower gastrointestinal system. A sigmoidoscopy allows the physician to visualize the anus, rectum, large intestine, and appendix.

A sigmoidoscopy is performed with a sigmoidoscope, which can be rigid (metal) or flexible (plastic). All sigmoidoscopes are equipped with a light source and a magnifying lens that gives the physician a clear view of the sigmoid structure. To provide better access to the sigmoid colon, an obturator, a firm plastic device, is attached within the hollow tubing of the sigmoidoscope. A few inches of the tapered end of the obturator extend beyond the tube, facilitating entry past the anal sphincter. Both instruments are lubricated and threaded into the rectum. The obturator is then removed by pulling it straight out of the opposite end of the sigmoidoscope. The sigmoidoscope is left in place, providing a clear view of the sigmoid colon.

Rectal Suppositories

If rapid absorption of a medication without the risk of GI upset is an issue, suppositories are a good option. The rectal mucosa are ideal for absorption due to the high vascularity of the membranes. When medication is introduced via the rectum, it is also not altered, as it would be by gastric juices. The ideal time to insert a rectal suppository is immediately after a bowel movement and when the patient can remain lying down in a supine position for at least 20 minutes.

PROCEDURE 24-1 Assist with a Colon Endoscopic/Colonoscopy Exam

Theory

Because of the personal nature of this invasive test, the patient may need your encouragement to discuss any concerns with the physician. You may prepare the Informed Consent form, and the physician or nurse secures the patient signature after discussing the procedure and risks. You will also give the patient pre-colonoscopy preparation instructions and post-colonoscopy care instructions.

Before the colonoscopy:

- The physician will order a cathartic to be administered at different intervals during the day before the procedure.
- The physician will order a high intake of fluids to prevent dehydration, unless there is a medical contraindication.
- The physician will order a clear-liquids-only diet for the day before surgery.
- The following are *prohibited* from the beginning of the preparation day until after the colonoscopy:
  - milk, dairy products, and solid food
  - fruit juices with pulp
  - any liquids that are red or purple
    After the colonoscopy:
- The physician will provide additional information relating to the procedure(s) performed during the colonoscopy.
- If specimens are taken for analysis, the physician will inform you when to expect the biopsy results. The physician may discuss diagnosis during the recovery period or during a later office visit.
- The physician will discuss postoperative care that may include the following:
  1. During the first 12–24 hours, restrict activities and driving until the effects of the sedative or anesthetic have worn off, restrict weight lifting, and take plenty of fluids, a soft diet, and pain control if needed.
  2. During days 2–14, expect some very minor bleeding in the stool, shift to a high-fiber diet, and take Metamucil or Citrucel if necessary to promote regular bowel movements. Take Milk of Magnesia if you do not have a bowel movement within 72 hours, and drink plenty of fluids.
- Recommendations will be given for a repeat colonoscopy or Hemoccult stool test.

Materials

- 2 pairs of nonsterile gloves
- instrument for viewing, depending on procedure being performed
- water-soluble lubricant
- patient drapes and gown
- sterile cotton-tipped applicators, for collection of fecal samples
- suction device
- sterile biopsy forceps
- disposable or sterile rectal speculum
- specimen containers with lab requisition form, as needed
- disposable tissue
- biohazard container
- patient chart

Competency

(**Conditions**) With the necessary materials, (**Task**) you will be able to set up an exam room and assist the physician with a colon endoscopic procedure (**Standards**) within the time frame designated by the instructor.

1. Gather all needed supplies.
2. Identify the patient and explain the procedure. Verify that the patient has followed pre-exam instructions regarding foods, medications, and activities to avoid, such as enemas. The patient should be asked to empty the bladder prior to the exam.
3. Give the patient drapes and a gown and instructions on proper gown opening placement.
4. Take the patient's vital signs.
5. Assist the patient to the table and position him or her for the exam.
6. Wash your hands and put on gloves.
7. Assist the physician by handing him or her supplies as requested. To ease equipment entry into the anal canal, the physician will use an anal speculum. A suction device may be required to remove any fecal matter that obstructs the physician's view. If polyp tissue samples are needed, the physician will use sterile biopsy forceps.
8. To ease any discomfort, instruct the patient to breathe slowly and deeply. Observe the patient for any change in vitals, increased pain level, or other undue reactions.
9. After the physician has collected the necessary samples, you will place them in sterile specimen containers.
10. When the physician has completed the examination, cleanse the patient's anal area with tissues.
11. Remove the gloves, wash your hands, and assist the patient into a recovery position.
12. While the patient is resting, recheck vital signs. Invasive procedures often cause a drop in blood pressure.
13. Once the blood pressure is stable, allow the patient to get off the exam table and get dressed.
14. Complete laboratory forms. Seal the specimen containers in an appropriate biohazard-labeled transport bag.
15. When the patient has been released from the room, wash your hands, put on new gloves, and disinfect the area. A disposable speculum should be discarded into a biohazardous container; a stainless steel speculum should be prepared for autoclaving.
16. Document the procedure in the patient's chart.

continued

PROCEDURE 24-1 Assist with a Colon Endoscopic/Colonoscopy Exam *(continued)*

Patient Education

Give the patient verbal and written instructions for care after this invasive procedure. The patient should report any undue effects, such as fainting, dizziness, loss of appetite, or rectal bleeding. Advise the patient to refrain from intense physical activity until directed by a physician.

Charting Example

08/05/XX 7:30 PM *Assisted in colon endoscopic procedure. Patient vital signs monitored and remained stable. Patient reported no feelings of faintness, dizziness, or discomfort following the procedure. Specimens collected and sent to laboratory. Anita Estrada, RMA*

PROCEDURE 24-2 Assist with a Sigmoidoscopy

Theory

During a sigmoidoscopy, the physician may occasionally need to distend the walls of the colon for easier viewing by introducing air into the colon via an inflation bulb, or insufflator, attached to the scope. This part of a sigmoidoscopy is uncomfortable and sometimes painful. To help ease discomfort, coach the patient to take slow, deep breaths.

Sigmoidoscopies can be performed with disposable or sterile equipment.

Materials

- sigmoidoscope
- insufflator
- water-soluble lubricant
- patient drapes and gown
- sterile cotton-tipped applicators
- suction device
- sterile biopsy forceps, as directed by physician
- disposable or sterile rectal speculum
- specimen containers with lab requisition form, as needed
- disposable tissue
- chucks pads
- water basin
- 500 ml of warmed water
- gloves
- biohazard container
- patient chart

Competency

(**Conditions**) With the necessary materials, (**Task**) you will be able to set up an exam room and assist the physician with a sigmoidoscopy procedure (**Standards**) within the time frame designated by the instructor.

1. Gather all needed supplies.
2. Identify the patient and explain the procedure. Verify that the patient has followed pre-exam instructions regarding foods, medications, and activities to avoid and performed an enema. The patient should be asked to empty the bladder prior to the exam for greater comfort.
3. Give the patient drapes and a gown and instructions on proper gown opening placement.
4. Take the patient's vital signs.
5. Assist the patient to the table and position for the exam.
6. Place a chucks pad, examination pad, or other absorbent material under the patient's perineal area.
7. Wash your hands and put on gloves.
8. Assist the physician as needed.
9. Attach the light source and insufflator to the sigmoidoscope, but do not turn on the light until the physician is ready to use it. The light generates heat the longer it is on and can potentially burn the patient.
10. To ease the patient's discomfort, instruct him or her to breathe slowly and deeply. Observe the patient for any change in vitals, increased pain level, or other undue reactions.
11. When the physician has completed the examination, cleanse the patient's anal area with tissues.
12. Remove the gloves, wash your hands, and assist the patient into a recovery position.
13. While the patient is resting, recheck vital signs. Invasive procedures often cause a drop in blood pressure.
14. Once the blood pressure is stable, allow the patient to get off the exam table and get dressed.
15. Complete the laboratory forms and send samples to be examined.
16. When the patient has been released from the room, wash your hands, put on new gloves, and disinfect the area.
17. Document the procedure in the patient chart.

Patient Education

When air is introduced into the gastrointestinal tract, it can cause mild discomfort or even pain for some patients. After

PROCEDURE 24-2 **Assist with a Sigmoidoscopy** *(continued)*

the procedure, instruct the patient to lie in the supine position to relieve this discomfort. Placing a pillow across the abdomen or between the knees can also help relieve gastric pressure. Encourage the patient to find the most comfortable position that will allow the passing of excess gas. Do not recommend that the patient take any gas-relief medication.

Charting Example

08/05/XX 7:30 PM Assisted in sigmoidoscopy procedure. Patient vital signs monitored and remained stable. Patient reported no feelings of faintness, dizziness, or discomfort following the procedure. Specimens collected and sent to laboratory. Lisa Kim, RMA

PROCEDURE 24-3 **Insert a Rectal Suppository**

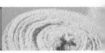

Theory

For patients who are experiencing extreme nausea or are unable to tolerate GI medications, rectal suppositories are often prescribed for medication administration.

Materials

- physician-prescribed rectal suppository
- water-soluble lubricant
- tissues
- biohazardous container
- disposable gloves
- patient instructions
- patient chart

Competency

(**Conditions**) With the necessary materials, (**Task**) you will be able to correctly administer a rectal suppository (**Standards**) within the time allotted by the instructor.

1. Verify the patient's identification and check for allergies.
2. Verify the physician's medication order.
3. Collect all necessary supplies.
4. Explain the procedure to the patient.
5. Wash your hands and put on gloves.

6. Ask the patient to remove all clothing from the waist area down.
7. Assist the patient into a Sims position and provide proper drapes (Figure 24-10 ◆).
8. Take the protective foil wrap from the suppository and carefully smooth any rough or jagged edges. Lubricate the suppository with the water-soluble lubricant.
9. Expose the patient's buttocks.
10. Holding the suppository in one hand, lift the upper buttock with your other hand, exposing the anus (Figure 24-11 ◆).
11. Firmly guide the suppository into the anus with your index finger, past any fecal masses and the internal sphincter. This will prevent it from being expelled (Figure 24-12 ◆)

Figure 24-11 ◆ Lift the upper buttock, exposing the anus

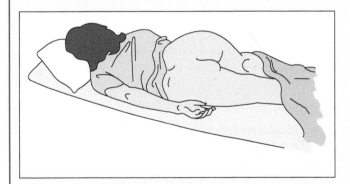

Figure 24-10 ◆ Assist patient into Sims position.

continued

. PROCEDURE 24-3 **Insert a Rectal Suppository** *(continued)*

12. With a tissue, apply firm pressure on the anus for 1–2 minutes to allow the medication to be retained. Discard the tissue into the biohazardous container.

13. With another tissue, wipe away any excess lubricant or fecal matter from the anus and discard the tissue into the biohazardous container.

14. Instruct the patient to get into a comfortable position and rest for 30 minutes as the medication is absorbed.

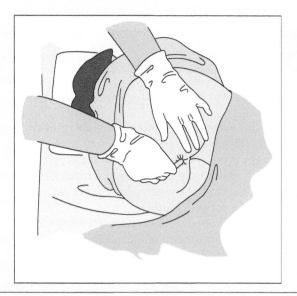

Figure 24-12 ◆ Insert the suppository.

15. Clean the area, providing a new drape if necessary, and dispose of all materials in the biohazardous container.

16. Remove the gloves and wash your hands.

17. Document the procedure in the patient chart.

Patient Education

Inform the patient of the time frame in which the medication takes effect. The patient may need to rest in a comfortable position while the medication is absorbed, as directed by office protocol. Also inform the patient of any side effects that may be experienced, such as flatulence or anal leakage. Some medications may also cause dizziness. Patients taking medication known to cause excessive sleepiness or dizziness should be monitored carefully and assisted when moving off the exam table. These patients will also require someone to drive them home, as it would be unsafe for them to operate a motor vehicle.

Charting Example

08/05/XX 7:30 PM Dulcolax 15 mg rectal suppository administered for relief of constipation. Patient advised to call office in 24 hours to report effectiveness. Alex Rodriguez, RMA

Patient Instruction in Nutrition

As a medical assistant you may be responsible for providing patients with information about special diets. Many offices have printed dietary plans available for distribution to patients. You should be familiar with the various dietary options and review the prescribed diet with the patient. Some common diets are described in Table 24-11.

Therapeutic Diets

In addition to providing dietary information, it may be necessary to refer the patient to a dietitian. A dietitian works with the patient to plan a diet that both meets medical needs and appeals to the patient's taste. Therapeutic diets are prescribed to alleviate symptoms and manage medical treatment. Some disorders that may benefit from a therapeutic diet are hypertension, hypercholesteremia, diabetes mellitus, and some gastrointestinal disorders. For example, eliminating foods high in sodium controls fluid retention that may be responsible for a patient's hypertension. Reducing foods high in cholesterol or cholesterol-forming agents may lower blood cholesterol and slow the progression of atherosclerosis. The American Heart Association, American Cancer Society, and American Diabetic Association all offer dietary recommendations for these medical conditions and for overall healthier eating habits. The guidelines of two of the groups are listed in Table 24-12.

Another area in which you can be helpful to patients concerns simple, common-sense treatments for common digestive problems:

Nausea

- Eat crackers slowly, in small amounts
- Keep the eyes open.
- Avoid head movements.
- Avoid milk and milk products.
- Avoid high-fat foods.
- Drink flat carbonated water or soft drinks (soda).

TABLE 24-11 SPECIAL DIETS

Name or Type of Diet	Reason for Diet	Dietary Concepts
Clear liquid diet	May be prescribed as a preoperative diet, postoperative diet, prep diet for certain diagnostic tests, or to treat GI upsets	Broth, tea, Jell-O; apple juice and cranberry juice occasionally allowed
Liquid diet (full liquid diet)	May be prescribed as a preoperative diet, postoperative diet, prep diet for certain diagnostic tests, or to treat GI upsets	Clear liquids, milk, custards, ice cream, fruit juices, eggnog, milkshakes
Soft diet	May be prescribed postoperatively to reduce strain on GI system or for certain gastrointestinal disorders	Foods containing very little roughage, no raw fruits or vegetables, no gas-forming foods, and reduced or no spices
Mechanical soft diet	Prescribed when mastication is difficult or impossible.	Pureed, chopped, or ground foods
High-fiber diet	Provides bulk in GI tract as an aid to elimination	Fruits, vegetables, whole-grain cereals, green leafy vegetables, deep yellow fruits and vegetables, members of cabbage family, and decreased fat and salt intake
Low-fiber diet	Elimination of high-fiber foods that may irritate intestinal mucosa and diverticulosis	No nuts, seeds, fruits or vegetables with skins (peas, corn, plums) or a high fiber content (whole grains, cabbage, celery)
Bland diet	Elimination of foods that may irritate gastric mucosa	No spices, fried foods, substances containing caffeine, pepper, chili, alcohol, and high-fiber foods
Elimination diet	Determination of food substances that may be causing an allergic response	One or two foods eliminated for a period of time to see if allergic response abates
Diabetic diet	Control of blood glucose levels in the diabetic patient. Usually includes controlling caloric intake and reducing simple sugars.	Balanced diet containing complex carbohydrates, monounsaturated fats, five servings of dark-colored vegetables or fruits daily, six servings of whole grains daily, two weekly servings of fish, reduced salt intake, avoidance of saturated fats.
Low-fat or low-cholesterol diet	Reduction of blood levels of lipids and cholesterol	Reduced intake of foods high in cholesterol and saturated fats
Reduced-calorie diet	Weight loss	Reduced calories while maintaining nutritional status
Low-sodium diet	Hypertension, heart problems, kidney disorders	Additional salt withheld from diet
Infant and pediatric diets	Provision of nutrients necessary for growth	High protein, vitamins, minerals, other nutrients
Diet for pregnancy and lactation	Provision of adequate calories and nutrients to support growing fetus and nursing infant	High protein, additional calcium and iron
Geriatric diet	Dentition, activity, and medication needs of geriatric patients	Softer or pureed food, fewer calories for less active patients, lower carbohydrates for diabetic patients, low-sodium diet for patients with CHF
High-energy diet	Prevention of fluctuating levels of blood sugar	Higher intake of raw or lightly cooked vegetables, fresh fruit, beans, nuts, whole grains, fish, free-range chicken, herb teas; exclusion of coffee, tea, alcohol, most meats; three regularly spaced meals and two snacks

TABLE 24-12 THERAPEUTIC DIETS

Heart-Healthy Dietary Guidelines (AHA)

■ Maintain a daily fat intake of 30% of total calories or less, distributed as follows:
   ■ Saturated fatty acids (the "bad" type) less than 10% of total calories
   ■ Polyunsaturated fats (the "good" type) less than 10% of total calories
   ■ Monounsaturated fats (the "good" type) less than 15% of total calories
■ Avoid products made with white flour. Substitute whole-grain products.
■ Replace granola and other cereals made with coconut or palm oil with whole-grain cereals low in fat and sugar but high in fiber.
■ Avoid deep-fried vegetables. Eat steamed or baked dark-green leafy vegetables.
■ Avoid cream, butter, margarine, lard, mayonnaise, and salad dressings.
■ Substitute skim, low-fat, or 1% milk products for whole milk, condensed milk, and evaporated milk.
■ Avoid whole-milk cheeses, processed cheeses, cheese spreads, and cream cheese. Substitute low- or nonfat hard cheese, low-fat cottage cheese, and part-skim ricotta cheese.
■ Avoid coconuts, coconut products, and dried fruits with sodium preservatives. Substitute fresh and frozen fruit without added sugar.
■ Instead of goose and duck, organ meats, or fried and processed meats, choose lean beef, veal, pork, and lamb.
■ Avoid smoked, fried, or salted fish, tuna packed in oil, sardines, anchovies, oysters, and crab. Substitute fresh or frozen fish, clams, scallops, and lobster.

American Cancer Society Dietary Guidelines

■ Include more high-fiber foods in the diet (fruits, vegetables, and whole-grain products).
■ Increase your intake of dark-green and yellow fruits and vegetables, broccoli, cabbage, brussels sprouts, kohlrabi, and cauliflower.
■ Limit your intake of processed, salt-cured, smoked, and nitrite-cured foods (bacon and smoked sausage).
■ Reduce total fat intake, especially animal fats.
■ Maintain a healthy weight.
■ Limit your intake of alcoholic beverages.

Vomiting

- Avoid food or fluids for one hour after emesis.
- Freshen the mouth by rinsing with water.
- Sip a soft drink in small amounts after one hour.
- When able to resume eating, start with bland foods.

Diarrhea

- Drink clear liquids.
- Use sports drinks to replace glucose and electrolytes.
- Avoid alcohol.
- Eat cultured yogurts.

Constipation

- Increase fluid intake.
- Increase fiber in the diet.
- Avoid milk, cheese, and other dairy products.
- Increase your level of exercise, including walking.
- *Do not* ignore the urge to defecate. Respond in a timely manner.
- Establish and maintain a daily routine for defecation.

REVIEW

Chapter Summary

- The gastrointestinal system is primarily responsible for nourishing the body. Salivation, mastication, and the process of digestion break food down into nutritional substances. Habits of good nutrition help the body maintain a strong immune system, healthy energy levels, and mental alertness. During times of altered health, a healthy nutritional status can speed recovery.

- Obtaining and recording the medical history and vital signs are an MA's routine functions in a gastroenterology or proctology medical office. The MA records specific symptoms, assists the physician in examinations and procedures, arranges appointments for diagnostic tests and procedures, and provides patient instruction.

- The gastrointestinal system or digestive tract is composed of the alimentary canal and accessory organs. The upper digestive tract begins at the mouth and goes on to the pharynx, esophagus, stomach, and duodenum. The lower digestive tract includes the small intestine and large intestine, cecum, appendix, sigmoid portion, rectum, and anus. The small intestine is made up of the duodenum, jejunum, and ileum. The large intestine comprises the cecum, ascending colon, transverse colon, descending colon, and sigmoid regions of the colon, terminating at the rectum. The accessory organs are the pancreas, liver, gallbladder, and connecting ducts.

- The major functions of the GI system are digestion, alimentation, and elimination. The digestion process is divided into ingestion, mastication, deglutination, digestion, and absorption. Elimination is the process of excretion.

- Healthy living habits help prevent disease as well as the additive effects of poor nutritional status upon a disease condition.

- Food is required for the growth and repair of body tissues, for the regulation of different body processes, and for heat production. Individuals fulfill their dietary needs based on

such factors as cultural and religious background, financial resources, and appetite.

- The basic components of nutrition are carbohydrates, proteins, fats, minerals, vitamins, fiber, and water. Carbohydrates are the primary source of energy and are primarily found in fruit, breads and cereals, pasta products, rice, and potatoes. Fats and proteins are also a source of energy. Fats aid in growth and development by providing fatty acids, and proteins build and renew body tissues.

- Vitamins are required components for metabolism and growth and development. Minerals help in specific regulatory processes, tissue development and repair, blood clotting, muscle contractions, and nervous system impulse conduction. Fiber is important to intestinal health and the prevention of intestinal diseases. Water regulates body temperature, lubricates joints, carries nutrition to and waste materials from body cells, and aids in other body processes.

- Weight management is best achieved by maintaining a balance between caloric intake and caloric expenditure. Obesity, a symptom of caloric intake greater than required caloric needs, is both a cause and a result of medical conditions.

- The MyPyramid is an educational tool developed by the USDA to assist healthy Americans over 2 years of age to maintain good eating habits.

- The pyramid lists the recommended servings of different food groups to meet daily nutritional needs. Alternate versions of the Food Pyramid address specific groups such as Asian, Latin, Mediterranean, vegetarian, the elderly, and children ages 2 through 6. Persons with medical needs require the professional assistance of dietitians and physicians to design optimum diets.

- The physiological functioning of the gastrointestinal system decreases as an individual ages. Functioning is also affected by past and present medical conditions, medications, and

Chapter Summary (continued)

social interaction. Establishing wellness habits early in life prevents malnutrition, obesity, inactivity, and the advancement or development of medical and dental conditions later. The nutritional status of an individual as he or she ages can affect or cause medical conditions. The elderly should be encouraged to eat high-nutrition foods and maintain or increase physical activity, which in turn increases appetite, mobility, physical endurance and immune response.

■ Food allergies and food intolerances occur in both children and adults. Food allergy reactions result from a hypersensitivity of the immune system to certain kinds of food substances. Persons with food allergies often have a genetic predisposition and a history of other allergies.

■ Diseases of the GI system include inflammatory conditions, obstructive conditions, infectious disorders, disorders due to increased or decreased peristalsis, circulatory or hemorrhagic disorders, congenital disorders, functional disorders, neoplasms, parasitic invasion, and food poisoning. Various diagnostic procedures may be ordered, some of which are performed in the office setting, including palpation, auscultation, visualization of the abdomen, blood tests, upper and lower GI series, stool specimen studies, and others.

■ Disease conditions result from and are the cause of altered nutritional states. For example, heart disease, hypertension, and atherosclerosis often result from dietary intake of foods high in fats and cholesterol. Prolonged nausea and vomiting are often responsible for electrolyte imbalances due to excessive loss of fluids. Parasitic infestation and infections result from the ingestion of contaminated food and/or water.

■ Colonoscopies are performed to assess healthy or disease states of the colon.

■ Warning signs of GI problems include nausea, vomiting, hematemesis, coffee ground emesis, diarrhea, constipation, bright red blood in stools, black stools, abdominal pain and distension, dyspepsia, anorexia, flatulence, and dysphagia.

■ Disorders or conditions of the GI tract may be classified as abnormal function, anatomical and congenital abnormalities, infections, food poisoning, inflammation, malignancies, vascular-related conditions, and conditions of the accessory digestive organs.

■ The medical assistant provides patients with information regarding special diets. It is customary for offices to have printed diets available for distribution to patients.

Chapter Review Questions

Multiple Choice

1. Which of the following terms means "difficulty swallowing"?
   A. hematemesis
   B. dyspepsia
   C. dysphagia
   D. hepatomegaly

2. The lower GI tract includes all of the following except:
   A. duodenum
   B. small intestine
   C. large intestine
   D. sigmoid

3. The upper GI tract includes all of the following except:
   A. pharynx
   B. cecum
   C. esophagus
   D. duodenum

4. The alimentary canal is composed of how many layers?
   A. 2
   B. 3
   C. 0
   D. 4

5. The parietal peritoneum covers which two organs?
   A. upper and lower intestines
   B. stomach and intestines
   C. esophagus and small intestine
   D. rectum and esophagus

6. The duct opening into the duodenum that releases bile and pancreatic enzymes is the:
   A. ampulla of Vater
   B. pancreatic duct
   C. common hepatic duct
   D. common bile duct

7. *Mastication* means:
   A. swallowing
   B. elimination
   C. chewing
   D. ingestion

8. Which of the following is *not* involved in the initial breakdown of food?
   A. teeth
   B. cheeks
   C. tongue
   D. esophagus

9. How many essential amino acids are there?
   A. 11
   B. 8
   C. 10
   D. 4

Chapter Review Questions (continued)

10. How many amino acids can be produced by the body?
    A. 11
    B. 8
    C. 6
    D. 4

True/False

T F 1. LDLs transport fats manufactured in the liver to body cells.

T F 2. HDLs transport fats from body cells to the liver.

T F 3. Lipoproteins contain cholesterol.

T F 4. Dietary fiber is a carbohydrate that takes the longest to digest, making a person feel full longer.

T F 5. Complex carbohydrates are sugars found in natural sources such as fruit and honey.

Short Answer

1. What is a calorie?

2. How much energy is released through the metabolism of 1 gram of carbohydrate, 1 gram of protein, and 1 gram of fat?

3. According to the American Cancer Society, who should have colonoscopies for cancer screening?

4. Which procedure is often used to treat obstructive conditions involving the small intestine?

5. What is the function of the organs and ducts of the biliary tract?

Research

1. Research the different types of vegetarian diets, such as full vegan.

2. Research the top five diet trends of the year. How are they similar? How are they different? What is the main "promise" of each?

Externship Application Experience

A patient sitting in the exam room states that he is feeling nauseous and very uncomfortable. What should you do?

Resource Guide

American College of Gastroenterology (ACG)
P.O. Box 3099
Alexandria, VA 22302
www.acg.gi.org

American Dental Association
211 E Chicago Ave.
Chicago, IL 60611-2678
www.ada.org

American Dietetic Association
216 W. Jackson Blvd.
Chicago, IL 60606-6995
800-877-1600
www.eatright.org

American Dietetic Association Foundation
120 South Riverside Plaza, Suite 2000
Chicago, IL 60606
1-800-877-1600
www.adaf.org

American Gastroenterology Association
493 Del Ray Ave.
Bethesda, MD 20814
301-654-2055
www.gastro.org

Food Allergy and Anaphylaxis Network
10400 Eaton Place, Suite 107
Fairfax, VA 22030
800-929-4040
www.foodallergy.org

National Institute of Allergy and Infectious Diseases
National Institutes of Health
U.S. Department of Health and Human Services
Bethesda, MD 20892
www.niaid.nih.gov

U.S. National Library of Medicine
National Institutes of Health
www.nlm.nih.gov

MedMedia
www.prenhall.com/frazier

More on this chapter, including interactive resources, can be found on the Student CD-ROM accompanying this textbook and on the Companion Website at www.prenhall.com/frazier.

Objectives

After completing this chapter, you should be able to:

- Spell and define the medical terminology in the chapter.
- Define the role of the medical assistant in the orthopedic office.
- Describe the anatomy and physiology of the bones and skeleton.
- Describe the anatomy and physiology of muscles.
- Discuss congenital, degenerative, infectious, malignant, and traumatic musculoskeletal conditions.
- List and describe diagnostic procedures for musculoskeletal conditions.
- Explain how splints and braces are used.
- Describe different types of casts and cast application.
- Describe major physical therapy modalities, including thermodynamics.
- Discuss ambulation modalities, including walking with crutches, a cane, and a walker.
- Explain the use of prostheses in orthopedics.
- Discuss proper body mechanics.

Orthopedics and Physical Therapy

Case Study

Xavier is restocking the exam rooms at the urgent care center where he works after a midafternoon rush of patients. Just as he is finishing, Jorge Ramirez hops in, assisted by two of his friends. Jorge explains that he was playing a game of touch football with his friends when he was tackled and twisted his ankle. It started swelling immediately, is very painful to move, and cannot bear any weight. Xavier directs Jorge's friends to assist him onto the X-ray table so the ankle can be checked for a fracture.

After the initial exam and X-ray by the physician, Jorge is told a fracture cannot be ruled out due to the swelling. The doctor says he will refer Jorge to an orthopedic specialist. In the meantime, prior to the appointment, Jorge is to wear an air brace for support and use crutches. It is Xavier's responsibility to teach him the proper technique for crutch use.

MedMedia

www.prenhall.com/frazier

Additional interactive resources and activities for this chapter can be found on the Companion Website. For videos, audio glossary, legal and ethical scenarios, job scenarios, quizzes, games, virtual tours, and activities related to the content of this chapter, please access the accompanying CD-ROM in this book.

 Assets Available:

Audio Glossary
Legal and Ethical Scenario: *Orthopedics and Physical Therapy*
On the Job Scenario: *Orthopedics and Physical Therapy*
Video Scenario: Crutch Instruction
Multiple Choice Quiz
Games: Crossword, Strikeout and Spelling Bee
3D Virtual Tour: Muscular System: Head & Neck; Muscular System: Hip & Thigh; Muscular System: Leg & Foot; Muscular System: Lower Limb; Muscular System: Pelvis (Female); Muscular System: Arm & Shoulder; Muscular System: Trunk & Abdomen; Muscular System: Upper Limb
Drag and Drop: Muscular System: Muscle structures, Muscles of the Anterior, Muscles of the Posterior

Medical Terminology

amphiarthrosis—condition of slight joint movement in all directions

arthritis—inflammation of a joint

articular—pertaining to a joint

atony—lack of normal tone or strength in a muscle

atrophy—decrease in size of normal muscle mass

axillary—pertaining to the axilla (armpit)

body mechanics—procedures for standing and efficient body movement, including lifting, pushing, or pulling, that prevent injury and maintain required energy levels for long employment

bursa (plural: bursae)—a sac filled with synovial fluid that reduces friction and provides ease of movement between tendons and ligaments, ligaments and bone, and other tissues

bursitis—inflammation of bursa(e)

cartilage—smooth, elastic connective tissue that covers the ends of the bones

cast—a plaster or fiberglass device used to immobilize a body part

compress—folded piece of material used to apply dry or moist heat or cold therapeutic applications

cryotherapy—the use of cold applications to prevent or reduce swelling and pain

diarthrosis—condition of bone joints moving freely

endosteum—membrane lining the inner portion and marrow cavity of the bone

hematopoiesis—formation of blood cells

ligament—a tough, elastic tissue that connects ends of bones

neoplasia—abnormal cell development

orthopedics—the study and treatment of diseases and disorders of the musculoskeletal system

osteoblast—a precursor cell in bone formation

periosteum—a fibrous membrane covering the outside of bone tissue

prosthesis (plural: prostheses)—artificial replacement for a body part

range of motion—the full extent of any joint potential for movement, including actions such as flexion, extension, circumduction, adduction, and abduction

✚ MEDICAL ASSISTING COMPETENCIES

CAAHEP ENTRY-LEVEL COMPETENCIES FOR CMA	ABHES ENTRY-LEVEL COMPETENCIES FOR RMA
■ Identify and respond to issues of confidentiality. ■ Perform within legal and ethical boundaries. ■ Demonstrate knowledge of federal and state health-care legislation and regulations. ■ Perform hand washing. ■ Dispose of biohazardous materials. ■ Practice Standard Precautions. ■ Use methods of quality control. ■ Perform telephone and in-person screening. ■ Obtain vital signs. ■ Obtain and record patient history. ■ Prepare and maintain examination and treatment areas. ■ Prepare patient for and assist with routine and specialty examinations. ■ Prepare patient and assist with minor procedures, treatments, and minor surgery. ■ Apply pharmacology principles to prepare and administer oral and parenteral medications. ■ Maintain medication and immunization records.	■ Project a positive attitude. ■ Maintain confidentiality at all times. ■ Be a "team player." ■ Be cognizant of ethical boundaries. ■ Exhibit initiative. ■ Adapt to change. ■ Evidence a responsible attitude. ■ Be courteous and diplomatic. ■ Conduct work within scope of education, training, and ability. ■ Interview and take a patient history. ■ Prepare patients for and assist physician with routine and specialty examinations and treatments and minor office surgery. ■ Apply principles of aseptic techniques and infection control. ■ Prepare and maintain examination and treatment area. ■ Collect and process specimens. ■ Dispose of biohazardous materials. ■ Practice Standard Precautions. ■ Prepare and administer oral and parenteral medications as directed by the physician. ■ Maintain medication and immunization records.

Introduction

Orthopedics is the study of the musculoskeletal system: the bones, muscles, joints, ligaments, tendons, and nerves. The bones of the skeletal system give the body its shape and support and also protect internal organs. The muscles cover the skeleton and move the different parts of the body. All parts of the musculoskeletal system are subject to disease and trauma.

An orthopedic surgeon is a surgical physician who specializes in the diagnosis and treatment of musculoskeletal conditions. Physicians in this practice are often called orthopedists or orthopods.

The Medical Assistant's Role in the Orthopedic Office

As a medical assistant in an orthopedic office, you should be familiar with the anatomy, terminology, and disorders and diseases of the musculoskeletal system. You will have a variety of tasks, depending on the area of the medical office to which you are assigned:

Medical Terminology *(continued)*

reduction—the process of open or closed manipulation that returns bony ends to correct anatomical position before healing

soak—procedure in which the total body or body part is immersed in water for heat or cold therapeutic applications

splint—a temporary orthopedic device used to immobilize, restrain, and support any extremity of the body

synarthrosis—condition of absent joint movement

tendon—tough, elastic tissue that connects muscle to bone

tetany—painful, intense, spasmodic muscle contractions

thermodynamics—the use of cryotherapy or thermotherapy for therapeutic treatment

thermotherapy—the use of heat application to increase circulation to an area and promote healing

Abbreviations

AKA—above knee amputation

BEA—below elbow amputation

BKA—below knee amputation

C1—cervical vertebra number 1 (number identifies 1-7 of cervical vertebrae)

Ca—calcium

DJD—degenerative joint disease

Fx—fracture

L1—lumbar vertebra number 1 (number identifies 1-5 of lumbar vertebrae)

LLE—left lower extremity

LLL—left lower leg

LS—lumbosacral

LUE—left upper extremity

PT—physical therapy

RA—rheumatoid arthritis

RLE—right lower extremity

RLL—right lower leg

ROM—range of motion

RUE—right upper extremity

T1—thoracic vertebra number 1 (number identifies 1-12 of thoracic vertebrae)

COMPETENCY SKILLS PERFORMANCE

1. Demonstrate assisting with a cast application.
2. Demonstrate assisting with cast removal.
3. Demonstrate assisting a patient with cold compress application.
4. Demonstrate assisting a patient with hot compress application.
5. Demonstrate assisting with therapeutic ultrasonography.
6. Demonstrate fitting a patient for axillary crutches.
7. Demonstrate assisting a patient with crutch walking.
8. Demonstrate assisting a patient using a cane.
9. Demonstrate assisting a patient using a walker.
10. Demonstrate assisting a patient in a wheelchair to and from an examination table.

■ obtaining and recording medical history, vital signs, and specific symptoms as reported by the patient

■ assisting the physician in examinations and procedures

■ placing X-ray films on the radiograph viewbox for the physician

■ instructing the patient about undressing, and providing a gown and drape

■ assisting the patient in ambulating or moving to and from the examination table

■ arranging appointments for diagnostic tests and procedures

■ providing patients with supportive and ambulation devices, including crutches, canes, and wheelchairs

■ instructing patients and family members in proper **body mechanics** and **thermodynamic** treatments

■ providing information on community resources for orthopedic patients such as rehabilitation, transportation, and mobility services, and physical therapy

The Anatomy and Physiology of the Musculoskeletal System

The musculoskeletal system is composed of bones and muscles. The skeleton provides the framework for the body, allowing the individual to stand erect, and protects the internal organs. Muscles facilitate the movement of the various bones and joints of the skeleton.

Bones

The skeleton can be divided into axial and appendicular sections (Figure 25-1 ◆). The axial skeleton consists of bones in the head and trunk, such as the cranial, facial, and ear bones; the vertebrae of the spinal column; the sternum; and the ribs. The spinal column consists of cervical, thoracic, lumbar, sacral, and coccygeal sections. It serves as an anchor for the head and extremities and provides structure for the positions of sitting, standing, and lying.

The appendicular section of the skeleton consists of the extremities and the shoulder and hip framework to which the extremities are attached. Examples of upper-division appendicular skeleton bones are the clavicle, scapula, humerus, radius, ulna, carpals, metacarpals, and phalanges of the fingers. The lower-division appendicular skeleton contains the pelvic bones, femur, patella, fibula, tibula, tarsals, metatarsals, and phalanges of the toes.

The skeleton is composed of 206 bones. These bones are classified according to structure (Figure 25-2 ◆).

■ Long bones are located in the thigh, lower leg, upper arm, lower arm, and digits.

■ The wrists and ankles consist of short bones that enable more specific movement.

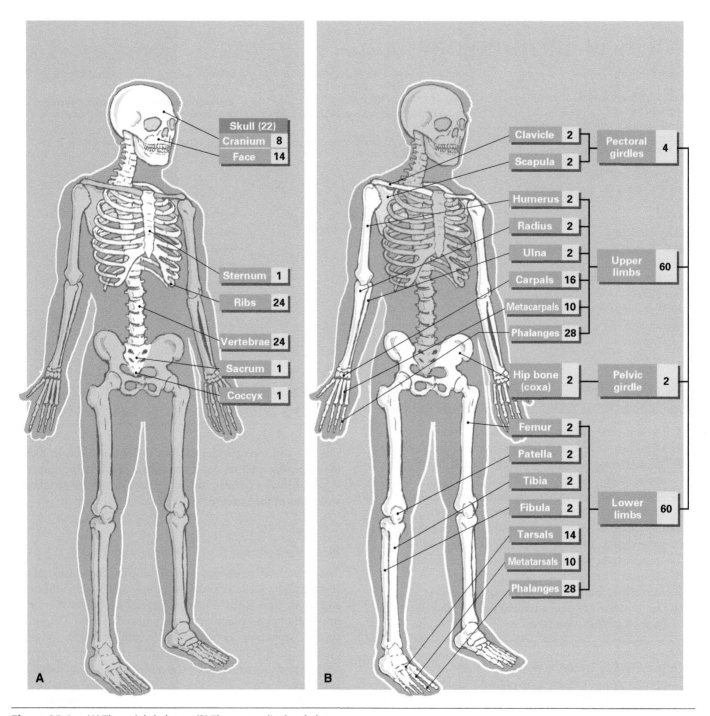

Figure 25-1 ◆ (A) The axial skeleton; (B) The appendicular skeleton

- Flat bones include the shoulder bones (scapulae), ribs, and pelvic bones.
- Sesamoid bones, which are formed within **tendons** or joint capsules, include the patella, also known as the kneecap.

The bones come together to form joints and serve as points of attachment for muscles, thereby making movement possible. Bone tissue also serves as a repository for calcium (**Ca**) and other mineral reserves. When calcium blood levels are low, such as during low dietary supply, bone tissue releases calcium into the blood.

The outside layer of bone is covered with a membrane called **periosteum** (Figure 25-3 ◆). **Cartilage,** a strong and flexible connective tissue, helps to reduce friction between the moving bones and serves as a shock absorber. Cartilage is also found in the tip of the nose, the pinna (outer ear), and the larynx and trachea. The periosteum layer contains **osteoblasts** for bone tissue formation, blood and lymphatic vessels, and nerve fibers.

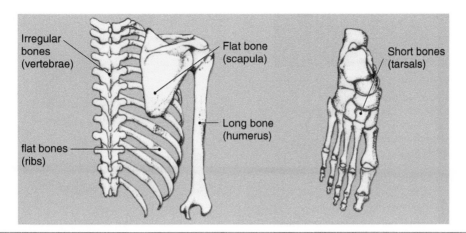

Figure 25-2 ◆ Classification of bones

The **endosteum** membrane lines the inner marrow cavity of the bone. Blood cells (RBCs and WBCs) are formed in the ends of long bones and the center of other bones, a process called **hematopoiesis.** Yellow marrow, made up largely of fat tissue, is found in the long, central portion of the bone. Bone tissue undergoes reabsorption and formation (bone metabolism) as the body progresses through the life stages of growth and aging. When bone reabsorption is greater than bone formation, such as in an older person, the risk of fracture increases.

Joints

A joint, or articulation, is the point at which two bones meet. Joints are classified according to the tissue construction between the bones and the amount of movement allowed by each joint.

- Cartilaginous joints are slightly movable because of the cartilage between the bones. They exhibit a type of movement called **amphiarthrosis.** There is no joint cavity. An example of a cartilaginous joint is the pubic symphysis between the pelvic bones; there are also cartilaginous joints between the vertebrae bodies of the spine.
- Fibrous joints, such as the sutures of the skull, are made of fibrous tissue. These joints exhibit **synarthrosis,** or no movement, because of the connective tissue between the bones. There is no joint cavity.
- Synovial joints are freely movable (**diarthrosis**) and have a joint cavity with anatomical structures to support full movement. They are found in the neck, shoulders, arms, hands, hips, legs, and feet. Synovial fluid secreted within

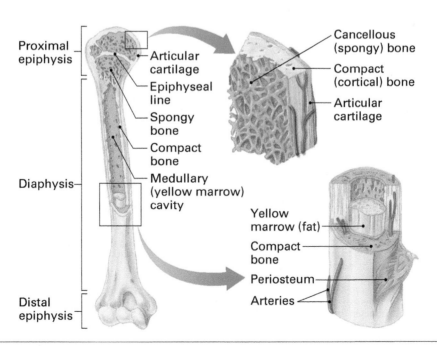

Figure 25-3 ◆ Bone and its anatomy

Keys to Success
THE IMPORTANCE OF CALCIUM

Calcium is essential to many body functions:

■ It is important for blood clotting (coagulation).
■ It helps nerves and muscles to function normally, including the myocardial muscle of the heart.
■ It is essential for healthy bone growth and metabolism.
■ It provides rigidity in bones and teeth.
■ It is necessary for lactation.
■ It serves as an activating enzyme for other chemical reactions in the body.
■ It maintains the permeability of cellular membrane.

Calcium deposits are stored in the bones, but may be released to the bloodstream when blood levels are low. The parathyroid glands (behind the thyroid gland) are responsible for regulating blood levels of dissolved calcium.

A deficiency of blood calcium may result in brittle bones and teeth, rickets, osteoporosis in the postmenopausal female, increased incidence of dental cavities, **tetany,** muscle twitching, convulsions, bleeding problems, or **atony** of the heart muscle. Blood levels of calcium are increased by dietary intake only if an activating substance such as vitamin D is available. Calcium supplements should therefore be accompanied by sources of vitamin D.

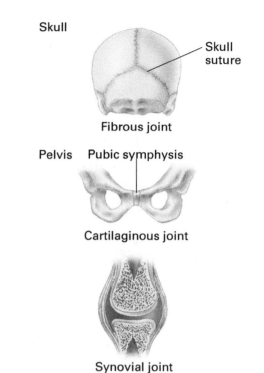

Figure 25-4 ◆ Types of joints found in the body

the joint cavity lubricates the joint. The bone surfaces of these joints are covered with **articular** cartilage for protection and ease of movement. Some synovial joints, called **bursae,** contain sacs filled with synovial fluid. In health, bursae help to ease movement of the often stressed joint. In disease, bursae become inflamed, a condition called **bursitis.** Synovial joints are also covered and protected by a joint capsule of connective tissue that joins with the outer layer, or periosteum, of the bone. Bones of synovial joints are held together by fibrous connective tissue called **ligaments.**

There are several types of synovial joints (Figure 25-4 ◆). They are capable of many different types of movement (Table 25-1 and Figure 25-5 ◆).

TABLE 25-1 SYNOVIAL JOINT MOVEMENTS

Name of Movement	Description	Examples
Flexion	Decreasing the angle of the joint	Bending the lower arm toward the shoulder or making a fist by bending the fingers in toward the palm of the hand
Extension	Opposite of flexion; increasing the angle of the joint	Opening a closed fist to straighten the fingers or unfolding a bent elbow to straighten an arm
Adduction	Bringing the joint toward the body's midline	Moving an arm toward the body
Abduction	Moving the joint away from the body's midline	Moving an arm away the body
Circumduction	Combination of flexion, extension, adduction, and abduction, accomplished by drawing a circle with an extremity	Rotating the distal portion of the arm while the proximal end remains fixed
Rotation	Turning the bone joint upon its own axis	Turning the head upon the first cervical vertebra
Supination	Describes movements of the hand, spine, and foot, referring to the spine or bony portion of the hand, spine, or foot in the dominant position (it is helpful to remember "supine on spine")	Having the palm facing upward when it is extended away from the body
Pronation	Describes movements of the hand, spine, and foot, referring to the soft tissue of the hand, palm, or abdomen in the dominant position	Having the palm facing downward when it is extended away from the body
Inversion	Turning inward	Turning the foot inward
Eversion	Turning outward	Turning the foot outward
Plantar flexion	Flexing of the foot with toes pointed downward and arch exaggerated	Ballet dancing on the toes

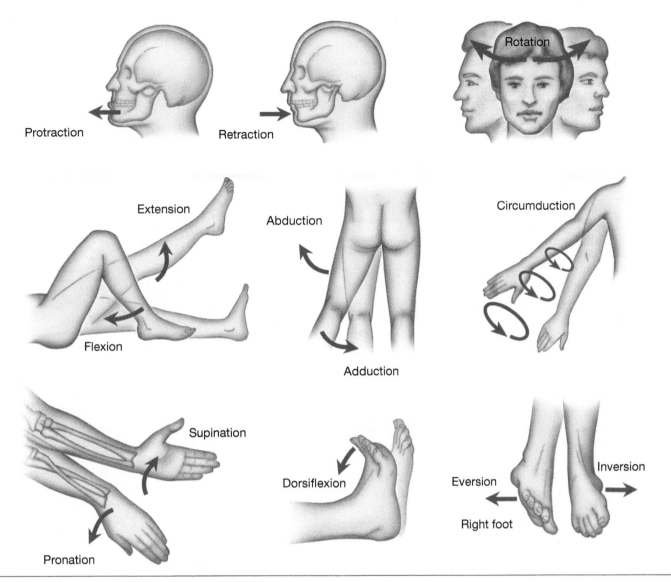

Figure 25-5 ◆ Range of motion exercises

- The ball-and-socket joint allows free movement in many directions from its central point. It is found in the shoulders and hips where they connect to the axial skeleton.
- The condyloid joint allows for two-way movement. It is found at the junction of the skull occipital bone and the first cervical bone, and at the junction of the metacarpal joint and the first phalanx of each finger.
- The gliding joint allows for the gliding of one bone over the surface of another. The wrist and ankle are gliding joints.
- The hinge joint allows for extension or flexion of joints in the knee, elbow, fingers, and toes.
- The pivot joint facilitates internal or external rotation. This joint is found between the first and second cervical vertebrae and at the proximal ends of the radius and ulna in the arm.

- The saddle joint allows for two-way joint movement like the condyloid joint, but with deeper articulating movement between surfaces. An example of this type of joint is found between the metacarpal bone of the thumb and the wrist.

Range of motion (ROM) is the full degree of movement a joint is capable of (Figure 25-5). When a patient is immobile for any length of time, joint range of motion and muscle strength diminish. Range-of-motion exercises are prescribed to maintain joint flexibility and muscle strength. Active range of motion is performed by the patient without any help. Passive range of motion is performed by another person for the patient. Joint contractures and muscle **atrophy** may result when ROM is not prescribed and performed for patients who are immobile for extended periods of time.

Muscles

A muscle is tissue composed of fibers that have the ability to contract and relax, facilitating the movement of body parts and organs. There are three kinds of muscle tissue in the body: skeletal, smooth, and cardiac. This chapter addresses the functions, disorders, and/or insults to skeletal muscle. Muscles are attached to bones by connective tissue known as tendons and contract when they are stimulated by the nervous system.

Muscles help to maintain an upright posture and generate heat by shivering when the body responds to cold. Other functions include a wide range of movements, from opening and closing the eyes to running and throwing a ball, from digesting food to enlarging the thoracic cavity. Muscle tissue is stimulated by voluntary or involuntary muscle control. Smooth and cardiac muscle tissue are classified as involuntary, and skeletal muscle is classified as voluntary (Figure 25-6 ◆ and Table 25-2).

Involuntary muscles are controlled by the autonomic nervous system. Individuals cannot control involuntary responses such as the ongoing process of peristalsis or the beating of the heart. Cardiac muscle usually responds to a stimulus that originates at the sinoatrial (SA) node. The path of neuromuscular conduction spreads through and down the normal channel of electrical conduction to stimulate cardiac muscle contraction and relaxation. Different stimuli such as trauma, excitement, or a medical condition can affect whether the impulse originates in the SA node or in any of the other individual cardiac muscle cells of the atria, nodal region, or ventricles. The property of automaticity, belonging only to the cardiac cells, explains why the heart can beat slowly, fast, or irregularly, according to the location of the initiated cardiac impulse.

Voluntary muscles respond to individual control as well as autonomic nervous system control. The action of skeletal muscles under voluntary control can be changed. For example, a person walking can decide to run. Skeletal muscles can also respond involuntarily—for instance, the action of jerking the hand back after touching a hot pan.

The Contraction of Muscle Cells

A nerve cell contacts the muscle cell at the neuromuscular junction. Between the nerve cell and muscle cell is a small space called a synaptic gap (Figure 25-7 ◆). A stimulus causes the release from the neuron of neurotransmitters that excite and prompt a response from the muscle fiber, or cell. Neurotransmitters, including acetylcholine and others, are stored in nerve ending vesicles until stimulated to release and carry the electrical impulse across the synaptic gap. The neurotransmitter chemicals attach to receptors of the muscle cell that spread the electrical impulse along the entire muscle cell.

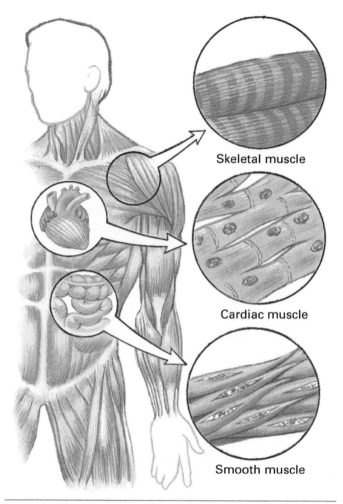

Figure 25-6 ◆ Types of muscles

Skeletal muscle

Cardiac muscle

Smooth muscle

TABLE 25-2 SMOOTH, CARDIAC, AND SKELETAL MUSCLES		
Smooth	**Cardiac**	**Skeletal**
■ Line the walls of blood vessels, respiratory tree, and hollow organs ■ Move involuntarily and produce peristalsis	■ Line the walls of the heart ■ Involuntary reaction to nervous system stimulation results in pumping of heart and pulsation of vessels	■ Attached to bones and responsible for movement of the body and extremities
■ Single nucleus	■ Single nucleus	■ Movements are voluntary (consciously controlled) ■ Multiple nuclei
■ Appear smooth when examined microscopically	■ Appear striated (striped) and have branching interconnections when examined microscopically	■ Long, heavily striated cells
■ Contract in response to neurological electrical impulse, hormonal influence, exercise, medications	■ Contract in response to neurological electrical impulse, hormonal influence, exercise, medications	■ Contract in response to neurological electrical impulse, hormonal influence, exercise, medications

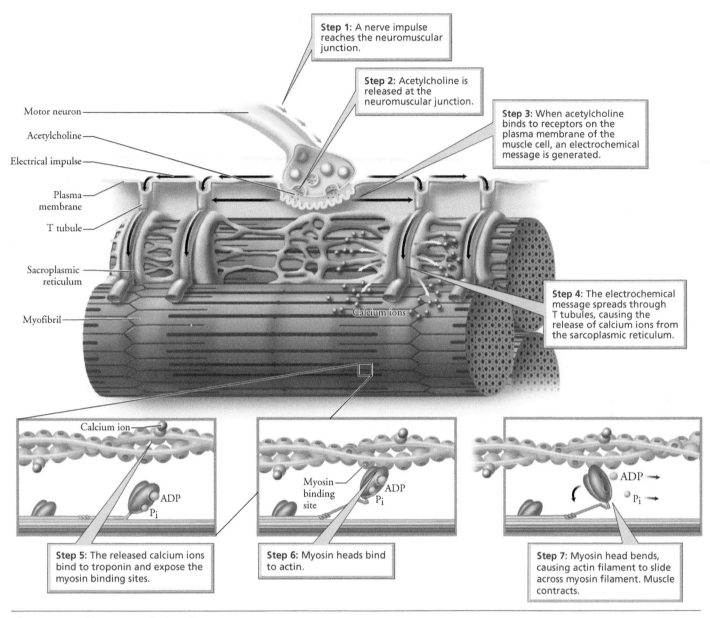

Step 1: A nerve impulse reaches the neuromuscular junction.

Step 2: Acetylcholine is released at the neuromuscular junction.

Step 3: When acetylcholine binds to receptors on the plasma membrane of the muscle cell, an electrochemical message is generated.

Motor neuron

Acetylcholine

Electrical impulse

Plasma membrane

T tubule

Sacroplasmic reticulum

Myofibril

Calcium ions

Step 4: The electrochemical message spreads through T tubules, causing the release of calcium ions from the sarcoplasmic reticulum.

Calcium ion

ADP
P$_i$

Step 5: The released calcium ions bind to troponin and expose the myosin binding sites.

Myosin binding site

ADP
P$_i$

Step 6: Myosin heads bind to actin.

ADP →
P$_i$ →

Step 7: Myosin head bends, causing actin filament to slide across myosin filament. Muscle contracts.

Figure 25-7 ◆ Neuromuscular junction

When all elements of the neuromuscular system are healthy and functioning properly, the transmission of the nervous impulse results in contraction. In certain disease conditions, degeneration of the neuromuscular systems occurs. For example, Parkinson's disease results from a deficiency of the neurotransmitter dopamine, muscular dystrophy from the death of muscle fibers, and multiple sclerosis from demyelination (destruction of the myelin sheath present on some neurons) (∞ see Chapter 28 for information on neuromuscular disorders).

Good health can prevent or inhibit the progression of neuromuscular diseases. A well-balanced diet provides vitamins and other nutrients that promote proper growth and development and help protect the neuromuscular system. Exercise enhances the circulation and transport of nutrition and oxygen to the cells and waste materials from the cells. It improves muscle tone and

prevents muscles from atrophying. Exercise also strengthens bone tissue, thereby lowering the risk of fractures. Additionally, medical checkups, for health maintenance or management of neuromuscular symptoms, promote optimal health.

Common Musculoskeletal Diseases and Disorders

Conditions encountered in the orthopedic office can be classified as congenital, degenerative, infectious, and malignant or traumatic (Tables 25-3, 25-4, and 25-5). Another way to classify them is by the anatomical structure affected: bones, joints, or muscles.

Common musculoskeletal diseases may involve muscles and bones of the body as a whole, the spine, the joints, or other connective tissue such as ligaments and cartilage. Others arise as the result of genetic predisposition.

TABLE 25-3 CONGENITAL AND DEVELOPMENTAL MUSCULOSKELETAL CONDITIONS

Condition	Signs and Symptoms	Cause	Diagnosis	Treatment
Clubfoot	Anterior aspect of foot of newborn is adducted and inverted, and potential for standing with foot flat is nil	Unknown; possibly congenital	Visual examination, manipulation, radiographs	Splinting in early months of life; if unsuccessful, surgical intervention may be required to straighten ankles and feet
Congenital hip dysplasia	Hip joint unstable due to abnormal development; folds of thigh in newborn uneven and one femur appears shorter during visual examination	Cause usually unknown or uncertain; possibly fetal position such as in breech presentation or softening of ligaments due to maternal hormones	Visual examination after birth, confirmed by imaging studies	Application of device to stabilize joint in proper position; if unsuccessful, surgical intervention may be required
Kyphosis	Outward curve of spine, usually in thoracic region; "hump" noted in upper spine, sometimes accompanied by pain and decreased mobility of spine	Etiology unknown in children; may be developmental, result of tumors, tuberculosis of the spine, or ankylosing spondylitis; in postmenopausal females, cause is frequently osteoporosis	Visual examination, imaging studies	Exercises, braces, and eventually surgical intervention for nonresponsive cases
Scoliosis	Lateral curve to spine, with one shoulder or hip higher than the other; often insidious onset; pain, occasional shortness of breath; occurs more frequently in adolescents	Etiology in some cases unknown; in others, cause may be uneven leg lengths, muscle degeneration, or vertebral deformity	Visual diagnosis, confirmed by imaging studies	Exercises, muscle electrostimulation, and braces; if unsuccessful, surgical intervention, fusion of vertebrae, possible implantation of instrumentation to secure spine in proper alignment
Lordosis (swayback)	Increased inward (anterior-posterior) curvature to the lower spine	Cause may be dependent on age of onset; may be developmental in children and degenerative in older children and adults; osteoporosis may be responsible in menopausal and post-menopausal females.	Visual examination, confirmed by imaging studies	Exercises and braces; if unsuccessful, fusion of affected vertebrae along with instrumentation
Muscular dystrophy	Progressive, degenerative weakening of muscles; onset in childhood; deterioration of muscle tissue is followed by eventual immobility and contractures	Generally considered genetic	Extensive family medical history; muscle biopsy and EMGs help confirm diagnosis	No cure at present, but exercise, PT, braces, and surgery help maintain child's ability to walk and move limbs; most children succumb before adulthood
Myasthenia gravis	Chronic weakness of muscles; initial onset usually in facial muscles, progressing to other muscles; droopy eyelids, difficulty swallowing often first symptoms; eventually progresses to paralysis	Possibly autoimmune disorder	Physical examination EMG; Tensilon test confirms involvement of acetylcholine receptors	Drug therapy including anticholinesterase medications, possibly corticosteroids; remissions are possible

Congenital conditions such as clubfoot and congenital hip dysplasia are present at birth. During development and throughout the growth periods, kyphosis, lordosis, and scoliosis, called developmental conditions, may occur. Some people have predispositions to certain conditions that are not observable at birth but are still present in underlying tendencies. Muscular dystrophy is a genetically transmitted disease. This progressive atrophy of skeletal muscles, with insidious loss of muscle strength, has no cure and leads to eventual death. Myasthenia gravis has an onset later in life as the individual experiences loss of muscle strength and function.

Degeneration of different areas of the musculoskeletal system occurs at various stages in life and affects numerous structures. **Arthritis** is the inflammation and degeneration of joint structures and appears as osteoarthritis or rheumatoid arthritis. Another form is gouty arthritis, which results from

the improper metabolism of uric acid and the deposit of urate crystals in the joint spaces. Bursitis is an inflammatory process in the bursae or tissue surrounding the joints. In osteoporosis, bone loses density, predisposing the patient to a higher risk of fracture as the bones become porous. Osteomalacia literally means the softening of bone, with deformities and increased flexibility of the bone tissue. Carpal tunnel syndrome and other related conditions are the result of repetitive trauma. Fibromyalgia—muscle pain accompanied by sleep disturbances—has no known etiology and no known cure, and is difficult to diagnose.

Infectious musculoskeletal conditions include Lyme disease and osteomyelitis. Lyme disease is a bacterial infection that develops from the bite of an infected deer tick. Osteomyelitis is an inflammation of bone tissue, caused by bacteria and usually following a traumatic insult or a surgical procedure.

TABLE 25-4   DEGENERATIVE AND INFLAMMATORY MUSCULOSKELETAL CONDITIONS

Condition	Signs and Symptoms	Cause	Diagnosis	Treatment
Osteoarthritis	Gradual onset of joint pain with edema and limited range of motion; muscles around affected joint become weak; bone spurs may be observed with imaging studies	Cause unknown; may be connected to aging process or follow insult to joint area	Physical examination, history, imaging studies	Drug therapy, including NSAIDs and steroids; exercise, heat applications provide pain relief
Rheumatoid arthritis	Deformed, painful joints; may become systemic, affecting many joints throughout body	Cause unknown at present; may be autoimmune response	Physical examination, history, imaging studies	Drug therapy, including NSAIDs and steroids; exercise, heat applications provide pain relief
Gout	Form of arthritis that normally affects great toe or fingers; pain and swelling in affected joints and possible limited movement	Deposits of uric acid crystals in joint spaces because of failure to fully metabolize purines in foods	Physical examination of joints, imaging studies; confirmed by urate crystals in joint fluid aspirate; elevated blood levels of uric acid may be indicator	Drug therapy including NSAIDs; rest to affected joint to relieve pain; avoidance of foods high in purine content
Bursitis	Inflammation of bursae in synovial tissue of joint; pain in joint area accompanied by limited range of motion	Repetitive motion to joint, friction in bursal space, or systemic disorders may lead to inflammatory condition	Imaging studies, physical examination	Resting affected joint, moist heat applications alternating with cold applications; drug therapy, including corticosteroids or NSAIDs
Osteoporosis	Usually asymptomatic until fracture occurs in older age, particularly to females; loss of height possible	Loss of calcium in bones, often after menopause as estrogen levels decrease	Blood serum studies, CT scan, bone scan, DEXA scans	Exercise helps to slow progress; drug therapy options are calcium and Vitamin D, hormone replacement therapy, or drugs such as Fosamax, Actonel, or Boniva.
Osteomalacia, rickets, softening of bone	Soft bones that deform during growth, bend easily or are brittle and painful; weakness	Vitamin D deficiency and loss of calcium; lack of sunlight	Bone scans and other imaging studies; blood tests including serum levels of calcium, alkaline phosphatase and Vitamin D; bone biopsy	Supplemental Vitamin D, calcium and phosphorus; exposure to sunlight for synthesis of natural Vitamin D.
Fibromyalgia	Chronic muscle pain, often accompanied by joint stiffness and tenderness; associated symptoms include fatigue, sleep disturbances, concentration problems, depression	Cause unknown at present; smoking tends to aggravate symptoms	Physical examination and tests to rule out other musculoskeletal conditions; tenderness in 11 of 18 specific trigger points indicates fibromyalgia	Improvement in sleep patterns, often with drug therapy; NSAIDs and muscle relaxants; exercise and relaxation techniques to relieve pain; no known cure at present.
Carpal tunnel syndrome	Chronic burning or aching pain in muscles and joint soft tissue	Cause unknown at present often trauma, infection; or emotional stress may precede onset	Pain in hand and wrist when median nerve is tapped indicates presence of trapped nerve; history and physical examination	Surgical release of compression on median nerve
Herniated disk	Severe pain in back area where disk is located; pain usually has sudden onset and is often sharp, radiating down to buttocks and thighs; possible muscle weakness of leg	Repetitive trauma or sudden impact; often caused by incorrect body mechanics when lifting heavy objects	Patient history and physical examination; MRI or radiographs confirm disk is protruding from normal area of spinal column and pressing on spinal cord and nerves	Rest and anti-inflammatory medication; surgical intervention to either trim bulging portion or remove entire disk
Tendonitis	Nonspecific pain along pathway of tendon or at its attachment	Injury to tendon or repetitive movement of tendon and joint	History and physical examination	Rest, drug therapy with NSAIDs or other anti-inflammatory drugs, cold therapy

TABLE 25-5 INFECTIOUS MUSCULOSKELETAL CONDITIONS

Condition	Signs and Symptoms	Cause	Diagnosis	Treatment
Lyme disease	Fever, chills, fatigue, headache, joint and muscle pain; characteristic itchy rash surrounding a red circle in early stages; untreated infection leads to arthritic-type pain, possible abnormalities in nervous system and/or cardiac arrhythmias	Infection spread by bite of a deer tick infected with the spirochete *Borrelia burgdorferi*	Patient history, physical examination revealing typical target lesion; skin biopsy revealing presence of spirochete confirms condition	Prompt removal of offending tick is essential; oral antibiotics in initial or early stages and IV in advanced stages; antipyretics to relieve fever
Osteomyelitis	Pain and tenderness in bone; fever; patient tends to guard against movement of the bone. Possible bone trauma or a surgical procedure preceding infection	Bacterial invasion of bone tissue or bone marrow may result from insult to bone tissue during surgical or traumatic event. Usual causative organism is staphylococci	Blood cultures and culture of aspirate or drainage confirms presence of offending microorganism	Antibiotic therapy; extensive infections may require surgical removal of infected tissue

Neoplasia

Neoplasia and/or malignant musculoskeletal conditions may involve any of the structures of the system—bone, cartilage or muscle—and usually take the form of tumors. Not all abnormal tissue growths (neoplasia) are malignant; some may be benign. Benign bone tumors are called osteomas.

Pain is a common factor in both benign and malignant tumors, often accompanied by swelling or growth. When a joint is affected, range of motion may be reduced. Diagnosis is often achieved through imaging studies; biopsy is required for positive differentiation of tumor origin and composition.

Malignant bone tumors usually occur in young people and affect the ends of the bones. Chemotherapy is administered to shrink a tumor prior to surgical removal. Primary carcinomas of the bone are called osteogenic sarcomas. Secondary or other forms of bone malignancy are the result of metastasis from primary malignancy sites. The bone destruction from metastatic carcinoma is quite painful, and fractures of the involved bone are frequent.

Rhabdomyosarcomas are rare, highly malignant tumors of muscle tissue. Early surgical removal is recommended. Many tumors metastasize before they are discovered and prognosis is not favorable.

Traumatic Musculoskeletal Conditions

Trauma to the musculoskeletal system includes insults to the bones in the form of fractures, soft-tissue insults to ligaments and tendons, and insults to the muscles. Sports injuries and motor vehicle accidents account for many traumatic musculoskeletal insults. Fractures resulting from falls are fairly common among the elderly.

Fractures

Fractures result from traumatic insult and challenge to the integrity of the bone structure. They take many forms, depending on the location of the traumatic insult, the type of insult, and the health status of the individual (Table 25-6).

Other Traumatic Conditions

Sprains, strains, dislocations, severed tendons, and torn meniscus in the knee are some of the soft-tissue injuries that involve the musculoskeletal system.

■ A sprain, or acute partial tear of a ligament, occurs as the result of a traumatic insult to the muscle, tendon, or ligament surrounding a joint. Careful questioning of the patient helps to ascertain the mechanism of injury, often a twisting action from a fall or partial fall. Severe pain is usually felt immediately, followed by swelling and discoloration. If a leg, ankle, or foot is injured, it is usually very difficult, if not impossible, to bear weight on it. Sprains to the upper appendages are usually characterized by limited range of motion or restricted movement. Imaging studies verify a sprain and rule out fracture. Treatment consists of immobilizing the joint.

■ A strain, or the overstretching of a muscle, tendon, or ligament, also occurs when a muscle is used or stretched beyond its normal capacity. In addition to pain, the individual may experience numbness or loss of feeling in the affected area, weakness, and reduced function. Edema is common. Cool therapy, usually with ice, helps to reduce swelling and relieve pain.

■ A dislocation involves a bone being displaced or separated from a joint and is usually the result of a traumatic insult. A subluxation is an incomplete or partial dislocation. A dislocation is painful, the joint appears deformed, and the range of motion is limited, if not absent. Dislocation can affect the shoulders, elbows, hand and finger joints, hips, knees, ankles, and toes. A serious dislocation of the vertebrae may cause damage to the spinal cord. Blood vessels and nerves may be injured, edema is spontaneous, and tissue is damaged. Imaging studies confirm the diagnosis. Dislocations must be reduced by manipu-

TABLE 25-6 TYPES OF FRACTURE

Name	Description	Usual Sites Affected
Avulsion	Fragment of a fractured bone is torn away with the muscle or ligament	Appendages; often occurs when clothing or a digit are entangled during the traumatic event
Comminuted fracture	Crushing or splintering of the bone	Long bones and any other bone vulnerable to crushing
Compound fracture	Open wound over the ends of the fractured bones; often an end of the bone is visible	Long bones
Compression	Collapse of the bone due to pressure exerted on it	Spinal vertebrae
Depression	Fragments or portions of bone pressed down in the skull and into the brain and surrounding tissue	Head, usually the result of acceleration-deceleration insult
Displaced fracture	Bone ends out of alignment	Long bones
Greenstick fracture	Bone partially bent and partially broken, like a twig or branch of a tree	Long bones, usually the arms; often occurs in children
Impacted fracture	One end of a fractured bone driven or wedged into the other end of the same bone	Long bones and bones of wrists, elbows, shoulders, ankles, knees and hips
Longitudinal fracture	Fracture parallel with the long axis of the bone, usually running along part of the length of the bone	Long bones
Nondisplaced fracture	Bone ends remain in alignment	Any bone
Oblique fracture	Fracture runs obliquely across the bone	Long bones
Pathological fracture	Result of insult to diseased or weakened bone that normally would not cause a fracture in healthy bone tissue	Any bone, particularly of the spine and hips
Simple fracture	Skin intact over the fracture	Any bone
Spiral fracture	Fracture follows a helical pattern, twisting around the axis of the bone	Long bones
Transverse fracture	Fracture crosses the bone at a 90° angle to the bone's axis	Long bones

lation or by surgical intervention. Depending on the joint involved, immobilization is generally required.

- A severed tendon generally also involves a laceration or acute tear to the surrounding tissue. Since tendons connect bone to muscle, severing renders the connected part unable to move. The tendons usually affected are those in the hands, fingers, forearms, feet, toes, and calves of the legs. Occasionally the tendon is torn rather than severed with a sharp object.
- A torn meniscus (cartilage in the knees and other joints) often results from a fall, but could also result from a twisting motion or a sports injury. The patient experiences pain, edema, limited range of motion, and a limited ability to bear weight. Arthroscopy is performed as an outpatient procedure to examine and often repair the damage. Upon discharge, the patient ambulates with the aid of crutches. The patient receives a prescription for pain medication along with instructions to elevate the extremity and apply ice intermittently.

Amputation

Amputation—the total or partial removal of a limb or digit—may be the result of trauma or of disease process. An accidental amputation may be complete, or a surgical procedure may be required to completely sever the body part or revise the remaining stump and close the wound. Often a traumatic amputation is the result of a crushing, tearing or incising event. Impaired circulation resulting from compromised arteries, peripheral vascular disease, tumors, infection or other disease processes leads to ischemia to the tissue and necrosis, making amputation necessary.

After an amputation, the individual may feel pain or other sensations in the area where the amputated part had been, as if it were still attached. This feeling is referred to as phantom limb or phantom pain. Damage to the sensory nerves during amputation is difficult to treat but may diminish with time.

After the stump has healed, rehabilitation of the affected limb, with a **prosthesis** and patient training, is recommended.

Diagnostic Procedures

In conjunction with the physical examination and the patient's description of symptoms, diagnostic procedures are performed to rule out or confirm diagnoses of musculoskeletal conditions (Table 25-7). Noninvasive diagnostic screening includes radiographs and most bone scans and CT scans. (When ordered by the physician, bone scans and CT scans can become invasive with the injection of contrast medium.) Arthrograms, myelograms, electromyograms, biopsies, and blood studies are invasive diagnostic procedures.

While most major fractures receive treatment at emergency facilities, many may be treated in the orthopedic office. Displaced, compound, avulsed, and other types of fractures usually receive surgical intervention at an emergency or urgent care center, and the patient has been referred to the orthopedic office for follow-up care. Radiographs and imaging studies are usually required to make a diagnosis. Most orthopedic clinics and offices have an imaging department on site.

TABLE 25-7 DIAGNOSTIC PROCEDURES FOR MUSCULOSKELETAL DISORDERS	
Radiograph	X-ray image of various body structures, used to detect fractures or other abnormalities based on the density of tissues
CT scan (Computed Axial Tomography)	Cross-sectional images in fine detail that assist in diagnosis of tumors, lesions, and other soft-tissue anatomical abnormalities
Arthrogram	Fluoroscopic examination of the internal aspects of the joint, accomplished by injecting contrasting medium into the joint capsule
Myelogram	Injection of a contrast medium into the spinal canal to diagnose/confirm intervertebral disc disorders
Bone scan	Imaging technique to evaluate bone density, bone growth, bone tumors, and other bone disease patterns
Electromyogram (EMG) and nerve conduction velocity studies	Diagnostic test to measure muscle contraction as a result of electrical stimulation (nerve conduction); evaluates the passage of nervous system impulses to and through the muscle and the muscular response
Bone and muscle biopsy	Removal of tissue samples to identify cancerous and benign neoplasms and other pathogenic conditions
Serum calcium (blood levels of calcium), serum phosphorus, serum alkaline phosphatase	Test for increased or decreased levels of blood calcium, phosphorus, or alkaline phosphatase to diagnose various bone and muscle diseases

Treatment of Musculoskeletal Conditions in the Orthopedic Office

The correction of a fracture, in which the bone fragments are realigned, is called **reduction.** A closed reduction is performed by external manipulation, and an open reduction is done through surgery.

Fractures are generally immobilized with **splints,** braces, or **casts.** Ambulation or mobility devices such as crutches and canes are prescribed as well. The MA often assists with procedures and patient education in these treatments as well as in physical therapy, particularly heat and cold treatments. Sutures or staples sometimes have to be removed and dressings inspected and replaced.

Splints and Braces

Splints are temporary devices used post-trauma primarily to prevent movement of the affected extremity(ies), including bones and joints, and to prevent further insult until the physician has assessed the extent of the injury (Figure 25-8 ◆). Sometimes a splint is used for post-reduction in place of a cast.

A brace is usually a more permanent device that provides support for a weak muscle or joint and allows it to function normally. With specialized padding, braces can provide corrective alignment for patients with scoliosis, congenital hip dysplasia,

Figure 25-8 ◆ Splints and accessories for musculoskeletal injuries

and other conditions. Braces can often be removed temporarily to allow observation of the affected area and hygiene care.

? — Critical Thinking Question 25-1—

Xavier must give information and instructions to the patient, Jorge, who is in pain and will probably not remember most of their conversation in the morning. What is the best approach Xavier can take to make certain Jorge understands his instructions for ankle care, using the brace, and his orthopedic appointment?

Casts

Casts are solid, rigid, cylindrical casings that immobilize joints or body parts and facilitate the healing of fractures, of joints with or without surgery, and of anatomical deformities without surgery. There are two basic types of casting materials (Figure 25-9 ◆). Traditionally, casts have been made of plaster. Today newer synthetic casts made of fiberglass, polyester, or cotton are more commonly used. Both types have benefits and drawbacks.

- Plaster casts are heavier, may soften or crumble with moisture, and can crack or break. Plaster casts are more easily molded to the body part, so immobilization is more effective.
- Synthetic casts are lighter in weight, are not affected by moisture, and usually do not crack or break. They dry more quickly than plaster casts and are less likely to dent and create a pressure area. However, synthetic casts are not flexible and do not mold to the body part, they are more expensive, and the rougher surface can tear clothing and scratch the skin.

Cast Application

Casts are applied and removed by the orthopedist with the help of the medical assistant or specially trained technician. The MA prepares the treatment room with equipment and supplies, assists the physician as instructed and trained, provides printed instructional materials to the patient, and schedules appointments and referrals.

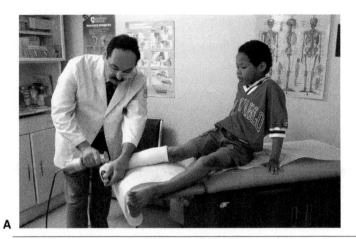
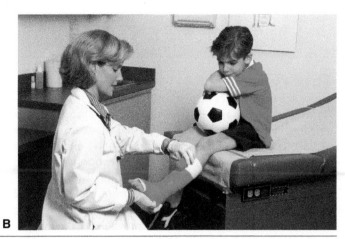

Figure 25-9 ◆ (A) Plaster cast; (B) Synthetic cast
Source: Michal Heron Photography

Before the cast is applied, X-rays are taken to assess the extent of the fracture. The physician performs reduction on the fracture and realigns the bone(s). The physician inspects the skin for lesions, redness, and bruises. The skin must be clean and dry for cast application. Either the physician or the MA does the cleansing.

After the cast has been applied, radiograph films are taken again to confirm that the ends of the bone are correctly aligned. Observe exposed areas for circulation, sensation, and movement. The instructions in Table 25-8 help patients care for their casted limbs at home.

TABLE 25-8 PATIENT INSTRUCTIONS: CAST CARE

Immediate Care Instructions

■ Elevate the casted limb above heart level for the first 24-48 hours to prevent swelling and reduce pain.
■ Move the toes or fingers frequently to maintain joint and muscle mobility.
■ Cold dry therapy in the form of ice bags may be applied at the local area of injury for 20 minutes per hour to reduce swelling. The cast should be protected from water damage.
■ With a plaster cast, avoid weight-bearing activity for 24 hours. With a synthetic cast, avoid activity for one hour.

General Care Instructions

■ To avoid injuring the skin, do not force anything under the cast.
■ Keep the cast dry. If the synthetic cast becomes wet, blot it dry, then sweep a blow-dryer on low or cool setting back and forth across the area.
■ Check the skin around the cast for signs of redness, sores, or swelling. Report any such findings to the physician.
■ Do not trim or break the cast. Notify the physician about any broken or loose areas.
■ Follow the exercise instructions prescribed by the physician or physical therapist to maintain muscle tone while the extremity is immobilized.
■ Follow the schedule for return appointments.
■ Report the following symptoms:

  ● Numbness or tingling in the fingers or toes.
  ● Blue, pale, or cold fingers or toes
  ● Increased pain or swelling that is not helped with elevation or rest.
  ● Pain or burning under the cast.
  ● Drainage or foul odor coming from the cast.
  ● Sores around the edge of the cast.
  ● Fever, chills, nausea, or vomiting.

PROCEDURE 25-1 **Assist with Fiberglass Cast Application**

Theory

There are many types of casts and many reasons for application. The physician will determine which is the most suitable for the patient's needs. Casts can be made from plaster of Paris, fiberglass, plastics, other synthetic materials, or fabric. If the cast must remain in place 24 hours a day for an extended period of time, fiberglass is generally used. Fiberglass is strong, lightweight, and waterproof. However, if the patient needs to wear the cast only when using the limb, the physician may choose to make a removable cast from synthetic materials that can be attached to the limb with Velcro straps. Air casts are fabric sleeves that fit over the injured limb and are inflated with air to immobilize the area. They can be used for a short time, depending on how much the limb is used.

Materials

- rolls of fiberglass casting material
- stockinette
- padding
- tape
- blunt/sharp nose scissors (for cutting material)
- warm tap water
- basin (2–4 liter)
- bandage
- gloves
- stool or low chair for support (if casting a foot or lower leg)
- patient drapes

Competency

(**Conditions**) With the necessary materials, you will be able to (**Task**) assist with the application of a fiberglass cast (**Standards**) correctly within the time frame designated by the instructor.

1. Assist the patient to the exam room and into a comfortable position. Explain that the patient should be comfortable to avoid having to shift the body weight during the lengthy casting process.
2. Identify the patient and verify the physician's orders.
3. Explain the procedure.
4. Wash your hands and put on gloves.
5. Cleanse and inspect the area to which the cast will be applied. Note any open wounds, bruising, or excessive swelling and report these to the physician.
6. Drape the patient to protect clothing.
7. Open one package of fiberglass material. Do not open the other packages until they are needed, to prevent waste.
8. Hand the physician the materials requested. If your clinic allows medical assistants to perform casting, cut the stockinette to fit the area.
9. Cover the affected body part with the stockinette, making sure it is smooth against the patient's skin and extends 1–2 inches beyond where the cast will end (Figure 25-10 ◆). If the stockinette is allowed to wrinkle or become bulky, it may cause a pressure sore on the patient's skin.
10. If you are casting the ankle, cut away excess wrinkled stockinette from the bend in the front of the ankle (Figure 25-11 ◆).
11. Use a spiral bandage turn to cover the casting area with padding (Figure 25-12 ◆). Apply extra padding to any bony areas.
12. Soak the inner layer of fiberglass tape in the basin of warm water (Figure 25-13 ◆). The tape material will be activated on contact with the water, so only wet as much as you need at a time.
13. The physician will roll and form the cast to the patient.
14. Roll the excess stockinette over the edges of the casting material to form a smooth edge.

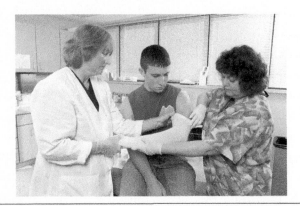

Figure 25-10 ◆ Apply stockinette to area that cast will cover.

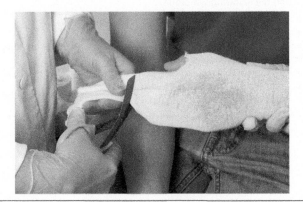

Figure 25-11 ◆ Cut away excess stockinette.

PROCEDURE 25-1 **Assist with Fiberglass Cast Application** *(continued)*

15. Open the package of outer fiberglass tape for the physician (Figure 25-14 ◆).
16. The physician will shape and smooth the cast or may direct you to do so (Figure 25-15 ◆).
17. Clean up the work station.
18. Remove the gloves and wash your hands.
19. Document the procedure in the patient chart.

Patient Education

Provide the patient with verbal and written cast care instructions to help ensure compliance. Make appointments or referrals for follow-up care.

Charting Example

01/26/XX 8:00 am Application of fiberglass cast to patient's left forearm. Fingertips checked for capillary refill, movement, and circulation. Patient sent to X-ray to verify correct bone alignment. Stacy Robbins, CMA

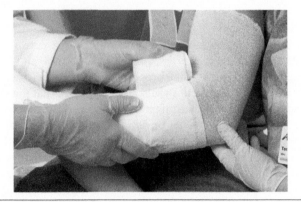

Figure 25-12 ◆ Use a spiral bandage turn to cover the casting area with padding.

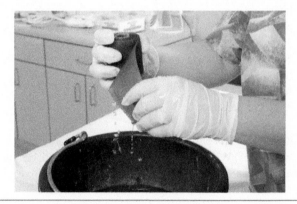

Figure 25-13 ◆ Soak the inner layer of fiberglass tape in the basin of warm water.

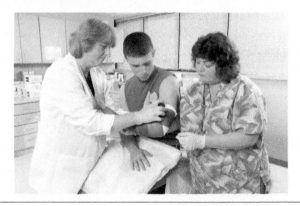

Figure 25-14 ◆ Open and apply an outer layer of fiberglass tape.

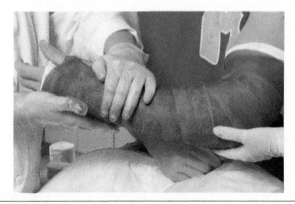

Figure 25-15 ◆ Assist in shaping the cast, as directed by the physician.

—Critical Thinking Question 25-2—

What signs and symptoms should Xavier tell Jorge to watch for as his ankle heals? What can Jorge do to relieve some of the pain of his injury?

Cast Removal

When the normal healing period has passed, the physician orders a radiograph to confirm that the cast may be removed. The physician usually performs the cast removal but occasionally delegates the task to a specially trained clinical staff person.

PROCEDURE 25-2 Assist with Cast Removal

Theory

A cast cutter is used in a procedure known as *bivalving the cast*. Cuts are made on two sides, and the cast is then pried apart with a cast spreader (Figure 25-16 ◆). The cast padding and stockinette are cut away with bandage scissors. Occasionally bivalving is done within the first few days after cast application to reduce pressure and pain on traumatized tissue. In this case the cast may need to be replaced.

Materials

■ cast-cutting device
■ cast spreader
■ bandage scissors
■ heavy-duty bag in which to discard cast materials
■ patient drape
■ 500 ml basin
■ 500 ml of warm water
■ hypoallergenic soap
■ towel
■ hypoallergenic lotion

Competency

(**Conditions**) With the necessary materials, you will be able to (**Task**) assist in the removal of a cast (**Standards**) correctly within the time frame designated by the instructor.

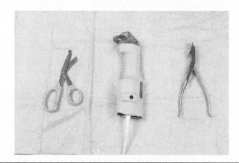

Figure 25-16 ◆ Cast cutter and cast spreader

1. Making certain that the limb is properly supported, make two cuts along the medial and lateral side of the long axis of the cast (Figure 25-17 ◆).
2. Pry the cast apart with a cast spreader.
3. Carefully remove the two halves of the cast.
4. Cut away the stockinette and padding with the large bandage scissors.
5. Wash the previously casted area with hypoallergenic soap.
6. Dry the skin and apply a gentle skin lotion.
7. Provide the patient with written and verbal instructions for care of the limb.
8. Make an appointment for physical therapy as directed by physician.

Patient Education

The patient may be apprehensive about the cast-cutting device. Explain that the cutter blade vibrates but does not spin. The patient will feel some pressure and warmth as the cutter vibrates. The patient should also be advised that the skin under the cast will appear lighter in color and possibly wrinkled, and muscle tone may be noticeably decreased. Reassure the patient that physical therapy will help in regaining lost muscle tone and strength and that skin color and appearance will gradually return to normal with exposure to air and sunlight.

Charting Example

01/26/XX 8:00 am Patient came in for removal of left arm cast. Successful removal performed. Patient reports weakness in limb but no adverse effects. Appointment for physical therapy initiated. Lawrence Graham, RMA

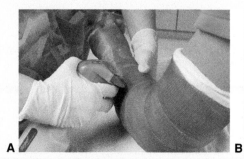
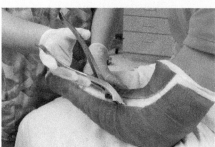

Figure 25-17 ◆ (A) Cut the medial and lateral side of the long axis of the cast; (B) Spread the cast.

Physical Therapy Modalities

Many physicians refer patients to physical therapists not only for therapy but for instruction in the use of assistive devices and thermodynamic applications (Table 25-9). Other physicians ask the medical assistant to provide patient teaching. You may be required to measure and fit the patient for crutches and/or to instruct the patient in the use of crutches, canes, and walkers. Other assignments may include instructing the patient in the therapeutic use of heat and cold, assisting in the evaluation of the patient's range of motion, and explaining proper body mechanics.

Thermodynamics

Thermodynamics consists of heat (**thermotherapy**) or cold (**cryotherapy**) applications that promote healing and prevent further tissue injury to areas affected by trauma, infection, and inflammation (Figure 25-18 ◆). The physician prescribes the appropriate treatment. You will be responsible for application in the medical office and patient instruction for self-care at home.

Heat dilates blood vessels and increases circulation. It can also speed up the localized formation of pus, also known as suppuration. The rate of healing is improved by increased oxygen

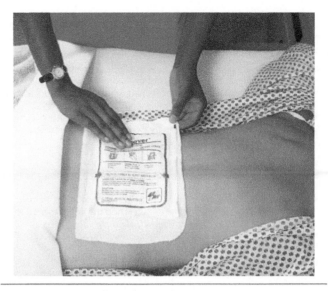

Figure 25-18 ◆ Applying heat and ice

and nutrition to the cells and the removal of the waste products of metabolism and inflammation. Heat relaxes the muscles and can reduce pain.

Cold constricts blood vessels, reducing blood flow and the leakage of fluid into tissues. By reducing swelling and stimulating nerve receptors, cold also acts as a temporary anesthetic, reducing discomfort and pain. In the early stages of infection, cold application can inhibit microbial growth and activity. For traumatic injury, with some exceptions, cold is usually applied for the first 24 to 48 hours to decrease swelling and pain, and heat is usually applied thereafter to increase circulation and healing.

In moist applications, water-immersed material is held against the skin. Thermodynamic treatments are applied for short, intermittent intervals (15 to 30 minutes) to prevent the reversal of the intended therapeutic effects. Covering the pack or other application prevents discomfort and pressure that might cause tissue damage and a breakdown in skin integrity.

Patients with neurological impairment due to aging or a medical condition, such as diabetes, may be more susceptible to harm from a thermodynamic treatment because they may not be aware that it is too hot or too cold and injuring the skin. In addition to providing verbal and written instructions to the patient, you may need to advise a family member or friend regarding potential complications from heat and cold applications.

The most common types of heat and cold application are the heating pad, hot **compress**, hot **soak**, ice bag, cold compress, and chemical hot or cold pack.

- In a heating pad, wires conduct electrical energy that is converted into heat.
- A hot compress increases circulation, suppuration, and infectious drainage. If a compress is used on an open wound, sterile technique and supplies must be used to prevent the introduction of pathogens.
- Hot soaks serve the same purposes as compresses. The affected body area is immersed in water or a medicated solution.

TABLE 25-9 PHYSICAL THERAPY MODALITIES

Therapy	Description and Purpose
Cryotherapy	■ Also known as cold therapy ■ Constricts blood vessels; slows circulation to affected area; reduces swelling, inflammation, and pain; decreases body temperature ■ Dry cryotherapy: ice collars, ice-filled gloves, or other forms of commercial or improvised ice bags ■ Moist cryotherapy: cold compresses
Exercise therapy	■ Improves joint flexibility, muscle tone, strength, and mobility ■ Should be monitored by a physician or physical therapist
Hydrotherapy	■ Affected part is immersed in a whirlpool or container of water ■ Water exercise takes place in swimming pools or spas, directed by a physical therapist trained in hydrotherapy
Massage	■ Stimulates circulation and promotes healing ■ Helps to relieve muscle spasms, soreness, and tightness, and to restore motion and function to the body part
Range of motion (ROM) exercises	■ Prescribed by the physician and defined by the physical therapist ■ Improve flexibility and mobility ■ Active ROM exercises are performed by the patient without assistance; passive ROM exercises are performed by the patient with assistance from another person
Thermotherapy	■ Increases circulation to the area for greater comfort and healing ■ Moist thermotherapy: hot soaks or compresses ■ Dry thermotherapy: heat lights, infrared lights, light bulbs, and heating pads
Ultrasound	■ Vibrates tissues, generates heat, promotes circulation

TABLE 25-10 PATIENT INSTRUCTION: MOIST AND DRY, HEAT AND COLD APPLICATIONS

Dry Heat Application: Heating Pad

- A heating pad uses electrical current to produce dry heat. Safety precautions must be followed to avoid overheating or electric shock. Inspect the heating pad for broken wires, do not use safety pins to hold the ends together or to attach the pad to bed linens, and inspect the cord for integrity.
- Cover the pad with a protective covering. Set the temperature as prescribed by the physician and place the pad on the area to be treated. The pad should feel warm but not uncomfortable.
- Do *not* turn the heating pad control to a higher temperature for more warmth. Doing so could cause serious burns.
- Call the physician if you notice increased swelling and redness or if pain increases.

Moist Heat Application: Hot Soak

- Wash and dry your hands before and after the treatment.
- Assemble a basin of very warm water or prescribed solution. The temperature should be between 105 and 110 degrees Fahrenheit (41–44 degrees Celsius).
- Immerse the body part gradually in the water or solution. To maintain the temperature of the soak, remove some water/solution and replace it with hotter water/solution every few minutes. Add the liquid toward the edge of the basin, away from rather than close to the immersed body part.
- Immerse the part for approximately 20 minutes.
- Call the physician if you notice increased swelling and redness or if pain increases.
- Clean and air-dry the basin for the next treatment.

Dry Cold Application: Ice Bag

- Fill an ice bag 1/2 to 2/3 full with small pieces of ice. Expel enough air to make the ice bag flexible.
- Cover the ice bag and lightly mold it to the treatment area. It may be slightly uncomfortable for a short time until skin sensitivity has adjusted.
- Remove the ice bag after 20 to 30 minutes. The skin may feel numb.
- Call the physician if the skin is pale, mottled blue, or very numb; if the pain becomes more intense; or if swelling or redness increases.
- Refill the ice bag and change the protective covering as necessary. Repeat the procedure as directed by the physician.
- If you do not have an ice bag, you may substitute a covered bag of frozen vegetables.

Dry Heat or Cold Application: Chemical Pack

- Follow the directions on the chemical pack to activate it. Generally this involves shaking the chemical crystals to the bottom of the bag, firmly squeezing and breaking the smaller inner bag of water, and shaking the bag to thoroughly mix the contents.
- Cover the pack with a protective cover and place it on the affected area for the prescribed period of time.
- Dispose of the pack as recommended by the manufacturer.

- Ice bags are used initially to treat pain and swelling.
- Cold compresses are used in the same ways as ice bags but conform more easily to the area being treated. They are also effective for treating eye injuries, headaches, and the jaws after dental extraction.

- Chemical cold or hot packs do not require cleaning, require very little storage space, and are flexible, easily activated, and disposable.

Patient instructions for the safe use of thermodynamic devices are listed in Table 25-10.

PROCEDURE 25-3 Assist the Patient with Cold Application/ Cold Compress

Theory

Cold applications cause the contraction of involuntary muscles, act as a vasoconstrictor, numb sensory nerve endings, and slow the inflammatory process. Inform the patient that although the cold application will prevent further swelling, it will not reduce swelling that is already present, which must be treated later with heat therapy. Cold compresses are generally ordered for application in 3- to 5-minute increments, with short breaks for tissue recovery. The skin should be monitored for redness and increased pain.

Materials

- water
- 4 × 4 gauze pads or other absorbent material, or washcloths
- waterproof pad
- waterproof wrap (plastic bag or plastic wrap)

- basin
- ice cubes

Competency

(**Conditions**) With the necessary materials, you will be able to (**Task**) apply a cold compress (**Standards**) correctly within the time frame designated by the instructor.

1. Wash your hands.
2. Identify the patient and verify the physician's order.
3. Explain the procedure to the patient.
4. Fill the basin with ice and water and soak the gauze pads or washcloths.
5. Wring out the compress so it is damp but not dripping.
6. Place the compress on the patient's injured body part and wrap it with plastic wrap to protect the patient's clothing.

PROCEDURE 25-3 Assist the Patient with Cold Application/ Cold Compress *(continued)*

7. Check the compress every 3–5 minutes, replacing it with a colder compress as needed. Remove water as necessary from the basin and add more ice to keep the water cold.
8. After applying compresses for the time specified by the physician, remove them and dry the affected area. Call the physician if you notice increased swelling and redness, or if the pain intensifies.
9. Launder the linens or place them in the appropriate laundry hamper, according to office protocol, and clean the room.
10. Wash your hands and document the procedure.

Patient Education
Physicians often prescribe cold compresses to be administered at home. Instruct the patient on the duration and frequency of application to avoid further injury or irritation to the skin.

Charting Example
01/26/XX 8:00 am Application of cold compress to left wrist for 20 minutes. Patient reports decrease in pain and swelling post application. Patient has been given written and verbal instructions for continued cold application at home. Tammy Lee, CMA

PROCEDURE 25-4 Assist the Patient with Hot Moist Application/ Hot Compress

Theory
Heat therapy increases circulation in the area to which it is applied, causes the muscles to relax, and helps tissues begin repair. Heat applications are often used to relieve tissue congestion or shorten the healing time of a sprained joint. Be sure to give clear written and verbal instructions to the patient, as heat can also be harmful. Prolonged exposure to heat can reduce the skin's resistance to injury. Extreme heat can cause severe nerve damage and burns.

Materials
- water
- digital or disposable strip thermometer
- 4 × 4 gauze pads or other absorbent material, or washcloths
- waterproof pad
- waterproof wrap (plastic bag or plastic wrap can be used)
- basin

Competency
(**Conditions**) With the necessary materials, you will be able to (**Task**) apply a cold compress (**Standards**) correctly within the time frame designated by the instructor.

1. Wash your hands.
2. Identify the patient and verify the physician's order.
3. Explain the procedure to the patient.
4. Fill the basin with water heated to 105–110 degrees F, as verified with the thermometer, and soak the gauze pads.
5. Wring out the pads or washcloths until damp but not dripping.

6. Place the waterproof pad under the injured body part. Apply the compress to the patient's injured body part and wrap with plastic wrap to protect clothing. Ask the patient to confirm that the temperature is comfortable but not burning (Figure 25-19 ◆).
7. Check the compress every 3–5 minutes, replacing it with a warmer compress as needed. Call the physician if you notice increased swelling and redness, or if pain increases.
8. After applying the compress for the time specified by the physician, remove it and dry the affected area.
9. Launder the linens or place them in the appropriate laundry hamper, according to office protocol, and clean the room.
10. Wash your hands and document the procedure.

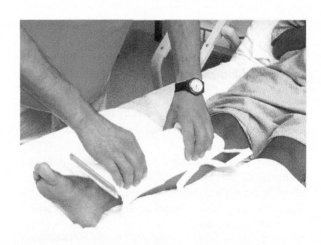

Figure 25-19 ◆ Apply a hot compress to the patient's leg.

continued

PROCEDURE 25-4 **Assist the Patient with Hot Moist Application/Hot Compress** *(continued)*

Patient Education

Physicians often prescribe hot compresses to be administered at home. Instruct the patient on the duration and frequency of application to avoid further injury or irritation to the skin.

Charting Example

11/16/XX 4:00 pm Application of hot compress to right ankle for 20 minutes. Patient reports decrease in pain and swelling post application. Patient has been given written and verbal instructions for continued hot application at home. Bonnie Barkley, CMA

Ultrasonography

Ultrasound therapy is performed by a trained therapist with an ultrasound machine, a special gel that allows ultrasound waves to be conducted through the skin, and an applicator. Ultrasound waves, with frequencies that cannot be heard by the human ear, penetrate deep into muscle tissue and are converted to heat.

Ultrasound therapy can be used to treat chronic pain or acute muscle injuries, such as sprains or strains. It relaxes the muscles and increases the elasticity of tendons and ligaments. Ultrasound also increases circulation, which speeds the healing process.

PROCEDURE 25-5 **Assist with Therapeutic Ultrasonography**

Theory

The ultrasound machine creates a steady vibration when placed in contact with the skin and a coupling agent. The ultrasonic waves vibrate the muscles and tissue, increasing blood flow and speeding recovery. Ultrasonic waves travel best through water, so they penetrate muscles and tissues more deeply than bone, which has almost no water content. Extra care must be taken when passing the machine over bony structures.

Materials

- ultrasound gel (coupling agent)
- ultrasound machine
- tissue
- patient chart

Competency

(**Conditions**) With the necessary materials, you will be able to (**Task**) assist with therapeutic ultrasonography (**Standards**) correctly within the time frame designated by the instructor.

1. Prepare the equipment and identify the patient.
2. Verify the physician's orders for duration and frequency of treatment.
3. Explain the procedure and encourage the patient to inform you of any pain or discomfort.
4. Have the patient remove clothing from the area to be treated.
5. Apply warmed ultrasonic gel to the area to be treated and to the applicator head.
6. Set the machine at the lowest treatment setting and increase gradually as needed. Set the timer to the specified treatment time.

7. Place the applicator head firmly against the patient's skin and move the applicator in a circular motion at a speed of 2 inches per second. Keep the applicator head in contact with the patient's skin and moving at all times when the machine is running.
8. When the set time has expired, the machine will shut off automatically.
9. Return the intensity control back to zero.
10. Wipe the ultrasonic gel from the patient's skin and assist with dressing if necessary.
11. Wash your hands and document the procedure in the patient's chart.

Patient Education

Ultrasound therapy should be soothing and relaxing. The patient should not feel any burning, pressure, or other discomfort. Any adverse reactions should be reported immediately. The patient should also be advised to avoid heavy lifting or quick movement with the treated muscles until advised by a physician, because they are more susceptible to injury immediately following therapy.

Charting Example

10/04/XX 6:00 pm Ultrasonic treatment of left levator scapula area on setting of 3 intensity for 12 minutes. Patient is instructed to return for treatment three times per week for the next three weeks. Patient tolerates treatment well and reports pain relief and decreased muscle spasm. Leslie Miller, RMA

Assistive Aids for Ambulation

Assistive aids for ambulation include **axillary** crutches and forearm crutches (also known as Lofstrand crutches); standard and legged canes; and standard and rolling walkers. The decision to use crutches, a cane, or a walker depends on various factors, including the patient's muscular coordination and weight-bearing capability and the type and severity of the physical impairment.

Crutches

Crutches remove or reduce weight bearing from one or both legs and transfer it to the arms and upper chest. The typical crutch is made of aluminum or wood and can be adjusted for hand placement and axillary height (Figure 25-20 ◆). Crutches are equipped with padded armrests, hand grips, and rubber tips to prevent sliding. Lofstrand crutches are used primarily by patients with cerebral palsy or paraplegia.

Axillary crutches that fit the patient properly are very important for his or her safety, comfort, and recovery. Crutches that are too short or too long will create balance problems and unsafe conditions that may further injure the patient, who may then avoid ambulation altogether. The physician may instruct the patient to see a physical therapist or convalescent aid provider for crutch fitting and instruction, or an MA may perform both functions.

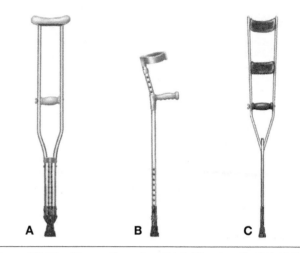

Figure 25-20 ◆ Types of crutches: (A) Axillary crutch; (B) Lofstrand or forearm crutch; (C) Canadian or elbow crutch

Patients who use crutches should be taught the safest and most efficient way to walk with them. There are several different gaits, or step patterns, a patient can use, depending on his or her condition (Table 25-12).

PROCEDURE 25-6 Demonstrate Measuring for Axillary Crutches

Theory

The goal of measuring for axillary crutches is to ensure the correct length and hand grip placement. Crutches that are too long are difficult to use because the patient cannot use shoulder force to push the body off the ground. The patient may experience axillary pain and subsequent crutch palsy, a sign of neurological damage characterized by muscular weakness of the lower arm, wrist, and hand. With crutches that are too short, the patient is bent forward, raising the risk of back pain.

The first step in proper measurement is to assist the patient to a standing position. The crutch tip should be placed 2 inches in front of the foot and 4 to 6 inches from the lateral aspect. The height of wooden crutches is adjusted by removing a bolt and wing nut from a lower central piece and sliding the central piece up or down. When the correct height is established, the bolt and wing nut are replaced and tightened. Aluminum crutches are adjusted by pushing in a spring button to allow sliding and, at the correct height, popping the button into a locked position. The last step is to place the hand grip so the patient's hand is flexed 30 degrees. The bolt and wing nut for the hand grip are removed, the grip is slid to the correct position, and then the bolt and wing nut are replaced and tightened. The patient should wear the same shoes (with nonskid soles) when being measured for the crutches and when using them.

Instruct the patient to observe for signs that crutch height may need to be adjusted. Back pain; weakness in the lower arm, wrist, and hand; inability to keep the back straight and avoid leaning forward; or general awkwardness in using the crutches are all signs that the handgrip and/or central strut should be adjusted.

Materials

- patient chart
- order for axillary crutches
- adjustable axillary crutches

Competency

(**Conditions**) With the necessary materials, you will be able to (**Task**) measure for axillary crutches (**Standards**) correctly within 20 minutes.

1. Wash your hands and gather the necessary materials.
2. Identify the patient and escort him or her to the treatment area.
3. Assist the patient, with shoes on, to a standing position. With the crutch armrests under the patient's axillae, adjust the crutches first for height and then for hand position, using the following criteria: (a) a space of two fingerwidths between the axilla and the crutch armrest; (b) body weight

continued

PROCEDURE 25-6 **Demonstrate Measuring for Axillary Crutches** *(continued)*

supported by the hands on the hand grips; and (c) crutch tip placement approximately 2 inches in front of the foot and 4 to 6 inches from the lateral aspect.

4. After the crutches have been correctly measured and fitted to the patient, provide verbal and written instruction about general guidelines, crutch gait, and symptoms of improper fit.
5. Document the procedure and prepare the treatment area for the next patient.

Patient Education

See patient instructions in Table 25-11.

Charting Example

08/23/XX 10:45 A.M. 23-year-old male seen for severely sprained Lt ankle. Physician splinted and ordered crutch walking with follow-up appointment in two weeks. Pt fitted for crutches with two-fingerwidth space between axilla and armrest, body support on wrists, and crutches approx 5 inches from the foot. Patient instructed on symptoms of improper crutch fitting, and instruction given on the three-point gait. Appointment scheduled for two-week return visit. John Young, CMA

TABLE 25-11 PATIENT INSTRUCTION: GUIDELINES FOR WALKING WITH CRUTCHES

General Guidelines

- Practice arm strengthening exercises regularly before and during the early stages of crutch walking.
- Practice the crutch gait prescribed by the physician before leaving the medical office, physical therapy department, outpatient treatment center, or convalescent aid supplier.
- Keep the back straight to maintain correct body posture, prevent back strain, and maintain balance.
- Look ahead when walking. Do *not* look at your feet.
- Nonskid shoes will provide stability when crutch walking.
- When crutch walking, body weight should be on the hand grips, and the armrests should be against the sides of the rib cage.
- Be aware of your environment and enlist the support of others to remove obstacles that might cause falls, including dark areas, throw rugs, and wet floors.
- Extra padding may be applied to the hand grips and shoulder rests, although the crutches may then need to be adjusted for height and hand placement.
- Dry crutch tips can become wet. Replace crutch tips that become smooth.
- Check the bolts and wing nuts frequently to make sure they are tight.
- Report symptoms of numbness, tingling, and weakness in the arms, wrists, or hands.

Four-Point Gait (Figure 25-21 ◆)

Start in the tripod position (crutch 4 to 6 inches in front of the foot and 4 to 6 inches to the lateral aspect) with your feet approximately a foot apart for balance (you may widen the base distance if you have a large frame). The sequence of steps is:

- Right crutch forward.
- Left foot forward.
- Left crutch forward.
- Right foot forward.
- Repeat.

Three-Point Gait (Figure 25-22 ◆)

Start in the tripod position with the feet base distance apart. The sequence of steps is

- Move the affected leg forward with the crutches.
- Balancing on the crutches, move the unaffected leg forward.
- Repeat.

Two-Point Gait (Figure 25-23 ◆)

Start in the tripod position with the feet base distance apart. The sequence of steps is:

- Move the left crutch and right foot forward at the same time.
- Move the right crutch and left foot forward at the same time.
- Repeat.

Swing Gait (Figure 25-24 ◆)

Start in the tripod position with the feet base distance apart. The sequence of steps for the swing-to gait is:

- Move both crutches forward.
- Lift and swing the extremities to the crutches.
- Repeat.

For the swing-through gait:

- Move both crutches forward.
- Lift and swing the extremities to and past the crutches.
- Repeat.

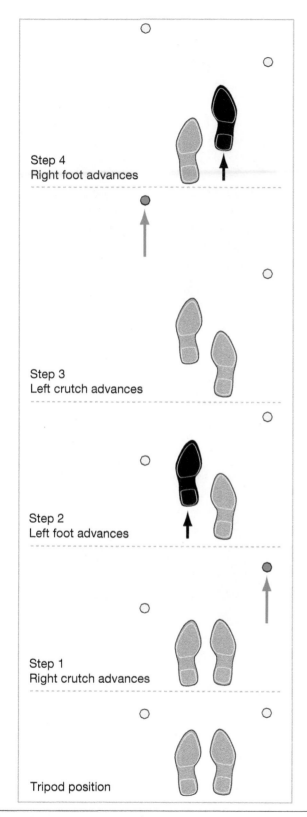

Figure 25-21 ◆ Four-point gait

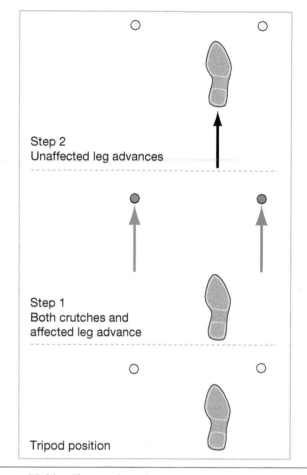

Figure 25-22 ◆ Three-point gait

- Patients with degenerative joint disease, impaired muscle coordination, muscle spasticity, or muscle weakness may be taught the four-point gait, the most stable gait.
- The three-point gait is for patients who can bear weight on only one leg, such as patients with fractures, sprains, amputations, or lower leg inflammations, or during post-surgical healing. Good upper arm strength and muscular coordination are required.
- The two-point gait is similar to the four-point gait, but with fewer steps. It is used by patients with better balance and muscular coordination who can bear more weight.
- Swing-to and swing-through gaits are used by those with lower extremity injuries or disabilities. These gaits require very strong arms and good muscular coordination.

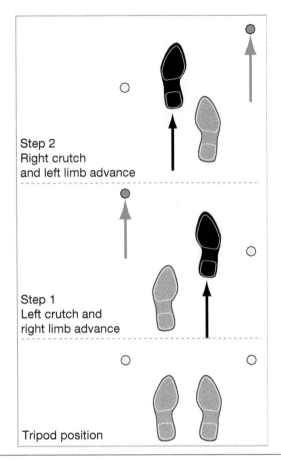

Figure 25-23 ◆ Two-point gait

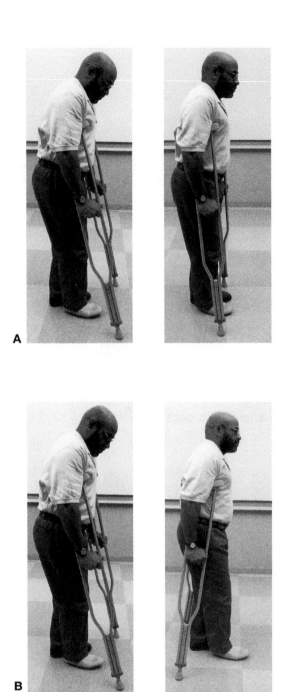

Figure 25-24 ◆ Swing gaits: (A) Swing-to gait; (B) Swing-through gait

Patients using assistive ambulation aids should be made aware of certain safety considerations. The patient or caregiver should monitor the rubber safety tips for replacement needs. All screws or connections should be regularly checked. Patients and their caregivers should be observant of the surrounding environment to avoid falls and injury. Two common hazards are throw rugs and dim lighting.

Canes

Canes are also commonly used as assistive ambulation devices by patients with one-sided weakness, such as hemiparesis, joint impairment, or other neuromuscular conditions. All canes consist of a grip handle, a pole portion, and rubber-tipped footing or legs (Figure 25-25 ◆) The standard cane has one rubber-tipped leg and is used by patients who require very little support for walking. The three-footed tripod cane and four-footed quad cane provide additional walking stability and support. Tripod and quad canes can stand alone as patients momentarily remove the hand to manage other activities, such as opening a door. However, tripod and quad canes are considered bulkier and harder to move because of their extra feet.

Walkers

Walkers are another common assistive device. They are used by patients who need more support, have symptoms of poor balance and weakness, or have had hip or knee replacement surgery. Because the walker provides a larger base of support than the cane or crutch, patients generally feel more secure during walking. However, the walker can slow ambulation and is more cumbersome to maneuver in some situations. Correct walker height is slightly below the patient's waistline.

PROCEDURE 25-7 Assist a Patient with Crutch Walking

Theory

The goal of proper patient instruction in the use of crutches is to reduce the risk of injury and accident in the patient's home and during day-to-day activities. Crutches provide support for greater mobility and allow for a wide range of gait patterns and speed. Several types of crutches are available: platform, forearm (or Lofstrand), and axillary. The type of crutches prescribed depends on the injury and the patient's ability and physical limitations.

Axillary crutches are the most commonly prescribed crutches. They are ideal for physically strong patients who need them only for a short time. Axillary crutches are easily transported, stored, and adjusted. They are easy to maneuver on unstable surfaces, such as stairs, or in tight spaces.

Forearm crutches are prescribed for patients who require crutches permanently or for a long period of time. They are built with a hard plastic or metal sleeve that fits around the patient's forearm. The patient's body weight is supported on the hand grips below the arm cuffs. Forearm crutches are shorter and provide less stability than axillary crutches and require a longer training session.

The platform crutch is most often recommended for elderly patients who cannot grip the handgrips of forearm crutches or support their weight on their hands or wrists with axillary crutches. The platform crutch has a platform attached to the top with a handgrip. The crutch is adjusted so that the patient's forearm rests on the platform, with the arm bent at a 45-degree angle. The forearm bears all the weight but does not provide much stability. Platform crutches require strength

and coordination, and it may be difficult for some patients to learn proper technique.

Materials

▪ crutches correctly fitted to the patient

Competency

(**Conditions**) With the necessary materials, you will be able to (**Task**) assist a patient with crutch walking (**Standards**) correctly within 20 minutes.

1. Inspect the crutches for correctly fitted arm pads, tight wing nuts, and comfortable handgrips.
2. Instruct the patient to relax the injured knee and keep it slightly bent to avoid touching the foot to the ground.
3. Instruct the patient in the crutch-walking gait ordered by the physician (see Table 25-11).
4. Have the patient practice taking several steps to ensure correct technique.

Patient Education

See patient instructions in Table 25-11.

Charting Example

08/23/XX 10:45 A.M. Patient instructed on proper crutch walking and how to inspect the crutches for wear and tear. Patient correctly demonstrated knowledge of crutch use. Maurice Ellis, RMA

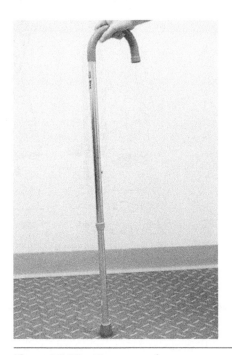
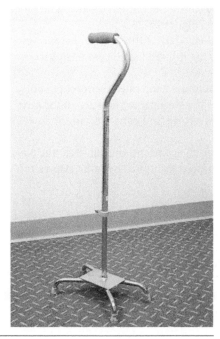

Figure 25-25 ◆ Two types of canes

PROCEDURE 25-8 Assist a Patient in Using a Cane

Theory

To measure for the correct cane height, instruct the patient to stand upright without leaning and to flex the elbow approximately 30 degrees. The grip handle of the cane should be located at the greater trochanter of the femur neck to maximize stability and support.

Materials

- single-tipped cane as ordered by physician
- gait belt

Competency

(**Conditions**) With the necessary materials, you will be able to (**Task**) instruct a patient on correct cane use (**Standards**) within the time frame allowed by the instructor.

1. Identify the patient and explain why instruction in cane use is necessary.
2. Wash your hands.
3. Verify the type of cane the patient and physician have agreed on and assemble equipment.
4. Make sure the suction tip on the cane is in good condition.
5. Place the gait belt snugly around the patient's waist, tucking any excess length into the belt.
6. Place the cane tip 4–6 inches to the side of the patient's foot, on the patient's stronger, unaffected side. Adjust the cane so that the handle grip is level with the patient's hip and the patient's elbow is flexed at a 20- to 30-degree angle.
7. Stand on the patient's weaker side with a firm underhand grip on the gait belt.
8. Instruct the patient to move the injured leg and cane forward simultaneously (Figure 25-26 ◆).
9. The patient should then advance the stronger leg and rest it slightly in front of the injured leg. Repeat this process.
10. Going up stairs:
    - Instruct the patient to use hand rails whenever possible.
    - The patient moves the stronger leg forward to the next step while the injured leg and cane rest on the lower step.
    - With a firm grip on the cane and the handrail, the patient moves the injured leg up to the same step as the uninjured leg.
    - Repeat as needed.
11. Going down stairs:
    - The patient steps down with the uninjured leg and the cane.
    - The injured leg follows to the same step.

Patient Education

During the early stages of using the cane, the patient may have to think through the sequence, but practice will make it second nature. The patient should be careful not to attempt too much at first, especially on stairs, in unfamiliar conditions, or when he or she is home alone.

Charting Example

05/23/XX 10:45 A.M. Patient arrived for cane adjustments and walking instructions post knee replacement surgery. Single-tip cane was adjusted to patient's hip joint. Patient was instructed on ambulating on flat surfaces and going up and down stairs. Patient successfully demonstrated understanding of instructions. Dawn Maynard, CMA

Figure 25-26 ◆ Instruct the patient to move the injured leg and cane forward simultaneously.

PROCEDURE 25-9 Assist a Patient in Using a Walker

Theory

Patients who have the strength to support their body weight but have difficulty keeping their balance may use a walker to get around and maintain their independence. The patient should wear good, supportive walking shoes and loose-fitting, comfortable clothing.

Materials

- walker
- gait belt

Competency

(**Conditions**) With the necessary materials, you will be able to (**Task**) teach a patient how to use a walker (**Standards**) correctly within the time frame allowed by the instructor.

1. Identify the patient and explain why instruction in using a walker is necessary.
2. Wash your hands.
3. Place a gait belt snugly around the patient's waist. Tuck any excess belt length under the belt near the hip.
4. Position the patient inside the walker. Adjust the height of the walker as needed. The patient's arms should be flexed at a 30-degree angle when resting on the hand grips.
5. Stand behind and slightly to the side of the patient, with an underhand grip on the gait belt.
6. Instruct the patient to move the walker directly ahead until the back supports of the walker are even with the patient's toes (Figure 25-27 ◆).
7. Instruct the patient to grip the handles firmly and step toward the walker with the stronger leg first, then the other leg.
8. Repeat: The patient moves the walker first, then moves toward the walker.
9. Watch the patient for signs of fatigue. Some walkers are equipped with platforms on which the patient can sit to rest.

Patient Education

At first the patient may have to think the sequence through, but practice will make it second nature. For stability and support, remind the patient to move the feet when the walker is stationary and to move the walker when the feet are stationary. The family can help the patient adjust to using the walker by rearranging furniture as necessary and removing loose carpets, cords, or other hazards from the patient's home.

Charting Example

08/23/XX 10:45 A.M. Patient assisted with use of her new walker. Patient practiced ambulating around the clinic. Patient states she is "comfortable" using the walker on her own. Steve Sanders, RMA

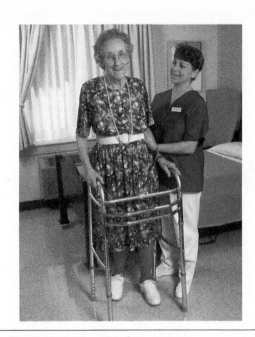

Figure 25-27 ◆ Using a walker for support

Prostheses

Prostheses replace not only extremities and joints but also diseased tissues and organs, often temporarily. Today there are prostheses for the heart, breasts, kidney, skin, blood vessels, blood, and teeth. Lighter-weight, stronger, more durable materials have made joint replacement possible for patients of all ages. Artificial limbs look more natural. Surgical techniques have been modified so they are less traumatic for the patient. As an example, a lateral approach for knee replacement, rather than the traditional frontal approach, has eliminated incising major muscles, thereby reducing pain and recovery time.

Caduceus Chronicle
THE PRATICE OF AMPUTATION

■ Throughout human history, amputation has been performed to treat injured, diseased, and deformed tissue. War has been the main force behind the development of advanced amputation procedures and prosthetic devices. Improvements in anesthesia, ligature (suturing), and antiseptic techniques were also factors, as were religious practices.

■ Some of the gods worshipped by the Peruvians, Aztecs, and Celts during prehistoric times have been identified as amputees. When amputation was performed as a punishment, it was done with an ax (used like a guillotine), and no anesthesia was given. When it was performed as curative surgery, plant extracts with healing and analgesic properties were administered. Hot oil, cautery (burning and scarring), smoke, honey, and wine were used as antiseptics.

■ Hippocrates (fifth century B.C.E.) proposed using ligatures to tie off bleeders. In his time, limbs were amputated to treat injuries, gangrene, tumors, and deformities.

■ During the Dark Ages, the surgical techniques used by the Romans and Greeks were discarded for more primitive practices such as limb crushing, dipping in hot oil, burning with hot irons, and amputation with the guillotine axe. Most patients died from blood loss; others died from infection.

■ During the Renaissance, both scientific advances and surgical practices rediscovered from earlier times led to the development of prosthetic devices. Linen ligatures were reintroduced as a substitute for cautery to close wounds. Conditions were not always ideal for surgery, however, and surgeons often performed without tourniquet, anesthesia, or skilled assistance. Ligature of bleeding vessels was not always effective. Because of the time limitations imposed by potential hemorrhage (30 seconds to amputate and 3 minutes to complete the surgical closure), many surgeons preferred direct cautery of major vessels.

■ In the late eighteenth century, Joseph Lister, a Scottish surgeon, developed antiseptic surgical technique and used catgut instead of hemp and silk for suturing.

■ The development of prosthetic devices in the United States was spurred by the high number of amputees in World War II.

Body Mechanics

Health-care personnel lift and move supplies and equipment as part of the job. To prevent musculoskeletal injuries and maintain health and safety, team members must practice proper body mechanics. One of the most basic principles is to keep the back straight when sitting, standing, and walking. Twisting the body can weaken or injure the back and lead to long-term, chronic back problems. Avoid twisting while lifting. Bending at the hips and knees with the back straight uses the strongest muscles of the body, the upper thighs.

It is also important to always maintain the center of gravity within the body. When standing straight, keep the feet about 12 inches apart. Hold objects close to the body when lifting or lowering them to prevent back injury and conserve energy. Push, pull, or roll objects rather than lifting or lowering them when possible, thereby using the weight of the body as leverage and keeping the center of gravity within the body. Avoid reaching too far when pushing, pulling, or rolling objects to maintain the center of gravity. Continue to keep the back straight and to bend at the knees and hips until the moving task is completed.

The principles of body mechanics should also be followed when transferring patients from a chair or wheelchair to an examination table and vice versa, when assisting a patient to a sitting or standing position, and when assisting the physician with procedures. Using proper body mechanics can prevent injury to yourself and to the patient. Follow these guidelines during a wheelchair transfer.

■ Know the patient's level of functioning, both physical and mental, before transferring to an examination table, or vice versa. You may need to call on another staff member if the patient is unable to help.

■ Keep the wheelchair brakes on during the transfer to keep it from rolling.

■ If possible, remove armrests or leg attachments, which may act as obstacles in the transfer.

■ Help the patient to stand. Holding him or her close to your center of gravity, pivot or guide the patient into position for sitting in the wheelchair or on the examination table. Some employers require the use of safety belts when lifting or transferring patients to help prevent back injury to the employee.

Although proper body mechanics are emphasized for employee health and safety, they also prevent injury to other workers and patients. (∞ Body mechanics are more fully discussed in Chapter 5.)

PROCEDURE 25-10 Assist a Patient in a Wheelchair to and from an Exam Table

Theory

Patients may present to the office in a wheelchair and not have the strength or mobility to move themselves to an examination table. You should be able to physically transfer these patients in a way that is effective and safe for both you and the patient.

Materials

- gait belt
- long-handled stool (if exam table is not equipped with pull-out step)

Competency

(**Conditions**) With the necessary materials, you will be able to (**Task**) transfer a patient from a wheelchair to an examination table and from an examination table to a wheelchair (**Standards**) correctly within the time frame allowed by the instructor.

To transfer the patient from a wheelchair to an exam table:

1. Identify the patient and explain what you are going to do.
2. Wash your hands.
3. Position the wheelchair so that the patient is sitting with his or her strongest side next to the examination table.
4. Lock the wheelchair brakes.
5. Place the gait belt snugly around the patient's waist, making certain the belt is tight enough that it will not slip and put unnecessary pressure on the ribs. Tuck any excess belt length under the belt.
6. If the wheelchair allows, remove the foot rests. If not, move them as far out as possible to avoid hitting your shins against them during the transfer.
7. Standing directly in front of and as close to the patient as possible, grip the gait belt with both hands in an underhand grip. Bend at the knees and hips to avoid back strain.
8. If the patient is able, have him or her grip the arm rests and push off at the same time that you lift, for added leverage. If possible, the patient can also assist by pushing upward with his or her legs.
9. With the patient now standing, have him or her place the stronger leg on the stool or exam table step, and together you will lift as the patient steps up (Figure 25-28 ◆).
10. Have the patient place one hand on the table and guide him or her to a sitting position.
11. Move the wheelchair out of the way.

To transfer the patient back to the wheelchair:

1. After identifying the patient, explaining the procedure, and washing your hands, place the stool (if the exam table does not have a step) next to the exam table.

2. Place the wheelchair next to the exam table with the brakes locked.
3. With a firm underhand grip on the gait belt, assist the patient to a standing position. If the patient is able, have him or her push off with the legs and arms.
4. Once the patient is steady on the step or stool, have him or her step to the floor with the stronger leg.
5. Have the patient take small steps backward until the backs of the knees touch the wheelchair.
6. Ask the patient to reach back and place the hands on the wheelchair armrests for support. Bending at the hips and knees, slowly lower the patient to the chair.
7. Help the patient adjust to a comfortable position in the wheelchair.
8. Replace the foot rests.

Patient Education

Make sure the patient understands the importance of moving with you as you lift and turn him or her, to avoid injury.

Charting Example

02/10/XX 3:15 P.M. Patient arrived for yearly physical and was successfully transferred to the exam table using a single-person transfer method and gait belt. Heather Brown, RMA

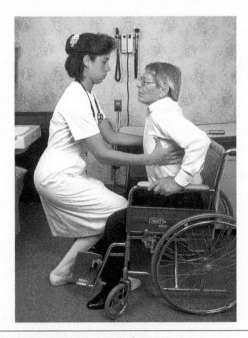

Figure 25-28 ◆ Wheelchair transfer

REVIEW

- Orthopedics is the study of the musculoskeletal system: bones, muscles, joints, ligaments, tendons, and nerves. An orthopedic surgeon specializes in the diagnosis and treatment of musculoskeletal conditions.

- The MA obtains and records medical history and vital signs, notes any obvious deformities, assists the physician in examinations and procedures, and instructs and assists the patient as necessary. The MA may also provide patients with ambulation devices, including crutches, canes, and wheelchairs, and provide instruction about proper body mechanics and thermodynamic treatments.

- The bones and muscles provide a framework for the body, help the individual to stand erect, protect internal organs, and make movement possible. Bone tissue serves as a repository for calcium reserves. Cartilage, a connective tissue, helps reduce friction between moving bone surfaces. The outside layer of bone is covered with a membrane called periosteum, which contains osteoblasts for bone tissue formation, blood and lymphatic vessels, and nerve fibers. The inner marrow cavity of the bone is lined with endosteum.

- Red bone marrow contains hematopoietic tissue in which precursor blood cells are manufactured. Yellow marrow is found in the long central portion of the bone. Bone tissue undergoes reabsorption and formation throughout life. When bone reabsorption is greater than bone formation, such as in an aging person, the risk of fractures rises.

- The skeleton consists of the axial skeleton (bones in the head and trunk) and appendicular skeleton (extremities and shoulder and hip framework for the attachment of the extremities). Bones are classified according to structure: long bones (thigh, lower leg, upper arm, lower arm, digits), short bones (wrists and ankles), flat bones (scapula, ribs, pelvic bones), and sesamoid bones (patella).

- Range of motion (ROM) is the total degree of movement a joint is capable of. When a patient is immobile for any length of time, joint range of motion and muscle strength diminish. Range-of-motion exercises maintain joint flexibility and muscle strength.

- Muscles are attached to bones by connective tissue called tendons and contract in response to nervous system stimulation.

- Musculoskeletal conditions seen in the orthopedic office are congenital, degenerative, infectious, malignant, or traumatic. They may also be classified by the anatomical structure affected: bones, joints, or muscles. Common musculoskeletal diseases involve the body as a whole, the spine, the joints, or the collagen. Some diseases are characterized by genetic predisposition.

- Congenital conditions are present at birth (for example, clubfoot and congenital hip dysplasia). Developmental conditions occur as the individual progresses into adulthood, such as kyphosis, lordosis, and scoliosis. Muscular dystrophy is the result of genetically transmitted disease. Myasthenia gravis may be an autoimmune disorder.

- Degeneration of different areas of the musculoskeletal system comprises another group of conditions. Arthritis is inflammation and degeneration of the joint structures. Three types are osteoarthritis, rheumatoid arthritis, and gouty arthritis. Bursitis is an inflammatory process in the bursae, or tissue surrounding the joints. Osteoporosis occurs as bone density diminishes and the bones become porous and susceptible to fracture. Osteomalacia is the softening of bone tissue, with deformities and increased flexibility. Carpal tunnel syndrome is the result of repetitive trauma. Fibromyalgia, with symptoms of muscle pain and sleep disturbance, has an unknown etiology and no known cure.

- Infectious musculoskeletal conditions include Lyme disease, the result of the bite of an infected deer tick, and osteomyelitis, inflammation of the bone tissue.

- Fractures result from traumatic insult and take many forms, depending on type and location and the individual's health status. Types of fractures include comminuted, compound, simple, compression, depression, displaced, nondisplaced, greenstick, impacted, longitudinal, oblique, transverse, spiral, and pathological fractures, as well as avulsions. Insults to joints, tendons, ligaments, and muscle tissue are other types of trauma.

- Neoplasia and/or malignant musculoskeletal conditions may affect any of the structures of the system, usually in the form of tumors. Not all abnormal tissue growths in the system are malignant. Pain, swelling, growth, and reduced range of motion are some symptoms. Chemotherapy is administered to shrink tumors prior to surgical removal. Rhabdomyosarcomas are rare malignant tumors of muscle tissue that should be surgically removed as early as possible.

- Sprains occur as the result of traumatic insult to the muscle, tendon, or ligament surrounding a joint. Strains result from the overuse or overstretching of a muscle. Dislocations involve a bone being displaced or separated from the joint and are usually the result of a traumatic insult. A severed tendon leaves the connected part unable to move. A torn meniscus may result from a fall, a twisting motion, or a sports injury.

- Many physicians refer patients to physical therapists for therapy and instruction in the use of assistive devices and thermodynamics, but sometimes the MA may provide patient instruction. The MA may measure and fit the patient for crutches, instruct the patient about the therapeutic use of heat and cold, assist in evaluating the patient's range of motion, or explain proper body mechanics.

- Thermodynamics involves the use of heat (thermotherapy) or cold (cryotherapy) applications to promote healing and prevent further tissue injury in areas affected by trauma, infection, and inflammation. Heat, by virtue of increasing circulation, increases nutrition to cells and carries away waste products. Cold constricts blood vessels, reduces leakage of fluid into tissues, acts as a temporary anesthetic, and reduces the number of pathogens in the area. Devices used in heat

Chapter Summary (continued)

or cold therapy include heating pads, chemical hot or cold packs, ice bags, and cold or hot moist soaks or compresses.

■ Assistive aids for ambulation include axillary crutches and forearm crutches (Lofstrand crutches); standard, tripod, and quad canes; and standard and rolling walkers. Special safety guidelines must be followed when assistive aids are used.

■ To prevent musculoskeletal injury and maintain health and safety, health-care team members must practice proper body mechanics such as keeping the back straight when sitting, standing, and walking; bending at the hips and knees and keeping objects close to the body when lifting and lowering them; and maintaining the center of gravity within the body.

Chapter Review Questions

Multiple Choice

1. Which of the following terms means "decrease in the size of normal muscle mass"?
   A. atony
   B. atrophy
   C. axillary
   D. articular

2. Which of the following is *not* part of the axial skeleton?
   A. clavicle
   B. sternum
   C. cranium
   D. ribs

3. Which of the following is *not* part of the appendicular section of the skeleton?
   A. scapula
   B. femur
   C. ulna
   D. facial bones

4. The type of membrane covering the outside layer of bone is:
   A. cartilage
   B. osteoblast
   C. periosteum
   D. endosteum

5. Which of the following means "no movement of a joint"?
   A. bursae
   B. diarthrosis
   C. amphiarthrosis
   D. synarthrosis

6. The type of fracture that results in the crushing or splintering of the bone is the:
   A. compression fracture
   B. compound fracture
   C. comminuted fracture
   D. depression fracture

7. A fractured bone that is partially bent and partially fractured is called:
   A. greenstick
   B. displaced
   C. comminuted
   D. impacted

8. Which of the following is *not* a soft-tissue knee injury?
   A. sprain
   B. avulsion
   C. torn meniscus
   D. severed tendon

9. Which of the following terms means "overstretching of a muscle, tendon, or ligament"?
   A. severed
   B. sprain
   C. dislocation
   D. strain

10. An imaging technique used to evaluate bone density is the:
    A. myelogram
    B. bone scan
    C. arthrogram
    D. radiograph

True/False

T F   1. The correction of a fracture is called *reduction*.

T F   2. Surgical intervention is not necessary for compound, avulsed, or displaced fractures.

T F   3. Cotton is a common material that can be used to make a cast.

T F   4. Thermotherapy includes both moist and dry applications.

T F   5. Heat can be used to speed up the localized formation of pus.

Short Answer

1. What is a compression fracture?

2. Which physical therapy modality vibrates tissue, generates heat, and promotes circulation?

3. What are the two types of thermodynamic applications?

4. The correct placement of the crutch pad is how many inches below the armpit?

5. What is the best gait for patients who need crutches but can bear weight on only one leg?

Research

1. In your local area, are there orthopedic physicians who specialize in pediatrics as well as geriatrics?

2. Are there physical therapists in your community who specialize in sports-related injuries and rehabilitation?

Externship Application Experience

As an extern, you have been sent into a room to prepare a 10-year-old boy for the removal of an arm cast. You prepare the materials and equipment with the mother and child present. When the patient sees the cast saw and orthopedic vacuum, he screams, "Don't cut off my arm!" How will you prepare the patient and mother for the cast removal?

Resource Guide

American Academy of Orthopedic Surgeons
6300 N. River Rd.
Rosemont, IL 60018-4262
1-800-346-AAOS
www.aos.org

American Lyme Disease Foundation
Mill Pond Offices
293 Route 100
Somers, NY 10389
1-914-277-6970
www.aldf.com

American Physical Therapy Association
1111 N. Fairfax St.
Alexandria, VA 22314-1488
1-800-999-2782
www.apta.org

Arthritis Foundation
PO Box 7669
Atlanta, GA 30357-0669
1-800-283-7800
www.arthritis.org

Muscular Dystrophy Association
3300 E. Sunrise Drive
Tucson, AZ 85718
1-800-572-1717
www.mdausa.org

National Osteoporosis Foundation
1232 22nd Street, NW
Washington, DC 20037-1292
1-202-223-2226
www.nof.org

National Rehabilitation Information Center
4200 Forbes Blvd
Lamham, MD 20706
1-800-346-2742
www.naric.com

MedMedia
www.prenhall.com/frazier

More on this chapter, including interactive resources, can be found on the Student CD-ROM accompanying this textbook and on the Companion Website at www.prenhall.com/frazier.

Objectives

After completing this chapter, you should be able to:

- Spell and define the medical terminology in this chapter.
- Discuss the medical assistant's role in the obstetric/gynecology medical office.
- Discuss the anatomy and physiology of the female reproductive system.
- Explain the menstrual cycle and menopause.
- Describe common disorders and conditions related to the menstrual cycle.
- List and describe the different methods of contraception.
- Explain some of the causes of female infertility.
- Discuss the processes of pregnancy and childbirth.
- List the information required for a complete obstetrical history.
- Explain common complications of pregnancy.
- Discuss the benefits and drawbacks of breastfeeding and formula feeding.
- List and describe disease conditions related to the female reproductive system.
- Explain how to assess vaginal bleeding.
- List and describe sexually transmitted diseases affecting women.
- Discuss disorders and conditions that affect the breasts.
- Discuss patient assessment in the OB/GYN office.
- Describe the various diagnostic procedures performed in the OB/GYN office.
- List and explain different treatment modalities for OB/GYN patients.
- Discuss psychological interventions for various OB/GYN conditions.

Obstetrics and Gynecology

Case Study

Sydney Jackson, RMA, is taking phone calls one afternoon when she receives a frantic message from Tina Blakely, a 72-year-old patient. Mrs. Blakely is concerned about recent news reports linking hormone replacement therapy to breast cancer and has stopped her medication. Now she is experiencing multiple symptoms and would like to know if there are any nonpharmaceutical therapies she can take.

MedMedia
www.prenhall.com/frazier

Additional interactive resources and activities for this chapter can be found on the Companion Website. For videos, audio glossary, legal and ethical scenarios, job scenarios, quizzes, games, virtual tours, and activities related to the content of this chapter, please access the accompanying CD-ROM in this book.

 **Assets Available:**

Audio Glossary
Legal and Ethical Scenario: *Obstetrics and Gynecology*
On the Job Scenario: *Obstetrics and Gynecology*
Video Scenario: Assisting in Gynecology Exams
A & P Quiz : The Reproductive System
Multiple Choice Quiz
Games: Crossword, Strikeout and Spelling Bee
3D Virtual Tour: Reproductive System: Female Reproductive System
Drag & Drop: Reproductive System: Ovulation; Reproductive System: Female Reproductive System

Medical Terminology

amniocentesis—procedure in which a needle is inserted into the amniotic sac to withdraw amniotic fluid for testing; used to identify genetic abnormalities, often neural tube deficits and Down syndrome, in the fetus; also used to determine the sex of the fetus

cervix—entrance to the uterus

colostrum—fluid secreted by the breasts after delivery, before milk production, that contains antibodies and provides the infant with immunological protection

effacement—thinning of the cervix during the labor process

embryo—initial physical stage of human development following fertilization of the ovum until the end of the seventh or eighth week

endometrium—lining of the uterus

fetus—human child in utero from embryonic stage until birth

fundal height—height of the fundus from the top of the symphysis pubis to the highest point at the top of the uterus; used to estimate the size of the fetus

gravida—combining form meaning a pregnant female or pregnancy

gynecology—branch of medicine pertaining to the female reproductive system, diseases, and disorders

gynecologist—physician specializing in the medical care of the female reproductive system, diseases, and disorders

menarche—onset of menses or menstrual cycle during adolescence

menopause—cessation of menses

menses—cyclic shedding of the uterine lining (endometrium) when fertilization of the ovum does not occur

obstetrician—physician specializing in the medical care of women during pregnancy, including prenatal, delivery, and postnatal care

obstetrics—branch of medicine pertaining to the medical care of women during pregnancy, including prenatal, delivery, and postnatal care

ovum (plural: ova)—human gamete (egg)

Pap Smear (Papanicolaou test)—A screening test to aid in the detection of cervical/uterine cancer and caner precursors.

para—combining form signifying the number of deliveries after the 20th week of gestation

✚ MEDICAL ASSISTING COMPETENCIES

CAAHEP ENTRY-LEVEL COMPETENCIES FOR CMA	ABHES ENTRY-LEVEL COMPETENCIES FOR RMA
▪ Perform telephone and in-person screening. ▪ Obtain vital signs. ▪ Obtain and record patient history. ▪ Prepare and maintain examination and treatment areas. ▪ Prepare patient for and assist with routine and specialty examinations. ▪ Prepare patient for and assist with procedures, treatments, and minor office surgeries. ▪ Screen and follow up test results.	▪ Interview and record patient history. ▪ Prepare patients for procedures. ▪ Apply principles of aseptic techniques and infection control. ▪ Take vital signs. ▪ Prepare and maintain examination and treatment area. ▪ Prepare patient for and assist physician with routine and specialty examinations and treatments and minor office surgeries. ▪ Use quality control. ▪ Collect and process specimens. ▪ Screen and follow up patient test results. ▪ Prepare and administer oral and parenteral medications as directed by physician. ▪ Maintain medication and immunization records. ▪ Dispose of biohazardous materials. ▪ Practice Standard Precautions. ▪ Perform electrocardiograms. ▪ Perform respiratory testing. ▪ Perform telephone and in-person screening.

Introduction

The **OB/GYN** practice focuses on the female reproductive system. **Obstetrics** focuses specifically on pregnancy and childbirth. Many pregnancies progress without complications and the infant is delivered spontaneously, without difficulty. The expectant mother and developing **fetus** are monitored throughout the pregnancy during routine **prenatal** visits. The expectant parents are provided with information regarding pregnancy, labor and delivery **(L & D)**, **postnatal** or **postpartum (PP)** care, and parenting. The **obstetrician** assists the mother during a normal vaginal delivery and with any surgical intervention that may be required if complications arise.

The **gynecology** practice addresses diseases and disorders of the female reproductive system. These conditions include ovarian, tubal, uterine, and vaginal disorders. Sexual dysfunction and sexually transmitted diseases are also treated. Fertility problems may be addressed by either the obstetrician or the **gynecologist.** Assisting women in dealing with normal life cycle changes is another goal of the OB/GYN practice.

The Medical Assistant's Role in the OB/GYN Office

As a medical assistant in an OB/GYN office you will assist with obtaining the patient history, paying special attention to OB/GYN-related information. You will obtain vital signs according to office protocol and assist the physician with physical examinations, including pelvic exams, and obtaining **Pap smears** and other specimens. You may also assist with other procedures the physician may perform.

Medical Terminology *(continued)*

perineum—area between the vaginal orifice and the anus

postnatal/postpartum—after childbirth

prenatal—prior to birth

zygote—the fertilized ovum created by the union of the male and female sex cells (sperm and ovum)

Abbreviations

AFT—alpha-fetoprotein

BSE—breast self-exam

C-section—cesarean section

EDC—estimated date of confinement

EDD—expected date of delivery

FHT—fetal heart tones

g—gravida (followed by number for each pregnancy experienced)

L & D—labor and delivery

LH—luteinizing hormone

LMP—last menstrual period

OB/GYN—obstetrics and gynecology

PMS—premenstrual syndrome

PP—postpartum

p—para (followed by number for each birth of a fetus over 20 weeks gestation)

UCG—urine chorionic gonadotropin

COMPETENCY SKILLS Performance

1. Assist with a prenatal exam.
2. Demonstrate patient instruction in breast self-examination.
3. Assist the physician in the performance of a pelvic examination and Pap test.
4. Demonstrate performance of a urine pregnancy test.
5. Assist with cryosurgery.

Normal prenatal visits include obtaining and recording the patient's weight and blood pressure and checking a urine specimen for protein and sugar. Urine pregnancy tests (**UCG**) are done on the initial visit and any visit when the patient reports vaginal bleeding.

Patient teaching involving the breast self-exam (**BSE**) is often delegated to the medical assistant. You may also be expected to give the patient information regarding nutritional requirements during pregnancy and lactation and to discuss breast and formula feeding options. Other important information for the patient and her partner addresses labor and delivery, prenatal classes, and caring for the newborn infant.

The Anatomy and Physiology of the Female Reproductive System

The female reproductive system consists of the following structures (Figure 26-1 ◆).

- Ovaries: The two ovaries are small almond-shaped structures located bilaterally in the lower aspect of the pelvis, beside the uterus, in a fold of the broad ligament. The process of ovulation occurs when the ovaries produce and release an egg, or **ovum,** in response to stimulation by the follicle-stimulating hormone. Hormones produced by the ovary control the entire reproductive process: the menstrual cycle, its onset (**menarche**), the fertility cycle and

menses, and the cessation of menses (**menopause**). At the moment of birth, the ovaries contain all the eggs that will be needed throughout a woman's child-bearing years.

- Fallopian tubes: Two fallopian tubes are also bilaterally located in the pelvis. Their distal aspect is close to the ovaries, and at their dorsal aspect they connect to the uterus. The ova travel through the fallopian tubes from the ovaries to the uterus. The fallopian tubes are also the route the sperm travels to meet the ovum and fertilize it. The distal portions of the fallopian tubes have fingerlike projections called *fimbriae* that move to capture the egg and direct it into the tube for its journey to the uterus.
- Uterus: A hollow pear-shaped organ centered in the pelvis, the uterus is the internal female organ of reproduction. It is composed of three layers: the **endometrium,** or internal lining; the myometrium, the middle muscular layer; and the perimetrium, the outermost layer, composed of serous connective tissue. The endometrium is sensitive to hormonal influence and is where the fertilized egg is implanted for growth and development. When pregnancy does not occur, the endometrium is shed and menses begin.
- Vagina: The vagina is the tube-like portion of the reproductive tract extending from the outer opening (vaginal orifice) to the cervix. During the process of natural birth, the fetus must pass through this birth canal, often referred to as the vaginal vault.
- Cul-de-sac: The cul-de-sac is located directly behind the cervix and is a highly sensitive area.

Other structures associated with the female reproductive system comprise the external genitalia (Figure 26-2 ◆). *Vulva* is the collective term for these external structures.

- Labia majora: the outer lips of the vagina
- Labia minora: the smaller inner structures of the vagina
- Bartholin's glands: glands on either side of the vaginal orifice that produce mucus to lubricate the vagina
- Clitoris: erectile tissue anterior to the vaginal orifice and in front of the urethral meatus
- **Perineum:** area between the vaginal orifice and the anus

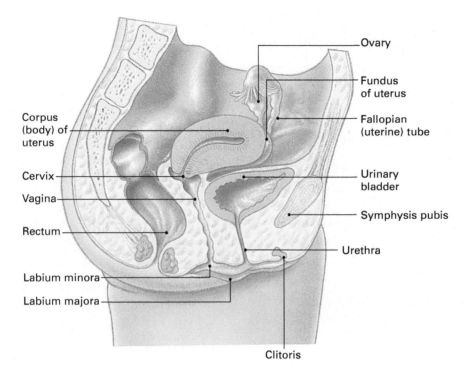

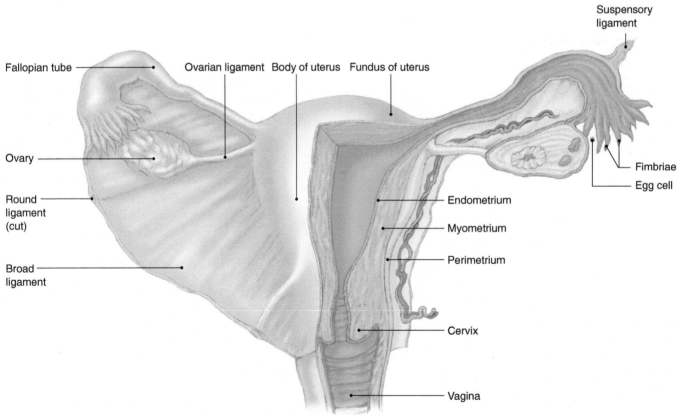

Figure 26-1 ◆ Female organs of reproduction

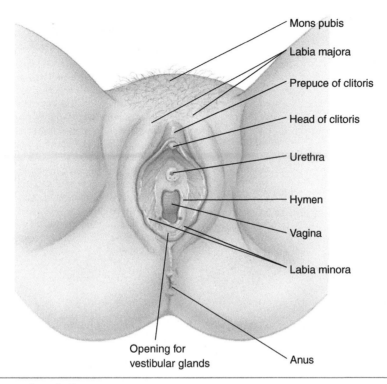

Mons pubis
Labia majora
Prepuce of clitoris
Head of clitoris
Urethra
Hymen
Vagina
Labia minora
Opening for vestibular glands
Anus

Figure 26-2 ◆ The female external genitalia

Anatomy and Physiology of the Female Breast

The female breasts, also known as mammary glands, develop during puberty but remain nonfunctional until the end of a pregnancy. Following birth, **colostrum** and the milk that follows serve as the source of the newborn's nutrition and passive immunity. Breastfeeding also establishes an emotional bond between mother and child.

Each mammary gland is composed of lobes containing fatty and glandular tissue and lactiferous (milk) ducts (Figure 26-3 ◆). On the exterior of each breast, in the center of the areola, the nipple is the convergence of the lactiferous ducts. With the birth of the child, a hormone called prolactin is secreted, thereby causing the glandular tissue to secrete colostrum, then breast milk, into the lactiferous ducts. The infant's sucking stimulates the release of oxytocin, a hormone that causes the lactiferous ducts to contract and release the milk, a process known as *milk letdown* or the *letdown reflex*. Breast milk production can be maintained for several months by continuous breastfeeding or by breast pumping.

The Menstrual Cycle

As the young female develops physically and approaches adolescence, hormonal changes stimulate the onset of menses and the menstrual cycle. Menarche signals the beginning of the female's reproductive capability. Hormones control the development, maturation, and release of ova for fertilization and

implantation. If the ovum is not fertilized or the zygote is not implanted, the endometrial lining is shed as menstrual flow to prepare the uterus for the next potential pregnancy.

Normal menstruation is based on a 28-day cycle, also referred to as a lunar month. The onset of a menstrual period, or menses, is considered the first day of the cycle (Figure 26-4 ◆). The menstrual period normally lasts around five days, during which the disintegrated cells of the endometrium are shed in a bloody fluid with glandular secretions and blood cells. This process is usually followed by the repair of the endometrium, the release of estrogen by the maturing graafian follicles, also known as ovarian follicles, and the maturation of another ovum during days 6 to 13 of the cycle. Just before ovulation, or the release of the egg, on approximately the fourteenth day, secretion of luteinizing hormone (**LH**) sharply increases. The ovarian follicle ruptures (ovulation), and the follicle is transformed into a corpus luteum. The corpus luteum is responsible for producing some estrogen and large amounts of progesterone, which causes the endometrium and uterine blood vessels to thicken in anticipation of a potential pregnancy. As ovulation occurs and the ovum is released, waving fimbriae at the distal end of each fallopian tube assist in moving the ovum through peritoneal fluid toward the mouth of the fallopian tube. The journey of the ovum from fallopian tube to uterus takes about five days and would not occur without the propelling movement of cilia within the tube. If fertilization does not occur, the corpus luteum deteriorates, and levels of estrogen and progesterone decrease. This drop in hormone

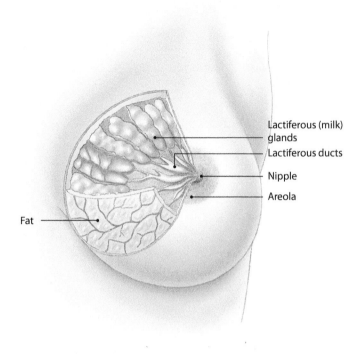

Lactiferous (milk) glands

Lactiferous ducts

Nipple

Areola

Fat

Figure 26-3 ◆ The female breast

levels is a signal to the body to begin the menses and prepare for the next cycle.

Menopause, or the cessation of the menses, usually occurs between the ages of 45 and 55. This expected, normal condition occurs because of aging and the decline of ovarian function. Menopause also occurs after a surgical procedure called a hysterectomy. Hormone replacement therapy (HRT) is one possible treatment for the symptoms of menopause. The physician should discuss the benefits and risks of HRT and other treatments with the menopausal patient and allow her to make an informed decision about whether to treat the symptoms. It is common for women undergoing the physical changes of menopause to feel too embarrassed to discuss their condition. Provide emotional support and reassurance that this is a normal condition.

？— Critical Thinking Question 26-1–

How should Sydney handle the phone call from Mrs. Blakely? How can she reassure her and offer support until Mrs. Blakely can speak to the physician? Should Sydney offer suggestions for nonpharmaceutical therapy?

Menstrual Disorders

Disorders relating to the menstrual cycle include dysmenorrhea, amenorrhea, menorrhagia, metrorrhagia, mittelschmertz, and premenstrual syndrome (**PMS**) (Table 26-1). Causes are varied, as are the treatments.

Keys to Success
THE DEBATE OVER HORMONE REPLACEMENT THERAPY

Recent research into hormone replacement therapy (HRT) has created a great deal of controversy. HRT had previously been recommended for post-menopausal women to help alleviate symptoms such as vaginal dryness, hot flashes, mood swings, sleep problems, and panic attacks. HRT was also recommended to prevent heart attacks and osteoporosis. Estrogen alone was prescribed for women who had undergone hysterectomies; progestin (progesterone) was prescribed in combination with estrogen for women who still had a uterus.

Recent studies suggest that hormone replacement therapy, especially the estrogen-progestin combination, increases a woman's risk for breast cancer. Many physicians have recommended that their patients discontinue combination therapy. Any decisions regarding HRT should be discussed by the patient, her partner, and the physician before a final decision is made. This discussion should include information regarding risks and benefits.

Contraception

The OB/GYN office provides information on contraception as well as prescriptions for contraceptive drugs and devices. Contraception, or birth control, may be achieved by various methods, including barriers, chemical contact, hormonal control, intrauterine devices, surgical sterilization, and periodic sexual abstinence. The use of contraception does not guarantee prevention of pregnancy. Although various contraceptive methods have established effectiveness rates, human factors, such as the consistency of correct use, and hormonal factors, such as those relating to breastfeeding, may affect the results and lead to unintended pregnancies.

Barrier methods of birth control are designed to prevent the sperm from entering the cervix, traveling through the uterus to the fallopian tube, and fertilizing the ovum. Barriers include condoms, diaphragms, and cervical caps, which are usually made of latex. In addition to blocking fertilization, condoms also help to protect against the spread of STDs by preventing contact between the causative organism and the mucous membrane of the vagina. Barriers are usually the least expensive method of contraception. One drawback, however, is the inconvenience of inserting the diaphragm into the vagina, positioning the cervical cap on the cervix, or placing the condom on the penis before sexual intercourse.

Contraception may be achieved by contact between sperm and a chemical spermicide. Spermicides are available in foam, jelly, or cream form and may be purchased in drugstores or other stores without a prescription. They are recommended for use with diaphragms and cervical caps to make these devices more effective, but they may also be used alone, inserted into the vagina following sexual intercourse for moderate efficacy.

Another chemical intervention is vaginal irrigation or douching with solutions that create unfavorable conditions for the survival of sperm. Douching also washes out many sperm remaining in the vagina following intercourse.

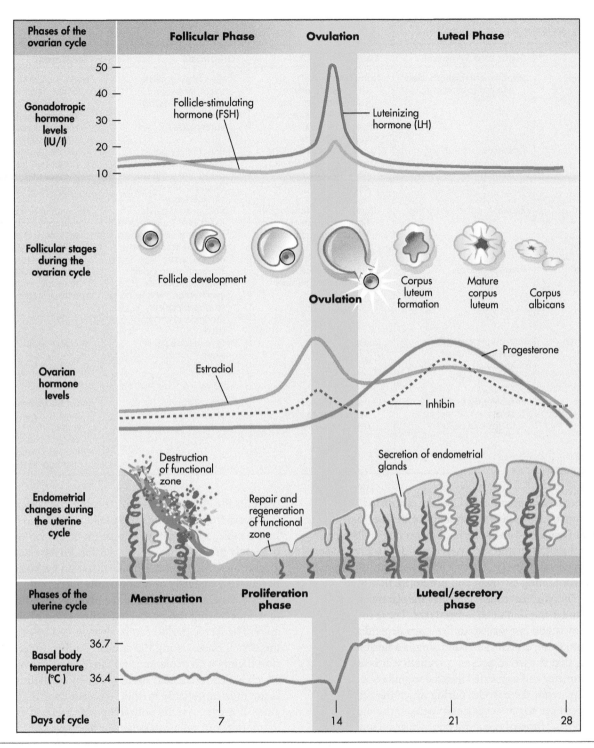

Figure 26-4 ◆ The menstrual cycle

TABLE 26-1 MENSTRUAL DISORDERS

Condition	Signs and Symptoms	Cause	Diagnosis	Treatment
Dysmenorrhea	Painful menstruation, often referred to as "cramps"	Normal hormonal changes, underlying conditions including endometriosis, pelvic infection, fibroids, cervical stenosis	Patient history, pelvic exam, ultrasound exams, laparoscopy, and finally surgery (D&C)	NSAIDS, contraceptives (oral or dermal patches), treatment of endometriosis, surgical approach to treating fibroids and cervical stenosis
Amenorrhea	Absence of menses for longer than six months	Pregnancy; loss of muscle mass due to anorexia nervosa or excessive exercise	Patient history, pelvic . exam, ultrasound exams, blood and urine studies, biopsy of uterine and cervical tissue	Often no treatment prescribed; hormone therapy may be used after ruled out pregnancy
Menorrhagia	Excessive or heavy menses	Uterine fibroids (etiology of fibroids unknown), pelvic inflammatory disease, tumors	Patient history, pelvic exam, ultrasound exams, blood and urine studies, biopsy of uterine and cervical tissue	Depending on cause: hormone replacement, treatment of pelvic inflammatory disease, removal of tumors
Metrorrhagia	Irregular menses	Uterine tumors or foreign bodies in uterus	Patient history, pelvic exam, ultrasound exams, blood and urine studies, biopsy of uterine and cervical tissue	Hormone replacement, D & C to restore endometrium to normal status
Mittelschmertz	Pain during ovulation in one side of lower abdomen that usually subsides within 12 hours	Cause unknown	Patient history, pelvic exam	Mild analgesics
Premenstrual syndrome (PMS)	Irritability, depression, breast tenderness prior to onset of period	Cause unknown; may be due to cyclic hormone deviation	Patient history, physical exam	Individualized treatment may include dietary alterations (reduction of salt, sugar, alcohol, and caffeine intake), exercise, stress management

Hormonal contraception includes the oral form (birth control pills), hormonal implants, intradermal patches, Norplant, Nuvaring or Depo-Provera injections. Birth control pills contain estrogen and progestin and are taken every day to prevent the ovaries from releasing an egg. A recent advance is the intradermal patch, also containing estrogen and progestin, that is changed every week. The Norplant concept involves the placement of progestin rods under the skin of the upper arm. These rods release progestin slowly and last for two or five years depending on the number of rods implanted. The NuvaRing is a flexible contraceptive ring that is used to prevent pregnancy. It is about two inches in diameter and is inserted into the vagina once a month. It is kept in place for three weeks, during which the ring releases a synthetic estrogen to protect against pregnancy for one month. Depo-Provera is a form of progestin that is injected intramuscularly every three months.

Another form of contraception is the intrauterine device (IUD). The physician inserts the IUD through the cervix into the uterus, where it prevents the fertilized egg from implanting in the uterine wall. IUDs may remain in place for up to ten years and require removal by a physician.

Contraception by surgical sterilization is usually permanent. Tubal ligation is a surgical procedure in which both fallopian tubes are ligated (tied off), usually with a laser, and both ends of each tube are cauterized. This procedure can be done with a laparoscope through a small abdominal incision and is often performed within two days after delivery. Tubal ligation prevents the egg from traveling through the fallopian tube and the sperm from traveling up the fallopian tube to meet the egg. In the male, a vasectomy, or ligation of the vas deferens, permanently prevents the sperm transfer during ejaculation. Surgical reversals to reestablish a fertilization pathway in the male or female are usually only minimally successful.

Periodic sexual abstinence involves avoiding sexual intercourse during the probable fertile period of the menstrual cycle. The fertile period can be determined by monitoring the menstrual cycle; taking the female's body temperature, which rises slightly with ovulation; and interpreting the vaginal mucus, which is clear, slick, and stretchy during ovulation. Abstinence is the most unreliable method of birth control. In some religions, however, it is the only acceptable method. Be careful not to impose your religious beliefs or feelings about birth control on the patient.

Infertility

An area of the OB/GYN practice that closely parallels contraception is fertility concerns, specifically the inability of the female to conceive. Obstetricians and gynecologists are both qualified to address fertility problems, but some choose to specialize in fertility.

The term *infertility* is used to describe partners who are under the age of 35 and have actively tried to conceive, without medical assistance, for 1 year without a resulting pregnancy.

For couples over the age of 35, the time frame is shortened to 6 months. The term primary infertility refers to couples who have never achieved a pregnancy, while secondary infertility refers to infertility that affects couples after one or both have achieved a viable pregnancy.

Fertility issues are broken down into percentages of which partner is the most likely result of the inability to conceive. Currently fertility issues are 40% female factor, 40% male factor, 10% combined factor, and 10% unknown origin.

Some OB/GYN practitioners choose to only treat female issues, while others will run the necessary tests on both partners.

If neither partner has no previous successful pregnancies or caused a pregnancy, and there is no medical reason to suspect either partner, the male factors are the first to be tested and ruled out due to the simplicity and noninvasive testing approaches. The testing for male factors is a simple blood test to check hormone levels and a semen analysis through a donated sperm sample. By microscopically examining the semen, the physician can verify if there is sufficient sperm, the sperm are mobile (no double tails, missing tails, double heads, etc.), the ejaculate is the correct viscosity, checking the total morphology and motility. If male factor is diagnosed there are multiple treatment options or even the possibility for the couple to explore donor sperm options.

Donor sperm options are also an option for women wishing to become single-parents or for same sex couples to achieve a pregnancy.

Testing for female fertility issues are much more complex and costly. Multiple issues can arise in the female anatomy: are the ovaries producing enough estrogen and progesterone? Is an egg being produced? Is the uterine lining adequate to support a fertilized egg? Can the uterus and cervix support a pregnancy? Can the ovum travel through the fallopian tubes? Is the cervical mucus thin enough to allow sperm passage into the uterus? Women can suffer from one or more fertility issues. To test female issues the physician may choose to start with a complete blood analysis to determine if hormonal levels are normal. Specifically a blood analysis can test for LH, FSH, Progesterone, TSH and Prolactin as well as a variety of STDs that may have been contracted without showing symptoms. LH stands for luteinizing hormone, which aids in triggering the female body to ovulate or the male to produce testosterone. FSH is follicle-stimulating hormone. High levels may indicate a low egg reserve, especially in older women, while a low FSH level may indicate the woman is not ovulating at all. Low progesterone levels may indicate the body can not ovulate. The thyroid functioning is checked with the TSH testing, to determine if it is over- or under-functioning. Either may affect the menstrual cycle and ability to ovulate. Prolactin is a by product of the pituitary gland that can also affect the woman's ability to ovulate.

Once it is determined that the woman is ovulating and there are no male factors, the practitioner must determine if there are structural abnormalities. This can be done through a variety of tests such as; an ultrasound of the pelvis to determine if follicle development is normal, a Hysterosalpingogram in which a contrast dye is injected via the vagina to check that

the cervix opens, the uterus and fallopian tubes are free of damage or structural problems. A much more invasive test is a laparoscopy, in which the uterus and fallopian tubes are viewed from surgical incisions in the abdomen. The laparoscopy can determine if there is scarring from pelvic inflammatory disease, endometriosis, or uterine fibroids. If those conditions are present, the practitioner can remove them during the viewing procedure.

If fertility issues are present there are multiple medical advancements to help with these family building challenges. Patients should be aware that most testing and infertility treatments are not covered by insurance. The patient should verify all financial responsibilities with their insurance carrier and practitioner prior to treatment.

Some religions and cultures regard the treatment of fertility problems as improper. Again, the patient's feelings and beliefs must be respected.

Pregnancy and the Birth Process

The release of an ovum from the ovary is the first step in the female reproductive process. If the ovum is fertilized by a sperm in the fallopian tube, a **zygote** is formed. As it divides and grows, it is transformed into an **embryo.** The embryo completes the journey through the fallopian tube to the uterus, where it implants itself in the endometrium. If conditions are favorable, the implanted embryo develops and grows into a fetus. It normally takes 38 to 40 weeks for the fetus to mature (Figure 26-5 ◆).

Delivery

In a normal delivery, the **cervix,** or mouth of the uterus, dilates and begins **effacement,** and uterine contractions propel the fetus through the vagina and into the external environment (Figure 26-6 ◆). Many of the movements the fetus makes as it travels down the birth canal stimulate its breathing after delivery.

Keys to Success
CALCULATING THE EXPECTED DATE OF DELIVERY

The normal gestational period is 266 days, or 38 weeks, from the date of conception. The expected date of delivery (**EDD**), also called the estimated date of confinement (**EDC**), can be estimated using Nagele's Rule or the lunar method. To use Nagele's Rule, take the date of onset of the last period, subtract 3 months, then add 1 year and 7 days. If the date of onset is June 5, 2007, for example, the EDD would be March 12, 2008. To calculate EDD with the lunar method, add 9 months to the date of onset of last period, then add 7 days to that new date. Again, for a date of onset of June 5, 2007, the EDD would be March 12, 2008. Both methods yield the same result; preference depends on which is easier for the user.

Many wheel-type charts are available for calculating EDD and are used in the OB office. If the exact date of fertilization is known, 38 weeks are added to that date. Ultrasounds of the pelvis and developing fetus are also fairly accurate in establishing the age of the fetus. (This method is not available in all locations, however, and may be too expensive for some patients.)

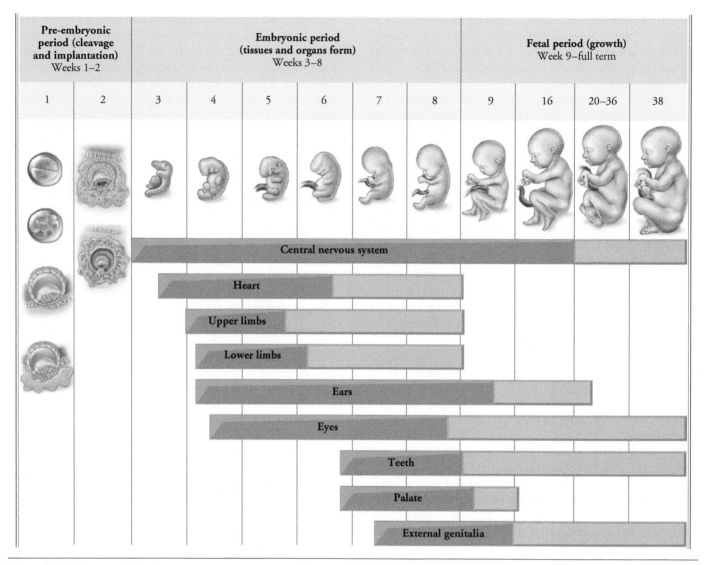

Pre-embryonic period (cleavage and implantation) Weeks 1–2		Embryonic period (tissues and organs form) Weeks 3–8						Fetal period (growth) Week 9–full term			
1	2	3	4	5	6	7	8	9	16	20–36	38

Central nervous system

Heart

Upper limbs

Lower limbs

Ears

Eyes

Teeth

Palate

External genitalia

Figure 26-5 ◆ Stages of development

If the fetus is not in a head-down (cephalic) presentation, or if it shows signs of distress during labor, the physician may elect to perform a **C-section** to prevent fetal death. In this procedure, a surgical incision is made either midline in the abdomen or lower on the abdomen and into the uterus to deliver the baby.

Obstetrical History

Routine prenatal visits are usually scheduled once a month until the seventh month. If the physician feels the patient should be seen more often because of emerging problems for the mother or fetus, visits may be more frequent. After the seventh month, the expectant mother is seen every two or three weeks, then every week in the final month. A nurse practitioner often manages routine visits.

The routine prenatal visit includes measuring the patient's weight and blood pressure and checking a urine specimen for protein and glucose. Fetal heart tones (**FHT**) and the fetal position are also assessed, and the physician measures **fundal height.** Other areas that may be addressed, depending on the clinical progression of the pregnancy and the condition of the mother, include dietary modifications as well as instruction on labor and delivery, breastfeeding, and postpartum visits.

During the initial visit, you will obtain an obstetrical history of the patient. Important information includes the following:

- date of the last menstrual period (**LMP**)
- age at the onset of menses (menarche)
- frequency and duration of menstrual periods and estimated amount of blood loss during periods (slight, moderate, heavy)
- pain, if any, during menstrual period

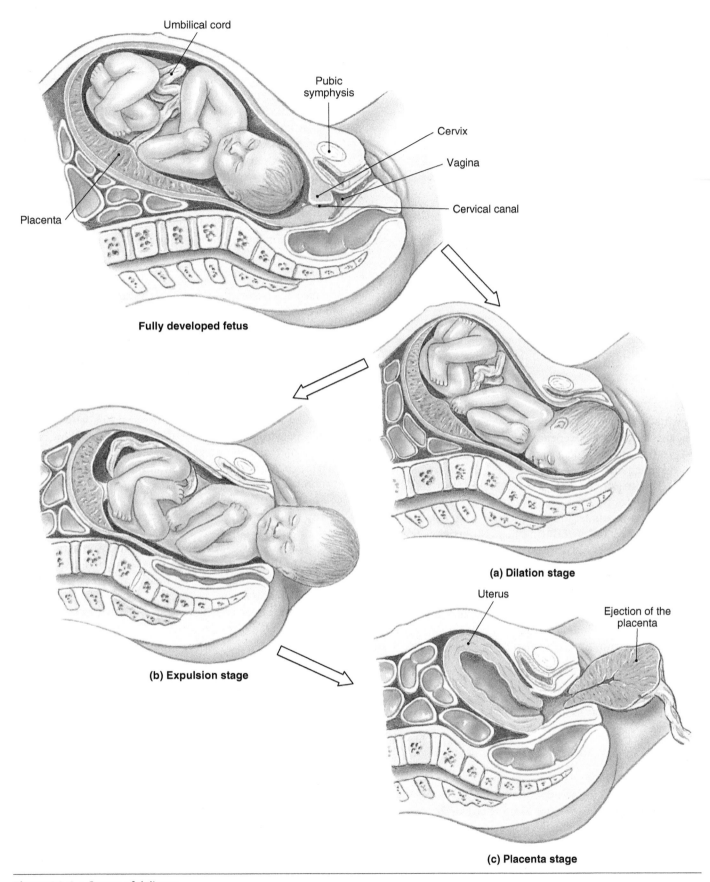

Fully developed fetus

(a) Dilation stage

(b) Expulsion stage

(c) Placenta stage

Figure 26-6 ◆ Stages of delivery

- total number of pregnancies (**gravida, g**)
- number of live births (fetus born alive and of gestational age of viability, or **para, p**)
- number of multiple pregnancies
- number of stillbirths
- number of miscarriages or abortions (spontaneous or induced)
- infants born with congenital defects
- age at cessation of menses (menopause)
- surgical procedures, if any
- history of any sexually transmitted disease
- dates of last mammogram and Pap smear
- medications, including birth control pills (BCP), vitamins and aspirin
- method of contraception
- breastfeeding, if there is a history of previous pregnancies
- blood type (if the patient has no documentation for blood type, in particular the Rh factor, a blood type test will be ordered)

Complications of Pregnancy

Most pregnancies progress through the normal gestational period without complications. Difficulties do arise, however, that create a danger for the fetus, mother, or both, such as hyperemesis gravidarum; spontaneous abortion or miscarriage; ectopic or tubal pregnancy; hydatidiform mole; toxemia, either pre-eclampsia or eclampsia; placenta previa; abruptio placenta; and premature labor and delivery (Table 26-2).

A history of previous or current medical conditions such as hypertension, hypothyroidism, hyperthyroidism, or diabetes mellitus presents a challenge to the obstetrical team. Gestational diabetes requires close monitoring during the pregnancy, delivery, and postpartum period. The neonate also requires prompt assessment for consequences of any of these conditions.

Breastfeeding

Breastfeeding is a matter of personal choice. Both breastfeeding and formula feeding have their advantages. Breast milk provides

---

PROCEDURE 26-1 Assist with a Prenatal Exam

Theory

The first prenatal appointment may be an exciting or terrifying visit for a woman, depending on whether the pregnancy was intentional. The physician will confirm or deny a suspected pregnancy during this visit.

The first prenatal appointment takes more time than subsequent routine visits and includes several blood tests, manual examinations, and consultation with the physician. Information established during this visit includes how far along the pregnancy has progressed, onset of menses, duration and amount of flow, any cycle problems, previous pregnancies or complications, previous births or complications, and all other obstetrical history. It is important to offer the patient guidelines for a healthy pregnancy, such as the safest amount of weight gain, nutritional guidelines, vitamin and mineral requirements, and substances and activities to avoid.

Materials

- EDD calculator
- full Pap and pelvic exam setup
- gloves
- patient's chart

Competency

(**Conditions** With the necessary materials, you will be able to (**Task**) assist with a prenatal exam (**Standards**) correctly within the time limit set by the instructor.

1. Verify the patient's identification.
2. Explain the tests that will be done as a baseline to compare to in the later stages of pregnancy.
3. Measure the patient's height and weight.

4. Depending on your office requirements, you may be asked to take a complete physical history of the patient. Obtain her menstrual history (age of onset, duration, flow rate, and intervals) and pregnancy history (number of pregnancies, number of live births, number of miscarriages, number of abortions).
5. Obtain a urine sample to run a UA.
6. Supply the patient with a paper gown and appropriate drape materials. Instruct the patient to undress completely and don the gown with the opening in front so that the practitioner may perform a breast exam. The patient should also be instructed on how to appropriately cover herself with the provided drape.
7. Assist the physician with the Pap and pelvic examination as required by office protocol.

Patient Education

It is important that the patient understand the importance of proper nutrition and which foods to avoid. If the patient qualifies, there are government programs that provide assistance to ensure a healthy pregnancy and delivery.

Charting Example

04/28/XX 9:41 AM Patient came in for confirmation of pregnancy and baseline testing. Pregnancy confirmed and patient was given prenatal package containing information about HIV and STD testing, Quad-screen testing for genetic disorders, and a prescription for prenatal vitamins. Copy placed in chart. Patient was asked about hospital preference and is undecided. Patient received paperwork for Lamaze class and nutritional guidelines. Payton Ferraro, CMA.

TABLE 26-2 COMPLICATIONS OF PREGNANCY

Condition	Signs and Symptoms	Cause	Diagnosis	Treatment
Hyperemesis gravidarum ("morning sickness")	Often first sign of pregnancy; nausea and/or vomiting; generally resolves as pregnancy progresses	Changes in hormone levels	Patient history of vomiting in the morning early in pregnancy	IV replacement of fluids and electrolytes in case of severe vomiting
Spontaneous abortion or miscarriage	Vaginal bleeding during early phases that results in termination of pregnancy	Etiology unknown; suggested causes include genetic fetal abnormality, hormonal imbalances, incompetent cervix, infection, immunological responses	Uterine bleeding, cramping, expulsion of products of conception from uterus	D&C if bleeding is severe to remove all products of conception from uterus
Ectopic or tubal pregnancy	Severe pain in pelvic area, usually vaginal bleeding, signs of shock	Zygote implants in area other than endometrium (usually fallopian tube but also ovary, outer wall of uterus, intestine, vaginal vault); in fallopian tube grows into embryo and causes tube to rupture	Patient history, pelvic exam, signs of shock	Immediate intervention: surgical termination of pregnancy, treatment of shock, replacement of lost fluids
Hydatidiform mole	Growth of abdomen but no fetal heart tones; bright vaginal bleeding during third month after cessation of menses	Error in conception involving chorionic villi; mass of vesicles develops and mimics early stages of pregnancy	Ultrasound	Mole may be expelled spontaneously, otherwise surgical removal; patient at risk for choriocarcinoma
Toxemia: preeclampsia is milder form, with no convulsions; can progress to more severe form, eclampsia, when convulsions occur	Sudden changes in blood pressure, weight, nausea, vomiting, headache, dizziness or spots before the eyes, edema in face, hands, and feet; usually affects primaparas under 18 or over 35; onset of convulsions (eclampsia) may trigger abruptio placentae	Sudden hypertension in last trimester	Routine urine testing and blood pressure monitoring	Dietary changes in early stages (low sodium, adequate protein); hospitalization if condition cannot be controlled and to avoid convulsions; delivery usually resolves condition quickly. Termination of pregnancy by induction or surgical intervention is the only cure. Preeclampsia requires close monitoring and often hospitalization; eclampsia is serious and requires constant monitoring.
Abruptio placentae	Sudden onset of abdominal pain, bright vaginal bleeding that may be copious; signs of shock, rigid and tight abdomen, fetal distress	Placenta prematurely separates from wall of uterus	Patient history, exam, ultrasound studies indicating location of placenta, vaginal bleeding	C-section to save mother's life and possibly child's life
Placenta previa	Painless vaginal bleeding during second and third trimester	Placenta implanted across cervical os or low in uterus close to cervical os	Patient history, exam, ultrasound studies showing location of placenta and vaginal bleeding	Bed rest often allows mother to carry baby to term; delivery by C-section
Premature labor	Labor before gestational period of 36 weeks; contractions, rupture of amniotic sac, vaginal bleeding or spotting, cervical effacement and dilation	Etiology often unknown; causes may include maternal infection, illness, injury, surgical procedures, incompetent cervix, placenta previa, placenta abruptio, toxemia, or presence of multiple fetuses.	Patient history, examination, fetal and uterine monitoring, observation of contractions by watching fundus	Restricted activities or bed rest; medications to slow or stop contractions; delivery if amniotic sac breaks to prevent infection; neonatal team present to care for high-risk premature infant

the infant with immunity to certain diseases and a readily available supply of nutrition that is always the correct temperature. The baby's suckling stimulates further milk production, and with continued breastfeeding the mother can usually produce adequate milk indefinitely. The APA (American Pediatric Association) recommends 12 months at minimum. For optimum milk production, the mother requires good nutrition and adequate fluid intake. A drawback to breastfeeding is that the mother must be available to nurse the baby on a regular basis or pump her breasts to obtain milk for the infant to be fed with a bottle. It takes some new mothers a while to develop the breastfeeding technique. Patient instruction is important in this area. The mother should never feel pressured into doing something she does not feel comfortable doing.

Formula feeding allows the mother more freedom to leave her infant in someone else's care. Bottle feeding provides a way to measure the calories and amount of liquid the infant is taking in. However, formula is expensive and requires preparation, while breast milk is essentially free and immediately available.

Gynecological Diseases and Disorders

The female reproductive system is prone to several diseases or conditions. Any structure in the system may be affected. For example, the ovaries may develop cysts or carcinoma. The fallopian tubes may be the site of an infectious process, scarring, and subsequent obstruction. The uterus is vulnerable to endometriosis, pelvic inflammatory disease, fibroids, and endometrial cancer. The cervix may be affected by infection, carcinoma, or dysplasia. The vagina is susceptible to vaginitis and uterine prolapse. Cystoceles and rectoceles also occur in the vaginal area.

Table 26-3 describes some of the common conditions of the female reproductive system that you are likely to encounter in the OB/GYN office. Table 26-4 lists risk factors and points of instruction for the patient concerning cervical and uterine cancer.

Assessing Vaginal Bleeding

A primary symptom of problems in the female reproductive tract is vaginal bleeding other than during the regular menstrual period. Abnormal bleeding can occur at any age. In the very young female, from infancy until puberty and menarche, vaginal bleeding may be an indication of sexual abuse. (Bleeding in the sexually and physically mature child-bearing adult or elderly female may also result from sexual abuse.)

Vaginal bleeding other than normal menses in the female who has passed menarche may indicate a hormonal imbalance or a pathology in the reproductive tract. During pregnancy vaginal bleeding is an abnormal occurrence and requires prompt assessment for the cause.

When a patient reports abnormal vaginal bleeding, even an unusually heavy menstrual flow, the actual amount lost, as well as its color, must be determined. You may need to ask the patient questions such as these:

- Describe the flow. Is it spotty or continuous?
- What type of pad or sanitary napkin are you using—a mini-pad or maxi-pad? Do you use tampons?

Keys to Success
CULTURAL CONSIDERATIONS ABOUT BREASTFEEDING

In many cultures, new mothers are expected to breastfeed their infants. Other societal pressures may also affect a new mother's decision whether to breastfeed. Some mothers are unable to breastfeed because of various health and emotional problems. As a medical assistant, you should accept the patient's decision in a nonjudgmental way.

- How much blood is present? Is the pad spotted or saturated? How much of the pad is covered?
- How long does it take to saturate the pad? How frequently does it need to be changed?
- Describe the color of the blood. Is it dark, light pink and watery, or bright red?

Document on the chart the patient's description of the type and amount of blood flow. This information enables the physician to estimate the amount of blood lost.

Sexually Transmitted Diseases

Both OB and GYN offices care for patients with contagious diseases that are transmitted through sexual contact, commonly referred to as sexually transmitted diseases (STDs) or venereal diseases (Table 26-5). STDs may be experienced by either the male or female and are transmitted during sex by blood, semen, and vaginal secretions.

Breast Disorders and Conditions

The female breast is prone to a number of conditions that may be seen in the OB/GYN office. Fibrocystic changes, mastitis, carcinoma, diminutive size, and massive size are examples. Some patients may wish to discuss the necessity of monthly breast self-exams and regular mammogram screenings. Those anticipating either breast reduction or augmentation procedures may seek additional information or reassurance.

Many females connect the size and shape of their breasts with their sexuality. For other women, the ability to bear children is essential to their self-esteem and femininity. Encouraging the female patient to vocalize her concerns and listening in a nonjudgmental way promotes a more positive outlook.

Hormonal changes during the menstrual cycle can cause changes in breast tissue. Fibrocystic changes are usually responses to hormone stimulation. Progesterone may cause an increase in fluid in the breast tissue, creating tenderness and an uncomfortable feeling. Fibrous tissue and cysts develop, and lumps may be felt upon palpation. Manual examination of the breasts, accompanied by a mammogram, is helpful in ruling out carcinoma. Caffeine is thought to aggravate the cystic condition, and avoiding or limiting caffeine intake is encouraged. A firm, supporting bra may also afford some relief and comfort. The most important aspect of the condition is ruling out breast cancer.

A small, painless lump in the breast is often the first sign of breast cancer (Table 26-6). The lump may be discovered by the female during a monthly breast self-exam or by the physician during a routine or annual physical. A mammogram is helpful in the diagnosis, but a biopsy is necessary to confirm it. Suggested treatment usually involves excision of the lesion and surrounding tissue by either lumpectomy or mastectomy. Lymph nodes may be removed and examined for the presence of malignant cells. Additional treatment may include chemotherapy and/or radiation.

Breast reduction is done for the female with extremely pendulous breasts that cause pain and discomfort, usually in

TABLE 26-3 DISEASES AND DISORDERS OF THE FEMALE REPRODUCTIVE SYSTEM

Condition	Signs and Symptoms	Cause	Diagnosis	Treatment
Ovarian cyst	Pain in one side of lower abdomen, possible vaginal bleeding; may be cyclic or may enlarge and rupture unless surgically removed	Often no known etiology; some caused by normal functioning of ovary from ovarian follicle or corpus luteum; some may be result of infectious process; others may be malignant	Patient history, exam, ultrasound, laparoscopy	Some resolve on their own; others require surgical removal
Pelvic inflammatory disease (PID)	Fever, chills, foul-smelling vaginal discharge, severe pelvic pain, backache, tender abdomen	Bacterial invasion of vagina and pelvic cavity, often caused by STDs	Patient history, exam, elevated white blood cell count, tender abdomen	Antibiotics; scarring often irreversible
Endometriosis	Pain caused by microscopic bleeding of displaced endometrial tissue; most attacks subside after menopause	Endometrial tissue displaced to other tissue in reproductive system or into abdominal cavity, where it implants, grows, and continues to respond to hormonal changes	Patient history, exam, laparoscopy	Hormones, surgical removal of ovaries, D&C
Uterine fibroids	Vaginal bleeding, heavy menstrual periods, pelvic pain and pressure	Benign fibrous growths or tumors of myometrium	Patient history, exam, ultrasound studies, laparoscopy, D&C	Surgical removal of fibroids (for women still planning to become pregnant), hysterectomy (for women no longer desiring children)
Vaginitis	Vaginal discharge, often yellow and foul-smelling	Inflammation of vagina, usually caused by *Trichomonas* infection	Patient history, exam, positive culture of vaginal smears	Antibiotics, antifungal medications, steroid creams
Uterine prolapse	Pressure in pelvic region, difficulty urinating	Uterus drops from normal suspension in pelvis into vagina; may protrude from vaginal orifice; caused by weakened pelvic muscles and ligaments	Patient history, pelvic exam, visualization of uterus protruding from vaginal canal	Minor prolapse helped by exercises that strengthen muscles of pelvic floor, weight loss; surgical repair
Cystocele	Frequent urination, urgency, incontinence, pressure	Downward displacement of urinary bladder into vagina; caused by weakened muscles in pelvic floor, often result of childbearing and aging	Patient history, pelvic exam	Exercises to strengthen pelvic floor muscles, surgical repair
Rectocele	Incontinence of flatus and stool	Downward displacement of rectum into vagina; caused by weakened muscles in pelvic floor, often result of childbearing and aging	Patient history, pelvic exam	Surgical repair
Ovarian cancer	Symptoms not specific for ovarian cancer: lower back pain, constipation, lower abdominal discomfort, irregular menstrual periods	Etiology unknown	History, exam revealing pelvic adnexal mass, laparoscopic exam, elevated tumor markers	Surgical removal if possible, chemotherapy
Uterine or endrometrial cancer	Vaginal "spotting" or bleeding in early stages, pain later	Etiology unknown; possibly caused by overexposure to estrogen, including postmenopausal HRT	Biopsy and staging with imaging procedures to determine extent of metastasis	Surgical excision and radiation
Cervical cancer	Often asymptomatic; bloody vaginal discharge bleeding between and menstrual periods; cervical lesions may be noted during visual pelvic exam	Possibly exposure to human papillomavirus; other causes not yet identified	Pelvic exam, Pap smear, biopsy	Surgical excision of lesion, followup chemotherapy and/or radiation (Note: vaccine for HPV is now available)
Labial cancer	Nodule or ulcer on labia, pruritis, burning, dysuria, possible enlarged lymph nodes	Unknown cause; occurs more often in females over age 60; history of herpes virus, multiple sexual partners, cigarette smoking; prior history of reproductive system cancers	Biopsy and evaluation for metastasis	Surgical excision of lesion and surrounding tissue; chemotherapy for systemic involvement

TABLE 26-4 RISK FACTORS AND EDUCATION RELATING TO CERVICAL AND UTERINE CANCER

Risk Factors

- A family history of various cancers, particularly breast, uterine, and cervical.
- Promiscuous sexual behavior.
- Frequent vaginal infections.
- Nonsurgical menopause.

Education

- An annual pelvic exam and Pap test are recommended after age 18 or when sexual activity has begun, whichever is earlier.
- The patient should report a family history of ALL cancers to the physician, particularly breast, uterine, and cervical.
- The patient should not douche or engage in sexual relations within 48 hours of the Pap test.
- Further examinations are required when abnormal symptoms are present, including: pelvic or vaginal pain; vaginal discharge other than bleeding; abnormal bleeding such as heavy, scanty, or spotting, or at times other than during the monthly menstrual period; changes in the breasts such as a new lump or mass; or lack of pregnancy without contraceptives during the childbearing years.

TABLE 26-6 RISK FACTORS AND EDUCATION RELATING TO BREAST CANCER

Risk Factors

- Female gender
- Increasing age, particularly over 50
- Ethnicity: non-Hispanic women have the highest incidence, and African American women have the highest mortality rate
- Early onset of menarche
- Later age of first full-term pregnancy (30 and over)
- Later onset of menopause (over 55)
- Personal medical history of abnormal breast changes
- Personal medical history of breast cancer
- Use of birth control pills or HRT (hormone replacement therapy)
- Obesity and physical inactivity
- High alcohol intake
- Family history of breast cancer or other associated cancers
- Radiation exposure, particularly to the chest

Education

- Monthly breast self-examination. Any breast changes such as newly found lumps, swelling, dimpling, skin retraction, or unusual nipple discharge should be evaluated by a physician.
- Routine professional breast examination.
- Routine mammography as determined by the physician based on risk factors and medical/family history.

the shoulders, neck, and back. As a cosmetic procedure, breasts may be reduced to allow the female to wear normal clothes. A reconstructive process for medical purposes may be covered by insurance. Many patients require counseling to adjust to their new image.

The female with small breasts may seek breast augmentation. Implants come in a variety of shapes and types. Implants all come in a form made of Elastomer, which is a rubber-like silicone material. The implant can be filled with gel, saline, silicone/saline combination, PVP-Hydrogel, or even natural plant oil. The shape of the implant can be round or anatomic, also known as teardrop shape. Breast implants have been available since 1976, but it was not until 1992 that they were regulated by the FDA as medical devices. Patients are advised that complications are possible, including pain, capsular contractures, and infection. Any patient who desires a surgical alteration in appearance may benefit from counseling before and after the procedure.

TABLE 26-5 SEXUALLY TRANSMITTED DISEASES

Condition	Signs and Symptoms	Causative Agent	Diagnosis	Treatment
Candidiasis	Irritation, itching, thick white vaginal discharge; often occurs in immunocompromised patients or following antibiotic therapy	*Candida albicans*	Microscopic examination	Antifungal creams or suppositories, including myconazole, clotrimazole, nystatin
Chlamydia	Usually asymptomatic before complications	*Chlamydia trachomatis*	Swab cultures, Giemsa stain, serologic testing for antibodies	Oral antibiotics, including doxycycline and erythromycin
Genital herpes	Painful, blister-like lesions in genital region; systemic influenza symptoms, including fever, headache, swollen glands; possible painful urination	Herpes simplex virus type 2 (HSV 2)	Observation of lesions, tissue culture	No cure; symptom relief with antiviral medications such as acyclovir, famcyclovir, and valacyclovir
Genital warts (condylomata acuminata)	Warts on genitalia; burning, itching lesions	Human papillomavirus (HPV)	Observation of warts, potential biopsy to rule out cancer/carcinoma	Chemical or surgical removal
Gonorrhea	Purulent discharge from GU tract; painful urination; occasionally asymptomatic	*Neisseria gonorrhoeae*	Gram stain of discharge	Antibiotics (penicillin, tetracycline, ceftriaxone)
Syphilis	Painless chancre(s) on genitalia	*Treponema pallidum*	Microscopic examination of smear with causative organism	Penicillin G
Trichomoniasis	Mainly asymptomatic; possible profuse green-yellow discharge	*Trichomonas vaginalis*	Wet prep slide and microscopic visualization of causative organism; urinalysis	Anti-infective medications

Theory

It is important for women to learn and practice monthly breast self-examination. Breast cancer has a high mortality rate in women with or without risk factors. During their lifetime, 12 percent of women will receive a diagnosis of breast cancer. Over 8 percent will be women without risk factors. Early diagnosis and treatment of malignancies increase survival rates. Patients should be taught how to reduce risk factors and encouraged to follow a preventive and healthier lifestyle.

Women who practice monthly breast self-examinations are more likely to seek medical treatment when they notice breast changes. Changes in appearance and tissue density may be subtle or obvious. Breast lumps may or may not be malignant, but medical management is necessary to monitor and treat the patient for changes that may become malignant later. You will use printed materials, videos, and artificial breast models to educate the patient. It is important to emphasize consistent times and techniques for the monthly exam to ensure that it is performed thoroughly and correctly. Breast inspection is done with the patient standing in front of a mirror, with her arms in different positions, then lying flat or on her side. She should start with the same breast and follow the same palpation search pattern (vertical strip, wedge, or circular) each time, to ensure that all areas are examined. Palpation is done in small, circular motions with the fingertip pads, which are more sensitive to abnormalities or differences in tissue.

Materials

- Patient chart
- Educational materials such as patient brochures or breast models

Competency

(**Conditions**) With the necessary materials, (**Task**) you will be able to instruct the patient in the performance of breast self-examination (**Standards**) correctly within 30 minutes.

1. Wash your hands and gather the necessary supplies.
2. Escort the patient to the patient education area.
3. Emphasize the following habits for the monthly self-exam.
   A. Premenopausal women should perform the examination about one week after the menstrual period, when the breasts are not swollen. Postmenopausal women should select a specific date of the month.
   B. Perform a visual inspection while standing in front of a mirror. With the arms hanging at the sides, above the head, or forward, away from the body, or with the hands positioned on the hips, observe for bilateral similarities or differences, for color or texture changes in the skin and nipples, and for nipple discharge (Figure 26-7 ◆).
   C. Examine each breast in side-lying and flat positions, starting with the same breast each time (Figures 26-8 ◆) For the flat position, place a pillow under the shoulder on each side.
   D. Palpate each breast with the fingertip pads of the opposite hand, using a dime-sized, circular motion (Figure 26-9 ◆). Use the same search pattern of vertical strip, wedge, or circle search for both breasts.
   E. Finish the breast examination by squeezing for nipple discharge and palpating the breast into the axillary area.
   F. Report any abnormalities or changes to the physician.
4. Document your patient instruction in breast self-examination. Note the patient's level of understanding.
5. Perform any necessary cleaning of teaching models and store for the next patient use.

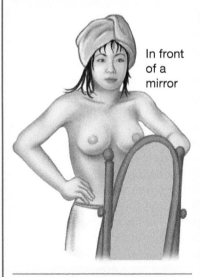

Figure 26-7 ◆ Perform a visual inspection while standing in front of a mirror.

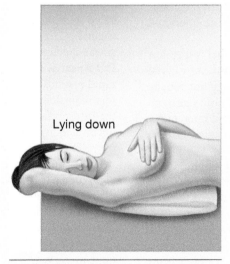

Figure 26-8 ◆ Patient in side-lying position for breast self-exam.

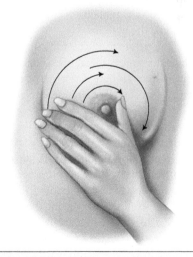

Figure 26-9 ◆ Palpate each breast in a circular motion.

continued

PROCEDURE 26-2 Instruct the Patient in Breast Self-Examination *(continued)*

Patient Education

Reinforce patient education materials with verbal instruction and demonstration. Ask the patient to perform a return demonstration. Encourage questions.

Charting Example

6/7/XX 11:00 AM Patient given written materials, verbal instruction, and demonstration on breast self-examination. Patient gave return demonstration correctly without questions. Edward Lee, RMA.

Routine Assessment

Assessment of the female patient in the medical office includes the following:

- taking a complete history: menstrual, obstetrical, surgical, and drug therapy history
- measuring weight and height, blood pressure, and temperature (if infection may be present)
- performing a UCG for women of child-bearing age and capability
- assessing vaginal bleeding

The pelvic exam and the Pap test are usually performed annually and are routine before oral or dermal forms of birth control are prescribed or prescriptions are renewed. A pelvic exam must be performed when vaginal bleeding, pelvic pain, and/or discharge is present. You will assist both the patient and the physician during the exam.

Diagnostic Procedures

Many diagnostic tests are typically performed in the OB/GYN office. You may perform certain tests or assist the physician with others.

- Urine tests can be used to determine if a patient is pregnant. Urine specimens from pregnant patients are tested for the presence of protein and glucose (sugar). The presence of

PROCEDURE 26-3 Assist the Physician in the Performance of a Pelvic Examination and Pap Test

Theory

Breast and pelvic exams help to assess the patient's health and diagnose disease conditions. Although both procedures are performed at the annual gynecological examination, specific patient symptoms or presenting complaints may warrant one examination without the other. Your role is to assist the physician as well as to explain the procedure and provide emotional support to the patient.

The pelvic examination consists of a visual inspection of the external genitalia, bimanual pelvic and rectal-vaginal examinations, and the Pap test. The patient should not douche or engage in sexual intercourse during the 48 hours prior to the Pap test. Douching alters the vaginal pH, and intercourse may cause inflammatory changes that affect the quality of the specimen and the accuracy of the test results.

In addition to gathering vital signs and weight, documenting details of the reason for the office visit, and charting allergies, you will ask the patient to void to prevent the discomfort of a full bladder during the examination. A general explanation of the procedure will also alleviate some of the patient's fear and anxiety. Generally, you will instruct the patient to change into a gown and place a cover across the body from the waist down. You will also provide privacy for the patient to change. You may need to stay and offer assistance to some patients during changing or positioning for the procedure.

As the physician performs the Pap test, the bimanual exam, and the rectal-vaginal examination, in that order, you must anticipate his or her needs and have materials prepared ahead of time to ensure that the procedure continues in a professional, efficient manner.

There are two different methods for obtaining specimens during a Pap and pelvic examination: the slide method and the thin-prep method. In the slide method, slides are labeled with the patient's identification and the letters *V* (for vaginal), *C* (cervical), or *E* (endocervical) to indicate where the smear specimen was obtained. Correlating the results of the Pap smear with the location will ensure more accurate and rapid diagnosis and treatment. When completing the laboratory requisition, indicate information that would be helpful to the interpretation of results, such as abnormal bleeding or hormonal, thyroid, steroid, and digitalis medications.

The thin-prep method involves collecting the specimen from the posterior fornix by scraping it with a plastic spatula. When a sufficient sample has been collected on the spatula, the spatula is rinsed by swirling for approximately 10 minutes in a solution specific for the thin-prep procedure. The vial of solution is then closed tightly and sent to the cytology department as soon as possible. Methanol-based solutions preserve the patient cells for approximately 3 weeks at room temperature.

The physician inserts the vaginal speculum to observe the vagina and cervix and obtain the Pap smears. After withdrawing the speculum, the physician lubricates the index and middle fingers of a gloved hand and inserts the fingers into the

PROCEDURE 26-3 Assist the Physician in the Performance of a Pelvic Examination and Pap Test *(continued)*

vagina while pressing on the lower abdomen with the other hand. This bimanual technique is used to palpate the uterus and ovaries to assess normalcy or changes that might indicate a disease condition (Figure 26-10 ◆). Last, for the rectal-vaginal examination, the physician inserts one gloved finger into the vagina and the gloved finger of the other hand into the rectum to assess for normalcy or disease conditions of the fallopian tubes, ovaries, ligaments of the uterus, and other pelvic organs. Hemorrhoids, fissures, or fistulas may also be diagnosed during the rectal-vaginal examination.

Materials

- Patient chart
- Examination gloves
- Water-soluble lubricant
- Physician's gown and eye protection
- Vaginal speculum
- Gooseneck or other light source
- Slide container, glass slides, marker to label slides, and slide fixative for Pap smear
- Cervical/spatula scraper
- Cotton-tipped applicators
- Lab requisition form

Competency

(**Conditions**) With the necessary materials, (**Task**) you will be able to assist the physician during the performance of a pelvic examination and Pap test (**Standards**) correctly within 30 minutes.

1. Wash your hands and assemble the equipment. Label the slide containers with patient information. Label the frosted edge of each slide with patient information and the location from which the specimen was taken.
2. Identify the patient and escort her to the examination room. Obtain the mensuration required by the physician (usually weight, temperature, blood pressure, pulse, and respirations).
3. Interview the patient for the following information:
   A. chief complaint (reason for visit)
   B. medications and known allergies
   C. start date of last menstrual period
   D. date of most recent Pap smear
4. Explain the procedure to the patient.
5. Before the procedure, assist the patient to the bathroom to void.
6. When the patient returns to the examination room, instruct her to remove clothing from the waist down. Assist as necessary. Provide a drape for the body from the waist down. If a breast examination is also to be performed, the patient will need to completely disrobe. Provide a gown cover for the chest area as well. The patient may sit on the examination table or lie comfortably until the physician arrives.
7. When the physician is present, assist the patient into a supine/dorsal recumbent position if a breast exam is to be performed. Slide the patient toward the stirrups and into the lithotomy position for the remainder of the pelvic examination and the Pap test.
8. Observe the patient's tolerance of the procedure and hand the slides, cervical/spatula scraper, and cotton-tipped

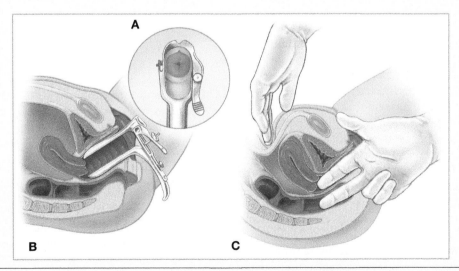

Figure 26-10 ◆ (A) and (B) The physician performs a pelvic examination of a female patient using a vaginal speculum; (C) Bimanual technique

continued

PROCEDURE 26-3 Assist the Physician in the Performance of a Pelvic Examination and Pap Test (continued)

applicators to the physician for the Pap smear. After the physician has placed the specimen on the slides, immediately spray or apply ethyl alcohol liquid fixative. Give the physician water-soluble lubricant for the pelvic examination.

9. When the procedure has been completed, assist the patient to a sitting position. Leave the room to allow her to dress in private, or assist if necessary.

10. Remove the used implements to the cleaning area. Dispose of disposable and biohazardous materials in the appropriate containers. Wash your hands.

11. Transport the labeled specimen to the laboratory, or arrange for transport, with the appropriate lab requisitions. Assist the patient with the scheduling of additional procedures, if necessary.

12. Document the patient's response to the procedure, any future appointments, and other patient information, including prescriptions or patient instruction.

Patient Education

If this is the patient's first visit for an annual pelvic examination, instruct her as to office procedure and her responsibility in scheduling subsequent visits. Also instruct her to call the office if any unusual vaginal or lower abdominal problems occur.

Charting Example

03/29/XX 2:30 PM Explained procedure to patient. Patient sent to bathroom to empty bladder. Patient required no assistance during examination. Instructions given to call office in two weeks for results and/or appointment in two weeks. Patient filled out reminder postcard for next year's appointment. Kimberly Rainer, RMA.

Keys to Success
CULTURAL CONSIDERATIONS

In some cultures, female patients are prohibited from disrobing in view of others. A woman may not be examined by a male physician, or the husband must be present in the room during any examination or treatment. These customs must be honored. The physician will generally provide guidance in how to handle this situation.

protein may indicate impending toxemia of pregnancy; elevated glucose levels may indicate gestational diabetes. These screening procedures are performed along with weight and blood pressure measurement.

■ A colposcopy is a special examination of the vagina and cervix with an optical magnifying instrument. It allows for a microscopic view of the cervix. The physician usually performs the cervical biopsy during this procedure when a Pap smear report indicates cervical dysplasia.

■ Patients experiencing heavy or unusual bleeding may have blood tests for hemoglobin and hematocrit.

■ During the course of the pregnancy, specific diagnostic testing may be ordered. A routine blood test is alpha-fetoprotein (**AFT**) screening for possible neural tube defects, performed between the fifteenth and eighteenth weeks. If results are elevated above acceptable levels, additional testing includes ultrasound examination and **amniocentesis.**

■ Glucose tolerance testing is now becoming routine as a part of the prenatal screening process and is useful in the detection of gestational diabetes.

■ The use of ultrasound during a pregnancy as well as to assess gynecological conditions is becoming more common. The age and sex of the fetus and possible congenital

conditions are often determined during an ultrasonic examination (∞ see Chapter 16). Ultrasounds are performed prior to and during amniocentesis, to determine the location of the placenta and fetal structures. After the area is anesthetized with local anesthetic, a needle is introduced into the uterus to withdraw a sample of amniotic fluid that is then analyzed in the laboratory.

■ Pap smears are performed as a screening process for cervical cancer. During a pelvic examination, the physician uses a special, thin wooden cervical spatula and a cervical brush to obtain cells from the cervix and the cervical canal. These cells are sent to a laboratory, where they are examined for the presence of cancer cells. Annual Pap smears help to detect cervical cancer in its early stages.

Treatment Modalities

Dysplasia of the cervix may be treated in a number of ways. The abnormal tissue is destroyed by chemicals (silver nitrate) or electricity (cautery). Another treatment method is cryocauterization, cellular destruction by cold (in this case, freezing with liquid nitrogen).

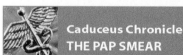

Caduceus Chronicle
THE PAP SMEAR

Dr. George Papanicolaou, a Greek physician who immigrated to the United States, first presented his research work on the use of cell scrapings to diagnose cervical cancer in 1928. By the late 1940s the Pap smear was widely accepted as a screening method for the early stages of cervical cancer. Since then the Pap test has become a routine gynecological procedure for millions of women, and deaths from cervical cancer have been greatly reduced.

PROCEDURE 26-4 Perform a Urine Pregnancy Test

Theory

When a pregnancy occurs, the placenta begins to develop, providing a filter between the mother and fetus for the remainder of the pregnancy. The placenta secretes a hormone called human chorionic gonadotropin (hCG) into the blood serum or urine. In a urine test, it is the presence of this hormone that confirms a pregnancy.

Pregnancy tests are one of the few diagnostic tools that can be purchased over-the-counter for patient use at home. Many pregnancy tests are so sensitive to the hormone hCG that a pregnancy can be detected as early as five days after conception. Any test performed at home should be evaluated by a medical office.

Materials

- gloves
- urine sample
- hCG test
- hCG positive urine control
- hCG negative urine control
- timer
- disinfectant
- patient chart

Competency

(**Conditions**) With the necessary materials, you will be able to (**Task**) test a patient's urine for the presence of hCG (**Standards**) within 5 minutes.

1. Assemble all necessary equipment.
2. Wash your hands and put on gloves.
3. Follow the manufacturer's directions for using the negative control serum.
4. Follow the manufacturer's directions for using the positive control serum.
5. When you are satisfied that the tests are reliable, test the patient's urine sample.

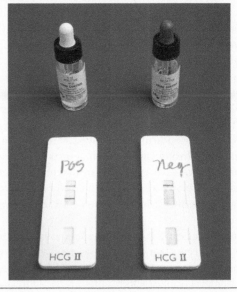

Figure 26-11 ◆ A urine pregnancy control test- positive and negative

6. Report the results to the physician (Figure 26-11 ◆).
7. Disinfect the work area.
8. Document the test and results in the patient's chart.

Patient Education

Keep in mind that not every pregnancy is a planned or positive event. Be sympathetic to the patient's needs and have appropriate contact numbers available for reference to counselors or other professionals.

Charting Example

04/28/XX 9:41 AM hCG urine test performed. Patient tested positive and was given results by Dr. King. Bryan Gross, RMA.

Gynecological surgical procedures are usually done in a clinical or hospital setting and include dilatation and curettage, laparoscopic procedures, tubal ligations and abdominal or vaginal hysterectomies, oophorectomies, and/or salpingectomies. Surgical intervention to suspend a prolapsed uterus or repair a cystocele or rectocele are other gynecological procedures. Obstetrical procedures include episiotomy (incision in the perineum to facilitate delivery of the infant) and C-section (Cesarean section).

- Dilatation and curettage (D&C) is a surgical procedure in which the cervix is dilated and the lining of the uterus

(endometrium) is scraped with a curette. This procedure is performed to obtain tissue for diagnosis of some uterine diseases, to treat prolonged or painful uterine bleeding, or to empty the uterus of products of conception (usually after a miscarriage).

- Laparoscopic procedures are surgical procedures performed with a laparoscope to view internal body structures with very small incisions. Organs and tissue can be removed or repaired by this method, which does not involve a surgical opening into the abdominal cavity.
- A tubal ligation is a surgical procedure in which both fallopian tubes are ligated, usually with a laser, and both

ends of each tube are cauterized. This procedure can be done through a small abdominal incision with a laparoscope and is often performed within two days post delivery. A tubal ligation is a permanent form of contraception, as it prevents the sperm from meeting the egg for fertilization. Reversal is generally not successful, although there are recorded instances of females conceiving after a tubal ligation.

- A hysterectomy is the surgical removal of the uterus. In a total abdominal hysterectomy (or bilateral salpingo-oophorectomy), the surgeon removes the uterus, cervix, both fallopian tubes, and both ovaries. In a vaginal hysterectomy the uterus is removed through the vagina rather than through an abdominal incision. Some physicians elect to leave a cervical stump intact, and sometimes one ovary or a portion of an ovary is left to produce female hormones. Menses cease with the removal of the uterus.
- An oophorectomy is the surgical removal of one ovary. The remaining ovary continues to ovulate regularly, menses continue, and the female can achieve pregnancy. In a bilateral oophorectomy, often referred to as surgical menopause, both ovaries are removed. The female no longer ovulates, hormones are not produced to stimulate the normal menstrual cycle, and menses cease. Many physicians order hormone replacement therapy to begin while the patient is in the recovery room to prevent or reduce symptoms of surgical menopause.

- A salpingectomy is the surgical removal of one fallopian tube. Bilateral salpingectomy is the removal of both tubes.
- A & P repair (anterior and posterior repair) is a procedure to correct a cystocele and a rectocele.
- A cesarean section (C-section) is a surgical procedure in which an incision is made either midline in the abdomen or lower on the abdomen and into the uterus to deliver the baby. This procedure is performed when the infant is too large to pass through the mother's pelvis, when it is in fetal distress, when the mother's life is in danger and immediate delivery is mandatory, or when the mother has had previous C-sections.
- An episiotomy is an incision made in the perineum to facilitate the delivery of an infant.

Cryosurgery

Cryosurgery is a technique that uses liquid nitrogen, which has an extremely low temperature, to freeze tissue so that it dies and sloughs off, to be replaced eventually by healthy tissue. Cryosurgery is performed to treat cervicitis, cervical erosion, and venereal warts.

PROCEDURE 26-5 Assist with Cryosurgery

Theory

Cryosurgery is performed with the patient in the lithotomy position. It is an uncomfortable procedure, and the patient should be made as comfortable as possible. Offer the patient a pillow for her head and remind her to take slow, deep breaths. Once she is in position, the physician will swab the cervix to remove mucus. The liquid nitrogen probe will be placed against the affected area as the liquid nitrogen flows over the area and freezes the tissue. The patient will feel pain similar to menstrual cramps. She should remain still and continue slow, deep breathing for pain control.

Materials

- gloves
- patient drapes
- light source
- liquid nitrogen
- vaginal speculum
- sterile specimen container (if needed)
- patient chart

Competency

(**Conditions**) With the necessary materials, you will be able to (**Task**) assist with a cryosurgery (**Standards**) within the time limits set by the instructor.

1. Verify the patient's identification.
2. Explain the procedure to the patient.
3. Wash your hands and put on gloves.
4. If necessary, assist the patient in undressing from the waist down. Provide proper patient drapes.
5. When the patient is undressed and draped, assist her into the lithotomy position.
6. Assist the physician as needed.
7. Reassure the patient that as the probe moves over the affected tissue and the liquid nitrogen freezes and kills the tissue, she will feel some discomfort, similar to menstrual cramping. The discomfort should not be unbearable, however.
8. After the procedure, assist the patient to a seated position and help her dress as needed.
9. Clean and disinfect the room.

Patient Education

Instruct the patient in post-cryosurgery care:

- Expect a heavy discharge for up to four weeks. It should have a clear, watery consistency.
- Cleanse the perineal area often.
- Use only sanitary napkins, not tampons or other devices that must be inserted, such as silicone cups.
- Remain on full cervical/pelvic rest for four weeks—no douching, tampon use, or sexual intercourse.

PROCEDURE 26-5 **Assist with Cryosurgery** *(continued)*

- Report any signs of infection such as vomiting, foul-smelling discharge, pain, or fever.
- The next menstrual cycle will be heavier than usual. This is normal.

Charting Example

04/28/XX 9:41 AM Cryosurgery performed for chronic cervicitis. Patient reported slight cramping for 20-30 minutes and was monitored. Vital signs remained stable and patient was released home. Patient received postoperative care instructions, both verbal and written. Diane Edwards, CMA

Psychological Considerations

Many psychologically sensitive issues are addressed in the OB/GYN office. It is important to listen with compassion to patients and their families as they present with various problems. Consider the following examples:

- Couples attempting to achieve a successful pregnancy or experiencing fertility problems often undergo a severe emotional, physical, and financial drain.
- Hormonal changes during the menstrual cycle, such as PMS, may disrupt the patient's emotional stability.

Menopause also has a tendency to create emotional turmoil.
- The diagnosis of cancer of any of the female reproductive structures not only intensifies the fear of death but also stimulates feelings of loss of femininity.
- Parents who have multiple fetuses or infants from the same pregnancy may face a myriad of stressful problems.
- The single mother faces many challenges. Understanding and tolerance are crucial when dealing with this patient.

Caduceus Chronicle
THE EVOLUTION OF THE MODERN DELIVERY ROOM AND BIRTHING CENTERS

In the late nineteenth century, most babies in the United States were born at home, where family and friends surrounded the mother and a midwife assisted her. With the advent of chloroform anesthesia, women in labor were encouraged to go to a hospital for the birth. As obstetric medicine progressed and other forms of anesthesia were developed, the mother generally went through labor in the hospital labor room, surrounded by medical personnel, and the expectant father was banished to the waiting area. The mother was often heavily sedated and restrained in the delivery room during the birth. The sedative often passed through to the fetus, resulting in a groggy newborn who had to be watched closely for the first 24 hours. The mother, also groggy, was typically unable to care for the baby for the first day or so, and the baby was kept in the newborn nursery.

In the 1940s an English physician, Dr. Grantly Dick-Reed, promoted the use of self-hypnosis and relaxation techniques during labor to break the cycle of fear, tension, and pain. Many women who used this technique were able to labor and give birth without pain medications.

In the early 1950s Dr. Fernand Lamaze, a French obstetrician, promoted "painless childbirth" through prenatal classes, relaxation and breathing techniques, and the involvement of the father as "coach" in the labor and delivery process. The mother remained fully awake, and the father was allowed to hold his newborn child. Rooming-in became the norm as both parents were involved in caring for the infant in the mother's room.

Parents now insist on full involvement in the birthing process. Although many babies are still born in a sterile hospital environment, more and more are being born in birthing centers or at home. Family members and midwives attend many of these births. The father or another family member may cut the umbilical cord and siblings can be present during the birth. In the past 100 years, the birthing process has come full circle.

Chapter Summary

- The OB/GYN practice focuses on the female reproductive system. Obstetrics specifically addresses pregnancy and childbirth. The expectant mother and developing fetus are monitored throughout the pregnancy during routine prenatal visits. The obstetrician assists the mother during a normal vaginal delivery and with any surgical intervention in the course of the delivery. The gynecology practice addresses diseases and disorders of the female reproductive system. Either the obstetrician or the gynecologist may address fertility problems.

- The medical assistant in the OB/GYN office obtains the patient's OB/GYN history and vital signs, assists the physician with pelvic examinations (including obtaining the Pap smear and other specimens), and instructs the patient in breast self-examination, nutritional requirements, labor and delivery, breast and formula feeding, and caring for the newborn infant.

- Mammary glands develop during puberty but remain nonfunctional until the end of a pregnancy. Following birth, colostrum and breast milk are the sources of nutrition and passive immunity for the newborn.

- As the female approaches adolescence, hormonal changes stimulate the onset of menses (menarche). Hormones influence the development, maturation, and release of an ovum (egg) for fertilization and implantation. If the egg is not fertilized or the fertilized egg is not implanted, menstrual flow takes place to cleanse, or shed, the endometrial lining and prepare the uterus and body for the next potential pregnancy.

- Menopause, or the cessation of the menses, usually occurs at 45 to 55 years of age because of aging and the decline of ovarian function. A surgical procedure called a hysterectomy also induces menopause.

- Disorders relating to the menstrual cycle include dysmenorrhea (painful menstruation), amenorrhea (lack of menstruation), menorrhagia (heavy menses), metrorrhagia (irregular menses), mittelschmertz (pain during ovulation), and premenstrual syndrome (PMS).

- The OB/GYN office provides contraception information and prescriptions. Contraception, or birth control, may be achieved with barriers, chemical contact, hormonal control, intrauterine devices, surgical sterilization and periodic sexual abstinence.

- Couples having difficulty conceiving are diagnosed with an infertility problem. Treatment varies but can include hormone treatment for the female to stimulate release of ova, as well as in-vitro fertilization and implantation.

- During the initial prenatal visit, an obstetrical history is obtained, including such information as age at menarche, frequency and duration of menstrual periods, total number of pregnancies, surgical procedures, sexually transmitted diseases, dates of last mammogram and Pap smear, blood type, medications, and so on.

- The routine prenatal visit includes measuring blood pressure and weight, checking the urine specimen for protein and glucose, and assessing fetal heart tones (FHT) and fetal position. The physician measures fundal height. Other areas may be addressed as well, depending on the clinical progression of the pregnancy and the mother's condition.

- Most pregnancies progress without complications. Problems that may arise include hyperemesis gravidarum; spontaneous abortion or miscarriage; ectopic or tubal pregnancy; hydatidiform mole; toxemia, either pre-eclampsia or eclampsia; placenta previa; abruptio placenta; and premature labor and delivery.

- Conditions affecting the female reproductive system include ovarian, tubal, uterine, or vaginal disorders, as well as sexual dysfunction and sexually transmitted diseases. Any structure in the system may be the site of the disorder.

- Cancer of the female reproductive system includes ovarian cancer, uterine or endometrial cancer, cervical cancer, labial cancer, and breast cancer. Screening for cervical cancer is routinely done with a Pap smear, breast cancer screening with monthly breast self-examinations and annual mammograms. A physical examination (pelvic or breast) and a biopsy confirm the diagnosis. Some blood tests may indicate the presence of cancer cells. Treatment in most cases includes surgical excision, chemotherapy, and/or radiation.

- Ovarian cysts, pelvic inflammatory disease, endometriosis, uterine fibroids, uterine prolapse, cystocele, and rectocele are other gynecological diseases and disorders. Sexually transmitted diseases (STDs) or venereal diseases affect both males and females and are transmitted during sex by blood, semen, or vaginal secretions.

- The female breast is prone to fibrocystic changes, mastitis, carcinoma, diminutive size, and pendulous size. A small painless lump in the breast often is the first sign of breast cancer, which is further diagnosed by mammogram and confirmed by biopsy. Treatment is usually lumpectomy or mastectomy, chemotheraphy, and/or radiation. All women should learn and practice monthly breast self-examination to detect the first signs of breast cancer.

- Breast reduction is performed on extremely pendulous breasts to relieve pain and discomfort or as a cosmetic procedure. Small breasts may be augmented with implants.

- Diagnostic procedures include urine tests, colposcopies, fetal ultrasounds, phlebotomy testing, and amniocentesis.

- Cervical dysplasia may be treated by cautery or cryocauterization. Gynecological surgical procedures in a clinic or hospital setting include D & C, laparoscopic procedures, tubal ligations, abdominal or vaginal hysterectomies, oophorectomies and/or salpingectomies, surgical fixation for suspension of a prolapsed uterus, and repair of cystocele or rectocele. Obstetrical procedures include episiotomy and C-section.

- Psychological issues are also addressed in the OB/GYN office. It is important to listen to patients and their families and provide emotional support.

Chapter Review Questions

Multiple Choice

1. The lining of the uterus is called a/an:
   A. menses
   B. menarche
   C. endometrium
   D. colostrum

2. The practice of gynecology addresses:
   A. STDs
   B. vaginal disorders
   C. sexual disorders
   D. all of the above

3. The internal lining of the uterus is called a/an:
   A. endometrium
   B. myometrium
   C. perimetrium
   D. cervimetrium

4. The projections on the distal portions of the fallopian tubes are called:
   A. Bartholin's glands
   B. fimbriae
   C. perineum
   D. myometrium

5. The glands on either side of the vaginal orifice are known as:
   A. lactiferous
   B. perineum
   C. Bartholin's glands
   D. fimbriae

6. Which of the following hormones is responsible for the secretion of colostrum in the breasts?
   A. prolactin
   B. oxytocin
   C. estrogen
   D. progesterone

7. The union of male and female sex cells produces a/an:
   A. ovum
   B. zygote
   C. fetus
   D. embryo

8. A woman who has not menstruated for more than six months has a condition called:
   A. dysmenorrhea
   B. mittelschmertz
   C. metrorrhagia
   D. amenorrhea

9. Cervical disorders include:
   A. PID
   B. dysplasia
   C. endometriosis
   D. fibroids

10. Often the first sign of breast cancer is:
    A. a small, painless lump
    B. a small, painful lump
    C. a large, painless lump
    D. a large, painful lump

True/False

T F   1. Fibrocystic disease, mastitis, and cancer are all breast disorders.

T F   2. Breast implants have been available since 1978, but it was not until 1990 that they were regulated by the FDA as medical devices.

T F   3. During their lifetime, 12 percent of women will receive a diagnosis of breast cancer.

T F   4. The pelvic examination consists of a visual inspection of the external genitalia, bimanual pelvic and rectal-vaginal examinations, and the Pap test.

T F   5. Slides prepared during a Pap smear should be labeled with the patient's identification and the letters *V* (for vaginal), *C* (cervical), or *E* (external) to indicate where the smear specimen was obtained.

Short Answer

1. List three ways in which dysplasia of the cervix is treated.

2. What is the medical term for the surgical removal of one ovary?

3. For which two substances are urine specimens from pregnant patients tested?

4. What is a colposcopy?

5. What is the difference between uterine prolapse and cystocele?

Research

1. Where in your local area can pregnant women locate a doula?

2. Are there support groups in your community for women with breast cancer?

3. In your state, at what age can a minor legally obtain birth control without the consent of her parents?

Externship Application Experience

As an extern, you escort a married Muslim woman to the examination room. She is accompanied by her husband. As you attempt to obtain her medical history, her husband answers all your questions. After instructing her to remove her clothing and put on a patient gown, you leave the room. Five minutes later you return and find the woman sitting in a chair completely dressed. You ascertain that her husband will not allow the male physician to examine his wife. What do you do?

Resource Guide

American Cancer Society
1599 Clifton Rd
Atlanta, GA 30329
1-800-ACS-2345
www.cancer.org

American College of Obstetricians and Gynecologists (ACOG)
409 12 St S.W., PO Box 96920
Washington, DC 20090-6920
1-800-673-8444
www.acog.com

Endometriosis Association
8585 N. 76th Place
Milwaukee, WI 53223
1-800-992-3636 or 414-355-2200
www.endometriosisassn.org

Chicago Office
1 Oakbrook Terrace #808
Oakbrook Terrace, IL 60181
1-630-627-9270

National Alliance of Breast Cancer Associations
9 E. 37th St., 10th floor
New York, NY 10016
www.nabco.org

North American Menopause Society
PO Box 94527
Cleveland, OH 44101
216-844-8748
info@menopause.org

Planned Parenthood Federation of America, Inc.
434 W. 33rd St
New York, NY 10001
212-541-7800
www.ppfa.org/ppfa

MedMedia
www.prenhall.com/frazier

More on this chapter, including interactive resources, can be found on the Student CD-ROM accompanying this textbook and on the Companion Website at www.prenhall.com/frazier.

Objectives

After completing this chapter, you should be able to:

- Spell and define the medical terminology in this chapter.
- Define the medical assistant's role in a pediatric specialty office.
- Discuss the physical and developmental factors relating to the age of the child.
- List the procedures that may be performed during a well-child visit.
- Explain the role of growth measurement in the routine or well-child visit.
- List recommended child immunizations and possible side effects.
- Discuss common contagious diseases of childhood.
- List and describe childhood disorders caused by neural tube defects.
- List and describe congenital heart conditions that affect children.
- List and describe common pediatric blood disorders.
- List and describe diagnostic procedures used with pediatric patients.
- Describe different techniques used to position and secure the child for examination and treatment.
- Describe pediatric urine specimen collection.

Pediatrics

Case Study

Lucas has just finished checking in his first patient of the afternoon, a 6-month-old girl, and is preparing to weigh her. After the mother removes the child's diaper, Lucas observes a thick, raised rash. The mother explains that her daughter has had a diaper rash that "just won't go away" and that when she gave her the prescribed medication, thick white patches appeared in the child's mouth. So the mother stopped giving the medication after the first couple of days.

MedMedia
www.prenhall.com/frazier

Additional interactive resources and activities for this chapter can be found on the Companion Website. For videos, audio glossary, legal and ethical scenarios, job scenarios, quizzes, and games related to the content of this chapter, please access the accompanying CD-ROM in this book.

 **Assets Available:**

Audio Glossary
Legal and Ethical Scenario: *Pediatrics*
On the Job Scenario: *Pediatrics*
Video Scenario: Pediatrics
Multiple Choice Quiz
Games: Crossword, Strikeout and Spelling Bee

Medical Terminology

acyanotic—pertaining to an absence of cyanosis

cyanotic—characterized by cyanosis, or a blue tint in the skin, which indicates reduced blood oxygen

fontanelle—"soft spot" on the cranium of a newborn or infant; area of the skull that is not covered by bone at birth but where the cranial bones eventually come together, allowing for the growth of the brain and skull

lavage—washing out of a cavity

pediatrician—physician who specializes in treating children from birth to age 20

pediatrics—medical specialty that focuses on the care and treatment of children from birth through age 20

Abbreviations

FAS—fetal alcohol syndrome

MMR—measles-mumps-rubella vaccine

RSV—respiratory syncytial virus

VIS—vaccination information sheet

✚ MEDICAL ASSISTING COMPETENCIES

CAAHEP ENTRY-LEVEL COMPETENCIES FOR CMA	ABHES ENTRY-LEVEL COMPETENCIES FOR RMA
■ Identify and respond to issues of confidentiality.	■ Project a positive attitude.
■ Perform within legal and ethical boundaries.	■ Maintain confidentiality at all times.
■ Demonstrate knowledge of federal and state health-care legislation and regulations.	■ Be a "team player."
	■ Be cognizant of ethical boundaries.
■ Perform hand washing.	■ Exhibit initiative.
■ Dispose of biohazardous materials.	■ Adapt to change.
■ Practice Standard Precautions.	■ Evidence a responsible attitude.
■ Use methods of quality control.	■ Be courteous and diplomatic.
■ Perform microbiology testing.	■ Conduct work within scope of education, training, and ability.
■ Screen and follow up test results.	■ Practice Standard Precautions.
■ Obtain vital signs.	■ Use quality control.
■ Prepare patient for and assist with routine and specialty examinations.	■ Dispose of biohazardous materials.
■ Prepare patients for and assist with procedures, treatments, and minor office surgeries.	■ Take vital signs.
	■ Prepare patients for procedures.
■ Apply pharmacology principles to prepare and administer oral and parenteral medications.	■ Assist physician with examinations and treatments.
■ Maintain medication and immunization records.	■ Prepare and administer medications as directed by physician.
	■ Maintain medication records.

Introduction

A **pediatrician** is a physician who specializes in treating children from birth to age 20. A primary care physician may also see pediatric patients. Early care is important for the evaluation of growth and development as well as for disease prevention and diagnosis. A **pediatrics** practice involves wellness and illness, and visits are categorized as well child or sick child. A well-child visit comprises health maintenance, including routine inoculations. During a sick-child visit, symptoms are assessed and treatment is prescribed. Additional checkups may be required for school, sports, or camp.

The Medical Assistant's Role in Pediatrics

As a medical assistant in a pediatric office, you will:

- Obtain the child's health and developmental history
- Take and record vital signs
- Measure and record growth

- Assist parents in undressing the child if necessary
- Assist the physician during the physical examination and treatment
- Help the parents restrain the child if necessary
- Obtain a urine specimen
- Administer medication injections and immunizations

Children ages zero through 20 go through many changes over time. A child's ability to understand medical care and treatment is based on his or her developmental, mental, and emotional stages. As an MA, you must be sensitive to emotions such as fear, mistrust, and embarrassment. Listen to the parent or guardian and respect his or her instincts and observations. Presenting symptoms may be subtle. A parent's finely tuned understanding of the child can provide vital clues, such as changes in the child's appetite, sleep habits, cry, mental alertness and energy levels, and fussiness. Avoid labeling a seriously concerned and anxious parent or guardian as neurotic or overbearing.

A parent or guardian should be allowed and encouraged to stay with the child unless his or her presence hinders effective care. When necessary, the parent or guardian may be asked to leave or be escorted from the room.

Never take a child from the parent. When weighing a child, ask the parent to place the child on the scales and stand nearby, reassuring the child. If the child can be held during a portion of the examination, encourage the parent do so. Show the parent how to hold the child during the examination.

Never tell a child "This will not hurt" when a potentially painful procedure is about to be done. Always be truthful. Reassure the parent or guardian about the procedure.

Consider how big and threatening you may look to a child. Whenever possible, get down to the child's eye level when conversing. Sitting in a chair while obtaining the history is helpful.

If a child feels uncomfortable and threatened when clothing needs to be removed, provide covering in the form of a drape, gown, or sheet. Let the child keep a security blanket or any other security item he or she has brought along, such as a stuffed animal or doll; it is an excellent source of comfort.

COMPETENCY SKILLS PERFORMANCE

1. Perform and record measurements of height, weight, head, and chest circumference.
2. Perform and record pediatric vital signs and vision screening.
3. Maintain medication and immunization records.
4. Perform urine collection with a pediatric urine collection bag.

Physical, Developmental, and Emotional Growth of a Child

Every child progresses through a sequence of stages in the growth process (Figures 27-1 ◆ through 27-7 ◆):

- Fetus or embryo: from conception to birth
- Neonate or newborn: birth to 4 weeks
- Infant: 4 weeks to 1 year
- Toddler: 1 to 3 years
- Preschool (early childhood): 3 to 6 years
- School age (late childhood): 6 to 12 years, or puberty
- Adolescence: 12 years or puberty to beginning of adult stage

Factors that influence physical growth include heredity, racial and ethnic characteristics, gender, environment (prenatal and postnatal), and hormonal balance.

Prenatal factors that can cause harm or delays in the normal physical growth of a child include the mother's drug or alcohol use, smoking, physical injury, poor diet, and infection with rubella. Illnesses or injury during childhood may also affect the progression of normal development.

Certain physical, developmental, and emotional growth stages have been found to be common to specific age groups (Table 27-1).

Monitoring Growth Development

Measuring growth and keeping growth records for the pediatric patient is important. The physician uses growth patterns to observe normal physical development or diagnose diseases. Growth charts are usually part of a child's medical file and are updated on each visit. Charts for growth record keeping are developed by the National Center for Health Statistics (NCHS)

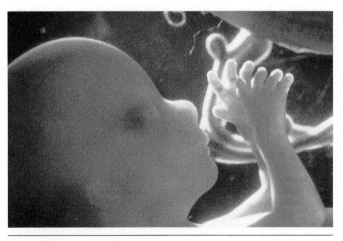

Figure 27-1 ◆ Fetus at four months
Source: Petit Format/Nestle/Photo Researchers, Inc.

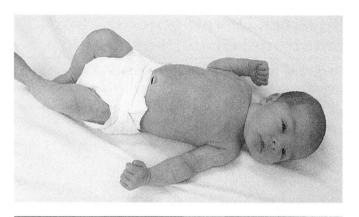

Figure 27-2 ◆ Newborn: birth to 4 weeks

Figure 27-3 ◆ Infant: 4 weeks to 1 year
Source: Michal Heron Photography

Figure 27-4 ◆ Toddler: 1 to 3 years
Source: Michal Heron Photography

along with the CDC's National Center for Chronic Disease Prevention and Health Promotion. These charts are colored with a blue background for boys and a pink background for girls. They are specific for age groups as well as length-for-age and weight-for-age percentiles; head-circumference-for-age and weight-for-length percentiles; body-mass-index-for-age percentiles and weight-for-stature percentiles (∞ see Appendix G, Growth Charts). The age groups are birth to 36 months and two to 20 years.

Figure 27-5 ◆ Preschool: 3 to 6 years
Source: Michal Heron Photography

Figure 27-6 ◆ School-age (late childhood): 6 to 12 years, or puberty
Source: Michal Heron Photography

Keys to Success
CIRCUMCISION

A procedure usually performed in the hospital shortly after birth is circumcision, in which the foreskin on an infant boy is surgically removed. The presurgical diagnosis is phimosis (condition in which the foreskin cannot be pushed back over the glans penis). Traditionally a routine procedure on most male babies, circumcision now involves an informed decision by the parents.

The Jewish faith mandates that the male infant be circumcised on the seventh day after birth. A rabbi routinely performs the procedure as part of a religious ceremony and family celebration. The medical office may become involved if an infection or other postoperative complication develops.

Figure 27-7 ◆ Adolescence: 12 years or puberty to beginning of adult stage
Source: Michal Heron Photography

TABLE 27-1 NORMAL OR EXPECTED CHILD DEVELOPMENT

Infant:

- Begins to smile at 6 weeks.
- Rolls from stomach to back at 10 weeks.
- Gains strength to raise head from a supine position.
- Begins to recognize sounds and make associations.
- Sits without support at 6 to 8 months.
- Begins to crawl, stand, and take steps at 8 to 12 months.
- Begins to develop language skills with simple words.

Toddler:

- Strength develops to include climbing and running.
- Coordination (including manual dexterity) improves.

(continued)

TABLE 27-1 NORMAL OR EXPECTED CHILD DEVELOPMENT (cont.)

- Continues to process information through senses.
- Continues to develop communication and speech skills.
- Begins to develop small motor skills and finger dexterity.
- Begins to develop independence.

Preschooler:

- Begins to mimic older children and adults.
- Becomes more independent.
- Enhances communication techniques.
- Talks in simple, complete sentences.
- Can dress and undress self.

School-age child:

- Eye and body coordination improves.
- Makes choices.
- Feels guilt and shame.
- Can experience emotional withdrawal or shyness.

Preadolescent or teenager:

- Develops secondary sex characteristics.
- Strives for independence.
- Experiences puberty and self-image changes.

Stages of emotional or personality development

- Infancy, birth to 1 year—sense of trust
- Toddler, 1 to 3 years—sense of autonomy
- Preschool, 3 to 6 years—sense of initiative
- School age, 6 to 12 years—sense of industry
- Adolescence, 12 years—sense of identity
- Late adolescence, sense of intimacy

TABLE 27-2 WELL-CHILD VISIT SCHEDULE

First Year of Life	Second Year of Life	After Two Years of Age
2 weeks 1 month 2 months 4 months 6 months 9 months 12 months (one year)	15 months 18 months	Annually Preschool check

- Measuring weight and height
- Measuring head and chest circumference
- Taking temperature, pulse, respirations, and in older children, blood pressure
- Testing range of motion (ROM) of limbs, head, and neck
- Testing pupil reaction
- Checking ears, nose, and throat
- Checking cardiac and respiratory status
- Palpating the abdomen

  Depending on the child's age, other assessments include:

- Ambulation (walking or moving about freely)
- Gait
- Scoliosis (curvature of the spine)
- Musculoskeletal abnormalities in the feet and legs
- Dental eruptions

Routine Visits (Well-Baby Checks)

Inoculations and well-baby or well-child checks account for many of the visits to the pediatric office (Table 27-2).

Procedures performed during a well-baby visit may include the following:

Measuring Growth

Growth is measured to evaluate the child's developmental patterns. A newborn's length, weight, and head circumference are one such measure. When growth patterns are abnormal, further assessment and diagnostic testing are performed to determine the cause.

PROCEDURE 27-1 Perform and Record Measurements of Height or Length, Weight, and Head and Chest Circumference

Theory

A platform scale is used to weigh an infant. Cover it with a paper protector to prevent cross-contamination between patients. Balance the scale with the protector in place. Set the scale to zero before the weight is taken. Infants are generally weighed without clothing or diaper as standard office policy.

Measuring the infant's length requires the help of the parent or guardian. Some exam tables are equipped with length scales, or the exam table is marked. Ask the parent or guardian to hold the infant's head at the zero mark. With the legs straightened, hold the infant's feet at right angles to the exam table.

Length is measured to approximately 2 years of age. When a child can stand on the stadiometer (device used to measure height) with minor help from the parent, the exam table is no longer necessary.

Head circumference is measured during the first three years of life. Use a plastic or paper tape measure at the greatest round distance of the head. Do *not* use a cloth measuring tape, because it can stretch and measurements would not be accurate.

continued

PROCEDURE 27-1 Perform and Record Measurements of Height or Length, Weight, and Head and Chest Circumference *(continued)*

Infant chest circumference is not routinely measured, except when respiratory or cardiac abnormalities are suspected.

An infant can move quickly and suddenly. Watch the infant from the periphery of your vision and take the measurements quickly. Keep a hand within reach of the infant to prevent accidental falls when weighing or measuring.

Materials
- plastic or paper tape measure
- infant or platform scale
- stadiometer
- growth charts
- patient chart

Competency
(**Conditions**) With the necessary materials, (**Task**) you will be able to measure the child's length (height), weight, and head and/or chest circumference (**Standards**) correctly within 15 minutes.

1. Wash your hands and gather equipment and supplies.
2. Identify the parent or guardian with the child and guide them to the treatment area.
3. Remove all clothing except the diaper before weighing.
4. Weigh the child on the platform scale (Figure 27-8 ◆).
5. Record the weight on the growth charts and/or progress notes within the child's chart.
6. Wash your hands.

7. Move or ask the parent or guardian to move the child to the exam table.
8. Measure the length of the child (Figure 27-9 ◆).
9. Record the height on the growth charts and/or progress notes within the child's chart.
10. Measure the child's head circumference (Figure 27-10 ◆).
11. Record the head circumference on the growth charts and/or progress notes within the child's chart.
12. Measure the child's chest circumference, if necessary (Figure 27-11 ◆).
13. Record the chest circumference on the growth charts and/or progress notes within the child's chart.
14. Tell the physician that the child is ready.
15. After the physician has examined the child, tell the parent or guardian to redress the child.
16. Dispose of disposables.
17. Clean the room.
18. Wash your hands.
19. Prepare the room for the next patient.

Patient Education
Tell the parent or guardian the purpose of growth measurements. Encourage questions.

Charting Example
09/23/XX 9:00 a.m. Wt. 15 lbs 9 oz, Ht 26 in., head circumference 42 cm. Results given to physician for evaluation. Vaiden Breen, CMA

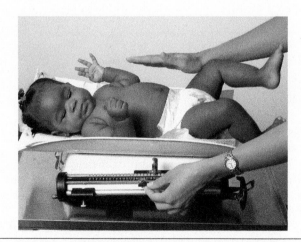

Figure 27-8 ◆ Weigh the infant on the balance baby scale.

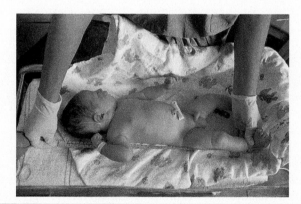

Figure 27-9 ◆ Measure the length of the newborn.

PROCEDURE 27-1 Perform and Record Measurements of Height or Length, Weight, and Head and Chest Circumference *(continued)*

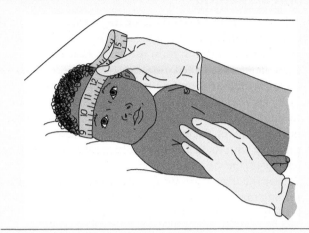

Figure 27-10 ◆ Measure the head circumference of the infant.

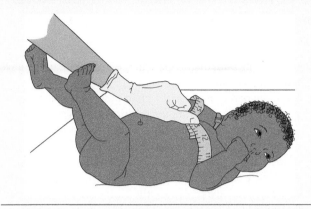

Figure 27-11 ◆ Measure the chest circumference of the infant.

PROCEDURE 27-2 Perform and Record Pediatric Vital Signs and Vision Screening

Theory

When taking pediatric vital signs, be sure to have the correct size equipment for the child. Temperature readings on an infant are most accurately obtained anally, although axillary readings may also be taken. If the child is older than 2, an aural temperature may be obtained. For a child is younger than 2, avoid using a tympanic thermometer. The reading may be incorrect by several degrees due to impacted cerumen or chronic ear infections. Oral temperatures are taken only on children age 5 years and older, who can understand directions and will not bite the thermometer.

The pulse of a child is taken at the apex of the heart, without clothing. Although the pulse can be felt at the brachial artery, the apex gives a more reliable pulse rate.

When counting a child's respirations, which are normally irregular, count for one full minute. Count an infant's respirations by watching the rise and fall of the chest as well as the abdomen.

Blood pressure is not normally taken on an infant unless it is specifically requested by the physician. After the age of 3, blood pressure is normally taken once per year to establish a baseline reading.

When children require a vision check to rule out abnormalities, you will use an Allen chart, E chart, or Snellen chart. If the child is old enough to recognize shapes but not directions, use an Allen chart, which features sailboats, hearts, stars, and other easily recognized shapes. For a child old enough to know direction but not the alphabet, you can use the E chart, which is a series of Es pointing in different directions. For children older than 5, most offices use the standard Snellen chart for vision testing.

Materials
■ pediatric blood pressure cuff
■ Snellen E chart
■ watch with a sweeping second hand
■ digital thermometer
■ patient chart

Competency
(**Conditions**) With the necessary materials, (**Task**) you will be able to measure a child's temperature, pulse, respirations, and blood pressure and perform a vision screening test (**Standards**) correctly within 15 minutes.

continued

PROCEDURE 27-2 Perform and Record Pediatric Vital Signs and Vision Screening *(continued)*

Pulse, Respirations, Axillary Temperature, and Blood Pressure

1. Gather equipment and supplies. Wash your hands.
2. Identify the patient and explain the procedure to the parent or guardian.
3. Have the parent disrobe the child down to the diaper.
4. Place the child in the supine position or allow him or her to remain in the parent's lap for greater compliance.
5. Locate the apex of the heart by feeling for the fifth intercostal space to the left of the sternum on the midclavicular line.
6. Make sure the stethoscope head is warmed and place it on the space, listening for the "lub-dub" of the heart. Count for one minute (each lub-dub equals one beat).
7. Record the results.
8. Place your hand on the child's chest and count inspirations and expirations for one minute. The rise and fall of the chest is counted as one breath.
9. Record the results.
10. Take the temperature probe and apply a disposable sheath.
11. Place the probe in the infant's axillary space, holding the child's arm down close to his or her side.
12. Wait for the beep to indicate the reading has been completed, then dispose of the probe cover.
13. Record the results.
14. If the physician orders that blood pressure be taken, follow the directions for taking an adult BP reading. Palpate the blood pressure first to avoid overinflating the cuff. Make sure the cuff size is correct for the patient size (Figure 27-12 ◆).
15. Record the results.

Vision Screening

16. Take the child to the vision screening area, accompanied by the parent. Explain the chart and ask the child to stand at the correct distance from the chart. (Each chart indicates the recommended distance.)
17. Have the child cover one eye and read as many lines as possible (Figure 27-13 ◆). If the child misses two objects, directions, or letters in a single line, stop the test and record the line number. For example, if the child reads line 20/20 correctly with the left eye but misses multiple letters on line 20/15, the vision would be 20/20 in the left eye.
18. Repeat the procedure for the other eye, then both eyes reading together.
19. Record the results in the patient's chart.

Patient Education

Explain to the parent or guardian the purpose of vital signs and vision screening. Encourage questions.

Charting Example

09/23/XX Pediatric vital signs obtained and given to the physician for review. Pediatric E chart vision test administered. Results recorded: 20/15 OD, 20/20 OS, 20/20 OU. Damion Frank, RMA

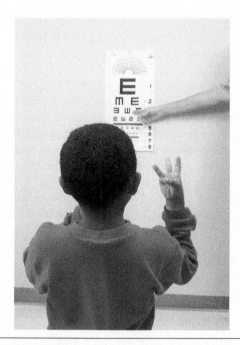

Figure 27-13 ◆ Have the child cover one eye and read as many lines as possible.

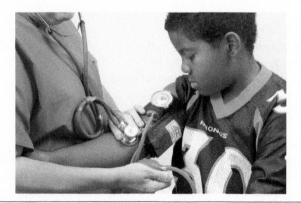

Figure 27-12 ◆ Take the child's blood pressure.

Immunizations

Children in the United States are routinely inoculated against such diseases as chickenpox, measles, mumps, and smallpox (Figure 27-14 ◆). Recent additions to routine vaccinations include hepatitis B and haemophilus b (HiB). Booster injections are recommended by the American Academy of Pediatrics (∞ See Appendix H for the CDC Recommended Childhood and Adolescent Immunization Schedule). Epidemics of childhood contagious diseases have a tendency to occur among college students when booster injections are not rigorously scheduled and administered.

Immunizations have dramatically reduced the frequency of many childhood illnesses and the transfer of disease to other children and adults. But it is important to alert parents to potential side effects. Vaccinations commonly cause such reactions as fever, rash, redness, and swelling at the vaccination site. Seizures and severe allergic reactions are much rarer side effects. Be sure to forward parents' questions about the benefits and risks of immunizations to the physician.

The American Academy of Pediatrics recommends that an immunization record (**VIS**) be a permanent part of a child's chart. This record documents the date, type, and site of each immunization; the manufacturer, lot number, and date of

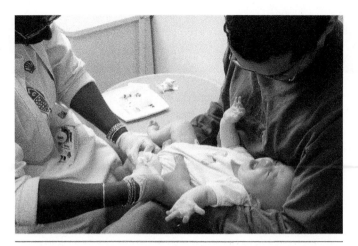

Figure 27-14 ◆ Infant receiving a vaccination

expiration of the immunization product; the parents' consent; and the initials of the person administering the immunization.

Storing Vaccines

The potency of vaccines depends on the proper refrigerator or freezer temperature, as stated in the manufacturer's directions. Vaccines are transported inside an insulated cold container with

---

PROCEDURE 27-3 Perform Documentation of Immunizations, Both Stored and Administered

Theory

Review the information from the vaccine package insert or from other sources, such as the *Physician's Desk Reference* (*PDR*) or CDC. Know the purpose of the medication, precautions, potential side effects or adverse reactions, correct route for administration, and storage requirements. The National Childhood Vaccine Injury Act of 1988 requires that benefit and risk information about immunizations be given to the parent or legal guardian and that consent to proceed be given by the parent or legal guardian before the child is vaccinated.

Encourage the parent to stay and help when the vaccine is administered. Discourage comments that imply the medical staff is "bad" because they are giving the painful injection. Establishing trust is an important part of the child's visit.

Before any immunization, it is important to obtain the medical history from the parent or guardian. Ask about any known allergies and recent illnesses. The physician will review this information and form an assessment before immunizing. Due to the cost of vaccinations, it is fairly common for a physician to refer patients to the Public Health Department for free or low-cost vaccinations.

After the immunization has been given, record the information. Include in the child's immunization record the date and the initials of the staff member who gave the immunization. The physician's name and number are sometimes recorded as

well. In the child's chart, record the date and time of immunization, product name, lot number and expiration date, manufacturer, injection site and/or route given, and the signature of whoever administered the vaccination.

Materials

- vaccine information sheets (VIS)
- vaccination dosage
- sterile gloves
- patient chart

Competency

(**Conditions**) With the necessary materials, (**Task**) you will be able to provide the parent or guardian instruction and give childhood immunizations (**Standards**) correctly within 45 minutes.

1. Wash your hands. Gather the equipment and supplies.
2. Identify the parent or guardian with the child and guide them to the treatment area.
3. Ask the parent or guardian about the child's recent health and if there is medical history that would exclude the child temporarily or permanently from any of the immunizations.
4. Provide vaccine information sheets for each immunization to be given.

continued

PROCEDURE 27-3 Perform Documentation of Immunizations, Both Stored and Administered *(continued)*

5. Take and record the child's vital signs.
6. After the physician has seen the patient, wash your hands and put on sterile gloves.
7. Administer the immunizations.
8. Dispose of sharps or biohazardous materials in the appropriate containers.
9. Wash your hands.
10. Document on the child's immunization record for the parent or guardian and on the child's chart.

Patient Education

Educate the parent or guardian about possible side effects of each immunization. The child may be given antipyretics and analgesics as directed by the physician during the first day or two after the immunizations. Instruct the parent or guardian to call the physician during office hours or the emergency room after hours for any symptoms that are worsening or of concern.

Charting Example

08/20/XX 8:00 a.m. Child seen for 12-month well-child visit. Mother stated that insurance has paid maximum benefits for immunizations and she cannot afford immunizations. Physician gave phone number of public health department for free immunizations. Heather Brown, CMA

cold packs. The container is placed on the front passenger seat of the vehicle for safety. Upon delivery, immediately move the vaccines to a freezer or refrigerator as required. Refrigerator temperatures must be kept between 35° and 46°F; the safest temperatures are between 41° and 46°F if the refrigerator door is opened frequently. Freezer temperatures should be kept below 5°F. Temperatures should be checked and logged twice daily. It is mandatory that the office keep a month's stock ahead of projected needs and have a back-up plan for emergencies in which power for the refrigerator or freezer may be lost. An emergency generator may be used, or the vaccines may be moved to a hospital, fire station, or other facility.

Common Pediatric Diseases and Conditions

A common complaint during a well-baby checkup is a diaper rash that has not responded to regular treatment. Nonresponsive diaper rash may have a fungal origin and require prescription medications. Frequent diaper changing, gentle cleansing, and gentle handling of the dry, irritated perianal skin are also recommended. After washing, patting the skin dry gently or using a hair dryer *only* on a cool setting will help ease the discomfort of the condition. The medication treats the fungal infection. If oral thrush, an often parallel condition, is also present, a prescription for an oral suspension to coat the white patchy mucous membranes of the mouth is prescribed.

Candida albicans is a fungus that can result from an immunodeficiency-related disease or from overuse of antibiotics. Young, and sometimes older, infants can display signs of oral thrush or a rash of the perianal area that will not resolve without medication.

? — Critical Thinking Question 27-1—

After the physician has diagnosed oral thrush combined with a yeast infection, what should Lucas explain to the mother so that the condition is correctly treated?

One of the most common medical conditions that affect infants and toddlers is otitis media (ear inflammation). Fussiness and pulling at the ear or sitting with the head held to one side are often indications of the condition. (∞ Refer to Chapter 19 for a complete discussion of otitis media.)

The condition responsible for the most lost school time is asthma. Asthma is usually the result of an allergic response. The child experiences shortness of breath (SOB) and usually wheezes. (∞ See Chapter 18 for a complete discussion of asthma.)

Respiratory conditions are common in children. Two respiratory diseases that are of major concern are respiratory syncytial virus (RSV) pneumonia and cystic fibrosis. RSV starts as a mild upper-respiratory infection. As it progresses downward into the lungs, pneumonia develops. Symptoms include fever, coughing, dyspnea, and lethargy. Contact with the respiratory secretions of an infected person is the usual source of the infection. A microscopic exam of a specimen obtained by nasal **lavage** confirms the presence of the virus. Keeping the child hydrated is important, and supplemental oxygen may be required. Fever is treated with antipyretics.

Cystic fibrosis, a genetic metabolic disorder, involves a chronic dysfunction of the exocrine glands. A thick, sticky mucous secretion is produced by the exocrine glands, blocking the ducts. Tissues most frequently affected include the lungs, digestive system (particularly the pancreas), and sweat glands.

Certain contagious diseases are common among children, particularly school-age children. More serious childhood conditions are neural tube defects, congenital heart conditions, and blood disorders. Treatment is required immediately for most of these conditions.

Common Contagious Diseases of Childhood

Thanks to routine preventive inoculations, the common contagious diseases of childhood are far less prevalent now than they were 50 years ago (Table 27-3). These diseases include chickenpox (*herpes varicella*), measles (rubeola), rubella (German measles), mumps (parotitis), whooping cough (pertussis),

Keys to Success
NEW INFORMATION ON AUTISM

Autism is a mental disorder with symptoms of diminished language, social, and emotional development. The child is described as introverted (withdrawn from reality), often incapable of appropriate social interaction with family and other caregivers. Recent research findings from the University of California suggest that abnormally rapid brain growth during infancy may be a clue for early diagnosis and treatment. Usually, autism is rarely diagnosed before 2 or 3 years of age.

polio, and diphtheria. Smallpox, once considered extinct globally, is now considered a possible terrorist threat.

TABLE 27-3 COMMON PREVENTABLE CONTAGIOUS DISEASES

Disease	Symptoms	Diagnosis	Vaccine
Chickenpox ■ Caused by herpes varicella, highly contagious virus ■ Spread by droplets from respiratory tract or direct contact with blisters ■ Virus can be reactivated later in life as herpes zoster (shingles)	■ Blister-like vesicles over body, starting at head and moving downward	■ Patient presenting symptoms	■ Live varicella virus vaccine
Diphtheria ■ Caused by the bacteria *Corynebacterium diphtheriae* ■ Spread by airborne droplets from an infected person's respiratory tract ■ May damage heart or central nervous system (CNS)	■ False membrane develops in throat and interferes with breathing	■ Patient presenting symptoms	■ Diphtheria-pertussis-tetanus (DPT)
Haemophilus influenza type B ■ Occurs mostly in children under age 5 ■ Causes acute respiratory infections ■ Can cause infections of the blood, bones, joints, and head, and bacterial meningitis ■ Can be fatal	■ Fever ■ Nausea and vomiting (N&V) ■ Loss of appetite ■ Irritability ■ Headache ■ Bulging **fontanelles** ■ Stupor ■ Seizures ■ Pneumonia ■ Meningitis ■ Septic arthritis	■ Patient presenting symptoms	■ Haemophilus B conjugate vaccine (HiB)
Hepatitis B ■ Caused by a virus ■ Spread by blood and body fluids ■ May cause death	■ Jaundice ■ Anorexia ■ N&V ■ Joint pain ■ Flulike symptoms ■ Liver damage ■ Liver failure	■ Patient presenting symptoms ■ Blood studies	■ Hepatitis B vaccine (recombinant)
Measles (rubeola) ■ Caused by a virus ■ Spread by airborne droplets	■ Fine rash over the body ■ Fever ■ Malaise ■ Eye problems ■ Otitis ■ Pneumonia ■ Encephalitis	■ Patient presenting symptoms	■ Measles-mumps-rubella (**MMR**) vaccine

continued

TABLE 27-3 COMMON PREVENTABLE CONTAGIOUS DISEASES (*Continued*)

Disease	Symptoms	Diagnosis	Vaccine
Rubella (German measles) ■ Caused by a virus ■ Spread by direct contact with infected persons and nasal or oral secretions ■ Can cause birth defects if pregnant mother contracts the disease	■ Fine rash over body ■ Fever	■ Patient presenting symptoms	■ MMR; immunity confirmed with rubella titer
Mumps (infectious parotitis) ■ Caused by a virus ■ Spread by direct contact with salivary secretions of infected person ■ Male sterility possible if contracted as an adult	■ Swollen parotid glands ■ Fever ■ Diarrhea ■ Malaise ■ Difficulty swallowing	■ Patient presenting symptoms	■ MMR
Pertussis (whooping cough) ■ Spread by direct contact or airborne droplets ■ Complications include pneumonia, atelectasis, otitis, and convulsions	■ Dry, harsh cough with spasms ■ Fever ■ Dyspnea	■ Patient presenting symptoms	■ DPT injections (series of three)
Poliomyelitis ■ Caused by one of three polio viruses that enter body through the mouth ■ Transmitted in feces of infected individuals ■ Respiratory system affected by paralysis followed by muscle atrophy ■ Post-polio syndrome may occur as late as 30 years post-infection	■ Fever ■ Malaise ■ Headache ■ Paralysis ■ N&V	■ Patient presenting symptoms	■ Trivalent live oral form (Sabin) ■ Inactivated poliovirus vaccine (Salk), given under the skin
Smallpox ■ Caused by a virus ■ Once thought to be completely eradicated worldwide; now may be used as terrorist weapon ■ Usually fatal	■ Pustule-like blisters on the skin.	■ Patient presenting symptoms	■ Smallpox vaccine
Tetanus ■ Caused by *Clostridium tetani* entering the body through puncture wound or open skin ■ CNS may become involved, resulting in death if not treated aggressively	■ Headaches ■ Fever ■ Muscle spasms	■ Patient presenting symptoms	■ Tetanus diphtheria (Td) or DPT vaccines ■ Tetanus antitoxin ■ Tetanus toxoid

Caduceus Chronicle
SMALLPOX

An English physician, Edward Jenner (1749–1823), first used the term *virus*. Jenner developed a smallpox vaccination in 1796 to immunize individuals against cowpox. The weakened dose of vaccine stimulates the creation of antibodies that will attack a specific invading microorganism.

As a result of Jenner's pioneering work in the field of immunization, smallpox became the first contagious disease to be eradicated by vaccination. Recent information about the storage of the smallpox virus in laboratories around the world has raised concern about use of the virus as a bioterrorist weapon.

Congenital Neurological Disorders/Neural Tube Defects

Neural tube defects are congenital disorders that occur when an embryo's neural tube fails to close during development (Table 27-4). Spinal fusion disorders are spina bifida occulta, meningocele, and myelomeningocele. Cranial fusion disorders are hydrocephalus, microencephaly, and anencephaly.

Congenital Heart Conditions

Congenital heart conditions are easily identified at birth or before birth by prenatal ultrasound examination (Table 27-5).

TABLE 27-4 CONGENITAL NEUROLOGICAL DISORDERS			
Disorder	**Symptoms**	**Diagnosis**	**Treatment**
Spina bifida occulta ■ Failure of neural tube to close ■ Usually located in lumbar region with no displacement or insult to the spinal cord	■ Dimpling or depression of skin over affected lumbar region, often with tuft of hair over site	■ Patient presenting symptoms	■ No intervention; close observation for any signs of neurological symptoms
Meningocele ■ Congenital hernia that results in meninges (membranes) protruding through a defect in skull or spinal column ■ Good prognosis if surgery is successful	■ Apparent bulging over spinal column, usually in lumbar region	■ Patient presenting symptoms ■ Imaging studies	■ Surgery to close opening in vertebral column
Myelomeningocele ■ Form of spina bifida in which a portion of spinal cord and membranes protrude ■ Many patients require intense physical care and often do not survive into teen years	■ Deformity in lumbar region of spinal column ■ Possible paralysis ■ Possible loss of bowel and bladder function	■ Patient presenting symptoms	■ Surgery to protect exposed spinal nerves and cord ■ Supportive care for any paralysis or bowel and bladder dysfunction
Hydrocephalus ■ Accumulation of cerebrospinal fluid (CSF) within brain and skull ■ May be result of developmental error, trauma, infection, or blood clot developing during or shortly after delivery ■ If surgery is performed before permanent neurological damage occurs, child has a good prognosis ■ Requires continual observation for neurological symptoms that signal reduced or impaired functioning of shunt	■ Enlargement of skull, with bulging fontanelles	■ Patient presenting symptoms	■ Surgery to insert shunt to drain excess fluid into circulatory system
Microencephaly ■ Abnormally small brain ■ Most patients die in infancy	■ Small head	■ Patient presenting symptoms ■ Imaging studies	■ Supportive care
Anencephaly ■ Cranial vault missing, and very little cerebral tissue present ■ Most patients are stillborn or die during neonatal period	■ Posterior cranial vault small or absent	■ Patient presenting symptoms ■ Imaging studies	■ Supportive care

Some conditions are caused by failure of fetal circulation to convert to normal cardiac circulation after birth. Others are caused by developmental anomalies. There are two classes of congenital heart conditions. **Acyanotic** conditions include ventricular septal defect (VSD), patent ductus arteriosus (PDA), coarctation of the aorta, and atrial septal defect. Tetralogy of Fallot and transposition of the great arteries are **cyanotic** conditions.

Blood Disorders

Disorders affecting the blood that are seen in pediatric patients include anemia, leukemia, and lead poisoning (Table 27-6).

Other Conditions

Some conditions are passed on to the fetus by a mother with a history of substance abuse. A baby with fetal alcohol syndrome (**FAS**) often shows retarded growth in height, weight, and mental capacity. A few days after birth, the baby suffers from alcohol withdrawal. Any neurological damage cannot be reversed, so most treatment involves supportive care. A "crack baby"—a baby whose mother took crack cocaine during the pregnancy—is very irritable and may also show growth retardation. Many of these children have severe emotional and behavioral problems later in life.

TABLE 27-5 CONGENITAL HEART CONDITIONS

Condition	Patient Symptoms	Diagnosis	Treatment
Ventricular septal defect (VSD) ▪ Opening in septum between right and left ventricles, resulting in shunting of blood from left to right side of heart	▪ Heart murmur ▪ Increased heart rate ▪ Increased respiratory rate ▪ Failure to gain weight ▪ Restlessness ▪ Irritability	▪ Patient presenting symptoms	▪ Surgery to repair or patch ventricular septum
Patent ductus arteriosus (PDA) ▪ Failure of ductus arteriosus to close after birth, which causes shunting of oxygenated blood to lungs ▪ Good prognosis with prompt medication or surgery	▪ Heart murmur ▪ Retarded growth ▪ Signs of heart failure	▪ Patient presenting symptoms	▪ Antiprostaglandin to inhibit prostaglandin synthesis ▪ Surgery to close patent ductus arteriosus
Coarctation of the aorta ▪ Portion of aorta is narrowed, restricting blood flow from left ventricle ▪ Fair prognosis with prompt surgery	▪ Left ventricular failure ▪ Pulmonary edema (swelling) ▪ Decreased pulse in legs ▪ Rapid heart rate ▪ Dyspnea	▪ Patient presenting symptoms	▪ Surgery recommended to remove the coarctation
Atrial septal defect ▪ Opening in atrial septal wall ▪ Good prognosis with prompt surgery	▪ Fatigue ▪ SOB ▪ Respiratory infections	▪ Patient presenting symptoms	▪ Surgery to repair wall
Tetralogy of Fallot ▪ Combination of ventricular septal defect, pulmonary stenosis, displacement of aorta to the right, and right ventricular hypertrophy ▪ Fair prognosis with prompt and successful surgery	▪ Cyanosis ("blue baby") ▪ Hypoxia ▪ Tachycardia ▪ Tachypnea ▪ Dyspnea ▪ Seizures	▪ Patient presenting symptoms	▪ Immediate surgery to correct defect
Transposition of the great arteries ▪ Aorta and pulmonary artery reversed as they exit the heart ▪ Variable prognosis with immediate surgery	▪ Cyanosis ▪ Tachypnea ▪ Heart failure ▪ Imaging studies	▪ Patient presenting symptoms	▪ Prostaglandins to keep ductus arteriosus open until surgery ▪ Surgery to repair defect

A common digestive disease in children is infestation with helminths, or parasitic intestinal worms. Toxocariasis (roundworm) and enterobiasis (pinworm) infestations are caused by the transfer of larvae by unclean hands and nails to the mouth.

In both cases, the larvae are swallowed and hatch in the intestines. Roundworm infestation can cause symptoms of cough, fever, nausea and vomiting, weight loss, or hepatomegaly (enlargement of the liver).

Diagnostic Procedures

Diagnostic procedures that may be performed in the pediatrics office include urinalysis, strep screens, hemoglobin and hematocrit, and for culture and sensitivity (C&S). The physician may order blood drawn for a blood lead level and/or theophylline level. Some physicians may perform a lumbar puncture on a child with a fever of unknown origin.

Positioning and Securing the Child for Examination and Treatment

As an MA, you will be responsible for positioning and securing the child for an examination or procedure. When possible,

Keys to Success
TAPE TEST FOR WORM/EGG COLLECTION

A classic sign of roundworm and pinworm infestation is scratching of the anus. A microscopic examination of the stool confirms the presence of eggs or worms.

An easy method for collecting the worms is to place clear tape across the rectum when the child goes to bed. The worms have a tendency to migrate to the anus and are trapped on the tape. Examining the tape early the next morning reveals the worms.

Another method of confirming an infestation is to shine a flashlight on the child's anus in the dark. Often the worms can be seen around the anus.

Treatment consists of an antihelminthic regimen for the entire family and laundering all bedding in hot water with bleach, if possible.

TABLE 27-6 BLOOD DISORDERS

Disorder	Symptoms	Diagnosis	Treatment
Anemia ■ Several possible causes, but in children commonly caused by iron deficiency and poor diet ■ Breast milk may have low iron if mother did not take prenatal supplement	■ Pale skin ■ Weakness ■ Fatigue ■ SOB	■ Patient presenting symptoms ■ Physical examination ■ Hemoglobin (hgb) test ■ Hematocrit (HCT) test	■ Fortified formula for infants ■ Iron supplements for prenatal care ■ For older children, proper diet with good sources of iron such as egg yolks and fortified cereals ■ Vitamin and mineral supplements for older children
Leukemia ■ Abnormal increase in white blood cells ■ Variable prognosis with treatment	■ Fatigue ■ Aching ■ Infection ■ Enlarged lymph nodes	■ Patient presenting symptoms ■ Blood studies ■ Lymph biopsy	■ Chemotherapy ■ Bone-marrow transplant
Lead Poisoning ■ Caused by lead in the environment ■ Can affect physical and mental development ■ Sources include lead-based paint, water from lead pipes, lead salts in certain foods, ceramic food containers painted with lead-based paint, food grown in contaminated soil, playing in contaminated soil or sand, and older vinyl mini-blinds ■ Leaded gasoline emissions and seepage are main cause of soil and sand contamination ■ Neurological damage cannot be reversed	■ Loss of appetite ■ Vomiting ■ Irritability ■ Difficulty walking ■ Stumbling ■ Anemia ■ Weakness ■ Colic ■ Peripheral neuritis ■ Possible mental retardation ■ Headache ■ Stupor ■ Convulsions ■ Coma	■ Patient presenting symptoms ■ Environmental history ■ Blood studies ■ Urine studies	■ Removing source ■ Chelating agents to remove lead from blood ■ Supportive treatment

involve the parent. Show the parent how to hold and restrain the child and then help the parent to do so.

Position 1: for examining the ears

1. Ask the parent to hold the child upright against his or her body.
2. The child's arms and legs should be tucked in under the parent's arms. The child's head should be turned to the side and held firmly against the parent's chest.
3. Gently turn the child's head and continue holding when the physician examines the other ear.

Position 2: for examining the ears, eyes, nose, and throat

1. Lay the child on the exam table.
2. Ask the parent to hold both of the child's arms against the child's head, grasping the hands together above the head. You may need to gently hold the child's body down on the exam table.
3. Gently turn the child's head from side to side so the physician may examine each ear.

Mummy restraint method: used when it is not possible for the parent to hold the child but the child must be completely restrained. This method may be adapted to expose an arm or leg.

1. Place the child's arms at his or her sides with the hands open and palms against the body (Figure 27-15 ◆).

2. Wrap the sheet from one side and enclose the arm (Figure 27-16 ◆).
3. Continue wrapping the sheet. Wrap the other end of the sheet around the child and secure it. (Figure 27-17 ◆). The child is now fully restrained, ready for medication.

Papoose board method:

1. Pad the board well (Figure 27-18 ◆).
2. Ask the parent to place the child on the board.
3. Secure the child with the restraining straps and board fasteners (Figure 27-19 ◆).

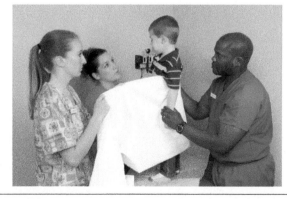

Figure 27-15 ◆ Place the child's arms at sides with palms against the body.

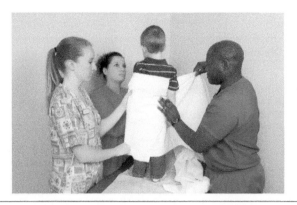

Figure 27-16 ◆ Wrap the sheet from one side and enclose the arm.

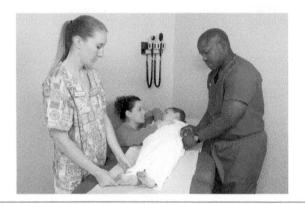

Figure 27-17 ◆ The child is now ready for medication.

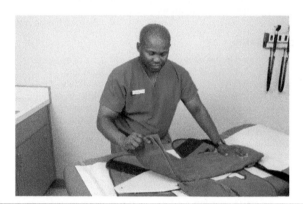

Figure 27-18 ◆ Papoose board method: pad the board well.

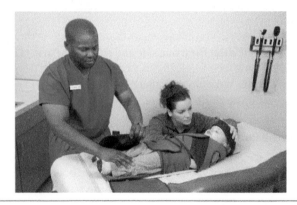

Figure 27-19 ◆ Secure the child.

For extensive procedures, a sedative may be administered to the child.

Pediatric Urine Collection

Urine samples are tested for the presence of blood, glucose, acetone, bilirubin, protein, drugs or hormones, and microorganisms. The specific gravity and pH of the urine may need to be determined. Because the newborn, infant, or toddler cannot physically or mentally follow directions to urinate into a sterile specimen container, you may need to attach a urine collection bag, or the physician may perform a catheterization.

PROCEDURE 27-4 Perform Urine Collection with a Pediatric Urine Collection Bag

Theory

It is important that a urine specimen collected with a collection bag be a recent urination. A fresh specimen provides more accurate information for correct diagnosis and treatment. For example, an old specimen may contain bacterial growth above what might have been present at the time of urination. Transport the specimen immediately to the laboratory for proper storage if it is not processed immediately.

Cleansing the skin is also crucial for obtaining accurate information (∞ see Chapter 15). Microorganisms on the skin may contaminate the urine specimen. To contain the urine specimen in the collection bag, you must create a wrinkle-free seal when you remove the adhesive covers from the tabs and place the bag on the skin. The tight seal is particularly important in the pediatric patient with oliguria (scanty urine production).

Materials

- urine collection bag for newborn or pediatric patient
- sterile gloves
- sterile container with label
- cotton balls
- prepackaged sterile cleansing swabs or towelettes
- laboratory requisition form
- patient chart

Competency

(**Conditions**) With the necessary materials, (**Task**) you will be to collect a urine specimen in a urine collection bag (**Standards**) correctly within 40 minutes.

1. Wash your hands. Gather the equipment and supplies.
2. Identify the parent or guardian with the child and guide them to the treatment area. Explain the procedure to the parent or guardian.

3. Put on sterile gloves.
4. Remove the diaper and dispose of it in the appropriate container.
5. Wipe the child's genital area with sterile towelettes or cleansing swabs. For boy infants, wipe around and away from the urinary meatus. For girl infants, wipe from the clitoris toward the rectal area. Repeat the wipe with a separate towelette or cleansing swab a second and third time to cleanse the area immediately surrounding the urinary meatus, then cleanse the wider surrounding area.
6. Dry the cleansed area with dry cotton balls.
7. Remove the adhesive tabs of the urine collection bag and apply the bag to the genital area securely, without gaps between the tabs and the skin (Figure 27-20 ◆).
8. Diaper the child.
9. Wash your hands.
10. Instruct the parent or guardian to encourage the infant or toddler to drink or nurse.
11. Recheck the diaper every 20 minutes until a specimen is obtained in the bag.
12. Wash your hands and put on sterile gloves.
13. Remove the urine collection bag. Place the bagged urine specimen in the sterile cup and cover the container tightly.
14. Diaper the child.
15. Remove the gloves and wash your hands.
16. Prepare the container label and laboratory requisition.
17. Transport or arrange for transport of the specimen to the laboratory.
18. Document the procedure in the child's chart.
19. Dispose of biohazardous materials in the proper containers.
20. Clean the area.
21. Wash your hands.

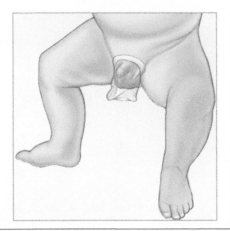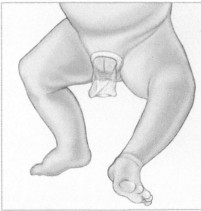

Figure 27-20 ◆ Applying urine collection bags on a male and female infant.

continued

PROCEDURE 27-4 Perform Urine Collection with a Pediatric Urine Collection Bag *(continued)*

Patient Education

Instruct the parent or guardian to increase the child's fluid intake to stimulate urine production. It may be necessary to explain that the urine collection bag is preferred, but the physician may choose to catheterize the child. If the parent or guardian is very anxious, it is often wise to avoid describing too many details. Explain only as much as the parent needs to understand and assist the child through the medical evaluation process.

Charting Example

09/27/XX 2:35 p.m. One-year-old female with history of 101° fever for two days. Mother states child is fussy, not drinking, and urine is darker than normal. Urine collection bag applied per physician order and office procedure. Shane Washington, RMA
09/27/XX 3:15 p.m. Urine collection bag removed and placed in sterile urine container. Urine is dark yellow and smells strong. Laboratory requisition sent with labeled urine specimen. Shane Washington, RMA

Keys to Success
ADMINISTERING LIQUID MEDICATIONS

Liquid medications are often prescribed for children. These require special care. A child's body uses and excretes medications differently than an adult's or elderly person's does. Because pediatric dosages are different, medical and other clinical staff must calculate and double-check for accuracy.

It may be tempting for a parent or guardian to use a household teaspoon or tablespoon to measure a liquid medication. Part of your instruction must be the importance of measuring with the spoons or cups supplied by the pharmacist or the manufacturer. For example, it is common to give a child an over-the-counter (OTC) medication, such as acetaminophen. This medication can be administered by drops or liquid. Giving 5 ml of acetaminophen drops on a regular schedule or 150 mg/kg could be toxic for the child, causing liver damage and even death. Instruct parents to read and follow directions carefully.

REVIEW

- The pediatric practice offers an MA a variety of tasks: obtaining and recording the child's health, developmental history, and vital signs; measuring and recording growth; assisting the parents or guardian and the physician with the child; obtaining a urine specimen; and administering medications, injections, and immunizations.
- An important role for the MA is to be aware of the needs and concerns of the parent or guardian and the child. Fear, mistrust, anxiety, and embarrassment are all common emotions. Listening can provide valuable information about the child.
- Growth measurement is usually part of a child's file and is vital information because it can indicate normal and abnormal growth.
- While inoculations and well-baby and child checks are a major part of office visits, diaper rash, thrush, ear inflammation, and asthma are also common.
- Common contagious diseases are more easily controlled today by preventive inoculations. Diseases include chickenpox,

measles, German measles, mumps, whooping cough, polio, and diphtheria. Vaccinations for hepatitis B and haemophilus b have been added to routine immunizations.
- Serious respiratory conditions, RSV and cystic fibrosis, require immediate care.
- Neural tube disorders are congenital. They occur when the embryo's neural tube fails to close. There are two categories: spinal and cranial fusion. There is no cure.
- Acyanotic and cyanotic are the two classifications of congenital heart disorders.
- Anemia, leukemia, and lead poisoning are all serious blood disorders.
- Fetal alcohol syndrome and drug-affected babies are more likely to show retarded growth and neurological damage. Often they experience severe emotional and behavioral problems later in life.
- Diagnostic procedures that may be performed include strep screens, urinalysis, hemoglobin and hematocrit, and C&S.

Chapter Review Questions

Multiple Choice

1. Which of the following is an acceptable way to handle an anxious parent?
   A. Ask the parent to leave the room and calm down.
   B. Take the child away from the parent, so you have control of the child.
   C. Show the parent how to hold the child during the exam.
   D. Tell the child and parent "It won't hurt."

2. When you weigh an infant, you must:
   A. swab the platform scale before using it
   B. watch the infant because he or she can move suddenly
   C. set the platform scale to -.05
   D. leave the infant's diaper on for comfort

3. Liquid acetaminophen drops can be administered:
   A. only as directed
   B. in a 5 ml dosage
   C. in a 6 ml dosage
   D. in a 7 ml dosage

4. The "mummy" restraint method involves:
   A. the parent holding the child's hands on the child's chest
   B. using a board
   C. tucking the infant's arms and legs under the parent's arms
   D. wrapping a sheet around a child

5. Which one of the following is a spinal fusion disorder?
   A. cystic fibrosis
   B. anencephaly
   C. meningocele
   D. RSV

6. Hydrocephalus is treated by surgically:
   A. closing the opening
   B. inserting a shunt
   C. protecting the exposed spinal cord
   D. repairing the septal wall

7. Which one of the following is a cyanotic congenital heart condition?
   A. transposition of the great arteries
   B. patent ductus arteriosus
   C. coarctation of the aorta
   D. atrial septal defect

8. Anemia in an older child is most often caused by:
   A. taking supplements
   B. drinking too much soda
   C. exercising too little
   D. eating a poor diet

9. A urine specimen from a toddler must be:
   A. obtained only by catheterization
   B. recent for an accurate laboratory result
   C. stored at room temperature
   D. done as soon as the child wakes in the morning

Chapter Review Questions (continued)

10. Immediately after removing the urine collection bag, you must:
    A. put the specimen into a sterile cup, but leave unsealed
    B. put the specimen into a sterile cup and seal
    C. take the bag to the laboratory sealed
    D. take the bag to the laboratory unsealed

True/False

T F 1. The medical assistant can have a role in physically restraining a child.

T F 2. There are two categories of visits to a pediatrician's office: well child or sick child.

T F 3. Children are too young to understand medical procedures, so it is best to lie to them and tell them "it won't hurt" so that they don't try to wiggle away from you.

T F 4. *Infant* is the term used for a baby from birth to 4 weeks old.

T F 5. Each child grows at his or her own individual speed, according to family genetics, so measurements are not important and not done at each visit.

Short Answer

1. What is phimosis?

2. What are the two age groups into which NCHS and CDC charts are divided?

3. Why should you place a paper protector on a platform scale before weighing an infant?

4. At what age can you begin taking a child's temperature orally?

5. Pulling at the ear or sitting with the head held to one side may be indications of what condition in a toddler or infant?

Research

1. Is there a crisis nursery or other organization in your community that provides respite care for children?

2. How many children will be injured or killed this year as a result of poor supervision in the bathtub?

Externship Application Experience

A mother refuses the first immunization series for her child during the first well-child checkup. As a medical assistant, how do you respond?

Resource Guide

American Academy of Allergies, Asthma, and Immunology
611 E. Wells
Milwaukee, WI 53202
1-800-822-ASMA
www.aaaai.org

Cystic Fibrosis Foundation
6931 Arlington Road
Bethesda, MD 20814-5200
1-800 FIGHT-CF
www.cff.org

National Easter Seal Society, Inc.
230 W. Monroe, Ste 1800
Chicago, IL 60606-4802
1-800-221-6872
www.easter-seals.org

MedMedia
www.prenhall.com/frazier

More on this chapter, including interactive resources, can be found on the Student CD-ROM accompanying this textbook and on the Companion Website at www.prenhall.com/frazier.

Objectives

After completing this chapter, you should be able to:

- Spell and define the medical terminology in this chapter.
- Identify the medical assistant's role in the neurology/neurosurgery practice.
- Discuss the anatomy and physiology of the central nervous system.
- Discuss the anatomy and physiology of the peripheral nervous system.
- Describe the structures that make up a nerve cell, or neuron.
- Discuss the functions of the various divisions of the nervous system.
- Discuss the various methods of neurological assessment.
- Explain how the Glasgow Coma Scale and lumbar punctures are used in neurological assessment.
- Describe common diseases and disorders of the central nervous system: CVA, TIA, epilepsy, ALS, Parkinson's disease, multiple sclerosis, amyotrophic lateral sclerosis, headache, infectious conditions, head trauma, spinal cord injuries, and disk disorders.
- Describe common diseases and disorders of the peripheral nervous system: Bell's palsy, trigeminal neuralgia, and shingles.

Neurology

Case Study

Dawn Benedict, RMA, is performing initial questioning with a patient, Milo Stevens, for a consultation regarding back pain. Dawn learns that Milo has recently had what he describes as an allergic reaction that caused a rash on his back, near the axial area on the right side. The patient states that at first he thought the blisters were acne and that his girlfriend helped him "pop" a few. Further questioning reveals that Milo's intense back pain started around the same time Milo had varicella as a child.

Medical Terminology

affect—emotional expression associated with facial and body behaviors

aura—warning of impending seizure

cephalgia—diffuse acute or chronic pain in any part of the head, commonly known as *headache*

clonic—alternating muscular contraction and relaxation

contrecoup—event on the opposite side, injury in which traumatic impact on the head is strong enough to make the brain strike the opposite side of the cranium and bounce back to strike the impacted side

decerebrate posture—posture characteristic of brain injury in which the patient is rigid, with head retracted and arms and legs extended

decorticate posture— posture characteristic of brain injury in which the patient is rigid, with clenched fists, flexed arms, and extended legs

dermatome—specific area of skin stimulated by a segment of the spinal cord

exacerbation—increasing severity and recurrence of symptoms

hemiparesis—loss of nerve and muscle function on one side of the body

innervate—stimulate

neuralgia—sharp nerve pain

neurology—study of the nervous system

neuron—nerve cell; basic unit of the nervous system

neurotransmitter—chemicals that aid in the transmission of electrical impulses from one neuron, or nerve cell, to the next

nuchal rigidity—severe and painful rigidity of the neck in which the head is bent forward toward the chest

palsy—tremors; temporary or permanent loss of ability to control or make muscle movement

paraplegia—loss of sensation and motor activity (paralysis) of the lower trunk and lower extremities

postictal—pertaining to the period immediately following a seizure

prodromal—pertaining to symptoms during the period immediately preceding onset of a disease condition

➕ MEDICAL ASSISTING COMPETENCIES

CAAHEP ENTRY-LEVEL COMPETENCIES FOR CMA	ABHES ENTRY-LEVEL COMPETENCIES FOR RMA
■ Identify and respond to issues of confidentiality. ■ Perform within legal and ethical boundaries. ■ Demonstrate knowledge of federal and state health-care legislation. ■ Perform hand washing. ■ Dispose of biohazardous materials. ■ Practice Standard Precautions. ■ Obtain vital signs. ■ Obtain and record patient history. ■ Prepare and maintain examination and treatment areas. ■ Apply pharmacology principles to prepare and administer oral and parenteral medications. ■ Maintain medication and immunization records. ■ Instruct individuals according to their needs. ■ Provide instruction for health maintenance and disease prevention. ■ Identify community resources.	■ Project a positive attitude. ■ Maintain confidentiality at all times. ■ Be a "team player." ■ Be cognizant of ethical boundaries. ■ Exhibit initiative. ■ Adapt to change. ■ Evidence a responsible attitude. ■ Be courteous and diplomatic. ■ Conduct work within the scope of education, training, and ability. ■ Be impartial and show empathy when dealing with patients. ■ Adapt what is said to the recipient's level of comprehension. ■ Serve as a liaison between the physician and others. ■ Interview effectively. ■ Use appropriate terminology. ■ Recognize and respond to verbal and nonverbal communication. ■ Adapt to individualized needs.

Introduction

Neurology is a branch of medicine that specializes in the diagnosis and treatment of diseases of the nervous system. Conditions affecting the brain, spinal cord, and peripheral nervous system are addressed by neurologists. Neurosurgeons treat neurological conditions requiring surgical intervention, such as traumatic insult to the brain, spinal cord, and peripheral nerves; the presence of a foreign body; tumor or abscess in these structures; and pressure from intracranial hemorrhage. Neurosurgery may also provide pain relief as well as relief from the tremors of parkinsonism.

The Medical Assistant's Role in Neurology and Neurosurgery

There are numerous opportunities for the medical assistant in neurology and neurosurgery offices. Many of these opportunities are in the administrative arena; however, clinical positions are generally available as well.

As a medical assistant in a neurology office, you may be responsible for obtaining a preliminary history and information pertaining to the current office visit. You will assess and record vital signs, assist the neurologist with the patient examination, assist the patient as required, document the examination on the patient's chart, provide patient instruction, and make and confirm appointments for any additional diagnostic tests.

In a neurosurgical office you will have many of the same responsibilities. In addition, when a surgical procedure is to be scheduled, you will either obtain precertification and schedule the

Medical Terminology   *(continued)*

projectile vomiting—vomiting with uncontrollable force

pyogenic—pus-forming

quadriplegia—paralysis of the entire
trunk and all four extremities

tonic—pertaining to muscular tension

Abbreviations

ALS—amyotrophic lateral sclerosis

CNS—central nervous system

CSF—cerebrospinal fluid

CVA—cerebrovascular accident

EEG—electroencephalography/electroen-
cephalogram

LP—lumbar puncture

PNS—peripheral nervous system

TIA—transient ischemic attack

procedure or coordinate it with the surgical scheduling department. You will obtain consent for the procedure according to office policy and instruct the patient and/or family about any
presurgical testing or procedures. Following surgical procedures,
you may remove sutures, staples, or drains and apply appropriate
dressings.

COMPETENCY SKILLS PERFORMANCE

1. Perform assessment of mental status.
2. Perform assessment of mood and behavior.
3. Assist in the neurological exam.
4. Assist with a lumbar puncture.
5. Assist in preparing a patient for an electroencephalogram.

The Anatomy and Physiology of the Nervous System

A healthy nervous system coordinates the homeostatic reactions of body systems to internal and external stimuli. ∞ As
you learned in Chapter 7, homeostasis is the ability of a living
organism to adjust to continually changing internal and external environments for optimum functioning and survival. For
example, shivering and diaphoresis are homeostatic reactions to
changes in external environment and internal body temperature. When the body senses a cold external environment, the
neurological system causes skin blood vessels to constrict and
reduce heat loss. Shivering and the resulting voluntary muscle
contractions and movement generate heat. Conversely, when
the body senses a warm external environment, the neurological system causes skin blood vessels to dilate and allow heat loss
and diaphoresis, or sweating. When the nervous system cannot
adjust to changing internal and external environments, serious
conditions may result, such as hypothermia or hyperthermia
in response to temperature changes.

The nervous system has two anatomical divisions (Figure
28-1 ◆):

■ Central nervous system (**CNS**)
■ Peripheral nervous system (**PNS**)

The Central Nervous System

The central nervous system, consisting of the brain and spinal
cord, maintains control of the peripheral nervous system and
integrates information between the two divisions. The brain
and spinal cord are protected by outer bony structures known
as the cranium and vertebral column, respectively. The
meninges, extending from the brain to cover the entire length
of the spinal cord, form a protective, watertight sheath around
the spinal cord known as the cerebrospinal canal. The meninges
consist of three protective layers:

■ Dura mater: a tough membrane that forms the outer and
thickest layer
■ Arachnoid meninges: the middle covering, which resem-
bles a spiderweb
■ Pia mater: the innermost layer, attached directly to the
brain and spinal cord tissues

Cerebrospinal fluid (**CSF**) supports and cushions the
brain and spinal cord and protects them from infection and
trauma. CSF is produced within the ventricles (spaces within
the cerebrum) and circulates through the brain and spinal cord
and into the subarachnoid space between the arachnoid and
pia mater layers.

The three major areas of the brain are the cerebrum, cerebellum, and brain stem. (∞ The functions of the different areas
of the brain are discussed further in Chapter 29.)

■ The outer layer of the cerebrum, or cerebral cortex, consists of six thin layers of gray matter containing many
millions of neuron cell bodies. The cerebral interior contains white matter and myelinated axons. The cerebrum
controls intelligence, learning and memory, reasoning
and judgment, and emotions, and interprets voluntary
muscle and sensory activities.
■ The cerebellum, also containing an outer layer of gray
matter and inner layer of white matter nerve tracts,
coordinates the activities of brain structures that control running and walking, maintaining posture and balance, and motor activities such as eating, dressing,
writing, riding a bicycle, and tracking movement with
the eyes.

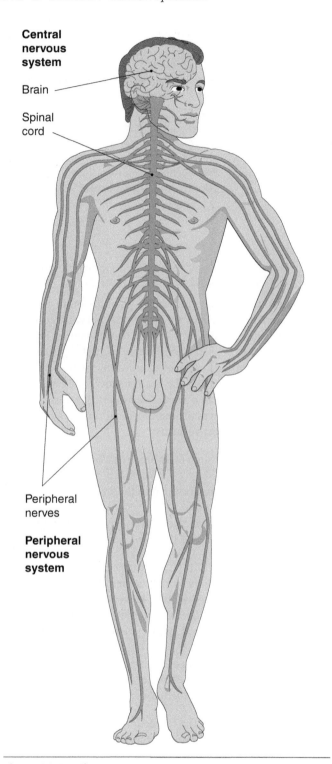

Central nervous system

Brain

Spinal cord

Peripheral nerves

Peripheral nervous system

Figure 28-1 ◆ The nervous system

■ The brain stem, consisting of the midbrain, pons, and medulla oblongata, is composed mainly of white matter and is responsible for regulating vital body functions such as respiration and heart rate.

The Peripheral Nervous System

The peripheral nervous system consists of cranial nerves, spinal nerves, and sympathetic and parasympathetic nerves. Cranial nerves originate from the base of the brain and distribute nervous system impulses mainly to the head and neck. They function in vision, hearing, smelling, the movement of eye muscles and pupil size, facial expression, chewing and tongue movements, and sensations of the head and face. There are 12 pairs of cranial nerves (Table 28-1). The cranial nerve number indicates the order of origination from the base of the brain, and the word name indicates the end distribution of the impulse or function of the nerve.

There are 31 pairs of spinal nerves, which originate from the spinal cord. They carry impulses to and from the brain.

The sympathetic and parasympathetic nerves comprise the autonomic nervous system, which is part of the peripheral nervous system. These nerves regulate all involuntary homeostatic functions and responses, including peristalsis, breathing, blinking, and hormonal and chemical activities.

The Neuron

The functional unit of the nervous system is the **neuron,** or nerve cell (Figure 28-2 ◆). Each neuron contains a cell body with a nucleus and other typical cellular components, an axon,

TABLE 28-1 THE CRANIAL NERVES		
Nerve	**Location of Receptors**	**Function**
I. Olfactory	Nasal mucosa	Sense of smell
II. Optic	Retina	Vision
III. Oculomotor	External eye muscles except superior oblique and lateral rectus	Eye movements, regulation of pupil size, accommodation, proprioception
IV. Trochlear	Superior oblique	Eye movements, proprioception
V. Trigeminal	Skin and mucosa of head and teeth	Sensations of head and face, chewing, proprioception
VI. Abducens	Lateral rectus	Abduction of the eye
VII. Facial	Taste buds of anterior two-thirds of the tongue	Facial expression, taste, secretion of saliva and tears
VIII. Vestibulocochlear	■ Vestibular branch: semicircular canals and vestibule	Balance and equilibrium
	■ Cochlear or auditory branch: organ of Corti in the cochlear duct	Hearing
IX. Glossopharyngeal	■ Pharynx: pharynx, taste buds and other receptors of posterior third of tongue	Sensations and movements of the tongue, saliva secretion
	■ Carotid: carotid sinus and carotid body	
X. Vagus	Pharynx, larynx, carotid body, thoracic and abdominal viscera	Sensations and movements of organs supplied
XI. Accessory	Trapezius and sternocleido-mastoid	Shoulder movements, turning of the head, movements of viscera, voice production
XII. Hypoglossal	Tongue muscles	Tongue movements

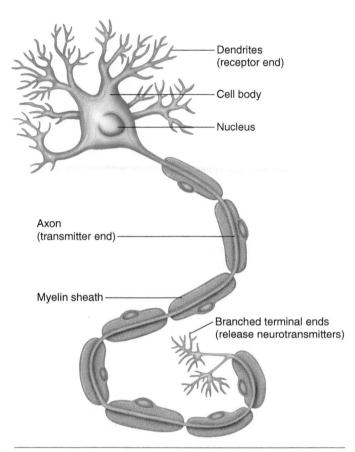

- Dendrites (receptor end)
- Cell body
- Nucleus
- Axon (transmitter end)
- Myelin sheath
- Branched terminal ends (release neurotransmitters)

Figure 28-2 ◆ The functional unit of the nervous system is the neuron.

and dendrites. Dendrites are fibers that receive impulses from other neurons and carry them to the cell body. The axon, or tail, of the neuron transmits impulses away from the cell body to other neurons, or to neuromuscular junctions. The conduction path of each nervous system impulse travels from the dendrite, through the nerve cell body, continues along the axon, and crosses the synaptic gap to the next dendrite.

Some neurons are protected by a thick, fatty covering called the myelin sheath. Cells with a very thin, almost nonexistent myelin sheath are referred to as unmyelinated. When the conduction path of unmyelinated or myelin fibers is interrupted by disease process, inflammation, or trauma, neurological symptoms include slow or altered gait, altered speech or mental process, or inability to control movements.

The myelinated fiber tissue of dendrites and axons is called white matter because the heavier myelin covering is white. Nerve cell body tissue is called gray matter. Bundles of nerve cell fibers within the central nervous system are known as tracts, and outside the central nervous systems are known as nerves.

Nerve cells are classified by the direction of relayed impulses in relation to the CNS.

- Afferent, or sensory, neurons carry impulses toward the brain and spinal cord.
- Efferent, or motor, neurons carry impulses away from the CNS to the muscles.

- Interneurons, or central neurons, relay information within the CNS.

Axon branches secrete chemical messengers called **neurotransmitters** that transmit electrical impulses across the synaptic gap. Neurotransmitters function to cause or inhibit reactions of the connected neuron(s). (∞ For a discussion of the role of neurotransmitters in mental disorders, refer to Chapter 29.)

Neuroglia, connective tissue cells of the nervous system, support, protect, and assist in the repair of nerve cells. Neuroglia also act as phagocytes for the nervous system and regulate the fluid composition between cells.

Functions of the Nervous System

The two physiological divisions of the nervous system are:

- Somatic, or voluntary, system: controlled by conscious thought; an example is climbing stairs, which requires conscious thought
- Autonomic, or involuntary, system: responsible for automatic reactions; an example is increased heart and respiratory rates in response to perceived threats

The autonomic nervous system is further divided into sympathetic ("fight-or-flight") and parasympathetic ("brakes") homeostatic nerves (Table 28-2). These two divisions work against each other to control the body's internal functions during normal activity as well as stressful or traumatic periods. Normally, every sympathetic reaction stimulates a physiological response of increased energy and activity, and the body recovers with a slowing or opposing parasympathetic response. The sympathetic nervous system reaction is also known as the "fight-or-flight" response because it engages the nervous system to respond quickly to perceived danger, with increased heart rate, respirations, metabolism, and other physiological reactions. The parasympathetic nervous system later applies the "brakes" to slow and return the body to normal physiological functioning.

In addition to parasympathetic and sympathetic reactions, reflexes also help to protect the body. A reflex is an automatic, rapid neuromuscular reaction to a specific stimulus.

TABLE 28-2 EXAMPLES OF SYMPATHETIC AND PARASYMPATHETIC REACTIONS

Sympathetic "Fight-or-Flight"	Parasympathetic "Brakes"
■ Faster, stronger heartbeat	■ Slower, calmer heartbeat
■ Decreased peristalsis of digestive tract	■ Increased peristalsis of digestive tract
■ Dilation of pupils	■ Constriction of pupils
■ Increased respiratory rate and dilated bronchi	■ Decreased respiratory rate and constricted bronchi
■ Increased circulation to skeletal muscles and respiratory system	■ Decreased circulation to skeletal muscles and respiratory system
■ Increased skin perspiration	■ Decreased circulation to skin
■ More glucose released by the liver	■ Less bladder activity

Spinal reflexes do not involve coordination with the brain. They include blinking, pulling a hand from a hot pan handle, or reaching out to prevent an off-balance fall. Stretch reflexes, on the other hand, require coordination with the brain. In a stretch reflex, such as the knee-jerk reflex, a muscle is quickly stretched and contracted. Eliciting reflex responses is a simple way to evaluate for neurological disease processes.

Assessing the Neurological System

Assessment of the central neurological system involves different evaluations to locate a deficit in the system. Areas that are assessed are mental status and speech, mood or emotional state, cognitive functioning, level of consciousness, and sensory and motor functions involving the cranial, spinal, and peripheral nerves.

Assessment of mental status usually consists of observation and specific questions such as "What is your name?" "How old are you?" "Do you know where you are?" "What is today's date?" "Who is the president of the United States?" and "Where do you live?" Observation includes noting how long it takes for the patient to respond, the appropriateness of the answers, and whether the patient makes eye contact.

Another assessment area is the individual's mood and behavior. Once again, the presence or absence of eye contact is noted. Does the individual appear sad or happy? Is he or she smiling or frowning? Is the posture straight or slumping? Does the patient have a flat **affect**? Is the patient crying? Does he or she appear angry? Responses that are not typical are noted. If the individual is groggy or unconscious, the Glasgow Coma Scale is used to assess the level of consciousness. A patient who enters the office on his or her own and talks with the staff in an appropriate manner is said to be alert and responding appropriately.

Sensory and motor function assessment is usually performed by the physician or nurse practitioner. A common assessment for motor skills of the hands and fingers is the grip response, in which the patient squeezes the examiner's fingers with both hands (Figure 28-3 ◆). If the grips appear to be unequal, the assessment is documented as "Grips unequal with weakness noted in the right/left side." Assessment of the legs and feet involves having the patient, in the supine or sitting position, push both feet up and down against the examiner's hands. In other common evaluations, the patient is asked to close the eyes and touch the nose with the index finger, walk with the eyes looking straight ahead, and stand on one foot, then the other. A thorough history may indicate another underlying pathology that could cause the patient's inability to perform all the requested tasks.

Sensory abilities are often evaluated by touching the patient's skin in various areas of the body, with a piece of gauze or other item, and asking the patient to close the eyes and state where he or she is being touched. A sterile safety pin may be used to prick the skin in this test. Olfactory senses are assessed by asking the patient to identify different odors.

Deep tendon reflexes are assessed by using a rubber reflex hammer to sharply strike a particular tendon at the site of a joint. This action provokes a spinal-mediated jerk response. Absent or diminished reflexes are indicative of nerve insult. Common sites evaluated this way are the elbows, knees, and posterior aspect of the ankles.

Head and facial injuries may affect the motor function of the six muscles controlling eye movement. These muscles and the nerves that **innervate** them are assessed by having the patient hold the head still, then look up, look down, look to the side, and follow the examiner's finger or pen as it moves around the normal field of vision. The innervation of the cranial nerve (III) oculomotor is to the superior rectus muscle that causes the eye to look up, to the inferior rectus muscle that causes the eye to look down, to the medial rectus muscle that causes the eye to rotate medially, and to the inferior oblique muscle that causes the eye to roll, look up, and look to the side. Cranial nerve VI, the abducens, innervates the lateral rectus muscle and causes the eyes to rotate laterally. Cranial nerve IV, the trochlear nerve, innervates the superior oblique muscle that causes the eye to roll, look down, and look to the side.

Another assessment of neurological function involves cranial nerve function. Areas tested are eye movement, visual acuity, sense of smell, movement of facial muscles on command, taste perception, and hearing.

The Glasgow Coma Scale

The Glasgow Coma Scale (∞ see Chapter 23) is a standardized system for the rapid assessment of brain activity, level of consciousness, possible insults to the brain, and possible outcome. Three responses are assessed: eye response, verbal response, and motor response. Each response is assigned a numerical value, and the three values provide an estimate of the injury.

The best score is noted for each portion of the response scale—for example, E2V2M4. Although it is a dependable rapid evaluation, the Glasgow Coma Scale is only a part of the neurological assessment.

Lumbar Punctures

Lumbar punctures (**LP**) are performed as a diagnostic procedure to evaluate the status of the cerebrospinal fluid and to measure the pressure within the cerebrospinal canal (Figure

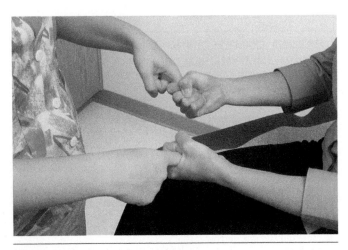

Figure 28-3 ◆ Performing a grip test

PROCEDURE 28-1 Assist in a Neurological Exam

Theory

As a medical assistant you may be responsible for interviewing patients prior to the physician's physical exam. You will evaluate and record any unusual changes in the patient's behavior—for example, in personal grooming habits and communication skills. As you conduct the interview, pay attention to what the patient is saying and how he or she is saying it. Is the speech slurred? Does the patient fumble for the right words? Is the patient making sense?

When assisting the physician with a neurological exam, you will help the patient assume the correct testing positions and having all instruments ready for use. For example, if the patient is being testing on the Glasgow Coma Scale for damage to the olfactory nerve, you will need to have objects with familiar scents available.

Materials

- reflex hammers
- penlight
- pinwheel
- tongue blade
- tuning fork
- ophthalmoscope
- cold object, as determined by physician
- warm object, as determined by physician
- scent object (coffee grounds, for example), as determined by physician
- patient drapes as determined by office protocol
- patient chart

Competency

(**Conditions**) With the necessary materials, (**Task**) you will be able to assist with a neurological exam (**Standards**) correctly, within the time frame determined by the instructor.

1. Wash your hands and gather equipment and supplies.
2. Interview the patient according to office protocol. Ask standard questions such as:
   A. What is your full name?
   B. Who is the current president of the United States?
   C. What is the date, including the month and year?
3. If your office protocol requires patients to change into cotton shorts and a tank top shirt, assist the patient as necessary.
4. Provide patient drapes as needed.
5. Follow office protocol for assisting the patient into the required positions. If the physician tests reflexes with a hammer first, assist the patient into a seated position on the exam table. Have the patient remove socks and shoes in preparation for testing the Babinski reflex.
6. After the physician has finished reflex testing, assist the patient to dress, as needed. Escort the patient to the gait-and-movement testing area.
7. Document any changes in the patient chart.

Patient Education

Tell the patient what to expect from the tests, any discomfort that may be experienced, and when test results will be ready. Encourage questions.

Charting Example

09/23/XX 2:30 p.m. Patient arrived for neurological testing, appearing disheveled. Patient was unshaven but stated he is not growing a beard. Clothes were wrinkled and unwashed, which is unusual for this patient. Patient was asked several orientation questions and could not identify self or correct time and place. Physician notified of results. Maurice Holmes, CMA

28-4 ◆). Pressure is measured with a device called a *manometer*, which is attached to the hub of a needle inserted into the cerebrospinal canal. Laboratory examination and culture and sensitivity of the CSF may reveal the presence of red blood cells, white blood cells, protein, glucose, or microorganisms. Interpreting these test results is helpful in the diagnosis of disorders and diseases of the central nervous system.

Electroencephalography

An electroencephalogram (**EEG**) records electrical impulses in the brain created when brain cells communicate with each other. Electroencephalography is a valuable tool in diagnosing brain death, brain tumors, epilepsy, and other brain conditions. Occasionally an EEG is ordered to evaluate a sleep disorder, in which case the test is performed in a sleep center, generally in a hospital.

The pattern, height, length, and rate of brain waves are unique to each person, like a brain "fingerprint." The brain-wave activity of the brain is recorded as a written tracing by the EEG machine. The EEG technician attaches electrodes to the scalp and to an amplifier that amplifies the patient's brain waves more than a million times. The technician looks for three distinct types of waves. The occipital alpha wave is an indicator of healthy brain function. This wave comes from the back of the head. Delta waves are normally found in infants and during deep sleep. They are slow, irregular waves that are rarely found in waking adults. A decrease in brain activity shows up as a theta wave, which is a slow, rhythmic wave.

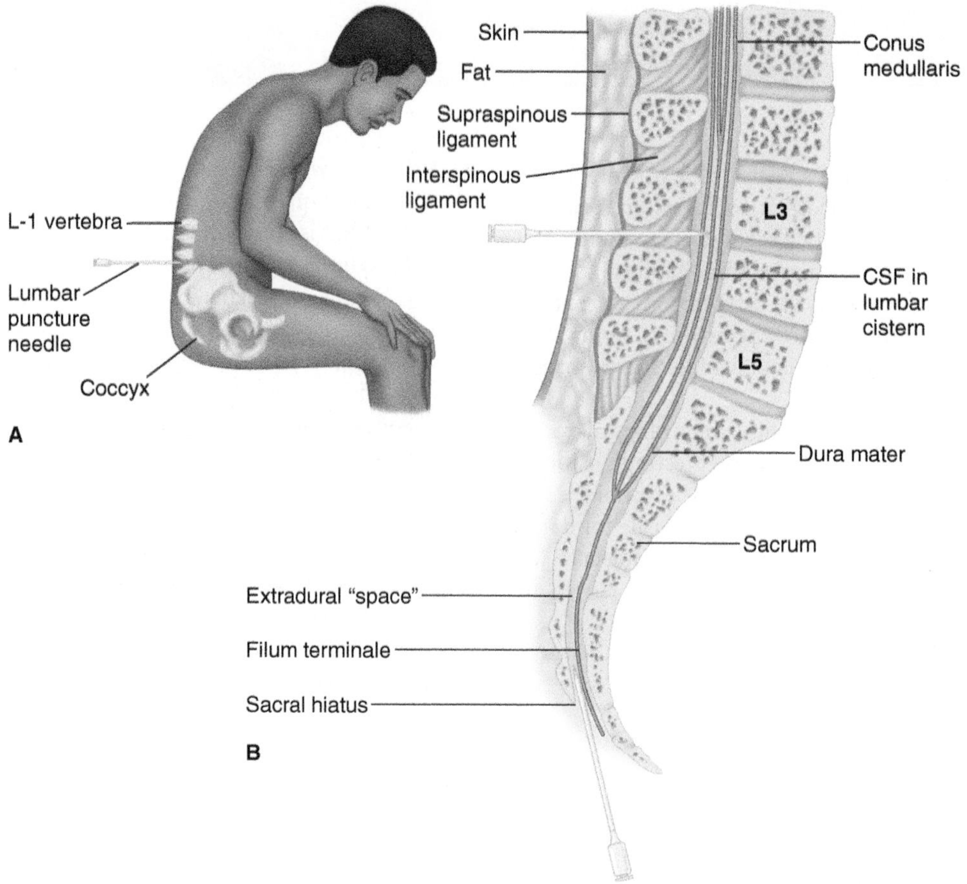

Figure 28-4 ◆ (A) Lumbar puncture; (B) Section of the vertebral column showing the spinal cord and membranes

PROCEDURE 28-2 Assist with a Lumbar Puncture

Theory

A lumbar puncture is a delicate procedure done under sterile technique in the physician's office. Most offices that perform lumbar punctures set aside a special room for this procedure, which requires that the patient remain at the clinic for several hours. Depending on your office protocol, it may be your responsibility to continuously monitor the patient's vital signs and alert the family of the patient's status. Family members are sometimes allowed to stay with the patient during the postoperative time.

Materials

- lumbar puncture kit: iodine antiseptic, iodine applicator, adhesive bandages, spinal puncture needle, 4 testing tubes
- patient drape
- BP cuff, sized appropriately for the patient
- manometer
- xylocaine1-2%
- syringe and needle for anesthetic
- sterile gloves
- gauze sponges
- fenestrated drape

Competency

(**Conditions**) With the necessary materials, (**Task**) you will be able to assist the physician with a lumbar puncture to obtain CSF (**Standards**) correctly within the time determined by the instructor.

1. Identify the patient and explain the procedure. Reinforce the need for postoperative care.
2. Verify that the patient has signed a consent form and that it has been filed in the chart.
3. Have the patient empty his or her bowel and bladder.
4. Obtain the patient's vital signs.
5. Wash your hands, put on gloves, and set up a tray using sterile technique.
6. With the iodine in the kit, disinfect the puncture site (L3 and L4).

PROCEDURE 28-2 Assist with a Lumbar Puncture *(continued)*

7. Have the patient lie on his or her left side and curl into the fetal position. Provide drapes for patient comfort.
8. Assist the physician as necessary in swabbing the patient with antiseptic and placing a fenestrated drape.
9. Assist the physician in aspirating the xylocaine.
10. To avoid potential trauma to the spinal cord, assist the patient in maintaining the fetal position.
11. While the physician is taking a pressure reading, remind the patient to breathe evenly and avoid talking. If the physician requests, assist the patient in straightening his or her legs to get a true pressure reading.
12. Place a gauze pad with firm pressure over the puncture site to absorb any bleeding.
13. After the fluid has been collected, tighten the sample tubes and fill out a lab order form. Correctly label the samples for analysis.
14. Move the patient to the recovery area.
15. Clean and disinfect the treatment area.
16. Remove the gloves and wash your hands.
17. Document the procedure in the patient's chart.

Patient Education

The patient should be instructed to remain in a prone position for 3–4 hours to allow the CSF to be replenished and the puncture site to heal. Make sure the patient understands the importance of not rushing through this vital healing process. The patient should not attempt to sit upright for extended periods, and excessive movement can cause spinal headaches and potential damage. In addition, the patient should increase fluid intake to replace the lost fluid. Any tingling, numbness, paralysis, or severe headaches should be reported immediately.

Charting Example

09/23/XX 9:00 A.M. Lumbar puncture performed by Dr. J. Lee. 3 vials of CSF obtained and sent to laboratory for testing. Patient tolerated procedure well, BP remained stable, checked every 15 minutes for 3 hours post-procedure. Patient was given verbal and written instructions to increase fluid intake, remain flat for 3-4 hours, and report any headaches, fever, bleeding, numbness, paralysis, or tingling. Kathleen Graham, RMA

PROCEDURE 28-3 Prepare a Patient for an Electroencephalogram

Theory

The EEG technician will ask the patient to remain motionless in a comfortable position, generally lying supine or in a reclining chair, while 16 to 25 electrodes are attached to the scalp. The electrodes are flat metal disks that are applied with a washable paste or adhesive. The placement of electrodes does not require shaving.

There is very little risk involved in performing an EEG. Although the EEG machine records electrical activity in the brain, the patient should be informed that no electricity will pass into the body, and there is no danger of electrocution. The patient should not feel anything during the procedure. If the patient is prone to seizures, which is a common reason for ordering an EEG, the portion of the test involving flashing lights may trigger this response. The EEG technician has been specially trained for this event should it occur.

To ensure an accurate reading, the patient must follow certain pretesting instructions, such as eliminating caffeine, avoiding smoking and other stimulants, and discontinuing certain medications. It may be your job to ensure that the patient has read, understood, and can comply with all pretesting requirements.

Materials

■ EEG machine
■ electrodes
■ approved EEG electrode adhesive

Competency

(**Conditions**) With the necessary materials, (**Task**) you will be able to assist the physician with an EEG (**Standards**) correctly, within the time determined by the instructor.

1. Identify the patient. Explain the procedure and why the physician has ordered it. Try to allay any anxiety the patient might be feeling.
2. Verify that the patient has followed pretesting procedures—avoiding caffeine and other stimulants and eating a well-balanced diet to avoid hypoglycemia.
3. Instruct the patient to remain absolutely motionless during the baseline reading. Even tongue or eyelid movements will alter the baseline.
4. Connect the electrodes to the patient's scalp with the appropriate adhesive.

continued

PROCEDURE 28-3 Prepare a Patient for an Electroencephalogram (continued)

5. If a sleep EEG has been ordered, the patient should not alter his or her sleeping patterns and avoid using sleep aids.

6. The patient will be shown flickering lights to stimulate the brain. This activity will be recorded by the technician.

7. Remove the electrodes from the patient's scalp. If the patient has been lying supine for the exam, help him or her to a sitting position. The patient should remain seated for a minimum of 1 minute to avoid dizziness caused by orthostatic hypotension.

8. Document the procedure in the patient's chart.

Patient Education

Make sure the patient understands that although the machine records electrical activity within the brain, there is no risk of electrocution. Reinforce that there should be no pain or discomfort during the examination.

Charting Example

06/17/XX 10:00 a.m. EEG performed by Dr. J. Lee. Patient verified she did not use stimulants 48 hours prior to appointment and had a well-balanced meal. Patient tolerated the procedure well and will be given the test results by Dr. Lee. Jason Santos, RMA

Disorders and Diseases of the Central Nervous System

CNS diseases and disorders involve the brain and the spinal cord. Cerebral vascular accidents account for a great portion of conditions affecting the brain. Cerebrovascular disease (CVD) is usually a result of atherosclerosis of the cerebral arteries, which deprives the brain of oxygen and is one cause of dementia (∞ see Chapter 17 for a discussion of atherosclerosis). Traumatic insults are another major cause. Other conditions affecting the CNS include epilepsy, multiple sclerosis, Parkinson's disease, and disk disorders.

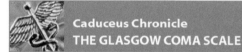

Caduceus Chronicle
THE GLASGOW COMA SCALE

After World War II, it was believed that neurosurgical treatment could do little to affect the outcome of most head injuries. Improvements in intensive care and resuscitation techniques made it possible to save the lives of more and more head injury patients, however, and pathological and post-mortem studies revealed that disability could be limited if head injuries were treated early and appropriately. Intensive care physicians wanted to know which treatments would provide better clinical outcomes and which patients had a better chance for partial or total recovery.

These concerns led Bryan Jennett, MD, and others at the University Department of Neurosurgery and the Institute of Neurological Sciences in Glasgow, Scotland, to conduct studies with the Glasgow Coma Scale, first published in 1974. The original scale was designed to use standardized terms to avoid ambiguity in patient assessments. It was also devised to measure three domains: eye opening, verbal responses, and motor response. If a patient was unable to participate in one domain, two others remained for an accurate neurological assessment. For example, a patient who could not speak might be capable of eye or motor responses. A tool developed for research in severe head injuries became the standard tool for neurological assessment.

Cerebrovascular Accidents

Cerebrovascular accidents (**CVA**), also referred to as strokes, may be the result of three vascular conditions in the brain (Figure 28-5 ◆).

- An embolus may lodge in an artery, causing an occlusion and depriving distal brain tissue supplied by that artery of oxygen and nutrition.
- A thrombus may occlude an artery and block distal circulation.
- A vessel rupture, usually from an aneurysm, may hemorrhage into the brain tissue. Malignant hypertension may also cause the rupture.

Regardless of the cause, prompt assessment and intervention are necessary to prevent permanent brain damage or death.

Symptoms of CVA vary, depending on the pathology, location, and extent of the event. Commonly, the person complains of headache and loss of nerve and muscle function on one side of the body (**hemiparesis**). Speech difficulties are typical, and the patient may appear confused. Loss of consciousness is an ominous sign.

CVAs are considered life threatening. Patients are transported to an emergency facility where anticoagulant and thrombolytic agents are administered to increase blood flow to the

Keys to Success
ASPIRIN THERAPY

To reduce the debilitating effects of CVA from thrombus or embolus, the medical community is advocating immediate self-intervention by chewing a single adult-dose aspirin. This is also recommended for anyone displaying the symptoms of a TIA or heart attack.

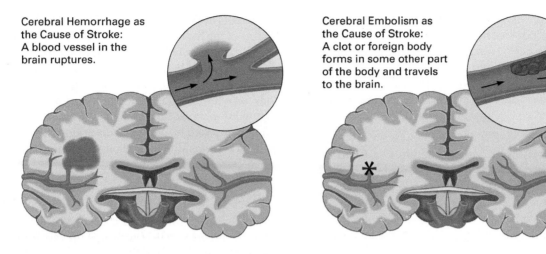

STROKE

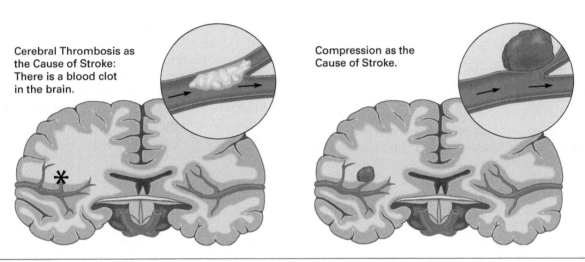

Figure 28-5 ◆ Causes of stroke

affected area. When the insult is the result of a "bleed," surgery may be performed to halt the hemorrhage. Surgery may also be required to reduce pressure on the brain caused by edema. Prognosis is unpredictable and varies according to the type, location, and extent of the insult.

Transient Ischemic Attack

Transient ischemic attacks (**TIA**), caused by brief periods of reduced blood flow to the cerebrum, exhibit symptoms similar to but often less severe than those of a cerebral vascular accident. TIAs usually resolve within 24 hours with little or no residual affects. They are considered a warning sign of possible impending CVA.

Epilepsy

Epilepsy is a chronic disorder characterized by seizure activity in the form of involuntary muscular contractions. The etiology is variable. One possible cause is the electrical disruption of normal brain activity by chemical imbalances, including alcohol withdrawal, poisoning or drug toxicity, eclampsia (severe toxemia of pregnancy), metabolic disease conditions such as diabetes, and the accumulation of waste products in blood when kidneys are not functioning properly. Other causes are CNS infections, CVA, or trauma to the brain.

Seizures occur randomly, as brain impulses are chaotic. Three types of epilepsy seizures are grand mal, petit mal, and status epilepticus.

■ The most severe **tonic-clonic** seizures are typical of grand mal epilepsy. Patients frequently experience a warning of impending seizure, called an **aura.** Auras may take the form of distinct odors, special sounds, dizziness, spots before the eyes, tingling in the fingers or toes, and/or loss of consciousness. The seizures are bilaterally symmetrical, involve the entire body, and have no local onset. Following the seizure, the individual is usually unconscious for a brief time and later has no memory of the event. This is called a **postictal** state.

- In petit mal epilepsy, the person, usually a child, experiences brief periods—a few seconds—of unconsciousness. These fleeting periods may go unnoticed as the child blinks or stares briefly into space.
- Status epilepticus is a series of repetitive seizures during which the patient does not regain consciousness. This is a true medical emergency that requires prompt intervention.

Diagnosis of epilepsy is based on a history of recurrent seizure activity, EEG, MRI, and CT scan. Treatment involves anticonvulsant drug therapy, education about the condition, and counseling. For status epilepticus, anticonvulsants are administered to stop the seizures and reduce the possibility of cerebral hypoxia or anoxia and the resulting permanent or fatal damage.

There is no cure for epilepsy. Prognosis is variable, depending on the patient's response to the drug therapy. Compliance is critical to a positive outcome (Figure 28-6 ◆).

Amyotrophic Lateral Sclerosis

Amyotrophic lateral sclerosis (**ALS**), also known as Lou Gehrig's disease, is a progressive neuromuscular disease with fatal outcome. The cause is unknown. Muscle weakness and minor involuntary muscular contractions of the arms and hands are early symptoms. The condition progresses to complete loss of neuromuscular function, and the patient requires a ventilator to breathe and tube feedings to compensate for the inability to chew and swallow. But cognitive ability is not affected. Diagnosis is confirmed by EMG and biopsy. Treatment is supportive until death occurs.

Parkinson's Disease

Parkinson's disease is a degenerative condition of the brain characterized by muscular rigidity and **palsy,** or tremors. This slowly progressing chronic condition typically has onset in later life.

Fine tremors of the hands are noted, followed by the shaking or nodding of the head. Movements become slower and the facial muscles stiffen. Ambulation becomes a shuffling gait.

The cause of Parkinson's is unknown, but there is a deficiency in the production of the neurotransmitter dopamine. While not a cure, drug therapy with L-dopa and anti-cholinergic drugs helps to replace the missing dopamine. Patients are encouraged to avoid alcohol consumption. Physical therapy is helpful in relieving stiffness and muscle cramps. At present there is no known cure for this debilitating disease.

Multiple Sclerosis

Multiple sclerosis (MS), also a chronic disorder, is characterized by the progressive destruction of the myelin sheath of the nerve and progressive disability. The specific cause is unknown; however, immune, viral, and genetic etiologies have been suggested. Transient motor and sensory disturbances occur and are variable in location, depending on the location of the myelin sheath damage. The vision may become impaired and muscles may weaken. **Exacerbation** is common.

Diagnosis of MS is based on a physical examination, history, CSF analysis, CT scans, and MRIs of the CNS. The goal of treatment is to relieve symptoms and avert exacerbation of the condition. Drug therapy includes the use of adrenocorticotropic hormones. Patients are encouraged to avoid stress and extreme temperatures. There is no known cure for MS and prognosis is variable, depending on the involvement and location of the insulted myelin sheath.

Headache

Headache, also known as **cephalgia,** is diffuse acute or chronic pain occurring in any part of the head. Often the cause is not identifiable; however, the pain results from the irritation of sensory nerve endings in the head or neck. The individual may describe the pain as diffuse, dull, aching, sharp, acute, intense, throbbing, or almost unbearable.

Diagnosis is determined from history and physical examination. Imaging and neurological studies, including EEG, help to identify the underlying pathology and rule out severe pathology. Analgesic drug therapy helps to relieve pain, and stress reduction and massage may be helpful as well.

Migraine headaches are intense, throbbing, and incapacitating. They are thought to be the result of changes in cerebral blood flow—vasoconstriction followed by vasodilation of the arterioles. **Prodromal** symptoms are common, such as photophobia, tinnitus, flashing lights, and cravings for sweets or certain foods. Treatment includes bed rest in a darkened room, analgesics, ergot preparations, and relaxation exercises. Prophylaxis with beta-blockers may be helpful.

Infectious Conditions of the Central Nervous System

Infectious or inflammatory conditions that affect the central nervous system include encephalitis, meningitis, and brain abscess.

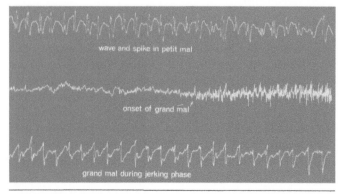

wave and spike in petit mal

onset of grand mal

grand mal during jerking phase

Figure 28-6 ◆ Seizure activity
Source: Science Source/Photo Researchers, Inc.

Encephalitis

Encephalitis is inflammation of the brain. It can be caused by a virus that is often transmitted to humans from birds or horses via mosquito bite. It may also be a sequela of viral infections such as mumps, measles, chickenpox, influenza, rubella, and mononucleosis. Another form of encephalitis is caused by infection with the herpes simplex virus and has the highest mortality rate when left untreated. Encephalitis caused by the West Nile virus (WNV) occurred only rarely in the United States until recently. Today this form of encephalitis has reached endemic proportions as the virus spreads across the country and into Canada and Mexico.

Symptoms of encephalitis include classic infectious CNS symptoms such as headache, fever, malaise, lethargy, visual disturbances, nausea and vomiting, and decreased level of consciousness. The disease progresses rapidly, causing **nuchal rigidity** (stiff neck), seizures, and loss of consciousness.

Diagnosis is confirmed with a patient history, physical examination, blood tests, and CSF analysis. Treatment involves drug therapy with antiviral agents, steroids, antipyretics, and anticonvulsants, with body system support. Prognosis is variable, depending on the causative agent, the extent and duration of the infection, the age and physical condition of the patient, and the patient's response to treatment.

Eradicating mosquito breeding sites is a primary preventive measure against encephalitis. Mosquito bites can be avoided by installing screens in doors and windows and by using insect repellents and wearing long-sleeved shirts and long pants outdoors.

Meningitis

Meningitis is an inflammation of the meninges, the coverings of the brain and spinal cord. The causative microorganism may be viral or bacterial. Common bacterial agents are *Hemophilus influenzae* type B, *Streptococcus pneumoniae,* and *Neisseria meningitidis.*

As with other CNS disorders, patients with meningitis experience headache, fever, dizziness, blurred vision, and motor problems. A common symptom is nuchal rigidity, indicated when the patient resists any movement of the head. Meningitis is considered a medical emergency and requires prompt diagnosis and aggressive treatment. Vigorous antibiotic therapy and support of systems are the treatments of choice. Prognosis is variable and depends on how quickly diagnosis and treatment are provided.

Brain Abscess

Infectious microorganisms that migrate to the brain from other infections in the body may cause a brain abscess (Figure 28-7 ◆). These **pyogenic** microorganisms may be in encapsulated or free form in the brain tissue. Body infections with a tendency to move to the brain are sinusitis, otitis media, mastoiditis, endocarditis, and pneumonia.

A patient with a brain abscess has a fever and often complains of a headache. Neurological symptoms vary, depending on the location and extent of the abscess. In addition to headache and fever, dizziness, syncope, drowsiness, visual problems, nausea and vomiting, hemiplegia, pallor, and slowed heart rate or respiratory effort are characteristic symptoms. The eyes usually look to the insult.

Imaging studies, including radiographs of the skull, CT scans, and cerebral angiography, are combined with examination of the CSF and measurement of the pressure in the cerebrospinal canal to arrive at a diagnosis. Treatment consists of aggressive antibiotic therapy and support of body systems. Outcome is variable.

Brain Tumors

Tumors of the brain arise from abnormal cell development and are benign or malignant. A malignant tumor may be the primary or secondary metastatic site. As it grows, the tumor exerts pressure on nearby tissues and causes signs and symptoms.

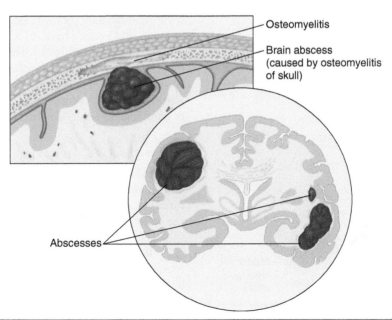

Figure 28-7 ◆ Abscesses of the brain

Symptoms include headache, vomiting, and changes in vision, balance and coordination, and muscle strength. Speech, personality, and mental function may also be affected. Diagnostic testing includes MRI, CT scan, EEG, lumbar puncture and examination of CSF, and biopsy of excised tissue. Treatment is primarily surgical to remove the tumor, but can also include chemotherapy and radiation. Other medications are prescribed to reduce or eliminate symptoms created by the pressure or to relieve symptoms associated with chemotherapy, radiation, or the progression of the disease.

Head Trauma

Head injuries are often classified as open or closed. In open head injuries, the skull is fractured and the skin is broken. In closed head injuries, the cranium is not fractured.

Symptoms of head injuries include altered levels of consciousness and mental status, unequal pupils, blood or fluid coming from the ears or nose, severe head pain, alterations in vital signs, dizziness, blurred vision, ringing in the ears, and **projectile vomiting.**

Brain injuries may also have an effect on a patient's posture. It should be noted if the patient displays **decerebrate or decorticate posture**.

Direct brain injuries such as lacerations, punctures, and bruises are caused by the fragments or edges of fractured cranial bones. Indirect brain injuries are the result of the impact of the brain on the cranium when force is applied to the skull. Hematomas, concussions, and contusions are indirect brain injuries.

Hematomas are collections of blood that form above or between the meninges (Figures 28-8 ◆ and 28-9 ◆). An epidural or extradural hematoma is above the dura mater, just under the cranial bones. A subdural hematoma lies under the dura mater and above the arachnoid meninges. Some hematomas resolve spontaneously with bed rest, while others may require surgical intervention. The extent and duration of the hematoma

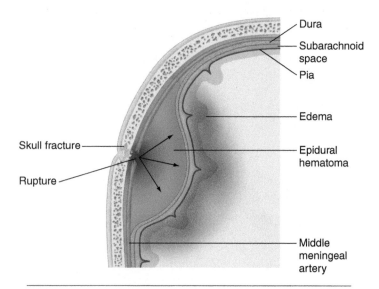

Figure 28-8 ◆ Extradural hematoma

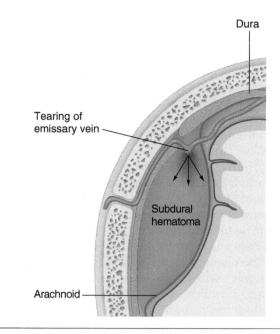

Figure 28-9 ◆ Subdural hematoma

as well as its resolution determine whether there are any residual effects.

Concussions and Contusions

A concussion is caused by a blow to the head or an acceleration/deceleration type of injury. The force is transferred through the skull to the brain with no detectable or permanent structural damage. The victim may feel dizzy, often complains of a headache, and may temporarily lose consciousness. Brief, temporary amnesia is not uncommon. The insult usually resolves spontaneously with no residual effects.

A contusion, a more severe form of head injury, is a bruise in the brain where blood vessels are ruptured. The impact is strong enough to make the brain strike the opposite side of the cranium and bounce back, striking the impacted side. This is termed a **contrecoup** injury. Hematomas may form, and increasing intracranial pressure often causes the individual to lose consciousness. Other symptoms of head injury may be present. Rest is prescribed along with monitoring of vital signs and level of consciousness. Surgical intervention may be necessary.

Spinal Cord Injuries

The vertebrae in the spinal column are separated by intervertebral disks. Insults to the spinal cord may be the result of fractured vertebrae, the dislocation of vertebrae, or other trauma to the vertebral column. These create pressure or edema on the spinal cord and exiting spinal nerves.

Paraplegia, the loss of sensation and motor activity (paralysis) of the lower trunk and lower extremities, is caused by injury to the spinal cord in the thoracic or lumbar region. Ambulatory function may be decreased or completely lost, and control of bowel and bladder function is impaired.

Quadriplegia, the paralysis of the entire trunk and all four extremities, is caused by an insult to the spinal cord in the cervical area. Respiration may be impaired and require mechanical assistance.

Diagnosis of a spinal cord injury is confirmed by observation, physical examination, and history of the insult. Neurological assessment combined with imaging studies helps to identify the location and possible source of the paralysis. Treatment involves reducing pressure on the spinal cord and spinal nerves. Stabilization of fractures and other injuries helps to prevent extension of the insult. Prognosis is variable, but permanent damage to the nerves is possible, as destroyed nerve tissue does not regenerate. Rehabilitation is encouraged.

Impotence is often a side effect for a male patient with a spinal cord injury. Mechanical and drug-based methods for achieving an erection should be explored. Counseling and referrals to a specialist are helpful.

Disk Disorders

Insult to the intervertebral disks from trauma or degenerative disease is one cause of back pain. The cervical and lumbar disks are the most vulnerable, since the cervical and lumbar vertebrae are not held in place by the rib cage as the thoracic vertebrae are. Traumatic insult to the spinal column, whether from a fall, an acceleration-deceleration injury or poor body mechanics when lifting, may squeeze the disk or cause it to bulge or herniate. In a degenerative disease, the disk deteriorates. Regardless of the cause, the damaged disk exerts pressure on the spinal cord and/or the spinal nerves in that region. This pressure causes pain and can lead to loss of function in the area of the body supplied by the compromised nerve.

Imaging studies, patient history, and neurological examination aid in diagnosis. It is not always possible to resolve disk problems. Pain usually dictates the course of treatment. Some bulging disks may resolve spontaneously with rest; others may require surgical intervention. Pain relief may be achieved with rest, drug therapy, physical therapy, or, if necessary, surgery. Prognosis is variable, depending on the cause, location, and extent of the insult.

Sciatica, also known as *spinal stenosis,* is the narrowing of the vertebral canal. The resulting compression of the spinal cord and connecting nerves within the canal cause back and radiating leg pain. Some patients experience numbness in these areas. Increased activity worsens the symptoms. The cause of sciatica may be arthritis or aging. Diagnostic studies include MRI, CT,

X-rays, and myelogram. Medications to reduce pain and inflammation are prescribed. A period of bed rest, applications of heat or cold therapy, and massage may help ease the pain. Surgery is performed only in cases of increasing weakness or debilitating pain.

Diseases of the Peripheral Nervous System

Peripheral nervous system disorders include Bell's palsy, trigeminal neuralgia, and shingles. These acute, nonprogressive conditions affect the cranial and spinal nerves.

Bell's Palsy

Bell's palsy is a disorder of the seventh cranial nerve (also called the facial nerve), which is the peripheral nerve supplying the facial muscles. The individual experiences a sudden onset of unilateral facial paralysis, often awakening with one side of the face drooping, in particular the mouth. Sensation on the affected side is diminished or absent.

The etiology of this disorder is unknown, although it may follow a viral infection. Diagnosis is based on observation, physical examination, and history of time of onset and duration of condition. Treatment consists of steroid drug therapy. Resolution may occur spontaneously, or residual effects may remain indefinitely. The patient is warned to use caution when eating and drinking, as sensations of heat and pain are absent. Many physicians recommend patching the eye on the affected side during sleep to prevent corneal abrasions that might otherwise occur because the eye cannot feel pain.

Trigeminal Neuralgia

Like Bell's palsy, trigeminal **neuralgia** (also called *tic douloureux*) has a sudden onset and is generally unilateral. The region of the face affected is supplied by the fifth cranial nerve, the trigeminal nerve. The pain is extremely sharp and can be intermittent. One branch or all three branches of the trigeminal nerve may be involved.

The etiology of trigeminal neuralgia is unknown. Diagnosis is based on observation, physical examination, and history. Treatment involves analgesic drug therapy. As a last resort, surgical intervention is performed to cut the nerve and stop the transmission of sensory impulses.

Shingles (Herpes Zoster)

Shingles occurs when the herpes varicella-zoster virus, which remains in a dormant state within the body following a case of chickenpox, is reactivated. Often triggered by emotional or physical stress, this condition is characterized by intense pain and small blisters that follow the affected **dermatome(s)** under the skin. The affected area is often hypersensitive to the touch, and the pain can be burning and tingling. Most incidences are unilateral and do not cross the midline.

Keys to Success
EYE MOVEMENTS IN HEAD INSULTS

Insults to the head, whether traumatic or infectious, have some symptoms in common. Often the eyes look toward the insult, especially when the insult is greater on one side than the other. Therefore, observation of eye movement—or lack thereof—is helpful in the diagnosis of cerebral insult.

The trained clinician recognizes the typical blister-type eruptions and the pattern of distribution along the nerve routes, which, combined with a history of chickenpox infection, confirm the diagnosis. Drug therapy comprises antiviral medications, steroids, analgesics, sedatives, and antipyretics. If the blisters become infected, antibiotics are prescribed. The condition usually resolves in less than a month. Recurrences seldom occur. If the pain persists longer than a month and the blisters have cleared, the condition is termed post-herpetic neuralgia.

Shingles is not contagious to people who have had chickenpox, but those who have never had chickenpox are at risk for developing it after exposure to the herpes varicella-zoster virus. There is no know prevention at this time; however, research is ongoing in the area of preventive vaccines.

— Critical Thinking Question 28-1—

What the patient thought was an allergic reaction may in fact be shingles, given the pain level and past history of varicella. What information can Dawn give the patient? How should Dawn handle the information that the patient's girlfriend ruptured some of the blisters?

REVIEW

Chapter Summary

- The central nervous system consists of the brain and spinal cord. The peripheral nervous system consists of cranial nerves, spinal nerves, and the sympathetic and parasympathetic nerves of the autonomic nervous system.
- The neuron is the functional unit of the nervous system. It is made up of a nerve cell body, an axon, and dendrites. Nervous system impulses cross the synaptic gap between neurons via neurotransmitters.
- The nervous system has two physiological divisions: the somatic or voluntary system, controlled by conscious thought, and the autonomic or involuntary system, controlled by homeostatic reactions of the body to sympathetic and parasympathetic stimuli. The sympathetic nervous system prepares the body for the "fight or flight" response to perceived dangers. The parasympathetic system applies the "brakes" to return the body to its normal physiological state.
- Neurological assessment utilizes a variety of tools to evaluate mental status, speech, mood or emotional state, cognitive functioning, level of consciousness, and sensory and motor functions. The Glasgow Coma Scale is a standardized system used to rapidly assess brain activity, level of consciousness, possible insults to the brain, and possible outcome based on eye, verbal, and motor responses. Lumbar punctures are a diagnostic procedure involving the analysis of cerebrospinal fluid.
- A CVA, or stroke, may be caused by an embolus, thrombus, or vessel rupture. Symptoms include headache, loss of unilateral nerve and muscle function, speech difficulties and confusion, and possible loss of consciousness.
- Transient ischemic attacks exhibit symptoms similar to those of a CVA. TIAs usually resolve within 24 hours with little or no residual effects.
- Epilepsy is characterized by seizures. Tonic-clonic seizures are observed in grand mal epilepsy. Petit mal seizures are brief periods of unconsciousness. Status epilepticus, repetitive seizures from which the patient does not regain consciousness, is a medical emergency requiring prompt intervention with anticonvulsive drugs.
- Parkinson's disease is a chronic degenerative condition of the brain characterized by muscular rigidity and palsy (tremors). Multiple sclerosis, also a chronic disorder, results in the progressive destruction of the myelin sheath of the nerve and progressive disability.
- A headache, or cephalgia, is diffuse acute or chronic pain occurring in any part of the head when sensory nerve endings in the head or neck are irritated. Migraine headaches may be caused by changes in cerebral blood flow.
- Head trauma can be classified as an open head injury (skull is fractured and skin is broken) or a closed head injury (skull is not fractured). Direct brain injuries (lacerations, punctures, bruises) are caused by fragments or edges of fractured cranial bones. Indirect brain injuries include hematomas, concussion, and contusion. Hematomas are collections of

Chapter Summary (continued)

blood above the meninges (epidural) or between the dura mater and arachnoid meninges (subdural).

■ A concussion is the result of a blow to the head or an acceleration/deceleration injury. A contusion is a bruise to the brain in which blood vessels are ruptured.

■ Spinal cord injuries may result in paraplegia or quadriplegia. Injuries may be caused by fractured or dislocated vertebrae or other trauma to the vertebral column.

■ Infectious conditions of the CNS include encephalitis, meningitis, and brain abscess. Encephalitis, inflammation of the brain, is usually caused by a virus or may be a sequela of a

viral infection. Meningitis is an inflammation of the meninges caused by a virus or bacteria. Infectious microorganisms that migrate to the brain from other infections in the body may cause brain abscess.

■ Diseases of the peripheral nervous system include Bell's palsy, trigeminal neuralgia, and shingles (herpes zoster). Bell's palsy is characterized by a sudden onset of unilateral facial paralysis. Trigeminal neuralgia also has a sudden onset and is generally unilateral. Shingles occurs when a dormant herpes varicella-zoster virus in the body is reactivated.

Chapter Review Questions

Multiple Choice

1. Which of the following terms means "sharp nerve pain"?
   A. neuron
   B. neurodynia
   C. neuralgia
   D. nuchal rigidity

2. Which of the following terms refers to a tough membrane that forms on the outer layer of the meninges?
   A. arachoid meninges
   B. dura mater
   C. pia mater
   D. contra mater

3. The nervous system has how many anatomical divisions?
   A. 2
   B. 1
   C. 3
   D. 4

4. Amyotrophic lateral sclerosis (ALS) is also known as:
   A. grand mal seizures
   B. multiple sclerosis
   C. Parkinson's disease
   D. Lou Gehrig's disease

5. Shingles occurs when _____ is reactivated in the patient's system.
   A. hepatitis A virus
   B. *Streptococcus pneumoniae*
   C. trigeminal neuralgia
   D. herpes varicella-zoster

True/False

T F 1. Infectious conditions of the CNS include encephalitis, meningitis, and brain abscess.

T F 2. Encephalitis, or inflammation of the brain, is usually caused by a virus or may be a sequela of a viral infection.

T F 3. Symptoms of shingles include headache, loss of unilateral nerve and muscle function, speech difficulties and confusion, and possible loss of consciousness.

T F 4. Tumors of the brain arise from abnormal cell development and are benign or malignant.

T F 5. There are 34 pairs of spinal nerves, which originate from the spinal cord.

T F 6. The spinal nerves carry impulses to and from the brain.

T F 7. Taste perception is one of many tests for neurological function.

T F 8. A concussion is more severe than a contusion.

T F 9. Peripheral nervous system disorders include Bell's palsy, trigeminal neuralgia, and shingles.

T F 10. The inferior rectus muscle causes the eye to look up, and the superior rectus muscle causes the eye to look down.

Short Answer

1. An assessment of neurological function involves cranial nerve function. Which areas are tested?

2. What are the three vascular conditions in the brain that cause CVA, or stroke?

3. What is the Glasgow Coma Scale?

4. Name three types of epilepsy seizures.

5. Which organs are affected by meningitis?

Research

1. Recent studies suggest that college-bound teens are more likely to contract meningitis while living in dormitories. Where in your community are vaccinations for meningitis offered?

2. What is the Romberg test, and how would a medical assistant assist the physician in performing this test?

Externship Application Experience

A patient comes to the reception desk with a possible diagnosis of shingles. Children are playing in the same area. What are the implications of allowing this patient to wait in the reception area with children and other adult patients? What is the appropriate action to take?

Resource Guide

American Academy of Neurology
1080 Montreal Ave.
St. Paul, MN 55116
1-800-879-1960
www.aan.com

American Association of Neurosurgery
5550 Meadowbrook Drive
Rolling Meadows, IL 60008
1-888-566-2267
www.neurosurgery.org

American Neurological Association
5841 Cedar Lake Rd., Suite #204
Minneapolis, MN 55416
956-545-6284
www.aneuroa.org

National Multiple Sclerosis Society
733 Third Ave.
New York, NY 10017
1-800-344-4867
www.nationalmssociety.com

National Parkinson Foundation
1501 N.W. 9th Avenue / Bob Hope Road
Miami, FL 33136-1494
1-800-327-4545
www.parkinson.org

National Spinal Cord Injury Association
6701 Democracy Blvd., Suite 300-9
Bethesda, MD 20817
301-588-6959
www.spinalcord.org

National Stroke Association
9707 E. Easter Lane
Englewood, CA 80112
1-800-strokes
www.stroke.org

MedMedia
www.prenhall.com/frazier

More on this chapter, including interactive resources, can be found on the Student CD-ROM accompanying this textbook and on the Companion Website at www.prenhall.com/frazier.

Objectives

After completing this chapter, you should be able to:

- Spell and define the medical terminology in the chapter.
- Identify the medical assistant's role in the mental health field.
- Discuss the cognitive functions of the brain.
- Discuss the concept of mental wellness.
- Describe the symptoms and treatment of schizophrenia.
- Describe the symptoms and treatment of various mood disorders.
- Describe the symptoms and treatment of personality disorders.
- Describe the symptoms and treatment of anxiety disorders.
- Describe the forms, symptoms, and treatment of somatoform disorders.
- Explain gender identity disorder.
- Describe mental retardation.
- Describe the forms, symptoms, and treatment of dementia.
- List and describe common mental disorders that originate in childhood.
- Describe disorders related to substance use.
- Explain how mental disorders are assessed and diagnosed.
- List the general treatments for mental disorders.

Mental Health

Case Study

Michael Yager, CMA, is doing a brief rotation in a mental health clinic. He is taking patient information when he meets Yolanda, a high school senior who has brought her 23-year-old brother in for a follow-up on his recent diagnosis of schizophrenia. While speaking to Yolanda, Michael observes several cuts on her forearms. Yolanda quickly folds her arms when she realizes he has noticed the marks.

Sensing her apprehension, Michael asks Yolanda how her family is coping with the new diagnosis and the changes in her brother. He asks if she has spoken to a counselor or if she would like to. After several minutes of conversation, Yolanda admits that she often cuts herself to deal with the stress of her brother's illness for her and her family. She says the cutting provides relief, and she has sometimes thought that killing herself would be better for her parents because they constantly worry and fight about how to pay for medications, mental health support, and supervision for her brother. Her mother often cries and says she will never be able to retire and travel with her husband because her son will have to live with them forever, "cheating" them out of their golden years, grandchildren, and freedom.

Yolanda tells Michael that she does not wish to speak to anyone about this and makes Michael promise not to tell the physician either. After all, she says, she is not a patient at this clinic, "so it's no one's business."

www.prenhall.com/frazier

Additional interactive resources and activities for this chapter can be found on the Companion Website. For audio glossary, legal and ethical scenarios, job scenarios, quizzes, and games related to the content of this chapter, please access the accompanying CD-ROM in this book.

 **Assets Available:**

Audio Glossary
Legal and Ethical Scenario: *Mental Health*
On the Job Scenario: *Mental Health*
Multiple Choice Quiz
Games: Crossword, Strikeout and Spelling Bee

Medical Terminology

addiction—repetitive and dependent behavior usually involving legal or illegal substance abuse

affect—the observable emotional reaction associated with an experience

antidepressant—medication used to treat depression

antipsychotic—medication used to treat psychotic episodes

comorbid—denoting coexisting, unrelated medical diseases or conditions

dementia—diminished mental or cognitive functioning with onset after the age of 18 years

dependence—state of addiction to certain drugs; rapid physical withdrawal can cause life-threatening and even fatal reactions

phobia—irrational, obsessive fear of an object, situation, or activity

psychiatrist—medical doctor or physician specializing in the medical treatment of mental illness

psychiatry—branch of medicine that deals with diagnosis, treatment, and prevention of mental disorders

psychologist—specialist in the field of psychology, therapy, and research

psychology—science dealing with normal and abnormal mental processes and behavior

psychosis—abnormal mental coping of the individual who is out of touch with reality

psychotherapeutic—alleviating symptoms of anxiety, depression, and psychosis

psychotherapy—treatment of mental disorders with talk therapy, or counseling

psychotropic—affecting psychic function, behavior, experience, or emotions

tolerance—requiring greater amounts of a substance to achieve the desired effect

✚ MEDICAL ASSISTING COMPETENCIES

CAAHEP ENTRY-LEVEL COMPETENCIES FOR CMA	ABHES ENTRY-LEVEL COMPETENCIES FOR RMA
■ Identify and respond to issues of confidentiality.	■ Project a positive attitude.
■ Perform within legal and ethical boundaries.	■ Maintain confidentiality at all times.
■ Demonstrate knowledge of federal and state health-care legislation and regulations.	■ Be a "team player."
	■ Be cognizant of ethical boundaries.
■ Perform telephone and in-person screening.	■ Exhibit initiative.
	■ Adapt to change.
■ Obtain and record patient history.	■ Evidence a responsible attitude.
■ Prepare and maintain examination and treatment areas.	■ Be courteous and diplomatic.
■ Apply pharmacology principles to prepare and administer oral and parenteral medications.	■ Conduct work within scope of education, training, and ability.
	■ Interview and take a patient history.
■ Maintain medication and immunization records.	■ Prepare and maintain examination and treatment area.
	■ Prepare and administer oral and parenteral medications as directed by the physician.
	■ Maintain medication and immunization records.

Introduction

Psychiatry is the branch of medicine that focuses on the diagnosis, treatment, and prevention of mental disorders. **Psychology** deals with normal and abnormal mental processes and behavior. It is the study of the mind, its functional processes, and its relationship to behavior and environmental processes. Patients with mental disorders may be treated by either a **psychiatrist** or a **psychologist**, or by other specialists in the field.

- The psychiatrist, a medical doctor with special training in the field of psychiatry, diagnoses and treats mental disorders. Treatment may consist of therapy sessions, drug therapy, or electroshock therapy.
- The psychologist has a doctorate in psychology. Psychologists may specialize in clinical or behavioral psychology, child psychology, development psychology, industrial and organizational psychology, educational psychology, social psychology, or forensic psychology. They do not prescribe medications.
- Social workers usually deal with family or behavioral problems.
- Family and marriage counselors are licensed professionals who specialize in couples and family therapy.
- Child therapists specialize in mental health issues concerning children.
- Substance abuse counselors treat individuals with substance abuse history and promote awareness of substance abuse in the general community.
- Correctional rehabilitative counselors usually work within the criminal justice system to counsel prisoners.
- Vocational training counselors assist individuals in finding appropriate vocations and receiving the training to achieve their goals.

Abbreviations

ADHD—attention-deficit hyperactivity disorder

DSM-IV—Diagnostic and Statistical Manual of Mental Disorders

MAO—monamine oxidase

OCD—obsessive compulsive disorder

ODD—oppositional defiance disorder

PD—personality disorder

PTSD—post-traumatic stress disorder

SAD—seasonal affective disorder

SSRI—selective serotonin reuptake inhibitors

The Medical Assistant's Role in the Mental Health Field

In the field of mental health, many of the opportunities for medical assistants are in the administrative arena, but clinical positions are often available as well (Table 29-1). The psychiatrist may want a patient's weight and certain vital signs obtained. You may be assigned to help a patient complete information forms, schedule appointments for diagnostic testing or other services, or obtain precertification. If you work with substance abuse counselors, you may be responsible for obtaining specimens for screening.

The Anatomy and Physiology of Cognitive Functioning

The brain is a complex organ consisting of many types of neurons and neurotransmitters. Each neuron may be connected by a single synapse, or synaptic gap, to thousands of other synapses for the purpose of communicating the commands of the brain, body, and behavior functions. Neurotransmitters are chemicals that aid in the transmission of electrical impulses from one neuron, or nerve cell, to the next. The neurotransmitter must be received by a receptor on the next neuron in order for a nervous system transmission to cross the synaptic gap. Each neuron may produce a number of neurotransmitters that may be specific or react with many different types of receptors. As the brain processes conscious and unconscious thoughts and memories, the neurons undergo changes that affect the physical structure and chemical substances released by the synaptic gaps. These changes affect the conduction of neuroelectrical impulses and ultimately affect behavior.

The brain maintains the body's homeostasis by reacting to sensory inputs, including emotions and thoughts, with processing and interpretation. Brain impulses signal the autonomic nervous, musculoskeletal, endocrine, and other body systems to respond. As the brain processes different sensory inputs, it prioritizes and places them in different types of memory storage. For example, an image is seen and transmitted

---

TABLE 29-1   GENERAL GUIDELINES FOR MENTAL HEALTH CARE PROVIDERS

1. Remember that expectations and prejudices complicate communication with the client.
2. You are the *only* person that you can control.
3. Know yourself. This is the most critical aspect of communication with any person.
4. Subtle things about a person's behavior, physical characteristics, and communication style affect our responses to others. Sometimes, we are influenced by things of which we are not aware. What you hear, see, smell, and feel on your first encounter with someone sets up your impression and response to that person.
5. Know which behaviors or traits in others trigger automatic feelings of like and dislike in you.
6. Learn about your biases in communication styles or behavioral patterns. You will probably always have these biases, but you can learn to manage your behavior toward another person's style or behavior.
7. Develop a skill for recognizing your immediate feelings toward others, and develop a set of responses that work in dealing with the situation or person without judgment.
8. Do not judge your clients. You do not have to like your clients, and they do not have to like you. Your goal is to help your clients and to do so fairly. Remember patients' rights.
9. All clients deserve respect and fair treatment.

10. You work in a mental health treatment setting to meet the needs of the client—*not your needs.*
11. Deal with your feelings with someone you trust, *not* with the client. Clients should not help you manage your feelings.
12. Examine your feelings *before* you react.
13. Learn to accept the fact that you do not have to be right; you can "win" even when you appear defeated. Winning an argument with a client is not important, nor is it therapeutic or permissible to argue with clients.
14. You can agree to disagree with others.
15. Remember that the client has to be in agreement with a goal to work on that goal.
16. Feelings are feelings. They are neither right nor wrong, good nor bad. Clients should feel free to tell you their true feelings.
17. People are entitled to feel what they feel. Your job is to help them manage the behavior that results from those feelings.
18. Remember that clients are reacting to illness, hospitalization, loss of control, and fear.
19. Know that people respond to situations with a set of behavioral responses that they have learned throughout life. These may not be healthy responses. The goal is to help the patient to develop healthy coping behaviors.

Source: Miele, Carole G., and England, Teresa, From Nursing Assistant to Clinical Care Associate, 1st Edition ©1999. Reprinted by permission of Pearson Education, Inc. Upper Saddle River, NJ.

from the retina to the thalamus, then to the visual cortex in the occipital lobe of the brain. Simultaneously, the neuron transmissions are analyzed for visual characteristics, such as form and color, as they are analyzed and stored as expressed and implied visual memories, and as memories of the emotional experience. This rapid communication through the neuroelectrical circuitry of the brain is accomplished by excitatory amino acid neurotransmitters such as glutamate and by inhibitory neurotransmitters such as gamma aminobutyric acid and glycine.

In addition to excitatory and inhibitory neurotransmitters, there are modulatory neurotransmitters, such as neuropeptides and purines (for example, adenosine), monoamines (norepinephrine, dopamine, serotonin, histamine), and acetylcholine. Neuropeptides and purines aid or inhibit the communication of the neuroelectrical circuitry. Monoamines and acetylcholine function in several ways:

- They determine a person's wakefulness or sleepiness, motivation, and attention span.
- They determine which stimuli are to be stored in memory and the level and type of emotional significance to be attached to each memory.
- They relay emotional feelings throughout the brain that help the patient determine whether to approach, avoid, repeat, fear, cry, or feel neutral in response to events.

Antidepressants, **antipsychotics**, and other medications utilize the actions of monoamine neurotransmitters to affect emotion and thought processing.

The anatomical regions of the brain are as follows.

- The two cerebral hemispheres contain the frontal, parietal, temporal, and occipital lobes; the basal ganglia; and the cerebral cortical area covering all lobes. The cerebral hemispheres control all the body's voluntary, and some involuntary, activities. Specifically, motion is controlled by the frontal lobes, sensation by the parietal lobes, hearing by the temporal lobes, and vision by the occipital lobes. The basal ganglia are involved in the processing and memory storage of emotions associated with rewarding behaviors such as drinking, eating, and sexual intercourse. The cerebral cortical area is where information from different cortical lobe regions is combined, providing input for logic and planning.
- The middle portion of the brain contains the thalamus, hypothalamus, and hippocampus. The thalamus is a relay station and is also important to perception and pleasure. The hypothalamus, located on the underside of the thalamus, is the master control for the autonomic nervous system. It controls hormone secretion, body temperature, and emotions. The hippocampus acts as a gateway for the passage of new memories into areas of permanent storage in the brain. In addition to converting short-term memory to permanent long-term memory, the hippocampus plays a role in recalling spatial relationships.

- The cerebellum is located on the posterior aspect of the brain. It is responsible for equilibrium and both involuntary and voluntary muscle control. The effects of alcohol on the cerebellum can be seen in the staggering of an intoxicated person.
- The brain stem comprises the pons and medulla and extends into the spinal cord. The pons controls wakefulness, mental alertness, and sleepiness states. As the lowest part of the brainstem, the medulla (medulla oblongata) regulates the heart rate, respirations, blood pressure, and reflexes, including coughing, sneezing, swallowing, and vomiting.

Mental Wellness

Mental wellness is a state of being. It is not necessarily an absence of mental problems but rather a capacity to cope in healthy ways with the pressures of daily living. A positive outlook on life as well as a strong support system, such as family and friends, are helpful. High self-esteem, personal growth, positive relationships with others, and a sense of purpose are also considered elements of mental well-being. Influences on mental health include family life, occupation or working life, and social interactions.

General Mental Disorders

Mental illness affects many families and still carries a stigma among many people. Prior to the advent of antipsychotic drugs of the phenothiazine type in the 1950s, individuals with schizophrenia, for example, were locked away in mental hospitals, often restrained in straitjackets. The new drugs made schizophrenic patients more amenable to treatment and helped return them to society as productive citizens and responsible family members. Antidepressants and other **psychotherapeutic** medications have also improved the outlook for many who previously would have been locked away in mental institutions, abandoned by their families, dismissed from their jobs, and labeled "crazies" or "mental cases."

Research indicates that many mental disorders are caused by a chemical imbalance in the brain. Other causes include heredity and genetic factors, environment, gender, and life experiences. Some mental disorders have no identifiable etiology and no absolute course of treatment. General classifications of mental disorders include schizophrenia, mood disorders, personality disorders, anxiety disorders, somatoform disorders, and gender identity disorder.

Schizophrenia

Disordered or disorganized thinking, inappropriate **affect**, unpredictable behavior, and visual or auditory hallucinations are all symptoms of schizophrenia (Figure 29-1 ◆). The affected person is often out of touch with reality and has difficulty functioning in a normal situation. No definite etiology has been identified; heredity, environment, and stress may be factors. Schizophre-

Figure 29-1 ◆ Example of someone suffering from a thought disorder

Mad Kate, 1806-07 (oil on canvas) by Henry Fuseli (1741–1825) Goethe Museum, Frankfurt/Bridgeman Art Library, London/New York

nia has devastating effects not only on the patient but on the family as well.

Schizophrenia is treated with antipsychotic medications such as phenothiazines (Thorazine, Compazine, and Mellaril), Haldol, Prolixin, Risperdal, Seroquel, and Zyprexia. Taking medications as prescribed usually controls most symptoms. Family support is also helpful in preventing relapses. See Table 29-2 for intervention strategies for patients who are hallucinating or delusional.

?—Critical Thinking Question 29-1—
What advice and support can Michael offer Yolanda to help her deal with her brother's newly diagnosed condition?

Mood Disorders

Mood disorders involve disturbances in mood level or affect and are the most common mental disorders. Major depressive disorder and bipolar disorder are two mood disorders.

Caduceus Chronicle
TREATMENT OF THE MENTALLY ILL

The treatment of persons with mental disorders has not always been humane. In primitive cultures such persons were thought to be possessed by evil spirits that had to be driven out. But the early Greeks and Romans viewed mental disorders as natural phenomena and treated them with opium, music, good nutrition, hygiene, and physical activity.

In the centuries after the fall of the Roman Empire, mental illness was again considered a form of possession. Families and the church attempted to provide care, but many of the afflicted ended up locked in prisons or asylums where they were beaten, starved, and tortured. They were considered incompetent and defective, and it was common practice to display them in cages for the public's amusement. During the 1300s in London, the Bethlehem Royal Hospital—popularly called Bedlam—was established for those who had no other lodging. Through the centuries, the hospital became a place in which the mentally ill—also called "the insane" or "lunatics"— were confined. The term *bedlam* has come to mean a place or state of great noise and confusion.

Benjamin Rush, who is considered the first U.S. psychiatrist, opened the first psychiatric hospital in Williamsburg, Virginia, in 1769. In the nineteenth century, the social reformer Dorothea Dix crusaded for the humane treatment of mental patients. She helped to open more than 30 hospitals for the mentally ill and indigent.

The next major efforts on behalf of the mentally ill came after World War I. Returning veterans suffered from many psychological problems, and some observers postulated that many of these symptoms had a medical origin. Great strides were made during the 1940s and 1950s, when new drugs were used to alleviate many symptoms. But it was soon clear that these "miracle drugs" were not a permanent cure.

The introduction of phenothiazine drugs, for the treatment of psychosis, and antidepressant drugs and lithium, for bipolar disorders, has made it possible for people with these disorders to function in society. As a result, mental hospitals are becoming a thing of the past. The recognition and acceptance of mental illness as treatable has vastly improved the prognosis for millions of people. However, the stigma of mental illness lingers today.

Major Depressive Disorder

Major depressive disorder often is referred to as major, acute, or severe depression. The depressed individual experiences an overwhelming sadness, hopelessness, and despair; has difficulty sleeping and no appetite; feels worthless; and thinks frequently of suicide as an escape from an intolerable situation. A flat affect may be observed.

There is no specific cause for major depressive disorder. However, it is believed that chemical imbalances in the neurotransmitters of the brain, specifically serotonin, may be responsible for the depressive reaction. Devastating life experiences may trigger a strong emotional response. Triggering factors may include unresolved grief, loss of a loved one, loss of a job, loss of a body part or function, and other severe, cruel, and relentless losses. Situational depression often resolves on its own, but care providers must be on the alert for symptoms of potential suicide.

Treatment often includes drug therapy with antidepressant medications: monoamine oxidase (**MAO**) inhibitors, tricyclics, and selective serotonin reuptake inhibitors (**SSRI**). Many of these drugs have serious side effects, and it may take two weeks or more for the condition to improve. Suicidal individuals require constant monitoring and a controlled environment until the crisis stage has been resolved (Table 29-3).

TABLE 29-2 INTERVENTION STRATEGIES FOR PATIENTS WHO ARE HALLUCINATING OR DELUSIONAL

1. Communication may be difficult with patients who are experiencing hallucinations because they may talk out loud to themselves, may make gestures or movements that are sudden and startling, or may accuse you or others of saying or doing things that you know are untrue.
2. Never argue or agree with these false perceptions or accusations because when the patient is in a realistic state of thinking, he or she may remember these events. The patient will think you are untrustworthy yourself and will no longer trust you. Even when patients are not in contact with reality, they know that they are experiencing unique perceptions and sensations. Your agreeing that you hear, feel, or see something that is not real will not make this person feel at ease or self-assured.
3. Most hallucinations are frightening or threatening to the person who is having them.
4. The behavior that you see is in response to these threats and fears. Patients need to know that you and the treatment team are working to keep them safe.
5. They need to know that you do not see, hear, or feel what they are experiencing. Simply state, "I know you think you hear your mother's voice, but I don't," or, "I know that you feel bugs crawling on your skin, but I don't see any bugs on you."
6. Initially, you want to investigate the nature of the hallucinations and help the treatment team understand what the patient is experiencing.
7. Once this has been established, do not continue to focus on the false perceptions and sensations.
8. Instead, help the patient to stay focused on reality and eventually divert the thinking to what is real. You may say something like, "I heard what you are experiencing and it must feel terrible, but I am here to help you think about things that we both know are going on around us. Let's talk about _____."
9. Sometimes, patients are plagued by auditory hallucinations, and they are unable to get the voices out of their heads. Try to help the patient focus on your voice. Say something like, "The voices that you are hearing are making you uncomfortable, so try listening to me instead of these voices."
10. It may sound strange, but sometimes you can help distract the patient from the voices by singing with the patient. Let's face it, you can't sing and listen to voices at the same time.
11. Do not allow the patient who is hallucinating to spend too much time alone. This only gives the patient more time to focus on the voices.
12. Sometimes, the voices may tell patients that they are evil and must die. Patients who hallucinate hostile voices may make attempts to injure, mutilate, or kill themselves because they are acting on the wishes of the hallucinations.
13. At times, people who respond to hallucinations and delusions are threatening to you and others.
14. You must be aware of the person's personal space and keep a distance that is safe for you and the patient. If you get too close or touch the person, you may be perceived as a threat. The person could strike out or hit you because you have invaded his or her personal space.
15. Patients who have paranoid delusions often feel threatened by others. When this is the case, they may threaten to strike staff or other patients. Pay attention to the body language and the verbal messages of people with delusions.
16. When someone who is extremely suspicious of others says, "Get away from me," it is often quite different in tone and intention than the depressed patient who asks to be left alone.
17. If someone who is hallucinating or has delusional thinking says, "Leave me alone," take it seriously. Do not get in this patient's way. Keep a close watch on the patient, but do not attempt to get too close or to explore for reasons.
18. Patients who have delusions of persecution or have paranoid thinking may think that you and the hospital or treatment facility are trying to harm them. They may not eat the food because it could be poisoned. They may refuse medication because they think it is poisoned. They will be argumentative and cannot be persuaded to believe that you want to help them.
19. Do not test the food for this patient. This will only strengthen the belief that even you consider that their delusion is true. Logical thought tells you that if you are willing to eat the food, it must be safe, but this patient's thought process is not logical.
20. Sometimes, you can help this patient to trust the food or medicine by using prepackaged foods and medications.
21. Foods like milk in a carton, canned soda, wrapped sandwiches, and pudding and gelatin in a package are safe to this person. Packaged medications are supplied in unit doses by pharmaceutical companies.
22. Never argue with a delusional thought. Simply state what you believe or know to be true.
23. It is more important to get this patient to say how the delusional thought influences his or her feelings than to argue with the illogical or unreasonable thought process. "So, you think that the food is poisoned. What do you do when you are hungry?" or "You think that the staff wants to kill you. This must be frightening. How can we help you to feel safe?"
24. Always consider your safety and the safety of the patient, other patients, and the staff when a patient is not in contact with reality. The person has a very serious illness that is causing him or her torment and needs your help. You cannot help people if you allow them to hurt you, themselves, or others.
25. Whenever you feel unsafe, other staff and patients probably do too. Let the nurse in charge or supervisor know what you feel.
26. Trust your instincts.

Source: Miele, Carole G.; and England, Teresa, From Nursing Assistant to Clinical Care Associate, 1st Edition ©1999. Reprinted by permission of Pearson Education, Inc. Upper Saddle River, NJ.

Suicide attempts or expressed suicidal thoughts are cries for help. Table 29-4 lists the typical symptoms of someone contemplating suicide. Occasionally, however, there are no overt symptoms or warning signs. When symptoms *are* present, the individual should not be left alone but should be assisted to a medical or mental health facility until an evaluation, referral, and treatment plan are developed and initiated.

? —Critical Thinking Question 29-2
What should Michael tell Yolanda about her self-inflicted injuries and her request that he promise not to tell anyone else? Is he bound by a patient–provider oath?

Postpartum Depression

Postpartum depression is a frequent phenomenon in the first few days or weeks after childbirth. It ranges in severity from crying spells or "new baby blues" through sadness and despair to **psychosis**, with potentially devastating outcomes. The new mother has feelings of inadequacy and worries about caring for her new infant. She experiences fatigue, loss of appetite, and often a flattened affect and avoids social interaction.

Sudden changes in hormonal balance during and after the birth process along with new infant care responsibilities are thought to trigger the depressive response. Sleep deprivation also plays a role in the condition.

Health-care providers and family members should be alert for symptoms and should make efforts to assist the new

TABLE 29-3 CONSTRUCTIVE APPROACHES TO CARING FOR PATIENTS WHO ARE DEPRESSED

1. Provide interactions and attention that are not associated with compliance or pleasing others' wishes or rules. Often, depressed people do not share their feelings because of the distorted perception that they have nothing to give in return for the "favor" of listening to them.

2. Know that you will identify with the person's depression. When you are emotionally engaged by the client's sadness, you may begin to feel sad yourself. Guard against internalizing the sadness because you will be less therapeutic if you internalize the client's sadness.

3. You will not be helpful if you are also overwhelmed by the person's pain. You may feel sad and empathize with these feelings, especially after the individual has shared his or her emotional pain.

4. Avoid making statements like "I know just how you feel" or "Everything will be all right" or "Just trust in the Lord. He will heal your pain." While these statements express sympathy for the person's sadness, they do not help to make anyone feel better. They also make the person feel that you view the problem as trivial. They may convey that the problems in this client's life are not important enough to warrant what the person is feeling.

5. You do not know just how the client feels. You are not in the client's life situation.

6. Do not try to minimize the depressed patient's problems, even though the complaints may seem simple to solve. To this person, the problems are very real and may feel insurmountable. When you minimize the problem or the reason for the depression, it does not make the person feel better. It makes the feelings worse. "I must really be inadequate if I can't solve this little problem."

7. Tolerate silences. When you are trying to communicate with people who feel very depressed, there will be many periods of silence. The person may not have enough energy to speak. Thoughts and ideas may come slowly.

8. Your ability to tolerate silences tells the depressed person that you care and that you are willing to accept the person "as is."

9. If the client says to you, "Don't bother to talk to me. I don't have anything to say," or asks, "Why bother with me? I'm hopeless," let the person know it's okay not to talk and that you want to sit with him or her quietly for a while. If the client wants to talk, he or she can, and if not, it's okay.

10. Often, people who are depressed feel devalued and have low self-esteem. Sit with the person in silence to demonstrate that this is time well spent. Quiet time assures the client that you are interested and that you care.

11. Tell the client that you will set aside 10 minutes to spend with him or her. "We can sit quietly or have a conversation; I will respect your need for silence." When the 10 minutes are almost up, remind the person that you have just a few minutes left. If nothing is said throughout the entire period of time, simply thank the client for sitting with you. Tell the patient that at a specific hour you will come back and spend another 10 minutes. Be specific about where you will meet.

12. Be sure to return at the stated time. This builds trust. If something prevents you from keeping the appointment, let the patient know you didn't forget your appointment, and explain what kept you away.

13. Do not probe the client for information about the depression. Many questions will make the person feel anxious and unable to answer. This reinforces the client's feelings of inadequacy.

14. When you ask questions the client cannot answer, let the client know it's acceptable not to have an answer: "You can answer that question when you've had more time to think about it."

15. If the client has a tendency to magnify negative aspects of a situation or a task he or she is asked to perform, try to shift the focus to a positive outcome. Shift the focus by emphasizing strategies for solving the problem rather than dwelling on the problem itself. "I know that _____ is a problem—this is one way of resolving this type of problem."

16. Look for and try to help the person find the positive aspects of his or her life. Do not exaggerate strengths. Look for real strengths. "You lost your job, and this was a job you held for _ years. That is a significant amount of time in one position. You must have been a productive employee for those years."

17. Give genuine praise for efforts made to accomplish activities of daily living (ADLs) or tasks. Do not give false praise. The person will know it is not real.

18. If the patient has not gotten out of bed for several days, offer praise when this behavior occurs. Say something like, "It's good to see you out of bed."

19. When patients cannot accept praise directly, offer it indirectly. Instead of telling the patient, tell another person so that the patient can hear your statement but does not have to directly accept your compliment.

20. When the patient tends to overdramatize everything, use this equation:

$$action = benefits\ obtained \div risks\ to\ be\ taken$$

In other words, if you ask Mr. Jenkins to get out of bed and he says, "I can't do it," try this: "How badly would you say you feel staying in bed? Rate it on a scale of 0 to 10, with 10 being the worst feeling you have ever experienced." If Mr. Jenkins says any number, there is nothing to lose. If he says 10, say something like, "If staying in bed feels like a 10, try getting out of bed, and we will evaluate how that feels. It can't be worse than a 10."

21. Help the person to realistically look at the action or task you want the person to perform. Evaluate the task in terms of the client's worst fear or what could happen. Help the patient to separate realistic consequences from self-imposed suffering. Present the positive and negative aspects of accomplishing the task. "If you get out of bed and feel worse, you will at least know that you have tried. You may find that it doesn't feel any worse. You will have accomplished something you haven't tried to do in several days, and that's a start. If it feels worse, then we can discuss going back to bed."

22. With depression, the person often avoids activity because he or she feels incapable of completing the task or fears failure. Help the person to look at the extremes on a scale of 0 to 10.

23. Be alert to clues of suicidal ideation, and examine these with the nurse. Suicidal ideation refers to thoughts or ideas of suicide or of killing oneself. An individual may be thinking of suicide as a means of ending his or her emotional pain.

24. Clues may include saying goodbye to significant others, making peace for wrong doings, talking about death as an option, giving away possessions, writing lists of things to do, suddenly appearing happy or "fleeting to health," and asking to be discharged. Fleeting to health refers to a sudden appearance of improvement from the depressed state. The person is said to "flee" to a healthy state when nothing has changed or improved in the person's life or mental condition. It is often used in association with the depressed client who has a sudden change in mood and behavior.

25. People who have made a plan for suicide usually feel a sense of accomplishment, and this may improve their mood and energize their behavior. Be alert to sudden improvements in the mood and energy level of depressed patients. This may be a danger signal. When people are extremely depressed, they usually do not have the organization of thought or the energy level to form a plan for suicide or to act on it.

26. When the energy level and thought organization of the depressed patient improves, he or she is more likely to attempt suicide.

27. If a patient discusses suicide, do not be afraid to ask about these thoughts. Asking about suicide does not give the person the idea to commit the act. Chances are the option of suicide has already been considered.

28. It is more important to find out if the patient is thinking about suicide than to avoid the topic.

29. If a patient expresses suicidal ideas, ask about a plan: "Have you thought of a plan for suicide?" If the person says yes, ask, "What are you considering as a plan?"

30. A patient who has a plan is serious. Even if the person has not thought of a plan but mentions the idea of suicide, *tell your supervisor.*

31. If you ask a question about suicide or a suicidal plan, you *cannot* promise to keep the response a secret, no matter how important

(continued)

TABLE 29-3 CONSTRUCTIVE APPROACHES TO CARING FOR PATIENTS WHO ARE DEPRESSED *(continued)*

you think it is for the patient to share suicidal thoughts. This is worth repeating: You must inform the nurse stat.

32. Whenever any client says, "Promise that you will keep this a secret," you must tell the patient that you *cannot* keep any secrets because the secret could be vital to their health and well-being. Say something like this, "I really want you to tell me your thoughts, but I cannot promise that I won't get anyone involved in your treatment," or "If it is important to your safety or health, I cannot keep the secret; it is up to you to tell me."

33. If you promise to keep a secret and then find out that the person has ideas of suicide or homicide or that the person has been a victim of abuse or has abused others or that the person has committed a crime, you must tell the person in charge. Now, you are caught in the bind of having to break a promise to a patient. You must tell the patient that someone in authority on the treatment team must know about this "secret." You risk losing the patient's trust when this happens. It is better to tell the patient up front that you cannot promise to keep a secret; this is for the patient's benefit.

34. People who express suicidal thoughts are often ambivalent about the wish to die and the wish to live. Ambivalence means having two opposite thoughts and feelings at the same time. It is like sitting on the fence and thinking, "Should I jump, or should I just sit here?"

35. It is important to allow the person time to discuss this ambivalence: "You say you want to die, and you are questioning this; tell me about wanting to live."

36. Patients who express suicidal thoughts and patients who have made suicide attempts are placed on special precautions. You must follow your agency's policy and procedures for "suicide watch" or "suicide precautions."

37. These special precautions could mean keeping the patient in eyesight at all times, making rounds on the patient every 15 minutes, documenting the patient's whereabouts and condition every 15 minutes on the rounds sheet, or a one-to-one observation.

38. The treatment team will determine the level of the precautions. If you are assigned, you must adhere closely to these policies.

39. A one-to-one observation means that one staff member is assigned to stay with the patient at all times. This means that you never leave the patient alone, that you stay within an arm's length of the patient, even when he or she is sleeping or in the bathroom or shower. Always follow your agency's procedure, and take this one-on-one observation very seriously.

40. Safety is the primary issue with all patients and especially patients who are thinking about suicide.

41. Every suicide attempt is a cry for help.

Source: Miele, Carole G.; and England, Teresa, From Nursing Assistant to Clinical Care Associate, 1st Edition ©1999. Reprinted by permission of Pearson Education, Inc. Upper Saddle River, NJ.

mother. Intervention is important to prevent tragic outcomes, including suicide or infanticide. Most cases resolve quickly when understanding and support are provided, but antidepressant medications may be required.

Seasonal Affective Disorder

Seasonal affective disorder (**SAD**) occurs during the winter months when days are shorter and sunlight is limited. This cyclic form of depression usually has an onset during the autumn months, continues through winter, and eases in the spring. Symptoms include excessive sleepiness and lengthened sleep periods, increased appetite, weight gain, and loss of energy. Phototherapy and exposure to as much natural daylight as possible are used to treat this seasonal depression.

Bipolar Disorder

Bipolar disorder is also referred to as manic-depressive disorder. Intense mood swings are the defining characteristic. During the "manic phase," the individual is highly outgoing, energetic, excited, even euphoric. The need for sleep is minimal, and the thought process is often disturbed and disconnected. The bipolar patient displays bizarre behavior in attitude, dress, and judgment; may spend money to excess; and expresses grandiose thoughts. During the depressive phase, the mood changes to one of sadness and flat affect, with loss of appetite and sleep disturbances. Communication is avoided and activity levels decrease. Suicide is always a concern during the depressive phase.

While this condition may have familial tendencies, alterations in neurotransmitter levels are usually the cause. As with acute depression, various life situations may trigger bipolar episodes. Treatment involves drug therapy to stabilize neurotransmitter levels.

Personality Disorders

Personality disorders (**PDs**) are characterized by behaviors that deviate from accepted and standard patterns of inappropriate behavior. The ten PDs are divided into three classifications, or clusters (Table 29-5).

- Cluster A is also referred to as the Odd Cluster and includes paranoid, schizoid, and schizotypical personalities. Cluster A individuals appear odd and eccentric.
- Cluster B, or the Dramatic Cluster, includes borderline and antisocial personality disorders, narcissistic disorder, and histrionic disorder. Behavior is emotional, dramatic, or erratic.
- Cluster C, the Anxious Cluster, includes avoidant, dependent, and obsessive-compulsive (**OCD**) personality disorders. Individuals appear fearful and anxious.

The etiology of personality disorders is unknown. Although symptoms of PD begin in adolescence, diagnosis should not be confirmed until adulthood. During the assessment process, it is important to distinguish PDs from delusional and psychotic disorders.

Treatment of personality disorders depends on the symptoms. The individual is taught coping mechanisms. Drug therapy for **comorbid** conditions may be helpful.

TABLE 29-4 SYMPTOMS AND WARNING SIGNS OF CONTEMPLATED SUICIDE

- Prolonged depression with episodes of crying, sadness, helplessness, hopelessness, fatigue, weight loss, change in bowel habits toward constipation, and poor concentration
- Episodes of uncharacteristic behavior
- Sudden mood swings, especially to calmness and even happiness
- A vacant stare
- A change in eating and sleeping patterns
- A lack of interest in and withdrawal from social activities
- Reduced interest in sexual activity
- Giving away prized possessions

TABLE 29-5 CLASSIFICATIONS AND SYMPTOMS OF PERSONALITY DISORDERS

Cluster A	
Paranoid Personality Disorder	Extreme distrust and suspicion of others; belief that others are deliberately trying to exploit, deceive, or harm the individual.
Schizoid Personality Disorder	Flat affect; indifference and detachment; relationships are few and unsatisfying.
Schizotypical Personality Disorder	Similarity to schizoid personality disorder; superstition, paranoia, and anxiety or depression.
Cluster B	
Antisocial Personality Disorder	Total disregard for the rights of others and of the law, failure to conform to social norms, aggression, manipulation, and reckless behavior.
Borderline Personality Disorder	Volatile and unstable relationships characterized by anger, despair, and feelings of rejection and abandonment; poor self-image; impulsive and manipulative behavior.
Histrionic Personality Disorder	Constant need for attention, approval, and reassurance; overly dramatic and theatrical behavior.
Narcissistic Personality Disorder	Pathologic self-love or grandiose self-admiration; exaggerated sense of importance; lack of empathy; tendency to exploit others; rage or humiliation when criticized.
Cluster C	
Avoidant Personality Disorder	Fear of criticism, disapproval or rejection; poor self-image; avoidance of social involvement.
Dependent Personality Disorder	Passivity; reliance on others for decision making; reluctance to disagree with others out of fear of disapproval.
Obsessive-Compulsive Personality Disorder	Preoccupation with orderliness, details and perfection; extreme mental and interpersonal control; tendency to make lists but never complete a task.

Anxiety Disorders

Anxiety is a common reaction that most people experience at some point in their lives. When a physical threat is perceived, anxiety is a natural response. When a reduction in the threat level is not apparent, anxiety can become both a physiologic and psychological condition. Anxiety disorders include generalized anxiety disorder and panic disorder, phobic disorder, obsessive-compulsive disorder, and post-traumatic stress disorder.

Generalized Anxiety Disorder and Panic Disorder

Generalized anxiety disorder, or "free-floating anxiety," is a constant state of anxiety with no apparent cause. Affected individuals worry constantly and find decision making difficult.

Physiologic symptoms include difficulty sleeping, hypertension, diarrhea, and tense muscles.

Panic disorder is characterized by a sudden onset of unexplained and severe anxiety that terminates in panic. A person with panic disorder claims to sense impending doom and often expresses the fear that he or she is dying. Physiologic symptoms may consist of trembling, dyspnea, palpitations, chest pain, and dizziness. Panic attacks occur on a regular basis and can become disabling.

Phobic Disorder

Phobic disorder is an unusual fear or anxiety concerning a specific object, situation, or activity that in reality does not present any danger. The fear progresses to the point where it controls the person's life as he or she strives to avoid the feared object or situation altogether. Table 29-6 lists typical **phobias**.

Obsessive-Compulsive Disorder

Unrelenting but unwelcome thoughts and obsessions as well as repeated, compulsive actions are the main feature of obsessive-compulsive disorder. The unsolicited thoughts may be sexual fantasies, or they may revolve around causing harm to others. The person's anxiety is often reinforced by feelings of "going crazy" or "losing my mind." Compulsive, senseless actions or rituals temporarily relieve the anxiety and reduce the stress level. Repeated, excessive hand washing is one example of an OCD symptom.

As with other anxiety disorders, it is not always possible to identify the cause of an OCD. Treatment usually involves drug therapy augmented by **psychotherapy**.

Post-Traumatic Stress Disorder

Post-traumatic stress disorder (**PTSD**) is characterized by a delayed response to a traumatic event. The event may be a natural disaster such as an earthquake or hurricane, war, terrorist attack,

TABLE 29-6 SOME COMMON PHOBIAS

Achluophobia	Fear of darkness
Acrophobia	Fear of heights
Agoraphobia	Overwhelming symptoms of anxiety that occur on leaving home; a form of social phobia.
Algophobia	Fear of pain
Arachnophobia	Fear of spiders
Bacteriophobia	Fear of bacteria
Claustrophobia	Fear of closed spaces
Dentophobia	Fear of dentists
Entomophobia	Fear of insects
Felinophobia	Fear of cats
Hematophobia	Fear of blood
Hydrophobia	Fear of water
Iatrophobia	Fear of physicians
Keraunophobia	Fear of thunder and lightning
Melissophobia	Fear of bees
Ophidiophobia	Fear of snakes
Pathophobia	Fear of disease
Pteromerhanophobia	Fear of flying
Pyrophobia	Fear of fire
Thanatophobia	Fear of death
Xenophobia	Fear of strangers
Zoophobia	Fear of animals

fire, rape, abuse, car accident, or other kinds of accidents. When personal safety has been compromised in any way, the traumatic shock may precipitate PTSD.

Onset of PTSD may be immediate or delayed. Symptoms include anxiety, denial of the event, fear of being in the proximity of the event, nightmares, flashbacks, reduced appetite, weight loss, and loss of interest in normal activities. Many individuals with PTSD create a safe environment by isolating themselves from society. This condition, which has existed for centuries, was identified and named in the twentieth century when war veterans in great numbers exhibited the symptoms.

Drug therapy is helpful in establishing better sleep patterns. Psychological therapy is directed to helping the patient overcome the traumatic memories and deal with situations and environments that trigger the reaction (Table 29-7). Some cases resolve spontaneously.

Somatoform Disorders

Physical symptoms with no underlying organic etiology are typical of a somatoform disorder. The affected individual has no conscious control over these feelings. Somatization disorder, conversion disorder, hypochondriasis, and factitious disorders are all somatoform disorders.

Somatization Disorder

The condition called somatization disorder is characterized by pain or physical symptoms of illness in more than four body regions or systems and no underlying pathology. These chronic, recurring, multiple complaints have an onset before age 30. Diagnostic tests reveal no cause. Psychotherapy is the usual treatment.

Conversion Disorder

An extremely stressful situation precipitates the onset of conversion disorder, once called hysteria. Physical symptoms—paralysis, tremors, mutism (inability to speak), shortness of breath, difficulty swallowing, nausea, vomiting, temporary blindness, or seizures—create an escape from the situation. The possibility of underlying physical causes must be eliminated. Most of these incidents resolve when the stressful situation has passed. Treatment usually involves psychotherapy.

Hypochondriasis

Individuals who report pain and symptoms that have no physiologic basis may be diagnosed with hypochondriasis. Although the symptoms are vague, the individuals actually experience them, and negative test results do not allay their fears. They move from physician to physician, looking for one who will verify that a medical condition exists. This abnormal preoccupation with the state of their health can be incapacitating, creating social and occupational dilemmas.

When it has been positively confirmed that there is no underlying pathology, psychotherapy may be helpful. However, it is likely to be rejected by the individual as unnecessary.

TABLE 29-7 THERAPEUTIC APPROACHES TO REDUCE ANXIETY

1. Remember that the person's behavior is aimed at reducing his or her anxiety.
2. The behavior that is displayed is telling others that something needs to be done. The person may be too anxious to make a decision about what to do with this feeling.
3. Unfamiliar and new surroundings and situations can produce anxious behavior. Anxiety increases when the person doesn't know what is expected.
4. Provide concise, clear, and simple directions.
5. Tell the person what is expected and what to expect from a situation or procedure. Tell the individual what is going to happen with each step or what will happen next.
6. Sometimes, what you are asking the person to do is causing anxiety.
7. The person may feel uncertain of what you are asking. Ask the individual what information he or she needs to proceed.
8. When you perceive that a patient is anxious, make a process statement about your perception: "You seem anxious or uncertain about what is happening." A process statement is stating what may be the underlying emotion rather than focusing on the obvious or observed behavior.
9. Allow the individual time to respond. Do not try to rush responses or actions when someone is anxious because this will only increase the anxiety.
10. It may be helpful to give directions about what to do rather than to ask the individual.
11. If you are involved in a discussion with someone who becomes nervous about a topic, it may be helpful to move the discussion off the "hot" topic. You might say, "We don't have to talk about this now. We can talk about this when you feel ready."
12. If there are time constraints, gently let the person know the expected time frame. Sometimes, compulsive actions and rituals cause delay. The client may need to handwash after every step of getting dressed or may need to check the locks and lights numerous times before leaving the room or building.
13. Try not to interrupt a compulsion or ritual because this is what the person feels he or she must do to manage anxiety. When you take away the opportunity to act out the ritual or compulsive behavior, you increase the anxiety.
14. Rituals and compulsions need to be controlled when they are harmful to the patient. If a client handwashes one hundred times a day, the healthy state of the skin might be in jeopardy.
15. Compulsive behavior must be withdrawn gradually. A plan to manage the compulsive behavior is provided by the patient's therapist and doctor.
16. Don't check your watch too often when you are helping an anxious person to communicate feelings or to prepare for an event.
17. Be aware of your frustration with these compulsions and rituals. Do not demonstrate your frustration to the client. This increases the anxiety and the need for the ritual.
18. Get the client started ahead of time so that neither of you becomes frustrated.
19. Do not tell this person about events too far in advance, as this will give him or her more to worry about. Tell the patient in enough time to give direction, to answer questions, and to prepare for the event or procedure.
20. Use a matter-of-fact or businesslike tone of voice when you are assisting someone who is anxious. A cheerful, overly friendly tone or a demanding or bossy attitude can overwhelm the person and will increase anxiety. The individual will wonder what is expected and what must be done in return for your friendliness. If you are demanding, the patient will feel that you cannot manage this display of anxious behavior.
21. It will take time for the anxious person to trust you and to recognize that your only interest is his or her well-being.
22. Your patience, calmness, and assurance of safety will build trust.
23. Do not expect anything in return for your efforts. The person's anxiety will prevent recognition of your efforts to help.

Source: Miele, Carole G.; and England, Teresa, From Nursing Assistant to Clinical Care Associate, 1st Edition ©1999. Reprinted by permission of Pearson Education, Inc. Upper Saddle River, NJ.

Factitious Disorders

Factitious disorders are intentional and fraudulent. Malingering, for example, is the faking or exaggeration of symptoms and complaints for personal and financial gain. Munchausen syndrome is another factitious disorder. Individuals with this syndrome have an extensive knowledge of disease processes and actually injure themselves or ingest or inject a toxic substance to create an illness. Their goal is personal attention from others. Munchausen syndrome by proxy occurs when a child under the care of the individual is administered a toxic substance to create an illness. The caregiver, generally the mother, then seeks medical attention for the child. The resulting personal attention is the caregiver's "reward."

Diagnosis of factitious disorders is difficult as the individual moves from facility to facility seeking care. When this condition is confirmed, psychotherapy may be helpful.

Gender Identity Disorder

Occasionally an individual experiences gender confusion. A gender identity disorder is characterized by feelings of belonging to the opposite sex, of discomfort or unhappiness in the biological gender role. Girls take on male characteristics, activities, and attire, while boys exhibit a preference for what are considered girls' activities and dress. Low self-esteem and social isolation may accompany these feelings. As the individuals reach maturity, they may take steps to realize their gender preference, including hormonal therapy and sex-change surgery. Psychological counseling helps many patients lead close-to-normal lives in their new gender roles. It also helps when family members recognize the condition as an illness and accept the gender change.

Mental Retardation

Mental retardation occurs as the result of an interruption in the intellectual growth of the child, during prenatal development or the birth process or after birth. Genetic aberrations and inborn errors of metabolism, exposure of the mother and fetus to infection, and any compromise to the oxygen and nutritional supply to the developing brain are possible causes.

Observation of a possible developmental disability is confirmed with standardized testing instruments such as Stanford-Binet, Wechsler Intelligence Scales for Children, and the Kaufman Assessment Battery for Children. The final diagnosis must be made before the age of 18 and must include deficiencies in behavioral areas as well as intellectual function.

Children with mental retardation show signs of lower-than-normal acquisition of intellectual and interpersonal skills. Behavioral performance in the areas of self-care, hygiene, safety, self-direction, and communication is at a lower level than expected for the age group. The children are often not diagnosed until they have problems in school. Many are educable, however, and are encouraged to learn coping and independent living skills. Others who are more severely impaired may require custodial care.

There is no cure or drug therapy for mental retardation, as the compromised brain cells cannot be replaced or repaired. Any concurrent mental disorders should be addressed and treatment options explored and implemented.

Keys to Success
UNDERSTANDING STANFORD-BINET

The Stanford-Binet scale is a standardized test used to assess the intelligence and cognitive abilities of children and young adults. It provides schools and treatment facilities with a beginning point for a child's therapy or education. Results are reported in a numerical format:

110 to 90—average
90 to 70—below average
70 to 50—mild retardation
50 to 35—moderate retardation
35 to 20—severe retardation
below 20—profound retardation

Dementia

Dementia is reduced mental or cognitive functioning that has an onset after the age of 18. Causes of dementia include Alzheimer's disease, vascular compromise, traumatic insult, and the aging process. Vascular disease, trauma, tumors, metabolic conditions, toxins, infections, or organic diseases may be responsible for the interruption of blood flow to the brain. As with mental retardation, symptoms are varied and may have sudden or subtle onset.

Alzheimer's Disease

Alzheimer's disease usually has an insidious inset. In this progressive degenerative disease of the brain, mental and physical functioning is reduced. Early signs include gradual loss of short-term memory, inability to concentrate or to learn new things, and progressively more severe personality changes. Communication becomes difficult, and the individual displays restlessness and disorientation. As the disease progresses, the patient may become hostile and combative. Motor skills also decline and eventually the patient is bedridden.

The onset of Alzheimer's usually occurs after the age of 60, and incidence is greater among the aging. No identifiable cause has yet been found. Diagnosis is difficult. Once symptoms indicate the onset of Alzheimer's, all other organic brain disorders must be ruled out. Recent advances in imaging studies make it possible to visualize an Alzheimer's-affected brain. On autopsy, neurofibrillary tangles and senile plaques and deposits of amyloid material are found in the brain tissue.

There is no cure for Alzheimer's. Treatment is supportive, with drug therapy to enhance memory and reduce anxiety and depression. As symptoms progress, custodial care may be required. Throughout the disease process, therapy is helpful for both the patient and the family to deal with the symptoms and projected outcome of the disorder.

Vascular Dementia

Vascular dementia may be the result of decreased blood flow to the brain. Often atherosclerosis causes narrowed or stenosed arteries and prevents normal oxygenation of cerebral tissue. Typical symptoms of dementia are loss of intellectual faculties, memory lapses, and personality changes. This often progressive condition creates anxiety, depression, and irritability. As the individual ages, the condition usually worsens and the patient loses interest in personal hygiene, appearance, and surrounding activities.

As with Alzheimer's, there is no cure for vascular dementia. Surgical procedures to remove the offending plaque help to prevent further damage from oxygen deprivation by increasing blood flow to the brain tissue and may arrest the progression of the condition. Drug therapy to increase blood flow to the cerebral arteries may be helpful. However, once brain cells have been destroyed, they cannot be replaced. Custodial care may be required. Consistency in care and environment is essential for optimum effect, and counseling is helpful for both the family and the individual.

Dementia due to Head Trauma

Dementia as the result of decreased blood flow to the brain may be caused by a traumatic insult to the skull and brain. The insult may be a closed or open head injury and includes fractures of the skull, hematomas, concussions, and contusions. As in vascular dementia, reduced blood flow leads to decreased oxygenation and nutrition to the brain cells, which die as a result of ischemia.

The symptoms of this type of dementia are similar to those of vascular dementia, except for the insidious onset of the latter. Most cases of severe traumatic insult have an abrupt onset as pressure builds in the cranium or the blood flow is acutely diminished. Treatment is directed to reducing pressure on the brain and in stopping bleeding from the tissue. As with other forms of dementia, once brain cells die from ischemia, there is no way to restore function. Treatment is supportive. Drug therapy relieves concurrent psychological circumstances. Consistency in care and daily routines is essential for optimal outcome. Counseling of the individual and the family are helpful in coping with the situation.

Mental Disorders Occurring during Childhood

Certain childhood disorders are considered mental disorders. These include, but are not limited to:

- Learning disorders, including stuttering, a communication disorder
- Pervasive development disorders, of which the most common is autistic spectrum disorder
- Attention-deficit hyperactivity disorder (**ADHD**), which is not specifically a childhood disorder but has its onset during childhood
- Oppositional defiant disorder (**ODD**), a significant childhood disorder that usually predicts poor outcomes such as dropping out of school, delinquency, and substance abuse

Children with any of these disorders, described in Table 29-8, may be seen by a psychiatrist or psychologist for initial

TABLE 29-8 MENTAL DISORDERS THAT OCCUR IN CHILDHOOD			
Condition	**Signs and Symptoms**	**Cause**	**Treatment**
Learning disorders, including communication disorders	Child learns in nonstandard manner; has normal or superior intelligence but functions at lower level than expected, usually in one area such as reading or math; often has low self-esteem as a result. Stuttering: abnormal speech pattern in which words or sounds are repeated or prolonged.	Often unidentifiable; possibly abnormality in cognitive processing, or problems with vision, hearing, memory, language comprehension, or attention mechanisms. Stuttering: may be familial tendency; occurs mostly in boys; exacerbated by anxiety in parents and others.	Tutoring; drug therapy for hyperactivity; speech therapy for stuttering, or problem may resolve on its own.
Pervasive development disorders	Lack of emotion, nonverbal communication, social interaction, eye contact; poor or absent verbal skills; resistance to physical contact; withdrawal and obsessive behavior before age 3.	Unknown; occurs more often in males.	Behavioral therapy that includes parents and teaches child adaptive responses; community resources for family.
Attention-deficit hyperactivity disorder	Onset before age 7 but can persist into adulthood; persistent inattention, impatience, hyperactivity, impulsivity; difficulty concentrating; fidgeting, excessive talking.	Unknown etiology; tendency to run in families.	Drug therapy, behavior therapy.
Oppositional defiant disorder	Argumentative behavior, defiance of adult supervision or guidance, tendency to blame others.	ADHD, stress related to parents and family, negative parent temperament, negative child temperament, ineffective child management.	Early treatment with drugs (Risperdal and Zyprexia) and psychotherapy; committed parental involvement and stable home environment; generally poor outcome otherwise.

evaluation. Other mental health care providers may eventually be involved in treatment.

Substance-Related Disorders

Substance abuse occurs among people from every educational, professional, ethnic, racial, and social background. The economic cost to society is immeasurable. **Tolerance, dependence,** and **addiction** are often the end results of abuse, as well as destruction of the family unit and social relationships. Criminal activity is another possible outcome.

Substance-related disorders involve alcohol, prescription drugs, and other drugs (Table 29-9).

- Alcohol abuse applies to all forms of alcohol, such as beer, liquor, wine, coolers, and spirits. Some addicts have been known to go so far as to drink after-shave lotion, some cough and cold medications, or vanilla, which contain a tiny amount of alcohol.
- Prescription drugs are subject to abuse, particularly those with **psychotropic** qualities. Analgesics, sedatives, stimulants, and mood-altering drugs are among the drugs commonly abused. Inhalants and other chemical substances may also be abused.
- Illegal substances frequently abused include cannabis, hallucinogens, designer drugs, and natural and synthetic

opioids. Other, nonillegal substances that are readily available are caffeine and nicotine.

These substances have the capacity to alter behavior, impair judgment, and create medical problems. Social and family relationships suffer and may deteriorate. Operating machinery and motor vehicles while under the influence of mood-altering drugs causes accidents, injuries, and even catastrophic events. When drug use is suspected in any of these events, drug screening may be performed.

The treatment and outcome of all substance abuse are variable, depending on the substance being abused and the client's cooperation and support systems. Drug therapy and psychotherapy are usually part of the treatment plan. The patient may be placed in a detoxification center or other controlled environment; however, success rates are unpredictable.

Patients going through substance withdrawal and others with psychological problems may experience periods of anger and angry behavior. Health-care providers must be alert to impending angry behavior and use constructive approaches to help manage that anger and provide safety for themselves, the patient, and any others in the surrounding environment. You may find the suggestions in Table 29-10 to be helpful for such situations.

TABLE 29-9   SUBSTANCES THAT ARE COMMONLY ABUSED

Classification	Substance	Use	Medical Use	Tolerance	Physical Dependence	Psychological Dependence
Sedatives	Alcohol	Reduce tension	No	Yes	Yes	Yes
	Barbiturates	Relax in social situations, cause relaxation and sleep	Yes	Yes	Yes	Yes
Stimulants	Amphetamines ■ Speed ■ Crank ■ Dexedrine ■ Methamphetamine	Increase feelings of confidence and alertness, decrease fatigue, stay awake, increase endurance, stimulate sex drive	Yes	Yes	No	Yes
	Cocaine		No	Minimal	No	Yes
	Crack cocaine		Yes	Yes	Yes	Yes
Narcotics	Opium, heroin, morphine, Demerol, Dilaudid, hydrochloride, Percodan, codeine	Reduce physical pain, reduce anxiety and tension, aid sleep	Yes (except heroin)	Yes	Yes	Yes
	Methadone	Treatment for heroin addiction	Yes	Yes	Yes	Yes
Hallucinogens	Marijuana, hashish, peyote, LSD, PCP	Relax; change mood, thoughts, and behavior; "mind expansion," "tripping"	No (THC, the active ingredient in marijuana, is used to reduce nausea associated w/terminally ill patients)	No	No	Yes
Tranquilizers (antianxiety drugs)	Librium, Valium, Ativan, Serax, Zanax	Reduce anxiety, induce sleep	Yes	Yes	Yes	Yes

Source: Miele, Carole G,; and England, Teresa, From Nursing Assistant to Clinical Care Associate, 1st Edition ©1999. Reprinted by permission of Pearson Education, Inc. Upper Saddle River, NJ.

TABLE 29-10 CONSTRUCTIVE APPROACHES TO PATIENTS EXHIBITING ANGRY BEHAVIOR

1. Remember that the person may be reacting to frustration that is beyond his or her impulse control. The anger may be misplaced and may have nothing to do with you.
2. Sometimes, the patient displays this anger because of the belief that you can and will handle it to help him regain control.
3. *Always pay attention to your feelings and intuition when you feel threatened by a hostile or physically threatening person.* If you feel physically threatened, get help before attempting to control the outburst.
4. If you sense that the person is acting out because he or she is threatened by hallucinations or delusional thinking, try to reassure the client that he or she is safe. Assure the client that you do not want to cause him or her harm.
5. Set limits on behavior, not feelings. Let the person know that you recognize the anger or frustration but that you cannot allow this person to hurt others.
6. Be willing to accept the person and the feelings, not the behavior.
7. Do not get drawn into an argument. If you do, the patient has "one up on you." The client has caused you to lose your temper and self-control. Anytime you argue or lose your temper with a patient, the patient wins. You are there to teach appropriate and healthy coping skills. You are perceived in a negative and unprofessional way when you forget this fact. You can expect that patients will not be able to act rationally, but *you* are expected to be rational.
8. Remain in control. Be aware of your body language, voice tone, and volume. The louder you get, the louder the client needs to be to dominate the situation.
9. Try to reduce the possibility of an audience. Try to remove the client to an area where others cannot see his or her loss of control. When the situation is over, the person will be embarrassed. The client may be angry with you because you let other clients see the display of hostility.
10. Do not attempt to do this alone. Have other staff help you to remove the person to a more private area.
11. If the client is physically violent, you or other clients could be injured.
12. When the available staff assemble to manage the violent or potentially violent client, you *must* plan your actions. Determine who will verbally direct the situation. Plan for the real possibility that the client will not cooperate with directions. Determine the number of staff needed, and decide how each staff member will respond to control the client's violent behavior.
13. Remember that other clients will be frightened by the hostile outburst. They want to see that the staff is in control of the person and situation.
14. Try to determine the reason for the outburst. Ask questions in a matter-of-fact but controlled tone of voice.
15. Do not engage the person in explaining this behavior in the heat of the moment.
16. If the patient identifies that you are frightened and uncomfortable, don't say, "I am not afraid," if you are. Simply state that his or her language or behavior is threatening and that you want to help him or her regain control.
17. Examine your attitude. Patients are very perceptive of rejection and hostility. Talk about your feelings with a neutral person to cool down before you face the patient again.
18. Be safe, and believe threats.
19. Get help from other staff. Follow the guidelines and procedures of the facility for controlling physical threats or actual acts of violence.
20. Keep a safe distance from a patient who is verbally threatening. Do not stand too close.
21. Make process statements rather than judgments. Say, "You are angry because you didn't get ____," rather than, "You didn't get ____, so now you are acting out to get ____."
22. First, try to deal with the fact that the person is angry. Then move on to find out why.
23. Sometimes, demanding behavior is in the form of passive, whining behavior that demands your reassurance and support. You may begin to feel that nothing you do for this client is satisfactory.
24. The client may try to control the amount of time that you spend with him or her. This person views the amount of time spent as an indication of personal worth.
25. Let the person know that you are interested and concerned by providing frequent and short interactions.
26. Whining is a style of passively demanding attention. When this is the case, give praise and spend more time with the individual when he or she is not whining. Assess the situation, and find out what the need is. Attend to the need, not the whining behavior.
27. Be kind and courteous, but set limits. Be specific about the amount of time you are prepared to provide.
28. If the person wants something *now* and you cannot do it now or the need is not immediate, tell the person when you will have time to meet the request. Do not say, "I will do this later." Explain when later is: "I will be able to help you with this at 1:00 P.M."
29. Process behavior that doesn't make sense to you with other staff so that, as a team, you will understand the possible underlying reasons for the behavior. *All behavior has a purpose.*

Source: Miele, Carole G., and England, Teresa, From Nursing Assistant to Clinical Care Associate, 1st Edition ©1999. Reprinted by permission of Pearson Education, Inc. Upper Saddle River, NJ.

Assessment and Diagnosis

The diagnosis and treatment of mental disorders consist of an initial mental health intake questionnaire (Table 29-11), a mental status examination (Table 29-12), and a treatment plan (Table 29-13). Drug therapy, psychotherapy, counseling, group therapy, stress reduction therapy, and relaxation techniques are common

Keys to Success
COMMUNITY SERVICES FOR MENTAL HEALTH CLIENTS

Patients with a history of mental disorders are often unemployed and have no income, no permanent residence, no means of travel, no health insurance, and no way to pay for mental health services and medications. Patients who *do* have insurance may find that coverage is limited. Elderly parents of mentally challenged or disabled children may need assistance in planning for their long-term care. As a medical assistant you should be aware of community and social service agencies to which you can refer these clients.

TABLE 29-11 SUGGESTED QUESTIONS FOR MENTAL HEALTH INTAKE

1. Reason for visit or counseling
2. History of counseling/therapy
3. Positive outcomes of previous therapy—what helped or didn't help?
4. Medication history
5. Health issues, physical history
6. Any family history of mental illness
7. Family status and history
8. Support systems available
9. School and work history
10. History of substance use or abuse, personally or family
11. Legal issues
12. Military history
13. History of sexual abuse
14. Sexuality history

TABLE 29-12 SUGGESTED MENTAL STATUS EXAMINATION

1. Is the patient oriented to time, person, place, situation?
2. Does the patient exhibit normal or abnormal memory?
3. Does the patient exhibit appropriate insight?
4. Does the patient exhibit appropriate judgment and thinking?
5. Has the patient experienced hallucinations or delusions? ("Do you hear or see things others say are not there?")
6. Has the patient had suicidal thoughts? If so, what does the patient report the thoughts to be?
7. Does the patient report thoughts of homicide?
8. Does the patient express a plan for suicide or homicide?
9. Does the patient have a history of previous suicide attempts?
10. Is there a family history of suicide?

TABLE 29-13 TREATMENT PLAN

- Develop the treatment plan with input from the client.
- Determine if therapy will be on an inpatient or outpatient basis, and whether it will be daily, weekly, biweekly, or monthly.
- Set treatment goals. What does the patient expect to get out of treatment? How will things be different in 6 months?

treatments for some mental disorders. It is important to include the client in goal setting and decision making related to treatment.

The *Diagnostic and Statistical Manual of Mental Disorders IV* (**DSM-IV**) is the reference manual used by mental health providers to diagnose a wide range of mental disorders. The DSM-IV establishes and updates standard criteria for diagnosis.

Standard Treatments for Mental Disorders

The treatment of mental disorders today is twofold: medication and therapy. Once the patient is assessed and a diagnosis is established, a treatment plan is developed. Many disorders respond to drug therapy alone, and many respond to therapy/counseling. However, many more require the combined actions of drug therapy and counseling or psychotherapy. Some conditions are the result of insult to the brain, especially deprivation of oxygen and nutrition, and the only treatment is supportive care. Disorders caused by chemical imbalance in the brain are treated with drugs, psychotherapy, counseling, group therapy, stress reduction therapy, and relaxation techniques. Those caused by heredity and genetic factors may have no absolute course of treatment. As with other types of disorders and conditions, there may be no identifiable cause and no definitive course of treatment.

REVIEW

Chapter Summary

- In the mental health setting, the psychiatrist or psychologist is the primary provider of treatment for mental health disorders. Social workers, family and marriage counselors, child therapists, substance abuse counselors, correctional rehabilitative counselors, and vocational training counselors may also be called on.
- Neurons, or nerve cells, of the brain are connected by synaptic gaps. Each neuron may produce a number of neurotransmitters that may be specific or react with many different types of receptors. As the brain develops and processes thoughts and memories, the neurons undergo changes that affect the physical structure and chemical substances released by the synaptic gaps. These changes ultimately affect behavior.
- Mental wellness is characterized by healthy methods of coping with the pressures of daily living. A positive outlook, strong support systems, strong self-esteem, personal growth, positive relationships, and a purpose in life are all elements of mental well-being.

- General classifications of mental disorders include schizophrenia, mood disorders, personality disorders, anxiety disorders, somatoform disorders, and gender identity disorder. Many mental disorders are caused by a chemical imbalance in the brain and are treated with drugs, psychotherapy, counseling, group therapy, stress reduction therapy, and relaxation techniques. Causes include heredity and genetic factors, environment, gender, and life experiences. Some mental disorders have no identifiable etiology and no absolute course of treatment.
- Symptoms of schizophrenia are disordered or disorganized thinking, inappropriate affect, unpredictable behavior, and visual or auditory hallucinations. Heredity, environment, and stress are possible causes. Schizophrenia is treated with antipsychotic medications.
- Mood disorders involve alterations in mood level. Major depressive disorder is treated with antidepressant medications. Postpartum depression can occur following childbirth. Seasonal affective disorder occurs as daylight hours decrease.

Chapter Summary (continued)

Bipolar disorder, or manic-depressive disorder, is characterized by intense mood swings. Alterations in neurotransmitter levels are the usual cause, and drug therapy the usual treatment.

■ Personality disorders (PD) are divided into three classifications or clusters. Cluster A includes paranoid, schizoid, and schizotypical personalities. Cluster B includes borderline and antisocial personalities, narcissistic disorder, and histrionic disorder. Cluster C includes avoidant, dependent, and obsessive compulsive personality disorders. The etiology of PDs is unknown. Therapy helps patients develop coping mechanisms. Drugs may be prescribed for comorbid conditions.

■ Anxiety is a common reaction to perceived threats but may become a physiologic and psychological condition. Anxiety disorders include generalized anxiety disorder and panic disorder, phobic disorder, obsessive-compulsive disorder, and post-traumatic stress disorder.

■ Physical symptoms with no underlying organic etiology are characteristic of a somatoform disorder. Somatization disorder, conversion disorder and hypochondriasis are somatoform disorders. Factitious disorders include malingering, Munchhausen syndrome, and Munchhausen syndrome by proxy. Symptoms are contrived in hopes of personal gain, with no confirmed medical condition.

■ The individual with gender identity disorder feels uncomfortable or unhappy in his or her biological role.

■ Other mental conditions are caused by lack of oxygen to the brain, genetic aberration, or illness or insult affecting the brain tissue. Mental retardation occurs as the result of an interruption in the child's intellectual growth before, during, or after birth. Dementia is reduced mental or cognitive functioning that has its onset after the age of 18. It may occur as the result of a traumatic insult to the skull and brain that reduces blood flow, oxygenation, and nutrition to the brain.

■ Alzheimer's is a progressive degenerative disease of the brain that affects mental and physical functioning. The usual onset is after the age of 60. There is no identifiable cause and no cure.

■ Vascular dementia may be the result of decreased blood flow to the brain. Typical symptoms are loss of intellectual faculties, memory lapses, and personality changes. The condition usually worsens with age, and there is no cure.

■ Mental disorders that occur in childhood include learning disorders, pervasive development disorder (autistic disorder), attention-deficit hyperactivity disorder, and oppositional defiant disorder. Children with learning disorders tend to function at a lower-than-expected level because of an abnormality in cognitive processing or problems with vision, hearing, memory, language comprehension, and attention.

■ Substance-related disorders involve alcohol, prescription drugs, and other drugs. Tolerance, dependence, addiction, and destruction of the family unit and social relationships are often the end results. Drug therapy, psychotherapy, and possible commitment to a detoxification center or other controlled environment are part of the treatment.

■ The *Diagnostic and Statistical Manual of Mental Disorders IV* (DSM-IV) is the reference manual used by mental health providers to diagnose mental disorders.

Chapter Review Questions

Multiple Choice

1. The term that means "abnormal mental coping of the individual who is out of touch with reality" is:
   A. phobia
   B. psychotropic
   C. psychotherapeutic
   D. psychosis

2. Which of the following is a medical doctor with special training in the field of psychiatry?
   A. psychologist
   B. psychiatrist
   C. social worker
   D. counselor

3. In addition to excitatory and inhibitory neurotransmitters, there are modulatory neurotransmitters such as:
   A. acetylcholine
   B. neuropeptides and purines
   C. monoamines
   D. all of the above

4. A patient who reports pain and symptoms with no physiologic basis may be diagnosed with:
   A. hypochondriasis
   B. personality disorder
   C. malingering
   D. ADD

5. The mental disorder characterized by disordered or disorganized thinking, inappropriate affect, unpredictable behavior, and visual or auditory hallucinations is:
   A. depression
   B. bipolar disorder
   C. schizophrenia
   D. multiple personality

True/False

T F 1. A psychologist has a doctorate in psychology.

T F 2. Benjamin Rush, who is considered the first U.S. psychiatrist, opened the first psychiatric hospital in Williamsburg, Virginia, in 1769.

T F 3. The onset of PTSD is always delayed.

Chapter Review Questions (continued)

T F   4. A psychologist can prescribe medications for patients.

T F   5. The cerebral hemispheres control all the body's voluntary, and some involuntary, activities.

T F   6. Seasonal affective disorder (SAD) is a cyclic form of depression.

T F   7. Typical symptoms of dementia are loss of intellectual faculties, memory lapses, and personality changes.

T F   8. Neurotransmitters are chemicals that aid in the transmission of electrical impulses from one neuron to the next.

T F   9. Tolerance, dependence, and addiction are often the end results of substance abuse.

T F 10. The cerebellum is located on the posterior aspect of the brain.

Short Answer

1. What is another term for major, acute, or severe depression?

2. List the 10 personality disorders.

3. What is the probable cause of vascular dementia?

4. Name two factitious disorders.

5. What is the purpose of the Stanford-Binet Scale?

Research

1. What age groups have the highest level of suicide attempts? Does this information surprise you? Why or why not?

2. In your community, where would family members affected by mental illness (their own or another family member's) find support?

Externship Application Experience

As an extern, you have a brief rotation in a mental health facility. Other students are verbally mocking a male schizophrenic patient who is yelling at a water fountain. The students are openly calling the patient "crazy," "fruitcake," "nutso," and "dummy." What should you do?

Resource Guide

American Psychiatric Association
www.psych.org

American Psychological Association
www.apa.org

National Depressive Manic Depression Association
1-800-826-3632
www.ndmda.org

National Institute of Mental Health
www.nimh.nih.gov

National Alliance for the Mentally Ill
1-800-950-6264
www.nami.org

 MedMedia
www.prenhall.com/frazier

More on this chapter, including interactive resources, can be found on the Student CD-ROM accompanying this textbook and on the Companion Website at www.prenhall.com/frazier.

Oncology

Case Study

Marilyn has been doing her externship in an oncology office, where she is responsible for taking patient histories and vital signs and assisting the physician. A 45-year-old female patient, Ruth Dillan, asks Marilyn about colorectal cancer. Ruth is concerned because she has experienced a change in her bowel habits and has a strong family history of cancer. Both of her sisters and her mother were diagnosed with cancer in recent years. As worried as she is, however, Ruth has canceled one previous appointment for screening because she is apprehensive about the embarrassment and discomfort of the testing procedures. Ruth asks Marilyn what her chances are of developing cancer. She also asks for specifics about the screening.

Objectives

After completing this chapter, you should be able to:

- Spell and define the medical terminology in this chapter.
- Identify the medical assistant's role in the oncology office.
- Describe the different types of malignant neoplasms.
- List and describe routine cancer screening tests.
- Explain tumor markers and how they are used in cancer diagnosis.
- Discuss the staging and grading of malignancies.
- Discuss the role of chemotherapy in cancer treatment.
- Discuss the use of radiation in cancer treatment.
- Discuss the role of surgical intervention in cancer treatment.
- Discuss hormone therapy and immunotherapy as cancer treatments.
- Explain some of the side effects of cancer treatment.
- Describe some recent advances in cancer research.
- Explain hospice care for terminally ill patients.
- Describe the cancer prevention lifestyle.

MedMedia

www.prenhall.com/frazier

Additional interactive resources and activities for this chapter can be found on the Companion Website. For audio glossary, legal and ethical scenarios, job scenarios, quizzes, and games related to the content of this chapter, please access the accompanying CD-ROM in this book.

Assets Available:

Audio Glossary
Legal and Ethical Scenario: *Oncology*
On the Job Scenario: *Oncology*
Multiple Choice Quiz
Games: Crossword, Strikeout and Spelling Bee

➕ MEDICAL ASSISTING COMPETENCIES

CAAHEP ENTRY-LEVEL COMPETENCIES FOR CMA	ABHES ENTRY-LEVEL COMPETENCIES FOR RMA
■ Identify and respond to issues of confidentiality. ■ Perform within legal and ethical boundaries. ■ Demonstrate knowledge of federal and state health-care legislation and regulations. ■ Perform hand washing. ■ Dispose of biohazardous materials. ■ Practice Standard Precautions. ■ Use methods of quality control. ■ Perform telephone and in-person screening. ■ Obtain vital signs. ■ Obtain and record patient history. ■ Prepare and maintain examination and treatment areas. ■ Prepare patient for and assist with routine and specialty examinations. ■ Prepare patient and assist with minor procedures, treatments, and minor surgery. ■ Apply pharmacology principles to prepare and administer oral and parenteral medications. ■ Maintain medication and immunization records.	■ Project a positive attitude. ■ Maintain confidentiality at all times. ■ Be a "team player." ■ Be cognizant of ethical boundaries. ■ Exhibit initiative. ■ Adapt to change. ■ Evidence a responsible attitude. ■ Be courteous and diplomatic. ■ Conduct work within scope of education, training, and ability. ■ Interview and take a patient history. ■ Prepare patients for and assist physician with routine and specialty examinations and treatments and minor office surgery. ■ Apply principles of aseptic techniques and infection control. ■ Prepare and maintain examination and treatment area. ■ Collect and process specimens. ■ Dispose of biohazardous materials. ■ Practice Standard Precautions. ■ Prepare and administer oral and parenteral medications as directed by the physician. ■ Maintain medication and immunization records.

Medical Terminology

benign—noncancerous or noninvasive

cancer—general term for various malignant neoplasms

chemotherapy—treatment of disease and infection with chemical agents; in cancer treatment, use of chemical agents to selectively kill cancer cells

hospice—holistic care of terminally ill patients in a home or homelike setting

malignant—cancerous, invasive, and destructive

metastasis—spread of a disease to adjacent and distal tissues and organs

neoplasm—new growth or tumor

oncology—branch of medicine that deals with the study, diagnosis, and treatment of tumors and cancer

remission—complete or partial disappearance of the clinical characteristics of chronic or malignant disease

tumor—growth characterized by progressive and uncontrolled production of cells

tumor marker—substance produced by tumor cells that can be measured and monitored in blood serum levels to indicate progression of metastases and/or effectiveness of cancer chemotherapy

Introduction

Oncology is the study of **tumors** and **cancer,** which are characterized by uncontrolled cell growth. General types of cancer include carcinomas, sarcomas, lymphomas, leukemias, and melanomas.

Every year 1.3 million Americans are diagnosed with cancer. Twenty-five percent of U.S. deaths (500,000 a year) are caused by cancer. The prevalence of various types of cancer has spurred ongoing research into the nature and causes of this dreaded disease, which in turn has led to important advances in its treatment. Information campaigns have educated the public about lifestyle habits—such as wearing sunscreen and not smoking—that can help reduce the chances of contracting certain types of cancer.

The Medical Assistant's Role in the Oncology Practice

The medical assistant performs several essential functions in an oncology medical practice:

- Obtaining the medical history and vital signs
- Assisting the oncologist as necessary in patient examination and procedures

- Instructing the patient in the removal of clothing before a physical examination and providing a gown and drape
- Providing patients with information on community resources
- Arranging appointments for other tests and procedures
- Collecting specimens, including blood

The Classification and Physiology of Cancers

Cell division and reproduction in the body usually occur at a controlled rate. Cancer, or malignancy, is caused by the rapid and uncontrollable development and reproduction of abnormal cells. These cells take on a different character from the original, normal cell (Figure 30-1 ◆). Abnormal cell growth of this kind is referred to as **malignant** or life-threatening cell growth. As the growth advances, normal cells are deprived of nutrition and crowded out of their normal environment.

The original malignant growth is called the primary site. **Metastasis** creates secondary sites elsewhere in the body. Malignant **neoplasms** are classified according to the type of tissue invaded (Table 30-1).

Benign tumors result from slow growth, and their cellular structure is close to that of adjacent cells. Benign tumor cells are differentiated; that is, they resemble the tissue of origin. These tumors do not necessarily cause symptoms when they are small, but they can cause compression of surrounding tissues and organs as they enlarge. Most benign tumors can be surgically excised, as most are encapsulated and do not invade surrounding tissue. If the entire tumor is removed, it usually does not recur.

Malignant tumors, also known as cancer, cause symptoms when they invade (often by cell migration through blood and lymph circulation) and destroy local, adjacent, and distal sites of tissue and organs (Table 30-2). When metastasis has occurred, total eradication becomes more difficult, and recurrence is a common problem.

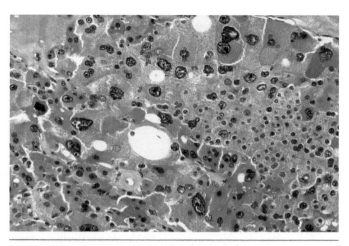

Figure 30-1 ◆ Human cancer cells and tissue
Source: Biophoto Associates/Photo Researchers, Inc.

Cancer has several possible causes:

- Repeated exposure to carcinogens over a long period of time, such as those inhaled during smoking (lung cancer) and certain physical agents such as radiation
- Genetic cellular mutations due to aging
- Immune system diseases such as AIDS, which causes lymphomas
- Hormones, as in breast cancer
- Certain viruses such as human papillomavirus, a possible precursor to cervical cancer

Radiation disrupts DNA and cellular replication. In the form of ultraviolet rays, x-rays, and radioactive materials, it can be carcinogenic. Overexposure to the sun's UV rays raises the risk of basal, squamous, and melanoma skin cancer. Greater amounts of skin pigmentation provide greater protection from the harmful effects of ultraviolet rays; thus, fair-skinned people with higher exposure to the sun are at greater risk of skin cancer.

TABLE 30-1 MALIGNANT NEOPLASMS		
Type of Neoplasm	**Tissue of Origin**	**Associated Conditions**
Carcinoma	Epithelial cells	Basal cell carcinoma, squamous cell carcinoma
Glioma	Nervous system, incuding the brain, spinal cord, and nerve tissues	Neurogenic sarcoma, neuroblastoma, glioblastoma, malignant meningioma
Leukemia	Blood precursors (stem cells) in the bone marrow	Acute lymphocytic leukemia, chronic lymphocytic leukemia, acute mylogenous leukemia, chronic mylogenous leukemia
Lymphoma	Lymphoid tissue and lymph vessels	Lymphangiosarcoma, lymphangioendothelioma, malignant lymphoma, lymphosarcoma, reticulum cell sarcoma, Hodgkin's lymphoma, non-Hodgkin's lymphoma
Melanoma	Melanin-producing cells	Malignant melanoma
Sarcoma	Supportive tissue including muscle, cartilage, and bone	Osteogenic sarcoma, angiosarcoma, leiomyosarcoma, rhabdomyosarcoma

TABLE 30-2 DIFFERENCES BETWEEN BENIGN AND MALIGNANT TUMORS

Benign Tumors (Figure 30-2 ◆)	Malignant Tumors (Figure 30-3 ◆)
Tumor cells appear similar to normal cells.	Tumor cells do not resemble normal cells.
Tumor cells are differentiated.	Tumor cells are undifferentiated.
Tumor cells exhibit slow growth.	Tumor cells exhibit rapid growth.
Tumor cells grow adjacent to each other.	Tumor cells infiltrate surrounding tissue.
Tumor expands but does not destroy tissue.	Tumor growth causes ulceration and necrosis of tissue.
Tumor is smooth and movable as a unit.	Tumor is irregularly shaped and more difficult to move.
Tumor recurrence is rare after surgical excision.	Tumor recurrence is common after surgical excision.
Symptoms are related to tumor location, size, and compression on tissue or organs.	Symptoms are related to tumor location, size, and compression, which cause severe pain, cachexia (weight loss), and death.

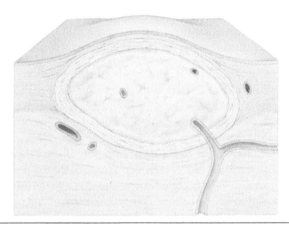

Figure 30-2 ◆ Benign tumor
Source: Dorling Kindersley Media Library

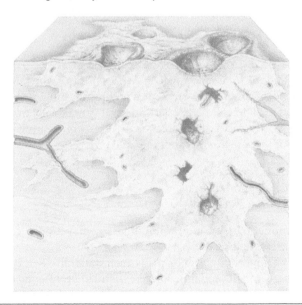

Figure 30-3 ◆ Malignant tumor
Source: Dorling Kindersley Media Library

The incidence of cancer has a tendency to rise with age. Often a silent invader, it may not be diagnosed until it has progressed to an advanced stage. It takes on many forms and has variable outcomes, depending on the tissue or area of the body involved and the degree to which the cancer has metastasized at the time of diagnosis.

Specific types of cancers are discussed in other chapters of this book.

Diagnostic Procedures

In general, the detection, diagnosis, and treatment of cancer in an early stage offer a better prognosis and a greater chance for cure. Public education about the signs and symptoms of cancer is designed to encourage individuals to seek medical evaluation earlier (Table 30-3). Prognosis is usually reported statistically as the percentage of patients with that cancer who are still alive after a certain period of time. The patient may be cured of the disease, in **remission**, or still undergoing treatment.

Cancer detection employs general and specific techniques of physical examination, medical history-taking, and laboratory screening tests. Screening examinations can detect cancers of the breast, rectum, colon, prostate, cervix, testis, tongue, mouth, and skin early, when treatment is more likely to succeed. These cancers account for approximately half of all new cancer cases.

If cancer is suspected, additional diagnostic investigation is achieved with imaging techniques (mammograms, ultrasonograms, MRIs, PET scans) and most decisively by biopsy of the lesion. Blood tests are used to evaluate hormone levels and tumor markers.

TABLE 30-3 CANCER WARNING SIGNALS

The American Cancer Society lists the following seven danger signs and symptoms of cancer:

1. Unusual bleeding or discharge
2. A lump or thickening in the breast or elsewhere
3. A sore that does not heal
4. Change in bowel or bladder habits
5. Persistent hoarseness or cough
6. Persistent indigestion or difficulty swallowing
7. Change in a wart or mole

The ABCDs of Abnormalities in Warts or Moles:

Asymmetry: half of the mole does not match the other half
Border: the edges of the mole are irregular
Color: the color of the mole is not uniform
Diameter: the diameter of the mole is greater than 6 mm

The Early Warning Signs of Breast Cancer:

■ A lump that can be seen in the breast or felt within the breast
■ Changes in the breast's skin color or texture
■ A depression or dimpling of the skin of the breast
■ Changes in the appearance of the nipple, such as retraction or inversion (pulling in)
■ Bloody or spontaneous discharge of any color from the nipple
■ Swelling of the breast or of the lymph nodes (in the armpit)

Routine Diagnostic Screening

Routine diagnostic screening for cancer includes the following tests:

- Colorectal screening: A fecal screening for occult blood is recommended on a yearly basis. Physicians generally order a flexible sigmoidoscopy or colonoscopy every three years after the age of 50. However, a different recommendation may be made, based on medical history, presenting symptoms, and family history.
- Barium enema or lower gastrointestinal X-ray studies.
- Mammogram screening: Mammograms are generally prescribed yearly after the age of 40, but the patient's medical history, presenting symptoms, and family history may dictate a different recommendation. Medicare, a federally sponsored health-care plan for senior citizens over 65, chronically disabled patients, and patients with end-stage renal disease, pays for annual mammograms.
- Pap smear and pelvic examination: These are generally ordered annually for sexually active females for life. Medicare covers these procedures only every two years.
- PSA screening and digital rectal examination: These are usually prescribed for males annually after the age of 50. Medicare will only pay annually for PSA screening.

?— Critical Thinking Question 30-1

Even though Ruth is not yet in the 50-year-old age bracket, should she still be tested for colorectal cancer?

Tumor Markers

Tumor markers, also referred to as *cancer markers*, are proteins, hormones, and other substances produced by tumors and released into the blood. They are used as screening tools to determine the progress of cancer treatment or the recurrence of a tumor. Tumor marker blood studies are usually ordered after a tumor has been diagnosed. Routine use of tumor markers in the diagnostic arena includes PSA screening tests for males and Pap smears for females.

Tumor markers for various forms of cancer include CA19-9, a marker for colorectal, gastric, and pancreatic cancer; CA125, a marker for ovarian cancer as well as for cancer of the uterus, cervix, lung, breast, and digestive tract; and carcinoembryonic antigen, a marker for colorectal cancer, especially when it has metastasized.

These markers are not always an indication of cancer cell or tumor activity. They are only used to monitor tumor growth. Tumor markers may be elevated in benign conditions such as inflammatory bowel disease, pancreatitis, liver disease, endometriosis, pelvic inflammatory disease, menstruation, and inflammation of the pleura.

Staging and Grading Malignant Tumors

Malignancies are staged and graded to determine the prognosis and optimum course of treatment for each patient. Staging identifies the type of cancer and the degree to which it has metastasized. It evaluates the size and extent of the primary tumor, the extent of lymph node involvement, and the extent and number of metastases at distant sites. The most commonly used staging system is the TNM system.

- The letter T indicates the size, depth, and location of the primary tumor. The letter or number following the T indicates the nature of the condition. X means that assessment of the primary tumor cannot be accomplished; 0 means that there is no indication of a primary tumor; and the numbers 1, 2, 3, or 4 indicate increasing degrees of tumor extension from local, limited involvement to metastasis into adjacent tissues.
- The letter N indicates nodal (lymph node) involvement. The letter X following means that assessment of the lymph nodes regional to the tumor cannot be assessed; 0 means there is no indication of lymph node involvement; and the numbers 1 to 4 indicate increasing metastasis into the lymph nodes.
- The letter M indicates distant metastasis. An X following means that no distant metastasis can be assessed; 0 means that no distant metastasis has been found; and 1 means that distant metastasis has been determined.

When the TNM staging has been completed, the tumor is designated stage I, II, III, or IV, indicating the prognosis. For example, T2 N2 M0 Stage II would be a good prognosis, whereas T4 N4 M1 Stage IV would indicate less potential for successful treatment and/or survivability.

Grading refers to the differentiation of the cancer cells. Well-differentiated cancer cells retain some of the features of the cells of origin. This grade of cancer signifies a better prognosis than one in which the cells are poorly differentiated and no longer resemble the cells of origin. The latter grade of cancer is usually in a more advanced stage. Grading involves the microscopic evaluation of biopsy tissue. A laboratory pathologist examines the tissue for growth rate and degree of cellular differentiation.

Cancer Treatment

The outlook for a cancer patient is more positive when the cancer is diagnosed at an early stage and prompt intervention is initiated. The complete eradication of cancer cells from the body is the goal of cancer treatment. At present, treatment consists of three major methods:

- Chemotherapy
- Radiation therapy
- Surgical removal

Hormonal therapy and immunotherapy may also be considered treatment methods.

There is no cure for many metastatic diseases, but the same treatment modalities may be useful in prolonging or improving the quality of the patient's life. Even after the patient has achieved remission, he or she must be followed closely for several years. Micrometastases that are not eradicated with systemic therapy can lead to eventual recurrence of the cancer.

Critical Thinking Question 30-2

Ruth is concerned about being embarrassed and uncomfortable. She has also canceled a previous appointment. How should Marilyn approach this situation?

Chemotherapy

Single or combination **chemotherapy**, in conjunction with other drug therapy, is used effectively to attack the malignancy at different stages of the cancer cell life cycle Figure 30-4 ◆.

Several types of antineoplastic agents are used in chemotherapy: alkalating agents, antimetabolites, hormones and hormone antagonists, antitumor antibiotics, plant extracts with antineoplastic activity, and miscellaneous anticancer drugs (Table 30-4). Each therapeutic approach is unique, specific to the patient, and may involve one drug, two or more drugs from the same class, or two or more drugs from multiple classes. In the first round of therapy, the maximum tolerable dose is administered to kill as many cancer cells as possible (Figure 30-5 ◆).

Chemotherapeutic treatment is a challenge as the drugs may cause uncomfortable and undesirable side effects. All the body systems can be affected. Recent advances, however, have reduced some of the undesirable effects.

Radiation

Radiation X-rays are used to diagnose and treat cancer (Figure 30-6 ◆). Radioactive materials may also be injected or implanted into the body. Radiation therapy destroys tumors while protecting healthy tissue as much as possible. However, it does not always accomplish these goals, usually because of where the tumor is located, and normal, healthy cells are destroyed as well. Also, some cancerous tumors are not affected by safe doses of radiation. Side effects of radiation therapy are hair loss, nausea and vomiting, stomatitis, and internal radiation burns.

Surgery

Surgery alone is only curative for early-stage tumors. Usually, more than one treatment option is employed. Surgery is important for the treatment of solid cancers and is often used in the staging evaluation as well. As a treatment modality, the goal is either cure or palliative symptom control. When surgery is employed as a curative measure, the surgeon tries to achieve negative margins around the tumor, meaning that a certain amount of normal tissue is removed along with the tumor to ensure the entire tumor is removed. If negative margins are not achieved, surgery must be performed again or another type of treatment must be tried. At the time of surgery, the regional lymph nodes may be evaluated in order to determine if the cancer cells have entered the lymphatic system and invaded the nodes. Affected nodes are generally removed. Palliative surgery is performed to relieve troublesome symptoms such as obstruction. Relief can be achieved by tumor resection, bypass, stenting (placing a mesh tube in a vessel to maintain its patency), or laser ablation (removing a growth with laser).

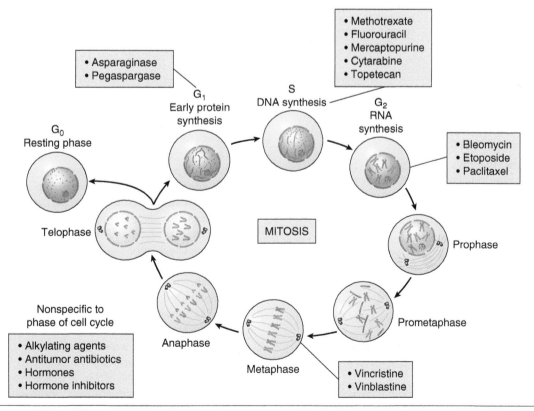

Figure 30-4 ◆ Antineoplastic agents

TABLE 30-4 ANTINEOPLASTIC DRUGS

Class of Drugs and Common Examples	Mode of Action	Type of Cancer Treated	Side Effects
Alkalating agents: Cytoxan, Leukeran, Alkeran, Emcyt, Zanozar, Myleran, Temodar, Ifex, Mustargen, Platinol, Praplatinoxu	Alter the structure of DNA in cancer cells, preventing them from functioning normally	Hodgkin's disease, non-Hodgkin's lymphoma, leukemias, multiple myeloma, and cancer of the breasts, ovaries, lungs, pancreas, testicles, brain, and bladder	Bone marrow depression with reduction in blood cell formation, RBCs, WBCs, and platelets; effects on epithelial cells lining GI tract, with nausea and vomiting
Antimetabolites: methotrexate, floxuridine, flurouracil, Cytosar, Gemzar, Leustatin, thiogantine	Similar in structure to essential nutrients and nucleic acids required for cellular growth; block chemical pathways of growth of normal building blocks of the cells, slowing their growth and killing many cancer cells	Leukemia, choriocarcinoma, lymphoma, and cancer of the testicles, breasts, colon, rectum, stomach, pancreas, and lungs; topical (fluorouracil) for basal cell carcinoma	Immunosuppressant action, nausea, vomiting, and anorexia
Hormones and Hormone Antagonists: corticosteroids, estrogen, progestin, and androgens	Usually given as a palliative measure	Glucocorticocoids for leukemias, Hodgkin's, and lymphomas; testosterone for breast cancer; progestin for breast cancer; estrogen for prostate and testicular cancer	
Antitumor Antibiotics: Rubex, Blenoxane, Cosmegan, Cerubidine, Doxil, Ellence, Idamycin, Mutamycin, Valstar	Interact with DNA similarly to alkalating agents	Lymphoma, sarcomas, Kaposi's sarcoma, Wilms' tumor, leukemias, and cancer of the breasts, lungs, testicles, thyroid, bladder, rectum, and ovaries	Similar to those of alkalating agents
Plant Extracts with Antineoplastic Activity: Oncovin, Velban, Navelbine, Taxotere, Taxol, Hycamtin, VePesid, Vumon, Camptosar	Block cell reproduction by impeding cell division	Hodgkin's disease, lymphoma, Wilms' tumor, leukemia, and cancer of the breasts, lungs, ovaries, testicles, colon, and rectum	Lowered resistance to infection, bruising or bleeding, anemia, sore mouth and taste change, diarrhea, malaise and weakness, hair loss, aching joints and muscles, skin changes including rash, numbness or tingling in hands or feet, headaches, allergic reactions, nausea and vomiting
Miscellaneous Anticancer Drugs: tamoxifen	Tamoxifen is an antiestrogenic agent that blocks estrogen receptor in cancer cells	Breast cancer	Nausea and vomiting, hot flashes, vaginal discharge, uterine bleeding, fluid retention and thrombus; may cause increased rate of uterine cancer.

Hormone Therapy and Immunotherapy

The use of hormone therapy and immunotherapy in the treatment of cancer is continually evolving. Hormone therapy can be effective in hormone-dependent cancers such as breast cancer and prostate cancer. It may involve the following:

- The administration of drugs that suppress hormone synthesis, such as luteinizing hormone-releasing hormone (LHRH) antagonists or aromatase inhibitors, which are used to treat prostate cancer.
- The administration of drugs that block the action of hormones, such as the estrogen receptor modulator tamoxifen, used to treat breast cancer.
- The surgical removal of hormone-producing glands, such as oophorectomy and orchiectomy.

Immunotherapy, also known as biotherapy, is used in combination with chemotherapy or radiation therapy to build the body's immune system to help fight the cancer. This treatment, still considered experimental, may be administered during the early stages of the disease. Immunotherapy methods include cancer vaccines, monoclonal antibody therapy, and nonspecific, primary, and adjuvant immunotherapy.

Cancer vaccines are similar in application theory to traditional vaccines. Each cancer vaccine contains entire or partial cancer cells or antigens and works to increase the immune response against cancer cells in the body. Cancer vaccinations have not yet been approved for use in the United States.

Monoclonal antibodies are designed to target certain products of cancer cells that are not found in normal cells. The monoclonal antibody is an antibody clone mass-produced in a laboratory setting (as opposed to in the body, in response to antigen presence). When the monoclonal antibody is combined with a B cell that has recognition for a specific antigen, the antibody continues to reproduce and support the immune system. Some monoclonal antibody therapies are still in clinical trial, and others are approved for use in treating specific cancers. Some antibodies currently approved for use are trastuzumab (Herceptin), used for certain breast cancers, and rituximab (Rituxan), used for lymphoma.

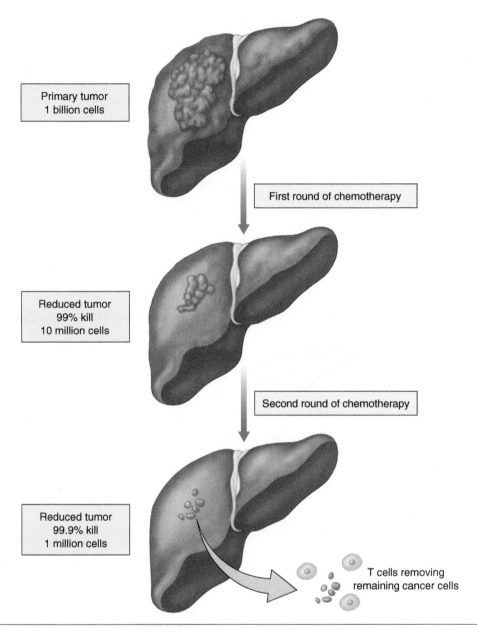

Primary tumor
1 billion cells

First round of chemotherapy

Reduced tumor
99% kill
10 million cells

Second round of chemotherapy

Reduced tumor
99.9% kill
1 million cells

T cells removing
remaining cancer cells

Figure 30-5 ◆ In the first round of therapy, the maximum tolerable dose is administered to kill as many cancer cells as possible

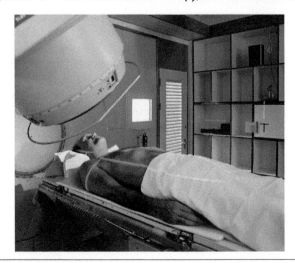

Figure 30-6 ◆ Radiation therapy
Source: Photolibrary.com

Nonspecific immunotherapy can be used as a primary treatment but is often used as adjuvant, or assistive, therapy to other cancer treatments. Cytokines, used in nonspecific immunotherapy, are naturally occurring hormones that regulate the growth and activity of blood and immune system cells. They can also be created in the lab. Cytokines boost the immune system and reduce the side effects of other cancer treatments, including chemotherapy and radiation. They are administered by subcutaneous, intramuscular, or intravenous routes.

Side Effects of Cancer Treatment

Advances in radiation and chemotherapy have diminished the need for radical surgery. But radiation and most anticancer drugs have significant side effects that require constant surveillance and management. Pain management at every stage is a major concern and includes generous use of analgesics and noninvasive techniques that promote relaxation and distraction. Terminally ill persons can be referred to hospice care for compassionate, holistic case management.

One aspect of cancer treatment that is becoming more important as a greater number of patients are being cured is the consequence of therapy. Chemotherapy and radiation therapy are very toxic not only to cancer cells, but to the body in general. Some of the effects of this toxicity are not seen until many years following therapy. Patients are predisposed to develop other malignancies, especially lymphomas and leukemias. The effects can be even more dramatic in children. Growth retardation and cognitive impairment may result. However, cancer therapies are constantly evolving and methods are being developed that may have fewer long-term side effects.

Recent Developments in Cancer Treatment

Recent cancer research has explored the areas of angiogenesis inhibitors and genetic causes. One new approach is based on "starving" a tumor. Experimental studies have shown that inhibiting the growth of new blood vessels that feed the tumor (angiogenesis) causes the tumor to shrink. Since 1994, two angiogenesis inhibitors, angiostatin and endostatin, have produced positive results in mice. Experimental treatments are being performed on humans.

Certain forms of cancer are inherited, such as Wilms' tumor and retinoblastoma; other forms of cancer develop from genetic mutation tendencies that cause common cancers, such as colon cancer and breast cancer, to run in families. Thus, much of the current research is focused on cancer at its genetic roots. Scientists are also investigating genetic switches that cause healthy cells to become disorderly. It has been observed that broken genes can send cells into spirals of cancerous growth. Such genes are proposed targets for therapy.

One recent advance in radiation therapy is particle beam treatment. Higher and more accurately focused doses of neutron energy minimize the side effects of the radiation.

Hospice and Emotional Support

The diagnosis of cancer in any form has a huge impact on the life of the patient and the family. A greatly feared disease, cancer often affects the patient's psychological as well as physical well-being. Many patients elect to fight the disease. Others decide there is no reason to attempt a cure as the cure is often worse than the disease. Religious beliefs, or the absence thereof, may have an impact on the patient's outlook. In all cases the understanding support of family, friends, and health care professionals is essential.

Hospice is the holistic care of terminally ill patients in a home or home-like setting. The philosophy of hospice is to provide quality, palliative care to patients during the final phase of life. Most patients are cancer patients, but hospice care is available to any patient with a terminal condition. Although the emphasis is on the patient, family needs are also addressed. Disease symptoms are managed with nursing-related care, medications, and nutritional support. Pain management integrates emotional, spiritual, and other therapies.

The hospice team is made up of professionals, paraprofessionals, and volunteers who aid the patient and family in holistic terminal care. The team coordinates input from the physician, nurse, chaplain, social worker, home health care workers, and volunteers. Team members help patients and their families address physical, social, emotional, and financial needs.

The Cancer Prevention Lifestyle

Some risk factors predisposing a person to cancer can be modified, but others cannot. For example, inherited tendencies cannot be altered. On the other hand, avoiding promiscuous sexual behavior is effective at preventing AIDS and human papillomavirus, the causes of lymphomas and cervical cancer, respectively. Unhealthy lifestyles are likely to increase cancer risk. Healthier lifestyles build the immune system, which fights foreign substances that invade the body, including cancer cells.

Practicing a healthy lifestyle requires education and commitment. The following measures are all part of an effective cancer prevention lifestyle.

- Eliminate tobacco products, both smoking and chewing.
- Avoid secondhand tobacco smoke and other carcinogens.
- Avoid promiscuous sexual behavior and the sharing of contaminated needles.
- Reduce your intake of animal fat. Eat foods high in fiber.
- Eat several servings a day of food from plant sources (vegetables and fruits).
- Limit your intake of alcoholic beverages.
- Exercise regularly and maintain a normal weight.
- Conduct monthly self-examinations (breasts in females, testicles in males) for lumps and abnormal lesions.
- Inspect your skin regularly for changes in pigmentation, lesions, and abnormal growths.
- Apply sunscreen prior to sun exposure. Wear a wide-brimmed hat and long sleeves when you anticipate being out in the sun for extended periods.

REVIEW

- Oncology is the study of malignancies or cancerous growths, including carcinomas, sarcomas, lymphomas, leukemias, and melanomas. Cancer is the rapid and uncontrolled growth and reproduction of abnormal cells. The original malignant growth is the primary site. When a tumor metastasizes, the new sites are known as secondary sites.
- Possible causes of cancer include repeated exposure to carcinogens, genetic cellular mutations due to aging, disease conditions that weaken the immunity system, and certain hormones and viruses. Benign, or nonmalignant, tumors can cause serious symptoms and physiological problems as they grow in size and compress surrounding tissues.
- Detection, diagnosis, and treatment of cancer in earlier stages allow a better prognosis and chance for cure. Screening tests are available for cancers of the breast, rectum, colon, prostate, cervix, testis, tongue, mouth, and skin. Routine diagnostic tests include Pap smears, mammograms, colorectal screening, PSA screening, and others.
- Tumor markers may indicate cancer cell or tumor activity, but are primarily used to monitor tumor growth. Staging identifies the type of cancer and degree of metastasis. Grading determines cellular differentiation and the resulting prognosis.
- The major types of cancer treatment are chemotherapy, radiation therapy, and surgical removal. They may be used alone or in combination. Combination treatments attack the replication cycle of cancer cells at different times and are often more effective if the patient can tolerate them. Hormonal therapy and immunotherapy are other possible treatments.
- Both radiation and chemotherapy have serious side effects that must be monitored and managed. As cancer therapies advance, however, some side effects are reduced as well.
- Hospice programs provide long-term integrated, palliative care to terminally ill patients.
- Although genetic tendencies toward certain cancers cannot be altered, a cancer prevention lifestyle can help prevent other types of cancer, such as cancer of the lungs, breasts, and skin.

Chapter Review Questions

Multiple Choice

1. The classification *benign* means:
   A. cancerous
   B. noninvasive
   C. invasive
   D. destructive

2. What percentage of U.S. deaths (500,000 a year) are caused by cancer?
   A. 20%
   B. 10%
   C. 15%
   D. 25%

3. Benign tumors result from:
   A. slow growth
   B. rapid growth
   C. normal growth
   D. all of the above

4. Radiation disrupts:
   A. cellular replication
   B. a and c
   C. DNA
   D. none of the above

5. All of the following statements about malignant tumors are true except:
   A. Tumor cells are undifferentiated.
   B. Tumors are smooth and movable as a unit.
   C. Tumors exhibit rapid growth.
   D. Tumor cells resemble normal cells.

True/False

T F 1. Tumor markers are always an indication of cancer cell or tumor activity.

T F 2. PSA exam and tests are usually prescribed for males annually after the age of 50.

T F 3. Each cancer vaccine contains entire or partial cancer cells or antigens and works to increase the immune response against cancer cells in the body.

T F 4. Oncology is the study of malignancies or cancerous growths, including carcinomas, sarcomas, lymphomas, leukemias, and melanomas.

T F 5. Cancer, or malignancy, is caused by the slow and controllable development and reproduction of abnormal cells.

T F 6. All cancerous tumors are affected by safe doses of radiation.

T F 7. Hormone therapy has not proven to be effective in hormone-dependent cancers such as breast cancer and prostate cancer.

Chapter Review Questions (continued)

T F 8. Benign tumor recurrence is common after surgical excision.

T F 9. Tumor markers, or cancer markers, are proteins, hormones, and other substances produced by tumors and released into the blood.

T F 10. Mammograms are generally prescribed yearly after the age of 50.

Short Answer

1. What is the term for the holistic care of terminally ill patients in a home or home-like setting?

2. In tumor staging, what does the letter T indicate?

3. What is the difference between staging and grading?

4. List three possible causes of cancer.

5. Name the three major methods of cancer treatment.

Research

1. Is there a support group for breast cancer survivors in your community?

2. In your community, where would a patient find a support group for prostate cancer survivors?

Externship Application Experience

A middle-aged woman visits the medical office. She tearfully states that she has found a lump in her breast. She says, "I'm going to die." What should you do?

Resource Guide

American Cancer Society
1599 Clifton Road NE
Atlanta, GA 30329-4251
404-320-3333 or 800-227-2345
Fax 404-329-7791
www.cancer.org

Cancer Care Incorporated, National Office
275 7th Avenue, 22nd Floor
New York City, NY
212-712-8080 or 800-813-HOPE
Fax 212-712-8495
www.cancercare.org

National Cancer Institute of National Institutes of Health
www.nci.nih.gov/cancerinformation/cancertype/

Cancer Information Service
304-599-1496
800-4-CANCER
Fax 304-599-1552
www.cancer.gov

MedMedia
www.prenhall.com/frazier

More on this chapter, including interactive resources, can be found on the Student CD-ROM accompanying this textbook and on the Companion Website at www.prenhall.com/frazier.

Objectives

After completing this chapter, you should be able to:

- Spell and define the medical terminology in this chapter.
- Explain the medical assistant's role in a geriatric medical office.
- Discuss the physical changes that take place during aging.
- Explain the psychological aspects of aging.
- Discuss the social components of the aging process.
- Discuss the nutritional needs and problems of the aging person.
- Discuss the economic impact of aging.
- List various cultural views on the place of the elderly in society.
- Describe measures to promote health in geriatric patients.

Geriatrics

Case Study

Elora, an RMA, checks in a patient, Alex Romey, and notices that he is wearing a T-shirt with a slogan that reads: "Do it yourself—I'm retired!" When Elora comments on its humor, Alex explains that this is his last week of work and he plans to wear a different joke shirt each day.

Elora notices that as Alex continues to talk about his past jobs and upcoming retirement, he appears less excited, stops smiling, and starts to look worried. Elora wants to make sure he is prepared for this transition, so she takes a few extra minutes to ask some important questions.

MedMedia
www.prenhall.com/frazier

Additional interactive resources and activities for this chapter can be found on the Companion Website. For videos, audio glossary, legal and ethical scenarios, job scenarios, quizzes, and games related to the content of this chapter, please access the accompanying CD-ROM in this book.

 **Assets Available:**

Audio Glossary
Legal and Ethical Scenario: *Geriatrics*
On the Job Scenario: *Geriatrics*
Video Scenario: A Medicare Mystery
Multiple Choice Quiz
Games: Crossword, Strikeout and Spelling Bee

Medical Terminology

assisted living facility—alternative to long-term care in a nursing home, often the choice for individuals who do not require the 24-hour care provided by skilled nursing facilities

extended care facility—facility that provides 24-hour nursing care; also called nursing home or long-term care facility

geriatrics—science focusing on the aging process; in health care, specialty that deals with the disorders of the aging population and their treatment

hemiplegia—paralysis of one side of the body

Medicare—federal health insurance program for those over the age of 65, the disabled, and those with end-stage renal disease

Medigap insurance—insurance for Medicare recipients that covers deductibles and allowable payments not covered by Medicare

orthostatic hypotension—sudden decrease in blood pressure when an individual rises too quickly from a sitting position, usually resulting in light-headedness

paraplegia—paralysis of the lower portion of the body

presbycusis—hearing deficiency normally associated with aging

presbyopia—vision deficiency normally associated with aging

short-term memory—memory of recent events

Abbreviations

CHF—Congestive Heart Failure

LRI—lower respiratory infection

URI—upper respiratory infection

⊕ MEDICAL ASSISTING COMPETENCIES

CAAHEP ENTRY-LEVEL COMPETENCIES FOR CMA	ABHES ENTRY-LEVEL COMPETENCIES FOR RMA
■ Identify and respond to issues of confidentiality.	■ Project a positive attitude.
■ Perform within legal and ethical boundaries.	■ Maintain confidentiality at all times.
■ Demonstrate knowledge of federal and state health-care legislation and regulations.	■ Be a "team player."
■ Perform hand washing.	■ Be cognizant of ethical boundaries.
■ Dispose of biohazardous materials.	■ Exhibit initiative.
■ Practice Standard Precautions.	■ Adapt to change.
■ Use methods of quality control.	■ Evidence a responsible attitude.
■ Perform telephone and in-person screening.	■ Be courteous and diplomatic.
■ Obtain vital signs.	■ Conduct work within scope of education, training, and ability.
■ Obtain and record patient history.	■ Interview and take a patient history.
■ Prepare and maintain examination and treatment areas.	■ Prepare patients for and assist physician with routine and specialty examinations and treatments and minor office surgery.
■ Prepare patient for and assist with routine and specialty examinations.	■ Apply principles of aseptic techniques and infection control.
■ Prepare patient and assist with minor procedures, treatments, and minor surgery.	■ Prepare and maintain examination and treatment area.
■ Apply pharmacology principles to prepare and administer oral and parenteral medications.	■ Collect and process specimens.
■ Maintain medication and immunization records.	■ Dispose of biohazardous materials.
	■ Practice Standard Precautions.
	■ Prepare and administer oral and parenteral medications as directed by the physician.
	■ Maintain medication and immunization records.

Introduction

Life expectancies of different population groups vary, depending on social, economic, environmental, physical, and genetic factors. The average life expectancy in the United States is 76 years. As life expectancy rates continue to rise, it is projected that in the year 2020 16% of the population will be over the age of 65.

The aging process begins at birth, but becomes more intense during middle age. **Geriatrics** is a medical practice specializing in the treatment and care of older or aging individuals. Some physicians classify themselves as specialists in geriatrics, but most physicians other than pediatricians have geriatric patients in their practice. Patients visiting the medical office may come from independent or **assisted living facilities**. Patients unable to travel may be seen by the physician in a long-term or **extended care facility**, usually on a monthly basis.

The Medical Assistant's Role in the Geriatric Office

As in other specialty medical offices, the medical assistant obtains and charts the patient's history, vital signs, and other pertinent information according to office policy. An important aspect of the MA's role is listening carefully to the patient.

1. Role-play sensorimotor changes of the elderly.

Depending on office policy, you may assist aging patients by providing information about community resource agencies that assist the elderly. Local Councils on Aging are a valuable resource that offer social activities and group trips, information sessions, and transportation to grocery stores, shopping centers, and medical care facilities. Many of these agencies also offer financial seminars or services and self-improvement classes.

All patients should be encouraged to document their wishes regarding the extent of medical intervention they desire when they are no longer able to speak for themselves. ∞ Advance directives, durable power of attorney, and living wills are discussed in Chapter 4. The medical office can be a source of printed information for patients and their families.

The Aging Process

The aging process is an integration of physical, social, and psychological events. Social, economic, and nutritional factors have an effect as well. Some factors—stress, disease, depression—accelerate the process. Others—a healthy diet, exercise, social interaction—can promote a healthier, longer life.

Physical Aspects of Aging

Changes in physical appearance are usually the most obvious changes caused by the aging process. The skin becomes drier, thinner, and less elastic, and it tears easily. Age spots and other changes in pigmentation appear. Wrinkles develop and the skin sags as fat cells and collagen are lost (Figure 31-1 ♦). Dark circles may appear under the eyes, and the eyelids may droop. Hair loss may be total, as in alopecia, or it may involve gradual thinning. In females, supportive tissue is lost in the breasts, which tend to sag as a result. The abdomen thickens in both males and females.

Figure 31-1 ♦ Elderly skin

All body systems feel the impact of the aging process.

- The cardiovascular system ages in more than one way. Plaque on vessel walls causes narrowing of the lumen and loss of elasticity. Blood pressure rises, increasing the workload of the heart. The heart itself often enlarges with the greater workload. It becomes less efficient at pumping blood, circulating nutrients and oxygen, and removing waste from body cells. CHF may result. This sequence moves on to the lungs, which may have experienced some degenerative or disease changes and become less elastic. The exchange of gases through respiration may require greater effort. Higher blood pressure also affects the kidneys or leads to sclerosing in the vessels in the kidneys, resulting in impaired kidney function and related consequences.

- An aging circulatory system contributes to **orthostatic hypotension** when the patient moves too quickly from a resting to an active position.

- Cumulative trauma to all body tissues causes aches and pains, accompanied by reduced range of motion and activity. Muscle tone declines, joints become arthritic and less mobile, and bones are at greater risk for brittleness and breaking due to inactivity. Wear and tear and natural deterioration take their toll on the spinal disks, and the individual stoops and becomes shorter. Hips, knees, ankles and feet are less limber and do not function as well. The fingers become stiff, and the joints are often swollen.

- The sense of taste, particularly sweet and salty, declines. Vision may be blurred or diminished, and hearing may become impaired. Sensation may also be diminished, which can present certain hazards. For example, an older individual is less able to feel the burning of an overly hot heating pad.

- As the immune system declines, the body is more susceptible to disease conditions that exacerbate the aging process.

- As the nervous system ages, the individual finds it harder to control conscious movement. **Short-term memory** may gradually diminish, and custodial care may become necessary.

- The GI tract has a tendency to slow, resulting in constipation. Spasms of the bladder cause urgency, a prolapsed bladder may lead to infections or incontinence, loss of muscle tone in the sphincter often results in incontinence, and an enlarged prostate may cause urinary retention, frequency, or nocturia.

- Response time to stimuli is diminished. Tragedies result when elderly drivers fail to respond appropriately in a difficult situation or become confused about the accelerator and brake pedals. Suggesting that the elderly patient stop driving is a task that often falls to the health-care provider. It is important for the medical assistant to document any discussion with the patient concerning a potentially unsafe situation.

Table 31-1 is a summary of physiological changes in the elderly.

TABLE 31-1 COMMON PHYSIOLOGIC CHANGES IN THE OLDER ADULT

System	Changes	Common Conditions
Cardiac	Decreased cardiac output and efficiency; decreased elasticity of vessel walls, resulting in poor circulation and edema	CHF, hypertension, orthostatic hypotension
Endocrine	Increased incidence of metabolic disease, decreased hormonal function, impaired ability to heal	Diabetes type II, thyroid disorders, menopause
Gastrointestinal	Changes in metabolic rate, changes in bowel habits, decreased peristalsis, decreased production of saliva, difficulty chewing and swallowing, loss of teeth, decreased appetite	Cholelithiasis, pernicious anemia, increased drug side effects and adverse interactions with other medications, peptic ulcers, gastroesophageal reflux disease, and colon cancer
Integumentary	Skin: thinning, dryness, decreased elasticity, increased pigmentation (age spots); decreased functioning of sweat and sebaceous glands, adding to dryness; reduced number of fat cells, resulting in often feeling cold (hypothermia); brittle, tough nails; gray or white hair because of loss of pigment; thinning hair or baldness	Seborrheic keratosis, skin tears, photosensitivity, bruising, inability to tolerate temperature extremes, decreased sensitivity to pain, delayed wound healing
Mental Health	Higher incidence of depression due to loneliness, loss of spouse and friends, decreased socialization, loss of sense of usefulness, changes in sleeping patterns	Depression, suicidal thoughts, social isolation
Muscular	Decreased muscle tone and muscle mass, decreased elasticity of ligaments and tendons	Decreasing strength and endurance, related to inactivity, muscle atrophy and fewer muscle cells
Nervous	Diminished sense of touch, pain, temperature, taste, smell, sight (including depth, color, night vision), hearing (delayed auditory response, damage to ossicles, sensoneural damage to auditory nerve); decreased equilibrium and coordination; impaired short-term memory and forgetfulness; slower processing of nervous system impulses; diminished brain size and increased loss of brain cells	Diminished pain perception, touch-related injuries; decreased visual acuity (visual fields, peripheral vision, depth perception, dark adaptation, color discrimination, **presbyopia**), **presbycusis**, (central deafness, conduction deafness), slower musculoskeletal and mental reactions, greater incidence of falls, cerebrovascular accidents (CVA), **paraplegia**, **hemiplegia**, memory problems, dementia, delirium
Respiratory	Decreased lung capacity, diminished tone in chest wall muscles and diaphragm	Higher risk of contracting **URI** and **LRI**, including pneumonia; advancing stages of emphysema
Skeletal	Softening of the bones, decline in joint flexibility, changes in vertebrae, changes in feet	Osteoporosis, fractures, arthritis, pain on ambulation, shrinking of height
Urinary	Impaired kidney function, diminished bladder tone and sphincter control	Decrease in urinary output, incontinence

Keys to Success
LISTENING TO THE GERIATRIC PATIENT

Some statements by aging patients demonstrate the complexity and physical effects of aging.
■ An 84-year-old female victim of rape tells the emergency department nurse, "If I had my hearing aid in, I would have heard him come in the house. If I had my glasses on, I would have been able to see him. If I had my teeth in, I could have bitten him."
■ A 70-year-old male states, "The bones don't work, the ears don't hear, the teeth are falling out, and I can't urinate."
■ A 75-year-old female says, "I can't button my clothes, I can't tie my shoes, I can't wear my wedding ring any more because my finger joint is too big, I can't walk in the grocery store without leaning on a grocery cart, I can't open a jar, I can't pick up my granddaughter, and I hurt all the time."
■ Two elderly men are discussing how aging is affecting their lives. One comments, "I feel like a baby. I have no teeth, no hair, and I have to wear a diaper or I mess my pants." Listen carefully to what patients report and record it in their charts.

Social and Psychological Aspects of Aging

Social and psychological changes occur as many elderly become more dependent on others for care and financial help. They lose their spouse or companion, other family members, and friends. Retirement often means losing regular social interaction as well as a sense of purpose. Many retired people become socially isolated and lonely. They must also grapple with a fear of illness and death.

—Critical Thinking Question 31-1–
What can Elora do to assist the patient during his transition from employment to retirement?

Circulation problems caused by changes in heartbeat or blood supply to the brain may lead to impaired mental functioning. Symptoms of Alzheimer's disease may begin to surface during the aging process. Alzheimer's disease may require long-term or custodial care.

Changes in financial resources and an inability to cope with the physical demands of home upkeep often lead to a change in residence. Familiar surroundings and lifetime attachments are left behind, and the person must learn to cope with the new environment. This major change is often a devastating event for an older person and may lead to depression and occasionally suicide.

An additional impact on social well-being is the often drastic role change that accompanies older age. Self-reliant, independent individuals who have spent most of their lives in a caretaker role suddenly become dependent on their children or others for their care and living arrangements.

Conversations with elderly patients provide clues to their mental status and psychological needs. Elderly persons who have symptoms as the result of a medical condition, a nutritional deficit, or noncompliance with medication administration are sometimes labeled "senile." Patients, especially older patients, should have a complete medical assessment before any psychological diagnosis is made.

Various groups and organizations provide social activities for senior citizens (Figure 31-2 ◆). Local Councils on Aging offer social events and trips. The Red Hat Society is an organization offering activities for women over 50. Other organizations are associated with previous employers or occupations. Many gather for breakfast or lunch, thus providing both social contact and a nutritious meal.

Nutritional Aspects of Aging

Nutrition is an important aspect of geriatric care. Many factors contribute to a declining nutritional status:

Figure 31-2 ◆ Various groups provide social activities for senior citizens

Caduceus Chronicle
FOUNTAIN OF YOUTH

The search for the "Fountain of Youth" has gone on for centuries. Juan Ponce de Leon, a Spanish explorer, landed at St Augustine, Florida, in 1513, seeking a source of water that would keep him eternally young. According to Florida legend, he discovered such a fountain near St. Augustine. But history reveals that he never did find the Fountain of Youth, nor did he reach the island of Bimini, where he believed the fountain to be located.

Today's Fountain of Youth is a marketing concept aimed at the aging segment of the population. Cosmetics are sold with the promise that they will restore a youthful appearance. Botox injections are given to reduce wrinkles in the face. Plastic surgery provides face-lifts, and liposuction removes body fat and restores youthful figures. Medications help prevent hair loss. The search for the Fountain of Youth continues.

PROCEDURE 31-1 Role-Play Sensorimotor Changes of the Elderly

Theory

Americans are living longer and longer. In the year 2000, more than 35 million Americans were older than 65 years. This number is expected to grow to 30% of the total population by the year 2030. As the size of the aging population grows, the need for health care will grow as well. There will be a greater need for health-care professionals who specialize in diseases and disorders of the elderly.

The process of aging has physiological, psychological, and social aspects. The elderly undergo changes in their physical appearance and their ability to cope with their environment. The loss of hearing, taste, smell, and mobility can lead to depression. These changes in sensorimotor abilities impact how the elderly interact with their environment.

Materials
- 2 pairs of laboratory goggles

- yellow tissue paper (such as gift wrap)
- pastel-colored candy
- Vaseline
- earmuffs
- black construction paper
- swimming goggles with one lens blacked out
- heavy dishwashing gloves
- long (50" or more) belt
- walker
- tongue depressors
- ace bandages
- regular print newspaper
- coins (pennies and dimes)
- button-front shirts
- textbook
- tape
- gallon jug of water

continued

PROCEDURE 31-1 **Role-Play Sensorimotor Changes of the Elderly** *(continued)*

Competency

(**Conditions**) With the necessary materials, (**Task**) you will be able to understand the changes that aging patients undergo (**Standards**) within the time determined by the instructor.

1. Vision loss:
   a. Put on the swimming goggles and wait for your partner's directions.
   b. Have your partner stand out of the line of vision and give directions to cross the room and pick up a specific textbook.
2. Vision loss accompanied by hearing loss:
   a. Continue to wear the swimming goggles and put on the earmuffs.
   b. Have your partner stand out of the line of sight and tell you to retrieve a different textbook.
3. Difficulty distinguishing colors:
   a. Remove the goggles and earmuffs. Put on the laboratory goggles, which should be covered with yellow paper to simulate yellowing of the lens.
   b. Have your partner spread the pastel candy on a table and give you directions to pick up specific colors and quantities of each color.
4. Difficulty focusing:
   a. Put on a set of lab goggles that have been smeared with Vaseline.
   b. Without speaking, your partner must get you to walk a specific distance using hand signals.
5. Loss of peripheral vision:
   a. While wearing goggles with black construction paper taped to the sides, have your partner stand out of your line of vision and give you directions to follow.
   b. Have your partner lead you through several turns and doors if possible.
6. Aphasia and partial paralysis:
   a. Bend one arm at the elbow, with your fingertips touching your shoulder. Have another student wrap the ace bandage around your arm, securing it in this position. Bend one leg at the knee with your foot near your buttocks. Have another student secure your leg in place with the belt. Finally, have someone tape your mouth shut.
   b. Your partner should stand several feet away. Communicate to your partner that you need to go to the bathroom.
7. Loss of dexterity:
   a. Put on the dishwashing gloves and try to button a shirt, tie your shoes, and pick up the coins off a flat surface.
8. Problems with mobility:
   a. Use a walker to move across the room.
   b. When you have traveled 2 feet, have your partner hand you a gallon of water to carry.

Patient Education

This exercise will help you better understand the changes that elderly patients are or will be going through.

- Loss of teeth, with a resulting difficulty chewing food
- Poorly fitting dentures
- Decreased secretions and impaired digestive process
- Diminished sensitivity of taste buds
- Solitude during mealtime, eliminating the socialization so helpful in food intake
- Reduced funds for nutritious food
- Inability or diminished desire to prepare meals
- Loss of desire to eat because of depression

Economic Aspects of Aging

The 65th birthday is a dreaded event for many. Our culture has set this age as a rite of passage from activity and regular employment to retirement. Many people look forward to retirement with great anticipation, only to be devastated when the day finally arrives. They feel a loss of identity, self-worth, and financial stability.

Of great concern to the aging population is health insurance. On retirement or at the age of 65, health-care insurance through an employer is usually no longer available. Ideally, it is replaced by Medicare, the government-sponsored health-care program. The **Medicare** system was established in 1965 for those over the age of 65, the disabled, and those with end-stage renal disease (ESRD). During their working years, a Medicare tax is deducted from the reported earnings of most individuals, along with the Social Security deduction.

In the three-month period prior to an individual's 65th birthday, he or she receives information about how to apply for Social Security and Medicare benefits. The individual is eligible for Medicare on the first day of the month of the 65th birthday. The Medicare premium is deducted automatically from the monthly Social Security payment.

Plan B of the program is elective coverage for outpatient services. If selected, the cost of this option is deducted from each month's Social Security check. Medicare covers 80% of allowable claim costs after the annual deductible has been met.

On January 1, 2006, a drug coverage plan, Medicare D, was offered to Medicare beneficiaries, also for a monthly premium. Anyone on Medicare is entitled to drug coverage regardless of income; no one can be denied for health reasons. Enrollment is voluntary, but if the beneficiary does not enroll during the open enrollment period, a penalty may be imposed at the time of enrollment.

Various plans are available; the choice is up to the Medicare beneficiary. In the basic Medicare Part D plan, the beneficiary pays a deductible, the first $250 of prescription costs. After that is paid, most plans reimburse 75% of prescription costs between $251 and $2,500. The beneficiary then pays the next $2,850 in drug costs. After spending a total of $3,600 out of pocket for the year, the beneficiary pays 5% of drug costs and the plan picks up the rest for the year.

Many pharmacies and senior citizen organizations offer assistance in choosing plans that provide coverage for the beneficiary's particular drug prescriptions. Not all drugs are covered, and plans vary in cost and benefits provided. The use of generic drugs is encouraged when appropriate. Medicare beneficiaries are encouraged to seek help by calling 1-800-633-4227, the Medicare Helpline, or checking the Medicare website, www.medicare.gov.

Medigap insurance is sold by private insurance companies to cover the allowable costs not reimbursed by Medicare. Different options are available, and regardless of the insurance company, coverage is the same according to the plan selected. It is important that the individual reaching the age of 65 make a decision about contracting for Medigap insurance, as all companies must accept the individual for coverage during the six months following the 65th birthday and cannot refuse to cover any preexisting conditions. They may refuse to provide coverage to a new applicant over 65 1/2, however. Medical offices should help older patients obtain information regarding Medicare and Medigap so they can make informed decisions about their future insurance coverage.

Social Security is another federal program for retired Americans. When the Social Security system was implemented in 1935, the age of eligibility for retirement benefits was set at 65 (the earliest qualifying age for Social Security benefits is now 62 years). Social Security was designed as a supplement for retired individuals, those with qualifying disabilities, those unable to work because of a physical disability, and those with end-stage renal disease. Spouses of individuals eligible for Social Security benefits also qualify for benefits when they reach the qualifying age. Those born before January 1, 1938, were eligible for full benefits based on the payments they made throughout their working years. A graduating age schedule applies to those born after January 1, 1938, who also have to work longer to qualify for retirement benefits. Widows and dependent children may be eligible for some benefits as well. It is important to note that eligibility is not automatic; payments must be made into the Social Security program for a minimum of 40 working quarters. Information on Social Security is available online at www.socialsecurity.gov.

Many people retire at 65, others are forced into retirement early, and others continue to work after the age of 65. Some choose to work part-time to supplement their income, while others attempt to live on the fixed income typical of retirement. Many are forced to choose between the essentials of survival (food and shelter) and the medicines they need to stay healthy. Medical care providers should be sensitive to these realities and be alert for signs of financial difficulty, particularly when the patient's health is affected. Many physicians give their Medicare patients pharmaceutical samples when prescribing a new medication. It is an economical way to assess the effect of a drug before prescribing a maintenance regimen. As a medical assistant, you should also become familiar with services in your community that offer financial and other assistance to the elderly.

﹖—Critical Thinking Question 31-2—

What can Elora do to make certain the patient has the necessary resources for his retirement and future health-care coverage?

Cultural Views of Aging

Societal values around the world are reflected in the treatment of the elderly. Table 31-2 lists some of these perspectives on the place of older people in society.

TABLE 31-2 VARIOUS CULTURAL VIEWS OF THE ELDERLY	
Islamic	■ Honor, respect, and stature increase with age. ■ Elders enjoy positions of authority in the family and society. ■ Nursing homes are rare because Muslims care for elderly family members. ■ The eldest son typically cares for the elderly parents.
Chinese	■ Grandparents enjoy a close relationship with their children and grandchildren. ■ The eldest son typically cares for the elderly parents. ■ It is considered shameful not to care for elderly parents.
Indian	■ Elders are respected for their wisdom and often counsel the younger generations. ■ Elders enjoy authority and power and typically control family wealth and arrangement of marriages. ■ Caring for the elderly transmits traditional values and is important to one's status in the afterlife.
Japanese	■ The concept of reciprocity involves being cared for by parents and later caring for the parents. ■ Elders are revered as senior advisors for the family and are given freedom from family duties. ■ The elderly view caring for grandchildren as an honor.
Latino	■ The elderly are considered resources to keep younger generations linked to past traditions. ■ Daughters are expected to care for elderly parents far more than sons are. ■ The elderly do not expect to live with their children, but do expect attention and/or assistance. ■ Elders actively help with the needs of other family members, including child care.
Korean	■ Parents are respected and cared for to preserve the family's honor. ■ Health care and financial support are provided by the children.
Native American	■ Elders are respected for their knowledge and wisdom. ■ The elderly pass tradition and cultural values to younger generations. ■ It is a family responsibility to care for the elderly. ■ Grandmothers who are not cared for by their children believe they should have done a better job raising them.
Dominant American	■ In an individualistic society, it is embarrassing for the elderly to require assistance. ■ The elderly consider it more desirable to live separately from their children and lead separate lives.

Promoting Health Among the Elderly

Nutrition is a health concern for many elderly. One way to improve the nutritional status of older individuals is to assist them in enrolling in a local "Meals on Wheels" program. This program may differ from community to community, but its basic service is to deliver hot meals and perform regular home visits to provide socialization and check on the status of homebound persons. Your local Council on Aging will have information on this program and other food resources.

With the continued increase in the elderly population, many private companies have started to address the concerns unique to aging adults. Living in their home with a caregiver who is scheduled to stop by, help with chores, shopping and companionship are an option. There are also unique living communities that cater specifically to the elderly population. These communities often have a recreational center for group activities, on-site health care facility, and aides to help with home maintenance and everyday chores, all while allowing the privacy of living in an individual apartment. There are numerous possibilities available for as much or as little additional help that the elderly patient may need, and the medical assistant should have contact lists available to the patient for researching these possibilities.

Physical activity is another important aspect of the aging process. Many of the elderly become less active and should be encouraged to include some type of moderate exercise, such as walking, in their daily routine as appropriate. Malls and school gyms provide a fairly safe environment for walking. Patients should be cautioned, however, to consult with their physician before beginning an exercise program.

The elderly are prone to falls. They should be encouraged to eliminate throw rugs in their homes and keep all areas well lit. A grab bar can be of great help moving in and out of the bathtub. Railings or banisters should be installed along steps and stairways. Other safety and assistive devices that can help older individuals maintain their independence (Figure 31-3 ◆) are:

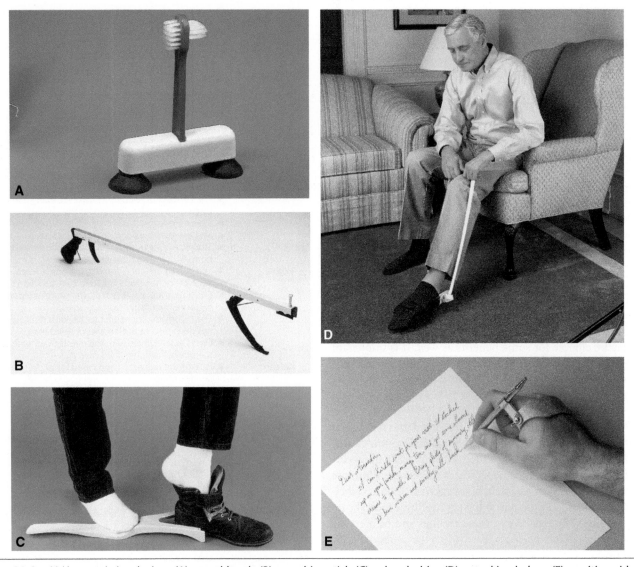

Figure 31-3 ◆ Various assistive devices: (A) a toothbrush; (B) a reaching stick; (C) a shoe holder; (D) a stocking helper; (E) a writing aid

Keys to Success
MYTHS AND MISCONCEPTIONS ABOUT AGING

Certain common beliefs about aging are more accurately seen as myths and misconceptions. Among these are the beliefs that getting older guarantees:
- A decline in activity and enjoyment of life
- Loss of sexuality and capacity for intimacy
- A decline in mental function
- Loss of independence
- Abandonment by family
- Loss of ability to contribute to society
- Mandatory retirement
- Financial insecurity
- Loneliness and depression

You can better serve older patients by ignoring these stereotypes about growing older.

- Wheelchairs
- Crutches, standard and quad canes
- Walkers
- Handrails and grab bars

- Shower benches and bathtub seats
- Elevated toilet seats and portable commodes
- Extended reachers or grabbers
- Velcro fasteners
- Medication containers with adapted lids
- Large-print and audio books
- Helper dogs
- Adequate lighting with reduced glare
- Grooming, bathing, and dressing devices
- Eating devices

It has been estimated that only 20 to 30% of the elderly are familiar with the Internet. Many have no access to computers. Assisting these individuals to locate facilities that offer help or guidance in this area is a valuable service you can offer.

It is important that you become familiar with the normal changes that accompany aging. As part of total patient care, you will help older patients identify these changes and how to address or cope with them in order to improve their overall quality of life.

REVIEW

Chapter Summary

- Geriatrics is a medical specialty that focuses on the care and treatment of older or aging patients.
- The aging process becomes more intense during middle age. Physical changes are complex and affect all body systems. The skin becomes thinner and drier, and age spots may appear. The GI tract slows, resulting in constipation. Urinary incontinence or retention may become a problem. Vision and hearing problems are common. Blood vessels become less elastic. High blood pressure increases the workload of the heart, which often enlarges and becomes less effective in its pumping function. The lungs are less elastic and respiration requires greater effort. The bones are affected by osteoporosis and other degenerative changes.
- Social and psychosocial changes can include retirement, decreased physical and social activity, lower income, greater dependence on others, social isolation and loneliness, loss of spouse or companion, and a change in living arrangements.

- Nutrition is an important aspect of geriatric care. Nutritional status can be affected by health problems, loss of teeth, mealtime solitude, and lower income. Meals on Wheels and other similar programs are a valuable resource for the elderly.
- A concern of the elderly is health insurance. Medicare, the government-sponsored health-care program, replaces employer-provided insurance for many. Medigap insurance is sold by private insurance companies to cover allowable costs not reimbursed by Medicare. Medical offices should help patients obtain information regarding both insurance programs.
- Medical care providers should be alert for signs of financial difficulty among older patients, especially when health is affected.
- Different cultures have different views on aging and the treatment of elders.
- Promoting healthy habits to improve the quality of life for older patients, such as a nutritious diet and moderate exercise, should be a goal of the medical office.

Chapter Review Questions

Multiple Choice

1. Which of the following means "hearing deficiency normally associated with aging"?
   A. hemiplegia
   B. presbyopia
   C. paraplegia
   D. presbycusis

2. The average life expectancy in the United States is:
   A. 79 years
   B. 67 years
   C. 87 years
   D. 76 years

3. What percentage of the U.S. population will be over the age of 65 in the year 2020?
   A. 16%
   B. 18%
   C. 20%
   D. 14%

4. An enlarged prostate can cause all of the following except:
   A. urinary frequency
   B. urinary retention
   C. CHF
   D. nocturia

5. The federal health-care program established in 1965 to serve those over age 65, the disabled, and those with ESRD was:
   A. Medicaid
   B. Medicare
   C. Social Security
   D. IRA

6. As part of their daily routine, the elderly should be encouraged to:
   A. avoid exercise
   B. engage in strenuous exercise
   C. include moderate exercise
   D. sleep as much as possible

7. The United States culture has set this age as a rite of passage from work to retirement:
   A. 65
   B. 70
   C. 55
   D. 60

8. Which of the following is *not* a qualifying factor for Medicare?
   A. ESRD
   B. presbyopia
   C. disability
   D. age greater than 65

9. The drug coverage plan offered in 2006 was Medicare Part:
   A. B
   B. C
   C. D
   D. A

10. The Social Security system was implemented in:
    A. 1935
    B. 1925
    C. 1945
    D. 1955

True/False

T F 1. Social Security benefits are automatic.

T F 2. The minimum number of working hours for Social Security eligibility is 40 working quarters.

T F 3. Spouses of individuals eligible for Social Security benefits do not qualify at any age.

T F 4. The best way to improve nutritional status of older individuals is to insist that they eat only prepared meals from a restaurant or take-out.

T F 5. It is estimated that only 40% of the elderly are familiar with the Internet.

T F 6. Computers are getting less and less expensive as technology improves, so most elderly people now own one.

T F 7. The aging process becomes more intense during middle age.

T F 8. Aging causes the skin to become thicker and more leathery.

T F 9. Korea has the most independent elderly generation, with the majority living alone.

T F 10. *Alopecia* is a condition of total loss of hair.

Short Answer

1. What substance forms on blood vessel walls, causing a loss of elasticity and leading to high blood pressure?

2. Name three gastrointestinal changes that take place in elderly adults.

3. What is the term for the condition that occurs when an elderly patient moves too quickly from a resting to an active position?

4. How is the Medicare system funded?

5. List three factors that contribute to declining nutritional status among the elderly.

Research

1. Is there a Red Hat Society in your local area?

2. Is there a special society for men of retirement age in your community?

Externship Application Experience

A man brings his elderly mother to the medical office because of a recent history of light-headedness and unsteadiness when standing. He interrupts her as she speaks and insists on answering questions for her. What should you do to obtain the history from the patient herself?

Resource Guide

Administration on Aging
Washington, DC 20201
202-619-0724
www.aoa.gov

American Association of Retired Persons (AARP)
601 E Street NW
Washington, DC 20049
1-800-424-3410
www.aarp.org

American Geriatrics Society
350 Fifth Avenue, Suite 801
New York, NY 10118
212-308-1414
www.americangeriatrics.org

Meals on Wheels Association of America
1414 Prince Street, Suite 302
Alexandria, VA 22314
703-548-5558
www.mowaa.org

National Council on Aging (NCOA)
300 D Street, SW
Suite 801
Washington, DC 20024
202-479-1200
www.ncoa.org

United Seniors Association Inc.
3900 Jamestown Road, #450
Fairfax, VA 22030
1-800-877-2872
www.unitedseniors.org

MedMedia

www.prenhall.com/frazier

More on this chapter, including interactive resources, can be found on the Student CD-ROM accompanying this textbook and on the Companion Website at www.prenhall.com/frazier.

Nontraditional Medicine

Chapter 32   Alternative Medicine

My name is Suzanne Bitters and I am a Registered Medical Assistant. In 1991, having to make a decision to change my direction in life, my cousin handed me a medical assisting textbook telling me, "You are going to love this field." Within a month I was enrolled and starting my new path in life.

I started in the field, getting myself an externship with an internal medicine physician. The doctor was willing to bring me on with no experience. Throughout my time in his practice, I learned professionalism, compassion, as well as the skills necessary to be an accomplished medical assistant. In 1997, I was able to fulfill my promise as I was hired as a medical assisting instructor as well as externship coordinator. Over my nine years teaching, I have in fact helped many students change their lives for the better: Teaching students that they are capable of impacting their patient's lives for the better, and teaching students that this field is never limited except by one's own ambitions.

I retired from teaching and am currently working in a cancer research facility. My position as phlebotomist is again at the forefront, breaking new ground for up-and-coming phlebotomists.

The facility took a chance on me, never having hired a MA/Phlebotomist. They are utilizing all of my skills in ways they did not realize when then hired me. I am on the Emergency Response Team (as well as training the ERT in CPR/FA); I work with the safety committee to make sure all of the labs are OSHA compliant as well as equipped with the most up-to-date safety equipment; I am training the researchers in patient confidentiality/HIPAA compliance; I am able to do vital signs on donors if the research needs it; I write proper protocol to be followed; and I work one-on-one with the researchers in development of their projects, from discussing the techniques needed to take the perfect specimen to which additive in the tubes will provide the right reaction needed to further their cancer research.

Making the decision to become a medical assistant so many years ago was the best decision I ever made. Wanting to be something that my children could be proud of, all of the life issues that came up, all of the hard work and self-doubt that had to be overcome to bring me to this point in my life—I would not change one second of every day.

CHAPTER 32

Alternative Medicine

Case Study

Leslie's patient has come in for a follow-up appointment after completing treatments for a recent motor vehicle accident. During her vitals and assessment, the patient mentions that although she has finished her physical therapy, her neck muscles still get tight and she gets headaches. She also mentions that she would be very interested in an alternative therapy, such as massage, because she is not comfortable with the long-term use of muscle relaxants and other narcotics.

Objectives

After completing this chapter, you should be able to:

- Spell and define the medical terminology in the chapter.
- List and describe the five NCCAM classifications of complementary and alternative medicine.
- Describe some types of alternative medicine: Ayurveda, homeopathy, naturopathy, and acupuncture.
- Explain the basic principle of biofeedback.
- Explain how aromatherapy and herbal medicine are used.
- Describe some types of manipulative and body-based therapies: hydrotherapy, acupressure, chiropractic, Craniosacral Therapy, exercise, reflexology, and massage.
- Explain the principle behind energy therapies.

MedMedia
www.prenhall.com/frazier

Additional interactive resources and activities for this chapter can be found on the Companion Website. For audio glossary, legal and ethical scenarios, job scenarios, quizzes, and games related to the content of this chapter, please access the accompanying CD-ROM in this book.

 Assets Available:

Audio Glossary
Legal and Ethical Scenario: *Nontraditional Medicine*
On the Job Scenario: *Nontraditional Medicine*
Multiple Choice Quiz
A & P Quiz: The Muscular System; The Skeletal System
Games: Crossword, Strikeout and Spelling Bee

⊕ MEDICAL ASSISTING COMPETENCIES

CAAHEP ENTRY-LEVEL COMPETENCIES FOR CMA	ABHES ENTRY-LEVEL COMPETENCIES FOR RMA
▪ Identify and respond to issues of confidentiality.	▪ Project a positive attitude.
▪ Perform within legal and ethical boundaries	▪ Maintain confidentiality at all times.
▪ Demonstrate knowledge of federal and state health-care legislation and regulations.	▪ Be a "team player."
	▪ Be cognizant of ethical boundaries.
	▪ Exhibit initiative.
▪ Perform hand washing.	▪ Adapt to change.
▪ Dispose of biohazardous materials.	▪ Evidence a responsible attitude.
▪ Practice Standard Precautions.	▪ Be courteous and diplomatic.
▪ Use methods of quality control.	▪ Conduct work within scope of education, training, and ability.
▪ Perform telephone and in-person screening.	▪ Interview and take a patient history.
▪ Obtain vital signs.	▪ Apply principles of aseptic techniques and infection control.
▪ Obtain and record patient history.	▪ Prepare and maintain examination and treatment area.
▪ Prepare and maintain examination and treatment areas.	▪ Dispose of biohazardous materials.
	▪ Practice Standard Precautions.

Introduction

Over the last few decades, many alternative forms of medicine have found their way into the U.S. health-care system. Some have been accepted by the mainstream medical community, but others have been rejected or are regarded with skepticism.

Health-care consumers are interested in pain relief and, if possible, a cure for their ailments. They are far more educated today about the range of treatments available to them, and many turn to complementary and alternative medicine (**CAM**) when conventional methods fail to meet their needs. They weigh the benefits of conventional medicine, which is sometimes invasive or has undesirable side effects, against the benefits of complementary or alternative methods that are more holistic and usually incorporate natural products and healthy lifestyle habits. Many physicians recommend alternative therapies for their patients to enhance their general health and well-being or to complement conventional treatment.

Alternative medicine has become so popular and in many instances so promising that the government has created the National Center for Complementary and Alternative Medicine (NCCAM). Ongoing scientific studies at NCCAM and elsewhere focus on the safety and effectiveness of alternative therapies.

As a medical assistant, you should be aware of the various forms of CAM. When taking a patient history, you will need to gather and document information regarding the patient's use of any alternative or complementary medicines or treatments. Harmful interactions may result when conventional and alternative medicine are used simultaneously. You will also direct the patient's questions about complementary and alternative therapies to the physician.

Medical Terminology

alternative medicine—systems of medical options varying from traditional medicine, chosen by individuals in place of regularly prescribed modalities and including certain diagnostic procedures and/or accepted and regularly prescribed treatment modalities; examples are aromatherapy, massage therapy, acupuncture, faith healing, and therapeutic touch

complementary medicine—systems of medical options varying from traditional medicine, chosen by individuals along with regularly prescribed modalities; examples include use of herbal remedies such as saw palmetto to promote prostate health

essential oils—oils extracted from flowers and herbs and integrated into an oil base for use in aromatherapy

integrative medicine—systems of medical options that incorporate forms of alternative medicine, complementary medicine, and traditional medicine

Abbreviations

CAM—complementary and alternative medicine

Complementary and Alternative Medical Systems

Complementary and alternative therapies are not new concepts; many have been in active use for thousands of years. According to NCCAM, "Complementary and alternative medicine, as defined by NCCAM, is a group of diverse medical and health care systems, practices, and products that are not presently considered to be a part of conventional medicine." **Complementary medicine** works together with conventional medical treatment. An example is massage therapy or relaxation techniques used in combination with pain medication. **Alternative medicine**, such as homeopathy, is practiced in place of conventional medical treatment. **Integrative medicine** incorporates conventional, complementary, and alternative therapies to treat medical conditions. Aromatherapy, reflexology, and music therapy used together in one session are an example of integrative medicine.

NCCAM has classified the various forms of complementary and alternative medicine (CAM) into five categories:

- Alternative medicine: homeopathic and naturopathic medicine, traditional Chinese medicine, Ayurveda
- Mind–body interventions: cognitive behavioral therapy, biofeedback, prayer, meditation, and therapies incorporating art, music, and dance
- Biologically based therapies: aromatherapy, herbal medicine
- Manipulative and body-based methods: acupressure, osteopathic and chiropractic manipulation, hydrotherapy, bodywork, Craniosacral Therapy, exercise, reflexology, various forms of massage
- Energy therapies: biofield therapies, biomagnetic-based therapies

Some of these therapies are described below.

Alternative Medicine

Alternative methods of diagnosis and treatment have been used for centuries. Many of the concepts of ancient as well as nineteenth- and twentieth-century medicine are now recognized as having validity. An example is the use of leeches to eat dead tissue and clean wounds. Nontraditional medical concepts have their origins in cultures all over the world. The Asian medical tradition has contributed several important concepts in alternative medicine, such as acupuncture, acupressure, and the use

Caduceus Chronicle
NON-TRADITIONAL CONCEPTS

Traditionally, the mainstream medical community has not trusted therapies that have not been and supported by scientific evidence. The terms *complementary medicine* and *alternative medicine* came into use in the 1970s. Prior labels for nontraditional therapies included *fringe medicine*, *medical cultism*, *quackery*, *irregular medicine*, and *sectarian medicine*.

of herbs, that are gaining popularity and recognition in the West. This chapter will introduce some of the alternative and complementary practices used today.

Ayurveda

Ayurveda is an ancient healing practice that originated in India. The Sanskrit word *Ayurveda* means "knowledge of life." Ayurvedic practice does not directly treat disease, but focuses on prevention of disease by promoting the return and maintenance of good health. It consists of exercise, nutritional counseling, massage, meditation, and herbal treatments. Ayurveda operates on two principles:

- The mind influences the operation of the body. Negative thoughts can create or aggravate illness. Positive thoughts assist in the return and maintenance of good health.
- Each individual has a specific body type, called *prakriti*, that affects the specific direction of treatment.

According to Ayurvedic principles, the body is made up of *dhatus* (tissues), *malas* (waste products), and *doshas* (energetic forces). The body operates according to the balance of three *doshas*. The *pitta* controls body metabolism, the *kapha* manages the musculoskeletal system, and the *vata* is responsible for cardiovascular, respiratory, digestive, and nervous system functions. The three *doshas,* or *tridoshas,* assist with the creation of all the tissues of the body and remove waste products. They influence all movements, all transformations, all sensory functions, and many of the other activities of the human body and mind. The goal of treatment is to balance the three *doshas*.

The *vata* is the most important of the three *doshas*. *Vata* is the main driver or mover of the body, including the other two *doshas*, the tissues, and the waste products. If the *vata* becomes sufficiently imbalanced, it can throw another *dosha* off balance. If it causes both *pitta* and *kapha* to become imbalanced, this is called a tridoshic imbalance and is the most difficult to overcome.

There are no licensing or accrediting boards for the practice of Ayurveda in the United States. Practitioners with a Bachelor of Ayurveda Medical Studies degree can practice as consultants but not as medical doctors.

Homeopathy

Homeopathic treatment involves the use of natural remedies made from plant, animal, or mineral substances to stimulate the immune system and strengthen the body's healing processes. Homeopathy is based on the theory that "like cures like"—that large doses of certain substances cause symptoms but smaller, highly diluted doses cure them. Homeopathic remedies are diluted to different strengths, and the practitioner determines which strength to prescribe based on an assessment of the patient. Homeopathy remains a controversial treatment that has not been substantiated by scientific research.

A medical doctor (MD), doctor of osteopathy (DO), or dental surgeon (DDS) can become a Diplomate in Homeopathy (DHt) by passing a written and practical exam. To receive a CCH (Certified in Classical Homeopathy) credential, a candidate must complete 500 hours of training, one to two years experience, and pass a written and practical exam.

Naturopathy

Naturopathy is an eclectic approach that helps the body heal itself by treating psychological, physical, and genetic factors in addition to the disease process. A naturopath may use any of the following approaches: nutritional and lifestyle counseling, acupuncture, exercise, hydrotherapy, osteopathy, homeopathy, herbal medicine, and others.

Naturopaths are licensed primary care practitioners. They determine the cause of the illness, educate the patient about a healthier lifestyle, and select the best treatment. They also refer patients to other health-care professionals as necessary.

Four years of naturopathic medical school are required to become a Doctor of Naturopathic Medicine (ND). Some states require passing a state or national board examination.

Acupuncture

Acupuncture is an important component of traditional Chinese medicine that has been practiced for over 5,000 years. The insertion of very thin needles into predetermined sites stimulates changes in heart rate, blood pressure, brain activity, blood chemistry, and the immune and endocrine systems (Figure 32-1 ◆). Acupuncture helps the body naturally regulate red and white blood cell counts and raise endorphin production. Some health problems or disease processes are treated by as few as one acupuncture treatment; others require many treatments. There is little risk from acupuncture. It is often used in conjunction with conventional medicine for pain management, asthma, drug addiction (illegal, narcotic, alcohol, and nicotine), stroke, and other conditions.

Some private insurance and Medicaid programs reimburse for acupuncture, especially in the treatment of back pain. In most states acupuncturists are licensed separately, but in a few states practitioners of acupuncture must be medical doctors.

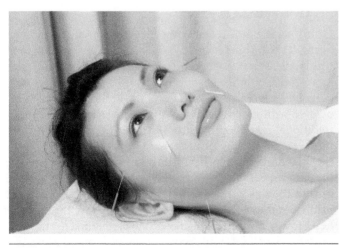

Figure 32-1 ◆ A client receiving acupuncture treatment
Source: MIXA/Alamy

Mind–Body Interventions

The focus of mind–body medicine is the ways in which a person's mental, emotional, social, and spiritual health directly affects his or her physiological health. This holistic approach uses techniques that enhance the mind's ability to influence body function and symptoms. For example, positive thinking, along with laughter and personal contact, help to release endorphins, the body's natural antipain mediators.

Biofeedback

Biofeedback is the process of training the client in relaxation, visualization, and meditation techniques. During these activities, body functions such as blood pressure, heart rate, muscle tension, and brain waves are electronically monitored by a biofeedback machine. Audible signals from the machine help the client learn to consciously control his or her body systems and responses. Eventually, the client learns to use the relaxation techniques without biofeedback monitoring. This program has been particularly effective in stress management and has been used to treat migraine headaches, depression, insomnia, and other conditions.

There is no state licensing for biofeedback practitioners. The Biofeedback Certification Institute of America and other groups offer certification.

Biologically Based Therapies

Natural substances such as herbs, foods, vitamins, and essential oils are the basis for biologically based therapies.

Aromatherapy

Essential oils extracted from flowers and herbs are used in aromatherapy. This branch of herbal healing has been practiced since ancient times, when aromatic plants were burned to drive out evil spirits and purify the air. René Maurice Gattefosse, a French chemist, experimented with essential oils and published his findings in 1928 in a book called *Aromatherapy*.

Aromatherapy affects the autonomic nervous system and stimulates the release of chemicals that are responsible for relaxation and the reduction of pain. Some essential oils have antibacterial or anti-inflammatory properties. Certain oils may be prescribed for complaints such as colds and flu, sinusitis, migraine headaches, insomnia, digestive problems, and muscle aches and pains. Rosemary oil is used for muscle relaxation and pain relief. Jasmine oil helps ease depression, eucalyptus oil and oil of wintergreen relieve congestion, lavender oil relieves anxiety and improves sleep, and peppermint oil relieves nausea and aids in digestion. Lemon, orange, and other citrus oils improve the mood and mental alertness.

Essential oils are extracted in a steam distillation process. They may be added to lotions used in massage treatments. Therapeutic scents can be diffused into the air with spray bottles, diffusers, and baths.

It is important to remember that although aromatherapy is usually considered safe, it is a complementary therapy

TABLE 32-1 COMMON HERBS USED FOR MEDICINAL PURPOSES

Herb	Reported Properties and Benefits	Herb	Reported Properties and Benefits
Angelica	astringent, diuretic, anti-inflammatory, expectorant, tonic	Lavender	antispasmodic, antidepressive, hypotensive; relieves stress, headaches, depression; promotes sleep
Bayberry	astringent, antidiarrheal, diaphoretic; stimulates circulatory system, reduces fever, reduces sore throat symptoms (gargle), relieves colitis symptoms	Licorice	expectorant, antispasmodic, anti-inflammatory, antihepatotoxic, laxative
		Mustard	irritant, stimulant, diuretic, emetic
Chamomile	anti-inflammatory, antispasmodic, antimicrobial, antianxiety; relieves insomnia, neuralgia, vertigo, motion sickness, stress	Myrrh	antimicrobial, astringent, expectorant; effective in treating mouth infections, pharyngitis, sinusitis, laryngitis, boils, and wound infections
Echinacea	antimicrobial; stimulates immune response to bacterial and viral invasions; increases phagocytosis and white blood cell count	Peppermint	anti-inflammatory, antispasmodic, antiemetic, antimicrobial, analgesic; relieves tension and anxiety
Eucalyptus	antimicrobial, antispermatic, expectorant	Rhubarb root	laxative, astringent
Garlic	antimicrobial, antispasmodic, diaphoretic, hypotensive; improves cardiovascular function and lowers blood cholesterol	Rosemary	antispasmodic, antidepressive, antimicrobial, rubofacient
		St. John's wort	anti-inflammatory, astringent; provides pain relief, sedation; relieves anxiety and tension
Ginseng	stimulant, tonic	Saw palmetto	diuretic, urinary antiseptic; tones and strengthens male reproductive and urinary system; relieves symptoms of hyperplasia of the prostate gland
Gingko	reduces vertigo, headache, tinnitus, anxiety, depression; improves memory, concentration, alertness; dilates blood vessels and increases cardiovascular circulation	Tea (or ti) tree	antimicrobial on the skin
		Valerian	antispasmodic, hypnotic, sedative, hypotensive
Goldenseal	antimicrobial, anti-inflammatory, laxative, expectorant, astringent (especially on mucous membranes)	Vervain	nerve tonic, sedative, antispasmodic, diaphoretic, hypotensive; reduces stress, tension, depression, fever
		Witch hazel	astringent, anti-inflammatory
Horehound	expectorant, antispasmodic; relaxes smooth muscles, especially in bronchi and respiratory tract	Yarrow	diaphoretic, urinary antiseptic; lowers fever, dilates peripheral vessels and reduces blood pressure; aids in digestive process

and should not be used as a substitute for conventional medical care. Essential oils can be quite potent, and some carry potential side effects.

There are no licensing requirements or accrediting boards for the practice of aromatherapy in the United States. Schools usually have their own certification standards.

Herbal Medicine

Throughout history, herbs have been used to treat disease and prevent illness. In the twentieth century the medicinal use of herbs declined as synthetic drugs took their place in conventional medicine. Many people are now turning to natural herbal medicine again.

Herbs are chosen according to their properties and are usually used in combination with other holistic treatments. Some herbs are said to counteract the effects of poor nutrition, stress, and lack of exercise. Others may help repair, strengthen, and rebuild body tissues. Much of the evidence is anecdotal, however. Scientific research has not validated many of the claims of therapeutic benefits to be derived from herbs. Individuals taking herbal supplements should do so with caution. Although side effects are uncommon, they should be discussed with the physician.

There are no herbal medicine licensing or accrediting boards in the United States. In addition, there are no controls or standards for herbal products. The FDA has not given its stamp of approval to any of these products.

Some herbs and their reported benefits are briefly described in Table 32-1. Keep in mind that these benefits have not necessarily been verified.

Manipulative and Body-Based Methods

Hydrotherapy is a body-based method that uses water to treat disease. Bodywork is a broad term referring to the hands-on manipulation of the musculoskeletal system to promote healing, energy flow, pain reduction, relaxation, and improved health. The following techniques fall into this category: acupressure, Alexander Technique, chiropractic, craniosacral therapy, Feldenkrais Method, foot reflexology, lymphatic massage, Rolfing, shiatsu, sports massage, Swedish massage, Trager approach, and trigger point therapy.

Hydrotherapy

Hydrotherapy, also called water therapy, is available in many forms. It can be offered in a swimming pool, sauna, steam bath, whirlpool, Jacuzzi, or hot tub, or in the form of a hot/cold pack, ice massage, or moist heat pack. Hydrotherapy increases flexibility and strength and accelerates the healing process. It can be used with individuals who cannot withstand the rigors of traditional exercise programs. In conventional medicine, hydrotherapy is usually an addition to physical therapy.

Hydrotherapy by heat stimulates circulation and relaxes the muscles, but prolonged exposure to heat can have the effects of cold therapy. Hydrotherapy by cold reduces swelling and pain, but prolonged application of cold can have the effects of heat therapy. Hydrotherapy-induced hyperthermia has not been proven to be effective. In theory, the body develops a fever, inhibits the reproduction of microorganisms, and increases antibody production. Hyperthermia, if it used at all, should not be induced in the elderly or the very young, who are very sensitive to high temperatures.

Acupressure

Acupressure, or shiatsu, is a traditional Chinese bodywork technique. It is a form of massage and is based on a concept similar to acupuncture. The goal of acupressure is to relieve discomfort by promoting greater balance and circulation of fluids and metabolic energies in the body. Normally, a healing energy or current known as *chi* circulates through body meridians. If it is blocked, disease results. Pressure and massage are applied with the fingers, thumbs, palms, and elbows at appropriate pressure points, often some distance from where the symptom appears. This technique relaxes the involved muscle or tissue, thereby reducing or eliminating pain.

Although there are no state licensing requirements for the practice of acupressure, patients should seek a practitioner who has graduated from an accredited school.

Chiropractic

In chiropractic treatment, manipulation and alignment of the spine promote optimum health of the spinal cord and nervous system. Chiropractic treatment corrects misalignments of the spinal column that cause pain, decreased agility, and illness. In addition to vertebral manipulation, massage therapy, heat, cold, and ultrasound may be applied to relieve tension and spasm. Treatment sessions may also include nutrition and exercise counseling.

All states require chiropractors to be licensed. To become a Doctor of Chiropractic (DC), one must graduate from an accredited school and pass national and state board exams.

Craniosacral Therapy

In Craniosacral Therapy, gentle pressure is applied to the areas of the craniosacral system (skull, face, mouth, spine, sacrum, connecting membranes for the cranium and sacrum, and cerebrospinal fluid) to treat tension in these areas and promote CNS health. Following treatment, it is not unusual for the client to experience some worsening of symptoms from pressure changes that occur during manipulation. Overall, the treatment can lead to a general state of relaxation.

Craniosacral Therapy was developed by John Upledger, an osteopathic physician. No licensing is required to practice Craniosacral Therapy, although the appropriate training and practical and written exams must be completed.

Exercise

All forms of exercise promote health and raise the level of body functioning. The primary focus of exercise can be cardiovascular or endurance training, stretching, or weight training. Cardiovascular training improves the functioning of the cardiovascular and respiratory systems. Activities such as walking, running, dancing, and swimming improve aerobic capacity and physical endurance. Stretching increases joint flexibility. Weight training strengthens bones and muscles. Exercise approaches

can include any of the following: hydrotherapy, yoga, qigong, tai chi, chiropractic, polarity therapy, and the Trager approach.

Reflexology

Reflexology restores the body's natural energy flow by stimulating specific reflex points on the foot or hand (Figure 32-2 ◆). Applying pressure to these points can restore function to the areas connected to each point, or zone. Although there are no state licensing requirements for the practice of reflexology, a certification program followed by a written and practical exam are recommended.

Massage

Massage is the manipulation of muscle and soft tissue to induce relaxation, relieve pain, and promote healing. Done correctly, massage enhances the client's sense of well-being. Types of massage include lymphatic massage, sports massage, and Swedish massage.

Although massage has a number of benefits, there are certain conditions for which it is not appropriate: intoxication, treatment with certain medications, localized tissue inflammation, hematoma, cancer, and others.

Lymphatic Massage

A person with an illness or a sedentary lifestyle may suffer from fatigue and lowered metabolism as a result of the accumulation of waste products in the body. When a healthy flow of lymphatic fluids is restored, waste materials and infectious organisms are more efficiently removed. Lymphatic massage applies pressure and manipulates the muscles to improve the functioning of the lymphatic system. Practitioners massage an area lightly and repeatedly until a small amount of lymphatic fluid surfaces on the skin, then proceed to the next area. Joints are also massaged. A specific order is followed to direct lymphatic flow to the lymph nodes.

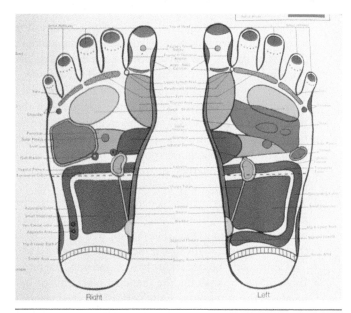

Figure 32-2 ◆ Reflexology points on the sole of the foot
Source: Andrew McClenaghan/Photo Researchers, Inc.

Lymphatic massage may not be appropriate if certain conditions exist such as aneurysms, hematomas, tissue damage, or bacterial inflammations.

To perform lymphatic massage, the practitioner must be trained and certified as a Certified Manual Lymph Drainage Therapist (CMLDT). Training in an allied health profession is prerequisite to entering this program.

Sports Massage

Sports massage involves the use of therapeutic massage before, during, and after engagement in sporting activities. Many athletes and sports teams employ a massage therapist or physical therapist who applies massage techniques to loosen up the muscles and relieve fatigue prior to a sporting event. Massage therapy can prepare the athlete for peak performance, reduce muscle tension, promote flexibility, relieve any swelling or edema present, and prevent injuries. During and after the event, the therapist is available to assess any insults to the body and employ massage to promote the healing of strained muscles and keep them in good condition.

Every sporting activity makes different demands on the athlete and uses muscle groups in different ways. The sports massage therapist uses specific techniques to meet different requirements.

Swedish Massage

Swedish massage focuses on general relaxation, stimulating circulation, and enhancing muscle tone. It is effective in reducing muscle tightness. Swedish massage makes use of five main strokes.

- *Effleurage* consists of long, gliding strokes starting at the neck and working down to the base of the spine or from the shoulder down to the fingertips. On the limbs, strokes are directed toward the heart, assisting the blood and lymphatic flow. Effleurage is performed with the whole hand or the thumb pads.
- When performing *petrissage,* the therapist gently lifts muscles up and away from the bones, then follows with a gentle rolling and squeezing action. Kneading and compressing motions, including squeezing, rolling, and pressing, enhance deeper circulation. The goal of petrissage is to increase circulation by clearing toxins from muscle and nerve tissue.
- *Friction,* the most penetrating massage stroke, involves deep circular or transverse movements made with the thumb pads or fingertips. The deep circular movement is performed near joints and other bony areas. Friction breaks down adhesions, or knots, that result when muscle fibers bind together during the healing process, thereby promoting more flexible joints and muscles.
- *Tapotement* is a series of brisk percussive movements. The hands of the therapist alternately strike or tap the muscles, with an invigorating effect. The tapping may be done with the side of the hand, the tips of the fingers, or a closed fist. This technique is used to release tension and muscle spasms.
- In *vibration,* or shaking, the therapist places his or her hands on the limbs or back and performs several seconds of rapid shaking. The goal of this technique is to boost circulation and increase the power of the muscles.

Caduceus Chronicle
SOME IMPORTANT DATES IN THE HISTORY OF CAM

- The earliest documented source of acupuncture theory is *Huang Di Nei Jing (Yellow-Emperor's Inner Classic),* from the second century BCE.
- Homeopathy, developed in the 1790s by German physician Samuel Hahnemann, was brought to the United States in 1825 by Dr. Hans Gram.
- The *Caraka Samhita,* written 200 to 400 BCE in India, documented the oral tradition of Ayurveda.
- The term *naturopathy* was coined in the late nineteenth century. The therapy is a combination of ancient and early modes of healing, including Ayurvedic, Taoist, Hippocratic, Roman Empire, Germanic homeopathy, English botanical medicine, Native American spiritual guidance, and early American spinal manipulation.
- The term *aromatherapy* was coined in 1928 by René Maurice Gattefosse, a French chemist, in his book *Aromatherapy.*
- The term *biofeedback* was first used in 1969 to describe the concept of using physiological feedback and learning to change physiological reaction and behavior.

—Critical Thinking Question 32-1—
What do you think would be the best way for Leslie's patient to find the type of massage that would be most beneficial for her needs?

Energy Therapies

Energy therapies work with the electromagnetic fields that are believed to surround the human body, called biofields. In some energy therapies, such as Reiki, qi gong, and Therapeutic Touch, the biofields are manipulated with the hands. Bioelectromagnetic-based therapies are characterized by more unconventional methods, such as the use of pulsed fields and magnetic fields. It has not been scientifically proven that these so-called biofields exist.

Reiki is a complementary therapy in which a trained practitioner places his or her hands on or above a specific body area and transfers what is called "universal life energy" to the patient. That energy is believed to provide strength, harmony, and balance, which are essential to the treatment of health disturbances. The therapy is derived from ancient Buddhist practice and involves a total of 15 hand positions covering all body systems.

Therapeutic Touch is a noninvasive, holistic approach to healing that attempts to stimulate the receiver's own powers of recuperation. This modern form of laying-on-of-hands is based on the principle of an energy exchange between people. Therapeutic Touch is believed to reduce or eliminate pain, promote healing, and bring about a relaxation response. Therapeutic Touch is based on the concept that a "human energy field" extends beyond the skin and flows in balanced patterns in health; in illness or injury, it is used up and/or unbalanced. Practitioners of Therapeutic Touch believe they have the ability to restore health by sensing and adjusting these energy fields.

Therapeutic Touch is one of the most visible and popular nontraditional healing techniques practiced by nurses. It is also controversial, and its positive effect may be a result of the positive energy generated by the practitioner.

Chapter Summary

- In recent years, alternative, complementary, and integrative therapies have gained popularity and, in some cases, acceptance by the medical community. These forms of medicine have been practiced for many centuries and in many cultures. As a medical assistant you should be familiar with the various therapies offered in your community. Always question patients about any alternative form of treatment they may be receiving. Document this information, and be careful not to chastise patients for seeking intervention by any of these methods.

- Alternative treatment modalities such as aromatherapy, massage therapy, acupuncture, faith healing, and therapeutic touch are practiced in place of conventional treatments. Complementary medicine, such as the use of herbal remedies, is used in combination with conventional, regularly prescribed modalities. Integrative medicine brings together conventional, complementary, and alternative therapies to treat medical conditions.

- Ayurveda, homeopathy, naturopathy, and acupuncture are forms of alternative medicine. Ayurveda, an ancient healing practice originating in India, focuses on preventing disease by promoting the return and maintenance of good health. It involves exercise, nutritional counseling, massage, meditation, and herbal treatments. Homeopathy is based on the concept that "like cures like" and uses natural remedies made from plant, animal, or mineral substances to stimulate the body's immune system and healing processes. Naturopathy, an eclectic approach, promotes the concept of the body healing itself and addresses psychological, physical, and genetic factors in addition to the disease process. Acupuncture an important component of traditional Chinese medicine that has been practiced for over 5,000 years. The insertion of very thin needles into predetermined sites stimulates changes in heart rate, blood pressure, brain activity, blood chemistry, and the immune and endocrine systems.

- Other forms of alternative medicine are mind–body interventions, such as biofeedback, and biologically based therapies that feature natural substances such as herbs, foods, vitamins, and essential oils.

- Manipulative and body-based methods include hydrotherapy, acupressure, chiropractic, craniosacral therapy, exercise, reflexology, and different forms of massage.

- Hydrotherapy, or water therapy, is available in many forms, such as sauna, steam bath, hot/cold packs, and ice massage. Hydrotherapy increases flexibility and strength and is useful for individuals who cannot withstand the rigors of traditional exercise programs.

- Acupressure, or shiatsu, is a form of massage based on the concept of healing energy or current (*chi*) circulating through body meridians. If *chi* is blocked, disease results. Pressure and massage are applied at pressure points to dissolve obstructions and reduce or eliminate pain.

- Chiropractic treatment consists of manipulating and aligning the spine to promote optimum health of the spinal cord and nervous system. Craniosacral therapists apply gentle pressure to the craniosacral system to relieve tension in these areas and promote CNS health.

- All forms of exercise promote health and improve body functioning. The primary focus can be cardiovascular or endurance training, stretching, or weight training.

- Reflexology restores the body's natural energy flow by stimulating specific reflex points on the foot or hand.

- Massage, the manipulation of muscle and soft tissue, induces relaxation, relieves pain, and promotes healing. Lymphatic massage is based on the theory that fatigue and lowered metabolism result from the accumulation of waste products in the body. Lymphatic massage improves the functioning of the lymphatic system, thereby removing waste materials and infectious organisms more efficiently. Sports massage involves the application of therapeutic massage before, during, and after engagement in sporting activities. It reduces muscle tension, promotes flexibility, relieves swelling or edema, and prevents injuries. Swedish massage focuses on general relaxation, stimulation of circulation, and enhancing muscle tone. The five main strokes in Swedish massage are effleurage, petrissage, friction, tapotement, and vibration or shaking.

- Energy therapies work with biofields, the electromagnetic fields believed to surround the human body. In some energy therapies, such as Reiki, qi gong, and Therapeutic Touch, the biofields are manipulated with the hands. Other, more unconventional methods rely on the use of pulsed fields and magnetic fields.

- The efficacy of some alternative, complementary, and integrative therapies is not supported by scientific evidence. Most insurance plans do not cover these therapies, but they continue to be popular with a growing number of health-care consumers.

Chapter Review Questions

Multiple Choice

1. The government branch that controls and evaluates the claims of alternative medicine is:
   A. NCCAM
   B. CAMCC
   C. NCAM
   D. CAM

2. An herb is used as an astringent, diuretic, anti-inflammatory, expectorant, and tonic is:
   A. echinacea
   B. bayberry
   C. chamomile
   D. angelica

3. An herb used for its antimicrobial, antispermatic, and expectorant properties is:
   A. chamomile
   B. bayberry
   C. eucalyptus
   D. echinacea

4. An herb known to lower blood cholesterol is:
   A. witch hazel
   B. lavender
   C. garlic
   D. goldenseal

5. Manipulation and alignment of the spine are the basis of the treatment called:
   A. chiropractic
   B. lymphatic massage
   C. reflexology
   D. Swedish massage

6. A body-based therapy that uses water to treat disease is:
   A. acupressure
   B. hydrotherapy
   C. chiropractic
   D. Craniosacral Therapy

7. A therapy that restores the body's natural energy flow by stimulating specific reflex points on the foot or hand is:
   A. chiropractic
   B. acupressure
   C. reflexology
   D. Craniosacral therapy

8. The massage stroke that consists of long, gliding strokes is:
   A. effleurage
   B. friction
   C. petrissage
   D. tapotenment

9. The massage stroke called *friction* consists of:
   A. rapid shaking
   B. kneading and compression
   C. tapping or striking
   D. deep circular movements

10. Massage is not appropriate for conditions such as:
   A. fatigue
   B. localized tissue inflammation
   C. muscle tightness
   D. muscle adhesions

True/False

T F 1. Acupressure, osteopathic, and chiropractic therapies are manipulative and body-based methods.

T F 2. Alternative medicine incorporates conventional, complementary, and alternative therapies to treat medical conditions.

T F 3. According to Ayurvedic principles, the body is made up of dhatus, malas, and doshas.

T F 4. Practitioners with a Bachelor of Ayurveda Medical Studies degree can practice as consultants and medical practitioners.

T F 5. Homeopathic medical treatment uses natural remedies that are all diluted to the same strength.

T F 6. To receive a CCH credential, a candidate must complete 250 hours of training, two to three years experience, and pass written and practical exams.

T F 7. Naturopaths are licensed primary care practitioners.

T F 8. Acupuncture is a traditional Japanese medicine that has been practiced for over 5,000 years.

T F 9. Acupuncture helps the body naturally regulate red and white blood cell counts.

T F 10. Some essential oils possess antibacterial and anti-inflammatory properties.

Short Answer

1. What are essential oils?

2. Which traditional Chinese therapy is used in the treatment of back pain?

3. List the five main strokes used in Swedish massage.

Research

1. Is there a practitioner of hydrotherapy in your community?

2. Is there a practitioner of Ayurveda near you?

Externship Application Experience

A patient comes to you and explains that he has decided not to proceed with the traditional cancer treatments of chemotherapy and medications. A family member has given him a copy of the movie *My Life,* starring Michael Keaton and Nicole Kidman, about a man who attempts to treat his cancer and prepare for death with alternative therapy. How do you respond?

Resource Guide

ACUPRESSURE

American Organization for Bodywork Therapies of Asia (AOBTA)
Laurel Oak Corporate Center, Suite 408
1010 Haddenfield Road
Voorhees, NJ 08043
856-782-1616
www.aobta.org

ACUPUNCTURE/HERBAL MEDICINE

National Acupuncture and Oriental Medical Alliance
14637 Starr Road, SE
Olalla, WA 98359
253-851-6896
www.acuall.org

National Commission for Certification of Acupuncturists (NCCA)
1424 16th Street, NW, Suite 501
Washington D. C. 20036

ALEXANDER TECHNIQUE

North American Society of Teachers of the Alexander Technique (NASTAT)
3010 Hennepin Avenue S., Suite 10
Minneapolis, MN 55408
www.alexandertech.com

AROMATHERAPY

Aromatherapy
836 Hanley Industrial Court
St. Louis, MO 63144

Flower Essence Society
PO BOX 459
Nevada City, CA 95959
800-736-9222
www.flowersociety.org

Nelson Bach USA
Educational Programs
100 Research Drive
Wilmington, MA 01887

AYURVEDA

Ayurvedic Institute
11311 Menaul NE, Suite A
Albuquerque, NM 87112

BIOFEEDBACK

Association for Applied Psychophysiology and Biofeedback
10200 W. 44th Avenue, Suite 304
Wheat Ridge, CO 80033

Biofeedback Certification Institute of America
255 W. 98th St
New York, NY 10025
212-222-5665
www.biof.com

CHIROPRACTIC

American Chiropractic Association
1701 Clarendon Boulevard
Arlington, VA 22209
800-986-4636
www.amerchiro.org

CRANIOSACRAL THERAPY

The Upledger Institute, Inc.
11211 Prosperity Farms Road
Palm Beach Gardens, FL 33410-3487
800-233-5880
www.upledger.com

FELDENKRAIS METHOD

Feldenkrais Guild
3611 SW Hood Ave, Suite 100
Portland, OR 97201
800-775-2118

HATHA YOGA

International Association of Yoga Therapists
20 Sunnyside Avenue, Suite A243
Mill Valley, CA 94941

HERBAL MEDICINE

American Holistic Medical Association
6728 Old McLeon Village Drive
McLeon, VA 22101

National Acupuncture and Oriental Medicine Alliance
14637 Starr Road, SE
Olalla, WA 98359

HOLISTIC DENTISTRY

Holistic Dental Association
PO Box 5007
Durango, CO 81301
970-259-1091
www.holisticdental.org

Resource Guide (continued)

**International Academy of Oral Medicine
and Toxicology, IAOMT**
PO Box 608531
Orlando, FL 32860-8531
407-298-2450
www.iaomt.org

HOMEOPATHY
National Center for Homeopathy
801 N. Fairfax Street, Suite 306
Alexandria, VA 22314

HYDROTHERAPY
Aquatic Exercise Association
PO BOX 1609
Nokomis, FL 34274

HYPNOTHERAPY/HYPNOTISM
American Board of Hypnotherapy
16842 Von Karman Avenue, Suite 475
Irvine, CA 92606

American Society of Clinical Hypnosis
2200 East Devon Avenue, Suite 291
Des Plaines, IL 60018

**International Medical and Dental Hypnotherapy
Association**
4110 Edgeland, Suite 800
Royal Oak, MI 48073-2285

National Guild of Hypnotists
PO Box 308
Merrimack, NH 03054

LYMPHATIC MASSAGE
Dr. Vodder School, North America
PO Box 5701
Victoria, British Columbia
Canada V8R 658

**North American Vodder Association of Lymphatic
Therapy**
356 Waterbury Drive
East Lake, OH 44095

NATUROPATHY
American Association of Naturopathic Physicians
2366 Eastlake Avenue, Suite 322
Seattle, WA 98102

NUTRITIONAL COUNSELING
American Association of Nutritional Consultants
810 South Buffalo Street
Warsaw, IN 46580

American Dietetic Association
216 West Jackson Boulevard, Suite 800
Chicago, IL 60606-6995

Ayurvedic Institute
11311 Menaul NE, Suite A
Albuquerque, NM 87112

National Acupuncture and Oriental Medicine Alliance
14637 Starr Road, SE
Olalla, WA 98359

REFLEXOLOGY
International Institute of Reflexology
5650 First Avenue, North
St. Petersburg, FL 33710

MedMedia
www.prenhall.com/frazier

More on this chapter, including interactive resources, can be found on the Student CD-ROM accompanying this textbook and on the Companion Website at www.prenhall.com/frazier.

Appendices

The Patient Care Partnership: Understanding Expectations, Rights, and Responsibilities

When you need hospital care, your doctor and the nurses and other professionals at our hospital are committed to working with you and your family to meet your health-care needs. Our dedicated doctors and staff serve the community in all its ethnic, religious, and economic diversity. Our goal is for you and your family to have the same care and attention we would want for our families and ourselves.

The sections explain some of the basics about how you can expect to be treated during your hospital stay. They also cover what we will need from you to care for you better. If you have questions at any time, please ask them. Unasked or unanswered questions can add to the stress of being in the hospital. Your comfort and confidence in your care are very important to us.

What to Expect During Your Hospital Stay

- **High quality hospital care.** Our first priority is to provide you the care you need, when you need it, with skill, compassion, and respect. Tell your caregivers if you have concerns about your care or if you have pain. You have the right to know the identity of doctors, nurses, and others involved in your care, and you have the right to know when they are students, residents, or other trainees.

- **A clean and safe environment.** Our hospital works hard to keep you safe. We use special policies and procedures to avoid mistakes in your care and keep you free from abuse or neglect. If anything unexpected and significant happens during your hospital stay, you will be told what happened, and any resulting changes in your care will be discussed with you.

- **Involvement in your care.** You and your doctor often make decisions about your care before you go to the hospital. Other times, especially in emergencies, those decisions are made during your hospital stay. When decision making takes place, it should include:

  ▶ *Discussing your medical condition and information about medically appropriate treatment choices.* To make informed decisions with your doctor, you need to understand:

- The benefits and risks of each treatment.
- Whether your treatment is experimental or part of a research study.
- What you can reasonably expect from your treatment and any long-term effects it might have on your quality of life.
- What you and your family will need to do after you leave the hospital.
- The financial consequences of using uncovered services or out-of-network providers.

Please tell your caregivers if you need more information about treatment choices.

▶ *Discussing your treatment plan.* When you enter the hospital, you sign a general consent to treatment. In some cases, such as surgery or experimental treatment, you may be asked to confirm in writing that you understand what is planned and agree to it. This process protects your right to consent to or refuse a treatment. Your doctor will explain the medical consequences of refusing recommended treatment. It also protects your right to decide if you want to participate in a research study.

▶ *Getting information from you.* Your caregivers need complete and correct information about your health and coverage so that they can make good decisions about your care. That includes:
- Past illnesses, surgeries, or hospital stays.
- Past allergic reactions.
- Any medicines or dietary supplements (such as vitamins and herbs) that you are taking.
- Any network or admission requirements under your health plan.

▶ *Understanding your health-care goals and values.* You may have health-care goals and values or spiritual beliefs that are important to your well-being. They will be taken into account as much as possible throughout your hospital stay. Make sure your doctor, your family, and your care team know your wishes.

▶ *Understanding who should make decisions when you cannot.* If you have signed a health-care power of attorney stating who should speak for you if you become unable to make health-care decisions for yourself, or a "living will" or "advance directive" that states your wishes about end-of-life care, give copies to your doctor, your family, and your care team. If you or your family need help making difficult decisions, counselors, chaplains, and others are available to help.

- **Protection of your privacy.** We respect the confidentiality of your relationship with your doctor and other caregivers, and the sensitive information about your health and health care that are part of that relationship. State and federal laws and hospital operating policies protect the privacy of your medical information. You will receive a Notice of Privacy Practices that describes the ways that we use, disclose, and safeguard patient information and that explains how you can obtain a copy of information from our records about your care.

- **Preparing you and your family for when you leave the hospital.** Your doctor works with hospital staff and professionals in your community. You and your family also play an important role in your care. The success of your treatment often depends on your efforts to follow medication, diet, and therapy plans. Your family may need to help care for you at home.

  You can expect us to help you identify sources of follow-up care and to let you know if our hospital has a financial interest in any referrals. As long as you agree that we can share information about your care with them,

we will coordinate our activities with your caregivers outside the hospital. You can also expect to receive information and, where possible, training about the self-care you will need when you go home.

- **Help with your bill and filing insurance claims.** Our staff will file claims for you with health-care insurers or other programs such as Medicare and Medicaid. They also will help your doctor with needed documentation. Hospital bills and insurance coverage are often confusing. If you have questions about your bill, contact our business office. If you need help understanding your insurance coverage or health plan, start with your insurance company or health benefits manager. If you do not have health coverage, we will try to help you and your family find financial help or make other arrangements. We need your help with collecting needed information and other requirements to obtain coverage or assistance.

While you are here, you will receive more detailed notices about some of the rights you have as a hospital patient and how to exercise them. We are always interested in improving. If you have questions, comments, or concerns, please contact _____.

Pharmacology: Medical Abbreviations

Medical Abbreviation	Meaning
a.a. or aa	Of each
a.c.	Before food, before meals
a.d.	Right ear
ad	To, up to
a.m.	Morning
Aq	Water
aq. ad	Add water up to
Aqua. Dist., DW	Distilled water
a.s	Left ear
a.t.c.	Around the clock
a.u.	Each ear
b.i.d.	Twice a day
c̄	With
Caps	Caplets, capsules
CSA	Federal Controlled Substances Act
DEA	Drug Enforcement Administration
dil.	Dilute
disp.	Dispense
div.	Divide
d.t.d.	Give of such doses
Elix.	Elixir
f, fl.	Fluid
f, ft.	Make, let it be made
g., G, gm	Gram
gtt.	Drops
h	Hour, at the hour of
h.s.	At bedtime, at hour of sleep
i.m., IM	Intramuscular
Inj., INJ	Injection
i.v., IV	Intravenous
i.v.p., IVP	Intravenous push
IVPB	Intravenous piggyback
l	Left
L	Liter
LIQ	Liquid

Medical Abbreviation	Meaning
mcg.	Microgram
mEq.	Milliequivalent
mg.	Milligram
ml.	Milliliter
NS	Normal Saline
o.d.	Right eye
o.s.	Left eye
OTC	over-the-counter
o.u.	Each eye
p.c.	After food, after meals
PDR	Physician's Drug Reference
p.o.	By mouth
p.r.n.	As needed
q	Each, every
q.d.	Each day
q.h.	Each hour
q.i.d.	Four times a day
q.s.	A sufficient quantity
q.s. ad	Add a sufficient amount to make
s	Without
SC, subc, subq, s	Subcutaneously
ss	Half
Stat.	Immediately
Supp.	Suppository
Syr.	Syrup
Tab	Tablet
tbsp.	Tablespoon
t.i.d.	Three times a day
top	Topically
tsp.	Teaspoon
Ung	Ointment
USP-NF	U.S. Pharmacopeia and National Formulary
ut dict., u.d	As directed

Normal Blood Values/Disease Conditions Evaluated for Abnormal Values

Test	Normal Value Range (Conventional)	Normal Value Range (SI units)	Possible Indications
Ammonia (NH_3) - diffusion	20–120 mcg/dl	12–70 mcmol/L	Abnormal levels of ammonia in the body are used to investigate severe changes in mood and consciousness and to help diagnose the cause of a coma of unknown origin.
Ammonia Nitrogen	15–45 µg/dl	11–32 µmol/L	The test for ammonia nitrogen is nonspecific and does not indicate a cause. Higher than normal levels simply indicate the body is not effectively metabolizing and eliminating ammonia.
Amylase	35–118 IU/L	0.58–1.97 mckat/L	The normal level of amylase will depend on the method used to collect the data. An increase level may indicate several disorders of the digestive and reproductive systems or cancer of the pancreas. Tubal pregnancies will also cause a rise in the amylase levels. Decreased amylase levels may indicate damage to the pancreas and kidneys.
Anion gap ($Na^+-[Cl^- + HCO_3^-]$) (P)	7–16 mEq/L	7–16 mmol/L	A determination of electrolytes in the blood fluid. Abnormal readings indicate a variety of factors. The test is non-specific and only tells the physician that there is cause for additional testing. Some factors that cause an abnormal anion gap reading are uncontrolled diabetes, starvation, kidney damage, and ingestion of potentially toxic substances such as antifreeze, excessive amounts of aspirin, or methanol.

Bicarbonate
  Arterial
  Venous
	
	21–28 mEq/L
	22–29 mEq/L
		
		21–28 mmol/L
		22–29 mmol/L
			See *Carbon dioxide content* below

Bilirubin:
  Conjugated (direct)
  Total
	
	0.2 mg/dl
	0.1–1 mg/dl
		
		4 mcmol/L
		2–18 mcmol/L
			Increased levels of bilirubin may be an indication of some kind of blockage of the liver or bile duct, hepatitis, trauma to the liver, a drug reaction, or long-term alcohol abuse or some inherited disorders, such as Gilbert's, Rotor's, Dubin-Johnson, Crigler-Najjar, which will cause an increase in levels. Increased levels of bilirubin in newborns is a critical situation as excessive levels kill developing brain cells and may lead to mental retardation.

Test	Normal Value Range Conventional	Normal Value Range SI units	Possible Indications
Calcitonin	< 100 pg/ml	< 100 ng/L	Increased levels of calcitonin in combination with a thyroid biopsy may be an indication of C-cell hyperplasia.
Calcium, Total: Calcium, Ionized:	8.6–10.3 mg/dl 4.4–5.1 mg/dl	2.2–2.74 mmol/L 1–1.3 mmol/L	Increased levels of calcium in the body indicate an inability to metabolize the intake. This can be due to several factors: hyperthyroidism, sarcoidosis, tuberculosis, excess Vitamin D intake, kidney transplant, and high protein levels (for example, if a tourniquet is used for too long while blood is collected). In this case, free or ionized calcium remains normal.
Carbon dioxide content (plasma)	21–32 mmol/L	21–32 mmol/L	Higher or lower than normal CO_2 levels indicate a problem losing or retaining fluid—disrupting the acid-base balance, which can be an indication of several disorders.
Carcinoembryonic antigen	< 3 ng/ml	< 3 mcg/L	CEA is a protein that is found in embryonic tissues. Increased CEA levels can indicate some non-cancer-related conditions of inflammation of internal organs. Pregnant women who smoke tend to have embryos that have increased levels of CEA. In a normally healthy infant all detectable levels of CEA are gone by birth.
Chloride	95–110 mEq/L	95–110 mmol/L	Increased levels of chloride may indicate dehydration or increased blood sodium. Decreased levels of chloride occurs with prolonged vomiting, chronic diarrhea, emphysema, or other chronic lung disease, and with loss of acid from the body.
Coagulation screen Bleeding time Prothrombin time Partial thrombo-plastin time (activated) Protein C Protein S	3–9.5 min 10–13 sec 22–37 sec 0.7–1.4 μ/ml 0.7–1.4 μ/ml	180–570 sec 10–13 sec 22–37 sec 700–1400 U/ml 700–1400 U/ml	Indicates an inability of the body to develop adequate clotting factors or the inability to produce the correct amount of clotting factors.
Copper, total	70–160 mcg/dl	11–25 mcmol/L	Indication of liver disease
Corticotropin (ACTH: adreno-corticotropic hormone)—0800 hr	< 60 pg/ml	< 13.2 pmol/L	This test is used in conjunction with cortisol to determine if a patient has Cushing's syndrome or Addison's disease.
Cortisol 0800 hr 1800 hr 2000 hr	5–30 mcg/dl 2–15 mcg/dl 50% of 0800 hr	138–810 nmol/L 50–410 nmol/L 50% of 0800 hr	Abnormal levels in coritsol may indicate Cushing's syndrome or Addison's disease.

Test	Normal Value Range Conventional	Normal Value Range SI units	Possible Indications

Creatine kinase
  Female
  Male
	
	20–170 IU/L
	30–220 IU/L
		
		0.33–2.83 mckat/L
		0.5–3.67 mckat/L
			Creatine kinase is an enzyme found in the heart, brain, skeletal muscle, and other tissues. The body has specific types of CK to indicate which muscles are affected.

Creatinine kinase isoenzymes, MB fraction	0–12 IU/L	0–0.2 mckat/L	Depending on the ratio, the CK-MB fraction will indicate some form of muscle damage. The specific ratio can indicate if the muscle damage is cardiac or skeletal.
Creatinine	0.5–1.7 mg/dl	44–150 mcmol/L	Increased creatinine levels indicate a disorder with kidney function. Creatinine can also increase temporarily as a result of muscle injury. Low levels of creatinine are not common. They may been seen in persons with decreased muscle mass, such as comatose patients. Normal pregnancy will cause the creatinine levels to drop and are not a cause for concern.

Follicle-stimulating hormone (FSH)
  Female
  Midcycle
  Men
	
	2–13 mIU/ml
	5–22 mIU/ml
	1–8 mIU/ml
		
		2–13 IU/L
		5–22 IU/L
		1–8 IU/L
			Increased levels of FSH and LH (luteinizing hormone) are consistent with primary ovarian failure, which is when ovaries themselves fail. In men this may be an indication of testicular developmental defects or injury.
			
			Decreased levels of FSH and LH are an indication of secondary ovarian failure, which results in a problems with the pituitary or hypothalamic gland. In men this may be an indication of hypothalamic disorders.

Glucose, fasting	65–115 mg/dl	3.6–6.3 mmol/L	Indicates diabetes or pre-diabetes.
Glucose Tolerance Test (Oral) 2 hour	(mg/dl) Normal fasting		Indicates diabetes or pre-diabetes.
Post-drink: Impaired tolerance Indicates diabetes	65–99 < 140 mg/dl 140–199 mg/dl > 200 mg/dl		
Haptoglobin	44–303 mg/dl	0.44–3.03 g/L	If the haptoglobin levels are decreased in combination with several other tests, it may be an indication of hemolytic anemia. Haptoglobin will be elevated in many inflammatory diseases, such as ulcerative colitis, acute rheumatic disease, heart attack, and severe infection.

Test	Normal Value Range Conventional	Normal Value Range SI units	Possible Indications
Fibrinogen	200–400 mg/dl	2–4 g/L	Lower than normal fibrinogen levels indicate that the person may not be able to form a stable blood clot after injury. Chronically low levels may indicate an inherited condition such as afibrinogenemia, or to an acquired condition such as liver disease, malnutrition, or some types of cancer. Higher than normal levels of fibrinogen may indicate acute infections, breast, kidney, or stomach cancer, chronic DIC, inflammatory disorders, myocardial infarction, stroke, or trauma. Fibrinogen concentrations may rise sharply in any condition that causes inflammation or tissue damage.
Hematocrit (Hct)			Decreased hematocrit level indicates anemia, such as iron deficiency, but may have other causes such as vitamin or mineral deficiencies, recent bleeding, liver cirrhosis, and malignancies.
Female	35%–46%	0.36–0.446 fraction of 1	
Male	40.0%–50.0%	0.4–0.503 fraction of 1	
Hemoglobin A_{1C}	40.0%–50.0% of total	0.053–0.075	Abnormally high levels of hematocrit may be an indication of dehydration and can be easily cured by increased fluid intake.
			Polycythemia vera—greater than normal number of red blood cells in a person can also cause a prolonged increase in the hematocrit levels. Higher than normal hematocrit levels are also seen in persons with chronic pulmonary conditions or lung damage. The person's bone marrow will increase production of red blood cells to supply the body with oxygen in response to a lacking pulmonary system.
Hemoglobin (Hb)			Low levels of Hb are an indication of anemia. Some types of anemia are treated with iron, folic acid, or vitamin B_{12} or B_6 supplements.
Female	11.6–15.5 g/dl	121–153 g/L	
Male	13.7–16.7 g/dl	138–175 g/L	It is normal for women of childbearing age to have temporary decreases during menstrual periods and pregnancy.
Leukocyte count (WBC)	3800–9800/mcl	$3.8–9.8 \times 10^9$/L	Infections usually cause increased WBC counts and may be treated with antibiotics. Leukemias (blood cancer) require chemotherapy and other treatments.
Erythrocyte count (RBC)			A low ESR can indicate polycythemia, extreme leukocytosis, and some protein abnormalities.
Female	$3.8–5.2 \times 10^6$/mcl	$3.8–5.2 \times 10^{12}$/L	
Male	$4.3–5.7 \times 10^6$/mcl	$4.3–5.7 \times 10^{12}$/L	
Erythrocyte sedimentation rate (sedrate, ESR)			Elevated ESR level is an indication of inflammation, anemia, infection, pregnancy, and advanced age.
Female	30 mm/hr	30 mm/hr	
Male	mm/hr	20 mm/hr	

Test	Normal Value Range Conventional	Normal Value Range SI units	Possible Indications
Leukocytes (WBC)	K/uL		Raised levels may indicate infections, inflammation, or cancer. Decreased levels may indicate autoimmune conditions, some severe infections, bone marrow failure, and congenital marrow aplasia. Decreased levels may also occur with certain medications such as methotrexate.
Lymphocytes	of WBC		Chronic high levels may indicate lymphocytic leukemia.
Lipase	7–60 units/L @ 37 C	7–60 units/L @ 37 C	High lipase levels, with abdominal pain, may indicate acute pancreatitis, slightly raised levels can indicate kidney disease, salivary gland inflammation, or peptic ulcer disease.
Lipids Total cholesterol Borderline high High	< 200 mg/dl 200–239 mg/dl 240–above		A person with high cholesterol has more than twice the risk of coronary heart disease as someone whose cholesterol is below 200 mg/dL.
HDL High	> 60 mg/dl < 40 mg/dl (men) < 50 mg/dl (women)		Low HDL is considered a major risk factor for heart disease.
LDL High	< 100 mg/dl > 130 mg/dl		If you don't have coronary heart disease or diabetes and have one or no risk factors, your LDL goal is less than 160 mg/dL. If you don't have coronary heart disease or diabetes and have two or more risk factors, your LDL goal is less than 130 mg/dL. If you do have coronary heart disease or diabetes, your LDL goal is less than 100 mg/dL.
Triglycerides High	> 150 mg/dl > 200 mg/dl and above		Normal triglyceride levels vary by age and sex. A high triglyceride level combined with low HDL cholesterol or high LDL cholesterol seems to speed up atherosclerosis (the buildup of fatty deposits in artery walls). Atherosclerosis increases the risk for heart attack and stroke. (Info on lipids from the American Heart Association)
PSA 0–54 yrs 55–59 yrs 60–64 yrs 65–69 yrs 70 plus yrs	0.00–2.50 ng/ml 0.00–3.40 ng/ml 0.00–4.10 ng/ml 0.00–5.10 ng/ml 0.00–5.60 ng/ml		PSA is a test indicating the level of protein cells the prostate is producing. The higher the PSA number, the more likely prostate cancer is present. Age, hormonal factors, and medications can alter the test results so a high PSA alone is not a cancer indicator.
TSH	0.40–5.00 IU/ml		A high TSH result is often due to some type of acute or chronic thyroid dysfunction that causes the thyroid to be underactive. Although rare, a high TSH can be an indication of secondary hyperthyroidism, which is a problem with the pituitary gland. A low TSH result can indicate an overactive thyroid gland.

Test	Normal Value Range Conventional	Normal Value Range SI units	Possible Indications
Urea, plasma (BUN)	8.5–25 mg/dl	2.9–8.9 mmol/liter	Increased BUN levels may be due to acute or chronic kidney disease, damage, or failure. Conditions that result in reduced blood flow to the kidneys, such as a recent heart attack, will also result in an increased BUN. Low BUN level are rarely detected because they result from diseases or symptoms, such as dehydration or starvation, that do not warrant a BUN test.
Urinalysis pH Specific gravity	5.0–7.5 1.001–1.030	5.0–7.5 1.001–1.030	Specific gravity is an indication of how well the kidneys are filtering waste products. Reduced specific gravity can indicate diabetes insipidus, certain renal diseases, excess fluid intake, or diabetes mellitus. Raised specific gravity can indicate dehydration, adrenal insufficiency, nephrosis, congestive cardiac failure, or liver disease.

AAMA Role Delineation Chart (2003) and Correlation of Text to AAMA Role Delineation Chart

Medical Assistant Role Delineation Chart

Administrative

ADMINISTRATIVE PROCEDURES

- Perform basic administrative medical assisting functions
- Schedule, coordinate, and monitor appointments
- Schedule inpatient/outpatient admissions and procedures
- Understand and apply third-party guidelines
- Obtain reimbursement through accurate claims submission
- Monitor third-party reimbursement
- Understand and adhere to managed care policies and procedures
- * *Negotiate managed care contracts*

PRACTICE FINANCES

- Perform procedural and diagnostic coding
- Apply bookkeeping principles
- Manage accounts receivable
- * *Manage accounts payable*
- * *Process payroll*
- * *Document and maintain accounting and banking records*
- * *Develop and maintain fee schedules*
- * *Manage renewals of business and professional insurance policies*
- * *Manage personnel benefits and maintain records*
- * *Perform marketing, financial, and strategic planning*

Clinical

FUNDAMENTAL PRINCIPLES

- Apply principles of aseptic technique and infection control
- Comply with quality assurance practices
- Screen and follow up patient test results

DIAGNOSTIC ORDERS

- Collect and process specimens
- Perform diagnostic tests

PATIENT CARE

- Adhere to established patient screening procedures
- Obtain patient history and vital signs
- Prepare and maintain examination and treatment areas
- Prepare patient for examinations, procedures, and treatments
- Assist with examinations, procedures, and treatments
- Prepare and administer medications and immunizations
- Maintain medication and immunization records
- Recognize and respond to emergencies
- Coordinate patient care information with other health-care providers
- Initiate IV and administer IV medications with appropriate training and as permitted by state law

General

PROFESSIONALISM

- Display a professional manner and image
- Demonstrate initiative and responsibility
- Work as a member of the health-care team
- Prioritize and perform multiple tasks
- Adapt to change
- Promote the CMA credential
- Enhance skills through continuing education
- Treat all patients with compassion and empathy
- Promote the practice through positive public relations

COMMUNICATION SKILLS

- Recognize and respect cultural diversity
- Adapt communications to individual's ability to understand
- Use professional telephone technique
- Recognize and respond effectively to verbal, nonverbal, and written communications
- Use medical terminology appropriately
- Utilize electronic technology to receive, organize, prioritize and transmit information
- Serve as liaison

LEGAL CONCEPTS

- Perform within legal and ethical boundaries
- Prepare and maintain medical records
- Document accurately
- Follow employer's established policies dealing with the health-care contract
- Implement and maintain federal and state health-care legislation and regulations
- Comply with established risk management and safety procedures
- Recognize professional credentialing criteria
- * *Develop and maintain personnel, policy, and procedure manuals*

INSTRUCTION

- Instruct individuals according to their needs
- Explain office policies and procedures
- Teach methods of health promotion and disease prevention
- Locate community resources and disseminate information
- * *Develop educational materials*
- * *Conduct continuing education activities*

OPERATIONAL FUNCTIONS

- Perform inventory of supplies and equipment
- Perform routine maintenance of administrative and clinical equipment
- Apply computer techniques to support office operations
- * *Perform personnel management functions*
- * *Negotiate leases and prices for equipment and supply contracts*

* **Denotes advanced skills.**

Reprinted with permission of the American Association of Medical Assistants.

Correlation of Text to AAMA Role Delineation Chart (2003)

		Clinical			General/Transdiciplinary				
Ch	Text	Fundamental Principles	Diagnostic Orders	Patient Care	Professionalism	Communication Skills	Legal Concepts	Instruction	Operational Functions
1.	The Medical Assistant Profession in Health Care				X	X	X	X	
2.	Interpersonal Communication			X	X	X	X	X	
3.	Patient-Centered Care		X	X		X			
4.	Considerations of Extended Life		X	X		X	X		
5.	The Clinical Environment and Safety in the Medical Office	X		X	X	X	X	X	X
6.	The Clinical Visit: Office Preparation and the Patient Encounter	X	X	X	X	X	X	X	
7.	Medical Asepsis	X	X	X	X	X	X	X	
8.	Surgical Asepsis	X	X	X	X	X	X	X	
9.	Pharmacology and Medication Administration	X	X	X	X	X	X	X	X
10.	Vital Signs	X	X	X	X	X	X	X	
11.	Minor Surgery	X	X	X	X	X	X	X	
12.	Diagnostic Procedures	X	X	X	X	X	X	X	
13.	Microscopes and Microbiology	X	X	X	X	X	X	X	
14.	Hematology and Chemistry		X	X					
15.	Urology and Nephrology		X	X		X		X	
16.	Medical Imaging	X	X	X	X	X	X	X	
17.	Cardiology and Cardiac Testing		X	X		X		X	

		Clinical				General/Transdiciplinary			
Ch	Text	Fundamental Principles	Diagnostic Orders	Patient Care	Professionalism	Communication Skills	Legal Concepts	Instruction	Operational Functions
18.	Pulmonology and Pulmonary Testing		✗	✗		✗		✗	
19.	EENT		✗	✗		✗		✗	
20.	Immunology and Allergies		✗	✗		✗		✗	
21.	Dermatology		✗	✗		✗		✗	
22.	Endocrinology		✗	✗		✗		✗	
23.	Emergency Care	✗		✗	✗	✗		✗	
24.	Gastroenterology and Nutrition		✗	✗		✗		✗	
25.	Orthopedics and Physical Therapy		✗	✗		✗		✗	
26.	Obstetrics and Gynecology		✗	✗		✗		✗	
27.	Pediatrics		✗	✗		✗		✗	
28.	Neurology		✗	✗		✗		✗	
29.	Mental Health		✗	✗		✗		✗	
30.	Oncology		✗	✗		✗		✗	
31.	Geriatrics		✗	✗		✗		✗	
32.	Alternative Medicine		✗	✗		✗		✗	

CAAHEP Standards for Curriculum and Correlation of Text to CAAHEP Standards

The tasks that medical assistants perform include, but are not limited to, those that are presented on this list. In order for students to attain the Entry-Level Competencies for the Medical Assistant, the curriculum must include, but not necessarily be limited to, the following:

a. Anatomy and Physiology

1. Anatomy and physiology of all the body systems
2. Common pathology/diseases
3. Diagnostic/treatment modalities

b. Medical Terminology

1. Basic structure of medical words
2. Word building and definitions
3. Applications of medical terminology

c. Medical Law and Ethics

1. Legal guidelines/requirements for health care
2. Medical ethics and related issues
3. Risk management

d. Psychology

1. Basic principles
2. Development stages of the life cycle
3. Hereditary, cultural, and environmental influences

e. Communication

1. Principles of verbal and nonverbal communication
2. Recognition and response to verbal and nonverbal communication
3. Adaptations for individualized needs

4. Applications of electronic technology
5. Fundamental writing skills

f. Medical Assisting Administrative Procedures

1. Basic medical office functions
2. Bookkeeping and basic accounting
3. Insurance and coding
4. Facility management

g. Medical Assisting Clinical Procedures

1. Aspesis and infection control
2. Specimen collection and processing
3. Diagnostic testing
4. Patient care
5. Pharmacology
6. Medical emergencies
7. Principals of radiology

h. Professional Components

1. Personal attributes
2. Job readiness
3. Workplace dynamics
4. Allied health professions and credentialing

i. Externship

1. A minimum of 160 contact hours
2. Placement in an ambulatory health-care setting

Reprinted with permission from Accrediting Bureau of Health Education Schools—www.CAAHEP.org

Correlation of Text to CAAHEP Standards for Curriculum

Ch	Text	Anatomy & Physiology	Medical Terminology	Medical Law & Ethics	Psychology	Communication Oral & Written	Medical Assisting Administrative Procedures	Medical Assisting Clinical Procedures	Professional Components	Externship
1.	The Medical Assistant Profession in Health Care		✗						✗	
2.	Interpersonal Communication		✗	✗	✗	✗	✗		✗	
3.	Patient-Centered Care	✗	✗	✗	✗	✗		✗	✗	
4.	Considerations of Extended Life	✗	✗	✗	✗	✗		✗	✗	
5.	Clinical Environment and Safety in the Medical Office		✗	✗	✗	✗			✗	
6.	The Clinical Visit: Office Preparation and Patient Encounter	✗	✗	✗	✗	✗		✗	✗	
7.	Medical Asepsis	✗	✗	✗	✗	✗		✗		
8.	Surgical Asepsis	✗	✗	✗	✗	✗		✗		
9.	Pharmacology and Medication Administration	✗	✗	✗	✗	✗		✗		
10.	Vital Signs	✗	✗	✗	✗	✗		✗		
11.	Minor Surgery	✗	✗	✗	✗	✗		✗	✗	
12.	Diagnostic Procedures		✗	✗	✗	✗		✗		
13.	Microscopes and Microbiology	✗	✗	✗	✗	✗		✗		
14.	Hematology and Chemistry	✗	✗	✗	✗	✗		✗		
15.	Urology and Nephrology	✗	✗		✗			✗		
16.	Medical Imaging		✗	✗	✗	✗		✗		
17.	Cardiology and Cardiac Testing	✗	✗		✗			✗		

Ch	Text	Anatomy & Physiology	Medical Terminology	Medical Law & Ethics	Psychology	Communication Oral & Written	Medical Assisting Administrative Procedures	Medical Assisting Clinical Procedures	Professional Components	Externship
18.	Pulmonology and Pulmonary Testing	✗	✗	✗	✗			✗		
19.	EENT	✗	✗	✗	✗			✗		
20.	Immunology and Allergies	✗	✗	✗	✗			✗		
21.	Dermatology	✗	✗	✗	✗			✗		
22.	Endocrinology	✗	✗	✗	✗			✗		
23.	Emergency Care	✗	✗	✗	✗	✗		✗	✗	
24.	Gastroenterology and Nutrition	✗	✗	✗	✗			✗		
25.	Orthopedics and Physical Therapy	✗	✗	✗	✗			✗		
26.	Obstetrics and Gynecology	✗	✗	✗	✗			✗		
27.	Pediatrics	✗	✗	✗	✗			✗		
28.	Neurology	✗	✗	✗	✗			✗		
29.	Mental Health	✗	✗	✗	✗			✗		
30.	Oncology	✗	✗	✗	✗			✗		
31.	Geriatrics	✗	✗	✗	✗			✗		
32.	Alternative Medicine	✗	✗	✗	✗			✗		

Registered Medical Assistant (RMA)
AMT Medical Assisting Task List

MEDICAL ASSISTING TASK LIST

The various tasks that medical assistants perform include, but are not necessarily limited to, those on the following list. The tasks presented in this inventory are considered by American Medical Technologists to be representative of the medical assisting job role. This document should be considered dynamic, to reflect the medical assistant's evolving role with respect to contemporary health care. Therefore, tasks may be added, removed, or modified on an on-going basis.

Medical Assistants that meet AMT's qualifications and pass a certification examination are **certified** as a Registered Medical Assistant (RMA).

I. GENERAL MEDICAL ASSISTING KNOWLEDGE

A. Anatomy and Physiology
1. Body systems
2. Disorders and diseases of the body

B. Medical Terminology
1. Word parts
2. Medical terms
3. Common abbreviations and symbols
4. Spelling

C. Medical Law
1. Medical law
2. Licensure, certification, and registration

D. Medical Ethics
1. Principles of medical ethics
2. Ethical conduct
3. Professional development

E. Human Relations
1. Patient relations
2. Interpersonal skills
3. Cultural diversity

F. Patient Education
1. Identify and apply proper communication methods in patient instruction
2. Develop, assemble, and maintain patient resource materials

II. ADMINISTRATIVE MEDICAL ASSISTING

A. Insurance
1. Medical insurance terminology
2. Various insurance plans
3. Claim forms
4. Electronic insurance claims
5. ICD-9/CPT Coding applications
6. HIPAA mandated coding systems
7. Financial applications of medical insurance

B. Financial Bookkeeping
1. Medical finance terminology
2. Patient billing procedures
3. Collection procedures
4. Fundamental medical office accounting procedures
5. Office banking procedures
6. Employee payroll
7. Financial calculations and accounting procedures

C. Medical Secretarial – Receptionist
1. Medical terminology associated with receptionist duties
2. General reception of patients and visitors
3. Appointment scheduling systems
4. Oral and written communications
5. Medical records management
6. Charting guidelines and regulations
7. Protect, store and retain medical records according to HIPAA regulations
8. Release of protected health information adhering to HIPAA regulations
9. Transcription of dictation
10. Supplies and equipment management
11. Medical office computer applications
12. Compliance with OSHA guidelines and regulations of office safety

8/05

III. CLINICAL MEDICAL ASSISTING

A. Asepsis
1. Medical terminology
2. State/Federal universal blood borne pathogen/body fluid precautions
3. Medical/Surgical asepsis procedure

B. Sterilization
1. Medical terminology associated with sterilization
2. Sanitization, disinfection, and sterilization procedures
3. Record keeping procedures

C. Instruments
1. Specialty instruments and parts
2. Usage of common instruments
3. Care and handling of disposable and re-usable instruments.

D. Vital Signs / Mensurations
1. Blood pressure, pulse, respiration measurements
2. Height, weight, circumference measurements
3. Various temperature measurements
4. Recognize normal and abnormal measurement results

E. Physical Examinations
1. Patient history information
2. Proper charting procedures
3. Patient positions for examinations
4. Methods of examinations
5. Specialty examinations
6. Visual acuity / Ishihara (color blindness) measurements
7. Allergy testing procedures
8. Normal / abnormal results

F. Clinical Pharmacology
1. Medical terminology associated with pharmacology
2. Commonly used drugs and their categories
3. Various routes of medication administration
4. Parenteral administration of medications (Subcutaneous, Intramuscular, Intradermal, Z-Tract)
5. Classes or drug schedules and legal prescriptions requirements for each
6. Drug Enforcement Agency regulations for ordering, dispensing, storage, and documentation of medication use
7. Drug Reference books (PDR, Pharmacopeia, Facts and Comparisons, Nurses Handbook)

American Medical Technologists
10700 W. Higgins Road
Rosemont, Illinois 60018
Phone: (847) 823-5169 – Fax: (847) 823-0458
Website: www.amt1.com

G. Minor Surgery
1. Surgical supplies and instruments
2. Asepsis in surgical procedures
3. Surgical tray preparation and sterile field respect
4. Prevention of pathogen transmission
5. Patient surgical preparation procedures
6. Assisting physician with minor surgery including set-up
7. Dressing and bandaging techniques
8. Suture and staple removal
9. Biohazard waste disposal procedures
10. Instruct patient in pre- and post-surgical care

H. Therapeutic Modalities
1. Various standard therapeutic modalities
2. Alternative/complementary therapies
3. Instruct patient in assistive devices, body mechanics and home care

I. Laboratory Procedures
1. Medical laboratory terminology
2. OSHA safety guidelines
3. Quality control and assessment regulations
4. Operate and maintain laboratory equipment
5. CLIA waived laboratory testing procedures
6. Capillary, dermal and venipuncture procedures
7. Office specimen collection such as: Urine, throat, vaginal, wound cultures – stool, sputum, etc
8. Specimen handling and preparation
9. Laboratory recording according to state and federal guidelines
10. Adhere to the M A Scope of Practice in the laboratory

J. Electrocardiography
1. Standard, 12 Lead ECG Testing
2. Mounting techniques for permanent record
3. Rhythm strip ECG monitoring on Lead II

K. First Aid
1. Emergencies and first aid procedures
2. Emergency crash cart supplies
3. Legal responsibilities as a first responder

Growth Charts

Growth charts are usually part of a child's medical file and are updated on each visit. Charts for growth record keeping are developed by the National Center for Health Statistics (NCHS) along with the CDC's National Center for Chronic Disease Prevention and Health Promotion. These charts are colored with a blue background for boys and a pink background for girls. They are specific for age groups as well as length-for-age and weight-for-age percentiles; head-circumference-for-age and weight-for-length percentiles; body-mass-index-for-age percentiles and weight-for-stature percentiles. The age groups are birth to 36 months and two to 20 years.

The following pages show growth charts specific to length-for-age and weight-for-age percentiles for boys and girls birth to 36 months, and body-mass-index-for-age percentiles for boys and girls two to 20 years. For additional growth charts, visit the CDC website at www.cdc.gov/growthcarts.

Birth to 36 months: Boys
Length-for-age and Weight-for-age percentiles

NAME _____

RECORD # _____

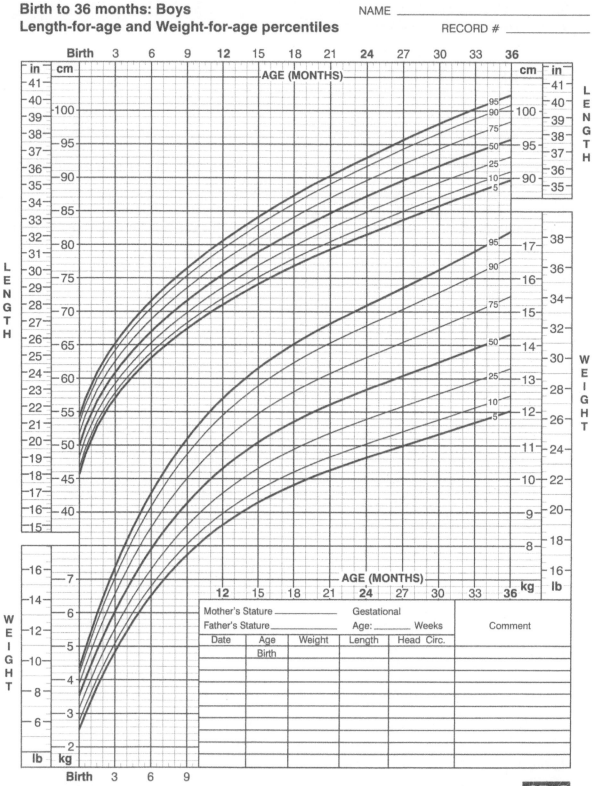

Published May 30, 2000 (modified 4/20/01).
SOURCE: Developed by the National Center for Health Statistics in collaboration with
the National Center for Chronic Disease Prevention and Health Promotion (2000).
http://www.cdc.gov/growthcharts

SAFER · HEALTHIER · PEOPLE™

Birth to 36 months: Girls
Length-for-age and Weight-for-age percentiles

NAME _____

RECORD # _____

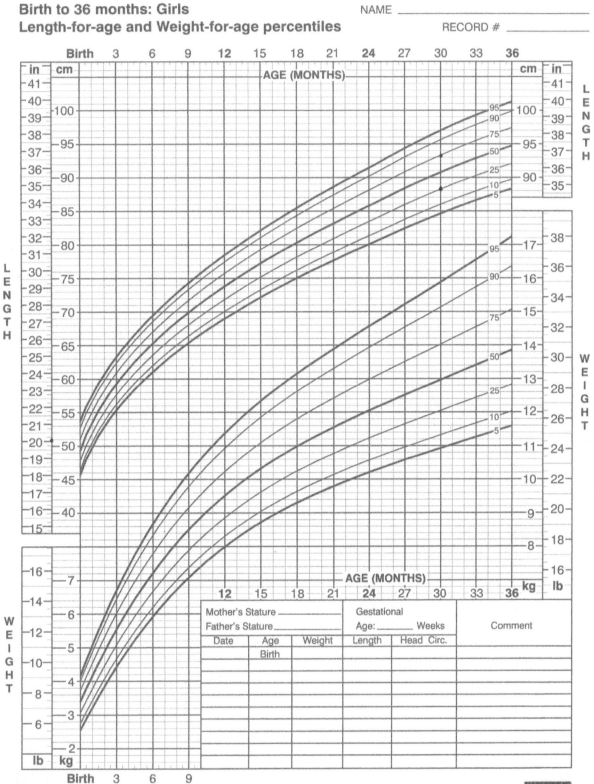

Mother's Stature			Gestational		
Father's Stature			Age: _____ Weeks		Comment
Date	Age	Weight	Length	Head Circ.	
	Birth				

Published May 30, 2000 (modified 4/20/01).
SOURCE: Developed by the National Center for Health Statistics in collaboration with
the National Center for Chronic Disease Prevention and Health Promotion (2000).
http://www.cdc.gov/growthcharts

SAFER · HEALTHIER · PEOPLE™

2 to 20 years: Boys
Body mass index-for-age percentiles

NAME _____

RECORD # _____

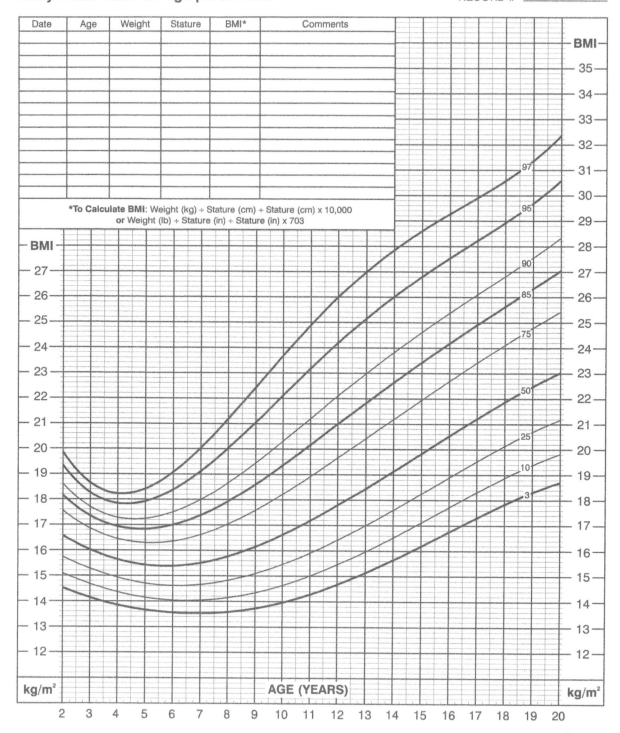

Date	Age	Weight	Stature	BMI*	Comments

*To Calculate BMI: Weight (kg) ÷ Stature (cm) ÷ Stature (cm) x 10,000
or Weight (lb) ÷ Stature (in) ÷ Stature (in) x 703

AGE (YEARS)

Published May 30, 2000 (modified 10/16/00).
SOURCE: Developed by the National Center for Health Statistics in collaboration with
the National Center for Chronic Disease Prevention and Health Promotion (2000).
http://www.cdc.gov/growthcharts

SAFER · HEALTHIER · PEOPLE™

2 to 20 years: Girls
Body mass index-for-age percentiles

NAME

RECORD # _____

Date	Age	Weight	Stature	BMI*	Comments

***To Calculate BMI**: Weight (kg) ÷ Stature (cm) ÷ Stature (cm) x 10,000
or Weight (lb) ÷ Stature (in) ÷ Stature (in) x 703

BMI

97
95
90
85
75
50
25
10
3

AGE (YEARS)

kg/m²   kg/m²

2 3 4 5 6 7 8 9 10 11 12 13 14 15 16 17 18 19 20

Published May 30, 2000 (modified 10/16/00).
SOURCE: Developed by the National Center for Health Statistics in collaboration with
the National Center for Chronic Disease Prevention and Health Promotion (2000).
http://www.cdc.gov/growthcharts

SAFER · HEALTHIER · PEOPLE™

Immunization Schedules

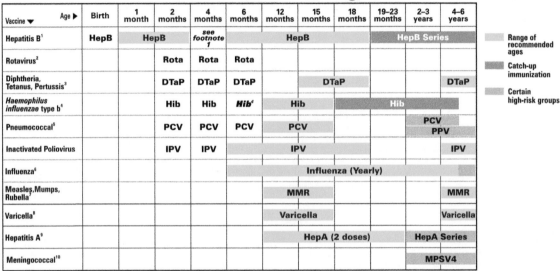

DEPARTMENT OF HEALTH AND HUMAN SERVICES • CENTERS FOR DISEASE CONTROL AND PREVENTION

Recommended Immunization Schedule for Ages 0–6 Years UNITED STATES • 2007

Vaccine ▼ Age ▶	Birth	1 month	2 months	4 months	6 months	12 months	15 months	18 months	19–23 months	2–3 years	4–6 years
Hepatitis B[1]	HepB	HepB		see footnote 1		HepB				HepB Series	
Rotavirus[2]			Rota	Rota	Rota						
Diphtheria, Tetanus, Pertussis[3]			DTaP	DTaP	DTaP		DTaP				DTaP
Haemophilus influenzae type b[4]			Hib	Hib	Hib[4]	Hib		Hib			
Pneumococcal[5]			PCV	PCV	PCV	PCV				PCV / PPV	
Inactivated Poliovirus			IPV	IPV		IPV					IPV
Influenza[6]						Influenza (Yearly)					
Measles, Mumps, Rubella[7]						MMR					MMR
Varicella[8]						Varicella					Varicella
Hepatitis A[9]						HepA (2 doses)				HepA Series	
Meningococcal[10]										MPSV4	

Legend:
- Range of recommended ages
- Catch-up immunization
- Certain high-risk groups

This schedule indicates the recommended ages for routine administration of currently licensed childhood vaccines, as of December 1, 2006, for children through age 6 years. For additional information see www.cdc.gov/nip/recs/child-schedule.htm. Any dose not administered at the recommended age should be administered at any subsequent visit when indicated and feasible. Additional vaccines may be licensed and recommended during the year. Licensed combination vaccines may be used whenever any components of the combination are indicated and other components of the vaccine are not contraindicated and if approved by the Food and Drug Administration for that dose of the series. Providers should consult the respective ACIP statement for detailed recommendations. Clinically significant adverse events that follow immunization should be reported to the Vaccine Adverse Event Reporting System (VAERS). Guidance about how to obtain and complete a VAERS form is available at www.vaers.hhs.gov or by telephone, 800-822-7967.

1. Hepatitis B vaccine (HepB). *(Minimum age: birth)*
  At birth:
- Administer monovalent HepB to all newborns prior to hospital discharge.
- If mother is HBsAg-positive, administer HepB and 0.5 mL of hepatitis B immune globulin (HBIG) within 12 hours of birth.
- If mother's HBsAg status is unknown, administer HepB within 12 hours of birth. Determine the HBsAg status as soon as possible and if HBsAg-positive, administer HBIG (no later than age 1 week).
- If mother is HBsAg-negative, the birth dose can only be delayed with physician's order and mothers' negative HBsAg laboratory report documented in the infant's medical record.

  Following the birth dose:
- The HepB series should be completed with either monovalent HepB or a combination vaccine containing HepB. The second dose should be administered at age 1–2 months. The final dose should be administered at age ≥24 weeks. Infants born to HBsAg-positive mothers should be tested for HBsAg and antibody to HBsAg after completion of 3 or more doses in a licensed HepB series, at age 9–18 months (generally at the next well-child visit).

  4-month dose of HepB:
- It is permissible to administer 4 doses of HepB when combination vaccines are given after the birth dose. If monovalent HepB is used for doses after the birth dose, a dose at age 4 months is not needed.

2. Rotavirus vaccine (Rota). *(Minimum age: 6 weeks)*
- Administer the first dose between 6 and 12 weeks of age. Do not start the series later than age 12 weeks.
- Administer the final dose in the series by 32 weeks of age. Do not administer a dose later than age 32 weeks.
- There are insufficient data on safety and efficacy outside of these age ranges.

3. Diphtheria and tetanus toxoids and acellular pertussis vaccine (DTaP). *(Minimum age: 6 weeks)*
- The fourth dose of DTaP may be administered as early as age 12 months, provided 6 months have elapsed since the third dose.
- Administer the final dose in the series at age 4–6 years.

4. *Haemophilus influenzae* type b conjugate vaccine (Hib). *(Minimum age: 6 weeks)*
- If PRP-OMP (PedvaxHIB® or ComVax® [Merck]) is administered at ages 2 and 4 months, a dose at age 6 months is not required.
- TriHiBit® (DTaP/Hib) combination products should not be used for primary immunization but can be used as boosters following any Hib vaccine in ≥12 months olds.

5. Pneumococcal vaccine. *(Minimum age: 6 weeks for Pneumococcal Conjugate Vaccine (PCV); 2 years for Pneumococcal Polysaccharide Vaccine (PPV))*
- Administer PCV at ages 24-59 months in certain high-risk groups. Administer PPV to certain high-risk groups aged ≥2 years. See *MMWR* 2000; 49(RR-9):1-35.

6. Influenza vaccine. *(Minimum age: 6 months for trivalent inactivated influenza vaccine (TIV); 5 years for live, attenuated influenza vaccine (LAIV)*
- All children aged 6–59 months and close contacts of all children aged 0–59 months are recommended to receive influenza vaccine.
- Influenza vaccine is recommended annually for children aged ≥59 months with certain risk factors, healthcare workers, and other persons (including household members) in close contact with persons in groups at high risk. See *MMWR* 2006; 55(RR-10):1-41.
- For healthy persons aged 5–49 years, LAIV may be used as an alternative to TIV.
- Children receiving TIV should receive 0.25 mL if aged 6–35 months or 0.5 mL if aged ≥3 years.
- Children aged <9 years who are receiving influenza vaccine for the first time should receive 2 doses (separated by ≥4 weeks for TIV and ≥6 weeks for LAIV).

7. Measles, mumps, and rubella vaccine (MMR). *(Minimum age: 12 months)*
- Administer the second dose of MMR at age 4–6 years. MMR may be administered prior to age 4–6 years, provided ≥4 weeks have elapsed since the first dose and both doses are administered at age ≥12 months.

8. Varicella vaccine. *(Minimum age: 12 months)*
- Administer the second dose of varicella vaccine at age 4–6 years. Varicella vaccine may be administered prior to age 4–6 years, provided that ≥3 months have elapsed since the first dose and both doses are administered at age ≥12 months. If second dose was administered ≥28 days following the first dose, the second dose does not need to be repeated.

9. Hepatitis A vaccine (HepA). *(Minimum age: 12 months)*
- HepA is recommended for all children at 1 year of age (i.e., 12–23 months). The 2 doses in the series should be administered at least 6 months apart.
- Children not fully vaccinated by age 2 years can be vaccinated at subsequent visits.
- HepA is recommended for certain other groups of children including in areas where vaccination programs target older children. See *MMWR* 2006; 55(RR-7):1-23.

10. Meningococcal polysaccharide vaccine (MPSV4). *(Minimum age: 2 years)*
- Administer MPSV4 to children aged 2–10 years with terminal complement deficiencies or anatomic or functional asplenia and certain other high risk groups. See *MMWR* 2005;54 (RR-7):1-21.

The Childhood and Adolescent Immunization Schedule is approved by:
Advisory Committee on Immunization Practices www.cdc.gov/nip/acip • American Academy of Pediatrics www.aap.org • American Academy of Family Physicians www.aafp.org

SAFER • HEALTHIER • PEOPLE™

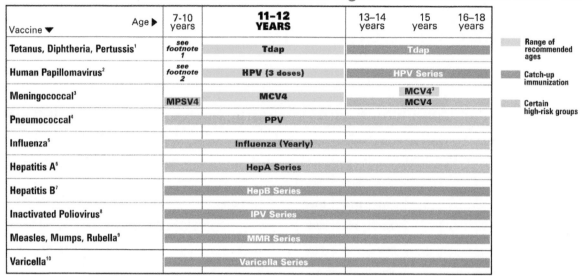

DEPARTMENT OF HEALTH AND HUMAN SERVICES • CENTERS FOR DISEASE CONTROL AND PREVENTION

Recommended Immunization Schedule for Ages 7–18 Years UNITED STATES • 2007

Vaccine ▼ / Age ►	7-10 years	11–12 YEARS	13–14 years	15 years	16–18 years
Tetanus, Diphtheria, Pertussis[1]	see footnote 1	Tdap	Tdap		
Human Papillomavirus[2]	see footnote 2	HPV (3 doses)	HPV Series		
Meningococcal[3]	MPSV4	MCV4		MCV4[3] / MCV4	
Pneumococcal[4]		PPV			
Influenza[5]		Influenza (Yearly)			
Hepatitis A[6]		HepA Series			
Hepatitis B[7]		HepB Series			
Inactivated Poliovirus[8]		IPV Series			
Measles, Mumps, Rubella[9]		MMR Series			
Varicella[10]		Varicella Series			

- Range of recommended ages
- Catch-up immunization
- Certain high-risk groups

This schedule indicates the recommended ages for routine administration of currently licensed childhood vaccines, as of December 1, 2006, for children aged 7–18 years. For additional information see www.cdc.gov/nip/recs/child-schedule.htm. Any dose not administered at the recommended earlier age should be administered at any subsequent visit when indicated and feasible. Additional vaccines may be licensed and recommended during the year. Licensed combination vaccines may be used whenever any components of the combination are indicated and other components of the vaccine are not contraindicated and if approved by the Food and Drug Administration for that dose of the series. Providers should consult the respective ACIP statement for detailed recommendations. Clinically significant adverse events that follow immunization should be reported to the Vaccine Adverse Event Reporting System (VAERS). Guidance about how to obtain and complete a VAERS form is available at www.vaers.hhs.gov or by telephone, 800-822-7967.

FOOTNOTES

1. **Tetanus and diphtheria toxoids and acellular pertussis vaccine (Tdap).**
   (Minimum age: 10 years for BOOSTRIX® and 11 years for ADACEL™)
   - Administer at age 11–12 years for those who have completed the recommended childhood DTP/DTaP vaccination series and have not received a Td booster dose.
   - Adolescents 13–18 years who missed the 11–12 year Td/Tdap booster dose should also receive a single dose of Tdap if they have completed the recommended childhood DTP/DTaP vaccination series.

2. **Human papillomavirus vaccine (HPV).** *(Minimum age: 9 years)*
   - Administer the first dose of the HPV vaccine to females at age 11–12 years.
   - Administer the second dose 2 months after the first dose and the third dose 6 months after the first dose.
   - Administer the HPV vaccine series to females at age 13–18 years if not previously vaccinated.

3. **Meningococcal vaccine.** *(Minimum age: 11 years for meningococcal conjugate vaccine (MCV4); 2 years for meningococcal polysaccharide vaccine (MPSV4))*
   - Administer MCV4 at age 11–12-years and to previously unvaccinated adolescents at high school entry (~15 years of age).
   - Administer MCV4 to previously unvaccinated college freshmen living in dormitories; MPSV4 is an acceptable alternative.
   - Vaccination against invasive meningococcal disease is recommended for children and adolescents aged ≥2 years with terminal complement deficiencies or anatomic or functional asplenia and certain other high risk groups. See *MMWR* 2005;54 (RR-7):1-21. Use MPSV4 for children aged 2–10 years and MCV4 or MPSV4 for older children.

4. **Pneumococcal polysaccharide vaccine (PPV).**
   (Minimum age: 2 years)
   - Administer for certain high-risk groups. See *MMWR* 1997; 46(RR-08); 1–24 and *MMWR* 2000; 49(RR-9):1-35.

5. **Influenza vaccine.** *(Minimum age: 6 months for trivalent inactivated influenza vaccine (TIV); 5 years for live, attenuated influenza vaccine (LAIV)*

   - Influenza vaccine is recommended annually for persons with certain risk factors, healthcare workers, and other persons (including household members) in close contact with persons in groups at high risk. See *MMWR* 2006; 55(RR-10);1-41.
   - For healthy persons aged 5–49 years, LAIV may be used as an alternative to TIV.
   - Children aged <9 years who are receiving influenza vaccine for the first time should receive 2 doses (separated by ≥4 weeks for TIV and ≥6 weeks for LAIV).

6. **Hepatitis A vaccine (HepA).** *(Minimum age: 12 months)*
   - The 2 doses in the series should be administered at least 6 months apart.
   - HepA is recommended for certain other groups of children including in areas where vaccination programs target older children. See *MMWR* 2006; 55(RR-7):1-23.

7. **Hepatitis B vaccine (HepB).** *(Minimum age: birth)*
   - Administer the 3-dose series to those who were not previously vaccinated.
   - A 2-dose series of Recombivax HB® is licensed for 11–15 year olds.

8. **Inactivated poliovirus vaccine (IPV).** *(Minimum age: 6 weeks)*
   - For children who received an all-IPV or all-oral poliovirus (OPV) series, a fourth dose is not necessary if third dose was administered at age ≥4 years.
   - If both OPV and IPV were administered as part of a series, a total of 4 doses should be given, regardless of the child's current age.

9. **Measles, mumps, and rubella vaccine (MMR).**
   (Minimum age: 12 months)
   - If not previously vaccinated, administer 2 doses of MMR during any visit with ≥4 weeks between the doses.

10. **Varicella vaccine.** *(Minimum age: 12 months)*
    - Administer 2 doses of varicella vaccine to persons without evidence of immunity.
    - Administer 2 doses of varicella vaccine to persons aged ≤13 years at least 3 months apart. Do not repeat the second dose, if administered ≥28 days following the first dose.
    - Administer 2 doses of varicella vaccine to persons aged ≥13 years at least 4 weeks apart.

The Childhood and Adolescent Immunization Schedule is approved by:
Advisory Committee on Immunization Practices www.cdc.gov/nip/acip • American Academy of Pediatrics www.aap.org • American Academy of Family Physicians www.aafp.org
SAFER • HEALTHIER • PEOPLE™

Answers to Case Study Critical Thinking Questions

CHAPTER 1

CTQ 1-1: Should Janet continue to allow her patients to call her "Nurse"? Why or why not? Can she be held civilly or criminally liable if she knowingly continues to do so?

Answer: To avoid confusion and to promote trust and pride in her title, Janet should never allow her patients to call her "Nurse." If they do, she can gently correct them and explain the difference between an MA and an RN. Janet can be held legally and civilly liable for intentionally misrepresenting her job title and educational background.

CTQ 1-2: Can Janet apply to take the AAMA exam at one of the three times offered this year? Why or why not? If not, explain what steps she might have to take to become eligible.

Answer: Because Janet has never attended an accredited medical assistant school, she would not be eligible to sit for the AAMA exam. She should research her educational options and find a school that is either CAAHEP or ABHES accredited, as required by the AAMA. When she has completed her education, she can submit her transcripts and sit for the exam.

CHAPTER 2

CTQ 2-1: How should Oksana have greeted the patient who walked up to her desk? What steps should she have taken before patients arrived to appear more professional and competent?

Answer: Oksana should have greeted her patient with "Good morning," "Good afternoon," or "Good evening," followed by "How may I help you?" or a similar statement conveying interest in the patient and a willingness to help. Oksana needs to remember that patients are not an interruption of her work, but the reason for her job.

As a general rule, it is never appropriate to eat or have uncovered beverages at the reception area. You cannot predict when the phone will ring or someone may walk up and need to speak with you. You should eat only on designated breaks and in the appropriate area. Medical offices are becoming more and more computerized, so it may be office policy that no open containers are allowed at desks to avoid possible damage to computers.

CTQ 2-2: Do you think Oksana's posture affects her tone of voice and the way she delivers her message to the caller? Should she have asked the callers if they could be placed on hold so that she could return to the patient at the desk?

Answer: Posture positively or negatively affects one's tone of voice. Medical assistants should practice correct posture to convey professionalism. If the patient at the desk was being helped first, Oksana should politely excuse herself, answer the telephone, ask the callers if they can be placed on hold, and return to helping the patient at the desk.

CHAPTER 3

CTQ 3-1: In the case study, why do you think the patient looked confused when he noticed that Marina was smoking? Why do you think Marina felt guilty or uneasy about being seen by her patient while smoking? How would you feel if the person teaching you healthy habits and encouraging you did not follow his or her own advice?

Answer: The patient was mostly confused by Marina's smoking because Marina works in the health-care field, in naturopathy, and gives patients advice on healthy lifestyle choices. Marina felt guilty about being seen smoking because it is her job to counsel patients against such behavior, and she might have felt like a hypocrite for not following her own advice.

There is a growing trend among employers to refuse to hire smokers or allow smokers to extern at their offices. It is a proven fact that smokers cost more overall than nonsmokers in terms of workdays missed because of smoking-related illnesses and hospitalizations.

CHAPTER 4

CTQ 4-1: How should Ori try to educate his mother about the process of organ donation?

Answer: Ori should ask his physician for informational brochures to take home to his mother. She may be more receptive to learning about organ donation in the comfort of her own home and at her own pace.

CTQ 4-2: As you read in the case study, Ori's mother believes that hospitals save money if they let patients die and harvest organs later. Explain why the hospital cannot receive monetary compensation for organs. Also explain the difference between time frames in cold ischemic and warm ischemic donations.

Answer: The hospital does not benefit from "letting a person die" because there is no guarantee that the organs can and will be used in donation. Due to the specific time lines, organs may not all be ideal for donation by the time an emergency situation is managed and the next of kin have been notified. The hospital absorbs the physician's fees and other related costs of organ donation surgery.

According to the Uniform Anatomical Gift Act, the hospital cannot receive compensation for harvested organs. Furthermore, the physician doing the harvesting cannot be the physician who pronounces the patient dead.

CHAPTER 5

CTQ 5-1: Ian wants to save time and get to the reception area as quickly as possible. But what is the proper procedure for storing personal food items and medications in an office environment?

Answer: It is a violation of OSHA safety standards to store edible items with medications. Ian and all employees should never place personal items in a medication refrigerator. The risk of contaminating both the food and the medications is too great.

CTQ 5-2: Once Ian is on the scene with Cora, who is assessing the patient's vital signs and status, what should he do next?

Answer: Cora is attending to the patient's most immediate needs, so Ian should call 911 or the local area's emergency response number to ensure advanced care will be on the way.

CTQ 5-3: After the situation in the reception area has been taken care of and the patient is no longer in need of medical assistance, how should the incident be recorded, and by whom?

Answer: Cora should document the incident as regulated by office procedures. The documentation should always include the nature of the situation, who was present, who offered aid, and the patient's identity, if known. If the person who received aid was not a patient, Cora should follow office protocol for storing this information. Some offices create a "dummy chart," and others might keep this information in a master file with all incident reports that occur in a certain timeframe.

CHAPTER 6

CTQ 6-1: What is the proper protocol for Alexis to follow after discovering the soiled chart? Who is responsible for the chart?

Answer: A patient's chart is a legal document in which all treatments and outcomes are recorded. It contains important, irreplaceable information. The situation must be addressed with the office manager or physician, who will know the proper protocol for recreating the documents that were soiled.

CTQ 6-2: Do you think the situation in the case study should be reported to the office manager or physician? Why or why not?

Answer: Alexis needs to take responsibility for her actions. The soiled chart must be recreated in a way that will protect the physician against possible malpractice lawsuits in the future. Recreating the chart may involve contacting the laboratory, hospital, or referring physician and asking for an additional copy of the stained reports. If the reports were created by the physician Alexis works for, he will have to decide the best way to recreate them. If they were computer generated, they may be reprinted. If a transcriptionist typed them, they might have been saved on a disk. Ultimately everyone in the office is responsible for the patient's chart.

CHAPTER 7

CTQ 7-1: How do you think Gloria's actions make her patient feel? How much time do you think Gloria really saved by not washing her hands and then not removing the gloves and washing her hands again?

Answer: The patient might feel uncomfortable or rushed, or might even feel like an inconvenience to Gloria. Proper hand washing takes only a few minutes, but it earns the patient's trust and confidence.

CTQ 7-2: In the scenario in the case study, who has been put at risk of possible exposure to strep A by Gloria's actions?

Answer: Gloria's careless actions have put several people at risk: the next person to touch the door handle, the receptionist who took the lab order form, the coworker who may place the pen in his or her mouth, and anyone else who comes in direct contact with surfaces Gloria may have touched with her contaminated gloves.

CTQ 7-3: How would you feel if you were a patient and Gloria enters the exam room and does not wash her hands before examining you?

Answer: This answer will vary from student to student.

CHAPTER 8

CTQ 8-1: In the case study, is the surgical instrument that Ian placed last, with noticeable moisture on it, considered sterile? Could the moisture possibly indicate that the autoclave is not working properly or that the cycle was not completed properly?

Answer: If the autoclave is run properly, there is no moisture on the instruments at the end of the cycle. Moisture attracts pathogens, so the instrument must be autoclaved again. The autoclave should be checked for mechanical failures or possible operator errors.

CTQ 8-2: Ian left the room to take a phone call after dropping one last instrument on the sterile field. When he reenters the room, is the setup still considered sterile?

Answer: When Ian left the room to answer the phone call without covering the sterile field, he left it open to possible contamination. Ian cannot be certain that the instruments were not touched, so he must start the procedure over with a completely new setup.

CHAPTER 9

CTQ 9-1: Heidi notes that Claire has been receiving medication refills even though she has missed her follow-up appointments. How would you handle this situation?

Answer: This is generally a simple situation that has been made complex by the patient's pregnancy.

First, Heidi should verify who refilled the prescription. Then she should ask if Claire has mentioned taking Zantac to Dr. Wittig, who was not the prescriber. After gathering this information, Heidi can talk to Dr. Wittig about office protocol for allowing continued refills when patients miss follow-up appointments.

CTQ 9-2: Claire has not been seen in Dr. Wittig's office for the past 10 months and is now 7 months pregnant. Dr. Wittig may not be aware that Claire is pregnant and has continued taking Zantac, which may be contraindicated during pregnancy. Now that Heidi is aware of this situation, how should she proceed?

Answer: Heidi should first verify with the patient that she has indeed been taking Zantac twice a day during her pregnancy. She can look up contraindications for Zantac during pregnancy in the *PDR*. Heidi should make sure Dr. Wittig is aware of the patient's continuing use of Zantac.

CHAPTER 10

CTQ 10-1: Knowing that a normal pulse pressure is between 30 mmHg and 50 mmHg, what should Chelsea do next?

Answer: Chelsea should switch arms and take another blood pressure reading. It is possible the patient has an auscultatory gap due to hypertension, or Chelsea may find that she is correct and there is an abnormal blood pressure. Double-checking abnormal findings is always a good idea.

CTQ 10-2: Chelsea heard two distinct blood pressure readings in the same arm. How should she record this in the patient's chart?

Answer: What Chelsea actually heard was an auscultatory gap, common in hypertensive patients. Chelsea should write down exactly what she heard and question her physician/employer about it later. This will be a good learning experience for her.

CHAPTER 11

CTQ 11-1: Latesha cannot locate the signed informed consent that Gwen "knows" she had the patient sign and promised to bring to Latesha later. How should Latesha handle this situation?

Answer: Even though Gwen is certain that she had the patient sign a consent form, Latesha should verify that it has been done. If the patient is already in the office, there is no harm in having him or her sign a second form. At the very least, Latesha should offer to go back to Gwen's desk to get the form and place it in the patient's chart so that she can be certain that correct protocol has been followed.

CTQ 11-2: Latesha observed Gwen cleaning the room but not sanitizing it or confirming that the counters were disinfected. What should Latesha do?

Answer: The quick cleanup is hazardous to the patient's health and unacceptable practice. Latesha should politely ask Gwen where the disinfectants are kept and should clean and disinfect the room herself so that she knows it has been done properly.

CHAPTER 12

CTQ 12-1: Jason is scheduling a patient for a laboratory procedure to be done at another location. He has offered the patient several appointment times, but she has rejected each one, saying she has too many other things she needs to do. How should Jason handle this?

Answer: Depending on the kinds of tests that need to be done and the time requirements, Jason should offer the patient specific appointment times. Instead of continuing to list several options, he can ask, "Do mornings or afternoons work better for you?" and follow with "What days of the week are best for you?" This will help save time and avoid frustration.

CTQ 12-2: Jason has called the patient several times this week to make a follow-up appointment to review test results. The physician has specified that she does not want the patient to receive the test results over the phone. But the patient has not returned any of Jason's calls. What can he do?

Answer: Jason should alert the physician and send a certified letter to the patient's home. It is possible that the patient has gone on vacation or is out of town, but a certified letter requesting an appointment for follow-up care protects the physician from a possible lawsuit.

CHAPTER 13

CTQ 13-1: The sample of *Staphyloccus aureus* taken from the toddler's rash confirms the physician's diagnosis of impetigo. Irene knows what the pathogen will look like and that it will be gram-positive even before she begins the microscopic exam. How does she know this?

Answer: Irene has been working in the microbiology department for several months and

remembers that all staph infections stain gram-positive. She knows the pathogen's shape based on its scientific name.

CTQ 13-2: Irene confirms that the patient is positive for an *E. coli* infection in her bladder. What are some possible causes for the bladder infection?

Answer: *E. coli* is the primary cause of UTIs because it is normally found in feces. Patients who do not wipe properly, front to back, are at risk for transferring the pathogen forward to the vaginal opening. Once the pathogen is in the vaginal area, it can spread farther up into the bladder and cause an infection.

CHAPTER 14

CTQ 14-1: Kathleen is assuming that because the brick-top tube does not contain additives, it will be fine to obtain the prothrombin time sample in. Why is this incorrect?

Answer: Blood-draw tube order is critical to proper testing of blood samples. Mixing up the order of tubes or which tubes samples are drawn in can invalidate results or contaminate other samples. Specifically, prothrombin and other hematology tests must be drawn in light-blue tubes containing EDTA.

CHAPTER 15

CTQ 15-1: When Gina's patient mentions her urinary frequency and painful urination, what can Gina do to relieve some of her nervousness?

Answer: Gina should inform the patient that there are many treatments that are safe and will give her relief. Gina should also explain the dangers of allowing a possible infection to continue.

CTQ 15-2: Given the patient's complaint, what tests do you think Gina should prepare to perform?

Answer: Gina should always verify what tests the physician would like to have performed on the patient. A urine dip with Chemstrips is standard for all pregnant women, so Gina should continue to perform that test as ordered. She should also keep the unused portion of urine for any additional tests the physician may order.

CHAPTER 16

CTQ 16-1: Olivia's previous experience with X-rays has made her comfortable with patient preparation, gowning, and draping instructions. The X-ray technician has been ordered to take chest X-rays of a female patient who is believed to have pneumonia. The patient is elderly and has come to the appointment alone. She needs help removing her clothing and getting the drape set up and is not steady enough on her feet to stand alone in the X-ray room. What instructions or assistance should Olivia give her?

Answer: Prior to beginning the exam, Olivia should make certain that the patient understands why an X-ray is being taken. Then Olivia can explain the X-ray procedure, what clothing needs to be removed, and how the patient will be positioned. Olivia should offer to stay in the room with the patient if she cannot stand unassisted or feels uncomfortable with only the male X-ray technician in the room.

CTQ 16-2: The patient tells Olivia that she is not steady on her feet and would like to have Olivia assist her during the X-ray procedure. What precautions should Olivia take to avoid unnecessary exposure to radiation?

Answer: Olivia should wear a half-apron because only the patient's chest is being X-rayed.

CHAPTER 17

CTQ 17-1: Knowing that Ray has a history of cardiac surgery and is planning to have dental surgery, what should Rachel's response to his presenting symptoms be?

Answer: With the symptoms that the patient is presenting, in combination with his previous cardiac surgery, endocarditis is a concern. Rachel should chart the patient's complaints and symptoms accurately so that the doctor has all the necessary information to assess the situation. The patient will probably need to take prophylactic antibiotics before future dental surgeries. Rachel can explain why and how that should be done as the physician directs.

CHAPTER 18

CTQ 18-1: Keera has been given the directions for obtaining a sputum sample and has observed the technique being performed. Now that it is her turn, what precautions should she take?

Answer: Patients are asked to cough forcefully and bring the sputum up from deep within the lungs. Coughing propels droplets and other infectious material on the person collecting the sample. Keera should wear the correct PPE: gown, gloves, and face mask with eye shield.

CTQ 18-2: Keera has just instructed the patient in the correct way to use a metered dose inhaler (MDI). What other instructions or methods should she mention to the patient?

Answer: Keera should tell the patient that to get the most effective dosage and therefore save money on MDI prescriptions, instructions must be followed very carefully. Keera should also make sure the patient understands the signs and symptoms of oral thrush, which is a common side effect of inhaler misuse.

CHAPTER 19

CTQ 19-1: The college student who has come in for a Snellen test wears contact lenses. With her left eye, the patient can read to the 20/20 line, making only two errors. With her right eye, she can only read to the 20/40 line and makes three errors. How should Stacy record these results?

Answer: Stacy should record the vision as O.S. 20/20-2 and O.D. 20/50, noting on the chart that the patient wears corrective lens.

CTQ 19-2: The young girl with sand in her eye is frightened about having her eye flushed. She squeezes her eye shut and will not hold still. What are Stacy's options?

Answer: Stacy should explain the procedure in age-appropriate language, assuring the child that the procedure will not hurt and will make her eye feel better. She should also explain that it is very important that she not move while Stacy is cleaning her eye. Stacy can also ask the parent or guardian to assist in holding the child still.

CTQ 19-3: What items should Stacy lay out for the physician so that he can remove the toy from the child's nose?

Answer: The physician will need the proper PPE, such as gloves and a face shield, a light source to get a clear visual of the foreign body, a nasal speculum to gain access, and forceps to grip the object.

CHAPTER 20

CTQ 20-1: What precautions should Eric take when setting up the patient with AIDS for examination by the physician?

Answer: Regardless of what the chart states, it is important to treat every patient as possibly infected when performing any tasks that put you at risk for infection. The rash is located on the right and left flanks, so Eric should instruct the patient on disrobing from the waist up and provide a drape if he would like to use it.

CTQ 20-2: Before Eric assists the doctor in performing a prick skin test, he must explain the four methods of diagnostic allergy testing. Because the child being tested is a minor, what else does Eric need to do?

Answer: Because the child is a minor, the parent will have to sign a consent form as well as any insurance forms that may or may not cover allergy testing. The methods that may be used to test for a pet allergy are: 1) intradermal, with small amounts of potential antigen under the skin; 2) skin patch, putting a patch soaked with the potential antigen on the skin; and 3) scratch test, placing the potential antigen into a scratch made on the skin. The physician determines the most effective method of testing.

CHAPTER 21

CTQ 21-1: The mother is very concerned that her children may have lice and is under the impression that they will be labeled "dirty" or that she will be seen as an unfit mother. In addition, she has assumed that all lice are the same and attach to all types of hair. What should Manny tell her about the different kinds of head lice and how they're transmitted?

Answer: Manny can start by explaining that there actually three types of lice, which attach to different areas based on several factors. Head lice are very common and are easily spread among schoolchildren via hats, combs, brushes, and coats. Body lice are a different species and are spread through poor hygiene and close body contact. Pubic lice spread via sexual contact.

CTQ 21-2: The teenage girl with the mole admits to sunbathing regularly in the summer at the lake and describes her mole only as "suspicious." What questions should Manny ask her regarding this condition? What advice should he give?

Answer: Manny should ask the patient to describe what she mean by "suspicious." Using the ABCD rules of mole appearance, he should ask: What color is the mole? Is it evenly colored? What size is the mole? What do the edges look like? Have any of these characteristics changed? If so, when and how? In addition, the patient should be warned about the dangers of long-term sun exposure and educated in the proper use of sun protection.

CHAPTER 22

CTQ 22-1: Mr. Wiat is apparently unaware of how adult-onset diabetes occurs and what the treatment options are. How should Charles educate him?

Answer: Charles should spend a significant amount of time with this patient. He will need to discuss his lifestyle choices, how they may have contributed to his current condition, and the changes he will need to make. He should ask several open-ended questions to verify that Mr. Wiat understands. To reinforce the information, Charles should also provide reading materials Mr. Wiat can take home and review. Charles should document their conversation in the patient's chart and list the additional resources he has provided Mr. Wiat.

CTQ 22-2: Mr. Wiat seems to be in denial about his condition and how his lifestyle may cause additional health problems and even death. How should Charles proceed in educating him?

Answer: In addition to the discussion about diabetes and the reading materials Charles has provided, Charles may suggest that Mr. Wiat seek additional support in the community through a diabetic counselor who can help him with coping mechanisms, diet and nutrition, equipment, and further education.

CHAPTER 23

CTQ 23-1: What questions should Ariko ask Brenna regarding the accident and the child's behavior?

Answer: To provide the physician with an accurate report, Ariko should ask: 1) Is Brenna certain there is no visible injury to the head or extremities, such as bruising, bleeding, or swelling? 2) How is the child reacting? Is she slow, sluggish, or able to talk or walk without assistance? If she has not moved herself, it is important that Brenna not move her to avoid furthering a neck or spinal cord injury. 3) Is the child feeling sleepy? Does she want to take a nap or go to bed? 4) Is there any nausea or vomiting?

CTQ 23-2: After Ariko has collected all the information on the accident as reported by Brenna, how should she advise Brenna?

Answer: Head and neck injuries are a serious matter. Without proper evaluation by a physician, it is impossible to diagnose or rule out a concussion over the phone. A head injury can cause intracranial bleeding, which may take up to 24 hours to produce symptoms. The victim should avoid strenuous activity or taking pain medications that can mask the symptoms and make it more difficult to correctly diagnose. Common symptoms to watch for are nausea, vomiting, sluggishness, confusion, irritability, persistent headache, blurred vision, and seizure activity. Ariko should advise Brenna to watch for those symptoms in her child and relay any other recommendations from the physician. The physician may recommend that the parent take the child to an ER for further evaluation because children cannot adequately describe symptoms that may indicate a serious underlying condition.

CHAPTER 24

CTQ 24-1: What questions should Reggie ask Serena about her newfound interest in vegetarianism so that he can more accurately assess her nutritional needs?

Answer: Reggie should ask Serena what type of vegetarianism she is interested in. To accurately assess her nutritional needs, he needs to know if she is cutting out meat alone, meat and fish, meat and dairy, or all animal products.

CTQ 24-2: Once Reggie has established what type of vegetarian Serena would like to become, how should he proceed to help her reach her nutritional as well as lifestyle goals?

Answer: Once Serena has established what types of animal products she would like to avoid, Reggie can give her a list of foods to help her maintain adequate protein intake. Depending on her dietary choices, Serena could eat soybeans and other beans, eggs, and dairy products. Reggie should also give Serena brochures and reliable website addresses that will help her understand the role of protein in a balanced diet, such as building and repairing tissue.

CHAPTER 25

CTQ 25-1: Xavier must give information and instructions to the patient, Jorge, who is in pain and will probably not remember most of their conversation in the morning. What is the best approach Xavier can take to make certain Jorge understands his instructions for ankle care, using the brace, and his orthopedic appointment?

Answer: Different people have different styles of learning. Some learn best by hearing, some by seeing, and others by doing. Xavier should

carefully explain each step of self-care, how to use the brace, and why an appointment has been made with another provider. He should ask Jorge if he has any questions. In addition, Xavier should give Jorge written instructions to reinforce his verbal instructions so that Jorge can review them at his leisure when he is feeling better in a few days. Xavier should also instruct Jorge on whom to call should an emergency arise.

CTQ 25-2: What signs and symptoms should Xavier tell Jorge to watch for as his ankle heals? What can Jorge do to relieve some of the pain of his injury?

Answer: Xavier should give Jorge a printed list of signs and symptoms to watch for, as directed by the physician. The list should include measures to relieve discomfort and the signs and symptoms that require immediate medical attention.

CHAPTER 26

CTQ 26-1: How should Sydney handle the phone call from Mrs. Blakely? How can she reassure her and offer support until Mrs. Blakely can speak to the physician? Should Sydney offer suggestions for nonpharmaceutical therapy?

Answer: Sydney should assure Mrs. Blakely that the latest findings do not mean that everyone who takes hormones will develop cancer. Mrs. Blakely should be offered an appointment to discuss treatment options with the physician, including nonpharmacuetical treatments. Sydney should not offer advice of any kind unless it has been approved by the physician.

CHAPTER 27

CTQ 27-1: After the physician has diagnosed oral thrush combined with a yeast infection, what should Lucas explain to the mother so that the condition is correctly treated?

Answer: Lucas should explain, without accusation, that the entire course of medication must be taken, even if symptoms subside. If it is not, the child may develop resistance to the medication, which will make further treatment more difficult.

CHAPTER 28

CTQ 28-1: What the patient thought was an allergic reaction may in fact be a shingles outbreak given her pain level and past history of varicella. What information can Dawn give the patient? How should Dawn handle the information that the patient's boyfriend ruptured some of the blisters?

Answer: Dawn should explain what shingles is and how it is related to varicella. By breaking the skin's integrity and releasing fluid from the blister, Dawn's boyfriend could potentially have infected himself. The boyfriend should be given information on signs and symptoms of infection.

CHAPTER 29

CTQ29-1: What advice and support can Michael offer Yolanda to help her deal with her brother's newly diagnosed condition?

Answer: It is clear that Yolanda is in great need of support and professional help. If she does not wish to see a therapist at a mental health clinic, she may feel more comfortable speaking to a school counselor. Regardless of where she receives help, she should be offered the support to protect her mental well-being.

CTQ 29-2: What should Michael tell Yolanda about her self-inflicted injuries and her request that he promise not to tell anyone else? Is he bound by a patient–provider oath?

Answer: Michael should recognize the self-inflicted injuries as a cry for help and alert the physician so that the situation can be properly assessed and it can be determined if Yolanda is a danger to herself. Michael is not bound by a patient–provider oath, as he is not a physician. He should explain that he cannot legally honor Yolanda's request of secrecy and that it is out of concern for her well-being that he must tell the physician. He should assure Yolanda that she will get the help she needs.

CHAPTER 30

CTQ 30-1: Even though Ruth is not yet in the 50-year-old age bracket, should she still be tested for colorectal cancer?

Answer: It is up to the physician to make the decision to test, but because Ruth has a strong family history of cancer she is at potentially greater risk. It will be very important for Ruth to monitor her health closely with the help of her physician.

CTQ 30-2: Ruth is concerned about being embarrassed and uncomfortable. She has also canceled a previous appointment. How should Marilyn approach this situation?

Answer: Marilyn should inform Ruth about what the test will entail so she will know what to expect and be less apprehensive. Marilyn should also discuss the missed appointment and find out the reason for it. Ruth may be taking a "head in the sand" approach, trying to ignore the symptoms so she will not have to face the possibility of a cancer diagnosis.

CHAPTER 31

CTQ 31-1: What can Elora do to assist the patient during his transition from employment to retirement?

Answer: Elora can politely ask the patient what he plans to do with his free time. Does he have any hobbies? Does he plan to travel? Elora can also give him information on support groups and local community activities designed for individuals of retirement age that he may not be aware of.

CTQ 31-2: What can Elora do to make certain the patient has the necessary resources for his retirement and future health-care coverage?

Answer: Elora should give the patient some brochures on Social Security and Medicare. Alex may already have them, but making certain is a good idea. He may want to ask about recent changes in Medicare or clear up confusion about his Social Security benefits.

CHAPTER 32

CTQ 32-1: What do you think would be the best way for Leslie's patient to find the type of massage that would be most beneficial for her needs?

Answer: There are many different types of massage and many possible settings. Questions the patient should ask herself are: 1) Do I prefer a female or male therapist, or does gender matter? 2) What are my time commitments? Would mornings, afternoons, or evenings work best for me? 3) Do I prefer a softer-touch or a firmer touch? 4) How comfortable am I with being unclothed? (Some therapies can be done on a fully clothed client, and others cannot.) Answering questions like these will help patients tailor the therapy experience to best suit their needs.

abrasion (ah-BRAY-zhun)—open wound in which the outer layer of skin is scraped away, leaving underlying tissue exposed

absorption (ab-SORP-shun)—passage of digested food products through the wall of the intestine into the bloodstream

accommodation (ah-kom-oh-DAY-shun)—the adjustment of the lens of the eye to various distances

acuity (ah-KYOO-ih-tee)—keenness or sharpness

acute (ah-KYOOT)—sharp, severe, sudden; having a sudden onset and usually of short duration

acyanotic (A-sigh-ah-NOH-tik)—pertaining to an absence of cyanosis

addiction (ah-DICK-shun)—repetitive and dependent behavior usually involving legal or illegal substance abuse

aerobe—organism able to survive and grow only in the presence of oxygen

affect (AF-fekt)—emotional expression associated with facial and body behaviors

afferent nerves (AFF-er-ent)—sensory nerves that carry impulses to the central nervous system

alimentary canal (al-ih-MEN-tar-ree)—tube-like structure of the gastrointestinal system that originates in the mouth and terminates at the anus

alimentation (al-ih-MEN-tay-shun)—entire process of providing nourishment to the body that includes mastication, swallowing, digestion, and absorption

aiquot—representative sample of a well-mixed specimen

allergen (ah-LER-jin)—substance that is not necessarily harmful, such as dust or eggs, but that produces a hypersensitive reaction in some individuals

alternative medicine—systems of medical options varying from traditional medicine, chosen by individuals in place of regularly prescribed modalities and including certain diagnostic procedures and/or accepted and regularly prescribed treatment modalities; examples are aromatherapy, massage therapy, acupuncture, faith healing, and therapeutic touch

aveolus (plural: alveoli) (al-VEE-oh-lus)—microscopic air sacs that are the primary unit of gas exchange in the lungs

Ambu bag (AM-boo bag)—bag-valve-mask unit used to provide ventilation to a non-breathing patient or to assist ventilations for a patient whose breathing (respiratory effort) is inadequate to support life

amino acids —(ah-MEE-no) chief components of protein, synthesized in the body and obtained from the diet

amniocentesis (am-nee-oh-sen-TEE-sis)—procedure in which a needle is inserted into the amniotic sac to withdraw amniotic fluid for testing; used to identify genetic abnormalities, often neural tube deficits and Down syndrome, in the fetus; also used to determine the sex of the fetus

amphiarthrosis (am-fee-ARTH-roh-sis)—condition of slight joint movement in all directions

amplitude (AM-plih-tood)—abundance, amount, extent, fullness, or size

anaerobe—organism that survives and grows in the absence of oxygen

analgesic (an-al-JEE-zik)—pain reducing

anaphylaxis (an-ah-fih-LAK-sis)—severe allergic reaction

anastomosis (ah-nas-toh-MOH-sis)—surgical joining of two tubular structures

anesthesia (an-ess-THEE-zee-ah)—partial or complete loss of sensation

aneurysm (AN-yoo-rizm)—weakening and dilation of an artery

angina (AN-jeye-nah)—left-sided chest pain brought on by exertion

angiography (AN-jee-awg-rah-fee)—radiograph of the vessels usually with contrast medium

angioplasty (AN-jee-oh-plas-tee)—procedure in which a balloon on the distal aspect of a cardiac catheter is inflated to compress plaque against coronary artery walls, increasing the lumen of the artery

ankylosis (ang-kih-LOH-sis)—condition of joint immobility

anorexia (an-oh-REK-see-ah)—diminished desire to eat or diminished appetite

anterior (an-TEE-ree-or)—toward the front

antibody (AN-tih-bawd-ee)—substance produced by the body in response to a specific antigen

anticoagulant (an-tee-koh-AG-yoo-lant)—substance that inhibits blood clot formation

antidepressant (an-tee-dee-PRES-ant)—medication used to treat depression

antigen (AN-tih-jen)—foreign substance that stimulates the production of antibodies against it when it is introduced into the body

antipsychotic (an-tee-sy-KAWT-ik)—medication used to treat psychotic episodes

antipyretic (AN-tih-pi-ret-ik)—fever reducing

antiseptic (an-tih-SEP-tick)—agent that inhibits the growth and reproduction of microorganisms

anuria (an-YOO-ree-ah)—absence of urine

anus (AY-nal)—terminal aspect of the gastrointestinal tract through which dietary waste is expelled

anxiety (ang-ZY-eh-tee)—fear of the unknown; a feeling of fear or worry about the future

apex (AY-pex)—pointed end of the ventricles

apical (ay-pih-ih-kal)—at the apex of the heart

apnea (AP-nee-ah)—inability to breathe

appendage (A-pen-dij)—anything attached to a larger or major body part

approximation—joining together of surgical wound edges

arrhythmia (ah-RITH-mee-ah)—absence of rhythm

arteriosclerosis (ar-tee-ree-oh-skleh-ROH-sis)—arterial hardening caused by the buildup of atherosclerotic plaque

arthritis (ar-THRY-tis)—inflammation of a joint

arthrography (ar-THRAWG-rah-fee)—radiographic examination of a joint

articular (ar-TIK-yoo-lar)—pertaining to a joint

artifact appearance of electrical activity or waveforms from sources outside the heart

asepsis (ay-SEP-sis), surgical practice that keeps objects and areas sterile or free from microorganisms using sterile technique

aseptic (ay-SEP-tick)—without germs (literally, without sepsis)

aseptic technique—technique used before and during sterile procedures to prevent microorganism contamination and the possibility of infection; also known as sterile technique

assisted living facility—alternative to long-term care in a nursing home, often the choice for individuals who do not require the 24-hour care provided by skilled nursing facilities

asthma (AZ-mah)—lung disease characterized by wheezing and shortness of breath; often caused by an allergic response; also known as reversible airways obstruction

asystole (aa-SIS-tole)—absence of cardiac activity; cardiac standstill, without systole

atherosclerosis (ar-TEER-ee-oh-skleh-ROH-sis)—buildup of plaque in the arteries over a period of years

atony (ay-TO-nee)—lack of normal tone or strength in a muscle

atrium (plural: atria) (AY-tree-um)—right or left upper chamber of the heart

atrophy (AT-roh-fee)—decrease in size of normal muscle mass

audiologist (AW-dee-AWL-oh-jist)—professional trained to assess hearing levels

audiometry (AW-dee-AWM-eh-tree)—measuring and testing hearing acuity

augmented lead (AWG-men-TED)—unipolar lead, one positive electrode; has very low voltage and must therefore be augmented by the electrocardiograph to equal the voltage of the other leads

aura (AW-ruh)—warning of impending seizure

aural (AW-ral)—pertaining to the ear

auscultation (AWS-kul-TAY-shun)—listening to various areas of the body

autoclave (aw-to-CLAVE) device used to sterilize instruments under steam and pressure

autoclave load wrapped or unwrapped instruments, packs, and supplies placed in an autoclave to be sterilized

autoimmunity (AW-toh-ih-MYOON-ih-tee)—body's negative reaction to its own cells

automaticity—ability of the heart to initiate and maintain rhythmic activity without the nervous system

avulsion (ah-VUL-shun)—open wound in which skin or tissue is torn loose or pulled completely from underlying tissue

axillary (AK-sil-air-ee)—pertaining to the axilla (armpit); under the arm

bactericidal (bak-TEER-ih-side-al)—capable of killing or destroying bacteria

benign (bee-NINE)—noncancerous or noninvasive

bilirubin (BIL-ih-ROO-bin)—substance formed by breakdown of hemoglobin

binocular (bih-NOK-yoo-lar)—having two eyepieces (on a microscope)

blood pressure—pressure the blood exerts on the vessel walls as a result of the pumping action of the heart

bloodborne pathogens—pathogens carried in the bloodstream

body mechanics—procedures for standing and efficient body movement, including lifting, pushing, or pulling, that prevent injury and maintain required energy levels for long employment

body substance isolation (BSI)—procedures, equipment, and supplies used to prevent the transmission of communicable diseases by preventing direct contact with all body substances such as blood, body fluids, drainage from wounds, feces, urine, sputum, and saliva

bolus (BOH-lus)—mass of masticated food that is swallowed

bradycardia (BRAD-ee-KAR-dee-ah)—heart rate below 60 beats per minute (BPM)

bronchiole (BRONG-kee-ole)—airway less than 1 mm in diameter

bronchitis (brong-KY-tis)—lung disease characterized by large volumes of pulmonary secretions and air trapping; can be chronic or acute in nature

bronchodilator (BRONG-koh-DY-lay-tor)—medication that dilates the walls of the bronchi

bronchus (plural: bronchi) (brong-KUSS)—one of two primary airways that branch into the lungs

bursa (plural: bursae) (BER-sah)—a sac filled with synovial fluid that reduces friction and provides ease of movement between tendons and ligaments, ligaments and bone, and other tissues

bursitis (ber-SIGH-tis)—inflammation of bursa(e)

cadaver—a dead body used for dissection, study, and tissue samples

calorie (also called small calorie)—energy released from the metabolism of proteins, fats, and carbohydrates; amount of heat required to raise 1 gram of water 1 degree Celsius

cancer—general term for various malignant neoplasms

cannula (KAN-yoo-lah)—tube or sheath

carbohydrates—simple and compound sugars that are the primary source of energy for metabolism

cardiac catheterization (KAR-dee-ak) (KATH-eh-ter-ih-ZAY-shun)—diagnostic procedure in which a catheter is threaded through a major artery back to the heart through the aorta; catheter may be threaded into the left ventricle or into the coronary arteries

cardiomegaly (KAR-dee-oh-MEG-ah-lee)—enlarged heart

cardiomyopathy (KAR-dee-oh-my-AWP-ah-thee)—diseases of the myocardium

carditis (KAR-DI-tis)—inflammation of the heart

carrier—person who has the capacity to transmit a disease and is usually unaware of infection

cartilage (KAR-tih-lij)—smooth, elastic connective tissue that covers the ends of the bones

cast—a plaster or fiberglass device used to immobilize a body part

cauterization (kaw-ter-ih-ZAY-shun)—destruction of tissue with a caustic, electric current, hot iron, or by freezing

Centers for Disease Control (CDC)—agency of the Public Health Operating Division of the U.S. Department of Health and Human Services that studies and monitors diseases and disease prevention and works to protect public health and safety

centrifuge (SEN-tri-fuj)—instrument that spins substances at high speed to separate them into layers according to density

cephalgia (SEF-al-AL-jee-ah)—diffuse acute or chronic pain in any part of the head, commonly known as *headache*

cerebral (sa-REE-bral)—pertaining to the cerebrum, the forepart of the brain

cerumen (sa-ROO-men)—earwax; waxy substance secreted in external ear canal

cervix (SER-viks)—entrance to the uterus

charting—documentation of all the events of a patient's visit

chemical name—official pharmaceutical name for a drug based on its chemical composition

chemotherapy (KEE-moh-THAIR-ah-pee)—treatment of disease and infection with chemical agents; in cancer treatment, use of chemical agents to selectively kill cancer cells

chime (KIME)—mixture of partially digested food and enzymes that enters the small intestines

cholecystography (koh-lee-sis-TOG-rah-fee)—radiograph of the gallbladder, using oral contrast; often referred to as gallbladder series

cholesterol (koh-LES-ter-all)—steroid alcohol formed in the liver and also found in plant and animal fats; may be responsible for fatty deposits of plaque in blood vessels

chronic (KRAW-nik)—of long duration, often with slow progression

cilia (SIL-ee-ah)—hairlike processes projecting from the epithelial cells

clonic (CLAWN-ik)—alternating muscular contraction and relaxation

closed wound—wound that involves trauma to the underlying tissue without a break in the skin or mucous membrane or exposure of the underlying tissue

coagulation (koh-ag-YOU-late-shun)—blood clot formation

cold sterilization (ster-ih-lih-ZAY-shun)—sterilization with a chemical sterilant, performed when heat cannot be used

collagen (KAWL-lah-jen)—fibrous connective tissue

colonoscopy (KOH-lon-AWS-koh-pee)—visual examination of the colon using a colonoscope

colostomy (koh-LOSS-toh-mee)—surgically created opening connecting the colon to the abdominal surface for fecal evacuation

colostrum (kuh-LOS-trum)—fluid secreted by the breasts after delivery, before milk production, that contains antibodies and provides the infant with immunological protection

comorbid—denoting co-existing, unrelated medical diseases or conditions

complementary medicine—systems of medical options varying from traditional medicine, chosen by individuals along with regularly prescribed modalities; examples include use of herbal remedies such as saw palmetto to promote prostate health

complete protein (kem-PLEET PRO-teen)—protein containing all the essential amino acids

compress (kom-PRES)—folded piece of material used to apply dry or moist heat or cold therapeutic applications

conduction (kon-DUK-shun)—heat transfer by direct contact through fluids, solids, or other substances

conduction system (con-DUK-shun) (sĭs'tĕm)—wiring and paths that initiate and maintain rhythmic contraction of the myocardium

conductivity (con-DUK-tiv-I-tee)—ability of a cardiac cell to transfer impulses to the next cell, allowing all areas of the heart (myocardium) to depolarize at one time

contamination—making a sterile field unclean or having pathogens placed in it

contractility—ability of the heart muscle to shorten or reduce in size

contraindication—condition for which a drug should be administered

contrecoup—(KON-tra-coo) event on the opposite side, injury in which traumatic impact on the head is strong enough to make the brain strike the opposite side of the cranium and bounce back to strike the impacted side

controlled substance (or schedule drug)—drug identified by the Federal Controlled Substances Act as having a potential for abuse; requires strict adherence to procedures for storage, prescription, administration, and disposal

controlled substances—narcotics, stimulants, and certain sedatives

convection (kon-VEKT-shun)—heat transfer by air

coronary artery bypass (KOR-ah-nair-ee) (AR-toh-ree)—surgery in which the ischemia or obstruction in the coronary arteries is bypassed with a graft of a vessel

coronary artery disease (KOR-ah-nair-ee) (AR-toh-ree)—condition in which the coronary arteries are narrowed by constriction caused by plaque buildup

crescentic—crescent-shaped; term used to describe abnormalities found on biopsy of the kidney in rapidly progressive glomerulonephritis

cryosurgery (KRY-oh-SER-jer-ee)—freezing lesions with nitrous oxide

cryotherapy (KRY-oh-THAIR-ah-pee)—the use of cold applications to prevent or reduce swelling and pain

cryptorchism (also cryptorchidism) (krip-TOHR-kiz-em)—a condition in which one or both of the testes fail to descend into the scrotal sac during fetal development

cutting—using a knife or surgical scissors to separate or divide tissues

cyanosis (sigh-ah-NOH-sis)—bluish tint in skin or mucous membrane, usually appearing in fingernail beds, oral mucous membranes, and circumoral tissue (tissue surrounding the mouth) and indicating excessive deoxygenated hemoglobin or reduced hemoglobin in the blood

cyanotic (sigh-ah-NOH-tik)—characterized by cyanosis, or a blue tint in the skin, which indicates reduced blood oxygen

cystitis (sis-TY-tis)—inflammation of the urinary bladder

deaf—unable to hear, or having a diminished sense of hearing

debris (de-BREE)—organic or inorganic extraneous material that interferes with the proper functioning or cleaning of supplies or equipment

decerebrate posture—posture characteristic of brain injury in which the patient is rigid, with head retracted and arms and legs extended

decibel (DES-ih-bel)—unit for measuring the intensity of sound

decontamination—use of physical means or chemical agents to remove, inactivate, or destroy pathogens on a surface or object to the point where they are no longer capable of transmitting infectious disease, thereby rendering the surface or object safe for handling, use or disposal.

decorticate posture—posture characteristic of brain injury in which the patient is rigid, with clenched fists, flexed arms, and extended legs

degenerative (dee-JEN-er-ah-tiv)—impaired in function or condition over time

dementia (dee-MEN-she-ah)—diminished mental or cognitive functioning with onset after the age of 18 years

dependence (dee-PEN-dens)—state of addiction to certain drugs; rapid physical withdrawal can cause life-threatening and even fatal reactions

depolarization (dee-POHL-ar-ih-ZAY-shun)—condition in which the cardiac cell environment becomes positive

dermatitis (DER-mah-TY-tis)—skin inflammation

dermatologist (DER-mah-TALL-oh-jist)—physician who specializes in the treatment of skin diseases and conditions

dermatology (DER-mah-TALL-oh-jee)—study and treatment of integumentary system diseases and conditions

dermatome (DER-mah-tohm)—specific area of skin stimulated by a segment of the spinal cord

dermatophytoses (DER-mah-to-FI-to-ses)—superficial fungal infections of the skin and its appendages

dermis (DER-mis)—middle layer of the skin

diagnosis (DY-ag-NOH-sis)—conclusion made about the patient's condition by interpretation of data

dialysis (dy-AL-ih-sis)—cleansing of waste products from the blood with a dialysis machine, or dialyzer

diaphoresis (DY-ah-foh-REE-sis)—profuse sweating

diaphragm (DY-ah-fram)—primary muscle of breathing; separates chest and abdominal cavities

diarthrosis (DY-ar-THROH-sis)—condition of bone joints moving freely

diastole (dy-AS-tole)—period of ventricular relaxation

diastolic (dy-ah-STOL-ik)—pertaining to relaxation of the heart muscle; lowest reading of the blood pressure

digestion (DY-jest-shun)—physical and chemical conversion of food into substances that can be used by the body

diluent (dh-LOO-ent)—diluting agent

disinfection—method of decontamination that destroys or inhibits pathogenic microorganisms but does not kill spores and some viruses; used sometimes as an alternative to autoclave sterilization

dissection (dy-SEK-shun)—cutting into smaller parts for study and analysis of each part

distal (diss-TALL)—away from the center

distal tubule (DISS-tal)—farthest tubule from the glomerulus

drug—any substance capable of producing a change in function when administered to a living organism; commonly, a term for a substance used to treat or prevent disease; in the medical office, synonymous with the term *medication*

dumb—unable to speak

dyscrasia (dis-KRAY-zee-ah)—abnormal blood or bone marrow condition, such as leukemia

dysfunction (dis-FUNK-shun)—abnormal or impaired function

dyspepsia (dis-PEP-see-ah)—painful digestion

dysphagia (dis-FAY-jee-ah)—difficulty swallowing

dysphasia (dis-FAY-zee-ah)—difficulty speaking

dyspnea (DISP-nee-ah)—difficulty breathing

dysrhythmia (dis-RITH-mee-ah)—abnormal, irregular, or disturbed heart rhythm

ecchymosis (EK-ih-MOH-seezsis)—bruise; area of bleeding under the skin

echocardiogram (EK-oh-KAR-dee-oh-gram)—type of sonogram used to study the internal structures of the heart

effacement (eh-FAYS-ment)—thinning of the cervix during the labor process

efferent nerves (EFF-er-ent)—motor nerves that carry impulses from the central nervous system to the peripheral nervous system

ejection fraction—measurement of the fraction of the total amount (volume) of blood filling the ventricle that is ejected during the ventricular contraction

electrolytes (ee-LEK-troh-lites)—substances present in the bloodstream, cells, and tissues that are involved in homeostatic changes in acid-base balance, movement of tissue fluid, and activities of the cells and cellular walls

electromyography (ee-LEK-troh-my-AWG-rah-fee)—procedure in which a needle is inserted into muscle tissue to record electrical activity

elimination (ee-LIM-ih-NAY-shun)—expulsion of waste products from the body

embolism (EM-boh-lizm)—condition in which an embolus that is moving through the vascular system becomes lodged in a vessel

embolus (plural: emboli) (EM-boh-lus)—mass of material or tissue in a vessel; may be a blood clot, air, fat, bone fragments, bacterial clumps, amniotic fluid, or other materials

embryo (EM-bree-oh)—initial physical stage of human development following fertilization of the ovum until the end of the seventh or eighth week

emesis (EM-eh-sis)—regurgitation of partially digested food from the stomach; vomit

empathy—understanding of and sensitivity to the feelings, thoughts, and experiences of others

emphysema (EM-fih-SEE-mah)—disease of chronic airways obstruction (COLD) in which air is trapped; usually caused by either smoking or heredity

emulsification (ee-MUL-sih-fih-KAY-shun)—transformation of ingested particles of fat into small globules with bile

endocarditis (EN-doh-kar-DY-tis)—inflammation of the endocardium

endocrine glands (EN-doh-krin)—glands that secrete and release hormones directly into the bloodstream; also known as ductless glands

endometrium (en-doh-MEE-tree-um)—lining of the uterus

endorphin (en-DOR-fin)—proteins in the brain that have analgesic properties

endoscope (en-doh-SKOPE)—fiber-optic instrument used to visualize the internal aspect of the GI tract

endosteum (en-doh-STEE-um)—membrane lining the inner portion and marrow cavity of the bone

epidemiology (ep-ih-DEE-mee-awl-oh-jee)—branch of science that studies the incidence, spread, and control of disease in a population

epidermis (EP-ih-DER-mis)—outermost layer of the skin

epistaxis (ep-ih-STAKS-is)—nosebleed

epithelial (ep-ih-THEE-lee-al)—pertaining to the epithelium (cells covering the external and internal surfaces of the body)

essential oils—oils extracted from flowers and herbs and integrated into an oil base for use in aromatherapy

eukaryotes (yoo-CARE-ce-oats)—group of microorganisms, such as fungi and parasites, that have organized nuclear material and organelles to assist in reproduction

eupnea (YOOP-nee-ah)—normal breathing

exacerbation (eg-ZAS-er-BAY-shun)—increasing severity and recurrence of symptoms

excitability—response of cardiac cell to electrical stimulus

exocrine glands (EK-soh-krin)—glands that secrete substances through ducts, such as sweat glands

extended care facility—facility that provides 24-hour nursing care; also called nursing home or long-term care facility

fats—food component that is a source of energy and aids in growth and development by providing fatty acids

feces (FEE-seez)—waste product of digestion that is expelled through the rectum and anus

fetus (FEE-tus)—human child in utero from embryonic stage until birth

fiber—nondigestible substances found in food, such as cellulose and pectin, that provide bulk and roughage for the evacuation of fecal waste

fibrillation (FIB-rih-LAY-shun)—irregular contractions of the heart; ECG shows waveforms without definite pattern or shape. Atrial fibrillation: Atria are quivering and do not have a forceful beat to push blood into ventricles. Ventricular fibrillation: Lethal arrhythmia; ventricles are quivering and do not contract with force to push blood into aorta. Rhythm is chaotic, with no recognizable P waves, QRS complexes, or T waves; without immediate intervention and conversion of rhythm, asystole will follow.

fistula (FIS-tyoo-lah)—abnormal tube-like structure connecting one body structure to another or to the surface of the body

flank (flanc)—region in the lateral aspect of the midback, between the ribs and the upper border of the ilium

flatulence (FLAT-yoo-lents)—excessive gas or air generated in the stomach or intestinal tract

fluoroscopy (floor-AWS-koh-pee)—radiographic study in which structures are visualized in motion

focus (plural: foci) (FOH-kus)—specific site; the origin of an electrical cardiac impulse

follicle (FAWL-ih-kl)—small hollow or cavity with secretory functions (e.g., hair follicle, ovarian follicle, gastric follicle, etc.)

fomites (FOH-mites)—nonliving objects that may transmit infectious material

fontanelle (FAWN-tah-NEL)—"soft spot" on the cranium of a newborn or infant; area of the skull that is not covered by bone at birth but where the cranial bones eventually come together, allowing for the growth of the brain and skull

fundal height (FUN-dal)—height of the fundus from the top of the symphysis pubis to the highest point at the top of the uterus; used to estimate the size of the fetus

gastric (GAS-trik)—pertaining to the stomach

gastroenterology (gas-troh-en-ter-ALL-oh-jee)—the study of diseases affecting the gastrointestinal tract

gastroscopy (gas-TRAWS-koh-pee)—visual examination of the stomach using a gastroscope

generic (nonproprietary) name—pharmaceutical name for a medication, often a shortened chemical name; used by all manufacturers that produce the medication; never capitalized

geriatrics (JAIR-ee-AT-riks)—science focusing on the aging process; in health care, specialty that deals with the disorders of the aging population and their treatment

germicide (JER-mih-side)—agent used to kill germs

glomerulonephritis (gloh-mair-yoo-loh-neh-FRYE-tis)—inflammation and possible infection of the glomerulus

glomerulus (gloh-MAIR-yoo-lus)—tuft or cluster of capillaries inside the capsule of the nephron

glucometer (gloo-koh-MEAT-er)—instrument used to measure blood glucose levels

gluconeogenesis (gloo-kon-ee-oh-JEN-ch-sis)—conversion of noncarbohydrate sources stored in the liver into glucose

-gravida (GRAV-ih-dah)—combining form meaning a pregnant female or pregnancy

gynecologist (guy-neh-KOL-oh-jist)—physician specializing in the medical care of the female reproductive system, diseases, and disorders

gynecology (guy-ne-KOL-oh-jee)—branch of medicine pertaining to the female reproductive system, diseases, and disorders

hematemesis (HEE-mah-TEM-ah-sis)—vomiting of blood, an indication of bleeding in upper GI tract

hematocrit (hee-MAT-oh-krit)—volume of RBCs in a given volume of blood, expressed as a percent of total blood volume

hematology (HEE-mah-TAWL-oh-jee)—study of blood

hematopoiesis (HEE-mah-toh-poy-EE-sis)—formation of blood cells

hematopoietic (HEE-mah-toh-poy-etic)—pertaining to normal blood cell development in the bone marrow

hematuria (HEE-mah-TYOO-ree-ah)—blood in the urine

hemiparesis (hem-ee-par-EE-sis)—loss of nerve and muscle function on one side of the body

hemiplegia (hem-ee-PLEE-jee-ah)—paralysis of one side of the body

hemoglobin (hee-moh-GLOH-bin)—iron-containing substance found in RBCs whose function is to carry oxygen from the lungs throughout the body

hemolytic (HEE-moh-LIT-ik)—pertaining to the breakdown of RBCs

hemoptysis (hee-MAWP-tih-sis)—coughing up blood from the respiratory tract

hemostasis (hee-moh-STAY-sis)—process by which the body spontaneously stops bleeding and maintains the blood in a fluid state within the vascular compartment

hemostat (HEE-moh-stat)—instrument used to stop blood flow

hepatomegaly (HEP-ah-toh-MEG-ah-lee)—enlargement of the liver

homeostasis (HOH-mee-oh-STAY-sis)—interaction between body systems that maintains optimum body function

hormones (HOR-mohnz)—chemical messengers secreted by the endocrine glands

hospice (HAWS-pis)—facility or program that provides care for the terminally ill and their families in a home setting or hospice center

hydronephrosis (high-droh-neh-FROH-sis)—enlargement of the kidney caused by retention of urine due to an obstruction

hyperglycemia (hy-per-gly-SEE-mee-ah)—condition in which blood glucose is elevated above normal

hypertension (hy-per-TEN-shun)—continued elevation of blood pressure above normal

hyperthermia (hu-per-THERM-ee-a)—condition in which body temperature is much higher than normal for a prolonged period of time

hypoglycemia (hy-poh-gly-SEE-mee-ah)—condition in which blood glucose is below normal

hypotension (hy-poh-TEN-shun)—below-normal blood pressure

hypothalamus (hy-poh-THAL-ah-mus)—very small structure in the midbrain, below the thalamus, that controls many body functions and endocrine processes

hypothermia (hy-poh-THERM-ee-a)—condition in which body temperature is below normal for a prolonged period of time

hypoxemia (hy-pawk-SEE-mee-ah)—reduced oxygen content in the blood

ileostomy (ill-ee-OSS-toh-mee)—surgical opening of the ileum onto the surface of the abdomen for the elimination of fecal material

immunity (im-YOO-nih-tee)—ability to resist disease

immunocompetence (im-yoo-noh-COM-petence)—body's ability to fight infection; capacity for normal immune response

immunodeficiency (im-yo-noh-deh-FISH-en-see)—inability of the immune system to function normally to protect the body from infection

immunohematology (im-yoo-noh-HEE-mah-TAWL-oh-jee)—study of antigens, antibodies, and their interactions

implied consent—agreement implied by the patient for examination and treatment when presenting for a routine visit; also, in an emergency, consent that it is assumed the patient would give if the patient could do so

incision (in-SIZH-un)—open wound with smooth edges made with a knife or other sharp object

incomplete protein—protein lacking one or more of the essential amino acids

incontinence (in-CON-tih-nens)—involuntary leakage of urine or feces

incubation—period of time between exposure to infection and the appearance of symptoms

indigestion (in-dy-JES-chun)—inability to digest, often with pain in the gastrointestinal (GI) tract

infection (in-FEK-shun)—invasion of the body by a pathogenic microorganism

informed consent—consent given by a patient after all potential treatments and outcomes have been discussed for a specific medical condition, including risks and possible negative outcomes

innervate—stimulate

inspection (in-SPEK-shun)—visual examination of both the external surface of the body and the interior portions of body cavities

integrative medicine—systems of medical options that incorporate forms of alternative medicine, complementary medicine, and traditional medicine

integumentary (in-TEG-you-men-tair-ee)—pertaining to the skin, hair, and nails

integumentary system (in-TEG-yoo-MEN-tair-ee)—the skin and its supporting structures (nails, hair, and sebaceous and sweat glands)

interatrial septum (in-ter-AY-tree-al SEP-tum)—wall between the right and left atria

internodal pathway—the three tracts that carry the electrical impulse as it leaves the SA node, transmit the impulse to the AV node, and distribute it throughout the atria; the three divisions are the anterior, middle, and posterior divisions

interphalangeal (IN-ter-fah-LAN-jee-al)—between the joints of the fingers or toes

interventricular septum (in-ter-ven-TRIK-yoo-lar SEP-tum)—wall between the right and left ventricles

intradermal (IN-trah-DER-mal)—between the layers of the skin

intraocular (in-trah-AWK-yoo-lar)—within the eye

intraoperative—pertaining to patient care during surgery

intrinsic factor—substance secreted by the gastric mucosa that is necessary for the absorption of vitamin B_{12} and the development of RBCs

ischemic (is-KEYH-mee-ik)—pertaining to a decreased blood supply to tissue due to impaired circulation to the organ or part

isoelectric line—flat, horizontal line on an ECG strip representing the beginning and ending point of all waves of the ECG cycle

jaundice (JAWN-dis)—yellowing of skin and mucous membranes resulting from deposit of bile pigment; usually a symptom of a biliary disease process

keratin (KAIR-ah-tin)—tough protein substance found in hair, nails, and horny tissue

keratinocyte (KAIR-ah-tin-oh-site)—any skin cell that produces keratin, the hard protein material found in the skin, hair, and nails

kidney (KID-nee)—one of two-bean shaped organs located retroperitoneally that filter blood, remove waste products, and manufacture urine

kilocalorie—1000 calories; amount of heat required to raise 1 kilogram of water 1 degree Celsius

laceration (LAS-er-aa-shun)—open wound in which the skin and underlying tissue are torn and skin integrity is broken

laryngologist (lar-in-JOL-oh-jist)—physician specializing in disorders and diseases of the throat

lavage (la-VAZH)—washing out of a cavity

lesion (LEE-shun)—tissue abnormality that may be hard or soft, small or large, flat or raised, crusted or filled with fluid or pus, and, when associated with skin, on or within the skin tissue

ligament (LIG-ah-ment)—a tough, elastic tissue that connects ends of bones

lipids (LIP-ids)—fat-related substances not soluble in water (triglycerides, fats, oils, phospholipids, sterols)

lithotripsy (LITH-oh-trip-see)—breaking up a renal calculus with ultrasound waves aimed at the calculus from outside the body

local anesthesia (LOH-kal) (AN-es-thee-zee-ah)—absence of feeling or pain in a localized area of tissue without the loss of consciousness

lower gastrointestinal tract (GAS-troh-in-TES-tih-nal) (TRAKT)—small and large intestines,

malignant (mah-LIG-nant)—cancerous, invasive, and destructive

malignant hypertension (mah-LIG-nant) (hy-per-TEN-shun)—rapidly developing, severe elevation of blood pressure, often fatal

malnutrition (MAL-noo-TRISH-un)—condition of excess or deficient nutrient and caloric intake

mammogram (MAM-moh-gram)—radiograph of breast tissue

Mayo stand—stand that holds a flat metal tray for setting up a sterile field for instruments and supplies; usually has an open side that allows it to be moved over a gurney or table

medical asepsis—the practice of reducing the number of pathogens and the transmission of disease; also known as clean technique

Medicare—federal health insurance program for those over the age of 65, the disabled, and those with end-stage renal disease

Medigap insurance—insurance for Medicare recipients that covers deductibles and allowable payments not covered by Medicare

megakaryocytes (meg-ah-KAIR-ee-oh-sites)—large bone marrow cells that play an important role in the production of platelets in the bone marrow

melanin (MEL-ah-nin)—pigment (color) in the skin and hair

melanocytes (mel-AN-oh-sights)—cells that produce melanin

melena (me-LEE-nah)—black, tarry stools

menarche (men-ARSH)—onset of menses or menstrual cycle during adolescence

menopause (MEN-oh-pawz)—cessation of menses

menses (MEN-seez)—cyclic shedding of the uterine lining (endometrium) when fertilization of the ovum does not occur

mensuration (men-ser-AY-shun)—measurement

metabolism (meh-TAB-oh-lizm)—process of changing nutrients from food into substances for anabolic or catabolic activity

metastasis (meh-TASS-tah-sis)—spread of a disease to adjacent and distal tissues and organs

microbiology—the study of microorganisms

microorganism—organism that can be viewed under a microscope, but not by the naked eye

mineral (MIN-er-al)—element essential to every cell, naturally occurring in nature, and used by the body in the processes of blood clotting, muscle contraction, and nervous system impulse conduction

mitral valve prolapse (MY-tral VALV PROH-laps)—valvular disorder in which cusps of mitral valve prolapse into right atrium, failing to close and resulting in back pressure into left atrium

monocular—having one eyepiece (on a microscope)

morphology (mor-FAWL-oh-jee)—the study of shape or form; in microbiology, a method of classifying bacteria according to shape

multifocal—originating from more than one area or focus

mycology (my-CALL-oh-jee)—study of fungi, such as yeast and molds

myelography (MY-eh-LAWG-rah-fee)—radiographs of the spinal cord using a contrast medium

myocardial infarction (my-oh-CAR-dee-al in-FARC-shun)—death of myocardial tissue due to obstructed blood supply to the tissue

myocarditis (my-oh-car-DYE-tis)—inflammation of the myocardium

nasal septum (NAY-zal SEP-tum)—cartilage wall that divides the nasal cavity

neoplasia (NEE-oh-PLAY-zee-ah)—abnormal cell development

neoplasm (NEE-oh-plazm)—new growth or tumor

nephrologist (neh-FRAWL-oh-jist)—physician specializing in the treatment of kidney diseases and conditions

nephrology (neh-FRAWL-o-jee)—study of the kidney and the diseases that affect it

nephrons (NEF-rawnz)—microscopic tubular structures of the kidney

neuralgia (nyoo-RAL-jee-ah)—sharp, stabbing, or burning pain that occurs along the course of a nerve

neuritis (nyoo-RY-tis)—inflammation of a nerve or nerves

neurology (nyoo-RAWL-oh-jee)—study of the nervous system

neuron (NOOR-on)—nerve cell; basic unit of the nervous system

neurotransmitter (noo-roh-TRANS-mit-ter)—chemicals that aid in the transmission of electrical impulses from one neuron, or nerve cell, to the next

nocturia (nok-TOO-ree-ah)—increased urine output at night

noncritical—pertaining to objects that do not touch the patient or touch only intact skin

noninvasive (non-in-VAY-siv)—pertaining to a procedure or technique that does not require entry into the body by incision or inserting an instrument

nonpathogen (non-PATH-oh-jen)—harmless organism that does not cause disease

normal flora—generally harmless microorganisms common in the human body

nosocomial infection (NOS-oh-koh-mee-al) (in-FEK-shun)—infection resulting from the hospitalization of a patient

nuchal rigidity (NOO-kal)—severe and painful rigidity of the neck in which the head is bent forward toward the chest

obesity (oh-BEE-sih-tee)—excess body weight 20 to 30 percent above average for gender, age, and height, with abnormal amounts of body fat

obstetrician (awb-steh-TRISH-an)—physician specializing in the medical care of women during pregnancy, including prenatal, delivery and postnatal care

obstetrics (awb-STET-riks)—branch of medicine pertaining to the medical care of women during pregnancy, including prenatal, delivery, and postnatal care

ocular—pertaining to the eye; also, the microscope's eyepiece

oliguria (ol-ig-YOO-ree-ah)—diminished urine output, less than 400 ml per day

oncology (ong-KALL-oh-jee)—branch of medicine that deals the study, diagnosis, and treatment of tumors and cancer

open wound—break in the skin or mucous membrane that exposes underlying tissues

ophthalmologist (OFF-thal-MAWL-oh-jist)—physician who specializes in the treatment of eye diseases and disorders

ophthalmoscope (off-THAL-moh-skohp)—instrument used to examine the eyes

opportunistic pathogen (AWP-or-too-NIS-tik PATH-oh-jen)—normally nonpathogenic microorganism that causes disease in a host whose immune resistance has been lowered by certain disorders or treatments

optician (op-TISH-un)—trained professional who grinds lenses, inserts the lenses into frames, and fits the patients' glasses

optometrist (op-TAWM-eh-trist)—licensed professional (Doctor of Optometric Medicine) who examines eyes, tests for visual acuity, and prescribes and adapts lens for patients

oral (AW-ral)—by mouth

organ—a group of tissues making up a structure that has a particular function in the body

organelle—a very small organ-functioning unit within a living cell; mitochondria organelles are responsible for the metabolism of lipids and the synthesis (building) of proteins

orthopedics (or-thoh-PEE-diks)—the study and treatment of diseases and disorders of the musculoskeletal system

orthopnea (or-THAWP-nee-ah)—ability to breathe only in a standing or upright sitting position

orthostatic hypotension (or-thoh-STAT-ik hy-poh-TEN-shun)—sudden decrease in blood pressure when an individual rises too quickly from a sitting position, usually resulting in light-headedness

osteoblast (AWS-tee-oh-blast)—a precursor cell in bone formation

otic (O-tik)—pertaining to the ear

otolaryngologist (OH-toh-LAIR-in-GAWL-oh-jist)—physician who specializes in the treatment of ear and throat diseases

otologist (O-tol-o-jist)—physician who specializes in the treatment of ear diseases

otorhinolaryngologist (OH-toh-RY-noh-LAIR-in-GAWL-oh-jist)—physician who specializes in ear, nose, and throat diseases

otoscope (OH-toh-skohp)—instrument used to examine the ears

over-the-counter medications—nonprescription medications that can be purchased anywhere without a physician's prescription; examples include antacids, cold remedies, and aspirin

overweight—general term for early stage of excess body weight above standard for gender, age, and height

ovum (plural: ova) (OH-vum)—human gamete (egg)

palliative (PAL-ee-ah-tiv)—relieving pain or discomfort

palpation (pal-PAY-shun)—examination involving touch; examiner uses the hands and fingers to feel both the surface of the body (for abnormalities or irregularities) and various organs (for size, location, and tenderness) and feel generally for masses or lumps and assessing the texture and temperature of the tissue

palpitations (pal-pih-TAY-shuns)—irregular and often erratic heartbeat felt by the patient

palsy (PAWL-zee)—tremors; temporary or permanent loss of ability to control or make muscle movement

-para (PAIR-ah)—combining form signifying the number of deliveries after the 20th week of gestation

paraplegia (pair-ah-PLEE-jee-ah)—loss of sensation and motor activity (paralysis) of the lower trunk and lower extremities

parasitology (PAIR-ah-si-TAWL-oh-jee)—branch of biology that studies parasites

patent (PAY-tent)—open

pathogen (PATH-oh-jen)—disease-causing microorganism

pathogenicity—ability of an organism to cause disease

pediatrician (pee-dee-ah-TRISH-an)—physician who specializes in treating children from birth to age 20

pediatrics (pee-dee-AT-riks)—medical specialty that focuses on the care and treatment of children from birth through age 20

percussion (per-KUSH-un)—examination consisting of tapping the fingertips lightly but sharply against the body to assess the size and location of underlying organs

pericarditis (pair-ee-kar-DY-tis)—inflammation of the pericardium

perineum (pair-ah-NEE-um)—area between the vaginal orifice and the anus

periorbital edema—abnormal, excessive fluid surrounding the eye that usually occurs in the morning upon waking

periosteum (pair-ee-AH-stee-um)—a fibrous membrane covering the outside of bone tissue

peristalsis (pair-ih-STAL-sis)—rhythmic, involuntary, wavelike motion in the hollow tubes of the body that assists the passage of contents

personal protective equipment (PPE)—protective clothing and equipment such as gloves, gowns, and masks that are worn to prevent contamination by blood and other body fluids

petechiae (peh-TEE-kee-eye)—small hemorrhages under the skin

phagocytic (FAG-oh-sit-ick)—having the ability to ingest particulate material, such as bacteria

phagocytosis (FAG-oh-sy-toh-sis)—the engulfing and destruction of microorganisms or foreign matter by phagocytic cells

pharmacology—the study of drugs and their effects on the human body

phlebotomist (fleh-BAWT-oh-mist)—individual trained to draw blood

phlebotomy (fleh-BAWT-oh-mee)—process of blood collection, sometimes defined as "an incision into a vein"

pH—measurement of hydrogen ion concentration in a substance or solution; a pH of 7.0 is considered neutral, below 7.0 is considered acidic, and above 7.0 is considered alkaline

phobia (FOH-bee-ah)—irrational, obsessive fear of an object, situation, or activity

photometer (foh-TOHM-eh-ter)—instrument used to measure the intensity of light rays; an electronic component of many instruments

plasma (PLAZ-mah)—liquid portion of anticoagulated blood

plasmapheresis (PLAZ-mah-feh-REE-sis)—daily replacement of blood plasma in the body with other fluids or donated plasma for two or more weeks

polyps (POLL-ips)—fingerlike growths on the mucous membranes throughout the body

polyuria (pol-ee-YOO-ree-ah)—excessive urine production and frequent, urgent, and excessive urinary output

portal hypertension (POR-tal hy-per-TEN-shun)—condition of increased blood flow pressure through the blood vessels of the liver (portal circulation), often caused by cirrhosis of the liver or compression of the hepatic blood vessels

postictal (post-IK-tal)—pertaining to the period immediately following a seizure

postnatal/postpartum (post-NAY-tal)—after childbirth

postoperative (post-op) (post-OP-er-ah-tiv)—pertaining to patient care following surgery

practitioner—a person who practices in a profession, such as medicine

precordical lead—ECG lead that views the heart in a horizontal plain

premature ventricular contraction (PVC)—a beat that comes early in the cardiac cycle, is not preceded by a P wave, and has a widened and distorted QRS complex; sometimes referred to as premature ventricular complex or premature ventricular beat (PVB)

prenatal (pree-NAY-tal)—prior to birth

preoperative (pre-op) (pree-OP-er-ah-tiv)—pertaining to preparation before surgery

presbycusis (PREZ-bee-ah-KOO-sis)—hearing deficiency normally associated with aging

presbyopia (prez-bee-OH-pee-ah)—vision deficiency normally associated with aging

proctology (prok-TALL-oh-jee)—medical practice specializing in disorders of the rectum and anus

prodromal—pertaining to symptoms during the period immediately preceding onset of a disease condition

prognosis (prawg-NOH-sis)—an outcome prediction for the course of a disease and patient recovery (literal meaning: knowledge before)

projectile vomiting—vomiting with uncontrollable force

prokaryote (pro-CARE-ee-oat)—group of microorganisms, such as bacteria, that lack an organized nucleus and cytoplasmic organelles

prostatitis (PRAWS-tah-TY-tis)—inflammation and/or infection of the prostate gland

prosthesis (plural: prostheses) (praws-THEE-sis)—artificial replacement for a body part

protein (PROH-teen)—food component composed of amino acids; provides a source of energy and assists in building and renewing body tissues

proteinuria (PROH-tee-NYOO-ree-ah)—presence of abnormally large amounts of protein in the urine

proximal tubule (PRAWK-sih-mal TOO-byool)—tubule closest to glomerulus

psychiatrist (sigh-KY-ah-trist)—medical doctor or physician specializing in the medical treatment of mental illness

psychiatry (sigh-KY-ah-tree)—branch of medicine that deals with diagnosis, treatment, and prevention of mental disorders

psychologist (sigh-KALL-oh-jist)—specialist in the field of psychology, therapy, and research

psychology (sigh-KALL-oh-jee)—science dealing with normal and abnormal mental processes and behavior

psychosis (sigh-KOH-sis)—abnormal mental coping of the individual who is out of touch with reality

psychotherapeutic (sigh-koh-THAIR-ah-pew-tik)—alleviating symptoms of anxiety, depression, and psychosis

psychotherapy (sigh-koh-THAIR-ah-pee)—treatment of mental disorders with talk therapy, or counseling

psychotropic (sigh-koh-TROW-pik)—affecting psychic function, behavior, experience, or emotions

pulmonary function testing (PUL-moh-nair-ee)—testing performed to evaluate airflow and lung volume

purulent (PYOOR-yoo-lent)—containing pus

pyelonephritis (pye-eh-loh-neh-FRYE-tis)—inflammation and/or of the pelvis of the kidney

pyogenic (pye-oh-JEN-ik)—pus-forming

pyuria (py-YOO-ree-ah)—pus in the urine

quadriplegia (kwod-rih-PLEE-jee-ah)—paralysis of the entire trunk and all four extremities

radial (RAY-dee-al)—at the wrist over the radial artery

radiation (ray-dee-AY-shun)—radiant energy

radiograph (rah-dee-O-gahf)—developed x-ray film

radiography (ray-dee-OG-rah-fee)—study or practice of radiology using x-rays

radiologist (rah-dee-ALL-oh-jist)—physician who specializes in radiology

radiology (ray-dee-ALL-oh-jee)—medical specialty that uses radiant energy forms, ultrasound, and magnetic waves to study, diagnose, and treat disease and injury

radiolucent (ray-dee-oh-LOO-cent)—easily penetrated by x-rays

radiopaque (ray-dee-oh-PAYK)—capable of obstructing the passage of x-rays

range of motion—the full extent of any joint potential for movement, including actions such as flexion, extension, circumduction, adduction, and abduction

reactive (ree-AK-tiv)—able to respond to a stimulus

reduction (ree-DUK-shun)—the process of open or closed manipulation that returns bony ends to correct anatomical position before healing

referred pain—pain that is felt in a different area from the injured or diseased part of the body

remission (rih-MISH-un)—complete or partial disappearance of the clinical characteristics of chronic or malignant disease

renal (REE-nal)—pertaining to the kidney

renal calculus (plural: calculi) (REE-nal) (KAL-kyoo-lus)—kidney stone

repolarization (ree-POHL-ar-ih-ZAY-shun)—return of the cardiac cell to the resting state

rhinologist (ry-NAWL-oh-jist)—physician who specializes in the treatment of nasal passage and sinus diseases

rhythm—time interval between pulses or breaths

risk factor—condition or situation that makes a person particularly vulnerable to certain diseases or disorders

sanitization (san-ih-ty-ZA-shun)—method of decontamination that reduces the numbers of microorganisms on an object or surface; removes organic material from equipment or instruments and must be performed before disinfection and sterilization

saturated fats—fats derived from animal sources that are solid at room temperature

sebaceous glands (see-BAY-shus)—small glands in the dermis that secrete sebum, usually through ducts that empty into the hair follicles

sepsis (SEP-sis)—febrile state characterized by pathogens in the bloodstream

sequela (plural: sequelae) (see-KWELL-ah)—outcome

serology (seer-HL-oh-gee)—laboratory science in which blood serum is tested for the presence of antibodies

serum (SEER-um)—liquid portion that remains when the blood has been allowed to clot

short-term memory—memory of recent events

side effect—effect other than the therapeutic effect

sign—that which can be seen, heard, measured, or felt by the examiner

sinoatrial (SA) node (sigh-noh-AY-tree-al)—pacemaker of the heart

soak—procedure in which the total body or body part is immersed in water for heat or cold therapeutic applications

sonography (soh-NAWG-rah-fee)—use of ultrasound waves to view internal body structures

spectrophotometric (SPEK-troh-foh-tom-met-rick)—the measurement or estimate of the amount of color in a solution

sphygmomanometer (sfig-moh-mah-NOM-eh-ter)—instrument used to measure blood pressure

splint—a temporary orthopedic device used to immobilize, restrain, and support any extremity of the body

spore—capsule formed by some bacteria as a protective shell during their resting state; under favorable conditions the bacteria become active again

Standard Precautions—precautions that replace Body Substance Isolation and Universal Precautions in institutional health-care settings such as hospitals and nursing homes; the first level of care combines Universal and Body Substance Isolation Precautions, and the second consists of Transmission-based Precautions

staph (STAFF)—*Staphylococcus*

status epilepticus (STAT-us EP-ih-LEP-tih-kus)—continuous seizure activity

stenosis (steh-NOH-sis)—narrowing or constriction of a passage

stent—device implanted in a vessel to maintain its patency (openness)

sterilant—chemical sterilizing agent

sterile—free from all living microorganisms and bacterial spores

sterile field—microorganism-free environment used during procedures to prevent contamination by pathogens

sterilization—process of destroying all microbial forms of life, for which the autoclave is most commonly used

sterilization indicator—different forms of tape or inserts (strips or tubes, for example) that provide verification of an autoclave's effectiveness

stethoscope (STETH-oh-skohp)—instrument used to listen to sounds within the body

strep—*Streptococcus*

subcutaneous (sub-kyoo-TAY-nee-us)—under the epidermal and dermal layers of the skin

subcutaneous tissue (sub-kyoo-TAY-nee-us)—deepest layer of the skin

sublingually (sub-LING-gwa-lee)—under the tongue

symptom (SIMP-tum)—a perceptible change in the body related by the patient

synarthrosis (sihn-ar-THROS-is)—condition of absent joint movement

systole (SIS-tole)—contraction of the myocardium

systolic (sis-TOL-ik)—pertaining to contraction of the heart; highest reading of the blood pressure

tachycardia (tak-ee-CAR-dee-ah)—heart rate above 100 beats per minute (BPM)

tachypnea (ta-kip-NEE-ah)—rapid breathing

temperature—measurement of body heat produced and lost during metabolism, respiration, elimination, and environmental fluctuation

tendon (TEN-dun)—tough, elastic tissue that connects muscle to bone

testis (**plural: testes,** also called testicle) (TES-tis)—oval structure in the scrotal sac that produces sperm

tetany (TET-ah-nee)—painful, intense, spasmodic muscle contractions

therapeutic effect—the desired or intended effect

thermodynamics—the use of cryotherapy or thermotherapy for therapeutic treatment

thermometer—instrument used to measure body temperature

thermotherapy (ther-moh-THAIR-ah-pee)—the use of heat application to increase circulation to an area and promote healing

thromboembolism (throm-boh-EM-boh-lizm)—obstruction of a blood vessel by a thrombus

thrombosis (THROM-boh-sis)—condition of having a blood clot in a blood vessel

thrombus (plural: thrombi) (THROM-bus)—blood clot in the vessel that can form an obstruction in the vessel

tissue (TISH-yoo)—a group of cells that act together for a particular body function

tolerance (TAHL-er-ans)—requiring greater amounts of a substance to achieve the desired effect

tonic (TAWN-ik)—pertaining to muscular tension

total parenteral nutrition (par-EN-ter-all) (NEW-try-shun)—nutrition ingested by means other than oral intake

toxic effect—potential harmful or life-threatening effect

trade (brand, proprietary) name—name registered by a manufacturer for use only by that manufacturer; has a registered trademark symbol; first letter is always capitalized

Transmission-based Precautions—care based on symptoms of disease and transmission method of the pathogen, such as contact, droplet, air, vector, or common vehicle

triage (TREE-azh)—sorting and setting priorities for treatment for patients who are on the phone or at the reception desk

triglycerides—chief form of fat found in foods

trigone (TRY-gohn)—triangular area in floor of urinary bladder where ureters enter and urethra exits

tumor (TOO-mor)—growth characterized by progressive and uncontrolled production of cells

tumor marker—substance produced by tumor cells that can be measured and monitored in blood serum levels to indicate progression of metastases and/or effectiveness of cancer chemotherapy

turbidity (TUR-bid-i-tee)—cloudiness, lack of clarity

turgor (TER-gor)—normal appearance of the skin and its ability to return to normal after being pinched

ultramicroscopic—requiring magnification with an electron microscope to be seen

ultrasonic cleaning—use of ultrasound waves to loosen contaminants

ultrasound (ULL-trah-sound)—use of high frequency sound waves being projected and bounced back to the transmitter resulting in an image being projected

unifocal—originating from same area or focus

Universal Precautions—the CDC's original guidelines for preventing the transmission of AIDS and other blood-borne diseases

unsaturated fats—fats derived from plant sources that are liquid at room temperature

upper gastrointestinal tract (GAS-troh-in-TES-tih-nal)—oral cavity (mouth), esophagus, duodenum, and stomach

ureter (YOO-ree-ter)—tube leading from the kidney to the urinary bladder

urethra (yoo-REE-thrah)—tube leading from urinary bladder to outside the body

urinalysis (YOO-rih-NAL-ih-sis)—visual and chemical examination of the urine

urinary bladder (YOO-rih-nair-e BLAD-er)—receptacle for urine that has been manufactured by the kidneys

urinary meatus (YOO-rih-nair-e mee-AY-tus)—external sphincter of the urethra

urobilinogen—derivative substance formed by conversion of direct bilirubin by bacteria in the intestinal tract

urologist (yoo-RALL-oh-jist)—physician who specializes in treating urinary system diseases and conditions and conditions involving the male reproductive system

urology (yoo-RALL-oh-jee)—study of the urinary system in males and females and the diseases that affect it

venipuncture (VEEN-ih-punk-cher)—method of obtaining venous blood for analysis of hematology and chemistry studies

venous (VEE-nus)—pertaining to blood vessels that carry blood toward the heart

ventricle (VEN-trik-el)—right or left lower chamber of heart

virology—specialized branch of microbiology that studies viruses and associated diseases

viruses—ultramicroscopic, nonliving organisms classified as microorganisms because they contain DNA or RNA and are capable of parasitic metabolism and reproduction

vitamins—components required for metabolism, growth, and development

x-ray—form of electromagnetic radiation that travels in waves at the speed of light and can penetrate matter and produce a visible image on film

zygote (ZEYE-goat)—the fertilized ovum created by the union of the male and female sex cells (sperm and ovum)

Numbers in italics refer to figures; those followed by t refers to tables.